TRADEMARKS AND UNFAIR COMPETITION

ASPEN CASEBOOK SERIES

TRADEMARKS AND UNFAIR COMPETITION

LAW AND POLICY
FIFTH EDITION

Graeme B. Dinwoodie
Global Professor of Intellectual Property Law
IIT Chicago-Kent College of Law

Mark D. Janis
Professor of Law
Robert A. Lucas Chair in Law
Indiana University Maurer School of Law

Wolters Kluwer

Published by Wolters Kluwer in New York.

Wolters Kluwer Legal & Regulatory U.S. serves customers worldwide with CCH, Aspen Publishers, and Kluwer Law International products. (www.WKLegaledu.com)

To contact Customer Service, e-mail customer.service@wolterskluwer.com, call 1-800-234-1660, fax 1-800-901-9075, or mail correspondence to:

Wolters Kluwer
Attn: Order Department
PO Box 990
Frederick, MD 21705

Printed in the United States of America.

3 4 5 6 7 8 9 0

ISBN 978-1-4548-7105-7

Library of Congress Cataloging-in-Publication Data

Names: Dinwoodie, Graeme B., author. | Janis, Mark D., author.
Title: Trademarks and unfair competition : law and policy / Graeme B.
  Dinwoodie, Global Professor of Intellectual Property Law, IIT Chicago-Kent
  College of Law; Mark D. Janis, Professor of Law, Robert A. Lucas Chair in
  Law, Indiana University Maurer School of Law.
Description: Fifth edition. | New York : Wolters Kluwer, [2018] | Series:
  Aspen casebook series | Includes bibliographical references and index.
Identifiers: LCCN 2018027394 | ISBN 9781454871057
Subjects: LCSH: Trademarks—Law and legislation—United States. |
  Competition, Unfair—United States. | LCGFT: Casebooks (Law)
Classification: LCC KF3180 .D56 2018 | DDC 346.7304/880264—dc23
LC record available at https://lccn.loc.gov/2018027394

About Wolters Kluwer Legal & Regulatory U.S.

Wolters Kluwer Legal & Regulatory U.S. delivers expert content and solutions in the areas of law, corporate compliance, health compliance, reimbursement, and legal education. Its practical solutions help customers successfully navigate the demands of a changing environment to drive their daily activities, enhance decision quality and inspire confident outcomes.

Serving customers worldwide, its legal and regulatory portfolio includes products under the Aspen Publishers, CCH Incorporated, Kluwer Law International, ftwilliam.com and MediRegs names. They are regarded as exceptional and trusted resources for general legal and practice-specific knowledge, compliance and risk management, dynamic workflow solutions, and expert commentary.

We dedicate this book to our advisers on what consumers think. You are all inherently distinctive. . . .

Isa, David, Christine, Davy, Maya, and Brian

Graeme

Julie, Aimee, Katie, and Kyle

Mark

Summary of Contents

CONTENTS

8 NON–CONFUSION-BASED TRADEMARK LIABILITY THEORIES

PREFACE TO FIFTH EDITION

We are pleased to introduce the Fifth Edition of Trademarks and Unfair Competition: Law and Policy. We are especially pleased that the Fifth Edition will be made available in a more modestly-priced, looseleaf format. We sincerely hope that the looseleaf format will prove to be convenient for instructors and students, and we hope that the reduced cost will provide at least a little relief for students' budgets.

This edition follows the core structure of prior editions, but reflects two emerging themes in U.S. trademark law. The first is the intersection between free speech and trademark rules. The most obvious illustration of the intersection is the Supreme Court's opinion in *Tam* finding the "disparagement" provision of the Lanham Act to be inconsistent with the First Amendment, and the Federal Circuit's follow-on decision in *Brunetti*, both of which appear in Chapter 5. But there are other examples, including the increased attention to *Rogers v. Grimaldi* as the standard by which to limit the enforcement of trademark rights against expressive uses (Chapter 9), and questions about the constitutionality of dilution by tarnishment (Chapter 8).

The second theme concerns the content of unfair competition law under Lanham Act Section 43(a), and particularly the extent to which rules that apply to registered rights also apply to unregistered rights enforced through Section 43(a) actions. The *Tam* decision, and other cases (such as *Belmora*, covered in Chapter 6), have brought renewed attention to this longstanding puzzle. This development is relatively inchoate (compared to the free speech challenges, which have been more developed and quite prominent), but we have tried to flag the issue where appropriate.

Instructors who are familiar with past editions will notice that the Fifth Edition strives to maintain the strong points of its predecessors. We have continued our tradition of extensively covering functionality (Chapter 3), an area of trademark jurisprudence that is increasingly important in view of the expanded interest in design protection (especially outside the trademark regime) and which we believe encourages students to develop a critical approach to the field from early in the course. We have also retained an emphasis on international and comparative aspects of trademark law, integrating those materials with the pertinent discussion of domestic law. And we have remained attentive to the impact on trademark law of shifts in online business practices and social media usage.

We have appreciated the help of many individuals in preparing this new edition of the book. Professor Janis benefitted from the efforts of research assistants Alyssa Deckard, Evan Glass, and Ryan McDonnell, and administrative support from the Center for Intellectual Property Research at the Indiana University Maurer School of Law. Professor Dinwoodie is very grateful for the research assistance provided by Shannon Bezner. And, as always, we greatly appreciate the comments we have received from users of the book, both students and fellow trademark professors. We hope that you will continue to offer us your reactions.

Statutory materials, and supplemental materials covering developments that post-date publication of the book, can be found online at http://www.indiana.edu/~tmlaw/.

Graeme B. Dinwoodie
Mark D. Janis

July 2018

PREFACE TO FIRST EDITION

Trademark and unfair competition law impinges upon every aspect of human activity—the social, the commercial, the political . . . and the Elvis. As you'll see from the first chapter, the law of trademarks is a study in the dynamics of popular culture. Trademark law is about beer, clothes, cars, cologne, laundry detergent, and what goes through people's minds when they shop at the mall or on the Internet. More thematically, it is about encouraging and preserving investments in goodwill and identity while preserving freedom in the popular discourse. It is about protecting consumers from being misled, and about encouraging producers to maintain consistent quality in their goods and services. These are the themes of this book, and popular culture is the backdrop.

This book is also about change. Because popular culture mutates so rapidly (and often capriciously), trademark law experiences enormous evolutionary pressures. Today, those pressures are causing profound changes in the structure and doctrine of trademark and unfair competition law. The most exciting, most contested changes of late have sprung from three sources: the revolution in electronic commerce, the contemporary obsession with image, and globalization. The revolution in electronic commerce has brought us disputes over domain name ownership, and a host of Internet practices (such as protest websites and pop-up ads) that raise issues of control over trade reputation or the nature of online competition. The contemporary obsession with image has engendered debates over what uses of trademarks should be permitted without the consent of the trademark owner. And the frequently nonverbal character of image has translated into disagreements over the protection of nontraditional source-identifiers such as product design. Finally, reflecting the increasingly global nature of society, these disputes are no longer confined within national borders, and the policy consequences of trademark decisions are no longer felt only in the domestic sphere. We have emphasized these developments throughout the book.

Despite these profound changes in trademark and unfair competition law, we have organized the materials according to a traditional understanding of intellectual property systems. The book proceeds on the basis of broad topics, into which we have sought to integrate new and exotic subjects alongside their more traditional counterparts. Thus, we address, in order, trademark creation, trademark scope and enforcement, and trademark transactions. This approach is more bold than it may seem, and it raises a number of challenging questions about the seemingly ad hoc progression of recent trademark law. For instance, as to the creation of rights, this arrangement might cause a reader to question why rules for recognition of one type of trademark subject matter (e.g., word marks) should differ from rules for recognition of another (e.g., trade dress). Similarly, concerning the scope and enforcement of rights, this arrangement may lead a reader to consider how the trademark dilution cause of action (introduced into federal law almost a decade ago) and the new cybersquatting cause of action (introduced in late 1999) align with other, traditional enforcement theories. Finally, our grouping of topics in a "transactions" unit that addresses transfer, licensing, franchising, and limits on the commercial exploitation of trademarks is designed to make students see the connections among issues that face transactional intellectual property lawyers on a daily basis. We believe that our integration of new law and traditional principles within a single conception of the field is unique, and hopefully more accessible to students, judges, legislators, and others who think about trademark law and policy.

A word about the format of the book. We are believers in the traditional case method of teaching, and so the book consists primarily of cases. We aren't believers in severe editing of cases. As former litigators, we tend to think that issues like procedure, facts, and evidence actually matter, and heavy editing can too often preclude proper discussion of these topics. Where we have edited original materials, this is indicated by ellipses or bracketed explanatory phrases. We have indicated deletions of citations by the bracketed abbreviation [cit.]. We have omitted most footnotes without indication; those that remain retain their original numbering.

We also have included a series of problems that challenge the reader to apply and extend the principles developed in the main cases and notes. A number of the problems are drawn from real-life examples. Others, such as any that portray the two of us as heroic, might possibly be embellished.

We have many people to thank for their contributions to this project. We benefited from the insights of several anonymous reviewers, whose names are Professors Julie Cohen, Tom Cotter, Lydia Loren, and Marshall Leaffer, along with a few others who are truly anonymous. We also benefited greatly from comments received from several trademark law professors, including Professors Graeme Austin, Barton Beebe, and Tim Holbrook, who used the materials in manuscript form. Students in our classes at Chicago-Kent College of Law and the University of Iowa College of Law offered helpful comments. Kati Jumper provided phenomenal secretarial support through many, many years' worth of drafts. Iowa students Kate Cox, Lynda Fitzpatrick, Paula Fritsch, Rob Hodgson, and Scott Timmerman, and Chicago-Kent students Jessica Kaiser, Christopher Kaiser, Aashit Shah, and Sheng Wu provided excellent research assistance. Thanks to our publishers, particularly Carol McGeehan, for encouraging us to pursue our vision of how best to teach trademark and unfair competition law. Finally, we could not have done any of this without the support of our respective families: Professor Janis is particularly grateful to Julie, Aimee, Katie, and Kyle; Professor Dinwoodie owes much more than can be conveyed by an acknowledgment to Isa, David, Christine, Davy, and Brian. Professor Janis is also especially grateful for the friendship of his colleague Professor Hillary Sale. And he apologizes in advance to his Brother Billy (he tried to change names to protect the innocent, but Professor Dinwoodie wouldn't let him).

Graeme B. Dinwoodie
Mark D. Janis

May 2004

Foundations and Purposes of Trademark and Unfair Competition Law

INTRODUCTION TO TRADEMARK AND UNFAIR COMPETITION LAW

A. SOURCES AND NATURE OF TRADEMARK RIGHTS

*You can break 6 of the 10 commandments in America, but please,
Thou Shalt not Violate the Brand.*

> —David Brooks, *No Sex Magazines Please, We're Wal-Mart
> Shoppers*, N.Y. TIMES, May 11, 2003, at WK 14.

But what's a Brand? What's a Violation? Who is Thou? Trademark and unfair competition law contains many nuances, all of which provide greater content to David Brooks' basic proposition. By the conclusion of this book, we hope you will have discovered what caused Brooks to give trademarks almost religious significance in twenty-first-century America—a significance increasingly afforded to trademarks throughout the world, for that matter. The rules of trademark and unfair competition law determine in large part whether Brooks' proposition is correct. And as you see trademark and unfair competition policy unfold throughout the book, you should also ask whether we adopt the appropriate (or an inappropriate) degree of reverence for brands.

In this introductory chapter, however, we will first consider the historical and constitutional foundations of trademark and unfair competition law, which will allow us an early discussion of the nature of trademark rights (a subject to which we will periodically return). Trademark rights have long been recognized and protected at common law in the United States, although most significant trademark law is now created at the federal level. Yet the United States Supreme Court's first major opinion on trademark law did not signal an auspicious beginning for federal protection.

THE TRADE-MARK CASES
100 U.S. 82 (1879)

Mr. Justice MILLER delivered the opinion of the Court:

The three cases whose titles stand at the head of this opinion are criminal prosecutions for violations of what is known as the trade-mark legislation of Congress. . . . In all of them the judges of the circuit courts in which they are pending have certified to a difference of opinion on what is substantially the same question; namely, are the acts of Congress on the subject of trade-marks founded on any rightful authority in the Constitution of the United States?

The entire legislation of Congress in regard to trade-marks is of very recent origin. It is first seen in sects. 77 to 84, inclusive, of the act of July 8, 1870, entitled "An Act to revise, consolidate, and amend the statutes relating to patents and copyrights." 16 Stat. 198. The part of this act relating to trade-marks is embodied in chap. 2, tit. 60, sects. 4937 to 4947, of the Revised Statutes.

It is sufficient at present to say that they provide for the registration in the Patent Office of any device in the nature of a trade-mark to which any person has by usage established an exclusive right, or which the person so registering intends to appropriate by that act to his exclusive use; and they make the wrongful use of a trade-mark, so registered, by any other person, without the owner's permission, a cause of action in a civil suit for damages. Six years later we have the act of Aug. 14, 1876 (19 Stat. 141), punishing by fine and imprisonment the fraudulent use, sale, and counterfeiting of trade-marks registered in pursuance of the statutes of the United States, on which the [cases before us are founded].

The right to adopt and use a symbol or a device to distinguish the goods or property made or sold by the person whose mark it is, to the exclusion of use by all other persons, has been long recognized by the common law and the chancery courts of England and of this country, and by the statutes of some of the States. It is a property right for the violation of which damages may be recovered in an action at law, and the continued violation of it will be enjoined by a court of equity, with compensation for past infringement. This exclusive right was not created by the act of Congress, and does not now depend upon it for its enforcement. The whole system of trade-mark property and the civil remedies for its protection existed long anterior to that act, and have remained in full force since its passage.

These propositions are so well understood as to require neither the citation of authorities nor an elaborate argument to prove them.

As the property in trade-marks and the right to their exclusive use rest on the laws of the States, and, like the great body of the rights of person and of property, depend on them for security and protection, the power of Congress to legislate on the subject, to establish the conditions on which these rights shall be enjoyed and exercised, the period of their duration, and the legal remedies for their enforcement, if such power exist at all, must be found in the Constitution of the United States, which is the source of all powers that Congress can lawfully exercise.

In the argument of these cases this seems to be conceded, and the advocates for the validity of the acts of Congress on this subject point to two clauses of the Constitution, in one or in both of which, as they assert, sufficient warrant may be found for this legislation.

The first of these is the eighth clause of sect. 8 of the first article. That section, manifestly intended to be an enumeration of the powers expressly granted to Congress, and closing with the declaration of a rule for the ascertainment of such powers as are necessary by way of implication to carry into efficient operation those expressly given, authorizes Congress, by the clause referred to, "to promote the progress of science and useful arts, by securing for limited times, to authors and inventors, the exclusive right to their respective writings and discoveries."

As the first and only attempt by Congress to regulate the *right of trade-marks* is to be found in the act of July 8, 1870, to which we have referred, entitled "Act to revise, consolidate, and amend the statutes relating to *patents* and *copyrights*," terms which have long since become technical, as referring, the one to inventions and the other to the writings of authors, it is a reasonable inference that this part of the statute also was, in the opinion of Congress, an exercise of the power found in that clause of the Constitution. It may also be safely assumed that until a critical examination of the subject in the courts became necessary, it was mainly if not wholly to this clause that the advocates of the law looked for its support.

Any attempt, however, to identify the essential characteristics of a trade-mark with inventions and discoveries in the arts and sciences, or with the writings of authors, will show that the effort is surrounded with insurmountable difficulties.

The ordinary trade-mark has no necessary relation to invention or discovery. The trade-mark recognized by the common law is generally the growth of a considerable period of use, rather than a sudden invention. It is often the result of accident rather than design, and when under the act of Congress it is sought to establish it by registration, neither originality, invention, discovery, science, nor art is in any way essential to the right conferred by that act. If we should endeavor to classify it under the head of writings of authors, the objections are equally strong. In this, as in regard to inventions, originality is required. And while the word *writings* may be liberally construed, as it has been, to include original designs for engravings, prints, etc., it is only such as are original, and are founded in the creative powers of the mind. The writings which are to be protected are *the fruits of intellectual labor*, embodied in the form of books, prints, engravings, and the like. The trade-mark may be, and generally is, the adoption of something already in existence as the distinctive symbol of the party using it. At common law the exclusive right to it grows out of its *use*, and not its mere adoption. By the act of Congress this exclusive right attaches upon registration. But in neither case does it depend upon novelty, invention, discovery, or any work of the brain. It requires no fancy or imagination, no genius, no laborious thought. It is simply founded on priority of appropriation. We look in vain in the statute for any other qualification or condition. If the symbol, however plain, simple, old, or well-known, has been first appropriated by the claimant as his distinctive trade-mark, he may by registration secure the right to its exclusive use. While such legislation may be a judicious aid to the common law on the subject of trade-marks, and may be within the competency of legislatures whose general powers embrace that class of subjects, we are unable to see any such power in the constitutional provision concerning authors and inventors, and their writings and discoveries.

The other clause of the Constitution supposed to confer the requisite authority on Congress is the third of the same section, which, read in connection with the granting clause, is as follows: "The Congress shall have power to regulate commerce with foreign nations, and among the several States, and with the Indian tribes."

The argument is that the use of a trade-mark—that which alone gives it any value—is to identify a particular class or quality of goods as the manufacture, produce, or property of the person who puts them in the general market for sale; that the sale of the article so distinguished is commerce; that the trade-mark is, therefore, a useful and valuable aid or instrument of commerce, and its regulation by virtue of the clause belongs to Congress, and that the act in question is a lawful exercise of this power.

Every species of property which is the subject of commerce, or which is used or even essential in commerce, is not brought by this clause within the control of Congress. . . .

The question . . . whether the trade-mark bears such a relation to commerce in general terms as to bring it within congressional control, when used or applied to the classes of commerce which fall within that control, is one which, in the present case, we propose to leave undecided. We adopt this course because when this court is called on in the course of the administration of the law to consider whether an act of Congress, or of any other department of the government, is within the constitutional authority of that department, a due respect for a co-ordinate branch of the government requires that we shall decide that it has transcended its powers only when that is so plain that we cannot avoid the duty. . . .

Governed by this view of our duty, we proceed to remark that a glance at the commerce clause of the Constitution discloses at once what has been often the subject of comment in this court and out of it, that the power of regulation there conferred on Congress is limited to commerce with foreign nations, commerce among the States, and commerce with the Indian tribes. While bearing in mind the liberal construction, that commerce with foreign nations means commerce between citizens of the United States and citizens and subjects of foreign nations, and commerce among the States means commerce between the individual citizens of different States, there still remains a very large amount of commerce, perhaps the largest, which, being trade or traffic between citizens of the same State, is beyond the control of Congress.

When, therefore, Congress undertakes to enact a law, which can only be valid as a regulation of commerce, it is reasonable to expect to find on the face of the law, or from its essential nature, that it is a regulation of commerce with foreign nations, or among the several States, or with the Indian tribes. If not so limited, it is in excess of the power of Congress. If its main purpose be to establish a regulation applicable to all trade, to commerce at all points, especially if it be apparent that it is designed to govern the commerce wholly between citizens of the same State, it is obviously the exercise of a power not confided to Congress.

We find no recognition of this principle in the chapter on trade-marks in the Revised Statutes. We would naturally look for this in the description of the class of persons who are entitled to register a trade-mark, or in reference to the goods to which it should be applied. If, for instance, the statute described persons engaged in a commerce between the different States, and related to the use of trade-marks in such commerce, it would be evident that Congress believed it was acting under the clause of the Constitution which authorizes it to regulate commerce among the States. So if, when the trade-mark has been registered, Congress had protected its use on goods sold by a citizen of one State to another, or by a citizen of a foreign State to a citizen of the United States, it would be seen that Congress was at least intending to exercise the power of regulation conferred by that clause of the Constitution. But no such idea is found or suggested in this statute. Its language is: "Any person or firm domiciled in the United States, and any corporation created by the United States, or of any State or Territory thereof," or any person residing in a foreign country which by treaty or convention affords similar privileges to our citizens, may by registration obtain protection for his trade-mark. There is no requirement that such person shall be engaged in the kind of commerce which Congress is authorized to regulate. It is a general declaration that anybody in the United States, and anybody in any other country which permits us to do the like, may, by registering a trade-mark, have it fully protected. So, while the person registering is required to furnish "a statement of the class of merchandise, and the particular description of the goods comprised in such class, by which the trade-mark has been or is intended to be appropriated," there is no hint that the goods are to be transported from one State to another, or between the United States and foreign countries. . . .

It is therefore manifest that no such distinction is found in the act, but that its broad purpose was to establish a universal system of trade-mark registration, for the benefit of all who had already used a trade-mark, or who wished to adopt one in the future, without regard to the character of the trade to which it was to be applied or the residence of the owner, with the solitary exception that those who resided in foreign countries which extended no such privileges to us were excluded from them here. . . .

While we have, in our references in this opinion to the trade-mark legislation of Congress, had mainly in view the act of 1870, and the civil remedy which that act provides, it was because the criminal offences described in the act of 1876 are, by their express terms, solely referable to frauds, counterfeits, and unlawful use of trade-marks which were registered under the provisions of the former act. If that act is unconstitutional, so that the registration under it confers no lawful right, then the criminal enactment intended to protect that right falls with it.

The questions in each of these cases being an inquiry whether these statutes can be upheld in whole or in part as valid and constitutional, must be answered in the negative; and it will be

So certified to the proper circuit courts.

HANOVER STAR MILLING CO. v. METCALF

240 U.S. 403 (1916)

Mr. Justice PITNEY delivered the opinion of the Court:

. . .

The redress that is accorded in trademark cases is based upon the party's right to be protected in the good will of a trade or business. The primary and proper function of a trademark is to identify the origin or ownership of the article to which it is affixed. Where a party has been in the habit of labeling his goods with a distinctive mark, so that purchasers recognize goods thus marked as being of his production, others are debarred from applying the same mark to goods of the same description, because to do so would in effect represent their goods to be of his production and would tend to deprive him of the profit he might make through the sale of the goods which the purchaser intended to buy. Courts afford redress or relief upon the ground that a party has a valuable interest in the good-will of his trade or business, and in the trade-marks adopted to maintain and extend it. The essence of the wrong consists in the sale of the goods of one manufacturer or vendor for those of another.

This essential element is the same in trade-mark cases as in cases of unfair competition unaccompanied with trade-mark infringement. In fact, the common law of trade-marks is but a part of the broader law of unfair competition. [cit.]

Common-law trade-marks, and the right to their exclusive use, are, of course, to be classed among property rights, *Trade-mark Cases*, 100 U.S. 82, 92, 93; but only in the sense that a man's right to the continued enjoyment of his trade reputation and the good-will that flows from it, free from unwarranted interference by others, is a property right, for the protection of which a trade-mark is an instrumentality. As was said in the same case (p. 94), the right grows out of use, not mere adoption. In the English courts it often has been said that there is no property whatever in a trade-mark, as such. [cit.] But since in the same cases the courts recognize the right of the party to the exclusive use of marks adopted to indicate goods of his manufacture, upon the ground that "A man is not to sell his own goods under the pretense that they are the goods of another man; he cannot be permitted to practise such a deception, nor to use the means which contribute to that end. He cannot therefore be allowed to use names, marks, letters, or other *indicia*, by which he may induce purchasers to believe, that the goods which he is selling are the manufacture of another person"; it is plain that in denying the right of property in a trade-mark it was intended only to deny such property right except as appurtenant to an established business or trade in connection with which the mark is used. This is evident from the expressions used in these and other English cases. Thus, in *Ainsworth v. Walmsley* L. R. 1 Eq. 518, 524, Vice Chancellor Sir Wm. Page Wood said: "This court has taken upon itself to protect a man in the use of a certain trade-mark as applied to a particular description of article. He has no property in that mark *per se*, any more than in any other fanciful denomination he may assume for his own private use, otherwise than with reference to his trade. If he does not carry on a trade in iron, but carries on a trade in linen, and stamps a lion on his linen, another person may stamp a lion on iron; but when he has appropriated a mark to a particular species of goods, and caused his goods to circulate with this mark upon them, the court has said that no one shall be at liberty to defraud that man by using that mark, and passing off goods of his manufacture as being the goods of the owner of that mark."

In short, the trade-mark is treated as merely a protection for the good-will, and not the subject of property except in connection with an existing business. The same rule prevails generally in this country, and is recognized in the decisions of this court. . . .

MISHAWAKA RUBBER & WOOLEN MFG. CO. v. S.S. KRESGE CO.

316 U.S. 203, 205 (1942)

The protection of trade-marks is the law's recognition of the psychological function of symbols. If it is true that we live by symbols, it is no less true that we purchase goods by them. A trade-mark is a merchandising short-cut which induces a purchaser to select what he wants, or what he has been led to believe he wants. The owner of a mark exploits this human propensity by making every effort to impregnate the atmosphere of the market with the drawing power of a congenial symbol. Whatever the means employed, the aim is the same—to convey through the mark, in the minds of potential customers, the desirability of the commodity upon which it appears. Once this is attained, the trade-mark owner has something of value. If another poaches upon the commercial magnetism of the symbol he has created, the owner can obtain legal redress. . . .

YALE ELECTRIC CORP. v. ROBERTSON

26 F.2d 972, 973-74 (2d Cir. 1928)

The law of unfair trade comes down very nearly to this—as judges have repeated again and again—that one merchant shall not divert customers from another by representing what he sells as emanating from the second. This has been, and perhaps even more now is, the whole Law and the Prophets on the subject, although it assumes many guises. . . . [An owner's] mark is his authentic seal; by it he vouches for the goods which bear it; it carries his name for good or ill. If another uses it, he borrows the owner's reputation, whose quality no longer lies within his own control. This is an injury, even though the borrower does not tarnish it, or divert any sales by its use; for a reputation, like a face, is the symbol of its possessor and creator, and another can use it only as a mask. And so it has come to be recognized that, unless the borrower's use is so foreign to the owner's as to insure against any identification of the two, it is unlawful. [cit.]

PRESTONETTES, INC. v. COTY

264 U.S. 359 (1924)

[Justice Holmes dealt with an allegation of trademark infringement arising from Prestonettes' use of the trademark COTY in label information on Prestonettes perfume and powder products. The label truthfully represented that COTY perfume was an ingredient in Prestonettes' products. Justice Holmes rejected the trademark infringement allegation.]

[W]hat new rights does the trade mark confer? It does not confer a right to prohibit the use of the word or words. It is not a copyright. . . . A trade mark only gives the right to prohibit the use of it so far as to protect the owner's good will against the sale of another's product as his. . . . When the mark is used in a way that does not deceive the public we see no such sanctity in the word as to prevent its being used to tell the truth. It is not taboo.

[Justice Holmes refused to accept the proposition that a trademark might confer on its owner the "naked right . . . to prohibit the defendant from making even a collateral reference to the [owner's] mark."]

NOTES AND QUESTIONS

1. *Trademark timeline.* Congress took the hint offered by the Supreme Court in *The Trade-Mark Cases.* Subsequent trademark legislation, most prominently the Act of 1905 and the 1946 Lanham Act, extended federal trademark protection only to marks used in interstate commerce. The Lanham Act contained important innovations, but was in many important respects a codification of state common law trademark principles. *See* Robert C. Denicola, *Some Thoughts on the Dynamics of Federal Trademark Legislation and the Trademark Dilution Act of 1995,* 59 Law & Contemp. Probs. 75, 79-80 (1996) ("Putting aside statutory innovations directly linked to the public notice provided by the Act's registration system, the Lanham Act codifie[d] the basic common law principles governing both the subject matter and scope of protection."). The Lanham Act remains the basic trademark statute today, though it has been amended since 1946 on several occasions. Although many of these amendments were in the nature of technical amendments, some were extremely significant. We will encounter them throughout the casebook. The most comprehensive reform of the Lanham Act occurred in 1988, with the Trademark Law Revision Act of 1988 (effective November 16, 1989), which substantially revised trademark registration procedures. In 1995, Congress created a federal cause of action for dilution of trademarks, codified in Section 43(c) and discussed in Chapter 8, *infra.* One notable feature of much recent legislative activity has been the influence of international obligations in bringing about these reforms (indeed, this motivation also influenced some provisions of the original Lanham Act). Changes were made to the Lanham Act in 1993 to implement the North American Free Trade Agreement (NAFTA), in 1994 to implement the Agreement on Trade-Related Aspects of Intellectual Property (the TRIPS Agreement), in 1998 to implement the Trademark Law Treaty (the TLT), and in 2002 to implement the Madrid Protocol Concerning the International Registration of Marks. Much commercial activity is now international, especially where that activity occurs online, and thus international trademark law has become extremely important. It remains a cardinal premise of international trademark law, however, that, despite the internationalization of commerce, trademark rights remain territorial in nature. French trademark rights, for example, must be acquired and maintained separately from U.S. rights, although international trademark agreements attempt in a number of ways to reduce the difficulties that flow from separate national rights. This book incorporates international developments throughout all the topics that we discuss. A fuller trademark timeline appears as Figure 1-1, *infra* page 39.

2. *The Lanham Act as codified.* The Lanham Act is reproduced in its current form in the Statutory Supplement to this book. There are two standard ways to refer to Lanham Act provisions: either by their Lanham Act section designations (e.g., Lanham Act §32) or by their corresponding U.S. Code section designations (e.g., 15 U.S.C. §1114). In this book, we use both types of section designation.

3. *Federal law and state law.* Most of the cases in this book relate to federal trademark law. But unlike copyright and patent law, where Congress has preempted state law, state trademark and unfair competition law does exist. *See* Mark P. McKenna, *Trademark Law's Faux Federalism, in* Intellectual Property and Common Law (Balganesh ed., Camb. Univ. Press, 2013). And in several ways it has been influential: Until the Federal Trademark Dilution Protection Act of 1995, for example, trademark owners would bring confusion-based infringement claims under federal law and dilution claims under state laws (over half the states had dilution laws). *See* Chapter 8 *infra.* And, publicity rights are accorded by state, rather than federal, law. *See* Chapter 11, section B, *infra.* But most principles of substantive state trademark law are consistent with principles being developed under federal law. We identify in the book the most significant areas of difference.

4. *The triadic structure of the mark.* Professor Barton Beebe has suggested that trademarks have a "triadic structure":

> Though perhaps not altogether consciously, trademark commentary has traditionally conceived of the trademark as a three-legged stool, consisting of a signifier (the perceptible form of the mark), a signified (the semantic content of the mark, such as the goodwill or affect to which the signifier refers), and a referent (the product or service . . . to which the mark refers). . . .
>
> [Beebe describes the "triadic structure of the mark" as follows.] First, the trademark must take the form of a "tangible symbol." When courts speak of the trademark as, in the Third Circuit's lexicon, a "signifier of origin" . . . they mean to refer specifically to the perceptible form of the mark. Some courts use the more general term "symbol." Second, the trademark must be used in commerce to refer to goods or services. These goods or services constitute the trademark's referent. . . . Third and finally, the trademark must "identify and distinguish" its referent. Typically, it does so by identifying the referent with a specific source and that source's goodwill. This source and its goodwill constitute the trademark's signified.
>
> The triadic structure is also apparent in the syntax of trademark talk, which tends to refer to a signifier x for a referent y (e.g., the trademark "FORD for cars" or the trademark "ACE for hardware, but not for bandages") and, in doing so, implies the existence of a third, unmentioned variable, z, the source of the product and the goodwill associated with that source.

Barton Beebe, *The Semiotic Account of Trademark Doctrine and Trademark Culture, in* TRADEMARK LAW AND THEORY: A HANDBOOK OF CONTEMPORARY RESEARCH 45-47 (Dinwoodie & Janis eds., 2008). Is this account consistent with the characterization of trademarks in the preceding excerpts from judicial opinions?

5. *The nature of trademarks.* In *The Trade-Mark Cases*, the Supreme Court commented that trademark rights were "a property right for the violation of which damages may be recovered in an action at law." What about trademarks makes them "property"? What is it that trademark rights are protecting? Is there any significance to calling trademarks "property"? Doctrinally? Rhetorically? *See* Lionel Bently, *From Communication to Thing: Historical Aspects of the Conceptualization of Trademarks as Property, in* TRADEMARK LAW AND THEORY: A HANDBOOK OF CONTEMPORARY RESEARCH 3 (Dinwoodie & Janis eds., 2008) (questioning the rhetorical strength of the "property" label in explaining expansion of trademark rights).

6. *The role of registration.* In *The Trade-Mark Cases*, the Court notes that "this exclusive right was not created by the act of Congress, and does not now depend upon it for its enforcement." That is, in the United States, trademark rights exist at common law. Registration is an important part of trademark law, which we will discuss in Chapter 5. But trademark rights may exist without registration. Indeed, the substantive rights afforded to an unregistered trademark owner under Section 43(a) of the Lanham Act (such an action for infringement of an unregistered trademark is often denominated as an action for "unfair competition") are largely coextensive with those available to the owner of a registered mark bringing a trademark infringement action under Section 32 of the Lanham Act. *See* S. Rep. No. 79-1333, at 4 (1946). And causes of action more recently enacted under Section 43(c) (dilution) and Section 43(d) (against cybersquatting) are available to protect registered and unregistered marks alike. Whether the protection of unregistered marks *should* be the same as that afforded registered marks under the Lanham Act is an important question, however. The possibility that marks denied registration by virtue of statutory prohibitions might still have protection under the common law (enforced via Section 43(a)) is considered further in Chapter 5.

7. *Criminal law.* Although *The Trade-Mark Cases* involved a criminal indictment under trademark legislation, most (indeed, almost all) of the cases that we will study involve civil liability. In what circumstances and for what reasons might you expect the criminal law to address the use of trademarks?

NOTE: TRADEMARKS . . . AND COPYRIGHTS AND PATENTS

As the Court explained in *The Trade-Mark Cases*, the other principal pieces of federal intellectual property legislation have been enacted pursuant to Article I, Section 1, Clause 8 (the Copyright and Patent Clause) of the United States Constitution. Both copyrights and patents are rights granted in order to incentivize creative and innovative conduct (and investment therein). While these rights thus benefit the authors and inventors who own the copyrights and patents, respectively, the ultimate purpose of copyright and patent law is public access to a richer and more diverse array of creative products. A central dilemma in both copyright and patent law is how much protection is required to provide sufficient incentive to create without unduly restricting public access.

Copyright protection initially attached to maps, charts, and books, but now extends to "original works of authorship fixed in a tangible medium of expression." Most notably, paintings, motion pictures, music, audio recordings, software, and plays are also protected by copyright. To obtain protection, the works must be original; this is, however, a very low standard. The work must simply be independently created and display a minimal degree of creativity. *See Feist Pub. v. Rural Tel. Serv. Co., Inc.*, 499 U.S. 340, 345 (1991). Even if the work passes this threshold and receives protection, that protection extends only to the expression in the work, not to the ideas contained therein. This elusive distinction between ideas and expression is extremely important in ensuring, among other things, that copyright does not impede the freedom of expression of third parties or provide the author of a work with a monopoly on a basic idea.

Although copyright comes into being automatically upon fixation in a tangible medium, it typically lasts only for the life of the author plus seventy years. Copyrights are awarded in the first instance to the author of the work, who according to the U.S. Supreme Court, "as a general rule, . . . [is] the party who actually creates the work." *Cmty. for Creative Non-Violence v. Reid*, 490 U.S. 730, 737 (1989). Where a work is created by an employee within the scope of his or her employment, the employer is treated as the author and owns the copyright. This so-called work for hire doctrine also confers authorship status on persons who commission another party to create certain types of copyrighted work. The copyright can, in any event, be transferred. The copyright owner, whether the author or a subsequent owner, is accorded the exclusive right to make copies of the work, prepare adaptations of the work, distribute copies of the work to the public, or publicly perform or display the work.

Although U.S. copyright law traditionally required the owner to register the work and to include a copyright notice on any copies of the work distributed to the public, these requirements (so-called copyright formalities) were abolished in 1989 with the entry into effect of the Berne Convention Implementation Act. International copyright law (as embodied in the Berne Convention for the Protection of Literary and Artistic Works) forbids the availability of copyright being conditioned on compliance with formalities. There remain good reasons for the copyright owner to place a copyright notice on copies of its work, and registration is a prerequisite for U.S. authors seeking to bring an infringement action. But neither notice nor registration is strictly relevant to the existence of the copyright.

Patents are granted to the inventor of innovative technology. As in copyright, the subject matter that is potentially patentable now has few limits. Patents are granted for subject matter ranging from software to biotechnology to drugs to mechanical inventions to processes. Like copyrights, patent rights are limited in duration (indeed, the Copyright and Patent Clause requires that copyright and patent rights are "for limited times"). Patents exist for twenty years from the date of the filing of the patent application. But patent rights only arise upon issuance of a patent, which requires application to the Patent and Trademark Office, and the process from application to issuance ordinarily takes eighteen months or more.

Patents are more exclusive than copyrights in two different ways. First, to obtain a patent, the applicant must show that its invention is novel, nonobvious, and useful, as well as comply with a variety of statutory disclosure requirements; it is therefore a right less readily conferred than copyright, for which the originality threshold is quite low. Second, however, the rights that the successful patentee acquires are far broader (the exclusive right to make, sell, use, offer for sale, or import the claimed invention) than those obtained by the copyright owner. The precise scope of rights that the patent owner obtains is determined by the invention that is claimed in the patent (in a part of the patent document called, perhaps obviously, "the claims"). Thus, the patentee (or his lawyer) has the capacity greatly to affect the rights that the patentee acquires.

We will return to the differences between copyright and patent, on the one hand, and trademark rights, on the other hand, in Chapters 2 and 3. *See also* Figure 1-2, *infra* page 40. As subject matter increasingly is susceptible to protection under two or more regimes, regulating that overlap has become important. *See generally Bonito Boats, Inc. v. Thunder Craft Boats, Inc.*, 489 U.S. 141 (1989); *Dastar v. Twentieth Century Fox Film Corp.*, 539 U.S. 23 (2003).

B. THE NATURE OF UNFAIR COMPETITION LAW

As the *Hanover Star Milling* Court suggested, historically, in the United States, trademark protection has existed as an important aspect of a larger body of law, namely unfair competition law: It is unfair competition to pass off your goods as those of another producer by using a trademark confusingly similar to that of the other producer. But unfair competition law might, under certain conceptions of that body of law, extend far more broadly than trademark infringement.

INTERNATIONAL NEWS SERVICE v. ASSOCIATED PRESS

248 U.S. 215 (1918)

Mr. Justice PITNEY:

[Associated Press (AP) published news reports in early editions of newspapers on the East Coast. International News Service (INS), a competitor in the gathering and distribution of news, copied the AP reports and relayed them to its member newspapers in the Midwest and on the West Coast, who occasionally received the reports even before West Coast newspapers with whom AP had a relationship. AP sought an injunction prohibiting INS from "copying news from . . . early editions of complainant's newspapers and selling this, either bodily or after rewriting it, to [its] customers." A majority of the Supreme Court upheld the grant of a preliminary injunction prohibiting the defendant from distributing or publishing AP's reports for the short period of time necessary to avoid appropriation of the commercial value of the reports.]

Defendant [INS] insists that when, with the sanction and approval of complainant [AP], and as the result of the use of its news for the very purpose for which it is distributed, a portion of complainant's members communicate it to the general public by posting it upon bulletin boards so that all may read, or by issuing it to newspapers and distributing it indiscriminately, complainant no longer has the right to control the use to be made of it; that when it thus reaches the light of day it becomes the common possession of all to whom it is accessible; and that any purchaser of a newspaper has the right to communicate the intelligence which it contains to anybody and for any purpose, even for the purpose of selling it for profit to newspapers published for profit in competition with complainant's members.

The fault in the reasoning lies in applying as a test the right of the complainant as against the public, instead of considering the rights of complainant and defendant, competitors in business, as between themselves. The right of the purchaser of a single newspaper to spread knowledge of its contents gratuitously, for any legitimate purpose not unreasonably interfering with complainant's right to make merchandise of it, may be admitted; but to transmit that news for commercial use, in competition with complainant—which is what defendant has done and seeks to justify—is a very different matter. In doing this defendant, by its very act, admits that it is taking material that has been acquired by complainant as the result of organization and the expenditure of labor, skill, and money, and which is salable by complainant for money, and that defendant in appropriating it and selling it as its own is endeavoring to reap where it has not sown, and by disposing of it to newspapers that are competitors of complainant's members is appropriating to itself the harvest of those who have sown. Stripped of all disguises, the process amounts to an unauthorized interference with the normal operation of complainant's legitimate business precisely at the point where the profit is to be reaped, in order to divert a material portion of the profit from those who have earned it to those who have not; with special advantage to defendant in the competition because of the fact that it is not burdened with any part of the expense of gathering the news. The transaction speaks for itself and a court of equity ought not to hesitate long in characterizing it as unfair competition in business.

The underlying principle is much the same as that which lies at the base of the equitable theory of consideration in the law of trusts—that he who has fairly paid the price should have the beneficial use of the property. [cit.] It is no answer to say that complainant spends its money for that which is too fugitive or evanescent to be the subject of property. That might, and for the purposes of the discussion we are assuming that it would, furnish an answer in a common-law controversy. But in a court of equity, where the question is one of unfair competition, if that which complainant has acquired fairly at substantial cost may be sold fairly at substantial profit, a competitor who is misappropriating it for the purpose of disposing of it to his own profit and to the disadvantage of complainant cannot be heard to say that it is too fugitive or evanescent to be regarded as property. It has all the attributes of property necessary for determining that a misappropriation of it by a competitor is unfair competition because contrary to good conscience. . . .

It is to be observed that the view we adopt does not result in giving to complainant the right to monopolize either the gathering or the distribution of the news, or, without complying with the copyright act, to prevent the reproduction of its news articles; but only postpones participation by complainant's competitor in the processes of distribution and reproduction of news that it has not gathered, and only to the extent necessary to prevent that competitor from reaping the fruits of complainant's efforts and expenditure, to the partial exclusion of complainant and in violation of the principle that underlies the maxim *sic utere tuo*, etc.

It is said that the elements of unfair competition are lacking because there is no attempt by defendant to palm off its goods as those of the complainant, characteristic of the most familiar, if not the most typical, cases of unfair competition. [cit.] But we cannot concede that the right to equitable relief is confined to that class of cases. In the present case the fraud upon complainant's rights is more direct and obvious. Regarding news matter as the mere material from which these two competing parties are endeavoring to make money, and treating it, therefore, as *quasi* property for the purposes of their business because they are both selling it as such, defendant's conduct differs from the ordinary case of unfair competition in trade principally in this that, instead of selling its own goods as those of complainant, it substitutes misappropriation in the place of misrepresentation, and sells complainant's goods as its own.

DASTAR CORP. v. TWENTIETH CENTURY FOX FILM CORP.

539 U.S. 23 (2003)

The Lanham Act was intended to make "actionable the deceptive and misleading use of marks," and "to protect persons engaged in . . . commerce against unfair competition." 15 U.S.C. §1127. While much of the Lanham Act addresses the registration, use, and infringement of trademarks and related marks, §43(a), 15 U.S.C. §1125(a) is one of the few provisions that goes beyond trademark protection. As originally enacted, §43(a) created a federal remedy against a person who used in commerce either "a false designation of origin, or any false description or representation" in connection with "any goods or services." 60 Stat. 441. As the Second Circuit accurately observed with regard to the original enactment, however—and as remains true after the 1988 revision—§43(a) "does not have boundless application as a remedy for unfair trade practices," *Alfred Dunhill, Ltd. v. Interstate Cigar Co.*, 499 F.2d 232, 237 (1974). "[B]ecause of its inherently limited wording, §43(a) can never be a federal 'codification' of the overall law of 'unfair competition,'" 4 J. McCarthy, Trademarks and Unfair Competition §27:7, p. 27-14 (4th ed. 2002), but can apply only to certain unfair trade practices prohibited by its text.

NOTES AND QUESTIONS

1.   INS *as the foundation for a dynamic law of unfair competition.* The language, if not the narrow holding, of the *INS* majority opinion by Mr. Justice Pitney appears capable of sustaining a very broad range of unfair competition claims. But you will find that *INS* is rarely invoked successfully in modern litigation. *But see Associated Press v. All Headline News Corp.*, 608 F. Supp. 2d 454 (S.D.N.Y. 2009) (permitting a claim for misappropriation of "hot news" to proceed under New York common law where the defendant's dissemination of reports of breaking news to its subscribers involved copying news reports prepared by the Associated Press, removing the identification of the Associated Press as author, and distributing the story under the defendant's banner). Most of the cases in this book that involve claims denominated as "unfair competition" will in fact be actions for infringement of unregistered marks brought under Section 43(a) of the Lanham Act; these are frequently referred to as actions for "unfair competition" or "infringement of unregistered trademarks" or "common law trademark infringement." (When unfair competition actions are essentially actions for infringement of an unregistered trademark, the elements of the cause of action are largely the same as in an action for infringement of a

registered trademark under Section 32.) As *Dastar* illustrates, although unfair competition law encompasses more than what is traditionally thought of as trademark infringement, U.S. unfair competition law has not, at least under Section 43(a) of the Lanham Act, moved far beyond trademark-like claims. This stands in contrast to unfair competition law in many foreign, especially civil law, jurisdictions, where courts have used unfair competition claims to provide relief in a much wider range of competitive contexts. Why do you think U.S. law has been so cautious in this regard?

2.   *Unfair competition law: defining the tort.* Why did the *INS* Court find that the defendant's conduct amounted to unfair competition? What limiting condition, if any, is there in the Court's reasoning? Section 43(a) is the principal provision of the Lanham Act designed to protect against acts of unfair competition. In the excerpt from *Dastar*, what limits does the Court place on actions for unfair competition under Section 43(a)? We will read the *Dastar* opinion in full in Chapter 2. Although the Court's opinion is somewhat ambiguous, you will discover there that the Court arguably suggests two other limiting rationales on unfair competition actions: First, certain actions for unfair competition under Section 43(a) should not be recognized where they would conflict with provisions of copyright law; and, second, certain actions for unfair competition under Section 43(a) should not be recognized where they would allow plaintiffs to circumvent limits imposed by other Supreme Court case law on causes of action for trademark infringement. Do these different limiting rationales make sense? Should a trademark possibly receive a different scope of protection under the unfair competition provisions of the Lanham Act than under the formal infringement provisions? Despite a growing assimilation of the scope of trademark infringement and federal unfair competition protection under Section 43(a)(1)(A), courts continue to find room for claims under Section 43(a)(1)(A) that do not involve trademark infringement proper. *See, e.g., Schlotzsky's, Ltd. v. Sterling Purchasing & Nat'l Distribution Co., Inc.*, 520 F.3d 393 (5th Cir. 2008). Review Section 43(a)(1)(A). What "unfair trade practices" referenced by the *Dastar* Court might fall within the statutory proscription notwithstanding that they do not involve trademark infringement proper?

3.   *The relationship between trademark and unfair competition laws.* As suggested in note 1 above, the elements of the cause of action that is called "unfair competition" (but is in substance a claim for infringement of an unregistered trademark) are largely the same as in an action for infringement of a registered trademark. The effect of that proposition has been largely to assimilate the two causes of action. Yet, there have been recent indications that some courts might approach an unfair competition claim under Section 43(a) of the Lanham Act differently than a claim for infringement of a registered trademark under Section 32. For example, in *Belmora LLC v. Bayer Consumer Care AG*, 819 F.3d 697 (4th Cir. 2016), excerpted in Chapter 6, the Court of Appeals for the Fourth Circuit noted that "[]it is important to emphasize that this is an unfair competition case, not a trademark infringement case," and vacated the decision of the lower court because it had "conflated the Lanham Act's infringement provision in §32 . . . with unfair competition claims pled in this case under §43(a)." As you proceed, you should be alert to the possibility that unfair competition actions under Section 43(a) might—or perhaps should—be more clearly distinct from an action for infringement of a registered mark under Section 32, and consider the consequences of such an approach.

4.   *Trademark and unfair competition law: the values.* The broader tort of unfair competition is impossible to define in the abstract with any degree of precision. Its outer boundaries are set not only by concerns of consumer protection but also by notions of commercial morality, and these considerations inevitably infuse trademark law. As you read the cases throughout this book, consider the values that appear to be influencing courts' determinations. Are they "trademark values" or some other set of values? Are "trademark

values" different from "unfair competition" values? *See* Mark P. McKenna, *The Normative Foundations of Trademark Law*, 82 NOTRE DAME L. REV. 1839 (2007) (suggesting that protecting producers against diversion of trade, rather than protecting consumers against confusion per se, motivated the historical development of trademark law). *But cf.* César Ramirez-Montes, *A Re-Examination of the Original Foundations of Anglo-American Trademark Law*, 14 MARQ. INTELL. PROP. L. REV. 91 (2010) (arguing that the original purpose of early trademark law was to balance the interests of consumers and producers).

C.   PURPOSES OF TRADEMARK LAW

In the United States, two primary justifications have traditionally been offered in support of trademark protection: to "protect the public so that it may be confident that, in purchasing a product bearing a particular trademark which it favorably knows, it will get the product which it asks for and wants to get"; and to ensure that "where the owner of a trademark has spent energy, time, and money in presenting to the public the product, he is protected in his investment from its misappropriation by pirates and cheats." S. Rep. No. 1333, 79th Cong., 2d Sess. 3 (1946). In recent years, as trademark law has expanded in reach, scholars have renewed discussion of the theoretical basis for, and public policies underlying, trademark rights. Law and economics scholars have explicitly grounded trademark protection in economic efficiency, and these arguments have resonated with many courts, including the U.S. Supreme Court. *See Qualitex Co. v. Jacobson Prods. Co.*, 514 U.S. 159, 163-64 (1995).

Section 45 of the Lanham Act, the principal statute in the field, contains a statement of purpose. It provides that "the intent of this chapter is to regulate commerce within the control of Congress by making actionable the deceptive and misleading use of marks in such commerce; to protect registered marks used in such commerce from interference by State, or territorial legislation; to protect persons engaged in such commerce against unfair competition; to prevent fraud and deception in such commerce by the use of reproductions, copies, counterfeits, or colorable imitations of registered marks; and to provide rights and remedies stipulated by treaties and conventions respecting trademarks, trade names, and unfair competition entered into between the United States and foreign nations."

DANIEL M. McCLURE, TRADEMARKS AND COMPETITION: THE RECENT HISTORY*

59 Law & Contemp. Probs. 13, 28-33 (1996)

Trademark infringement cases have shown the slow evolution of legal doctrine since the 1970s. As trademark law matures and as the courts develop precedent interpreting the Lanham Act, established legal doctrines tend to take on a certain sanctity. Thus, "likelihood of confusion" between two marks by consumers has become the hallmark concept litigated in trademark infringement cases. Likewise, in determining the initial validity of a trademark, the traditional trademark legal doctrine [*see* Chapter 2, *infra*] assessing marks as generic/descriptive/suggestive/arbitrary has not changed substantially. However, because such decisions concentrate so heavily on the facts of a particular case, and because this legal doctrine tends to become formalistic and conceptualistic, there is much room for judicial discretion. As legal realism has taught us, judicial discretion is exercised within the context of broader political and intellectual trends of the times. Therefore, as society and the courts

---

have become more politically conservative, the trend in infringement cases has been toward greater protection for trademarks within the general doctrinal confines of the Lanham Act. The theoretical underpinning for expanded protection has been the economic theories of the Chicago School.

Just as the Chicago School theorists have come to dominate thinking in antitrust law, so has the Chicago School influenced the development of basic trademark law. Even though many courts do not explicitly assess economic issues in deciding trademark cases,[106] the Chicago School approach has had an undeniable impact on trademark cases across the board. In most instances, that impact has been supportive of existing trademark legal doctrine and trademark protection generally.

The approach of the Chicago School to trademarks was reflected judicially in two Seventh Circuit opinions in 1985 authored by two judges who are leaders of the Chicago School, Judges Frank Easterbrook and Richard Posner. In the first case, *Scandia Down* [*Corp. v. Euroquilt, Inc.*, 772 F.2d 1423 (7th Cir. 1985), *cert. denied*, 475 U.S. 1147 (1986),] Judge Easterbrook took the opportunity to describe succinctly the economic benefit that the Chicago School sees in trademarks:

> Trademarks help consumers to select goods. By identifying the source of the goods, they convey valuable information to consumers at lower costs. Easily identified trademarks reduce the costs consumers incur in searching for what they desire, and the lower the costs of search the more competitive the market. A trademark also may induce the supplier of goods to make higher quality products and to adhere to a consistent level of quality.

In *Scandia*, the Seventh Circuit explained aspects of traditional trademark doctrine in economic terms. The first issue addressed by the Court was whether the words "Down Shop[pe]" used with Scandia's logo of a goose was "merely descriptive" [of the plaintiff's down products shop] (in which case protection would be denied) or "arbitrary" or "suggestive" (in which case Scandia's mark would be protected). The Seventh Circuit sided with Scandia and affirmed the lower court's assessment of the evidence that the mark was protectable. The second issue in the case was whether the trademark of the competitor, Euroquilt, was "confusingly similar" to Scandia's trademark. Again, the Seventh Circuit affirmed the trial court's determination of likelihood of confusion. Significantly, Judge Easterbrook analyzed these issues in economic terms: "Confusingly similar marks make consumers' task in searching for products harder." Judge Easterbrook drew the comparison to antitrust cases "where retailers may try to take a free ride on the services provided by their rivals." By enjoining trademark infringement, the "free rider" effect could be prevented. However, Judge Easterbrook emphasized that a trademark holder could not obtain rights to merely descriptive words because that would constitute "a free ride on the language."

. . .

---

106. The Restatement has recognized the general principle that trademark infringement actions are an exception to the general principle of non-liability for injury caused by one competitor as a result of free competition and that trademark law requires a balancing of the public interest:

> The rules governing the protection of trademarks must also be responsive to the public interest in fostering vigorous competition. In defining protectable subject matter and in delineating the scope of exclusive rights, the law cannot neglect the legitimate interest of other competitors. In some cases the recognition of exclusive rights in favor of a particular seller may undermine the ability of other sellers to communicate useful information to consumers or deprive competitors of access to product features necessary for effective competition.

Restatement (Third) of Unfair Competition §1 cmt. e (1995).

In *W.T. Rogers* [*Co. v. Keene*, 778 F.2d 334 (7th Cir. 1985),] Judge Posner announced that "competition is not impaired by giving each manufacturer a perpetual 'monopoly' of his identifying mark" if he has chosen a "distinctive" trademark where the available names are "for all practical purposes infinite." Judge Posner noted that "generic" names are not subject to trademark protection because the manufacturer there "is trying to monopolize a scarce input, for there usually are only one or two words in common usage to describe a given product (such as 'car' and 'automobile'). . . ."

Significantly, these Chicago School judicial opinions purport to expressly reject a formalistic or conceptualistic approach to trademark protection. Although finding in favor of protection and essentially justifying pre-existing legal doctrines, the Seventh Circuit took pains to avoid reaching a decision deductively from the concepts and language familiar to trademark lawyers. In its place, the Seventh Circuit applied a very pragmatic economic analysis.

> We have said before that "arbitrary," "suggestive," and the other words in the vocabulary of trademark law may confuse more readily than they illuminate . . . , a caution litigants should take seriously before arguing cases so that everything turns on which word we pick. It is better to analyze trademark cases in terms of the functions of trademarks. . . .

These Chicago School judicial decisions have been accompanied by a series of journal articles in support of the economic theory of trademark protection. The most influential articles, *The Economics of Trademark Law* and *Trademark Law: An Economic Perspective*, were by two of the leading lights of the Chicago School, William Landes and Richard Posner. The appeal of the Chicago School economic theory is that it has the capacity to provide an all-encompassing and unifying approach to virtually every legal issue in trademark law. The function of trademark law is reduced to a single goal of economic efficiency to maximize wealth. Much of existing trademark legal doctrine can then be "explained" in terms of the economic function of trademarks. This economic approach places less emphasis on other ideas that have historically been viewed as animating goals of trademark law, such as commercial morality, preventing consumer deception, and protecting a trademark owner's business goodwill from misappropriation. The Chicago School approach purports to subsume these varied ideas in a single economic theory.

NOTES AND QUESTIONS

1. *The convergence of the dual purposes of trademark law.* As you read the cases throughout the book, consider how these separate interests—of the purchasing public and of producers—are each served by classical trademark protection. When might these interests diverge? As we proceed through the course, you should periodically revisit the question whether modern trademark law developments are driven to a greater or lesser extent by divergent consumer and producer interests (and which should triumph, if they conflict).

2. *Alternatives to trademark law.* If trademark protection did not exist, how might these goals of providing consumers with information regarding products and encouraging the production of quality products be pursued? Are these goals that are worthy of pursuit? Would the alternative mechanisms be superior?

D.   MODERN MARKETING AND TRADEMARK LAW

An awareness of popular culture and contemporary consumer experiences (that is, some sense of context) is relevant to an appreciation of trademark and unfair competition law.

Courts and scholars have long debated how trademark law should adapt to the changing social and economic role of trademarks in contemporary society. In recent times, they have sought to address how legal principles can or should take account of the broader communicative significance of trademarks in an increasingly image-conscious culture. Likewise, the means by which the commercial value of trademarks is exploited have multiplied, and the enhanced value of trademarks has prompted some to frame discussion of trademarks in terms of "property" rights rather than consumer protection. As we saw above, this might challenge traditional understandings of trademark rights in the United States.

JERRE B. SWANN, DILUTION REDEFINED FOR THE YEAR 2002

92 Trademark Rep. 585, 586-618 (2002) *

II.   THE TRANSITION OF BRANDS FROM AN AGRICULTURAL TO AN INDUSTRIAL ECONOMY

For much of this country's history there was little need for trademarks. . . . While the industrial revolution had begun in this country early in the Nineteenth Century, the economy as of the 1870s was still principally agrarian, and it was still cheaper to make than to buy many goods. Many families were thus units of production, not of consumption, and because the distance between a product and its guarantor typically was small, trademarks were not reputational requirements (proxies for personal proximity). Everyone knew the only two blacksmiths in town, and even products imported into the community were locally certified—the country store owner, not Nabisco (or then "Uneeda"), stood behind the crackers in the barrel.

In the late Nineteenth Century, however, the nation experienced huge gains in productivity from the advent of the electric motor and of railroads, and between 1870 and 1920, the percentages of total urban population, and of the workforce engaged in agriculture, dramatically reversed themselves.

> "On or about December 1910," Virginia Woolf once said, "human character changed." This hyperbole contains a kernel of truth. Around the turn of the century a fundamental cultural transformation occurred. . . . [Whereas] the older culture [had been] suited to a production-oriented society of small entrepreneurs[,] the newer culture epitomized a consumption-oriented society dominated by [large] corporations.

What were then principally manufacturer marks, and what trademark lawyers would call source marks, emerged: e.g., Kodak and Kraft. As the distance between promisor and product grew, consumers turned to a species—Pillsbury or Hormel—as the guarantor of a genus of goods, flour or ham. . . .

III.   THE ADVENT OF THE INFORMATION AGE

[W]e have entered a new age, the Age of Information, leaving behind the industrial revolution and its source/quality based brands. More "information," indeed, has been

---

* Copyright 2002, Jerre B. Swann; International Trademark Association.

produced in the last 30 years than in the previous 5000, and in such an environment, brands have become among the most powerful communicators in our vocabulary.

Few strong brands today have source- and quality-limited messages. TIDE, CHEER and IVORY SNOW do not identify different detergent manufacturers—they all, in fact, come from Procter & Gamble—and each transmits not a general, but a specific and very different cleaning signal—TIDE "is so powerful, it cleans down to the fiber," CHEER is for all temperatures and IVORY SNOW is "99 and 44/100ths percent pure and thus mild for baby clothes." Each has its own distinct image.

There are still "manufacturer" brands that, technically, remain engaged in source/quality genus/species competition: consumers, e.g., buy soup from CAMPBELL'S. That name, however, now connotes more than just one company's liquid consumable—it means (in the consumer's mind, in fact, owns), "M'm! M'm! Good!" COKE no longer merely sells cola; COKE sells refreshment. KODAK no longer merely sells film; KODAK sells a "Kodak moment." CAMPBELL'S, COKE and KODAK are promises, not as to a producer, but as to the fulfillment of a perception; strong, singular brands today are trustmarks, not as to source, but as to sensation.

In the information age, many products and sources have merged into brands that generate immediate mental images. Today, we instantly know what to expect from ABSOLUT, BUDWEISER and GALLO.

> Consumers are richer today (and can proceed with greater efficiency and confidence) in the presence of CAMAY, JOY, SECRET and SURE than if confronted by P&G bar soap and liquid soap, and P&G deodorant for women and for men.

Today, many strong, singular trademarks are "integrated holistic experiences."

In an information age, even more than in earlier times, consumers adopt and use the "shortest, simplest word" that will call to mind a product they want to talk about, and modern marks have become hugely informative "data clusters" that "reduce [to a minimum a] customer's costs of shopping and making purchasing decisions." Brands may give us a positive inkling as to a proprietor[58] or a premier provenance,[59] but modern trademarks are equally or more likely to convey, among a multitude of other messages, personality,[60] purpose,[61] performance,[62] preparation,[63] properties,[64] price,[65] position[66] and panache.[67] "A unique brand name and cohesive brand identity are probably the most powerful pieces of information for consumers," and a single brand can communicate product attributes and imagery, user and usage imagery, and functional, experiential and symbolic benefits. Amid, indeed, a compulsion to achieve economies, I submit that few plants operate as efficiently in producing goods, as do strong brands in telling about them.

---

58. JEEP® is a trademark of the DaimlerChrysler Corporation.
59. JACK DANIELS is Tennessee sippin' whiskey.
60. SONY is innovative.
61. GATORADE replaces fluids.
62. CREST fights cavities.
63. COKE has secret ingredients.
64. VOLVO is safe.
65. MOTEL 6 is economical.
66. DOMINOS means delivery.
67. RITZ CARLTON is luxurious.

In the information age, consumers even use brands to convey information about themselves.

"Many persons purchase branded goods for the purpose of demonstrating to others that they are consumers of the particular goods"—in other words, to impress others. . . . They advertise themselves (much as sellers of goods advertise the goods) by wearing clothes, jewelry, or accessories that tell the world that they are people of refined . . . taste or high income.

A brand that today only denotes source and quality is thus often lacking in added attributes or content that consumers now want, demand and need.

In the information age, brands have become, quite simply, the most consumer friendly symbols in our society. Not only do they communicate the features and benefits of a product that the consumer cannot see, but they help the consumer avoid risk; assist the consumer in satisfying emotional, social and self-expressive needs; reduce the consumer's economic and *emotional* costs of finding a product he wants; and provide a wider array of both product points and *reasonable* price points. Moreover, because brands truly are "hostages" in consumers' minds, they incentivize owners to meet tomorrow's expectations as well as they met yesterday's.

Likewise, brands are among the most valuable assets that a company, particularly one that sells consumer experience goods, can possess. They afford access to consumers' minds; enhance advertising; open channels of trade; create expansion opportunities; provide resilience; and are repositories of loyal customers. Pioneer brands afford an air of authenticity, and a host of brands can themselves create a reason to buy: an American Express card, e.g., evokes "quality and prestige, available to only the most select group of consumers." "Products can be reverse engineered, processes can be copied, senior management can change jobs, but a strong, [singular] brand—a carefully nurtured cognitive network of brand-authentic associations—will remain unique."

Brands, as one astute observer has noted, have thus moved from being "*signals*" triggering specific source and quality responses to being "*symbols*" generating a broader array of associations and images. . . .

VII. COGNITIVE PSYCHOLOGY

C. The Vulnerabilities of Modern Marks

. . .

Some brands are transformative:

[O]pening a Tiffany package will feel different from opening a Macy's package—the feeling will be more intense, more special. Further, the wearing of a Tiffany bracelet may even make the wearer feel more attractive and confident. . . . The associations of prestige and quality are hypothesized to actually change the use experience. . . .

TIFFANY should thus have concerns far beyond confusion if "Tiffany blue" boxes are adopted by a chain of perfumeries.

Other brands tap into emotional and self-expressive needs:

A cook using WILLIAMS-SONOMA kitchen equipment to host a dinner will enhance his reputation among guests who value quality housewares. Not only will he garner the functional, use-benefit of the cookware, and enjoy the emotional benefit of cooking well with quality equipment, but he also will express himself subtly as someone who can afford the best and who merits the admiration of his guests for his good taste and a presumed culinary aptitude.

Any interference with consumers' associations with, or feelings about, such a brand would undermine its essence. Confusion of the mark's meaning, indeed, would be more detrimental than confusion of the mark.

Still other brands "for many people, . . . serve the function that fraternal, religious and service organizations used to serve—to help people define who they are and then help them communicate that definition to others." HARLEY-DAVIDSON owners enjoy a social experience rooted in the brand, and the APPLE users group provides a forum for devotees to exchange information and obtain advice for problems. Such brands are cultural icons, each with its own gestalt and charisma, and consumers "don't [just] buy [them]; they join them. [They] bond to a brand, and one generation . . . can lead you to the next." "The *psychological* response to a brand can [thus] be as important as the *physiological* response to the product." . . .

Frequently, above, I have referred to brand "images," but TIFFANY, APPLE, WILLIAMS-SONOMA, HARLEY-DAVIDSON, VIAGRA, MICHELIN, ROLEX and MONTBLANC are more than "images"—temporal impressions created by an advertising campaign. Each is a total identity: each has its own personality; each has known benefits and attributes, both functional and personal, that foster a relationship; and each has the trustworthiness to deliver on its promises. A mere trademark is just another word—it is frequently flat and difficult to recall among the tens of thousands of words floating around in memory; a strong, singular brand, on the other hand, assumes rounded, human proportions and is immediately accessible. While Judge Hand thus correctly noted that a source/quality symbol of his day was an "authentic seal," it is far truer of a brand "identity" of today that "[i]f another uses it, he [*necessarily*] borrows the owner's reputation." . . .

Moralists among us, of course, sometimes decry experiential marketing—the creation of images and identities that generate (and satisfy) expectations beyond the functional characteristics of the product itself. As, however, the renown[ed] humanistic psychologist Abraham Maslow has theorized, we are not controlled by mechanical forces or instinctual impulses, but actively strive to reach our highest potential, and, in order of priority, are motivated to fill:

1. physiological needs (food, water, air, shelter, sex);
2. safety and security needs (protection, order, stability);
3. social needs (affection, friendship, belonging);
4. ego needs (prestige, status, self-respect); and
5. self-actualization (self-fulfillment).

To the extent that brands can assist us in scaling the last three rungs of the ladder, they create, to repeat, "perceptions" that consumers rightfully "value." Consumers thus logically, rationally and *emotionally* are interested in more than quality and price, and I submit that their mental as well as their physical expectations are entitled to insulation.

ALEX KOZINSKI, TRADEMARKS UNPLUGGED

68 N.Y.U. L. Rev. 960, 961-75 (1993) *

. . . There's a growing tendency to use trademarks not just to identify products but also to enhance or adorn them, even to create new commodities altogether. There was a time when the name of a shirt's manufacturer was discreetly sewn inside the collar. Izod and Pierre Cardin changed all that, making the manufacturer's logo an integral part of the

---

product itself. Do you like a particular brand of beer? Chances are you can buy a T-shirt that telegraphs your brand loyalty. Some people put stickers on their cars announcing their allegiance to the Grateful Dead. Go figure.

It's a pretty good deal all around. The consumer gets a kick out of it, and the manufacturer gets free advertising, solidifying its name recognition and reinforcing brand loyalty. What's more, it's lucrative—not merely in enhancing sales of the product, but also as a separate profit center. Think, for example, how much money is made in products associated with sports teams and blockbuster movies.

When trademarks are used in this way, they acquire certain functional characteristics that are different from—and sometimes inconsistent with—their traditional role as identifiers of source. Where trademarks once served only to tell the consumer who made the product, they now often enhance it or become a functional part of it. This trend raises questions about whether—and to what extent—the law should protect trademarks when they are pressed into service as separate products. . . .

[T]rademarks play a significant role in our public discourse. They often provide some of our most vivid metaphors, as well as the most compelling imagery in political campaigns. Some ideas—"it's the Rolls Royce of its class," for example—are difficult to express any other way. That's no accident. Trademarks are often selected for their effervescent qualities, and then injected into the stream of communication with the pressure of a firehose by means of mass media campaigns. Where trademarks come to carry so much communicative freight, allowing the trademark holder to restrict their use implicates our collective interest in free and open communication.

So long as trademark law limits itself to its traditional role of avoiding confusion in the marketplace, there's little likelihood that free expression will be hindered. Whatever first amendment rights you may have in calling the brew you make in your bathtub "Pepsi" are easily outweighed by the buyer's interest in not being fooled into buying it. But once you get past the confusion rationale—as I think we should—trademark law loses this built-in first amendment compass. . . . [O]ur vision of the world and of ourselves is shaped by the words we use and by the images that fill our fantasies. The words and images of trade are an important part of this panorama. What starts out as a trademark or slogan quickly spills over into a political campaign, a *Saturday Night Live* skit, a metaphor, a cultural phenomenon, an everyday expression—and occasionally a fixed part of the language. Looking back in recent history, for example, "Where's the Beef" and Joe Isuzu are perhaps the only memorable aspects of the 1984 and 1988 presidential campaigns. Think back further to a time when it seemed like everyone in the country would bring a thumb and two fingers to their lips, blow off a kiss, and, in their worst Italian accent, say, "Try it, you'll like it." Or a few years later, when everyone thought they were the soul of wit when they pointed to some large object like a car or a house and drawled out, "I can't believe I ate the whole thing." How many others can you think of? "This Bud's for you." "It takes two hands to handle a Whopper." "Just do it." Even as we speak, there's a federal judge who runs around the country telling anyone who is willing to listen that a lot of tort cases can be resolved by a rule of law he calls the Toyota Principle: "You asked for it—you got it." . . .

The point is that any doctrine that gives people property rights in words, symbols, and images that have worked their way into our popular culture must carefully consider the communicative functions those marks serve. The originator of a trademark or logo cannot simply assert, "It's mine, I own it, and you have to pay for it any time you use it." Words and images do not worm their way into our discourse by accident; they're generally thrust there by well-orchestrated campaigns intended to burn them into our collective consciousness. Having embarked on that endeavor, the originator of the symbol necessarily—and justly—must give up some measure of control. The originator must understand that the mark or symbol or image is no longer entirely its own, and that in some sense it also belongs to all those other minds who have received and integrated it. This does not imply a total loss of control, however, only that the public's right to make use of the word or image must be considered in the balance as we decide what rights the owner is entitled to assert.

NOTES AND QUESTIONS

1. *The role of trademarks (descriptively).* Several of the excerpts above suggest different understandings of the role trademarks play in our society (principally, for consumers) and hint at the developing debate about whether trademarks are "property." What role do you think trademarks play in our society? Are the characteristics of trademarks discussed in the articles excerpted such that they should be treated as "property"? Does this matter? To help answer these questions, ask yourself what role the following terms (all of which are, or are claimed to be, trademarks) play in our culture. To what extent do these terms communicate things to you? What meaning do you take from seeing or hearing them? How does use of these terms help or hinder you as you go about your daily business?

- COKE
- TRUMP
- UBER
- DELTA
- WAL-MART
- KATE SPADE

2. *The meaning of "broader meaning."* Is Swann correct regarding the meaning of brands? David Brooks has likewise argued:

> Some countries have national poets, like Pushkin or Goethe, but [America has] national brands. We have companies that have carved out such clear identities for themselves that you can practically treat them as characters in a novel. Imagine, for example, what would happen if Trader Joe, the leading man of morally upscale groceries, married Ann Taylor, the heroine of Protestant woman's wear.

David Brooks, *No Sex Magazines Please, We're Wal-Mart Shoppers*, N.Y. TIMES, May 11, 2003, at WK 14.

Assuming that Swann, Brooks, and Kozinski are correct in noting the broader role that trademarks play in modern society, how should trademark law respond? Does this counsel in favor of stronger protection for trademarks, or weaker protection? Should trademark law preserve all meaning that a trademark has? Scholars of marketing discuss the concept of "brand" in very broad terms. Should a "brand" encompass meaning that we should not recognize as "trademark" meaning and thus leave unprotected? What harms, if any, would ensue from limiting the meaning that trademark law protects? What harms, if any, would ensue from imposing no limit on the meaning that trademark law protects?

3. *Assumptions of rationality?* Neoclassical economics relies on assumptions of rational behavior. What weight, if any, should trademark law give to neurological studies on consumer behavior suggesting that shopping is anything but rational?

4. *The role of trademark law (normatively).* To what extent should trademark law seek to shape the role that trademarks play in society? Should trademark law react to changes in the use of trademarks by consumers and producers, or should trademark law proactively seek to induce certain consumer values or attitudes? If it should be a proactive body of law, how should it shape those values? What role should trademarks play in

modern society? *See generally* Graeme B. Dinwoodie, *Trademarks and Territory: Detaching Trademark Law from the Nation-State*, 41 Hous. L. Rev. 885, 961-63 (2004) (the distinction between reactive and proactive lawmaking); Graeme B. Dinwoodie, *The Seventh Annual Honorable Helen Wilson Nies Memorial Lecture on Intellectual Property Law: The Trademark Jurisprudence of the Rehnquist Court*, 8 Marq. Intell. Prop. L. Rev. 187, 209 (2004) (same in context of trademark fair use).

   5.   *Merchandising and brand awareness programs.* Producers are engaging in increasingly extensive efforts to promote and strengthen brand awareness. These include the sale of collateral, promotional materials bearing the same mark that the producer uses on its core products. However, the sale and distribution of promotional merchandise is, as we will see later, now a lucrative economic activity in its own right that is in large part sustained by trademark law. For example, in a long-running dispute between John Deere and rival garden equipment manufacturer MTD Products, testimony showed:

> In addition to its agricultural products, Deere has licensed third parties to make and sell "collateral goods" such as golf shirts, jackets, t-shirts, coffee mugs, toys, fishing lures, dinnerware, serving trays and ink pens with the intention, among other things, of creating awareness for Deere's "core products," *i.e.*, its agricultural and consumer outdoor power equipment. In 1995, Deere formed a "Trademark Administration Group" to "expand and promote the use of the John Deere name and trademark in nontraditional products and services" and in conjunction with the Group's formation, increased its emphasis on the production and marketing of "collateral goods." All of these collateral products display the John Deere name and/or the leaping deer symbol as well as the green and yellow color combination. By 2002, the annual sales of John Deere collateral goods amounted to approximately $200 million. Deere claims that its sale of collateral goods has promoted awareness of John Deere trademarks and has caused the public to further associate the green and yellow color combination with Deere. In addition to the collateral goods, Deere has promoted its name and trademarks in various other ways including sponsoring a NASCAR racing car and team and sponsoring the John Deere Classic Golf Tournament.

Deere & Co. v. MTD Holdings Inc., 70 U.S.P.Q.2d (BNA) 1009, 1012 (S.D.N.Y. 2004). What costs and benefits does society reap from facilitating merchandising activity? Does your answer change depending on whether the merchandising activity is closely related to the producer's core goods or services? For example, would you wish to treat merchandising by Rihanna differently than merchandising activities by John Deere? What about universities, which rely on merchandising to fund many of their activities?

GRAEME B. DINWOODIE, (NATIONAL) TRADEMARK LAWS AND THE (NON-NATIONAL) DOMAIN NAME SYSTEM

21 U. Pa. J. Int'l Econ. L. 495, 497-505 (2000)

   [What are] the characteristics of the [domain name system?] Domain names are the unique addresses assigned to particular computers that are connected to the Internet. Without such unique addresses, computers would not be able to send packets of information to the correct location.[4] The naming system, and the history of its development, are well explained elsewhere.[5] For our current purposes, four aspects of the system are pertinent.

---

   4. The actual Internet addresses (Internet Protocol addresses) are unique numbers, each with an assigned corresponding unique name in order to deal with the frailty of human memory. Thus, the Internet address of the University of Pennsylvania is actually 128.91.2.28, but it is easier to remember the name that corresponds to that number, namely, *www.upenn.edu.*

First, domain names currently say very little about the nature or location of the domain name registrant. Every domain name has a top-level domain name (the suffix at the end of the domain name) that will consist of either a generic top-level domain name (such as .edu or .com)[6] or a country code (such as .uk, for the United Kingdom, or .it, for Italy).[7] But, as presently constituted, even the top-level domain name is not determinative of the nature or location of the registrant in question. Although the registrars responsible for country code registers may impose residency requirements, domain names are available in the generic top-level domains regardless of physical location and many country code registrars are not insistent on residency requirements.[10] And, while the four principal generic top-level domains [openly available in 2000] were once indicative of the nature of the domain name's owner (.edu signified educational institutions, .gov was found at the end of government agency addresses, .com was used by commercial enterprises, and .mil was restricted to military users), the expansion of users and an open registration system have reduced the value of the suffix as an indicium of the nature of the user (except for .edu, .gov, and .mil).

Second, and related to the lack of connection between address and location, because the accreditation of registrars is performed by a single body, ICANN,[13] there is close to (but not complete)[14] uniformity of registration practices among registrars, at least with respect to the generic top-level domains. Third, within each top-level domain, there cannot be two identical names, or computers would not know where to send information. Thus, while there may be separate domain name registrations of apple.com and apple.net, there cannot be two domain name registrations of apple.com. Finally, domain names [in the most lucrative generic top-level domains] are registered on a first-come, first-served basis. There can only be one apple.com, and it goes to the first person to register it. The only check, on initial application, is whether an identical name is already registered in that domain. . . .

[D]omain names . . . challenge the conceptual boundaries of trademark law. To see the ways in which this is so, let's briefly explore the conceptual boundaries of trademark law. . . . The scope of U.S. trademark rights was limited both by reference to the products on which the mark was used and by reference to the geographic area in which the mark was used. . . . [E]ach of these limits . . . reflected a desire to restrain the activities of legitimate

---

5. *See generally* Joseph P Liu, *Legitimacy and Authority in Internet Coordination: A Domain Name Case Study*, 74 IND. L.J. 587 (1999) (discussing the history of domain name system and proposals for reform).

6. The present generic top-level domain names include .edu, .com, .gov, .org, .net, .int, and .mil. [*Ed. Note:* Since this article was published, ICANN has created a variety of new top-level domains, many of which are sponsored by a private agency (e.g., aero for the air transport industry). It has also created so-called internationalized domains.]

7. The administration of country code top-level domains is delegated by ICANN (performing the functions formerly performed by the Internet Assigned Numbers Authority to authorities ("managers") in the relevant country). . . .

10. Some country code domains have become attractive for reasons unrelated to geography. For example, doctors in the United States are purchasing names in the Moldova country code domain, namely, .md. . . .

13. ICANN is a not-for-profit corporation that was created by the U.S. government to operate the domain name system, among other things, in accordance with parameters set by the Commerce Department. *See* Management of Internet Names and Addresses, 63 Fed. Reg. 31,741 (proposed June 10, 1998).

14. The flexibility that causes slightly different practices among registrars reflects the notion that the system of registering generic top-level domain names would benefit from competition in the registration process. This was an important part of the shift from administration of the system by Network Solutions, Inc. [Before the U.S. government established ICANN, responsibility for registering .com domain names—the most valuable names—lay with Network Solutions, Inc. (to whom the government had outsourced the job).]

traders only to the extent necessary to further the two primary purposes of trademark law. If the products upon which the mark was used were wholly different from those of the first mark owner, the public would not purchase the goods of the second producer, believing them to be those of the first producer. Thus, although Apple owns the mark APPLE for personal computers, a manufacturer of shoes could use the mark APPLE on shoes without affecting the goodwill established by the Apple company or deceiving consumers in their purchasing decisions. DOMINO's is used for both pizzas and sugar without harm to either company (despite efforts to suggest otherwise). To use an example on the services side, United Airlines and United Van Lines each own trademark rights in the mark UNITED, for airline services and moving services, respectively.

Limits on the geographic scope of rights were similarly motivated: if Apple computer did not use its mark in State A, then consumers in State A would not come to associate the mark APPLE with the products made by the Apple company, and thus the use of the term—even by another computer producer—would not confuse consumers or endanger any consumer perceptions of the quality of the product of the Apple company (because there are no such perceptions). . . . The domain name system presents a series of conflicts with these basic principles of U.S. trademark law. There can only be one united.com;[29] should that domain name be granted to the airline or the moving company, or should prior trademark ownership be irrelevant? What is the geographic scope of use where a trademark is used as a domain name: has the user now made use of the mark globally, potentially causing the acquisition of rights in all use-based systems and infringement of rights in all countries where the mark is owned by another? . . .

The domain name system, and its operation apart from the trademark system, will also require the courts to develop new responses to old questions. For example, how does one assess confusion in cyberspace? The courts must construct a cyberconsumer, whose purchasing and browsing habits clearly encompass the use of domain names as well as trademarks in the searching process.[32] And, if use retains any importance in the system of trademark protection, then how does one assess whether a trademark is being "used" in cyberspace: is registration of a domain name the "use of a mark in commerce" sufficient either to acquire trademark rights or (if that mark is owned by another) to infringe trademark rights? Again, this will require courts to apply classical principles with an eye to new consumer practices. Whether and to what extent domain names will serve as trademarks is not a question of abstract philosophy, but a matter of how consumer practices and comprehension develop in cyberspace. Even in the last few years, consumer attitudes about what a domain name signifies have changed; trademark law must reflect those changes. . . .

NOTES AND QUESTIONS

1. *The role of domain names.* As we will see throughout the book, domain names are acquired and dealt with differently from trademarks. Many domain names consist of a trademarked term (e.g., *www.coke.com*), although they need not do so. What role do

---

29. The extent to which this remains a problem may depend on the maintenance of the current architecture of the Internet. For example, where more than one trademark holder (or other person) has a legitimate claim to united.com, that address may take the user to a registrar-administered site listing (and linking to the sites of) all claimants to the UNITED name, relegating those users to concurrent use of united.com and exclusive use only of some other configuration including "united."

32. These habits may, however, change as technological options for cybersearching grow. The use of keywords, available with different browsers, for example, altered the reliance of consumers on domain names. *See* Andy Johnson-Laird, *Looking Forward, Legislating Backward?*, 4 J. SMALL & EMERGING BUS. L. 95 (2000).

domain names play in our society? To what extent do domain names communicate things to you? What meaning do you take from seeing or hearing them? How do you use them as you go about your daily business?

2. *New top-level domains.* As suggested in footnote 6 of the Dinwoodie article, ICANN has in recent years been open to the creation of new generic top-level domains. That strategy has, however, met with substantial resistance from trademark owners. One aspect of this expansion of gTLDs is that ICANN has granted (after a bidding process) applications for domains based on brands (e.g., .CANON). How do you think this will change the relationship between marks and domain names?

3. *Domain names and trademarks.* The excerpt from Professor Dinwoodie's article suggests ways in which conflicts exist between the rules governing domain names and the rules governing trademarks. Why are the rules different? What functions does each serve? To what extent do the purposes underlying the regulation of each differ?

4. *Domain names and international agreements.* Some of the problems identified by Professor Dinwoodie are international in nature. The problems of multiple owners of the same mark become even more acute when one considers all potential owners of APPLE marks throughout the world, all of which might be accessible in the United States because of the ubiquity of the Internet. Thus, some of the dilemmas that territorial rights generate in an increasingly unterritorial world have been addressed at the international level. For example, in 1999, the World Intellectual Property Organization adopted a nonbinding resolution on the meaning of the concept of "use" on the Internet, which we will discuss in detail in Chapters 4 and 6.

E.   AN ILLUSTRATION

We will conclude this introductory chapter with a case that exemplifies the rich variety of trademark, unfair competition, and related theories of liability that are typically brought to bear in the cases that we will encounter. As you read the case, consider the interplay between the infringement theories advanced by the plaintiff, and identify the social harms that the different causes of action seek to redress. What are the premises that underlie the theories of harm? What values counsel in the plaintiff's favor, and which would be vindicated by holding for the defendant? We'll deal with these and other questions (as well as the variety of substantive trademark law rules referenced by the court) at different stages throughout the book. The case is also representative of many of the cases you'll read in this book, in that it deals with highbrow, sophisticated culture,* as well as the marketing and consumption of certain popular beverages.**

ELVIS PRESLEY ENTERPRISES, INC. v. CAPECE
950 F. Supp. 783 (S.D. Tex. 1996), rev'd, 141 F.3d 188 (5th Cir. 1998)

GILMORE, District Judge:

I.   BACKGROUND

Elvis Presley Enterprises ("EPE") is a Tennessee corporation formed in 1981 under the terms of a testamentary trust created by Elvis Presley ("Presley"). EPE is the assignee and registrant of all trademarks, copyrights, and publicity rights belonging to the Presley

---

* Meaning Elvis.
** Including the "Love Me Blenders."

estate, including over a dozen United States federal trademark registrations and common law trademarks of Presley's name and likeness. None of these marks, however, are registered service marks for use in the restaurant and tavern business. EPE's exclusive rights are marketed through a licensing program which grants licensees the right to manufacture and sell Elvis Presley merchandise worldwide. Products range from t-shirts to juke boxes. Merchandise sales have generated over $20 million in revenue in the last five years and account for the largest percentage of EPE's annual earnings. In addition, EPE operates a mail order business and several retail stores at Graceland, the Elvis Presley home in Memphis, Tennessee, including two restaurants and an ice cream parlor. EPE recently announced plans to open an Elvis Presley night club in 1997 on Beale Street in Memphis and is also currently exploring the possibility of opening similar establishments throughout the world.

In April of 1991, Barry Capece ("Capece"), operating through the now dormant limited partnership, Beers 'R' Us, opened a night-club on Kipling Street in Houston, Texas, named "The Velvet Elvis." The name, "The Velvet Elvis," referring to one of the more coveted velvet paintings, was selected for the powerful association it immediately invokes with a time when lava lamps, velvet paintings, and bell bottoms were popular. Capece intended the bar to parody an era remembered for its sensationalism and transient desire for flashiness. By taking bad, albeit once widely popular, art and accentuating it with gallery lights and by showcasing decor which mocks society's idolization of less than scrupulous celebrities, Capece ridiculed a culture's obsession with the fleeting and unimportant. His biting criticism provides his patrons with a constant reminder not to take themselves nor the world they live in too seriously. . . .

[In 1992, the PTO issued Capece a federal trademark registration for the service mark "VELVET ELVIS" for use in the restaurant and tavern business. Although the Kipling Street nightclub closed in 1993, Capece obtained financial backing to reopen the club on Richmond Street, Houston.] In July [1994], EPE sent a cease and desist letter to Capece, threatening legal action if the bar opened with EPE's trademark, "Elvis," in its name. Capece was "All Shook Up." Despite the warning letter, however, the Richmond Street "Velvet Elvis" opened for business in August of 1994.

The bar currently serves a wide selection of liquors, including premium scotches, bourbons, and tequilas. Food is available and menu items range from appetizers to complete entrees. "The Velvet Elvis" also claims to be the first cigar bar in Houston, specializing in high quality cigars. "The Velvet Elvis's" decor, consistent with its theme, features velvet paintings along with a widely divergent assortment of eclectic art. In addition to the velvet Elvis painting in the back lounge, velvet portraits of Stevie Wonder, Chuck Berry, Bruce Lee, and a collection of velvet nudes are hung throughout the bar. Also a part of the bar's decor are lava lamps, cheap ceramic sculptures, beaded curtains, and vinyl furniture. A painting of the Mona Lisa exposing her breasts hangs prominently in the front room. Centerfolds from Playboy magazines dating back to the sixties completely cover the walls of the men's room. Reminders of Elvis Presley, including numerous magazine photographs and a statue of Elvis playing the guitar, were at one time amongst the bar's decorations, but have since been replaced with art work unrelated to Elvis or his music but equally as reminiscent of the forgotten era the bar attempts to mimic.

Pictures and references to Elvis Presley were also used in advertisements promoting the establishment until 1995. A number of ads contained actual pictures of Elvis Presley. Some ads made direct references to the deceased singer or Graceland using phrases such as "The King Lives," "Viva la Elvis," or "Elvis has *not* left the building." Others, while avoiding explicit references to Elvis or his persona, boldly displayed the "Elvis" portion of "The Velvet Elvis" insignia with an almost unnoticeable "Velvet" appearing alongside in smaller script. The bar's menu bears a caption, "The King of Dive Bars." A frozen drink, "Love Me Blenders," is served in the bar and the menu features items such as peanut butter and banana sandwiches, and "Your Football Hound Dog."

Plaintiff claims that the focal point of the bar's name, decor, and advertisements is Elvis Presley. To protect its exclusive right to license the commercial use of Elvis Presley's name, image, and likeness, Plaintiff filed suit against [the partnership through which Capece operated the bar] and Capece, as owner of "The Velvet Elvis" service mark, on April 21, 1995. Plaintiff sued Defendants for unfair competition, trademark infringement, and dilution, under both the common law and the Lanham Act, 15 U.S.C. §1051 et seq. (1994), and for infringement of its common law and corresponding statutory right of publicity. . . .

Defendants, on the other hand, maintain that Plaintiff is merely a victim of "Suspicious Minds. . . ." Because the bar is meant and viewed as a parody, Defendants also argue that use of its service mark has not yet nor will in the future cause confusion as to the identity of the bar's owners, sponsors, or affiliates. Defendants claim that all possibility of confusion or dilution of Plaintiff's trademarks is negated with the customer's immediate appreciation of the bar's parodic message.

II.   UNFAIR COMPETITION AND TRADEMARK INFRINGEMENT

. . .

To prevail on its trademark infringement and unfair competition claims under the Lanham Act, Plaintiff needs to demonstrate that Defendants' use of "The Velvet Elvis" service mark and the image, likeness, and other indicia of Elvis Presley was likely to cause confusion in the mind of the ordinary consumer as to the source, affiliation, or sponsorship of Defendants' bar. [cit.] The focus is whether a defendant's use of a mark and image creates a "'likelihood that an appreciable number of ordinarily prudent purchasers are likely to be misled, or indeed simply confused, as to the source of the goods in question.'" [cit.] Liability is established if the evidence demonstrates that consumers will mistakenly believe the goods or services in dispute actually originated with the plaintiff or if it appears that plaintiff may have sponsored or otherwise approved of defendant's use. [cit.] The governing standard for common law trademark infringement and unfair competition is the same "likelihood of confusion" test applied to claims brought under the Lanham Act. [cit.]

Although the standards are similar, there is a fundamental distinction between trademark infringement and unfair competition. [cit.] Trademark law is based on a relatively narrow principal [sic] as compared to its frequent companion unfair competition—its goal is to provide the holder of a trademark the exclusive right to use a phrase, word, symbol, image, or device to identify and distinguish his product. [cit.] Unfair competition, on the other hand, is much more encompassing. . . . Due to this difference, there may be some instances where "a defendant is guilty of competing unfairly without having technically infringed." [cit.]

In this circuit, courts have relied on the following list of factors in determining whether a defendant's use of a mark or image creates a likelihood of confusion:

(1)   the type of trademark alleged to have been infringed;
(2)   the similarity of design between the two marks;
(3)   the similarity of the products or services;
(4)   the identity of the retail outlets and purchasers;
(5)   the identity of the advertising medium utilized;
(6)   the defendant's intent; and
(7)   evidence of actual confusion.

[*Conan Properties, Inc. v. Conans Pizza, Inc.*, 752 F.2d 145, 149 (5th Cir. 1985).] This list is neither exhaustive nor exclusive. In fact, "[t]he absence or presence of any one factor ordinarily is not dispositive; indeed, a finding of likelihood of confusion need not be supported by even a majority of the seven factors." *Id.* at 150. Further, the Court is not limited to the factors enunciated in *Conan* to determine likelihood of confusion and is free to consider other relevant evidence of confusion. [cit.] An additional factor that impacts the analysis in this case is whether Defendants' attempt to parody the Elvis era and the eclectic bars of the sixties successfully eliminated the potential for a customer to be misled or whether it simply increased the likelihood of confusion. . . .

The Court will first analyze whether Defendants' use of the Elvis name in its service mark and Elvis memorabilia as bar decor is likely to create consumer confusion. Defendants' employment of the image, likeness, and other indicia of Presley in advertisements will be addressed separately.

A.   [DEFENDANTS'] SERVICE MARK AND BAR DECOR

1.   Type of Trademark (Strength of the Mark)

The "type" of trademark refers to the "strength" of the trademark and its ability to invoke an immediate association in the consumer's minds with a plaintiff's goods. [cit.] The stronger the mark the broader the protection it is afforded. [cit.] The strength of the mark "refers to the distinctiveness of the mark, or more precisely, its tendency to identify the goods sold under the mark as emanating from a particular, although possibly anonymous, source." [cit.] . . .

. . . Defendants concede that the worldwide fame and almost instantaneous recognition that the Elvis or Elvis Presley name has acquired enhance Plaintiff's claim that its trademark is a strong mark. "The more deeply a plaintiff's mark is embedded in the consumer's mind, the more likely it is that the defendant's mark will conjure up the image of the plaintiff's product instead of that of the junior user." [cit.]

Even though Plaintiff's widely recognized trademarks are deserving of protection, this fact alone does not support a finding of confusion. Confusion is avoided when the defendant uses the plaintiff's mark as a part of a parody, jest, or societal commentary. [cit.] Parody has been defined as a subtly humorous, imitative form of criticism, which provides "social benefit by shedding light on an earlier work, and in the process, creating a new one." . . . Because "the keystone of parody is imitation," a successful parodist must conjure up enough of the original to "convey two simultaneous—and contradictory—messages: that it is the original, but also that it is not the original but instead a parody." . . .

Defendants' use of the service mark "The Velvet Elvis" when combined with the bar's gaudy decor form an integral part of Defendants' parody of the faddish, eclectic bars of the sixties. The phrase "velvet Elvis" has a meaning in American pop culture that is greater than the name, image, or likeness of Elvis Presley. The phrase symbolizes tacky, "cheesy," velvet art, including, but not limited to velvet Elvis paintings. Here, the image of Elvis, conjured up by way of velvet paintings, has transcended into an iconoclastic form of art that has a specific meaning in our culture, which surpasses the identity of the man represented in the painting. That image is confirmed upon entering the bar. Plaintiff's own witnesses testified that despite their thoughts about the bar's name, they immediately realized the tacky bar they had just encountered was in no way associated or affiliated with EPE. The humorous jab at the trends of the sixties is almost overpowering and readily apparent with one quick look around a lounge cluttered with tasteless art, long strand beads, and a lighted disco ball conspicuously hung from the ceiling. The customer's recognition and appreciation of Defendants' parody decreases the probability of confusion that would otherwise result from use of a trade name which partially incorporates a relatively strong mark. [cit.] Thus, the Court finds that while Plaintiff's mark is entitled to protection, it is doubtful that its inclusion within the name "The Velvet Elvis" will mislead consumers into believing that the bar is affiliated or somehow associated with EPE. Nor will customers mistake "The Velvet Elvis" for an EPE owned or sponsored business because Elvis related items are used in the bar's decor. This factor therefore weighs against finding a likelihood of confusion exists both with respect to Defendants' use of "The Velvet Elvis" service mark and Elvis memorabilia as bar decor.

2.   Degree of Similarity Between the Two Marks

. . .

As a general rule, "a subsequent user may not avoid likely confusion by appropriating another's entire mark and adding descriptive or non-distinctive matter to it." [J. Thomas McCarthy, Trademarks and Unfair Competition, §23.15[8] (4th ed. 1996)]. An exception to the general rule is found where the marks in their entireties convey two different meanings. *Long John Distilleries, Ltd. v. Sazerac Co.*, 426 F.2d 1406, 1407 (1970) (holding "Long John" and "Friar John" not substantially similar because the marks communicate very different ideas). The Court finds Defendants' service mark falls within this narrow category of exception because each party's mark creates a very different overall impression. Plaintiff's trademarks obviously refer to the legendary singer, Elvis Presley and products of his image and likeness marketed through EPE and its licensees. The term "The Velvet Elvis," on the other hand, is symbolic of a faddish art style that belongs to the culture that created it. It has no specific connection with the singer other than the coincidence of its use to portray him. Marked dissimilarity in the meaning of two marks can be determinative and weigh against a finding of confusion under this factor. . . . The Court finds any similarity between the marks is outweighed by their strikingly different meanings. Accordingly, the Court finds the lack of similarity between the two marks weighs against a finding of confusion.

3.   Similarity of Products or Services

"The greater the similarity between products and services, the greater the likelihood of confusion." [cit.] Direct competition between the parties is not necessary for infringement to occur. Rather, "the gist of the action [for trademark infringement] lies in likelihood of confusion to the public." [cit.] Confusion may exist "when the sponsor or maker of one business product might naturally be assumed to be the maker or sponsor of another business or product," although the parties' products or services are non-competitive. [cit.] In addition, a trademark owner has a definite interest in "preserving avenues of expansion" and is entitled to protection in related fields where the possibility for future growth exists even though he had not entered that particular area at the time the infringement action is brought. [cit.] Thus, protection is extended in cases where it is clear that the plaintiff intends to expand his sales efforts to compete directly with the defendant or it is possible that the public will assume or perceive that an expansion of the plaintiff's operations has in fact occurred although there is no evidence of the plaintiff's expectation to do so. [cit.]

The evidence produced at trial showed that Defendants' bar caters to a young, "hip" crowd, providing patrons with a place to socialize. A customer can go to "The Velvet Elvis" to eat, drink, watch one of many television sets, or smoke a cigar in the bar's smoking room. At the present time, EPE does not provide services comparable to those of "The Velvet Elvis," although it currently operates two family oriented restaurants, one of which serves beer. EPE's operations are based on the sale of Elvis Presley merchandise. Its on-site eateries and ice cream parlors are a byproduct of the commercialization of Graceland rather than a venture into the restaurant business. Plaintiff has, however, indicated its intention to enter Defendants' field and plans to open an "Elvis Presley's" nightclub in Memphis sometime in 1997. Also, Debbie Johnson, General Manager of EPE, testified that an international chain of Elvis Presley restaurant/nightclubs with an Elvis motif is currently under contemplation.

While the Court finds the majority of Plaintiff's revenue is derived from a merchandising market unrelated to the service market Defendants occupy, there is some overlap between the parties' present services. Both parties do in fact operate restaurants, although the businesses are not directly competitive due to the very different clientele and purposes of the respective establishments. As the Plaintiff has presented testimony of its immediate plans to open a Memphis nightclub and future intent to open a chain of similar bars throughout the world, this factor might favor Plaintiff, were it not for the relative clarity of "The Velvet Elvis'" parodic purpose. . . . [T]his Court concludes that "The Velvet Elvis" is a successful parody. Defendants' bar is sufficiently dissimilar from any establishment EPE currently operates or has plans to operate in the future to prevent confusion as to the bar's source or origin. . . .

6.   Defendants' Intent

"[I]f the mark was adopted with the intent of deriving benefit from the reputation of [the senior user] that fact alone 'may be sufficient to justify the inference that there is confusing similarity.'" . . . [T]he proper focus "is whether defendant had the intent to derive benefit from the reputation or goodwill of plaintiff." [cit.]

The Court does not find that Defendants had an improper intent when adopting "The Velvet Elvis" as its establishment's name and service mark. Capece testified that the name refers to a particular type of painting and gaudy decor that was characteristic of bars during the sixties. In fact, he claims he was looking at a velvet Elvis painting when he determined that the name would be fitting for the kind of tacky, "cheesy," bar he had envisioned. His intent was to parody a time or concept from the sixties—the Las Vegas lounge scene, the velvet painting craze and perhaps indirectly, the country's fascination with Elvis. By furnishing his bar with tasteless, tacky decor similar to that seen in a typical sixties nightclub, his intent was not only to mock what was once considered the height of sophistication and class but also to provide critical commentary on society as a whole. Reference to Elvis Presley is indirect, yet use of his name is an essential part of the parody because the term, "velvet Elvis," has become a synonym for garish, passe black velvet art. Any association between Elvis and velvet art is attributable to the public's linking Elvis Presley with this particular art form and not to any aspect of Elvis' persona cultivated by Plaintiff for the purpose of achieving national prominence. . . .

[T]his Court finds that, due to the clarity of Defendants' parody, use of the service mark, "The Velvet Elvis," was not intended to cause confusion among consumers as to the source or sponsorship of Defendants' bar.

7.   Actual Confusion

Regarding this last factor, the Fifth Circuit stated that "[t]here can be no more positive or substantial proof of the likelihood of confusion than proof of actual confusion." [cit.] It is well settled, however, that the plaintiff is not required to prove any instances of actual confusion in order to be entitled to a finding of a likelihood of confusion. [cit.] However, an absence of actual confusion after a long period of concurrent use of the marks raises a presumption against a likelihood of confusion in the future. . . .

In an attempt to prove actual confusion, Plaintiff offered the testimony of four witnesses. Three of the four witnesses were members of the Elvis Presley fan club in Austin, Texas. These fan club members were all women ranging in age from mid-forties to early seventies. They had been shown samples of ads for "The Velvet Elvis" one month before trial and had the opportunity to visit the bar the day before testifying. The first woman, an Elvis fan since age seven and a five time visitor to Graceland, testified that she was offended by the nude paintings of women and the audacity of the bar's owner to hang these paintings in the same room with pictures of Elvis. The second woman, who had an extensive collection of Elvis memorabilia and had been to Graceland twenty-five times, testified that she was also not pleased to see Elvis's memorabilia in a bar, much less a bar that openly displayed portraits of nude women. The third woman, who was the President of the Austin Elvis Presley Fan Club and claimed to have been to Graceland between forty and fifty times, was likewise offended by the nudity in the decor and was disappointed to have Elvis's name associated with an establishment of this type. The fourth witness was a man who had been to both "The Velvet Elvis" bars. He testified that when first visiting the original "The Velvet Elvis," he initially thought he might be able to buy some Elvis merchandise. He quickly realized, though, upon closer inspection of the bar's decor, that the bar had nothing to do with Elvis Presley. Consistently, each witness acknowledged that once inside "The Velvet Elvis" and given an opportunity to look around, each had no doubt that the bar was not associated or in any way affiliated with EPE.

In addition, Plaintiff was not able to produce evidence of customer complaints or other instances of confusion although "The Velvet Elvis" had been in business at the Richmond Avenue location for more than two years. In fact, Carol Butler, Director of Worldwide Licensing for EPE since July of 1994, testified that she was not aware of any complaints or inquiries from customers, licensees, or employees of EPE regarding the sponsorship of "The Velvet Elvis" or EPE's connection to the Houston establishment. Capece, who oversaw the bar's day to day operations, also testified that he was never contacted or asked whether "The Velvet Elvis" was affiliated, endorsed, or licensed by EPE. Based on the evidence presented, the Court concludes that there was an insufficient showing of actual confusion to allow this factor to weigh in Plaintiff's favor. An absence of actual confusion after a period of concurrent use by Plaintiff and Defendants of their respective marks supports the Defendants' position and raises a presumption . . . against a likelihood of confusion in the future. [cit.]

After reviewing the evidence presented, the Court concludes that Defendants' service mark, "The Velvet Elvis," as currently used, and Defendants' use of Elvis memorabilia as bar decor does not create a likelihood of customer confusion under either the Lanham Act or the common law. Accordingly, the Court finds this aspect of Plaintiff's infringement claim to be without merit.

B.   The Advertisements

The Court reaches a different conclusion with respect to the use of Elvis imagery and indicia of his persona in Defendants' advertisements. The ads clearly lack a recognizable connection with Defendants' parodic purpose. Pictures and images of Elvis Presley would, to the ordinary customer without knowledge of the underlying parody, leave the distinct impression that the bar's purpose was to pay tribute to Elvis Presley or to promote the sale of EPE related products and services. Consequently, use of this type of advertisement can only indicate a marketing scheme based on the tremendous drawing power of the Presley name and its ability to attract consumer interest and attention. Further, without the backdrop of parodic meaning, these ads and their continued circulation will cause confusion, leading customers to wonder if they might find memorabilia of their beloved singer somewhere behind the doors of "The Velvet Elvis." The Court also finds ads which overemphasize the "Elvis" portion of "The Velvet Elvis" service mark to have a comparable effect. The meaning conveyed by the composite mark, "The Velvet Elvis," is lost when the word "Elvis" is overemphasized and dominates a much smaller "Velvet." This transmuted display of Defendants' service mark focuses attention on "Elvis" instead of the meaning of the combined words "The Velvet Elvis" and what they represent together, creating a definite risk that consumers will identify the bar with Presley or EPE.

Plaintiff also presented evidence that this style of advertising did in fact confuse consumers as to the source of the bar's sponsorship. About one month before trial, Plaintiff's counsel showed each witness a sample of Defendants' previous advertisements. They all testified that the ads' use of pictures and images of Elvis led them to believe that "The Velvet Elvis" was connected or otherwise affiliated with Elvis Presley and EPE. Because "there can be no more positive or substantial proof of the likelihood of confusion than proof of actual confusion," the Court concludes that Defendants' ads, published between 1992 and 1995, were confusing and misleading. [cit.] Accordingly, the Court finds Defendants' former advertisements which depicted the image and likeness of Elvis, made explicit references to Elvis, or overemphasized the "Elvis" segment of "The Velvet Elvis" service mark to be actionable infringement and conduct amounting to unfair competition, violative of both the common law and Lanham Act.

III.   DILUTION

Plaintiff also requests relief under the Federal Trademark Dilution Act of 1995. [15 U.S.C.A. §1125(c)]. . . .

The dilution theory grants "protection to strong, well-recognized marks even in the absence of a likelihood of confusion" and depends neither upon a showing of a competitive relationship nor a certain degree of correlation or association between the parties goods or services. McCarthy, *supra*, §§24.13[1][b], 24.13[1][c]. The goal of dilution theory is to eliminate any "risk of an erosion of the public's identification of [a] very strong mark with the plaintiff alone" and to prevent another user from "diminishing [a mark's] distinctiveness, uniqueness, effectiveness and prestigious connotations." [cit.]

[The court noted that dilution can be shown in two ways—either through blurring or tarnishment, and the plaintiff claimed both blurring ("the gradual whittling away or dispersion of the identity and hold upon the public mind of the mark or name by its use upon non competing goods") and tarnishment had occurred in this case. After concluding that no blurring occurred because of the lack of similarity between the marks and because of the humorous nature of the defendant's use, the court considered the tarnishment theory.]

B.   TARNISHMENT

Tarnishment generally arises when "a plaintiff's trademark is linked to products of shoddy quality, or is portrayed in an unwholesome or unsavory context likely to evoke unflattering thoughts about the owner's product." *[S]ee Dallas Cowboys Cheerleaders, Inc. v. Pussycat Cinema, Ltd.*, 604 F.2d 200, 205 (2d Cir. 1979) (Dallas Cowboy Cheerleader uniforms used in sexually depraved movie). . . .

Regardless of the context, however, a finding of dilution by tarnishment must be supported by evidence that the plaintiff's mark will suffer negative associations from the defendant's use. [cit.] There has been no evidence in this case to indicate that Defendants' service mark has had an actionable impact on the image cultivated by either the "Elvis" or "Elvis Presley" trademarks.

Plaintiff bases its tarnishment claim on the unsupported assumption that Defendants' use of the Elvis name in association with a tacky bar that indiscriminately displays explicit and almost pornographic paintings of nude women has tainted the wholesome image of

Elvis and EPE sponsored products and services. The Court finds, however, without any evidence to the contrary, that nude portraits hung in a bar for the purpose of mocking the tasteless decor of the sixties does not inspire negative or unsavory images of Elvis or Elvis related products or services in the minds of EPE customers. Furthermore, the nude pictures and the bar's intentional tackiness are an obvious part of the parody and are associated, to the extent any association is made, for purposes of the parody only, rather than for creating a permanent derogatory connection in the public's mind between the two businesses. [cit.] Although "The Velvet Elvis" might be considered by some customers to be in poor taste, the Court is convinced that it is not likely to prompt an unsavory or unwholesome association in consumers' minds with the "Elvis" or "Elvis Presley" trademarks. Absent such a showing, a tarnishment claim cannot be sustained.

IV.   RIGHT OF PUBLICITY

Plaintiff claims that Defendants' use of the name, image, likeness, and other indicia of Elvis for the purposes of trade constitutes an appropriation of Elvis Presley's right of publicity. As owner of the exclusive rights in the identity of Elvis, Plaintiff seeks redress for a violation of its common law right as well as its corresponding statutory rights under . . . Texas law. . . .

Under Texas law a person is specifically prohibited from using:

> without the written consent of a person who may exercise the property right, a deceased individual's name, voice, signature, photograph, or likeness in any manner, including: (1) in connection with products, merchandise or goods; or (2) for purpose of advertising, selling, or soliciting the purchase of products, merchandise, goods or services.

Tex. Prop. Code §26.011 (Vernon 1984 & Supp. 1996). A prima facie case requires proof that (1) the defendant has appropriated another's identity and (2) is using it for trade or commercial benefit. [cit.] . . .

Unquestionably, use of pictures or images of Elvis in "The Velvet Elvis" advertisements is an unlawful appropriation of the identity of Elvis Presley. Elvis is clearly identifiable and the only distinguishable purpose of the ads is to exploit the persona of Elvis for commercial advantage. Defendants admitted as much when they expressed a willingness at trial to be permanently enjoined from using similar advertisements in the future. The mention of Graceland or use of phrases in ads that are linked inextricably to the identity of Elvis as a celebrity, such as "Elvis has left the building" is also violative of Plaintiff's publicity rights. . . .

Use of Elvis memorabilia as decor, on the other hand, does not amount to any violation as it is not intended for the purpose of advertising, selling, or soliciting the purchase of products, merchandise, goods or services. In other words, the function of the memorabilia is not to promote a product or capitalize on the personality of Elvis himself but rather to recreate an era of which Elvis was a public part. In fact, with the exception of the now infamous velvet Elvis portrait, Defendants have removed most of the Elvis related objects with no apparent effect on the bar's message or success. Likewise, the Court finds the menu's use of the expression "King of Dive Bars" and its incorporation of peanut butter and banana sandwiches as a menu item are not actionable. While it may be true that Elvis enjoyed peanut butter and banana sandwiches, this fact alone will not support a claim for violation of the Plaintiff's right of publicity. To trigger infringement the plaintiff must be clearly identifiable from use of the item or phrase in question. [cit.] Such is not the case here.

Additionally, the Court finds Defendants' use of the service mark, "The Velvet Elvis," does not amount to an unauthorized commercial exploitation of the identity of Elvis Presley. The service mark represents an art form reflective of an era that Elvis helped to shape. "The Velvet Elvis" became a coined phrase for the art of velvet paintings and was adopted by Defendants for this reason—not because of its identification with Elvis Presley. Elvis's association with velvet paintings was not a product of his own doing nor can it be considered a part of the character or personality of Elvis that Plaintiff has the right to control. [T]his phrase is not the thumbprint, work product, or tangible expression of Elvis Presley's celebrity identity. The mere association of a phrase or expression with a celebrity without the intent or effect of exploiting his identity or persona is insufficient cause for a violation of publicity rights.

Even assuming a violation of Plaintiff's right of publicity, Defendants' use of "The Velvet Elvis" as its service mark should be protected expression under the First Amendment. . . .

Finally, Plaintiff also accuses Defendants of violating its right of publicity by selling a frozen drink called "Love Me Blenders" and a food item named "Your Football Hound Dog." The Court finds that the connection with Elvis's hit songs "Love Me Tender" and "Hound Dog" is an obvious attempt at humor and plays a supporting part in the overall parody. Its use, therefore, is not actionable. . . .

Thank you. Thank you very much.

NOTES AND QUESTIONS

1. *Cross-references.* The *Elvis Presley* case touches on many of the theories that we will discuss in this book in greater detail. For example, we will explore the likelihood-of-confusion analysis in Chapter 7, the dilution theory in Chapter 8, the parody "defense" in Chapter 9, and the right of publicity in Chapter 11.

2. *Validity and infringement.* We discuss the creation and validity of trademarks in Part II, and the scope of protection in Part III, of this book. Did the defendant in *Elvis Presley* challenge the validity of the plaintiff's marks? If not, why not? What does this tell you about the nature of trademark rights?

3. *Interests protected by trademark law.* What harms to the Presley estate is the plaintiff concerned about? What interests is it seeking to vindicate?

4. *The focus of trademark law.* The defendant argued that "[b]ecause the bar is meant and viewed as a parody, . . . use of its service mark has not yet nor will in the future cause confusion as to the identity of the bar's owners, sponsors, or affiliates." Which should be more important to trademark law—whether the bar was meant or viewed as a parody? Which is more important to unfair competition law?

5. *Judicial values.* McClure suggested above that "because . . . decisions [on validity and infringement] concentrate so heavily on the facts of a particular case, and because this legal doctrine tends to become formalistic and conceptualistic, there is much room for judicial discretion. As legal realism has taught us, judicial discretion is exercised within the context of broader political and intellectual trends of the times." What values appear to be driving the district court judge here? Which values cut in which direction?

6. *Different theories of liability.* The *Elvis Presley* court appears to group many of the different theories of liability together. Why does it do that? Which theories does it treat differently and why?

7.   *On appeal.* Conducting a de novo review of the district court's likelihood-of-confusion analysis, the Fifth Circuit reversed. *Elvis Presley Enterprises, Inc. v. Capece*, 141 F.3d 188 (5th Cir. 1998). The Fifth Circuit took a very different approach *inter alia* to Capece's claim of parody, concluding (consistent with doctrinal rules regarding parody in the copyright context):

> The Defendants' parody of the faddish bars of the sixties does not require the use of EPE's marks because it does not target Elvis Presley; therefore, the necessity to use the marks significantly decreases and does not justify the use. Capece himself conceded that the Defendants could have performed their parody without using Elvis's name. Without the necessity to use Elvis's name, parody does not weigh against a likelihood of confusion in relation to EPE's marks. It is simply irrelevant. As an irrelevant factor, parody does not weigh against or in favor of a likelihood of confusion, and the district court erred in relying upon parody in its determination of the likelihood of confusion.

Id. at 200. Why should parody be relevant (or irrelevant) to trademark infringement liability?

8.   *Federal jurisdiction and appeal routes.* The U.S. Patent and Trademark Office (PTO), a federal administrative entity, takes original jurisdiction over applications for federal trademark registration. Individual trademark examiners have responsibility for the initial registrability decision. Applicants who are dissatisfied with the examiner's decision can appeal to an administrative tribunal, the Trademark Trial and Appeal Board (TTAB), composed of administrative law judges who sit in panels. *See* 15 U.S.C. §1070. The TTAB takes evidence and renders opinions much in the nature of a judicial body. You will encounter a few TTAB opinions in this book.

Applicants who are dissatisfied with the TTAB's decision can appeal to court. The relevant statutory provision, 15 U.S.C. §1071, provides two options: the applicant can appeal directly to the Court of Appeals for the Federal Circuit (CAFC); or, alternatively, the applicant can institute a civil action against the PTO in a district court (ordinarily the District Court for the District of Columbia). Most applicants prefer the CAFC, perhaps because of the perception that the CAFC has substantial intellectual property expertise owing to its role as the exclusive appellate authority in patent cases. The alternative route, civil suit in the district court, does have one advantage: The suit is on a de novo record, so the applicant (and the PTO, for that matter) may supplement the record with additional expert witness testimony, documentary evidence, and so forth.

Suits for registered trademark infringement (Section 32 of the Lanham Act), or for other causes of action under the Lanham Act (Section 43(a) unfair competition, 43(c) dilution, and 43(d) cybersquatting) can be instituted in federal district court. *See* 15 U.S.C. §1121(a). Appeals in such cases proceed through the regular appeal route—i.e., to regional appellate courts, then by certiorari to the Supreme Court. This differs from the appellate regime for patent cases, in which a specialized court—the CAFC—takes predominant appellate jurisdiction. Accordingly, federal trademark rights may be subject to conflicting legal standards issuing from various regional appellate bodies.

Although this suggests two separate routes by which trademark issues reach appeal courts, the two paths can and often do converge. In many actions involving registered trademarks, the target of the lawsuit may put in issue the validity of the trademark registration. The Lanham Act empowers courts to review registration validity and order cancellation of registrations where warranted. 15 U.S.C. §1119.

We will note the peculiarities of particular procedural postures as we encounter them throughout the book. For a graphic representation of appeal routes, *see* Figure 1-3, *infra* page 42.

FIGURE 1-1

A Trademark Timeline

Date	*Development*
1870	Congress enacts the first statute providing for federal trademark registration.
1879	The United States Supreme Court strikes down the 1870 Act as unconstitutional in *The Trademark Cases*.
1881	Congress enacts a very limited response to *The Trademark Cases*, with a statute that provides for registration of marks used in commerce with foreign nations and Indian tribes (but not interstate commerce).
1905	Congress enacts a statute permitting registration of marks used in interstate commerce, but registrable marks are in essence limited to those categories that we would now describe as inherently distinctive (then called "technical trademarks").
1946	The Lanham Act is enacted, providing for federal registration of marks used in commerce, and liberalizing the rules regarding registrable marks.
1958	The Trademark Trial and Appeal Board (TTAB) is created to hear appeals from ex parte refusals by the PTO to register a mark, and to hear the trial of *inter partes* proceedings.
1962	Section 32 (the principal infringement provision governing registered marks) is amended to eliminate the requirement that confusion had to be of "purchasers as to the source of origin of such goods or services."
1982	The Court of Customs and Patent Appeals (C.C.P.A.), which hears appeals from the TTAB, is replaced by the Court of Appeals for the Federal Circuit (CAFC), which assumes that same appellate jurisdiction.
1984	The Trademark Counterfeiting Act of 1984 enhances the remedies available against counterfeiters.
1988	The Trademark Law Revision Act of 1988 (TLRA), effective November 16, 1989, substantially revises the Lanham Act: it introduces the intent-to-use (ITU) system into U.S. law, makes a variety of amendments designed to keep the register uncluttered, rewrites Section 43(a) to reflect judicial developments, and expands Section 43(a) to cover product disparagement claims under the rubric of false advertising.
1993	The Lanham Act is amended in minor ways to implement the North American Free Trade Agreement (NAFTA).
1994	The Lanham Act is amended in minor ways to implement the Agreement on Trade-Related Aspects of Intellectual Property (TRIPS).
1995	The Federal Trademark Dilution Protection Act of 1995, effective January 16, 1996, enacts Section 43(c) of the Lanham Act and creates a federal cause of action for dilution.
1998	The Trademark Law Treaty Implementation Act of 1998, effective October 30, 1999, amends several registration-related provisions of the Lanham Act to comply with the Trademark Law Treaty (TLT), which sought to harmonize registration formalities worldwide.
1999	The Anticybersquatting Consumer Protection Act of 1999 enacts Section 43(d) of the Lanham Act and creates a cause of action for cybersquatting.
2003	The Lanham Act is amended to enable the United States to adhere to the Madrid Protocol.
2006	The Trademark Dilution Revision Act of 2006 makes multiple reforms to Section 43(c) and abrogates the Supreme Court's *Victoria's Secret* decision.

FIGURE 1-2
A Comparison of Copyright, Patent, and Trademark

The figure below sets out a basic comparison of the principal features of copyright, patent, and trademark law. As you will see throughout the book (and also if you study copyright or patent law), there are exceptions and nuances that cannot be reflected in this format. For example, trademark rights may be acquired by foreign applicants based upon parallel foreign registrations without use in commerce. *See* Chapter 4 *infra*. And famous marks get a broader scope of protection. *See* Chapter 8 *infra*. But this chart illustrates the basic differences and similarities among the three primary forms of intellectual property.

	Copyright	*Utility Patent*	*Trademark*
Protectable subject matter	Works of authorship	Any process, machine, manufacture, or composition of matter, or improvement thereof	Any symbol or device that is capable of identifying the source of goods
Primary threshold for protection	Originality	Novelty, nonobviousness, utility, and adequate disclosure	Distinctiveness
Principal exclusions from protection	Ideas, facts	Abstract ideas, products of nature	Functional matter, generic terms
How to acquire rights	Fixation in a tangible medium of expression	Obtaining a patent from the PTO	Using the mark in commerce
Duration	Life of the author plus 70 years	20 years from filing	As long as the mark is used and is distinctive
Required formalities	None	No rights prior to grant of patent	None
Form of notice	© with year of publication and name of owner	"Patent" or "pat." and patent number (after grant of patent)	® or "Reg. U.S. Pat. & Tm. Off." (after registration), or "TM" or "SM" (before registration)
Benefits of complying with optional formalities	Registration required to sue for infringement of U.S. works: notice and registration affect remedies	Notice affects remedies	Notice affects remedies

(*continued*)

FIGURE 1-2. (*contd.*)

	Copyright	*Utility Patent*	*Trademark*
Scope of principal rights acquired	Exclusive right to make copies of the work	Right to exclude others from making, using, offering for sale, selling, or importing the invention	Right to stop the unauthorized use of the same or similar mark in ways that are likely to cause consumer confusion
International protection	Protected without formalities in most countries (under the law of the country in question)	Obtained by securing rights on a country-by-country basis, or through a centralized mechanism such as the Patent Cooperation Treaty or the European Patent Convention	Rights obtained on a country-by-country basis, or through a centralized registration mechanism such as the Madrid Protocol

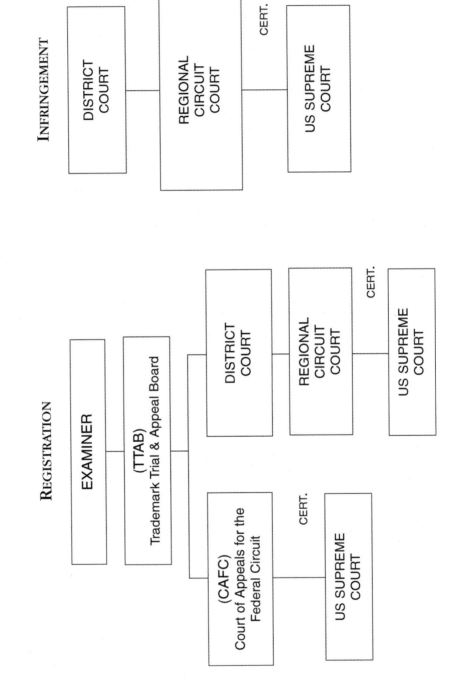

FIGURE 1-3
Appeal Routes

II

CREATION OF TRADEMARK RIGHTS

DISTINCTIVENESS

The existence of trademark rights is an issue that arises in many different areas of trademark law and in several procedural contexts. Obviously, a plaintiff bringing an action for infringement of a mark (whether registered or unregistered) must show the existence of a trademark. Thus, the issue will be litigated in many infringement cases. Similarly, an applicant for a federal trademark registration must demonstrate to the United States Patent and Trademark Office (PTO) that its claimed trademark exists. And where a third party seeks to oppose or cancel the grant of a trademark registration (two procedures discussed in more detail in Chapter 5), the issue is often put in play. Thus, each of the elements we discuss in the next three chapters pervades the practice of trademark law.

Most of the elements that a producer must show to establish trademark rights can be identified from the definitions found in the Restatement (Third) of Unfair Competition (1995) and in Section 45 of the Lanham Act (which is the definitions section of the trademark statute). The next three chapters (Chapters 2-4) will expand upon each of those requirements. Parse the definitions below, and extract from them the prerequisites to trademark protection. More concretely, what do you need to be able to say about CREST, a name under which toothpaste is sold, before you can say that it is a trademark? To what extent do those prerequisites, or the definitions themselves, reflect or flow inevitably from the purposes of trademark law discussed in Chapter 1?

RESTATEMENT (THIRD) OF UNFAIR COMPETITION (1995)

Section 9

A trademark is a word, name, symbol, device, or other designation, or a combination of such designations, that is distinctive of a person's goods or services and that is used in a manner that identifies those goods or services and distinguishes them from the goods or services of others. A service mark is a trademark that is used in connection with services.

LANHAM ACT

Section 45

The term "trademark" includes any word, name, symbol, or device, or any combination thereof . . . used by a person . . . to identify and distinguish his or her goods, including a unique product, from those manufactured or sold by others and to indicate the source of the goods, even if that source is unknown.

The term "service mark" means any word, name, symbol, or device, or any combination thereof . . . used by a person . . . to identify and distinguish the services of one person, including a unique service, from the services of others and to indicate the source of the services, even if that source is unknown. . . .

The terms "trade name" and "commercial name" mean any name used by a person to identify his or her business or vocation.

NOTES AND QUESTIONS

1. *The role of registration.* The full definition of "trademark" in Section 45 of the Lanham Act also makes reference to source-identifiers that a producer has a "bona fide intent to use in commerce." This part of the definition relates to questions of trademark registration. In the United States, trademark rights as such are not acquired through registration. Registration is an important part of the trademark system, and we will study the registration process and issues related thereto in Chapter 5. But the general premise of U.S. law is that registration of a trademark merely recognizes the trademark rights that exist at common law (through *use* of a symbol to identify the source of goods). In most other countries, trademark rights are secured through registration. The trademark systems in these countries are, not surprisingly, referred to as registration-based systems; the U.S. trademark system remains use-based. Although the United States is in a small minority on this issue, the use/registration divide lies at the heart of many international trademark debates.

2. *Trade names.* Historically, the term "trade name" was often used to refer to a subset of trademarks that were protected only upon proof of secondary meaning, but modern parlance draws a firmer distinction between trademarks and trade names. Review the definitions from the Lanham Act. What is the difference between a trademark and a trade name? As we will discuss in Chapter 5, trademarks can be registered with the PTO. Trade names cannot be registered with the PTO, but may be protected under the unfair competition provision of the federal trademark statute (Section 43(a) of the Lanham Act).

3. *Trademarks versus service marks.* As the Restatement and Section 45 definitions point out, the term "trademark" refers to a source-identifier for goods, and the term "service mark" refers to a source-identifier for services. Routine promotional activities that a trademark owner might undertake in connection with his or her goods do not separately qualify as "services." *In re Dr. Pepper Co.*, 836 F.2d 508 (Fed. Cir. 1987) (refusing to register PEPPER MAN as a service mark for the asserted service of promoting applicant's DR. PEPPER soft drink via contests).

In many situations, it is not necessary to distinguish between trademarks and service marks; the same rules will apply to both. *See* Lanham Act §3 ("Subject to the provisions relating to the registration of trademarks, so far as they are applicable, service marks shall be registrable, in the same manner and with the same effect as are trademarks, and when registered they shall be entitled to the protection provided in this chapter in the case of trademarks.").

In the trademarks/unfair competition literature, the term "trademark" is often used as an umbrella term for any source-identifier. The same is true of the term "mark." *See* Lanham Act Section 45 (stating that "[t]he term 'mark' includes any trademark, service mark . . ." and continuing on to list other types of marks). In this book, we will adopt the prevalent usage of "trademark" and "mark" as an umbrella term, and we will identify situations where the distinction between service marks and trademarks matters.

4. *Certification and collective marks.* Two other types of mark are identified by the Lanham Act. A certification mark is a mark "used by a person other than its owner . . . to certify regional or other origin, material, mode of manufacture, quality, accuracy, or other characteristics of such person's goods or services or that the work or labor on the goods or services was performed by members of a union or other organization." 15 U.S.C. §1127.

Although courts have held that certification marks could (and still can) be protected at common law, the Lanham Act for the first time permitted federal registration of such marks. *See* 15 U.S.C. §1054. For example, the GOOD HOUSEKEEPING SEAL OF APPROVAL is a certification mark that can only be used by manufacturers whose products comply with the standards of quality and safety established by the Good Housekeeping Institute. The certification mark is owned by the Institute, but is used on the goods of persons *other than* the Institute. Certification marks are frequently used by producers of wines and foodstuffs from a particular region (e.g., PARMA for ham, or IDAHO for potatoes) to vouch for the fact that the food in question originates from the relevant locale and has been manufactured or produced or grown in a particular way or with particular ingredients.

The term "collective mark" was created by the Lanham Act in 1946, and means a trademark or service mark used by "the members of a cooperative, an association, or other collective group or organization . . . and includes marks indicating membership in a union, an association, or other organization. . . ." 15 U.S.C. §1127. At common law, the names of organized clubs or churches were protected under principles of unfair competition. The Lanham Act permitted their federal registration.

A.   The Spectrum of Distinctiveness

ABERCROMBIE & FITCH CO. v. HUNTING WORLD, INC.
537 F.2d 4 (2d Cir. 1976)

Friendly, Circuit Judge:
[Plaintiff sold various items of clothing under the mark SAFARI. The defendant marketed its rival clothing products under marks that used SAFARI either alone or in combination with other words. When the plaintiff sued for infringement, the district court dismissed the complaint and canceled the plaintiff's federal registrations. On appeal, the Second Circuit was required *inter alia* to assess the validity of plaintiff's claimed marks.]

II

It will be useful at the outset to restate some basic principles of trademark law, which, although they should be familiar, tend to become lost in a welter of adjectives.

The cases, and in some instances the Lanham Act, identify four different categories of terms with respect to trademark protection. Arrayed in an ascending order which roughly reflects their eligibility to trademark status and the degree of protection accorded, these classes are (1) generic, (2) descriptive, (3) suggestive, and (4) arbitrary or fanciful. The lines of demarcation, however, are not always bright. Moreover, the difficulties are compounded because a term that is in one category for a particular product may be in quite a different one for another,[6] because a term may shift from one category to another in light of differences in usage through time,[7] because a term may have one meaning to one group of users and a different one to others, and because the same term may be put to different uses with respect to a single product. In various ways, all of these complications are involved in the instant case.

A generic term is one that refers, or has come to be understood as referring, to the genus of which the particular product is a species. At common law neither those terms which were generic nor those which were merely descriptive could become valid trademarks. . . .

---

6. To take a familiar example "Ivory" would be generic when used to describe a product made from the tusks of elephants but arbitrary as applied to soap.

7. *See, e.g., Haughton Elevator Co. v. Seeberger*, 85 U.S.P.Q. 80 (1950), in which the coined word "Escalator," originally fanciful, or at the very least suggestive, was held to have become generic.

While . . . the Lanham Act makes an important exception with respect to those merely descriptive terms which have acquired secondary meaning, see §2(f), 15 U.S.C. §1052(f), it offers no such exception for generic marks. The Act provides for the cancellation of a registered mark if at any time it "becomes the common descriptive name of an article or substance," §14(c). This means that even proof of secondary meaning, by virtue of which some "merely descriptive" marks may be registered, cannot transform a generic term into a subject for trademark. [N]o matter how much money and effort the user of a generic term has poured into promoting the sale of its merchandise and what success it has achieved in securing public identification, it cannot deprive competing manufacturers of the product of the right to call an article by its name. [cit.] The pervasiveness of the principle is illustrated by a series of well known cases holding that when a suggestive or fanciful term has become generic as a result of a manufacturer's own advertising efforts, trademark protection will be denied save for those markets where the term still has not become generic and a secondary meaning has been shown to continue. [cit.] A term may thus be generic in one market and descriptive or suggestive or fanciful in another.

The term which is descriptive but not generic stands on a better basis. Although §2(e) of the Lanham Act, 15 U.S.C. §1052, forbids the registration of a mark which, when applied to the goods of the applicant, is "merely descriptive," §2(f) removes a considerable part of the sting by providing that "except as expressly excluded in paragraphs (a)-(d) of this section, nothing in this chapter shall prevent the registration of a mark used by the applicant which has become distinctive of the applicant's goods in commerce" and that the Commissioner may accept, as prima facie evidence that the mark has become distinctive, proof of substantially exclusive and continuous use of the mark applied to the applicant's goods for five years preceding the application. "[C]ommon descriptive name," as used in §§14(c) and 15(4), refers to generic terms applied to products and not to terms that are "merely descriptive." In the former case any claim to an exclusive right must be denied since this in effect would confer a monopoly not only of the mark but of the product by rendering a competitor unable effectively to name what it was endeavoring to sell. In the latter case the law strikes the balance, with respect to registration, between the hardships to a competitor in hampering the use of an appropriate word and those to the owner who, having invested money and energy to endow a word with the good will adhering to his enterprise, would be deprived of the fruits of his efforts.

The category of "suggestive" marks was spawned by the felt need to accord protection to marks that were neither exactly descriptive on the one hand nor truly fanciful on the other[,] a need that was particularly acute because of the bar in the Trademark Act of 1905 . . . on the registration of merely descriptive marks regardless of proof of secondary meaning. [cit.] Having created the category the courts have had great difficulty in defining it. Judge Learned Hand made the not very helpful statement:

> It is quite impossible to get any rule out of the cases beyond this: That the validity of the mark ends where suggestion ends and description begins.

Franklin Knitting Mills, Inc. v. Fashionit Sweater Mills, Inc., 297 F. 247, 248 (2 Cir. 1923), *aff'd per curiam*, 4 F.2d 1018 (2 Cir. 1925), a statement amply confirmed by comparing the list of terms held suggestive with those held merely descriptive in 3 Callmann, Unfair Competition, Trademarks and Monopolies §71.2 (3d ed.). Another court has observed, somewhat more usefully, that:

> A term is suggestive if it requires imagination, thought and perception to reach a conclusion as to the nature of goods. A term is descriptive if it forthwith conveys an immediate idea of the ingredients, qualities or characteristics of the goods.

Stix Products, Inc. v. United Merchants & Manufacturers Inc., 295 F. Supp. 479, 488 (S.D.N.Y. 1968)—a formulation deriving from *General Shoe Corp. v. Rosen*, 111 F.2d 95, 98 (4 Cir. 1940). Also useful is the approach taken by this court in *Aluminum Fabricating Co. of Pittsburgh v. Season-All Window Corp.*, 259 F.2d 314 (2 Cir. 1958), that the reason for restricting the protection accorded descriptive terms, namely the undesirability of preventing an entrant from using a descriptive term for his product, is much less forceful when the trademark is a suggestive word since, as Judge Lumbard wrote, 259 F.2d at 317:

> The English language has a wealth of synonyms and related words with which to describe the qualities which manufacturers may wish to claim for their products and the ingenuity of the public relations profession supplies new words and slogans as they are needed.

If a term is suggestive, it is entitled to registration without proof of secondary meaning. Moreover, as held in the *Season-All* case, the decision of the Patent Office to register a mark without requiring proof of secondary meaning affords a rebuttable presumption that the mark is suggestive or arbitrary or fanciful rather than merely descriptive.

It need hardly be added that fanciful or arbitrary terms[12] enjoy all the rights accorded to suggestive terms as marks—without the need of debating whether the term is "merely descriptive" and with ease of establishing infringement.

In the light of these principles we must proceed to a decision of this case.

III

We turn first to an analysis of [plaintiff's] trademarks to determine the scope of protection to which they are entitled. We have reached the following conclusions: (1) applied to specific types of clothing 'safari' has become a generic term . . . ; (2) 'safari' has not, however, become a generic term for boots or shoes; it is either "suggestive" or "merely descriptive." . . .

It is common ground that [plaintiff] could not apply 'Safari' as a trademark for an expedition into the African wilderness. This would be a clear example of the use of 'Safari' as a generic term. What is perhaps less obvious is that a word may have more than one generic use. The word 'Safari' has become part of a family of generic terms which, although deriving no doubt from the original use of the word and reminiscent of its milieu, have come to be understood not as having to do with hunting in Africa, but as terms within the language referring to contemporary American fashion apparel. These terms name the components of the safari outfit well-known to the clothing industry and its customers: the 'Safari hat,' a broad flat-brimmed hat with a single, large band; the 'Safari jacket,' a belted bush jacket with patch pockets and a buttoned shoulder loop; when the jacket is accompanied by pants, the combination is called the 'Safari suit.' Typically these items are khaki-colored.

This outfit, and its components, were doubtless what Judge Ryan had in mind when he found that "the word 'safari' in connection with wearing apparel is widely used by the general public and people in the trade." The record abundantly supports the conclusion that many stores have advertised these items despite [plaintiff's] attempts to police its mark. . . .

---

12. As terms of art, the distinctions between suggestive terms and fanciful or arbitrary terms may seem needlessly artificial. Of course, a common word may be used in a fanciful sense; indeed one might say that only a common word can be so used, since a coined word cannot first be put to a bizarre use. Nevertheless, the term "fanciful," as a classifying concept, is usually applied to words invented solely for their use as trademarks. When the same legal consequences attach to a common word, i. e., when it is applied in an unfamiliar way, the use is called "arbitrary."

What has been thus far established suffices to support the dismissal of the complaint with respect to many of the uses of 'Safari' by [the defendant]. . . .

RESTATEMENT (THIRD) OF UNFAIR COMPETITION (1995)

Section 13

A word, name, symbol, device, or other designation, or a combination of such designations, is "distinctive" . . . if:

(a) the designation is "inherently distinctive," in that, because of the nature of the designation and the context in which it is used, prospective purchasers are likely to perceive it as a designation that, in the case of a trademark, identifies goods or services produced or sponsored by a particular person, whether known or anonymous, . . . ; or
(b) the designation, although not "inherently distinctive," has become distinctive, in that, as a result of its use, prospective purchasers have come to perceive it as a designation that identifies goods, services, businesses, or members in the manner described in Subsection (a). Such acquired distinctiveness is commonly referred to as "secondary meaning."

NOTES AND QUESTIONS

1. *The role of distinctiveness and the distinctiveness lenses.* Review the definition of "trademark" at the beginning of this chapter. Why is distinctiveness a prerequisite to trademark protection? What are the reasons for the different treatment of arbitrary, fanciful, suggestive, descriptive, and generic marks? *See* Graeme B. Dinwoodie, *Reconceptualizing the Inherent Distinctiveness of Product Design Trade Dress*, 75 N.C. L. Rev. 471, 500-04 (1997) (suggesting and analyzing the two rationales underlying the distinctiveness spectrum). In answering this question, think not only about the consequences of protecting marks in these different categories, but also about the extent to which protecting marks in these categories would serve the purposes of trademark law. To make this exercise more concrete, consider whether to grant trademark protection to the following marks (or possible marks):

- APPLE for personal computers;
- SPEEDY for a mail courier service;
- EXTRA-STRONG for over-the-counter pain killers;
- ONE for perfume designed to be worn by either men or women;
- WHOLE WHEAT for whole wheat bread.

2. *Different kinds of distinctiveness.* Section 45 of the Lanham Act requires a trademark "to identify and distinguish his or her goods . . . from those manufactured or sold by others and to indicate the source of the goods, even if that source is unknown." Does this definition suggest that a trademark might identify goods in several different ways? Professor Barton Beebe has drawn on semiotic theory to suggest that trademarks might possess both "source distinctiveness" and "differential distinctiveness." *See* Barton Beebe, *The Semiotic Analysis of Trademark Law*, 51 UCLA L. Rev. 621 (2004). He writes that source distinctiveness describes the extent to which the trademark is "distinctive *of* source," whereas differential distinctiveness measures the extent to which the trademark is "distinctive *from* other trademarks." COKE for carbonated soft drinks is clearly distinctive: which of Beebe's forms of distinctiveness does it possess? Can a trademark do one without the other? What types of distinctiveness (either Beebe's or other types) does the statutory definition encompass? *Cf. In re Bayer AG*, 488 F.3d 960 (Fed. Cir. 2007).

   3.   *Registration and protectability.* Judge Friendly notes that "the cases, and in some instances the Lanham Act, identify four different categories of terms with respect to trademark protection." The provisions in the Lanham Act that refer to certain of these categories, and which are mentioned by Judge Friendly, relate to the registration of trademarks (or the cancellation of trademark registrations). More specifically, Section 2 of the Lanham Act (15 U.S.C. §1052) lists the grounds upon which trademark registrations may be denied, and Section 14 (15 U.S.C. §1064) lists the grounds on which a registration may be canceled. But there is an obvious parallel between the rules that determine whether trademark protection exists under the Lanham Act and those that govern whether a trademark registration should be granted under that statute. After all, as noted above, in the United States trademark registration is conceptualized as the recognition of trademark rights that exist at common law. Indeed, in 1992, Justice Stevens suggested that the protection of unregistered marks under Section 43(a) of the Lanham Act "is properly understood to provide protection in accordance with the standards for registration in §2." *Two Pesos Inc. v. Taco Cabana, Inc.*, 505 U.S. 763, 784 (1992). As we proceed, you should consider the extent to which Justice Stevens is correct that standards for *protection* under Section 43(a) mirror the standards for *registration* under Section 2 (and whether that should be the case). But Justice Stevens is clearly correct that, as a general proposition, the standards for protectability and registration are the same. The possibility that marks denied registration by virtue of statutory prohibitions might still have protection under the common law (enforced via Section 43(a)) is considered further in Chapter 5.

   4.   *Common descriptive (i.e., generic) terms.* Judge Friendly identifies the following categories of terms: (1) generic, (2) descriptive, (3) suggestive, and (4) arbitrary or fanciful. In his opinion, he quotes a statutory provision that refers to "common descriptive terms" (as opposed to "merely descriptive terms"). As Judge Friendly notes, that phrase—"common descriptive term"—was used by the statute to refer to generic terms. To avoid confusion, Congress eventually amended Section 14 such that the term "generic" (rather than "common descriptive") is now used in the statute.

   5.   *Two paths to distinctiveness.* Section 13 of the Restatement divides protected (i.e., distinctive) marks into marks that are inherently distinctive and marks that have acquired distinctiveness (i.e., have secondary meaning). How does the *Abercrombie* spectrum fit with the Restatement explanation: that is, which marks on the *Abercrombie* spectrum are inherently distinctive?

   6.   *Marks for goods and services.* Notice the way that trademark lawyers identify marks: The Coca-Cola Company owns the trademark COKE for carbonated soft drinks. This highlights the limited nature of trademark rights; they symbolize the goodwill attaching to the product they identify. It also illustrates why distinctiveness analysis must focus on the relationship between the identifier and the product it identifies. One cannot assess "how distinctive IVORY is" without knowing the goods for which it purports to act as a trademark. Thus, the mark BRILLIANT for garbage bags would probably be classified differently from BRILLIANT for diamonds.

   7.   *Selecting trademarks.* Assume that you are counsel to a well-known baby products company (LOCKWOOD'S) that has developed a new form of food seal that will help to make baby food containers tamperproof (or at least make it obvious if someone has tried to tamper with the seal on the container). Similar goods are already on the market, but are less reliable and of a relatively low quality. Your client wants to emphasize the quality of its product and also its ability to guarantee safety in ways that current products cannot. The marketing department has suggested three marks under which it might market the product:

SAFEKIDS; LOCKWOOD'S SAFESEAL; and TAMPERNO. Based upon your reading thus far, which mark would you wish your client to adopt? If you were to suggest any other alternative marks that you would like (from a trademark perspective) to have the company consider, what would they be? What about ZEEM? How do you believe the marketing department would react to that suggestion?

8. *Archaic usage*. Although marks that are descriptive can now be protected (and registered) as trademarks upon proof of secondary meaning, it was not always so. Prior to the Lanham Act in 1946, in essence only so-called technical trademarks (what we now call inherently distinctive marks) could be protected and registered under trademark law. Descriptive marks could effectively be protected upon proof of secondary meaning only under principles of unfair competition (not trademark) law. Indeed, under this early twentieth-century case law, marks that were not technical trademarks were called "trade names." *See* J. THOMAS MCCARTHY, TRADEMARKS AND UNFAIR COMPETITION LAW §4.5 (2002) ("[I]n archaic usage, the term 'trade name' was used to designate terms in that category of marks which required proof of secondary meaning for legal protection."). As we discussed above, the term "trade name" now has a different meaning.

9. *Examples of fanciful and arbitrary marks.* Developing a feel for where a mark might be placed on the distinctiveness spectrum can be assisted not only by considering the rationales for the different categories, but also to some extent by reviewing prior determinations. A word of caution is in order, however. Distinctiveness determinations are notoriously fact-specific, and it is not difficult to find decisions that are hard to reconcile. However, both the TMEP and the McCarthy treatise helpfully (in different sections) list illustrations of marks found by the PTO or courts to be properly classified as fanciful, arbitrary, suggestive, descriptive, or generic. It is worth briefly perusing these lists (which are found in TMEP § 1209.01 and McCarthy, §§ 11:8, 11:13, 11:24, 11:72 and 12:18-19). In particular, you may find it useful to compare the marks in the different lists. For present purposes, we have set out below a few illustrations of marks that have been found to be fanciful or arbitrary. (If you want the cites for the different examples, review the above-cited sections of the TMEP or McCarthy). We include other illustrative listings later in this chapter when we examine the line between suggestive and descriptive marks, and then the descriptive/generic line.

Marks Found to be Fanciful	Marks Found to be Arbitrary
CLOROX for bleach	CONGRESS for spring water
EXXON for oil and gasoline products	GAP for wearing apparel
KODAK for photographic supplies	OMEGA for watches
VIAGRA for erectile dysfunction drug	MUSTANG for motel
CUTICURA for toilet soap	VICTORIA'S SECRET for lingerie and clothing
ODOL for mouthwash	LAMBDA for computer equipment

B.   DESCRIPTIVENESS AND SECONDARY MEANING

ZATARAIN'S, INC. v. OAK GROVE SMOKEHOUSE, INC.

698 F.2d 786 (5th Cir. 1983)

GOLDBERG, Circuit Judge:

This appeal of a trademark dispute presents us with a menu of edible delights sure to tempt connoisseurs of fish and fowl alike. At issue is the alleged infringement of two trademarks, "Fish-Fri" and "Chick-Fri," held by appellant Zatarain's, Inc. ("Zatarain's"). The district court held that the alleged infringers had a "fair use" defense to any asserted infringement of the term "Fish-Fri" and that the registration of the term "Chick-Fri" should be cancelled. We affirm.

I.   FACTS AND PROCEEDINGS BELOW

A.   The Tale of the Town Frier

Zatarain's is the manufacturer and distributor of a line of over one hundred food products. Two of these products, "Fish-Fri" and "Chick-Fri," are coatings or batter mixes used to fry foods. These marks serve as the entree in the present litigation.

Zatarain's "Fish-Fri" consists of 100% corn flour and is used to fry fish and other seafood. "Fish-Fri" is packaged in rectangular cardboard boxes containing twelve or twenty-four ounces of coating mix. The legend "Wonderful FISH-FRI®" is displayed prominently on the front panel, along with the block Z used to identify all Zatarain's products. The term "Fish-Fri" has been used by Zatarain's or its predecessor since 1950 and has been registered as a trademark since 1962.

Zatarain's "Chick-Fri" is a seasoned corn flour batter mix used for frying chicken and other foods. The "Chick-Fri" package, which is very similar to that used for "Fish-Fri," is a rectangular cardboard container labelled "Wonderful CHICK-FRI." Zatarain's began to use the term "Chick-Fri" in 1968 and registered the term as a trademark in 1976.

Zatarain's products are not alone in the marketplace. At least four other companies market coatings for fried foods that are denominated "fish fry" or "chicken fry." Two of these competing companies are the appellees here, and therein hangs this fish tale.

Appellee Oak Grove Smokehouse, Inc. ("Oak Grove") began marketing a "fish fry" and a "chicken fry" in March 1979. Both products are packaged in clear glassine packets that contain a quantity of coating mix sufficient to fry enough food for one meal. The packets are labelled with Oak Grove's name and emblem, along with the words "FISH FRY" or "CHICKEN FRY." Oak Grove's "FISH FRY" has a corn flour base seasoned with various spices; Oak Grove's "CHICKEN FRY" is a seasoned coating with a wheat flour base.

Appellee Visko's Fish Fry, Inc. ("Visko's") entered the batter mix market in March 1980 with its "fish fry." Visko's product is packed in a cylindrical eighteen-ounce container with a resealable plastic lid. The words "Visko's FISH FRY" appear on the label along with a photograph of a platter of fried fish. Visko's coating mix contains corn flour and added spices.

Other food manufacturing concerns also market coating mixes. Boochelle's Spice Co. ("Boochelle's"), originally a defendant in this lawsuit, at one time manufactured a seasoned "FISH FRY" packaged in twelve-ounce vinyl plastic packets. Pursuant to a settlement between Boochelle's and Zatarain's, Boochelle's product is now labelled "FISH AND VEGETABLE FRY." Another batter mix, "YOGI Brand® OYSTER SHRIMP and FISH FRY," is also available. Arnaud Coffee Corporation ("Arnaud") has manufactured and marketed "YOGI Brand" for ten to twenty years, but was never made a party to this litigation. A product called "Golden Dipt Old South Fish Fry" has recently entered the market as well.

B.   Out of the Frying Pan, into the Fire

[Zatarain's filed a complaint against Oak Grove and Visko's on June 19, 1979, alleging trademark infringement and unfair competition under the Lanham Act. The United States District Court for the Eastern District of Louisiana concluded that the mark FISH FRI was protectable, because although it was merely descriptive, there was evidence demonstrating secondary meaning. Nevertheless, the court held that defendants were not liable for trademark infringement, because their use of the mark was shielded by the fair use doctrine, which enables competitors in certain circumstances to make use of a trademarked term in order fairly and in good faith to describe their own product. *See infra* Chapter 9. The district court also concluded that plaintiff's mark CHICK-FRI was merely descriptive and there was no evidence establishing secondary meaning; thus, the court granted the defendants' counterclaim that the registration of CHICK-FRI be canceled under Section 37.]

Battered, but not fried, Zatarain's appeals from the adverse judgment on several grounds. First, Zatarain's argues that its trademark "Fish-Fri" is a suggestive term and therefore not subject to the "fair use" defense. . . .* Zatarain's [also] urges that the district court erred in cancelling the trademark registration for the term "Chick-Fri" because Zatarain's presented sufficient evidence to establish a secondary meaning for the term. For these reasons, Zatarain's argues that the district court should be reversed. . . .

III.   THE TRADEMARK CLAIMS

A.   BASIC PRINCIPLES

1.   *Classifications of Marks*

The threshold issue in any action for trademark infringement is whether the word or phrase is initially registerable or protectable. [cit.] Courts and commentators have traditionally divided potential trademarks into four categories. A potential trademark may be classified as (1) generic, (2) descriptive, (3) suggestive, or (4) arbitrary or fanciful. These categories, like the tones in a spectrum, tend to blur at the edges and merge together. The labels are more advisory than definitional, more like guidelines than pigeonholes. Not surprisingly, they are somewhat difficult to articulate and to apply. [cit.]

A *generic* term is "the name of a particular genus or class of which an individual article or service is but a member." [cit.] A generic term connotes the "basic nature of articles or services" rather than the more individualized characteristics of a particular product. [cit.] Generic terms can never attain trademark protection. [cit.] . . . Such terms as aspirin and cellophane have been held generic and therefore unprotectable as trademarks. *See Bayer Co. v. United Drug Co.*, 272 F. 505 (S.D.N.Y. 1921) (aspirin); *DuPont Cellophane Co. v. Waxed Products Co.*, 85 F.2d 75 (2d Cir. 1936) (cellophane).

A *descriptive* term "identifies a characteristic or quality of an article or service," [cit.] such as its color, odor, function, dimensions, or ingredients. *American Heritage*, 494 F.2d at 11. Descriptive terms ordinarily are not protectable as trademarks, . . . ; they may become valid marks, however, by acquiring a secondary meaning in the minds of the consuming public. *See* 15 U.S.C. §1052(f). Examples of descriptive marks would include "Alo" with reference to products containing gel of the aloe vera plant, *Aloe Creme Laboratories, Inc. v. Milsan, Inc.*, 423 F.2d 845 (5th Cir. 1970), and "Vision Center" in reference to a business offering optical goods and services. [cit.] As this court has often noted, the distinction between descriptive and generic terms is one of degree. . . .

A *suggestive* term suggests, rather than describes, some particular characteristic of the goods or services to which it applies and requires the consumer to exercise the imagination in order to draw a conclusion as to the nature of the goods and services. [cit.] A suggestive mark is protected without the necessity for proof of secondary meaning. The term "Coppertone" has been held suggestive in regard to sun tanning products. *See Douglas Laboratories, Inc. v. Copper Tan, Inc.*, 210 F.2d 453 (2d Cir. 1954).

Arbitrary or *fanciful* terms bear no relationship to the products or services to which they are applied. Like suggestive terms, arbitrary and fanciful marks are protectable without proof of secondary meaning. The term "Kodak" is properly classified as a fanciful term for

---

* *Ed. Note:* Whether the fair use defense is available with respect to a suggestive mark is discussed *infra* in Chapter 9.

photographic supplies [cit.]; "Ivory" is an arbitrary term as applied to soap. *Abercrombie & Fitch*, 537 F.2d at 9 n.6.

2.   *Secondary Meaning*

As noted earlier, descriptive terms are ordinarily not protectable as trademarks. They may be protected, however, if they have acquired a secondary meaning for the consuming public. The concept of secondary meaning recognizes that words with an ordinary and primary meaning of their own "may by long use with a particular product, come to be known by the public as specifically designating that product." *Volkswagenwerk Aktiengesellschaft v. Rickard*, 492 F.2d 474, 477 (5th Cir. 1974). . . .

B.   "Fish-Fri"[3]

1.   *Classification*

Throughout this litigation, Zatarain's has maintained that the term "Fish-Fri" is a suggestive mark automatically protected from infringing uses by virtue of its registration in 1962. Oak Grove and Visko's assert that "fish fry" is a generic term identifying a class of foodstuffs used to fry fish; alternatively, Oak Grove and Visko's argue that "fish fry" is merely descriptive of the characteristics of the product. The district court found that "Fish-Fri" was a descriptive term identifying a function of the product being sold. Having reviewed this finding under the appropriate "clearly erroneous" standard, we affirm. [cit.]

We are mindful that "[t]he concept of descriptiveness must be construed rather broadly." [cit.] Whenever a word or phrase conveys an immediate idea of the qualities, characteristics, effect, purpose, or ingredients of a product or service, it is classified as descriptive and cannot be claimed as an exclusive trademark. *[S]ee Stix Products, Inc. v. United Merchants & Manufacturers, Inc.*, 295 F. Supp. 479, 488 (S.D.N.Y. 1968). Courts and commentators have formulated a number of tests to be used in classifying a mark as descriptive.

A suitable starting place is the dictionary, for "[t]he dictionary definition of the word is an appropriate and relevant indication 'of the ordinary significance and meaning of words' to the public." [cit.] *Webster's Third New International Dictionary* 858 (1966) lists the following definitions for the term "fish fry": "1. a picnic at which fish are caught, fried, and eaten; . . . 2. fried fish." Thus, the basic dictionary definitions of the term refer to the preparation and consumption of fried fish. This is at least preliminary evidence that the term "Fish-Fri" is descriptive of Zatarain's product in the sense that the words naturally direct attention to the purpose or function of the product.

The "imagination test" is a second standard used by the courts to identify descriptive terms. This test seeks to measure the relationship between the actual words of the mark and the product to which they are applied. If a term "requires imagination, thought and perception to reach a conclusion as to the nature of goods," [cit.] it is considered a suggestive term. Alternatively, a term is descriptive if standing alone it conveys information as to the characteristics of the product. In this case, mere observation compels the conclusion that a product branded "Fish-Fri" is a prepackaged coating or batter mix applied to fish prior to cooking. The connection between this merchandise and its identifying terminology is so close and direct that even a consumer unfamiliar with the product would doubtless have an idea of its purpose or function. It simply does not require an exercise of the imagination to deduce that "Fish-Fri" is used to fry fish. [cit.] Accordingly, the term "Fish-Fri" must be considered descriptive when examined under the "imagination test."

---

3. We note at the outset that Zatarain's use of the phonetic equivalent of the words "fish fry"—that is, misspelling it—does not render the mark protectable. *Soweco*, 617 F.2d at 1186 n.24.

A third test used by courts and commentators to classify descriptive marks is "whether competitors would be likely to need the terms used in the trademark in describing their products." *Union Carbide Corp. v. Ever-Ready, Inc.*, 531 F.2d 366, 379 (7th Cir. 1976). A descriptive term generally relates so closely and directly to a product or service that other merchants marketing similar goods would find the term useful in identifying their own goods. [cit.] Common sense indicates that in this case merchants other than Zatarain's might find the term "fish fry" useful in describing their own particular batter mixes. While Zatarain's has argued strenuously that Visko's and Oak Grove could have chosen from dozens of other possible terms in naming their coating mix, we find this position to be without merit. As this court has held, the fact that a term is not the only or even the most common name for a product is not determinative, for there is no legal foundation that a product can be described in only one fashion. [cit.] There are many edible fish in the sea, and as many ways to prepare them as there are varieties to be prepared. Even piscatorial gastronomes would agree, however, that frying is a form of preparation accepted virtually around the world, at restaurants starred and unstarred. The paucity of synonyms for the words "fish" and "fry" suggests that a merchant whose batter mix is specially spiced for frying fish is likely to find "fish fry" a useful term for describing his product.

A final barometer of the descriptiveness of a particular term examines the extent to which a term actually has been used by others marketing a similar service or product. [cit.] This final test is closely related to the question whether competitors are likely to find a mark useful in describing their products. [A] number of companies other than Zatarain's have chosen the word combination "fish fry" to identify their batter mixes. Arnaud's product, "Oyster Shrimp and Fish Fry," has been in competition with Zatarain's "Fish-Fri" for some ten to twenty years. When companies from A to Z, from Arnaud to Zatarain's, select the same term to describe their similar products, the term in question is most likely a descriptive one.

The correct categorization of a given term is a factual issue [cit.]; consequently, we review the district court's findings under the "clearly erroneous" standard of Fed. R. Civ. P. 52. [cit.] The district court in this case found that Zatarain's trademark "Fish-Fri" was descriptive of the function of the product being sold. Having applied the four prevailing tests of descriptiveness to the term "Fish-Fri," we are convinced that the district court's judgment in this matter is not only not clearly erroneous, but clearly correct.

2.   *Secondary Meaning*

Descriptive terms are not protectable by trademark absent a showing of secondary meaning in the minds of the consuming public. To prevail in its trademark infringement action, therefore, Zatarain's must prove that its mark "Fish-Fri" has acquired a secondary meaning and thus warrants trademark protection. The district court found that Zatarain's evidence established a secondary meaning for the term "Fish-Fri" in the New Orleans area. We affirm.

The existence of secondary meaning presents a question for the trier of fact, and a district court's finding on the issue will not be disturbed unless clearly erroneous. [cit.] . . .

In assessing a claim of secondary meaning, the major inquiry is the consumer's attitude toward the mark. The mark must denote to the consumer "a single thing coming from a single source," *Coca-Cola Co. v. Koke Co.*, 254 U.S. 143, 146 (1920); [cit.], to support a finding of secondary meaning. Both direct and circumstantial evidence may be relevant and persuasive on the issue.

Factors such as amount and manner of advertising, volume of sales, and length and manner of use may serve as circumstantial evidence relevant to the issue of secondary meaning. [cit.] While none of these factors alone will prove secondary meaning, in combination they may establish the necessary link in the minds of consumers between a product and its source. It must be remembered, however, that "the question is not the *extent* of the promotional efforts, but their *effectiveness* in altering the meaning of [the term] to the consuming public." [cit.]

Since 1950, Zatarain's and its predecessor have continuously used the term "Fish-Fri" to identify this particular batter mix. Through the expenditure of over $400,000 for advertising during the period from 1976 through 1981, Zatarain's has promoted its name and its product to the buying public. Sales of twelve-ounce boxes of "Fish-Fri" increased from 37,265 cases in 1969 to 59,439 cases in 1979. From 1964 through 1979, Zatarain's sold a total of 916,385 cases of "Fish-Fri." The district court considered this circumstantial evidence of secondary meaning to weigh heavily in Zatarain's favor.

In addition to these circumstantial factors, Zatarain's introduced at trial two surveys conducted by its expert witness, Allen Rosenzweig. In one survey, telephone interviewers questioned 100 women in the New Orleans area who fry fish or other seafood three or more times per month. Of the women surveyed, twenty-three percent specified Zatarain's "Fish-Fri" as a product they "would buy at the grocery to use as a coating" or a "product on the market that is especially made for frying fish." In a similar survey conducted in person at a New Orleans area mall, twenty-eight of the 100 respondents answered "*Zatarain's* Fish-Fri'" to the same questions.[8]

The authorities are in agreement that survey evidence is the most direct and persuasive way of establishing secondary meaning. *Vision Center*, 596 F.2d at 119; *Aloe Creme Laboratories*, 423 F.2d at 849; [cit.]. The district court believed that the survey evidence produced by Zatarain's, when coupled with the circumstantial evidence of advertising and usage, tipped the scales in favor of a finding of secondary meaning. Were we considering the question of secondary meaning *de novo*, we might reach a different conclusion than did the district court, for the issue is close. Mindful, however, that there is evidence in the record to support the finding below, we cannot say that the district court's conclusion was clearly erroneous. Accordingly, the finding of secondary meaning in the New Orleans area for Zatarain's descriptive term "Fish-Fri" must be affirmed.

3.   The "Fair Use" Defense

[The court decided that even though the plaintiff's term "Fish-Fri" was protectable, the defendants' use of the term was protected under the "fair use" doctrine. We will discuss the fair use defense *infra* in Chapter 9.]

C.   "Chick-Fri"

1.   Classification

[The court concluded that sufficient evidence existed to support the district court's finding that "Chick-Fri" is a descriptive term.]

2.   Secondary Meaning

The district court concluded that Zatarain's had failed to establish a secondary meaning for the term "Chick-Fri." We affirm this finding. The mark "Chick-Fri" has been in

---

8. The telephone survey also included this question: "When you mentioned 'fish fry,' did you have a specific product in mind or did you use that term to mean any kind of coating used to fry fish?" To this inartfully worded question, 77% of the New Orleans respondents answered "specific product" and 23% answered "any kind of coating." Unfortunately, Rosenzweig did not ask the logical follow-up question that seemingly would have ended the inquiry conclusively: "Who makes the specific product you have in mind?" Had he but done so, our task would have been much simpler.

use only since 1968; it was registered even more recently, in 1976. In sharp contrast to its promotions with regard to "Fish-Fri," Zatarain's advertising expenditures for "Chick-Fri" were mere chickenfeed; in fact, Zatarain's conducted no direct advertising campaign to publicize the product. Thus the circumstantial evidence presented in support of a secondary meaning for the term "Chick-Fri" was paltry.

Allen Rosenzweig's survey evidence regarding a secondary meaning for "Chick-Fri" also "lays an egg." The initial survey question was a "qualifier": "Approximately how many times in an average month do you, yourself, fry *fish* or *other seafood*?" Only if respondents replied "three or more times a month" were they asked to continue the survey. This qualifier, which may have been perfectly adequate for purposes of the "Fish-Fri" questions, seems highly unlikely to provide an adequate sample of potential consumers of "Chick-Fri." This survey provides us with nothing more than some data regarding fish friers' perceptions about products used for frying chicken. As such, it is entitled to little evidentiary weight.

[The court affirmed the district court's finding that the term "Chick-Fri" lacks secondary meaning.]

3. Cancellation

Having concluded that the district court was correct in its determination that Zatarain's mark "Chick-Fri" is a descriptive term lacking in secondary meaning, we turn to the issue of cancellation. The district court, invoking the courts' power over trademark registration as provided by section 37 of the Lanham Act, 15 U.S.C. §1119 (1976), ordered that the registration of the term "Chick-Fri" should be cancelled. The district court's action was perfectly appropriate in light of its findings that "Chick-Fri" is a descriptive term without secondary meaning. We affirm. . . .

V.   CONCLUSION

And so our tale of fish and fowl draws to a close. We need not tarry long, for our taster's choice yields but one result, and we have other fish to fry. Accordingly, the judgment of the district court is hereby and in all things *affirmed*.

RESTATEMENT (THIRD) OF UNFAIR COMPETITION (1995)

Section 13, Comment (e)

[S]econdary meaning does not connote a subordinate or rare meaning. It refers instead to a subsequent significance added to the original meaning of the term. . . .

Secondary meaning may be established by either direct or circumstantial evidence. Testimony from individual consumers is clearly relevant to the existence of secondary meaning, but the lack of a representative sample of consumers often undermines its probative value. Surveys of prospective purchasers, if properly formulated and conducted, can be particularly persuasive. Proof of actual consumer confusion caused by another's use of the designation is also evidence of secondary meaning, since if the designation is not distinctive, use by another will not result in confusion. . . .

The length of time the designation has been in use is also relevant. Although secondary meaning may sometimes be inferred from evidence of long and continuous use, no particular length of use is required. In some cases distinctiveness is not acquired even after an extended period of time; in others it may be acquired soon after adoption. Section 2(f) of the Lanham Act, 15 U.S.C.A. §1052(f), permits but does not require the Patent and Trademark Office to accept as prima facie evidence of distinctiveness proof of "substantially exclusive and continuous use" for five years. Advertising and other promotional efforts resulting in increased public exposure for the designation may also support an inference of secondary meaning. It is the likely effect rather than the effort invested in such activities, however, that is determinative, and the expenditure of substantial sums in advertising does not in itself create protectable rights. Advertisements that emphasize the source significance of the designation through prominent use of the term or symbol or that invite consumers to "look for" the designation when selecting goods, for example, are more likely to generate secondary meaning than are more descriptive advertising uses.

The physical manner in which the designation is used with the goods, services, or business can also affect the likelihood that the designation will acquire secondary meaning. A designation that is relatively inconspicuous or that is used only in conjunction with other trademarks may be less likely to acquire secondary meaning than a more prominently displayed designation. Similarly, prominent use of a designation in the manner typical of a trade name, such as its appearance on signs or correspondence, can emphasize its association with the particular business more clearly than less conspicuous uses.

Concurrent use of a term by competitors is relevant as tending to negate the existence of secondary meaning. If the term has been used in a descriptive sense or as part of a trademark or trade name by numerous sellers in the market, it is unlikely to become associated exclusively with a single producer.

The significance of the designation to prospective purchasers may also be demonstrated by the nature of its use in newspapers, popular magazines, or dictionaries, at least when the product is marketed to the general public. The significance of the term to professionals in the trade such as dealers or retailers is also relevant, although it may not be accorded substantial weight if the goods or services are marketed primarily to nonprofessionals.

Proof that a competing seller has intentionally copied a designation previously used by another is often accepted as evidence of secondary meaning on the theory that the copying was motivated by a desire to benefit from confusion with the prior user. The strength of the inference may be diminished, however, by other credible motives for the copying. Thus, if the designation is plainly descriptive and equally applicable to the products of both sellers, or consists of a feature that is functional or that otherwise enhances the value of the product for reasons unrelated to any alleged source significance, evidence of intentional copying may carry little weight on the issue of secondary meaning.

NOTES AND QUESTIONS

1. *Distinctiveness lenses revisited.* Review the four different tests used by the court to determine whether FISH-FRI was a descriptive term. Why is each of these tests relevant to the question of descriptiveness? Are they all relevant for the same reason? Whose interests are being protected by the four different inquiries that the court makes in determining descriptiveness? The third test used by the court asks "whether competitors would be likely to need the terms used in the trademark in describing their products." The fourth test considers "the extent to which a term actually has been used by others marketing a similar service or product." In what ways are these tests different? Should one be more relevant than the other in assessing distinctiveness? *See* Graeme B. Dinwoodie, *Reconceptualizing the Inherent Distinctiveness of Product Design Trade Dress*, 75 N.C. L. Rev. 471, 503-04 (1997). Is it possible to consider "whether competitors would be likely to need the terms used" without considering subjective consumer perceptions?

2. *Descriptiveness of what?* A mark will be treated as descriptive if it is descriptive of any of the features of a product in respect of which rights are claimed. Likewise, the Federal

Circuit has stressed that a mark will be regarded as descriptive, and denied registration, if it is descriptive of any of the services for which registration is sought. *See In re The Chamber of Commerce of the United States*, 675 F.3d 1297, 1301 (Fed. Cir. 2012) (affirming descriptiveness rejection because NATIONAL CHAMBER described at least one service within the application).

3. *Suggestive/descriptive.* Why is it preferable for the plaintiff to have its mark classified as suggestive rather than descriptive? For descriptive marks, the plaintiff can acquire rights by showing that its mark has established secondary meaning. Why is this still a second-best option?

4. *Misspelling.* In assessing the distinctiveness of the plaintiff's FISH-FRI mark, the court examines the dictionary meaning of the term "fish fry." The dictionary contains no entry under "fish fri." Why does the court ignore the different spelling of the plaintiff's mark? *Cf. Miller Brewing Co. v. Jos. Schlitz Brewing Co.*, 605 F.2d 990, 996 (7th Cir. 1979) (ordering cancellation of registration of LITE for low-calorie beer on grounds that the term "light" was generic).

5. *Repeated terms.* How would you classify CAESAR! CAESAR! for salad dressings? Assume that CAESAR for salad dressings would be (at best) descriptive. Would your answer change if the PTO had previously issued registrations for PIZZA! PIZZA! for pizzas and restaurant services? *See In re Litehouse Inc.*, 82 U.S.P.Q.2d (BNA) 1471 (TTAB 2007).

6. *Online evidence.* The *Zatarain's* court notes the role of dictionaries in classifying a word mark and cites a definition from Webster's Third New International Dictionary. What relevance would you attach to an entry in Wikipedia? (Wikipedia describes itself as follows: "Wikipedia is an encyclopedia written collaboratively by many of its readers. It uses a special type of website, called a wiki, that makes collaboration easy. Lots of people are constantly improving Wikipedia, making thousands of changes an hour, all of which are recorded on article histories and recent changes. Inappropriate changes are usually removed quickly." *http://en.wikipedia.org/wiki/Wikipedia:Introduction.*) *See In re Grand Forest Holdings Inc.*, 78 U.S.P.Q.2d (BNA) 1152 (TTAB 2006) (citing to Wikipedia in classifying FREEDOM FRIES for frozen french fries); *see also infra* Problem 2-2 (discussing Word Spy).

What about online evidence generally? In *In re Bayer AG*, 488 F.3d 960 (Fed. Cir. 2007), the examiner rejected the application for ASPIRINA for analgesic products as descriptive and cited in support, inter alia, a "Google search engine report showing the first ten 'hits' for ASPIRINA. The report [included] a small amount of Spanish text with each of the ten search results. . . ." What weight should be given to "search engine results," which list the relevant websites and include excerpts from the sites that include the search term? What about a printout of the entire web page where the search term is used? *See id.*

7. *Similarity and association: closeness to unprotected terms.* In *In re Bayer AG, supra*, the Federal Circuit affirmed the finding of the TTAB that the term ASPIRINA for analgesic products was descriptive because of, *inter alia*, its similarity to the term ASPIRIN, which (in the United States) had long been treated as generic for the same goods. The majority affirmed the Board's finding that "ASPIRINA and ASPIRIN are sufficiently close in appearance, sound and meaning that '[t]he mere addition of the letter "A" at the end of the generic term "aspirin" is simply insufficient to transform ASPIRINA into an inherently distinctive mark for analgesics.'" *Id.* at 964-65. Is similarity to an unprotected term the proper test of distinctiveness? *See id.* (Newman, J., dissenting). What does similarity measure? Are there broader policy concerns that support the majority's conclusion and reasoning? Is analysis of similarity consistent with the approach of the *Zatarain's* court? If so, where would the approach of the Fifth Circuit allow for consideration of the similarity of ASPIRIN and ASPIRINA?

8. *Applying the* Zatarain's *tests.* In *Zobmondo Entertainment, LLC v. Falls Media, LLC*, 602 F.3d 1108, 1116-17 (9th Cir. 2010), Falls Media claimed rights in the mark WOULD YOU RATHER . . . ? for board games incorporating questions that pose strange or undesirable choices. The Ninth Circuit reviewed the trial court's application of the imagination test (described by the court as the "primary criterion" for determining distinctiveness in the Ninth Circuit) and the competitors' needs test:

> The first, and clearly the most-used, test is known as the "imagination" test. . . . For example, the mark "ENTREPRENEUR" as applied to a magazine was descriptive, not suggestive, because "an entirely unimaginative, literal-minded person would understand the significance of the reference." [cit.] On the other hand, "ROACH MOTEL" [for roach traps] was held suggestive because "an ordinary consumer having read or heard on television the words 'roach motel' would remember the conception . . . a fanciful abode for roaches in an establishment normally frequented by human [travelers]." *Am. Home Prods. Corp. v. Johnson Chem. Co.*, 589 F.2d 103, 107 (2d Cir. 1978). . . .
>
> The district court determined that the imagination test indicated that "WOULD YOU RATHER . . . ?" is merely descriptive as a matter of law because it requires "no imaginative or interpretive leap to understand that this phrase is the main aspect of the game to which it is affixed." Falls Media argues that the district court erred because multistage reasoning is needed to link the mark to the "essential nature of these products [namely,] . . . that the choices are ridiculous, bizarre . . . and [limited to two options]."
>
> We reject Falls Media's argument in part. The imagination test does not ask what information about the product *could* be derived from a mark, but rather whether "a mental leap is *required*" to understand the mark's relationship to the product. [*Rudolph Int'l, Inc. v. Realys, Inc.*, 482 F.3d 1195, 1198 (9th Cir. 2007)] (quotation omitted and emphasis added). Our prior precedent makes it clear that merely descriptive marks need not describe the "essential nature" of a product; it is enough that the mark describe some aspect of the product. [cit.]
>
> But we conclude that the district court erred in concluding that the imagination test indicates that "WOULD YOU RATHER . . . ?" is merely descriptive as a matter of law. We cannot look the entire mark up in a dictionary; there is no literal meaning of the "WOULD YOU RATHER . . . ?" phrase, given that the words precede an ellipse; one may infer that there is a question, but only imagination can tell us that the question will serve up a bizarre or humorous choice. . . . When we give all reasonable inferences to Falls Media, and credit its evidence as true, we conclude that the imagination test is inconclusive by itself to determine if the challenged mark is descriptive or suggestive of a board game.
>
> [T]he second test . . . the competitors' needs test is related to the imagination test, "because the more imagination that is required to associate a mark with a product or service, the less likely the words used will be needed by competitors to describe their products or services." [cit.]
>
> [D]rawing all inferences in favor of Falls Media, the competitors' needs test strongly favored Falls Media's argument that "WOULD YOU RATHER . . . ?" is suggestive. Falls Media proffered significant evidence suggesting that its competitors do not need to use "WOULD YOU RATHER . . . ?" to fairly describe their products. Perhaps most important is the experience of Zobmondo itself. Zobmondo identified 135 possible alternative names for its game during development. Also, Zobmondo marketed and sold its game and a related book for a period of time without using the phrase "WOULD YOU RATHER . . . ?" (instead using the name "The Outrageous Game of Bizarre Choices"), and another board game company used the name "Would You Prefer?" during the same time period. These titles are not linguistically inferior to "WOULD YOU RATHER . . . ?". Cf. [*Entrepreneur Media, Inc. v. Smith*, 279 F.3d 1135, 1143 (9th Cir. 2002)] (observing that others need the term "entrepreneur" because "[w]e are not aware of . . . any synonym for the word"). In the face of this evidence, credited as true on summary judgment, it's difficult to say that Zobmondo necessarily needs to use "WOULD YOU RATHER . . . ?" for its version of the board game of bizarre or humorous choices.

The Ninth Circuit also found the evidence of third-party use to be insufficiently one-sided to support summary judgment. In reviewing that third-party use, the court commented that the "statement [by Pressman, the person who optioned the game,] that 'WOULD YOU RATHER . . . ?' is *more* descriptive than 'Zobmondo' does not exclude the possibility that it is still suggestive, nor does Pressman's comment that 'WOULD YOU RATHER . . . ?' gives a person a 'good idea' of what the game is about; a mark can be suggestive and still convey information about a product. . . ." Do you agree with the Ninth Circuit's conclusion regarding the classification of WOULD YOU RATHER . . . ? for board games? Does its classification sit well with the court's prior decisions regarding ENTREPRENEUR and ROACH MOTEL (mentioned in the excerpt above)? Would you need to know more to answer this question?

9. *Foreign evidence.* In *Bayer*, the examiner had also cited a number of stories that resulted from a search on the term ASPIRINA on the NEXIS database. The majority found that the use of term ASPIRINA in these stories could be probative of the meaning of ASPIRINA, even if the stories appeared in foreign publications, noting that:

> Information originating on foreign websites or in foreign news publications that are accessible to the United States public may be relevant to discern United States consumers' impression of a proposed mark. . . . The probative value, if any, of foreign information sources must be evaluated on a case-by-case basis. Because of the association of the proposed mark ASPIRINA with a pharmaceutical product, the growing availability and use of the internet as a resource for news, medical research results, and general medical information, we find that the foreign publication evidence in this record carries some probative value with respect to prospective consumer perception in the United States.

In contrast, the majority declined to give any weight to the thirty-four foreign trademark registrations held by the claimant for the term ASPIRINA for analgesic products, including several from Spanish-speaking countries. Is the majority correct that information on foreign websites should be relevant to a determination of the inherent distinctiveness of a claimed mark while foreign registrations should not? Judge Newman, in dissent, would have regarded such registrations as potentially relevant, but her discussion of the relevance of foreign registrations appears premised on ASPIRINA being a "well-known mark." The policy basis for that doctrine and its conceptual basis are discussed *infra* in Chapter 6, section C.

10. *Competitors' needs.* In applying the third test for assessing descriptiveness, the court "suggests that a merchant whose batter mix is specially spiced for frying fish is likely to find 'fish fry' a useful term for describing his product." A rival producer of carbonated drinks would surely find it "useful" to market its dark-colored carbonated soft drinks under the term COKE. How is this use different from the use of "fish fry" envisaged by the *Zatarain's* court?

11. *Distinctiveness evidence.* If a mark is classified as descriptive, how much evidence of secondary meaning is required to overcome that assessment? What is the significance of the statement in *Abercrombie* that the distinctiveness "categories, like the tones in a spectrum, tend to blur at the edges and merge together"? *See Royal Crown Co., Inc. v. The Coca-Cola Co.*, __ F.3d ___ (Fed. Cir. June 20, 2018) ("[T]he applicant's burden of showing acquired distinctiveness increases with the level of descriptiveness; a more descriptive term requires more evidence of secondary meaning") (*quoting In re Steelbuilding.com*, 415 F.3d 1293, 1300 (Fed. Cir. 2005)). In *New Colt Holding Corp. v. RJG Holdings of Fla., Inc.*, 312 F. Supp. 2d 195, 208 (D. Conn. 2004), the court noted that unsolicited media coverage of the plaintiff's design (in which it claimed trade dress rights) that stretched back for decades was less probative than more recent evidence. The relevant period for determining secondary meaning was when defendants entered the market. Does the approach of the *New Colt* court make sense? In other respects, the plaintiff might prefer to rely on evidence that is inevitably recent. Thus, in *General Motors Corp. v. Lanard Toys, Inc.*, 468 F.3d 405 (6th Cir. 2006), the defendant argued that because, with marks that are not inherently distinctive, secondary meaning must be proven before the first allegedly infringing use of the trademark, survey evidence that plaintiff developed after the defendant's first use (i.e., when the plaintiff became aware of potential infringement) should not be admissible. *See infra* Problems 2-1 and 4-1. How might you reconcile the proposition about when the plaintiff must show secondary meaning with the fact that courts have historically favored the use of consumer surveys

as a means of showing secondary meaning? *See General Motors*, 468 F.3d at 419; *cf. Bay State Sav. Bank v. Baystate Fin. Servs.*, 484 F. Supp. 2d 205 (D. Mass. 2007) (dismissing relevance of late-conducted survey). What weight would you give to a survey conducted five years *before* the date at which an applicant alleged it has acquired secondary meaning? *See Royal Crown Co., Inc. v. The Coca-Cola Co.*, __ F.3d ___ (Fed. Cir. June 20, 2018).

12.   *Circumstantial evidence based on use of mark as part of a larger phrase.* In *E.T. Browne Drug Co. v. Cococare Prods., Inc.*, 538 F.3d 185 (3d Cir. 2008), the plaintiff claimed that the mark COCOA BUTTER FORMULA for beauty products had acquired secondary meaning, and relied on circumstantial evidence in the form of long use, substantial sales, and extensive advertising. The Third Circuit was unpersuaded by this evidence:

> Browne has introduced no evidence indicating that it ever used "Cocoa Butter Formula" as a standalone term in marketing or packaging. Instead, it always used the term connected with the "Palmer's," forming the phrase "Palmer's Cocoa Butter Formula." For example, Browne's lotion bottles bore logos with "Palmer's" immediately above the words "Cocoa Butter Formula," creating one visual presentation for the consumer. The marketing and sales evidence thus likely would raise a reasonable inference that "Palmer's Cocoa Butter Formula" has gained secondary meaning in the minds of the public.
>
> But Browne wants to do something more complicated: it wants to establish that a portion ("Cocoa Butter Formula") of the larger term ("Palmer's Cocoa Butter Formula") has acquired an independent secondary meaning. Nothing in the record would allow a jury to evaluate the strength of the term "Cocoa Butter Formula" independently from the larger term including "Palmer's." We thus conclude . . . that the marketing and sales evidence provided by Browne does not create a reasonable inference that "Cocoa Butter Formula" has acquired secondary meaning.

Id. at 200. Do you agree with the court's unwillingness to give any weight to the circumstantial evidence presented by the plaintiff? *Cf. Case C 353/03, Société des produits Nestlé SA v. Mars UK*, [2005] E.T.M.R. 96 (ECJ 2005) (distinctiveness of phrase HAVE A BREAK can be acquired through its use as part of the registered mark HAVE A BREAK . . . HAVE A KIT-KAT). If this reasoning is correct, how could the plaintiff in *Browne Drug* have shown that COCOA BUTTER FORMULA had acquired secondary meaning? *See* 538 F.3d at 200-01.

13.   *Relevance of accompanying text.* What is the relevance of text that appears alongside the mark on promotional materials? In 2014, the North Carolina Lottery Commission introduced new scratch-off lottery games available on the first Tuesday of each month. The applicant sought to register FIRST TUESDAY for lottery cards and scratch cards for playing lottery games. It submitted specimens, including the promotional materials reproduced below, that have explanatory text such as "[n]ew scratch-offs" or "[n]ew scratch-offs the first Tuesday of every month." How does the explanatory text affect your assessment of the mark? *See In re North Carolina Lottery*, 866 F.3d 1363 (Fed. Cir. 2017).

14.   *Survey evidence of secondary meaning in* Zatarain's. The *Zatarain's* court found the survey by the plaintiff's expert somewhat unpersuasive. The court described the following question as "inartfully worded": "When you mentioned 'fish fry,' did you have a specific product in mind or did you use that term to mean any kind of coating used to fry fish?" Why was this question inartfully worded? Do you agree with the court that asking (as a follow-up) "Who makes the specific product you have in mind?" would have ended the inquiry conclusively? How would you attack the value of a survey that, as its first question, asked, "What company do you think puts out these products?" *See Straumann Co. v. Lifecore Biomedical Inc.*, 278 F. Supp. 2d 130, 138 (D. Mass. 2003).

15. *Constructing surveys.* Surveys are relevant at several stages of trademark analysis. In addition to proving secondary meaning, they are most notably used in assessing infringement. From the discussion in *Zatarain's*, what "traps" might an expert conducting a survey fall into? That is, which aspects of the construction of the survey are most important? If an applicant for a registration has conducted a survey to assess likely confusion between its mark and that of an alleged infringer (which is common, as we will discuss more fully in Chapter 7), how relevant might that same survey be to proof of secondary meaning? Consider the evidence relevant to secondary meaning identified in the Restatement. Would it depend upon the type of survey? In *Parks LLC v. Tyson Foods, Inc.*, 863 F.3d 220 (3d Cir. 2017), the plaintiff's survey expert had used a so-called *Squirt* survey, in which two products are placed side by side, often with other products that serve as controls, and participants are asked questions to determine if confusion exists as to the source of the products. In particular, the survey presented an image of both the plaintiff's PARKS product and the defendant's PARK'S FINEST product (below). Would you give weight to confusion suggested by this survey in proving acquired distinctiveness? (Note that there are other survey methods, typically used with stronger marks, that do not show the plaintiff's product to the survey participant; *see infra* Chapter 7.)

16. *Secondary meaning test.* Courts frequently quote a 1938 decision of the United States Supreme Court in articulating what must be shown to establish secondary meaning. In particular, those courts state that in order to establish a secondary meaning for a term, a plaintiff "must show that the primary significance of the term in the minds of the consuming public is not the product but the producer." *Kellogg Co. v. National Biscuit Co.*, 305 U.S. 111, 118 (1938). Does this test comport with your understanding of the term "secondary meaning"? Does it capture the change that a descriptive term undergoes in order to fall within Section 13(b) of the Restatement?

In *Royal Crown Co., Inc. v. The Coca-Cola Co.*, __ F.3d __ (Fed. Cir. June 20, 2018), Coca-Cola sought to prove the secondary meaning of COKE ZERO by relying on a survey that asked consumers whether they "associated" the term ZERO with the products of one or more companies. What weight would you give to such a survey? *Cf. Société Des Produits Nestlé SA v. Cadbury UK Ltd* [2017] EWCA Civ 358 (CA) (UK) at [77] ("the Court of Justice of the EU has held that it is not sufficient for the applicant to show that a significant proportion of the relevant class of persons recognise and associate the mark with the applicant's goods. However, to a non-trade mark lawyer, the distinction between, on the one hand, such recognition and association and, on the other hand, a perception that the goods designated by the mark originate from a particular undertaking may be a rather elusive one.").

17.   *Validity and scope.* Even though the plaintiff in *Zatarain's* succeeded in demonstrating the validity of its FISH-FRI mark, the defendant ultimately prevailed (because of the defense of fair use). The *validity* of a mark does not afford the proprietor of the mark absolute property rights in the term. The *scope of rights* acquired by a trademark holder (meaning the range of conduct that the plaintiff can restrain by assertion of its valid trademark rights) is dealt with in Chapters 6-9. The fair use defense, in particular, is dealt with in Chapter 9.

18.   *Section 37 jurisdiction.* Once it concluded that CHICK-FRI was descriptive and possessed no secondary meaning, the court in *Zatarain's* invoked Section 37 of the Lanham Act to order the cancellation of the registration for that mark. In order to create jurisdiction in the federal courts under Section 37, however, at least one court has concluded that a federal registration must already have been issued. That is to say, the court cannot prematurely interfere in the registration process by ordering the PTO to reject a pending application. *See Johnny Blastoff Inc. v. Los Angeles Rams Football Co.*, 48 U.S.P.Q.2d (BNA) 1385 (E.D. Wis. 1998), *aff'd*, 188 F.3d 427 (7th Cir. 1999). The evidentiary effect of an issued registration in infringement proceedings is discussed *infra* in Chapter 5. What other relief can courts order under Section 37? Recall the facts of *E.T. Browne Drug Co.*, *supra* note 12, where the court held that the mark COCOA BUTTER FORMULA for beauty products, in which plaintiff claimed rights, was descriptive and had not acquired secondary meaning. Can the court order the PTO to place a disclaimer on the plaintiff's federal registration on PALMER'S COCOA BUTTER FORMULA for beauty products?

Suppose that, after filing suit, Zatarain's became concerned that Oak Grove would ultimately succeed in showing that Zatarain's' marks lacked distinctiveness. If Zatarain's unilaterally covenanted not to sue Oak Grove for Oak Grove's currently-used marks, and Zatarain's voluntarily dismissed its infringement claims, could Oak Grove still press forward with its distinctiveness challenge? That is, does Section 37 provide an independent basis for jurisdiction? Does it matter whether Oak Grove asserted its distinctiveness challenge as a counterclaim as opposed to an affirmative defense to infringement? *See Nike, Inc. v. Already, LLC*, 133 S. Ct. 721 (2013).

19.   *Disclaimers.* In *In re Louisiana Fish Fry Prods., Ltd.*, 797 F.3d 1332 (Fed. Cir. 2015), the applicant sought to register LOUISIANA FISH FRY PRODUCTS BRING THE TASTE OF LOUISIANA HOME! (along with a design) for seafood sauce mixes. The PTO required the applicant to disclaim FISH FRY PRODUCTS on the ground that it was either generic or merely descriptive without secondary meaning. In *Royal Crown Co., Inc. v. The Coca-Cola Co.*, __ F.3d ___ (Fed. Cir. June 20, 2018), the manufacturer of DIET RITE PURE ZERO soft drinks opposed efforts by the Coca-Cola Company to register COKE ZERO for soft drinks. The only relief that the opposer sought was to require the applicant to disclaim the term ZERO; it did not argue that, if Coca-Cola disclaimed ZERO, the registration should not be allowed. *See* Lanham Act, Section 6(a). Why might this be significant?

20. *Examples of suggestive and descriptive marks.* As noted earlier in this Chapter, developing a feel for where a mark might be placed on the distinctiveness spectrum can be assisted to some extent by reviewing prior determinations. Subject to the caution noted there, we have set out below a few illustration of marks that have been found to be suggestive or descriptive. (If you want the cites for the different examples, review the sections of the TMEP and McCarthy cited earlier; the McCarthy treatise contains a much longer list of illustrations, and is worth perusing.)

Marks Found to be Suggestive	Marks Found to be Descriptive
AT A GLANCE for calendars	AMERICA'S BEST POPCORN! for popcorn
SPRAY 'N VAC for aerosol rug cleaner	CAR-FRESHNER auto air deodorizer
CYCLONE for wire fence	FROSTY TREATS for frozen desserts and ice cream
GLASS DOCTOR for glass repair service	FIRST BANK for banking services
HABITAT for home furnishings	HOLIDAY INN for motel
7-ELEVEN for food store chain	INTELLIGENT for vehicle tires
IT'S A 10 for hair care products	JOY for detergent
WET ONES pre-moistened wet wipes	KING SIZE clothing for larger men
WE SMILE MORE for motel services	LIGHTS for low tar and nicotine cigarette
SNEAKER CIRCUS for retail shoe store	OATNUT for bread containing oats and nuts
ACTION SLACKS for pants	P.M. for night-time analgesic/sleep-aid
CLASSIC for auto washing services	SHEAR PLEASURE for beauty salon
CURV for permanent wave solution	TWENTY FOUR HOUR FITNESS for fitness facility
GOBBLE GOBBLE for processed turkey meat	YOUR CLOUD for computer storage services

As you review these lists, consider how clear is the line that the doctrine draws between descriptive and suggestive marks. Would you support assimilating descriptive and suggestive marks, and (if so) why? *See* Jake Linford, *The False Dichotomy Between Suggestive and Descriptive Trademarks*, 76 OHIO STATE L.J. 1367 (2015).

IN RE OPPEDAHL & LARSON, LLP

373 F.3d 1171 (Fed. Cir. 2004)

RADER, Circuit Judge:

The Trademark Trial and Appeal Board (Board) affirmed the United States Patent and Trademark Office's (PTO's) refusal to register the mark patents.com to appellant Oppedahl & Larson, LLP. Because the proposed mark is merely descriptive under 15 U.S.C. §1052(e)(1), this court affirms.

I

[Appellant filed an intent-to-use application to register the mark patents.com. The PTO refused to register the mark based on a finding that the mark was merely descriptive of applicant's goods, i.e., software for tracking patent applications and issued patents. In particular, the PTO found that the term "patents" merely describes a feature of the goods, and the term ".com" is a top level domain indicator (TLD) without any trademark significance. The appellant did not allege acquired distinctiveness.]

II

This court reviews the Board's legal determinations de novo and its factual findings for substantial evidence. *See In re Dial-A-Mattress Operating Corp.*, 240 F.3d 1341, 1344 (Fed. Cir. 2001). The Board's placement of a mark on the fanciful-suggestive-descriptive-generic continuum is a question of fact, which this court reviews for substantial evidence. *See In re Nett Designs, Inc.*, 236 F.3d 1339, 1341 (Fed. Cir. 2001). . . .

With respect to marks that include TLDs, the Trademark Manual of Examining Procedure (TMEP) instructs:

1209.03(M) DOMAIN NAMES [R-2]

If a proposed mark includes a TLD such as ".com", ".biz", ".info", the examining attorney should present evidence that the term is a TLD, and, if available, evidence of the significance of the TLD as an abbreviation (*e.g.* ".edu" signifies an educational institution, ".biz" signifies a business). Because TLDs generally serve no source-indicating function, their addition to an otherwise unregistrable mark typically cannot render it registrable. *In re CyberFinancial.Net, Inc.*, 65 USPQ2d 1789, 1792 (TTAB 2002) ("Applicant seeks to register the generic term 'bonds,' which has no source-identifying significance in connection with applicant's services, in combination with the top level domain indicator '.com,' which also has no source-identifying significance. And combining the two terms does not create a term capable of identifying and distinguishing applicant's services."). . . . *See also Goodyear*, 128 U.S. at 602 (the incorporation of a term with no source-indicating function into an otherwise generic mark cannot render it registrable). For example, if a proposed mark is composed of merely descriptive term(s) combined with a TLD, the examining attorney must refuse registration on the Principal Register under Trademark Act §2(e)(1), 15 U.S.C. §1052(e)(1), on the ground that the mark is merely descriptive. *See* TMEP §1215.04.

TMEP §1209.03(m) (3d ed. 2003).

In appellant's view, the PTO has erred by, in effect, cutting off the TLDs before evaluation of the consumer's impression of the mark. Appellant argues that the anti-dissection policy outlined in *Dial-A-Mattress* should apply to domain name marks as well. In short, appellant simply asserts that the Board should consider a domain designation as part of the mark as a whole.

The law requires that a mark be "considered in its entirety." [cit.] In *Dial-A-Mattress*, this court required the Board to consider marks using telephone area codes, i.e., "1-888-MATRESS," as a whole to determine the commercial impression of the mark. *Dial-A-Mattress*, 240 F.3d at 1345-46. Even though the area code (888) standing alone was "devoid of source-indicating significance," the analysis in *Dial-A-Mattress* required the Board to weigh the entire commercial impression, including the (888) prefix, when assessing the registrability of the mark. *Id.*

In *Dial-A-Mattress*, this court did not say, however, that the Board cannot ascertain the meaning of each of the words or components that make up the entire mark. In considering a mark as a whole, the Board may weigh the individual components of the mark to determine the overall impression or the descriptiveness of the mark and its various components. [cit.] Thus, the PTO may properly consider the meaning of "patents" and the meaning of ".com" with respect to the goods identified in the application. However, if those two portions individually are merely descriptive of an aspect of appellant's goods, the PTO must also determine whether the mark as a whole, i.e., the combination of the individual parts, conveys any distinctive source-identifying impression contrary to the descriptiveness of the individual parts.

This court does not read the PTO's policy to include an absolute prohibition on the possibility that adding a TLD to a descriptive term could operate to create a distinctive mark. Instead the TMEP states that "TLDs *generally* serve no source-indicating function, [and] their addition to an otherwise unregistrable mark *typically* cannot render it registrable." TMEP §1209.03(m) (3d ed. 2003) (emphasis added). This language certainly leaves open the possibility that in unique circumstances a TLD could perform a source-indicating function. The PTO has not applied a bright-line rule that the addition of a TLD to an otherwise descriptive term will never under any circumstances affect the registrability of a mark. Such a rule would be a legal error.

The PTO has offered the analysis in the *Goodyear* case as applicable in this case. Thus, in this case, the PTO uses that analysis to argue that ".com" possesses no source-identifying characteristics just as "Co." and "Corp." did not affect registrability in *Goodyear*. Although not a perfect analogy, the comparison of TLDs (i.e., ".com," ".org," etc.) to entity designations such as "Corp." and "Inc." has merit. The commercial impression created by ".com" is similar to the impression created by "Corp." and "Co.," that is, the association of a commercial entity with the mark. TLDs, however, can convey more than simply the organizational structure of the entity that uses the mark. For example, TLDs immediately suggest a relationship to the Internet. Thus, the per se rule in *Goodyear* that "Corp.," etc. never possess source-indicating significance does not operate as a per se rule, but more as a general rule, with respect to TLDs.

During oral argument in this case, this court discussed a hypothetical case that might illustrate that a TLD could affect the descriptiveness or registrability of a proposed mark. Under the hypothetical, a company seeks to register the mark tennis.net for a store that sells tennis nets. The applicant openly states that it does no business on the Internet and has no intention to ever use the Internet. This hypothetical applicant's mark consists of a descriptive term—"tennis"—and a TLD—".net." The ".net" portion alone has no source-identifying significance. The hypothetical mark as a whole, as is immediately apparent, produces a witty double entendre relating to tennis nets, the hypothetical applicant's product. Arguably, the attachment of the TLD to the other descriptive portion of the mark could enhance the prospects of registrability for the mark as a whole. This hypothetical example illustrates that, although TLDs will most often not add any significant source-identifying function to a mark, a bright-line rule might foreclose registration to a mark with a TLD component that can demonstrate distinctiveness.*

Appellant offers another hypothetical, Amazon.com, to argue that the addition of ".com" will generally, if not always, add source-identifying significance. According to appellant, saying the word "Amazon" to a person on the street may conjure images of a river or a fierce female warrior. In the hypothetical, however, the entire mark Amazon.com changes the impression to invoke an online retailer. This hypothetical, however, has a serious flaw in the context of this case. The Board must, of course, determine the commercial impression of a mark in the proper context of the goods or services associated with that mark. *See* 15 U.S.C. §1052(e)(1) (2000). In its proper context, appellant's proposed hypothetical yields a different result. In context, appellant's hypothetical would state, "I bought this book from Amazon," and "I bought this book from Amazon.com." In that setting, the addition of ".com" adds no source-identifying significance, which is likely to be the case in all but the most exceptional case.

The "Amazon" hypothetical also illustrates another principle that the Board properly recognized, namely that TLD marks may obtain registration upon a showing of distinctiveness. Thus Amazon.com may well denote the source of services of an on-line retailer (rather than a used car dealer or some other association) because the mark has acquired that secondary meaning. The Board properly left that door open for this patents.com mark as well.

---

* This court does not presume to decide whether this mark is registrable under the Lanham Act or enforceable under common law principles. Rather this example serves merely as an illustration of the way a TLD might enhance the distinctiveness of a mark. The hypothetical might even raise questions about misdescriptiveness or other problems. This court does not presume to offer an advisory opinion on any of these issues.

In this case, the Board concluded that ".com" conveys to the public that the mark is owned or used by a commercial entity or business. To support that conclusion, the Board cites various dictionary definitions indicating that ".com" is an abbreviation for "company" used in Internet addresses. Appellant argues that domain name registries no longer enforce the use of particular TLDs based on the type of entity seeking to register the domain name, i.e., ".com" for companies and ".org" for non-profit organizations. Regardless of the current state of Internet governance, the Board is correct that the overall impression of ".com" conveys to consumers the impression of a company or commercial entity on the Internet. "Any competent source suffices to show the relevant purchasing public's understanding of a contested term, including . . . dictionary definitions." *Dial-A-Mattress*, 240 F.3d at 1345. Accordingly, substantial evidence supports the Board's conclusion that ".com" indicates a commercial entity. Moreover, under *Goodyear*, as qualified above, that impression bears no trademark significance. The dictionary definitions in the record also establish that ".com" conveys the use of the Internet in association with the mark. Appellant's identification of goods includes the use of the Internet. Accordingly, ".com" is descriptive of this feature of the goods listed in the application.

Substantial record evidence also supports the Board's finding that "patents" is descriptive of a feature of the appellant's goods. Appellant's website shows that it offers software to track, *inter alia*, patent applications and issued patents using the Internet. Tracking patents falls within the scope of the goods identified in the application, i.e., "tracking records." Thus, the term "patents" describes a feature of the goods offered.

The Board also concluded that the combination of "patents" and ".com" does not render the mark as a whole distinctive and registrable. The Board reached this conclusion based on its application of the *Goodyear* analysis, i.e., finding that ".com" holds no source-indicating significance just as "Corp." [holds none]. An analysis of the commercial impression of the mark as a whole as required under the analysis stated above still yields the same result on this record.

Appellant asserts that domain names are inherently distinctive because they can only be associated with one entity or source at a time. The simple fact that domain names can only be owned by one entity does not of itself make them distinctive or source identifying. Telephone numbers and street addresses are also unique, but they do not by themselves convey to the public the source of specific goods or services. Thus, this court declines to adopt a per se rule that would extend trademark protection to all Internet domain names regardless of their use. Trademark law requires evaluation of a proposed mark to ascertain the commercial impression conveyed in light of the goods or services associated with the mark, not a simple check for ownership of an Internet address.

Appellant's goods include patent tracking software by means of the Internet. The term patents.com merely describes patent-related goods in connection with the Internet. The two terms combined do not create a different impression. Rather, the addition of ".com" to the term "patents" only strengthens the descriptiveness of the mark in light of the designation of goods in the application. "Patents" alone describes one feature of the goods—that of tracking patent applications and issued patents. Adding ".com" to the mark adds a further description of the Internet feature of the identified goods. Thus, appellant's argument to consider the mark as a whole only strengthens the descriptiveness finding.

III

When examining domain name marks, the PTO must evaluate the commercial impression of the mark as a whole, including the TLD indicator. The addition of a TLD such as ".com" or ".org" to an otherwise unregistrable mark will typically not add any source-identifying significance, similar to the analysis of "Corp." and "Inc." in *Goodyear Rubber*

Manufacturing Co., 128 U.S. at 602. This, however, is not a bright-line, per se rule. In exceptional circumstances, a TLD may render an otherwise descriptive term sufficiently distinctive for trademark registration. In this case, the mark patents.com, as a whole, is merely descriptive of appellant's goods. The decision of the Board is affirmed.

BOOKING.COM B.V. v. MATAL

278 F. Supp. 3d 891 (E.D. Va. 2017)

BRINKEMA, District Judge:

Plaintiff Booking.com B.V. ("Booking.com" or "plaintiff") filed this civil action challenging the denial by the Trademark Trial and Appeal Board ("TTAB") of the United States Patent and Trademark Office ("USPTO") of four trademark applications involving the mark "BOOKING.COM" for [travel agency services and making hotel reservations]. One of the applications was for the word mark and three were for stylized versions of the mark. For each of the applications, the TTAB found plaintiff's marks ineligible for registration as trademarks because it concluded that BOOKING.COM is generic for the services identified in the applications or, alternatively, that it is merely descriptive and lacks acquired distinctiveness.

I.   BACKGROUND

[The examiner refused registration for each application on the basis that the mark is generic as applied to the relevant services and, in the alternative, that the mark is merely descriptive and that plaintiff had failed to establish acquired distinctiveness. The TTAB affirmed the four refusals of registration. Plaintiff then filed a civil action under 15 U.S.C. §1071(b) against the USPTO Director ("the USPTO Director"), and the USPTO (collectively "defendants"), challenging the USPTO's denial of registration of the four applications. The parties filed the administrative record from the USPTO proceedings and both sides produced new evidence on the questions of genericness and descriptiveness.]

II.   DISCUSSION

A.   STANDARDS OF REVIEW

A trademark applicant "dissatisfied with the decision" of the [USPTO, including the TTAB,] has two remedies under the Lanham Act: either "appeal to the United States Court of Appeals for the Federal Circuit," see 15 U.S.C. §1071(a), or file a civil action against the USPTO Director in federal district court, see 15 U.S.C. §1071(b). Under §1071(a), an appeal to the Federal Circuit is taken "on the record" before the USPTO, id. §1071(a)(4), and the USPTO's factual findings will be upheld if they are supported by "substantial evidence." [cit.] In contrast, in a civil action under §1071(b), "the district court reviews the record de novo and acts as the finder of fact." [cit.] Placement of a mark on the generic-descriptive-suggestive-fanciful continuum is a question of fact. *In re Dial-a-Mattress Operating Corp.*, 240 F.3d 1341, 1344 (Fed. Cir. 2001).

Upon the motion of a party, the district court must admit the USPTO record and give it the "same effect as if originally taken and produced in the suit." §1071(b)(3). "[T]he district court may, in its discretion, 'consider the proceedings before and findings of the [USPTO] in deciding what weight to afford an applicant's newly-admitted evidence.'" *Kappos v. Hyatt*, 566 U.S. 431 (2012) [cit.]. The district court also "has authority independent of the [USPTO] to grant or cancel registrations." [cit.]

. . .

B. Analysis

Although plaintiff filed four trademark applications, neither plaintiff nor defendants contend that the stylized elements described in those applications affect the protectability of the mark. Instead, the parties focus on the word mark BOOKING.COM and on where along the generic-descriptive-suggestive-fanciful continuum the mark is situated. Therefore, rather than addressing each application individually, the Court will disregard the stylized elements and focus on the appropriate categorization of the word mark BOOKING. COM. . . .

1. The Framework of the Lanham Act

[T]he Lanham Act identifies four categories of marks. . . . "A generic mark refers to the genus or class of which a particular product [or service] is a member and can never be protected." [cit.] Examples include Light Beer for ale-type beverages and Thermos for vacuum-insulated bottles. [cit.] A descriptive mark "describes a function, use, characteristic, size, or intended purpose" of the product or service, such as 5 Minute glue and the Yellow Pages telephone directory. [cit.] "Marks that are merely descriptive are accorded protection only if they have acquired a secondary meaning [also called 'acquired distinctiveness'], that is, if in the minds of the public, the primary significance of a product [or service] feature or term is to identify the source of the product [or service] rather than the product [or service] itself." Id. (internal citations omitted). Although eligible for protection in some instances, descriptive marks are considered weak marks. *Shakespeare Co. v. Silstar Corp. of Am.*, 110 F.3d 234, 239-40 (4th Cir. 1997). Suggestive marks, such as Coppertone for sunscreen and Orange Crush for orange flavored soda, "connote, without describing, some quality, ingredient, or characteristic of the product [or service]." [cit.] Marks that are "comprised of words in common usage" but "do not suggest or describe any quality, ingredient, or characteristic of the goods [or services] they serve, are said to have been arbitrarily assigned." [cit.] Examples of arbitrary marks include Tea Rose brand flour and Apple for computers. Lastly, fanciful marks are "in essence, made-up words expressly coined for serving as a trademark," such as Clorox for a bleach product and Kodak for photography-related products. [cit.] Because the "intrinsic nature" of suggestive, arbitrary, and fanciful marks "serves to identify a particular source of a product [or service]," these categories "are deemed inherently distinctive and are entitled to protection." [cit.]

2. Genericness

i. "Booking"

[The USPTO's argument that BOOKING.COM is generic rested primarily on its view of the meaning of "booking." The court accepted that, by itself, the word "booking" is generic for the classes of hotel and travel reservation services recited in plaintiff's applications.]

ii. Top-Level Domains

The finding that "booking" is a generic term does not end the analysis because the mark at issue is BOOKING.COM. Therefore the Court must consider whether the term resulting from combining "booking" with ".com" remains generic. . . . Plaintiff argues that ".com" should be read as a top-level domain (TLD), in the same family as ".net," ".org," and ".edu." A TLD can be contrasted with a second-level domain (SLD), which is the next level of organization in the domain name hierarchy. For example, in "booking.com," "booking" is the SLD and ".com" is the TLD. According to plaintiff, the combination of "booking" and ".com" signals a domain name, which is a unique identifier capable of indicating the source of a product or service. The defendants, on the other hand, argue that ".com" is merely a term that denotes services offered via the Internet, and point to Federal Circuit cases holding that a TLD has no source identifying significance.

Although Federal Circuit case law on trademark is not controlling in this jurisdiction, it is persuasive authority. Because the parties acknowledge that there is no Fourth Circuit precedent regarding the source identifying significance of a TLD, the reasoning of the Federal Circuit, which has addressed the role of TLDs in at least five cases, is a helpful starting point; however, it is important to appreciate that all of these opinions arose in §1071(a) proceedings, in which the Federal Circuit reviewed the TTAB's decisions regarding genericness and descriptiveness for substantial evidence, which is a more deferential standard than the de novo review applicable in this civil action brought under §1071(b).

The Federal Circuit first addressed the legal effect of combining a SLD consisting of a generic word (henceforth "generic SLD") and a TLD in *In re Oppedahl & Larson LLP*, 373 F.3d 1171 (Fed. Cir. 2004). There, the USPTO found that PATENTS.COM was generic for software that allowed consumers to track the status of U.S. trademark and patent applications. . . . Before the Federal Circuit, the applicant argued that domain name marks were inherently distinctive and therefore all such marks were entitled to registration. The Federal Circuit rejected this argument and affirmed the USPTO, reasoning that "[t]elephone numbers and street addresses are also unique, but they do not by themselves convey to the public the source of specific goods or services." Nevertheless, the Federal Circuit cautioned that "a bright-line rule that the addition of a TLD to an otherwise descriptive term will never under any circumstances affect the registratibility [sic] of a mark" would "be a legal error," concluding that the USPTO's policy was not a bright-line rule.

The Federal Circuit's next TLD case, *In re Steelbuilding*, 415 F.3d 1293 (2005), is the only case in which the Federal Circuit reversed the TTAB's finding that a domain name was generic, although it ultimately sustained the USPTO's denial of registration [on the alternative basis] that the mark was descriptive for [computerized online retail services in the field of pre-engineered metal buildings and roofing systems] and that the applicant had failed to meet its burden of proving acquired distinctiveness. In a separate opinion that diverged from *Oppedahl & Larson*'s conclusion that TLDs generally serve no source identifying function, Judge Linn argued that "[i]n the Internet world, domain-name recognition is a form of source identification" and argued that the case should be remanded to the TTAB for a reassessment of the evidence. Id. at 1301 (Linn, J., concurring-in-part and dissenting-in-part).

[The Federal Circuit's next case involved the mark HOTELS.COM for services consisting of providing information for others about temporary lodging. The Federal Circuit concluded that the Board's finding that HOTELS.COM is generic was supported by substantial evidence. Likewise, the Federal Circuit affirmed a judgment that denied registration to MATTRESS.COM for services identified as "online retail store service in the field of mattresses, beds, and bedding" on the basis of genericness. *In re 1800Mattress.com IP, LLC*, 586 F.3d 1359, 1361 (Fed. Cir. 2009).]

Although the Court recognizes the persuasive force of Federal Circuit cases, a number of factors caution against crediting these precedents here. From a chronological perspective, the Federal Circuit's first TLD case, *Oppehahl & Larson*, which held that "TLDs generally serve no source-indicating function," was decided in 2004 when the internet was in its infancy and norms regarding domain names were just taking root. Subsequent opinions have undermined *Oppehahl & Larson*'s reasoning by recognizing that a TLD indicates a domain name and "domain-name recognition is a form of source identification." *Steelbuilding*, 415 F.3d at 1301 (Linn, J., concurring-in-part and dissenting-in-part). There also appears to be a tension between the Federal Circuit's statement that a per se rule that TLDs cannot be source identifying would be "legal error," *Oppedahl & Larson*, 373 F.3d at 1177, and the outcomes of these cases, which show that the USPTO's guidance on TLDs functions as a per se rule. [cit.] [] *Steelbuilding* is a notable exception, but as Professor McCarthy explains, this case "muddied the waters" and appears to be based on an "erroneous" characterization of STEELBUILDING.COM. [cit.]

Beyond the tension within the cases, the Federal Circuit's TLD precedents also demonstrate the difficulty of distinguishing between generic and descriptive marks, an indeterminacy evidenced both by the anomalous holding in *Steelbuilding* and the multiple cases in which examining attorneys denied registration based on descriptiveness only to be affirmed by TTAB decisions concluding that the mark was actually generic. [cit.] As discussed below, because "categorizing trademarks is necessarily an imperfect science," *Fortune Dynamic, Inc. v. Victoria's Secret Stores Brand Mgmt., Inc.*, 618 F.3d 1025, 1033 (9th Cir. 2010), it would be imprudent to adopt a sweeping presumption denying trademark protection to a whole category of domain name marks in the absence of robust evidence that public ownership of this language is necessary for consumers and competitors to describe a class of products or services—evidence that does not appear in the Federal Circuit cases. Most importantly, in each of these TLD cases the Federal Circuit reviewed TTAB decisions under the deferential substantial evidence standard, a point that was repeatedly emphasized in the cases. [cit.] By contrast, under §1071(b) this Court is required to conduct a de novo review. For all these reasons, this Court declines to rely on the Federal Circuit's precedents regarding TLDs and will treat this question as an issue of first impression. And, for the reasons developed below, the Court concludes that, when combined with an SLD, a TLD generally has source identifying significance and the combination of a generic SLD and a TLD is generally a descriptive mark that is protectable upon a showing of acquired distinctiveness.

To illustrate this conclusion, it is helpful to consider the Federal Circuit's reasoning in a case involving telephone numbers as marks. In 2001, before the Federal Circuit first confronted the issue of TLDs, it held that the mark 1-888-M-A-T-R-E-S-S was protectable as a descriptive mark. *In re Dial-a-Mattress*, 240 F.3d 1341, 1346 (Fed. Cir. 2001). In that case, the applicant applied to register 1-888-M-A-T-R-E-S-S as a service mark for "telephone shop-at-home retail services in the field of mattresses." The examining attorney rejected the mark as generic for the relevant services or, in the alternative, as a descriptive mark with insufficient evidence of acquired distinctiveness. The TTAB affirmed both rationales. On appeal to the Federal Circuit, Dial-a-Mattress conceded that the area code in the mark was devoid of source identifying significance by itself and that the word "mattress," no matter how creatively spelled, was generic for retail services in the field of mattresses; however, it argued that, considered in its entirety, the mark was not generic. The Federal Circuit agreed, holding that although area codes have no source identifying significance by themselves and the term "mattress" was generic, the combination of an area code and a generic term (1-888-MATRESS) was source identifying. Specifically, it was descriptive, as it indicated that "a service relating to mattresses [was] available by calling the telephone number." Yet, even though the telephone mnemonic was source identifying, the Federal Circuit explained that the applicant still needed to establish "acquired secondary meaning" (also termed "acquired distinctiveness") in order to register the descriptive mark.

The reasoning in *Dial-a-Mattress* maps seamlessly onto TLDs. Although a TLD, like an area code, has no source identifying significance by itself, in combination with a SLD, it indicates a domain name, which, like a telephone number, is unique. Moreover, like the mnemonic phone number 1-888-M-A-T-R-E-S-S, the combination of a TLD and a generic SLD creates a descriptive mark by indicating that services relating to the generic SLD are available by accessing the domain name. Finally, whether such a mark is entitled to trademark protection depends on whether the applicant can demonstrate that it has acquired distinctiveness. In short, TLDs generally do have source identifying value when used in conjunction with an SLD and a mark comprised of a generic SLD and a TLD is generally a descriptive mark entitled to trademark protection if the mark holder can establish acquired distinctiveness.

Defendants resist this conclusion. Beyond invoking the Federal Circuit cases, defendants' argument that a TLD does not have identifying significance relies principally on the Supreme Court's 1888 decision in *Goodyear's Rubber Mfg. Co. v. Goodyear Rubber Co.*, 128 U.S. 598, 602 (1888), which held that adding terms such as "Corp.," "Inc.," and "Co." to a generic term does not add any trademark significance to an otherwise unregistrable mark. By analogy, defendants argue that "[a]dding '.com' to a generic term does not create a composite that is capable of identifying source, just as Plaintiff would not have created a protectable mark by adopting the designation 'Booking Company.'" This analogy is unhelpful because *Goodyear's* reasoning regarding corporate designators does not apply with equal force to domain names. As the Supreme Court explained in *Goodyear*, the use of a corporate designation had no source identifying value because it "only indicates that the parties have formed an association or partnership to deal in [particular] goods, either to produce or to sell them." By contrast, adding a TLD such as ".com" to a generic SLD does more than indicate that a company offers services via the internet; it indicates a unique domain name that can only be owned by one entity. In this respect, unlike a corporate designation, a TLD that functions as part of a domain name does have source identifying significance.

Defendants further argue that the public understands that a mark comprised of a generic SLD combined with a TLD is generic for that class of goods or services; however, they provide no evidence to support this position other than citations to the aforementioned Federal Circuit decisions. As will be discussed below, defendants' evidence shows that the public understands that such a mark represents a unique domain name indicating to consumers that the proprietor of the domain name provides goods or services relating to the generic term.

Next, citing *Advertise.com, Inc. v. AOL Adver., Inc.*, 616 F.3d 974, 980 (9th Cir. 2010), defendants raise the policy argument that recognizing the source identifying significance of TLDs would create "a per se rule—in contravention of the Lanham Act—that the combination of '.com' with any generic term renders it protectable." . . . This argument overreaches. Acknowledging that combining a TLD with a generic SLD can produce a source identifying domain name is not tantamount to finding that all domain name marks are protectable. Rather, a generic SLD combined with a TLD creates a descriptive mark that is eligible for protection only upon a showing of acquired distinctiveness. Importantly, acquired distinctiveness is a much higher bar than uniqueness and requires an evidentiary showing that "in the minds of the public, the primary significance of a . . . term is to identify the source of the product rather than the product itself." *Inwood Labs., Inc. v. Ives Labs.*, 456 U.S. 844, 851 n.11 (1982). In the trademark context, "source" does not refer to the location where a good or service may be found, e.g., at the website associated with a domain name, but to the "producer." *Kellogg*, 305 U.S. at 118. Therefore, domain name marks composed of a generic SLD and TLD, will be eligible for protection only when the applicant can show that "the primary significance" of the mark in the minds of the relevant consumers is the producer. Such a showing is only possible where the owner of the mark has developed strong brand recognition.

The second policy concern raised by defendants is that granting trademark protections to domain names with a generic SLD would prevent competitors from using the generic term in their domain names, hampering their ability to communicate the nature of their services. [The court noted that "although the USPTO has registered marks with what it determined are descriptive SLDs, such as WORKOUT.COM, ENTERTAINMENT. COM, and WEATHER.COM, this has not stopped competitors from using the words 'workout,' 'entertainment,' or 'weather' in their domain names. To the contrary, such related domain names abound and many, such as MIRACLEWORKOUT.COM, WWW. GOLIVE-ENTERTAINMENT.COM, and CAMPERSWEATHER.COM, have actually been afforded trademark protection by being registered on the Principal Register."]

In addition, the descriptive nature of domain name marks with a generic SLD will significantly limit the protection they receive, thereby safeguarding competition and public use. It is axiomatic that "descriptive terms qualify for registration as trademarks only after taking on secondary meaning . . . with the registrant getting an exclusive right not in the original, descriptive sense, but only in the secondary one associated with the markholder's goods." *KP Permanent Make-Up*, 543 U.S. at 122. Beyond the circumscribed protection afforded to descriptive marks, competitors are also protected by the likelihood of confusion standard. As the Supreme Court emphasized in *KP Permanent Make-Up*, the party charging infringement bears the burden of proving that a competitor's use of a mark is likely to confuse consumers. [Likelihood of confusion is particularly difficult to prove for descriptive marks because they are considered "weak" marks.] As the Supreme Court has explained, "[i]f any confusion results" from descriptive fair use "that is a risk the plaintiff accepted when it decided to identify its product with a mark that uses a well known descriptive phrase." This principle is equally true in the context of domain names and will preclude holders of marks comprised of a generic SLD and a TLD from preventing competitors from using the generic term in other domain names.

Defendants' third policy concern, which again proves more imagined than real, is that granting trademark protection to domain names with generic SLDs would deprive competitors of the right to describe their goods and services as what they are. . . . Defendants appear to suggest that plaintiff's competitors need to be able to describe themselves as "booking.coms." Although concerns about monopoly are one of the animating forces behind the prohibition on registering generic marks, because each domain name is unique the Court is unpersuaded that the threat of monopoly applies with equal force to domain names.[10] Further, the monopoly argument appears to assume that certain terms must be left in the public commons because they have descriptive value and are needed by consumers and competitors alike; however, no evidence in this record supports the view that domain names are used as descriptive terms for classes of services. To the contrary, the record is replete with evidence that consumers are predisposed to think that a domain name refers to a particular entity. [cit.] By this same logic, plaintiff's competitors, such as Expedia and Travelocity, have no incentive to describe themselves as "booking.coms" because this risks diverting customers to the website of their competitor. In short, there is no evidence in this record indicating that permitting registration of a domain names with a generic SLD would result in the monopolization of descriptive terms that must be left free for public use.

---

10. In rejecting plaintiff's applications, the TTAB observed that "[a]s domain name registrations are not perpetual, [the plaintiff] may be supplanted as the registrant of that Internet address or may voluntarily transfer its domain name registration to another." A practical problem might arise if the plaintiff let the domain name registration lapse or transferred it but wanted to continue using the mark; however, because a trademark right would only enhance plaintiff's incentive to maintain its registration the Court need not concern itself with this remote possibility. In addition, this concern applies equally to personal names and alphanumeric telephone numbers, both of which are eligible for trademark protection.

Recognizing that the policy concerns regarding generic terms are a poor fit for marks comprised of a generic SLD and a TLD, the next question is whether the dual purposes of the Lanham Act—protecting consumers and incentivizing brand development—militate for or against protection. Generally, the consumer protection rationale favors trademark protection because brands minimize the information costs of purchasing decisions. [cit.] Although trademark rights are disfavored when they would cause consumer confusion or impede competition, [cit.] because domain names are inherently unique and the scope of protection afforded to a domain name with a generic SLD will be narrow, the risk of consumer confusion or anticompetitive monopolies is remote. Rather, the evidence in this record shows that consumers are primed to perceive a domain name as a brand which militates for, not against, trademark protection for domain names. In addition, because online goods and services are a significant and ever-growing part of the economy, granting trademarks to producers who primarily offer goods and services online and brand themselves based on their domain name favors the interest of consumers by limiting the prospect of deception and confusion. Incidentally, this also protects the good will generated by producers, often at great effort and expense, and thereby incentivizes brand development.[11] In sum, the rationales animating the Lanham Act are aligned with the conclusions that TLDs are generally source identifying and that a mark composed of a generic SLD and a TLD is a descriptive mark eligible for protection upon a showing of acquired distinctiveness.

iii.   Evidence of Public Understanding Regarding Genericness

[The court proceeded to consider evidence of the public's understanding of BOOKING.COM, including public usage and a so-called *Teflon* survey (*see infra* page 96, note 8) that revealed that 74.8 percent of respondents identified BOOKING.COM as a brand name rather than a generic term. The court concluded that the most striking feature of record was the absence of evidence indicating that the consuming public uses the term BOOKING.COM to refer to a class of services. The court thus found that the relevant consuming public primarily understood that BOOKING.COM does not refer to a genus; rather it is descriptive of services involving "booking" available at that domain name. And, because "booking" was a broad enough term to refer to both hotel and travel reservation services, the court found that BOOKING.COM was "descriptive of both the Class 39 and Class 43 services described in plaintiff's applications."]

3.   *Acquired Distinctiveness*

As with any descriptive mark, BOOKING.COM is eligible for protection only upon a showing of secondary meaning or acquired distinctiveness. [cit.] To make this showing, the burden shifts to the applicant to demonstrate that "in the minds of the public, the primary significance of a product feature or term is to identify the source of the product rather than the product itself." *Inwood Labs.*, 456 U.S. at 851 n.11 . . . *Perini Corp. v. Perini Constr., Inc.*, 915 F.2d 121, 125 (4th Cir. 1990) ("Secondary meaning is the consuming public's

---

11. At first glance, it may not be immediately apparent why plaintiff, which uses a unique domain name as its mark, needs trademark protection; however, in the absence of protection, competitors could capitalize on plaintiff's goodwill by expropriating its brand identifiers by, for example, adopting a similar domain name and using the stylized elements of plaintiff's mark or advertising with a hyperlink labeled "Booking.com" that opened a different domain name. Without trademark protection, plaintiff might have some recourse in unfair competition and related torts, but outcomes in this area of law are difficult to predict and leave much to judicial discretion, increasing plaintiff's business risk and leaving consumers more vulnerable to misinformation regarding plaintiff's brand.

understanding that the mark, when used in context, refers, not to what the descriptive word ordinarily describes, but to the particular business that the mark is meant to identify.").

Proof of secondary meaning requires a "rigorous evidentiary" showing and courts consider six factors: "(1) advertising expenditures; (2) consumer studies linking the mark to a source; (3) sales success; (4) unsolicited media coverage of the product; (5) attempts to plagiarize the mark; and (6) the length and exclusivity of the mark's use." *Perini*, 915 F.2d at 125. Secondary meaning exists if a "substantial portion" of the relevant consuming public associates the term with the particular business, id., and the applicant bears the burden of proof, *U.S. Search, LLC v. U.S. Search.com, Inc.*, 300 F.3d 517, 525-26 (4th Cir. 2002).

. . .

[i]   Evidence of Acquired Distinctiveness

With respect to advertising, plaintiff has submitted evidence of the number of visual impressions of BOOKING.COM by consumers. Although the secondary meaning test refers to "advertising expenditures," *Perini*, 915 F.2d at 125, the Court is satisfied that the number of visual impressions is equally, if not more, probative of secondary meaning because it more closely approximates the number of consumers who have been exposed to a brand. Plaintiff aired BOOKING.COM branded television commercials that received 1.3 billion visual impressions from U.S. customers in 2015 and 1.1 billion impressions in 2016. Its internet advertisements during these years received 212 million and 1.34 billion visual impressions from U.S. customers, respectively. And its 2015 movie theater advertisements received approximately 40 million visual impressions from U.S. customers. This is compelling evidence of plaintiff's advertising efforts and is considerably more wide-reaching than the evidence used to satisfy the first factor in other Fourth Circuit cases. See *Resorts of Pinehurst, Inc. v. Pinehurst Nat'l Corp.*, 148 F.3d 417, 421-22 (4th Cir. 1998) (finding that the markholder had made "considerable advertising efforts and expenditure of money toward developing a reputation and goodwill" for its mark through a "nationwide marketing campaign" that involved "placing advertisements in numerous national golf publications such as Golf and Golf Digest magazines" and aggressively "seeking out major professional golf tournaments").

As to the second factor . . . [Plaintiff relies] on the *Teflon* survey conducted by Poret, which indicated that 74.8 percent of consumers of online travel services recognize BOOKING.COM as a brand. Although primarily used to determine whether a mark is generic, *Teflon* surveys are also a generally accepted way of measuring secondary meaning. [cit.] In this Circuit, "survey evidence is generally thought to be the most direct and persuasive way of establishing secondary meaning." *U.S. Search, LLC*, 300 F.3d at 526 n.13. And Professor McCarthy has identified survey evidence as one of a handful of types of direct evidence of consumer understanding—along with consumer testimony—as compared to the other secondary meaning factors, which offer circumstantial evidence of brand recognition. [cit.] Because plaintiff's *Teflon* survey is the only evidence in the record that speaks directly to how consumers understand plaintiff's mark, it weighs heavily in the secondary meaning analysis and the survey's finding that approximately three out of four consumers recognize BOOKING.COM as a brand indicates strong brand awareness. See *IDV N. Am., Inc. v. S & M Brands, Inc.*, 26 F. Supp. 2d 815, 823 (E.D. Va. 1998) (holding that BAILEYS liqueurs had secondary meaning, based in part upon a "51% consumer awareness rating").

The third factor, record of sales success, is also well-established. Plaintiff's public filings reflect that its U.S. customers conduct billions of dollars' worth of transactions each year, and, as of 2013, plaintiff's total transaction value, both in the United States and abroad, was over $8 billion, which is substantially higher than the sales success in other cases where courts in this Circuit have found secondary meaning. See, e.g., *Worsham Sprinkler Co. v. Wes Worsham Fire Prot., LLC*, 419 F. Supp. 2d 861, 869-72 (E.D. Va. 2006) (citing annual revenues averaging $18-20 million); *IDV N. Am., Inc.*, 26 F. Supp. 2d at 823 (finding that BAILEYS liqueurs' $1 billion in sales over the course of a decade supported a finding of secondary meaning). In addition, plaintiff's mobile app, which can be used to search for hotels and make reservations, was downloaded approximately 1 million times in 2014, 1.9 million times in 2015, and 2.5 million times in 2016, which offers additional, circumstantial evidence of sales success and consumer brand recognition.

The fourth factor is unsolicited media coverage. In 2015 and 2016 the number of news articles published in the United States referencing BOOKING.COM was over 600 and 650, respectively. This compares very favorably to other cases where courts have found that media coverage demonstrated that a brand had achieved public prominence. *Washington Speakers Bureau, Inc. v. Leading Authorities, Inc.*, 33 F. Supp. 2d 488, 496-97 (E.D. Va. 1999), aff'd, 217 F.3d 843 (4th Cir. 2000) (relying on evidence that a "news database search offered by [the markholder] disclosed hundreds of articles specifically referring to [the service] and its activities").

Plaintiff identifies no evidence of the fifth factor, attempts to plagiarize the mark. But, a party need not prove all six factors and the Fourth Circuit has concluded that secondary meaning can exist even when "no attempts to plagiarize the mark were shown." *Perini*, 915 F.2d at 126.

With respect to the sixth factor, length and exclusivity of use, plaintiff, which has been offering "online hotel reservation service" since 1996, operated from "1996 to June 2006 using the mark BOOKINGS. In June 2006, [plaintiff] modified its mark to BOOKING. COM and has been providing services under that mark since then." Eleven years of uninterrupted use, in conjunction with the other factors, weighs in favor of secondary meaning. See *Teaching Co. Ltd. P'ship v. Unapix Entm't, Inc.*, 87 F. Supp. 2d 567, 579-80 (E.D. Va. 2000) (finding that secondary meaning existed in a mark that had been used without interruption for eight years).

In addition, there is no evidence in the record that "any other party offering travel agency services refers to itself as a 'Booking.com.'" [D]efendants point to fifteen third-party websites that include "booking.com" or "bookings.com," and one might argue that this is evidence that plaintiff has not enjoyed exclusive use. This argument fails because the mere existence of a registered domain name or even a website does not equate to its use as a "mark." "[A] domain name does not become a trademark or service mark unless it is also used to identify and distinguish the source of goods or services." [cit.] Out of the millions of domain names, only a fraction play the role of a mark. Indeed, the websites associated with the domain names cited by the defendants identify their services not by reference to their domain name but by phrases such as "Dream Vacation Booking" and "Vacation Home Booking." Further, . . . these websites are not actually referring to themselves as "booking.coms," therefore they are not using the term either descriptively or as a mark.

Finally, plaintiff has adduced evidence of its substantial social media following. As of 2016, over 5 million consumers had "liked" BOOKING.COM on Facebook and over 100,000 "followed" BOOKING.COM on Twitter. Although this evidence does not directly relate to any of the *Perini* factors, those factors are non-exhaustive, *Shammas v. Rea*, 978 F. Supp. 2d 599, 612 (E.D. Va. 2013), and, just as unsolicited media coverage offers circumstantial evidence of consumer awareness of a brand, the size of a producer's social media following is indicative of the number of consumers who are familiar with a brand, interested in receiving additional information about it, and presumably tend to feel goodwill toward the producer.

In the face of this evidence, defendants argue that "although [p]laintiff has provided documents related to its commercial success, they do not demonstrate actual market recognition of 'booking.com' as a source indicator." This argument ignores the direct evidence of consumer understanding established by plaintiff's Teflon survey and appears to challenge the very nature of the secondary meaning test, which acknowledges that five of the six factors—advertising expenditures, sales success, media coverage, attempts to plagiarize, and exclusivity of use—are all circumstantial evidence. Professor McCarthy acknowledges direct evidence "is not a requirement and secondary meaning can be, and most often is, proven by circumstantial evidence." [cit.] In addition, it defies logic to suggest that billions of consumer impressions through advertising, billions of dollars in sales, and over 1,000 newspaper articles have no bearing on whether consumers understand BOOKING.COM to be a source of reservation services.[19]

[ii]   Class Specific Analysis

[U]nfortunately, the evidence does not clearly differentiate between Class 39—travel agency services—and Class 43—hotel reservation services. Plaintiff's evidence often speaks simply of BOOKING.COM, and, where it does differentiate, it refers only to plaintiff's hotel reservation services. . . . In light of the total absence of evidence that either the consuming public, or even Booking.com's officers, associate BOOKING.COM with travel agency services, plaintiff has failed to carry its burden of establishing secondary meaning as to Class 39.

Conversely, the record demonstrates strong evidence of secondary meaning for Class 43 on five of the six secondary meaning factors: Plaintiff has established the existence of an extensive nationwide advertising campaign; a strong public perception that BOOKING.COM is a brand identifier, as evidenced by the Teflon survey; robust consumer sales; voluminous unsolicited media coverage; and a decade of exclusive use. This evidence is more than sufficient to demonstrate that "in the minds of the public, the primary significance of" BOOKING.COM "is to identify the source of the product rather than the product itself," and that plaintiff's mark is entitled to protection for the services identified in Class 43, as a descriptive mark.

III.   CONCLUSION

The question of whether a TLD has source identifying significance is a question of first impression in this Circuit. After carefully reviewing the Federal Circuit's precedent on this issue, the purposes of the Lanham Act, and the competition-protecting features built into the structure of trademark law, the Court has concluded both that a TLD generally has source identifying significance and that a mark composed of a generic SLD and a TLD is usually a descriptive mark eligible for protection upon a showing of secondary meaning. Applying these holdings to the facts of this case, the Court holds that BOOKING.COM is a descriptive mark and that plaintiff has carried its burden of demonstrating the mark's secondary meaning as to the hotel reservation services described in Class 43 but not as to the travel agency services recited in Class 39.

---

19. Defendants also argue that "[u]se of a company name does not demonstrate consumer recognition as a brand." Defendants identifies no legal basis for drawing a distinction between a company name and a brand, nor is the Court aware of any. See *Sara Lee*, 81 F.3d at 464 (recognizing that EXXON, POLAROID, and APPLE, all the names of major companies, are also brands). Such a distinction might make sense in certain contexts. For example, consumer recognition of the company name Procter & Gamble would not necessarily be probative of consumer recognition of its brands, such as DAWN for dish soap. But, here, the company name and the brand name BOOKING.COM are one and the same.

NOTES AND QUESTIONS

1. *TLDs and source identification.* As a descriptive matter, is the statement in the TMEP correct that "TLDs generally serve no source-indicating function"? Does that depend on the TLD in question? What about ".aero," which is reserved for aviation-related sites? What about fake TLDs? If a suffix looks like a TLD, should it be treated as one? For example, what about a service designed to assist in memorializing loved ones that was offered under the mark FRIENDS.RIP? Do the same considerations apply to county code top-level domains (e.g., ".us," ".uk," or ".tv") as apply to generic top-level domains (e.g., ".edu" and ".com")? How should the approach of trademark law to the relevance of generic top level domains in assessing distinctiveness change now that ICANN is in the process of rolling out domains based on brands (e.g., .CANON)? That process and the disputes that it has engendered are discussed in Chapter 8.

2. *Web-related prefixes.* Does the policy stated in the TMEP reflect the likely reaction to the "www" prefix? That is, does "www" act as a source-identifier? How would you classify the mark WWW.IMBLEDONNEWS.COM for a tennis results service?

3. *Secondary meaning in the online environment.* In assessing secondary meaning, what weight should be given to the fact that the mark in which the applicant claims rights is also the applicant's domain name? What about the fact that the bulk of the applicant's advertising expenditures was online (e.g., the purchase of banner ads or keyword-triggered sponsored links)? What weight would you give to the fact that each day 200 new users and 200 repeat users logged on to an applicant's website (at an address consisting of the claimed mark) to request price quotes? *See In re Steelbuilding.com*, 415 F.3d 1293 (Fed. Cir. 2005) (Linn, J., concurring in part and dissenting in part); *see also In re Country Music Ass'n, Inc.*, 100 U.S.P.Q.2d (BNA) 1824 (TTAB 2011) (discussing relevance of placement of mark owner's advertisement in paid advertising listings on search engine results page). What weight should courts give to the number of "likes" a product's Facebook page had received?

C. GENERIC TERMS

As explained in the *Abercrombie & Fitch* case, generic terms receive no protection as trademarks. This was true at common law, and the principle is also reflected in PTO practice and in the Lanham Act. The PTO will deny registration for generic terms, and the statute expressly provides that a registration can be canceled at any time on the ground that the mark registered is in fact generic. *See* 15 U.S.C. §1064(3). Thus, like all distinctiveness issues, the generic status of a claimed mark can be raised in infringement litigation or in proceedings before the PTO. There is considerable case law on the question of generic terms, although not all of it is crystal clear. Terms may be generic in two ways. Terms might be (inherently) generic by virtue of their natural relationship to the products with which they are used (for example, BEER for beer); these terms never possess any trademark significance. Alternatively, terms that have trademark significance (i.e., identify the source of a product) may become generic by virtue of common usage. ASPIRIN is an example of a term that once was protected as a trademark but which became generic because of public usage. As you read the materials that follow, consider whether the public policies underlying genericism apply with as much force to both categories of generic terms. And ask yourself whether the doctrinal tests and rules that courts have developed can be applied as easily to both categories. *Cf. Gimix, Inc. v. JS & A Group, Inc.*, 699 F.2d 901, 905 (7th Cir. 1983) (suggesting that the tests applicable may vary depending upon whether the mark has prior trademark significance); *Miller Brewing Co. v. Jos. Schlitz Brewing Co.*, 605 F.2d 990 (7th Cir. 1979) (same).

FILIPINO YELLOW PAGES, INC. v. ASIAN JOURNAL PUBS., INC.

198 F.3d 1143 (9th Cir. 1999)

O'SCANNLAIN, Circuit Judge:

[Plaintiff ("FYP") was the publisher of a directory called the *Filipino Yellow Pages*. AJP published the *Filipino Consumer Directory*. These directories competed in the California market. AJP periodically used the term "Filipino Consumer Yellow Pages" in print advertisements directed at potential advertisers. On August 2, 1996, FYP filed a complaint against AJP in the Central District of California alleging, *inter alia*, trademark infringement and unfair competition. AJP moved for summary judgment, arguing that the term "Filipino Yellow Pages" is generic and as such incapable of trademark protection. In opposing the motion for summary judgment, FYP contended that "Filipino Yellow Pages," rather than being generic, is protectable under trademark law as a descriptive mark with a secondary meaning in the minds of consumers (i.e., as specifically referring to FYP's telephone directory). The district court granted AJP's motion for summary judgment, holding that the term "Filipino Yellow Pages" was generic. FYP appealed.]

II

. . .

A

Before proceeding to the merits, a word on the burden of persuasion is appropriate. In cases involving properly registered marks, a presumption of validity places the burden of proving genericness upon the defendant. *See* 15 U.S.C. §1057(b) ("A certificate of registration of a mark . . . shall be prima facie evidence of the validity of the registered mark. . . ."). If a supposedly valid mark is not federally registered, however, the plaintiff has the burden of proving nongenericness once the defendant asserts genericness as a defense. [cit.] The case at bar involves a claimed mark that is unregistered; FYP has not yet been successful in its attempts to register "Filipino Yellow Pages" with the PTO. Thus FYP, as trademark plaintiff, bears the burden of showing that "Filipino Yellow Pages" is not generic.

B

. . .

In determining whether a term is generic, we have often relied upon the "who-are-you/what-are-you" test: "A mark answers the buyer's questions 'Who are you?' 'Where do you come from?' 'Who vouches for you?' But the [generic] name of the product answers the question 'What are you?'" *Official Airline Guides, Inc. v. Goss*, 6 F.3d 1385, 1391 (9th Cir. 1993) (quoting 1 J. Thomas McCarthy, *Trademarks and Unfair Competition* §12.01 (3d ed. 1992)). Under this test, "[i]f the primary significance of the trademark is to describe the *type of product* rather than the *producer*, the trademark [is] a generic term and [cannot be] a valid trademark." [cit.]

Here the parties do not dispute that "Filipino" and "yellow pages" are generic terms. The word "Filipino" is a clearly generic term used to refer to "a native of the Philippine islands" or "a citizen of the Republic of the Philippines." *Webster's Ninth New Collegiate Dictionary* 462 (1986). The term "yellow pages" has been found to be a generic term for "a local business telephone directory alphabetized by product or service." [cit.] The district court further noted, as shown by FYP's application for trademark registration, that the PTO requires the use of a disclaimer regarding rights to the term "yellow pages" whenever it is used as part of a registered trademark.

The issue then becomes whether combining the generic terms "Filipino" and "yellow pages" to form the composite term "Filipino Yellow Pages" creates a generic or a descriptive term. AJP argues, and the district court concluded, that "Filipino Yellow Pages" is generic based on this court's analysis in *Surgicenters of America, Inc. v. Medical Dental Surgeries Co.*, 601 F.2d 1011 (9th Cir. 1979). In *Surgicenters*, we held that the term "surgicenter" was generic and that the plaintiff's registered service mark had to be removed from the trademark register. In our discussion in *Surgicenters*, we summarized (but did not explicitly adopt) the analysis of the district court in that case, which reasoned that "surgicenter," created by combining the generic terms "surgery" and "center," retained the generic quality of its components. *Id.* at 1015. We distinguished "surgicenter" from the composite term "Startgrolay" upheld as a valid mark for poultry feed, by noting that the combination of terms in "surgicenter" did not constitute a "deviation from normal usage" or an "unusual unitary combination." *Id.* at 1018. Nowhere in *Surgicenters* did we hold, however, that a composite term made up of generic components is automatically generic unless the combination constitutes a "deviation from normal usage" or an "unusual unitary combination."

In reaching our conclusion of genericness in *Surgicenters*, we placed significant but not controlling weight on the dictionary definitions and generic nature of "surgery" and "center." We explained that "[w]hile not determinative, dictionary definitions are relevant and often persuasive in determining how a term is understood by the consuming public, the ultimate test of whether a trademark is generic." *Id.* at 1015 n.11. But we also based our genericness finding upon detailed information in some 45 exhibits that, taken collectively, suggested that the consuming public considered the composite term "surgicenter" to mean a surgical center generally speaking, as opposed to a surgical center maintained and operated by the plaintiff specifically. *See id.* at 1017. These exhibits included letters from potential consumers and several publications that used the term "surgicenter" in a clearly generic sense. The finding of genericness in *Surgicenters* cannot be separated from the uniquely well-developed record in that case. [cit.]

In this case, the district court cited *Surgicenters* for the proposition that "a combination of two generic words is also generic, unless the combination is a 'deviation from natural usage' or an 'unusual unitary combination.'" The court then stated that "[u]nder this analysis, the term 'Filipino Yellow Pages' seems to be neither a 'deviation from natural usage,' nor an 'unusual unitary combination.'" The district court's reading of *Surgicenters* appears somewhat troubling insofar as it oversimplifies our opinion. First, it overlooks our explicit recognition that "words which could not individually become a trademark may become one when taken together." 601 F.2d at 1017 (internal quotation marks omitted). Second, it effectively makes dictionary definitions the crucial factor in assessing genericness, even though *Surgicenters* makes clear that such definitions are "not determinative" and that the "ultimate test" of genericness is "how a term is understood by the consuming public." *Id.* at 1015 n.11. Finally, it severs our *Surgicenters* analysis from its unique factual context, in which a wealth of exhibits supported a finding that the term "surgicenter" was generic even when taken as a whole (as opposed to the sum of generic parts).

Furthermore, reading the *Surgicenters* opinion for the rather broad (and somewhat reductionist) principle that "a generic term plus a generic term equals a generic term" would give rise to an unnecessary conflict between that decision and several other cases, decided both before and after *Surgicenters*, in which we have adopted a more holistic approach to evaluating composite terms. . . .

[S]everal pre- and post-*Surgicenters* cases have announced what could be described as an "anti-dissection rule" for evaluating the trademark validity of composite terms. *Official Airline Guides, Inc.*, 6 F.3d at 1392 (noting that under this rule, "the validity and distinctiveness of a composite trademark is determined by viewing the trademark as a whole, as it appears in the marketplace"). When *Surgicenters* is examined in light of these later cases, it becomes clear that *Surgicenters* should not be read overbroadly to stand for the simple proposition that "generic plus generic equals generic." . . .

In light of the foregoing discussion, the district court here may have oversimplified matters somewhat when it stated that "[t]he Ninth Circuit has held that a combination of two generic words is also generic, unless the combination is a 'deviation from natural usage' or an 'unusual unitary combination.'" Any arguable imprecision in the district court's application of *Surgicenters* was harmless, however, because the term "Filipino Yellow Pages" would be unprotectible in any event.

In finding "Filipino Yellow Pages" generic, the district court did not rely solely upon the generic nature and presence in the dictionary of "Filipino" and "yellow pages." The district court also considered other evidence tending to suggest that "Filipino Yellow Pages," even when considered as an entire mark, is generic with respect to telephone directories. The district court took note of the following facts: (1) [an officer of the plaintiff] himself appeared to use the term "Filipino Yellow Pages" in a generic sense in [an earlier] Shareholders' Buy Out Agreement with [an officer of the defendant], when he "agree[d] not to compete in the Filipino Directory (Filipino Yellow Pages) [market] in California"; (2) FYP did not bring suit to challenge the marketing of [an unrelated] second *Filipino Yellow Pages* to the Filipino-American community on the East Coast; and (3) a *Los Angeles Times* article, in discussing a trend toward specialized yellow pages, appeared to use the term in a generic sense; the article referred to a directory published by one Virgil Junio as "his Filipino yellow pages" instead of using the actual title of Junio's publication.

These three pieces of evidence are not as weighty as the 45 exhibits presented in *Surgicenters*, in which the record established generic use of the term "surgicenter" by *Newsweek* magazine, six medical publications, and the Department of Health, Education and Welfare. [cit.] An important difference between *Surgicenters* and the instant case should be noted, however. The mark at issue in *Surgicenters* was a federally registered mark, and thus the burden of proving genericness rested upon the party challenging the mark's validity. [cit.] The mark at issue in this case, in contrast, is not registered; thus FYP, as trademark plaintiff, must prove that "Filipino Yellow Pages" is *not* generic. It does not appear that FYP has offered evidence of nongenericness sufficient to rebut even the fairly modest evidence of genericness offered by AJP. In light of the evidence presented by AJP, it would seem that under the "who-are-you/what-are-you" test, the term "Filipino Yellow Pages" is generic. If faced with the question "What are you?", FYP's *Filipino Yellow Pages*, AJP's *Filipino Consumer Directory*, and the *Filipino Directory of the U.S.A. and Canada* could all respond in the same way: "A Filipino yellow pages." Giving FYP exclusive rights to the term "Filipino Yellow Pages" might be inappropriate because it would effectively "grant [FYP as] owner of the mark a monopoly, since a competitor could not describe his goods as what they are." *Surgicenters*, 601 F.2d at 1017 (internal quotation marks omitted). . . .

Affirmed.

MIL-MAR SHOE CO., INC. v. SHONAC CORP.

75 F.3d 1153 (7th Cir. 1996)

FLAUM, Circuit Judge:

[Mil-Mar Shoe Company, Inc. ("Mil-Mar"), the owner of a chain of shoe stores under the name "Warehouse Shoes," sought a temporary restraining order and a preliminary injunction to prevent Shonac from using the name "DSW Shoe Warehouse" to designate the retail shoe store that Shonac announced would be opened in the Greater Milwaukee area. After a hearing on the matter, the district court granted the preliminary injunction, enjoining Shonac from using "DSW Shoe Warehouse," "Shoe Warehouse," or any other name confusingly similar to "Warehouse Shoes" in the Greater Milwaukee area. The Court of Appeals reversed.]

The essential difference between "generic" terms and "descriptive" terms was and is the degree of distinctiveness, and thus their relative ability to serve as a source-identifier of particular goods and services. Because generic use implies use consistent with common understanding, we have often looked to dictionaries as a source of evidence on genericness. [cit.]

Webster's Third New International Dictionary defines the noun "warehouse" as follows:

> **1:** a structure or room for the storage of merchandise or commodities: **a:** a wholesale establishment of the service type in which large inventories are carried **b:** a wholesale establishment operated by a chain store organization **c:** a place for the storing of surplus or reserve stocks of merchandise by a retail store **d:** a public institution for the storing of goods for others **2** *Brit.:* retail store.

WEBSTER'S THIRD NEW INTERNATIONAL DICTIONARY 2576 (1993).

The word "warehouse," as it is being used by both Mil-Mar and Shonac, thus would seem to potentially fit both the 1(a) and the 1(b) definitions. Both companies run chain stores that sell large inventories of goods (i.e., shoes) at wholesale, or at least "discounted," prices. Furthermore, the second definition, "retail store," obviously fits the stores at issue. Mil-Mar strenuously argues against this dictionary evidence, pointing out that the "retail store" definition is a *British* use of the word. . . . Mil-Mar would have us believe that *Americans* simply do not use the word "warehouse" to refer to retail store. Yet the evidence presented to the district court by Shonac, showing widespread use of "warehouse" to refer to retail stores, decisively rebuts any such claim.

When the district court considered the evidence on genericness, it seemed to focus upon the fact that the *primary* meaning of warehouse, the one that appears first in the dictionaries, is that of a large structure used for storage—not that of a retail store. It also noted that "warehouse" has multiple dictionary meanings.[11] The court concluded: "As such, the term 'Warehouse Shoes' does not appear to be subject to one common public understanding so as to be considered generic." Mil-Mar emphasizes the primary definition of "warehouse" and the image that first comes to mind when the word "warehouse" is mentioned—generally not a retail store. However, no principle of trademark law mandates that only the primary definition of a word can qualify as generic. In fact, we have previously found that "light" and its phonetic equivalent "lite" are generic when used to describe a type of beer, *Miller Brewing* [*Co. v. G. Heileman Brewing Co. Inc.*, 561 F.2d 75,] 80-81, even though the most common adjectival meaning of "light" has to do with weight. We recognized that "light" and "lite," as applied to beer, could refer to color, flavor, body, alcoholic content, or a combination of these characteristics. *Id.* It did not matter that such common, accepted uses of "light" were not listed first and were not the only definitions in the dictionary. The question is whether the term is being *used* in a common or generic sense, not whether a *particular* use represents the most common use of that term. The district court's legal error in this regard infected its conclusion that "Warehouse Shoes" was not generic.

---

11. It is somewhat unclear which factor was decisive for the district court: that the primary definition of "warehouse" was not that of a retail store or the bare fact that "warehouse" has multiple meanings. In either case, we determine that the district court was incorrect in inferring that such a finding mandated the conclusion that "Warehouse Shoes" was not generic.

Shonac put on evidence that, nationally, over 8000 retail stores use the word "warehouse" in their names. Such names include: Furniture Warehouse, Warehouse Electronics, Just Plants Warehouse, Jewelry Warehouse, Mattress Warehouse, Carpet Warehouse, Warehouse Carpet, Warehouse Fragrances, Auto Parts Warehouse, Tire Warehouse, Bedding Warehouse, Warehouse Liquors, Pasta Warehouse, Warehouse Antiques, Warehouse Furniture and Bedding, Warehouse Fabrics, Warehouse Carpet & Tile, Warehouse Beer & Wine, The Clothing Warehouse, Bridal Warehouse, Wallpaper Warehouse, Book Warehouse, etc. Such widespread retail usage indicates that the American public commonly understands the term "warehouse" to apply to retail stores that sell any of a wide range of products. [cit.] When consumers hear the word "warehouse" in the retail context, as in the names listed above, they generally expect goods to be sold in high volume, from a relatively large store, at discount prices. The word "warehouse" is thus being used generically to denote a particular type or genus of retail store.

Significant use of a term by competitors in the industry has traditionally been recognized, along with dictionary evidence, as indicating genericness. *Miller Brewing*, 561 F.2d at 80; 2 J. Thomas McCarthy, McCarthy on Trademarks and Unfair Competition §12.02[7][b] (3d ed. 1995). Shonac has presented evidence that hundreds of retail shoe stores use some form of either "Shoe Warehouse" or "Warehouse Shoes" in their names. Although none of these stores were competing directly with Mil-Mar's "Warehouse Shoes" stores in the Greater Milwaukee area, and thus Mil-Mar had no incentive or standing to challenge these names, the breadth of the use nationally by other shoe retailers further substantiates our ultimate conclusion that both "Shoe Warehouse" and "Warehouse Shoes" are generic. . . .

We acknowledge that the genericness issue is a closer call with "Warehouse Shoes" than with "Shoe Warehouse." At first glance, it appears that "warehouse" is functioning as an adjective in Mil-Mar's "Warehouse Shoes," which makes it seem more descriptive. An easy "noun versus adjective" test to signify a mark as either generic or descriptive, respectively, does not, however, adequately characterize the law of this circuit,[14] nor would such a simplistic approach adequately embody fundamental principles of trademark law. The fact that "light" and "lite" were being used as adjectives to describe beer did not defeat our conclusion that "light beer" and "lite beer" were generic terms that could not garner trademark protection. *Miller Brewing*, 561 F.2d at 80 ("The fact that 'light' is an adjective does not prevent it from being a generic or common descriptive word.")[.] The word "warehouse" in both "Warehouse Shoes" and "Shoe Warehouse" plays the same role as the words "light" and "lite" do when they modify "beer." "Warehouse Shoes" and "Shoe Warehouse" both signify a particular type, category, or genus of retail stores: large stores that sell shoes in high volume at discount prices. . . .

While Mil-Mar would have us believe that placing the word "warehouse" first in the name makes all the difference, this argument simply does not hold up. The substantial number of other retailers, including many shoe retailers, who position the word "warehouse" first in their names belies any attempt to draw much significance from such placement. In fact, one court has already held that the name "Warehouse Foods" is generic. *Warehouse Foods, Inc. v. Great Atlantic and Pacific Tea Co.*, 223 U.S.P.Q. 892, 893 (N.D. Fla. 1984) (noting that the phrase has been "widely used in the trade as a generic designation for a type

---

14. McCarthy remarks: "A rule of thumb sometimes forwarded as distinguishing a generic name from a descriptive term is that generic terms are nouns and descriptive terms are adjectives. However, this 'part of speech' test does not accurately describe the case law results." 2 McCarthy, §12.02[5].

of food store"). We leave open the possibility that changing the order of terms in a name or phrase may make the difference between genericness and trademark potential.[16] Indeed, inverting word order often completely changes meaning. We simply find that, as the terms are used by the parties, "Warehouse Shoes" means the same thing as "Shoe Warehouse," and both terms are generic. The district court clearly erred when it found that "Warehouse Shoes" was not generic.

HAUGHTON ELEVATOR CO. v. SEEBERGER
85 U.S.P.Q. (BNA) 80 (Comm'r Pat. 1950)

MURPHY, Assistant Commissioner:

This is an appeal from the decision . . . sustaining the petition of the Haughton Elevator Company to cancel the trade mark "ESCALATOR," Registration No. 34,724, issued May 29, 1900, to Charles D. Seeberger, assigned to the Otis Elevator Company, and duly renewed May 29, 1930. . . .

The Examiner . . . sustained the petition for cancellation and recommended that the registration be canceled on the ground that the term "escalator" has become a [generic term] to both the general public and to engineers and architects and that, to them, the term not only does not mean a moving stairway made by the Respondent but rather means any moving stairway without reference to the maker thereof.

He further held "that the Respondent not only has not been successful in preventing the use of the term 'escalator' from becoming a [generic] name, but, by its own use thereof as a generic term, has given assent to such use."

On careful consideration of the record in this case, it appears . . . that the term "escalator" is recognized by the general public as the name for a moving stairway and not the source thereof. It further appears that Respondent has used the term as a [generic] term instead of an indication of origin, in a number of patents which have been issued to them and has also so used the name in their advertising matter which has appeared in magazines addressed to the trade which would be likely prospective customers for such devices. Thus, in the *Architectural Forum* for March 1946, appears an advertisement beginning as follows: "Otis elevators Otis escalators." From this it is seen that the word "escalators" is used generically . . . and without any trade mark significance just as is the word "elevators." Also, in the same magazine for January, 1946, . . . appears the advertisement of the Otis Elevator Company with the name "OTIS," in a circle, prominently displayed near the middle of the page, beneath which is this notation in bold letters: "THE MEANING OF THE OTIS TRADEMARK." Beneath this, in part, is the following:

> To the millions of daily passengers on the Otis elevators and escalators, the Otis trademark or name plate means safe, convenient, energy-saving transportation.
> To thousands of building owners and managers, the Otis trademark means the utmost in safe, efficient economical elevator and escalator operation.

It is obvious to me from this advertisement that the trade mark emphasis is on the word "Otis" and its significant mark because here, again, the word "escalator" or "escalators" is

---

16. In cases like this one, where inversion does not change meaning, the genericness of the inverted term essentially depends upon how large the cognitive leap is from the inverted term ("Warehouse Shoes") to the more common formulation ("Shoe Warehouse"). Because the word "warehouse" is so commonly placed first in the names of retail stores generally and shoe stores specifically, we find that the cognitive leap in this case is a mere hop and that "Warehouse Shoes" is no less generic than "Shoe Warehouse."

written in small letters and in the same manner and same context as the word "elevator" or "elevators" which obviously has no trade mark significance.

It also appears that the Otis Elevator Company had two responsible representatives on the committee which prepared the "Standard Safety Code for Elevators, Dumbwaiters and Escalators.". . . In this model code, "escalator" is defined as a moving inclined continuous stairway or runway used for raising or lowering passengers. Throughout, the word "escalator" is used descriptively without any indication that it designates origin of the type of device under consideration. It does not appear that any protest was made by the Otis Elevator Company or their representatives on the committee to the generic and descriptive use of the word "escalator." Thus the course of conduct of the Respondent was such as to cause the mark of "escalator" to lose its significance as an indication of origin.

Upon careful consideration of the record, I am not convinced that the examiner erred in sustaining the petition for cancellation and in recommending that Registration No. 34,724 be canceled.

MURPHY DOOR BED CO., INC. v. INTERIOR SLEEP SYS., INC.

874 F.2d 95 (2d Cir. 1989)

MINER, Circuit Judge:

. . .

At the turn of this century, William Lawrence Murphy invented and manufactured a bed that when not in use could be concealed in a wall closet. By using a counter-balancing mechanism, the bed could be lowered from or raised to a closet in a wall to which the bed is hinged. In 1918, the United States Patent Office granted Mr. Murphy a patent for a "pivot bed," which was substantially similar to the wall bed. Mr. Murphy incorporated in New York in 1925 as the Murphy Door Bed Company and began to sell the wall bed under the name of "Murphy bed." Since its inception, the Murphy Co. has used the words Murphy and Murphy bed as its trademark for concealed beds. Other manufacturers of wall beds generally describe their products as "wall beds," "concealed beds," "disappearing beds," "authentic adjustable hydraulic beds" and the like, but rarely as Murphy beds. In fact, at least twice, when independent companies marketed their products as Murphy beds, Murphy complained to them and, as a result, the companies refrained from further deliberate use of the term Murphy bed.

On March 23, 1981, and again on November 16, 1982, the Patent and Trademark Office ("PTO") denied the Murphy Co.'s application to register the Murphy bed trademark. The PTO examining attorney explained that the words "Murphy bed" had become generic and that the phrase Murphy bed was "merely descriptive of a characteristic of the goods." In August 1984, the Trademark Trial and Appeal Board ("TTAB") affirmed the denial of registration. [cit.] The TTAB noted that "Murphy bed has for a long period of time been used by a substantial segment of the public as a generic term for a bed which folds into a wall or a closet." [cit.]

In December 1981, Frank Zarcone, on behalf of [Interior Sleep Systems, Inc. (ISS)] and himself, entered into a distributorship agreement with the Murphy Co. and became the exclusive distributor of the Murphy bed in the four Florida counties of Broward, Dade, Palm Beach and Monroe. [After termination of this agreement, a third party ordered 109 Murphy beds from Zarcone. Zarcone previously had filled similar orders with beds of the Murphy Co. To fill this order, however, Zarcone delivered beds designated as Murphy bed Model SL 60/80 but that were, in fact, manufactured by one of his companies. The Murphy Co. sued, *inter alia*, for trademark infringement and unfair competition.]

The district court found that Murphy had shown that the term Murphy bed had secondary meaning—i.e., that the term symbolized a particular business, product or company—and thus was protectable. As a result, the court assigned to defendants the burden of proving that the term somehow had been transformed into a generic phrase. The defendants did not sustain their burden, in the view of the court. Defendants now claim that the court improperly placed the burden of proof upon them, arguing that, instead, Murphy should have been required to prove that the trademark was not generic.

A term or phrase is generic when it is commonly used to depict a genus or type of product, rather than a particular product. [cit.] When a term is generic, "trademark protection will be denied save for those markets where the term still has not become generic and a secondary meaning has been shown to continue." [cit.] We have held that "the burden is on plaintiff to prove that its mark is a valid trademark . . . [and] that its unregistered mark is not generic." *Reese Publishing Co. v. Hampton Int'l Communications, Inc.*, 620 F.2d 7, 11 (2d Cir. 1980).

As the Murphy mark is unregistered, *Reese* suggests that the district court erred in shifting the burden of proof to the defendants. However, the words at issue in *Reese*, "Video Buyer's Guide," were of common use before the product developer applied them to his product, whereas here, the term Murphy bed was created for its purpose by the manufacturer and only thereafter was it adopted by the public as a matter of common use. *See Gimix v. JS & A Group, Inc.*, 699 F.2d 901, 905 (7th Cir. 1983) (differentiating between term in common usage before application to product and coinage of term to suit product that is later expropriated). It was this genericness of an "invented" term that Learned Hand addressed when determining whether "aspirin," a coined word, had been so adopted by the lay public as to become generic. *See Bayer Co. v. United Drug Co.*, 272 F. 505, 509 (S.D.N.Y. 1921); *see also King-Seely Thermos Co. v. Aladdin Indus., Inc.*, 321 F.2d 577, 579 (2d Cir. 1963) (widespread use of the word "thermos," despite having been invented by plaintiff for description of vacuum bottle, created genericness); *DuPont Cellophane Co. v. Waxed Products Co.*, 85 F.2d 75, 81 (2d Cir.) (expropriation by public of word "cellophane" created genericness), *cert. denied*, 299 U.S. 601 (1936). We find this distinction important and hold that where the public is said to have expropriated a term established by a product developer, the burden is on the defendant to prove genericness. Thus, critical to a trial court's allocation of proof burdens is a determination of whether the term at issue is claimed to be generic by reason of common usage or by reason of expropriation. This presumption of nongenericness of a product name in the case of apparent public expropriation is justified by the commercial protection a developer of innovations deserves.

The Murphy Co. was the first to employ the word Murphy to describe a bed that could be folded into a wall closet. It is claimed that over time the public adopted, or, rather, expropriated, the term Murphy bed as a synonym for any bed that folds into a closet. Accordingly, the district court was correct in placing the burden of proof of genericness upon the defendants. We find, however, that [the defendant] Zarcone did indeed establish the genericness of the term Murphy bed.

The following factors combined lead us to conclude that Zarcone showed at trial that today the term Murphy bed, in the eyes of "a substantial majority of the public," *King-Seely*, 321 F.2d at 579, refers to a species of beds that can fold into a wall enclosure. First, the decision of the PTO, and certainly the TTAB, is to be accorded great weight. [cit.] The district court explicitly rejected the decisions of the PTO and TTAB finding genericness, despite acknowledging their persuasive force. Second, the term Murphy bed is included in many dictionaries as a standard description of a wall-bed. *See, e.g.*, Webster's Third New International Dictionary 1489 (1981). While dictionary definitions are not conclusive proof of a mark's generic nature, they are influential because they reflect the general public's perception of a mark's meaning and implication. *See Gimix*, 699 F.2d at 905. Third, Zarcone introduced as evidence numerous examples of newspaper and magazine use of the phrase Murphy bed to describe generally a type of bed. Again, such evidence is not proof positive, but it is a strong indication of the general public's perception that Murphy bed connotes something other than a bed manufactured by the Murphy Co. [cit.]

In finding a lack of genericness, the district court was influenced by Murphy's efforts at policing its mark. The court noted with approval instances where Murphy complained to those who had used the term Murphy bed to describe beds not necessarily produced by Murphy. However, when, as here, the mark has "entered the public domain beyond recall," policing is of no consequence to a resolution of whether a mark is generic. *King-Seely*, 321 F.2d at 579.[2]

Because we find that the evidence presented at trial demonstrated the genericness of the term Murphy bed, the claim for trademark infringement must fail. . . .

[The court, however, offered the Murphy Co. relief under broader principles of unfair competition. Zarcone advertised the wall beds that he manufactured as "Murphy Bed Co. of America, Inc.—Original Wall-Bed Systems" and "The New Murphy Beds . . . Original Wall Bed Systems." The court held that "even though 'original' might refer to the genus of design rather than to a bed manufactured by the Murphy Co., there is no doubt that the public generally would associate the term 'original' with the first company to manufacture Murphy beds, the Murphy Co. As the district court found, Zarcone intentionally represented his product as plaintiff's wall bed. That is unfair competition. *See King-Seely*, 321 F.2d at 581 ('thermos' held to be generic but defendants prohibited from using term 'genuine' or 'original').")]

BLINDED VETERANS ASS'N v. BLINDED AMERICAN VETERANS FOUND.

872 F.2d 1035 (D.C. Cir. 1989)

RUTH BADER GINSBURG, Circuit Judge:

[The Blinded Veterans Association (BVA or the Association), a nonprofit organization founded in 1945 by a group of blinded World War II veterans, sought to enjoin the Blinded American Veterans Foundation (BAVF or the Foundation), another nonprofit corporation founded in September 1985 by three former officials of BVA, from using the words "blinded" and "veterans" in its name and from using the initials "BVA" as an acronym. The court held that BVA's name (whether the full name or the acronym) is not a protectable trademark because the term "blinded veterans" is generic.]

II

. . .

Even if "blinded veterans" is generic, BVA asserts, BAVF may be enjoined from passing itself off as BVA. Case law in this area is not perspicuous; there is, however, support for BVA's contention. For the reasons stated herein, we conclude that BVA may, dependent

---

2. Indeed, the only evidence that even arguably supports the view that the mark was not generic is the circumstance that other manufacturers did not use the term "Murphy bed" to describe their beds. However, that fact is not sufficient to support a conclusion that the mark is not generic, especially since Murphy's action in policing the mark might well have deterred other manufacturers from using the term Murphy bed in describing their products.

upon further proceedings in the district court, succeed in obtaining limited relief to prevent BAVF from passing off.

If the name of one manufacturer's product is generic, a competitor's use of that name, without more, does not give rise to an unfair competition claim under section 43(a) of the Lanham Act. *See Liquid Controls Corp. v. Liquid Control Corp.*, 802 F.2d 934, 939 (7th Cir. 1986). Nevertheless, such a claim "might be supportable if consumer confusion or a likelihood of consumer confusion arose from the failure of the defendant to adequately identify itself as the source of the product." *Id.* (citing *Miller Brewing Co. v. Jos. Schlitz Brewing Co.*, 605 F.2d 990, 997 (7th Cir. 1979)); *see also Technical Publishing Co. v. Lebhar-Friedman, Inc.*, 729 F.2d 1136, 1142 (7th Cir. 1984); [cit.]. Analogously, if an organization's own name is generic, a competitor's subsequent use of that name may give rise to an unfair competition claim if the competitor's failure adequately to identify itself as distinct from the first organization causes confusion or a likelihood of confusion. *See Liquid Controls*, 802 F.2d at 939-40 (suggesting that "Liquid Controls Corp." could have valid claim against "Liquid Control Corp." if there were more evidence of confusion than merely misdirected mail).

In either situation, the subsequent competitor cannot be prevented from using the generic term to denote itself or its product, but it may be enjoined from passing itself or its product off as the first organization or its product. Thus, a court may require the competitor to take whatever steps are necessary to distinguish itself or its product from the first organization or its product. In the paradigm case, *Kellogg Co. v. National Biscuit Co.*, 305 U.S. 111 (1938), for example, the Supreme Court held that the term "shredded wheat" is generic; the National Biscuit Company therefore was not entitled to exclusive use of the term. *Id.* at 116. Because National Biscuit had been the only manufacturer of shredded wheat for many years, however, the public had come to associate the product and the term "shredded wheat" with that company. The Court therefore stated that the Kellogg Company, which also produced a shredded wheat cereal, could be required to "use reasonable care to inform the public of the source of its product." *Id.* at 119;[19] *see also, e.g., Singer Mfg. Co. v. June Mfg. Co.*, 163 U.S. 169, 204 (1896) (holding that "Singer" had become generic denotation of type of sewing machine, but requiring that defendant not use the word on its product or in advertisements "without clearly and unmistakably stating . . . that the machines are made by the defendant, as distinguished from the sewing machines made by the Singer Manufacturing Company"); *Metric & Multistandard Components Corp. v. Metric's, Inc.*, 635 F.2d 710, 714 (8th Cir. 1980) (finding "metric" generic designation of metric industrial supplies, but nevertheless concluding that section 43(a) of Lanham Act had been violated because mark had become so associated with plaintiff that defendant's use of it created likelihood of confusion); *King-Seeley Thermos Co. v. Aladdin Indus., Inc.*, 321 F.2d 577, 581 (2d Cir. 1963) (finding "thermos" generic denotation of vacuum-insulated container, but affirming requirement that defendant distinguish its product from plaintiff's by preceding "thermos" with "Aladdin's," by using only the lower case "t", and by never using the words "original" or "genuine" in describing its product); *DuPont Cellophane Co. v. Waxed Prods. Co.*, 85 F.2d 75, 80, 82 (2d Cir. 1938) (finding "cellophane" generic denotation of cellulose transparent wrappings, but requiring defendant to identify itself as source of product in certain instances

---

19. The Court further said that "[f]airness requires that [Kellogg exercise its right to use the name 'Shredded Wheat'] in a manner which reasonably distinguishes its product from that of [National Biscuit]." 305 U.S. at 120. The Court then determined that Kellogg had sufficiently distinguished its product by selling it in cartons different from National Biscuit's in size, form, and color, with a different label, a different number of biscuits in each carton, and the name "Kellogg" displayed prominently. *Id.* at 120-21.

to avoid confusion with plaintiff's product);[20] [cit.]; *cf. Miller Brewing Co. v. Jos. Schlitz Brewing Co.*, 605 F.2d 990, 997 (7th Cir. 1979) (rejecting claim of passing off because defendant had adequately identified itself as source of product by preceding generic name of product, "Light Beer," with producer's name, "Schlitz," and had not engaged in potentially confusion-generating practices such as using a similar label or misleading advertisements).[21]

   Under the approach set forth in these cases, a court will not act to remedy or prevent "confusion generated by a mere similarity of names." *Liquid Controls*, 802 F.2d at 940; *see also Standard Paint Co. v. Trinidad Asphalt Mfg. Co.*, 220 U.S. 446, 461 (1911) (rejecting passing off claim because any confusion resulted solely from likeness of generic terms "rubbero" and "ruberoid" and not from any acts of defendant that might cause confusion). If a consumer confuses two manufacturers' shredded wheat cereal, for example, because both products share the same name and the consumer has a general appetite for crunchy pillow-shaped wheat biscuits, there is no cause for judicial action. Such confusion results merely from the manufacturers' concurrent use of a generic term to designate their products, and the late entrant into the shredded wheat field cannot be said to have engaged in unfair competition. If, however, the consumer associates "shredded wheat" with a particular manufacturer, perhaps because that manufacturer enjoyed a de facto (or de jure) monopoly for many years, there is a risk that the consumer may erroneously assume that any product entitled "shredded wheat" comes from that manufacturer.[22] A second manufacturer may increase the risk of confusion by, for example, using a similar label, similar packaging, misleading advertisements, or simply by failing to state the product's source. Only when there is a likelihood that the newcomer might thus pass its product off as the

---

   20. In *Kellogg* and *Singer*, the plaintiffs' patents on the products had expired. Upon expiration of the patents, the Supreme Court held in both cases, the right to make the products passed to the public. [cit.] In *King-Seeley Thermos* and *DuPont Cellophane*, the courts held that formerly exclusive trademark rights had been lost because the terms "thermos" and "cellophane," respectively, had become generic. *King-Seeley Thermos*, 321 F.2d at 579; *DuPont Cellophane*, 85 F.2d at 80-81. A court's authority to require competitors to distinguish themselves or their products is not limited, however, to instances in which the plaintiff once enjoyed an exclusive legal right to make a product or to use a particular name. *But cf. Liquid Controls*, 802 F.2d at 940 (distinguishing *King-Seeley Thermos* and *DuPont Cellophane* on this ground). Regardless of *how* a generic term becomes associated with a particular source, once it does, late-coming competitors may be required to distinguish themselves or their products sufficiently to prevent confusion. *See Brown Chem. Co. v. Meyer*, 139 U.S. 540, 547 (1890) (holding, in case not involving expired patent or lost trademark, that defendant had right to use generic words "Iron Bitters" "*unless he uses them in such connection with other words or devices as to operate as a deception upon the public*") (emphasis added). . . .
   21. One commentator explains the results in some of these cases as predicated on the terms' "dual usage": one portion of the relevant market recognized a term as the mark of a particular source, whereas another portion used the term generically. *See* MCCARTHY §12:16 at 565-68. Although this explanation accurately accounts, in part, for some of the judgments, *see, e.g., DuPont Cellophane*, 85 F.2d at 82 (requiring that defendant attach disclaimer only when dealing with consumers who associate "cellophane" with DuPont), it is underinclusive. In neither *Kellogg* nor *Singer*, for example, did the Supreme Court base its holding on a division in the public's understanding of the terms. Rather, the term in each case had a "dual usage" in another sense: the public in general used each term generically, but it also associated each term with a particular company because that company had been the only manufacturer for a long period. *See, e.g., Kellogg*, 305 U.S. at 118; *Singer*, 163 U.S. at 186-87.
   22. Commentators sometimes refer to this association between a generic term and one particular source, arising normally from that source's monopoly for an extended period, as "de facto secondary meaning." *See, e.g.,* MCCARTHY §12:15 at 562-65. A generic term that acquires de facto secondary meaning is still not afforded trademark protection. *See id.* Nevertheless, as the cases cited above establish, a generic term with de facto secondary meaning may be protected against passing off, *e.g.,* by requiring fair notice that a newcomer's product or service does not come from the original source.

original manufacturer's may a court require the newcomer to distinguish its product or to notify consumers explicitly that its product does not come from the original manufacturer.

In speaking of "passing off," we do not mean to insinuate that the complaining party must prove intent on the part of the passer off. Because passing off developed as an offshoot of the common law of fraud and deceit, some courts in the past required proof that the defendant intended to deceive consumers. *See, e.g., O. & W. Thum Co.*, 245 F. at 621 ("The essence of unfair competition consists in palming off, either directly or indirectly, one person's goods as the goods of another, and this, of course, involves an intent to deceive."); [cit.]. Today, however, the predominant view is that, "[w]hen used in connection with passing off, the term 'fraud' is understood to mean the result of the defendant's act, i.e., deception of the public, rather than his intent." [cit.] Intent to deceive, nevertheless, retains potency; when present, it is probative evidence of a likelihood of confusion. [cit.]

Although the district court did not credit the testimony advanced by BAVF concerning the Foundation's conception, that court reported no conclusion, drawn from the evidence, that BAVF passed itself off as BVA. The court stated only that it disbelieved BAVF's president's testimony that it "never occurred" to him that BAVF's name was similar to BVA's and that BAVF did not plan to compete with BVA:

> The Court . . . finds that BAVF was deliberately named, and presently refuses to change its name, to enable it to capitalize upon the association in the mind of the charitable public between the words "blinded" and "veterans" (and the understandable sympathy they engender), and, thus, to compete with [BVA] for the funds of those inclined to give to such a cause.

680 F. Supp. at 444-45. The Lanham Act, of course, does not proscribe competition per se. Nor is the competition described by the district court unfair merely because BAVF intended to capitalize upon the public's sympathetic association of the words "blinded" and "veterans." Only if BAVF was capitalizing on the public's association of "blinded" and "veterans" with BVA, and therefore reaping the benefits of BVA's goodwill, would the Foundation's actions constitute unfair competition.

True, the district court's opinion is somewhat ambiguous on this score. In a footnote, for example, the district court adverted to the evident similarity of BAVF's original logo — "'BAV' in large type, followed by the word 'foundation' in small-type subscript" — to BVA's logo. *Id.* at 445 n.1. The court also noted that, while the Foundation "professes to be concerned with veterans' 'sensory disabilities' generally, its founders selected a name which adverts only to blindness." *Id.* Although these findings, along with the fact that BAVF's founders all had worked for BVA, *suggest* that BAVF's founders purposely sought to create confusion, the court did not expressly find so.

Moreover, even if BAVF's founders had intended to pass BAVF off as BVA, such an intent, although probative, would not conclusively establish unfair competition. [cit.] Ultimately, to succeed on its passing off claim, BVA must prove that the likely *effect* of BAVF's actions is to induce the public to think that BAVF is BVA. The evidence now in the record appears insufficient to establish this type of confusion. The district court noted that local CFC authorities had confused BAVF and BVA in processing their applications to be listed as beneficiary organizations in 1986, that BVA's name is often misstated by intending contributors even without the compounding presence of BAVF, and that college students in three experiments were unable to distinguish between the parties' names. To prevail in this action, however, it is not enough for BVA to show confusion that is the natural consequence of the two organizations' use of generic names. *See Liquid Controls*, 802 F.2d at 940 (proof falls short if it does not show confusion results or is likely to result "from anything other than the similarity of names"). What is essential, we underscore, is evidence that people associate "blinded veterans" with BVA per se[24] and that, because of specific actions by BAVF that increase the risk of confusion, people are likely to think BAVF is BVA.

Taking into account the opacity of some of the decisional law in this area, and the district court's understandable but incorrect assumption that trademark protection was available, we think it proper to permit the parties to submit additional evidence trained on the question whether people are likely to think that BAVF is actually BVA. [cit.] It would fill out and sharpen the record to prove (or disprove), for instance, that people who have contributed to BVA in the past have contributed, or are likely to contribute, to BAVF thinking it was BVA, or that people familiar with BVA's long service on behalf of blinded veterans are likely to think any group with a name containing "blinded veterans" or with the letters "B" "A" and "V" in its logo is the same as, or is associated with, BVA. BVA need not show actual confusion, we emphasize, but actual confusion is probative evidence that consumers are *likely* to confuse the two entities. [cit.]

If the district court, on remand, finds from the evidence that BAVF is passing itself off as BVA, the court may order that BAVF distinguish itself from BVA to avoid confusion. This case obviously differs from *Kellogg* and other cases cited above because it involves the name of an organization rather than the name of a particular product. This difference precludes such a ready remedy as attaching the manufacturer's name to the generic name of the product. The district court could, however, require BAVF to attach a prominent disclaimer to its name alerting the public that it is not the same organization as, and is not associated with, the Blinded Veterans Association. *See N. Hess' Sons, Inc. v. Hess Apparel, Inc.*, 738 F.2d 1412, 1413-14 (4th Cir. 1984) (approving injunction allowing defendant apparel shop to sell shoes provided it state prominently in all of its advertising for one year, and display a sign in its show area indefinitely, alerting customers that it was not affiliated with plaintiff shoe store); *Warner Bros. Pictures v. Majestic Pictures Corp.*, 70 F.2d 310, 312-13 (2d Cir. 1934) (requiring defendant to accompany title of motion picture, which included generic term "Gold Diggers," with producer's name and disclaimer stating that the picture was not based on the play or plaintiff's motion picture entitled "The Gold Diggers"); *Barton v. Rex-Oil Co.*, 2 F.2d 402, 406-07 (3d Cir. 1924) (allowing defendant to use term "Dye and Shine" in competition with plaintiff's "Dyanshine" provided defendant add affirmative, prominent disclaimer stating that his product was not that of plaintiff); [cit.]. Alternatively, the court could order that BAVF adopt another name containing the term "blinded veterans" that is less likely to confuse. Either remedy would assist BVA to retain, and reap the benefits of, the goodwill it has built up over the years, while allowing BAVF to appeal, fairly, to the public's general desire to aid blinded veterans. *Cf. King-Seeley Thermos*, 321 F.2d at 581 (noting that requiring producer's name to accompany generic name of product would strike proper balance between defendant's interest in using generic term and plaintiff's and public's interest in avoiding confusion).

CONCLUSION

"Blinded veterans" is a generic term; BVA's name and logo therefore are not entitled to trademark protection. . . . BVA may be entitled to protection against passing off, however. If the district court determines that people will likely think that BAVF *is* BVA, it can fashion equitable relief in accordance with the considerations set forth in this opinion.

---

24. Because we have ruled out the question of trademark protection, BVA is not called upon to show "secondary meaning" in that setting. BVA nevertheless must show, analogously, what has been called "de facto secondary meaning" — *i.e.*, that people associate the generic term "blinded veterans" with BVA. *See supra* note 22.

NOTES AND QUESTIONS

1.   *The prohibition against protection for generic terms.* For what reasons does trademark law withhold protection from generic terms? What were the consequences that the court feared from granting trademark rights to the plaintiff in *Mil-Mar Shoe*? How would the plaintiff in that case, its competitors and shoe consumers, have changed their behavior if the plaintiff had prevailed? Would these changes be socially harmful?

2.   *Statutory and other tests.* Section 14 of the Lanham Act, which lists the grounds upon which a registration may be canceled, *see infra* Chapter 5, provides in subsection (3):

> A registered mark shall not be deemed to be the generic name of goods or services solely because such mark is also used as a name of or to identify a unique product or service. The primary significance of the registered mark to the relevant public rather than purchaser motivation shall be the test for determining whether the registered mark has become the generic name of goods or services on or in connection with which it has been used.

This language was added to the Lanham Act by the Trademark Clarification Act of 1984, Pub. L. No. 98-620, §102, 98 Stat. 3335, after an aberrant decision of the Ninth Circuit in *Anti-Monopoly, Inc. v. General Mills Fun Group, Inc.*, 684 F.2d 1316 (9th Cir. 1982), emphasized consumer motivation in assessing whether the term MONOPOLY for a board game was generic. The Ninth Circuit had held the term to be generic because a survey revealed that most purchasers wanted the game MONOPOLY but did not care who made it. The statutory standard in Section 14(3) overrules the approach of the Ninth Circuit. *See also* 15 U.S.C. §1127 (definition of "abandoned").

The "primary significance" language is often traced to the decision of the United States Supreme Court in *Kellogg v. National Biscuit Co.*, 305 U.S. 111, 118 (1938), where the Court stated that to show secondary meaning the plaintiff must show "that the primary significance of the term in the minds of the consuming public is not the product but the producer." Although the Court strictly used the "primary significance" language in discussing the doctrine of secondary meaning, it is often cited in judicial analyses of whether a term is generic (perhaps because the *Kellogg* Court was proceeding on the premise that the term at issue—"shredded wheat"—was generic). Is the "primary significance" test sufficient to effectuate the policy concerns that underlie the genericism doctrine (and the distinctiveness inquiry in general)? Should it be relevant whether competitors could call their products by some other name? *See A.J. Canfield Co. v. Honickman*, 808 F.2d 291, 306 (3d Cir. 1986). For a discussion of *Kellogg*, *see* Graeme B. Dinwoodie, *The Story of* Kellogg v. National Biscuit Company*: Breakfast with Brandeis, in* INTELLECTUAL PROPERTY STORIES 220 (Dreyfuss & Ginsburg eds., 2005) (tracing the evolution of language from *Kellogg* to Section 14).

3.   *Identifying the relevant class of goods.* The PTO often frames the genericness analysis as a two-step inquiry: "First, what is the genus of goods or services at issue? Second, is the term sought to be registered or retained on the register understood by the relevant public primarily to refer to that genus of goods or services?" *H. Marvin Ginn Corp. v. Int'l Ass'n of Fire Chiefs, Inc.*, 782 F.2d 987, 989 (Fed.Cir.1986)*; Princeton Vanguard, LLC v. Frito-Lay North Am., Inc.*, 786 F.3d 960, 965 (Fed. Cir. 2015). The comments to the Restatement suggest that "a term that denominates a sub-category of a more general class, such as 'light' used with beer or 'diet' with cola, is also generic." Restatement (Third) of Unfair Competition §15, cmt. a (1995). How should a court go about identifying the relevant class (or subclass) of goods in which to analyze the term in question? As we will see in Chapter 5, the claim that a term is generic can be raised in the context of a trademark registration application. Might the process of identifying the relevant class of goods be conducted differently when the issue is before the PTO in the registration context than before a court in an infringement proceeding? (Consider what evidence would be available to inform the analysis in both of these contexts.) If the Coca-Cola Company, manufacturers of COKE ZERO soft drinks with fewer than five calories, applied to register COKE ZERO for "beverages, namely soft drinks," would you assess whether the term is generic for soft drinks by reference to "soft drinks" or "zero-calorie soft drinks"? Would it matter? *See Royal Crown Co., Inc. v. The Coca-Cola Co.*, __ F.3d ___ (Fed. Cir. June 20, 2018). In *Royal Crown*, the Federal Circuit vacated a TTAB ruling that COKE ZERO was not generic because the Board "failed to consider that 'a term can be generic for a genus of goods or services if the relevant public . . . understands the term to refer to a *key aspect* of that genus.'" *In re Cordua Rests., Inc.*, 823 F.3d 594, 603 (Fed. Cir. 2016) (emphasis added). The Court noted (again quoting *Cordua*) that: "the test is not only whether the relevant public would itself use the term to describe the genus, but also whether the relevant public would understand the term to be generic. Any term that the relevant public understands to refer to the genus . . . is generic"; and, that "a term is generic if the relevant public understands the term to refer to *part of the claimed genus of goods or services*, even if the public does not understand the term to refer to the broad genus as a whole." In the *Cordua* case, the Court of Appeals had suggested that "pizzeria" would be "generic for restaurant services, even though the public does not understand the term to refer to the broad class of restaurants as a whole; the public need only understand that the term refers to "a particular sub-group or type of restaurant rather than to all restaurants." *Cordua Rests., Inc.*, 823 F.3d at 605. With that guidance in mind, on remand to the Board would you find the term ZERO in the claimed mark COKE ZERO to be generic? *See Royal Crown*, at 13-14 ("[T]he Board must examine whether the term ZERO, when appended to a beverage mark, refers to a key aspect of the genus. ZERO need not be equated by the general public with the entire broad genus [applicant] claims in order for the term to be generic. The Board therefore must consider whether ZERO is generic because it refers to a key aspect of at least a sub-group or type of the claimed beverage goods. The Board must make this determination by considering the facts that the genus of goods for which [Coca-Cola] seeks registration of its marks clearly encompasses zero calorie beverages as a sub-group, and that [Coca-Cola] only proposed to use ZERO in combination with beverage marks that offer zero calorie versions thereof.")

4. *Defining the consumer universe.* What is the relevant consumer universe in determining the "primary significance" of the term alleged to be generic? *See, e.g., Ross-Whitney Corp. v. Smith Kline & French Laboratories*, 207 F.2d 190 (9th Cir. 1953) (assessing status of term used on a prescription drug by looking at the understanding of physicians rather than patients). If a term is generic in one market but not another, a court may craft an injunction permitting use by the defendants of the term in one market but not the other. *See Bayer Co. v. United Drug Co.*, 272 F. 505 (S.D.N.Y. 1921) (enjoining defendant's use of ASPIRIN in sales to physicians but finding the term generic with respect to consumers).

5. *New product markets.* How well does the "primary significance" test work when the "operative question is whether a new product name, even if it does tend to indicate the producer or source of the product, *must nonetheless* be considered a product genus or type, rather than merely a product brand"? *Genesee Brewing Company, Inc. v. Stroh Brewing Co.*, 124 F.3d 137, 144 (2d Cir. 1997). To deal with this problem, the Third Circuit has formulated a test, complementary to the primary significance test:

> If a producer introduces a product that differs from an established product class in a particular characteristic, and uses a common descriptive term of that characteristic as the name of the product, then the product should be considered its own genus. Whether the term that

identifies the product is generic then depends on the competitors' need to use it. At the least, if no commonly used alternative effectively communicates the same functional information, the term that denotes the product is generic. If we held otherwise, a grant of trademark status could effectively prevent a competitor from marketing a product with the same characteristic despite its right to do so under the patent laws.

A.J. Canfield Co. v. Honickman, 808 F.2d 291, 305-06 (3d Cir. 1986). In the *Genesee Brewing* case, the Second Circuit adopted the same test to determine that the term HONEY BROWN as applied to ales is generic. *See Genesee Brewing Co., Inc. v. Stroh Brewing Co.*, 124 F.3d 137 (2d Cir. 1997).

   6. *Misspellings, acronyms, and foreign terms.* How should courts treat efforts to obtain trademark rights in terms that are abbreviations, acronyms, or misspellings of generic words? *See Welding Servs. Inc. v. Forman*, 509 F.3d 1351 (11th Cir. 2007) (plaintiff seeking protection for WSI, an acronym for the generic term "Welding Services Inc." for welding services); *see generally* Mary LaFrance, *Initial Impressions: Trademark Protection for Abbreviations of Generic or Descriptive Terms*, 45 Akron L. Rev. 201 (2012). How should a U.S. court assess whether a foreign word is a generic term? To what extent should it matter whether the term is generic in the foreign country whose language has been used? *See Otokoyama Co. Ltd. v. Wine of Japan Import, Inc.*, 175 F.3d 266, 270-72 (2d Cir. 1999) (mark unprotected in Japan); *cf. In re Bayer AG*, 488 F.3d 960 (Fed. Cir. 2007) (assessing descriptiveness of term ASPIRINA protected as a registered mark for analgesics in a number of Spanish-speaking countries, but similar to term ASPIRIN, long held to be generic for the same goods in the United States). Would your answer change if the term declared generic in the foreign country was in English? The Austrian Supreme Court has held that the term WALKMAN for portable cassette players was generic. (Unfortunately for Sony, a German dictionary had defined the term "walkman" as a common noun for portable cassette players, and Sony had apparently not taken action to have such definition retracted.) Should the PTO cancel Sony's U.S. trademark registration for that mark?

   7. *Generic terms and domain names.* As discussed above in *In re Oppedahl & Larson, LLP*, *supra* page 66, the mere addition of a TLD to a generic or descriptive term will rarely ensure trademark status. In *Advertise.com, Inc. v. AOL Advertising, Inc.*, 616 F.3d 974 (9th Cir. 2010), the Ninth Circuit held that ADVERTISING.COM was generic for online advertising services. The putative trademark owner had argued that "refusing to protect such marks will result in 'parasite' marks such as 'addvertising.com' diverting business from marks like ADVERTISING.COM." The Ninth Circuit was unimpressed, noting that "this is the peril of attempting to build a brand around a generic term." Moreover, the court feared that affording rights in ADVERTISING.COM would potentially allow the mark owner to control all combinations of the generic term with any TLD (e.g., ".com"; ".biz"; ".org"). Do you think this is a legitimate fear? On what would your answer depend? How does the prefix "I" before a generic term affect distinctiveness? How would you classify IPHONE for mobile phones? What about PHONE. COM for a website selling mobile phones?

   8. *Proving genericness with surveys.* In assessing whether a term is generic, courts often consider consumer surveys. The Third Circuit has summarized prevailing practice in a dispute concerning the protectability of COCOA BUTTER FORMULA for beauty products:

   Plaintiffs seeking to establish the descriptiveness of a mark often use one of two types of survey evidence. J. Thomas McCarthy, McCarthy on Trademarks and Unfair Competition (4th ed. 2008) [hereinafter McCarthy on Trademarks] describes a "Teflon survey" as "essentially a mini-course in the generic versus trademark distinction, followed by a test." 2 McCarthy on Trademarks §12:16. That survey runs a participant through a number of terms (such as "washing machine" and "Chevrolet"), asking whether they are common names or brand names. After the participant grasps the distinction, the survey asks the participant to categorize a number of terms, including the term at issue. *Id.* (discussing survey created for *E.I. DuPont de Nemours & Co. v. Yoshida Int'l, Inc.*, 393 F. Supp. 502 (E.D.N.Y. 1975)).

A "Thermos survey," on the other hand, asks the respondent how he or she would ask for the product at issue. If, to use the term under dispute in the case from which the survey gets its name, the respondents largely say the brand name ("Thermos") rather than the initial product category name ("Vacuum Bottle"), the survey provides evidence that the brand name ("Thermos") has become a generic term for the product category. 2 McCarthy on Trademarks §12:15 (discussing survey used in *American Thermos Prods. Co. v. Aladdin Indus., Inc.*, 207 F. Supp. 9 (D. Conn. 1962)). To put this in the terms of the primary significance test, the term would be generic because the consumers would be using it to refer to the product category rather than a producer who makes products within that product category.

[Plaintiff] Browne conducted a survey in this case that generally adheres to the "Thermos survey" model. The survey posed a number of open-ended questions asking respondents to "identify or describe the product category" in which its products fall. It asked each of the 154 valid respondents "[w]hat *word* or *words* would you use to *identify* or *describe* a skin care product which contains cocoa butter?" and "[i]f you needed to identify or describe a skin care product containing cocoa butter, what word or words would you use *instead of* or *in addition to just* saying cocoa butter, if any?" Neither "Cocoa Butter Formula" nor any form of the word "Formula" appeared among the respondents' answers.

. . .

Browne's survey does have non-trivial flaws. . . . Only 30% of valid respondents used a noun identifying the product genus (*e.g.*, lotion, cream). The majority of respondents either answered with an adjective describing the product class (*e.g.*, healing, moisturizing) or did not answer. This suggests that the questions confused many respondents. The survey may have caused this confusion by deviating from the standard "Thermos survey" model by asking respondents for terms describing the products in addition to asking (as a "Thermos survey" should) for terms identifying the products. The survey likely would have been strongest if it had asked respondents, as the "Thermos survey" also did, how they would ask at a store for the type of product at issue.

These flaws nonetheless do not deprive the survey of probative value. . . . It is premature for us now to conclude that the survey does not provide probative evidence that "Cocoa Butter Formula" is not generic. Browne could have performed a better survey. Indeed, it might have rued the survey's design flaws after a trial. But the survey is strong enough to allow Browne to survive summary judgment on the genericness issue.

E.T. Browne Drug Co. v. Cococare Prods., Inc., 538 F.3d 185, 195-97 (3d Cir. 2008). Which of the two standard survey methods—*Teflon* or *Thermos*—appears best suited to measuring whether a term is generic? In *DuPont* itself, in response to an argument by the defendant that its TEFLON mark for non-stick resin on a number of kitchen and other products had become generic, the trademark owner submitted a survey along the lines described by the Third Circuit. The results were that 68% of the survey respondents identified TEFLON as a brand name and 31% as a common name; the TEFLON mark was thus valid. For point of reference, here are the fuller results:

Name	Brand (%)	Common Name (%)	Don't Know (%)
STP	90	5	5
THERMOS	51	46	3
MARGARINE	9	91	1
TEFLON	68	31	2
JELLO	75	25	1
REFRIGERATOR	6	94	0
ASPIRIN	13	86	0
COKE	76	24	0

See E. I. DuPont de Nemours & Co. v. Yoshida Int'l, Inc., 393 F. Supp. 502, 528 n.54 (E.D.N.Y. 1975).

In contrast, in *American Thermos Products*, survey participants were asked what they would ask for in a store of they were looking for a "container that is used to keep liquids, like soup, coffee, tea and lemonade, hot or cold for a period of time". 75% of over 3,500 persons interviewed said "Thermos,", while 11% said "Vacuum Bottle". (Only about 12% thought that "Thermos" had some trademark significance). The court found the term generic.

In the *DuPont* case, the defendant submitted a survey to support its claim that TEFLON had become generic. This survey, which was based on the *Thermos* model, "was conducted among adult women, 90.6% of whom expressed awareness of 'kitchen pots and pans that have their inside surfaces coated by chemical substances to keep grease or food from sticking to them.' Of the aware respondents, 86.1% apparently mentioned only 'TEFLON' or 'TEFLON II' as their sole answer when asked, 'What is the name . . . or names of these pots and pans . . . ?' Further, 71.7% of the aware women gave only 'TEFLON' or 'TEFLON II' as the name they would use to describe the pots and pans to a store clerk or friend." *E. I. DuPont de Nemours & Co.*, 393 F. Supp. at 525. Does this affect your answer? Should TEFLON have been found generic? Or does this simply inform your assessment of the better test? For a thorough analysis of both "Thermos" and "Teflon" surveys, *see* E. Deborah Jay, *Genericness Surveys in Trademark Disputes: Evolution of Species*, 99 TRADEMARK REP. 1118 (2009). If a term is generic *ab initio*, no amount of survey evidence of distinctiveness will overcome that finding. *See Schwan's IP, LLC v. Kraft Pizza Co.*, 460 F.3d 971 (8th Cir. 2006). Is this too rigid a rule?

      9. *Proving genericness with circumstantial evidence.* Which of the following uses of a mark would be most persuasive evidence of whether a claimed mark was generic: use by the claimed mark owner in a patent application, uses by competitors in advertising material, uses by journalists writing for the general media, uses by writers in trade publications, uses by purchasers in corresponding with the claimed mark owner, and use as a defined term in a contract negotiated by the claimed mark owner and a bulk institutional purchaser. *See Colt Defense LLC v. Bushmaster Firearms, Inc.*, 486 F.3d 701, 706-07 (1st Cir. 2007). Would evidence of sales and advertising expenditure be relevant? *See Royal Crown Co., Inc. v. The Coca-Cola Co.*, __ F.3d ___ (Fed. Cir. June 20, 2018). In *Boston Duck Tours, LP v. Super Duck Tours, LLC*, 531 F.3d 1 (1st Cir. 2008), the plaintiff had for many years operated touring services in Boston under the mark BOSTON DUCK TOURS and had obtained a federal trademark registration for the composite phrase BOSTON DUCK TOURS (with the terms "duck" and "tours" disclaimed). The plaintiff offered its tours using renovated amphibious vehicles that had been first used by the army in World War II. These vehicles were called "DUKWS," which is commonly pronounced as "ducks." The defendant was a rival operator who began to offer similar services in Boston using amphibious vehicles that were larger and more modern than the original DUKW vehicles. The defendant adopted the mark SUPER DUCK TOURS for its tours and the plaintiff sued for trademark infringement. The defendant conceded that the composite phrase BOSTON DUCK TOURS was entitled to trademark protection, but argued that the phrase "duck tours" was generic. (In fact, thirty-six different companies offered tours in different cities of the United States using amphibious vehicles. Thirty-two of them used the word "duck" in their trade names, and ten used both "duck" and "tour.") The district court had rejected the defendant's argument and enjoined it from *inter alia* using the phrase "duck tours" as a trademark in association with its sightseeing tour service in the Boston area. The court held that the phrase common to both marks—"DUCK TOURS"—was not generic because the dictionary definition of "duck" did not include any reference to an amphibious boat. The defendant appealed. If you were counsel for the defendant, how would you deal with evidence of actual confusion among consumers regarding the two rival operators? If you were counsel for plaintiff, how would you use this evidence? How would you decide the appeal? *See* 531 F.3d 1. Even if the phrase "duck tours" is generic, how should that inform a court's analysis given the defendant's concession that the composite phrase "BOSTON DUCK TOURS" was entitled to trademark protection? Why should the court even consider the protectability of "DUCK TOURS"? *Cf. E.T. Browne Drug Co. v. Cococare Prods., Inc.*, 538 F.3d 185 (3d Cir. 2008). We will return to this question in Chapter 7, a fact that may offer some hints regarding where this consideration might affect a court's analysis.

   10. De jure *genericism.* The *Kellogg* opinion, discussed at length in the *Blinded Veterans* opinion and excerpted in Chapter 3, offers more than one rationale for why the term "SHREDDED WHEAT" should be treated as generic. Justice Brandeis suggests in some parts of the majority opinion that the term had come to identify a product type. But elsewhere in the opinion, he suggests that the term could be used freely by competitors (subject to obligations under unfair competition law) because under patent law those competitors had the right to copy the shape of the shredded wheat biscuit upon expiration of the plaintiff's patent, and thus had the concomitant right to use the term by which biscuits of that shape had come to be known. Might there be other contexts in which trademarks should be deemed generic *de jure* in order to buttress the defendant's rights under other intellectual property regimes? *See In re Pennington Seed, Inc.*, 466 F.3d 1053 (Fed. Cir. 2006) (plant varietal names held generic); *cf. In re Bayer AG*, 488 F.3d 960 (Fed. Cir. 2007) (Newman, J., dissenting) (noting that the PTO Solicitor argued that ASPIRINA for analgesics should be generic because ASPIRIN is generic for analgesics). What justifications exist for elevating the goals of those regimes over the confusion-avoidance goals of trademark law (assuming distinctiveness in fact can be demonstrated)?

   In December 2011, the French legislature adopted a provision precluding pharmaceutical producers from enjoining the unauthorized use of their marks by legitimate producers of generic pharmaceutical products after expiry of the pharmaceutical patent. This provision is not unlike one that was considered (but eventually dropped) in debates leading to the passage of the Lanham Act, effectively deeming certain marks to be generic as a matter of law. *See* Graeme B. Dinwoodie, *The Story of* Kellogg v. National Biscuit Company*: Breakfast with Brandeis, in* Intellectual Property Stories 220, 241-42 (Dreyfuss & Ginsburg eds., 2005).

   11. *Relief under Section 43(a).* What are the values that courts are seeking to effectuate (and to balance) when they grant relief to plaintiffs under the principles of unfair competition in Section 43(a) despite their determination that trademark protection is not available because the term used by the plaintiff is generic? *See King-Seeley Thermos Co. v. Aladdin Indus., Inc.*, 321 F.2d 577, 581 (2d Cir. 1963). Should this protection against unfair competition be available to all terms declared generic, or only to those that once had trademark significance? *See* Jerre B. Swann, *Genericism Rationalized*, 89 Trademark Rep. 639 (1999). Is there an appropriate distinction to be drawn between the different marks for which the courts have denied trademark but granted unfair competition protection? Are the *Murphy Door Bed* and *Blinded Veterans* opinions consistent on whether to treat generic terms differently depending on how those terms became generic?

   12. *Examples of generic terms.* As noted earlier in this Chapter, developing a feel for where a mark might be placed on the distinctiveness spectrum can be assisted to some extent by reviewing prior determinations. Subject to the caution noted there, we have set out below a few illustration of marks that were challenged as generic and noted the outcome. (If you want the cites for the different examples, review the sections of the TMEP and McCarthy cited earlier; the McCarthy treatise contains a much longer list of illustrations, and is worth perusing.)

Marks Found Not Generic	Marks Found to be Generic
BEER NUTS for flavored nuts	CUSH-N-GRIP for tool handles
BETTER BUSINESS BUREAU for business ethics organizations	DISCOUNT MUFFLERS for repair and replacement of auto mufflers
APPLE RAISIN CRISP for breakfast cereal	FOOTLONG for 12 inch long sandwich
PERKS for volume discount buying services	GOLD CARD for premium level credit card services
TRIM for manicuring implements	PRECISION CUTS for haircut services
INSTANT MESSENGER for real-time Internet communications	WELDING SERVICES for servicing welding equipment
SEATS for ticket reservation services	SOFTCHEWS for chewable medical tablets
HEROES for charitable services assisting surviving family of police and firefighters killed on duty	SCREENWIPE for anti-static cloth for cleaning computer and television screens

PROBLEM 2-1:   THE WINDOWS PRODUCT

WINDOWS is a registered trademark of the Microsoft Corporation. In the course of an infringement suit that Microsoft filed against the manufacturer of Lindows software (which enables programs written for Microsoft's WINDOWS operating system to run on the Linux operating system) seeking an injunction shutting down the Lindows.com website, a federal district court judge suggested that there were serious questions about the validity of the mark WINDOWS. The judge noted that there was widespread use of windows-related terms to describe graphical user interfaces as far back as the early 1980s (and even before Microsoft launched its own WINDOWS software in 1985). Is WINDOWS generic? What evidence would you need to answer that question? At what point in time should the "generic" status of WINDOWS be assessed? (This might affect whether one could call WINDOWS an example of a term that was "once a trademark; now generic"; is it instead a term "then generic, so never a trademark"?) For what products is the mark arguably generic? Microsoft argued that distinctiveness should be answered with respect to operating system software, rather than software products in general. Is Microsoft correct? For what purposes might Microsoft prefer a narrower product market, and for which purposes might it wish the judge to focus on a broader product market? If WINDOWS is generic, is Microsoft without a remedy? If WINDOWS is not generic, does the rival manufacturer have to stop using the term LINDOWS?

PROBLEM 2-2:   PREVENTING GENERICIDE

Trademark owners spend significant resources on ensuring that their employees, consumers, and the public use their trademark in ways that minimize the risk of "genericide" (i.e., their marks becoming generic). What kind of steps might a company take to prevent this problem? Google Technologies Inc. offers web searching services at www.google.com through its GOOGLE search engine. Word Spy, an online dictionary that compiles and defines new words occurring in contemporary media, contains the following entry:

> google. (GOO.gul) v. To search for information on the Web, particularly by using the Google search engine; to search the Web for information related to a new or potential girlfriend or boyfriend. —Googling pp.

Example Citation:

Still a rare practice among the online masses, **Googling** the one you (might) love is fairly common among the young, professional and Internet-savvy. "Everyone does it," said Jena Fischer, 26, a Chicago advertising executive. "And if [they say] they're not doing it, they're lying."—Nara Schoenberg, "Don't Go Into Date Blind; Singles Googling Before Canoodling," *Chicago Tribune*, April 2, 2001.

Backgrounder: Here's a citation illustrating the more general sense of the verb:

Dave Eggers, the 29-year-old author of "A Heartbreaking Work of Staggering Genius" and editor of the quarterly journal McSweeney's, will chat with folks at a private Denver residence on Tuesday. . . . Eggers is owner of probably the most Googled name out there right now.

— "Novelist Dave Eggers to speak in Denver," *The Denver Post*, September 10, 2000.

Lawyers for Google Technologies Inc. asked Word Spy to add the following text to its entry: "Note that Google™ is a trademark identifying the search technology and services of Google Technologies Inc." Is this sufficient? Would you seek other changes? *See* Google Rules for Proper Usage, www.google.com/permissions/trademark/rules.htm; *see also Elliott v. Google, Inc.*, 860 F.3d 1151 (9th Cir. 2017); Heather Schwedel, *Let's Uber. I'll Call a Lyft: Why conscientious consumers no longer want to use Uber, except as a verb*, Slate Dec. 14, 2017 (noting the use of UBER to mean ride-hailing apps). Is Word Spy the type of entity upon whose usages the company should focus? In assessing whether a mark has become generic, should a court give weight to a company's good faith efforts to avoid genericide? Trademark owners frequently make efforts to educate the public to make proper uses of their marks, such as the advertisement below run by Xerox.

For another example of a mark owner's attempt to preempt genericness, *see* Don't Say Velcro®, *https://www.youtube.com/watch?v=rRi8LptvFZY*; We ® Still VELCRO Brand, *www.velcro.com/about-us/dontsayvelcro*. Trigger warning: These are a mock music videos involving actual trademark lawyers singing and dancing (sort of). We know—you're roll-ing your eyes, while also secretly wishing that you were in them. If a competitor (or some other third party) behaves in ways that cause a mark to become generic, should the trade-mark holder possess a cause of action against that person? Why (or why not)? *Cf. Ty Inc. v. Perryman*, 306 F.3d 509 (7th Cir. 2002) (analyzing the assertion that third-party usage that threatens to cause a mark to become generic should be recognized as a form of dilution under Section 43(c). *See* Chapter 8).

PROBLEM 2-3:   WORD MARK DISTINCTIVENESS

Apply the *Abercrombie* distinctiveness spectrum to assess the distinctiveness of the fol-lowing word marks. Consider four questions:

(1)   What is your own reaction, as an "ordinary consumer," to the distinctiveness of the mark? Is it distinctive, and why?

(2)   What are the best arguments in favor of inherent or acquired distinctiveness? What additional information would you seek in order to bolster your case?

(3)   What are the best arguments against inherent or acquired distinctiveness? What additional information would you seek in order to bolster your case?

(4)   Can the reason(s) why you reached your conclusion on the distinctiveness of the mark be used to formulate a rule of thumb or doctrinal rule with respect to the type of mark in question (and what would that "type" be)? Trademark law contains many such rules or doctrines. *See* TMEP, § 1209.03.

  (1)   **CITIBANK** for banking services

  (2)   **SPEX** for optician's services; **JOY OF SPEX** for optician's services; **JOY OF SPEX IS THE JOY OF SIGHT** for optician's services

  (3)   **AMERICA'S BEST CHEW** for chewing tobacco

  (4)   **RED HOT BLUES** for spicy blue corn tortilla chips

  (5)   **HEY. BEER. MAN.** for beer products and related promotional goods

  (6)   **TWO ALL BEEF PATTIES SPECIAL SAUCE LETTUCE CHEESE PICKLES ONIONS ON A SESAME SEED BUN** for fast-food restaurant services

  (7)   **DRIVE SAFELY** for Volvo automobiles

  (8)   **ERGONOMIC** for ceiling fans

  (9)   **THE LONE RANGER** for a motion picture

(10)   **YO QUIERO TACO BELL!** for "Mexican" fast-food services

(11)   **PARTY AT A DISCOUNT!** for private party sevices

(12)   **BEAR** for cold-weather outerwear

(13)   **FDNY** for promotional items, such as clothing

(14)   **7-11** for retail convenience stores

(15)   **9-11** for T-shirts

(16)   **NRG** for coffee for use in single-service brewing machines

(17)   **"YOU'RE FIRED"** for entertainment services, filed on behalf of Donald Trump

(18)   **BRICK OVEN** for pizza

(19)   **#TACOTUESDAY** for restaurant services. (As you proceed through Part II of the casebook, you might consider what other doctrines of trademark law might present obstacles to the registration of hashtags as marks. *See* Alexandra Roberts, *Trademark Failure to Function*, 104 Iowa L. Rev. __ (2018) (forth-coming). How are such marks used differently than conventional marks? *See generally* Alexandra J. Roberts, *Tagmarks*, 105 Cal. L. Rev. (2017).)

As Problem 2-3 notes, many of the rationales that likely supported your assessment of the distinctiveness of the marks listed there are reflected in trademark doctrine. There are, however, dangers associated with detaching doctrine too quickly from the premises that generated the doctrine, as Judge Posner stresses in the following opinion. When are doctrinal rules most valuable, and when should we be willing to "limit them by their rationale"?

PEACEABLE PLANET, INC. v. TY, INC.

362 F.3d 986 (7th Cir. 2004)

Posner, Circuit Judge:

[Peaceable Planet and Ty both make plush toys in the shape of animals, filled with bean-like materials. In 1999, Peaceable Planet began selling a camel that it named "Niles." The name was chosen to evoke Egypt, which is largely desert. Peaceable Planet sold only a few thousand of its camels. In 2000, Ty (who makes Beanie Babies) began selling a camel also named "Niles." It sold a huge number of its "Niles" camels, precipitating a lawsuit.]

The district court ruled that "Niles," being a personal name, is a descriptive mark that the law does not protect unless and until it has acquired secondary meaning, that is, until there is proof that consumers associate the name with the plaintiff's brand. Peaceable Planet did not prove that consumers associate the name "Niles" with its camel.

The general principle that formed the starting point for the district court's analysis was unquestionably sound. A descriptive mark is not legally protected unless it has acquired secondary meaning. 15 U.S.C. §§1052(e), (f); [cit.]. . . . Had Peaceable Planet named its camel "Camel," that would be a descriptive mark in a relevant sense, because it would make it very difficult for Ty to market its own camel—it wouldn't be satisfactory to have to call it "Dromedary" or "Bactrian."

Although cases and treatises commonly describe personal names as a subset of descriptive marks, [cit.] it is apparent that the rationale for denying trademark protection to personal names without proof of secondary meaning can't be the same as the rationale just sketched for marks that are "descriptive" in the normal sense of the word. Names, as distinct from nicknames like "Red" or "Shorty," are rarely descriptive. "Niles" may evoke but it certainly does not describe a camel, any more than "Pluto" describes a dog, "Bambi" a fawn, "Garfield" a cat, or "Charlotte" a spider. (In the Tom and Jerry comics, "Tom," the name of the cat, could be thought descriptive, but "Jerry," the name of the mouse, could not be.) So anyone who wanted to market a toy camel, dog, fawn, cat, or spider would not be impeded in doing so by having to choose another name.

The reluctance to allow personal names to be used as trademarks reflects valid concerns (three such concerns, to be precise), but they are distinct from the concern that powers the rule that descriptive marks are not protected until they acquire secondary meaning. One of the concerns is a reluctance to forbid a person to use his own name in his own business. [cit.] Supposing a man named Brooks opened a clothing store under his name, should this prevent a second Brooks from opening a clothing store under his own (identical) name even though consumers did not yet associate the name with the first Brooks's store? It should not. [cit.]

Another and closely related concern behind the personal-name rule is that some names are so common—such as "Smith," "Jones," "Schwartz," "Wood," and "Jackson"—that consumers will not assume that two products having the same name therefore have the same source, and so they will not be confused by their bearing the same name. [cit.] If there are two bars in a city that are named "Steve's," people will not infer that they are owned by the same Steve.

The third concern, which is again related but brings us closest to the rule regarding descriptive marks, is that preventing a person from using his name to denote his business may deprive consumers of useful information. Maybe "Steve" is a well-known neighbor-hood figure. If he can't call his bar "Steve's" because there is an existing bar of that name, he is prevented from communicating useful information to the consuming public. [cit.]

The scope of a rule is often and here limited by its rationale. Or, to make the same point differently, one way of going astray in legal analysis is to focus on the semantics of a rule rather than its purpose. Case 1 might say that a personal name could not be trade-marked in the circumstances of that case without proof of secondary meaning. Case 2 might say that personal names cannot be trademarked without proof of secondary meaning but might leave off the qualifications implicit in the circumstances of the case. And then in Case 3 the court might just ask, is the trademark at issue a personal name? As we observed in *AM Int'l, Inc. v. Graphic Management Associates, Inc.*, 44 F.3d 572, 575 (7th Cir. 1995), "rules of law are rarely as clean and strict as statements of them make them seem. So varied and unpredictable are the circumstances in which they are applied that more often than not the summary statement of a rule—the terse formula that judges employ as a necessary shorthand to prevent judicial opinions from turning into treatises—is better regarded as a generalization than as the premise of a syllogism." The "rule" that personal names are not protected as trademarks until they acquire secondary meaning is a generalization, and its application is to be guided by the purposes that we have extracted from the case law. When none of the purposes that animate the "personal name" rule is present, and application of the "rule" would impede rather than promote competition and consumer welfare, an exception should be recognized. And will be; for we find cases holding, very sensibly—and with inescapable implications for the present case—that the "rule" does not apply if the public is unlikely to understand the personal name as a personal name. [cit.]

The personal-name "rule," it is worth noting, is a common law rather than statu-tory doctrine. All that the Lanham Act says about personal names is that a mark that is "primarily merely a surname" is not registrable in the absence of secondary meaning. 15 U.S.C. §§1052(e)(4), (f). There is no reference to first names. The reason for the surname provision is illustrated by the Brooks example. The extension of the rule to first names is a judicial innovation and so needn't be pressed further than its rationale, as might have to be done if the rule were codified in inflexible statutory language. Notice too the limitation implicit in the statutory term "primarily."

In thinking about the applicability of the rationale of the personal-name rule to the pres-ent case, we should notice first of all that camels, whether real or toy, do not go into business. Peaceable Planet's appropriation of the name "Niles" for its camel is not preventing some hap-less camel in the Sahara Desert who happens to be named "Niles" from going into the water-carrier business under its own name. The second thing to notice is that "Niles" is not a very common name; in fact it is downright rare. And the third thing to notice is that if it were a common name, still there would be no danger that precluding our hypothetical Saharan water carrier from using its birth name "Niles" would deprive that camel's customers of valuable information. In short, the rationale of the personal-name rule is wholly inapplicable to this case.

What is more, if one wants to tie the rule in some fashion to the principle that descrip-tive marks are not protectable without proof of second meaning, then one must note that "Niles," at least when affixed to a toy camel, is a suggestive mark, like "Microsoft" or "Business Week," or—coming closer to this case—like "Eeyore" used as the name of a donkey, . . . rather than being a descriptive mark. Suggestive marks are protected by trade-mark law without proof of secondary meaning. [cit.] Secondary meaning is not required because there are plenty of alternatives to any given suggestive mark. There are many more ways of suggesting than of describing. Suggestive names for camels include "Lawrence [of Arabia]" (one of Ty's other Beanie Babies *is* a camel named "Lawrence"), "Desert Taxi," "Sopwith" (the Sopwith Camel was Snoopy's World War I fighter plane), "Camelia," "Traveling Oasis," "Kamelsutra," "Cameleon," and "Humpy-Dumpy."

If "Niles" cannot be a protected trademark, it must be because to give it legal protection would run afoul of one of the purposes of the common law rule that we have identified rather than because it is a descriptive term, which it is not. But we have seen that it does not run afoul of any of those purposes. . . .

Treating the personal-name rule as a prohibition against ever using a personal name as a trademark (in the absence of secondary meaning) would lead to absurd results, which is a good reason for hesitating to press a rule to its logical limit, its semantic outer bounds. . . .

Ty argues . . . that "one competitor should not be allowed to impoverish the language of commerce by monopolizing descriptive names," and "there are a limited number of personal names that are recognized as such by the public." All true. But the suggestion that "Niles" belongs to the limited class of "recognized" names or that "Niles" is the only way to name a camel is ridiculous.

. . .

There is a town named "Niles" in Illinois and another one in Michigan, and this is a reminder of the importance of context in characterizing a trademark. "Apple" is a generic term when used to denote the fruit, but a fanciful mark (the kind that receives the greatest legal protection) when used to denote a computer. If a gas station in Niles, Michigan, calls itself the "Niles Gas Station," it cannot before the name acquires secondary meaning enjoin another firm from opening the "Niles Lumber Yard" in the town, on the ground that people will think that the firms are under common ownership. 15 U.S.C. §§1052(e)(2), (f); [cit.]. In a town named Niles, firms bearing the name are sharing a name that is too common to be appropriable without proof of secondary meaning. That is not the case when the name is applied to a camel. And while both Niles, Illinois, and Niles, Michigan, are fine towns, neither is the place of origin of the camel or identified with that animal in some other way.

We conclude that Peaceable Planet has a valid trademark in the name "Niles" as applied to its camel, and so the case must be returned to the district court [for decision in accordance with this opinion].

D.   DISTINCTIVENESS OF NONVERBAL IDENTIFIERS: LOGOS, PACKAGES, PRODUCT DESIGN, AND COLORS

1.   Different Tests, Different Standards?

Words can indicate source. Indeed, words remain the most common form of trademarks. But what of graphic symbols, or other nonverbal indicia? If we accept the possibility that nonverbal indicia might indicate source, we must then determine how to apply the distinctiveness regime to such indicia. The cases in this section reveal that the task has been a difficult one.

Consider the following Swoosh logo used to identify footwear sold by Nike.

To what extent do logos identify the source of products and thus act as trademarks? Or are they mere decorative touches? Does the fact that they are decorative affect their ability to act as trademarks? Is the number 22 emblazoned on a sweatshirt distinctive? *See J.M. Hollister, LLC v. American Eagle Outfitters*, No. 203CV703, 2005 WL 1076246 (S.D. Ohio May 5, 2005); *cf.* TMEP §1202.03 ("Subject matter that is merely a decorative feature does not identify and distinguish the applicant's goods and, thus, does not function as a trademark. A decorative feature may include words, designs, slogans or other trade dress. . . . Matter that serves primarily as a source-indicator, either inherently or as a result of acquired distinctiveness, and that is only incidentally ornamental or decorative, can be registered as a trademark."). What about a "smiley face"? *See id.* at §1202.03(a). If logos do potentially indicate source, how should one adjudicate whether they are distinctive? In particular, how should one adjudicate whether they are *inherently* distinctive? In what ways are words different from graphic identifiers such that the tests used for determining distinctiveness should be different for each? Are there other reasons why the distinctiveness of logo marks should be assessed differently from word marks?

In fact, it is clear that logos do serve as trademarks. The NIKE Swoosh mark is an extremely valuable mark. But determining the distinctiveness of less recognizable marks (especially as a matter of inherent distinctiveness) is not easy. Before we discuss the tests that courts have developed to assist in that determination, what is it about the NIKE Swoosh that makes you regard it as a source-identifier (if you do)? If Nike had used a blue square to mark products, would that be distinctive of NIKE products? What is different with the Swoosh?

Some courts sought to apply the *Abercrombie* spectrum discussed earlier in this chapter to determine the distinctiveness of logos and other nonverbal marks (such as the overall packaging of products). Does the *Abercrombie* test help you determine the distinctiveness of the NIKE Swoosh? Recall the purposes underlying the distinctiveness determination. Does the test help you to implement the purposes underlying the requirement of distinctiveness?

In *Seabrook Foods, Inc. v. Bar-Well Foods, Ltd.*, 568 F.2d 1342 (C.C.P.A. 1977), the Court of Customs and Patent Appeals was faced with the question whether the logo appearing on the packaging for frozen foods was distinctive. The packaging and logo are reproduced here.

The court fashioned a test for the inherent distinctiveness of logos that differed from *Abercrombie*, and which is still used by many courts and the PTO in helping to assess the distinctiveness of logos:

> In determining whether a design is arbitrary or distinctive this court has looked to whether it was a "common" basic shape or design, whether it was unique or unusual in a particular field, whether it was a mere refinement of a commonly adopted and well-known form of ornamentation for the goods, or whether it was capable of creating a commercial impression distinct from the accompanying words.

Id. at 1344. Do you think that this test is likely to be effective for determining the distinctiveness of the logo in question? What about the packaging as a whole? Do you think that the test could readily be adapted for determining the distinctiveness of other categories of nonverbal source indicators?

STAR INDUS., INC. v. BACARDI & CO. LTD.

412 F.3d 373 (2d Cir. 2005)

POOLER, Circuit Judge:

BACKGROUND

Plaintiff-appellant Star Industries, Inc. ("Star") produces alcoholic beverages including, of particular relevance to this appeal, the "Georgi" brand of vodkas. . . . Defendants-appellees Bacardi & Co. Ltd. and Bacardi U.S.A. (collectively "Bacardi") produce, import, and distribute "Bacardi" brand rums. . . .

In June 1996, inspired by the success of flavored vodkas introduced by leading international companies such as Stolichnaya, Star's president decided to develop an orange-flavored Georgi vodka. A new label [reproduced above] was designed, consisting of the traditional Georgi label, which contains a coat of arms and a logo consisting of stylized capital letters spelling "Georgi" on a white background, together with three new elements: an orange slice, the words "orange flavored," and a large elliptical letter "O" appearing below the "Georgi" logo and surrounding all of the other elements. The "O" was rendered as a vertical oval, with the outline of the "O" slightly wider along the sides (about one quarter inch thick) and narrowing at the top and bottom (about one eighth inch thick); the outline of the "O" is colored orange and decorated with two thin gold lines, one bordering the inside and one bordering the outside of the outline. Star was apparently the first company to distribute an orange-flavored alcoholic beverage packaged in a bottle bearing a large elliptical orange letter "O."

Star's hope was that, just as consumers of orange-flavored Stolichnaya vodka had begun referring to the vodka as "Stoli O," consumers would come to refer to orange-flavored Georgi vodka as "Georgi O." Accordingly, Star applied in 1996 to register "Georgi O" as a word trademark with the U.S. Patent and Trademark Office ("PTO"). Reasoning that consumers viewing the Georgi O label were likely to perceive the word "Georgi" as separate from the "O" design, and not as constituting a composite phrase, the PTO rejected Star's application. Between 1996 and 2002 Star promoted its new orange-flavored vodka, although it is unclear how vigorously, and it apparently had little success. Sales volume remained low. . . . No evidence in the record suggests that Georgi vodka has ever been commonly referred to by consumers as "Georgi O."

In 2000 Bacardi began to develop an orange-flavored rum, which it ultimately introduced nationally in 2001 under the name "Bacardi O." Bacardi's line of flavored rums originated in 1995 with "Bacardi Limon." Unlike Bacardi's other flavored rums, however, Bacardi O was produced and marketed bearing a distinct label consisting of the Bacardi logo and bat symbol above a large elliptical letter "O" against a clear background. . . . Like the Georgi "O," the Bacardi "O" was decorated with gold bordering, was colored in orange, and spanned most of the height of the bottle. Its appearance differed in certain respects from the Georgi "O" design, including lesser elongation, greater thickness, variable shading, and the use of a brighter variety of orange. . . .

After sending a cease and desist letter to Bacardi in September 2001, Star filed the instant lawsuit in May 2002. . . . In June 2003 Star applied with the PTO to register its "O" design.[1] [After a bench trial, the district court rejected Star's claims, holding Star's "O" design not protectable as a trademark, and holding in the alternative that, assuming the Georgi "O" design was a protectable trademark, such trademark was not infringed because Star's product was not likely to be confused with Bacardi's despite the similar "O" designs. On February 6, 2004, the PTO approved Star's application to register its "O" design.]

We conclude that the district court erred in holding Star's "O" design not protectable as a trademark. . . . However, as we agree with the district court that Star has not established a likelihood of confusion with Bacardi's product, we affirm the district court's judgment for appellees.

DISCUSSION

. . .

On appeal, Star does not purport to rely on a "secondary meaning" acquired by its "O" design, relying instead on inherent distinctiveness. "Common basic shapes" or letters are, as a matter of law, not inherently distinctive. *See Seabrook Foods, Inc. v. Bar-Well Foods, Inc.*, 568 F.2d 1342, 1344 (C.C.P.A. 1977) (implying that "'common' basic shape or design" is not inherently distinctive); [cit.]. However, stylized shapes or letters may qualify, provided the design is not commonplace but rather unique or unusual in the relevant market. [cit.] The guiding principle in distinguishing protectable from unprotectable marks is that no one enterprise may be allowed to attain a monopoly on designs that its competitors must be able to use in order to effectively communicate information regarding their products to consumers. *See* Restatement (Third) of Unfair Competition §13 cmts. b & d; [cit.]. Trademark protection of a sufficiently stylized version of a common shape or letter will not hamper effective

---

1. Unlike its 1996 PTO application which sought to register the word "Georgi O" as a trademark, Star now sought to register its stylized "O" design separately from the word "Georgi."

competition because competitors remain free to use nonstylized forms or their own alternative stylizations of the same shape or letter to communicate information about their products.

A design used in conjunction with other marks is separately protectable in its own right if it creates a separate and distinct impression from the impression created by the other marks. This will be true if either the mark is itself inherently distinctive, *see, e.g.*, *In re Servotronics, Inc.*, 156 U.S.P.Q. 592, 592 (T.T.A.B. 1968) (holding stylized letter "S" separately protectable from word in which it appeared); *In re W.B. Roddenbery Co.*, 135 U.S.P.Q. 215, 216 (T.T.A.B. 1962) (holding combination of gold circle and colored rectangle, utilized as background to applicant's advertisement for sour pickles, registrable separately from foreground elements), or if the consuming public has come to associate the separate mark in itself with the particular product, vesting it with its own distinct secondary meaning, *see* Restatement (Third) of Unfair Competition §13 cmt. d.

The district court held Star's "O" design not protectable on two grounds. First, the court held that the mark was not protectable separately from the other material appearing on the Georgi O label on the ground that there was a lack of evidence that it produced a separate impression among consumers. Second, the court held that the mark was not protectable because it was not inherently distinctive and Star had not demonstrated secondary meaning. A district court's findings that a mark is not protectable as inherently distinctive is a finding of fact that we generally review for clear error. [cit.] However, where the district court "base[d] its findings upon a mistaken impression of applicable legal principles," we are "not bound by the clearly erroneous standard." [cit.]

The district court erred when it described the Star "O" as a basic geometric shape or letter, and therefore rejected inherent distinctiveness and required a showing of secondary meaning. The Star "O" is not a "common basic shape" or letter, and the district court's holding to the contrary was premised on a misunderstanding of this trademark law concept. Unshaded linear representations of common shapes or letters are referred to as "basic." They are not protectable as inherently distinctive, because to protect them as trademarks would be to deprive competitors of fundamental communicative devices essential to the dissemination of information to consumers. However, stylized letters or shapes are not "basic," and are protectable when original within the relevant market. *See* [*Courtenay Communications Corp. v. Hall*, 334 F.3d 210, 215 n.3 (2d Cir. 2003)] (distinguishing case of mark consisting of word displayed with distinctive "typeface, color, and other design elements," which was protectable, from cases holding generic words not protectable). . . . Star's "O" is sufficiently stylized to be inherently distinctive and therefore protectable as a trademark. It is stylized with respect to shading, border, and thickness, and each of these design elements distinguishes it from the simple or basic shapes and letters that have been held unprotectable.

The Star "O" design had sufficient shape and color stylization to render it slightly more than a simply linear representation of an ellipse or the letter "O." It was, furthermore, a unique design in the alcoholic beverage industry at the time it was introduced. This suffices to establish its inherent distinctiveness and thus its protectability. Furthermore, the Star "O" design is protectable separately from the other design elements on the Georgi orange-flavored vodka label precisely because the "O" design is itself inherently distinctive. *See In re E.J. Brach & Sons*, 256 F.2d 325, 327 (C.C.P.A. 1958); *W.B. Roddenbery*, 135 U.S.P.Q. at 216. However, the extent of stylization was marginal at best. The outline of the "O," though not uniform, is ordinary in its slightly varying width, and the interior and exterior borders are also ordinary. The result is a "thin" or weak mark, which will be entitled to only limited protection. *See Libman Co. v. Vining Indus.*, 69 F.3d 1360, 1363 (7th Cir. 1995).

[The court then proceeded to consider whether the defendant's activities caused a likelihood of confusion, and found that the district court concluded correctly that confusion was not likely. Star therefore had not met its burden to prove trademark infringement. Thus the court affirmed the district court's judgment for defendants-appellees.]

AMAZING SPACES, INC. v. METRO MINI STORAGE

608 F.3d 225 (5th Cir. 2010)

KING, Circuit Judge:

Amazing Spaces, Inc., and Metro Mini Storage are rival self-storage businesses in Houston, Texas. Amazing Spaces brought this action against Metro . . . alleging infringement of a star design that it claims as a service mark. The district court concluded that the design was not a legally protectable mark and dismissed Amazing Spaces's claims on summary judgment. We agree that the design was not legally protectable, and we affirm the judgment dismissing Amazing Spaces's service mark infringement claims. However, we also conclude that the district court erred in dismissing Amazing Spaces's claims relating to infringement of its trade dress, and we reverse and remand for further proceedings.

I.   BACKGROUND

Amazing Spaces and Metro compete directly with each other in providing self-storage services in Houston, Texas. . . . Amazing Spaces claims, in connection with providing storage services, exclusive use rights in a design consisting of a raised, five-pointed star set within a circle (the "Star Symbol"). . . . Metro uses a similar star design on its buildings. . . .

Amazing Spaces was founded in 1998 by Scott and Kathy Tautenhahn, and it currently operates three storage facilities in the greater Houston area. . . . Landmark [Construction] was hired to build each of these facilities and, at Amazing Spaces's request, installed the Star Symbol under the peaks of the facilities' gabled roofs. Amazing Spaces has used the Star Symbol in its facilities' architecture and in its advertising, and it claims to have done so since at least April 1998. One trade magazine has recognized Amazing Spaces for its storage services, and the magazine displayed the Star Symbol in connection with the accompanying article. Amazing Spaces has also used the Star Symbol to designate the locations of its facilities on maps, and it claims to have directed customers—through telephone advertisements—to "look for the star."

The Star Symbol is registered as a service mark with the United States Patent and Trademark Office. [*See* Appendix A reproduced at bottom of opinion.] Prior to applying for registration, Amazing Spaces engaged a company to perform a database search to determine whether other storage companies had registered a similar star mark; the search revealed no such registrations. . . .

Landmark has also constructed self-storage facilities for Metro; these facilities feature a similar five-pointed-star-in-a-circle design (but not raised) on their gables. Despite Amazing Spaces's demand that Metro cease its use of a star, Metro continued to use its design and remodeled existing facilities to include the design. According to Amazing Spaces, this has caused confusion among its customers, who mistook Metro's facilities for new Amazing Spaces facilities. According to Kathy Tautenhahn, existing or prospective customers have inquired about whether new Amazing Spaces facilities had opened where Metro facilities were located. The record also includes a declaration from a customer to similar effect.

. . .

Metro moved for summary judgment on the ground that the Star Symbol was not a valid service mark. It argued primarily that the Star Symbol was not inherently distinctive and that Amazing Spaces could not establish that it had acquired secondary meaning. It supported this contention by presenting evidence that the same or a similar five-pointed star was used in commerce "in at least 63 different industries and businesses on buildings, property, and as part of logos" and on the buildings of "at least 28 other self-storage locations." [cit.] The court concluded that "[t]he ubiquitous nature of the five-pointed star set within a circle precludes a finding that it is inherently distinctive or that it can serve as an indicator of origin for a particular business," and that "the record d[id] not raise a fact issue material to determining whether the star mark has acquired distinctiveness through a secondary meaning."

. . .

III. DISCUSSION

A. THE STAR SYMBOL

. . .

2. *Inherent Distinctiveness*

["A] mark is inherently distinctive if 'its intrinsic nature serves to identify a particular source.'" . . . Inherent distinctiveness is attributable to a mark when the mark "almost automatically tells a customer that it refers to a brand and . . . immediately signal[s] a brand or a product source." . . . The parties disagree over not only the answer to whether the Star Symbol is inherently distinctive but also over the proper method for conducting the inquiry. Metro urges that the familiar *Abercrombie* test cannot be used to categorize the Star Symbol and instead asks that we apply the *Seabrook Foods* test to determine that the Star Symbol is not inherently distinctive. Amazing Spaces, by contrast, presses the application of the *Abercrombie* test, under which it claims the Star Symbol is inherently distinctive, and it argues alternatively that the Star Symbol is inherently distinctive under the *Seabrook Foods* test.

a. Abercrombie

. . .

[W]e agree with Metro that the Star Symbol resists categorization under the *Abercrombie* test, and we consequently do not rely on a rote application of its categories in determining whether the Star Symbol is inherently distinctive. . . .

As the district court discovered, the challenge of placing the Star Symbol into *Abercrombie*'s constellation of categories is a futile endeavor. . . .

The district court briefly probed the utility of applying the *Abercrombie* test and concluded that the Star Symbol did not fit as a generic, descriptive, or suggestive mark. [cit.] The district court first rejected the notion that the Star Symbol was generic because "[a] five-pointed star within a circle does not refer to a product or service provided by a self-storage company" and "[t]he evidence of widespread use of a five-point star or a five-point star set within a circle by many diverse businesses and government offices supports the conclusion that the star mark is not related to or a generic symbol for self-storage goods or services." It next determined that the Star Symbol was not descriptive because "[i]t does not identify a characteristic or quality of self-storage service, such as its function or quality." Nor was the Star Symbol suggestive, according to the district court, because "[t]here is no basis to conclude that a five-pointed star set within a circle suggests an attribute of self-storage services." We discern no flaws in the district court's analysis with respect to these three categories. However, the logical extension of the district court's analysis is the conclusion that the Star Symbol is arbitrary or fanciful, which under the *Abercrombie* test would render it inherently distinctive and thus entitled to protection. Yet the district court refused to so conclude, stating that "the star mark cannot be classified as arbitrary or fanciful unless it is inherently distinctive so as to serve as a source identifier for Amazing Spaces." It then turned to the *Seabrook Foods* test in conducting its inquiry into the Star Symbol's inherent distinctiveness.

We agree that the Star Symbol—indeed, any mark—lacks inherent distinctiveness if its intrinsic nature does not serve to identify its source. [cit.] Furthermore, as we have already indicated, we approve the district court's decision to apply a test other than *Abercrombie* in this case. However, we disagree somewhat with the district court's reasoning that a mark cannot be categorized as arbitrary or fanciful unless it is inherently distinctive. Under the *Abercrombie* test, it is the categorization of a mark that dictates its inherent distinctiveness, not the other way around. A rote application of the *Abercrombie* test yields the conclusion that the Star Symbol is an arbitrary or fanciful mark because it "'bear[s] no relationship to the products or services to which [it is] applied.'" [*Pebble Beach Co. v. Tour 18 I Ltd.*, 155 F.3d 526, 540 (5th Cir. 1998)] (quoting *Zatarains*, 698 F.2d at 791).[13] Were we to apply the *Abercrombie* test mechanically to the Star Symbol, without an eye to the question the test seeks to answer, we would be left with the conclusion that the Star Symbol is inherently distinctive. The district court, aware of that result, proceeded to apply the *Seabrook Foods* test.

Both the Supreme Court and scholars have questioned the applicability of the *Abercrombie* test to marks other than words. *See Wal-Mart Stores*, 529 U.S. at 210-13 (noting that the *Abercrombie* test was developed and applied "[i]n the context of word marks" and declining to apply it to a mark consisting of product design); *Qualitex*, 514 U.S. at 162-63 (referring to the *Abercrombie* test but not applying it to a mark consisting of a shade of color); Restatement §13 cmt. d, at 107 ("[U]nless the symbol or design is striking, unusual, or otherwise likely to differentiate the products of a particular producer, the designation is not inherently distinctive."); [cit.]; 2 [MCCARTHY ON TRADEMARKS AND UNFAIR COMPETITION] §11:2, at 11-7 ("Use of the spectrum of descriptive, suggestive, arbitrary and fanciful is largely confined to word marks. It is usually not suitable for nonword designations such as shapes and images making up trade dress."). We do not go so far as to hold that the *Abercrombie* test is eclipsed every time a mark other than a word is at issue. Instead, we hold that the *Abercrombie* test fails to illuminate the fundamental inquiry in this case: whether the Star Symbol's "'intrinsic nature serves to identify'" Amazing Spaces and its storage services. [cit.] For the answer to that question, we now turn to the *Seabrook Foods* test employed by the district court.

b.   Seabrook Foods

In contrast to the *Abercrombie* test, the *Seabrook Foods* test, articulated by the U.S. Court of Customs and Patent Appeals in 1977, applies expressly to marks consisting of symbols and designs:

> In determining whether a design is arbitrary or distinctive this court has looked to [1] whether it was a "common" basic shape or design, [2] whether it was unique or unusual in a particular field, [3] whether it was a mere refinement of a commonly-adopted and well-known form of ornamentation for a particular class of goods viewed by the public as a dress or ornamentation for the goods, or [4] whether it was capable of creating a commercial impression distinct from the accompanying words.

---

13. One commentator has noted that marks consisting of symbols and designs are typically arbitrary with respect to their associated goods and services where the marks are "nonrepresentational":

> Nonverbal and nonrepresentational designs and figures are perfectly acceptable as trademarks. Indeed, they have the advantage of being totally arbitrary, and so cannot be descriptive of the goods or services. The only problem which may be encountered is the question of whether such designs or figures are regarded by the public as identifying indicia or merely as decorations. Especially is this true of such simple figures as rectangles, diamonds, circles, triangles, or lines.

LOUIS ALTMAN & MALLA POLLACK, 3 CALLMAN ON UNFAIR COMPETITION, TRADEMARKS AND MONOPOLIES §18:24 (4th ed. 2010) (footnotes omitted). Under this reasoning, nonverbal marks—even though "arbitrary"—must still be shown to serve as identifying indicia. Professor McCarthy appears to share the view that such marks are arbitrary when they are nonrepresentational. *See* 1 MCCARTHY ON TRADEMARKS §7:36, at 7-91 ("A picture that is merely a representation of the goods themselves is regarded as merely descriptive of the goods.").

Seabrook Foods, 568 F.2d at 1344 (footnotes omitted).[14] The first three of the *Seabrook Foods* "'questions are merely different ways to ask whether the design, shape or combination of elements is so unique, unusual or unexpected in this market that one can assume without proof that it will automatically be perceived by customers as an indicator of origin—a trademark.'" *I.P. Lund Trading ApS v. Kohler Co.*, 163 F.3d 27, 40 (1st Cir. 1998) (quoting 1 MCCARTHY ON TRADEMARKS §8:13, at 8-58.5). As is true of the *Abercrombie* test, the *Seabrook Foods* test seeks an answer to the question whether a mark's "'intrinsic nature serves to identify a particular source.'" [cit.]

We agree with the assessment of the *I.P. Lund Trading* court and Professor McCarthy that the *Seabrook Foods* factors are variations on a theme rather than discrete inquiries. In *Star Industries v. Bacardi & Co.*, the Second Circuit noted that "'[c]ommon basic shapes' or letters are, as a matter of law, not inherently distinctive . . . , [but] stylized shapes or letters may qualify, provided the design is not commonplace but rather unique or unusual in the relevant market." 412 F.3d 373, 382 (2d Cir. 2005) (citing *Seabrook Foods*, 568 F.2d at 1344); [cit.]. This statement, turning on whether the symbol or design is "common," comprises, essentially, the first two *Seabrook Foods* factors. However, the third *Seabrook Foods* factor similarly asks whether a symbol or design is "common" in the sense that it is likely to be perceived by the public as ornamentation rather than a mark. *See Wiley v. Am. Greetings Corp.*, 762 F.2d 139, 142 (1st Cir. 1985) (equating a red heart shape on a teddy bear to "an ordinary geometric shape" because it "carrie[d] no distinctive message of origin to the consumer, . . . given the heart shape's widespread use as decoration for any number of products put out by many different companies"). A "common" symbol or design—lacking inherent distinctiveness—is the antithesis of a symbol or design that "'is so unique, unusual or unexpected in this market that one can assume without proof that it will automatically be perceived by customers as an indicator of origin—a trademark.'" *I.P. Lund Trading*, 163 F.3d at 40 (quoting 1 MCCARTHY ON TRADEMARKS §8:13, at 8-58.5); *accord* Restatement §13 cmt. d, at 107 ("Commonplace symbols and designs are not inherently distinctive since their appearance on numerous products makes it unlikely that consumers will view them as distinctive of the goods or services of a particular seller.").

The district court determined that the Star Symbol was "not a plain five-pointed star" but was instead "shaded and set within a circle," rendering it "sufficient[ly] styliz[ed]" to be "more than a common geometric shape." It then proceeded to conclude that the Star Symbol "[wa]s not inherently distinctive and d[id] not act as an indicator of origin for any self-storage business, including Amazing Spaces." It supported this assertion with a discussion of "[t]he ubiquitous nature of the five-pointed star set within a circle" in Texas, specifically its "use[] as a decoration or ornamentation on innumerable buildings, signs, roads, and products." The court concluded that this ubiquity—including use of the same or a similar star design in 63 industries businesses and 28 other self-storage locations—"preclude[d] a finding that [the Star Symbol wa]s inherently distinctive or that it c[ould] serve as an indicator of origin for a particular business."

Undoubtedly, the Star Symbol is stylized relative to an unshaded five-pointed star design not set within a circle. However, we disagree that the issue of stylization revolves around comparing a design's actual appearance to its corresponding platonic form. Instead, as discussed above, asking whether a shape is stylized is merely another way of asking whether the design is "commonplace" or "unique or unusual in the relevant market," *Star Indus.*, 412 F.3d at

---

14. [T]he district court omitted discussion of the fourth factor, which by its terms applies only when a party seeks trademark protection for a background design typically accompanied by words. [cit.] Similarly, we will not consider the fourth *Seabrook Foods* factor.

382, or whether it is "a mere refinement of a commonly-adopted and well-known form of ornamentation for a particular class of goods viewed by the public as a dress or ornamentation," *Seabrook Foods*, 568 F.2d at 1344.[18] The stylization inquiry is properly conceived of asking whether a particular symbol or design is stylized such that prospective purchasers of goods or services are likely to differentiate it from other, similar symbols or designs. *See Wiley*, 762 F.2d at 142 (holding that a red heart on a teddy bear "carrie[d] no distinctive message of origin to the consumer . . . given the heart shape's widespread use as decoration for any number of products put out by many different companies"); *Brooks Shoe Mfg. Co. v. Suave Shoe Corp.*, 716 F.2d 854, 858 (11th Cir. 1983) (holding that a design consisting of a "V," "7," or arrow on athletic shoes was common ornamentation such that it was not inherently distinctive); Restatement §13 cmt. d, at 107 ("The manner in which a symbol or design is used is also relevant to the likelihood that it will be perceived as an indication of source. In some instances a design is likely to be viewed as mere ornamentation rather than as a symbol of identification."); 1 McCarthy on Trademarks §3.3, at 3-11 ("Usually, if when viewed in context, it is not immediately obvious that a certain designation is being used as an indication of origin, then it probably is not. In that case, it is not a trademark."). The record evidence is replete with similar or identical five-pointed stars, both raised and set in circles, and used in similar manners, such that—notwithstanding the residual evidence of the presumption of validity—no reasonable jury could find that the Star Symbol is even a mere refinement of this commonly adopted and well-known form of ornamentation.[20] The Star Symbol is thus not "'so unique, unusual or unexpected in this market that one can assume without proof that it will automatically be perceived by customers as an indicator of origin—a trademark,'" *I.P.*

---

18. The parties dispute the scope of the "relevant market"—specifically, whether the district court correctly considered use of a similar or identical star design beyond the self-storage service industry. Amazing Spaces contends that we should limit our analysis to the self-storage services industry, while Metro argues that we may take into account uses of star designs in a larger context. The second *Seabrook Foods* factor refers to uniqueness or unusualness "in a particular field," and the Second Circuit has stated that a stylized design may be protectable when it "is not commonplace but rather unique or unusual in the relevant market," *Star Indus.*, 412 F.3d at 382. Similarly, the third factor refers to whether a mark is commonly used as ornamentation for a "particular class of goods." *Seabrook Foods*, 568 F.2d at 1344. In contrast, the First Circuit, in considering whether a red heart on the chest of a teddy bear was inherently distinctive, appeared to consider the broader use of red hearts in determining whether the use at issue was unique or unusual. *See Wiley*, 762 F.2d at 142. . . . Because a mark must distinguish one person's services from another, we agree that our inquiry is whether the Star Symbol identifies and distinguishes Amazing Spaces's self-storage services from others' self-storage services. This does not mean, however, that we must blind ourselves to uses beyond the self-storage services industry: the fact that the same or a similar star is used in countless other ways certainly bears on whether it is "likely that prospective purchasers will perceive [a given star design] as an indication of source" within a particular industry because a "[c]ommonplace symbol[']s . . . appearance on numerous products makes it unlikely that consumers will view [it] as distinctive of the goods or services of a particular seller." Restatement §13 cmt. d, at 107.

20. This is what differentiates the Star Symbol from the examples of registered marks containing stars that Amazing Spaces cites to support the protectability of five-pointed stars. The Dallas Cowboys star is stylized through the inclusion of a white border. The star in the Wal-Mart registration is a plain, five-pointed star, but the registered mark consists of more than just the star—the mark is the words "Wal" and "Mart" on either side of the star. The LanChile Airlines star is set against a circle that is 50% filled in, and it is adjacent to the words "LanChile Airlines." Finally, the USA Truck mark is a complex design consisting of a white star within a blue circle, set against a white rectangle with blue borders and a red stripe running across the middle. Each of these marks contains elements distinguishing it from the commonplace stars in the record. *See Union Nat'l Bank of Tex., Laredo, Tex.*, 909 F.2d at 848 n.25 (noting that the appropriate inquiry is whether the mark as a whole is protectable, not whether its component parts are individually protectable (citing *Estate of P.D. Beckwith v. Comm'r of Patents*, 252 U.S. 538 (1919)).

Lund Trading, 163 F.3d at 40 (quoting 1 MCCARTHY ON TRADEMARKS §8:13, at 8-58.5), and it "does not almost automatically tell a customer that it refers to a brand . . . [or] immediately signal a brand or a product source." [cit.] Because the Star Symbol does not, by "'its intrinsic nature[,] serve[] to identify a particular source,'" it is not inherently distinctive, and it can be protected only upon a showing of secondary meaning.

3.   Secondary Meaning

The parties disagree over whether the Star Symbol has acquired distinctiveness through secondary meaning. . . .

In the context of trade dress, we have articulated seven factors to consider in determining whether secondary meaning has been shown:

> (1) length and manner of use of the mark or trade dress, (2) volume of sales, (3) amount and manner of advertising, (4) nature of use of the mark or trade dress in newspapers and magazines, (5) consumer-survey evidence, (6) direct consumer testimony, and (7) the defendant's intent in copying the trade dress.

Smack Apparel, 550 F.3d at 476 (quoting *Pebble Beach*, 155 F.3d at 541). "In considering this evidence, the focus is on how it demonstrates that the meaning of the mark or trade dress has been altered in the minds of consumers." *Pebble Beach*, 155 F.3d at 541 (citing *Zatarains*, 698 F.2d at 795); *accord Zatarains*, 698 F.2d at 795 ("'[T]he question is not the *extent* of promotional efforts, but their *effectiveness* in altering the meaning of the term to the consuming public.'" (alteration omitted) (quoting *Aloe Creme Labs., Inc. v. Milsan, Inc.*, 423 F.2d 845, 850 (5th Cir. 1970))). We have consistently expressed a preference for "an objective survey of the public's perception of" the mark at issue. [cit.]

The district court considered the following evidence that Amazing Spaces claimed raise a fact issue regarding secondary meaning: (1) the Star Symbol was used for ten years; (2) Amazing Spaces had spent nearly $725,000 in advertising and promoting the Star Symbol; (3) Amazing Spaces had realized over $11.5 million in revenue since it first began using the Star Symbol; (4) Kathy Tautenhahn's statement in her declaration that the Star Symbol identifies Amazing Spaces's self-storage services; and (5) declarations of a customer and an alarm technician about confusion when seeing rival self-storage facilities (Metro and Community) that displayed symbols similar to the Star Symbol. The district court concluded that no fact issue was raised. It based this conclusion partly on the absence of survey evidence, but primarily on its determination that the remaining evidence was not probative regarding secondary meaning: the advertisements did not prominently display the Star Symbol but instead prominently featured the Peaks and Sky Symbol, and the declarations described confusion only in reference to the overall architecture of the facilities.

We agree with the district court that no fact issue has been raised regarding the existence of secondary meaning. [A]mazing Spaces's use of the Star Symbol has been primarily decorative and ornamental. Moreover, the record discloses that the Star Symbol was almost invariably used not as a stand-alone mark but was rather, as Amazing Spaces states in its brief, "an integral part of several marks that Amazing Spaces uses—indeed it is the one common element across its non-word marks." While this argument might support secondary meaning as to those other marks, it does not support secondary meaning as to the Star Symbol. *Cf. Taco Cabana Int'l, Inc. v. Two Pesos, Inc.*, 932 F.2d 1113, 1120 (5th Cir. 1991) ("[C]ompetitors may use individual elements in Taco Cabana's trade dress, but the law protects the distinctive totality."), *aff'd*, 505 U.S. 763. This logic extends to the advertising present in the record. While the Star Symbol (or a variation thereof) constitutes a minor piece of the Peaks and Sky Symbol, marks Amazing Spaces's locations on a map, or replaces the bullet in a bulleted list, it is virtually absent as a stand-alone mark from Amazing Spaces's advertising in the record. This predominant advertising use belies the force Amazing Spaces would attribute to its telephonic advertising directing customers to "look for the star." Nor does Amazing Spaces's volume of sales—to the extent that it applies to a service mark rather than a trademark, trade dress, or product design—reveal secondary meaning: the advertising attempted to attract customers using marks other than the Star Symbol.

We also agree with the district court's assessment that the two declarations evidencing consumer confusion do not bear on the secondary meaning of the Star Symbol. Shane Flores averred that he was confused by the appearance of a Metro facility's "use of a star logo in conjunction with the similarity in the architectural features and designs" and believed it to be an Amazing Spaces facility. Glen Gilmore averred similarly with respect to a [use by a third party that had since ceased]. While these instances of confusion may bear on Amazing Spaces's trade dress claims, they do not have relevance as to the secondary meaning of the Star Symbol itself. Amazing Spaces also claims that intentional copying has been shown because Metro constructed a facility that incorporated a star design after this lawsuit had been filed. But this chronology does not bear on whether Metro's use of a common design was intentional copying of Amazing Spaces's design. Amazing Spaces also contends that the district court placed undue emphasis on the lack of a survey. We have already noted this court's preference for survey evidence as proof of secondary meaning, and we also note that the other factors do not weigh in Amazing Spaces's favor. As Professor McCarthy has stated, "in a borderline case where it is not at all obvious that [a] designation has been used as a mark, survey evidence may be necessary to prove trademark perception." 1 McCarthy on Trademarks §3.3, at 3-8.

In conclusion, we agree with the district court's assessment that Amazing Spaces has failed to raise a fact issue regarding the existence of secondary meaning with respect to the Star Symbol. In light of the overwhelming evidence that the Star Symbol is not distinctive, we hold that it does not serve "to identify and distinguish the services of" Amazing Spaces.

. . .

B. Trade Dress Claims

Having concluded that the district court correctly held that the Star Symbol is not protectable as a mark, we next address whether the district court correctly dismissed Amazing Spaces's causes of action relating to its trade dress and facility design. Amazing Spaces asserts that [these] causes of action were improperly dismissed because they do not "rest entirely on whether the Star Logo is entitled to trademark protection." . . .

In addition to its claim that Metro had infringed its Star Symbol service mark, Amazing Spaces also brought claims for trade dress infringement under §43(a) of the Lanham Act and Texas common law. *See Blue Bell Bio-Med. v. Cin-Bad, Inc.*, 864 F.2d 1253, 1256 (5th Cir. 1989) ("The Lanham Act creates a cause of action for trade dress infringement. This action is analogous to the common law tort of unfair competition." (citing cases)). "Trade dress refers to the total image and overall appearance of a product and may include features such as the size, shape, color, color combinations, textures, graphics, and even sales techniques that characterize a particular product." . . .

Amazing Spaces is correct that, to protect the overall appearance of its facilities as trade dress, it need not establish that the Star Symbol is legally protectable. Amazing Spaces's claimed trade dress, unlike the Star Symbol, consists of the entirety of the facilities' design, including placement of the Star Symbol under the roof peaks. *See Taco Cabana Int'l*, 932 F.2d at 1120 ("[T]he existence of [non-distinctive] elements does not eliminate the possibility of inherent distinctiveness in the trade dress as a whole."). The district court limited discovery to the issue of the trademarkability of the Star Symbol, and Amazing Spaces was therefore unable to present its trade dress and unfair competition claims. We therefore reverse the dismissal of those claims and remand for further proceedings.

APPENDIX

Int. Cl.: 39

Prior U.S. Cls.: 100 and 105

Reg. No. 2,859,845

United States Patent and Trademark Office

Registered July 6, 2004

SERVICE MARK
PRINCIPAL REGISTER

AMAZING SPACES (TEXAS CORPORATION)
9040 LOUETTA ROAD, SUITE B
SPRING, TX 77379

FOR: STORAGE SERVICES, IN CLASS 39 (U.S.
CLS. 100 AND 105).

FIRST USE 4-0-1998; IN COMMERCE 4-0-1998.

SER. NO. 76-540,854, FILED 8-15-2003.

DOMINIC J. FERRAIUOLO, EXAMINING ATTOR-
NEY

NOTE

1. *Separate commercial impression*. In footnote 14 of the *Amazing Spaces* opinion, the court explained why it did not consider the fourth *Seabrook* factor ("separate commercial impression"). This is not unusual. Likewise, in *Forney Indus., Inc. v. Daco of Missouri*, 835 F.3d 1238 (10th Cir. 2016), the Tenth Circuit explained in a footnote that "we do not consider this factor because it does not relate to whether the trade dress is inherently distinctive, but instead 'to a different question: is the design really a separately registerable mark apart from any nearby words.'" Indeed, the court pointedly cited to the fact that in *Wal-Mart* the Supreme Court listed only the first three factors in describing the *Seabrook* test. Review the packaging in *Seabrook*, *supra* page 106. In concrete terms, what question does the fourth *Seabook* factor require you to ask? Is there an analogous consideration that should come into play in assessing the claimed secondary meaning of such marks? *Cf. Société Des Produits Nestlé SA v. Cadbury UK Ltd (KitKat shape)* [2017] EWCA Civ 358 (CA) (UK). ("it is legitimate . . .when assessing whether the applicant has proved [secondary meaning], to consider whether [consumers] would rely upon the sign as denoting the origin of the goods or services if it were used on its own").

2.   Expanding the Types of Nonverbal Marks

The types of nonverbal marks recognized by the courts and the Patent and Trademark Office have continued to expand over the years. Logos and packaging have long been treated as source-identifiers and thus protected under trademark or unfair competition law. But in recent years, colors, product designs, and other symbols have been protected and/or registered under trademark and unfair competition law.

In the early years of the Lanham Act, disputes under the Act largely involved producers claiming rights in words and two-dimensional logos that identified the source of their products and distinguished them from the goods of others. Over time, however, the categories of subject matter protected as trademarks grew to encompass the packaging or receptacles in which products were contained. This expansion in subject matter reflected the realization that consumers had come to identify and distinguish products by their packaging. Consumers clearly identified the carbonated soft drink produced by the Coca-Cola Company as much from the shape of the bottle in which it was contained as by the word COKE® emblazoned on the side of the bottle. Eventually, this acceptance of the growing bases for consumer identification led to the acknowledgment that the source of a product could be identified not only by the packaging in which it was contained (for example, the appearance of the box in which CROCS foam shoes are sold) but by the design of a product itself (for example, the very appearance of the CROCS shoes). The first recognition of this development at the federal appellate level came in 1976 from the Eighth Circuit in *Truck Equipment Service Co. v. Fruehauf Corp.*, where the court of appeals affirmed a successful infringement claim predicated upon the appearance of the hopper of a truck acting to identify its source. [Since then], courts have protected as trade dress the design features of an extensive range of products including kitchen appliances, sporting equipment, candies, bathroom fittings, sports cars, giant gumball machines, furniture, hardware items, fashion accessories, lamps, and even golf holes. Graeme B. Dinwoodie, *The Death of Ontology: A Teleological Approach to Trademark Law*, 84 Iowa L. Rev. 611, 621-22 (1999).

The vehicle for much of this expansion has been the protection of so-called trade dress under Section 43(a) of the Lanham Act. Historically, the term "trade dress" was used to refer to product packaging that identified the source of the product it packaged; the term "trademark" was conventionally reserved for situations where the identifier of a product's source was a word or pictorial symbol. But the significance of this terminology is now slight. *See Blau Plumbing, Inc. v. S.O.S. Fix-It, Inc.*, 781 F.2d 604, 608 (7th Cir. 1986) (concluding that there was "no substantive difference" between trade dress and trademarks). The terms are often used interchangeably and their usage tends to reflect the historical classification of different source-identifying subject matter rather than any different treatment under modern trademark law. (You might consider whether you agree with this last statement after you have read the Supreme Court cases below.)

In the last quarter of a century, the United States Supreme Court has issued three opinions addressing the question of the distinctiveness of nonverbal marks. We will discuss these cases in chronological order (with references to some other cases interspersed throughout). Has there been any evolution in the Court's views, or are the three opinions wholly consistent?

TWO PESOS, INC. v. TACO CABANA, INC.

505 U.S. 763 (1992), reh'g denied, 505 U.S. 1244 (1992)

Justice WHITE delivered the opinion of the Court:

The issue in this case is whether the trade dress[1] of a restaurant may be protected under §43(a) of the Trademark Act of 1946 (Lanham Act), based on a finding of inherent distinctiveness, without proof that the trade dress has secondary meaning.

I

Respondent Taco Cabana, Inc., operates a chain of fast-food restaurants in Texas. The restaurants serve Mexican food. The first Taco Cabana restaurant was opened in San Antonio in September 1978, and five more restaurants had been opened in San Antonio by 1985. Taco Cabana describes its Mexican trade dress as "a festive eating atmosphere having interior dining and patio areas decorated with artifacts, bright colors, paintings and murals. The patio includes interior and exterior areas with the interior patio capable of being sealed off from the outside patio by overhead garage doors. The stepped exterior of the building is a festive and vivid color scheme using top border paint and neon stripes. Bright awnings and umbrellas continue the theme."

In December 1985, a Two Pesos, Inc., restaurant was opened in Houston. Two Pesos adopted a motif very similar to the foregoing description of Taco Cabana's trade dress. Two Pesos restaurants expanded rapidly in Houston and other markets, but did not enter San Antonio. In 1986, Taco Cabana entered the Houston and Austin markets and expanded into other Texas cities, including Dallas and El Paso, where Two Pesos was also doing business.

In 1987, Taco Cabana sued Two Pesos in the United States District Court for the Southern District of Texas for trade dress infringement under §43(a) of the Lanham Act, 15 U.S.C. §1125(a) (1982 ed.), and for theft of trade secrets under Texas common law. The case was tried to a jury, which was instructed to return its verdict in the form of answers to five questions propounded by the trial judge. The jury's answers were: Taco Cabana has a trade dress; taken as a whole, the trade dress is nonfunctional; the trade dress is inherently distinctive; the trade dress has not acquired a secondary meaning in the Texas market; and the alleged infringement creates a likelihood of confusion on the part of ordinary customers as to the source or association of the restaurant's goods or services. Because, as the jury was told, Taco Cabana's trade dress was protected if it either was inherently distinctive or had acquired a secondary meaning, judgment was entered awarding damages to Taco Cabana. In the course of calculating damages, the trial court held that Two Pesos had intentionally and deliberately infringed Taco Cabana's trade dress.

The Court of Appeals ruled that the instructions adequately stated the applicable law and that the evidence supported the jury's findings. In particular, the Court of Appeals

---

1. The District Court instructed the jury: "'[T]rade dress' is the total image of the business. Taco Cabana's trade dress may include the shape and general appearance of the exterior of the restaurant, the identifying sign, the interior kitchen floor plan, the decor, the menu, the equipment used to serve food, the servers' uniforms and other features reflecting on the total image of the restaurant." The Court of Appeals accepted this definition and quoted from *Blue Bell Bio-Medical v. Cin-Bad, Inc.*, 864 F.2d 1253, 1256 (CA5 1989): "The 'trade dress' of a product is essentially its total image and overall appearance." It "involves the total image of a product and may include features such as size, shape, color or color combinations, texture, graphics, or even particular sales techniques." *John H. Harland Co. v. Clarke Checks, Inc.*, 711 F.2d 966, 980 (CA11 1983). . . .

rejected petitioner's argument that a finding of no secondary meaning contradicted a finding of inherent distinctiveness.

In so holding, the court below followed precedent in the Fifth Circuit. In *Chevron Chemical Co. v. Voluntary Purchasing Groups, Inc.*, 659 F.2d 695, 702 (CA5 1981), the court noted that trademark law requires a demonstration of secondary meaning only when the claimed trademark is not sufficiently distinctive of itself to identify the producer; the court held that the same principles should apply to protection of trade dresses. The Court of Appeals noted that this approach conflicts with decisions of other courts, particularly the holding of the Court of Appeals for the Second Circuit in *Vibrant Sales, Inc. v. New Body Boutique, Inc.*, 652 F.2d 299 (1981), cert. denied, 455 U.S. 909 (1982), that §43(a) protects unregistered trademarks or designs only where secondary meaning is shown. We granted certiorari to resolve the conflict among the Courts of Appeals on the question whether trade dress that is inherently distinctive is protectible under §43(a) without a showing that it has acquired secondary meaning. [cit.] We find that it is, and we therefore affirm.

II

The Lanham Act was intended to make "actionable the deceptive and misleading use of marks" and "to protect persons engaged in . . . commerce against unfair competition." §45. Section 43(a) "prohibits a broader range of practices than does §32," which applies to registered marks, *Inwood Laboratories, Inc. v. Ives Laboratories, Inc.*, 456 U.S. 844, 858 (1982), but it is common ground that §43(a) protects qualifying unregistered trademarks and that the general principles qualifying a mark for registration under §2 of the Lanham Act are for the most part applicable in determining whether an unregistered mark is entitled to protection under §43(a). See . . . *Thompson Medical Co. v. Pfizer Inc.*, 753 F.2d 208, 215-216 (CA2 1985); [cit.] . . .

The general rule regarding distinctiveness is clear: An identifying mark is distinctive and capable of being protected if it *either* (1) is inherently distinctive *or* (2) has acquired distinctiveness through secondary meaning. [cit.] It is also clear that eligibility for protection under §43(a) depends on nonfunctionality. [cit.] It is, of course, also undisputed that liability under §43(a) requires proof of the likelihood of confusion. [cit.]

The Court of Appeals determined that the District Court's instructions were consistent with the foregoing principles and that the evidence supported the jury's verdict. Both courts thus ruled that Taco Cabana's trade dress was not descriptive but rather inherently distinctive, and that it was not functional. None of these rulings is before us in this case, and for present purposes we assume, without deciding, that each of them is correct. In going on to affirm the judgment for respondent, the Court of Appeals, following its prior decision in *Chevron*, held that Taco Cabana's inherently distinctive trade dress was entitled to protection despite the lack of proof of secondary meaning. It is this issue that is before us for decision, and we agree with its resolution by the Court of Appeals. There is no persuasive reason to apply to trade dress a general requirement of secondary meaning which is at odds with the principles generally applicable to infringement suits under §43(a). . . .

Petitioner argues that the jury's finding that the trade dress has not acquired a secondary meaning shows conclusively that the trade dress is not inherently distinctive. The Court of Appeals' disposition of this issue was sound:

> "Two Pesos' argument—that the jury finding of inherent distinctiveness contradicts its finding of no secondary meaning in the Texas market—ignores the law in this circuit. While the necessarily imperfect (and often prohibitively difficult) methods for assessing secondary meaning address the empirical question of current consumer association, the legal recognition of an inherently distinctive trademark or trade dress acknowledges the owner's legitimate proprietary

interest in its unique and valuable informational device, regardless of whether substantial consumer association yet bestows the additional empirical protection of secondary meaning." 932 F.2d, at 1120, n.7.

Although petitioner makes the above argument, it appears to concede elsewhere in its brief that it is possible for a trade dress, even a restaurant trade dress, to be inherently distinctive and thus eligible for protection under §43(a). . . .

This brings us to the line of decisions by the Court of Appeals for the Second Circuit that would find protection for trade dress unavailable absent proof of secondary meaning. . . . In *Vibrant Sales, Inc. v. New Body Boutique, Inc.*, 652 F.2d 299 (1981), the plaintiff claimed protection under §43(a) for a product whose features the defendant had allegedly copied. The Court of Appeals held that unregistered marks did not enjoy the "presumptive source association" enjoyed by registered marks and hence could not qualify for protection under §43(a) without proof of secondary meaning. *Id.*, at 303, 304. The court's rationale seemingly denied protection for unregistered, but inherently distinctive, marks of all kinds, whether the claimed mark used distinctive words or symbols or distinctive product design. The court thus did not accept the arguments that an unregistered mark was capable of identifying a source and that copying such a mark could be making any kind of a false statement or representation under §43(a).

This holding is in considerable tension with the provisions of the Lanham Act. If a verbal or symbolic mark or the features of a product design may be registered under §2, it necessarily is a mark "by which the goods of the applicant may be distinguished from the goods of others," 60 Stat. 428, and must be registered unless otherwise disqualified. Since §2 requires secondary meaning only as a condition to registering descriptive marks, there are plainly marks that are registrable without showing secondary meaning. These same marks, even if not registered, remain inherently capable of distinguishing the goods of the users of these marks. Furthermore, the copier of such a mark may be seen as falsely claiming that his products may for some reason be thought of as originating from the plaintiff.

Some years after *Vibrant*, the Second Circuit announced in *Thompson Medical Co. v. Pfizer Inc.*, 753 F.2d 208 (1985), that in deciding whether an unregistered mark is eligible for protection under §43(a), it would follow the classification of marks set out by Judge Friendly in *Abercrombie & Fitch*. Hence, if an unregistered mark is deemed merely descriptive, which the verbal mark before the court proved to be, proof of secondary meaning is required; however, "[s]uggestive marks are eligible for protection without any proof of secondary meaning, since the connection between the mark and the source is presumed." [cit.] The Second Circuit has nevertheless continued to deny protection for trade dress under §43(a) absent proof of secondary meaning, despite the fact that §43(a) provides no basis for distinguishing between trademark and trade dress. See, *e.g.*, *Stormy Clime Ltd. v. ProGroup, Inc.*, 809 F.2d, at 974; *Union Mfg. Co. v. Han Baek Trading Co.*, 763 F.2d 42, 48 (1985); *LeSportsac, Inc. v. K Mart Corp.*, 754 F.2d 71, 75 (1985).

The Fifth Circuit was quite right in *Chevron*, and in this case, to follow the *Abercrombie* classifications consistently and to inquire whether trade dress for which protection is claimed under §43(a) is inherently distinctive. If it is, it is capable of identifying products or services as coming from a specific source and secondary meaning is not required. This is the rule generally applicable to trademarks, and the protection of trademarks and trade dress under §43(a) serves the same statutory purpose of preventing deception and unfair competition. There is no persuasive reason to apply different analysis to the two. The "proposition that secondary meaning must be shown even if the trade dress is a distinctive, identifying mark, [is] wrong, for the reasons explained by Judge Rubin for the Fifth Circuit in *Chevron*." *Blau Plumbing, Inc. v. S.O.S. Fix-It, Inc.*, 781 F.2d 604, 608 (CA7 1986). The Court of Appeals for the Eleventh Circuit also follows *Chevron, AmBrit, Inc. v. Kraft, Inc.*, 805 F.2d 974, 979 (1986), and the Court of Appeals for the Ninth Circuit appears to think that proof of secondary meaning is superfluous if a trade dress is inherently distinctive, *Fuddruckers, Inc. v. Doc's B.R. Others, Inc.*, 826 F.2d 837, 843 (1987).

It would be a different matter if there were textual basis in §43(a) for treating inherently distinctive verbal or symbolic trademarks differently from inherently distinctive trade dress. But there is none. The section does not mention trademarks or trade dress, whether they be called generic, descriptive, suggestive, arbitrary, fanciful, or functional. Nor does the concept of secondary meaning appear in the text of §43(a). Where secondary meaning does appear in the statute, 15 U.S.C. §1052 (1982 ed.), it is a requirement that applies only to merely descriptive marks and not to inherently distinctive ones. We see no basis for requiring secondary meaning for inherently distinctive trade dress protection under §43(a) but not for other distinctive words, symbols, or devices capable of identifying a producer's product.

Engrafting onto §43(a) a requirement of secondary meaning for inherently distinctive trade dress also would undermine the purposes of the Lanham Act. Protection of trade dress, no less than of trademarks, serves the Act's purpose to "secure to the owner of the mark the goodwill of his business and to protect the ability of consumers to distinguish among competing producers. National protection of trademarks is desirable, Congress concluded, because trademarks foster competition and the maintenance of quality by securing to the producer the benefits of good reputation." *Park 'N Fly*, 469 U.S., at 198, citing S. Rep. No. 1333, 79th Cong., 2d Sess., 3-5 (1946) (citations omitted). By making more difficult the identification of a producer with its product, a secondary meaning requirement for a nondescriptive trade dress would hinder improving or maintaining the producer's competitive position.

Suggestions that under the Fifth Circuit's law, the initial user of any shape or design would cut off competition from products of like design and shape are not persuasive. Only nonfunctional, distinctive trade dress is protected under §43(a). The Fifth Circuit holds that a design is legally functional, and thus unprotectible, if it is one of a limited number of equally efficient options available to competitors and free competition would be unduly hindered by according the design trademark protection. *See Sicilia Di R. Biebow & Co. v. Cox*, 732 F.2d 417, 426 (1984). This serves to assure that competition will not be stifled by the exhaustion of a limited number of trade dresses.

On the other hand, adding a secondary meaning requirement could have anticompetitive effects, creating particular burdens on the startup of small companies. It would present special difficulties for a business, such as respondent, that seeks to start a new product in a limited area and then expand into new markets. Denying protection for inherently distinctive nonfunctional trade dress until after secondary meaning has been established would allow a competitor, which has not adopted a distinctive trade dress of its own, to appropriate the originator's dress in other markets and to deter the originator from expanding into and competing in these areas.

[P]etitioner concedes that protecting an inherently distinctive trade dress from its inception may be critical to new entrants to the market and that withholding protection until secondary meaning has been established would be contrary to the goals of the Lanham Act. Petitioner specifically suggests, however, that the solution is to dispense with the requirement of secondary meaning for a reasonable, but brief, period at the outset of the use of a trade dress. If §43(a) does not require secondary meaning at the outset of a business' adoption of trade dress, there is no basis in the statute to support the suggestion that such a requirement comes into being after some unspecified time.

III

We agree with the Court of Appeals that proof of secondary meaning is not required to prevail on a claim under §43(a) of the Lanham Act where the trade dress at issue is inherently distinctive, and accordingly the judgment of that court is affirmed.

It is so ordered.

Justice STEVENS, concurring in the judgment:

As the Court notes in its opinion, the text of §43(a) of the Lanham Act, 15 U.S.C. §1125(a) (1982 ed.), "does not mention trademarks or trade dress." Nevertheless, the Court interprets this section as having created a federal cause of action for infringement of an unregistered trademark or trade dress and concludes that such a mark or dress should receive essentially the same protection as those that are registered. Although I agree with the Court's conclusion, I think it is important to recognize that the meaning of the text has been transformed by the federal courts over the past few decades. I agree with this transformation, even though it marks a departure from the original text, because it is consistent with the purposes of the statute and has recently been endorsed by Congress.

I

It is appropriate to begin with the relevant text of §43(a). [cit.] Section 43(a) provides a federal remedy for using either "a false designation of origin" or a "false description or representation" in connection with any goods or services. The full text of the section makes it clear that the word "origin" refers to the geographic location in which the goods originated. . . . For example, the "false designation of origin" language contained in the statute makes it unlawful to represent that California oranges came from Florida, or vice versa.

For a number of years after the 1946 enactment of the Lanham Act, a "false description or representation," like "a false designation of origin," was construed narrowly. The phrase encompassed two kinds of wrongs: false advertising and the common-law tort of "passing off." False advertising meant representing that goods or services possessed characteristics that they did not actually have and passing off meant representing one's goods as those of another. Neither "secondary meaning" nor "inherent distinctiveness" had anything to do with false advertising, but proof of secondary meaning was an element of the common-law passing-off cause of action. See, *e.g., G. & C. Merriam Co. v. Saalfield*, 198 F. 369, 372 (CA6 1912) ("The ultimate offense always is that defendant has passed off his goods as and for those of the complainant").

II

Over time, the Circuits have expanded the categories of "false designation of origin" and "false description or representation.". . . Although some have criticized the expansion as unwise, it is now "a firmly embedded reality." The United States Trade Association Trademark Review Commission noted this transformation with approval: "Section 43(a) is an enigma, but a very popular one. Narrowly drawn and intended to reach false designations or representations as to the geographical origin of products, the section has been widely interpreted to create, in essence, a federal law of unfair competition. . . . It has definitely eliminated a gap in unfair competition law, and its vitality is showing no signs of age."

[Justice Stevens noted that "whether we call the violation infringement, unfair competition, or false designation of origin, the test is identical—is there a 'likelihood of confusion?'" And he noted further that although, "consistent with the common-law background of §43(a), the Second Circuit has said that proof of secondary meaning is required to establish a claim that the defendant has traded on the plaintiff's goodwill by falsely representing that his goods are those of the plaintiff, . . . the Second Circuit has not explained why 'inherent distinctiveness' is not an appropriate substitute for proof of secondary meaning in a trade dress case. Most of the cases in which the Second Circuit has said that secondary meaning is required did not involve findings of inherent distinctiveness."]

III

[Justice Stevens concluded that "even though the lower courts' expansion of the categories contained in §43(a) is unsupported by the text of the Act, . . . it is consistent with the general purposes of the Act." In particular, he invoked the stated concerns of Congressman Lanham, who suggested that one way the dual goals of the statute (protecting legitimate business and consumers) could be accomplished was by creating uniform legal rights and remedies that were appropriate for a national economy. Although the protection of trademarks had once been entirely a State matter, trade was no longer local, and national legislation was necessary to secure to the owners of trademarks in interstate commerce definite rights.]

Congress has revisited this statute from time to time, and has accepted the "judicial legislation" that has created this federal cause of action. Recently, for example, in the Trademark Law Revision Act of 1988, 102 Stat. 3935, Congress codified the judicial interpretation of §43(a), giving its *imprimatur* to a growing body of case law from the Circuits that had expanded the section beyond its original language.

Although Congress has not specifically addressed the question whether secondary meaning is required under §43(a), the steps it has taken in this subsequent legislation suggest that secondary meaning is not required if inherent distinctiveness has been established.[17] First, Congress broadened the language of §43(a) to make explicit that the provision prohibits "any word, term, name, symbol, or device, or any combination thereof" that is "likely to cause confusion, or to cause mistake, or to deceive as to the affiliation, connection, or association of such person with another person, or as to the origin, sponsorship, or approval of his or her goods, services, or commercial activities by another person." 15 U.S.C. §1125(a). That language makes clear that a confusingly similar trade dress is actionable under §43(a), without necessary reference to "falsity." Second, Congress approved and confirmed the extensive judicial development under the provision, including its application to trade dress that the federal courts had come to apply.[18] Third, the legislative history of the 1988 amendments reaffirms Congress' goals of protecting both businesses and consumers with the Lanham Act. And fourth, Congress explicitly extended to any violation of §43(a) the basic Lanham Act remedial provisions whose text previously covered only registered trademarks. . . . These steps buttress the conclusion that §43(a) is properly understood to provide protection in accordance with the standards for registration in §2. These aspects of the 1988 legislation bolster the claim that an inherently distinctive trade dress may be protected under §43(a) without proof of secondary meaning.

---

17. "When several acts of Congress are passed touching the same subject-matter, subsequent legislation may be considered to assist in the interpretation of prior legislation upon the same subject." [cit.]

18. As the Senate Report explained, revision of §43(a) is designed "to codify the interpretation it has been given by the courts. Because Section 43(a) of the Act fills an important gap in federal unfair competition law, the committee expects the courts to continue to interpret the section. As written, Section 43(a) appears to deal only with false descriptions or representations and false designations of geographic origin. Since its enactment in 1946, however, it has been widely interpreted as creating, in essence, a federal law of unfair competition. For example, it has been applied to cases involving the infringement of unregistered marks, violations of trade dress and certain nonfunctional configurations of goods and actionable false advertising claims." S. Rep. No. 100-515, p. 40 (1988), [U.S. Code Cong. & Admin. News 1988, pp. 5577, 5605].

IV

In light of the consensus among the Courts of Appeals that have actually addressed the question, and the steps on the part of Congress to codify that consensus, *stare decisis* concerns persuade me to join the Court's conclusion that secondary meaning is not required to establish a trade dress violation under §43(a) once inherent distinctiveness has been established. Accordingly, I concur in the judgment, but not in the opinion, of the Court.

Justice THOMAS, concurring in the judgment:

Both the Court and Justice Stevens decide today that the principles that qualify a mark for registration under §2 of the Lanham Act apply as well to determining whether an unregistered mark is entitled to protection under §43(a). The Court terms that view "common ground," though it fails to explain why that might be so, and Justice Stevens decides that the view among the Courts of Appeals is textually insupportable, but worthy nonetheless of adherence. I see no need in answering the question presented either to move back and forth among the different sections of the Lanham Act or to adopt what may or may not be a misconstruction of the statute for reasons akin to *stare decisis*. I would rely, instead, on the language of §43(a).

Section 43(a) . . . codified, among other things, the related common-law torts of technical trademark infringement and passing off, which were causes of action for false descriptions or representations concerning a good's or service's source of production. [cit.]

At common law, words or symbols that were arbitrary, fanciful, or suggestive (called "inherently distinctive" words or symbols, or "trademarks") were presumed to represent the source of a product, and the first user of a trademark could sue to protect it without having to show that the word or symbol represented the product's source in fact. See, *e.g.*, *Heublein v. Adams*, 125 F. 782, 784 (CC Mass. 1903). . . . Trade dress, which consists not of words or symbols, but of a product's packaging (or "image," more broadly), seems at common law to have been thought incapable ever of being inherently distinctive, perhaps on the theory that the number of ways to package a product is finite. Thus, a user of trade dress would always have had to show secondary meaning in order to obtain protection. [cit.]

Over time, judges have come to conclude that packages or images may be as arbitrary, fanciful, or suggestive as words or symbols, their numbers limited only by the human imagination. . . . A particular trade dress, then, is now considered as fully capable as a particular trademark of serving as a "representation or designation" of source under §43(a). As a result, the first user of an arbitrary package, like the first user of an arbitrary word, should be entitled to the presumption that his package represents him without having to show that it does so in fact. This rule follows, in my view, from the language of §43(a), and this rule applies under that section without regard to the rules that apply under the sections of the Lanham Act that deal with registration.

Because the Court reaches the same conclusion for different reasons, I join its judgment.

NOTES AND QUESTIONS

1. *The holding in* Two Pesos. What precisely did the Court hold in *Two Pesos*? Are there any limits to its apparent holding that trade dress can be inherently distinctive? According to what test are courts instructed to determine whether trade dress is inherently distinctive? Which issues, if any, are left open by the Court?

2. *Rationale of* Two Pesos. Why did the Court reach its conclusion in *Two Pesos?* Statutory language? Statutory purpose? Trademark policy? Other considerations? Where did Justice Stevens and Justice Thomas differ from Justice White?

3. *The relationship between inherent distinctiveness and secondary meaning.* The trial court had accepted the jury's finding that the plaintiff's trade dress was inherently distinctive but possessed no secondary meaning in the Texas market. Is this logically possible (in a use-based system)? If it is logically possible, what does this tell you about the relationship between inherent distinctiveness and secondary meaning, and the ease with which each can be established?

4. *Secondary meaning in the making.* Because the petitioner recognized that a requirement of secondary meaning "imposed 'an unfair prospect of theft [or] financial loss' on the developer of fanciful or arbitrary trade dress at the outset of its use," it suggested that "such trade dress should receive limited protection without proof of secondary meaning." In particular, the petitioner argued that "such protection should be only temporary and subject to defeasance when over time the dress has failed to acquire a secondary meaning." This was a doctrine called "secondary meaning in the making," which had been floated in a few earlier lower court decisions. The Supreme Court rejected the doctrine:

> This approach is also vulnerable for the reasons given by the Court of Appeals. If temporary protection is available from the earliest use of the trade dress, it must be because it is neither functional nor descriptive, but an inherently distinctive dress that is capable of identifying a particular source of the product. Such a trade dress, or mark, is not subject to copying by concerns that have an equal opportunity to choose their own inherently distinctive trade dress. To terminate protection for failure to gain secondary meaning over some unspecified time could not be based on the failure of the dress to retain its fanciful, arbitrary, or suggestive nature, but on the failure of the user of the dress to be successful enough in the marketplace. This is not a valid basis to find a dress or mark ineligible for protection. The user of such a trade dress should be able to maintain what competitive position it has and continue to seek wider identification among potential customers.

QUALITEX CO. v. JACOBSON PRODUCTS CO., INC.
514 U.S. 159 (1995)

Justice BREYER delivered the opinion of the Court:

The question in this case is whether the Trademark Act of 1946 (Lanham Act), 15 U.S.C. §§1051-1127 (1988 ed. and Supp. V), permits the registration of a trademark that consists, purely and simply, of a color. We conclude that, sometimes, a color will meet ordinary legal trademark requirements. And, when it does so, no special legal rule prevents color alone from serving as a trademark.

I

The case before us grows out of petitioner Qualitex Company's use (since the 1950's) of a special shade of green-gold color on the pads that it makes and sells to dry cleaning firms for use on dry cleaning presses. In 1989, respondent Jacobson Products (a Qualitex rival) began to sell its own press pads to dry cleaning firms; and it colored those pads a similar green gold. In 1991, Qualitex registered the special green-gold color on press pads with the Patent and Trademark Office as a trademark. Registration No. 1,633,711 (Feb. 5, 1991). Qualitex subsequently added a trademark infringement count, 15 U.S.C. §1114(1), to an unfair competition claim, §1125(a), in a lawsuit it had already filed challenging Jacobson's use of the green-gold color.

Qualitex won the lawsuit in the District Court. But, the Court of Appeals for the Ninth Circuit set aside the judgment in Qualitex's favor on the trademark infringement claim because, in that Circuit's view, the Lanham Act does not permit Qualitex, or anyone else, to register "color alone" as a trademark. [However, the Court of Appeals upheld the judgment in Qualitex's favor under Section 43(a) of the Lanham Act. *See* 13 F.3d 1297 (9th Cir. 1994).]

The Courts of Appeals have differed as to whether or not the law recognizes the use of color alone as a trademark. Compare *NutraSweet Co. v. Stadt Corp.*, 917 F.2d 1024, 1028 (CA7 1990) (absolute prohibition against protection of color alone), with *In re Owens-Corning Fiberglas Corp.*, 774 F.2d 1116, 1128 (CA Fed. 1985) (allowing registration of color pink for fiberglass insulation), and *Master Distributors, Inc. v. Pako Corp.*, 986 F.2d 219, 224 (CA8 1993) (declining to establish *per se* prohibition against protecting color alone as a trademark). Therefore, this Court granted certiorari. We now hold that there is no rule absolutely barring the use of color alone, and we reverse the judgment of the Ninth Circuit.

II

The Lanham Act gives a seller or producer the exclusive right to "register" a trademark, 15 U.S.C. §1052 (1988 ed. and Supp. V), and to prevent his or her competitors from using that trademark, §1114(1). Both the language of the Act and the basic underlying principles of trademark law would seem to include color within the universe of things that can qualify as a trademark. The language of the Lanham Act describes that universe in the broadest of terms. It says that trademarks "includ[e] any word, name, symbol, or device, or any combination thereof." §1127. Since human beings might use as a "symbol" or "device" almost anything at all that is capable of carrying meaning, this language, read literally, is not restrictive. The courts and the Patent and Trademark Office have authorized for use as a mark a particular shape (of a Coca-Cola bottle), a particular sound (of NBC's three chimes), and even a particular scent (of plumeria blossoms on sewing thread). See, *e.g.*, Registration No. 696,147 (Apr. 12, 1960); Registration Nos. 523,616 (Apr. 4, 1950) and 916,522 (July 13, 1971); *In re Clarke*, 17 U.S.P.Q. 2d 1238, 1240 (TTAB 1990). If a shape, a sound, and a fragrance can act as symbols why, one might ask, can a color not do the same?

A color is also capable of satisfying the more important part of the statutory definition of a trademark, which requires that a person "us[e]" or "inten[d] to use" the mark

> "to identify and distinguish his or her goods, including a unique product, from those manufactured or sold by others and to indicate the source of the goods, even if that source is unknown."
> 15 U.S.C. §1127.

True, a product's color is unlike "fanciful," "arbitrary," or "suggestive" words or designs, which almost automatically tell a customer that they refer to a brand. *Abercrombie & Fitch Co. v. Hunting World, Inc.*, 537 F.2d 4, 9-10 (CA2 1976) (Friendly, J.); see *Two Pesos, Inc. v. Taco Cabana, Inc.*, 505 U.S. 763, 768 (1992). The imaginary word "Suntost," or the words "Suntost Marmalade," on a jar of orange jam immediately would signal a brand or a product "source"; the jam's orange color does not do so. But, over time, customers may come to treat a particular color on a product or its packaging (say, a color that in context seems unusual, such as pink on a firm's insulating material or red on the head of a large industrial bolt) as signifying a brand. And, if so, that color would have come to identify and distinguish the goods—*i.e.*, "to indicate" their "source"—much in the way that descriptive words on a product (say, "Trim" on nail clippers or "Car-Freshner" on deodorizer) can come to indicate a product's origin. See, *e.g.*, *J. Wiss & Sons Co. v. W. E. Bassett*

Co., 462 F.2d 567, 569 (1972); *Car-Freshner Corp. v. Turtle Wax, Inc.*, 268 F. Supp. 162, 164 (SDNY 1967). In this circumstance, trademark law says that the word (*e.g.*, "Trim"), although not inherently distinctive, has developed "secondary meaning." See *Inwood Laboratories, Inc. v. Ives Laboratories, Inc.*, 456 U.S. 844, 851, n.11 (1982) ("[S]econdary meaning" is acquired when "in the minds of the public, the primary significance of a product feature . . . is to identify the source of the product rather than the product itself"). Again, one might ask, if trademark law permits a descriptive word with secondary meaning to act as a mark, why would it not permit a color, under similar circumstances, to do the same?

We cannot find in the basic objectives of trademark law any obvious theoretical objection to the use of color alone as a trademark, where that color has attained "secondary meaning" and therefore identifies and distinguishes a particular brand (and thus indicates its "source"). In principle, trademark law, by preventing others from copying a source-identifying mark, "reduce[s] the customer's costs of shopping and making purchasing decisions," 1 J. McCarthy, McCarthy on Trademarks and Unfair Competition §2.01[2], p. 2-3 (3d ed. 1994) (hereinafter McCarthy), for it quickly and easily assures a potential customer that *this* item—the item with this mark—is made by the same producer as other, similarly marked items that he or she liked (or disliked) in the past. At the same time, the law helps assure a producer that it (and not an imitating competitor) will reap the financial, reputation-related rewards associated with a desirable product. The law thereby "encourage[s] the production of quality products," *ibid.*, and simultaneously discourages those who hope to sell inferior products by capitalizing on a consumer's inability quickly to evaluate the quality of an item offered for sale. [cit.] It is the source-distinguishing ability of a mark—not its ontological status as color, shape, fragrance, word, or sign—that permits it to serve these basic purposes. See Landes & Posner, Trademark Law: An Economic Perspective, 30 J. Law & Econ. 265, 290 (1987). And, for that reason, it is difficult to find, in basic trademark objectives, a reason to disqualify absolutely the use of a color as a mark. . . .

It would seem, then, that color alone, at least sometimes, can meet the basic legal requirements for use as a trademark. It can act as a symbol that distinguishes a firm's goods and identifies their source, without serving any other significant function. See U.S. Dept. of Commerce, Patent and Trademark Office, Trademark Manual of Examining Procedure §1202.04(e), p. 1202-13 (2d ed. May, 1993) (hereinafter PTO Manual) (approving trademark registration of color alone where it "has become distinctive of the applicant's goods in commerce," provided that "there is [no] competitive need for colors to remain available in the industry" and the color is not "functional"); see also 1 McCarthy §§3.01[1], 7.26, pp. 3-2, 7-113 ("requirements for qualification of a word or symbol as a trademark" are that it be (1) a "symbol," (2) "use[d] . . . as a mark," (3) "to identify and distinguish the seller's goods from goods made or sold by others," but that it not be "functional"). Indeed, the District Court, in this case, entered findings (accepted by the Ninth Circuit) that show Qualitex's green-gold press pad color has met these requirements. The green-gold color acts as a symbol. Having developed secondary meaning (for customers identified the green-gold color as Qualitex's), it identifies the press pads' source. And, the green-gold color serves no other function. (Although it is important to use *some* color on press pads to avoid noticeable stains, the court found "no competitive need in the press pad industry for the green-gold color, since other colors are equally usable.") Accordingly, unless there is some special reason that convincingly militates against the use of color alone as a trademark, trademark law would protect Qualitex's use of the green-gold color on its press pads.

III

Respondent Jacobson Products says that there are four special reasons why the law should forbid the use of color alone as a trademark. We shall explain, in turn, why we, ultimately, find them unpersuasive.

First, Jacobson says that, if the law permits the use of color as a trademark, it will produce uncertainty and unresolvable court disputes about what shades of a color a competitor may lawfully use. Because lighting (morning sun, twilight mist) will affect perceptions of protected color, competitors and courts will suffer from "shade confusion" as they try to decide whether use of a similar color on a similar product does, or does not, confuse customers and thereby infringe a trademark. Jacobson adds that the "shade confusion" problem is "more difficult" and "far different from" the "determination of the similarity of words or symbols."

We do not believe, however, that color, in this respect, is special. Courts traditionally decide quite difficult questions about whether two words or phrases or symbols are sufficiently similar, in context, to confuse buyers. They have had to compare, for example, such words as "Bonamine" and "Dramamine" (motion-sickness remedies); "Huggies" and "Dougies" (diapers); "Cheracol" and "Syrocol" (cough syrup); "Cyclone" and "Tornado" (wire fences); and "Mattres" and "1-800-Mattres" (mattress franchisor telephone numbers); [cit.]. Legal standards exist to guide courts in making such comparisons. See, *e.g.*, 2 McCarthy §15.08; 1 McCarthy §§11.24-11.25 ("[S]trong" marks, with greater secondary meaning, receive broader protection than "weak" marks.). We do not see why courts could not apply those standards to a color, replicating, if necessary, lighting conditions under which a colored product is normally sold. See Ebert, Trademark Protection in Color: Do It by the Numbers!, 84 T. M. Rep. 379, 405 (1994). Indeed, courts already have done so in cases where a trademark consists of a color plus a design, *i.e.*, a colored symbol such as a gold stripe (around a sewer pipe), a yellow strand of wire rope, or a "brilliant yellow" band (on ampules). [cit.]

Second, Jacobson argues, as have others, that colors are in limited supply. [cit.] Jacobsen claims that, if one of many competitors can appropriate a particular color for use as a trademark, and each competitor then tries to do the same, the supply of colors will soon be depleted. Put in its strongest form, this argument would concede that "hundreds of color pigments are manufactured and thousands of colors can be obtained by mixing." L. Cheskin, Colors: What They Can Do for You 47 (1947). But, it would add that, in the context of a particular product, only some colors are usable. By the time one discards colors that, say, for reasons of customer appeal, are not usable, and adds the shades that competitors cannot use lest they risk infringing a similar, registered shade, then one is left with only a handful of possible colors. And, under these circumstances, to permit one, or a few, producers to use colors as trademarks will "deplete" the supply of usable colors to the point where a competitor's inability to find a suitable color will put that competitor at a significant disadvantage.

This argument is unpersuasive, however, largely because it relies on an occasional problem to justify a blanket prohibition. When a color serves as a mark, normally alternative colors will likely be available for similar use by others. [cit.] Moreover, if that is not so—if a "color depletion" or "color scarcity" problem does arise—the trademark doctrine of "functionality" normally would seem available to prevent the anticompetitive consequences that Jacobsen's argument posits, thereby minimizing that argument's practical force.

The functionality doctrine, as we have said, forbids the use of a product's feature as a trademark where doing so will put a competitor at a significant disadvantage because the feature is "essential to the use or purpose of the article" or "affects [its] cost or quality."

Inwood Laboratories, Inc., 456 U.S., at 850, n.10. The functionality doctrine thus protects competitors against a disadvantage (unrelated to recognition or reputation) that trademark protection might otherwise impose, namely their inability reasonably to replicate important non-reputation-related product features. . . .

The upshot is that, where a color serves a significant non-trademark function—whether to distinguish a heart pill from a digestive medicine or to satisfy the "noble instinct for giving the right touch of beauty to common and necessary things," G. Chesterton, Simplicity and Tolstoy 61 (1912)—courts will examine whether its use as a mark would permit one competitor (or a group) to interfere with legitimate (nontrademark-related) competition through actual or potential exclusive use of an important product ingredient. That examination should not discourage firms from creating esthetically pleasing mark designs, for it is open to their competitors to do the same. See, *e.g.*, *W. T. Rogers Co. v. Keene*, 778 F.2d 334, 343 (CA7 1985) (Posner, J.). But, ordinarily, it should prevent the anticompetitive consequences of Jacobsen's hypothetical "color depletion" argument, when, and if, the circumstances of a particular case threaten "color depletion."

Third, Jacobson points to many older cases—including Supreme Court cases—in support of its position. In 1878, this Court described the common-law definition of trademark rather broadly to "consist of a name, symbol, figure, letter, form, or device, if adopted and used by a manufacturer or merchant in order to designate the goods he manufactures or sells to distinguish the same from those manufactured or sold by another." *McLean v. Fleming*, 96 U.S. 245, 254. Yet, in interpreting the Trademark Acts of 1881 and 1905, which retained that common-law definition, the Court questioned "[w]hether mere color can constitute a valid trade-mark," *A. Leschen & Sons Rope Co. v. Broderick & Bascom Rope Co.*, 201 U.S. 166, 171 (1906), and suggested that the "product including the coloring matter is free to all who make it," *Coca-Cola Co. v. Koke Co. of America*, 254 U.S. 143, 147 (1920). Even though these statements amounted to dicta, lower courts interpreted them as forbidding protection for color alone. . . .

These Supreme Court cases, however, interpreted trademark law as it existed *before* 1946, when Congress enacted the Lanham Act. The Lanham Act significantly changed and liberalized the common law to "dispense with mere technical prohibitions," S. Rep. No. 1333, 79th Cong., 2d Sess., 3 (1946), most notably, by permitting trademark registration of descriptive words (say, "U-Build-It" model airplanes) where they had acquired "secondary meaning." See *Abercrombie & Fitch Co.*, 537 F.2d, at 9 (Friendly, J.). The Lanham Act extended protection to descriptive marks by making clear that (with certain explicit exceptions not relevant here)

> "nothing . . . shall prevent the registration of a mark used by the applicant which has become distinctive of the applicant's goods in commerce." 15 U.S.C. §1052(f) (1988 ed., Supp. V).

This language permits an ordinary word, normally used for a non-trademark purpose (*e.g.*, description), to act as a trademark where it has gained "secondary meaning." Its logic would appear to apply to color as well. Indeed, in 1985, the Federal Circuit considered the significance of the Lanham Act's changes as they related to color and held that trademark protection for color was consistent with the

> "jurisprudence under the Lanham Act developed in accordance with the statutory principle that if a mark is capable of being or becoming distinctive of [the] applicant's goods in commerce, then it is capable of serving as a trademark." *Owens-Corning*, 774 F.2d, at 1120.

In 1988, Congress amended the Lanham Act, revising portions of the definitional language, but left unchanged the language here relevant. §134, 102 Stat. 3946, 15 U.S.C.

§1127. It enacted these amendments against the following background: (1) the Federal Circuit had decided *Owens-Corning*; (2) the Patent and Trademark Office had adopted a clear policy (which it still maintains) permitting registration of color as a trademark, see PTO Manual §1202.04(e) (at p. 1200-12 of the January 1986 edition and p. 1202-13 of the May 1993 edition); and (3) the Trademark Commission had written a report, which recommended that "the terms 'symbol, or device' . . . not be deleted or narrowed to preclude registration of such things as a color, shape, smell, sound, or configuration which functions as a mark," The United States Trademark Association Trademark Review Commission Report and Recommendations to USTA President and Board of Directors, 77 T. M. Rep. 375, 421 (1987); see also 133 Cong. Rec. 32812 (1987) (statement of Sen. DeConcini) ("The bill I am introducing today is based on the Commission's report and recommendations"). This background strongly suggests that the language "any word, name, symbol, or device," 15 U.S.C. §1127, had come to include color. And, when it amended the statute, Congress retained these terms. Indeed, the Senate Report accompanying the Lanham Act revision explicitly referred to this background understanding, in saying that the "revised definition intentionally retains . . . the words 'symbol or device' so as not to preclude the registration of colors, shapes, sounds or configurations where they function as trademarks." S. Rep. No. 100-515, at 44. (In addition, the statute retained language providing that "[n]o trademark by which the goods of the applicant may be distinguished from the goods of others shall be refused registration . . . on account of its nature" (except for certain specified reasons not relevant here). 15 U.S.C. §1052 (1988 ed., Supp. V).)

This history undercuts the authority of the precedent on which Jacobson relies. Much of the pre-1985 case law rested on statements in Supreme Court opinions that interpreted pre-Lanham Act trademark law and were not directly related to the holdings in those cases. Moreover, we believe the Federal Circuit was right in 1985 when it found that the 1946 Lanham Act embodied crucial legal changes that liberalized the law to permit the use of color alone as a trademark (under appropriate circumstances). At a minimum, the Lanham Act's changes left the courts free to reevaluate the preexisting legal precedent which had absolutely forbidden the use of color alone as a trademark. Finally, when Congress reenacted the terms "word, name, symbol, or device" in 1988, it did so against a legal background in which those terms had come to include color, and its statutory revision embraced that understanding.

Fourth, Jacobson argues that there is no need to permit color alone to function as a trademark because a firm already may use color as part of a trademark, say, as a colored circle or colored letter or colored word, and may rely upon "trade dress" protection, under §43(a) of the Lanham Act, if a competitor copies its color and thereby causes consumer confusion regarding the overall appearance of the competing products or their packaging, see 15 U.S.C. §1125(a) (1988 ed., Supp. V). The first part of this argument begs the question. One can understand why a firm might find it difficult to place a usable symbol or word on a product (say, a large industrial bolt that customers normally see from a distance); and, in such instances, a firm might want to use color, pure and simple, instead of color as part of a design. Neither is the second portion of the argument convincing. Trademark law helps the holder of a mark in many ways that "trade dress" protection does not. See 15 U.S.C. §1124 (ability to prevent importation of confusingly similar goods); §1072 (constructive notice of ownership); §1065 (incontestible status); §1057(b) (prima facie evidence of validity and ownership). Thus, one can easily find reasons why the law might provide trademark protection in addition to trade dress protection.

IV

Having determined that a color may sometimes meet the basic legal requirements for use as a trademark and that respondent Jacobson's arguments do not justify a special legal rule preventing color alone from serving as a trademark (and, in light of the District Court's here undisputed findings that Qualitex's use of the green-gold color on its press pads meets the basic trademark requirements), we conclude that the Ninth Circuit erred in barring Qualitex's use of color as a trademark. For these reasons, the judgment of the Ninth Circuit is

Reversed.

NOTES AND QUESTIONS

1. *"Trademark"/"trade dress."* The effect of *Two Pesos* and *Qualitex* was largely to assimilate what historically had been called "trademark" and "trade dress" protection. Yet, the *Qualitex* Court noted that "trademark law helps the holder of a mark in many ways that 'trade dress' protection does not." From the citations that the Court provides, it is clear that the Court means to say that *registration* of a nonverbal mark provides a variety of benefits that cannot be obtained by relying on Section 43(a) of the Lanham Act for protection of an unregistered nonverbal mark. (Recall that the precise question before the Court was whether color per se could be *registered*.) We will discuss those benefits further in Chapter 5.

2. *Qualitex and* Two Pesos. To what extent, if any, did *Qualitex* affirm or modify the holding of the Court three years earlier in *Two Pesos?*

3. *The need to use nonverbal marks.* Justice Breyer mentions one reason producers might want to use nonverbal marks such as color per se rather than verbal marks. Why do you think that the manufacturers of dry cleaning press pads wished to use a color mark rather than a word mark? To what extent are consumers relying more or less frequently on nonverbal marks and, if there is a shift in the extent of this reliance, what might be the cause or explanation?

4. *Protecting against over-protection.* The *Qualitex* Court was aware of the potential for over-broad protection as a result of its decision to permit the registration of color per se as a trademark. What concepts or doctrines does the Court rely upon to effectuate that concern? To what extent is the "subject matter" of trademark protection part of the safety net against over-broad protection?

3.   The Design/Packaging Distinction

a.   Post–Two Pesos *Circuit Split in the Test of Inherent Distinctiveness of Trade Dress*

After *Two Pesos*, courts sought with some difficulty to apply the holding of the case to different factual settings. Nothing changed after *Qualitex*. Courts struggled in particular to assess the distinctiveness of product design trade dress. Almost all courts read *Two Pesos* as applying to product design trade dress, thus permitting the possibility of inherently distinctive product design trade dress. But courts differed widely on the appropriate *tests* to be applied to determine the distinctiveness of product design trade dress.

Some courts continued to apply to product design claims the classical (*Abercrombie*) test used with respect to word marks. Others applied the *Seabrook* test, which called upon a court to consider whether a shape or packaging feature was "a common, basic shape or design, whether it [was] unique or unusual in a particular field, or whether it [was] a mere refinement of commonly adopted and well-known form of ornamentation for a particular class of goods viewed by the public as a dress or ornamentation for the goods." Can these tests be applied to determine the distinctiveness of the design of this penguin-shaped cocktail shaker?

Finally, in a third approach, "some courts concluded that while existing distinctiveness analysis might helpfully assist in an evaluation of the distinctiveness of product packaging, it was unhelpful in the case of product design, and thus developed different tests depending upon the category — design or packaging — into which the trade dress fell. . . . This final approach required the courts in question to develop new analytical devices with which to measure the distinctiveness of product design. The tests that they developed were unduly complex and tended to provide lesser trade dress protection for product designs than for packaging." Graeme B. Dinwoodie, *The Rational Limits of Trademark Law, in* UNITED STATES INTELLECTUAL PROPERTY: LAW AND POLICY 59 (Hansen ed., 2006). For example, in *Knitwaves, Inc. v. Lollytogs Ltd.*, 71 F.3d 996 (2d Cir. 1995), which involved the design of sweaters, the Court of Appeals for the Second Circuit held that in determining whether a product design is inherently distinctive, "we ask whether it is likely to serve primarily as a designator of origin of the product."

What characteristics of product design (as opposed to packaging or words) might cause these courts to develop different tests for product design? Why won't (or will) *Abercrombie* or *Seabrook* work for product designs? Do they work for packaging? Do you agree that the *Knitwaves* test would tend to provide lesser trade dress protection for product designs than for packaging? Should it?

b.   *The Protection of Packaging Trade Dress After* Two Pesos *and* Qualitex

Although the most contentious issue after *Two Pesos* and *Qualitex* was the protection of product design trade dress, it was also unclear what test should be applied to determine the inherent distinctiveness of packaging trade dress. Two years after the Second Circuit handed down *Knitwaves, Inc. v. Lollytogs Ltd.*, 71 F.3d 996 (2d Cir. 1995), in which it articulated a new test by which to determine the inherent distinctiveness of product design trade dress, the court was faced (not for the first time) with the question of what test should apply in the case of product packaging. In *Fun-damental Too, Ltd. v. Gemmy Indus. Corp.*, 111 F.3d 993 (2d Cir. 1997), Fun-damental asserted trade dress in the packaging (shown here) for its "Toilet Bank" product, a coin bank that resembled a flush toilet.

Defendant Gemmy argued that to determine inherent distinctiveness, the court should rely on the *Seabrook* test, not the standard distinctiveness spectrum from *Abercrombie*. The court declined to do so:

> We see no reason to abandon the *Abercrombie* distinctiveness spectrum in this case. Several reasons lead us to decline. First, we have expressly ruled that the *Abercrombie* classifications apply to packaging. *Paddington*, 996 F.2d at 583. Second, *Knitwaves* is a pure product configuration case, separate from product packaging, the category of trade dress at issue in this case. In *Knitwaves*, the trade dress lay in the product itself, rather than in a symbol — a trademark or packaging — associated with the product. It was therefore difficult to define some aspect or feature of the trade dress as "descriptive" or "arbitrary" in relation to the product. *See Knitwaves*, 71 F.3d at 1007-08. . . . In contrast, a store display of a product's packaging style creates an image of the product more readily separated from the product itself. Moreover, although there may be a finite set of ways to configure a product, the variety of packaging available for a given product is limited only by the bounds of imagination. These factors render packaging more suitable than product configuration for classification under the *Abercrombie* system as arbitrary or fanciful, suggestive, descriptive, or generic.
>
> Third, use of the *Abercrombie* test tracks the purpose of the Lanham Act to identify source. That is, it is consistent with the Supreme Court's emphasis on a trade dress' capacity to "identify a particular source of the product." *Two Pesos*, 505 U.S. at 771. While a more stringent test is necessary in the product configuration context, applying *Abercrombie* to product packaging serves the aims of the Lanham Act because consumers are more likely to rely on the packaging of a product than on the product's design as an indication of source. Restatement (Third) of Unfair Competition §16 cmt. b (1995). In contrast, over-inclusive protection of the product design risks conferring benefits beyond the intended scope of the Lanham Act and entering what is properly the realm of patent law. *See Fabrication Enters., Inc. v. Hygenic Corp.*, 64 F.3d 53, 59 n.4 (2d Cir. 1995). Thus, though the *Abercrombie* classifications were originally developed for analysis of word marks, we conclude that because of the endless number of product packaging options the *Abercrombie* test is appropriately applied in this trade dress case.

Thus, the court applied *Abercrombie*. However, many courts did (and still do) apply *Seabrook* instead of (or in addition to) *Abercrombie*. *See Yankee Candle, infra* page 144.

c. *The Supreme Court Enters the Fray: Product Design Trade Dress*

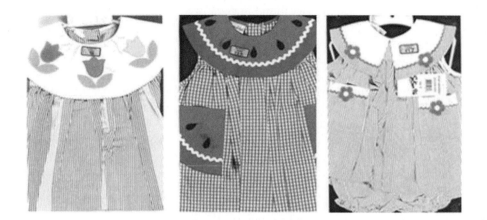

WAL-MART STORES, INC. v. SAMARA BROTHERS, INC.

529 U.S. 205 (2000)

Justice SCALIA delivered the opinion of the Court:

In this case, we decide under what circumstances a product's design is distinctive, and therefore protectible, in an action for infringement of unregistered trade dress under §43(a) of the Trademark Act of 1946 (Lanham Act), 60 Stat. 441, as amended, 15 U.S.C. §1125(a).

I

Respondent Samara Brothers, Inc., designs and manufactures children's clothing. Its primary product is a line of spring/summer one-piece seersucker outfits decorated with appliqués of hearts, flowers, fruits, and the like. A number of chain stores, including JC Penney, sell this line of clothing under contract with Samara.

Petitioner Wal-Mart Stores, Inc., is one of the nation's best known retailers, selling among other things children's clothing. In 1995, Wal-Mart contracted with one of its suppliers, Judy-Philippine, Inc., to manufacture a line of children's outfits for sale in the 1996 spring/summer season. Wal-Mart sent Judy-Philippine photographs of a number of garments from Samara's line, on which Judy-Philippine's garments were to be based; Judy-Philippine duly copied, with only minor modifications, 16 of Samara's garments, many of which contained copyrighted elements. In 1996, Wal-Mart briskly sold the so-called knock-offs, generating more than $1.15 million in gross profits.

In June 1996, a buyer for JC Penney called a representative at Samara to complain that she had seen Samara garments on sale at Wal-Mart for a lower price than JC Penney was allowed to charge under its contract with Samara. The Samara representative told the buyer that Samara did not supply its clothing to Wal-Mart. Their suspicions aroused, however, Samara officials launched an investigation, which disclosed that Wal-Mart and several other major retailers—Kmart, Caldor, Hills, and Goody's—were selling the knockoffs of Samara's outfits produced by Judy-Philippine.

After sending cease-and-desist letters, Samara brought this action in the United States District Court for the Southern District of New York against Wal-Mart, Judy-Philippine, Kmart, Caldor, Hills, and Goody's for copyright infringement under federal law, consumer fraud and unfair competition under New York law, and—most relevant for our purposes—infringement of unregistered trade dress under §43(a) of the Lanham Act, 15 U.S.C. §1125(a). All of the defendants except Wal-Mart settled before trial.

After a weeklong trial, the jury found in favor of Samara on all of its claims. Wal-Mart then renewed a motion for judgment as a matter of law, claiming, *inter alia*, that there was insufficient evidence to support a conclusion that Samara's clothing designs could be legally protected as distinctive trade dress for purposes of §43(a). The District Court denied the motion, and awarded Samara damages, interest, costs, and fees totaling almost $1.6 million, together with injunctive relief. The Second Circuit [found that the design trade dress was inherently distinctive and] affirmed the denial of the motion for judgment as a matter of law, and we granted certiorari.

II

The Lanham Act [in Section 2] provides for the registration of trademarks, which it defines in §45 to include "any word, name, symbol, or device, or any combination thereof [used or intended to be used] to identify and distinguish [a producer's] goods . . . from those manufactured or sold by others and to indicate the source of the goods. . . ." 15 U.S.C. §1127. . . . In addition to protecting registered marks, the Lanham Act, in §43(a), gives a producer a cause of action for the use by any person of "any word, term, name, symbol, or device, or any combination thereof . . . which . . . is likely to cause confusion . . . as to the origin, sponsorship, or approval of his or her goods. . . ." 15 U.S.C. §1125(a). It is the latter provision that is at issue in this case.

The breadth of the definition of marks registrable under §2, and of the confusion-producing elements recited as actionable by §43(a), has been held to embrace not just word marks, such as "Nike," and symbol marks, such as Nike's "swoosh" symbol, but also "trade dress"—a category that originally included only the packaging, or "dressing," of a product, but in recent years has been expanded by many courts of appeals to encompass the design of a product. See, *e.g.*, *Ashley Furniture Industries, Inc. v. Sangiacomo N. A., Ltd.*, 187 F.3d 363 (CA4 1999) (bedroom furniture); *Knitwaves, Inc. v. Lollytogs Ltd.*, 71 F.3d 996 (CA2 1995) (sweaters); *Stuart Hall Co., Inc. v. Ampad Corp.*, 51 F.3d 780 (CA8 1995) (notebooks). These courts have assumed, often without discussion, that trade dress constitutes a "symbol" or "device" for purposes of the relevant sections, and we conclude likewise. "Since human beings might use as a 'symbol' or 'device' almost anything at all that is capable of carrying meaning, this language, read literally, is not restrictive." *Qualitex Co. v. Jacobson Products Co.*, 514 U.S. 159, 162 (1995). This reading of §2 and §43(a) is buttressed by a recently added subsection of §43(a), §43(a)(3), which refers specifically to "civil action[s] for trade dress infringement under this chapter for trade dress not registered on the principal register." 15 U.S.C. §1125(a)(3) (1994 ed., Supp. V).

The text of §43(a) provides little guidance as to the circumstances under which unregistered trade dress may be protected. It does require that a producer show that the allegedly infringing feature is not "functional," see §43(a)(3), and is likely to cause confusion with the product for which protection is sought, see §43(a)(1)(A), 15 U.S.C. §1125(a)(1)(A). Nothing in §43(a) explicitly requires a producer to show that its trade dress is distinctive, but courts have universally imposed that requirement, since without distinctiveness the trade dress would not "cause confusion . . . as to the origin, sponsorship, or approval of [the] goods," as the section requires. Distinctiveness is, moreover, an explicit prerequisite for registration of trade dress under §2, and "the general principles qualifying a mark for registration under §2 of the Lanham Act are for the most part applicable in determining whether an unregistered mark is entitled to protection under §43(a)." *Two Pesos, Inc. v. Taco Cabana, Inc.*, 505 U.S. 763, 768 (1992) (citations omitted).

In evaluating the distinctiveness of a mark under §2 (and therefore, by analogy, under §43(a)), courts have held that a mark can be distinctive in one of two ways. First, a mark is inherently distinctive if "[its] intrinsic nature serves to identify a particular source." *Ibid*. In the context of word marks, courts have applied the now-classic test originally formulated by Judge Friendly, in which word marks that are "arbitrary" ("Camel" cigarettes), "fanciful" ("Kodak" film), or "suggestive" ("Tide" laundry detergent) are held to be inherently distinctive. See *Abercrombie & Fitch Co. v. Hunting World, Inc.*, 537 F.2d 4, 10-11 (CA2 1976). Second, a mark has acquired distinctiveness, even if it is not inherently distinctive, if it has developed secondary meaning, which occurs when, "in the minds of the public, the primary significance of a [mark] is to identify the source of the product rather than the product itself." *Inwood Laboratories, Inc. v. Ives Laboratories, Inc.*, 456 U.S. 844, 851, n.11 (1982).*

The judicial differentiation between marks that are inherently distinctive and those that have developed secondary meaning has solid foundation in the statute itself. Section 2 requires that registration be granted to any trademark "by which the goods of the applicant may be distinguished from the goods of others"—subject to various limited exceptions. 15 U.S.C. §1052. It also provides, again with limited exceptions, that "nothing in this chapter shall prevent the registration of a mark used by the applicant which has become distinctive of the applicant's goods in commerce"—that is, which is not inherently distinctive but has become so only through secondary meaning. §2(f), 15 U.S.C. §1052(f). Nothing in §2, however, demands the conclusion that *every* category of mark necessarily includes some marks "by which the goods of the applicant may be distinguished from the goods of others" *without* secondary meaning—that in every category some marks are inherently distinctive.

Indeed, with respect to at least one category of mark—colors—we have held that no mark can ever be inherently distinctive. *See Qualitex*, 514 U.S., at 162-163. . . .

It seems to us that design, like color, is not inherently distinctive. The attribution of inherent distinctiveness to certain categories of word marks and product packaging derives from the fact that the very purpose of attaching a particular word to a product, or encasing it in a distinctive packaging, is most often to identify the source of the product. Although the words and packaging can serve subsidiary function—a suggestive word mark (such as "Tide" for laundry detergent), for instance, may invoke positive connotations in the consumer's mind, and a garish form of packaging (such as Tide's squat, brightly decorated plastic bottles for its liquid laundry detergent) may attract an otherwise indifferent consumer's attention on a crowded store shelf—their predominant function remains source identification. Consumers are therefore predisposed to regard those symbols as indication of the producer, which is why such symbols "almost *automatically* tell a customer that they refer to a brand," *id*., at 162-163, and "immediately . . . signal a brand or a product 'source,'" *id*., at 163. And where it is not reasonable to assume consumer predisposition to take an affixed word or packaging as indication of source—where, for example, the affixed word is descriptive of the product ("Tasty" bread) or of a geographic origin ("Georgia" peaches)—inherent distinctiveness will not be found. That is why the statute generally excludes, from those word marks that can be registered as inherently distinctive, words

---

* The phrase "secondary meaning" originally arose in the context of word marks, where it served to distinguish the source-identifying meaning from the ordinary, or "primary," meaning of the word. "Secondary meaning" has since come to refer to the acquired, source-identifying meaning of a non-word mark as well. It is often a misnomer in that context, since non-word marks ordinarily have no "primary" meaning. Clarity might well be served by using the term "acquired meaning" in both the word-mark and the non-word-mark contexts—but in this opinion we follow what has become the conventional terminology.

that are "merely descriptive" of the goods, §2(e)(1), 15 U.S.C. §1052(e)(1), or "primarily geographically descriptive of them," see §2(e)(2), 15 U.S.C. §1052(e)(2). In the case of product design, as in the case of color, we think consumer predisposition to equate the feature with the source does not exist. Consumers are aware of the reality that, almost invariably, even the most unusual of product designs—such as a cocktail shaker shaped like a penguin—is intended not to identify the source, but to render the product itself more useful or more appealing.

The fact that product design almost invariably serves purposes other than source identification not only renders inherent distinctiveness problematic; it also renders application of an inherent-distinctiveness principle more harmful to other consumer interests. Consumers should not be deprived of the benefits of competition with regard to the utilitarian and esthetic purposes that product design ordinarily serves by a rule of law that facilitates plausible threats of suit against new entrants based upon alleged inherent distinctiveness. How easy it is to mount a plausible suit depends, of course, upon the clarity of the test for inherent distinctiveness, and where product design is concerned we have little confidence that a reasonably clear test can be devised. Respondent and the United States as *amicus curiae* urge us to adopt for product design relevant portions of the test formulated by the Court of Customs and Patent Appeals for product packaging in *Seabrook Foods, Inc. v. Bar-Well Foods, Ltd.*, 568 F.2d 1342 (1977). That opinion, in determining the inherent distinctiveness of a product's packaging, considered, among other things, "whether it was a 'common' basic shape or design, whether it was unique or unusual in a particular field, [and] whether it was a mere refinement of a commonly-adopted and well-known form of ornamentation for a particular class of goods viewed by the public as a dress or ornamentation for the goods." *Id.*, at 1344 (footnotes omitted). Such a test would rarely provide the basis for summary disposition of an anticompetitive strike suit. Indeed, at oral argument, counsel for the United States quite understandably would not give a definitive answer as to whether the test was met in this very case, saying only that "[t]his is a very difficult case for that purpose." Tr. of Oral Arg. 19.

It is true, of course, that the person seeking to exclude new entrants would have to establish the nonfunctionality of the design feature, see §43(a)(3), 15 U.S.C. §1125(a)(3) (1994 ed., Supp. V)—a showing that may involve consideration of its esthetic appeal, *see Qualitex, supra*, at 170. Competition is deterred, however, not merely by successful suit but by the plausible threat of successful suit, and given the unlikelihood of inherently source-identifying design, the game of allowing suit based upon alleged inherent distinctiveness seems to us not worth the candle. That is especially so since the producer can ordinarily obtain protection for a design that is inherently source identifying (if any such exists), but that does not yet have secondary meaning, by securing a design patent or a copyright for the design—as, indeed, respondent did for certain elements of the designs in this case. The availability of these other protections greatly reduces any harm to the producer that might ensue from our conclusion that a product design cannot be protected under §43(a) without a showing of secondary meaning.

Respondent contends that our decision in *Two Pesos* forecloses a conclusion that product-design trade dress can never be inherently distinctive. . . . *Two Pesos* unquestionably establishes the legal principle that trade dress can be inherently distinctive, but it does not establish that *product-design* trade dress can be. *Two Pesos* is inapposite to our holding here because the trade dress at issue, the decor of a restaurant, seems to us not to constitute product *design*. It was either product packaging—which, as we have discussed, normally *is* taken by the consumer to indicate origin—or else some *tertium quid* that is akin to product packaging and has no bearing on the present case.

Respondent replies that this manner of distinguishing *Two Pesos* will force courts to draw difficult lines between product-design and product-packaging trade dress. There will indeed be some hard cases at the margin: a classic glass Coca-Cola bottle, for instance, may constitute packaging for those consumers who drink the Coke and then discard the bottle, but may constitute the product itself for those consumers who are bottle collectors, or part of the product itself for those consumers who buy Coke in the classic glass bottle, rather than a can, because they think it more stylish to drink from the former. We believe, however, that the frequency and the difficulty of having to distinguish between product design and product packaging will be much less than the frequency and the difficulty of having to decide when a product design is inherently distinctive. To the extent there are close cases, we believe that courts should err on the side of caution and classify ambiguous trade dress as product design, thereby requiring secondary meaning. The very closeness will suggest the existence of relatively small utility in adopting an inherent-distinctiveness principle, and relatively great consumer benefit in requiring a demonstration of secondary meaning.

We hold that, in an action for infringement of unregistered trade dress under §43(a) of the Lanham Act, a product's design is distinctive, and therefore protectible, only upon a showing of secondary meaning. The judgment of the Second Circuit is reversed, and the case is remanded for further proceedings consistent with this opinion.

It is so ordered.

NOTES AND QUESTIONS

1. *The question before the Court.* In *Wal-Mart*, the Court granted certiorari on the question "[w]hat must be shown to establish that a product's design is inherently distinctive for purposes of Lanham Act trade-dress protection?" *See* 528 U.S. 808 (1999). Why is there little discussion in the Court's opinion of the case law discussing inherent distinctiveness of product design trade dress or of the issue presented in the petition for certiorari?

2. *Consistency with prior Supreme Court case law.* Do you agree with the reading of *Two Pesos* and *Qualitex* offered by the *Wal-Mart* Court? To what extent has the Court offered an elaboration upon the meaning of its earlier opinions? To what extent is the Court backtracking on its earlier opinions? Does the *Wal-Mart* Court look to the same sources as the *Two Pesos* and *Qualitex* Courts? What is the respective significance of statutory language, legislative history, trademark policy, or other concerns in each of the Court's decisions? How does the Court's concern for competition manifest itself in each of the three cases? *See* Graeme B. Dinwoodie, *The Seventh Annual Honorable Helen Wilson Nies Memorial Lecture on Intellectual Property Law: The Trademark Jurisprudence of the Rehnquist Court*, 8 Marq. Intell. Prop. L. Rev. 187 (2004) (suggesting various influences); Robert G. Bone, *Enforcement Costs and Trademark Puzzles*, 90 Va. L. Rev. 2099 (2004) (suggesting that trade dress law reflects attention to enforcement costs).

3. *Consistency with lower court approaches.* How is the test announced by the Court in *Wal-Mart* different from the approach of the Second Circuit in *Knitwaves, supra* page 133?

4. *Rationales for a secondary meaning requirement.* What are the reasons the Court imposed a secondary meaning requirement on product design trade dress claims? (You may find several variables or reasons in the opinion.) Are these reasons persuasive? To what extent do these reasons apply to other types of trademark?

5. *Assigning significance to categories.* Classical trademark distinctiveness analysis assigns marks to different categories (e.g., descriptive terms), which in turn affects the ability of those marks to receive protection absent secondary meaning. Is the Court simply saying that product design marks are, as a legal matter, to be treated as descriptive marks? Is the classification of a mark as descriptive (thus requiring secondary meaning for protection) different from classifying a mark as a product design (thus requiring the same proof for protection)?

6. *The design/packaging line.* The Court has now created a different rule for product design than for product packaging. How would you draw that line? Which considerations would be important? Consider the following possibilities: (a) the examples cited by the *Wal-Mart* Court of different types of mark, (b) the different variables that made the *Wal-Mart* Court treat design differently, or (c) a conceptual definition of what is a "design" and what is "packaging." *Cf.* Graeme B. Dinwoodie, *Reconceptualizing the Inherent Distinctiveness of Product Design Trade Dress*, 75 N.C. L. Rev. 471, 573-85 (1997).

7. *Color combinations.* In *Wal-Mart* the Court confirmed that color per se can be protected only upon proof of secondary meaning. What about combinations of colors? Can they be inherently distinctive? *Cf. Deere & Co. v. MTD Holdings Inc.*, 70 U.S.P.Q.2d (BNA) 1009 (S.D.N.Y. 2004) (green and yellow for farm equipment) *with Gateway, Inc. v. Companion Prods., Inc.*, 68 U.S.P.Q.2d (BNA) 1407 (D.S.D. 2003) (black and white cattle-like design for computer products), *aff'd*, 384 F.3d 503 (8th Cir. 2004), and *Deere & Co. v. FIMCO Inc.*, 239 F. Supp. 3d 964 (W.D. Ky. 2017) (green and yellow for farm equipment, again). If neither *Qualitex* nor *Wal-Mart* answers that question, what position would you take? In answering this question, consider the reasons advanced by the Supreme Court for its per se secondary meaning requirement for protecting color. In *Forney Indus., Inc. v. Daco of Missouri*, 835 F.3d 1238 (10th Cir. 2016), the plaintiff brought an action under Section 43(a) claiming trade dress rights in the following mark that it used on packaging for metalwork accessories:

> The Forney Color Mark is a combination and arrangement of colors defined by a red into yellow background with a black banner/header that includes white letters. More specifically, the Forney Color Mark includes red and yellow as the dominate [sic] background colors. Red typically starts at the bottom of the packaging, continues up the packaging and may form borders. Red may also be used in accents including but not limited to lettering. Yellow typically begins higher than the red and continues up the packaging. Yellow may also provide borders and be used in accents including but not limited to lettering. A black banner is positioned toward the top of the package label or backer card. Black may also be used in accents including but not limited to lettering. White is used in lettering and accents.

Could such a mark be inherently distinctive? The Tenth Circuit reviewed a number of cases where the color of packaging was involved and concluded that "in light of the Supreme Court's directive that a product's color cannot be inherently distinctive and its concern that inherent distinctiveness not be the subject of excessive litigation, we hold that the use of color in product packaging can be inherently distinctive (so that it is unnecessary to show secondary meaning) only if specific colors are used in combination with a well-defined shape, pattern, or other distinctive design." Do you agree? What concerns might you have with the mark claimed? *Cf. Société Des Produits Nestlé SA v. Cadbury UK*

Ltd [2013] EWCA Civ 1174 (UK) (denying trademark registration to "The colour purple (Pantone 2685C), as shown on the form of application, applied to the whole visible surface, or being the predominant colour applied to the whole visible surface, of the packaging of the [chocolate products]."

8. *Distinctiveness as a question of fact.* Classification of a term under *Abercrombie* is a question of fact. When the *Wal-Mart* case was before the Second Circuit, Judge Newman dissented from part of the court's opinion, including the part on the extent to which a court should give deference to jury determinations of distinctiveness. The allocation of parts of patent litigation between judge and jury has been the subject of much litigation during the last decade. Judge Newman suggested that it was important for courts to reconsider whether distinctiveness was an issue that had to be regarded as a question of law in trademark cases. Why might this be the case? *See Samara Bros., Inc. v. Wal-Mart Stores, Inc.,* 165 F.3d 120, 135-36 (2d Cir. 1998).

9. *"Some* tertium quid.*"* The Court distinguished *Two Pesos* by describing that case as involving "product packaging" (which the Court implies can be inherently distinctive) "or else some *tertium quid* that is akin to product packaging and has no bearing on the present case." Might there be other types of mark that one could categorize as "some *tertium quid*," such that the less demanding *Two Pesos* rule would apply? What is there about restaurant decor that warrants abrogation from the *Wal-Mart* rule? What is the test for assessing the inherent distinctiveness of trade dress that constitutes "some *tertium quid*"? *See Miller's Ale House Inc. v. Boynton Carolina Ale House LLC,* 702 F.3d 1312 (11th Cir. 2012).

10. *Seabrook as an alternative test?* The government refused at oral argument in *Wal-Mart* to answer questions regarding how *Seabrook* would be applied in the case before the Court. Would the *Seabrook* test have supported a finding of inherent distinctiveness in *Wal-Mart*? Is *Seabrook* still good law? *See In re Chippendales,* 622 F.3d 1346, 1357-58 (Fed. Cir. 2010). In *Chippendales,* the Federal Circuit applied *Seabrook,* describing it as a "four-part test," and suggesting that "if a mark satisfies any of the first three tests, it is not inherently distinctive." *See id.* at 1351. Is that how the Fifth Circuit applied the test in *Amazing Spaces?*

4. Trade Dress Protection After *Wal-Mart*

IN RE SLOKEVAGE

441 F.3d 957 (Fed. Cir. 2006)

Lourie, Circuit Judge:

BACKGROUND

[Joanne] Slokevage filed an application to register a mark on the Principal Register for "pants, overalls, shorts, culottes, dresses, skirts." Slokevage described the mark in her application as a "configuration" that consists of a label with the words "FLASH DARE!" in a V-shaped background, and cut-out areas located on each side of the label. The cut-out areas consist of a hole in a garment and a flap attached to the garment with a closure device. This trade dress configuration, which is located on the rear of various garments, is depicted [here].

Although Slokevage currently seeks to register a mark for the overall configuration of her design, she has already received protection for various aspects of the trade dress configuration. For example, she received a design patent for the cut-out area design. She also registered on the Supplemental Register[1] a design mark for the cut-out area. In addition, she registered the word mark "FLASH DARE!" on the Principal Register.

[The trademark examiner initially refused registration of the proposed mark *inter alia* on the ground that it constituted a clothing configuration that is not inherently distinctive. Slokevage chose not to submit evidence of acquired distinctiveness. The examiner made final his refusal to register the mark on the ground that the clothing configuration constitutes "product design/configuration," which cannot be inherently distinctive. The examiner noted that Slokevage's reference in her application to the trade dress as a "cut-away flap design" supported a determination that the configuration constitutes product design. Slokevage appealed the refusal of the examiner to register the trade dress configuration, and the Board affirmed the examiner's decision.]

DISCUSSION

. . .

As a preliminary matter, Slokevage argues that whether trade dress is product design or not is a legal determination, whereas the government asserts that it is a factual issue. The resolution of that question is an issue of first impression for this court. We conclude that the determination whether trade dress is product design is a factual finding because it is akin to determining whether a trademark is inherently distinctive or whether a mark is descriptive, which are questions of fact. *See, e.g.*, *Hoover Co. v. Royal Appliance Mfg. Co.*, 238 F.3d 1357, 1359 (Fed. Cir. 2001) ("The issue of inherent distinctiveness is a factual determination made by the board."); [cit.] Inherent distinctiveness or descriptiveness involves consumer perception and whether consumers are predisposed towards equating a symbol with a source. *See In re MBNA Am. Bank, N.A.*, 340 F.3d 1328, 1332 (Fed. Cir. 2003); *In re Nett Designs, Inc.*, 236 F.3d at 1341-42. Such issues are determined based on testimony, surveys, and other evidence as questions of fact. Determining whether trade dress is product design or product packaging involves a similar inquiry. *Wal-Mart*, 529 U.S. at 213 (discussing product packaging and design in the context of consumers' ability to equate the product with the source). We therefore will defer to the Board's finding on product design, affirming the Board if its decision is supported by substantial evidence. . . .

I.   TRADE DRESS AND PRODUCT DESIGN

On appeal, Slokevage argues that the Board erred in determining that the trade dress for which she seeks protection is product design and thus that it cannot be inherently distinctive. She asserts that the Board's reliance on the Supreme Court's decision in *Wal-Mart* to support its position that Slokevage's trade dress is product design is misplaced. In particular, she contends that *Wal-Mart* does not provide guidance on how to determine whether trade dress is product design. Moreover, she maintains that the trade dress at issue in *Wal-Mart*, which was classified as product design without explanation, is different from Slokevage's trade dress because the *Wal-Mart* trade dress implicated the overall appearance of the product and was a theme made up of many unique elements. Slokevage argues that her trade dress, in contrast, involves one component of a product design, which can be used with a variety of types of clothing. Slokevage further asserts that her trade dress is located

---

1. Pursuant to section 23 of the Lanham Act, the United States Patent and Trademark Office ("PTO") maintains a Supplemental Register for marks "capable of distinguishing applicant's goods or services and not registrable on the principal register." 15 U.S.C. §1091(a).

on the rear hips of garments, which is a location that consumers frequently recognize as identifying the source of the garment.

The PTO responds that the Board correctly concluded that Slokevage's trade dress is product design and that it properly relied on *Wal-Mart* for support of its determination. According to the PTO, in the *Wal-Mart* decision the Supreme Court determined that a design of clothing is product design. The PTO further asserts that the trade dress at issue in *Wal-Mart*, which was classified as product design, is similar to Slokevage's trade dress. The trade dress in *Wal-Mart* consists of design elements on a line of garments, and Slokevage's trade dress similarly consists of a design component common to the overall design of a variety of garments. The PTO notes that Slokevage's trade dress application refers to her trade dress as a "configuration" including a "clothing feature," and that "product configuration" is synonymous with "product design." The PTO also argues that under *Wal-Mart* product design cannot be inherently distinctive, the rationale being that consumers perceive product design as making the product more useful or desirable, rather than indicating source. According to the PTO, the trade dress at issue here makes the product more desirable to consumers, rather than indicates source. Finally, the PTO notes that even if it were a close case as to whether Slokevage's trade dress constitutes product design, the Court's opinion in *Wal-Mart* states that in "close cases," trade dress should be categorized as product design, thereby requiring proof of acquired distinctiveness for protection. 529 U.S. at 215.

We agree with the Board that Slokevage's trade dress constitutes product design and therefore cannot be inherently distinctive. . . .

Although the decision in *Wal-Mart* does not expressly address the issue of what constitutes product design, it is informative to this case because it provides examples of trade dress that are product design. The Court observed that a "cocktail shaker shaped like a penguin" is product design and that the trade dress at issue in that case, "a line of spring/summer one-piece seersucker outfits decorated with appliques of hearts, flowers, fruits, and the like" is product design. *Wal-Mart*, 529 U.S. at 207, 213. These examples demonstrate that product design can consist of design features incorporated into a product. Slokevage urges that her trade dress is not product design because it does not alter the entire product but is more akin to a label being placed on a garment. We do not agree. The holes and flaps portion are part of the design of the clothing—the cut-out area is not merely a design placed on top of a garment, but is a design incorporated into the garment itself. Moreover, while Slokevage urges that product design trade dress must implicate the entire product, we do not find support for that proposition. Just as the product design in *Wal-Mart* consisted of certain design features featured on clothing, Slokevage's trade dress similarly consists of design features, holes and flaps, featured in clothing, revealing the similarity between the two types of design.

In addition, the reasoning behind the Supreme Court's determination that product design cannot be inherently distinctive is also instructive to our case. The Court reasoned that, unlike a trademark whose "predominant function" remains source identification, product design often serves other functions, such as rendering the "product itself more useful or more appealing." *Wal-Mart*, 529 U.S. at 212, 213. The design at issue here can serve such utilitarian and aesthetic functions. For example, consumers may purchase Slokevage's clothing for the utilitarian purpose of wearing a garment or because they find the appearance of the garment particularly desirable. Consistent with the Supreme Court's analysis in *Wal-Mart*, in such cases when the purchase implicates a utilitarian or aesthetic purpose, rather than a source-identifying function, it is appropriate to require proof of acquired distinctiveness.

Finally, the Court in *Wal-Mart* provided guidance on how to address trade dress cases that may be difficult to classify: "To the extent that there are close cases, we believe that courts should err on the side of caution and classify ambiguous trade dress as product design, thereby requiring secondary meaning." 529 U.S. at 215. Even if this were a close case, therefore, we must follow that precedent and classify the trade dress as product design. We thus agree with the Board that Slokevage's trade dress is product design and therefore that she must prove acquired distinctiveness in order for her trade dress mark to be registered.

[*Affirmed.*]

YANKEE CANDLE COMPANY, INC. v. BRIDGEWATER CANDLE COMPANY, LLC

259 F.3d 25 (1st Cir. 2001)

Torruelia, Circuit Judge:

[Yankee Candle Company ("Yankee"), a leading manufacturer of scented candles, sued competitor Bridgewater Candle Company ("Bridgewater") on counts of, *inter alia*, copyright infringement and trade dress infringement under Section 43(a) of the Lanham Act. The district court granted summary judgment to Bridgewater on both claims. The court of appeals affirmed the district court's judgment with respect to the copyright claim and proceeded to consider the trade dress claim.

The district court had identified three ways in which Yankee claimed that Bridgewater had infringed its trade dress: (i) by copying Yankee's method of shelving and displaying candles in its stores, called the "Vertical Display System"; (ii) by copying the overall "look and feel" of Yankee's Housewarmer line of candles; and (iii) by copying the design of Yankee's merchandise catalog, specifically its one-fragrance-per-page layout.]

On appeal, Yankee argues that the district court erred in several ways. First, Yankee contends that the district court ignored its "combination" claim defining its trade dress as the *combination* of its Housewarmer series of labels, its choice of candle sizes and styles, its Vertical Design System, and its catalog layout. By disaggregating the features of its trade dress, says Yankee, the district court failed to analyze the "look and feel" of the entire Yankee product. Second, Yankee argues that the district court erroneously defined its trade dress as product design/configuration, and in so doing, proceeded directly to the question of secondary meaning without considering that the dress might be inherently distinctive. Third, Yankee argues that it introduced sufficient evidence of secondary meaning to survive summary judgment. . . . Although we agree with Yankee that the district court failed to address its combination claim as such and we entertain the possibility that the court incorrectly analyzed Yankee's claims under a product design/configuration rubric, we ultimately reach the same conclusion as the district court and affirm the grant of summary judgment, albeit using a different analysis. [cit.]

1. Yankee's Trade Dress

We begin by sketching Yankee's claimed trade dress, which we read on appeal as defined in two possible ways. First, Yankee suggests that its trade dress is a combination of: (i) the Vertical Display System; (ii) the catalog, with an emphasis on its "one fragrance per page" layout; (iii) its candle shapes and sizes; (iv) the quantities of candles it sells as a unit; and (v) the Housewarmer labels, specifically their inclusion of (a) a full-bleed photograph, (b) a superimposed title plate with gold edging and lettering on a white background, (c) a rectangular shape, and (d) a reflective border.[9] Alternatively, Yankee describes its trade dress as the elements common to its Housewarmer labels. . . .

2.   INHERENT DISTINCTIVENESS

a.   *The Combination Claim*

Yankee argues that the distinct combination of elements comprising its candle sizes and shapes, quantities sold, labels, Vertical Design System, and catalog stem from "arbitrary" choices and are thus "inherently distinctive" and entitled to trademark protection. *See Two Pesos*, 505 U.S. at 768 (inherently distinctive marks are entitled to protection). Certain types of trade dress, however, can never be inherently distinctive. *Wal-Mart*, 529 U.S. at 212-14 (product design/configuration cannot be inherently distinctive); *Qualitex Co. v. Jacobson Prods. Co.*, 514 U.S. 159, 162 (1995) (color cannot be inherently distinctive). We find that Yankee's combination claim falls under the category of product design/configuration, and thus Yankee must prove that the dress has attained secondary meaning in order for it to be protected under the Lanham Act. *Wal-Mart*, 529 U.S. at 215.

Yankee argues that because its products are candles, all the trappings associated with the sale of the candle—i.e., the candle-holders, the Vertical Display System, the labels, and the catalog—constitute product packaging, or at the very least a "*tertium quid* . . . akin to product packaging," categories of trade dress that may be inherently distinctive. *See Wal-Mart*, 529 U.S. at 215 (citing *Two Pesos*, 505 U.S. at 773).

Although, as we explain below, Yankee's Housewarmer *labels* are product packaging and thus may be inherently distinctive, when combined with actual candle features, candle containers, the catalog,[10] and the in-store display system, the claim is no longer clearly a product-packaging one. Nor can the claim be categorized as product design/configuration, as that term has generally been defined to be limited to features inherent to the actual physical product: here, the candles. *See Wal-Mart*, 529 U.S. at 212 (describing cocktail shaker shaped as penguin as a product design); *Lund*, 163 F.3d at 34-36 (kitchen faucets). We also do not see this claim as akin to the restaurant decor upheld as potentially inherently distinctive in *Two Pesos*, which the Supreme Court later described as a "*tertium quid* that is akin to product packaging." *Wal-Mart*, 529 U.S. at 215; [cit.] Yankee has not made a claim as to the overall appearance of an entire store, but has instead isolated certain characteristics of its candle display in stores. This strikes us as far closer to the design/configuration category.

---

9. We note that Yankee has not been entirely consistent in its definition of its trade dress in its appellate brief. At times, it appears that Yankee is arguing that individual *features* of its product line, namely its labels, its catalogues and its Vertical Display System, deserve trade dress protection. This was the analysis undertaken by the district court. At other points, however, Yankee disclaims such an approach. We note that the burden to clearly identify the trade dress at issue is on the plaintiff. *See, e.g., Landscape Forms v. Columbia Cascade Co.*, 113 F.3d 373, 381 (2d Cir. 1997). Moreover, at least one federal court has previously criticized Yankee for failing in this regard. *Yankee Candle Co. v. New England Candle Co.*, 14 F. Supp. 2d 154, 162 (D. Mass. 1998), *vacated pursuant to settlement*, 29 F. Supp. 2d 44 (D. Mass. 1998). After a careful review of the record, we conclude that Yankee has been sufficiently consistent as to these two descriptions of its trade dress for us to evaluate them on appeal.

10. We note that we are troubled by the inclusion of Yankee's catalog in its combination trade dress claim. A combination trade dress claim is one that includes a number of different features of a product or its packaging which, *taken together*, are potentially indicative of source. In this case, although the candles, their labels, and the Vertical Display System are all seen at the same time, the catalog is a separate item mailed to consumers at their homes. . . . At any rate, because we conclude that Yankee must establish that its combination has acquired secondary meaning, and has not in fact done so, whether the catalog is included or not in the combination claim is ultimately irrelevant.

The fact that Yankee points to particular aspects of the candles themselves, namely their shapes and sizes, only confirms our categorization.

In *Wal-Mart*, the Supreme Court instructed us how to deal with claims that were at the margin of product design/configuration: "To the extent that there are close cases, we believe that courts should err on the side of caution and classify ambiguous trade dress as product design, thereby requiring secondary meaning." 529 U.S. at 215. We follow that advice here. To prevail on its combination claim, Yankee must show that its trade dress has acquired secondary meaning.

b.   Labels

Yankee also claims that unique features of its Housewarmer labels constitute an inherently distinctive trade dress. The district court found that the labels were also product configuration/design, and thus could not be inherently distinctive as a matter of law. We disagree. Detachable labels are a classic case of product packaging, and therefore may be inherently distinctive. *See, e.g., Fun-Damental Too*, 111 F.3d at 1000-01. Although the district court did not determine whether the Housewarmer labels were inherently distinctive, we are convinced that the label elements highlighted by Yankee do not meet the inherent distinctiveness test of *Abercrombie & Fitch Co. v. Hunting World, Inc.*, 537 F.2d 4 (2d Cir. 1976). We therefore uphold the district court's grant of summary judgment on this basis.

[B]ecause the *Abercrombie* test was first applied to word marks, [cit.,] it may be difficult to apply to visual marks or trade dress, *Lund*, 163 F.3d at 39. The Supreme Court, however, has endorsed the use of the *Abercrombie* test in the evaluation of visual marks, as well as in the assessment of product packaging trade dress claims. *Id.* (citing *Two Pesos*, 505 U.S. at 768-69).

This Court, however, has noted that "[w]e do not believe that the Supreme Court's endorsement of the *Abercrombie* test in *Two Pesos* requires a strict application of the *Abercrombie* test in all contexts. . . ." *Id.* at 40. Instead, we have found it appropriate to supplement the somewhat bare-boned *Abercrombie* categories with the questions asked in *Seabrook Foods, Inc. v. Bar-Well Foods Ltd.*, 568 F.2d 1342 (C.C.P.A. 1977). In *Seabrook*, inherent distinctiveness was determined by reference to: (i) whether the design was a common or basic one; (ii) whether it was "unique or unusual" in the field; (iii) whether it was a refinement of a common form of ornamentation; and (iv) "whether it was capable of creating a commercial impression distinct from the accompanying words."[11] *Wiley v. Am. Greetings Corp.*, 762 F.2d 139, 141 (1st Cir. 1985) (quoting *Seabrook*, 568 F.2d at 1344). "In reality [the question is] whether the [dress] is so unique, unusual or unexpected in this market that it will automatically be perceived by customers as an indicator of origin." *Lund*, 163 F.3d at 40 (citing 1 J. McCarthy, *McCarthy on Trademarks and Unfair Competition* §8.13 (4th ed. 1996)); *see also McKernan v. Burek*, 118 F. Supp. 2d 119, 124 (D. Mass. 2000) (describing this question as the "*Lund* test" for inherent distinctiveness).

Furthermore, in evaluating the inherent distinctiveness of Yankee's packaging, we must consider the fact that although Yankee's Housewarmer labels have obvious similarities, they also differ significantly from one another, in that they necessarily display different pictures corresponding to their particular candle fragrance. In other words, Yankee seeks to protect features common to a set of labels, as opposed to a specific label common to a host of Yankee goods. A trade dress plaintiff seeking to protect a series or line of products faces

---

11. We note that other circuits may be less willing to apply this "gloss" on the *Abercrombie* test when product packaging is at issue. For example, despite noting that "[w]e are not so confident that the *Abercrombie* analysis is more naturally fit for product packaging cases" than is a *Seabrook*-like test, the Second Circuit has resisted the temptation to refine the *Abercrombie* test for visual marks or trade dress. *Landscape Forms*, 113 F.3d at 379.

a particularly difficult challenge, as it must show that the appearance of the several products is "sufficiently distinct and unique to merit protection." *Landscape Forms*, 113 F.3d at 380; *Jeffrey Milstein, Inc. v. Greger, Lawlor, Roth, Inc.*, 58 F.3d 27, 32-33 (2d Cir. 1995). Moreover, trade dress claims across a line of products present special concerns in their ability to artificially limit competition, as such claims are generally broader in scope than claims relating to an individual item. *Landscape Forms*, 113 F.3d at 381.

Yankee has focused on the "arbitrary" choices it made in designing its label, and has for this reason introduced into evidence numerous possibilities of alternative label designs. While we appreciate that there are many different potential ways of creating a candle label, we think Yankee's approach ignores the focus of the inherent distinctiveness inquiry. . . . Yankee's label is essentially a combination of functional and common features. *See Pubs. Int'l*, 164 F.3d at 341 (gold coloring is a prime example of aesthetic functionality, because it connotes opulence). Although such a combination may be entitled to protection where secondary meaning is shown, *Lund*, 163 F.3d at 37, it is less likely to qualify as inherently distinctive, *Jeffrey Milstein*, 58 F.3d at 32. While the particular combination of common features may indeed be "arbitrary," we do not think that any reasonable juror could conclude that these elements are so "unique and unusual" that they are source-indicative in the absence of secondary meaning. *Lund*, 163 F.3d at 40.

3. SECONDARY MEANING

Having concluded that neither trade dress claim made by Yankee qualifies for protection based on its inherent distinctiveness, we next address whether Yankee has introduced sufficient evidence to survive summary judgment on the question of secondary meaning. As evidence of secondary meaning,[12] Yankee points to: (i) its advertising campaign featuring pictures of its products with the claimed trade dress; (ii) its continuous and virtually exclusive use of its trade dress since 1995; (iii) its high sales figures for Housewarmer candles; (iv) evidence from Bridgewater's files indicating that retailers identify a resemblance between Bridgewater's styles and Yankee's; (v) testimony by a Bridgewater's sales agent as to the distinctiveness of the Yankee trade dress; (vi) testimony by Bridgewater and Yankee employees as to the distinctiveness of Yankee's claimed trade dress; (vii) evidence of actual consumer confusion between Bridgewater and Yankee products; and (viii) evidence of intentional copying by Bridgewater.

This Court has said that "[p]roof of secondary meaning entails vigorous evidentiary requirements." [cit.] The only direct evidence probative of secondary meaning is consumer surveys and testimony by individual consumers. *Id*. Although survey evidence is not required, "it is a valuable method of showing secondary meaning." *Lund*, 163 F.3d at 42. Yankee has introduced no survey evidence here.[13] Yankee also cites no evidence that individual consumers associate the particular features at issue with Yankee.[14]

---

12. With respect to the question of secondary meaning, Yankee does not clearly distinguish the evidentiary support for its label claim from that supporting its combination claim. For purposes of this analysis, we assume that the adduced evidence may be relevant to both aspects of its claimed trade dress. We note, however, that secondary meaning faces a higher threshold in a product design/configuration case. *See Lund*, 163 F.3d at 42; *Duraco*, 40 F.3d at 1435.

13. Yankee has cited surveys, taken by Bridgewater, indicating that Bridgewater's trade dress is substantially similar to Yankee's. Although this evidence, if admissible, would be probative of a likelihood of confusion, it does not indicate that Yankee's trade dress has acquired secondary meaning.

14. The evidence that Yankee's retailers and distributors viewed the trade dress as distinctive is not probative of secondary meaning. "[S]econdary meaning occurs when 'the primary significance [of the trade dress] *in the minds of the consuming public* is not the product but the producer.'" *Lund*, 163 F.3d at 42 (quoting *Kellogg v. Nat'l Biscuit Co.*, 305 U.S. 111 (1938)) (emphasis added). The opinions of retailers and distributors active in the scented candle field and extremely familiar with Yankee products [are] hardly evidence of whether the "consuming public" forms the same association.

Secondary meaning may also be proven through circumstantial evidence, specifically the length and manner of the use of the trade dress, the nature and extent of advertising and promotion of the trade dress, and the efforts made to promote a conscious connection by the public between the trade dress and the product's source. *See Boston Beer*, 9 F.3d at 182. Other factors may include the product's "established place in the market" and proof of intentional copying. *Lund*, 163 F.3d at 42. Yankee has introduced substantial evidence that the Housewarmer line of candles and corresponding display have been in circulation since 1995, that Yankee spends significant resources advertising its Housewarmer line, and that sales of Housewarmer candles have been extremely successful. However, in concluding that Yankee had not made a sufficient evidentiary showing of secondary meaning, the district court focused on the lack of evidence as to advertising of the *specific* trade dress claimed, as well as the lack of evidence demonstrating a conscious connection by the public between the claimed trade dress and the product's source.

We believe the district court emphasized the relevant issues in conducting its analysis of secondary meaning. Proof of secondary meaning requires at least *some* evidence that consumers associate the trade dress with the source. Although evidence of the pervasiveness of the trade dress may support the conclusion that a mark has acquired secondary meaning, it cannot stand alone. To find otherwise would provide trade dress protection for any successful product, or for the packaging of any successful product. *See Seabrook*, 568 F.2d at 1344 (evidence of sales volume may be relevant to secondary meaning, but "is not necessarily indicative"). Such an open standard hardly comports with the "vigorous" evidentiary showing required by this Court, nor does it comport with the purposes of trade dress protection, namely "to protect that which identifies a product's source." *Lund*, 163 F.3d at 35. In the absence of *any* evidence that the claimed trade dress actually *does* identify a product's source, the trade dress should not be entitled to protection.

That being said, Yankee argues that, because its advertising contained pictures of its products incorporating the claimed trade dress, it was the type of "look-for" advertising that can, on its own, support a finding of secondary meaning *See First Brands Corp. v. Fred Meyer, Inc.*, 809 F.2d 1378, 1383 (9th Cir. 1987). "Look-for" advertising is such that "encourages consumers to identify the claimed trade dress with the particular producer." *Thomas & Betts Corp. v. Panduit Corp.*, 65 F.3d 654, 662 (7th Cir. 1995). In other words, it is advertising that specifically directs a consumer's attention to a particular aspect of the product. To be probative of secondary meaning, the advertising must direct the consumer to those features claimed as trade dress. *Id.* Merely "featuring" the relevant aspect of the product in advertising is no more probative of secondary meaning than are strong sales; again, to provide protection based on extensive advertising would extend trade dress protection to the label (or to the combination claim) without any showing that the consumer associated the dress with the product's source. [cit.] The district court found that Yankee's advertising did not emphasize any particular element of its trade dress, and thus could not be probative of secondary meaning. We agree.

We also do not find Yankee's evidence of intentional copying probative of secondary meaning. First, to the extent Yankee seeks to use such evidence as secondary meaning of its *combination* trade dress, intent plays a particularly minor role in product design/configuration cases. *See, e.g., Duraco*, 40 F.3d at 1453 ("[A]ttempts to copy a product configuration [may] not be probative [because] the copier may very well be exploiting a particularly desirable feature, rather than seeking to confuse consumers as to the source of the product."). Given the highly functional nature of certain elements of Yankee's claimed combination trade dress, the concern that protection could prevent healthy competition in the scented candle field weighs heavily in this case.

The testimony that Bridgewater designers were, at times, told to make the labels look more like Yankee's is more troubling. *See Blau Plumbing, Inc. v. S.O.S. Fix-it, Inc.*, 781 F.2d 604, 611 (7th Cir. 1986) (defendant's belief that trade dress has acquired secondary meaning provides some evidence that it actually has acquired secondary meaning). However, the relevant intent is not just the intent to copy, but to "pass off" one's goods as those of another. *Id.* Given that Bridgewater prominently displayed its trade name on its candles, we do not think that the evidence of copying was sufficiently probative of secondary meaning.

In sum, Yankee has not introduced any of the direct evidence—surveys or consumer testimony—traditionally used to establish secondary meaning. Although it has introduced some of the circumstantial evidence often used to support such a finding, the lack of any evidence that actual consumers associated the claimed trade dress with Yankee, as well as the lack of evidence as to confusion on the part of actual consumers, renders this circumstantial evidence insufficient for a reasonable juror to find that the trade dress had acquired a secondary meaning. Yankee has not made the vigorous evidentiary showing required by this Court. The grant of summary judgment on Yankee's Lanham Act claim is affirmed.

NOTES AND QUESTIONS

1. *Definition of trade dress.* As the *Yankee Candle* court notes, modern courts may require careful (and consistent) definition of what plaintiffs claim as trade dress. Most trade dress cases are litigated under Section 43(a), so there is rarely a registration record to assist; most definitions are crafted in litigation. Although the court concludes, *see* n.10, that the definition is sufficiently consistent to be evaluated, the closeness of that question does still affect the court's analysis. In what way? For a discussion of the interests served by requiring specificity in trade dress definition, *see New Colt*, 312 F. Supp. 2d at 203-04 (citing *Yurman Design, Inc. v. PAJ, Inc.*, 262 F.3d 101, 117 (2d Cir. 2001)). Are there any dangers in requiring that a complaint provide a written description of the claimed trade dress, rather than relying on visual representation? *See id.* If the trade dress is defined during the course of the litigation, when precisely must the plaintiff offer a definition? *Cf. Maharishi Hardy Blechman Ltd. v. Abercrombie & Fitch Co.*, 292 F. Supp. 2d 535, 545-46 (S.D.N.Y. 2003). What advantages does this "claiming practice" offer over regimes such as design patent, where the patentee must include in its application drawings that effectively define the property right? Are there ways of controlling any potential for abuse that "late claiming" opens up? *See* Jeanne C. Fromer and Mark P. McKenna, *Claiming Design*, 167 U. Pa. L. Rev. __ (2018) (forthcoming). (You might consider by way of comparison how a design patentee might seek to expand the scope of the property right it defined during the application process. *See generally* Graeme B. Dinwoodie, Mark D. Janis and Jason Dumont, Trade Dress and Design Law (2d ed. 2018).)

2. *Family trade dress.* Courts are becoming particularly strict in their recognition of what is called "family trade dress," meaning a line of products with identical source-identifying design features. Indeed, in *Rose Art Indus., Inc. v. Swanson*, 235 F.3d 165, 173 (3d Cir. 2000), the Court of Appeals for the Third Circuit held that when the plaintiff in a trade dress action seeks protection under the Lanham Act for a series or line of products or packaging:

> [W]e will require [a] more stringent test before the non-functionality/distinctiveness/likelihood of confusion test is applied. A plaintiff, seeking protection for a series or line of products, must first demonstrate that the series or line has a recognizable and consistent overall look. Only after the plaintiff has established the existence of recognizable trade dress for the line or series of products should the trial court determine whether the trade dress is distinctive,

whether the trade dress is nonfunctional, and whether the defendant's use of plaintiff's trade dress is likely to cause consumer confusion.

What is the purpose of this additional threshold requirement? What is a "consistent overall look"? How many products should be considered in determining whether such a look exists? *See Keurig v. Strum Foods*, 769 F. Supp. 2d 699 (D. Del. 2011) (dismissing trade dress claim for failure to show a consistent overall look on packaging of single-serve coffee cartridges).

    3. *Strategic definition of trade dress.* Why might a plaintiff seek to define its trade dress broadly? What would be the advantages of a plaintiff defining its trade dress more narrowly?

    4. *The design/packaging line.* The *Yankee Candle* court defines product design cases as involving "features inherent to the actual physical product." Is this a workable definition? The court also suggests that "certain characteristics of [the] candle display in stores" may be closer to the design category than "the overall appearance of an entire store." Why might this be so? And, in classifying the labels as packaging, the court states that "detachable labels are a classic case of product packaging, and therefore may be inherently distinctive." Might there be a distinction between detachable and nondetachable labels? Between nondetachable labels and designs etched into the candles?

    5. *Determining distinctiveness.* In making its case for inherent distinctiveness, Yankee Candle emphasized the "arbitrary choices" that it made in designing its label and the fact that numerous alternative design possibilities existed. The court seemed unimpressed. Should these considerations be relevant? As regards its secondary meaning arguments, the court noted that a plaintiff relying on proving "secondary meaning faces a higher threshold in a product design/configuration case." This proposition has support in modern case law. Why might this be so? *See* Ingrida Karins Berzins, *Comment: The Emerging Circuit Split over Secondary Meaning in Trade Dress Law*, 152 U. PA. L. REV. 1661 (2004). Some courts still place great weight on intentional copying, even in product design cases where alternative explanations of copying are more likely. *See, e.g., Leviton Mfg. Co. v. Universal Sec. Instruments, Inc.*, 304 F. Supp. 2d 726 (D. Md. 2004). Despite this, one commentator noted that immediately post–*Wal-Mart*, "[i]n all the cases where secondary meaning [of a design] was found, the product designs in question had been in use for years, if not decades. . . ." Berzins, *supra*, at 1673. If this assessment is correct, has the *Wal-Mart* opinion had the effect that the Supreme Court sought? What about color combinations? Consider your university's school colors. How easy would it be for the university to show that those colors had acquired distinctiveness? *See Bd. of Supervisors for Louisiana State Univ. Agric. & Med. Coll. v. Smack Apparel Co.*, 550 F.3d 465 (5th Cir. 2008) ("We think this desire by consumers to associate with a particular university supports the conclusion that team colors and logos are, in the minds of the fans and other consumers, source indicators of team-related apparel. By associating the color and other indicia with the university, the fans perceive the university as the source or sponsor of the goods because they want to associate with that source.").

    6. *Limping trademarks.* More generally, how should the presence of a word mark on a product (whether on a label or etched into the product) affect a court's analysis of the distinctiveness of the design of that product? *Cf. E.T. Browne Drug Co. v. Cococare Prods., Inc.*, 538 F.3d 185, 200 (3d Cir. 2008); *Philips Elec. BV v. Remington Consumer Prods.*, [1998] RPC 283 (Ch. D. 1997) (Jacob, J.) (UK) (commenting that the product design mark for which the plaintiff (Philips) sought protection "has never been used by Philips as the sole means of identification of trade source. It has never been trusted by Philips to do this job on its own, a matter plainly relevant in considering acquired distinctiveness. It is at best a 'limping trade mark,' needing the crutch of [the word mark] 'Philishave'").

7. *Trade dress and services?* How would the mark depicted below for "adult enter-tainment services, namely exotic dancing for women," fare under the *Seabrook* test? *See In re Chippendales*, 622 F.3d 1346 (Fed. Cir. 2010).

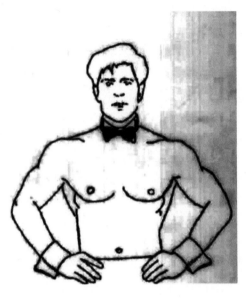

Can any costume be inherently distinctive of a service? In *In re Frankish Enters Ltd.*, 113 U.S.P.Q.2d 1964 (TTAB 2015), the Trademark Trial and Appeal Board held that "while trade dress in the nature of product design can never be inherently distinctive, prod-uct packaging trade dress and trade dress for services can be inherently distinctive." For the proposition that service trade dress can be inherently distinctive, the Board in *Frankish* cited *Two Pesos* (and *Chippendales*). Do you think that properly reads *Wal-Mart?*

The Board then applied *Seabrook* to find the image below of a monster truck inher-ently distinctive of "entertainment services in the nature of monster truck exhibitions":

The Board stressed that "applicant does not seek registration of its design for a *product*, it seeks registration of its 'fanciful, prehistoric animal' design for its monster truck exhibition *services*, and under *Two Pesos*, trade dress for services may be inherently distinctive." Are you persuaded by this distinction? Does it present any dangers? If a competitor manufactured trucks bearing the same design, could the applicant bring an infringement claim? You should reconsider this question after reading the materials in Chapter 7.

PROBLEM 2-4: CHEERIOS

General Mills filed an application to register the proposed mark shown below for "Toroidal-shaped, oat-based breakfast cereal":

The application stated that "The mark consists of the color yellow appearing as the predominant uniform background color on product packaging for the goods. The dotted outline of the packaging shows the position of the mark and is not claimed as part of the mark."

A specimen of the use of the proposed mark, submitted with the application, is shown below:

General Mills offers CHEERIOS brand cereal in a variety of flavors, not all of which are packaged in yellow.

General Mills argued that the purchasing public recognizes the color yellow on packages of toroidal (ring or doughnut-shaped) oat-based breakfast cereal as an indication that Applicant is the source of the cereal.

General Mills had sold CHEERIOS (originally called CHEERIOATS) since 1941 and has prominently featured the color yellow on the front of its boxes since the 1940s. At least as early as 1944, the color yellow also began to appear prominently on the back of the box and on other panels of the box. Although many variations of the artwork on the box appeared over the years, the overall trade dress of the box has been relatively consistent since the 1940s. Among the most consistent features has been prominent use of the word mark "Cheerios" (or "Cheerioats") displayed at the top of the front panel in a black, initial-capital typeface that is quite similar to today's typeface. Another relatively consistent feature is a photograph of a bowl of cereal occupying the center of the front panel.

In General Mills' print and television advertisements, the color yellow is noticeably featured not only on the cereal box but on backgrounds, props, clothing worn by actors and models, and in other ways. Television advertisements from 1994, 1995, and 1997 featured a musical jingle beginning with the words, "It's the big yellow box that everyone knows . . ." and ending with the tag line, "The one and only CHEERIOS." In a television spot of 1991, an actor refers nostalgically to "that yellow box."

General Mills' expert conducted a survey. The survey was administered by means of computer. Subjects were shown the image below and were told it was a "cereal box" and that "This box has been altered by removing the cereal brand name, logo, package images, and other package texts from the box."

Subjects were asked the following question ("Question 1"): "If you think you know, what brand of cereal comes in this box?" The question was formatted as shown below:

If you think you know, what brand of cereal comes in this box?

I don't know

On successive screens, subjects were asked the following questions:

What, in particular, makes you think the brand is "[Response to Q1]"?
Why do you think that? Anything else?
What is it about the cereal box that makes you associate it with "[Response to Q1]"?
Anything else?

The expert concluded that 48.3 percent of respondents associated the yellow box with the CHEERIOS brand. Nearly all respondents who made the association stated that the yellow color of the box was the reason for their response.

At least twenty-three cereal products are offered in packaging similar in color to that of CHEERIOS, including by major competitors of General Mills, although some of these are no longer on the U.S. market. These include the following:

The Examining Attorney argued that the proposed mark failed to function as a trademark because purchasers will perceive the color yellow merely as a decorative feature of the packaging for the goods, as they are accustomed to encountering cereal packages—even those for toroidal-shaped oat-based cereals—in a variety of colors, including yellow. According to the Examining Attorney, the variety of colors on cereal boxes preconditions a consumer into believing that the applied-for color (like other colors) serves primarily as a form of decoration (i.e., it has a primary purpose other than to indicate the source of the goods).

Do you agree? What weight would you give to the survey? What is the relevance of the nature of the packaging in which CHEERIOS are sold? What is the relevance of the competing cereal products? What weight would you give to the advertising (on which General Mills has spent millions of dollars)? What more might you want to know?

E.   THE EDGE OF TRADEMARK PROTECTION: SUBJECT-MATTER EXCLUSIONS?

The line of Supreme Court case law that we have discussed thus far in this chapter, and the *Qualitex* decision in particular, would appear to have rejected the notion that only certain types of subject matter can act and be protected as a trademark. "Almost anything is capable of carrying meaning," and thus acting as a trademark, according to *Qualitex*. To be sure, the *Wal-Mart* Court in particular suggests that we might analyze certain subject matter under different sets of rules. We might, for example, impose on color per se or product design a secondary meaning requirement. And, as you read the materials in the rest of this book, you should be alert to the possibility that other rules of trademark law might expressly or implicitly (on their face, or as applied) discriminate between different types of subject matter. (In Chapter 3, we will separately address the nonfunctionality requirement, which most acutely affects product designs.) But the basic proposition appears supported by what we have read thus far: Almost anything can be a trademark. This raises at least two questions. First, is this statement descriptively accurate? Do you believe that all subject matter can convey *trademark* meaning? Second, even if this is so, might there be countervailing policies that warrant excluding certain subject matter from being potential trademark subject matter? We address both topics in this concluding part of Chapter 2. Answering these two questions might also require us to confront a question raised in Chapter 1, namely whether trademark law should be proactive or reactive in determining what it should protect.

1.   Exotic Source-Identifiers

IN RE CLARKE
17 U.S.P.Q.2d (BNA) 1238 (TTAB 1990)

SIMMS, Board Member:

Applicant, Celia Clarke, doing business as Clarke's OSEWEZ, has appealed from the final refusal of the Trademark Examining Attorney to register applicant's asserted mark for "sewing thread and embroidery yarn." Applicant has described her mark in the "drawing" filed with her application as follows: "The mark is a high impact, fresh, floral fragrance reminiscent of Plumeria blossoms."

The Examining Attorney has refused registration on the ground that applicant's asserted mark does not function as a trademark because it does not identify or distinguish applicant's goods from those of others. In the initial refusal, the Examining Attorney observed that applicant's fragrance mark is analogous to other forms of product ornamentation in that it is not the type of matter which consumers would tend to perceive as an indication of origin. The Examining Attorney also refused registration on the basis that applicant's alleged mark was de jure functional, assertedly because of the competitive need for free access to pleasant scents or fragrances. In his appeal brief, the Examining Attorney withdrew the de jure functionality refusal.

In support of her attempt to register this fragrance mark, counsel for applicant submitted a declaration of applicant attesting to the fact that, to the best of her knowledge, no other company has ever offered any scented embroidery yarn or thread; that she has placed advertisements stressing the fact that her company is the source of sweet-scented embroidery products, known in the trade as Russian embroidery or punch embroidery; and that due to the success of her products, applicant is now a major source of yarn and thread and supplies dealers and distributors throughout the United States. Applicant also states that her company has received a great number of favorable and positive responses to her unique product and that, to the best of her knowledge, customers, dealers and distributors throughout the embroidery field recognize applicant as the source of scented embroidery yarn and thread. While maintaining that her fragrance is registrable as a mark because it is inherently distinctive of yarns and threads, no other manufacturer having sold such goods, applicant nevertheless argues that she has presented sufficient evidence of recognition of her asserted mark. Applicant concludes:

> Others are free to adopt any other scent for their yarns and threads, including floral scents such as that of a lily of the valley, a carnation or a rose to give but three examples. Surely people have come [to] distinguish these floral scents from one another, just as they can distinguish the color pink (for fiberglass insulation) from other warm colors such as red, orange, and yellow. Just as the registration of the color pink for fiberglass insulation has been held to not present a significant obstacle for competitors wishing to produce fiberglass insulation, so does the applicant's particular fragrance not present a significant obstacle to competitors wishing to offer scented yarns.

Applicant has made of record a complete sealed kit containing scented yarn and thread for making a scented skunk.

Expressing unawareness of any precedent dealing with the registrability of an arbitrary, nonfunctional scent, the Examining Attorney states that the most closely analogous determinations appear to be those dealing with colors as trademarks. The Examining Attorney concedes that there is no inherent bar to the registrability of an arbitrary, nonfunctional scent or fragrance and that this record discloses that the scent applicant has added to her product is not a natural or inherent feature of the goods and does not provide any utilitarian advantage. The Examining Attorney adds that, presumably, if applicant's scent does function to indicate origin, potential consumers may readily be able to distinguish among the vast array of scents in identifying competing sources of goods.

In support of his argument that applicant's fragrance mark is not of a character usually recognized by potential consumers as an indication of origin, he requests the Board to take judicial notice of the fact that there are pleasant, arbitrary and nonfunctional scents in a wide variety of products, including cosmetics and cleaning products, which have the sole purpose of making the use of those products more pleasant or attractive. Therefore, while applicant is the only source of scented yarn and thread, the Examining Attorney argues that potential consumers are unlikely to regard scent in any product as an indication of exclusive origin in view of their conditioning in the consumer product marketplace. The rarity of usage of fragrance as a feature of applicant's goods weighs against registration, according to the Examining Attorney. Rather, it is much more likely that consumers will regard the scent as a pleasant feature of the goods.

While the Examining Attorney concedes that the asserted fragrance may be registrable upon a convincing showing of trademark function, he maintains that applicant has not specifically promoted the *particular* scent as an indication of origin. Applicant's advertising makes reference to "Clarke's Distinctive Soft-Scented Yarns," but no reference is made to a specific fragrance. Nor does the advertising make any attempt, according to the Examining Attorney, to draw attention to the scent as an indicator of origin.

Upon careful review of this record, we believe that applicant has demonstrated that the scented fragrance does function as a trademark for her thread and embroidery yarn. Under the circumstances of this case, we see no reason why a fragrance is not capable of serving as a trademark to identify and distinguish a certain type of product. It is clear from the record that applicant is the only person who has marketed yarns and threads with a fragrance.[4] That is to say, fragrance is not an inherent attribute or natural characteristic of applicant's goods but is rather a feature supplied by applicant. Moreover, applicant has emphasized this characteristic of her goods in advertising, promoting the scented feature of her goods. Applicant has demonstrated that customers, dealers and distributors of her scented yarns and threads have come to recognize applicant as the source of these goods. In view of the unique nature of applicant's product, we do not believe that the failure of applicant to indicate in her promotional materials the specific scent or fragrance of her yarn (admittedly difficult to describe except in the manner that applicant has done so) is significant. In her advertisements and at craft fairs, applicant has promoted her products as having a scented nature. We believe that applicant has presented a prima facie case of distinctiveness of her fragrance mark. Compare *In re Star Pharmaceuticals, Inc.*, 225 USPQ 209 (TTAB 1985) (where applicant failed to demonstrate that the features (colors) sought to be registered had been promoted as a source indicator).

Decision: The refusal of registration is reversed.

NOTES AND QUESTIONS

1. *Sound marks.* General Electric Broadcasting Co., Inc. sought to register the following mark for radio broadcasting services:

> . . . a series of bells tolled during four hour sequences, beginning with one ring at approximately a first half hour and increasing in number by one ring at approximately each half hour thereafter.

What rule should apply to determine whether the mark is distinctive? Should the Trademark Office recognize inherent distinctiveness of sound marks? If so, what should be the test for inherent distinctiveness? *See In re General Elec. Broad. Co., Inc.*, 199 U.S.P.Q. (BNA) 560 (TTAB 1978); *Ride the Ducks, L.L.C. v. Duck Boat Tours, Inc.*, 75 U.S.P.Q.2d 1269 (E.D. Pa. 2005) (finding that a duck quacking sound used for amphibious sightseeing tours in Philadelphia was not inherently distinctive because it was a familiar noise, and that plaintiffs had shown insufficient evidence of secondary meaning). The Trademark Trial and Appeal

---

4. It should be noted that we are not here talking about the registrability of scents or fragrances of products which are noted for those features, such as perfumes, colognes or scented household products. Nor is this a case involving the question of descriptiveness of a term which identifies a particular fragrance of a product. In such cases it has been held that a term is unregistrable under Section 2(e)(1) of the Act if it merely describes an odor or other significant feature of the product. See *In re Gyulay* 820 F.2d 1216 (Fed. Cir. 1987) (APPLE PIE held merely descriptive since the term described the scent released by potpourri simmered in water.)

Board has held that the registration of sounds as trademarks for goods that make sound in their normal course of operation (such as alarms or telephones) is available only on a showing of secondary meaning. *See In re Vertex Grp. LLC*, 89 U.S.P.Q.2d (BNA) 1694 (TTAB 2009) (rejecting application for "a descending frequency sound pulse" for personal security alarms); *see also Nextel Commc'ns, Inc. v. Motorola Inc.*, 91 U.S.P.Q.2d (BNA) 1393 (TTAB 2009) (denying protection for cell phone "chirp"). The Board developed this formulation in trying to follow and adapt *Qualitex* and *Wal-Mart Stores* for "certain types of sound mark." *See Vertex*, 89 U.S.P.Q.2d at 1700. Should *Qualitex* and *Wal-Mart Stores* be limited to "certain types" of color marks or design marks?

   2.   *Comparative and international dimensions.* Article 15 of the TRIPS Agreement provides:

> Any sign, or any combination of signs, capable of distinguishing the goods or services of one undertaking from those of other undertakings, shall be capable of constituting a trademark. Such signs, in particular words including personal names, letters, numerals, figurative elements and combinations of colours as well as any combination of such signs, shall be eligible for registration as trademarks.

In some bilateral trade agreements, such as the U.S.-Korea agreement concluded in 2007, the United States has extracted an agreement from its trading partners that smell marks will be protectable trademark subject matter. In March 2012, the Canadian Intellectual Property Office reversed long-standing policy and began accepting registrations of sound marks. The decision was prompted by litigation involving the "Roaring Lion" sound mark used by Metro-Goldwyn-Mayer in its movies.

   3.   *Other exotic source-identifiers.* What limits should there be on what can act as a source-identifier and thus be protected as a trademark? What concerns or principles should guide the construction of limits? Consider whether the following symbols should be protected as trademarks. If not, why not?

- A video clip of a winged white horse resembling the mythic Pegasus, with wings flapping, for motion picture entertainment.
- The "gesture" of a consumer slapping his or her rear pocket, to signify the cost savings of shopping at a particular store, while speaking the words "That's ASDA price" (ASDA being the store in question).

Even if rights are recognized in exotic source-identifiers, proving a case for infringement and thus securing enforcement may present greater difficulties than with traditional marks. In light of these difficulties, do you agree with the observation by the *Qualitex* Court that obstacles like "shade confusion" (i.e., comparing the colors of the parties' products) should not preclude registration of nontraditional subject matter such as color per se as a trademark?

2.   Subject Matter Protected by Copyright

   As the subject matter of trademark protection has expanded, claims have increasingly been asserted that subject matter more traditionally the domain of copyright law (motion pictures, sound recordings, etc.) is acting as a trademark and should be protected under the Lanham Act against third-party uses. Sometimes these actions are brought under Section 43(a) of the Lanham Act and denominated as actions for unfair competition or "false endorsement" rather than for strict unregistered trademark infringement. We will examine the range of means for protecting trade identity (including claims under Section 43(a)) more fully in Chapter 11. However, these complaints often include an unregistered trademark claim or are framed in ways that resemble a trademark claim. And so we consider them here also.

At least three different scenarios might motivate a plaintiff to bring such a claim (regardless of how it is denominated). First, even if the plaintiff still owns copyright in the work in question, the scope of rights available under the Lanham Act differs from those under the Copyright Act and thus might potentially catch conduct permitted under the Copyright Act (e.g., because the Copyright Act contains an exemption that permits the defendant to do what it is doing). The trademark claim may also carry with it different remedies. Second, the plaintiff may not own the copyright in the work (if it ever did) either because of the copyright work-for-hire doctrine or because the copyright was transferred to another person. Third, copyright may not subsist in the work, because the work failed to meet the originality requirements of copyright law, because the term of copyright has expired, or because the work has fallen into the public domain because of failure to comply with formalities formerly imposed by U.S. copyright law (e.g., filing a renewal copyright application or attaching a copyright notice to published copies of the work). *See* Copyright Office Regulations, 37 C.F.R. § 202.1 (including as examples of works not subject to copyright "Words and short phrases such as names, titles, and slogans; familiar symbols or designs; mere variations of typographic ornamentation, lettering or coloring; mere listing of ingredients or contents").

OLIVEIRA v. FRITO-LAY, INC.

251 F.3d 56 (2d Cir. 2001)

Leval, Circuit Judge:

Astrud Oliveira, known professionally as Astrud Gilberto, appeals from the dismissal of her suit by the United States District Court for the Southern District of New York (Loretta A. Preska, *District Judge*). The defendants are Frito-Lay, Inc., a well-known seller of potato chips, and other entities engaged in the promotion of Frito-Lay products (collectively the "Defendants" or "Frito-Lay"). Among numerous claims, the complaint alleged that the defendants infringed her trademark rights under §43(a) of the Lanham Act by using a famous 1964 recording of Gilberto singing "The Girl from Ipanema" ("Ipanema") in a television commercial for Frito-Lay's baked potato chips [and engaged in trademark dilution under Section 43(c) by virtue of the same conduct]. . . . With respect to [the claim under Section 43(a)], the district court dismissed based on its conclusion that no reasonable jury could find that defendants' use of plaintiff's performance in their commercial implied an endorsement by plaintiff of Frito-Lay's potato chips. . . .

We affirm the dismissal of [that] Lanham Act claim for somewhat different reasons. . . .

BACKGROUND

1. Facts

In 1964, Gilberto recorded "Ipanema" accompanied by Stan Getz, on saxophone, and her then-husband, Joao Gilberto, on the guitar. The 1964 recording became world famous (the "1964 Recording").

In 1996, defendant Frito-Lay began to market "Baked Lays" Potato Crisps, a low-fat baked potato chip. It introduced the product with a thirty-second television advertisement created by its advertising agency, defendant BBDO Worldwide, Inc. The ad shows several famous models reclining by a swimming pool. The 1964 Recording of Ipanema plays in the background. . . .

"Ipanema" was written by Vinicius de Moraes and Antonio Carlos Jobim. Jobim registered the composition with the U.S. Copyright Office in 1963, and renewed the registration in 1991. Norman Gimbel composed the English lyrics for the song and registered a U.S. copyright for them in 1963, renewing in 1991. The 1964 recording at issue in this case was made for the recording company Verve, which is now a subsidiary of PolyGram Records, Inc. PolyGram Records claims to own the master of the recording. It distributes the recording, along with Gilberto's rendition of several other popular songs, on various albums and CDs under the Verve Records label.

In order to use the recording in the Baked Lays commercial, BBDO purchased the synchronization rights from Duchess Music Corporation on behalf of Jobim and Gimbel Music Group on behalf of Gimbel. BBDO also purchased a license to use the master recording from PolyGram Records. It paid more than $200,000 for the licenses. Apparently believing that Gilberto had retained no rights in the recording, BBDO did not seek her authorization to use it in the ad.

Gilberto was not involved in the production of the 1964 Recording other than as lead singer. She did not compose the music, write the lyrics, or produce the recording. According to her complaint, when recording the song, she did not sign any contract or release with the recording company or the producers; and she was not employed by them.

Gilberto received a Grammy award for the recording, which immediately became a smash hit and launched her now thirty-five year career in singing. She claims that as the result of the huge success of the 1964 Recording, and her frequent subsequent performances of "Ipanema," she has become known as The Girl from Ipanema and is identified by the public with the 1964 Recording. She claims as a result to have earned trademark rights in the 1964 Recording, which she contends the public recognizes as a mark designating her as a singer. She contends, therefore, that Frito-Lay could not lawfully use the 1964 Recording in an advertisement for its chips without her permission.

2. PROCEEDINGS BELOW

[The district court initially denied a motion to dismiss Gilberto's complaint of "false implied endorsement" under Section 43(a) of the Lanham Act because it was "not entirely implausible" that plaintiff could prove that the audience might interpret the inclusion of the 1964 Recording in the ad as implying Gilberto's endorsement of Baked Lays. However, the district court dismissed the dilution claim because, in the court's view, "there is no federal trademark protection for a musical work." Subsequently, defendants moved for summary judgment on the claim under Section 43(a) of the Lanham Act. In an opinion delivered from the bench on February 10, 2000, the district court granted the defendants' motion.]

DISCUSSION

On appeal, Gilberto challenges the dismissal of [*inter alia*] her claim for trademark infringement under the Lanham Act. . . .

1. LANHAM ACT

The district court granted summary judgment on Gilberto's Lanham Act claim on [the] ground [*inter alia* that] a factfinder could not reasonably find that the ad implied Gilberto's endorsement of Frito-Lay's product. . . .

To the extent Gilberto's claim depended on the theory of implied endorsement, we agree with the district court that a factfinder could not reasonably find an implied endorsement and affirm its judgment. Had Gilberto not amended the Lanham Act claim in her First Amended Complaint, which was captioned "False Implied Endorsement in Violation of 15 U.S.C. §1125(a)," and which seemed to rely solely on the implied endorsement theory, this reasoning might dispose of the Lanham Act claim. The Second Amended Complaint, however, broadened the Lanham Act claim. It expressly asserts that "Plaintiff's performance of her signature song . . . constitutes Plaintiff's unregistered trademark" and that the defendants' use of the recording of plaintiff's performance in its advertisement "capitalize[s] on Plaintiff's valuable reputation and good will and [is] likely to cause confusion or to deceive as to the affiliation, connection or association of Defendants with Plaintiff." These passages assert that Gilberto possesses a trademark in her 1964 performance, and the defendants made unauthorized use of her mark in their advertisement, causing likely consumer confusion.

Gilberto sought to support this theory in defending the motion for summary judgment by affidavits asserting that the song is her signature piece and the centerpiece of all her concert appearances, that the public associates her performance of Ipanema with her, and that she bills herself as "The Girl from Ipanema" and operates an informational website under that name.

The district court's ruling did not expressly address this branch of plaintiff's Lanham Act claim. The court did say in explaining its dismissal of the trademark *dilution* claim, under 15 U.S.C. §1125(c)(1), that "there is no federal trademark protection for a musical work," which may explain why the court found it unnecessary to address further plaintiff's trademark *infringement* claim. The court furnished no authority supporting its assertion that a musical work cannot serve as a trademark, but reasoned that the protection of a musical work "falls under the rubric of copyright, not trademark law."

If the court meant to dismiss the trademark infringement claim on the ground that a musical composition cannot serve as a trademark, we see no reason why this should be so. The fact that musical compositions are protected by the copyright laws is not incompatible with their also qualifying for protection as trademarks. Graphic designs, of course, may be protected by copyright; that does not make them ineligible for protection as trademarks. The Act defines a "trademark" as including "any word, name, symbol, or device, or any combination thereof used by a person . . . to identify and distinguish his or her goods . . . from those manufactured or sold by others and to indicate the source of the goods." 15 U.S.C. §1127. We can see no reason why a musical composition should be ineligible to serve as a symbol or device to identify a person's goods or services. In *Qualitex Co. v. Jacobson Products Co., Inc.*, 514 U.S. 159 (1995), the Supreme Court considered whether a color could serve as a mark. In deciding that it could, the Court reviewed the broadly inclusive language of the statutory definition and observed that the courts and the Patent and Trademark Office have authorized trademark protection for "a particular shape (of a Coca-Cola bottle), a particular sound (of NBC's three chimes), and even a particular scent (of plumeria blossoms on sewing thread)." *Id.* at 162. NBC's three chimes, which the Supreme Court referred to as "a particular sound," is of course not a single sound; it is three sounds, in a specified order, with a specified tempo, on a specified instrument—in short, a brief musical composition. For many decades it has been commonplace for merchandising companies to adopt songs, tunes and ditties as marks for their goods or services, played in commercials on the radio or television.[1] We can see no reason to doubt that such

---

1. A few famous examples over the years have been the William Tell Overture for the Lone Ranger (*see* Registration No. 2155923), "Sweet Georgia Brown" for the Harlem Globetrotters (*see* Registration No. 1700895), "My Beer Is Rheingold the Dry Beer," "See the U.S.A. in Your Chevrolet," "You Deserve a Break Today—at McDonalds," "Double your pleasure, double your fun with . . . Doublemint Gum," "Um, Um, good; Um, Um, good; that's what Campbell's soups are, um, um, good," "Try Wildroot Cream Oil, Charley. Start using it today," "When you see the three-ring-sign, Ask the man for Ballantine," "Chock Full o' Nuts is that heavenly coffee," "National Shoes ring the bell," Alka-Seltzer's "Plop plop, fizz fizz, oh what a relief it is," "Spud cigarettes are cooler than cool," as well as the theme songs of the "I Love Lucy" show, "The Honeymooners," "Sesame Street," "Mr. Rogers' Neighborhood," and "The Sopranos."

musical compositions serve as marks, protected as such by the Lanham Act. We do, however, affirm the district court's dismissal of the trademark infringement claim for a slightly different reason.

Dealing with a related question, a panel of our court considered whether a musical composition could serve as a trademark *for itself*, and concluded it could not. *See EMI Catalogue Partnership v. Hill, Holliday, Connors, Cosmopulos Inc.*, 228 F.3d 56, 64 (2d Cir. 2000). The court reasoned that granting to a song the status of trademark *for itself* would stretch the definition of trademark too far and would cause disruptions as to reasonable commercial understandings. *Id. Cf. Sinatra v. Goodyear Tire & Rubber Co.*, 435 F.2d 711, 712 (9th Cir. 1970) (rejecting claim by singer Nancy Sinatra that song she sang "has been so popularized by [Sinatra] that her name is identified with it; that she is best known by her connection with the song [and] that said song . . . has acquired a secondary meaning" such that another person could not sing it in a commercial).

For similar reasons, we conclude that, at least upon the showing made by Gilberto, the law does not accord her trademark rights in the recording of her signature performance. Plaintiff has not cited a single precedent throughout the history of trademark supporting the notion that a performing artist acquires a trademark or service mark signifying herself in a recording of her own famous performance. The "signature performance" that a widespread audience associates with the performing artist is not unique to Gilberto. Many famous artists have recorded such signature performances that their audiences identify with the performer. Yet in no instance was such a performer held to own a protected mark in that recording.

It is true, there are instances in which courts have protected the "persona" of an artist against false implication of endorsement generally resulting from the use of look-alikes or sound-alikes. *See, e.g., Waits v. Frito-Lay, Inc.*, 978 F.2d 1093, 1107 (9th Cir. 1992) (affirming judgment for plaintiff, Tom Waits, on false implied endorsement claim for use in a snack-food commercial of a singer who imitated plaintiff's gravelly singing style praising defendant's product); *White v. Samsung Elecs. Am., Inc.*, 971 F.2d 1395, 1400-01 (9th Cir. 1992) (holding there was genuine issue of material fact precluding summary judgment as to false implied endorsement claim brought by Vanna White, the hostess of the "Wheel of Fortune" game show, for use in an advertisement for VCRs of a look-alike caricature robot endorsing defendant's product); *Allen v. National Video, Inc.*, 610 F. Supp. 612, 627-28 (S.D.N.Y. 1985) (upholding actor Woody Allen's claim of false implied endorsement for use in an advertisement for video-rental stores of a look-alike renting videos from defendant). But these authorities do not help Gilberto. The use of her recorded song has not taken her persona, and the district court properly concluded that she could sustain no claim of implied endorsement.

We cannot say it would be unthinkable for the trademark law to accord to a performing artist a trademark or service mark in her signature performance. If Congress were to consider whether to extend trademark protection to artists for their signature performances, reasons might be found both for and against such an expansion. But for a court now to "recognize" the previously unknown existence of such a right would be profoundly disruptive to commerce. Numerous artists who could assert claims similar to Gilberto's would bring suit against entities that had paid bona fide license fees to all known holders of rights. Indeed, artists who had licensed users under their copyrights and had received fees for the copyright license could bring suits claiming additional compensation for infringement of trademark rights. Immense unforeseen liabilities might accrue, upsetting reasonable commercial expectations. We can see no justification for now altering the commercial world's understanding of the scope of trademark rights in this fashion.

We perceive no need in the interests of fairness to so expand the scope of trademark, because the law affords performing artists a number of other protections—even for performances made before the federal copyright statute was expanded in 1972 to cover sound recordings—including significant protections that may be secured by contract. We therefore affirm the district court's dismissal of the Lanham Act claim. . . .

CONCLUSION

The dismissal of Gilberto's Lanham Act claim is affirmed. [The court vacated the grant of summary judgment to the defendant on various state law claims, discussed in Chapter 11, and remanded the state law claims with an instruction to dismiss without prejudice so they could be repleaded in state court.]

NOTES AND QUESTIONS

1. *Distinguishing among song trademarks.* In footnote 1, the *Oliveira* court listed several examples of musical works that have served as trademarks. In what respects, if any, are these different from the mark claimed by Gilberto?

2. *The relevance of copyright protection.* In *Comedy III Prods. v. New Line Cinema*, 200 F.3d 593 (9th Cir. 2000), the plaintiffs (who claimed all intellectual property rights in The Three Stooges) brought an action under Section 43(a) of the Lanham Act objecting to the release of a motion picture that contained a thirty-second clip from The Three Stooges' short film, *Disorder in the Court. Disorder in the Court* was unprotected by copyright. The Ninth Circuit rejected the claim:

> Essentially, [plaintiff] is arguing that the clip at issue falls under the protection of the Lanham Act because it contains elements that in other contexts might serve as trademarks. Had New Line used the likeness of The Three Stooges on t-shirts which it was selling, [the plaintiff] might have an arguable claim for trademark violation. But we will not entertain this expedition of trademark protection squarely into the dominion of copyright law, to allow for Lanham Act coverage of a piece of footage taken directly from a film by The Three Stooges. [The] assertion that this clip is itself a collection of trademarks of The Three Stooges is unconvincing.

In what circumstances might a claim be viable under Section 43(a) notwithstanding the unavailability of copyright protection? *Cf. Nova Wines, Inc. v. Adler Fels Winery LLC*, 467 F. Supp. 2d 965 (N.D. Cal. 2006) (upholding trade dress infringement claims based on an image of Marilyn Monroe used on wine labels notwithstanding that copyright in the image belonged to third party and had been licensed to the defendant). For what reasons might one support a per se rule against the protection of copyrightable subject matter under the trademark statute? *See EMI Catalogue P'ship v. Hill, Holliday, Connors, Cosmopulos Inc.*, 228 F.3d 56 (2d Cir. 2000) (holding that a musical composition cannot be protected as "its own trademark" under the Lanham Act). Would it matter whether the subject matter (e.g., a musical composition) could have been protected by copyright? What if the work at issue is insufficiently original to merit any copyright protection? Should that cut in favor or against possible trademark protection? To what extent is it accurate to say that a trademark infringement action claiming trademark rights in a musical composition is seeking to protect the same subject matter as a copyright claim in that musical work? Do the different purposes of copyright and trademark law support or undermine the adoption of a per se rule barring trademark protection?

3. *Tying the scope of trademark law to copyright law.* One court has suggested a bright-line rule to the effect that "where a plaintiff's Lanham Act claim parallels his copyright infringement claim, a finding of no substantial similarity on the copyright claim precludes the Lanham Act claim." *Tiseo Architects, Inc. v. B&B Pools Serv. & Supply Co.*, 495 F.3d 344 (6th Cir. 2007) (claim for infringement of copyright and trade dress in architect's design of commercial building); *see also Romantics v. Activision Publ'g, Inc.*, 532 F. Supp. 2d 884, 889 (E.D. Mich. 2008) (noting that a "musical composition . . . cannot be protected as its own trademark under the Lanham Act. [cit.] In addition, the Lanham Act has been held not to permit a plaintiff to state a . . . claim predicated on the use of an allegedly distinctive 'signature' sound recording."). How does such a rule differ from the approach taken in *Oliviera*? Would you support such a rule? Note that the test of "substantial similarity" used to determine copyright infringement asks whether the two works at issue reveal a substantial similarity of "protected expression" (as opposed to, say, ideas or facts). You might reconsider this question after you have studied the materials on proving actionable confusion, *see infra* Chapter 7.

4. *Author names as trademarks.* Should the name of an author of a book be protected as a trademark? What policy reasons might counsel caution in recognizing such rights? Would it matter whether the book remained the subject of copyright protection? *See In re First Draft Inc.*, 76 U.S.P.Q.2d (BNA) 1183 (TTAB 2005).

5. *Expired copyrights.* If a trademark claim sought to restrain use of artwork previously protected by copyright but now in the public domain, would you support a per se rule barring protection? *See Frederick Warne & Co. v. Book Sales Inc.*, 481 F. Supp. 1191 (S.D.N.Y. 1979) (refusing to dismiss a Lanham Act claim brought by the publisher of the original Peter Rabbit books written and illustrated by Beatrix Potter against a rival publisher who copied the cover artwork, the copyright in which had expired). Would it matter why the work is in the public domain (e.g., failure to comply with formalities of U.S. copyright law, or because the term of copyright had expired)?

6. *Cartoon characters.* If copyright in the character Mickey Mouse (or, perhaps more strictly, the first copyrighted work containing the Mickey Mouse character) expires, should trademark law permit the Disney Company to restrain use of the character? *Cf.* J. Thomas McCarthy, Trademarks and Unfair Competition §6.11 (2002) ("[I]f the cartoon character has achieved trademark significance, one should not, even after expiration of the copyright, be able to take an image of the character and use it on merchandise if it is likely to cause confusion as to source, affiliation, or connection."), *with Comedy III Prods., Inc. v. New Line Cinema*, 200 F.3d 593, 596 (9th Cir. 2000), *and Leigh v. Warner Bros.*, 10 F. Supp. 2d 1371, 1381-82 (S.D. Ga. 1998) (noting the potential for "undermining copyright" by offering trade dress protection to a photograph used on the cover of a book), *aff'd in relevant part*, 212 F.3d 1210 (11th Cir. 2000).

7. *Affirmative rights under the Copyright Act?* Section 120 of the Copyright Act limits the scope of copyright in architectural works by providing that the copyright "does not include the right to prevent the making, distributing, or public display of pictures, paintings, photographs, or other pictorial representations of the work, if the building in which the work is embodied is located in or is ordinarily visible from a public place." Should this preclude a district court from granting an injunction under trademark law against the sale of posters of the Cleveland skyline showing the design of the Rock and Roll Hall of Fame (in which trade dress rights are claimed by the museum)? *See Rock & Roll Hall of Fame & Museum, Inc. v. Gentile Prods.*, 134 F.3d 749 (6th Cir. 1998). What if the rights asserted by the defendant flowed not from the Copyright Act but from a valid copyright license? *See Nova Wines, Inc. v. Adler Fels Winery LLC*, 467 F. Supp. 2d 965 (N.D. Cal. 2006) (holding that a valid copyright does not entitle the copyright holder or its licensee to infringe another's trade dress, "particularly . . . where [the] trade dress rights are considerably broader than the defendants' copyright interests at issue").

8.   *Accounting for different types of intellectual property rights.* To what extent should the existence of a per se rule against trademark protection for subject matter covered by other intellectual property rights vary depending upon the other intellectual property right in question? Should it matter whether the "other intellectual property right" is accorded under state or federal law? We will address the specific question of the overlap between patent and trade dress protection in the next chapter.

In 2003, the United States Supreme Court decided *Dastar v. Twentieth Century Fox.* That case most directly addresses the ability of plaintiffs to use Section 43(a) of the Lanham Act to remedy failure to attribute the source of a creative product. And we will discuss *Dastar* in that context. *See* Chapter 11. But the Court's opinion *may* have ramifications beyond that issue that pertain to the question we have just been discussing. That is to say, we believe the Court might be as concerned about alternative theories of protection under Section 43(a) and interface issues (here, with copyright law) as with the narrow doctrinal question of failure to attribute. You may disagree, but, for that reason, we introduce the case here, with the caveat that this case (like the last one) presents a set of facts that make it hardly a routine trademark case.

DASTAR CORP. v. TWENTIETH CENTURY FOX FILM CORP.

539 U.S. 23 (2003)

Justice SCALIA delivered the opinion of the Court:

In this case, we are asked to decide whether §43(a) of the Lanham Act, 15 U.S.C. §1125(a), prevents the unaccredited copying of a work. . . .

I

In 1948, . . . General Dwight D. Eisenhower completed Crusade in Europe, his written account of the allied campaign in Europe during World War II. Doubleday published the book, registered it with the Copyright Office in 1948, and granted exclusive television rights to an affiliate of respondent Twentieth Century Fox Film Corporation (Fox). Fox, in turn, arranged for Time, Inc., to produce a television series, also called Crusade in Europe, based on the book, and Time assigned its copyright in the series to Fox. The television series, consisting of 26 episodes, was first broadcast in 1949. . . . In 1975, Doubleday renewed the copyright on the book as the "'proprietor of copyright in a work made for hire.'" [cit.] Fox, however, did not renew the copyright on the Crusade television series, which expired in 1977, leaving the television series in the public domain.

In 1988, Fox reacquired the television rights in General Eisenhower's book, including the exclusive right to distribute the Crusade television series on video and to sub-license others to do so. Respondents SFM Entertainment and New Line Home Video, Inc., in turn, acquired from Fox the exclusive rights to distribute Crusade on video. SFM obtained the negatives of the original television series, restored them, and repackaged the series on videotape; New Line distributed the videotapes.

Enter petitioner Dastar. In 1995, Dastar decided to expand its product line from music compact discs to videos. Anticipating renewed interest in World War II on the 50th anniversary of the war's end, Dastar released a video set entitled World War II Campaigns in Europe. To make Campaigns, Dastar purchased eight beta cam tapes of the *original* version of the Crusade television series, which is in the public domain, copied them, and then edited the series. Dastar's Campaigns series is slightly more than half as long as the original Crusade television series. Dastar substituted a new opening sequence, credit page, and final closing for those of the Crusade television series; inserted new chapter-title sequences and narrated chapter introductions; moved the "recap" in the Crusade television series to the beginning and retitled it as a "preview"; and removed references to and images of the book. Dastar created new packaging for its Campaigns series and (as already noted) a new title.

Dastar manufactured and sold the Campaigns video set as its own product. The advertising states: "Produced and Distributed by: *Entertainment Distributing*" (which is owned by Dastar), and makes no reference to the Crusade television series. Similarly, the screen credits state "DASTAR CORP presents" and "an ENTERTAINMENT DISTRIBUTING Production," and list as executive producer, producer, and associate producer, employees of Dastar. The Campaigns videos themselves also make no reference to the Crusade television series, New Line's Crusade videotapes, or the book. Dastar sells its Campaigns videos to Sam's Club, Costco, Best Buy, and other retailers and mail-order companies for $25 per set, substantially less than New Line's video set.

In 1998, respondents Fox, SFM, and New Line brought this action alleging that Dastar's sale of its Campaigns video set infringes Doubleday's copyright in General Eisenhower's book and, thus, their exclusive television rights in the book. Respondents later amended their complaint to add claims that Dastar's sale of Campaigns "without proper credit" to the Crusade television series constitutes "reverse passing off"[1] in violation of §43(a) of the Lanham Act, 15 U.S.C. §1125(a), and in violation of state unfair-competition law. On cross-motions for summary judgment, the District Court found for respondents on all three counts, treating its resolution of the Lanham Act claim as controlling on the state-law unfair-competition claim because "the ultimate test under both is whether the public is likely to be deceived or confused." . . .

The Court of Appeals for the Ninth Circuit affirmed the judgment for respondents on the Lanham Act claim, but reversed as to the copyright claim and remanded. (It said nothing with regard to the state-law claim.) With respect to the Lanham Act claim, the Court of Appeals reasoned that "Dastar copied substantially the entire *Crusade in Europe* series created by Twentieth Century Fox, labeled the resulting product with a different name and marketed it without attribution to Fox[, and] therefore committed a 'bodily appropriation' of Fox's series." It concluded that "Dastar's 'bodily appropriation' of Fox's original [television] series is sufficient to establish the reverse passing off."[2] . . . We granted certiorari.

II

The Lanham Act was intended to make "actionable the deceptive and misleading use of marks," and "to protect persons engaged in . . . commerce against unfair competition." 15 U.S.C. §1127. While much of the Lanham Act addresses the registration, use, and infringement of trademarks and related marks, §43(a), 15 U.S.C. §1125(a), is one of the few provisions that goes beyond trademark protection. As originally enacted, §43(a) created a federal remedy against a person who used in commerce either "a false designation of origin, or any false description or representation" in connection with "any goods or services." 60 Stat. 441. As the Second Circuit accurately observed with regard to the original

---

1. Passing off (or palming off, as it is sometimes called) occurs when a producer misrepresents his own goods or services as someone else's. [cit.] "Reverse passing off," as its name implies, is the opposite: The producer misrepresents someone else's goods or services as his own. [cit.] [*Ed. Note:* Reverse passing off is dealt with in more detail in Chapter 11.]

2. . . . The copyright issue is still the subject of litigation, but is not before us. We express no opinion as to whether petitioner's product would infringe a valid copyright in General Eisenhower's book.

enactment, however—and as remains true after the 1988 revision—§43(a) "does not have boundless application as a remedy for unfair trade practices," *Alfred Dunhill, Ltd. v. Interstate Cigar Co.*, 499 F.2d 232, 237 (C.A.2 1974). "[B]ecause of its inherently limited wording, §43(a) can never be a federal 'codification' of the overall law of 'unfair competition,'" 4 J. McCarthy Trademarks and Unfair Competition §27:7, p. 27-14 (4th ed. 2002) (McCarthy), but can apply only to certain unfair trade practices prohibited by its text.

Although a case can be made that a proper reading of §43(a), as originally enacted, would treat the word "origin" as referring only "to the geographic location in which the goods originated," [cit.] the Courts of Appeals considering the issue, beginning with the Sixth Circuit, unanimously concluded that it "does not merely refer to geographical origin, but also to origin of source or manufacture," *Federal-Mogul-Bower Bearings, Inc. v. Azoff*, 313 F.2d 405, 408 (1963), thereby creating a federal cause of action for traditional trademark infringement of unregistered marks. [cit.] Moreover, every Circuit to consider the issue found §43(a) broad enough to encompass reverse passing off. [cit.] The Trademark Law Revision Act of 1988 made clear that §43(a) covers origin of production as well as geographic origin. Its language is amply inclusive, moreover, of reverse passing off—if indeed it does not implicitly adopt the unanimous court-of-appeals jurisprudence on that subject. [cit.]

Thus, as it comes to us, the gravamen of respondents' claim is that, in marketing and selling Campaigns as its own product without acknowledging its nearly wholesale reliance on the Crusade television series, Dastar has made a "false designation of origin, false or misleading description of fact, or false or misleading representation of fact, which . . . is likely to cause confusion . . . as to the origin . . . of his or her goods." §43(a). That claim would undoubtedly be sustained if Dastar had bought some of New Line's Crusade videotapes and merely repackaged them as its own. Dastar's alleged wrongdoing, however, is vastly different: it took a creative work in the public domain—the Crusade television series—copied it, made modifications (arguably minor), and produced its very own series of videotapes. If "origin" refers only to the manufacturer or producer of the physical "goods" that are made available to the public (in this case the videotapes), Dastar was the origin. If, however, "origin" includes the creator of the underlying work that Dastar copied, then someone else (perhaps Fox) was the origin of Dastar's product. At bottom, we must decide what §43(a)(1)(A) of the Lanham Act means by the "origin" of "goods."

III

The dictionary definition of "origin" is "[t]he fact or process of coming into being from a source," and "[t]hat from which anything primarily proceeds; source." Webster's New International Dictionary 1720-1721 (2d ed. 1949). And the dictionary definition of "goods" (as relevant here) is "[w]ares; merchandise." *Id.*, at 1079. We think the most natural understanding of the "origin" of "goods"—the source of wares—is the producer of the tangible product sold in the marketplace, in this case the physical Campaigns videotape sold by Dastar. The concept might be stretched (as it was under the original version of §43(a))[5] to include not only the actual producer, but also the trademark owner who commissioned

---

5. Under the 1946 version of the Act, §43(a) was read as providing a cause of action for trademark infringement even where the trademark owner had not itself produced the goods sold under its mark, but had licensed others to sell under its name goods produced by them—the typical franchise arrangement. See, *e.g.*, *My Pie Int'l, Inc. v. Debould, Inc.*, 687 F.2d 919 (CA7 1982). This stretching of the concept "origin of goods" is seemingly no longer needed: The 1988 amendments to §43(a) now expressly prohibit the use of any "word, term, name, symbol, or device," or "false or misleading description of fact" that is likely to cause confusion as to "affiliation, connection, or association . . . with another person," or as to "sponsorship, or approval" of goods. 15 U.S.C. §1125(a).

or assumed responsibility for ("stood behind") production of the physical product. But as used in the Lanham Act, the phrase "origin of goods" is in our view incapable of connoting the person or entity that originated the ideas or communications that "goods" embody or contain. Such an extension would not only stretch the text, but it would be out of accord with the history and purpose of the Lanham Act and inconsistent with precedent.

Section 43(a) of the Lanham Act prohibits actions like trademark infringement that deceive consumers and impair a producer's goodwill. It forbids, for example, the Coca-Cola Company's passing off its product as Pepsi-Cola or reverse passing off Pepsi-Cola as its product. But the brand-loyal consumer who prefers the drink that the Coca-Cola Company or PepsiCo sells, while he believes that that company produced (or at least stands behind the production of) that product, surely does not necessarily believe that that company was the "origin" of the drink in the sense that it was the very first to devise the formula. The consumer who buys a branded product does not automatically assume that the brand-name company is the same entity that came up with the idea for the product, or designed the product—and typically does not care whether it is. The words of the Lanham Act should not be stretched to cover matters that are typically of no consequence to purchasers.

It could be argued, perhaps, that the reality of purchaser concern is different for what might be called a communicative product—one that is valued not primarily for its physical qualities, such as a hammer, but for the intellectual content that it conveys, such as a book or, as here, a video. The purchaser of a novel is interested not merely, if at all, in the identity of the producer of the physical tome (the publisher), but also, and indeed primarily, in the identity of the creator of the story it conveys (the author). And the author, of course, has at least as much interest in avoiding passing-off (or reverse passing-off) of his creation as does the publisher. For such a communicative product (the argument goes) "origin of goods" in §43(a) must be deemed to include not merely the producer of the physical item (the publishing house Farrar, Straus and Giroux, or the video producer Dastar) but also the creator of the content that the physical item conveys (the author Tom Wolfe, or—assertedly—respondents).

The problem with this argument according special treatment to communicative products is that it causes the Lanham Act to conflict with the law of copyright, which addresses that subject specifically. The right to copy, and to copy without attribution, once a copyright has expired, like "the right to make [an article whose patent has expired]—including the right to make it in precisely the shape it carried when patented—passes to the public." *Sears, Roebuck & Co. v. Stiffel Co.*, 376 U.S. 225, 230 (1964); see also *Kellogg Co. v. National Biscuit Co.*, 305 U.S. 111, 121-122 (1938). "In general, unless an intellectual property right such as a patent or copyright protects an item, it will be subject to copying." *TrafFix Devices, Inc. v. Marketing Displays, Inc.*, 532 U.S. 23, 29 (2001). The rights of a patentee or copyright holder are part of a "carefully crafted bargain," *Bonito Boats, Inc. v. Thunder Craft Boats, Inc.*, 489 U.S. 141, 150-151 (1989), under which, once the patent or copyright monopoly has expired, the public may use the invention or work at will and without attribution. Thus, in construing the Lanham Act, we have been "careful to caution against misuse or over-extension" of trademark and related protections into areas traditionally occupied by patent or copyright. *TrafFix*, 532 U.S., at 29. "The Lanham Act," we have said, "does not exist to reward manufacturers for their innovation in creating a particular device; that is the purpose of the patent law and its period of exclusivity." *Id.*, at 34. Federal trademark law "has no necessary relation to invention or discovery," *Trade-Mark Cases*, 100 U.S. 82, 94 (1879), but rather, by preventing competitors from copying "a source-identifying mark," "reduce[s] the customer's costs of shopping and making purchasing decisions," and "helps assure a producer that it (and not an imitating competitor) will reap the financial, reputation-related rewards associated with a desirable product," *Qualitex Co.*

v. Jacobson Products Co., 514 U.S. 159, 163-164 (1995) (internal quotation marks and citation omitted). Assuming for the sake of argument that Dastar's representation of itself as the "Producer" of its videos amounted to a representation that it originated the creative work conveyed by the videos, allowing a cause of action under §43(a) for that representation would create a species of mutant copyright law that limits the public's "federal right to 'copy and to use'" expired copyrights, *Bonito Boats, supra*, at 165.

When Congress has wished to create such an addition to the law of copyright, it has done so with much more specificity than the Lanham Act's ambiguous use of "origin." The Visual Artists Rights Act of 1990, §603(a), 104 Stat. 5128, provides that the author of an artistic work "shall have the right . . . to claim authorship of that work." 17 U.S.C. §106A(a)(1)(A). That express right of attribution is carefully limited and focused: It attaches only to specified "work[s] of visual art," §101, is personal to the artist, §§106A(b) and (e), and endures only for "the life of the author," at §106A(d)(1). Recognizing in §43(a) a cause of action for misrepresentation of authorship of noncopyrighted works (visual or otherwise) would render these limitations superfluous. A statutory interpretation that renders another statute superfluous is of course to be avoided. [cit.]

Reading "origin" in §43(a) to require attribution of uncopyrighted materials would pose serious practical problems. Without a copyrighted work as the basepoint, the word "origin" has no discernible limits. A video of the MGM film Carmen Jones, after its copyright has expired, would presumably require attribution not just to MGM, but to Oscar Hammerstein II (who wrote the musical on which the film was based), to Georges Bizet (who wrote the opera on which the musical was based), and to Prosper Mérimée (who wrote the novel on which the opera was based). In many cases, figuring out who is in the line of "origin" would be no simple task. Indeed, in the present case it is far from clear that respondents have that status. Neither SFM nor New Line had anything to do with the production of the Crusade television series—they merely were licensed to distribute the video version. While Fox might have a claim to being in the line of origin, its involvement with the creation of the television series was limited at best. Time, Inc., was the principal if not the exclusive creator, albeit under arrangement with Fox. And of course it was neither Fox nor Time, Inc., that shot the film used in the Crusade television series. Rather, that footage came from the United States Army, Navy, and Coast Guard, the British Ministry of Information and War Office, the National Film Board of Canada, and unidentified "Newsreel Pool Cameramen." If anyone has a claim to being the *original* creator of the material used in both the Crusade television series and the Campaigns videotapes, it would be those groups, rather than Fox. We do not think the Lanham Act requires this search for the source of the Nile and all its tributaries.

Another practical difficulty of adopting a special definition of "origin" for communicative products is that it places the manufacturers of those products in a difficult position. On the one hand, they would face Lanham Act liability for *failing* to credit the creator of a work on which their lawful copies are based; and on the other hand they could face Lanham Act liability for *crediting* the creator if that should be regarded as implying the creator's "sponsorship or approval" of the copy, 15 U.S.C. §1125(a)(1)(A). In this case, for example, if Dastar had simply "copied [the television series] as Crusade in Europe and sold it as Crusade in Europe," without changing the title or packaging (including the original credits to Fox), it is hard to have confidence in respondents' assurance that they "would not be here on a Lanham Act cause of action," Tr. of Oral Arg. 35.

Finally, reading §43(a) of the Lanham Act as creating a cause of action for, in effect, plagiarism—the use of otherwise unprotected works and inventions without attribution—would be hard to reconcile with our previous decisions. For example, in *Wal-Mart Stores, Inc. v. Samara Brothers, Inc.*, 529 U.S. 205 (2000), we considered whether product-design trade dress can ever be inherently distinctive. Wal-Mart produced "knock-offs" of children's clothes designed and manufactured by Samara Brothers, containing only "minor modifications" of the original designs. *Id.*, at 208. We concluded that the designs could not be protected under §43(a) without a showing that they had acquired "secondary meaning," *id.*, at 214, so that they "'identify the source of the product rather than the product itself,'" *id.*, at 211 []. This carefully considered limitation would be entirely pointless if the "original" producer could turn around and pursue a reverse-passing-off claim under exactly the same provision of the Lanham Act. Samara would merely have had to argue that it was the "origin" of the designs that Wal-Mart was selling as its own line. It was not, because "origin of goods" in the Lanham Act referred to the producer of the clothes, and not the producer of the (potentially) copyrightable or patentable designs that the clothes embodied.

[The Court similarly concluded that respondent's theory would have permitted plaintiffs to succeed in two cases, *Bonito Boats*, 489 U.S. 141, and *TrafFix*, 532 U.S. 23, where the Court had in the recent past denied a plaintiff's claim. *See* Chapter 3 *infra*.]

In sum, reading the phrase "origin of goods" in the Lanham Act in accordance with the Act's common-law foundations (which were *not* designed to protect originality or creativity), and in light of the copyright and patent laws (which *were*), we conclude that the phrase refers to the producer of the tangible goods that are offered for sale, and not to the author of any idea, concept, or communication embodied in those goods. Cf. 17 U.S.C. §202 (distinguishing between a copyrighted work and "any material object in which the work is embodied"). To hold otherwise would be akin to finding that §43(a) created a species of perpetual patent and copyright, which Congress may not do. See *Eldred v. Ashcroft*, 537 U.S. 186, 208 (2003).

The creative talent of the sort that lay behind the Campaigns videos is not left without protection. The original film footage used in the Crusade television series could have been copyrighted, see 17 U.S.C. §102(a)(6), as was copyrighted (as a compilation) the Crusade television series, even though it included material from the public domain, see §103(a). Had Fox renewed the copyright in the Crusade television series, it would have had an easy claim of copyright infringement. And respondents' contention that Campaigns infringes Doubleday's copyright in General Eisenhower's book is still a live question on remand. If, moreover, the producer of a video that substantially copied the Crusade series were, in advertising or promotion, to give purchasers the impression that the video was quite different from that series, then one or more of the respondents might have a cause of action—not for reverse passing off under the "confusion . . . as to the origin" provision of §43(a)(1)(A), but for misrepresentation under the "misrepresents the nature, characteristics [or] qualities" provision of §43(a)(1)(B). For merely saying it is the producer of the video, however, no Lanham Act liability attaches to Dastar. . . .

Because we conclude that Dastar was the "origin" of the products it sold as its own, respondents cannot prevail on their Lanham Act claim. . . . The judgment of the Court of Appeals for the Ninth Circuit is reversed, and the case is remanded for further proceedings consistent with this opinion.

It is so ordered.

NOTES AND QUESTIONS

1. *Breadth of the holding.* Where does the term "origin" appear in Section 43(a)? Could you frame a cause of action under Section 43(a) that does not implicate the term "origin"? *Cf. Baden Sports, Inc. v. Molten USA, Inc.*, 556 F.3d 1300 (Fed. Cir. 2009) (rejecting efforts to squeeze a false attribution claim into Section 43(a)(1)(B)). If so, how significant is the *Dastar* decision? How broad is its holding? *See* Graeme B. Dinwoodie, *Concurrence and Convergence of Rights: The Concerns of the U.S. Supreme Court, in* CROSSING BORDERS: BETWEEN TRADITIONAL AND ACTUAL 19-20 (Grosheide & Brinkhof eds., 2005) ("If the *Dastar* rule is nominally grounded in interpretation of the term 'origin' or indeed in judges' amateur psychological speculation about consumer attitudes, the rule will continue to develop with only indirect significance for the development of a Court philosophy on cumulation" of different intellectual property rights.).

2. *The nature of the plaintiff's claim.* How would you characterize the plaintiff's claim? It would not appear to be a garden-variety claim for "trademark infringement." It would seem to be grounded in the failure to give proper credit.

3. *Claims left intact by the Supreme Court.* If its decision is read very broadly, the Court might be calling into question the applicability of the Lanham Act to subject matter the protection of which implicates copyright law. *Cf. Bach v. Forever Living Prods. U.S., Inc.,* 473 F. Supp. 2d 1110 (W.D. Wash. 2007) (permitting trademark claims based on rights in the name and title of a book and the trade dress of the book cover to proceed despite similar factual allegations underlying a claim for infringement of the copyright in the book's main character, its text, and a photograph contained therein). But the Court expressly noted that the plaintiff's "claim would undoubtedly be sustained if Dastar had bought some of New Line's Crusade videotapes and merely repackaged them as its own." Why would that claim be different? If a defendant scraped data from a website and hosted the data on the defendant's own website (without attribution), would *Dastar* preclude an action by the owner of the first website? Would it matter whether the data was copyrightable? *See Cvent, Inc. v Eventbrite, Inc.,* 739 F. Supp. 2d 927, 935-36 (E.D. Va. 2010). What did the Court mean by "repackaging them as its own"? *See Dutch Jackson IATG, LLC v. Basketball Mktg. Co.,* 846 F. Supp. 2d 1044 (E.D. Mo. 2012) (*Dastar* applied where defendant used plaintiff's song as part of soundtrack to DVD produced by defendant).

4. *Interpretation of the term "origin."* The Court says that "at bottom, we must decide what [is meant by] the 'origin' of 'goods'" and dismisses the plaintiff's claim based upon its interpretation of the term "origin" in Section 43(a). How does the Court go about determining the meaning of the term "origin of goods"? It offers various reasons for its interpretation. Is the Court's approach consistent with its approach to statutory interpretation in other recent Lanham Act cases? Several courts have also focused on language in the *Dastar* opinion to the effect that the "phrase 'origin of goods' . . . refers to the producer of the tangible goods that are offered for sale, and not to the author of any idea, concept, or communication embodied in those goods." As a threshold matter, such courts have dismissed the cause of action if the product that was the subject of the claim was not a "tangible good . . . offered for sale." *See Larkin Grp., Inc. v. Aquatic Design Consultants, Inc.,* 323 F. Supp. 2d 1121, 1126 (D. Kan. 2004) (discussing case law); *see also Tao of Sys. Integration, Inc. v. Analytical Servs. & Materials, Inc.,* 299 F. Supp. 2d 565 (E.D. Va. 2004) (proposal in which defendant was alleged to have incorporated plaintiff's ideas without authorization or attribution was not a good or service); *Bretford Mfg., Inc. v. Smith Sys. Mfg. Corp.,* 419 F.3d 576 (7th Cir. 2005) (use in sample product shown to potential customer). What difficulties might the reference to "tangible good" cause? *See Phoenix Ents. Partners LLC v. Rumsey,* 829 F. 3d 817 (7th Cir. 2016) (assuming that a digital file counts as a tangible good).

5. *Communicative versus other products.* Does the Court give a different meaning to the term "origin" when the good is a "communicative product"? If so, why? On what basis does it distinguish between "communicative products" and other products? If this distinction is of significance, then what is a "communicative product"? Is software a

communicative product? *See General Universal Sys., Inc. v. Lee*, 379 F.3d 131, 149 (5th Cir. 2004) (applying *Dastar* to software). Should *Dastar* apply to software, or should *Dastar* be limited to cases involving communicative products?

6. **Dastar *and trade dress claims.*** If Peter designed a range of popular furniture with a distinctive design, and Donnie copied the drawings thereof from Peter's catalog, would *Dastar* preclude a Lanham Act claim if Donnie presented the unauthorized copies of the drawings to potential purchasers as showing his furniture? *Cf. Bretford Mfg., Inc. v. Smith Sys. Mfg. Corp.*, 419 F.3d 576 (7th Cir. 2005); *Universal Furniture Int'l, Inc. v. Collezione Europa USA Inc.*, 618 F.3d 417 (4th Cir. 2010). Would your answer change if Donnie simply showed potential purchasers a page ripped from Peter's catalog showing the design (having removed any references to Peter on that page)? *See Victor Stanley, Inc. v. Creative Pipe, Inc.*, No. MJG-06-2662, 2011 WL 4596043 (D. Md. Sept. 30, 2011). Does your answer depend on the consequences of Donnie's conduct under copyright law? Does your answer depend on whether Donnie secures and fills purchase orders? Do any of your answers turn on the meaning of the word "origin"?

7. *Attribution and the right to copy.* The Court quotes the *Sears* and *Kellogg* Courts for the proposition that "the right to copy, and to copy without attribution, once a copyright has expired . . . passes to the public." In a decision five months earlier, the Court emphasized that the law at issue in *Sears* was a state law, and its holding did not restrict the ability of the federal Congress to enact protection. *See Eldred v. Ashcroft*, 537 U.S. 186, 202 n.8 (2003) ("A decision thus rooted in the Supremacy Clause cannot be turned around to shrink congressional choices"). And in *Kellogg*, the Court emphasized that the defendant's right to make the biscuits in the same pillow shape as did the plaintiff was conditional upon the defendant taking steps to distinguish it and its products. Not only did the *Kellogg* Court not articulate a right to copy without attribution, it affirmatively conditioned the right to copy on reasonable steps to avoid confusion. What caused the Court in *Dastar* to express the right as broadly as it did?

8. *The relevance of copyright protection.* What was the relevance of the copyright claim to the Court's analysis? Does the Court's rationale extend to the case where the work in question involved copyrightable subject matter but no copyright protection existed because of failure to meet the originality threshold? Lower courts have read *Dastar* broadly. The opinion has also been invoked by courts to bar reverse passing-off claims arising from the unauthorized use of copyright-protected works.

9. *The effect of the Visual Artists' Rights Act.* The Visual Artists' Rights Act (VARA), enacted in 1990, was intended to *create* rights not previously available at the federal level. Indeed, VARA was enacted in part to ensure U.S. compliance with international copyright obligations found in Article 6*bis* of the Berne Convention for the Protection of Literary and Artistic Works. That provision obliges the United States to provide authors of works with the right to be attributed as the author of their works. Until VARA, the United States claimed compliance with this obligation through a patchwork of state and federal claims, including the possibility of an action under Section 43(a) of the Lanham Act. What was the relevance of VARA to the Court's analysis? If Congress had not enacted VARA, would the Court have decided the case differently?

10. *Legislative response.* Could Congress legislatively reverse the Court's decision in *Dastar*? That is, to what extent are any of the Court's conclusions constitutionally grounded?

11. *Older case law.* In *Gilliam v. American Broadcasting Co.*, 538 F.2d 14 (2d Cir. 1976), the defendant had acquired the rights to show an episode of the British television show *Monty Python's Flying Circus* created by the plaintiffs. Before doing so, the defendant edited the recording to make the show more suitable for American audiences and to

accommodate commercial advertising. The plaintiffs sued under both copyright law and Section 43(a) of the Lanham Act (but in effect were seeking indirectly to vindicate their moral rights of integrity). The majority of the Second Circuit recognized that a claim could be stated under Section 43(a) if the edited version of the show was presented to American audiences; one judge on the appellate panel would have denied relief under Section 43(a) if an appropriate disclaimer were shown indicating that the edits had not been authorized by the plaintiffs. Would such a claim be viable after *Dastar*?

PROBLEM 2-5: *DASTAR* KARAOKE

Slep–Tone Entertainment produces and distributes karaoke accompaniment tracks under the trademark "Sound Choice." These tracks are designed for professional karaoke systems and include both audio and graphic (visual) components. The audio component is a re-recorded version of a popular song that omits the lead vocals, as those will be performed by the karaoke singer or singers. The graphic component displays the lyrics to the song as well as a variety of visual cues (including color coding and various icons) that are synchronized with the music in order to aid the singers. In addition to the Sound Choice trademark, Slep–Tone also claims ownership of a distinctive trade dress that distinguishes its tracks from those of its competitors. This trade dress includes the typeface, style, and visual arrangement of the song lyrics displayed in the graphic component of the accompaniment tracks; a display version of the Sound Choice mark that is itself typically shown with the song lyrics; and the style of entry cues that are displayed for karaoke singers to signal when they should begin to sing. Slep–Tone alleges that this trade dress is sufficiently recognizable to karaoke customers to enable them to distinguish a track produced by Slep–Tone and a track produced by a competitor. The defendant bar purchased Slep–Tone's karaoke tracks on compact discs and copied the tracks onto the hard drive of its karaoke equipment. This allows a machine to host hundreds or thousands of accompaniment tracks and does not require a user physically to insert a disc into the karaoke machine. Slep-Tone alleges that when the defendant plays unauthorized copies of Slep–Tone karaoke tracks at the pub, customers see Slep–Tone's Sound Choice mark and trade dress and believe they are seeing and hearing a legitimate, authentic Slep–Tone track. Slep–Tone characterizes the unauthorized copy of its track as a distinct good which the defendants are improperly "passing off" as a genuine Slep–Tone track. Does *Dastar* bar such a claim? *See Phoenix Ent. Partners, LLC v. Rumsey*, 829 F.3d 817 (7th Cir. 2016).

3

FUNCTIONALITY

A. AN INTRODUCTION TO THE CONCEPT OF FUNCTIONALITY

As trademark rights expanded to encompass new subject matter in general, and product designs or configurations in particular, courts (and the PTO) became concerned that trademark protection for this new subject matter might have substantial adverse consequences. The functionality doctrine has been a critical device in avoiding or mitigating those consequences.

In *Qualitex Co. v. Jacobson Products Co., Inc.*, 514 U.S. 159 (1995), *supra* Chapter 2, section D, the U.S. Supreme Court held that color per se could be registered as a trademark under the Lanham Act. In the course of addressing the respondent's argument that color per se could not be registered under the Lanham Act, the Supreme Court considered whether the functionality doctrine in any way provided guidance on that issue. In so doing, the Court explained the purpose of the functionality doctrine:

> The functionality doctrine prevents trademark law, which seeks to promote competition by protecting a firm's reputation, from instead inhibiting legitimate competition by allowing a producer to control a useful product feature. It is the province of patent law, not trademark law, to encourage invention by granting inventors a monopoly over new product designs or functions for a limited time, 35 U.S.C. §§154, 173, after which competitors are free to use the innovation. If a product's functional features could be used as trademarks, however, a monopoly over such features could be obtained without regard to whether they qualify as patents and could be extended forever (because trademarks may be renewed in perpetuity). *See Kellogg Co. v. National Biscuit Co.*, 305 U.S. 111, 119-120 (1938) (Brandeis, J.); . . . Functionality doctrine therefore would require, to take an imaginary example, that even if customers have come to identify the special illumination-enhancing shape of a new patented light bulb with a particular manufacturer, the manufacturer may not use that shape as a trademark, for doing so, after the patent had expired, would impede competition—not by protecting the reputation of the original bulb maker, but by frustrating competitors' legitimate efforts to produce an equivalent illumination-enhancing bulb. *See, e.g., Kellogg Co., supra*, 305 U.S. at 119-120 (trademark law cannot be used to extend monopoly over "pillow" shape of shredded wheat biscuit after the patent for that shape had expired).

Identify precisely the concern(s) articulated by the Court in *Qualitex*. Is there more than one such concern? On what grounds would it be improper for trademark law to be used to extend a monopoly over the shape of the light bulb after its patent had expired? What if the manufacturer had not obtained a patent on that shape? What dangers does the Court see resulting from extensive trade dress protection? You have read several cases in Chapter 2 in which trademark rights were claimed in product features. Are the Court's concerns justified? Are the concerns raised by trademark protection for product designs different from those raised by trademark protection for subject matter protected by copyright, discussed in the cases in Chapter 2, section E? Reconsider these questions as you read the cases in this chapter.

Through the years, a significant group of trademark law scholars has addressed the question of functionality. The single point upon which these scholars agree is that neither courts nor jurists have successfully formulated a consistent or workable approach to functionality. Disagreement centers on a variety of issues:

- The *rationales* underlying the functionality doctrine;
- The *test* for determining when a claimed mark is functional;
- The *scope* of the doctrine (in particular, does it extend to aesthetic features?);
- The *evidence* relevant to proof of functionality; and
- Whether existing functionality doctrine is *sufficient to effectuate* the rationales that undergird it.

Bear these questions in mind as we review the cases in this chapter.

The functionality doctrine was initially articulated in the courts. The doctrine has also been briefly addressed in the Lanham Act, though the statute still does not provide a definition or test of functionality. And, like so much of trademark law, the issue of functionality arises both in the process of seeking registration before the PTO and in litigating claims of infringement before the courts. Understanding the role of functionality in trademark law requires consideration of the different judicial and statutory forays into this area. In this chapter, we excerpt judicial opinions that have been issued both in the context of registration disputes and in infringement litigation. And, for reasons that we hope will become obvious, we include cases that precede and postdate explicit reference to functionality doctrine in the Lanham Act (which first occurred in 1998; *see* Trademark Law Treaty Implementation Act, Pub. L. No. 105-330, §201(a)(2) (1998)).

As formulated by many courts and by the PTO, one of the prerequisites for trademark protection is that the claimed mark be "nonfunctional." Accordingly, the doctrine of functionality is relevant to the establishment of trademark rights. Our decision (reflecting current law) to cover functionality doctrine at this stage should not, however, foreclose your asking whether there is a more appropriate part of trademark analysis at which the question of functionality should be considered. Indeed, we urge you to do so. *See* Graeme B. Dinwoodie, *The Death of Ontology: A Teleological Approach to Trademark Law*, 84 IOWA L. REV. 611 (1999) (arguing for a robust doctrine of functionality but proposing that the functionality of a mark under such a doctrine should not foreclose limited relief under principles of unfair competition law).

The leading modern United States Supreme Court decision on functionality is *TrafFix Devices, Inc. v. Marketing Displays, Inc.*, 532 U.S. 23 (2001). We will study that opinion (and case law applying it) in some detail. But a proper understanding of *TrafFix Devices*, and an appreciation of the questions that the Supreme Court leaves unanswered, first requires discussion of earlier case law.

IN RE MORTON-NORWICH PRODUCTS, INC.

671 F.2d 1332 (C.C.P.A. 1982)

RICH, Judge:

This appeal is from the ex parte decision of the United States Patent and Trademark Office (PTO) Trademark Trial and Appeal Board (Board), 209 USPQ 437 (TTAB 1980), in application serial No. 123,548, filed April 21, 1977, sustaining the examiner's refusal to register appellant's container configuration on the principal register. We reverse the holding on "functionality" and remand for a determination of distinctiveness.

BACKGROUND

Appellant's application seeks to register the following container configuration as a trademark for spray starch, soil and stain removers, spray cleaners for household use, liquid household cleaners and general grease removers, and insecticides:

Appellant owns U.S. Design Patent 238,655, issued Feb. 3, 1976, on the above configuration, and U.S. Patent 3,749,290, issued July 31, 1973, directed to the mechanism in the spray top.

The above-named goods constitute a family of products which appellant sells under the word-marks FANTASTIK, GLASS PLUS, SPRAY 'N WASH, GREASE RELIEF, WOOD PLUS, and MIRAKILL. Each of these items is marketed in a container of the same configuration but appellant varies the color of the body of the container according to the product. Appellant manufactures its own containers and stated in its application (amendment of April 25, 1979) that:

> Since such first use (March 31, 1974) the applicant has enjoyed substantially exclusive and continuous use of the trademark (i.e., the container) which has become distinctive of the applicant's goods in commerce.

The PTO Trademark Attorney (examiner), through a series of four office actions, maintained an unshakable position that the design sought to be registered as a trademark is not distinctive, that there is no evidence that it has become distinctive or has acquired a secondary meaning, that it is "merely functional," "essentially utilitarian," and nonarbitrary, wherefore it cannot function as a trademark. In the second action she requested applicant to "amplify the description of the mark with such particularity that *any portion* of the alleged mark considered to be non functional [sic] is incorporated in the description." (Emphasis ours.) She said, "The Examiner sees none." Having already furnished two affidavits to the effect that consumers spontaneously associate the package design with appellant's products, which had been sold in the container to the number of 132,502,000 by 1978, appellant responded to the examiner's request by pointing out, in effect, that it is the overall configuration of the container rather than any particular feature of it which is distinctive and that it was intentionally designed to be so, supplying several pieces of evidence showing several other containers of different appearance which perform the same functions. Appellant also produced the results of a survey conducted by an independent market research firm which had been made in response to the examiner's demand for evidence of distinctiveness. The examiner dismissed all of the evidence as "not persuasive" and commented that there had "still not been one iota of evidence offered that the subject matter of this application has been promoted as a trademark," which she seemed to consider a necessary element of proof. She adhered to her view that the design "is no more than a non-distinctive purely functional container for the goods plus a purely functional spray trigger controlled closure . . . essentially utilitarian and non-arbitrary. . . ."

BOARD OPINION

The board, citing three cases, stated it to be "well-settled" that the configuration of a container "may be registrable for the particular contents thereof if the shape is non-functional in character, and is, in fact, inherently distinctive, or has acquired secondary meaning as an indication of origin for such goods." In discussing the "utilitarian nature" of the alleged trademark, the board took note of photographs of appellant's containers for FANTASTIK spray cleaner and GREASE RELIEF degreaser, the labels of which bore the words, respectively, "adjustable easy sprayer" and "NEW! Trigger Control Top," commenting that "the advertising pertaining to applicant's goods promotes the word marks of the various products and the desirable functional features of the containers."

[In light of the above, and after detailed review of appellant's survey evidence without any specific comment on it, the board concluded that "the container for applicant's products, the configuration of which it seeks to register, . . . [is functional], and is therefore unregistrable, despite any de facto secondary meaning which applicant's survey and other evidence of record might indicate." The board noted that "not every word or configuration that has a de facto secondary meaning is protected as a trademark."]

ISSUES

The parties do not see the issues in the same light. Appellant and the solicitor agree that the primary issue before us is whether the subject matter sought to be registered—the configuration of the container—is "functional."

Appellant states a second issue to be whether the configuration has the capacity to and does distinguish its goods in the marketplace from the goods of others.

The solicitor contends that it would be "premature" for us to decide the second issue if we disagree with the PTO on the first issue and have to reach it, and that we should, in that event, remand the case so the board can "consider" it. Whether to remand is, therefore, an issue.

OPINION

As would be expected, the arguments made in this court are, except for the remand question, essentially the same as they were below. The question is not new and in various forms we have been over the ground before: is the design sought to be registered "functional"? There is a plethora of case law on this subject and it becomes a question of which precedents to follow here—and why. In our view, it would be useful to review the development of the principles which we must apply in order to better understand them. In doing so, it should be borne in mind that this is not a "configuration of *goods*" case but a "configuration of the *container* for the goods" case. . . .

A trademark is defined as "any word, name, symbol, or device or any combination thereof adopted and used by a manufacturer or merchant to *identify his goods* and distinguish them from those manufactured or sold by others" (emphasis ours). 15 U.S.C. §1127 (1976). Thus, it was long the rule that a trademark must be something other than, and separate from, the merchandise to which it is applied. *Davis v. Davis*, 27 F. 490, 492 (D. Mass. 1886). [cit.]

Aside from the trademark/product "separateness" rationale for not recognizing the bare design of an article or its container as a trademark, it was theorized that all such designs would soon be appropriated, leaving nothing for use by would-be competitors. . . .

This limitation of permissible trademark subject matter later gave way to assertions that one or more features of a product or package design could legally function as a trademark. [cit.] It was eventually held that the entire design of an article (or its container) could, without other means of identification, function to identify the source of the article and be protected as a trademark. *E.g., In re Minnesota Mining and Manufacturing Co.*, 51 CCPA 1546, 1547-48.

That protection was limited, however, to those designs of articles and containers, or features thereof, which were "nonfunctional." [cit.] This requirement of "nonfunctionality" is not mandated by statute, but "is deduced entirely from court decisions." *In re Mogen David Wine Corp.*, 328 F.2d 925, 932 (C.C.P.A. 1964) (Rich, J., concurring). It has as its genesis the judicial theory that there exists a fundamental right to compete through imitation of a competitor's product, which right can only be temporarily denied by the patent or copyright laws:

> If one manufacturer should make an advance in effectiveness of operation, or in simplicity of form, or in utility of color; and if that advance did not entitle him to a monopoly by means of a machine or process or a product or a design patent; and if by means of unfair trade suits he could shut out other manufacturers who plainly intended to share in the benefits of unpatented utilities . . . he would be given gratuitously a monopoly more effective than that of the unobtainable patent in the ratio of eternity to seventeen years. [*Pope Automatic Merchandising Co. v. McCrum-Howell Co.*, 191 F. 979, 981-82 (7th Cir. 1911).]

An exception to the right to copy exists, however, where the product or package design under consideration is "nonfunctional" and serves to identify its manufacturer or seller, and the exception exists even though the design is not temporarily protectable through acquisition of patent or copyright. Thus, when a design is "nonfunctional," the right to compete through imitation gives way, presumably upon balance of that right with the originator's right to prevent others from infringing upon an established symbol of trade identification.

This preliminary discussion leads to the heart of the matter—how do we define the concept of "functionality," and what role does the above balancing of interests play in that definitional process?

I.   FUNCTIONALITY DEFINED

Many courts speak of the protectability as trademarks of product and package configurations in terms of whether a particular design is "functional" or "nonfunctional." Without proper definition, however, such a distinction is useless for determining whether such design is registrable or protectable as a trademark, for the label "functional" has dual significance. It has been used, on the one hand, in lay fashion to indicate "the normal or characteristic action of anything," and, on the other hand, it has been used to denote a legal conclusion. *Compare In re Penthouse International Ltd.*, 565 F.2d 679, 681 (C.C.P.A. 1977) (If the product configuration "has a non-trademark function, the inquiry is not at an end; possession of a function and of a capability of indicating origin are not in every case mutually exclusive."), *with In re Mogen David Wine Corp.*, 328 F.2d *supra* at 933 (Rich, J., concurring) ("The Restatement appears to use the terms 'functional' and 'nonfunctional' as labels to denote the legal consequence: if the former, the public may copy; and if the latter, it may not. This is the way the 'law' has been but it is not of much help in deciding cases.").

Accordingly, it has been noted that one of the "distinct questions" involved in "functionality" reasoning is, "In what *way* is [the] subject matter functional or utilitarian, factually or legally?" *In re Honeywell, Inc.*, 497 F.2d 1344, 1350 (C.C.P.A. 1974) (Rich, J., concurring). This definitional division . . . leads to the resolution that if the designation "functional" is to be utilized to denote the *legal* consequence, we must speak in terms of de facto functionality and de jure functionality, the former being the use of "functional" in the lay sense, indicating that although the design of a product, a container, or a feature of either is directed to performance of a function, it *may* be legally recognized as an indication of source. De jure functionality, of course, would be used to indicate the opposite — such a design may not be protected as a trademark.

This is only the beginning, however, for further definition is required to explain *how* a determination of whether a design is de jure functional is to be approached. We start with an inquiry into "utility."

A.   *"Functional" Means "Utilitarian"*[1]

From the earliest cases, "functionality" has been expressed in terms of "utility." In 1930, this court stated it to be "well settled that the configuration of *an article having utility* is not the subject of trade-mark protection." (Emphasis ours.) *In re Dennison Mfg. Co.*, 39 F.2d 720, 721 (C.C.P.A. 1930) ([a]rbitrary urn or vase-like shape of reinforcing patch on a tag). [cit.] This broad statement of the "law," that the design of an article "having utility" cannot be a trademark, is incorrect and inconsistent with later pronouncements.

We wish to make it clear . . . that a discussion of "functionality" is *always* in reference to the design of the thing under consideration (in the sense of its *appearance)* and *not* the thing itself. One court, for example, paraphrasing Gertrude Stein, commented that "a dish is a dish is a dish." *Hygienic Specialties Co. v. H. G. Salzman, Inc.*, 302 F.2d 614, 621 (2d Cir. 1962). No doubt, by definition, a dish always functions as a dish and has its utility, but it is the appearance of the dish which is important in a case such as this, as will become clear.

Assuming the *Dennison* court intended that its statement reference an article whose *configuration* "has utility," its statement is still too broad. Under that reasoning, the design of a particular article would be protectable as a trademark only where the design was useless, that is, wholly unrelated to the function of the article. . . .

Most designs, however, result in the production of articles, containers, or features thereof which are indeed utilitarian, and examination into the possibility of trademark protection is not to the mere *existence* of utility, but to the *degree* of design utility. . . .

---

1. It is well known that the law of "functionality" has been applied in both a "utilitarian" sense and in terms of "aesthetics." *See e.g., Vuitton et Fils S.A. v. J. Young Enterprises, Inc.*, 644 F.2d 769 (9th Cir. 1981); *International Order of Job's Daughters v. Lindeburg and Co.*, 633 F.2d 912 (9th Cir. 1980). [cit.] Recognition of this provides an explanation for the statement that "the term 'functional' is not to be treated as synonymous with the literal significance of the term 'utilitarian.'" *J.C. Penney Co. v. H.D. Lee Mercantile Co.*, 120 F.2d 949, 954 (8th Cir. 1941). It will be so treated, however, where the issue is one of "utilitarian functionality" and not "aesthetic functionality." The PTO does not argue in this case that appellant's container configuration is aesthetically functional, notwithstanding appellant's argument that its design was adopted, in part, for aesthetic reasons.

Thus, it is the "utilitarian" *design* of a "utilitarian" *object* with which we are concerned, and the manner of use of the term "utilitarian" must be examined at each occurrence. The latter occurrence is, of course, consistent with the lay meaning of the term. But the former is being used to denote a *legal consequence* (it being synonymous with "functional"), and it therefore requires further explication.

B.   "Utilitarian" Means "Superior in Function (De Facto) or Economy of Manufacture," Which "Superiority" Is Determined in Light of Competitive Necessity to Copy

Some courts have stated this proposition in the negative. In *American-Marietta Co. v. Krigsman*, 275 F.2d 287, 289 (2d Cir. 1960), the court stated that "those features of the original goods that are not in any way essential to their use" may be termed "nonfunctional." But what does this statement mean? In the case at bar, for example, we cannot say that it means that the subject *design* is "functional" merely because a hollow body, a handhold, and a pump sprayer are "essential to its use." What this phrase must mean is not that the generic *parts* of the article or package are essential, but, as noted above, that the particular *design* of the whole assembly of those parts must be essential. This, of course, leaves us to define "essential to its use," which is also the starting place for those courts which have set forth in positive fashion the reasons they believe that some product or package designs are not protectable as trademarks and thus not registrable.

In *Luminous Unit Co. v. Williamson*, 241 F. 265 (N.D. Ill. 1917), the court noted that "the owner of a fixture, machine, or device, patented or unpatented, who has obtained a trade in it, may simply exclude others from taking away that trade when they deceive the purchasing public as to the origin of the goods sold by them." *Id.* at 268. The court went on to state an exception to this rule, which is the public right to copy those "[n]ecessary elements of mechanical construction, essential to the practical operation of a device, and which cannot be changed without either lessening the efficiency or materially increasing expense." *Id.* at 269. . . . Another court framed the issue this way: Is the subject matter "made in the form it must be made if it is to accomplish its purpose"? *Marvel Co. v. Tullar Co.*, 125 F. 829, 830 (S.D.N.Y. 1903).

Thus, it is clear that courts in the past have considered the public policy involved in this area of the law as, not the *right* to slavishly copy articles which are not protected by patent or copyright, but the *need* to copy those articles, which is more properly termed the right to compete *effectively*. Even the earliest cases, which discussed protectability in terms of exhaustion of possible packaging forms, recognized that the real issue was whether "the effect would be to gradually throttle trade." *Harrington v. Libby, supra* at 606.

More recent cases also discuss "functionality" in light of competition. One court noted that the "question in each case is whether protection against imitation will hinder the competitor in competition." *Truck Equipment Service Co. v. Fruehauf Corp.*, 536 F.2d 1210, 1218 (8th Cir. 1976). Another court, upon suit for trademark infringement (the alleged trademark being plaintiff's building design), stated that "enjoining others from using the building design [would not] inhibit competition in any way." *Fotomat Corp. v. Cochran*, 437 F. Supp. 1231, 1235 (D. Kan. 1977). This court has also referenced "hinderance of competition" in a number of the "functionality" cases which have been argued before it. [cit.] . . .

Given, then, that we must strike a balance between the "right to copy" and the right to protect one's method of trade identification, [cit.], what weights do we set upon each side of the scale? That is, given that "functionality" is a question of fact [cit.], what facts do we look to in determining whether the "consuming public has an interest in making use of [one's design], superior to [one's] interest in being [its] sole vendor"? *Vaughan Novelty Mfg. Co. v. G. G. Greene Mfg. Corp.*, 202 F.2d 172, 176 (3d Cir. 1953).

II.   DETERMINING "FUNCTIONALITY"

A.   In General

Keeping in mind, as shown by the foregoing review, that "functionality" is determined in light of "utility," which is determined in light of "superiority of design," and rests upon the foundation "essential to effective competition," *Ives Laboratories, Inc. v. Darby Drug Co.*, 601 F.2d 631, 643 (2d Cir. 1979), and cases cited *supra*, there exist a number of factors, both positive and negative, which aid in that determination.

Previous opinions of this court have discussed what evidence is useful to demonstrate that a particular design is "superior." In *In re Shenango Ceramics, Inc.*, 362 F.2d 287, 291 (C.C.P.A. 1966), the court noted that the existence of an expired utility patent which disclosed the *utilitarian advantage of the design* sought to be registered as a trademark was evidence that it was "functional." . . . It may also be significant that the originator of the design touts its utilitarian advantages through advertising.

Since the effect upon competition "is really the crux of the matter," it is, of course, significant that there are other alternatives available. Nims, *Unfair Competition and Trade-Marks* at 377; *compare Time Mechanisms, Inc. v. Qonaar Corp.*, 422 F. Supp. 905, 913 (D.N.J. 1976) ("the parking meter mechanism can be contained by housings of many different configurations"), *and In re World's Finest Chocolate, Inc.*, 474 F.2d 1012, 1014 (C.C.P.A. 1973) ("We think competitors can readily meet the demand for packaged candy bars by use of other packaging styles, and we find no utilitarian advantages flowing from this package design as opposed to others as was found in the rhomboidally-shaped deck involved in *Deister.*") . . . *with In re Honeywell, Inc.*, 532 F.2d at 182 (A portion of the board opinion which the court adopted noted that there "are only so many basic shapes in which a thermostat or its cover can be made," but then concluded that "[t]he fact that thermostat covers may be produced in other forms or shapes does not and cannot detract from the functional character of the configuration here involved.").

It is also significant that a particular design results from a comparatively simple or cheap method of manufacturing the article. In *Schwinn Bicycle Co. v. Murray Ohio Mfg. Co.*, 339 F. Supp. 973, 980 (M.D. Tenn. 1971), *aff'd*, 470 F.2d 975 (6th Cir. 1972), the court stated its reason for refusing to recognize the plaintiff's bicycle rim surface design as a trademark:

> The evidence is uncontradicted that the various manufacturers of bicycle rims in the United States consider it commercially necessary to mask, hide or camouflage the roughened and charred appearance resulting from welding the tubular rim sections together. The evidence represented indicates that the only other process used by bicycle rim manufacturers in the United States is the more complex and more expensive process of grinding and polishing.

. . .

B.   The Case at Bar

1.   The Evidence of Functionality

We come now to the task of applying to the facts of this case the distilled essence of the body of law on "functionality" above discussed. The question is whether appellant's plastic spray bottle is de jure functional; is it the best or one of a few superior designs available? We hold, on the basis of the evidence before the board, that it is not.

[Of] course, the spray bottle is highly useful and performs its intended functions in an admirable way, but that is not enough to render the *design* of the spray bottle—which is all that matters here—functional.

As the examiner appreciated, the spray bottle consists of two major parts, a bottle and a trigger-operated, spray-producing pump mechanism which also serves as a closure. We shall call the latter the spray top. In the first place, a molded plastic bottle can have an infinite variety of forms or designs and still *function* to hold liquid. No one form is *necessary* or appears to be "superior." Many bottles have necks, to be grasped for pouring or holding, and the necks likewise can be in a variety of forms. The PTO has not produced one iota of evidence to show that the shape of appellant's bottle was *required* to be as it is for any de facto functional reason, which might lead to an affirmative determination of de jure functionality. The evidence, consisting of competitor's molded plastic bottles for similar products, demonstrates that the same functions can be performed by a variety of other shapes with no sacrifice of any functional advantage. There is no necessity to copy appellant's trade dress to enjoy any of the functions of a spray-top container.

As to the appearance of the spray top, the evidence of record shows that it too can take a number of diverse forms, all of which are equally suitable as housings for the pump and spray mechanisms. Appellant acquired a patent on the pump mechanism, the drawings of which show it embodied in a structure which bears not the slightest resemblance to the appearance of appellant's spray top. The pictures of the competition's spray bottles further illustrate that no particular housing *design* is necessary to have a pump-type sprayer. Appellant's spray top, seen from the side, is rhomboidal, roughly speaking, a design which bears no relation to the shape of the pump mechanism housed within it and is an arbitrary decoration—no more de jure functional than is the grille of an automobile with respect to its under-the-hood power plant. The evidence shows that even the shapes of pump triggers can and do vary while performing the same function.

What is sought to be registered, however, is no single design feature or component but the overall composite design comprising both bottle and spray top. While that design must be *accommodated* to the functions performed, we see no evidence that it was *dictated* by them and resulted in a functionally or economically superior design of such a container.

Applying the legal principles discussed above, we do not see that allowing appellant to exclude others (upon proof of distinctiveness) from using this trade dress will hinder competition or impinge upon the rights of others to compete effectively in the sale of the goods named in the application, even to the extent of marketing them in *functionally* identical spray containers. The fact is that many others are doing so. Competitors have apparently had no need to simulate appellant's trade dress, in whole or in part, in order to enjoy all of the functional aspects of a spray top container. Upon expiration of any patent protection appellant may now be enjoying on its spray and pump mechanism, competitors may even copy and enjoy all of its functions without copying the external appearance of appellant's spray top.

If the functions of appellant's bottle can be performed equally well by containers of innumerable designs and, thus, no one is injured in competition, why did the board state that appellant's *design* is functional and for that reason not registrable?

2.   The Relationship Between "Functionality" and Distinctiveness

One who seeks to register (or protect) a product or container configuration as a trademark must demonstrate that its design is "nonfunctional," as discussed above, and that the design functions as an indication of source, whether inherently so, because of its distinctive nature, [cit.], or through acquisition of secondary meaning. These two requirements must, however, be kept separate from one another.

The issues of distinctiveness and functionality may have been somewhat intermixed by the board. . . .

. . . Whether in fact the design is "functional" requires closer and more careful scrutiny. We cannot say that there exists an inverse proportional relationship in all cases between distinctiveness of design and functionality (de facto or de jure). . . .

This court's past opinions which indicate that a particular design is "nonfunctional" because it is "arbitrary" are not to be construed as contrary to [our comments on this relationship]. [cit.] In this situation, "arbitrary" is not used in the typical trademark (distinctiveness) sense of the word. It is used to indicate a design which may have been selected without complete deference to utility and, thus, is most likely "nonfunctional." That is, it is used to indicate the opposite side of the "functional" coin, since a design can be inherently distinctive (the usual trademark law meaning of the word "arbitrary") and still be "functional." . . .

Reversed and Remanded.

NOTES AND QUESTIONS

1. *The* Morton-Norwich *approach.* What is the rationale for the functionality doctrine, according to the *Morton-Norwich* court? What is the test that the court applies? To what evidence does it look to determine the answer to the relevant question? Which of the evidentiary factors identified in *Morton-Norwich* appear to offer potential for expansive interpretation by courts?

2. *Limiting protection for designs: doctrinal vehicles.* What are the different doctrinal devices through which courts or the PTO might limit the protection of product designs under the trademark statute? Why might the classification of a design as "arbitrary" be relevant to its protection as a trademark? Why might the availability of alternative designs that perform the same function be relevant to the protection of a design as a trademark? Would it matter whether these alternative designs already existed in the marketplace or were simply possibilities? *See* Graeme B. Dinwoodie, *Reconceptualizing the Inherent Distinctiveness of Product Design Trade Dress,* 75 N.C. L. REV. 471, 600-02 (1997).

3. *Product design/product packaging.* Judge Rich stresses that "it should be borne in mind that this is not a 'configuration *of goods*' case but a 'configuration of the *container* for the goods' case." Should that affect the functionality doctrine? In *Wal-Mart, supra* Chapter 2, section D, the Supreme Court endorsed a different test by which to determine the distinctiveness of product design (as opposed to product packaging). Should we have different functionality doctrines for product configuration cases, on the one hand, and product container configuration cases, on the other? *See Speare Tools, Inc. v. Klein Tools, Inc.* 113 U.S.P.Q.2d (BNA) 1800 (E.D. Wis. 2014).

4. *The separateness argument.* The court notes that the "separateness" rationale for not recognizing trademark rights in the design of an article had eventually given way to a more liberal approach to design trademark protection. To what extent has that rationale resurfaced in other (recent) cases that we have read? Might it be relevant to some aspects of trademark analysis but not others?

5. *Balancing interests.* What interests or values cause the right to compete through imitation of a product unprotected by patent or copyright law to give way to the assertion of trademark rights? How should the interests served by trademark protection be balanced with the right to compete? The court concludes (pre–*Wal-Mart,* of course) that "a design can be inherently distinctive . . . and still be 'functional.'" What protection *is* available to a distinctive but functional design? What protection *should be* available?

6.   *Design patent protection.* The *Morton-Norwich* court mentions that the applicant owned a design patent on the configuration in question. Design patent protection is granted to new and nonobvious ornamental designs. *See* 35 U.S.C. §171 ("Whoever invents any new, original and ornamental design for an article of manufacture may obtain a patent therefor, subject to the conditions and requirements of this title."). A design must also meet a nonfunctionality requirement. From a review of Section 171, in what ways is the protection offered by a design patent in the United States different from that offered by U.S. trade dress law or copyright law? What explains those differences?

B.   THE SCOPE OF THE FUNCTIONALITY DOCTRINE

Consider the following hypothetical. Dinwoodie and Janis open a chocolate store in Chicago just in time for St. Valentine's Day. To attract the crowd of overly sentimental romantics who rush mindlessly to the stores on February 13, they decide to market chocolates in a red heart-shaped box. (Suppose, for the purpose of this hypothetical, that Dinwoodie and Janis were the first producers to package chocolates in a heart-shaped box; indeed, they only hit upon the idea after months of thought.) Quickly, the chocolate lovers (and just plain lovers) of Chicago come to associate the heart-shaped box with the chocolates produced by Dinwoodie and Janis. Would you be willing to grant Dinwoodie and Janis trademark protection in the heart-shaped box for chocolates? What concerns might this raise? Are these concerns addressed by the rules articulated by the *Morton-Norwich* court? What is the "function" of the box shape? If the *Morton-Norwich* rules (and factors) were applied to the shape of the box, what would be the result? What interests might support giving Dinwoodie and Janis trademark rights in the shape of the box for chocolates?

Most early applications of the functionality rule involved denial of protection to mechanical or utilitarian features of a product's trade dress. But, as the *Morton-Norwich* court hints in footnote 1, the doctrine of functionality soon expanded to deny protection to certain design features that were not utilitarian in the mechanical sense (i.e., were aesthetic). This doctrine of "aesthetic functionality" is derived from commentary to the first Restatement of Torts. *See* Restatement of Torts §742 cmt. a (1938) ("When goods are bought largely for their aesthetic value, their features may be functional because they definitely contribute to that value and thus aid the performance of an object for which the goods are intended."). But the judicial opinion regarded as the effective starting point for aesthetic functionality is *Pagliero v. Wallace China Co.*, 198 F.2d 339, 343 (9th Cir. 1952) (articulating rule that a design that was "an important ingredient in the commercial success" of a product was *de jure* functional and thus unprotected even if that feature was aesthetic). In that case, the decorative design of hotel china was held to be aesthetically functional because it was "an essential selling feature" of the product. Although the *Pagliero* standard was heavily criticized and is now rarely used by courts—the Ninth Circuit has itself retreated from its standard in *Pagliero*—the doctrine of aesthetic functionality has survived.

Consider whether the rationales for the functionality doctrine articulated in *Morton-Norwich* apply with as much force to the design features for which trademark rights are claimed in the following cases. Are there alternative rationales that support the doctrine in these cases? Is the doctrine of "aesthetic functionality" a separate doctrine from a doctrine of "utilitarian functionality"? Do we need different tests to determine the limits of trademark protection for "aesthetic" as opposed to "utilitarian" features? Is this a viable distinction?

WALLACE INT'L SILVERSMITHS, INC. v. GODINGER SILVER ART CO., INC.

916 F.2d 76 (2d Cir. 1990), cert. denied, 499 U.S. 976 (1991)

WINTER, Circuit Judge:

Wallace International Silversmiths ("Wallace") appeals from Judge Haight's denial of its motion for a preliminary injunction under Section 43(a) of the Lanham Act prohibiting Godinger Silver Art Co., Inc. ("Godinger") from marketing a line of silverware with ornamentation that is substantially similar to Wallace's GRANDE BAROQUE line. Judge Haight held that the GRANDE BAROQUE design is "a functional feature of 'Baroque' style silverware" and thus not subject to protection as a trademark. We affirm.

BACKGROUND

Wallace, a Delaware corporation, has sold sterling silver products for over one hundred years. Its GRANDE BAROQUE pattern was introduced in 1941 and is still one of the best-selling silverware lines in America. Made of fine sterling silver, a complete place setting costs several thousand dollars. Total sales of GRANDE BAROQUE silverware have exceeded fifty million dollars. The GRANDE BAROQUE pattern is fairly described as "ornate, massive and flowery [with] indented, flowery roots and scrolls and curls along the side of the shaft, and flower arrangements along the front of the shaft." Wallace owns a trademark registration for the GRANDE BAROQUE name as applied to sterling silver flatware and hollowware. The GRANDE BAROQUE design is not patented, but on December 11, 1989, Wallace filed an application for trademark registration for the GRANDE BAROQUE pattern. This application is still pending.

Godinger, a New York corporation, is a manufacturer of silver-plated products. The company has recently begun to market a line of baroque-style silver-plated serving pieces. The suggested retail price of the set of four serving pieces is approximately twenty dollars. Godinger advertised its new line under the name 20TH CENTURY BAROQUE and planned to introduce it at the Annual New York Tabletop and Accessories Show, the principal industry trade show at which orders for the coming year are taken. Like Wallace's silverware, Godinger's pattern contains typical baroque elements including an indented root, scrolls, curls, and flowers. The arrangement of these elements approximates Wallace's design in many ways, although their dimensions are noticeably different. The most obvious difference between the two designs is that the Godinger pattern extends further down the handle than the Wallace pattern does. The Wallace pattern also tapers from the top of the handle to the stem while the Godinger pattern appears bulkier overall and maintains its bulk throughout the decorated portion of the handle. Although the record does not disclose the exact circumstances under which Godinger's serving pieces were created, Godinger admits that its designers were "certainly inspired by and aware of [the Wallace] design when [they] created [the 20TH CENTURY BAROQUE] design."

On the afternoon of April 23, 1990, Leonard Florence of Wallace learned from a wholesale customer, Michael C. Fina Company, that Godinger had placed an advertisement for its 20TH CENTURY BAROQUE serving pieces in an industry trade magazine. George Fina, the company's president, said that he was "confused" when he saw what he believed to be a pattern identical to GRANDE BAROQUE being advertised by another company. He asked Mr. Florence whether Wallace had licensed the design to Godinger or whether "the Godinger product was simply a 'knock-off.'" Two days after this conversation, Wallace filed the complaint in the instant matter stating various federal trademark and state unfair competition claims. Wallace also filed a motion for a temporary restraining order and sought a preliminary injunction prohibiting Godinger from using the mark 20TH CENTURY BAROQUE or infringing the trade dress of Wallace's GRANDE BAROQUE product.

. . . [T]he district court held a hearing on Wallace's application for preliminary relief . . . [and] concluded that the GRANDE BAROQUE design was a "functional" feature of baroque-style silverware and thus ineligible for trade dress protection under Section 43(a) of the Lanham Act. In so holding, [Judge Haight] stated:

> In the case at bar, the "Baroque" curls and flowers are not "arbitrary embellishments" adopted to identify plaintiff's product. Instead, all the "Baroque" style silverware use essentially the same scrolls and flowers as a way to compete in the free market. The "Baroque" style is a line of silverware which many manufacturers produce. Just like the patterns on the chinaware in *Pagliero* [*v. Wallace China Co.*, 198 F.2d 339 (9th Cir. 1952)], the "Grande Baroque" design is a functional feature of "Baroque" style silverware.
>
> Wallace may well have developed secondary meaning in the market of "Baroque"-styled silverware. In fact, I assume for purposes of this motion that anyone that sees, for instance, five lines of Baroque silverware will single out the Wallace line as being the "classiest" or the most handsome looking and will immediately exclaim "Oh! That's the Wallace line. They make the finest looking 'Baroque' forks!" That is secondary meaning. However, that does not mean that plaintiff's design is subject to protection. The "Baroque" curls, roots and flowers are not "mere indicia of source." Instead, they are requirements to compete in the silverware market. This is a classic example of the proposition that "to imitate is to compete." *Pagliero, supra*, at 344. The designs are aesthetically functional.
>
> Accordingly, I conclude that plaintiff does not have a trade dress subject to the protection of the Lanham Act. . . .

He therefore . . . denied Wallace's motion for a preliminary injunction.

DISCUSSION

. . .

In order to maintain an action for trade dress infringement under Section 43(a) of the Lanham Act, the plaintiff must show that its trade dress has acquired secondary meaning — that is, the trade dress identifies the source of the product — and that there is a likelihood of confusion between the original trade dress and the trade dress of the allegedly infringing product. *LeSportsac, Inc. v. K Mart Corp.*, 754 F.2d 71, 75 (2d Cir. 1985). Even if the plaintiff establishes these elements, the defendant may still avoid liability on a variety of grounds, including the so-called functionality doctrine. Our present view of that doctrine is derived from the Supreme Court's dictum in *Inwood Laboratories*, stating that "[i]n general terms, a product feature is functional if it is essential to the use or purpose of the article or if it affects the cost or quality of the article." [*Inwood Laboratories, Inc. v. Ives Laboratories, Inc.*, 456 U.S. 844, 850 n.10 (1982)]. Our most recent elaboration of the doctrine was in [*Stormy Clime, Ltd. v. ProGroup, Inc.*, 809 F.2d 971 (2d Cir. 1987)], where Judge Newman stated:

> [T]he functionality inquiry . . . should [focus] on whether bestowing trade dress protection upon [a particular] arrangement of features "'will hinder competition or impinge upon the rights of others to compete effectively in the sale of goods.'" *Sicilia di R. Biebow & Co. v. Cox*, 732 F.2d 417, 429 (5th Cir. 1984) (quoting In re *Morton-Norwich Products, Inc.*, 671 F.2d 1332, 1342 (Cust. & Pat. App. 1982)).

Id. at 976-77. . . .

. . . Judge Haight found that the similarities between the Godinger and Wallace designs involved elements common to all baroque-style designs used in the silverware market. He noted that many manufacturers compete in that market with such designs and found that "[t]he 'Baroque' curls, roots and flowers are not 'mere indicia of source.' Instead, they are requirements to compete in the silverware market." Judge Haight concluded that "the 'Grande Baroque' design is a functional feature of 'Baroque' style silverware," relying on *Pagliero v. Wallace China Co.*, 198 F.2d 339 (9th Cir. 1952).

Although we agree with Judge Haight's decision, we do not endorse his reliance upon *Pagliero*. That decision allowed a competitor to sell exact copies of china bearing a particular pattern without finding that comparably attractive patterns were not available to the competitor. It based its holding solely on the ground that the particular pattern was an important ingredient in the commercial success of the china. *Id.* at 343-44. We [have] rejected *Pagliero* [before] and reiterate that rejection here. Under *Pagliero*, the commercial success of an aesthetic feature automatically destroys all of the originator's trademark interest in it, notwithstanding the feature's secondary meaning and the lack of any evidence that competitors cannot develop non-infringing, attractive patterns. By allowing the copying of an exact design without any evidence of market foreclosure, the *Pagliero* test discourages both originators and later competitors from developing pleasing designs. *See Keene Corp. v. Paraflex Industries, Inc.*, 653 F.2d 822, 824-25 (3d Cir. 1981).

Our rejection of *Pagliero*, however, does not call for reversal. Quite unlike *Pagliero*, Judge Haight found in the instant matter that there is a substantial market for baroque silverware and that effective competition in that market requires "use [of] essentially the same scrolls and flowers" as are found on Wallace's silverware. Based on the record at the hearing, that finding is not clearly erroneous and satisfies the requirement of *Stormy Clime* that a design feature not be given trade dress protection where use of that feature is necessary for effective competition. 809 F.2d at 976-77.

Stormy Clime [which involved protection for the design of jackets that included side-vents in the jackets] is arguably distinguishable, however, because it involved a design that had both aesthetic and utilitarian features. If read narrowly, *Stormy Clime* might be limited to cases in which trademark protection of a design would foreclose competitors from incorporating utilitarian features necessary to compete in the market for the particular product. In the instant case, the features at issue are strictly ornamental because they neither affect the use of the silverware nor contribute to its efficient manufacture. The question, therefore, is whether the doctrine of functionality applies to features of a product that are purely ornamental but that are essential to effective competition.

Our only hesitation in holding that the functionality doctrine applies is based on nomenclature. "Functionality" seems to us to imply only utilitarian considerations and, as a legal doctrine, to be intended only to prevent competitors from obtaining trademark protection for design features that are necessary to the use or efficient production of the product. *See Keene, supra* at 825 ("inquiry should focus on the extent to which the design feature is related to the utilitarian function of the product or feature"). Even when the doctrine is referred to as "aesthetic" functionality, it still seems an apt description only of pleasing designs of utilitarian features. Nevertheless, there is no lack of language in caselaw endorsing use of the defense of aesthetic functionality where trademark protection for purely ornamental features would exclude competitors from a market. *See, e.g.,* [*W.T. Rogers Co. v. Keene*, 778 F.2d 334, 347 (7th Cir. 1985)] ("Though a producer does not lose a design trademark just because the public finds it pleasing, there may come a point where the design feature is so important to the value of the product to consumers that continued trademark protection would deprive them of competitive alternatives[.]") (Posner, J.). . . .

We put aside our quibble over doctrinal nomenclature, however, because we are confident that whatever secondary meaning Wallace's baroque silverware pattern may have acquired, Wallace may not exclude competitors from using those baroque design elements necessary to compete in the market for baroque silverware. It is a first principle of trademark law that an owner may not use the mark as a means of excluding competitors from a substantial market. Where a mark becomes the generic term to describe an article, for example, trademark protection ceases. [cit.] Where granting trademark protection to the use of certain colors would tend to exclude competitors, such protection is also limited. *See First Brands Corp. v. Fred Meyer, Inc.*, 809 F.2d 1378 (9th Cir. 1987); J. THOMAS MCCARTHY, TRADEMARKS AND UNFAIR COMPETITION, §7:16 *et seq.* Finally, as discussed *supra*, design features of products that are necessary to the product's utility may be copied by competitors under the functionality doctrine.

Wallace's Grand Baroque Silverware

In the instant matter, Wallace seeks trademark protection, not for a precise expression of a decorative style, but for basic elements of a style that is part of the public domain. As found by the district court, these elements are important to competition in the silverware market. We perceive no distinction between a claim to exclude all others from use on silverware of basic elements of a decorative style and claims to generic names, basic colors or designs important to a product's utility. In each case, trademark protection is sought, not just to protect an owner of a mark in informing the public of the source of its products, but also to exclude competitors from producing similar products. We therefore abandon our quibble with the aesthetic functionality doctrine's nomenclature and adopt the Draft Restatement's view that, where an ornamental feature is claimed as a trademark and trademark protection would significantly hinder competition by limiting the range of adequate alternative designs, the aesthetic functionality doctrine denies such protection. See Third Restatement of the Law,

Unfair Competition (Preliminary Draft No. 3), Ch. 3, §17(c) at 213-14. This rule avoids the overbreadth of *Pagliero* by requiring a finding of foreclosure of alternatives while still ensuring that trademark protection does not exclude competitors from substantial markets.

Of course, if Wallace were able to show secondary meaning in a precise expression of baroque style, competitors might be excluded from using an identical or virtually identical design. In such a case, numerous alternative baroque designs would still be available to competitors. Although the Godinger design at issue here was found by Judge Haight to be "substantially similar," it is not identical or virtually identical, and the similarity involves design elements necessary to compete in the market for baroque silverware. Because according trademark protection to those elements would significantly hinder competitors by limiting the range of adequate alternative designs, we agree with Judge Haight's denial of a preliminary injunction.

Affirmed.

BRUNSWICK CORP. v. BRITISH SEAGULL LTD.
35 F.3d 1527 (Fed. Cir. 1994)

RADER, Circuit Judge:

[Mercury manufactured and sold marine outboard engines for over thirty years, and for most of that time, all Mercury outboard engines were black. Some of Mercury's advertisements focused on Mercury's "all black" color. Mercury engines were not, however, the only black outboard engines on the market during that time. In 1998, Mercury filed an application to register the color black for outboard engines on the Principal Register. British Seagull Ltd. and Outboard Marine Corp. (the opposers) filed Opposition Nos. 80,900 and 80,901. The Board considered the proposed mark's functionality.]

> [A]lthough the color black is not functional in the sense that it makes these engines work better, or that it makes them easier or less expensive to manufacture, black is more desirable from the perspective of prospective purchasers because it is color compatible with a wider variety of boat colors and because objects colored black appear smaller than they do when they are painted other lighter or brighter colors. The evidence shows that people who buy outboard motors for boats like the colors of the motors to be harmonious with the colors of their vessels, and that they also find it desirable under some circumstances to reduce the perception of the size of the motors in proportion to the boats.

British Seagull, Ltd. v. Brunswick Corp., 28 U.S.P.Q.2d 1197, 1199 (T.T.A.B. 1993).

[Accordingly, the Board concluded that the color black, applied to the engines, was *de jure* functional because of competitive need. Mercury appealed the Board's decision. The Court of Appeals for the Federal Circuit stressed that "contrary to Mercury's assertion, the test for de jure functionality does not involve inquiry into whether a particular feature is 'essential' to compete at all." Rather, "if the feature asserted to give a product distinctiveness is the best, or at least one, of a few superior designs for its de facto purpose, it follows that competition is hindered. *Morton-Norwich* does not rest on total elimination of competition in the goods." Thus, the Board did not err by basing its finding of *de jure* functionality on competitive need. The Court then turned to the facts of Mercury's application.]

Turning to the present case, the Board determined that "black, when applied to [Mercury's] outboard marine engines, is de jure functional because of competitive need." *British Seagull*, 28 U.S.P.Q.2d at 1199. The color black, as the Board noted, does not make the engines function better as engines. The paint on the external surface of an engine does not affect its mechanical purpose. Rather, the color black exhibits both color compatibility with a wide variety of boat colors and ability to make objects appear smaller. With these advantages for potential customers, the Board found a competitive need for engine manufacturers to use black on outboard engines. Based on this competitive need, the Board determined that the color was de jure functional. This court discerns no error in the Board's legal reasoning and no clear error in its factual findings.

This court's decision in [*In re Owens-Corning Fiberglass Corp.*, 774 F.2d 1116 (Fed. Cir. 1985)] does not compel a different result. In *Owens-Corning*, Owens-Corning sought to register the color pink as applied to its fibrous glass insulation. This court reversed the Board's refusal to register the color pink as Owens-Corning's trademark. The Board found that no other insulation manufacturer colored any of its products. The record revealed no reason to dye the insulation pink or any other color. Indeed, insulation in use is not open to general view at all. Owens-Corning alone undertook the additional, unnecessary step of coloring the insulation.

This court determined that no anti-competitive effects would follow from awarding Owens-Corning a mark for the color pink. . . .

This case, as the Board found, compels a different result. All outboard engine manufacturers color their products. These manufacturers seek colors that easily coordinate with the wide variety of boat colors. The Board found that the color black served this non-trademark purpose. In addition, the Board found that the color black serves the non-trademark purpose of decreasing apparent object size. The record showed that these features were important to consumers. Unlike the pink color in *Owens-Corning*, the Board found a competitive need for the color black. Thus, the Board concluded that registration of Mercury's proposed mark would hinder competition. This court discerns no clear error in the Board's findings.

[The court concluded that the Board properly considered whether alternative colors were available in order to avoid the fettering of competition. The court noted that "the functionality limitation on trademark protection properly subsumes any lingering policy concerns embodied in the 'color depletion theory,' [such that] [t]he theory is not a per se bar to registration of color marks." But, as a result, "if the use of color on the applicant's goods serves a non-trademark purpose that hinders competition, the de jure functionality doctrine precludes trademark protection."]

NOTES AND QUESTIONS

1. *Color and functionality.* In *Qualitex*, the Supreme Court acknowledged that color per se could be legally functional. The respondent had argued that color per se should not be registrable as a trademark because colors are in limited supply. It claimed that "if one of many competitors can appropriate a particular color for use as a trademark, and each competitor then tries to do the same, the supply of colors will soon be depleted . . . to the point where a competitor's inability to find a suitable color will put that competitor at a significant disadvantage." The Court acknowledged the concern for competition, but did not find it a reason to deny the possibility that some colors per se could be registered because if the color scarcity problem arose, the doctrine of functionality would be available to prevent any anticompetitive consequences.

2. *Relevant market.* The *Wallace* court appears to be concerned with ensuring competition. In what markets is the court analyzing competition? How did it identify the relevant market in which it sought to analyze competition? How would the plaintiff wish to define the relevant market for the court's analysis? The defendant? (Might the parties wish to define the market differently for the purposes of other aspects of trademark analysis?)

3.   *Separating the mark and the market.* Functionality doctrine reflects a concern that by ostensibly giving rights in a *mark*, trademark law might afford undue competitive advantages in a discrete *market*. To avoid this problem, trademark rights are denied in the claimed mark. If you are counsel for a producer claiming rights in a mark that may present this problem, what range of arguments might you adopt to persuade a court that granting rights in the mark will not provide an unwarranted competitive advantage in the market?

4.   *Different levels of need.* What level of competitive need (or what competitive effect) must be established to warrant a finding of functionality? According to the *Wallace* court? According to the *Brunswick* court? In what ways is the *Wallace* approach different from the test announced by the *Pagliero* court (and rejected by the *Wallace* court)?

5.   *Compatibility and standardization concerns.* Under the *Wallace* and *Brunswick* tests, what is the relevance of color compatibility? That is, if most consumers have purchased complementary goods that have to be a particular color to be compatible, is that relevant to the functionality inquiry? Does it matter whether consumers simply prefer that the goods be a particular color? Should functionality doctrine consider *why* consumers prefer the goods to be a particular color? In *Keene Corp. v. Paraflex Indus., Inc.*, 653 F.2d 822 (3d Cir. 1981), the Court of Appeals for the Third Circuit upheld a trial court's finding that the design of a luminaire was functional because there were only a limited number of configurations or designs for a luminaire that were architecturally compatible with the structures on which they were placed. Should there be a difference in the analysis of functionality depending on whether the defendant pleads color compatibility, shape compatibility, or style compatibility? What if the reason for compatibility is health-related rather than fashion-related: should those motivations affect the result? *See Shire US Inc. v. Barr Labs., Inc.*, 329 F.3d 348 (3d Cir. 2003) (finding that the shape and color of plaintiff's drugs were functional because use of the same shape and color by manufacturers of the equivalent generic drug enhances patient safety and compliance with the prescribed dosing regimen where the drugs in question were frequently dispensed by nonmedical intermediaries such as school secretaries).

6.   *The effect of functionality doctrine on eligible subject matter requirements.* Functionality doctrine serves to confine trademark rights for the reasons discussed above. But notice how the existence of the functionality doctrine allows courts to be more generous to trademark claimants as they analyze other questions relevant to the availability of trademark rights. In *Qualitex*, the Court rejected respondent's argument that color per se should not be registrable as a trademark because colors are in limited supply, noting:

> This argument is unpersuasive, however, largely because it relies on an occasional problem to justify a blanket prohibition. When a color serves as a mark, normally alternative colors will likely be available for similar use by others. *See, e.g., Owens-Corning*, 774 F.2d, at 1121 (pink insulation). Moreover, if that is not so — if a "color depletion" or "color scarcity" problem does arise — the trademark doctrine of "functionality" normally would seem available to prevent the anticompetitive consequences that Jacobson's argument posits, thereby minimizing that argument's practical force.

7.   *Relation to the genericness doctrine.* The *Wallace* court comments that it could "perceive no distinction between a claim to exclude all others from use on silverware of basic elements of a decorative style and claims to generic names, basic colors or designs important to a product's utility." Might there be a reason, in certain circumstances, to treat a generic product design differently from a functional product design? *Cf. Kendall Jackson*

Winery Ltd. v. E&J Gallo, 150 F.3d 1042, 1050-51 (9th Cir. 1998) (affirming jury verdict that the trade dress of plaintiff's wine bottles, which represented the "California look," was functional and nondistinctive). Are the interests at stake the same in both instances? *See* Graeme B. Dinwoodie, *Reconceptualizing the Inherent Distinctiveness of Product Design Trade Dress*, 75 N.C. L. REV. 471, 599-600 (1997).

C.   THE SUPREME COURT'S APPROACH TO FUNCTIONALITY

Over the years, the U.S. Supreme Court has issued a number of opinions that bear on the question of functionality. In this section, we first consider the Court's 1938 *Kellogg* opinion involving the shape of Shredded Wheat pillow-shaped biscuits. Many discussions of functionality start with this case, which at first glance has relatively little to say about functionality doctrine, but a good deal to say about the concerns underlying that doctrine. In recent years, the Supreme Court has increasingly referenced or developed the detailed doctrinal tests of functionality. In 1982, in *Inwood Laboratories, Inc. v. Ives Laboratories, Inc.*, 456 U.S. 844 (1982), the Court, in the course of considering the standards for appellate review of a district court's findings in a trademark case (*see infra* Chapter 7), noted in a footnote that "[i]n general terms, a product feature is functional if it is essential to the use or purpose of the article or if it affects the cost or quality of the article." *Id.* at 850, n.10. Thirteen years later, in *Qualitex Co. v. Jacobson Products Co., Inc.*, 514 U.S. 159 (1995), the Court offered more substantial analysis of the functionality doctrine, although again the doctrine was tangential to the main holding of the case. Finally, in 2001 the Court in *TrafFix Devices v. Marketing Displays* specifically addressed the doctrine. We will conclude this section by considering that opinion in detail.

KELLOGG CO. v. NATIONAL BISCUIT CO.
305 U.S. 111 (1938)

Mr. Justice BRANDEIS delivered the opinion of the Court:

This suit was brought in the federal court for Delaware by National Biscuit Company against Kellogg Company to enjoin alleged unfair competition by the manufacture and sale of the breakfast food commonly known as shredded wheat. The competition was alleged to be unfair mainly because Kellogg Company uses, like the plaintiff, the name shredded wheat and, like the plaintiff, produces its biscuit in pillow-shaped form.

Shredded wheat is a product composed of whole wheat which has been boiled, partially dried, then drawn or pressed out into thin shreds and baked. The shredded wheat biscuit generally known is pillow-shaped in form. It was introduced in 1893 by Henry D. Perky, of Colorado; and he was connected until his death in 1908 with companies formed to make and market the article. Commercial success was not attained until the Natural Food Company built, in 1901, a large factory at Niagara Falls, New York. In 1908, its corporate name was changed to "The Shredded Wheat Company"; and in 1930 its business and goodwill were acquired by National Biscuit Company.

Kellogg Company has been in the business of manufacturing breakfast food cereals since its organization in 1905. [Kellogg began manufacturing a product "whose form was somewhat like the product in question, but whose manufacture was different, the wheat being reduced to a dough before being pressed into shreds." Eventually, National Biscuit sued.]

In 1935, the District Court dismissed the bill. It found that the name "Shredded Wheat" is a term describing alike the product of the plaintiff and of the defendant; and that no passing off or deception had been shown. It held that upon the expiration of the Perky patent No. 548, 086 issued October 15, 1895, the name of the patented article passed into the public domain. [The Court of Appeals affirmed, then vacated and reversed upon rehearing. The Court of Appeals directed the District Court to enjoin Kellogg from "the use of the name 'Shredded Wheat' as its trade-name" and from "advertising or offering for sale its product in the form and shape of plaintiff's biscuit." Kellogg nevertheless persisted in selling its product, claiming that the injunction only prevented it from selling a product called "Shredded Wheat," in the form of plaintiff's product, accompanied by a graphic of a dish with biscuits in it. National Biscuit petitioned to "clarify" the injunction, and prevailed in the lower courts. The Supreme Court ultimately granted certiorari.]

The plaintiff concedes that it does not possess the exclusive right to make shredded wheat. But it claims the exclusive right to the trade name "Shredded Wheat" and the exclusive right to make shredded wheat biscuits pillow-shaped. It charges that the defendant, by using the name and shape, and otherwise, is passing off, or enabling others to pass off, Kellogg goods for those of the plaintiff. Kellogg Company denies that the plaintiff is entitled to the exclusive use of the name or of the pillow-shape; denies any passing off; asserts that it has used every reasonable effort to distinguish its product from that of the plaintiff; and contends that in honestly competing for a part of the market for shredded wheat it is exercising the common right freely to manufacture and sell an article of commerce unprotected by patent.

First. The plaintiff has no exclusive right to the use of the term "Shredded Wheat" as a trade name. For that is the generic term of the article, which describes it with a fair degree of accuracy; and is the term by which the biscuit in pillow-shaped form is generally known by the public. Since the term is generic, the original maker of the product acquired no exclusive right to use it. As Kellogg Company had the right to make the article, it had, also, the right to use the term by which the public knows it. [cit.] Ever since 1894 the article has been known to the public as shredded wheat. For many years, there was no attempt to use the term "Shredded Wheat" as a trade-mark. . . .

Moreover, the name "Shredded Wheat," as well as the product, the process and the machinery employed in making it, has been dedicated to the public. The basic patent for the product and for the process of making it, and many other patents for special machinery to be used in making the article, issued to Perky. In those patents the term "shredded" is repeatedly used as descriptive of the product. The basic patent expired October 15, 1912; the others soon after. Since during the life of the patents "Shredded Wheat" was the general designation of the patented product, there passed to the public upon the expiration of the patent, not only the right to make the article as it was made during the patent period, but also the right to apply thereto the name by which it had become known. As was said in *Singer Mfg. Co. v. June Mfg. Co.*, 163 U.S. 169, 185:

> It equally follows from the cessation of the monopoly and the falling of the patented device into the domain of things public that along with the public ownership of the device there must also necessarily pass to the public the generic designation of the thing which has arisen during the monopoly. . . .
>
> To say otherwise would be to hold that, although the public had acquired the device covered by the patent, yet the owner of the patent or the manufacturer of the patented thing had retained the designated name which was essentially necessary to vest the public with the full enjoyment of that which had become theirs by the disappearance of the monopoly.

It is contended that the plaintiff has the exclusive right to the name "Shredded Wheat," because those words acquired the "secondary meaning" of shredded wheat made at Niagara Falls by the plaintiff's predecessor. There is no basis here for applying the doctrine of secondary meaning. The evidence shows only that due to the long period in which the plaintiff or its predecessor was the only manufacturer of the product, many people have come to associate the product, and as a consequence the name by which the product is generally known, with the plaintiff's factory at Niagara Falls. But to establish a trade name in the term "shredded wheat" the plaintiff must show more than a subordinate meaning which applies to it. It must show that the primary significance of the term in the minds of the consuming public is not the product but the producer. This it has not done. The showing which it has made does not entitle it to the exclusive use of the term shredded wheat but merely entitles it to require that the defendant use reasonable care to inform the public of the source of its product.

The plaintiff seems to contend that even if Kellogg Company acquired upon the expiration of the patents the right to use the name shredded wheat, the right was lost by delay. . . . Those facts are without legal significance. Kellogg Company's right was not one dependent upon diligent exercise. Like every other member of the public, it was, and remained, free to make shredded wheat when it chose to do so; and to call the product by its generic name. The only obligation resting upon Kellogg Company was to identify its own product lest it be mistaken for that of the plaintiff.

Second. The plaintiff has not the exclusive right to sell shredded wheat in the form of a pillow-shaped biscuit—the form in which the article became known to the public. That is the form in which shredded wheat was made under the basic patent. The patented machines used were designed to produce only the pillow-shaped biscuits. And a design patent was taken out to cover the pillow-shaped form.[4] Hence, upon expiration of the patents the form, as well as the name, was dedicated to the public. As was said [in *Singer*, 163 U.S. at 185]: "It is self-evident that on the expiration of a patent the monopoly granted by it ceases to exist, and the right to make the thing formerly covered by the patent becomes public property. It is upon this condition that the patent is granted. It follows, as a matter of course, that on the termination of the patent there passes to the public the right to make the machine in the form in which it was constructed during the patent. We may therefore dismiss without further comment the complaint as to the form in which the defendant made his machines."

Where an article may be manufactured by all, a particular manufacturer can no more assert exclusive rights in a form in which the public has become accustomed to see the article and which, in the minds of the public, is primarily associated with the article rather than a particular producer, than it can in the case of a name with similar connections in the public mind. Kellogg Company was free to use the pillow-shaped form, subject only to the obligation to identify its product lest it be mistaken for that of the plaintiff.

Third. The question remains whether Kellogg Company in exercising its right to use the name "Shredded Wheat" and the pillow-shaped biscuit, is doing so fairly. Fairness requires that it be done in a manner which reasonably distinguishes its product from that of plaintiff.

Each company sells its biscuits only in cartons. The standard Kellogg carton contains fifteen biscuits; the plaintiff's twelve. The Kellogg cartons are distinctive. They do not resemble those used by the plaintiff either in size, form, or color. And the difference in the labels is striking. The Kellogg cartons bear in bold script the names "Kellogg's Whole Wheat Biscuit" or "Kellogg's Shredded Whole Wheat Biscuit" so sized and spaced as to

---

4. The design patent would have expired by limitations in 1909. In 1908 it was declared invalid by a district judge on the ground that the design had been in public use for more than two years prior to the application for the patent and theretofore had already been dedicated to the public.

strike the eye as being a Kellogg product. It is true that on some of its cartons it had a picture of two shredded wheat biscuits in a bowl of milk which was quite similar to one of the plaintiff's registered trade-marks. But the name Kellogg was so prominent on all of the defendant's cartons as to minimize the possibility of confusion.

Some hotels, restaurants, and lunchrooms serve biscuits not in cartons, and guests so served may conceivably suppose that a Kellogg biscuit served is one of the plaintiff's make. But no person familiar with plaintiff's product would be misled. The Kellogg biscuit is about two-thirds the size of plaintiff's; and differs from it in appearance. Moreover, the field in which deception could be practiced is negligibly small. Only 2½ per cent of the Kellogg biscuits are sold to hotels, restaurants and lunchrooms. Of those so sold 98 per cent are sold in individual cartons containing two biscuits. These cartons are distinctive and bear prominently the Kellogg name. To put upon the individual biscuit some mark which would identify it as the Kellogg product is not commercially possible. Relatively few biscuits will be removed from the individual cartons before they reach the consumer. The obligation resting upon Kellogg Company is not to insure that every purchaser will know it to be the maker but to use every reasonable means to prevent confusion.

It is urged that all possibility of deception or confusion would be removed if Kellogg Company should refrain from using the name "Shredded Wheat" and adopt some form other than the pillow-shape. But the name and form are integral parts of the goodwill of the article. To share fully in the goodwill, it must use the name and the pillow-shape. And in the goodwill Kellogg Company is as free to share as the plaintiff. [cit.] Moreover, the pillow-shape must be used for another reason. The evidence is persuasive that this form is functional—that the cost of the biscuit would be increased and its high quality lessened if some other form were substituted for the pillow-shape.

Kellogg Company is undoubtedly sharing in the goodwill of the article known as "Shredded Wheat"; and thus is sharing in a market which was created by the skill and judgment of plaintiff's predecessor and has been widely extended by vast expenditures in advertising persistently made. But that is not unfair. Sharing in the goodwill of an article unprotected by patent or trade-mark is the exercise of a right possessed by all—and in the free exercise of which the consuming public is deeply interested. There is no evidence of passing off or deception on the part of the Kellogg Company; and it has taken every reasonable precaution to prevent confusion or the practice of deception in the sale of its product.

. . .

Decrees reversed with direction to dismiss the bill.

Mr. Justice McReynolds and Mr. Justice Butler are of opinion that the decree of the Circuit Court of Appeals is correct and should be affirmed. To them it seems sufficiently clear that the Kellogg Company is fraudulently seeking to appropriate to itself the benefits of a goodwill built up at great cost by the respondent and its predecessors.

QUALITEX CO. v. JACOBSON PRODS. CO., INC.
514 U.S. 159 (1995)

Justice Breyer delivered the opinion of the Court:

[As discussed *supra*, in Chapter 2, in *Qualitex* the U.S. Supreme Court held that color per se could be registered as a trademark under the Lanham Act. In its opinion, however, the Court elaborated on its previous discussions of the functionality doctrine.]

Neither can we find a principled objection to the use of color as a mark in the important "functionality" doctrine of trademark law. The functionality doctrine prevents trademark law, which seeks to promote competition by protecting a firm's reputation, from instead inhibiting legitimate competition by allowing a producer to control a useful product feature. It is the province of patent law, not trademark law, to encourage invention by granting inventors a monopoly over new product designs or functions for a limited time, 35 U.S.C. §§154, 173, after which competitors are free to use the innovation. If a product's functional features could be used as trademarks, however, a monopoly over such features could be obtained without regard to whether they qualify as patents and could be extended forever (because trademarks may be renewed in perpetuity). *See Kellogg Co. v. National Biscuit Co.*, 305 U.S. 111, 119-20 (1938) (Brandeis, J.); *Inwood Laboratories, Inc. v. Ives Laboratories, Inc.*, 456 U.S. 844, 863 (1982) (White, J., concurring in result) ("A functional characteristic is 'an important ingredient in the commercial success of the product,' and, after expiration of a patent, it is no more the property of the originator than the product itself") (citation omitted). Functionality doctrine therefore would require, to take an imaginary example, that even if customers have come to identify the special illumination-enhancing shape of a new patented light bulb with a particular manufacturer, the manufacturer may not use that shape as a trademark, for doing so, after the patent had expired, would impede competition—not by protecting the reputation of the original bulb maker, but by frustrating competitors' legitimate efforts to produce an equivalent illumination-enhancing bulb. *See, e.g., Kellogg Co., supra,* at 119-20 (trademark law cannot be used to extend monopoly over "pillow" shape of shredded wheat biscuit after the patent for that shape had expired). This Court consequently has explained that, "[i]n general terms, a product feature is functional," and cannot serve as a trademark, "if it is essential to the use or purpose of the article or if it affects the cost or quality of the article," that is, if exclusive use of the feature would put competitors at a significant non-reputation-related disadvantage. *Inwood Laboratories, Inc., supra,* at 850, n.10. Although sometimes color plays an important role (unrelated to source identification) in making a product more desirable, sometimes it does not. And, this latter fact—the fact that sometimes color is not essential to a product's use or purpose and does not affect cost or quality—indicates that the doctrine of "functionality" does not create an absolute bar to the use of color alone as a mark. *See Owens-Corning,* 774 F.2d, at 1123 (pink color of insulation in wall "performs no non-trademark function"). . . .

The functionality doctrine, as we have said, forbids the use of a product's feature as a trademark where doing so will put a competitor at a significant disadvantage because the feature is "essential to the use or purpose of the article" or "affects [its] cost or quality." *Inwood Laboratories, Inc.,* 456 U.S. at 850, n.10. The functionality doctrine thus protects competitors against a disadvantage (unrelated to recognition or reputation) that trademark protection might otherwise impose, namely, their inability reasonably to replicate important non-reputation-related product features. For example, this Court has written that competitors might be free to copy the color of a medical pill where that color serves to identify the kind of medication (e.g., a type of blood medicine) in addition to its source. *See id.,* at 853, 858, n.20 ("[S]ome patients commingle medications in a container and rely on color to differentiate one from another"); *see also* J. Ginsburg, D. Goldberg & A. Greenbaum, Trademark and Unfair Competition Law 194-95 (1991) (noting that drug color cases "have more to do with public health policy" regarding generic drug substitution "than with trademark law"). And the federal courts have demonstrated that they can apply this doctrine in a careful and reasoned manner, with sensitivity to the effect on competition. Although we need not comment on the merits of specific cases, we note that lower courts have permitted competitors to copy the green color of farm machinery (because customers wanted their farm equipment to match) and have barred the use of black as a trademark on outboard boat motors (because black has the special functional attributes of decreasing the apparent size of the motor and ensuring compatibility with many different boat colors). *See Deere & Co. v. Farmhand, Inc.*, 560 F. Supp. 85, 98 (SD Iowa 1982), *aff'd*, 721 F.2d 253 (CA8 1983); *Brunswick Corp. v. British Seagull Ltd.*, 35 F.3d 1527, 1532 (CA Fed. 1994); *see also Nor-Am Chemical v. O.M. Scott & Sons Co.*, 4 U.S.P.Q.2d 1316, 1320 (ED Pa.1987) (blue color of fertilizer held functional because it indicated the presence of nitrogen). The Restatement (Third) of Unfair Competition adds that, if a design's "aesthetic value" lies in its ability to "confe[r] a significant benefit that cannot practically be duplicated by the use of alternative designs," then the design is "functional." Restatement (Third) of Unfair Competition §17, Comment *c*, pp. 175-76 (1993). The "ultimate test of aesthetic functionality," it explains, "is whether the recognition of trademark rights would significantly hinder competition." *Id.*, at 176.

The upshot is that, where a color serves a significant non-trademark function—whether to distinguish a heart pill from a digestive medicine or to satisfy the "noble instinct for giving the right touch of beauty to common and necessary things," G. Chesterton, Simplicity and Tolstoy 61 (1912)—courts will examine whether its use as a mark would permit one competitor (or a group) to interfere with legitimate (non-trademark-related) competition through actual or potential exclusive use of an important product ingredient. That examination should not discourage firms from creating aesthetically pleasing mark designs, for it is open to their competitors to do the same. *See, e.g., W.T. Rogers Co. v. Keene*, 778 F.2d 334, 343 (CA7 1985) (Posner, J.). But, ordinarily, it should prevent the anticompetitive consequences of Jacobson's hypothetical "color depletion" argument, when, and if, the circumstances of a particular case threaten "color depletion." . . .

TRAFFIX DEVICES, INC. v. MARKETING DISPLAYS, INC.

532 U.S. 23 (2001)

Justice KENNEDY delivered the opinion of the Court:

Temporary road signs with warnings like "Road Work Ahead" or "Left Shoulder Closed" must withstand strong gusts of wind. An inventor named Robert Sarkisian obtained two utility patents for a mechanism built upon two springs (the dual-spring design) to keep these and other outdoor signs upright despite adverse wind conditions. The holder of the now-expired Sarkisian patents, respondent Marketing Displays, Inc. (MDI), established a successful business in the manufacture and sale of sign stands incorporating the patented feature. MDI's stands for road signs were recognizable to buyers and users (it says) because the dual-spring design was visible near the base of the sign.

This litigation followed after the patents expired and a competitor, TrafFix Devices, Inc., sold sign stands with a visible spring mechanism that looked like MDI's. MDI and TrafFix products looked alike because they were. When TrafFix started in business, it sent an MDI product abroad to have it reverse engineered, that is to say copied. Complicating matters, TrafFix marketed its sign stands under a name similar to MDI's. MDI used the name "WindMaster," while TrafFix, its new competitor, used "WindBuster."

MDI brought suit under the Trademark Act of 1946 (Lanham Act), . . . against TrafFix for trademark infringement (based on the similar names), trade dress infringement (based on the copied dual-spring design) and unfair competition. TrafFix counterclaimed on antitrust theories. After the United States District Court for the Eastern District of Michigan considered cross-motions for summary judgment, MDI prevailed on its trademark claim for the confusing similarity of names and was held not liable on the antitrust counterclaim; and those two rulings, affirmed by the Court of Appeals, are not before us.

I

We are concerned with the trade dress question. The District Court ruled against MDI on its trade dress claim. [cit.] After determining that the one element of MDI's trade dress at issue was the dual-spring design [cit.], it held that "no reasonable trier of fact could determine that MDI has established secondary meaning" in its alleged trade dress [cit.]. In other words, consumers did not associate the look of the dual-spring design with MDI. As a second, independent reason to grant summary judgment in favor of TrafFix, the District Court determined the dual-spring design was functional. On this rationale secondary meaning is irrelevant because there can be no trade dress protection in any event. In ruling on the functional aspect of the design, the District Court noted that Sixth Circuit precedent indicated that the burden was on MDI to prove that its trade dress was nonfunctional, and not on TrafFix to show that it was functional (a rule since adopted by Congress, see 15 U.S.C. §1125(a)(3) (1994 ed., Supp. V)), and then went on to consider MDI's arguments that the dual-spring design was subject to trade dress protection. Finding none of MDI's contentions persuasive, the District Court concluded MDI had not "proffered sufficient evidence which would enable a reasonable trier of fact to find that MDI's vertical dual-spring design is *non*-functional." [cit.] Summary judgment was entered against MDI on its trade dress claims.

The Court of Appeals for the Sixth Circuit reversed the trade dress ruling. [cit.] The Court of Appeals held the District Court had erred in ruling MDI failed to show a genuine issue of material fact regarding whether it had secondary meaning in its alleged trade dress [cit.], and had erred further in determining that MDI could not prevail in any event because the alleged trade dress was in fact a functional product configuration. [cit.] The Court of Appeals suggested the District Court committed legal error by looking only to the dual-spring design when evaluating MDI's trade dress. Basic to its reasoning was the Court of Appeals' observation that it took "little imagination to conceive of a hidden dual-spring mechanism or a tri or quad-spring mechanism that might avoid infringing [MDI's] trade dress." [cit.] The Court of Appeals explained that "[i]f TrafFix or another competitor chooses to use [MDI's] dual-spring design, then it will have to find *some other way* to set its sign apart to avoid infringing [MDI's] trade dress." [cit.] It was not sufficient, according to the Court of Appeals, that allowing exclusive use of a particular feature such as the dual-spring design in the guise of trade dress would "hinde[r] competition somewhat." Rather, "[e]xclusive use of a feature must 'put competitors at a *significant* non-reputation-related disadvantage' before trade dress protection is denied on functionality grounds." [*Marketing Displays, Inc. v. TrafFix Devices, Inc.*, 200 F.3d 929, 940 (6th Cir. 1999)] (quoting *Qualitex Co. v. Jacobson Products Co.*, 514 U.S. 159, 165 (1995)). In its criticism of the District Court's ruling on the trade dress question, the Court of Appeals took note of a split among Courts of Appeals in various other Circuits on the issue whether the existence of an expired utility patent forecloses the possibility of the patentee's claiming trade dress protection in the product's design. 200 F.3d, at 939. *Compare Sunbeam Products, Inc. v. West Bend Co.*, 123 F.3d 246 (C.A.5 1997) (holding that trade dress protection is not foreclosed), *Thomas & Betts Corp. v. Panduit Corp.*, 138 F.3d 277 (C.A.7 1998) (same), *and Midwest Industries, Inc. v. Karavan Trailers, Inc.*, 175 F.3d 1356 (C.A. Fed. 1999) (same), *with Vornado Air Circulation Systems, Inc. v. Duracraft Corp.*, 58 F.3d 1498, 1500 (C.A.10 1995) ("Where a product configuration is a significant inventive component of an invention covered by a utility patent . . . it cannot receive trade dress protection"). To resolve the conflict, we granted certiorari. 530 U.S. 1260 (2000).

II

It is well established that trade dress can be protected under federal law. The design or packaging of a product may acquire a distinctiveness which serves to identify the product with its manufacturer or source; and a design or package which acquires this secondary meaning, assuming other requisites are met, is a trade dress which may not be used in a manner likely to cause confusion as to the origin, sponsorship, or approval of the goods. In these respects protection for trade dress exists to promote competition. As we explained just last Term, *see Wal-Mart Stores, Inc. v. Samara Brothers, Inc.*, 529 U.S. 205 (2000), various Courts of Appeals have allowed claims of trade dress infringement relying on the general provision of the Lanham Act which provides a cause of action to one who is injured when a person uses "any word, term name, symbol, or device, or any combination thereof . . . which is likely to cause confusion . . . as to the origin, sponsorship, or approval of his or her goods." 15 U.S.C. §1125(a)(1)(A). Congress confirmed this statutory protection for trade dress by amending the Lanham Act to recognize the concept. Title 15 U.S.C. §1125(a)(3) (1994 ed., Supp. V) provides: "In a civil action for trade dress infringement under this chapter for trade dress not registered on the principal register, the person who asserts trade dress protection has the burden of proving that the matter sought to be protected is not functional." This burden of proof gives force to the well-established rule that trade dress protection may not be claimed for product features that are functional. *Qualitex, supra*, at 164-165; *Two Pesos, Inc. v. Taco Cabana, Inc.*, 505 U.S. 763, 775 (1992). And in *Wal-Mart, supra*, we were careful to caution against misuse or overextension of trade dress. We noted that "product design almost invariably serves purposes other than source identification." *Id.*, at 213.

Trade dress protection must subsist with the recognition that in many instances there is no prohibition against copying goods and products. In general, unless an intellectual property right such as a patent or copyright protects an item, it will be subject to copying. As the Court has explained, copying is not always discouraged or disfavored by the laws which preserve our competitive economy. *Bonito Boats, Inc. v. Thunder Craft Boats, Inc.*, 489 U.S. 141, 160 (1989). Allowing competitors to copy will have salutary effects in many instances. "Reverse engineering of chemical and mechanical articles in the public domain often leads to significant advances in technology." *Ibid.*

The principal question in this case is the effect of an expired patent on a claim of trade dress infringement. A prior patent, we conclude, has vital significance in resolving the trade dress claim. A utility patent is strong evidence that the features therein claimed are functional. If trade dress protection is sought for those features the strong evidence of functionality based on the previous patent adds great weight to the statutory presumption that features are deemed functional until proved otherwise by the party seeking trade dress protection. Where the expired patent claimed the features in question, one who seeks to establish trade dress protection must carry the heavy burden of showing that the feature is not functional, for instance by showing that it is merely an ornamental, incidental, or arbitrary aspect of the device.

In the case before us, the central advance claimed in the expired utility patents (the Sarkisian patents) is the dual-spring design; and the dual-spring design is the essential feature of the trade dress MDI now seeks to establish and to protect. The rule we have explained bars the trade dress claim, for MDI did not, and cannot, carry the burden of overcoming the strong evidentiary inference of functionality based on the disclosure of the dual-spring design in the claims of the expired patents.

The dual springs shown in the Sarkisian patents were well apart (at either end of a frame for holding a rectangular sign when one full side is the base) while the dual springs at issue here are close together (in a frame designed to hold a sign by one of its corners). As the District Court recognized, this makes little difference. The point is that the springs are necessary to the operation of the device. The fact that the springs in this very different-looking device fall within the claims of the patents is illustrated by MDI's own position in earlier litigation. In the late 1970's, MDI engaged in a long-running intellectual property battle with a company known as Winn-Proof. Although the precise claims of the Sarkisian patents cover sign stands with springs "spaced apart," U.S. Patent No. 3,646,696, col. 4; U.S. Patent No. 3,662,482, col. 4, the Winn-Proof sign stands (with springs much like the sign stands at issue here) were found to infringe the patents by the United States District Court for the District of Oregon, and the Court of Appeals for the Ninth Circuit affirmed the judgment. *Sarkisian v. Winn-Proof Corp.*, 697 F.2d 1313 (1983). Although the Winn-Proof traffic sign stand (with dual springs close together) did not appear, then, to infringe the literal terms of the patent claims (which called for "spaced apart" springs), the Winn-Proof sign stand was found to infringe the patents under the doctrine of equivalents, which allows a finding of patent infringement even when the accused product does not fall within the literal terms of the claims. [cit.] In light of this past ruling—a ruling procured at MDI's own insistence—it must be concluded the products here at issue would have been covered by the claims of the expired patents.

The rationale for the rule that the disclosure of a feature in the claims of a utility patent constitutes strong evidence of functionality is well illustrated in this case. The dual-spring design serves the important purpose of keeping the sign upright even in heavy wind conditions; and, as confirmed by the statements in the expired patents, it does so in a unique and useful manner. As the specification of one of the patents recites, prior art "devices, in practice, will topple under the force of a strong wind." U.S. Patent No. 3,662,482, col. 1. The dual-spring design allows sign stands to resist toppling in strong winds. Using a dual-spring design rather than a single spring achieves important operational advantages. For example, the specifications of the patents note that the "use of a pair of springs . . . as opposed to the use of a single spring to support the frame structure prevents canting or twisting of the sign around a vertical axis," and that, if not prevented, twisting "may cause damage to the spring structure and may result in tipping of the device." U.S. Patent No. 3,646,696, col. 3. In the course of patent prosecution, it was said that "[t]he use of a pair of spring connections as opposed to a single spring connection . . . forms an important part of this combination" because it "forc[es] the sign frame to tip along the longitudinal axis of the elongated ground-engaging members." App. 218. The dual-spring design affects the cost of the device as well; it was acknowledged that the device "could use three springs but this would unnecessarily increase the cost of the device." *Id.*, at 217. These statements made in the patent applications and in the course of procuring the patents demonstrate the functionality of the design. MDI does not assert that any of these representations are mistaken or inaccurate, and this is further strong evidence of the functionality of the dual-spring design.

III

In finding for MDI on the trade dress issue the Court of Appeals gave insufficient recognition to the importance of the expired utility patents, and their evidentiary significance, in establishing the functionality of the device. The error likely was caused by its misinterpretation of trade dress principles in other respects. As we have noted, even if there has been no previous utility patent the party asserting trade dress has the burden to establish the nonfunctionality of alleged trade dress features. MDI could not meet this burden. Discussing trademarks, we have said "'[i]n general terms, a product feature is functional,' and cannot serve as a trademark, 'if it is essential to the use or purpose of the article or if it affects the cost or quality of the article.'" *Qualitex*, 514 U.S., at 165 (quoting *Inwood Laboratories,*

Inc. v. Ives Laboratories, Inc., 456 U.S. 844, 850, n.10 (1982)). Expanding upon the meaning of this phrase, we have observed that a functional feature is one the "exclusive use of [which] would put competitors at a significant non-reputation-related disadvantage." 514 U.S., at 165. The Court of Appeals in the instant case seemed to interpret this language to mean that a necessary test for functionality is "whether the particular product configuration is a competitive necessity." 200 F.3d, at 940. *See also Vornado*, 58 F.3d, at 1507 ("Functionality, by contrast, has been defined both by our circuit, and more recently by the Supreme Court, in terms of competitive need"). This was incorrect as a comprehensive definition. As explained in *Qualitex, supra*, and *Inwood, supra*, a feature is also functional when it is essential to the use or purpose of the device or when it affects the cost or quality of the device. The *Qualitex* decision did not purport to displace this traditional rule. Instead, it quoted the rule as *Inwood* had set it forth. It is proper to inquire into a "significant non-reputation-related disadvantage" in cases of aesthetic functionality, the question involved in *Qualitex*. Where the design is functional under the *Inwood* formulation there is no need to proceed further to consider if there is a competitive necessity for the feature. In *Qualitex*, by contrast, aesthetic functionality was the central question, there having been no indication that the green-gold color of the laundry press pad had any bearing on the use or purpose of the product or its cost or quality.

The Court has allowed trade dress protection to certain product features that are inherently distinctive. *Two Pesos*, 505 U.S., at 774. In *Two Pesos*, however, the Court at the outset made the explicit analytic assumption that the trade dress features in question (decorations and other features to evoke a Mexican theme in a restaurant) were not functional. *Id.*, at 767, n.6. The trade dress in those cases did not bar competitors from copying functional product design features. In the instant case, beyond serving the purpose of informing consumers that the sign stands are made by MDI (assuming it does so), the dual-spring design provides a unique and useful mechanism to resist the force of the wind. Functionality having been established, whether MDI's dual-spring design has acquired secondary meaning need not be considered.

There is no need, furthermore, to engage, as did the Court of Appeals, in speculation about other design possibilities, such as using three or four springs which might serve the same purpose. [cit.] Here, the functionality of the spring design means that competitors need not explore whether other spring juxtapositions might be used. The dual-spring design is not an arbitrary flourish in the configuration of MDI's product; it is the reason the device works. Other designs need not be attempted.

Because the dual-spring design is functional, it is unnecessary for competitors to explore designs to hide the springs, say, by using a box or framework to cover them, as suggested by the Court of Appeals. [cit.] The dual-spring design assures the user the device will work. If buyers are assured the product serves its purpose by seeing the operative mechanism that in itself serves an important market need. It would be at cross-purposes to those objectives, and something of a paradox, were we to require the manufacturer to conceal the very item the user seeks.

In a case where a manufacturer seeks to protect arbitrary, incidental, or ornamental aspects of features of a product found in the patent claims, such as arbitrary curves in the legs or an ornamental pattern painted on the springs, a different result might obtain. There the manufacturer could perhaps prove that those aspects do not serve a purpose within the terms of the utility patent. The inquiry into whether such features, asserted to be trade dress, are functional by reason of their inclusion in the claims of an expired utility patent could be aided by going beyond the claims and examining the patent and its prosecution history to see if the feature in question is shown as a useful part of the invention. No such claim is made here, however. MDI in essence seeks protection for the dual-spring design alone. The asserted trade dress consists simply of the dual-spring design, four legs, a base, an upright, and a sign. MDI has pointed to nothing arbitrary about the components of its device or the way they are assembled. The Lanham Act does not exist to reward manufacturers for their innovation in creating a particular device; that is the purpose of the patent law and its period of exclusivity. The Lanham Act, furthermore, does not protect trade dress in a functional design simply because an investment has been made to encourage the public to associate a particular functional feature with a single manufacturer or seller. The Court of Appeals erred in viewing MDI as possessing the right to exclude competitors from using a design identical to MDI's and to require those competitors to adopt a different design simply to avoid copying it. MDI cannot gain the exclusive right to produce sign stands using the dual-spring design by asserting that consumers associate it with the look of the invention itself. Whether a utility patent has expired or there has been no utility patent at all, a product design which has a particular appearance may be functional because it is "essential to the use or purpose of the article" or "affects the cost or quality of the article." *Inwood*, 456 U.S., at 850, n.10.

TrafFix and some of its *amici* argue that the Patent Clause of the Constitution, Art. I, §8, cl. 8, of its own force, prohibits the holder of an expired utility patent from claiming trade dress protection. [cit.] We need not resolve this question. If, despite the rule that functional features may not be the subject of trade dress protection, a case arises in which trade dress becomes the practical equivalent of an expired utility patent, that will be time enough to consider the matter. The judgment of the Court of Appeals is reversed, and the case is remanded for further proceedings consistent with this opinion.

It is so ordered.

NOTES AND QUESTIONS

1. *The functionality test after* TrafFix. The *TrafFix* opinion speaks to at least two primary issues: first, the test for functionality, upon which the Court had offered passing remarks in *Inwood* and *Qualitex*; and, second, the relevance of an expired utility patent to that analysis. As to the first question, the Court has confirmed that "in general terms, a product feature is functional . . . if it is essential to the use or purpose of the article or if it affects the cost or quality of the article." That is, the Court has endorsed the test for functionality first articulated in a footnote in *Inwood* and approved in *Qualitex*. In what ways is that test different from the tests applied in the other cases we have read in this chapter? For what reason did the Court conclude that MDI's dual-spring design feature was "essential to the use or purpose of the article in question or affects the cost or quality of the article"?

2. *Evidence.* In applying the *Inwood* test, is there a role for assessing competitive necessity? Is there a role for the number of available alternatives? *See* Graeme Dinwoodie, *Product Configuration Marks, Functionality, and the Supreme Court's Opinion in* TrafFix, 7 INT'L INTELL. PROP. L. & POL'Y 39-1 (2004). In what ways did the Court of Appeals for the Sixth Circuit err in its functionality analysis?

3. *The relevance of an expired patent.* The second (more particular) question addressed by the Court's opinion was the relevance of an expired utility patent to the functionality question. Here, the Court held that "a utility patent is strong evidence that the features claimed therein are functional." Why is this so? What was the Court's rationale for this rule? *See* Dinwoodie, *supra* (noting possible explanations for why the Court might have thought utility patent protection relevant to functionality determinations). Was the Court focused on the same concerns as it was when discussing functionality in *Qualitex*?

4. *Trigger for the evidentiary inference.* Does the mere existence of a patent on some part of the product in question trigger this evidentiary inference with respect to all design

features embodied in that product? In the case before it, the Court found that there was a "strong evidentiary inference of functionality based upon the disclosure of the dual-spring design in the claim of the expired patents," such design being "the central advance claimed in the expired utility patents" and "the essential feature of the [claimed] trade dress." Which aspect of the Court's description of the dual-spring design triggered the "strong evidentiary inference of functionality"? In addition to the characteristics noted above, how many other considerations or characteristics can you identify from the opinion that might have been important to the Court's inference of functionality? (Can you determine which of the Court's statements are descriptive of the facts, rather than prescriptive?)

5. *Overcoming the evidentiary inference.* The Court also concluded that the plaintiff in *TrafFix* had failed to overcome the inference of functionality that the expired patent generated. According to the Court, in what ways can a plaintiff overcome this evidentiary inference of functionality? How easy will it be to overcome this inference? Professor McCarthy has noted that the Court is somewhat careless in its use of intellectual property concepts in at least one of its hints about the ways in which the inference could be rebutted. In particular, he has argued that "the Supreme Court confused a patent claim with a patent disclosure." J. THOMAS MCCARTHY, TRADEMARKS AND UNFAIR COMPETITION §7:89 (4th ed. 2005). Indeed, although the Court observed that in "a case where a manufacturer seeks to protect arbitrary, incidental, or ornamental aspects of features of a product found in the patent claims, such as arbitrary curves in the legs or an ornamental pattern painted on the springs, a different result might obtain," it would be surprising to find such an arbitrary or ornamental feature recited in a utility patent claim (though it may well be that such features would be referenced in the patent's disclosure). However, the Seventh Circuit has since stressed that the language in the *TrafFix* opinion regarding the means by which a plaintiff could overcome the evidentiary inference is merely illustrative (a "for-instance"). *See Eco Mfg. LLC v. Honeywell Int'l Inc.*, 357 F.3d 649 (7th Cir. 2003) (suggesting technological change might also be relevant in showing that "what was once functional may . . . later be ornamental"). If the Seventh Circuit is correct, in what other ways might the inference be overcome? Is the "ornamentality" of the feature an appropriate consideration in any event?

6. *The "that is" language from* Qualitex. What is the significance of the other language regarding functionality found in the Court's *Qualitex* opinion? Are you persuaded by the Court's interpretation of what was at issue in *Qualitex* or by the Court's analysis of its *Qualitex* opinion? Does the *Inwood* test state the only inquiry that lower courts should make?

7. *Aesthetic functionality.* What is the test for aesthetic functionality after *TrafFix*? Is it the same as the test for functionality generally, or does the Court intend for the functionality of aesthetic features to be assessed differently from utilitarian or mechanical features? Is there a role for an assessment of competitive necessity? Is there a role for the number of available alternatives? Do you think that the Court's approach to aesthetic functionality is more or less generous to trade dress claimants than under the *Pagliero* standard (*supra* page 185) or the *Wallace* opinion?

8. *Terminology and the relationship between the different tests.* The terminology in functionality cases was confusing (and inconsistent) before *TrafFix* and it has not improved since. Some courts follow the lead of the *TrafFix* Court and describe the *Inwood* test as the "traditional" test of functionality, with the additional language from *Qualitex* described variously as constituting an "elaboration" or a "secondary test" or the "competitive necessity test." The relationship between the two tests is also unclear. The Supreme Court's opinion leaves open at least two ways to approach the "two tests of functionality." First, one could regard the two tests as separate filters, both of which any feature claimed to be nonfunctional must pass through to be protected. Second, one could regard the two tests as applicable to different types of features, *Inwood* to mechanical features and "competitive necessity" to

aesthetic features. *See* Graeme B. Dinwoodie, *Report of the United States, in* ADJUNCTS AND ALTERNATIVES TO COPYRIGHT (2002) ("while the *TrafFix Devices* opinion remains somewhat enigmatic, under one reading, the Court might be instructing courts to assess claims of functionality based upon mechanical utility primarily under the *Inwood* test (which might be called a test of mechanical necessity), and only claims of aesthetic functionality under a test of competitive necessity"). Consider this question as you read post-*TrafFix* cases below.

9.   *Reconciling past approaches.* Would Judge Rich (the author of the *Morton-Norwich* opinion) agree with the analysis of the Court in *TrafFix*? In particular, what approach would he take to the term "essential" as that term is used by the *TrafFix* Court? Does the *TrafFix* Court adhere to the understanding of the relationship between distinctiveness and functionality envisaged by Judge Rich? Would the spray bottle shape in *Morton-Norwich* have passed the *TrafFix* test? To what extent are the *Morton-Norwich* factors relevant after *TrafFix*? Would looking at those factors be consistent with the approach of the Supreme Court in *TrafFix*? If any of them are still relevant, is the weighting of the factors different?

10.   Kellogg *and* TrafFix. In *Kellogg*, the Court noted that "the pillow-shape must be used for another reason. The evidence is persuasive that this form is functional—that the cost of the biscuit would be increased and its high quality lessened if some other form were substituted for the pillow-shape." Would the *Kellogg* Court's conclusion be sustained under the *Qualitex/Inwood* test of functionality?

11.   *Constitutional dimensions.* The *TrafFix* Court declined to consider whether the Patent Clause of the Constitution prohibits the holder of an expired utility patent from claiming trade dress protection. However, some scholars have argued that a right to copy certain product designs is rooted in the Constitution. And many of the leading Supreme Court cases often cited in support of a right to copy contain references to the Copyright and Patent Clause of the Constitution. For example, the *Bonito Boats* Court noted that "the novelty and nonobviousness requirements of patentability embody a congressional understanding, implicit in the Patent Clause itself, that free exploitation of ideas will be the rule, to which the protection of a federal patent is the exception." Similarly, in *Compco*, the Court noted that the injunction against copying an unpatented article impermissibly "interfere[d] with the federal policy, found in Art. I, §8, cl. 8, of the Constitution and in the implementing federal statutes, of allowing free access to copy whatever the federal patent and copyright laws leave in the public domain." Yet none of the modern Supreme Court cases addressed directly the possible conflict between two federal laws (patent and trademark), and thus those decisions can be explained on other grounds (such as federal preemption of state laws) that make them distinguishable. But is there a constitutional right to copy? The arguments in favor of a constitutional right to copy also make frequent reference to *The Trade-Mark Cases, supra* Chapter 1. Review the Copyright and Patent Clause, and recall the Supreme Court's analysis in *The Trade-Mark Cases*. Can you frame an argument for a constitutional right to copy? What would be the content of that right (i.e., in what circumstances would it exist)? Note that *Sears* involved invalidated design and utility patents, *Compco* involved an invalidated design patent (and a rejected utility patent), *Kellogg* involved an invalidated design patent and an expired utility patent, *Singer* involved an expired utility patent, and *Bonito Boats* involved a wholly unpatentable (and never-patented) invention. This is a complex matrix. Does *Kellogg* support an absolute right to copy?

12.   *Institutional dilemmas.* Since 1982, regional appellate federal courts have been largely uninvolved in patent litigation. Appeals in patent cases are now heard by the Court of Appeals for the Federal Circuit. Thus, regional appellate courts are not practiced in the art of reading and construing patent documents. Should the Court of Appeals for the Federal Circuit assume exclusive jurisdiction in trademark cases where the availability of trade dress protection will be influenced by patent law? What arguments might support that

proposition? *See Midwest Indus., Inc. v. Karavan Trailers, Inc.*, 175 F.3d 1356 (Fed. Cir. 1999) (en banc) (deciding to apply its own law rather than the law of the regional circuit in determining whether patent law conflicted with trade dress rights in product designs).

    13. *Incontestability and functionality.* In 1998, Congress amended the Lanham Act to clarify that functionality could be asserted as a defense even in an action for infringement of a mark covered by an incontestable registration, and could be a ground for cancellation of a registration even after the passage of more than five years. *See* Trademark Law Treaty Implementation Act, Pub. L. No. 105-330, §201 (1998); *see also Wilhelm Pudenz, GmbH v. Littlefuse, Inc.*, 177 F.3d 1204 (11th Cir. 1999) (holding that this statutory provision was intended simply to clarify that the *Shakespeare Silstar* decision of the Fourth Circuit was flawed rather than to change the law). The 1998 amendments apply even to registrations that became incontestable prior to the effective date of the amendments. *See Eco Mfg. LLC v. Honeywell Int'l Inc.*, 357 F.3d 649, 653 (7th Cir. 2003).

    14. *European Union and Canadian comparisons.* The European Union Directive on Trademark Law, now implemented throughout the EU, contains provisions that approximate the functionality defense in U.S. law. The Court of Justice of the European Union has held that "where the essential functional characteristics of the shape of a product are attributable solely to the technical result, . . . [the functionality rule] precludes registration of a sign consisting of that shape, even if that technical result can be achieved by other shapes." Case C-299/99, *Philips v. Remington*, 2002 E.C.R. 1-5475. The Directive also excludes protection for signs which "consist exclusively of . . . the shape which gives substantial value to the goods." This approximates the concept of aesthetic functionality, but has not yet been interpreted by the Court of Justice in ways that clearly define its content. The Canadian Supreme Court has also taken a strict line on functional marks. *See Kirkbi AG v. Ritvik Holdings, Inc.*, [2005] 3 S.C.R. 302 (Can.) (relying in part on the existence of a prior utility patent to hold the design of the LEGO toy building block functional).

D.   POST-*TRAFFIX* APPLICATIONS OF THE FUNCTIONALITY DOCTRINE

    Many of the questions raised in the Notes and Questions following *TrafFix* have of course been addressed in case law since the Supreme Court's decision. But that case law has been somewhat inconsistent. As you read the cases in this section, reconsider the issues raised above and ask yourself whether the lower courts have clarified or modified the approach contained in *TrafFix*. One of the issues we raised above, *see supra* note 8, was whether the Court had established different tests for utilitarian and aesthetic features. In this section we have divided the lower court case law into cases primarily addressing utilitarian features, on the one hand, and aesthetic features, on the other hand. We do so in order to structure discussion; we do not intend to prejudge the issue of the relationship between the different tests of functionality.

1.   Utilitarian Features

VALU ENGINEERING, INC. v. REXNORD CORP.

278 F.3d 1268 (Fed. Cir. 2002)

Dyk, Circuit Judge:

    Valu Engineering, Inc. ("Valu") appeals a decision of the Trademark Trial and Appeal Board ("Board") sustaining Rexnord Corporation's ("Rexnord") opposition to registration of

Valu's cross-sectional designs of conveyor guide rails as trademarks on the Principal Register. . . . Because the Board correctly concluded that Valu's cross-sectional designs of conveyor guide rails are *de jure* functional, we *affirm* the Board's refusal to register Valu's designs. . . .

BACKGROUND

On February 25, 1993, Valu filed three applications seeking registration of conveyor guide rail configurations in ROUND, FLAT, and TEE cross-sectional designs as trademarks on the Principal Register. Conveyor guide rails are rails positioned along the length of the sides of a conveyor to keep containers or objects that are traveling on the conveyor from falling off the conveyor. Valu's ROUND, FLAT, and TEE cross-sectional designs are shown below.

For each cross-sectional design, Valu asserted a claim of acquired distinctiveness under 15 U.S.C. §1052(f). In each application, Valu specified the goods in connection with which Valu uses the marks in commerce as "Conveyor Guide Rails." The Examining Attorney approved the applications. Rexnord timely filed Opposition Nos. 94,922, 94,937, and 94,946, which the Board consolidated.

Rexnord alleged [*inter alia*] that all three guide rail designs were *de jure* functional and thus unregistrable. . . . The focus of the opposition as concerns functionality was on the "wet" areas of bottling and canning plants. Such areas are considered "wet" because the machinery, including conveyor guide rails, is frequently washed with disinfectants containing bactericides, such as chlorine, for sanitation and product spillage. Because these washing solutions are corrosive, the machinery in the wet areas are usually formed of noncorrosive materials, such as stainless steel and plastic.

The Board concluded that Valu's cross-sectional shapes were functional and not registrable, and sustained Rexnord's opposition on May 9, 2000. [cit.] The Board analyzed the functionality of Valu's guide rail configurations by applying the factors outlined by this court's predecessor in *In re Morton-Norwich Products, Inc.*, 671 F.2d 1332, 1340-41 (C.C.P.A. 1982). The Board focused its functionality analysis on the utilitarian advantages of Valu's guide rail configurations as they are used in a particular application, *i.e.*, the so-called "wet areas" of bottling and canning plants, and as they are composed of particular materials, *i.e.*, stainless steel and plastic. The Board determined that all four *Morton-Norwich* factors weighed in favor of a finding of functionality. Specifically, the Board found that: an abandoned utility patent application filed by Valu but rejected under 35 U.S.C. §103 "disclose[d] certain utilitarian advantages of [Valu's] guide rail designs, and that those advantages . . . result from the shape of the guide rail designs," [cit.]; Valu's advertising materials "tout the utilitarian advantages of [Valu's] guide rail design[s]," [cit.]; the "limited number of basic guide rail designs . . . should not be counted as 'alternative designs'" because they are "dictated solely by function," [cit.]; and Valu's guide rail designs "result[] in a comparatively simple or cheap method of manufacturing," [cit.]. Accordingly, the Board sustained Rexnord's opposition and refused to register Valu's guide rail designs. . . .

The primary issue on appeal is whether the Board erred in confining its functionality analysis to a particular use, rather than considering all potential uses for the marks. . . .

DISCUSSION

I.   JURISDICTION AND STANDARD OF REVIEW

We have jurisdiction over this appeal pursuant to 28 U.S.C. §1295(a)(4)(B) and 15 U.S.C. §1071(a).

Functionality is a question of fact, *Morton-Norwich*, 671 F.2d at 1340, and depends on the totality of the evidence. [cit.] We uphold the Board's factual findings unless they are unsupported by substantial evidence. *Dickinson v. Zurko*, 527 U.S. 150, 165 (1999). [cit.] Legal issues are reviewed without deference. [cit.]

II.   FUNCTIONALITY

Beginning at least with the decisions in *Kellogg Co. v. National Biscuit Co.*, 305 U.S. 111, 119-20 (1938), and *Morton-Norwich*, 671 F.2d at 1336-37, the Supreme Court and this court's predecessor have held that a mark is not registrable if the design described is functional, because "patent law, not trade dress law, is the principal means for providing exclusive rights in useful product features." *Elmer v. ICC Fabricating*, 67 F.3d 1571, 1580 (Fed. Cir. 1995). . . . Commentators share this view: "trademark law cannot properly make an 'end run' around the strict requirements of utility patent law by giving equivalent rights to exclude." J. Thomas McCarthy, 1 MCCARTHY ON TRADEMARKS AND UNFAIR COMPETITION §7:64, 7-147 (4th ed. 2001). . . .

Congress explicitly recognized the functionality doctrine in a 1998 amendment to the Lanham Act by making "functionality" a ground for *ex parte* rejection of a mark. 15 U.S.C. §1052(e)(5) (2000). Under this provision, a mark that comprises "*any matter* that, as a whole, is functional" is not entitled to trademark protection. *Id.* (emphasis added). Although the new statutory basis for refusal of registration does not apply in this case,[3] we note that the 1998 amendment was intended to "make explicit some of the current practices of the Patent and Trademark Office with respect to the trademark protection of matter that is wholly functional," and referred to the amendment as a "mostly technical," "housekeeping" amendment. See 105 Cong. Rec. S6572 (daily ed. June 18, 1998) (statement of Sen. Hatch).

III.   DEFINITION OF "FUNCTIONALITY"

To determine whether a particular product design is *de jure* functional, we have applied the [four] "Morton-Norwich factors." . . .

Because we have an obligation to apply the case law in effect at the time of decision, [cit.], we must determine whether the Supreme Court's recent decision in *TrafFix Devices, Inc. v. Marketing Displays, Inc.*, 532 U.S. 23 (2001) altered the *Morton-Norwich* factors. In order to understand the Supreme Court's decision in *TrafFix*, it is important to understand the background of *TrafFix* and the decisions on which the Court relied, namely *Inwood Laboratories, Inc. v. Ives Laboratories, Inc.*, 456 U.S. 844 (1982), and *Qualitex Co. v. Jacobson Products Co.*, 514 U.S. 159, 165 (1995).

---

3. The statute applies only to applications filed after October 30, 1998. Technical Corrections to Trademark Act of 1946, Pub. L. No. 105-330, §201(b), 112 Stat. 3064 (1998). The application in this case was filed on February 25, 1993.

[The Federal Circuit then summarized the Supreme Court's opinions in *Inwood,
Qualitex,* and *TrafFix,* noting in particular that in *TrafFix,*] the Court . . . reaffirmed
the "traditional rule" of *Inwood* that "a product feature is functional if it is essential to
the use or purpose of the article or if it affects the cost or quality of the article." *Id.*
The Court further held that once a product feature is found to be functional under this
"traditional rule," "there is no need to proceed further to consider if there is competitive necessity for the feature," and consequently "[t]here is no need . . . to engage . . . in
speculation about other design possibilities. . . . Other designs need not be attempted."
Id. at 1262.[4]

We do not understand the Supreme Court's decision in *TrafFix* to have altered the
Morton-Norwich analysis. As noted above, the *Morton-Norwich* factors aid in the determination of whether a particular feature is functional, and the third factor focuses on the
availability of "other alternatives." *Morton-Norwich,* 671 F.2d at 1341. We did not in the
past under the third factor require that the opposing party establish that there was a "competitive necessity" for the product feature. Nothing in *TrafFix* suggests that consideration
of alternative designs is not properly part of the overall mix, and we do not read the Court's
observations in *TrafFix* as rendering the availability of alternative designs irrelevant. Rather,
we conclude that the Court merely noted that once a product feature is found functional
based on other considerations[5] there is no need to consider the availability of alternative
designs, because the feature cannot be given trade dress protection merely because there
are alternative designs available. But that does not mean that the availability of alternative
designs cannot be a legitimate source of evidence to determine whether a feature is functional in the first place. We find it significant that neither party argues that *TrafFix* changed
the law of functionality, and that scholarly commentary has reached exactly the same conclusion that we have:

> In the author's view, the observations by the Supreme Court in *TrafFix* do not mean that the
> availability of alternative designs cannot be a legitimate source of evidence to determine in the
> first instance if a particular feature is in fact "functional." Rather, the Court merely said that
> once a design is found to be functional, it cannot be given trade dress status merely because
> there are alternative designs available. . . .
>   . . . The existence of actual or potential alternative designs that work equally well strongly
> suggests that the particular design used by plaintiff is not needed by competitors to effectively
> compete on the merits.

J. Thomas McCarthy, 1 McCarthy on Trademarks and Unfair Competition §7:75,
7-180-1 (4th ed. 2001). In sum, *TrafFix* does not render the Board's use of the *Morton-
Norwich* factors erroneous.

---

4. *TrafFix* suggests that there may be a requirement under *Qualitex* to inquire into a "significant
non-reputation-related disadvantage" in aesthetic functionality cases, because aesthetic functionality
was "the question involved in *Qualitex.*" 532 U.S. at 33. This statement has been criticized because
"aesthetic functionality was *not* the central question in the *Qualitex* case." J. Thomas McCarthy, 1
McCarthy on Trademarks and Unfair Competition §7:80, 7-198 (4th ed. 2001). We need not
decide what role, if any, the determination of a "significant non-reputation-related disadvantage"
plays in aesthetic functionality cases, because aesthetic functionality is not at issue here.

5. For example, a feature may be found functional where the feature "affects the cost or quality
of the device." *TrafFix,* 532 U.S. at 35.

IV.   Analysis Confined to a Single Application

The central question here is whether the Board improperly focused on a single application. Here, in its analysis of the four *Morton-Norwich* factors, the Board focused primarily on the utilitarian advantages of Valu's designs in a particular, competitively significant application, namely, as they are used in the wet areas of bottling and canning plants. Rather than considering all potential uses of the marks, the Board confined its analysis to this particular application, reasoning that "[a] finding of *de jure* functionality does not depend on a finding that applicant's design is *de jure* functional as applied to all possible industries and applications which might be encompassed by the identification of goods." Valu contends on appeal that the Board erred in confining its functionality analysis to a single use, arguing that the Board should have instead considered all possible and potential uses of the marks.

Valu also contends that the Board improperly confined its functionality analysis to Valu guide rails composed of specific materials, *i.e.*, stainless steel and plastic. The Board focused on these materials because it found that these are the only materials suitable for use in the wet areas of bottling and canning plants. Therefore, Valu's contention that the Board erred by focusing on particular materials is essentially the same as its contention that the Board erred by focusing on a particular application. Accordingly, both contentions collapse into a single issue: whether the Board erred in confining its functionality analysis to the wet areas of bottling and canning plants. This issue is apparently (and surprisingly) an issue of first impression both in this court and before the Board. We conclude that the Board properly limited itself to a single application.

An important policy underlying the functionality doctrine is the preservation of competition. As this court's predecessor noted in *Morton-Norwich*, the "effect upon competition 'is really the crux'" of the functionality inquiry, 671 F.2d at 1341, and, accordingly, the functionality doctrine preserves competition by ensuring competitors "the right to compete effectively." *Id.* at 1339. As we stated in *Brunswick Corp. v. British Seagull Ltd.*, 35 F.3d 1527, 1531 (Fed. Cir. 1994), "functionality rests on 'utility' which is determined in light of 'superiority of design,' and rests upon the foundation of 'effective competition.'" The importance of competition was reaffirmed in *Qualitex*, in which the Supreme Court focused on whether a feature "would put competitors at a significant non-reputation-related disadvantage." *Qualitex*, 514 U.S. at 165. And when discussing the policy behind limiting trade dress protection, the Supreme Court in *TrafFix* noted that "[a]llowing competitors to copy will have salutary effects in many instances." *TrafFix*, 532 U.S. 29.

Thus, in determining "functionality," the Board must assess the effect registration of a mark would have on competition. Although in examining likelihood of confusion, registrability "must be decided on the basis of the identification of goods set forth in the application regardless of what the record may reveal as to the particular nature of an applicant's goods," *Octocom Sys., Inc. v. Houston Computer Servs., Inc.*, 918 F.2d 937, 942 (Fed. Cir. 1990), for functionality purposes a narrower inquiry is appropriate. Requiring the Board to review the "entire universe" of potential uses of a contested mark in the recited identification of goods would seriously undermine the goals of the functionality doctrine. Functionality may be established by a single competitively significant application in the recited identification of goods, even if there is no anticompetitive effect in any other areas of use, since competitors in that single area could be adversely affected.

Such an approach is also supported by other considerations. A targeted Board analysis focusing on a single use deters applicants from claiming an overbroad identification of goods in order to defeat a functionality finding, and makes possible more efficient Board proceedings by eliminating the need to address each and every possible use of the challenged mark.

The statutory language of the newly enacted statute supports this result as well. Section 2(e)(5) prohibits registration of a mark that "comprises *any matter* that, as a whole, is functional."[6] 15 U.S.C. §1052(e)(5) (2000) (emphasis added). This suggests that if the Board identifies any competitively significant single use in the recited identification of goods for which the mark as a whole is functional, the Board should deny registration.

Substantial evidence supports the conclusion that the wet areas of bottling and canning plants are competitively significant. Valu urges that the Board made no findings on competitive significance of the wet areas of bottling and canning plants, and that the record is devoid of evidence on the subject. Instead, Valu steadfastly maintains that the "record says nothing" about the competitive significance of the wet areas of bottling and canning plants, and that "[t]he record is silent as to what, if any, competitive significance the 'wet areas' have." We agree that the Board made no findings on the issue, no doubt because Valu did not even raise the issue of significance below. But in fact Rexnord submitted substantial evidence showing that the wet areas of bottling and canning plants comprise a significant segment of the market for Rexnord's and Valu's guide rails. A Rexnord executive testified that the single biggest end users of Rexnord guide rail products are bottling and canning plants. The record shows that bottling, canning, and other plants that require sanitary filling of containers have wet areas, and that wet areas are a substantial portion of those conveyor lines. Valu's president testified that Valu's major customers include manufacturers that have "wet areas" in a substantial portion of their conveyor lines, where containers are filled with such products as food, beverages, shampoo, and cosmetics. A Rexnord expert testified that bottling and canning plant "wet areas" constitute a substantial portion of the conveyor lines, including the areas where the containers are filled, sealed, labeled, pasteurized, warmed, and cooled, and where the containers undergo the processes necessary for final packaging. Valu has not called our attention to any contrary evidence.

Even if the record failed to conclusively establish the competitive significance of that particular application, Rexnord made a *prima facie* showing that Valu's designs are functional as used in the wet areas of bottling and canning plants, and that the wet areas of bottling and canning plants are a competitively significant application. Where, as here, the opposer in a trademark opposition has made a *prima facie* showing of functionality, the burden shifts to the applicant to prove nonfunctionality. [cit.]

To prevail in a trademark opposition proceeding, the applicant must rebut the opposer's *prima facie* evidence of functionality with competent evidence. *See Smith*, 734 F.2d at 1484. The appropriateness of shifting the burden to the applicant in a trademark opposition proceeding is supported by the recent amendment to Section 43(a) of the Lanham Act, which shifts the burden of proving nonfunctionality of unregistered trade dress to the applicant-plaintiff in civil actions for trade dress infringement, even without a *prima facie* showing by the alleged infringer.[8] 15 U.S.C. §1125(a)(3) (2000).

In this case, Valu failed to refute Rexnord's *prima facie* showing of competitive significance. Thus, we find that the Board did not err in confining its functionality analysis to the wet areas of the plants.

---

6. The term "as a whole" existed under prior decisional law and refers to the entirety of the mark itself, rather than the entirety of the class of goods in connection with which the mark is used. *In re Teledyne Indus., Inc.*, 696 F.2d 968, 971 (Fed. Cir. 1982) (noting that functionality of a mark is properly determined by considering the mark as a whole, rather than dissecting the mark into its design features).

8. "In a civil action for trade dress infringement under this chapter for trade dress not registered on the principal register, the person who asserts trade dress protection has the burden of proving that the matter sought to be protected is not functional." 15 U.S.C. §1125(a)(3) (2000).

V.   APPLICATION OF *MORTON-NORWICH* FACTORS

Valu also challenges the Board's application of the *Morton-Norwich* factors. But this challenge is based almost entirely on Valu's contention that the Board improperly confined its functionality analysis to wet areas of the plants, an argument we have rejected. We agree with the Board that an abandoned patent application should be considered under the first *Morton-Norwich* factor, because an applied-for utility patent that never issued has evidentiary significance for the statements and claims made in the patent application concerning the utilitarian advantages, just as an issued patent has evidentiary significance. *See TrafFix.* We find that under the proper standard the Board's findings are supported by substantial evidence.

CONCLUSION

Because the Board's decision to confine its functionality analysis to a competitively significant application of Valu's guide rail designs was not legally erroneous, and because we find that the Board's finding that Valu's guide rails are *de jure* functional is supported by substantial evidence, the Board's refusal to register Valu's guide rail designs is *affirmed.* . . .

EPPENDORF-NETHELER-HINZ GMBH v. RITTER GMBH

289 F.3d 351 (5th Cir. 2002)

JONES, Circuit Judge:

[Eppendorf, a German company that manufactured medical and laboratory equipment, sought trade dress protection for a line of disposable pipette tips (so-called Combitips) and dispenser syringes capable of accurate and rapid "multiple dispensing" of liquids. After a jury trial finding infringement, the district court permanently enjoined the defendant from selling or marketing in the United States dispenser syringes or syringes of "a confusingly similar design" to Eppendorf's syringes. On appeal, the Court of Appeals for the Fifth Circuit concluded that Eppendorf failed to carry its burden of proving nonfunctionality and thus reversed the judgment of the district court. The Fifth Circuit offered an analysis of functionality law after *TrafFix.*]

It is clear that functional product features do not qualify for trade dress protection. However, the definition of "functionality" has not enjoyed such clarity. [cit.] In *TrafFix*, the Supreme Court recognized two tests for functionality. First, the Court recognized the "traditional" definition of functionality: "a product feature is functional, and cannot serve as a trademark, 'if it is essential to the use or purpose of the article or if it affects the cost or quality of an article.'" *TrafFix*, 532 U.S. at 32 (citations omitted). Under this traditional definition, if a product feature is "the reason the device works," then the feature is functional. *Id.* at 34. The availability of alternative designs is irrelevant. *Id.* at 33-34.

In addition to the traditional definition, *TrafFix* recognized a second test for functionality: "a functional feature is one the 'exclusive use of which would put competitors at a significant non-reputation-related disadvantage.'" *Id.* at 32 (quoting *Qualitex*, 514 U.S. at 165). This "competitive necessity" test for functionality is an expansion of the traditional test. *Id.* The Court emphasized, however, that the "competitive necessity" test is not "a comprehensive definition" of functionality. *Id.* at 33. The primary test for functionality is the traditional test, and there is no need to consider the "competitive necessity" test where a product feature is functional under the traditional definition. *Id.* at 33-35. . . .

[The Fifth Circuit acknowledged that before *TrafFix*, the Fifth Circuit had adopted a differently stated test of functionality (which the Fifth Circuit had, for several years, rather confusingly called its "utilitarian test" of functionality). That test was, according to the *Eppendorf* court, "virtually identical" to the competitive necessity test discussed in *TrafFix*. Accordingly, the court held that "*TrafFix* supersedes the definition of functionality previously adopted by this court" and that its competitive necessity test, though "still valid as a secondary test, is not a comprehensive definition of functionality." *TrafFix*, 532 U.S. at 32-33. "In light of *TrafFix*, the primary test for determining whether a product feature is functional is whether the feature is essential to the use or purpose of the product or whether it affects the cost or quality of the product." *Id.* The court concluded that the design of the fin features for which plaintiff sought protection was functional because it was undisputed that the fins provided necessary support for the flange (another part of the product).]

The only testimony offered by Eppendorf to prove non-functionality of the fins related to the existence of alternative design possibilities. Eppendorf's functionality expert testified that the appearance and number of fins could be changed without affecting the function of the fins. Eppendorf did not prove, however, that the fins are an arbitrary flourish which serve no purpose in the Combitips. Rather, Eppendorf's experts concede that fins of some shape, size or number are necessary to provide support for the flange and to prevent deformation of the product. Thus, the fins are design elements necessary to the operation of the product. Because the fins are essential to the operation of the Combitips, they are functional as a matter of law, and it is unnecessary to consider design alternatives available in the marketplace. *TrafFix*, 532 U.S. at 33-34.

Likewise, a careful review of the record demonstrates that Eppendorf failed to prove that the remaining [product] design elements are unnecessary, non-essential design elements. It is undisputed that: (1) The flange is necessary to connect the Combitip to the dispenser syringe; (2) The rings on the plunger head are necessary to lock the plunger into a cylinder in the dispenser syringe; (3) The plunger is necessary to push liquids out of the tip, and the ribs on the plunger stabilize its action; (4) The tips at the lower end of the Combitips are designed to easily fit into test tubes and other receptacles; (5) The size of the Combitip determines the dispensed volume, and size is essential to accurate and efficient dispensing; (6) The color scheme used on the Combitip—clear plastic with black lettering—enables the user easily to see and measure the amount of liquid in the Combitip, and black is standard in the medical industry; and (7) The stumps of the larger Combitips must be angled to separate air bubbles from the liquid and ensure that the full volume of liquid is dispensed. Thus, all eight design elements identified by Eppendorf are essential to the operation of the Combitips.

[The court concluded that although alternative designs are relevant to the test formerly applied by the Fifth Circuit (and now relevant only as a secondary test), "alternative designs are not germane to the traditional test for functionality. Each of the eight design elements identified by Eppendorf is essential to the use or purpose of the Combitips, and is not arbitrary or ornamental features [sic]. Therefore, no reasonable juror could conclude that Eppendorf carried its burden of proving non-functionality."]

JAY FRANCO & SONS, INC. v. FRANEK

615 F.3d 855 (7th Cir. 2010)

EASTERBROOK, Chief Judge:

The same year Huey Lewis and the News informed America that it's "Hip To Be Square," Clemens Franek sought to trademark the circular beach towel. His company, CLM Design, Inc., pitched the towel as a fashion statement—"the most radical beach fashion item since the bikini," declared one advertisement. "Bound to be round! Don't be square!" proclaimed another. CLM also targeted lazy sunbathers: "The round shape eliminates the need to constantly get up and move your towel as the sun moves across the sky. Instead merely reposition yourself."

The product enjoyed some initial success. Buoyed by an investment and promotional help from the actor Woody Harrelson (then a bartender on the TV show *Cheers*), CLM had sold more than 30,000 round beach towels in 32 states by the end of 1987. To secure its status as the premier circular-towel maker, the company in 1986 applied for a trademark on the towel's round design. The Patent and Trademark Office registered the "configuration of a round beach towel" as trademark No. 1,502,261 in 1988. But this was not enough to save CLM: Six years later it dissolved. The mark was assigned to Franek, who continues to sell circular towels.

In 2006 Franek discovered that Jay Franco & Sons, a distributor of bath, bedding, and beach accessories, was selling round beach towels. After settlement negotiations failed . . . Franco sued . . . Franek to invalidate his mark. . . . The district judge . . . granted summary judgment in Jay Franco's favor, and . . . Franek appeals from that judgment. . . .

One way to void a trademark is to challenge its distinctiveness. . . . But this type of invalidation is unavailable to Jay Franco. Franek (and before him CLM) has continuously used the round-towel mark since its 1988 registration. That makes the mark "incontestable," 15 U.S.C. §1065, a status that eliminates the need for a mark's owner in an infringement suit to show that his mark is distinctive. *See* 15 U.S.C. §1115(b); *Park 'N Fly, Inc. v. Dollar Park and Fly, Inc.*, 469 U.S. 189 (1985).

Unfortunately for Franek, incontestable marks are not invincible. The Lanham Act lists a number of affirmative defenses an alleged infringer can parry with; one is a showing that the mark is "functional." *See* §1115(b)(8); *Specialized Seating, Inc. v. Greenwich Industries, L.P.*, 616 F.3d 722, 724 (7th Cir. 2010) (discussing functionality and other ways to defeat incontestable marks). As our companion opinion in *Specialized Seating* explains, patent law alone protects useful designs from mimicry; the functionality doctrine polices the division of responsibilities between patent and trademark law by invalidating marks on useful designs. This was the route Jay Franco pursued. The district judge agreed, finding Franek's mark "functional" under the definition the Supreme Court gave that concept in *TrafFix Devices, Inc. v. Marketing Displays, Inc.*, 532 U.S. 23, 32-35 (2001). The judge got it right.

TrafFix says that a design is functional when it is "essential to the use or purpose of the device or when it affects the cost or quality of the device," 532 U.S. at 33, a definition cribbed from *Inwood Laboratories, Inc. v. Ives Laboratories, Inc.*, 456 U.S. 844, 850 n.10 (1982). So if a design enables a product to operate, or improves on a substitute design in some way (such as by making the product cheaper, faster, lighter, or stronger), then the design cannot be trademarked; it is functional because consumers would pay to have it rather than be indifferent toward or pay to avoid it. A qualification is that any pleasure a customer derives from the design's identification of the product's source—the joy of buying a marked good over an identical generic version because the consumer prefers the status conferred by the mark—doesn't count. That broad a theory of functionality would penalize companies for developing brands with cachet to distinguish themselves from competitors, which is the very purpose of trademark law. In short, a design that produces a benefit other than source identification is functional.

Figuring out which designs meet this criterion can be tricky. Utility patents serve as excellent cheat sheets because any design claimed in a patent is supposed to be useful. [cit.] For this reason, *TrafFix* held that expired utility patents provide "strong evidence that the features therein claimed are functional." [cit.] The parties in this case wrangle over the relevance of a handful of utility patents that claim circular towels. We need discuss only one

(No. 4,794,029), which describes a round beach towel laced with drawstrings that can be pulled to turn the towel into a satchel. This patent's first two claims are:

1. A towel-bag construction comprising: a non-rectangular towel;
    a casing formed at the perimeter of said towel;
    a cord threaded through said casing; and
    a section of relatively non-stretchable fabric of a shape geometrically similar to that of said towel attached with its edges equidistant from the edges of said towel.
    2. A towel-bag construction as set forth in claim 1 wherein said towel is circular in shape, whereby a user while sunbathing may reposition his or her body towards the changing angle of the sun while the towel remains stationary.

Claim 2 sounds like Franek's advertisements, which we quoted above. The patent's specification also reiterates, in both the summary and the detailed description, that a circular towel is central to the invention because of its benefit to lazy sunbathers.

Franek argues that claim 2 does not trigger the *TrafFix* presumption of functionality because his towel does not infringe the '029 patent. He notes that claim 2 incorporates claim 1 (in patent parlance, claim 1 is "independent" and claim 2 "dependent," see 35 U.S.C. §112) with the added condition that the towel be circular. An item can infringe a dependent claim only if it also violates the independent claim incorporated by the dependent claim. [cit.] Franek reasons that because his towel lacks a perimeter casing, drawstring, and non-stretchable section of fabric, it does not infringe claim 1, and thus cannot infringe claim 2. Even if his towel could infringe claim 2, Franek maintains that the claim is invalid because the towel-to-bag patent was sought in 1987, two years after Franek started selling a round beach towel, and thus too late to claim its invention. *See* 35 U.S.C. §102(b); [cit.].

Proving patent infringement can be *sufficient* to show that a trademarked design is useful, as it means that the infringing design is quite similar to a useful invention. *See Raytheon Co. v. Roper Corp.*, 724 F.2d 951, 959 (Fed. Cir. 1983). But such proof is unnecessary. Functionality is determined by a feature's usefulness, not its patentability or its infringement of a patent. *TrafFix*'s ruling that an expired patent (which by definition can no longer be infringed) may evince a design's functionality demonstrates that proof of infringement is unnecessary. If an invention is too useless to be patentable, or too dissimilar to a design to shed light on its functions, then the lack of proof of patent infringement is meaningful. Otherwise it is irrelevant. A design may not infringe a patented invention because the invention is obvious or taught by prior art, *see* 35 U.S.C. §§102(a), 103(a), but those and other disqualifers do not mean that the design is not useful. Just so here: Franek's towel may lack some of the components in claim 1 necessary to infringe claim 2, but claim 2's coverage of a circular beach towel for sunbathing is enough to signal that a round-towel design is useful for sunbathers. Each claim in a patent is evaluated individually, [cit.], each must be substantially different, [cit.], and each is presumed valid, 35 U.S.C. §282. We must therefore presume that the unique component in claim 2—the round shape of the towel—is useful.

Nor does it matter that the '029 patent application was filed two years after Franek began selling round towels. As we've explained, a patent's invalidity for a reason other than uselessness says nothing about the claimed design's functionality. And a design patented yesterday can be as good evidence of a mark's functionality as a design patented 50 years ago. Indeed, more recent patents are often better evidence because technological change can render designs that were functional years ago no longer so. *See Eco Manufacturing LLC v. Honeywell International Inc.*, 357 F.3d 649, 653 (7th Cir. 2003). The Court in *TrafFix* may have dealt only with *expired* utility patents, but the logic it employed is not limited to them.

To put things another way, a trademark holder cannot block innovation by appropriating designs that under-gird further improvements. Patent holders can do this, but a patent's life is short; trademarks can last forever, so granting trademark holders this power could permanently stifle product development. If we found Franek's trademark nonfunctional, then inventors seeking to build an improved round beach towel would be out of luck. They'd have to license Franek's mark or quell their inventiveness. That result does not jibe with the purposes of patent or trademark law.

This "strong evidence" of the round towel's functionality is bolstered by Franek's own advertisements, which highlight two functional aspects of the round beach towel's design. One, also discussed in the '029 patent, is that roundness enables heliotropic sunbathers—tanners who swivel their bodies in unison with the sun's apparent motion in order to maintain an even tan—to remain on their towels as they rotate rather than exert the energy to stand up and reposition their towels every so often, as conventional rectangular towels require.

Franek responds that whatever its shape (golden-ratio rectangle, square, nonagon) any towel can satisfy a heliotropic tanner if it has enough surface area—the issue is size, not shape. That's true, and it is enough to keep the roundness of his towel from being functional under the first prong of *TrafFix*'s definition ("essential to the use or purpose of the device") but not the second. For heliotropic sunbathers, a circle surpasses other shapes because it provides the most rotational space without waste. Any non-circle polygon will either limit full rotations (spinning on a normal beach towel leads to sandy hair and feet) or not use all the surface area (a 6' tall person swiveling on a 6' by 6' square towel won't touch the corners). Compared to other shapes that permit full rotations, the round towel requires less material, which makes it easier to fold and carry. That's evidence that the towel's circularity "affects the . . . quality of the device." (The reduction in needed material also suggests that round towels are cheaper to produce than other-shaped towels, though Franek contends that cutting and hemming expenses make them costlier. We express no view on the matter.)

But let us suppose with Franek—who opposed summary judgment and who is thus entitled to all reasonable inferences—that round towels are not measurably better for spinning with the sun. After all, other shapes (squircles, regular icosagons) are similar enough to circles that any qualitative difference may be lost on tanners. Plus, the ability to rotate 180 degrees may be an undesired luxury. Few lie out from dawn 'til dusk (if only to avoid skin cancer) and the daily change in the sun's declination means it will rise due east and set due west just twice a year, during the vernal and autumnal equinoxes. A towel shaped like a curved hourglass that allows only 150 or 120 degrees of rotation (or even fewer) may be all a heliotropic tanner wants. No matter. Franek's mark still is functional.

Franek's advertisements declare that the round towel is a fashion statement. Fashion is a form of function. A design's aesthetic appeal can be as functional as its tangible characteristics. *See Qualitex Co. v. Jacobson Products Co.*, 514 U.S. 159, 169-70 (1995); *Wal-Mart*, 529 U.S. at 214; *TrafFix*, 532 U.S. at 33; *W.T. Rogers Co. v. Keene*, 778 F.2d 334 (7th Cir. 1985); [cit.]; *Abercrombie & Fitch Stores, Inc. v. American Eagle Outfitters, Inc.*, 280 F.3d 619 (6th Cir. 2002). And many cases say that fashionable designs can be freely copied unless protected by patent law. *See, e.g., Bonito Boats, Inc. v. Thunder Craft Boats, Inc.*, 489 U.S. 141 (1989); *Sears, Roebuck & Co. v. Stiffel Co.*, 376 U.S. 225 (1964); *Compco Corp. v. Day-Brite Lighting, Inc.*, 376 U.S. 234 (1964); *Kellogg Co. v. National Biscuit Co.*, 305 U.S. 111 (1938); *Singer Manufacturing Co. v. June Manufacturing Co.*, 163 U.S. 169 (1896).

The chief difficulty is distinguishing between designs that are fashionable enough to be functional and those that are merely pleasing. Only the latter group can be protected, because trademark law would be a cruel joke if it limited companies to tepid or repugnant brands that discourage customers from buying the marked wares. We discussed this problem at length in *Keene*. [cit.] The Supreme Court broached the subject in *Qualitex* when it discussed the functionality of the green-gold color of a dry cleaning pad. Unwilling to say that the pad required a green-gold hue or was improved by it, the Court still thought that the color would be functional if its exclusive use by a single designer "would put competitors at a significant non-reputation-related disadvantage." [cit.] This is a problem for Franek's round-towel mark.

Franek wants a trademark on the circle. Granting a producer the exclusive use of a basic element of design (shape, material, color, and so forth) impoverishes other designers' palettes. *See, e.g., Brunswick Corp. v. British Seagull Ltd.*, 35 F.3d 1527 (Fed. Cir. 1994) (black color of boat engines is functional because it is compatible with boats of many different colors). *Qualitex*'s determination that "color alone, at least sometimes, can meet the basic legal requirements for use as a trademark" means that there is no per se rule against this practice. *See also Thomas & Betts Corp. v. Panduit Corp.*, 138 F.3d 277, 299 (7th Cir. 1998). The composition of the relevant market matters. But the more rudimentary and general the element—all six-sided shapes rather than an irregular, perforated hexagon; all labels made from tin rather than a specific tin label; all shades of the color purple rather than a single shade—the more likely it is that restricting its use will significantly impair competition. *See, e.g., Keene*, 778 F.2d at 343; [cit.]. Franek's towel is of this ilk. He has trademarked the "configuration of a round beach towel." Every other beach towel manufacturer is barred from using the entire shape as well as any other design similar enough that consumers are likely to confuse it with Franek's circle (most regular polygons, for example).

Contrast Franek's mark with the irregular hexagon at issue in *Keene* or the green-gold hue in *Qualitex*. Those marks restrict few design options for competitors. Indeed, they are so distinctive that competitors' only reason to copy them would be to trade on the goodwill of the original designer. *Cf. Service Ideas, Inc. v. Traex Corp.*, 846 F.2d 1118, 1123-24 (7th Cir. 1988) (purposeful copying of a beverage server's arbitrary design indicated a lack of aesthetic functionality). That's not so here. A circle is the kind of basic design that a producer like Jay Franco adopts because alternatives are scarce and some consumers want the shape regardless of who manufactures it. There are only so many geometric shapes; few are both attractive and simple enough to fabricate cheaply. *Cf. Qualitex*, 514 U.S. at 168-69 (functionality doctrine invalidates marks that would create color scarcity in a particular market). And some consumers crave round towels—beachgoers who prefer curved edges to sharp corners, those who don't want to be "square," and those who relish the circle's simplicity. A producer barred from selling such towels loses a profitable portion of the market. The record does not divulge much on these matters, but any holes in the evidence are filled by the *TrafFix* presumption that Franek's mark is functional, a presumption he has failed to rebut.

Franek chose to pursue a trademark, not a design patent, to protect the stylish circularity of his beach towel. *Cf. Kohler Co. v. Moen Inc.*, 12 F.3d 632, 647 (7th Cir. 1993) (Cudahy, J., dissenting) (calling Franek's mark a "horrible example[]" of a registered trademark that should have been a design patent). He must live with that choice. We cannot permit him to keep the indefinite competitive advantage in producing beach towels this trademark creates.

If Franek is worried that consumers will confuse Jay Franco's round beach towels with his, he can imprint a distinctive verbal or pictorial mark on his towels. [cit.] That will enable him to reap the benefits of his brand while still permitting healthy competition in the beach towel market.

Affirmed.

IN RE BECTON, DICKINSON AND COMPANY

675 F.3d 1368 (Fed. Cir. 2012)

CLEVENGER, Circuit Judge:

Becton, Dickinson and Company ("BD") appeals from the final decision of the Trademark Trial and Appeal Board ("Board") affirming the examining attorney's refusal to register BD's design of a closure cap for blood collection tubes as a trademark on the ground that the design is functional. . . . [W]e affirm the Board's conclusion that the mark as a whole is functional.

BD applied to register with the United States Patent and Trademark Office ("PTO") the following mark on the Principal Register for "closures for medical collection tubes":

U.S. Trademark Application Serial No. 77/254,637 (filed August 14, 2007). The application asserts acquired distinctiveness based on five years of substantially exclusive and continuous use in commerce. The required description of the mark, as amended, reads as follows:

> The mark consists of the configuration of a closure cap that has [1] an overall streamlined exterior wherein the top of the cap is slimmer than at the bottom and the cap features [2] vertically elongated ribs set out in combination sets of numerous slim ribs bordered by fatter ribs around most of the cap circumference, where [3] a smooth area separates sets of ribs. [4] The slim ribs taper at their top to form triangular shapes which intersect and blend together at a point where [5] a smooth surface area rings the top of the cap above the ribs, thus [6] extending the cap's vertical profile. At the bottom, [7] a flanged lip rings the cap and protrudes from the sides in two circumferential segments with the bottom-most segment having [8] a slightly curved contour. The matter in dotted lines is not claimed as a feature of the mark, but shows the tube on which the closure is positioned.

The numbers in brackets in the description above are not part of the trademark application, but were used by BD in conjunction with the following illustration to illustrate key features of the mark:

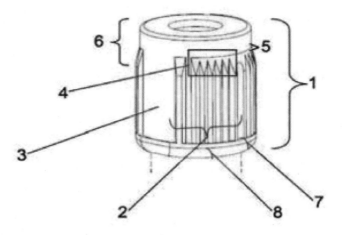

[The examining attorney refused registration under Section 1052(e)(5) on the basis, *inter alia*, that the cap design is functional. In response to an initial office action, BD submitted several of its utility and design patents, including U.S. Patent No. 4,741,446 (filed Dec. 29, 1986) ("the '446 patent"), samples of advertising materials, and copies of website printouts showing medical closure caps manufactured by other entities.] BD also submitted numerous advertising samples for its VACUTAINER® collection tubes with HEMOGARD™ closure—the brand name of the closure cap for which BD seeks registration. . . .

[On appeal, the] Board found that the proposed mark is a configuration of the outer shell portion of BD's HEMOGARD™ collection tube closure caps. [cit.] BD argued that its amended mark description and a numbered illustration in its reply brief set out the features of the cap design, but the Board explained that the features described in the amended description do not embody the mark in its entirety. [cit.] The Board saw additional elements not recited in the mark description, including the circular opening on the top of the cap. [cit.] Thus, the Board concluded that the proposed mark included all elements shown in the drawing except the tube, which was shown in dotted lines. [cit.]

The Board considered the four factors from *In re Morton-Norwich Prods., Inc.*, 671 F.2d 1332 (C.C.P.A. 1982), in finding that the cap design, considered in its entirety, is functional. . . .

In conducting the analysis, the Board gave less weight to less prominent features, such as the exact spacing or shape of the ribs, because it found them to be incidental to the overall adoption of those features and hardly discernible when viewing the mark. [cit.] In this regard, the Board relied on *Textron, Inc. v. International Trade Commission*, 753 F.2d 1019, 1025 (Fed. Cir. 1985), for the proposition that presence of non-functional features in a mark would not affect the functionality decision where the evidence shows the overall design to be functional. The Board concluded that the overall design is dictated by utilitarian concerns and that the "'overall composite design' engendered by [BD's] proposed mark is functional." [cit.] . . .

II

The functionality of a proposed mark is a question of fact. *In re Bose Corp.*, 476 F.3d 1331, 1334 (Fed. Cir. 2007); *Valu Eng'g, Inc. v. Rexnord Corp.*, 278 F.3d 1268, 1273 (Fed. Cir. 2002); [cit.]. . . .

Legal conclusions of the Board are reviewed de novo, but the factual findings of the Board are upheld unless they are unsupported by substantial evidence. [cit.] Evidence is substantial if a "reasonable person might find that the evidentiary record supports the agency's conclusion." [cit.] The possibility that two inconsistent conclusions may be drawn from the evidence does not preclude a Board finding from being supported by substantial evidence. [cit.] . . .

III

BD presents two challenges to the Board's conclusion that the mark as a whole is functional. Its lead argument posits legal error by the Board in its determination that certain features of the mark, which are admittedly non-functional, will not serve to remove the mark as a whole from the realm of functionality. BD asserts that the elongated shape of the closure cap, the spacing of the ribs and their particular shapes, as well as the design relationship of those features to the whole of the closure cap are the design embraced by the mark. As such, BD asserts that the scope of its mark is "extremely modest and limited." [cit.] BD does not contest that the ribs themselves are functional, as is the opening in the top of the closure cap. These prominent and important functional features, which are common to the closure caps made by BD's competitors, led the Board to conclude that admitted non-functional features could not save the mark from being deemed overall functional. BD contends that the Board committed reversible error by discounting the significance of the non-functional elements.

BD's secondary argument is that the Board's analysis of the *Morton-Norwich* factors is unsupported by substantial evidence. BD appreciates the more deferential standard of review we apply to its second argument.

A

BD's first argument fails to recognize that one object of the *Morton-Norwich* inquiry is to weigh the elements of a mark against one another to develop an understanding of whether the mark as a whole is essentially functional and thus non-registrable. Whenever a proposed mark includes both functional and non-functional features, as in this case, the critical question is the degree of utility present in the overall design of the mark. This court recognized as much in *Morton-Norwich*, where Judge Rich harked back to the design in *In re Deister Concentrator Co.*, 289 F.2d 496, 506 (C.C.P.A. 1961), in which the design was judged "in essence utilitarian." In *In re R.M. Smith, Inc.*, 734 F.2d 1482, 1484 (Fed. Cir. 1984), this court reiterated the importance of the "degree of utility" proposition, and explained how the distinction between de facto and de jure functionality gives shape to a court's inquiry into a mark's "degree of utility."

De facto functionality simply means that a design has a function, like the closure cap in this case. Such functionality is irrelevant to the question of whether a mark as a whole is functional so as to be ineligible for trademark protection. De jure functionality "means that the product is in its particular shape because it works better in this shape." [cit.] Further, as the Board recognized in this case, *Textron* instructs that where a mark is composed of functional and non-functional features, whether "an overall design is functional should be based on the superiority of the design as a whole, rather than on whether each design feature is 'useful' or 'serves a utilitarian purpose.'" [cit.] *Textron* cited as an example the Coca-Cola® bottle, noting that the bottle's significant overall non-functional shape would not lose trademark protection simply because "the shape of an insignificant element of the design, such as the lip of the bottle, is arguably functional." [cit.] Likewise, a mark possessed of significant functional features should not qualify for trademark protection where insignificant elements of the design are non-functional.

The foregoing authority makes clear that the Board committed no legal error by weighing the functional and non-functional features of BD's mark against each other. Our functionality precedent indeed mandates that the Board conduct such an assessment as part of its determination of whether a mark in its entirety is overall de jure functional. As the court explained in *Morton-Norwich*, "we must strike a balance between the 'right to copy' and the right to protect one's method of trade identification." [cit.] To decide as a matter of fact "whether the 'consuming public' has an interest in making use of [one's design], superior to [one's] interest in being [its] sole vendor," we are guided by the *Morton-Norwich* factors. [cit.]

B

. . .

BD challenges the Board's ultimate factual determination that the mark as a whole is functional by homing in on the Board's *Morton-Norwich* analysis, arguing that the Board's analysis lacks substantial evidence support. As to the first *Morton-Norwich* factor, the Board did not err in finding that this factor weighs in favor of finding functionality. In *TrafFix Devices, Inc. v. Marketing Displays, Inc.*, 532 U.S. 23, 31 (2001), the Supreme Court stated that "the disclosure of a feature in the claims of a utility patent constitutes strong evidence of functionality." As discussed by the Board, claim 4 of the '446 patent shows the utilitarian nature of at least two prominent features of BD's mark: (1) the two concentric circles at the top of the closure cap, which allow a needle to be inserted, and (2) the ribs, which serve as a gripping surface.

BD does not contest the Board's finding that the '446 patent teaches the functional benefits of two important features of its proposed mark. Rather it argues that those features, while disclosed in the '446 patent, were not themselves claimed in that patent. BD's argument lacks merit. *TrafFix* does not require that a patent claim the exact configuration for which trademark protection is sought in order to undermine an applicant's assertion that an applied-for mark is not de jure functional. Indeed, *TrafFix* teaches that statements in a patent's specification illuminating the purpose served by a design may constitute equally strong evidence of functionality. *See TrafFix*, 532 U.S. at 32-33, 34-35. The Board correctly read the '446 patent to indicate that at least two of the important elements of the proposed mark were functional.

BD argues that its design patents are persuasive evidence of the non-functionality of the closure caps' overall design. However, while evidence of a design patent may be some evidence of non-functionality under *Morton-Norwich*, "the fact that a device is or was the subject of a design patent does not, without more, bestow upon said device the aura of distinctiveness or recognition as a trademark." *R.M. Smith*, 734 F.2d at 1485 (citation omitted). Furthermore, the design patents BD claims as evidence of non-functionality do not reflect the specific design for which trademark protection is sought. Our law recognizes that the existence of a design patent for the very design for which trademark protection is sought "presumptively . . . indicates that the design is *not de jure* functional." *Morton-Norwich*, 671 F.2d at 1342 n.3. Absent identity between the design patent and the proposed mark, the presumption loses force, and the "similar" design patents lack sufficient evidentiary value to overcome the strong conclusion in this case that BD's utility patents underscore the functionality of significant elements of the proposed mark.

As to the second *Morton-Norwich* factor, substantial evidence supports the Board's assessment of BD's advertising. BD's advertising touts the utilitarian advantages of the prominent features of the mark, such as the top's circular opening (which maximizes the possible useful area of the opening), the side's ribs, and the bottom's flanged lip. The advertisements emphasize that the "ridges on the outer surface permit for a more secure grip," and praise the "enhanced handling features" that are "inherent in the design." The advertisements explain that the top's "plastic shield" is an "important design innovation that keeps the blood safely contained within the closure" and "encourages safer opening—discourages use of the thumb roll technique, which can result in spattering of the specimen," and that the "hooded feature of closure reduces the possibility of catching glove between stopper and tube on reclosing." Against this substantial evidence of functionality, BD offers two explanations, each of which we reject. First, BD argues that the designs shown in the advertisements are not exactly the same as the proposed mark's design. For purposes of an overall functionality assessment, this distinction is without a difference. While the spire-like tops of the ribs may not be shown in the advertisements, the arrangement of the ribs along the side of the top and the shape of the opening are sufficiently like the features of the claimed mark to show an identity of functionality between the articles shown in the advertising and the proposed mark's prominent features. Second, BD would characterize the advertisements as "look for" advertising—the kind that pulls out of an overall article a few features to catch the viewer's attention. Thus BD argues that its advertisements were not really intended to tout functional aspects of its design, but merely to cause the viewer to look at one part of a design in particular. This argument fails. Nothing in the text of the advertisements underscores this "look for" concept. Instead the advertisements taken as a whole are more than substantial evidence that the proposed mark as a whole is functional. Indeed, the enlarged photographs of parts of the device actually highlight the functional aspects of the mark.

As to the third factor, if functionality is found based on other considerations, there is "no need to consider the availability of alternative designs, because the feature cannot be given trade dress protection merely because there are alternative designs available." *Valu Eng'g*, 278 F.3d at 1276. Thus, since the patent and advertising evidence established functionality, the Board did not need to analyze whether alternative designs exist. Nonetheless, the Board did conduct this analysis and found that one of the proposed designs was irrelevant and the other two could not be characterized as alternative designs because they shared the same utilitarian features of BD's design. BD has not shown that this finding is unsupported by substantial evidence.

Finally, as to the fourth factor, there was little record evidence before the Board to establish whether the cap design results from a comparatively simple or inexpensive method of manufacture. The sole evidence in the record on this factor consists of the declarations of Jaeger and Newby, two BD witnesses, who both averred that the design features did not lower the cost of manufacture. Given this scarce evidence, the Board did not err in refusing to weigh this factor in its analysis.

In *New England Butt Co. v. International Trade Commission*, 756 F.2d 874 (Fed. Cir. 1985), we explained that the public policy underlying the rule that de jure functional designs cannot be protected as trademarks is "not the *right* to slavishly copy articles which are not protected by patent or copyright, but the *need* to copy those articles, which is more properly termed the right to compete *effectively*." *Id.* at 877 (citing *Morton-Norwich*, 671 F.2d at 1339). The record in this case shows that BD's competitors in the closure cap industry also feature ribs for sure gripping and similar functional openings on their products. The Board thus concluded that the record failed to establish that there are meaningful alternative designs for collection tube closure caps. [cit.] Substantial evidence supports this conclusion, which underscores the competitive need to copy the functional features of BD's proposed mark.

Because the Board committed no legal error in its assessment of the functionality of BD's proposed mark, and because substantial evidence supports the Board's findings of fact under the *Morton-Norwich* factors, we affirm the final decision of the Board.

LINN, Circuit Judge, dissenting:

Because the [Board] incorrectly applied the legal standards in assessing the functionality of the trademark of [BD], and because substantial evidence does not support the Board's conclusion of functionality, I respectfully dissent.

It is undisputed that certain individual features of BD's closure cap design are functional, but the evidence falls short in supporting a conclusion that the mark, as a whole and as shown in the drawing, is in essence utilitarian, and thus *de jure* functional. . . .

I agree with the majority that the degree of design utility must be considered in determining *de jure* functionality. [cit.] I part company with the majority, however, when it approves the Board's "weigh[ing] the elements of a mark against one another to develop an understanding of whether the mark as a whole is essentially functional and thus non-registrable." [cit.] The presence of functional features may be relevant, but not in the sense of comparing dissociated functional features against non-functional features. The proper inquiry is to examine the degree to which the mark as a whole is dictated by utilitarian concerns (functional or economic superiority) or is arbitrary ("without complete deference to utility"). *See Morton-Norwich*, 671 F.2d at 1338-39, 1342-43.

Weighing individual elements of a mark against each other is analytically contrary to the consideration of the mark as a whole. As this court has previously held, "[s]imply dissecting appellant's alleged trademark into its design features and attributing to each a proven or commonly known utility is not, without more, conclusive that the design, considered as a whole, is de jure functional and not registrable." *In re Teledyne Indus., Inc.*, 696 F.2d 968, 971 (Fed. Cir. 1982).

This court's decision in *Morton-Norwich* is instructive. . . . The examining attorney [in that case] rejected the mark on the basis that the design "is no more than a non-distinctive purely functional container for the goods plus a purely functional spray trigger controlled closure . . . essentially utilitarian and non-arbitrary." *Id.* at 1335. The Board similarly concluded that the mark "is dictated primarily by functional (utilitarian) considerations, and is therefore unregistrable." *Id.* (original emphasis omitted).

Our predecessor court reversed finding that the applicant sought to register "no single design feature or component but the overall composite design comprising both bottle and spray top." *Id.* at 1342. Thus, the degree of design utility was analyzed for the whole mark, not the dissociated functional elements. . . .

The facts in the present case are very much like those in *Morton-Norwich*. . . . As in *Morton-Norwich*, there is no evidence that the overall design of the BD closure cap is required to look the way it does or that the design is "the best or one of a few superior designs available." [cit.] The Board and the majority place principal focus on the function served by certain features of the mark, including, *inter alia*, the top's opening (to allow for the insertion of a needle), the ribs on the side of the cap (to allow for increased grip), and the bottom's flanged lip (to allow for a safer opening). These considerations relate to the *de facto* functionality of individual product features and not the *de jure* functionality of the overall design—whether the design as a whole must look this way to serve some identified function. In focusing on the functional attributes of individual components, the Board and the majority overlook the arbitrary nature of BD's overall design.

Even under the improper analysis accepted by the majority, if the individual attributes with recognized functions are examined, there is no support for the proposition that the form of those components was dictated by their function. There is no evidence that: (1) the hole in the top *must* be that particular shape and size for a needle to pass through the opening; (2) the side of the cap *must* possess horizontally spaced ribs in the precise shape, size, and spacing depicted in BD's design to provide for increased grip; or (3) the bottom lip *must* be flanged and tapered in the precise manner depicted to avoid being unsafe.

[W]hile the Board and the majority correctly cite the *Morton-Norwich* factors to determine the functionality of the overall design based on the evidence presented, [cit.], both the Board and the majority fail to consider the design as a whole in analyzing these factors. [cit.]

First, while the Board and the majority put great weight in the existence of a utility patent, [the '446 Patent], that patent fails to illuminate the functionality inquiry. The Supreme Court recognized that "[a] utility patent is strong evidence that the features therein claimed are functional." *TrafFix*, 532 U.S. at 29. However, the '446 Patent claims none of the features of BD's design mark. Specifically, the claims of the '446 Patent do not cover the appearance or pattern of the ridges, the flanged lip, or the top opening of BD's design. . . .

Second, the majority correctly notes that the advertisements tout the features of BD's design that serve a functional purpose, which weighs against a finding of non-functionality. [cit.] However, the advertisements do support the finding of non-functionality based on the third *Morton-Norwich* factor: the presence of alternative designs. While the majority finds no relevance in the fact that the designs featured in BD's advertisements were not exactly the same as the current mark, [cit.], this fact indicates the existence of alternative designs that are nonetheless functionally identical.

Addressing the third *Morton-Norwich* factor, the Board and the majority discounted the most probative evidence submitted in this case—the design patents and evidence of alternative designs. Because "the effect upon competition is really the crux of the matter, it is, of course, significant that there are other alternatives available." *Morton-Norwich*, 671 F.2d at 1341 (internal quotation omitted).

The three design patents noted by the majority are not identical to the specific design for which trademark protection is sought. [cit.] However, the fact that three distinct design patents were granted on similar, but not identical, designs performing the same overall function as the current design at issue suggests that the current design is not "made in the form it must be made if it is to accomplish its purpose." *Morton-Norwich*, 671 F.2d at 1339 (internal citation omitted). If a design patent can show that one design in a group of functionally identical alternative designs is non-functional, the entire class of arbitrary alternative designs is likely nonfunctional.

. . .

Further, the Board and the majority wholly disregarded the evidence submitted by BD of alternative designs utilized by BD's competitors. The majority is correct that there is no need to consider alternative designs when functionality has been established, [cit.]; however, "that does not mean that the availability of alternative designs cannot be a legitimate source of evidence to determine whether a feature is functional in the first place." *Valu Eng'g*, 278 F.3d at 1276. In this case, the Board disregarded two alternative designs—designs actually used by BD's competitors—because it found that they shared the same utilitarian features and were therefore not "alternative designs." [cit.] The disqualification of an alternative design because it shares the same utilitarian features is unsupported by law. *See Morton-Norwich*, 671 F.2d at 1342 ("[C]ompetitors may even copy and enjoy all of [the design's] *functions* without copying the external appearance of appellant's spray top." (emphasis added)). In fact, this evidence strongly suggests that BD's design is not functional because BD faces competition from products with similar functionality, yet differing designs. As in *Morton-Norwich*, BD's "[c]ompetitors have apparently had no need to simulate" BD's product design "in order to enjoy all of the *functional* aspects" of a closure cap. *Id.* at 1342 (emphasis in original). Any concern that BD will unfairly assert its mark against these competitors rings hollow when BD, in seeking protection of this mark, has already distinguished those designs of its competitors.

Finally, the Board may not ignore the fourth *Morton-Norwich* factor—whether the design results from a less expensive method of manufacture—when evidence was presented on it. There were undisputed statements from BD indicating that the design did not result from reduced costs of manufacture. This uncontroverted evidence should have been taken into consideration in the Board's weighing of the factors. While the majority characterizes this as "little record evidence," [cit.], it is evidence that must be considered nonetheless.

Because the Board committed legal error in failing to analyze the functionality of BD's mark as a whole and lacked substantial evidence for its findings, I would reverse the Board's decision on functionality. On the functionality determination, I therefore respectfully dissent. . . .

APPLE INC. v. SAMSUNG ELECTRONICS CO. LTD.
786 F.3d 983 (Fed. Cir. 2015)

Prost, Chief Judge:

BACKGROUND

Apple sued Samsung in April 2011. On August 24, 2012, the first jury reached a verdict that numerous Samsung smartphones infringed and diluted Apple's patents and trade dresses in various combinations and awarded over $1 billion in damages.

[T]he diluted trade dresses are Trademark Registration No. 3,470,983 ("'983 trade dress") and an unregistered trade dress defined in terms of certain elements in the configuration of the iPhone. [The District Court upheld the jury determinations over Samsung's post-trial motions.]

DISCUSSION

. . .

I.   Trade Dresses

The jury found Samsung liable for the likely dilution of Apple's iPhone trade dresses under the Lanham Act. When reviewing Lanham Act claims, we look to the law of the regional circuit where the district court sits. [cit.] We therefore apply Ninth Circuit law.

[I]t is necessary for us to determine first whether Apple's asserted trade dresses, claiming elements from its iPhone product, are nonfunctional and therefore protectable.

"In general terms, a product feature is functional if it is essential to the use or purpose of the article or if it affects the cost or quality of the article." *Inwood Labs., Inc. v. Ives Labs., Inc.*, 456 U.S. 844, 850 n.10 (1982). "A product feature need only have *some* utilitarian advantage to be considered functional." *Disc Golf Ass'n v. Champion Discs, Inc.*, 158 F.3d 1002, 1007 (9th Cir. 1998). A trade dress, taken as a whole, is functional if it is "in its particular shape because it works better in this shape." [*Leatherman Tool Corp. v. Cooper Indus.*, 199 F.3d 1009 (9th Cir. 1999).]

"[C]ourts have noted that it is, and should be, more difficult to claim product configuration trade dress than other forms of trade dress." Id. at 1012-13 (discussing cases). Accordingly, the Supreme Court and the Ninth Circuit have repeatedly found product configuration trade dresses functional and therefore non-protectable. . . .

Moreover, federal trademark registrations have been found insufficient to save product configuration trade dresses from conclusions of functionality. *See, e.g., Talking Rain Beverage Co. v. S. Beach Beverage*, 349 F.3d 601, 602 (9th Cir.2003) (affirming summary judgment that registered trade dress covering a bottle design with a grip handle was functional); *Tie Tech, Inc. v. Kinedyne Corp.*, 296 F.3d 778, 782–83 (9th Cir.2002) (affirming summary judgment that registered trade dress covering a handheld cutter design was functional). The Ninth Circuit has even reversed a jury verdict of non-functionality of a product configuration trade dress. See *Leatherman*, 199 F.3d at 1013 (reversing jury verdict that a trade dress on the overall appearance of a pocket tool was non-functional). Apple conceded during oral argument that it had not cited a single Ninth Circuit case that found a product configuration trade dress to be non-functional. . . .

The Ninth Circuit's high bar for non-functionality frames our review of the two iPhone trade dresses on appeal. While the parties argue without distinguishing the two trade dresses, the unregistered trade dress and the registered '983 trade dress claim different details and are afforded different evidentiary presumptions under the Lanham Act. We analyze the two trade dresses separately below.

A.   Unregistered Trade Dress

Apple claims elements from its iPhone 3G and 3GS products to define the asserted unregistered trade dress:

> a rectangular product with four evenly rounded corners; a flat, clear surface covering the front of the product; a display screen under the clear surface;
> substantial black borders above and below the display screen and narrower black borders on either side of the screen; and
> when the device is on, a row of small dots on the display screen, a matrix of colorful square icons with evenly rounded corners within the display screen, and an unchanging bottom dock of colorful square icons with evenly rounded corners set off from the display's other icons.

As this trade dress is not registered on the principal federal trademark register, Apple "has the burden of proving that the claimed trade dress, taken as a whole, is not functional. . . ." See 15 U.S.C. §1125(c)(4)(A).

Apple argues that the unregistered trade dress is nonfunctional under each of the *Disc Golf* factors that the Ninth Circuit uses to analyze functionality: "(1) whether the design yields a utilitarian advantage, (2) whether alternative designs are available, (3) whether advertising touts the utilitarian advantages of the design, and (4) whether the particular design results from a comparatively simple or inexpensive method of manufacture." See *Disc Golf*, 158 F.3d at 1006. However, the Supreme Court has more recently held that "a feature is also functional . . . when it affects the cost or quality of the device." See *TrafFix*, 532 U.S. at 32. The Supreme Court's holding was recognized by the Ninth Circuit as "short circuiting some of the *Disc Golf* factors." *Secalt* [*v. Wuxi Shenxi Const. Mach. Co.*, 668 F. 3d 677, 686-87 (9th Cir. 2012)]. Nevertheless, we explore Apple's contentions on each of the *Disc Golf* factors and conclude that there was insufficient evidence to support a jury finding in favor of non-functionality on any factor.

1.   Utilitarian Advantage

Apple argues that "the iPhone's physical design did not 'contribute unusually . . . to the usability' of the device." Apple further contends that the unregistered trade dress was "developed . . . not for 'superior performance.'" Neither "unusual usability" nor "superior performance," however, is the standard used by the Ninth Circuit to determine whether there is any utilitarian advantage. The Ninth Circuit "has never held, as [plaintiff] suggests, that the product feature must provide superior utilitarian advantages. To the contrary, [the Ninth Circuit] has suggested that in order to establish nonfunctionality the party with the burden must demonstrate that the product feature serves no purpose other than identification." *Disc Golf*, 158 F.3d at 1007 (internal quotation marks omitted).

The requirement that the unregistered trade dress "serves no purpose other than identification" cannot be reasonably inferred from the evidence. Apple emphasizes a single aspect of its design, beauty, to imply the lack of other advantages. But the evidence showed that the iPhone's design pursued more than just beauty. Specifically, Apple's executive testified that the theme for the design of the iPhone was:

> to create a new breakthrough design for a phone that was beautiful and simple and *easy to use* and created a beautiful, smooth surface that had a touchscreen and went right to the rim with the bezel around it and looking for a look that we found was beautiful and *easy to use* and appealing.

[Joint Appendix] 40722-23 (emphases added).

Moreover, Samsung cites extensive evidence in the record that showed the usability function of every single element in the unregistered trade dress. For example, rounded corners improve "pocketability" and "durability" and rectangular shape maximizes the display that can be accommodated. A flat clear surface on the front of the phone facilitates touch operation by fingers over a large display. The bezel protects the glass from impact when the phone is dropped. The borders around the display are sized to accommodate other components while minimizing the overall product dimensions. The row of dots in the user interface indicates multiple pages of application screens that are available. The icons allow users to differentiate the applications available to the users and the bottom dock of unchanging icons allows for quick access to the most commonly used applications. Apple rebuts none of this evidence.

Apple conceded during oral argument that its trade dress "improved the quality [of the iPhone] in some respects." It is thus clear that the unregistered trade dress has a utilitarian advantage. *See Disc Golf*, 158 F.3d at 1007.

2. Alternative Designs

The next factor requires that purported alternative designs "offer exactly the same features" as the asserted trade dress in order to show non-functionality. *Tie Tech*, 296 F.3d at 786 (quoting *Leatherman*, 199 F.3d at 1013-14). A manufacturer "does not have rights under trade dress law to compel its competitors to resort to alternative designs which have a different set of advantages and disadvantages." *Id.*

Apple, while asserting that there were "numerous alternative designs," fails to show that any of these alternatives offered exactly the same features as the asserted trade dress. Apple simply catalogs the mere existence of other design possibilities embodied in rejected iPhone prototypes and other manufacturers' smartphones. The "mere existence" of other designs, however, does not prove that the unregistered trade dress is non-functional. See *Talking Rain*, 349 F.3d at 604.

3. Advertising of Utilitarian Advantages

"If a seller advertises the utilitarian advantages of a particular feature, this constitutes strong evidence of functionality." *Disc Golf*, 158 F.3d at 1009. An "inference" of a product feature's utility in the plaintiff's advertisement is enough to weigh in favor of functionality of a trade dress encompassing that feature. Id.

Apple argues that its advertising was "[f]ar from touting any utilitarian advantage of the iPhone design. . . ." Apple relies on its executive's testimony that an iPhone advertisement, portraying "the distinctive design very clearly," was based on Apple's "product as hero" approach. The "product as hero" approach refers to Apple's stylistic choice of making "the product the biggest, clearest, most obvious thing in [its] advertisements, often at the expense of anything else around it, to remove all the other elements of communication so [the viewer] see[s] the product most predominantly in the marketing."

Apple's arguments focusing on its stylistic choice, however, fail to address the substance of its advertisements. The substance of the iPhone advertisement relied upon by Apple gave viewers "the ability to see a bit about how it might work," for example, "how flicking and scrolling and tapping and all these multitouch ideas simply [sic]." Another advertisement cited by Apple similarly displayed the message, "[t]ouching is believing," under a picture showing a user's hand interacting with the graphical user interface of an iPhone. Apple fails to show that, on the substance, these demonstrations of the user interface on iPhone's touch screen involved the elements claimed in Apple's unregistered trade dress and why they were not touting the utilitarian advantage of the unregistered trade dress.

4.   Method of Manufacture

The fourth factor considers whether a functional benefit in the asserted trade dress arises from "economies in manufacture or use," such as being "relatively simple or inexpensive to manufacture." *Disc Golf,* 158 F.3d at 1009.

Apple contends that "[t]he iPhone design did not result from a 'comparatively simple or inexpensive method of manufacture'" because Apple experienced manufacturing challenges. Apple's manufacturing challenges, however, resulted from the durability considerations for the iPhone and not from the design of the unregistered trade dress. According to Apple's witnesses, difficulties resulted from its choices of materials in using "hardened steel"; "very high, high grade of steel"; and, "glass that was not breakable enough, scratch resistant enough." These materials were chosen, for example, for the iPhone to survive a drop:

> If you drop this, you don't have to worry about the ground hitting the glass. You have to worry about the band of steel surrounding the glass hitting the glass. . . . In order to, to make it work, we had to use very high, high grade of steel because we couldn't have it sort of deflecting into the glass.

The durability advantages that resulted from the manufacturing challenges, however, are outside the scope of what Apple defines as its unregistered trade dress. For the design elements that comprise Apple's unregistered trade dress, Apple points to no evidence in the record to show they were not relatively simple or inexpensive to manufacture. [cit.]

In sum, Apple has failed to show that there was substantial evidence in the record to support a jury finding in favor of non-functionality for the unregistered trade dress on any of the *Disc Golf* factors. Apple fails to rebut the evidence that the elements in the unregistered trade dress serve the functional purpose of improving usability. Rather, Apple focuses on the "beauty" of its design, even though Apple pursued both "beauty" and functionality in the design of the iPhone. We therefore reverse the district court's denial of Samsung's motion for judgment as a matter of law that the unregistered trade dress is functional and therefore not protectable.

B.   *The Registered '983 Trade Dress*

In contrast to the unregistered trade dress, the '983 trade dress is a federally registered trademark. The federal trademark registration provides "prima facie evidence" of non- functionality. [cit.] This presumption "shift[s] the burden of production to the defendant . . . to provide evidence of functionality." Once this presumption is overcome, the registration loses its legal significance on the issue of functionality. Id. ("In the face of sufficient and undisputed facts demonstrating functionality, . . . the registration loses its evidentiary significance.").

The '983 trade dress claims the design details in each of the sixteen icons on the iPhone's home screen framed by the iPhone's rounded-rectangular shape with silver edges and a black background:

> The first icon depicts the letters "SMS" in green inside a white speech bubble on a green background;
>
> . . .
>
> the seventh icon depicts a map with yellow and orange roads, a pin with a red head, and a red-and-blue road sign with the numeral "280" in white;
>
> . . .
>
> the sixteenth icon depicts the distinctive configuration of applicant's media player device in white over an orange background.

'983 trade dress (omitting thirteen other icon design details for brevity).

It is clear that individual elements claimed by the '983 trade dress are functional. For example, there is no dispute that the claimed details such as "the seventh icon depicts a map with yellow and orange roads, a pin with a red head, and a red-and-blue road sign with the numeral '280' in white" are functional. Apple's user interface expert testified on how icon designs promote usability. This expert agreed that "the whole point of an icon on a smartphone is to communicate to the consumer using that product, that if they hit that icon, certain functionality will occur on the phone." The expert further explained that icons are "[v]isual shorthand for something" and that "rectangular containers" for icons provide "more real estate" to accommodate the icon design. Apple rebuts none of this evidence.

Apple contends instead that Samsung improperly disaggregates the '983 trade dress into individual elements to argue functionality. But Apple fails to explain how the total combination of the sixteen icon designs in the context of iPhone's screen-dominated rounded-rectangular shape—all part of the iPhone's "easy to use" design theme—somehow negates the undisputed usability function of the individual elements. Apple's own brief even relies on its expert's testimony about the "instant recognizability due to highly intuitive icon usage" on "the home screen of the iPhone." Apple's expert was discussing an analysis of the iPhone's overall combination of icon designs that allowed a user to recognize quickly particular applications to use. The iPhone's usability advantage from the combination of its icon designs shows that the '983 trade dress viewed as a whole "is nothing other than the assemblage of functional parts. . . ." See *Tie Tech*, 296 F.3d at 786 (quoting *Leatherman*, 199 F.3d at 1013). There is no "separate 'overall appearance' which is non-functional." Id. (quoting *Leatherman*, 199 F.3d at 1013). The undisputed facts thus demonstrate the functionality of the '983 trade dress. "In the face of sufficient and undisputed facts demonstrating functionality, as in our case, the registration loses its evidentiary significance." See id. at 783.

The burden thus shifts back to Apple. But Apple offers no analysis of the icon designs claimed by the '983 trade dress. Rather, Apple argues generically for its two trade dresses without distinction under the *Disc Golf* factors. Among Apple's lengthy citations to the record, we can find only two pieces of information that involve icon designs. One is Apple's user interface expert discussing other possible icon designs. The other is a citation to a print iPhone advertisement that included the icon designs claimed in the '983 trade dress. These two citations, viewed in the most favorable light to Apple, would be relevant to only two of the *Disc Golf* factors: "alternative design" and "advertising." But the cited evidence suffers from the same defects as discussed [above]. Specifically, the expert's discussion of other icon design possibilities does not show that the other design possibilities "offer[ed] exactly the same features" as the '983 trade dress. See *Tie Tech*, 296 F.3d at 786 (quoting

Leatherman, 199 F.3d at 1013-14). The print iPhone advertisement also fails to establish that, on the substance, it was not touting the utilitarian advantage of the '983 trade dress. The evidence cited by Apple therefore does not show the non-functionality of the '983 trade dress.

In sum, the undisputed evidence shows the functionality of the registered '983 trade dress and shifts the burden of proving non-functionality back to Apple. Apple, however, has failed to show that there was substantial evidence in the record to support a jury finding in favor of non-functionality for the '983 trade dress on any of the *Disc Golf* factors. We therefore reverse the district court's denial of Samsung's motion for judgment as a matter of law that the '983 trade dress is functional and therefore not protectable. . . .

[The court affirmed the judgment on design and utility patent issues.]

NOTES AND QUESTIONS

1. *Different applications of* Inwood. Do you have a good sense of how to apply the *Inwood* test? *See Moldex-Metric, Inc. v. McKeon Prods., Inc.*, 891 F.3d 878 (9th Cir. 2018) ("In *Inwood* and *TrafFix*, the Supreme Court did not explain what it takes for a feature to be 'essential to the use or purpose of a product.' And whether a feature is 'essential to the use or purpose of a product' is not always as apparent as it was in *TrafFix*, especially in cases such as this where the visibility of [plaintiff's] green color is not the 'central advance' of a utility patent and does not equate to the same 'strong evidence' of essentiality as the patents in *TrafFix*, and where the green color does not affect the cost of ear plugs as compared to the dual-spring device in *TrafFix* that was less expensive than an alternative three-spring device").

Note that the *Inwood* test itself contains two separate bases on which a mark might be held functional. In *In re Change Wind Corp.*, 123 U.S.P.Q.2d (BNA) 1453 (TTAB 2017), the TTAB found the design of a wind turbine to be functional. The Board reasoned as follows:

> Because the patent and advertisements disclosed *use*-related benefits, the lack of *cost*-related benefits does not undercut our finding of functionality. The Supreme Court has stated that "a product feature is functional, and cannot serve as a trademark, [1] if it is essential to the use or purpose of the article *or* [2] if it affects [a] the cost *or* [b] quality of the article." *TrafFix*, 58 USPQ2d at 1006 (citation omitted; emphasis and numbering added). Thus, a product feature can be found functional for affecting *either* the quality of the article *or* its cost. While evidence that a product feature makes the product cheaper to manufacture may be probative in showing functionality, evidence that it does not affect its cost is not necessarily proof of non-functionality. *In re N.V. Organon*, 79 USPQ2d 1639, 1646 (TTAB 2006). In other words, evidence that a design costs more, or has no impact on cost, is irrelevant if the design is found to work better.

In *Eco Mfg. LLC v. Honeywell Int'l Inc.*, 357 F.3d 649 (7th Cir. 2003), the Seventh Circuit suggested three ways in which the round shape of a thermostat could be functional, at least in principle:

> First, rectangular objects may clash with other architectural or decorative choices. . . . Second, round thermostats (and other controls) may reduce injuries, especially to children, caused by running into protruding sharp corners. Third, people with arthritis or other disabilities may find it easier to set the temperature by turning a large dial (or the entire outer casing of the device) than by moving a slider or pushing buttons on boxes. The record does not contain much along any of these lines. . . . Although the three possibilities we have mentioned do not show that roundness is "essential" to a thermostat, that's not required. *TrafFix* rejected an equation of functionality with necessity; it is enough that the design be useful. The Justices told us that a feature is functional if it is essential to the design *or* it affects the article's price or quality.

Do you agree with the Seventh Circuit's reading of *TrafFix*? Under *TrafFix* do you agree that the three possibilities raised by the Court might show functionality? *See also Dippin' Dots, Inc. v. Frosty Bites Distribution, LLC*, 369 F.3d 1197, 1206 (11th Cir. 2004) (finding size of the bead shape "contributes" to the product's creamy taste, which would be different in a larger "dot"); *cf. Gen. Motors Corp. v. Lanard Toys, Inc.*, 468 F.3d 405, 417 (6th Cir. 2006) (holding that having a function in mind when designing a product does not amount to that design being "essential" to the use or purpose of the article).

2. *Evidence and the relevance of alternatives.* In what ways has *TrafFix* altered the factors to which courts look in determining functionality? For example, do the *Morton-Norwich* factors contribute to answering the questions at the heart of the *TrafFix* test? Are they still relevant? Post-*TrafFix* courts take different views of the relevance of alternative designs. Clearly, alternatives will not of themselves undermine a functionality determination under *Inwood*. *See Antioch Co. v. W. Trimming Corp.*, 347 F.3d 150, 156 (6th Cir. 2003) ("[A] court is not *required* to examine alternative designs when applying the traditional test for functionality. . . . The traditional *Inwood* test for functionality is the main rule, and if a product is clearly functional under *Inwood*, a court need not apply the competitive-necessity test and its related inquiry concerning the availability of alternative designs."). However, some courts continue to stress the relevance of alternatives. *See, e.g., Eco Mfg. LLC v. Honeywell Int'l Inc.*, 357 F.3d 649 (7th Cir. 2003); *New Colt Holding Corp. v. RJG Holdings of Fla., Inc.*, 312 F. Supp. 2d 195, 214, 219 (D. Conn. 2004) (noting that "to the extent that Second Circuit law required consideration of design alternatives in all circumstances, that is no longer the law. However, under the present circumstances and given the nature of the product, the existence of design alternatives is helpful for determining whether a particular design is truly necessary to the way the revolver works"); *Moldex-Metric, Inc. v. McKeon Prods.*, 891 F.3d 878 (9th Cir. 2018); *Georgia-Pacific Consumer Prods. LP v. Kimberly-Clark Corp.*, 647 F.3d 723, 727-28 (7th Cir. 2011). Insofar as alternative designs *are* relevant, which opinion in *Becton, Dickinson* has the better of the arguments on whether designs tendered by the applicant constituted an "alternative" for the purposes of this analysis? Is the approach of the *Apple* court consistent with the approach of Judge Clevenger or Judge Linn in *Becton, Dickinson*? Likewise, the relationship between the *TrafFix* test and the Ninth Circuit *Disc Golf* factors, discussed in *Apple*, remains uncertain. In *Millennium Labs., Inc. v. Ameritox, Ltd.*, 817 F.3d 1123 (9th Cir. 2016), the Court of Appeals for the Ninth Circuit held that "the *Disc Golf* factors reflect the *Inwood* definition of functionality—'essential to the use or purpose of the article or if it affects the cost or quality of the article.'" *Id.* at 1129. As a result, the Ninth Circuit endorsed their continued use in the wake of *TrafFix*. *See Moldex-Metric, Inc. v. McKeon Prods., Inc.*, 891 F.3d 878 (9th Cir. 2018). Is the approach in *Apple* and *Millennium Labs* consistent with *TrafFix*?

3. *Functionality in design patent law.* Other intellectual property regimes that offer design protection have similar functionality doctrines, but the standards may be slightly different. One court has explained that

> although the general considerations of functionality are of course similar, the functionality doctrine in trademark law is quite distinct from the functionality determination in design patents. Although functionality will invalidate a design patent only when the design is "*dictated*" by the function, [cit.], a lesser showing of functionality is necessary to invalidate trademarks. Functionality will invalidate a trademark "if it is essential to the use or purpose of the article or if it affects the cost or quality of the article." *Qualitex*, 514 U.S. at 165 ("[A] product feature is functional . . . if exclusive use of the feature would put competitors at a significant non-reputation-related disadvantage."); *see also Telebrands Direct Response Corp. v. Ovation Communications, Inc.*, 802 F. Supp. 1169, 1177 (D.N.J. 1992) (remarking that "the more

rigorous standard of functionality required to defeat a design patent as opposed to a trade dress claim is reflected in the ownership term of the respective rights" in that the trade dress rights can be perpetual and design patents expire after a limited term). This is particularly true "in light of the Supreme Court's recent rulings which curtail trade dress protection by expanding the functionality doctrine." [cit.]

Spotless Enters., Inc. v. A & E Prods. Grp. L.P., 294 F. Supp. 2d 322, 350 (E.D.N.Y. 2003). Does this comparison help to define the contours of the *Inwood* trademark test by way of contrast with the design patent system? *See* Jason Du Mont & Mark D. Janis, *Functionality in Design Protection Systems*, 19 J. INTELL. PROP. L. 261 (2012) (explaining—and criticizing—some prevailing approaches to functionality in design protection systems).

    4. *Focus of analysis.* Whose product—plaintiff's or defendant's—should be analyzed in determining whether a design feature is "essential to the use or purpose of the article or affects its cost or quality"? In *Maker's Mark Distillery, Inc. v. Diageo N. Am., Inc.*, 102 U.S.P.Q.2d (BNA) 1693 (6th Cir. 2012), the plaintiff owned a federal registration for a "wax-like coating covering the cap of the bottle and trickling down the neck of the bottle in a freeform irregular pattern." The defendant argued that a "freeform wax coating protects the cork from air, moisture, and contaminants and preserves the contents of the bottle on *some* bottles of alcohol and that tendrils are a natural byproduct of such a coating." Plaintiff Maker's Mark argued that on its product an air- and liquid-tight twist cap—and not the registered trademark freeform wax coating—protects and preserves its product. The court noted that "[t]his is an unusual puzzle because in most cases the challenged trademark serves the same purpose on any product." Could a trademark be invalid on functionality grounds not because it is essential to the use or purpose of the trademark owner's product, but because it prevents a competitor from using the same feature in a useful way on the competitive product? If so, does the necessity of use by the defendant affect the question to be asked under the *Inwood* test or under the competitive necessity test (or both)? Would your answer change if Maker's Mark had patented its air- and liquid-tight twist cap?

    5. *The evidentiary inference and* Inwood. How does the rule articulated by the Supreme Court in *TrafFix* regarding the relevance of utility patents fit into the scheme of functionality tests that lower appellate courts are now articulating? *Cf. Moldex-Metric, Inc. v. McKeon Prods., Inc.*, 891 F.3d 878 (9th Cir. 2018) (distinguishing *TrafFix* because in case before court "the visibility of [plaintiff's] green color is not the 'central advance' of a utility patent and does not equate to the same 'strong evidence' of essentiality as the patents in *TrafFix* . . .").

    6. *The evidentiary inference: "central advance."* In *Leviton Mfg. Co. v. Universal Sec. Instruments, Inc.*, 304 F. Supp. 2d 726 (D. Md. 2004), the plaintiff asserted trade dress rights in the appearance of a ground fault circuit interrupting product that had been disclosed in a prior utility patent. The expired patent was, however, given little weight by the court in considering functionality because the "central advance" of the patent was its "unique switching mechanism and ability to fit into a wall receptacle" rather than the product's appearance. *Id.* at 736 ("*TrafFix* does not dictate a finding of functionality where a patent has been issued. Rather, the Court prohibits affording trade dress protection of the central advance of an existing patent."). If the evidentiary inference is triggered only when the design feature constitutes the "central advance," how are courts to determine the "central advance" in a patent?

    7. *The evidentiary inference: Where to look.* In addition to knowing *what* a court should look for in an expired patent (or an invention) in order to apply the *TrafFix* inference, it is also important to know *where* a court (or competitor) should look to determine whether a product design feature will be subject to the evidentiary inference of functionality. Where in the expired patent should a court look? In this regard, think back to the possible purposes underlying the rule the *TrafFix* Court announced. Where did the *Franco* and

Becton, Dickinson courts look? In *Fuji Kogyo Co. v. Pac. Bay Int'l, Inc.*, 461 F.3d 675 (6th Cir. 2006), the plaintiff argued that because the design feature in which trademark rights were asserted was not *claimed* in the relevant utility patent it should not create any inference of functionality suggested by the *TrafFix* Court. The Sixth Circuit thought that argument was well taken but found it unavailing because "the design departure [was] too slight" such that the plaintiff's patent claims would (hypothetically) have covered the defendant's design under a theory of infringement based upon the doctrine of equivalents (had the patent still been extant). The court was reinforced in this conclusion by language in the patent specification, which can be used to interpret the claims, and because the plaintiff had previously sought to assert its patent rights against a competitor making a similar design and thus could reasonably be estopped from claiming that its designs were not functional. Does the *Fuji Kogyo* court's reliance upon the fact that defendant's design would (hypothetically) have been covered under an equivalency theory had the patent still been extant provide an alternative standard to whether the feature was a "central advance"? Does the court's reference to estoppel effectuate a different purpose from that pursued by the Court in *TrafFix*?

In *Georgia-Pacific Consumer Prods. LP v. Kimberly-Clark Corp.*, 647 F.3d 723 (7th Cir. 2011), the plaintiff claimed trade dress rights in the quilted design of its toilet paper. The design had been the subject of several utility patents. The Seventh Circuit gave effect to the inference of functionality based on *TrafFix*, reasoning as follows:

> The parties agree that the essential feature of the trademarks is the Quilted Diamond Design, which is embossed on the toilet paper, giving it a quilt-like appearance. [cit.] Therefore, the question is whether the Quilted Diamond Design is also the "central advance" claimed in any of the utility patents. Unfortunately for [the plaintiff], all five utility patents disclose a diamond lattice design filled with signature bosses and claim the benefits of this design as the "central advance.". . . Each of the patents discusses the benefits of the Quilted Diamond Design. [Defendant] argues that this language is strong evidence of functionality. We agree.
>
> [Plaintiff] argues, however, that the Quilted Diamond Design is merely "incidental" under *TrafFix*. Accordingly, we will "[go] beyond" the patent claims to the specifications. *See TrafFix*, 532 U.S. at 34. The abstracts for the '639 and '156 patents state that "[t]he perceived *softness of embossed tissue can be increased greatly while avoiding nesting* when a particular pattern is embossed into the tissue." (Emphasis added.) The '776 abstract describes that patent as "[a]n embossed tissue having *improved bulk and puffiness* while being non-nesting by having a lattice pattern and at least two signature bosses." (Emphasis added.) And the '057 patent states that "[t]his invention relates to the discovery that *perceived softness of embossed tissue can be increased greatly while avoiding prior art nesting problems if a particular pattern is embossed into the tissue*." (Emphasis added.) So [plaintiff's] argument fares no better here; these abstracts all refer to the Quilted Diamond Design's utilitarian benefits of softness, bulk, and non-nesting.
>
> Moreover, the patents claim the Quilted Diamond Design as the "most preferred embodiment." (The preferred embodiment of the '057 patent is a lattice pattern of diamond cells filled with signature debossments; the most preferred embodiment for the '639 patent is a lattice comprised of "diamond shaped" cells filled with a "signature boss.") And while the preferred embodiment alone is not definitive of functionality, the language [plaintiff] uses in the preferred embodiment (a lattice pattern filled with hearts and flowers) matches the language in the claims (a lattice structure and diamond-shaped cells). As with the language in the specifications, the consistency in language between the preferred embodiment and the claims is evidence of functionality.
>
> Thus, reading the language of the patents, we find that the "central advance" claimed in the utility patents is embossing a quilt-like diamond lattice filled with signature designs that improves (perceived) softness and bulk, and reduces nesting and ridging. This is the same "essential feature" claimed in the trademarks. Thus, the language of the patents—the claims, abstracts, and preferred embodiment—is "strong evidence" that the Quilted Diamond Design is functional, and [plaintiff] has failed to offer evidence that the design is merely incidental.

Is this analysis consistent with how the *TrafFix* Court intended lower courts to use patents? Does it incorporate undue (or too little) patent technicality into trademark law?

For your reference, Section 112 of the Patent Act in relevant part reads as follows:

35 U.S.C. §112. SPECIFICATION

(a) The specification shall contain a written description of the invention, and of the manner and process of making and using it, in such full, clear, concise, and exact terms as to enable any person skilled in the art to which it pertains, or with which it is most nearly connected, to make and use the same, and shall set forth the best mode contemplated by the inventor of carrying out his invention.
(b) The specification shall conclude with one or more claims particularly pointing out and distinctly claiming the subject matter which the applicant regards as his invention.

In short, it is the claims of the patent that define its scope. The specification assists only in the interpretation of the claims. What is the relevance of Section 112 to the question of where to look?

Compare *Georgia-Pacific* with *McAirlaids, Inc. v. Kimberly-Clark Corp.*, 756 F.3d 307 (4th Cir. 2014). There, McAirlaids produced "airlaid," a textile-like material composed of cellulose fiber. Airlaid is used in a wide variety of absorbent goods, including medical supplies, hygiene products, and food packages. To make airlaid, cellulose fiber is shredded into "fluff pulp," which is arranged into loosely formed sheets. In contrast to most of its competitors, McAirlaids fuses these fluff pulp sheets through an embossing process that does not require glue or binders. McAirlaids patented its pressure-fusion process, and the resulting product. In this process, sheets of fluff pulp pass at very high pressures between steel rollers printed with a raised pattern. The rollers leave an embossing pattern on the resulting material, and the high-pressure areas bond the fiber layers into a textile-like product. In order for McAirlaids' fusion process to adequately hold together the airlaid, the embossed design must fall within certain general size and spacing parameters. McAirlaids has chosen a "pixel" pattern for its absorbent products: the high-pressure areas form rows of pinpoint-like dots on the material. McAirlaids registered this pattern as trade dress with the U.S. Patent and Trademark Office with the following description: "the mark is a [three dimensional] repeating pattern of embossed dots" used in various types of absorbent pads. McAirlaids sued Kimberly-Clark for trademark infringement after Kimberly-Clark began using a similar dot pattern on its GoodNites bed mats, an absorbent product manufactured in a manner different from McAirlaids' pads. The parties disputed whether McAirlaids' chosen embossing pattern was functional. The Court of Appeals for the Fourth Circuit distinguished *TrafFix* because:

> the utility patents in TrafFix protected the dualspring mechanism, which was the same feature for which MDI sought trade-dress protection. In contrast, McAirlaids's utility patents cover a process and a material, but do not mention a particular embossing pattern as a protected element. The Court in *TrafFix* acknowledged that "a different result might obtain" when "a manufacturer seeks to protect arbitrary, incidental, or ornamental aspects of features of a product found in the patent claims, such as arbitrary curves in the legs or an ornamental pattern painted on the springs." In such a case, the court must "examin[e] the patent and its prosecution history to see if the feature in question is shown as a useful part of the invention." Here, McAirlaids's patents cover a production process and a material, while the trade dress claimed is a particular pattern on the material that results from the process. Unlike in *TrafFix*, therefore, the pattern is not the "central advance" of any utility patent. Neither of McAirlaids's patents refer to a particular embossing pattern. Both patents reference line-shaped as well as point- or dotshaped pressure areas, but the patents also directly acknowledge that embossing studs of different shapes can be used, including lines, pyramids, cubes, truncated cones, cylinders, and parallelepipeds. In fact, the diagrams of [the relevant patent] show hexagonal shapes rather than circles. Therefore, while McAirlaids's patents do provide evidence of the dots' functionality, they are not the same "strong evidence" as the patents in *TrafFix*.

The court also concluded that "because the facts of this case are different from those presented to the Supreme Court in *TrafFix*, *TrafFix*'s holding about alternative designs is inapplicable here." Thus, in addressing the alleged factual disputes, the Court considered evidence of alternative designs. Did the Fourth Circuit properly apply *TrafFix*? In what ways might *Kellogg* be relevant to the case? What weight would you give to the fact that patents for other nonwoven products specify that dot-shaped patterns are preferred for embossed bonding, but such patents also indicate that many designs can also be used?

8. *The evidentiary inference: who should decide and how.* In the utility patent context, the Supreme Court has held that judges, not juries, should be responsible for construing the claims in a patent. *See Markman v. Westview Instruments, Inc.*, 517 U.S. 370 (1996); *Teva Pharms. USA, Inc. v. Sandoz, Inc.*, 135 S. Ct. 831 (2015) (acknowledging that subsidiary fact finding is sometimes necessary, especially when the claims contain technical terms). Indeed, most courts conduct special evidentiary proceedings ("*Markman* hearings") to establish the meaning of the claims. In *Fuji Kogyo*, because of the court's reliance on the scope of the patents, the plaintiff sought a remand to the district court to engage in proper construction of patent claims and equivalents analysis in line with the dictates of patent law. The court rejected that demand on the ground that the patents were being used merely as probative evidence. What should be the respective roles for judges and juries in making functionality determinations where an expired patent is involved? Does this question affect your view on the relative importance of the different devices through which trademark law defines the protection available for product design trade dress? *Cf. Samara Bros. v. Wal-Mart Stores, Inc.*, 165 F.3d 120 (2d Cir. 1998) (Newman, J., dissenting), *rev'd*, 529 U.S. 205 (2000).

9. *Venerable patents.* Given the reasons behind the "evidentiary inference," what weight would you give to an expired utility patent on a design that had issued over fifty years ago? *See Eco Mfg. LLC v. Honeywell Int'l Inc.*, 357 F.3d 649, 653 (7th Cir. 2003) (noting that "passage of time diminishes a utility patent's significance").

10. *The relevance of abandoned or rejected applications.* In what way is an abandoned utility patent application relevant to the question of functionality, as the Federal Circuit suggests in *Valu Engineering*? If it should be relevant, which of the purposes underlying the functionality doctrine is being effectuated? What if the design of the plaintiff's product is "closely related to a potentially patentable . . . process"? *See Incredible Techs., Inc. v. Virtual Techs., Inc.*, 284 F. Supp. 2d 1069, 1078 (N.D. Ill. 2003), *aff'd*, 400 F.3d 1007 (7th Cir. 2005). What should be the relevance of the fact that a plaintiff had tried, but failed, to secure a copyright registration on the design? *See Bonazoli v. R.S.V.P. Int'l, Inc.*, 353 F. Supp. 2d 218 (D.R.I. 2005).

11. *The relevance of related design and utility patents.* How should a design patent on the design claimed as a trademark affect analysis of functionality? *See Fuji Kogyo Co. v. Pac. Bay Int'l, Inc.*, 461 F.3d 675 (6th Cir. 2006) (noting that a design patent is presumptive evidence of nonfunctionality, but affording it little weight because of parallel utility patent on the product that created a presumption of functionality); *Secalt S.A. v. Wuxi Shenxi Constr. Mach. Co.*, 668 F.3d 677 (9th Cir. 2012) (emphasizing that the existence of a design patent on the feature for which trade dress protection is sought will not of itself overcome a presumption of functionality). Which of the opinions in *Becton, Dickinson* give appropriate weight to the design patent in that case?

12. *Changes in status.* Clearly, a design that is at one time distinctive might become functional. Can a design that is once held to be functional become nonfunctional? *See Adidas-America, Inc. v. Payless Shoesource, Inc.*, 546 F. Supp. 2d 1029, 1084-86 (D. Or. 2008) (accepting "that product features once deemed wholly functional can be transformed over time to non-functional, source-indicating features"). *Compare Eco Mfg. LLC v. Honeywell Int'l Inc.*, 357 F.3d 649 (7th Cir. 2003), *and In re Honeywell Inc.*, 8 U.S.P.Q.2d (BNA) 1600, 1604-05 (TTAB 1988), *with In re Honeywell, Inc.*, 532 F.2d 180, 182-83 (C.C.P.A. 1976). If the functional status of a mark can change, at what point in time should a court assess the functionality question? *See Adidas*, 546 F. Supp. 2d at 1085. Might that depend on whether the basis for the functionality determination was the existence of an expired utility patent? *Cf. In re Bose Corp.*, 81 U.S.P.Q.2d (BNA) 1748 (Fed. Cir. 2007). Should the approach to this last question parallel the treatment of generic terms? *See* Problem 2-1.

13. *Cumulation of rights.* The availability of trade dress protection for potentially patentable subject matter is often justified on the ground that the purposes of trademark law and patent law are different. That is, the different regimes protect different legal interests (rather than one regime extending perpetually the term of protection offered by the other to protect the same interest). To what extent is that true? If, in fact, trademark and patent law effectively protect the same interests, should we restrict cumulation of trademark and patent protection? Should we allow producers to use one intellectual property regime but not the other? Others justify cumulative protection on the ground that the scope of rights granted by trademark law is narrower than that afforded under patent law, and thus does not threaten to undermine patent law. (As we discuss the scope of trademark rights, *see infra* Chapters 7 and 8, reconsider the strength of this argument.) When these arguments are taken together, some scholars have suggested that because a trade dress claimant must demonstrate use in commerce, distinctiveness, nonfunctionality, and use by the defendant of (typically) a confusingly similar device, and because "none of these showings bears any relationship whatsoever to the prerequisites for utility patent protection, the proposition that an extension of trade dress protection somehow can 'extend' the protection previously afforded by a related utility patent is a *non sequitur*." Theodore H. Davis, Jr., *Directing* TrafFix: *A Comment on the Construction and Application of Utility Patent Claims in Trade Dress Litigation*, 54 FLA. L. REV. 229, 259 (2002). Are you persuaded that the concern about trade dress rights extending the life of patents is overstated?

14. *Derivative functionality.* In *Georgia-Pacific Consumer Prods. LP v. Kimberly-Clark Corp.*, 647 F.3d 723 (7th Cir. 2011), the plaintiff argued that even if the design of its toilet paper was functional as used on toilet paper, it was not functional as used on packaging. The Court of Appeals for the Seventh Circuit rejected that argument, affirming that if a product design is found to be functional, the accurate depiction of that product design is also functional. *Cf. supra* page 99 (discussing *de jure* genericism of the terms used to identify products covered by expired patents).

15. *Functional packaging.* Should the *TrafFix* test apply to the features of packaging that are alleged to be functional? *See Speare Tools, Inc. v. Klein Tools, Inc.*, 113 U.S.P.Q.2d (BNA) 1800 (E.D. Wis. 2014). Does *Wal-Mart v. Samara* bear on this question?

2.   Aesthetic Features

ABERCROMBIE & FITCH STORES, INC. v. AMERICAN EAGLE OUTFITTERS, INC.

280 F.3d 619 (6th Cir. 2002)

BOGGS, Circuit Judge:

[Abercrombie & Fitch (A&F or Abercrombie) brought a trade dress claim against American Eagle Outfitters (American) based upon the defendants' alleged copying of, *inter alia*, the designs of certain articles of clothing, its store setup, and its Quarterly catalog. The district court granted summary judgment in favor of American Eagle, reasoning that Abercrombie & Fitch had sought protection for something that did not constitute trade dress at all. The Court of Appeals for the Sixth Circuit affirmed the district court on the alternative grounds that the clothing designs were functional as a matter of law (and the defendant's catalog was not confusingly similar).]

In *TrafFix*, the Court identified two forms of functionality. The first, traditional functionality, deems a feature functional when "'it is essential to the use or purpose of the device or when it affects the cost or quality of the device.'" [cit.] *Qualitex* "[e]xpand[ed] upon the meaning of this phrase [by] observ[ing] that a functional feature is one the 'exclusive use of which would put competitors at a significant non-reputation-related disadvantage.'" *TrafFix*, 532 U.S. at 32 (quoting *Qualitex*, 514 U.S. at 165). But the competitive disadvantage comment did not displace the traditional functionality standard from *Inwood Laboratories*. Instead it explained the policy underlying the functionality doctrine in a way readily adaptable to the problem of aesthetic functionality, the issue presented in *Qualitex*. [cit.] Thus, the "significant non-reputation-related disadvantage" to competitors approach is the second form of trade dress functionality.

None of the design features that Abercrombie claims as its trade dress is essential to the use or purpose of the garments, catalog, and stores they adorn. The design features surely affect the cost and quality of the garments and the design of the catalog affects its cost and aesthetics (which determines, in part, its quality as a device for selling clothing), so a jury question exists as to whether the designs are functional in the traditional sense. However, no reasonable jury could deny the existence of a "significant non-reputation-related disadvantage" that would be imposed on competitors by protecting Abercrombie's claimed trade dress. That form of functionality governs the analysis of this case.[16]

The two most common "tests" of aesthetic functionality under the competition theory prove useful in this case. "The test for 'comparable alternatives' asks whether trade-dress protection of certain features would nevertheless leave a variety of comparable alternative features that competitors may use to compete in the market. If such alternatives do not exist, the feature is functional; but if such alternatives do exist, then the feature is not functional." [Mitchell M. Wong, *The Aesthetic Functionality Doctrine and the Law of Trade Dress Protection*, 83 Cornell L. Rev. 1116, 1144-45 (1998)] (noting that "[t]he comparable alternatives requirement may necessitate more than the mere existence of one alternative, and may instead require a number of alternatives from which competitors may choose") (footnotes omitted).[17] "The 'effective competition' test asks . . . whether trade dress protection for a product's feature would hinder the ability of another manufacturer to compete effectively in the market for the product. If such hinderance is probable, then the feature is functional and unsuitable for protection. If the feature is not a likely impediment to market competition, then the feature is nonfunctional and may receive trademark protection." *Id.* at 1149 (footnotes omitted).[18] The same principle applies to trade dress law. *See Two Pesos*, 505 U.S. at 768.

---

16. For quite some time, the circuits have disagreed about the most appropriate theory of functionality to use in aesthetic functionality cases. . . . Because the Supreme Court has . . . repeatedly followed the competition theory's approach in addressing the second form of functionality, *see TrafFix*, 532 U.S. at 32-33 (explaining *Qualitex*), we expressly adopt the competition theory of functionality.

17. The Seventh Circuit described the comparable alternatives problem thus: "a functional feature is one which competitors would have to spend money not to copy but to design around, as they would have to do if they wanted to come up with a nonoval substitute for a football. It is something costly to do without (like the hood [of a car] itself), rather than costly to have (like the statue of Mercury [decorating the hood])." *W.T. Rogers Co. v. Keene*, 778 F.2d 334, 339 (7th Cir. 1985).

18. As the Seventh Circuit explained: "[I]t would . . . be unreasonable to let a manufacturer use trademark law to prevent competitors from making pleasing substitutes for his own brand; yet that would be the effect of allowing him to appropriate the most pleasing way of configuring the product." *W.T. Rogers Co.*, 778 F.2d at 340. In this sense, functionality depends on "whether the feature . . . is something that other producers of the product in question would have to have as part of the product in order to be able to compete effectively in the market—in other words, in order to give consumers the benefits of a competitive market—or whether it is the kind of merely incidental feature which gives the brand some individual distinction but which producers of competing brands can readily do without." *Id.* at 346.

We turn first to Abercrombie's clothing designs.[19] Abercrombie's complaint itself identifies the functions of the design elements it selected: use of the word *performance* "convey[s] the image of an active line of . . . clothing"; use of the words *authentic, genuine brand, trademark*, and *since 1892* "convey the reliability of the . . . brand"; and so on. Use of these elements in combination with one another and with Abercrombie's trademarks on clothing bearing "primary color combinations . . . in connection with solid, plaid and stripe designs" and made from "all natural cotton, wool and twill fabrics" creates reliable rugged and/or athletic casual clothing drawn from a consistent texture, design, and color palette. Were the law to grant Abercrombie protection of these features, the paucity of comparable alternative features that competitors could use to compete in the market for casual clothing would leave competitors at a significant non-reputational competitive disadvantage and would, therefore, prevent effective competition in the market.

Giving Abercrombie a monopoly on the words it claims form part of its trade dress would hamstring any competitor's ability to convey the reliability of its own brand. The English language currently contains a limited list of synonyms for reliable and other words that convey a product's integrity. While Abercrombie designers deserve credit for using the company's age as a creative indicator of their products' reliability, few other verbal formulations adequately or efficiently convey this concept. The same is true of using suggestive symbols like lacrosse sticks and the ski patrol cross on clothing to convey the product's athletic nature or capacity to invoke images of athleticism. Producers have a limited range of sports and sporting equipment to choose from in attempting to convey this idea in this manner on clothing. Producers could go without such images or devise wholly new ways of conveying the athleticism concept in connection with casual clothing, but at present these features are ones that "competitors would have to spend money not to copy but to design around." *W.T. Rogers Co.*, 778 F.2d at 340. The lack of comparable alternatives to pleasing design features means that granting an injunction would deny consumers the benefits of a competitive market. In short, these design features are "something that other producers of the [casual clothing] have to have as part of the product in order to be able to compete effectively in the market . . . [it is not] the kind of merely incidental feature which gives the brand some individual distinction but which producers of competing brands can readily do without." *Id.* at 346.

Finally, Abercrombie is not saved by its characterization of its trade dress as the *combination* of different design features on its clothing: denying American or other producers the right to combine these functional design features with their own trademarks on clothing bearing certain generic designs (unspecified "solid, plaid, and stripe designs," without

---

19. For ease of reference, we here reprint the features Abercrombie claims comprise the trade dress of its garment designs: "a) use of the Abercrombie Marks, in particular the A & F trademark in universe bold condensed typeface; b) use of the word *performance* on labels and advertising and promotional material to convey the image of an active line of casual clothing; c) use of such words and phrases as *authentic, genuine brand, trademark*, [and] *since 1892* on labels and advertising and promotional material to convey the reliability of the Abercrombie Brand; d) use of the word *outdoor* on labels and advertising and promotional materials to convey the image of a rugged outdoor line of casual clothing; e) use of design logos, such as the ski patrol cross and lacrosse sticks, and product names for the types of clothing, such as '*field jersey*,' to convey the image of an athletic line of casual clothing; f) use of primary color combinations, such as red, blue, grey, tan and green in connection with solid, plaid and stripe designs, to create a consistent design and color palette; g) use of all natural cotton, wool and twill fabrics to create a consistent texture palette. . . ." Compl. ¶7. The last two features are obviously functional standing alone. And American has not directly copied the first feature, the use of Abercrombie's trademarks; it has used its own. It seems, then, that Abercrombie meant to define its trade dress as including some or many of the features labeled b) through e) in combination with the last two features and the producer's own trademark.

more, are indisputably generic) made from generic fabrics would undoubtedly force these competitors to spend money to design around Abercrombie's creations. There can be no dispute that preventing other producers from combining these design elements in the way Abercrombie does would prevent them from competing effectively in the market for casual clothing aimed at young people. No reasonable jury could find to the contrary. Remand for further proceedings in the district court on this question would be a waste of judicial resources, not to mention the parties' time and money.

We reach the same conclusion with respect to Abercrombie's claim of trade dress in its in-store display setups and use of college students as sales associates. Forbidding clothiers to use college students to sell garments to or for college-age people indubitably prevents them from effectively competing in the market for casual clothing directed at young people.

Abercrombie's catalog is a different matter entirely.[22] Of course, the Quarterly has certain functions, including "the creation of a cutting edge 'cool' Abercrombie image," and, presumably, selling clothes. But that does not make the catalog's overall design functional. Nor does the presence of many functional elements in the Quarterly's design. Even if the elements Abercrombie identifies were all separately functional, as American argued and the district court held, A&F's arrangement of these features can constitute more than the sum of its non-protectable parts. *See Publications Int'l, Ltd. v. Landoll, Inc.*, 164 F.3d 337, 341-43 (7th Cir. 1998) (holding various elements of a cookbook's design functional but recognizing that their appearance in concert could garner legal protection "unless it was the only way the product *could* look, consistent with its performing each of the product's functions optimally"). [cit.]

A&F has chosen to print its catalog on an unusual kind of paper, leaving competitors a variety of other paper options. The clothes offered for sale appear in "clothesline" or "cutout" form (the garments appear on the page as if hanging from a clothesline, *i.e.*, not on a model), while many catalogs show garments on a model or display them in other ways. Color bars are a useful mechanism for communicating the available selection of colors, but the same information can be provided in a handful of other ways. Abercrombie uses grainy images of exceptionally fit and attractive young people in outdoor (often collegiate) settings, alone and in groups, wearing more or less A&F clothing in ways that convey their allegiance to the brand while also seemingly attempting to create a sexual mystique about the wearer. The Quarterlies in the record rarely deviate from this pattern, but clothing retailers have an infinite variety of options for surrounding their clothes with pleasing or desirable imagery that avoids showing scantily clad college students in a grainy photograph. Finally, the record demonstrates that clothing catalogs have included so-called lifestyle editorial content for some time. But mail order retailers can still sell their clothes and create an aura about their products without including such content, although this method seems to have recently become a particularly effective way of creating demand. At the very least, the evidence in the record creates a genuine issue of material fact as to whether protection of the design features chosen by Abercrombie for its catalog leaves open sufficient comparable alternate methods of marketing clothing to young people by mail, such that granting

---

22. Again, for ease of reference, A&F describes its catalog's trade dress thus: "the creation of a cutting edge 'cool' Abercrombie image through photographs and advertising and promotional material . . . which presents the Abercrombie Brand and Trade Dress in a unique manner, namely, it features the Abercrombie Brand and Trade Dress in a 'cutout' or 'clothesline' style and uses color bars to illustrate the available colors of goods, while combining a consistent conceptual theme with a lifestyle editorial content of music, electronics, books, and magazine features and is printed on cougar vellum paper which is unique for a catalog." Compl. ¶7(h).

A&F a monopoly on its distinctive configuration would not hinder the ability of another manufacturer to compete effectively in the market. Here, the Seventh Circuit's verbal formulation of the issue seems particularly apt: "whether the [combination of] feature[s] . . . is something that other producers of the product in question would have to have as part of [their catalog] in order to be able to compete effectively in the market . . . or whether it is the kind of merely incidental [configuration] which gives the brand some individual distinction but which producers of competing brands can readily do without." *W.T. Rogers Co.*, 778 F.2d at 346.

Abercrombie claimed three "things" as its trade dress. Its clothing designs and its in-store presentation are not protectable because they are functional, despite their distinctiveness. As to the overall design of the A&F Quarterly, however, we will assume that it satisfies the distinctiveness and non-functionality conditions for protectability because, for purposes of the instant appeal, American conceded secondary meaning and the record evidence raises genuine issues as to the material fact of non-functionality. We therefore proceed to assess whether Abercrombie could prevail on its trade dress infringement claim.

[The court concluded that Abercrombie could not possibly have carried its burden of proving that American's catalog was confusingly similar to what it presumed was the protectable trade dress of Abercrombie's Quarterly.]

CHRISTIAN LOUBOUTIN S.A. v. YVES SAINT LAURENT AMERICA, INC.

696 F.3d 206 (2d Cir. 2012)

JOSE A. CABRANES, Circuit Judge:

. . .

BACKGROUND

[A designer of high-fashion women's footwear and accessories, Christian] Louboutin is best known for his emphasis upon the otherwise-largely-ignored outsole of the shoe. Since their development in 1992, Louboutin's shoes have been characterized by their most striking feature: a bright, lacquered red outsole, which nearly always contrasts sharply with the color of the rest of the shoe.

[The District court below commented that "whether inspired by a stroke of original genius or . . . copied from King Louis XIV's red-heeled dancing shoes, or Dorothy's famous ruby slippers in 'The Wizard of Oz,' or other styles long available in the contemporary market—including those sold by Yves Saint Laurent, Christian Louboutin deviated from industry custom. In his own words, this diversion was meant to give his line of shoes 'energy,' a purpose for which he chose a shade of red because he regarded it as 'engaging, flirtatious, memorable and the color of passion,' as well as 'sexy.'"]

Christian Louboutin introduced his signature footwear to the fashion market in 1992. Since then, his shoes have grown in popularity, appearing regularly on various celebrities and fashion icons. The District Court concluded . . . that "Louboutin [had] invested substantial amounts of capital building a reputation and good will, as well as promoting and protecting Louboutin's claim to exclusive ownership of the mark as its signature in women's high fashion footwear." . . . As a result of Louboutin's marketing efforts, the District Court found, the "flash of a red sole" is today "instantly" recognizable, to "those in the know," as Louboutin's handiwork.

On the strength of the fashion world's asserted recognition of the red sole, Louboutin on March 27, 2007 filed an application with the PTO to protect his mark (the "Red Sole

Mark" or the "Mark"). The trademark was granted in January 2008, and stated: "The color(s) red is/are claimed as a feature of the mark. The mark consists of a lacquered red sole on footwear." *Id.* at 449 (capitalization altered). The written description was accompanied by a diagram indicating the placement of the color:

In 2011, [Yves Saint Laurent America (YSL)] prepared to market a line of "monochrome" shoes in purple, green, yellow, and red. YSL shoes in the monochrome style feature the same color on the entire shoe, so that the red version is all red, including a red insole, heel, upper, and outsole. This was not the first time that YSL had designed a monochrome footwear line, or even a line of footwear with red soles; indeed, YSL maintains that since the 1970s it had sold such shoes in red and other colors.

. . .

[L]ouboutin filed this action on April 7, 2011, asserting [*inter alia*] claims under the Lanham Act for (1) trademark infringement and counterfeiting, (2) false designation of origin and unfair competition, and (3) trademark dilution. . . . Louboutin also sought a preliminary injunction preventing YSL from marketing, during the pendency of the action, any shoes, including red monochrome shoes, bearing outsoles in a shade of red identical to the Red Sole Mark, or in any shade which so resembles the Red Sole Mark as to cause confusion among consumers.

[In response, YSL asserted counterclaims including one seeking cancellation of the Red Sole Mark on the grounds, *inter alia*, that it is (1) not "distinctive," but instead merely "ornamental" and (2) functional.]

[T]he District Court held that, in the fashion industry, single-color marks are inherently "functional" and that any such registered trademark would likely be held invalid. The Court therefore held that Louboutin was unlikely to be able to prove that the Red Sole Mark was eligible for trademark protection, and denied Louboutin's motion for a preliminary injunction. This appeal followed.

. . .

DISCUSSION

. . .

III. The "Functionality" Defense

[T]wo forms of the functionality doctrine are relevant to us today: "traditional" or "utilitarian" functionality, and "aesthetic" functionality. Both forms serve as an affirmative defense to a trademark infringement claim.

A.   "Traditional" or "Utilitarian" Functionality

According to our traditional understanding of functionality, a product feature is considered to be "functional" in a utilitarian sense if it is (1) "essential to the use or purpose of the article," or if it (2) "affects the cost or quality of the article." *Inwood Labs.*, 456 U.S. at 850 n.10. A feature is essential "'if [it] is dictated by the functions to be performed'" by the article. *LeSportsac, Inc. v. K Mart Corp.*, 754 F.2d 71, 76 (2d Cir. 1985) (quoting *Warner Bros. Inc. v. Gay Toys Inc.*, 724 F.2d 327, 331 (2d Cir. 1983)).[13] It affects the cost or quality of the article where it "'permits the article to be manufactured at a lower cost' or 'constitutes an improvement in the operation of the goods.'"[14] *Id.* (quoting *Warner Bros., Inc.*, 724 F.2d at 331). A finding that a product feature is functional according to the *Inwood* test will ordinarily render the feature ineligible for trademark protection.

B.   "Aesthetic Functionality"

Generally, "[w]here [a product's] design is functional under the *Inwood* formulation there is no need to proceed further." *TrafFix Devices, Inc. v. Marketing Displays, Inc.*, 532 U.S. 23, 33 (2001) ("*TrafFix*"). Nevertheless, as the Supreme Court had held in 1995 in *Qualitex*, when the aesthetic design of a product is *itself* the mark for which protection is sought, we may also deem the mark functional if giving the markholder the right to use it exclusively "would put competitors at a significant non-reputation-related disadvantage," *Qualitex*, 514 U.S. at 165. This remains true even if there is "no indication that [the mark has] any bearing on the use or purpose of the product or its cost or quality." *TrafFix*, 532 U.S. at 33; *see Landscape Forms, Inc. v. Colum. Cascade Co.*, 70 F.3d 251, 253 (2d Cir. 1995) (when evaluating design trademarks we consider whether "certain features of the design are essential to effective competition in [the] particular market").

As set forth below, the test for aesthetic functionality is threefold: At the start, we address the two prongs of the *Inwood* test, asking whether the design feature is either "essential to the use or purpose" or "affects the cost or quality" of the product at issue. Next, if necessary, we turn to a third prong, which is the competition inquiry set forth in *Qualitex*. In other words, if a design feature would, from a traditional utilitarian perspective, be considered "essential to the use or purpose" of the article, or to affect its cost or quality, then the design feature is functional under *Inwood* and our inquiry ends. But if the design feature is not "functional" from a traditional perspective, it must still pass the fact-intensive *Qualitex* test and be shown not to have a significant effect on competition in order to receive trademark protection.

---

13. In *LeSportsac*, K Mart challenged the trade dress of a backpack composed of "parachute nylon and trimmed in cotton carpet tape with matching cotton-webbing straps. The zippers used to open and close the bags [we]re color coordinated with the bags themselves, and usually [we]re pulled with hollow rectangular metal sliders." *LeSportsac*, 754 F.2d at 74.

14. In *Warner Brothers*, we cited as examples *Kellogg Co. v. National Biscuit Co.*, 305 U.S. 111, 122 (1938), in which the pillow shape of a shredded wheat biscuit was deemed functional because the cost of the cereal would be increased and its quality lessened by any other form, and *Fisher Stoves Inc. v. All Nighter Stove Works, Inc.*, 626 F.2d 193, 195 (1st Cir. 1980), in which a two-tier woodstove design was deemed functional because it improved the operation of the stove. *See Warner Bros., Inc.*, 724 F.2d at 331.

i.   The Development of the Aesthetic Functionality Doctrine

. . .

Despite its apparent counterintuitiveness (how can the purely aesthetic be deemed functional, one might ask?), our Court has long accepted the doctrine of aesthetic functionality. *See, e.g., Warner Bros., Inc.,* 724 F.2d at 329-32 (distinctive color and symbols on toy car were not functional, and so were protectable as trade dress).[17] We have rejected, however, the circular "important ingredient" test formulated by the *Pagliero* court, which inevitably penalized markholders for their success in promoting their product. Instead, we have concluded that "Lanham Act protection does not extend to configurations of ornamental features which would *significantly* limit the range of competitive designs available." *Coach Leatherware Co. v. AnnTaylor, Inc.,* 933 F.2d 162, 171 (2d Cir. 1991) (emphasis added). Accordingly, we have held that the doctrine of aesthetic functionality bars protection of a mark that is "necessary to compete in the [relevant] market." *Villeroy & Boch Keramische Werke K.G. v. THC Sys., Inc.,* 999 F.2d 619, 622 (2d Cir. 1993).

ii.   A Modern Formulation of the Aesthetic Functionality Doctrine

In 1995, the Supreme Court in *Qualitex* gave its imprimatur to the aesthetic functionality doctrine, holding that "[t]he ultimate test of aesthetic functionality . . . is whether the recognition of trademark rights [in an aesthetic design feature] would significantly hinder competition." . . . Six years later, reiterating its *Qualitex* analysis, the Supreme Court in *TrafFix* declared that where "[a]esthetic functionality [is] the central question," courts must "inquire" as to whether recognizing the trademark "would put competitors at a significant non-reputation-related disadvantage." *TrafFix,* 532 U.S. at 32-33.

Although we have not recently had occasion to apply the doctrine of aesthetic functionality thus enunciated by the Supreme Court, it is clear that the combined effect of *Qualitex* and *TrafFix* was to validate the aesthetic functionality doctrine as it had already been developed by this Court in cases including *Wallace International Silversmiths, Stormy Clime,* and *LeSportsac. See Yurman Design, Inc. v. PAJ, Inc.,* 262 F.3d 101, 116 (2d Cir. 2001) (confirming, five months after the *TrafFix* decision, that a putative design trademark is "aesthetic[ally] functional[]," and therefore barred from trademark protection, if granting "the right to use [the mark] exclusively 'would put competitors at a significant non-reputation-related disadvantage'" (quoting *TrafFix,* 532 U.S. at 32)).

On the one hand, "'[w]here an ornamental feature is claimed as a trademark and trademark protection would significantly hinder competition by limiting the range of

---

17. The doctrine of aesthetic functionality remains controversial in our sister circuits, which have applied the doctrine in varying ways (and some not at all). For example, the Seventh Circuit has applied the doctrine of aesthetic functionality liberally, holding that "[f]ashion is a form of function." *See Jay Franco & Sons, Inc. v. Franek,* 615 F.3d 855, 860 (7th Cir. 2010). The Sixth Circuit recently discussed the doctrine, but made clear that it has not yet decided whether or not to adopt it. *See Maker's Mark Distillery, Inc. v. Diageo N. Am., Inc.,* 679 F.3d 410, 417-19 (6th Cir. 2012). The Ninth Circuit has applied the doctrine inconsistently. *See* 1 MᴄCᴀʀᴛʜʏ ᴏɴ Tʀᴀᴅᴇᴍᴀʀᴋs §7:80 (4th ed.) (collecting cases). The Fifth Circuit rejects the doctrine of aesthetic functionality entirely. *Bd. of Supervisors for La. State Univ. Agric. & Mech. Coll. v. Smack Apparel Co.,* 550 F.3d 465, 487-88 (5th Cir. 2008) (arguing that the Supreme Court has recognized the aesthetic functionality doctrine only in dicta, and that therefore the Fifth Circuit's long-standing rejection of the doctrine was not abrogated by *Qualitex* and *TrafFix*).

adequate alternative designs, the aesthetic functionality doctrine denies such protection.'" *Forschner Grp., Inc. v. Arrow Trading Co.*, 124 F.3d 402, 409-10 (2d Cir. 1997) (quoting *Wallace Int'l Silversmiths, Inc.*, 916 F.2d at 81). But on the other hand, "'distinctive and arbitrary arrangements of predominantly ornamental features that do *not* hinder potential competitors from entering the same market with differently dressed versions of the product are non-functional[,] and [are] hence eligible for [trademark protection].'" *Fabrication Enters., Inc.*, 64 F.3d at 59 (quoting *Stormy Clime*, 809 F.2d at 977) (emphasis added).

In short, a mark is aesthetically functional, and therefore ineligible for protection under the Lanham Act, where protection of the mark *significantly* undermines competitors' ability to compete in the relevant market. *See Knitwaves, Inc. v. Lollytogs Ltd.*, 71 F.3d 996, 1006 (2d Cir. 1995) (linking aesthetic functionality to availability of alternative designs for children's fall-themed sweaters); *Landscape Forms, Inc.*, 70 F.3d at 253 (holding that "in order for a court to find a product design functional, it must first find that certain features of the design are essential to effective competition in a particular market"). In making this determination, courts must carefully weigh "the competitive benefits of protecting the source-identifying aspects" of a mark against the "competitive costs of precluding competitors from using the feature." *Fabrication Enters., Inc.*, 64 F.3d at 59.

Finally, we note that a product feature's successful source indication can sometimes be difficult to distinguish from the feature's aesthetic function, if any. *See, e.g., Jay Franco & Sons, Inc. v. Franek*, 615 F.3d 855, 857 (7th Cir. 2010) (noting that "[f]iguring out which designs [produce a benefit other than source identification] can be tricky"). Therefore, in determining whether a mark has an aesthetic function so as to preclude trademark protection, we take care to ensure that the mark's very success in denoting (and promoting) its source does not itself defeat the markholder's right to protect that mark. *See Wallace Int'l Silversmiths, Inc.*, 916 F.2d at 80 (rejecting argument that "the commercial success of an aesthetic feature automatically destroys all of the originator's trademark interest in it, notwithstanding the feature's secondary meaning and the lack of any evidence that competitors cannot develop non-infringing, attractive patterns").

Because aesthetic function and branding success can sometimes be difficult to distinguish, the aesthetic functionality analysis is highly fact-specific. In conducting this inquiry, courts must consider both the markholder's right to enjoy the benefits of its effort to distinguish its product and the public's right to the "vigorously competitive market [ ]" protected by the Lanham Act, which an overly broad trademark might hinder. *Yurman Design, Inc.*, 262 F.3d at 115 (internal quotation mark omitted). In sum, courts must avoid jumping to the conclusion that an aesthetic feature is functional merely because it denotes the product's desirable source. *Cf. Pagliero*, 198 F.2d at 343.

iii.   Aesthetic Functionality in the Fashion Industry

We now turn to the *per se* rule of functionality for color marks in the fashion industry adopted by the District Court—a rule that would effectively deny trademark protection to any deployment of a single color in an item of apparel. [The] Supreme Court specifically forbade the implementation of a *per se* rule that would deny protection for the use of a single color as a trademark in a particular industrial context. *Qualitex* requires an individualized, fact-based inquiry into the nature of the trademark, and cannot be read to sanction an industry-based *per se* rule. The District Court created just such a rule, on the theory that "there is something unique about the fashion world that militates against extending trademark protection to a single color."

Even if *Qualitex* could be read to permit an industry-specific *per se* rule of functionality (a reading we think doubtful), such a rule would be neither necessary nor appropriate here. We readily acknowledge that the fashion industry, like other industries, has special concerns in the operation of trademark law; it has been argued forcefully that United States law does not protect fashion design adequately.[19] Indeed, the case on appeal is particularly difficult precisely because, as the District Court well noted, in the fashion industry, color can serve as a tool in the palette of a designer, rather than as mere ornamentation.

Nevertheless, the functionality defense does not guarantee a competitor "the greatest range for [his] creative outlet," [as the District Court suggested], but only the ability to fairly compete within a given market. *See Wallace Int'l Silversmiths, Inc.*, 916 F.2d at 81 ("It is a first principle of trademark law that an owner may not use the mark as a means of *excluding* competitors from a . . . market." (emphasis added)). The purpose of the functionality defense "is to prevent advances in functional design from being *monopolized* by the owner of [the mark] . . . in order to encourage competition and the broadest dissemination of useful design features." *Fabrication Enters., Inc.*, 64 F.3d at 58 (internal quotation marks omitted) (emphasis added).

In short, "[b]y focusing upon hindrances to legitimate competition, the [aesthetic] functionality test, carefully applied, can accommodate consumers' somewhat conflicting interests in being assured enough product differentiation to avoid confusion as to source and in being afforded the benefits of competition among producers." *Stormy Clime*, 809 F.2d at 978-79.

IV.   The Red Sole Mark

Having determined that no *per se* rule governs the protection of single-color marks in the fashion industry, any more than it can do so in any other industry, we turn our attention to the Red Sole Mark. As we have explained, we analyze a trademark infringement claim in two stages, asking first whether the mark "merits protection" and, second, whether the allegedly infringing use of the mark (or a similar mark) is "likely to cause consumer confusion." [cit.] The functionality defense (including the tripartite aesthetic functionality test) is an affirmative defense that we consider at the second stage of this analysis. *Stormy Clime, Ltd.*, 809 F.2d at 974.

. . .

---

19. The intellectual property protection of fashion design has been for years a subject of controversy among commentators. Some have proposed working within the confines of the current intellectual property system, while others have advocated that fashion design may be an appropriate area for sui generis statutory protection. *See generally* C. Scott Hemphill & Jeannie Suk, *The Law, Culture, and Economics of Fashion*, 61 Stan. L. Rev. 1147 (2009); *see also id.* at 1184-90. (Indeed, suggested legislation creating such protection has been considered several times by Congress, although not adopted. *See, e.g.*, Design Piracy Prohibition Act, H.R. 2033, 110th Cong. §2(c) (2007); Design Piracy Prohibition Act, S.1957, 110th Cong. §2(c) (2007).) Still other commentators have suggested that intellectual property protection of fashion design would be damaging to the industry and should be avoided. *See* Kal Raustiala & Christopher Sprigman, *The Piracy Paradox: Innovation and Intellectual Property in Fashion Design*, 92 Va. L. Rev. 1687, 1775-77 (2006). It is arguable that, in the particular circumstances of this case, the more appropriate vehicle for the protection of the Red Sole Mark would have been copyright rather than trademark. *See generally Kieselstein-Cord v. Accessories by Pearl, Inc.*, 632 F.2d 989, 993-94 (2d Cir. 1980) (addressing the broad issue of aesthetically functional copyrights and holding that decorative belt buckles that were used principally for ornamentation could be copyrighted because the primary ornamental aspect of the buckles was conceptually separate from their subsidiary utilitarian function); Laura A. Heymann, *The Trademark/Copyright Divide*, 60 SMU L. Rev. 55 (2007). However, because Louboutin has chosen to rely on the law of trademarks to protect his intellectual property, we necessarily limit our review to that body of law and do not further address the broad and complex issue of fashion design protection.

A.   Distinctiveness

. . .

Although a single color, standing alone, can almost never be inherently distinctive because it does not "almost automatically tell a customer that [it] refer[s] to a brand," *Qualitex*, 514 U.S. at 162-63, a color as used here is certainly capable of acquiring secondary meaning. . . .

We see no reason why a single-color mark in the specific context of the fashion industry could not acquire secondary meaning—and therefore serve as a brand or source identifier—if it is used so consistently and prominently by a particular designer that it becomes a symbol, "the primary significance" of which is "to identify the source of the product rather than the product itself." *Inwood Labs.*, 456 U.S. at 851 n.11; [cit.].

. . . The record before the District Court included extensive evidence of Louboutin's advertising expenditures, media coverage, and sales success, demonstrating both that Louboutin has created a "symbol" within the meaning of *Qualitex*, and that the symbol has gained secondary meaning that causes it to be "uniquely" associated with the Louboutin brand. [cit.] There is no dispute that Louboutin originated this particular commercial use of the lacquered red color over twenty years ago. As the District Court determined, in findings of fact that are supported by the record and not clearly erroneous, "Louboutin invested substantial amounts of capital building a reputation and good will, as well as promoting and protecting Louboutin's claim to exclusive ownership of the mark as its signature in women's high fashion footwear." And there is no dispute that Louboutin's efforts were successful "to the point where, in the high-stakes commercial markets and social circles in which these things matter a great deal, the red outsole became closely associated with Louboutin," and where unsolicited media attention to that red sole became rampant. . . .

In light of the evidence in the record, including extensive consumer surveys submitted by both parties during the preliminary injunction proceedings, and of the factual findings of the District Court, we think it plain that Louboutin's marketing efforts have created what the able district judge described as "a . . . brand with worldwide recognition." By placing the color red "in [a] context [that] seems unusual," *Qualitex*, 514 U.S. at 162, and deliberately tying that color to his product, Louboutin has created an identifying mark firmly associated with his brand which, "to those in the know," "instantly" denotes his shoes' source. These findings of fact by the District Court in addressing a motion for a preliminary injunction are not clearly erroneous. We hold that the lacquered red outsole, as applied to a shoe with an "upper" of a different color, has "come to identify and distinguish" the Louboutin brand, and is therefore a distinctive symbol that qualifies for trademark protection.

We further hold that the record fails to demonstrate that the secondary meaning of the Red Sole Mark extends to uses in which the sole *does not* contrast with the upper—in other words, when a red sole is used on a monochromatic red shoe. As the District Court observed, "[w]hen Hollywood starlets cross red carpets and high fashion models strut down runways, and heads turn and eyes drop to the celebrities' feet, lacquered red outsoles on *high-heeled, black shoes* flaunt a glamorous statement that *pops out* at once." *Louboutin*, 778 F. Supp. 2d at 448 (emphasis added). As clearly suggested by the District Court, it is the *contrast* between the sole and the upper that causes the sole to "pop," and to distinguish its creator.

The evidentiary record further demonstrates that the Louboutin mark is closely associated with contrast. . . . Of the hundreds of pictures of Louboutin shoes submitted to the District Court, only *four* were monochrome red. [cit.] And Louboutin's own consumer surveys show that when consumers were shown the YSL monochrome red shoe, of those consumers who misidentified the pictured shoes as Louboutin-made, nearly every one cited the red *sole* of the shoe, rather than its general red color. We conclude, based upon the record before us, that Louboutin has not established secondary meaning in an application of a red sole to a red shoe, but *only* where the red sole contrasts with the "upper" of the shoe. The use of a red lacquer on the outsole of a red shoe of the same color is not a use of the Red Sole Mark.

Because we conclude that the secondary meaning of the mark held by Louboutin extends only to the use of a lacquered red outsole that contrasts with the adjoining portion of the shoe, we modify the Red Sole Mark, pursuant to Section 37 of the Lanham Act, insofar as it is sought to be applied to any shoe bearing the same color "upper" as the outsole. We therefore instruct the Director of the Patent and Trade Office to limit the registration of the Red Sole Mark to only those situations in which the red lacquered outsole contrasts in color with the adjoining "upper" of the shoe.

In sum, we hold that the Red Sole Mark is valid and enforceable as modified. This holding disposes of the Lanham Act claims brought by both Louboutin and YSL because the red sole on YSL's monochrome shoes is neither a use of, nor confusingly similar to, the Red Sole Mark. We therefore affirm the denial of the preliminary injunction insofar as Louboutin could not have shown a likelihood of success on the merits in the absence of an infringing use of the Red Sole Mark by YSL.

B.   *Likelihood of Confusion and Functionality*

Having limited the Red Sole Mark as described above, and having established that the red sole used by YSL is not a use of the Red Sole Mark, it is axiomatic that we need not—and should not—address either the likelihood of consumer confusion or whether the modified Mark is functional.

AU-TOMOTIVE GOLD, INC. v. VOLKSWAGEN
OF AMERICA, INC.

457 F.3d 1062 (9th Cir. 2006)

McKeown, Circuit Judge:

This case centers on the trademarks of two well-known automobile manufacturers—Volkswagen and Audi. The question is whether the Lanham Act prevents a maker of automobile accessories from selling, without a license or other authorization, products bearing exact replicas of the trademarks of these famous car companies. Au-Tomotive Gold, Inc. ("Auto Gold") argues that, as used on its key chains and license plate covers, the logos and marks of Volkswagen and Audi are aesthetic functional elements of the product—that is, they are "the actual benefit that the consumer wishes to purchase"—and are thus unprotected by the trademark laws.

Accepting Auto Gold's position would be the death knell for trademark protection. . . . Taken to its limits, as Auto Gold advocates, this doctrine would permit a competitor to trade on any mark simply because there is some "aesthetic" value to the mark that consumers desire. This approach distorts both basic principles of trademark law and the doctrine of functionality in particular.

Auto Gold's incorporation of Volkswagen and Audi marks in its key chains and license plates appears to be nothing more than naked appropriation of the marks. The doctrine of aesthetic functionality does not provide a defense against actions to enforce the trademarks against such poaching. Consequently, we reverse the district court's grant of summary judgment in favor of Auto Gold on the basis of aesthetic functionality. . . .

BACKGROUND

Volkswagen and Audi are manufacturers of automobiles, parts and accessories that bear well-known trademarks, including the names Volkswagen and Audi, the encircled VW logo, the interlocking circles of the Audi logo, and the names of individual car models. The marks are registered in the United States and have been in use since the 1950s.

Auto Gold produces and sells automobile accessories to complement specific makes of cars, including Cadillac, Ford, Honda, Lexus, Jeep, Toyota, and others. In 1994, Auto Gold began selling license plates, license plate frames and key chains bearing Volkswagen's distinctive trademarks and, in 1997, began selling similar products bearing Audi's distinctive trademarks. . . .

According to Auto Gold, its goods serve a unique market. Consumers want these accessories "to match the chrome on their cars; to put something on the empty space where the front license tag would otherwise go; or because the car is a [Volkswagen or Audi], they want a [Volkswagen or Audi]-logo plate." Both Auto Gold and Volkswagen and Audi serve this market. . . .

[Volkswagen and Audi alleged, *inter alia*, that Auto Gold's activities constitute trademark infringement, trademark dilution, trademark counterfeiting, and unfair competition.] In ruling for Auto Gold, the district court found that "[t]he VW and Audi logos are used not because they signify that the license plate or key ring was manufactured or sold (i.e., as a designation of origin) by Volkswagen or Audi, but because there is a[n] aesthetic quality to the marks that purchasers are interested in having." Concluding that the marks were "protected under the aesthetic functionality doctrine," the district court . . . entered an order declaring that Auto Gold's "license plates, license plate frames and key chains displaying Volkswagen and Audi trademarks . . . are not trademark infringements and/or trademark counterfeiting." [Volkswagen and Audi appealed.]

ANALYSIS

. . .

A.   Trademark Law and Aesthetic Functionality

. . .

A functional product feature does not . . . enjoy protection under trademark law. [cit.] The Supreme Court has instructed that a feature is functional if it is "essential to the use or purpose of the article [or] affects [its] cost or quality." [cit.] [That] *Inwood Laboratories* definition is often referred to as "utilitarian" functionality, as it relates to the performance of the product in its intended purpose. Thus, "[t]he functionality doctrine prevents trademark law, which seeks to promote competition by protecting a firm's reputation, from instead inhibiting legitimate competition by allowing a producer to control a useful product feature." *Qualitex*, 514 U.S. at 164.

Extending the functionality doctrine, which aims to protect "useful" product features, to encompass unique logos and insignia is not an easy transition. Famous trademarks have assumed an exalted status of their own in today's consumer culture that cannot neatly be reduced to the historic function of trademark to designate source. Consumers sometimes buy products bearing marks such as the Nike Swoosh, the Playboy bunny ears, the Mercedes tri-point star, the Ferrari stallion, and countless sports franchise logos, for the appeal of the mark itself, without regard to whether it signifies the origin or sponsorship of the product. As demand for these marks has risen, so has litigation over the rights to their use as claimed "functional" aspects of products. *See, e.g., Vuitton et fils S.A. v. J. Young Enters., Inc.* 644 F.2d 769 (9th Cir. 1981) (reversing and remanding for trial a district court determination that the Louis Vuitton logo and trademarked purse material were functional). . . .

The results reached in these various aesthetic functionality cases do not easily weave together to produce a coherent jurisprudence, although as a general matter courts have been loathe to declare unique, identifying logos and names as functional. To understand how the concept of functionality applies to the case before us, broad invocations of principle are not particularly helpful. Instead, we find it useful to follow the chronological development and refinement of the doctrine. [The court then traced the development of the doctrine of aesthetic functionality from the 1938 Restatement of Torts, through *Pagliero*, and later Ninth Circuit case law rejecting *Pagliero* that dealt aesthetic functionality "a limiting but not fatal blow."]

The Supreme Court has yet to address aesthetic functionality as it applies to logos and insignia, in contrast to product features. The Court has, however, outlined the general contours of functionality and aesthetic functionality. . . .

The Court's most recent explication of aesthetic functionality is found in . . . *TrafFix Devices, Inc. v. Marketing Displays, Inc.*, 532 U.S. 23 (2001). . . . [T]he Court clarified *Qualitex*'s emphasis on competitive necessity and the overall test for functionality. . . .

[After quoting the Supreme Court's discussion of the *Inwood* test and the "significant non-reputation-related disadvantage" test, the Ninth Circuit continued.] The Court explained the interplay between these two statements of functionality. If a feature is functional under *Inwood Laboratories*, the inquiry ends and the feature cannot be protected under trademark law. [cit.] As the Court elaborated, "there is no need to proceed further to consider if there is a competitive necessity for the feature." [cit.] . . .

By contrast, the Court went on to suggest that "[i]t is proper to inquire into a 'significant non-reputation-related disadvantage' in cases of aesthetic functionality." . . .

[W]e read the Court's decision to mean that consideration of competitive necessity may be an appropriate but not necessary element of the functionality analysis. If a design is determined to be functional under the traditional test of *Inwood Laboratories* there is no need to go further to consider indicia of competitive necessity, such as the availability of alternative designs. *Accord Valu Eng'g, Inc. v. Rexnord Corp.*, 278 F.3d 1268, 1275-76 (Fed. Cir. 2002). However, in the context of aesthetic functionality, such considerations may come into play because a "functional feature is one the 'exclusive use of [which] would put competitors at a significant non-reputation-related disadvantage.'" [cit.] . . .

B. AESTHETIC FUNCTIONALITY AND AUTO GOLD'S USE OF VOLKSWAGEN AND AUDI'S PRODUCTS

So where do we stand in the wake of forty years of trademark law scattered with references to aesthetic functionality? After *Qualitex* and *TrafFix*, the test for functionality proceeds in two steps. In the first step, courts inquire whether the alleged "significant non-trademark function" satisfies the [*Inwood* definition]. If this is the case, the inquiry is over—the feature is functional and not protected.[8] [cit.] In the case of a claim of aesthetic

---

8. Our long-standing test for functionality largely excluded aesthetic considerations, instead asking: (1) whether the feature delivers any utilitarian advantage, (2) whether alternative designs are possible, (3) whether advertising touts utilitarian benefits of the feature, and (4) whether the feature results in economies in manufacture or use. Following *TrafFix* we reiterated [those] factors as legitimate considerations in determining whether a product feature is functional. *Talking Rain Beverage Co. v. South Beach Beverage Co*, 349 F.3d 601, 603-04 (9th Cir. 2003) (applying the four factors to conclude that a bottle design was utilitarian). We noted that "the existence of alternative designs cannot negate a trademark's functionality," but "may indicate whether the trademark itself embodies functional or merely ornamental aspects of the product."

functionality, an alternative test inquires whether protection of the feature as a trademark would impose a significant non-reputation-related competitive disadvantage. [cit.]

We now address the marks at issue in this case. Volkswagen and Audi's trademarks are registered and incontestable, and are thus presumed to be valid, distinctive, and non-functional. [cit.] Auto Gold, thus, must show that the marks are functional under the test set forth above. To satisfy this requirement, Auto Gold argues that Volkswagen and Audi trademarks are functional features of its products because "the trademark is the feature of the product which constitutes the actual benefit the consumer wishes to purchase." While that may be so, the fact that a trademark is desirable does not, and should not, render it unprotectable. Auto Gold has not shown that Volkswagen and Audi's marks are functional features of Auto Gold's products. The marks are thus entitled to trademark protection.

At the first step, there is no evidence on the record, and Auto Gold does not argue, that Volkswagen and Audi's trademarks are functional under the utilitarian definition in *Inwood Laboratories* as applied in the Ninth Circuit in *Talking Rain*. [cit.] That is to say, Auto Gold's products would still frame license plates and hold keys just as well without the famed marks. Similarly, use of the marks does not alter the cost structure or add to the quality of the products.

We next ask whether Volkswagen and Audi's marks, as they appear on Auto Gold's products, perform some function such that the "'exclusive use of [the marks] would put competitors at a significant non-reputation-related disadvantage.'" [cit.] As an initial matter, Auto Gold's proffered rationale—that the trademarks "constitute[] the actual benefit the consumer wishes to purchase"—flies in the face of existing caselaw. We have squarely rejected the notion that "any feature of a product which contributes to the consumer appeal and sale-ability of the product is, as a matter of law, a functional element of that product." *Vuitton*, 644 F.2d at 773. Such a rule would eviscerate the very competitive policies that functionality seeks to protect. This approach is consistent with the view of our sister circuits. [cit.]

Even viewing Auto Gold's position generously, the rule it advocates injects unwarranted breadth into our caselaw. *Pagliero, Job's Daughters*, and their progeny were careful to prevent "the use of a trademark to monopolize a design feature which, *in itself and apart from its identification of source*, improves the usefulness or appeal of the object it adorns." *Vuitton*, 644 F.2d at 774 (discussing *Pagliero*, 198 F.2d 339) (emphasis added). The concept of an "aesthetic" function that is non-trademark-related has enjoyed only limited application. In practice, aesthetic functionality has been limited to product features that serve an aesthetic purpose wholly independent of any source-identifying function. *See Qualitex*, 514 U.S. at 166 (coloring dry cleaning pads served non-trademark purpose by avoiding visible stains); *Publications Int'l, Ltd. v. Landoll, Inc.*, 164 F.3d 337, 342 (7th Cir. 1998) (coloring edges of cookbook pages served non-trademark purpose by avoiding color "bleeding" between pages); *Brunswick Corp. v. British Seagull Ltd.*, 35 F.3d 1527, 1532 (Fed. Cir. 1994) (color black served non-trademark purpose by reducing the apparent size of outboard boat engine); *Pagliero*, 198 F.2d at 343 (china patterns at issue were attractive and served non-trademark purpose because "one of the essential selling features of hotel china, if, indeed, not the primary, is the design").

It is difficult to extrapolate from cases involving a true aesthetically functional feature, like a box shape or certain uses of color, to cases involving well-known registered logos and company names, which generally have no function apart from their association with the trademark holder. The present case illustrates the point well, as the use of Volkswagen and Audi's marks is neither aesthetic nor independent of source identification. That is to say, there is no evidence that consumers buy Auto Gold's products solely because of their "intrinsic" aesthetic appeal. Instead, the alleged aesthetic function is indistinguishable from and tied to the mark's source-identifying nature.

By Auto Gold's strident admission, consumers want "Audi" and "Volkswagen" accessories, not beautiful accessories. This consumer demand is difficult to quarantine from the source identification and reputation-enhancing value of the trademarks themselves. . . . The demand for Auto Gold's products is inextricably tied to the trademarks themselves. *See Qualitex*, 514 U.S. at 170 (identifying "legitimate (*non-trademark-related*) competition" as the relevant focus in determining functionality) (emphasis added). Any disadvantage Auto Gold claims in not being able to sell Volkswagen or Audi marked goods is tied to the reputation and association with Volkswagen and Audi.

In the end, we take comfort that the doctrine of aesthetic functionality, as we apply it in this case, has simply returned from whence it came. The 1938 Restatement of Torts includes this reminder of the difference between an aesthetic function and a trademark function:

> A feature which merely associates goods with a particular source may be, like a trade-mark or trade name, a substantial factor in increasing the marketability of the goods. But if that is the entire significance of the feature, it is non-functional; for its value then lies only in the demand for goods associated with a particular source rather than for goods of a particular design.

Restatement of Torts §742, comment a (1938). Volkswagen and Audi's trademarks undoubtedly increase the marketability of Auto Gold's products. But their "entire significance" lies in the demand for goods bearing those nonfunctional marks. Today, as in 1938, such poaching is not countenanced by the trademark laws.

We hold that Volkswagen and Audi's marks are not functional aspects of Auto Gold's products. These marks, which are registered and have achieved incontestable status, are properly protected under the Lanham Act against infringement, dilution, false designation of source and other misappropriations. . . .

NOTES AND QUESTIONS

1. *Test of aesthetic functionality.* What is the test (or tests) being applied by the *Abercrombie & Fitch*, *Louboutin* and *Au-Tomotive Gold* courts to determine whether a feature is aesthetically functional? The *Louboutin* court refers to the test for aesthetic functionality variously as "tripartite" or "threefold." What are the three parts that the *Louboutin* court had in mind? In footnote 17, the *Louboutin* court notes that the Fifth Circuit has declined to recognise the doctrine of aesthetic functionality? Is this consistent with *Qualitex* and *TrafFix*?

2. *Aesthetic functionality and merchandising.* The arguments advanced by the defendant in *Au-Tomotive Gold* are routinely put forward in merchandising cases. But they rarely succeed. Despite the strong statements in both *Qualitex* and *TrafFix* supporting a robust doctrine of functionality, most courts appear unwilling to return to the notions of aesthetic functionality typified by *Pagliero*. For example, in *Bd. of Supervisors for La. State Univ. Agric. & Mech. Coll. v. Smack Apparel Co.*, 550 F.3d 465 (5th Cir. 2008), the Court of Appeals for the Fifth Circuit considered whether school colors were functional. The court applied both *TrafFix* tests, and found the claimed marks were not functional:

> The school colors and other indicia used here do not make the t-shirts "work." The t-shirts would function just as well as articles of clothing without the colors and designs. [Defendant] Smack's t-shirts are sold not because of any functionality in the marks Smack placed on them but rather because they bear the identifiable marks of the plaintiff Universities. The marks fail under the traditional test for functionality and are protectable.

Smack urges, however, that the Universities' colors on the t-shirts serve several functional purposes. It contends that the shirts allow groups of people to bond and show support for a philosophy or goal; facilitate the expression of loyalty to the school and a determination of the loyalties of others; and identify the wearer as a fan and indicate the team the fan is supporting. [The court rejected this argument.]

. . .

Furthermore, we believe application of the competitive necessity test does not require a different result. Smack contends that it will be placed at a significant non-reputation-related disadvantage if it "is unable to satisfy consumer demand for game day clothing that allows fans to conform to the crowd, or satisfy consumer demand for game day clothing that matches other items of clothing worn by the consumer." Smack has admitted that the colors and indicia on its shirts are designed to call the Universities to the mind of the fans, and it acknowledges in its brief that fans purchase t-shirts to wear to football games to show the colors of the team that the consumer is supporting. In other words, fans desire to wear the t-shirts precisely because they show the Universities' marks. The Court in *Qualitex* stressed that the focus of functionality is "legitimate (non-trademark-related) competition." But here any demand for Smack's t-shirts is inextricably tied to the Universities' trademarks themselves. We agree with the Ninth Circuit that "the fact that a trademark is desirable does not, and should not, render it unprotectable." [*Au-Tomotive*.] Smack's alleged competitive disadvantage in the ability to sell game day apparel relates solely to an inability to take advantage of the Universities' reputation and the public's desired association with the Universities that its shirts create. This is not an advantage to which it is entitled under the rubric of legitimate competition. We conclude that the district court correctly held that the marks at issue here are nonfunctional.

558 F.3d at 486-88.

3. *Aesthetic functionality and distinctiveness (again).* Early opinions developing the aesthetic functionality doctrine (such as *Pagliero*) often hint at suspicions that the design for which protection is claimed is not truly a mark, that is, that the design is not distinctive. A district court in the Ninth Circuit has read *Au-Tomotive Gold* in terms that likewise appeared to treat distinctiveness and aesthetic functionality as mutually exclusive conditions, which in light of liberal approaches to distinctiveness might substantially weaken the aesthetic functionality doctrine. *See Adidas-America, Inc. v. Payless Shoesource, Inc.*, 546 F. Supp. 2d 1029, 1083 (D. Or. 2008) (suggesting that "to the extent that the aesthetic functionality defense survives, it has been 'limited to product features that serve an aesthetic purpose *wholly independent of any source-identifying function*.' Thus, the aesthetic functionality doctrine is inapplicable where . . . Adidas seeks to prevent Payless from using a confusingly similar imitation of a trademark that is distinctive indicator of source") (citing *Au-Tomotive Gold*) (emphasis added by *Adidas* court). Thus, the court held that Adidas' three-stripe design for shoes was protectable. Do you agree with this reading of *Au-Tomotive Gold*? If that is what the Ninth Circuit held in *Au-Tomotive Gold*, would it be consistent with *TrafFix*? With the purpose of the aesthetic functionality doctrine?

4. *Relevant market.* What is the relevant market with respect to which the aesthetic functionality analysis should be conducted? Consider this statement from the Eleventh Circuit in *Dippin' Dots, Inc. v. Frosty Bites Distribution, LLC*, 369 F.3d 1197, 1203 n.7 (11th Cir. 2004):

[T]he color, shape, and size of dippin' dots are "aesthetic functions" that easily satisfy the competitive necessity test because precluding competitors . . . from copying any of these aspects of dippin' dots would eliminate all competitors in the flash-frozen ice cream market, which would be the ultimate non-reputation-related disadvantage. Therefore, [plaintiff's] argument that [the defendant] could still compete in the ice cream market by producing, e.g., soft-serve ice cream, which would not have many of the same functional elements as dippin' dots and thus would not infringe upon [plaintiff's] product trade dress, is unavailing. [Defendant] does not want to compete in the ice cream business; it wants to compete in the flash-frozen ice cream business, which is in a different market from more traditional forms of ice cream. *See* 3 Louis Altman, *Callmann on Unfair Competition, Trademarks and Monopolies* §19:7, at 79 (4th ed.

2003) (stating that "functionality . . . is not to be determined within the broad compass of different but interchangeable products; the doctrine of functionality is intended to preserve competition within the narrow bounds of each *individual* product market").

Does this offer sufficient guidance about how to determine the relevant market?

5.   *Evidence.* Courts have been comfortable considering alternative designs in assessing aesthetic functionality. *See, e.g., Yurman Design, Inc. v. Golden Treasure Imps., Inc.*, 275 F. Supp. 2d 506, 512 (S.D.N.Y. 2003) (jewelry designs). *Cf. Moldex-Metric, Inc. v. McKeon Prods., Inc.*, 891 F.3d 878 (9th Cir. 2018) ("Our cases reflect that, with some features, the availability of alternative designs becomes more important in assessing functionality. . . . Considering alternative designs is particularly probative of functionality in a color case like this one where the mark is more akin to the green-gold hue in *Qualitex* than to the dual-spring stand in *TrafFix*.")

6.   *Relationship between the tests.* Reconsider the question we asked in the immediate wake of *TrafFix*. What is the relationship between the *Inwood* test and the analysis of "competitive necessity" that appears to be at the heart of the "aesthetic functionality" test? There, we suggested that (1) they might be separate filters, both of which any feature claimed to be nonfunctional must pass through to be protected; or (2) each test may be applicable to different types of features, *Inwood* to mechanical features and "competitive necessity" to aesthetic features. Do you think you can now answer that question having read post-*TrafFix* cases? If the first approach is adopted (i.e., each design feature for which protection is sought must pass both tests), how does this fit with the apparent linking of the "competitive necessity" test and "aesthetic functionality" by the Court in *TrafFix*? Perhaps this linking can be seen merely as an acknowledgment that designs that appear to have no mechanical utility related to the purpose of the article are likely to pass the first, *Inwood*, test and thus stand or fall depending upon the competitive necessity test. *Cf. Dippin' Dots, Inc. v. Frosty Bites Distribution*, 369 F.3d 1197, 1203 (11th Cir. 2004) (noting the "two tests" for functionality and acknowledging that if the terms of the *Inwood* test are satisfied, there is no need to proceed further to consider whether the competitive necessity test, which is "generally applied in cases of aesthetic functionality," is satisfied). This treats the use of the adjectives "utilitarian" and "aesthetic" as simply labels for the *test* that a feature passes or fails, rather than as ontological classifications of the feature for which protection is sought. *Cf. Millenium Labs., Inc. v. Ameritax, Ltd.*, 817 F.3d 1123 (9th Cir. 2016). This would create a unitary analysis for functionality, *see* Graeme B. Dinwoodie, *The Death of Ontology: A Teleological Approach to Trademark Law*, 84 Iowa L. Rev. 611, 701-21 (1999) (advocating a broad "competitive need" test for aesthetic and utilitarian features alike), albeit one with two hurdles for any design to overcome. Would it make the functionality test easier to apply? (Note that the *Louboutin* court in footnote 17 of its opinion called *Franco* a case involving aesthetic functionality. We included *Franco* in our section on "utilitarian features.") Would it make it easier or harder for plaintiffs? Would it be consistent with *TrafFix* or any of the post-*TrafFix* cases you have read? What other issues remain open in functionality doctrine after *TrafFix*?

7.   *A simplified test?* In *In re Florists' Transworld Delivery, Inc.*, 106 U.S.P.Q.2d (BNA) 1784 (TTAB 2013), the Trademark Trial and Appeal Board affirmed the denial of the registration of the color black for packaging for flower arrangements. The Board's decision turned in large part on its analysis of competitive need. In a concurring opinion, Judge Bucher indicated some impatience with the existing case law and complex doctrinal categories. Instead, he said he would simply apply "first principles" and ask whether "the public interest is best served by refusing to permit a particular feature to be taken from the 'public domain,'" which would involve analysis of "whether the non-traditional indicator should remain permanently available for competitors to use freely." Are you attracted to this approach?

8. *Application of the aesthetic functionality doctrine to other subject matter?* Should the functionality doctrine be applied to trademark subject matter other than color per se, the design or configuration of goods, and packaging? *See Ford Motor Co. v. Lloyd Design Corp.,* 184 F. Supp. 2d 665 (E.D. Mich. 2002). Could a word mark be functional? What about a number mark, such as "23" for basketball uniforms? *Cf. GTFM, Inc. v. Solid Clothing Inc.,* 215 F. Supp. 2d 273 (S.D.N.Y. 2002) (considering whether the mark "05" emblazoned on athletic jerseys is functional).

9. *Marketing themes and the "look" of humans.* Abercrombie & Fitch is not alone in seeking to protect the particular "look" of its employees or advertising models from copying by others. There, the look in question ("pleasing or desirable imagery . . . showing scantily clad college students in a grainy photograph") was one feature of the catalogs used to sell Abercrombie & Fitch products. But the Hooters restaurant chain took the argument one step further, and argued that what the court called the "iconic Hooters Girl" (i.e., the waitresses of a somewhat consistent look who wear relatively skimpy tank tops and running shoes and serve food at Hooters restaurants) was part of its trade dress. *See HI Ltd. P'ship v. Winghouse of Fla., Inc.,* 347 F. Supp. 2d 1256, 1258 (M.D. Fla. 2004). Should the approach of trademark law differ as between the look of the models in promotional material and the look of employees? In any event, the court denied protection to Hooters, finding that the Hooters Girl was "the very essence of Hooters' business" and thus functional. Does this formulation capture the gist of the functionality inquiry? If not, how else might you deny trade dress protection on these facts? In *Haagen Dazs, Inc. v. Frusen Gladje Ltd.,* 493 F. Supp. 73, 75 (S.D.N.Y. 1980), the district court held that a marketing theme cannot constitute trade dress, and thus plaintiff could not obtain exclusive use of a Scandinavian name for its ice cream. Might this be a rule applicable to the trade dress in *HI Ltd. P'ship?* Can you express that rule in terms of a doctrine that we have already discussed? Or do you prefer the apparently simple rule that "a marketing theme cannot constitute trade dress"? How would *Two Pesos* be decided under that rule?

10. *Defining rights.* To what extent did the *Louboutin* court rely on the plaintiff's registration in defining its trademark rights? Based on the cases you have read to date, did the Second Circuit in *Louboutin* attribute the correct significance to the narrowed registration? Would (and should) the scope of Louboutin's rights be different under Section 43(a)? Could you define Louboutin's trademark in a way that protects the distinctiveness of the red sole mark while permitting appropriate competition? Did the Second Circuit achieve that?

11. *Registration and scope of rights.* To what extent *did* YSL *use* the Louboutin mark? Compare the question to the ways in which the defendant "used" the word marks of plaintiffs in cases you have read so far. Would it be correct to say that the plaintiff in *Louboutin* obtained a "thin" trademark? Is this a useful concept? (It has been deployed in copyright law.) What would be the essence of a "thin" trademark? *Cf. Moldex-Metric, Inc. v. McKeon Prods., Inc.,* 891 F.3d 878 (9th Cir. 2018) (noting that plaintiff "claims twelve Pantone colors it believes to be confusingly similar to its green earplug color. It is not clear from the record what portion of the color spectrum between green and yellow this includes, or what portion of the set of colors that facilitate safety checks [the alleged non-trademark functions served by the color] this includes"). After ordering the narrowing of Louboutin's registration, the Second Circuit affirmed the refusal of the District Court to enjoin YSL from selling the monochrome shoe. Should the court have instead remanded the case to the trial court for a determination of likely confusion based upon the narrowed registration? If a rival shoe manufacturer sold shoes with the color red covering most but not all of the sole (and a black upper), do you think the Second Circuit would entertain an infringement claim?

12.   *Designs "as a whole."* After *TrafFix*, some commentators expressed concern that the Court's opinion "casts a cloud over the principle that when a decision maker decides whether a product's overall configuration is functional, that configuration should be viewed in its entirety, and not as discrete individual design features." Harold R. Weinberg, *Trademark Law, Functional Design Features, and the Trouble with* TrafFix, 9 J. Intell. Prop. L. 1, 6 (2001). Are those concerns confirmed or alleviated by any of the decisions excerpted above? *Cf. Tie Tech, Inc. v. Kinedyne Corp.*, 296 F.3d 778, 786 (9th Cir. 2002) ("Where the plaintiff only offers evidence that the 'whole is nothing other than the assemblage of functional parts,' our court has already foreclosed this argument, holding that 'it is semantic trickery to say that there is still some sort of separate overall appearance which is non-functional.'"); *Logan Graphic Prods., Inc. v. Textus USA, Inc.*, 67 U.S.P.Q.2d (BNA) 1470, 1473 (N.D. Ill. 2003) (appropriate inquiry focuses on the overall trade dress).

PROBLEM 3-1:   THE HERSHEY BAR

Would you register the product configuration shown below for "candy, chocolate"? *See In re Hershey Chocolate and Confectionary Corporation*, Serial No. 77809223 (June 28, 2012). The applicant described the mark as "twelve (12) equally-sized recessed panels arranged in a four panel by three panel format with each panel having its own raised border within a large rectangle."

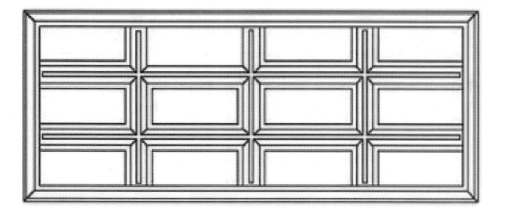

If the record showed that candy makers often embellish their candy bars with decorative elements and these raised borders and ridges decorate and embellish what otherwise would be a simple rectangular shape with a four by three pattern, would that affect your analysis? What else would you want to know? If Hershey's secured a registration, based upon *Louboutin*, what scope of rights would you expect it to obtain?

4

USE

The U.S. trademark system is "use"-based. The "use" requirement plays numerous roles. First, the "use in commerce" requirement ensures that the federal trademark regime remains within Congress's Commerce Clause powers. *See infra* section A.

Second, use determines who initially owns federal trademark rights. As a general rule, *actual* trademark use is a prerequisite for obtaining common law trademark rights protectable under Section 43(a) of the Lanham Act. In contrast, either actual or *constructive* trademark use in the United States, or specified activity overseas, may supply the basis for filing an application for a federal registration of a mark on the Principal Register. *See infra* sections B (actual use in the United States), C (constructive use in the United States), and D (activity overseas). Some cases on use present subtle questions about identifying the trademark "user." The issue often arises where trademarks are used in connection with informal organizations, such as musical groups and nonprofit organizations. *See infra* section E.

If use determines initial ownership, what happens when a user discontinues use? What happens when a user tolerates multiple third-party uses? *See infra* section F, dealing with trademark abandonment doctrines.

We leave for subsequent chapters (Chapters 7-9) a discussion of additional roles for the concept of "use" in the U.S. system, such as identifying the *types of use actionable* under the Lanham Act, and *fair* use as a defense to liability. When you reach those chapters, consider whether the standards of use that apply to the issues of acquisition and maintenance of rights do (or should) also apply to liability.

A. "USE" AS A JURISDICTIONAL PREREQUISITE

The Lanham Act specifies that only marks used "in commerce" can be the subject of federal trademark rights, reflecting constitutional concerns expressed in the *Trade-Mark Cases*, which we discussed in Chapter 1. The "in commerce" limitation appears in Lanham Act provisions governing both registered and unregistered rights. *See, e.g.,* Lanham Act §§1(a)(1), 32 (registered rights); Lanham Act §43(a)(1) (unregistered rights).

Consider the following illustration. Christian Faith Fellowship Church began selling caps and shirts marked with the phrase ADD A ZERO as part of a fundraising campaign to pay off the debt on its facility. The church is located in Illinois, within five miles of the Illinois–Wisconsin border, and has parishioners from both states. The church can show that it sold two ADD A ZERO–marked hats for $38.43 to Charlotte Howard, a Wisconsin resident. Has the church engaged in a use "in commerce" under the Lanham Act?

According to the Lanham Act definition, use in "commerce" encompasses "all commerce which may lawfully be regulated by Congress." Lanham Act §45; *United We Stand Am., Inc. v. United We Stand, Am., N.Y., Inc.,* 128 F.3d 86, 92-93 (2d Cir. 1997) ("commerce" in Lanham Act is coterminous with "commerce" in Commerce Clause). Under the Supreme Court's expansive modern Commerce Clause jurisprudence, Congress is empowered to regulate all activities that have a substantial effect on interstate commerce, even if the activities taken in isolation are arguably local in nature. *Wickard v. Filburn*, 317 U.S. 111, 120 (1942); *see also Taylor v. United States,* 136 S. Ct. 2074, 2081 (2016) (not necessary to prove that the defendant's conduct itself affected interstate commerce; only necessary to show that "defendant's conduct fell into a category of conduct that, in the aggregate, had the requisite effect"). There is no exception for *de minimis* activity. *See, e.g., Gonzales v. Raich*, 545 U.S. 1, 17 (2005) (*de minimis* cultivation and possession of marijuana falls within the reach of federal drug laws passed under the Commerce Clause); *Katzenbach v. McClung*, 379 U.S. 294 (1964) (single-state restaurant that ordered food from outside the state is operating in interstate commerce and thus can be regulated under the 1964 Civil Rights Act); *Heart of Atlanta Motel, Inc. v. United States*, 379 U.S. 241 (1964) (same, for a single-state motel that served some out-of-state travelers). Consistent with that approach, the Federal Circuit has refused to create a *de minimis* exception for assessing whether uses of a mark are "in commerce." *Larry Harmon Pictures Corp. v. Williams Restaurant Corp.*, 929 F.2d 662 (Fed. Cir. 1991) (mark BOZO'S for restaurant services was used in commerce where even a modest fraction of mark owner's business—15 percent —was with out-of-state customers).

In view of these cases, the church's claim to be acting in interstate commerce in the ADD A ZERO case is easy to resolve: The sale of the hats falls into the category of economic activity that, in the aggregate, undoubtedly could affect interstate commerce. Moreover, there is no need for any particularized showing that these two hats actually crossed state lines or themselves affected interstate commerce, and the arguably *de minimis* nature of the hat sales does not affect the outcome. *See Christian Faith Fellowship Church v. Adidas AG*, 841 F.3d 986 (Fed. Cir. 2016) (finding the in-commerce requirement to be satisfied). (The dispute arose when Adidas AG sought to register ADIZERO for clothing and received a rejection based on the church's ADD A ZERO registrations.) The *Christian Faith* case is representative. It will be the extremely rare case in which a mark owner will be unable to show evidence of a connection to interstate commerce sufficient to satisfy the "commerce" requirement, at least where domestic activities are involved. Where a mark owner's activities occur overseas, those activities might still be "in commerce" for Lanham Act purposes. We will return to that topic in Chapter 6, which takes up the territorial scope of U.S. trademark rights.

B.   ACTUAL "USE" AS A BASIS FOR ESTABLISHING RIGHTS

Long before the advent of the modern federal trademark regime, the common law of trademarks in the United States required trademark use as a precondition to trademark ownership. For example, in *Columbia Mill Co.*, the U.S. Supreme Court declared that "the exclusive right to the use of the mark or device claimed as a trade-mark is founded on priority of appropriation; that is to say, the claimant of the trade-mark must have been the first to use or employ the same on like articles of production." *Columbia Mill Co. v. Alcorn*, 150 U.S. 460, 463-64 (1893).

The reliance on a first-to-use regime distinguishes U.S. trademark law from other forms of intellectual property—such as U.S. patent law, which awards rights to the first inventor to file a patent application, even if the inventor has not put the invention into use. The use requirement also distinguishes U.S. trademark law from the trademark laws of many other jurisdictions, where registration, not use, is the basis for awarding rights. Is the U.S. system superior to a first-to-register system?

Why should U.S. trademark law employ a first-to-use approach? Is that approach necessary to effectuate the purposes of U.S. trademark law (as articulated in Chapter 1)? What about the rules of distinctiveness (explored in Chapter 2)? Do they depend on a use-based approach to trademark law?

We begin by studying actual use as a basis for claiming rights. In the cases and materials in section B.1 below, the general issue is whether a person claiming entitlement to rights in a certain mark has in fact adopted and used the mark. In section B.2, we explore the rules that govern *when* use is deemed to have occurred. This issue of priority of use most often arises when rivals are claiming rights in the same or similar marks.

Note that the requirements relating to actual use may differ depending on whether the claim is made to support registered rights (whether in an application before the PTO for registration or in an action for infringement based upon such a registration) or a claim of unregistered rights (normally arising in the context of a judicial proceeding alleging infringement). In addition, the requirements differ depending on whether the mark is used in connection with goods or with services. As you have seen from Chapters 2 and 3, these distinctions are often of little significance when the distinctiveness or functionality doctrines are at issue. By contrast, they can be dispositive when use is at issue.

1. Establishing Actual Use

In the modern U.S. trademark system, actual use is the *only* permissible basis for a claim of unregistered rights. *See, e.g., Ford Motor Co. v. Summit Motor Products, Inc.*, 930 F.2d 277, 292 (3d Cir. 1991) ("With respect to ownership of unregistered marks, the first party to adopt a trademark can assert ownership rights, provided it continuously uses it in commerce."). Actual use is one of *several* permissible bases for filing an application to claim registered rights. Section 1(a) of the Lanham Act specifies that actual use in commerce may serve as a filing basis for an application; Section 45 contains a definition of "use in commerce."

LANHAM ACT

Section 1 [15 U.S.C. §1051]

(a)

(1) The owner of a trademark used in commerce may request registration of its trademark on the principal register hereby established by paying the prescribed fee and filing in the Patent and Trademark Office an application and a verified statement, in such form as may be prescribed by the Director, and such number of specimens or facsimiles of the mark as used as may be required by the Director.

(2) The application shall include specification of the applicant's domicile and citizenship, the date of the applicant's first use of the mark, the date of the applicant's first use of the mark in commerce, the goods in connection with which the mark is used, and a drawing of the mark.

(3) The statement shall be verified by the applicant and specify that—

. . .

(C) the mark is in use in commerce . . .

. . .

LANHAM ACT

Section 45 [15 U.S.C. §1127]

The term "use in commerce" means the bona fide use of a mark in the ordinary course of trade, and not made merely to reserve a right in a mark. For purposes of this Act, a mark shall be deemed to be in use in commerce—

(1) on goods when—

(A) it is placed in any manner on the goods or their containers or the displays associated therewith or on the tags or labels affixed thereto, or if the nature of the goods makes such placement impracticable, then on documents associated with the goods or their sale, and

(B) the goods are sold or transported in commerce, and

(2) on services when it is used or displayed in the sale or advertising of services and the services are rendered in commerce, or the services are rendered in more than one State or in the United States and a foreign country and the person rendering the services is engaged in commerce in connection with the services.

NOTES AND QUESTIONS

1.   *When does the Section 45 definition of "use" apply?* The Section 45 definition of use clearly applies to determine whether an applicant for registered rights has made the use necessary to support a registration sought or granted under Section 1(a). Should courts also refer to the Section 45 definition to inform their decisions about whether actual use has been demonstrated in cases involving the assertion of unregistered rights (sometimes called "common law" trademarks)? Recall that those rights are typically vindicated through an action brought under Section 43(a) of the Lanham Act; registered rights granted after a Section 1(a) application are vindicated through an action under Section 32. The *Planetary Motion* case, excerpted below, comments on this question.

2.   *Structure of the Section 45 definition of "use in commerce."*   The Section 45 definition contains three components: (1) a preamble imposing requirements for all uses; (2) a two-part test applicable to uses in connection with goods; and (3) a slightly different two-part test applicable to uses in connection with services. The preamble states that a mark "shall be deemed to be in use in commerce" if the applicable two-part test is met. What does "deemed" mean—that a use is sufficient *only* if it meets the applicable two-part test, or that satisfying the applicable two-part test is sufficient, but is not the exclusive path for establishing actual use within the meaning of the preamble?

3.   *Construing the preamble language of the Section 45 definition—"bona fide"; "in the ordinary course of trade"; "not made merely to reserve a right in a mark."* The preamble language in the Section 45 definition was added in 1988. The legislative history makes clear that one primary reason was to abrogate the rule that mere "token" use provided a basis for a use-based application to register a mark, a topic that we discuss further in section C of this chapter (on constructive use). The legislative history also indicates Congress' understanding that the inclusion of the phrase "ordinary course of trade" allows for some variability from industry to industry. H.R. Rep. No. 1028, 100th Cong. 2d Sess. 15 (1988). Accordingly, infrequent sales of expensive or seasonal products might suffice if that is standard practice in a given industry, *id.*, as might uses made in test markets. S. Rep. No. 515, 100th Cong. 2d Sess. 44-45 (1988). In view of the legislative history, the PTO has suggested that in determining whether an applicant's activity amounts to a bona fide use in the ordinary course of trade, three factors may be considered: "(1) the amount of use; (2) the

nature or quality of the transaction; and (3) what is typical use within a particular industry." TMEP §901.02 (Oct. 2017). The legislative history also suggests that Congress expected the Section 45 definition to be interpreted "with flexibility." S. Rep. No. 515, 100th Cong. 2d Sess. 44-45 (1988). As you read the cases excerpted below, consider whether courts are implementing the legislative history's stated preference for a flexible approach.

4. *Services versus goods in the Section 45 definition.* Why is the part of Section 45 applicable to goods different from that for services? Should service mark cases receive a higher level of scrutiny for purposes of determining whether actual use has occurred?

5. *The Section 45 definition before and after 1988 reforms.* While the Section 45 preamble language was added in 1988, the provisions separately addressing the meaning of "use in commerce" for goods and for services did not change at that time. To what extent should pre-1988 case law on actual use be followed in a post-1988 analysis? The *Aycock* case below addresses this issue. *See also Custom Vehicles, Inc. v. Forest River, Inc.*, 476 F.3d 481 (7th Cir. 2007) (raising the issue).

6. *Policy basis for the use requirement.* What does the Section 45 definition tell us about the policy rationale for the use requirement? The Section 45 definition expresses an aversion to activities undertaken merely to reserve rights in a mark. But why do we care whether someone "reserves rights" in a mark? In a case involving rights in the mark STEALTH for baseball bats, an individual (the sole shareholder of Central Manufacturing) had purported to register the mark STEALTH for myriad products and had routinely failed to prove use in prior litigation. As the court portrayed it:

> Acting as a sort of intellectual property entrepreneur, [he] has federally registered scores of trademarks with the U.S. PTO (Central lists upwards of 50 that are actual or pending for just the "Stealth" mark), many containing everyday words that regularly pop up in commercial enterprise. When other companies or individuals inevitably make use of these words, [he] issues cease-and-desist letters in the hopes that the user will blanche at the prospect of litigation and either agree to pay him a "licensing fee" or yield to his claims of ownership and stop using the alleged mark altogether.

Cent. Mfg., Inc. v. Brett, 492 F.3d 876, 880 (7th Cir. 2007). (For those inclined toward baseball, Central was suing Hall-of-Famer George Brett.) Do trademark entrepreneurs pose a threat to competition?

Consider a related policy question: Should we require use to avoid the proliferation of trademark "thickets"? As Judge Posner wrote:

> We suppose that one sale of a $150 million airplane or yacht within the first six months might be sufficient use [to establish trademark rights] for it would be enough to seize the attention of the relevant market. See [cit.]; *New England Duplicating Co. v. Mendes*, 190 F.2d 415, 418 (1st Cir. 1951). But not one sale of a van. That sale would have been too obscure an event to alert any significant number of consumers that "Work-N-Play" had a definite referent (even if the name had been used in the sale); and until that happens, the creator of the mark should not be able to appropriate it. For such a practice, by creating a trademark thicket, would make it difficult for new producers to find suitable names for their products that had not already been appropriated to no worthier end than providing the premise for an infringement suit. . . . Unless, as in our yacht example, the product is unusually expensive, a single sale, followed by frenetic but futile efforts to make a second sale, hardly justifies allowing the seller to appropriate the mark, denying its use to sellers who can actually sell.

Custom Vehicles, Inc. v. Forest River, Inc., 476 F.3d 481, 485-86 (7th Cir. 2007). Is the notion of "seizing the attention of the market" reflected in any other trademark concepts that we have discussed? Do you agree with Judge Posner that courts should require a level of use that is sufficient to "seize the attention" of the market? Do you agree that dispensing with the requirement to seize the attention of the market would lead to the creation of "trademark thickets"? What is a trademark thicket? Note that the *Mendes* case cited by Judge Posner figures prominently in the *Planetary Motion* decision, excerpted below.

What other policy goals might a use requirement serve? A notice function? An evidentiary function?

PROBLEM 4-1: USE IN CONNECTION WITH GOODS

Suppose that your client *Z*, operating in the town of Big Sky (a small town in southwest Montana), produces a specialty wine for sale at grocery stores in Montana and Wyoming under the name BAD BISON. *Z* has a number of questions about whether its activities constitute a use in commerce under the Section 45 definition. As you address the questions, consider the importance of variables such as quantity of activity, quality (e.g., the purpose of the activity; the prominence of the mark), location of the activity, and common practices in the trade.

(1) Once *Z* has chosen the name BAD BISON, is the mark in actual use?

(2) If *Z* has received an order of shipping crates for the wine bearing the BAD BISON label, is the mark in actual use?

(3) If *Z* has advertised BAD BISON wine for sale on *Z*'s website, is the mark in actual use (even if no wine has yet been sold)?

(4) If *Z* has given away bottles of wine (labelled with the mark) to tourists passing through Montana on their way to Wyoming, is the mark in actual use?

(5) If *Z* has sold two bottles of wine (labelled with the mark) to his brother in Cody, Wyoming, at cost, is the mark in actual use?

(6) How many bottles of wine (if any) bearing the BAD BISON label would *Z* need to sell in order for the mark to be in actual use?

(7) If *Z* has shipped three cases of wine (in bottles labelled with the BAD BISON mark) to a grocery store in Wyoming, but the wine has not yet been sold, does this constitute actual use?

(8) Must *Z*'s activities each be analyzed individually for purposes of compliance with the Section 45 definition, or may you take into account the cumulation of activities? For example, would all of (1)-(5) taken together constitute actual use even if the activities taken individually do not?

The case below involves a claim of actual use in connection with services, as a basis for a claim of registered rights. Note the court's focus on the language of the Section 45 definition of "use in commerce," particularly paragraph 2, which defines use in connection with services.

AYCOCK ENGINEERING, INC. v. AIRFLITE, INC.
560 F.3d 1350 (Fed. Cir. 2009)

O'GRADY, District Judge (sitting by designation):

I.   BACKGROUND

[In the late 1940s, William Aycock attempted to build a flight chartering business under the name AIRFLITE. He planned to operate as a middleman between customers and air taxi operators. He would take reservation requests from customers via a toll-free number, and then would contact an air taxi operator to arrange a flight. He believed that he needed at least 300 air taxi operators to agree to participate in his system for the business to be operational.]

In the years after conceiving of the idea for his service, Mr. Aycock worked toward offering the service to the public. In the mid-1960s, he formed Aycock Engineering—the corporate entity under which his service would operate. He also sought and obtained two toll-free telephone numbers that the public could use to make reservations. In March of 1970, Mr. Aycock invited virtually all air taxi operators certified by the Federal Aviation Administration ("FAA") to join his operation by, inter alia, distributing flyers with in-depth information about his AIRFLITE service. He eventually entered into contracts with some of those air taxi service operators. Under these contracts, air taxi operators agreed to participate in the AIRFLITE service and even paid modest initiation fees to Mr. Aycock. Furthermore, Mr. Aycock filed a service mark application on August 10, 1970 for the term AIRFLITE, which was a term he had included in his advertisements. [Eventually, after agreeing to define the relevant services as "[a]rranging for individual reservations for flights on airplanes," Mr. Aycock received a registration. He renewed the registration in April 1994.]

Despite his efforts, Mr. Aycock's operation never got off the ground. While he estimated that he needed at least 300 air service operators under contract to make his service operational, Mr. Aycock never had more than twelve (4% of his minimum goal) under contract at any time throughout his company's history. And while Mr. Aycock advertised to air taxi operators, he never marketed the AIRFLITE service to the general public. More specifically, the record does not suggest that Mr. Aycock ever gave the public an opportunity to use the toll-free phone numbers to book reservations, or that he ever spoke with a member of the general public about making a reservation. Finally, and most notably, Mr. Aycock never arranged for a single passenger to fly on a chartered flight.

. . .

In 2001, Airflite, Inc., the Petitioner-Appellee, filed a petition for cancellation alleging, inter alia, that Aycock Engineering did not use its AIRFLITE mark prior to registration in connection with the services identified in its registration. In that proceeding, the TTAB agreed with Airflite, Inc. and cancelled the AIRFLITE registration, finding that Mr. Aycock failed to render the service described in its registration in commerce. [cit.] ("*TTAB Decision*").

II.   DISCUSSION

. . .

C.   Interpretation of the Recitation of Services in Mr. Aycock's Service Mark Application

[The court rejected Aycock's argument that creating contacts with a network of air taxi operators was itself the service at issue. This interpretation of the relevant services figured importantly in the court's conclusion about whether Aycock had engaged in use.]

D.   Use Requirement

[The court recited the Section 45 definition of "use in commerce" and noted the elements that are specific to service marks.]

E.   Use Requirement for Service Marks

[Because Aycock had filed before 1988, the pre-1988 statutory definition applied. However, the pertinent language relating to service marks had not changed, the court explained.] The use provision of the Lanham Act in force in 1970 stated that a service mark was in use in commerce "when it is used or displayed in the sale or advertising of services, and the services are rendered in commerce, or the services are rendered in more than one State or in this and a foreign country and the person rendering the services is engaged in commerce in connection therewith." Pub. L. No. 87-772, 76 Stat. 769 (1962). Therefore, like the current use requirement, a service mark applicant seeking to meet the pre-1989 version had to (1) use the mark in the sale or advertising of a service and (2) show that the service was either rendered in interstate commerce or rendered in more than one state or in this and a foreign country by a person engaged in commerce.

Courts, as well as the TTAB, have interpreted the pre-1989 statutory language in analogous cases. Without question, advertising or publicizing a service that the applicant intends to perform in the future will not support registration. *In re Cedar Point, Inc.*, 220 USPQ 533, 536 (TTAB 1983) (quoting *Intermed Commc'ns, Inc. v. Chaney*, 197 USPQ 501, 507-08 (TTAB 1977)); *Greyhound Corp. v. Armour Life Ins. Co.*, 214 USPQ 473, 474 (TTAB 1982). Instead, the advertising or publicizing must relate to "an existing service which has already been offered to the public." *Greyhound*, 214 USPQ at 474. Furthermore, "[m]ere adoption (selection) of a mark accompanied by preparations to begin its use are insufficient . . . for claiming ownership of and applying to register the mark." *Intermed*, 197 USPQ at 507; [cit.]. "At the very least," in order for an applicant to meet the use requirement, "there must be an open and notorious public offering of the services to those for whom the services are intended." *Intermed*, 197 USPQ at 507.

In *Intermed*, the TTAB rejected a service mark application for failing to meet the use in commerce requirement even where the applicant had performed many pre-application service-oriented activities involving the public. *Id.* at 508-09. The applicant in that case sought to register a mark intended to identify an international medical services operation. *Id.* at 502. The applicant's plan was to build the international service from an already operating United States–based medical service. *Id.* at 503. The applicant intended to, and did use the United States–based operation as a fundraising affiliate of the new international operation. *Id.* Additionally, the applicant communicated with and solicited the support of the Iranian government regarding the service before the application was filed. *Id.* The applicant also issued a detailed announcement using the service mark term before the filing date designed to inform and update individuals about the service's status. *Id.* Finally, and also before the date of application, the applicant hired a fundraising firm to raise money for the service. *Id.* at 508.

Despite these activities, the TTAB held that the applicant failed to meet the use requirement because the services described in the application were not "offered, promoted, advertised or rendered . . . in commerce." *Intermed*, 197 USPQ at 504. The TTAB stated that "[t]he statute requires not only the display of the mark in the sale or advertising of services but also the rendition of those services in order to constitute use of the service mark in commerce." *Id.* at 507-08. The TTAB further explained that adopting a mark accompanied by mere "preparations to begin its use" is insufficient for service mark registration, and that in order for the use requirement to be met, there must be "an open and notorious public offering of the services to those for whom the services are intended." *Id.*

In 1983, the TTAB again rejected a service mark application because it failed to meet the use requirement. *Cedar Point*, 220 USPQ at 533. In *Cedar Point*, the Cedar Point amusement park, which had been in business for decades, was preparing to open a new water park addition in mid-May of 1980. *Id.* at 535. One preparatory step taken by Cedar Point before opening day was the filing of a service mark application to register the mark "OCEANA" for its new water park service. *Id.* Cedar Point also distributed nearly 700,000 water park advertisement brochures containing the OCEANA mark during the months preceding the grand opening. *Id.*

The TTAB emphasized the fact that Cedar Point filed its service mark application with the USPTO before it opened the water park's doors and offered those services to the public. *Id.* at 535-36. The TTAB then explained that the use of a mark in connection with the advertising of services intended to be "available at some time in the future, but not yet available at the time of filing" does not qualify the mark for registration. *Id.* at 535. Therefore, Cedar Point's water park advertising campaign, which was ongoing at the time the application was filed, was insufficient on its own to support registration. *Id.* As a result, the TTAB held that the "applicant's mark 'OCEANA' was not in 'use in commerce' . . . at the time of the filing of [the] application" and that the application was thus void ab initio. *Id.* at 537.

Interestingly, Cedar Point filed for its service mark roughly one month before the scheduled opening of the new water park. *Id.* at 535. With the application date being so close to the opening date, it is indisputable that Cedar Point had taken numerous steps toward constructing the water park by the time the application was filed. Nevertheless, the TTAB found none of these preparatory steps sufficient to satisfy the use in commerce requirement.

The TTAB also addressed the use in commerce issue in the 1982 *Greyhound* case. *Greyhound*, 214 USPQ at 473. In that case, the applicant, a life insurance company, filed a service mark application in November of 1979. *Id.* at 474. Before the filing date, the applicant advertised its services by disseminating informational letters and posters using the service mark. *Id.* Despite this activity, the TTAB held that the service described in the application was not rendered in commerce and thus declared the application void ab initio. *Id.* at 475. The TTAB explained that "it is well settled that advertising of a service, without performance of a service, will not support registration. . . . The use in advertising which creates a right in a service mark must be advertising which relates to an existing service which has already been offered to the public." *Id.* at 474.

We find the reasoning of these cases persuasive. The language of the statute, by requiring that the mark be "used or displayed in the sale or advertising of services, and the services are rendered in commerce," makes plain that advertisement and actual use of the mark in commerce are required; mere preparations to use that mark sometime in the future will not do. Thus, we hold that an applicant's preparations to use a mark in commerce are insufficient to constitute use in commerce. Rather, the mark must be actually used in conjunction with the services described in the application for the mark.

F.   ANALYSIS

As explained above, Mr. Aycock's AIRFLITE service mark application can only meet the use requirement if (1) his AIRFLITE mark was "used or displayed in the sale or advertising of services," and (2) his AIRFLITE service was either "rendered in commerce" or rendered in more than one state or in this and a foreign country by a person engaged in commerce. 15 U.S.C. §1127 (2006). Because our determination under the second element is dispositive, we will not address the issue of whether Mr. Aycock's advertising was sufficient to meet the first element of the service mark use requirement.

In order to decide whether the second element is met, we must determine whether Mr. Aycock ever gave an intended customer the opportunity to use his AIRFLITE service. In other words, we must determine if Mr. Aycock made an open and notorious rendering, or offering, of his service to the public. *See Intermed*, 197 USPQ at 507. Upon review, we conclude that the TTAB's determination that Mr. Aycock failed to offer his service to the public is supported by substantial evidence, because he never gave anyone an opportunity to use his AIRFLITE service to make a charter flight reservation. Instead, Mr. Aycock merely took sporadic steps in preparing to offer his service to the public.

Specifically, Mr. Aycock formed Aycock Engineering, which was the corporate entity under which he intended to operate his AIRFLITE service. He also obtained two toll-free telephone numbers that he planned to provide for potential customers seeking to make flight reservations. The most notable step Mr. Aycock took toward offering his AIRFLITE service to the public came when he contracted with the air taxi operators. Under these contracts, air taxi operators agreed to participate in the AIRFLITE air taxi network by being available to provide flights for customers using the AIRFLITE service. These operators even paid modest initiation fees to Aycock in order to participate in the service.

But these activities, even taken together, do not constitute a service that falls within the scope of our definition of the recitation of services. As mentioned earlier, it is our view that the service described in Mr. Aycock's service mark application covers only the arranging of flights between an air taxi operator and a passenger, and not preparatory efforts to arrange a network of air taxi operators. The activities described above, however, were merely preparatory steps that Mr. Aycock took toward his goal of one day, as he described, operating a "communication service between persons desiring to charter aircraft" that "put[ ] individuals desiring air transportation in contact with people rendering that service." [cit.]

In order for Mr. Aycock to satisfy the use requirement, more was required. Mr. Aycock had to develop his company to the point where he made an open and notorious public offering of his AIRFLITE service to intended customers. *See Intermed*, 197 USPQ at 507. However, at no point in time did Mr. Aycock give a potential customer the chance to use his AIRFLITE service. He never arranged for a single flight between a customer and an air taxi operator. This is because Mr. Aycock, as stated in his deposition, believed he needed at least 300 air taxi operators under contract before his service could become operational. Reasonably, because he never had more than twelve air taxi operators under contract at any one time, Mr. Aycock chose not to open his doors to the public.

Furthermore, while the two toll-free telephone numbers he obtained could have been used at some point in time as a means of offering the service to the public, they were never actually used for this purpose. Nothing in the record suggests that Mr. Aycock ever gave potential customers an opportunity to use the phone lines to make flight reservations, or that a single customer seeking to book a flight actually called the toll-free number. The record also fails to indicate that Mr. Aycock, or anyone else associated with Aycock Engineering ever spoke with a member of the general public about making a flight reservation through the AIRFLITE service.

That Mr. Aycock advertised to, contracted with, and was paid by air taxi operators does not transform the service from its preparatory stages to being rendered in commerce. Instead, these actions were Mr. Aycock's attempts to build the service's infrastructure, which, when completed, could then be offered to the public (and thus "rendered in commerce").

Notably, Mr. Aycock set the goal of obtaining 300 air taxi operators by himself. He had the option of attempting to run his AIRFLITE service with the air taxi operators he had under contract when he applied for his service mark in 1970. Even though this approach likely would have led to a much smaller and less profitable operation than he originally intended, he could have met the use requirement had he taken this route.[11] Even

---

11. The success or profitability of the service once it is offered to the public is irrelevant in the use requirement analysis. Therefore, the use requirement can be met when a service that was open for business immediately fails. This reasoning does not apply, however, to services that failed during their preparatory stages and, as a result, were never offered to the public. The use requirement is not met in such instances.

more, because Mr. Aycock filed his service mark application before 1989, he had the "token use" option at his disposal. But he does not argue, and the facts do not show, that he ever attempted to make a token use of his AIRFLITE service.

In sum, the activities that Mr. Aycock performed throughout the process of building his AIRFLITE service at no point in time amounted to a rendering in commerce of the service described in his application. In addition, the service was never rendered in more than one state or in this and a foreign country by a person engaged in commerce. Therefore, we hold that Mr. Aycock's AIRFLITE service mark application did not meet the use requirement when he filed it in 1970 and is thus void ab initio.[12] Further, Mr. Aycock failed to meet the use requirement during any of his additional dealings with the USPTO that took place after 1970, including his 1994 renewal application.

. . .

Affirmed.

[Judge Newman's dissenting opinion is omitted.]

NOTES AND QUESTIONS

1. *How useful is the use requirement as a policy instrument?* Suppose Aycock had shown that he had booked one flight for a customer through his system—and the evidence suggests that this was a bona fide transaction. Would he then have satisfied the statutory requirements for use? If so, does this raise a question about the extent to which the use requirement is really advancing policy goals? If one flight would not have sufficed, how many would have been required? Does the statutory language provide the basis for your answer, or must you incorporate other considerations? Which considerations?

2. *The Section 45 definition: services "rendered in commerce."*   Does *Aycock* stand for the proposition that a party's activities preparing to render services—its "non-sales" activities—are given no significance in analyzing priority of use? In *Rearden LLC v. Rearden Commerce, Inc.*, 683 F.3d 1190, 1205 (9th Cir. 2012), a Ninth Circuit panel stated that

> evidence of actual sales, or lack thereof, is not dispositive in determining whether a party has established "use in commerce" within the meaning of the Lanham Act. Instead, we have acknowledged the potential relevance of non-sales activity in demonstrating not only whether a mark has been adequately displayed in public, but also whether a service identified by the mark has been "rendered in commerce."

15 U.S.C. §1127. The court concluded that "[a]ccordingly, even if a party completes the initial sale of its services only after its opponent has done so, that party still could establish prior use of the contested mark based on its prior non-sales activities." *Id.* at 1206. Is this consistent with *Aycock*?

3. *Does the Section 45 definition extend to "open and notorious" offers to render services in commerce?* In *Aycock*, the court observed that Mr. Aycock had not even made an "open and notorious public offering" of his services (seemingly borrowing language from the law of adverse possession). Suppose that Mr. Aycock had made such an offering,

---

12. We find it unfortunate that Mr. Aycock lost his AIRFLITE service mark after the USPTO granted him a registration over thirty years ago. But under the federal trademark and service mark registration system, no period of years exists beyond which a mark holder becomes immune from invalidation under the use requirement. This harsh reality may be offset by the common-law trademark doctrine, which provides a mark user with rights even if that user did not file an application with the USPTO.

without having actually rendered services. Should that be enough to satisfy the Section 45 definition of use in connection with services? In *Couture v. Playdom, Inc.*, 778 F.3d 1379 (Fed. Cir. 2015), the applicant sought to register the mark PLAYDOM for screenwriting and production services. The applicant had set up a website, at *www.playdominc.com*, which stated: "Welcome to PlaydomInc.com. We are proud to offer writing and production services for motion picture film, television, and new media. Please feel free to contact us if you are interested: *playdominc@gmail.com*." The web page included the notice: "Website Under Construction." No services under the mark were provided until after the application was filed. How would you decide the issue of actual use?

The next case, *Planetary Motion*, involves a claim of actual use of a mark in connection with goods, asserted as the basis for common law rights. As you read the case, consider what makes it so different from *Aycock*. The fact that it involves a claim to common law rights? A claim to rights in connection with goods? Is it because it simply involves better facts for the mark claimant than *Aycock* does?

PLANETARY MOTION, INC. v. TECHSPLOSION, INC.

261 F.3d 1188 (11th Cir. 2001)

RESTANI, Circuit Judge:

FACTS

. . .

I.   DEVELOPMENT AND DISTRIBUTION OF THE "COOLMAIL" SOFTWARE

In late 1994, Byron Darrah ("Darrah") developed a UNIX-based program (the "Software") that provides e-mail users with notice of new e-mail and serves as a gateway to the users' e-mail application. On December 31, 1994, Darrah distributed the Software over the Internet by posting it on a UNIX user site called "Sunsite," from which it could be downloaded for free. Darrah had named the Software "Coolmail" and this designation appeared on the announcement sent to the end-users on Sunsite as well as on the Software user-manual, both of which accompanied the release.

The Software was distributed without charge to users pursuant to a GNU General Public License that also accompanied the release.[*] A GNU General Public License allows users to copy, distribute and/or modify the Software under certain restrictions, e.g., users modifying licensed files must carry "prominent notices" stating that the user changed the files and the date of any change. After the release of the Software, Darrah received correspondence from users referencing the "Coolmail" mark and in some cases suggesting improvements. In 1995, Darrah released two subsequent versions of the Software under the same mark and also pursuant to the GNU General Public License.

In early 1995, a German company named S.u.S.E. GmbH sought permission from Darrah to include the Software in a CD-ROM package sold as a compilation of UNIX-based programs. Darrah consented and, pursuant to the GNU licensing agreement, S.u.S.E. distributed the Software in its compilation product and in subsequent versions thereof.

-----

* *Ed. Note:* The GNU project, described in detail at *www.gnu.org*, was organized to develop a UNIX-like operating system built on free software.

S.u.S.E. sold and continues to sell the software compilation in stores in the United States and abroad, as well as over the Internet.

[In July 1999, Darrah transferred all rights in the Coolmail software, including intellectual property rights, to plaintiff Planetary Motion, which operated an e-mail service under the "Coolmail" trademark.]

II. Launch of Techsplosion's "CoolMail" E-mail Service

In 1998, Appellant Carson formed Techsplosion, for the purpose of operating a business based on an e-mail service that he had developed. On April 16, 1998, Techsplosion began offering the e-mail service on the Internet under the mark "CoolMail." Two days later, Techsplosion activated the domain name "coolmail.to"[] Techsplosion delivered an e-mail solicitation under the "CoolMail" mark to approximately 11,000 members of the Paramount Banner Network, an Internet advertising network, also created and operated by Carson. Techsplosion charged no fee to subscribe to the service and generated revenues through the sale of banner advertisements on its web site.

[In 1999, Planetary Motion sued Techsplosion under Section 43(a) of the Lanham Act, alleging infringement of the claimed mark "Coolmail" for use in connection with e-mail services.]

DISCUSSION

. . .

I. Prior Use in Commerce

Under common law, trademark ownership rights are "appropriated only through actual prior use in commerce." *Tally-Ho, Inc. v. Coast Community College Dist.*, 889 F.2d 1018, 1022 (11th Cir. 1989) (citation omitted). Under the Lanham Act,[5] the term "use in commerce" is defined in relevant part as follows:

> the bona fide use of a mark in the ordinary course of trade, and not made merely to reserve a right in a mark. . . . [A] mark shall be deemed to be in use in commerce . . . on goods when (A) it is placed in any manner on the goods or their containers or the displays associated therewith or on the tags or labels affixed thereto, or if the nature of the goods makes such placement impracticable, then on documents associated with the goods or their sale, and (B) the goods are sold or transported in commerce. . . .

15 U.S.C. §1127. The district court found that because the statute is written in the disjunctive (i.e., "sale *or* transport"), Darrah's wide distribution of the Coolmail software over the Internet, even absent any sales thereof, was sufficient to establish ownership rights in the "CoolMail" mark. Appellants contend that "transport in commerce" alone—here, Darrah's free distribution of software over the Internet "with no existing business, no intent to form a business, and no sale under the mark"—is insufficient to create trademark rights. Appellants' argument lacks merit.

. . .

[T]he use of a mark in commerce . . . must be sufficient to establish *ownership rights* for a plaintiff to recover against subsequent users under section 43(a). *See New England Duplicating Co. v. Mendes*, 190 F.2d 415, 417-18 (1st Cir. 1951) (after finding "use

---

5. "In the absence of registration, rights to a mark traditionally have depended on the very same elements that are now included in the statutory definition: the bona fide use of a mark in commerce that was not made merely to reserve a mark for later exploitation." *Allard Enters., Inc. v. Advanced Programming Res., Inc.*, 146 F.3d 350, 357 (6th Cir. 1998). . . .

in commerce" jurisdiction predicate satisfied, court noted that "[t]he question remains whether the plaintiff has established that he was the 'owner' of the mark, for under [15 U.S.C. §1051] only the 'owner' of a mark is entitled to have it registered."). The court in *Mendes* set forth a two part test to determine whether a party has established "prior use" of a mark sufficient to establish ownership:

> [E]vidence showing, first, adoption, and, second, use in a way sufficiently public to identify or distinguish the marked goods in an appropriate segment of the public mind as those of the adopter of the mark, is competent to establish ownership, even without evidence of actual sales.

Id. at 418. [cit.]

Courts generally must inquire into the activities surrounding the prior use of the mark to determine whether such an association or notice is present. *See, e.g., Johnny Blastoff, Inc. v. L.A. Rams Football Co.*, 188 F.3d 427, 433 (7th Cir. 1999) ("The determination of whether a party has established protectable rights in a trademark is made on a case by case basis, considering the totality of the circumstances."), *cert. denied*, 528 U.S. 1188 (2000). Under the "totality of circumstances" analysis, a party may establish "use in commerce" even in the absence of sales. "[A]lthough evidence of sales is highly persuasive, the question of use adequate to establish appropriation remains one to be decided on the facts of each case. . . ." [*New West Corp. v. NYM Co. of Cal., Inc.*, 595 F.2d 1194, 1200 (9th Cir. 1979)] (quoting *Mendes*, 190 F.2d at 418). The court in *New West* recognized that "mere advertising by itself may not establish priority of use," but found that promotional mailings coupled with advertiser and distributor solicitations met the *Mendes* "public identification" ownership requirement. *Id.* at 1200. Thus, contrary to Appellants' assertions, the existence of sales or lack thereof does not by itself determine whether a user of a mark has established ownership rights therein. *Compare Marvel Comics Ltd. v. Defiant*, 837 F. Supp. 546, 549 (S.D.N.Y. 1993) (finding announcement of "Plasmer" title to 13 million comic book readers and promotion at annual trade convention sufficient to establish trademark ownership rights, notwithstanding lack of any sales) *with WarnerVision Entm't Inc. v. Empire of Carolina Inc.*, 915 F. Supp. 639, 645-46 (S.D.N.Y. [1996]) (finding toy manufacturer's promotional efforts insufficient to establish priority of use where only a few presentations were made to industry buyers, even though one resulted in a sale to a major toy retailer), *aff'd in part, vacated in part*, 101 F.3d 259 (2d Cir. 1996).[11]

Similarly, not every transport of a good is sufficient to establish ownership rights in a mark. To warrant protection, use of a mark "need not have gained wide public recognition," but "[s]ecret, undisclosed internal shipments are generally inadequate." *Blue Bell, Inc. v. Farah Mfg. Co.*, 508 F.2d 1260, 1265 (5th Cir. 1975). In general, uses that are *de minimis* may not establish trademark ownership rights. *See, e.g., Paramount Pictures Corp. v. White*, 31 U.S.P.Q.2d 1768, 1772-73 (Trademark Tr. & App. Bd. 1994) (finding no bona fide use in ordinary course of trade where mark was affixed to a game consisting of three pieces of paper and distributed for the purpose of promoting musical group).

We find that, under these principles, Darrah's activities under the "Coolmail" mark constitute a "use in commerce" sufficiently public to create ownership rights in the mark.

---

11. Courts applying the "totality of circumstances" approach routinely have found evidence of a few sales of goods to which the mark had been affixed insufficient to establish trademark ownership. For example, in [*Zazu Designs v. L'Oreal, S.A.*, 979 F.2d 499, 503-04 (7th Cir. 1992),] the plaintiff hair salon had sold a few bottles of shampoo bearing the mark "Zazu" both over the counter and mailed over state lines. The court found that such limited sales "neither link the Zazu mark with [the plaintiff's] product in the minds of consumers nor put other producers on notice." *Id.* at 503.

First, the distribution was widespread, and there is evidence that members of the targeted public actually associated the mark Coolmail with the Software to which it was affixed. Darrah made the Software available not merely to a discrete or select group (such as friends and acquaintances, or at a trade show with limited attendance), but to numerous end-users via the Internet. The Software was posted under a filename bearing the "Coolmail" mark on a site accessible to anyone who had access to the Internet. End-users communicated with Darrah regarding the Software by referencing the "Coolmail" mark in their e-mails. Appellants argue that only technically skilled UNIX users made use of the Software, but there is no evidence that they were so few in number to warrant a finding of *de minimis* use.

Third,* the mark served to identify the source of the Software. The "Coolmail" mark appeared in the subject field and in the text of the announcement accompanying each release of the Software, thereby distinguishing the Software from other programs that might perform similar functions available on the Internet or sold in software compilations. The announcements also apparently indicated that Darrah was the "Author/Maintainer of Coolmail" and included his e-mail address. The user manual also indicated that the Software was named "Coolmail." The German company S.u.S.E. was able to locate Darrah in order to request permission to use his Software in its product under the mark "Coolmail." Appellants do not assert that S.u.S.E. was unaware that the Software was called "Coolmail" when it contacted Darrah.

Fourth, other potential users of the mark had notice that the mark was in use in connection with Darrah's Software. . . . Planetary Motion was able to discover that Darrah was using the mark to designate his Software product.

Fifth, the Software was incorporated into several versions of a product that was in fact sold worldwide and specifically attributed ownership of the Software to Darrah under the "Coolmail" mark. Any individual using the S.u.S.E. product, or competitor of S.u.S.E., that wanted to know the source of the program that performed the e-mail notification function, could do so by referring to the user manual accompanying the product. There is no support for the argument that for a trademark in software to be valid, the mark must appear on the box containing the product incorporating it, that the mark must be displayed on the screen when the program is running, or that the software bearing the mark be a selling point for the product into which it is incorporated. There is no requirement that the public come to associate a mark with a product in any particular way or that the public be passive viewers of a mark for a sufficient public association to arise.

Sixth, software is commonly distributed without charge under a GNU General Public License. The sufficiency of use should be determined according to the customary practices of a particular industry. *See* S. Rep. 100-515 at 44 (1988) ("The committee intends that the revised definition of 'use in commerce' . . . be interpreted to mean commercial use *which is typical in a particular industry*.") (emphasis added). That the Software had been distributed pursuant to a GNU General Public License does not defeat trademark ownership, nor does this in any way compel a finding that Darrah abandoned his rights in trademark. Appellants misconstrue the function of a GNU General Public License. Software distributed pursuant to such a license is not necessarily ceded to the public domain and the licensor purports to retain ownership rights, which may or may not include rights to a mark.[16]

---

* *Ed. Note:* The court's opinion proceeds from "First" to "Third" without any intervening paragraph labeled "Second."

16. Because a GNU General Public License requires licensees who wish to copy, distribute, or modify the software to include a copyright notice, the license itself is evidence of Darrah's efforts to control the use of the "CoolMail" mark in connection with the Software.

NOTES AND QUESTIONS

1. *Revisiting the question: When does the Section 45 definition of "use in commerce" apply?* Aycock involves a claim to registered rights, and the court applies the Section 45 definition of use in commerce, producing a result that might seem harsh. *Planetary Motion* involves a claim to unregistered rights, and the court purports to apply the statutory rules, but engages in a "totality of the circumstances" analysis that seems to invite consideration of the equities. If the *Planetary Motion* court simply had parsed the Section 45 definition in conducting its analysis, would the case have come out the same way? If the *Aycock* court had channeled the *Planetary Motion* methodology in its analysis, would the case have come out the same way? Note that in footnote 5, the *Planetary Motion* court asserts that the statutory definition of use in commerce expresses the elements that have been traditionally required for a showing of use at common law. Based on *Aycock* and *Planetary Motion* alone, does the court's assertion appear to be correct? Should rules for actual use be the same for registered and unregistered marks? (In footnote 12, the *Aycock* court suggests that the statutory rules "may be offset by the common-law trademark doctrine.") Should they be the same when the PTO makes an assessment of whether to grant trademark rights as when a court is making that assessment in the context of infringement (whether of registered or unregistered rights)?

2. *"Totality of the circumstances" test.* Planetary Motion adopts the test for use from *Mendes* and suggests that the question of public identification under that test be assessed by evaluating the totality of the circumstances. Some other courts have also adopted the totality of the circumstances test, but have sought to connect it more directly to the Section 45 definition of use in commerce. For example, in *Rearden LLC v. Rearden Commerce, Inc.*, 683 F.3d 1190, 1205-06 (9th Cir. 2012), involving a service mark, a Ninth Circuit panel invoked the totality of the circumstances test and asserted that evidence presented under that test could be relevant to assessing both components of the Section 45 definition—i.e., whether the mark was "used or displayed in the sale or advertising of services," and whether the services were "rendered in commerce." For another example, *see FN Herstal S.A. v. Clyde Armory Inc.*, 838 F.3d 1071 (11th Cir. 2016), in which the mark owner (FN Herstal) had made sales of semi-automatic weapons bearing the mark to the military, but only later had started making sales to law enforcement and civilians. Applying *Planetary Motion*, the court found that the mark owner could rely on the date of the first military sales to establish priority. The sales were sufficiently public because the mark owner received widespread media attention. In addition, the mark owner engaged in extensive advertising and promotional activities in anticipation of the future release of the product to law enforcement personnel and civilians.

In *West Florida Seafood, Inc. v. Jet Restaurants, Inc.*, 31 F.3d 1122, 1125-26 (Fed. Cir. 1994), involving the mark FAST EDDIE's used in connection with restaurant services, the court may have been using a totality of the circumstances approach to use. The court asserted that in analyzing use, "one should look at the evidence as a whole, as if each piece of evidence were part of a puzzle which, when fitted together establishes prior use." Is the "totality of the circumstances" test really a test, or simply a euphemism for the exercise of unfettered (or barely fettered) judicial discretion? What values might guide the court in exercising its discretion? Would you expect other courts to adopt the totality of the circumstances test?

3. *Totality of the circumstances test applied to use in connection with services.* In *Chance v. Pac-Tel Teletrac Inc.*, 242 F.3d 1151 (9th Cir. 2001), the court invoked the "totality of the circumstances" test to assess use of a service mark, and also elaborated on the types of circumstances that might be relevant under that test:

> In applying this approach, the district courts should be guided in their consideration of non-sales activities by factors we have discussed, such as the genuineness and commercial character of the activity, the determination of whether the mark was sufficiently public to identify or distinguish the marked service in an appropriate segment of the public mind as those of the holder of the mark, the scope of the non-sales activity relative to what would be a commercially reasonable attempt to market the service, the degree of ongoing activity of the holder to conduct the business using the mark, the amount of business transacted, and other, similar factors which might distinguish whether a service has actually been "rendered in commerce."

Id. at 1159. Are there some circumstances that are more weighty than others? Does the *Planetary Motion* court give any clues that might help identify these especially relevant circumstances? Does the dictum from *Chance* quoted above do the job? If the totality of the circumstances test had been applied in *Aycock*, when (if ever) would use have occurred? If a manufacturer includes a mark in a tweet, does that constitute use in commerce sufficient to confer rights? *See Play Club by Cipriani*, Case No. D2013-1883 (WIPO 2014).

    4. *"Market penetration" as an alternative to the totality of the circumstances test?* Some courts have incorporated a "market penetration" analysis into their tests for actual use. *Lucent Info. Mgmt., Inc. v. Lucent Techs., Inc.*, 186 F.3d 311 (3d Cir. 1999); *see also Allard Enterprises, Inc. v. Advanced Programming Resources, Inc.*, 146 F.3d 350 (6th Cir. 1998) (appearing to combine a variety of principles, including market penetration, in assessing use). In *Lucent*, the court laid out a four-factor test "to determine whether the market penetration of a trademark in an area is sufficient to warrant protection: (1) the volume of sales of the trademarked product; (2) the growth trends (both positive and negative) in the area; (3) the number of persons actually purchasing the product in relation to the potential number of customers; and (4) the amount of product advertising in the area." 186 F.3d at 317 (quoting *Natural Footwear Ltd. v. Hart, Schaffner & Marx*, 760 F.2d 1383, 1398-99 (3d Cir. 1985)). Market penetration tests derive from cases in which the *geographic* scope of the trademark rights is in question. We deal with these cases in Chapter 6. In such cases, the trademark owner may have established actual use somewhere, but not necessarily in the *place* where the alleged infringer operates. Is the market penetration concept better left for ascertaining the respective geographic extent of uses among competing users who have each established initial actual uses? Is the market penetration test simply a reiteration of the "totality of the circumstances" approach?

    5. *Big player versus small.* Viewed in terms of practical commercial considerations, the "use" requirement can be formidable. If, for example, a local hardware store owner can establish trademark use only after selling thousands of branded hardware items, it may take the owner a considerable length of time to achieve legally effective "use." By contrast, a national hardware chain capable of saturating the market quickly with branded goods might quite easily (and quickly) be able to establish trademark use—and, hence, common law rights. This sort of disparity between large and small businesses is always a matter of concern for trademark law, to the extent that trademark rules may impair market entry by small businesses. How, if at all, should this observation affect the way that courts apply the test for actual use?

    Consider the *Planetary Motion* court's rationale for distinguishing *Heinemann v. General Motors Corp.*, 342 F. Supp. 203 (N.D. Ill. 1972), *aff'd*, 478 F.2d 1405 (7th Cir. 1973). There, Heinemann, an oil company employee who raced cars at county fairs as a hobby, used a mark on his car. Later, an automobile manufacturer independently adopted the same mark for a new car model. The court found that Heinemann had not established rights in the mark prior to the automobile company's doing so. There was evidence that Heinemann was attempting to reserve the mark for later use in connection with an auto repair shop, and (because racing was merely Heinemann's hobby) his usages were deemed sporadic. In *Planetary Motion*, by contrast, there was no evidence that Darrah was attempting to warehouse the mark, and the mark did pertain to Darrah's full-time profession. These distinctions were dispositive, according to the *Planetary Motion* court. Do you agree? Do you think *Aycock* was attempting to warehouse the mark at issue there?

PROBLEM 4-2:   ILLEGAL USES

(1) Professor Janis' Cousin Clem, who recently relocated to Colorado, applies to register HERBAL ACCESS for "retail store services featuring herbs." It turns out that one of the "herbs" sold in Cousin Clem's store is marijuana. Assume that Cousin Clem's marijuana sales are legal in Colorado, but not under federal law. Should the PTO reject Cousin Clem's application on the ground that his use in commerce is not lawful? Would it matter if the specimen of use shows the mark in proximity to a graphic of a green cross, which is associated with the organized medical marijuana industry? Does it make any difference that all of the other herbs sold in Cousin Clem's store are sold legally under federal law? Is it significant that federal law enforcement authorities have indicated that they will limit federal enforcement to activities such as distribution to minors and diversion of marijuana to states where its possession remains illegal? *See In re Morgan Brown*, 123 U.S.P.Q.2d (BNA) 1122 (TTAB 2016); *In re JJ206, LLC*, 120 U.S.P.Q.2d (BNA) 1568 (TTAB 2016). *See also FN Herstal S.A. v. Clyde Armory Inc.*, 838 F.3d 1071 (11th Cir. 2016) (discussing cases that have presented the unlawful use issue); *CreAgri, Inc. v. Usana Health Servs., Inc.*, 474 F.3d 626 (9th Cir. 2007).

(2) Assume that under the regulations of the Iowa State Department of Environmental Resources, beauty shop operators must file documents certifying that they are disposing of "hazardous biological waste" in a prescribed manner. The regulations specify that the certification must be "received by the Department before the beauty shop commences business"; uncertified businesses are subject to closure and fines. Fran opened HIGH PERFORMANCE, a beauty shop, in March 2017. The day after she opened, she mailed her certification to the Department. Unfortunately, due to an unexplained delay in the mails, the Department did not receive her certification until December 2017. Suppose that Fran files an application under Section 1(a) to register HIGH PERFORMANCE for beauty shop services, claiming March 2017 as the date of first use. Should the PTO reject Fran's application on the ground that her use in commerce was not lawful as of March 2017? Should there be a requirement that the PTO show that the violation was substantial and that there is a nexus between the use of the mark and the violation?

PROVING USE IN REGISTRATION PRACTICE

A mark owner filing a Section 1(a) (i.e., use-based) application for registration must include in the application a statement alleging actual use, and must submit a specimen of use. (These submissions are also required, albeit later in the process, for applicants who file intent-to-use applications under Section 1(b), as we will discuss in section C of this chapter.) Specimens are required "because they show the manner in which the mark is seen by the public." TMEP §904 (Oct. 2017). A specimen of a mark that is used with goods "is a label, tag, or container for the goods, or a display associated with the goods." 37 C.F.R. §2.56 (1). A service mark specimen is anything that "show[s] the mark as used in the sale or advertising of the services." 37 C.F.R. §2.56 (2). The specimen may be submitted electronically. TMEP §904.02(a) (Oct. 2017).

The examiner must assess the propriety of these submissions as a routine part of the examination process, and, consequently, many technical questions about actual use may arise. Trademark practitioners involved in the registration process should become familiar with the PTO's views on these questions, which can be found primarily in the TMEP and the decisions of the TTAB. This body of administrative jurisprudence also may be informative for courts deciding questions of actual use in litigation.

Examining Specimens Used on Goods

The affixation requirement. Early trademark cases insisted that actual use of a mark on goods could be evidenced only by a showing that the mark had been placed in direct physical contact with the goods. The Restatement explains this fixation with the affixation requirement:

> The law of trademarks originally recognized as "use" only the direct physical affixation of the designation to the goods marketed by the person claiming trademark rights. A designation that was not physically affixed to the goods could not be protected as a technical "trademark" in an action for trademark infringement. In part the reason was historical, since trademarks developed from medieval production marks that were affixed to goods manufactured by the local guilds. The requirement of physical affixation also served to facilitate proof of use by minimizing disputed issues of fact. A designation that was not protectable as a technical "trademark" because of the affixation requirement, however, could be protected in an action for unfair competition upon proof that it had become associated with the goods or services of the person seeking relief.

Restatement (Third) of Unfair Competition §18 cmt. d (1995) (internal cross-references omitted).

Displays "associated with" goods; website usage. The modern approach is considerably more forgiving, as the language of the Lanham Act definition and PTO regulations reflect. For example, use on a menu or on a point-of-sale display associated with the goods will suffice. *See, e.g., In re Marriott Corp.*, 459 F.2d 525 (C.C.P.A. 1972) (overturning a refusal to register TEEN TWIST for sandwiches, where applicant had used the mark on menus alongside a listing of the product's ingredients and a photo of the product); *cf. In re Kohr Brothers, Inc.*, 121 U.S.P.Q.2d (BNA) 1793 (TTAB 2017) (upholding a refusal to register where the submitted specimen was a small, seemingly temporary sign hung on the wall of a custard stand alongside a business license and health department certificate; this was not a display associated with the goods).

The advent of online commerce presented some challenges in applying these rules. Some older cases involving catalogue specimens of use had seemed to impose a per se requirement that any display must include a photograph of the goods. However, the Federal Circuit rejected any such requirement in more contemporary cases involving website specimens, ruling that a textual description of the goods may suffice where "the actual features or inherent characteristics of the goods are recognizable from the textual description, given that the more standard the product is, the less comprehensive the textual description need be." *In re Sones*, 590 F.3d 1282, 1289 (Fed Cir. 2009). The PTO now takes the view that a web page that displays a product can constitute a "display associated with the goods" if it: "(1) contains a picture or textual description of the identified goods; (2) shows the mark in association with the goods; and (3) provides a means for ordering the identified goods." TMEP §904.03(i) (Oct. 2017); *see also* TMEP §904.03(i)(A)-(D) (Oct. 2017) (providing sample website screenshots and accompanying analysis).

Examining Service Mark Specimens

The "direct association" requirement. The TTAB has traditionally held that a service mark specimen must demonstrate a "direct association" between the services and the mark sought to be registered. *In re Osmotica Holdings Corp.*, 95 U.S.P.Q.2d (BNA) 1666 (TTAB 2010) (website displaying applicant's mark in descriptions of applicant's drug delivery technologies did not establish the requisite direct association between the mark and applicant's consulting services relating to those technologies); *but cf. In re Advertising & Marketing Dev., Inc.*, 821 F.2d 614, 620 (Fed. Cir. 1987) (commenting that the "'direct association' test does not create an additional or more stringent requirement for registration" but rather is implicit in the statutory definition of a mark). Where a specimen shows the mark as used in *advertising* the services—for example, on the applicant's web page—the PTO takes the position that the specimen must contain an explicit reference to the services in order for the direct association requirement to be met. TMEP §1301.04(f)(ii) (Oct. 2017); *In re Florists' Transworld Delivery, Inc.*, 119 U.S.P.Q.2d (BNA) 1056, 1062 (TTAB 2016) (website acceptable as a specimen "if it shows the mark used in advertising the identified services and creates the required direct association by referring to the services and by showing the mark being used to identify and distinguish the services and their source"); TMEP §1301.04(h)(iv)(C) (Oct. 2017) (same). Where the specimen shows the mark as used in the *sale* of the services, no explicit reference to the services is required. "Rather, direct association may be indicated by the context or environment in which the services are rendered, or may be inferred based on the consumer's general knowledge of how certain services are provided or from the consumer's prior experience in receiving the services." TMEP §1301.04(f)(ii) (Oct. 2017); *see also In re WAY Media, Inc.*, 118 U.S.P.Q.2d (BNA) 1697, 1698 (TTAB 2016). For example, a screenshot of a software app that shows the mark as the services are performed by the app is likely to be an acceptable service mark specimen. TMEP §1301.04(h)(iv)(D) (Oct. 2017). For additional examples revealing the PTO's view on analyzing online usages of service marks, *see* TMEP §1301.04(i) (Oct. 2017).

Identifying the services in online settings; distinguishing services from software. In an online environment, where a firm engages its customers through its website software, the specimen (usually a screenshot of the firm's website) might present a question about whether the firm is rendering services or selling software. The answer could affect the actual use determination given that the statutory tests for use on goods and on services differ. The Federal Circuit has suggested that the services vs. software distinction should turn on factors such as whether the software "(1) is simply the conduit or necessary tool useful only to obtain applicant's services; (2) is so inextricably tied to and associated with the service as to have no viable existence apart therefrom; and (3) is neither sold separately from nor has any independent value apart from the services." *Lens.com v. 1-800 Contacts, Inc.*, 686 F.3d 1376 (Fed. Cir. 2012); *see also In re JobDiva, Inc.*, 843 F.3d 936, 941 (Fed. Cir. 2016) (rejecting any bright-line rule that a firm only provides services in the Lanham Act sense where it does something in addition to having its software render services). In *JobDiva*, the applicant operated a subscription-based website that provided an applicant tracking system for recruitment and human resources departments. The TTAB had concluded that *JobDiva* merely provided a software solution for its customers' personnel placement and recruitment needs, rather than providing "personnel placement and recruitment services" as specified in its application for registration. The Federal Circuit vacated and remanded. *Id.* at 942.

Specimens and the Concept of "Failure to Function" as a Mark

When examining an application for evidence of use, the examiner will necessarily consider whether the specimen shows that the mark actually identifies the applicant's goods or services, distinguishes them from those of others, and indicates source, in accord with the definition of a mark in Lanham Act §45. If the specimen fails to do so, the examiner may reject the application because the applied-for subject matter fails to function as a mark. *See* TMEP §1202.17(c) (Oct. 2017) (explaining the rationale for the failure-to-function rejection). For example, suppose the alleged mark is SPECTRUM for switches used in airplane cockpits, and the specimen is a point-of-purchase brochure that includes the phrase "Now with Voltage-Controlled Dimming and a SPECTRUM of Sunlight-Readable Colors." Should the examiner enter a failure-to-function rejection? Would it make a difference if the term "Spectrum" is in a different font and different color from the remainder of the text? *See In re Aerospace Optics Inc.*, 78 U.S.P.Q.2d (BNA) 1861 (TTAB 2006). A failure-to-function rejection is likely if the applied-for mark is deemed to be mere ornamentation, mere informational matter, a background design that does not create a separate commercial impression, or in certain other circumstances. *See* TMEP §904.07(b) (Oct. 2017) (listing these and other examples). The failure-to-function concept may also have roots in the concept of distinctiveness, as we saw in Chapter 2.

2.   Priority of Use

In the *Aycock* opinion, the focus was on whether Mr. Aycock ever established actual use. Determining that he had not, the court ruled that his registration was void *ab initio*. Accordingly, the court did not need to reach the issue of *when* actual use was established as between Mr. Aycock and Airflite, Inc.—that is, the issue of *priority of use*. Disputes about trademark use frequently revolve around questions of priority of use between competing claimants.

As we have seen, determining whether use has occurred is a fact-bound (and, hence, somewhat unpredictable) inquiry. Determining precisely *when* actual use occurred may likewise call for in-depth scrutiny of the facts, even in disputes involving relatively simple businesses. For example, consider the following chronology, in which a pizza restaurant owner *Z* operating in the town of Kalispell (a small town in northern Montana) plans to adopt the service mark MANLY MOOSE PIZZA for retail pizza sales, while rival owner *A* (also doing business in Kalispell) plans to adopt the service mark MACHO MOOSE PIZZA for retail pizza sales:

May 1: Z conceives of a name (MANLY MOOSE PIZZA) for a pizza restaurant.

May 3: Z creates a flyer bearing the MANLY MOOSE PIZZA mark and mails it to himself, intending to use the postmark as evidence of his date of first use.

May 5: Z leases retail space near a high school in Kalispell. The lease agreement specifies that *Z* intends to open a pizza restaurant under the name MANLY MOOSE PIZZA.

May 7: Z reserves the domain name manlymoosepizza.com and hires a designer to begin work on a website. The website is not operational until June.

May 10: Z travels to Alberta, Canada (not that far from Kalispell, at least as Montanans measure mileage), and distributes flyers announcing that MANLY MOOSE PIZZA is "Coming Soon" to the northern Montana/southern Alberta region.

May 13: Z distributes the same flyers around the high school in Kalispell.

May 15: Z orders and receives his first delivery of pizza boxes and napkins, both of which bear the MANLY MOOSE PIZZA mark. *Z* also installs a sign at the restaurant bearing the mark.

May 20: Z makes a token delivery of two pizza boxes (without pizzas in them) to a friend in Kalispell.

May 23: Z makes the first pizzas, packages them in boxes that bear the mark, and delivers them for free to a local social club in Kalispell.

May 24: A, without any prior publicity, sells 80 pizzas under the name MACHO MOOSE PIZZA from his restaurant at a meeting of the Friends of the Bob Marshall Wilderness Area, a volunteer group of several hundred members that regularly meets at *A*'s restaurant.

May 25: Z sells twelve pizzas under the MANLY MOOSE PIZZA name from his restaurant.

May 30: Z has an official grand opening (at which the mayor of Kalispell participates in a ribbon-cutting ceremony), and gives away 150 pizzas.

June 1: Z sells out his entire inventory of 350 pizzas (not surprising—it's the start of rodeo season).

June 5: Z's website becomes operational, and he begins taking orders via the website.

Word travels fast in a small town. Suppose that *A* and *Z* quickly learn of each other's activities and both claim unregistered rights in their respective marks, used in Kalispell. To sort out priority of use, a court would apply the principles that (1) an assertion of common law rights requires evidence of actual use; and (2) as between multiple actual users, the first to adopt and use obtains priority of use. As we have seen from the cases and materials above, a court might apply a totality of the circumstances approach, or might apply a more strict rendition of the Section 45 definition, to determine whether *A*'s May 24 sales constitute actual use of the mark, and whether any of *Z*'s pre-May 24 activities constitute actual use. (There are other potential complications. *See* Problem 4-3 for an exploration of what happens if the marks at issue are not inherently distinctive. *See* Chapter 6 for cases about what happens when the competing claimants for rights are not located in the same geographic region.) *See* Chapter 7 for a discussion of the analysis for determining whether the parties' respective marks are confusingly similar under Section 2(d).

Suppose instead that on June 10, *A* files a use-based application under Section 1(a) to register MACHO MOOSE PIZZA for retail pizza sales on the Principal Register, citing May 24 as the date of first use. In due course, *Z* opposes the registration (under procedures that we will describe in more detail in Chapter 5), asserting that *Z*'s activities prior to May 24 establish that *Z* has priority of use. In determining the priority of use question, the TTAB would start from the proposition that *A* is entitled to priority of use at least as of *A*'s application filing date (*see* Lanham Act §7, which we will discuss in more detail in section C *infra*). The TTAB would then apply the priority of use provision codified in Section 2(d), excerpted below. Note that it requires the TTAB to determine whether MANLY MOOSE PIZZA and MACHO MOOSE PIZZA so resemble one another as to be likely to cause confusion, and it also requires the TTAB to decide whether *Z*'s MANLY MOOSE PIZZA is a mark or trade name "previously used in the United States. . . ." (*See* Chapter 7 for the test for assessing whether the two marks are confusingly similar.) To make that latter determination, the TTAB would presumably apply *Aycock* and its strict approach to the Section 45 definition of use in commerce.

LANHAM ACT

Section 2(d) [15 U.S.C. §1052(d)]

No trademark by which the goods of the applicant may be distinguished from the goods of others shall be refused registration on the principal register on account of its nature unless it—

. . .

(d) Consists of or comprises a mark which so resembles a mark registered in the Patent and Trademark Office, or a mark or trade name previously used in the United States by another and not abandoned, as to be likely, when used on or in connection with the goods of the applicant, to cause confusion, or to cause mistake, or to deceive.

. . .

NOTES AND QUESTIONS

1. *Relative or absolute?*　When courts analyze use in order to determine priority of ownership in a case such as *Z v. A* of the pizza hypothetical, should they assess use against an absolute standard? Or should they rely on relative measures—that is, should the court compare the intensity of A's activities with the intensity of Z's and pick a priority "winner" accordingly? Is it possible that a court could conclude that neither of two competing parties has adequately evidenced actual use? What would be the consequence of such a finding?

   2.   *Scope of use and scope of priority—does use in connection with one set of goods establish priority of use for other types of goods?*   How should courts analyze priority of use disputes where the competing users' goods or services differ? For example, suppose that Z uses MANLY MOOSE for pizzas starting in 2010, and begins using MANLY MOOSE for beer in 2014. However, in 2013, A had already adopted MANLY MOOSE for beer. As between Z and A, who has priority of use? What if another party, W, adopts MANLY MOOSE for wine in 2012?

   3.   *"Analogous" use as a basis for claiming priority.* Under the so-called *Otto Roth* rule, an opposition or cancellation petitioner asserting a Section 2(d) prior use must show "proprietary rights" in the prior used mark. *Otto Roth & Co. v. Universal Foods Corp.*, 640 F.2d 1317, 1320 (C.C.P.A. 1981). In the Section 2(d) context, this notion of "proprietary rights" extends beyond trademark rights. This makes sense; Section 2(d)'s language states that a Section 2(d) argument may be based on a previously registered mark, or on a previously used mark *or trade name*. Indeed, the Federal Circuit has observed that an opposition or cancellation petitioner may base a Section 2(d) argument on "a prior registration, prior trademark or service mark use, prior use as a trade name, prior use analogous to trademark or service mark use, or any other use sufficient to establish proprietary rights." *Herbko Int'l, Inc. v. Kappa Books, Inc.*, 308 F.3d 1156 (Fed. Cir. 2002). *See also L. & J.G. Stickley Inc. v. Cosser*, 81 U.S.P.Q.2d (BNA) 1956, 1966 (TTAB 2007). A "prior use analogous to trademark or service mark use" means (1) "an open and notorious public use"; (2) "directed to the segment of the purchasing public for whom the services are intended"; and (3) carried out "in a manner . . . sufficient to inform or apprise prospective purchasers of the present or future availability of the adopter's service under the mark." *T.A.B. Systems v. Pactel Teletrac*, 77 F.3d 1372, 1376 (Fed. Cir. 1996) (quoting *Computer Food Stores, Inc. v. Corner Store Franchises, Inc.*, 176 U.S.P.Q. (BNA) 535 (TTAB 1973)). The alleged analogous use must (eventually) be followed by an actual use in order to serve as a basis for priority. *Am. Express Co. v. Goetz*, 515 F.3d 156 (2d Cir. 2008); *Westrex Corp. v. New Sensor Corp.*, 83 U.S.P.Q.2d (BNA) 1215, 1218 (TTAB 2007). For example, if a mark is displayed in a television commercial that features a montage of mysterious images without any explanation of the products or services being advertised (say, as a teaser to drive consumers to search online for more information), the commercial might be an example of an analogous use of a mark.

PROBLEM 4-3:   THE USE REQUIREMENT AND MERELY DESCRIPTIVE MARKS

   Implicit in the concept that trademark rights are owned by the first to use the mark is the concept that the use is a use of a symbol that satisfies the other requirements for serving as a mark (including, for example, distinctiveness). This poses no difficulty where the mark at issue is inherently distinctive (such as MANLY MOOSE for pizza sales): Between two users of identical marks on identical goods, the first in time wins priority under Section 2(d). But what of marks that acquire distinctiveness through secondary meaning? Suppose that Z begins selling SLEEK brand bicycle helmets in January 2017, while a competitor, Y, begins using the same term in connection with the same goods in November 2017. Suppose further that the mark is deemed merely descriptive of the goods. How should priority be determined? Strictly by the calendar (so that Z prevails), or by identifying the first user to achieve secondary meaning? If you choose the latter rule, note that it is likely to be difficult to identify a precise date on which a given party has achieved secondary meaning in a mark. Can you propose a refinement that might make the latter rule easier to apply?

PROBLEM 4-4:   TACKING

Problem Statement

Professor Janis' Brother Billy ingeniously parlayed two of his main recreational interests (loud noise and dirt) into a successful business: designing apparel for off-road, rough-terrain motorcycle racers. His company, O'Billy Racing, adopted and used the following "O'" logo in 2007:

In 2010, O'Billy redesigned the logo as follows:

In view of the following Background Readings, assess whether O'Billy can "tack" the use of its current 2010 logo back to the use of its 2007 logo. Should courts develop a different set of tacking rules for marks having a visual element? *See One Indus., LLC v. Jim O'Neal Distrib., Inc.*, 578 F.3d 1154 (9th Cir. 2009).

Background Readings

Courts have permitted tacking in "exceptionally narrow" circumstances. *Brookfield Commc'ns, Inc. v. West Coast Entm't Corp.*, 174 F.3d 1036 (9th Cir. 1999). In general, courts require that the prior mark be the "legal equivalent" of the later mark such that consumers would consider the two to be essentially the same. *Data Concepts, Inc. v. Digital Consulting, Inc.*, 150 F.3d 620, 623 (6th Cir. 1998); *Van Dyne–Crotty, Inc. v. Wear-Guard Corp.*, 926 F.2d 1156, 1159 (Fed. Cir. 1991).

The court in *Brookfield* discussed the rationale for permitting tacking:

> We agree that tacking should be allowed if two marks are so similar that consumers generally would regard them as essentially the same. Where such is the case, the new mark serves the same identificatory function as the old mark. Giving the trademark owner the same rights in the new mark as he has in the old helps to protect source-identifying trademarks from appropriation by competitors and thus furthers the trademark law's objective of reducing the costs that customers incur in shopping and making purchasing decisions. [cit.]
>
> Without tacking, a trademark owner's priority in his mark would be reduced each time he made the slightest alteration to the mark, which would discourage him from altering the mark in response to changing consumer preferences, evolving aesthetic developments, or new advertising and marketing styles. In *Hess's of Allentown, Inc. v. National Bellas Hess, Inc.*, for example, a department store ("Allentown") with trademark rights in the terms "Hess Brothers"

and "Hess" dating from 1899 began promoting itself in 1952 instead as "Hess's," largely because customers and employees commonly referred to the store as "Hess's" rather than "Hess Brothers" or "Hess." *See* 169 U.S.P.Q. 673, 674-75, 1971 WL 16482 (T.T.A.B. 1971). Another department store ("Bellas") first used "Hess" in its mark around 1932. In light of the fact that Allentown first used "Hess's" after Bellas commenced using "Hess," Bellas would have priority on the basis of the actual first use dates of those two marks. Even though Allentown had acquired over a half-century's worth of goodwill in the essentially identical marks "Hess" and "Hess Brothers," Allentown no longer had trademark rights in those terms because it had ceased using those marks when it adopted "Hess's." Nevertheless, the Trademark Board allowed the owner of "Hess's" to tack his first use date of "Hess Brothers" and "Hess" onto "Hess's" since those terms were viewed as identical by the public. *See id*. at 677.

The standard for "tacking," however, is exceedingly strict: "The marks must create the *same, continuing commercial impression*, and the later mark should not materially differ from or alter the character of the mark attempted to be tacked." *Van Dyne–Crotty*, 926 F.2d at 1159 (emphasis added) (citations and quotation marks omitted). In other words, "the previously used mark must be the *legal equivalent* of the mark in question or indistinguishable therefrom, and the consumer should consider both as the same mark." *Id*. (emphasis added); *see also Data Concepts*, 150 F.3d at 623 (adopting the *Van Dyne–Crotty* test). This standard is considerably higher than the standard for "likelihood of confusion". . . .

The Federal Circuit, for example, concluded that priority in "CLOTHES THAT WORK. FOR THE WORK YOU DO" could not be tacked onto "CLOTHES THAT WORK." *See Van Dyne–Crotty*, 926 F.2d at 1160 (holding that the shorter phrase was *not* the legal equivalent of the longer mark). The Sixth Circuit held that "DCI" and "dci" were too dissimilar to support tacking. *See Data Concepts*, 150 F.3d at 623-24. And the Trademark Board has rejected tacking in a case involving "American Mobilphone" with a star and stripe design and "American Mobilphone Paging" with the identical design, *see American Paging, Inc. v. American Mobilphone, Inc.*, 13 U.S.P.Q.2d 2036, 1989 WL 274416 (T.T.A.B. 1989), *aff'd*, 923 F.2d 869, 17 U.S.P.Q.2d 1726 (Fed. Cir. 1990), as well as in a case involving "PRO-CUTS" and "PRO-KUT," *see Pro-Cuts v. Schilz-Price Enterprises*, 27 U.S.P.Q.2d 1224, 1227, 1993 WL 266611 (T.T.A.B. 1993).

Brookfield, 174 F.3d at 1048-49 (refusing to permit MOVIEBUFF.COM to be tacked to THE MOVIE BUFF'S MOVIE STORE).

The commercial impression inquiry carried out in the course of the tacking analysis is to be decided by the fact finder. In 2015, the U.S. Supreme Court in *Hana Financial, Inc. v. Hana Bank*, 135 S. Ct. 907, 911 (2015), held that "application of a test that relies upon an ordinary consumer's understanding of the impression that a mark conveys falls comfortably within the ken of a jury." The Court reasoned that while the commercial impression test might be characterized as a mixed question of law and fact, such questions were usually reserved for juries. In addition, tacking cases are likely to be fact-intensive; they are unlikely to place the jury in the position of making general statements about the overarching legal standard for tacking. Finally, the argument that juries would behave unpredictably was not persuasive, given that the same argument could be made about the use of the jury in any setting. *See also Jack Wolfskin Ausrustrung fur Draussen GmbH & Co. v. New Millenium Sports, S.L.U.*, 797 F.3d 1363 (Fed. Cir. 2015) (applying the "continuing commercial impression" test).

In *Hana Financial*, a California firm (Hana Financial) adopted and used the mark HANA FINANCIAL for financial services in the United States in 1995. Hana Bank, based in Korea, had begun marketing its services to Korean expatriates in the United States in 1994 using a logo mark accompanied by "Hana Bank" rendered in Korean:

In 2002, Hana Bank began to use a mark composed of the same logo, accompanied by "Hana Bank" in English:

The District Court had instructed the jury on the commercial impression test for tacking, and the jury had rendered a verdict for the bank, apparently accepting the argument that the bank should be entitled to tack back to the 1994 use. Both the Ninth Circuit and Supreme Court affirmed.

The Court's ruling may have implications for a more significant question: whether the likelihood-of-confusion inquiry should be deemed a question of law or a question of fact, because the lower courts have treated tacking and likelihood of confusion as roughly analogous when considering the question of fact/question of law issue. *Hana Financial, Inc. v. Hana Bank*, 735 F.3d 1158, 1164 n.5 (9th Cir. 2014) (Ninth Circuit treated tacking as a question of fact, consistent with its treatment of likelihood of confusion); *Van Dyne-Crotty, Inc. v. Wear-Guard Corp.*, 926 F.2d 1156, 1159 (Fed. Cir. 1991) (Federal Circuit treated tacking as a question of law). However, the Court in *Hana* made no mention of these potential implications.

C.   CONSTRUCTIVE USE AS A BASIS FOR ESTABLISHING RIGHTS

As the materials in the preceding section reflect, in many circumstances, actual use is a burdensome precondition for acquiring trademark rights. That fact was recognized in U.S. law long ago, but it took a good deal of time before a consensus emerged on how to deal with the use requirement in a way that lightened the burden while preserving the use requirement as a guard against the warehousing of marks.

Prior to the 1989 reform legislation, the doctrine of "token use" emerged as one effort to strike an appropriate balance. Under that doctrine, mere token use—use at a level insufficient to qualify as actual use under the then-existing standards—was deemed acceptable to establish rights to file an application for registration. The token use doctrine was commendable as a pragmatic response, but questionable conceptually in a use-based trademark regime (especially in a system in which registration merely confirms the existence of common law rights).

Ultimately, Congress intervened, in the Trademark Law Revision Act (TLRA) of 1988, effective in 1989. In the TLRA, Congress changed the rules for use in several ways that are significant to the present discussion. First, Congress recognized a concept of "constructive use" for registration purposes, adding provisions enabling applicants to file for registration based on an "intent to use" a mark in commerce and providing that registration would be contingent on the "intent to use" (ITU) maturing into actual use. This was a dramatic conceptual change to U.S. trademark law. Additionally, having softened the use regime by the addition of the ITU provisions, Congress repudiated the doctrine of token use and tightened the definition of actual use, in the manner described *supra* in section B of this chapter. The following legislative history excerpt gives the Senate's version of the rationales for these statutory changes.

S. REP. NO. 100-515

100th Cong. 2d Sess., 4-6 (1988)

INTENT TO USE

S.1883 will improve the federal trademark registration system by eliminating the requirement that U.S. citizens and businesses, unlike their foreign counterparts, must use a mark in commerce before they can file an application to register it. The Lanham Act currently requires that a U.S. business or individual seeking to register a trademark in the United States first make use of the mark in interstate commerce before it can apply for registration.

Under current law, a trademark is considered to have been used when it is affixed to the product, its packaging, labels or hang tags and the product is sold or shipped in commerce. Similarly, a service mark is considered to have been used when the services are performed or advertised in commerce, such as by opening a hotel or a restaurant.

This requirement unfairly discriminates against U.S. citizens, as compared to foreign citizens, puts significant legal risks on the introduction of new products and services, and gives preference to certain industries over others, frequently disadvantaging small companies and individuals.

Today, the United States is the only developed country that requires use of a mark before an application for registration may be filed. Other countries, whose trademark laws are based on the common-law concept that rights in a mark are acquired by use, decided long ago that it is not in the interests of the business community to force businesspeople to use a mark before its protection could be assured. In 1938, the United Kingdom converted to an intent-to-use system, and Canada converted in 1954.

This disparity between U.S. law and that of most other countries results in foreign applicants having an advantage over U.S. applicants in obtaining trademark registration rights. U.S. treaty obligations, reflected in Section 44 of the Lanham Act, require that foreign applicants, relying upon a home country registration, may register in the United States, notwithstanding their lack of use of the mark anywhere in the world. Moreover, foreign applicants can obtain a filing priority in the United States corresponding to the date they file their home application. Under current interpretations, this means that while a U.S. applicant is required to use its mark before applying, foreign nationals can apply for and obtain a U.S. registration without first using a mark in the United States or anywhere else.

While it is impossible to measure the extent to which Americans are disadvantaged by the current system, the frequency with which foreign nationals avail themselves of the preference given them in Section 44 is noteworthy. As of March 1, 1988, approximately 7 percent, roughly 48,200, of the active applications and registrations in the U.S. Patent and Trademark Office claimed the benefits of Section 44. In addition, since 1983 the PTO has issued more than 17,700 Section 44 registrations to foreigners.

The Lanham Act's pre-application use requirement also creates unnecessary legal uncertainty for a U.S. business planning to introduce products or services into the marketplace. It simply has no assurance that after selecting and adopting a mark, and possibly making a sizable investment in packaging, advertising and marketing, it will not learn that its use of the mark infringes the rights another acquired through earlier use. In an age of national, if not global, marketing, this has a chilling effect on business investment. This effect is not merely theoretical, but is real. And it can be costly: Marketing a new product domestically often exceeds $30 million for a large company and can consume the life-savings of an individual or small entrepreneur.

Partially in recognition of the difficulties companies face in launching new products and services, and the sizable investments that may be at stake, regardless of a company's or individual's resources, the courts have sanctioned the practice of "token use." Token use is a contrived and commercially transparent practice—nothing more than a legal fiction. At the same time, token use is essential under current law because it recognizes present day marketing costs and realities; it reduces some of the legal and economic risks associated with entering the marketplace; and it nominally achieves the threshold "use" required to apply for federal registration and the creation of trademark rights in advance of commercial use.

Unfortunately, token use is not available to all businesses and industries. For example, it is virtually impossible to make token use of a trademark on a large or expensive product such as an airplane. The same is true for service industries (that is, hotels, restaurants, and banks) prior to opening for business. Similarly, it is difficult for small business and individuals to avail themselves of token use because they frequently lack the resources or the knowledge to engage in the practice. Token use is also troublesome for another reason. It allows companies to obtain registration based on minimal use. Often these companies change their marketing plans and subsequently do not make commercial use. The result is that the trademark register is clogged with unused marks, making the clearance of new marks more difficult and discouraging others from adopting and using marks which should otherwise be available.

Despite its numerous virtues, a registration system based on intent also carries some potential for abuse. A single business or individual might, for instance, attempt to monopolize a vast number of potential marks on the basis of a mere statement of intent to use the marks in the future. To minimize such risks, S.1883 requires the specified intent to be bona fide. This bona fide requirement focuses on an objective good-faith test to establish that the intent is genuine.

S.1883 addresses these problems and increases the integrity of the federal trademark registration system through the creation of a dual application system. It gives all applicants the choice of applying to register marks on the principal register on the basis of pre-application use in commerce, as they do now, or on the basis of a bona fide intention to use the mark in commerce. Since token use becomes unnecessary and inappropriate under the intent-to-use application system proposed by S.1883, the definition of "use in commerce" in Section 45 of the Act is strengthened to reflect this significant change in the law.

1.   Establishing Intent to Use

Under post-1988 law, applicants may now file applications for registration on the Principal Register based on a bona fide intent to use the mark (Lanham Act §1(b)), subject to the requirement to show actual use within a specified time after allowance (Lanham Act §1(d)).

LANHAM ACT
Section 1 [15 U.S.C. §1051]

. . .

(b) Application for bona fide intention to use trademark

(1) A person who has a bona fide intention, under circumstances showing the good faith of such person, to use a trademark in commerce may request registration of its trademark on the principal register hereby established by paying the prescribed fee and

filing in the Patent and Trademark Office an application and a verified statement, in such form as may be prescribed by the Director.

(2) The application shall include specification of the applicant's domicile and citizenship, the goods in connection with which the applicant has a bona fide intention to use the mark, and a drawing of the mark.

(3) The statement shall be verified by the applicant and specify—

(A) that the person making the verification believes that he or she, or the juristic person in whose behalf he or she makes the verification, to be entitled to use the mark in commerce;

(B) the applicant's bona fide intention to use the mark in commerce;

(C) that, to the best of the verifier's knowledge and belief, the facts recited in the application are accurate; and

(D) that, to the best of the verifier's knowledge and belief, no other person has the right to use such mark in commerce either in the identical form thereof or in such near resemblance thereto as to be likely, when used on or in connection with the goods of such other person, to cause confusion, or to cause mistake, or to deceive. Except for applications filed pursuant to section 44 [15 U.S.C. §1126], no mark shall be registered until the applicant has met the requirements of subsections (c) and (d) of this section.

(4) The applicant shall comply with such rules or regulations as may be prescribed by the Director. The Director shall promulgate rules prescribing the requirements for the application and for obtaining a filing date herein.

. . .

(d) Verified statement that trademark is used in commerce

(1) Within six months after the date on which the notice of allowance with respect to a mark is issued under section 13(b)(2) [15 U.S.C. §1063(b)(2)] to an applicant under subsection (b) of this section, the applicant shall file in the Patent and Trademark Office, together with such number of specimens or facsimiles of the mark as used in commerce as may be required by the Director and payment of the prescribed fee, a verified statement that the mark is in use in commerce and specifying the date of the applicant's first use of the mark in commerce and those goods or services specified in the notice of allowance on or in connection with which the mark is used in commerce. Subject to examination and acceptance of the statement of use, the mark shall be registered in the Patent and Trademark Office, a certificate of registration shall be issued for those goods or services recited in the statement of use for which the mark is entitled to registration, and notice of registration shall be published in the Official Gazette of the Patent and Trademark Office. Such examination may include an examination of the factors set forth in subsections (a) through (e) of section 2 [15 U.S.C. §1052]. The notice of registration shall specify the goods or services for which the mark is registered.

(2) The Director shall extend, for one additional 6-month period, the time for filing the statement of use under paragraph (1), upon written request of the applicant before the expiration of the 6-month period provided in paragraph (1). In addition to an extension under the preceding sentence, the Director may, upon a showing of good cause by the applicant, further extend the time for filing the statement of use under paragraph (1) for periods aggregating not more than 24 months, pursuant to written request of the applicant made before the expiration of the last extension granted under this paragraph. Any request for an extension under this paragraph shall be accompanied by a verified statement that the applicant has a continued bona fide intention to use the mark in commerce and specifying those goods or services identified in the notice of allowance on or in connection with which the applicant has a continued bona fide intention to use the

mark in commerce. Any request for an extension under this paragraph shall be accompanied by payment of the prescribed fee. The Director shall issue regulations setting forth guidelines for determining what constitutes good cause for purposes of this paragraph.

(3) The Director shall notify any applicant who files a statement of use of the acceptance or refusal thereof and, if the statement of use is refused, the reasons for the refusal. An applicant may amend the statement of use.

(4) The failure to timely file a verified statement of use under paragraph (1) or an extension request under paragraph (2) shall result in abandonment of the application, unless it can be shown to the satisfaction of the Director that the delay in responding was unintentional, in which case the time for filing may be extended, but for a period not to exceed the period specified in paragraphs (1) and (2) for filing a statement of use.

M.Z. BERGER & CO., INC. v. SWATCH AG

787 F.3d 1368 (Fed. Cir. 2015)

CHEN, Circuit Judge:

I. BACKGROUND

Berger is a business that manufactures, imports, and sells watches, clocks, and personal care products. On July 5, 2007, it filed an intent-to-use application at the Patent and Trademark Office (PTO), seeking to register the mark "iWatch" for over thirty different goods, each of which belongs to one of three general categories: watches, clocks, and goods related to watches and/or clocks (e.g., clock dials, watch bands, and watch straps).

The application included a declaration which states that Berger has "a bona fide intention to use or use through [Berger's] related company or licensee the mark in commerce on or in connection with the identified goods and/or services."

The PTO approved the application for publication on May 21, 2008. On October 22, 2008, Swatch AG (Swatch) filed a Notice of Opposition on the basis that "iWatch" is confusingly similar to its mark, "Swatch." Swatch later added a claim opposing the mark on ground that Berger lacked a bona fide intent to use the mark in commerce at the time Berger filed the application.

The Board assessed whether Berger had the requisite intent to use the iWatch mark by separately considering each of the three general categories of goods. [With respect to Berger's intent to use the iWatch mark on two of the categories, clocks and goods related to watches/clocks, the Board concluded that Berger lacked the requisite intent. Berger's owner and CEO, Bernard Mermelstein, testified that Berger never intended for the mark to be used for any goods other than watches, and Berger's paralegal testified that the related goods were listed merely to "leave all doors open."]

With respect to . . . watches, the Board also concluded that Berger lacked a genuine plan to commercialize the iWatch mark on such goods. The Board considered the documentary evidence of record but found that such evidence did not demonstrate intent because the documents related solely to prosecution of the trademark application. [The documents consisted of: (i) a trademark search performed by the paralegal; (ii) an internal email describing the substance of a discussion between the paralegal with the trademark examining attorney concerning the application; and (iii) a series of internal emails forwarding images of watches and a clock bearing the iWatch mark, which were apparently made in response to the examiner's request for additional information about how Berger planned to use the mark.] As for the testimonial evidence presented by Berger, the Board found that Berger's employees failed to tell a consistent story about the company's intent at the time the application was filed. [While some Berger employees testified that the images of the iWatch mark were from pictures of actual mockups, Mermelstein testified that no such mockups were made. Moreover, Berger's vice president of merchandising, Brenda Russo, testified about a conversation with a buyer in which she told the buyer that the watch would have interactive technological features, but Mermelstein testified that no conversations with any buyers took place, and Berger had told the PTO that watches bearing the iWatch mark would not have interactive features. In addition, Mermelstein testified that, as of 2010, three years after the application was filed, Berger had yet to figure out what type of watch it intended to sell with the iWatch mark, or even whether such a watch would have any particular features.] The Board lastly considered the company's long history in the watch business, but found that Berger's inaction with respect to a potential iWatch product diminished the value of such evidence. [In particular, Berger employees testified they had not previously made a watch with technological features, and admitted they never took any step toward developing any such features, either contemporaneous with the filing of the application or in the eighteen months thereafter.]

. . . Berger appealed the Board's decision to sustain the opposition. . . .

II. DISCUSSION

. . .

[The court determined that a lack of bona fide intent is a proper statutory ground on which to challenge a trademark application. The court then turned to the question of what "bona fide intention" means under Section 1(b) of the Lanham Act.]

There is no statutory definition of the term "bona fide," but the language is clear on its face that an applicant's intent must be "under circumstances showing the good faith of such person." *Id.* The reference to "circumstances showing the good faith" strongly suggests that the applicant's intent must be demonstrable and more than a mere subjective belief. Both the PTO and the leading treatise on trademark law have arrived at this same understanding. *See Lane*, 33 U.S.P.Q.2d at 1355; 3 *McCarthy on Trademarks* §19.14, at 19.48 ("Congress did not intend the issue to be resolved simply by an officer of the applicant later testifying, 'Yes, indeed, at the time we filed that application, I did truly intend to use the mark at some time in the future.'").

This interpretation is confirmed by the legislative history, where Congress made clear that whether an applicant's intent is "bona fide" should be assessed on an objective basis:

> Although "bona fide" is an accepted legal term, it can be read broadly or narrowly, subjectively or objectively, by a court or the Patent and Trademark Office. In connection with this bill, *"bona fide" should be read to mean a fair, objective determination of the applicant's intent* based on all the circumstances.

Senate Report at 24 (emphasis added); *see also id.* at 23 ("Bona fide intent is measured by objective factors."); House Report at 8-9 ("The use of the term 'bona fide' is meant to . . . require, based on an objective view of the circumstances, a good faith intention to eventually use the mark in a real and legitimate commercial sense."). In addition, an applicant's intent must reflect an intention to use the mark consistent with the Lanham Act's definition of "use in commerce":

> [T]he bona fide use of a mark in the ordinary course of trade, and not made merely to reserve a right in a mark.

15 U.S.C. §1127; *see also* Senate Report at 24-25 (quoting the definition). The applicant's intention to use the mark in commerce must have been "firm." Senate Report at 24.

Neither the statute nor the legislative history indicates the specific quantum or type of objective evidence required to meet the bar. Indeed, Congress expressly rejected inclusion of a statutory definition for "bona fide" in order to preserve "the flexibility which is vital to the proper operation of the trademark registration system." *Id.*[5]

Accordingly, we hold that whether an applicant had a "bona fide intent" to use the mark in commerce at the time of the application requires objective evidence of intent. 15 U.S.C. §1051(b)(1). Although the evidentiary bar is not high, the circumstances must indicate that the applicant's intent to use the mark was firm and not merely intent to reserve a right in the mark. *See id.* §1127; *see also* Senate Report at 24-25. The Board may make such determinations on a case-by-case basis considering the totality of the circumstances.

III. M.Z. BERGER'S APPEAL

A

Berger argues that it satisfied the minimal standard for intent, and that the Board improperly discounted Berger's evidence. Berger's arguments hinge on its belief that the Board should have found the intent requirement satisfied because Berger offered *some* objective evidence in support of its position. Viewed in isolation, the evidence Berger prefers to focus on could perhaps lead a reasonable fact-finder to conclude there was bona fide intent. As discussed above, however, all circumstances regarding an applicant's bona fide intent must be considered, including those facts that would tend to disprove that Berger had the requisite intent. 15 U.S.C. §1051(b)(1); *see also Lane*, 33 U.S.P.Q.2d at 1353 ("[W]hether an applicant has a bona fide intention . . . must be an objective determination based on *all* the circumstances." (emphasis added)).

Here, viewing the evidence as a whole, we find that substantial evidence supports the Board's conclusion. First, we agree with the Board that the documentary evidence offered by Berger appears to relate only to the prosecution of the trademark application. [The Board had cited *Research in Motion Ltd. v. NBOR Corp.*, 92 U.S.P.Q.2d (BNA) 1926, 1931 (T.T.A.B. 2009) ("If the filing and prosecution of a trademark application constituted a bona fide intent to use a mark, then in effect, lack of a bona fide intent to use would never be a ground for opposition or cancellation, since an *inter partes* proceeding can only be brought if the defendant has filed an application.").] The paralegal who performed the trademark search testified that such searches are routinely conducted before Berger files a trademark so that Berger does not waste time filing an application on an unavailable mark. It is undisputed that the internal email relaying the substance of a discussion with the trademark examining attorney also relates to the application. The other internal emails, which forwarded the images of two watches and a clock bearing the mark, were undisputedly submitted to the PTO in response to the trademark examining attorney's request for documents showing how the mark would be used.

Faced with conflicting statements from Berger witnesses about whether the images were created for prosecution or for business reasons evidencing intent, the Board exercised

---

5. The PTO has promulgated a rule specifying that an applicant's ongoing efforts to make use of a mark "may include product or service research or development, market research, manufacturing activities, promotional activities, steps to acquire distributors, steps to obtain governmental approval, or other similar activities." 37 C.F.R. §2.89(d). Although this rule relates to the required showing of "good cause" for an extension to file a statement of use, i.e., at a time after the initial filing, such evidence may also indicate sources of objective evidence of an applicant's bona fide intent to use the mark in commerce.

its discretion in crediting the testimony of Mr. Mermelstein, Berger's Rule 30(b)(6) witness, over that of other Berger employees. . . . We defer to the Board's determination of the weight and credibility of such evidence. [cit.] Having found that the documentary evidence was generated in relation to the trademark application, the Board reasonably determined that such images were likely created with an intention to advance the prosecution of the trademark application rather than an intention to move forward on an actual product in commerce.

> . . .

With respect to watches, the Board considered conflicting testimony about Berger's alleged meeting with a buyer, as well as whether the watch would be technological in nature. The Board was within its discretion to disagree with Berger's bottom-line position that it possessed a bona fide intent, given the inability of the Berger witnesses to pull together a consistent story on a number of issues, e.g., would the watch be technological, did actual physical samples exist, were potential customers ever consulted. Critically, Mr. Mermelstein all but conceded that Berger had not yet made a firm decision to use the mark in commerce at the time of its application. ("[I]f [Berger] decided to do a—either a technology watch or information watch or something that would have that type of characteristics that [iWatch] would be a good mark for it."). *See, e.g., Research in Motion,* 92 U.S.P.Q.2d at 1931 (applicant's stated belief that the mark would be "a good mark for future use" does not establish a bona fide intent to use).

We also find unavailing Berger's contention that the Board ignored Berger's history in the watch industry. The Board did consider Berger's past but noted that even though the iWatch mark was allegedly to be used with a "smart" watch, Berger had never made such a watch and took no steps following the application to develop such a watch. We find no error with the Board's determination that there was no nexus between Berger's general capacity to produce watches and the capacity required to produce a "smart" watch.

Ultimately, we find that the Board properly exercised its judgment as the trier of fact in assessing the evidence and concluding that Berger did not have a bona fide intent to use the mark at the time of its application. Berger's contention that the Board "missed the forest for the trees" by systematically discrediting each piece of evidence is misplaced. Quite to the contrary, the Board's opinion reflects that it carefully considered Berger's evidence and understandably found that Berger lacked "bona fide" intent to use the iWatch mark on the recited goods at the time of the application was filed.

The bar for showing a bona fide intent is not high. But in our view, considering the inconsistent testimony offered by Berger employees and the general lack of documentary support, substantial evidence supports the Board's conclusion that Berger's intent at the time of the application was merely to reserve a right in the mark, and not a bona fide intent to use the mark in commerce.

B

Berger also argues that the Board applied the wrong legal standard for bona fide intent, "because it insisted upon evidence that [Berger] had taken steps to promote, develop and market the iWatch mark at the time that it filed its original application." Berger argues that the Board's emphasis on objective evidence conflicts with the application and registration steps outlined in the PTO's administrative review process and regulations. In other words, Berger contends the Board erred by applying a more stringent threshold for bona fide intent than required by statute or by the PTO's regulations and procedures.

We disagree. Nowhere did the Board state that the applicable standard requires an applicant to have actually promoted, developed, and marketed the mark at the time of the application. Nor did the Board state that it applied such a standard. To the contrary, the

Board's opinion reflects that it reached its conclusions by considering all the relevant facts and circumstances, including those that indicated Berger lacked intent. This is indeed the proper inquiry under the Lanham Act. 15 U.S.C. §1051(b)(1) (intent to use must be "under circumstances showing the good faith of such person").

We also find that the Board's opinion is not inconsistent with PTO practice. The PTO is within its discretion to allow intent-to-use applications to proceed, at the time of filing, upon only a verified statement of bona fide intent to use. *See id.* §1051(b)(3)(B). However, the agency has the statutory authority to seek further evidence of the applicant's "bona fide" intent. *See id.* §1051(b)(1). Indeed, not only did the agency contemplate that an applicant's intent to use may be at issue in *inter partes* proceedings, but it reserved the right to make its own inquiry into the issue under appropriate circumstances:

> Generally, the applicant's sworn statement of a bona fide intention to use the mark in commerce will be sufficient evidence of good faith in the ex parte context. Consideration of issues related to good faith may arise in an inter partes proceeding, but the USPTO will not make an inquiry in an ex parte proceeding unless evidence of record clearly indicates that the applicant does not have a bona fide intention to use the mark in commerce.

Trademark Manual of Examining Procedure (TMEP) §1101.

We find that the Board did not err in its application of the standard for bona fide intent. As discussed *supra*, whether an applicant has a bona fide intent to use a mark in commerce is an objective inquiry based on the totality of the circumstances. The Board conducted such an inquiry.

[*Affirmed.*]

NOTES AND QUESTIONS

1. *Judicial role in defining bona fide intention and good faith.* As *Berger* reflects, it is largely up to the courts (and the TTAB) to elaborate on the concepts of bona fide intention and good faith. *See* United States Trademark Association, Trademark Law Revision Act of 1988 43 (1989) (comment on Section 1(b)) ("The term 'bona fide' is not defined in the Act because of the impossibility of identifying every factor that might be determinative of whether an applicant's intent is indeed bona fide at every stage of the registration process."). The legislative history does list scenarios in which bona fide intention may be called into doubt, including the following: filing many ITU applications for the same mark on a large number of products; filing many ITU applications for numerous marks for use on the same product; and repeatedly refiling ITUs to replace prior ITUs that have lapsed. S. Rep. No. 100-515, at 23-24 (1988). Notably, however, Congress rejected any flat numerical limit on the number of ITUs that a party could file for a single product or product line. S. Rep. No. 100-515, at 25. Does this leave too much discretion to the courts (and the TTAB)? Might it mean that some firms will benefit from the exercise of that discretion by getting away with at least a limited form of trademark hoarding? On the other hand, does *Berger* illustrate that where a court perceives strong evidence of bad faith, the court might exercise its discretion to require a showing of something akin to actual use?

2. *Corroborating bona fide intent to use.* If you were counseling an ITU applicant, what are some examples of documentary evidence that you would regard as sufficient to corroborate an intent to use? If an ITU applicant fails to produce corroborating documents, should the PTO rule that a prima facie case of no bona fide intent has been made out, such that the applicant must come forward with evidence explaining the lack of corroboration? *Spirits International B.V. v. S.S. Taris Zeytin Ve Zeytinyagi Tarim Satis Kooperatifleri Birligi*, 99 U.S.P.Q.2d (BNA) 1545 (TTAB 2011) (adopting this rule). Does the rule from *Spirits* reflect a suspicion that the ITU provisions may be too generous to applicants?

3. *Analyzing distinctiveness in the absence of use.* When an applicant files an ITU application, the trademark examiner may potentially examine the application twice: once when the applicant initially files, and again when the applicant perfects the ITU application by filing a statement of use (15 U.S.C. §1051(d)). In the initial examination stage, the examiner "must raise all possible issues." TMEP §1102.

Suppose that an applicant files an ITU application and, in the initial examination stage, the examiner determines that the mark is merely descriptive of the underlying goods or services. Assuming that the mark is not yet in use, the applicant would have no secondary meaning evidence to submit in response to the rejection, unless, perhaps, the applicant is already using the mark on other products. *See* TMEP §1212.09(a) (discussing proof by use on other goods). Should the ITU applicant be entitled to suspend the examination until the applicant perfects the ITU by filing an amendment or statement of use? *See In re Am. Psychological Ass'n*, 39 U.S.P.Q.2d (BNA) 1467 (Comm'r Pat. & Trademarks 1996) (refusing applicant's request to suspend examination).

4. *The rule against assigning ITU applications.* When Congress introduced the concept that constructive use could be a basis for a Lanham Act application for registration, it also amended the rules for assigning rights in applications. In particular, Congress prohibited applicants from assigning ITU applications prior to the filing of a verified statement of use under Section 1(d), "except for an assignment to a successor to the business of the applicant, or a portion thereof, to which the mark pertains, if that business in ongoing and existing." Lanham Act §10(a)(1). Why might Congress have introduced this prohibition?

5. *The future of the ITU system.* Do you agree with the following proposals?

> [P]erhaps it is now time to jump off the fence Congress has been straddling since 1988 and allow for registration *before* actual use of the mark, as is done in many foreign nations. A party could still forfeit that registration for failure to use after a specified period of time, if so challenged by another user, but until such a challenge, the party would have all the rights of a trademark registrant as provided by the Lanham Act. Such a change would eliminate the need for the evaluation of the applicant's statement of use and for the second examination of the mark itself.
>
> Congress should also consider statutorily eliminating or limiting the "use analogous to trademark use" doctrine, which allows one to oppose a registration based not on actual use before the application, but only on "use analogous" to such use. Perhaps it would make more sense to create a system where the first to file has priority, regardless of any promotional or other activities of another.
>
> Finally, Congress should consider providing some way in which an ITU applicant can establish its bona fide intention to use so that it will not be subject to easy challenges by opposers looking for a way to delay the ITU process. For example, Congress could impose on an opposer the burden of proving bad faith on the part of the applicant, rather than forcing the applicant to prove its own good faith.

Amy B. Cohen, *Intent to Use: A Failed Experiment?*, 35 U.S.F. L. Rev. 683, 724-25 (2001) (footnote omitted).

For other critiques, *see, e.g.*, Traci L. Jones, *Remedy Holes and Bottomless Rights: A Critique of the Intent-to-Use System of Trademark Registration*, 59 Law & Contemp. Probs. 159 (1996); Stephen L. Carter, *The Trouble with Trademark*, 99 Yale L.J. 759 (1990).

2.   Constructive Use Priority

The opportunity to use constructive use as a basis for filing an application for registration would mean little if the ITU applicant could not claim priority against other mark claimants based on the ITU filing. Sections 1(b) and 7(c), taken together, provide that when an applicant files an application stating that the applicant has a bona fide intent to use the mark, the mark is deemed to be in use as of the application filing date (a concept of "constructive use priority"). As the materials below indicate, constructive use priority introduces greater complexity into the U.S. trademark system because it opens up the possibility of priority contests in which some of the claimants are relying on actual use and others on constructive use.

LANHAM ACT

Section 7(c) [15 U.S.C. §1057(c)]

Contingent on the registration of a mark on the principal register provided by this Act, the filing of the application to register such mark shall constitute constructive use of the mark, conferring a right of priority, nationwide in effect, on or in connection with the goods or services specified in the registration against any other person except for a person whose mark has not been abandoned and who, prior to such filing—

(1) has used the mark;

(2) has filed an application to register the mark which is pending or has resulted in registration of the mark; or

(3) has filed a foreign application to register the mark on the basis of which he or she has acquired a right of priority, and timely files an application under section 44(d) [15 U.S.C. §1126(d)] to register the mark which is pending or has resulted in registration of the mark.

NOTES AND QUESTIONS

1. *Derogating from actual use.* Does the concept of constructive use priority as embodied in Section 7(c) suggest that the modern U.S. trademark system has broken radically from its traditional insistence on actual use as a basis for rights? Or only incrementally? Is the departure wise in view of the policy justifications that traditionally underlay the actual use requirement?

2. *Section 7(c) priority in PTO proceedings.*   The following chronologies illustrate the use of constructive use priority in PTO proceedings.

- "defensive" use of constructive use priority by an ITU applicant:

  A files ITU application.
  Z makes actual use.
  A's application is published for opposition.
  Z initiates opposition proceeding, asserting its actual use as the basis of a Section 2(d) bar.

Held: *A* is deemed to enjoy constructive use priority over *Z* in the opposition, *Zirco Corp. v. AT&T Co.*, 21 U.S.P.Q.2d (BNA) 1542, 1544 (TTAB 1991), but the PTO will not actually enter judgment in favor of the applicant until after the ITU application has been perfected and the mark is registered. Lanham Act §18 ("no final judgment shall be entered in favor of an applicant under section 1(b) before the mark is registered, if such applicant cannot prevail without establishing constructive use pursuant to section 7(c)"); Lanham Act §21(a)(4) (reciting the same rule for judgments in appeals from the PTO to the Court of Appeals for the Federal Circuit).

- "offensive" use of constructive priority by an ITU applicant:

  A files ITU application.
  Z makes actual use and files use-based application.
  Z's application is published for opposition.
  A initiates an opposition proceeding, asserting its constructive use date (i.e., its ITU application filing date) as the basis of a Section 2(d) bar.

  Held: *A* is deemed to enjoy constructive use priority over *Z* in the opposition. *Larami Corp. v. Talk to Me Programs Inc.*, 36 U.S.P.Q.2d (BNA) 1840, 1845 n.7 (TTAB 1995); *see also Salacuse v. Ginger Spirits Inc.*, 44 U.S.P.Q.2d (BNA) 1415 (TTAB 1997) (same, in a cancellation proceeding). Again, however, the PTO may not render a judgment for *A* until the ITU application is perfected and a registration issues.

3. *Section 7(c) priority in litigation.* Consider the following chronologies illustrating how Section 7(c) may apply in litigation.

- "defensive" use of constructive use priority by a Section 1(b) ITU application holder:

  A files ITU application.
  Z makes actual use.
  Z sues *A* in federal district court under Section 43(a), seeking to enjoin *A* from preparations to engage in use.

  Held: "[A]s long as an ITU applicant's privilege has not expired, a court may not enjoin it from making the use necessary for registration on the grounds that another party has used the mark subsequent to the filing of the ITU application. To permit such an injunction would eviscerate the ITU provisions and defeat their very purpose." *Warnervision Ent. Inc. v. Empire of Carolina, Inc.*, 101 F.3d 259, 262 (2d Cir. 1996).

- "offensive" use of constructive use priority by a registrant where the filing basis for the registration was Section 1(b) intent to use:

  A files ITU application.
  Z makes actual use.
  A's ITU application matures into a registration.
  A files a trademark infringement suit in federal district court against *Z*, seeking to enjoin *Z* from further use.

  Held: *A* is entitled to claim Section 7(c) constructive use priority to establish priority as of the filing date of the ITU application, which precedes *Z*'s actual use. This is a straightforward application of Section 7(c).

  What result if *A* had detected *Z*'s use and filed suit immediately, while the ITU application was still pending? *See Talk to Me Products, Inc. v. Larami Corp.*, 804 F. Supp. 555, 559-60 (S.D.N.Y. 1992), *aff'd*, 992 F.2d 469 (2d Cir. 1993) (refusing to allow an ITU applicant to rely on Section 7(c) to establish priority over an alleged infringer in an infringement lawsuit prior to the time that the ITU applicant files a 1(d) affidavit). Accordingly, a pending ITU application can be used offensively in PTO proceedings, but not in litigation. *Larami Corp. v. Talk to Me Programs, Inc.*, 36 U.S.P.Q.2d (BNA) 1840, 1845 n.7 (TTAB 1995) (citing legislative history to support the conclusion that Congress intended this result).

D.   Foreign Activity as a Basis for Establishing Rights

As the following materials indicate, Lanham Act §§44(d) and (e) establish that specified foreign activity may serve as a basis for establishing U.S. trademark rights. The "activity" referred to here is generally an overseas trademark application filing or registration, not actual overseas use. Thus, it is appropriate to think of these provisions as further examples of the concept of constructive use and constructive use priority. Provisions of the Lanham Act implementing the Madrid Protocol (discussed below) similarly may provide overseas applicants with an opportunity to use their domestic registrations to establish U.S. trademark rights.

Consider the following example as you read the materials below on Sections 44(d) and (e). *A*, a Canadian firm, owns a Canadian registration and files a U.S. trademark registration application for the same mark. *A* invokes Section 44(e) of the Lanham Act and bases its application on its Canadian registration, alleging only an intent to use the mark in U.S. commerce. It does not submit any evidence of actual use in U.S. commerce prior to the filing of the application. Is the U.S. application void ab initio?

LANHAM ACT
Section 44(e) [15 U.S.C §1126(e)]

A mark duly registered in the country of origin of the foreign applicant may be registered on the principal register if eligible, otherwise on the supplemental register in this chapter herein provided. Such applicant shall submit, within such time period as may be prescribed by the Director, a true copy, a photocopy, a certification, or a certified copy of the registration in the country of origin of the applicant. The application must state the applicant's bona fide intention to use the mark in commerce, but use in commerce shall not be required prior to registration.

NOTES AND QUESTIONS

1.   *International obligations.* Lanham Act §44(e) implements the so-called *telle quelle* obligation found in Art. 6 *quinquies* of the Paris Convention. What conditions must an applicant satisfy to take advantage of Section 44(e)? *See* Section 44(c).

2.   *Registration without evidence of use anywhere?* Should a foreign national filing under Section 44(e) be required at least to show use somewhere in the world, even if not in the United States, in order to perfect the claim to priority and the entitlement to registration? In *Crocker Nat'l Bank v. Canadian Imperial Bank of Commerce*, 223 U.S.P.Q. (BNA) 909 (TTAB 1984), the TTAB broke with prior practice to hold that Section 44 provides foreign nationals with an independent basis of registration, such that foreign nationals were under no obligation to prove use in Section 44 applications. What problems does this create?

3. *Evidence of U.S. use required to maintain U.S. rights.* Suppose that the foreign applicant succeeds in acquiring a U.S. registration on the Principal Register under Section 44(e), without demonstrating any actual use (or engaging in any) in the United States. The Federal Circuit has held that all registrants, including those who procured registrations under Section 44(e), are subject to the same rules for *maintaining* their registrations. Accordingly, non-use in the United States for an extended time may result in abandonment. *See infra* section F for a discussion of abandonment.

4. *U.S. rights based solely on overseas actual use?* U.S. courts have declared that "[i]t is well settled that foreign use is ineffectual to create trademark rights in the United States." *Fuji Photo Film Co. v. Shinohara Shoji Kabushiki Kaisha,* 754 F.2d 591, 599 (5th Cir. 1985) (citation omitted). This rule is less definitive than it sounds. For example, under the well-known mark doctrine, where a foreign mark becomes well known in the United States (despite having been "used" only overseas) such that U.S. consumers associate the mark with the foreign user, some courts may recognize priority in the *foreign* user. *See also* Graeme B. Dinwoodie et al., International Intellectual Property Law and Policy 175-215 (2d ed. 2008) (discussing the doctrine of "well-known" marks). We discuss the well-known marks doctrine in Chapter 6.

IN RE RATH

402 F.3d 1207 (Fed. Cir. 2005)

DYK, Circuit Judge:

. . .

BACKGROUND

Rath is a German citizen who applied to register the marks [DR. RATH and RATH] for goods and services including, *inter alia*, nutritional supplements, books, grains, and educational services. The applications were based upon ownership of a German trademark registration for the marks. [The examiner refused to register the marks on the ground that the marks were primarily merely surnames. Section 2(e)(4) of the Lanham Act, 15 U.S.C. §1052(e)(4), bars such marks from registration on the principal register, although Section 2(f) allows such marks to be registered if the applicant presents evidence of secondary meaning. (We discuss these doctrines in Chapter 5, section B.4.) The TTAB upheld the examiner's refusal to register, and the applicant appealed to the Federal Circuit.]

DISCUSSION

. . .

II

Rath does not appeal the Board's holdings that his marks are primarily merely surnames under the meaning of section 2(e)(4). Indeed, he specifically "concedes that the marks are primarily, merely surnames." [cit.] Rather, he argues that the surname rule is at odds with the Paris Convention as applied to those holding foreign registrations.

Rath invokes [the so-called *telle quelle* obligation found in] article 6*quinquies* of the Paris Convention, which addresses the protection of marks registered in one member country in other member countries. It states in pertinent part:

A(1) *Every trademark duly registered in the country of origin shall be accepted for filing and protected as is in the other countries of the Union, subject to the reservations indicated in this Article.*

Such countries may, before proceeding to final registration, require the production of a certificate of registration in the country of origin, issued by the competent authority. No authentication shall be required for this certificate.

. . .

B. *Trademarks covered by this Article may be neither denied registration nor invalidated except in the following cases:*

1. when they are of such a nature as to infringe rights acquired by third parties in the country where protection is claimed;

2. *when they are devoid of any distinctive character*, or consist exclusively of signs or indications which may serve, in trade, to designate the kind, quality, quantity, intended purpose, value, place of origin, of the goods, or the time of production, or have become customary in the current language or in the bona fide and established practices of the trade of the country where protection is claimed;

3. when they are contrary to morality or public order and, in particular, of such a nature as to deceive the public. It is understood that a mark may not be considered contrary to public order for the sole reason that it does not conform to a provision of the legislation on marks, except if such provision itself relates to public order.

Paris Convention for the Protection of Industrial Property, July 14, 1967, art. 6*quinquies*, 21 U.S.T. 1583, 1643-44 (emphases added).

Rath argues that he is exempt from the surname rule because it does not fall within any of the three enumerated exceptions to the registration of foreign marks within the Paris Convention, and he is therefore entitled to registration of his mark on the principal register. The PTO urges that surname marks are descriptive, and therefore "devoid of any distinctive character" within the meaning of the Paris Convention, such that no conflict exists between the requirements of the Lanham Act and the Paris Convention. We need not decide whether the surname rule conflicts with the Paris Convention because we find that the Paris Convention is not a self-executing treaty and requires congressional implementation.

III

It is well established that executory treaties (those treaties that are not self-executing) have no direct effect until implemented by domestic law. [cit.] Our predecessor court held that "[t]he Paris Convention was not . . . self-executing and required implementing legislation." *Kawai v. Metlestics*, 480 F.2d 880, 884 (Cust. & Pat. App. 1973). [The court noted that it was bound by all prior decisions of the C.C.P.A., regarded itself as bound by the decision of the C.C.P.A., and concluded that in any event the decision in *Kawai* was correct. Indeed, the court noted that the majority of other Courts of Appeals that have considered the issue have also held that the Paris Convention is not self-executing. The court found decisions to the contrary, such as *Vanity Fair Mills, Inc. v. T. Eaton Co.*, 234 F.2d 633, 640-41 (2d Cir. 1956) (stating that the Paris Convention is self-executing but does not create private rights for acts occurring in foreign countries), and *Davidoff Extension S.A. v. Davidoff Int'l, Inc.*, 221 U.S.P.Q. 465 (S.D. Fla. 1983), unpersuasive and not binding on it.]

IV

Rath alternatively argues that section 44(e) of the Lanham Act is congressional legislation implementing the Paris Convention, and that section 44(e) itself requires registration because the Paris Convention requires registration. Whatever the situation with respect to other sections of the Lanham Act, section 44(e) cannot be construed as Rath urges.

Section 44(e) of the Lanham Act provides:

(e) Registration on principal or supplemental register; copy of foreign registration.—A mark duly registered in the country of origin of the foreign applicant may be registered on the principal register *if eligible*, otherwise on the supplemental register herein provided. Such applicant shall submit, within such time period as may be prescribed by the Director, a certification or a certified copy of the registration in the county of origin of the applicant. The application must state the applicant's bona fide intention to use the mark in commerce, but use in commerce shall not be required prior to registration.

Lanham Act §44(e), 15 U.S.C. §1126(e) (2000) (emphasis added).

In cases of ambiguity, we interpret a statute such as section 44(e) of the Lanham Act as being consistent with international obligations. *Murray v. The Schooner Charming Betsy*, 6 U.S. (2 Cranch) 64 (1804); [cit.]. However, even assuming that the surname provision of the Lanham Act is inconsistent with the Paris Convention, section 44(e) is not susceptible to a construction that the surname rule is overcome where there has been an earlier foreign registration, and the *Charming Betsy* presumption is inapplicable. Congress did not simply adopt language incorporating the requirements of the convention in the Lanham Act. Rather, it provided for registration of a foreign mark "if eligible." A mark is not "eligible" for registration on the principal register under the statute unless it satisfies the section 2 requirements, including the surname rule.

The legislative history cited by the concurrence does not support a contrary conclusion. There is no question but that Congress generally intended section 44 of the Lanham Act to implement the Paris Convention. But this does not mean that Congress intended to do so in every respect or that it actually accomplished that objective in all respects or that it correctly understood the requirements of the Paris Convention in enacting section 44. There is simply no way to read this history as suggesting that Congress intended to require registration on the principal register despite United States eligibility requirements. If anything, the history confirms that the principal register was available to foreign registrants and United States citizens on equal terms—both had to meet the eligibility requirements of United States law.

V

What is apparent from the face of the statute is confirmed by the cases as well. The issue whether section 44 acts to excuse an applicant from proving the distinctiveness of a surname mark as to the applicant's goods arose in our earlier *Darty* case [*In re Etablissements Darty et Fils*, 759 F.2d 15 (Fed. Cir. 1985)]. . . . This court held that a foreign applicant who claimed priority based on a foreign filed application under section 44(d) of the Lanham Act was not excused from the surname rule. . . .

We specifically noted in *Darty* that "[s]ection 44(e) specifically directs issuance of registration on the Principal Register only 'if eligible.'" [cit.] The language of section 44(e) itself makes clear that the reference to eligibility pertains to eligibility for registration on the principal register, rather than eligibility under the Paris Convention. The leading treatise confirms this interpretation. McCarthy states that the requirement of eligibility necessarily means "that the mark is subject to all the recognized statutory bars to U.S. registration." 4 J. Thomas McCarthy, *McCarthy on Trademarks and Unfair Competition* §29:13 (4th ed. 2004). Section 2(e)(4) of the Lanham Act—prohibiting the registration of a mark that "is primarily merely a surname" on the principal register—is such an eligibility requirement. 15 U.S.C. §1052(e)(4).

Rejecting the relevance of *Darty*, Rath and the concurrence rely on various cases that suggest that the implementing legislation and the Paris Convention are coextensive. In this connection Rath, like the concurrence, relies primarily on the Board's decision in *Crocker National Bank v. Canadian Imperial Bank of Commerce*, 223 U.S.P.Q. 909 (TTAB 1984). But *Crocker* did not directly address the interpretation of the "if eligible" clause of section 44(e). The actual holding of *Crocker* "is that a foreign national qualified under §44(b) is entitled to an alternative basis for registration of a trademark registered in its country of origin without regard to whether such mark is in use prior to the application's filing date." *Id*. at 924.[7] Broader language in *Crocker* stated that the Paris Convention "establish[ed] a minimum standard for all member countries as to what grounds for refusal of registration of any mark duly registered in the country of origin can be imposed by the other countries" and

> that Section 44 is an independent provision, standing on its own feet with respect to applications for registration depending upon it and the conventions as the bases for United States registration, *except for such formal requirements and conditions for registration as are consistent with the purposes of the conventions and the implementing statute.*

Id. at 917, 920-21 (emphasis added). We have previously approved the holding in *Crocker* ("that regarding an application based on foreign registration under 15 U.S.C. §1126(e), [an] applicant need not meet the otherwise applicable statutory requirements regarding prior use of the mark") but not the broader language. *In re Compagnie Generale Mar.*, 993 F.2d 841, 843 n.3 (Fed. Cir. 1993).

. . .

Thus, we conclude that while section 44(e), like section 44(d), affects United States priority or prior use rules, it is impossible to read section 44(e) to require the registration of foreign marks that fail to meet United States requirements for eligibility. Section 44 applications are subject to the section 2 bars to registration, of which the surname rule is one. McCarthy at §29:13. Whether the surname rule conflicts with the requirements of the Paris Convention as applied to foreign registrants is a matter we need not decide.

[*Affirmed.*]

BRYSON, Circuit Judge, concurring:

I fully concur in Parts I, II, and III of the court's opinion. With respect to Parts IV and V, I concur only in the result. In Parts IV and V, the court holds that the Lanham Act overrides the requirements of the Paris Convention with respect to the rights of foreign registrants. The majority acknowledges that Congress sought to implement the Paris Convention through the Lanham Act but concludes, surprisingly, that Congress did not "accomplish[] that objective."

The question whether the Lanham Act should be read to conflict with and trump the Paris Convention is a difficult one that has significant potential implications for international intellectual property law. Because I do not believe it is necessary to decide that issue

---

7. At the time *Crocker* was decided, the statutory definition of a trademark required that the mark be previously used. 15 U.S.C. §1127 (1982 & Supp. II 1984). That definition was later amended, and now includes a mark that is used or a mark that a person has a bona fide intention to use in commerce. 15 U.S.C. §1127 (2000).

in this case, I would instead decide the case on the narrower ground that the Lanham Act and the Paris Convention are in accord as applied in this case.

[Judge Bryson found *Darty*'s discussion of the issue "terse and unenlightening" and thus continued with his analysis.]

I

The language of the Paris Convention, together with the language of the Lanham Act that adopts the Paris Convention, seems unequivocally to give foreign registrants rights unless their foreign registered marks fall within one of the express exceptions set forth in Article 6 of the Convention.

Article 6*quinquies* of the Paris Convention states, in its current version:

> Every trademark duly registered in the country of origin shall be accepted for filing and protected as is in the other countries of the Union.
> Trademarks covered by this Article may be neither denied registration nor invalidated except in the following cases: . . . when they are devoid of any distinctive character.

[cit.] Congress enacted the Lanham Act in large part to meet its obligation to protect the rights afforded registrants in the Paris Convention. [cit.] Section 45 of the Lanham Act makes that explicit: "The intent of this Act is to . . . provide rights and remedies stipulated by treaties and conventions respecting trademarks . . . entered into between the United States and foreign nations." 15 U.S.C. §1127. Section 44(b) of the Lanham Act further provides:

> Any person whose country of origin is a party to any convention or treaty relating to trademarks . . . to which the United States is also a party . . . shall be entitled to the benefits of this section under the conditions expressed herein to the extent necessary to give effect to any provision of such convention, treaty or reciprocal law, *in addition to* the rights to which any owner of a mark is otherwise entitled by this chapter.

15 U.S.C. §1126(b) (emphasis added). The clear import of that language is that the treaties to which the United States is a party, including the Paris Convention, may give foreign nationals greater trademark rights than are available to United States citizens. *See* Allan Zelnick, *Shaking the Lemon Tree: Use and the Paris Union Treaty*, 67 Trademark Rep. 329, 339 (1977) ("The very purpose of [Article 6*quinquies*] was to afford nationals of member states a right to request in all other member country states marks which nationals of the receiving country could not file in their home country.").

> . . .

In the 1984 *Crocker* case, the TTAB [held] that a showing of use was not required of foreign applicants because

> Section 44 is an independent provision, standing on its own feet with respect to applications for registration depending upon it and the conventions as the bases for United States registration, except for such formal requirements and conditions for registration as are consistent with the purpose of the conventions and implementing statute.

223 USPQ at 918. The Board concluded that Article 6*quinquies* of the Paris Convention "establish[ed] a minimum standard for all member countries as to what grounds for refusal of registration any mark duly registered in the country of origin can be imposed by the other countries." *Id.* at 920-21. Therefore, the Board reaffirmed the . . . principle . . . that the Lanham Act and the Paris Convention limit the substantive grounds on which the PTO can refuse a foreign trademark owner's application.

The *Crocker* decision continues to be good law. In *In re Compagnie Generale Maritime*, 993 F.2d 841 (Fed. Cir. 1993), this court addressed a case in which a foreign trademark applicant was denied United States registration of a mark based on geographical descriptiveness. This court first had to address whether *Crocker* set forth the controlling principles of law. We held that it did: "*Crocker National Bank* was governing case law at the time of [Compagnie Generale Maritime's] applications and still is today." *Id.* at 844 n.3. It is clear that the court in *Compagnie Generale* was well aware of *Crocker* and *Merry Cow*. As Judge Nies stated, *id.* at 857 (Nies, C.J., dissenting),

> [t]he *Crocker Bank* decision . . . adopted the view that a use requirement was a substantive ground of rejection . . . and that a foreign registration could be rejected only on the grounds recognized in the Convention itself. Those grounds, per *Crocker Bank*, are only those found in Article 6 [6*quinquies* of Lisbon text].

It is clear that Judge Nies, in dissent, understood that *Merry Cow* and *Crocker* set forth the governing law at the time, although she expressed the view that those cases should be overruled. *Id.* at 858.

. . .

Crocker has been criticized, and it may be that *Crocker* was not correctly decided. But the principle underlying that decision cannot be lightly disregarded, particularly in view of this court's endorsement of *Crocker* in the *Compagnie Generale* case. The majority states that we have approved of only the "holding" of *Crocker* and not the "broader language." To accept the result of *Crocker* without the rationale, however, makes little sense. *Crocker* did not simply state the prior use rule in a vacuum, but came to it only after a careful analysis of the history of the Paris Convention and Lanham Act.

. . .

II

. . .

While accepting that Congress intended section 44 to implement the Paris Convention, the majority notes that Congress may have failed to achieve that objective or failed to understand the requirements of the Paris Convention. Yet it seems inconceivable that Congress could specifically try to implement a piece of legislation, fail, and then labor for 60 years under the delusion that it had done so. That possibility seems especially unlikely since a "treaty will not be deemed to have been abrogated or modified by a later statute, unless such purpose on the part of Congress has been clearly expressed." *Cook v. United States*, 288 U.S. 102, 120 (1933). . . .

Pointing to the provision of section 44(e) that grants registration to foreign registrants "if eligible," the majority asserts that section 44 applicants must be "eligible" for registration under section 2 and therefore foreign registrations are subject to all of the section 2 bars to registration, regardless of whether those bars may violate the substantive provisions of international agreements such as the Paris Convention. That conclusion is surprising, particularly in light of the fact that Congress originally included such language in section 44(e) and expressly deleted it. . . . In light of that background, it seems unlikely that the words "if eligible" were intended to mean "registrable under section 2 of the Act," thus reinserting in shorthand form the very provision that had been purposefully omitted.

In light of (1) our treaty obligations; (2) the fact that section 44 was viewed as a distinct piece of legislation implementing those treaty obligations; (3) the legislative purpose behind the Lanham Act; and (4) our decision in *Compagnie Generale*, the term "if eligible" is more appropriately read to refer to the explicit eligibility requirements set forth in section

44(b), which incorporates the eligibility requirements of applicable international agreements, including the Paris Convention. In other words, the applicant must be a person whose country of origin is a party to a convention relating to trademarks, the restrictions set forth in section 44 must not apply, and registration must be allowable under the applicable conventions. In the event those requirements are satisfied, the person is "eligible" for the benefits conferred by section 44. In sum, the more natural reading of the "if eligible" language of section 44(e) is that it refers to eligibility under section 44 of the Lanham Act and thus incorporates the requirements of the Paris Convention for foreign applications.

III

Instead of adopting the position that the Paris Convention confers no rights on foreign registrants—a position not adopted by the TTAB and not argued by any party in this appeal—I would decide this case on the ground upheld by the Board and argued by the government: that the Paris Convention and the "primarily merely a surname" rule are not inconsistent. That approach makes it unnecessary to decide whether the requirements of section 2 of the Lanham Act prevail over the eligibility provisions of the Paris Convention.

Article 6*quinquies* permits nations that are parties to the convention to bar registration of marks that are "devoid of distinctive character" or merely descriptive because, for instance, they only designate the kind, intended purpose, or place of origin of the good. Surnames are a subset of "merely descriptive" marks. Courts have routinely conflated those two categories, but have nevertheless held that surnames fall into these categories. The overwhelming weight of authority is that surnames are both descriptive and void of distinction. Although the policies underlying the "primarily merely a surname" rule and the prohibition against registration of "merely descriptive" marks differ, *see Peaceable Planet, Inc. v. Ty, Inc.*, 362 F.3d 986 (7th Cir. 2004), the two have traditionally been closely associated and, in light of the historical treatment of the two, it is not unreasonable to regard the "devoid of any distinctive character" category of the Paris Convention as encompassing surnames. Accordingly, I would affirm the Board's decision on this narrow ground; I would not decide whether the Lanham Act and the Paris Convention can be read disparately with respect to foreign registrants, and whether foreign registrants have no rights under the Paris Convention unless those rights are also conferred by the Lanham Act.

NOTES AND QUESTIONS

1.   *Names as marks.* We have already seen a discussion of the issues surrounding the protectability of names as marks in *Peaceable Planet*, excerpted *supra* in Chapter 2. We will separately deal with name marks, and specifically with the bar against registering terms that are "primarily merely surnames," in Chapter 5 (section B.4). Note that the applicant in *Rath* did not contest the applicability of the surname bar.

2.   *The international interpretation of Article 6 quinquies.*   Judge Bryson reads the Lanham Act as being fully consistent with Article 6 *quinquies* of the Paris Convention. Complaints regarding compliance with the Paris Convention can now be pursued by World Trade Organization (WTO) member states before the WTO Dispute Settlement Body (DSB) because Article 2(1) of the TRIPS Agreement requires WTO member states to comply with Articles 1-12 of the Paris Convention. The Appellate Body of the DSB addressed the meaning of Article 6 *quinquies* in a complaint brought against the United States. *See* United States—Section 211 Omnibus Appropriations Act of 1998, Report of the Appellate Body, WT/DS176/AB/R (WTO 2002). There, the European Union challenged a U.S. law

restricting the ability to own and register trademarks that were similar to trademarks used in connection with a business that was confiscated at the time of the Cuban (Castro) revolution. The challenge was made under several provisions of the Paris Convention and the TRIPS Agreement, including Article 6 *quinquies* of the Paris Convention. The European Union argued that "Article 6 *quinquies* A(1) requires that a trademark duly registered in a country of origin that is a country of the Paris Union must be accepted for registration and protected 'as is' in every respect in other countries of the Paris Union, subject only to the specific exceptions set forth in that Article." The Appellate Body adopted a narrow reading of Article 6 *quinquies*, fearing that "if Article 6 *quinquies* A(1) were interpreted too broadly, the legislative discretion reserved for Members under Article 6(1) [to determine the conditions for filing and registration of trademarks in its domestic legislation] would be significantly undermined." Indeed, in passing, the Appellate Body mentioned that a contrary interpretation would mean that "a national of a Paris Union country could circumvent the 'use' requirements of a particular regime by registering in the jurisdiction that does not impose 'use' requirements." (Of course, the United States permits just that via the Section 44 mechanism, and thus may read Article 6 *quinquies* more generously than required.) Instead, the Appellate Body held that the obligation to register another trademark *telle quelle* relates only to the "form" of the trademark (and they found the challenged U.S. law to regulate only ownership). Under that reading by the Appellate Body, the obligations imposed by Article 6 *quinquies* surely allow the United States to deny an application on the grounds that the mark for which registration is sought is primarily merely a surname.

LANHAM ACT
Section 44(d) [15 U.S.C. §1126(d)]

An application for registration of a mark under sections 1, 3, 4, or 23 of this Act [15 U.S.C. §1051, 1053, 1054, or 1091] or under subsection (e) of this section filed by a person described in subsection (b) of this section who has previously duly filed an application for registration of the same mark in one of the countries described in subsection (b) shall be accorded the same force and effect as would be accorded to the same application if filed in the United States on the same date on which the application was first filed in such foreign country: *Provided*, that—

(1) the application in the United States is filed within six months from the date on which the application was first filed in the foreign country;

(2) the application conforms as nearly as practicable to the requirements of this Act, including a statement that the applicant has a bona fide intention to use the mark in commerce;

(3) the rights acquired by third parties before the date of the filing of the first application in the foreign country shall in no way be affected by a registration obtained on an application filed under this subsection;

(4) nothing in this subsection shall entitle the owner of a registration granted under this section to sue for acts committed prior to the date on which his mark was registered in this country unless the registration is based on use in commerce.

NOTES AND QUESTIONS

1. *Paris Convention, again.* Like Section 44(e), Section 44(d) implements an obligation found in the Paris Convention—in particular, in Article 4.

2.   *The concept of foreign priority.* Section 44(d) is a typical "foreign priority" provision. It provides that if a qualifying national (one who meets the requirements of Section 44(b)) who first files an application for registration of a mark in an eligible country later files an application for U.S. registration, the U.S. application will be treated as having been filed on the filing date of the foreign application, if the other requirements of Section 44(d) are satisfied. Among these other requirements, Section 44(d)(1) imposes a time limitation: The U.S. application must be filed within six months of the foreign application filing date. Section 44(d)(2) requires that the applicant file a statement of bona fide intention to use the mark "in commerce."

3.   *Section 44(d) as a filing basis, not a basis for registration.* Section 44(d) provides the applicant with a priority date, and for that reason is usually listed among the bases for filing an application to register a mark. However, an applicant who claims priority under Section 44(d) must still establish a basis for registration under Section 1(a), Section 1(b), or Section 44(e). *See* TMEP §1003.03 (Oct. 2017).

4.   *Effect on Section 7(c) constructive use priority date.* If the Section 44(d) requirements are satisfied, a foreign applicant receives a Section 7(c) constructive use priority date as of the date of the foreign priority filing. Thus, Section 7(c)(3) specifies that an applicant's claim to Section 7(c) priority is not effective as against another who previously filed a foreign application and timely files a U.S. application claiming Section 44(d) priority. For example, suppose:

> *A* (Canadian firm) files in Canada.
> *Z* (U.S. firm) uses the mark in the United States.
> *Z* files in the United States.
> *A* files in the United States within six months of the Canadian filing, properly claiming
> priority to the Canadian application under Section 44(d).

In this scenario, *A*'s U.S. application is treated as having been filed as of the Canadian filing date, and *A*'s Section 7(c) constructive use priority date is the Canadian filing date. Put another way, *Z*'s claim is subject to *A*'s rights based on the prior Canadian filing.

5.   *Pan-American Convention.* The General Inter-American Convention for Trademark and Commercial Protection (the "Pan-American Convention"), which is self-executing in the United States, also creates a form of priority for a national of a Convention country that owns the same mark in a Convention country (even if no use has been made of the mark in the United States). (The members of the Convention are Colombia, Cuba, Guatemala, Haiti, Honduras, Nicaragua, Panama, Paraguay, Peru, and the United States.) In particular, Article 7 allows nationals of a Convention country to challenge the use and registration of an interfering mark in another contracting country upon proof that the interfering party had knowledge of the existence and continuous use of the mark in the same class of goods, upon compliance with the requirements established by the domestic legislation in such country and by this Convention. *See Diaz v. Servicios de Franquicia Pardo's S.A.C.*, 83 U.S.P.Q.2d (BNA) 1320 (TTAB 2007) (holding that Article 7 provides a separate basis on which to assert priority). In *Diaz*, a Peruvian applicant (SFP) under Section 44(e) successfully invoked Article 7 to establish priority over the first user in the United States (Diaz) based on SFP's five-year-old Peruvian registration for the same mark when Diaz was aware of the SFP's Peruvian registration prior to his use in the United States. The Board rejected Diaz's argument that Section 44 of the Lanham Act abrogated Article 7, noting that the purpose of the Convention was to create a uniform system for the protection of foreign trademarks.

LANHAM ACT

Section 66 [15 U.S.C. §1141f]

(a) Requirement for request for extension of protection

A request for extension of protection of an international registration to the United States that the International Bureau transmits to the United States Patent and Trademark Office shall be deemed to be properly filed in the United States if such request, when received by the International Bureau, has attached to it a declaration of bona fide intention to use the mark in commerce that is verified by the applicant for, or holder of, the international registration.

(b) Effect of proper filing . . . [T]he proper filing of the request for extension of protection under subsection (a) shall constitute constructive use of the mark, conferring the same rights as those specified in section 1057(c) of this title, as of the earliest of the following:

    (1) The international registration date, if the request for extension of protection was filed in the international application.

    . . .

    (3) The date of priority claimed pursuant to section 1141g of this title.

Section 67 [15 U.S.C. §1141g]

The holder of an international registration with a request for an extension of protection to the United States shall be entitled to claim a date of priority based on a right of priority within the meaning of Article 4 of the Paris Convention for the Protection of Industrial Property if—

    (1) the request for extension of protection contains a claim of priority; and

    (2) the date of international registration or the date of the recordal of the request for extension of protection to the United States is not later than 6 months after the date of the first regular national filing (within the meaning of Article 4(A)(3) of the Paris Convention for the Protection of Industrial Property) or a subsequent application (within the meaning of Article 4(C)(4) of the Paris Convention for the Protection of Industrial Property).

NOTES AND QUESTIONS

1. *The Madrid Protocol.* The Madrid Agreement Concerning the International Registration of Marks, which dates back to 1891 (the "Madrid Agreement") and the Protocol Relating to the Madrid Agreement Concerning the International Registration of Marks (the "Madrid Protocol"), adopted in 1989, each establish a system under which trademark owners in member countries may secure trademark rights in other member countries by a single filing with their home country's trademark office. The United States never acceded to the Madrid Agreement, but it joined the Madrid Protocol in 2003. Under the Madrid Protocol Implementation Act (Lanham Act §§66 *et seq.*), and the implementing PTO regulations, trademark applicants from other Contracting Parties to the Protocol can file an international application with their respective trademark offices and "request an extension of protection of their international registration to the United States" (i.e., apply for a U.S. trademark registration), claiming the international registration as a filing basis in accord with Lanham Act §66. To initiate such a procedure, the applicant must have filed a trademark application in its home country, and this is the basis for the filing with the PTO

via the Madrid mechanism. In such a case, the International Bureau of WIPO (the World International Property Organization) will forward the request for extension of protection to the PTO, and the PTO will examine the request as it would any domestic application under Section 1, except that a registration may be issued without proof of use in the United States. Madrid applicants do, however, have to allege a bona fide intent to use.

2.   *Priority under the Madrid Protocol.* When an applicant files a U.S. application claiming a Section 66 filing basis (that is, when an applicant makes a request for extension of protection of an international registration to the United States in an international application), the international registration date serves as the filing date of the U.S. Section 66 application. However, Lanham Act §67 allows such an applicant the opportunity to claim priority to the filing date of the applicant's earliest overseas filing, provided that the applicant has requested extension of protection to the United States within six months of that overseas filing date.

3.   *The Madrid Protocol from the perspective of U.S.-based applicants.* In the notes above we have focused on how the Madrid Protocol might assist applicants who seek to use their overseas activities to establish priority for claiming trademark rights in the United States. The Madrid Protocol is (of course) also of potential benefit to U.S.-based applicants who want to rely on U.S. activity as the basis for a request for extension of protection to foreign countries. We discuss this topic in Chapter 5 regarding the U.S. registration process.

E.   "SURROGATE" USES

The previous sections dealt with whether a party's acts should be deemed to constitute a use for trademark purposes. In this section, we consider a slightly different question: *Who* is the user for trademark purposes? In some cases, the question is not especially robust. Consider the case of the owner of a small bar who devises a logo and then places the logo on his signs, menus, and advertisements. The bar owner is both creator and user of the mark. By contrast, consider the following scenarios:

1.   Professor Janis' Brother Billy, a faithful consumer of BLACK MULE malt liquor, devises a slogan (BLACK MULE — IT KICKS) and offers to sell it to Black Mule Brewers, Inc., the producers of the BLACK MULE product. They decline, but then adopt the slogan anyway, without paying Brother Billy.
2.   Brand Strategy Affiliates, Inc., a consulting company that develops brand names, proposes the name ARMADILLO for its client's proposed new sport utility vehicle. The client, the New Brighton Motor Co., begins using the name but never pays Brand Strategy.

In both scenarios, the party that developed the name or slogan is not the user. Yet U.S. trademark law grants trademark rights to the user, even to the exclusion of the creator. The creator is left to pursue alternative (non-trademark) remedies, if any are available.

In other cases, identifying who is the user may be the first step in an argument that we might term a "surrogate" use argument. Under the surrogate use argument as we conceive of it, trademark use by someone other than the trademark owner may inure to the trademark owner's benefit. Should U.S. law recognize surrogate trademark uses? Or, given the importance that U.S. law vests in the use requirement, should only a trademark owner's own uses "count" for purposes of establishing trademark rights?

Section 1 below considers the problem of attributing uses among affiliated entities or persons—whether trademark uses by partners inure to the benefit of the partnership; whether uses by members inure to the benefit of the organization to which the members belong; and so on. The concluding section explores whether uncoordinated uses by the public can inure to the benefit of a private trademark owner.

1.   Uses by Affiliates

Suppose that *S* Corp., a wholly-owned subsidiary of *P*, Inc., begins operating five restaurants in Iowa under the name GALACTIC BURGER in 1995. A year later, *P*, Inc. decides to open ten more restaurants in Iowa. Can *P*, Inc. claim priority of use for 1995, even though *S* Corp. undertook the 1995 uses?

Analogously, suppose that *P*, Inc. and *S* Corp. are related, not as corporate parent and subsidiary, but instead as franchisor and franchisee. If *S* begins operating GALACTIC BURGER restaurants in 1995 under the franchising arrangement, should those uses be attributed to *P*?

To answer the question, it may be helpful to reexamine some basic premises of trademark protection. We say that trademarks indicate source. If "source" means only "location" (i.e., the unique physical location from which the actual goods or services emanate) or "supplier identity," then we might conclude that *S*'s uses cannot be attributed to *P* no matter what the corporate or contractual relationship between the two. If "source" bears a broader meaning—i.e., if we treat physical location and supplier identity as only two of many attributes of source—then we might be more liberal about attributing *S*'s uses to *P*. For example, if quality level is an additional attribute of source, and *P* ensures that the quality level of trademarked goods sold through *S*'s restaurants is consistent with the quality level of trademarked goods sold through *P*'s restaurants, it would seem plausible to conclude that *S*'s uses inure to *P*'s benefit.

In the 1930s, U.S. courts began to move from the former, restrictive view of "source" to the latter, more generous view. The modern Lanham Act reflects the more generous approach through the doctrine of "related companies." Under Lanham Act §5 (15 U.S.C. §1055), the first use of a mark by an entity that is "controlled by the registrant or applicant for registration of the mark" inures to the benefit of the controlling entity. *See also* Lanham Act §45 (defining "related company" to mean "any person whose use of a mark is controlled by the owner of the mark with respect to the nature and quality of the goods or services or in connection with which the mark is used"). The related-companies doctrine as embodied in Lanham Act §5 requires a showing of a "substantial relationship" between the using entity and the controlling entity. *See Secular Orgs. for Sobriety, Inc. v. Ullrich*, 213 F.3d 1125 (9th Cir. 2000) (finding the requisite substantial relationship lacking where national organizers of not-for-profit entity had specifically encouraged autonomy on the part of local groups); *see also Estate of Coll-Monge v. Inner Peace Movement*, 524 F.3d 1341 (D.C. Cir. 2008) (holding that a nonprofit corporation could qualify as a "related company" such that use by the nonprofit could inure to the benefit of a controlling entity).

Under the modern approach, where a parent-subsidiary relationship is established, the subsidiary's use will ordinarily inure to the benefit of the parent under straightforward application of the related companies doctrine. *See, e.g., May Dep't Stores Co. v. Prince*, 200 U.S.P.Q. (BNA) 803 (TTAB 1978) (applying related-companies doctrine to parties in parent-subsidiary relationship); TMEP §1201.03(a) (stating that the party who controls quality will be expected to be the registration applicant).

Similarly, a licensee's use will ordinarily inure to the benefit of a licensor, where the license agreement (often contained within a franchising agreement) provides for adequate quality control on the part of the licensor. *See, e.g., United States Jaycees v. Philadelphia*

Jaycees, 639 F.2d 134 (3d Cir. 1981). *See also Watec Co. v. Liu*, 403 F.3d 645 (9th Cir. 2005) (concluding that U.S. licensee's use inured to benefit of Japanese licensor). Should the converse be true—i.e., may a licensee claim the benefit of the licensor's use for priority purposes? *See Julie A. Moreno v. Pro Boxing Supplies, Inc.*, 124 U.S.P.Q.2d (BNA) 1028 (TTAB 2017) (licensee Ms. Moreno sought to claim the benefit of licensor Deportes Casanova's use to establish priority over Pro Boxing Supplies in an opposition proceeding).

These principles are particularly important in franchising. A franchise arrangement is a contractual arrangement between one firm (the franchisor) and an investor from outside the firm (the franchisee). Trademarks are central to most franchises: The franchisor licenses its trademarks to the franchisee, which uses the marks at franchise outlets. Uses of the mark by the franchisees inure to the benefit of the franchisor.

As the following materials demonstrate, the appropriate outcome of an analysis of use becomes less clear as we move away from organizations that are formalized in terms of corporate ownership or in terms of contract. In more amorphous organizations—clubs, college fraternities, professional organizations, other nonprofits, and so forth—it may be difficult for a court to discern the existence of an affiliation, or the level of control accompanying that affiliation. Moreover, in such organizations, membership may routinely shift, or the organization might dissolve altogether and reappear in some slightly different incarnation, presenting additional use issues. *See also Southern California Darts Ass'n v. Zaffina*, 762 F.3d 921 (9th Cir. 2014) (holding that an unincorporated association that promoted competitive darts events could own rights in mark SOUTHERN CALIFORNIA DARTS ASSOCIATION).

PROBLEM 4-5: TRUTH IN ROCK

(1) Herb Reed founded "The Platters" in 1953, performing in and managing the group. Paul Robi joined the group in 1954, left the group in 1965 when he was jailed, and did not return to the group after his release from prison. Herb Reed continued to use the group name into the 1980s. In November 1988, Robi executed an "assignment" to his wife Martha, purporting to assign all of his rights in THE PLATTERS mark to Martha, who would manage another group called "The Platters" (not including any of the original members). Who has the better claim to trademark ownership, Robi or Reed? *Robi v. Reed*, 173 F.3d 736 (9th Cir. 1999).

In general, and in the absence of any agreements specifying otherwise, should courts rule that rights in a musical group's trademark attach to the individual group members? (Would that also mean that members of a group forfeit any interest in the group's trademark when they leave the group?) Or should courts rule that rights in a musical group's trademark attach to the person who is in a position to control the quality of the services— perhaps, say, the group's manager? *See HEC Enters., Ltd. v. Deep Purple, Inc.*, 213 U.S.P.Q. 991 (C.D. Cal. 1980) (involving the group Deep Purple); *Rick v. Buchansky*, 609 F. Supp. 1522 (S.D.N.Y. 1985); *Kingsmen v. K-Tel Int'l, Ltd.*, 557 F. Supp. 178 (S.D.N.Y. 1983) (involving the group that popularized the song "Louie, Louie"); *Boogie Kings v. Guillory*, 188 So. 2d 445, 448 (La. App. 1966) (applying Louisiana state law). *See also generally* Barbara Singer, *A Rose by Any Other Name: Trademark Protection of the Names of Popular Music Groups*, 14 HASTINGS COMM. & ENT. L.J. 331 (1992).

(2) Study the following legislation, Pennsylvania's "Truth in Music Advertising Act," 73 PA. CONS. STAT. §§611-15 (2006), which took effect in late April 2006. In relevant part, the Act provides as follows:

§613. PRODUCTION

It shall be unlawful for any person to advertise or conduct a live musical performance or production in this Commonwealth through the use of a false, deceptive or misleading affiliation, connection or association between a performing group and a recording group. This section does not apply if any of the following apply:

(1) The performing group is the authorized registrant and owner of a Federal service mark for that group registered in the United States Patent and Trademark Office.

(2) At least one member of the performing group was a member of the recording group and has a legal right by virtue of use or operation under the group name without having abandoned the name or affiliation with the group.

(3) The live musical performance or production is identified in all advertising and promotion as a salute or tribute.

(4) The advertising does not relate to a live musical performance or production taking place in this Commonwealth.

(5) The performance or production is expressly authorized by the recording group.

§614. RESTRAINING PROHIBITED ACTS

(a) Injunction.—Whenever the Attorney General or a district attorney has reason to believe that any person is advertising or conducting or is about to advertise or conduct a live musical performance or production in violation of section 3 and that proceedings would be in the public interest, the Attorney General or district attorney may bring an action in the name of the Commonwealth against the person to restrain by temporary or permanent injunction that practice.

In addition, the court may require the defendant to pay restitution to any "person in interest" and may impose a fine payable to the Commonwealth. 73 PA. CONS. STAT. §§614(b), 615. Compare this legislation with the federal proposal and evaluate whether either advances the goals of the trademark system. Does the Pennsylvania legislation raise any additional issues?

LYONS v. AM. COLLEGE OF VETERINARY SPORTS MED. & REHAB.

859 F.3d 1023 (Fed. Cir. 2017)

LOURIE, Circuit Judge:

BACKGROUND

Lyons is an equine veterinarian. In 1999, Lyons met Dr. Robert Gillette ("Gillette") at a conference where they discussed the prospect of forming a veterinary specialist organization ("VSO") for treating athletic animals. Gillette had published a similar proposal for board certification in canine medicine the previous year. For a VSO to become accredited by the American Veterinary Medical Association ("AVMA"), a group of veterinarians wishing to create the VSO must form an organizing committee and submit a letter of intent to the AVMA. Thus, between 1999 and 2002, Lyons, Gillette, and four other veterinarians formed an organizing committee, of which Gillette served as the chair. By at least as early as 2002, the committee began using the mark as the name of the intended VSO. In the winter of 2002, Lyons participated in drafting a letter of intent, which was later submitted to the AVMA, and worked with the organizing committee to create a petition to seek accreditation for its VSO. In early 2004, Lyons drafted proposed bylaws and articles of incorporation for the VSO, which she presented to the organizing committee. In July 2004, Lyons was dismissed from the organizing committee for reasons not relevant to this appeal.

Almost a year after her dismissal from the committee, Lyons sought registration of the mark on the Principal Register for "veterinary education services namely conducting classes, seminars, clinical seminars, conferences, workshops and internships and externships in veterinary sports medicine and veterinary rehabilitation" in International Class 41, based on her assertion of a bona fide intention to use the mark in commerce under 15 U.S.C. § 1051(b). The PTO denied her application on the ground that the mark was geographically descriptive. In March 2006, Lyons there-fore amended the application to seek registration on the Supplemental Register, based on actual use under 15 U.S.C. § 1091(a), alleging first use anywhere as of December 20, 1995 and first use in commerce at least as early as June 18, 1996. In May 2006, the PTO registered the mark on the Supplemental Register, Registration No. 3,088,963.

Meanwhile, the organizing committee, led by Dr. Gillette, had continued to work on the VSO petition for AVMA accreditation and submitted a first draft to the AVMA in November 2008. In 2009, the AVMA published the petition to its members in the *Journal of American Veterinary Medicine* and in its electronic newsletter. In 2010, the AVMA granted provisional recognition to the VSO, which was entitled the "American College of Veterinary Sports Medicine and Rehabilitation" ("the College") and incorporated as a Colorado non-profit organization in June 2011. The College administered its first certification test in 2012 and subsequently certified over 115 veterinarians in the specialty, established 13 active residency programs at veterinary colleges, and conducted annual meetings, conferences, and continuing education programs in collaboration with other AVMA-certified VSOs.

On April 25, 2011, the College petitioned to cancel Lyons's registration on the Supplemental Register on grounds of priority of use and likelihood of confusion under 15 U.S.C. § 1052(d), misrepresentation of source under 15 U.S.C. § 1064, and fraud. The cancellation proceeding was suspended for almost three years during the pendency of a civil action between the parties in the U.S. District Court for the District of Massachusetts, where Lyons alleged infringement of the mark by the College. On February 19, 2014, the district court issued a final order dismissing Lyons's claims because, *inter alia*, her claimed prior use did not cause the mark to acquire distinctiveness in the public mind. The district court ordered the PTO to reject Lyons's application for registration on the Principal Register, but declined to cancel her registration on the Supplemental Register.

After the district court's disposition, the Board refused Lyons's application for registration on the Principal Register, and resumed the cancellation proceeding relating to the registration on the Supplemental Register. The Board concluded that Lyons was not the owner of the mark, and that the underlying application for her registration on the Supplemental Register was void *ab initio*.

The Board explained that, although the cancellation proceeding was initially brought on grounds of likelihood of confusion, the "true issue [was] ownership of the mark" as between "a former organizing committee member and . . . the veterinary specialty organization she helped found." The Board analyzed three factors to determine ownership of the mark: (1) the parties' objective intentions or expectations; (2) who the public associates with the mark; and (3) to whom the public looks to stand behind the quality of goods or services offered under the mark. The Board found that all three factors favored the College.

First, the Board found that Lyons's interactions with the organizing committee were in the nature of "proposing and planning the formation of a [VSO]," not "providing the services herself." The Board noted Lyons's behavior in helping to draft the letter of intent, and in drafting the proposed bylaws and articles of incorporation—all toward forming a VSO under the name the organizing committee had already begun to use for the VSO, the "American College of Veterinary Sports Medicine and Rehabilitation" (i.e., the mark). The Board also pointed to the testimony of the other organizing committee members, who unanimously agreed that Lyons never indicated that she considered the mark to be her own or notified them that they were not to use the mark after her departure from the committee. In fact, the Board observed, the organizing committee believed that they had conceived of the mark themselves. Thus, the Board found that the objectively manifested intent of the parties weighed in favor of ownership by the College.

Second, the Board found that the relevant public associates the mark with the College, rather than with Lyons. The Board observed that the College had certified veterinarians in its specialty, had established residency programs, conducted annual conferences and meetings, maintained a public website, and is recognized as a specialty on the AVMA's website, accessible to the 80,000-plus veterinarian AVMA members. The Board explained that, while Lyons used the mark in a non-published document called "The Equine Excellence Initiative" as early as 1995, such use was "not use in commerce"—rather, it was "at most [] *de minimis* use that never acquired distinctiveness." In fact, the Board found that The Equine Excellence Initiative was written in the *future* tense—detailing Lyons's plans for the VSO she envisioned forming. The Board noted that Lyons does not employ any teachers, has no students, has not yet acquired any physical premises for offering her educational services, and has not certified any veterinarians, and that her nonprofit organization (formed before 1999) has no employees, volunteers, real estate, or significant assets. Furthermore, the Board reasoned, because of Lyons's participation in the organizing committee between 1999 and 2004, any actions by Lyons "from that point on," undertaken in the name of the "American College of Veterinary Sports and Rehabilitation Medicine" and resulting in acquired distinctiveness of the mark, inured to the benefit of the College.

Finally, the Board found that the relevant public looks to the College to stand behind the quality of the educational and certification services associated with the mark. The Board noted that veterinarians certified by the College "may hold themselves out as diplomates in an AVMA-approved specialty." Moreover, the Board continued, the College's very name—the American College of Veterinary Sports Medicine and Rehabilitation—carries with it the AVMA's "seal of approval" because almost all AVMA-certified specialties (and none that are not AVMA-certified) use the prefix "American College of Veterinary" in the VSO name. Thus, the Board concluded that the public would look to the College to stand behind the quality of the services associated with the mark, rather than to Lyons, "who left the American Veterinary Medical Association in 2005, abandoned all thought of obtaining a certification from that Association, has no students enrolled in educational courses offered under the mark, and has no certification program."

In sum, the Board concluded that all "indicia of ownership" point to the College rather than to Lyons, and that the application underlying her registration on the Supplemental Register was void *ab initio* because she never owned the mark.

Lyons timely appealed to this court. . .

DISCUSSION

I.

It is axiomatic in trademark law that ownership of a mark is predicated on priority of use in commerce. *See, e.g., Holiday Inn v. Holiday Inns, Inc.*, 534 F.2d 312, 319 n.6 (C.C.P.A. 1976) ("It is fundamental that ownership of a mark is acquired by use, not by registration."); *Application of Deister Concentrator Co.*, 289 F.2d 496, 501 (C.C.P.A. 1961) (emphasizing that registration of a mark under the Lanham Act does not "create ownership," but rather is "only evidence thereof").

Thus, registration by one who did not own the mark at the time of filing renders the underlying application void *ab initio. See, e.g., Holiday Inn*, 534 F.2d at 319 n.6 ("One must be the owner of a mark before it can be registered."); *Aycock Eng'g, Inc. v. Airflite, Inc.*, 560 F.3d 1350, 1357 (Fed. Cir. 2009) ("The registration of a mark that does not meet the use requirement is void ab initio.").

The statutory requirement for use in commerce applies to service marks as well as to trademarks. *Aycock Eng'g, Inc.*, 560 F.3d at 1357. Under the Lanham Act, a service mark is any "word, name, symbol or device, or any combination thereof used by a person, or which a person has a bona fide intention to use in commerce . . . to identify and distinguish the services of one person . . . from the services of others and to indicate the source of the services." 15 U.S.C. § 1127.

For service marks, the "use in commerce" requirement is met when: (1) a mark is "used or displayed in the sale or advertising of services"; and (2) either (i) the services are "rendered in commerce" or (ii) the services are "rendered in more than one State or in the United States and a foreign country and the person rendering those services is engaged in commerce in connection with the services." 15 U.S.C. § 1127. Therefore, to meet the use requirement for a service mark, an applicant must use the mark in *advertising or sale* of a service, and show that the service was *actually rendered* in interstate commerce or in more than one state, or in this and a foreign country, by a person engaged in commerce.

A framework has developed in situations such as the present, where there has been a departure from or change of membership in a group, and both the departing member and the remnant group claim ownership of the mark. *See, e.g.*, [*Wonderbread 5 v. Gilles*, 115 U.S.P.Q.2d 1296, 1297 (T.T.A.B. 2015)]; *see generally*, 2 J. Thomas McCarthy, McCarthy on Trademarks and Unfair Competition § 16:45 (4th ed. 2015).

For example, in *Wonderbread 5* the Board resolved a dispute regarding ownership of a band's name after the departure of one of its members. 115 U.S.P.Q.2d at 1297. Due to the absence of a formal agreement between the parties regarding ownership of the mark, the Board examined the "parties' statements and actions at the time" of the member's departure from the group. *Id.* at 1303. After finding that the evidence was inconsistent with the departing member's claim that he "owned the mark as an individual," the Board applied Professor McCarthy's two-step test as a "useful adjunct" to its preliminary findings based on the parties' objective manifestations. *Id.* at 1303, 1305. For ownership disputes arising out of changes of membership in musical groups, McCarthy frames the inquiry as whether the mark "identif[ies] the group regardless of its members." 2 McCarthy § 16:45. To answer that question, McCarthy proposed a two-part analysis: first, one determines whether the mark is "personal to the individual members or not"; and second, if it is not, then it must be determined "for what quality or characteristic the group is known and who controls that quality." *Id.* The Board rephrased McCarthy's two-step inquiry in its findings to mean that "the consuming public did not associate" the mark with the departing member, and the group, rather than any individual member, "controlled the quality or characteristic of the band." *Wonderbread 5*, 115 U.S.P.Q.2d at 1307. Thus, the Board determined that the band owned the mark, the departing member's application for registration was void *ab initio*, and the resulting registration was invalid. *Id.*

This case presents a similar scenario, where Lyons was a member of a group (the organizing committee) and, after her departure from the group, both Lyons and the remnant committee (now the College) claim ownership of a mark used by the group while Lyons was still a member.

II.

Although the College initiated this cancellation proceeding based on a likelihood of confusion and other grounds, the dispute in the case, as the Board found, centers on ownership of the mark, which in turn depends upon priority of use in commerce, *Holiday Inn*, 534 F.2d at 319.

In a priority dispute, the Board's determination whether a trademark has been appropriated by first use in commerce is a fact question that we review for substantial evidence. *See, e.g.*, *Aycock Eng'g, Inc.*, 560 F.3d at 1360 (upholding the Board's determination that the Appellant was not the first to use the service mark in commerce because that finding was "supported by substantial evidence").

On appeal, Lyons argues that the Board erred in finding that she did not own the mark at the time she filed her application because the evidence shows that she, not the College, was the first to use the mark in commerce. Lyons contends that she used the mark as early as 1995 in the fundraising document entitled "The Equine Excellence Initiative," which was "widely disseminated to the veterinary community, sport-horse industry, philanthropic organizations and the public." Lyons asserts that, since 1996, she has continuously used the mark in commerce to conduct classes, clinical seminars, educational conferences, and workshops; create internship and externships for veterinary students; create, present, publish, sell, and distribute education materials, including booklets, presentations, and student test materials; create advertising educational programs; maintain an interactive website for educational programs; publish scholarship guidelines and applications; certify veterinarians; and provide student scholarships. Since 1996, Lyons maintains, she has raised over two million dollars in grant support from fundraising conducted using the mark.

The College responds that the Board correctly determined that the three factors relevant to ownership all demonstrate that the College owns the mark. First, the College asserts that the objectively manifested intent of the parties was that the mark would be used to name the VSO, which is exactly what has transpired. Second, the College continues, the relevant public associates the mark with the College, not with Lyons, because the College has certified over 140 veterinarians in approximately 33 states and 14 countries, established 13 active residency programs, collaborated with other AVMA-accredited VSOs to organize conferences and professional meetings, and maintains an active website. Finally, the College argues that the public looks to the AVMA-accredited College to stand behind the quality of the education and certification services associated with the mark because those certified by the College may hold themselves out as AVMA-recognized specialists, whereas Lyons, on the other hand, cancelled her membership with the AVMA after being dismissed from the committee, abandoned plans to seek accreditation, and has no educational programs and no students.

We agree with the College that the Board correctly determined that Lyons does not own the mark.

First, we find no error in the legal framework the Board used to evaluate ownership. The Board noted that, although various sources delineate the relevant test using different language, they all substantively include three main factors to be considered in ownership disputes surrounding service marks as between a departing member and the remnant group: (1) the parties' objective intentions or expectations; (2) who the public associates with the mark; and (3) to whom the public looks to stand behind the quality of goods or services offered under the mark. We agree with the Board's articulation of the relevant factors and accept the legal framework it applied for resolving ownership disputes when there has been a departure from or change of membership in a group and, in the absence of a formal agreement governing ownership of the mark, both the departing member and the remnant group claim ownership of the mark.

Second, we conclude that the Board's findings regarding each of the three prongs of its analysis were supported by substantial evidence. We discuss the findings in turn.

A. The Parties' Collective Intent

The Board determined that the parties' objective expectations were that Lyons and the rest of the organizing committee would form an AVMA-accredited VSO entitled "American College of Veterinary Sports Medicine and Rehabilitation," not that Lyons would render her own personal services using the mark. Substantial evidence supports that finding.

The record shows that, even before meeting Gillette, Lyons intended to form an AVMA-accredited VSO entitled "American College of Veterinary Sports Medicine and Rehabilitation." Because the AVMA rules for accreditation require the formation of an organizing committee comprising a minimum of six members, some of them canine veterinarians, she reached out to Gillette and the other veterinarians to form the organizing committee. During her concerted action with the rest of the organizing committee, she held herself out to the AVMA as a member of the committee, acting on behalf of the intended VSO that she agreed to name the "American College of Veterinary Sports Medicine and Rehabilitation." At no point did she communicate to any of the other committee members her belief that she owned the mark, any prior use of the mark, or any objection to the committee naming the VSO after the mark. In fact, she testified of her expectation that, at the end of the AVMA recognition process, the VSO would be named The American College of Veterinary Sports Medicine and Rehabilitation.

Although some evidence may indicate Lyons's *subjective* belief that she owned the mark and would control the VSO once it was formed, her *objectively* manifested expectations contradict that notion. As the Board found, "[w]hatever secret reservations [Lyons] may have harbored were not reflected in her interactions with the other committee members." Thus, the collective expectation of the parties, as objectively manifested, was that Lyons and the rest of the organizing committee would form an AVMA-accredited VSO with a name that became the mark. The Board's determination to that effect was supported by substantial record evidence.

B. Who the Public Associates with the Mark

The Board next determined that the relevant public—the AVMA and veterinary community—associates the mark with the College, rather than with Lyons. The Board found that Lyons engaged in at most "*de minimis*" use of the mark, and that her use never rose to the level of use in commerce sufficient to "create an association in the minds of the purchasing public" between Lyons and the mark. The Board relied upon substantial record evidence to support that finding.

First, the document Lyons cites as her first use of the mark, The Equine Excellence Initiative, was written in the future tense, indicating Lyons's *future* plans to form a VSO with the name of the mark. J.A. 832–39. But we have held that mere preparation and publication of future plans do not constitute use in commerce.[1] *See, e.g., Aycock Eng'g,* 560 F.3d at 1360 ("[M]ere preparations to use [the] mark sometime in the future will not

---

1. Other aspects of the evidence pertaining to the Equine Excellence Initiative are problematic. Specifically, Lyons admits that she did not publish the Equine Excellence Initiative in a systematic or public way, that she did not maintain a mailing list or other documentation demonstrating to whom she sent the document, and that she has no evidence demonstrating that she sent it at all.

do. . . ."); *id.* at 1358 ("[T]he advertising or publicizing must relate to an existing service which has already been offered to the public." (internal quotation marks omitted)); *see also Intermed Commc'ns, Inc. v. Chaney*, 197 U.S.P.Q. (BNA) ¶ 501, 507 (T.T.A.B. Dec. 23, 1977) ("Mere adoption (selection) of a mark accompanied by preparations to begin its use are insufficient . . . for claiming ownership of . . . the mark.").

Second, the record shows that Lyons has never engaged in advertising or marketing expenditures for the mark and, prior to 2003, had never maintained a website for herself or her wholly-owned nonprofit organization, Homecoming Farms. In fact, according to the record, the first time the mark appeared online was in December 2002, when Gillette put the name of the VSO on the website he used for coordinating efforts of the organizing committee. Furthermore, the evidence indicates that Lyons has no employees or volunteers, no students enrolled in educational courses offered under the mark, and no certification program.

On the other hand, there is evidence that the College has certified at least 115 veterinarians, established 13 active residency programs in veterinary colleges, and conducted conferences and continuing education programs in collaboration with other AMVA-accredited VSOs. Furthermore, the AVMA published the committee's VSO petition to its 80,000-plus veterinarian members in the *Journal of American Veterinary Medicine* and in its electronic newsletter for the purpose of allowing its members to comment on it. Moreover, the College has obtained corporate sponsorships from companies in the veterinary industry and received considerable attention in the press. Finally, the College, not Lyons, is listed on the AVMA's website regarding the VSO bearing the mark.

As we have explained, the statute, 15 U.S.C. § 1127, requires both advertisement and actual use of the mark to satisfy the "use in commerce" requirement. *See Aycock Eng'g*, 560 F.3d at 1360 ("[A]dvertisement and actual use of the mark in commerce are required."); *see also Intermed*, 197 U.S.P.Q. at 507 (explaining that "[a]t the very least," in order to meet the use requirement, "there must be an open and notorious public offering of the services to those for whom the services are intended"); *id.* at 507–08 ("The statute requires not only the display of the mark in the sale or advertising of services but also the rendition of those services in order to constitute use of the service mark in commerce.").

Thus, substantial evidence supports the Board's finding that the relevant public looks to the College, not Lyons, for services in connection with the mark because Lyons's use of the mark has not created distinctiveness inuring to Lyons.

C. To Whom the Public Looks for Quality Control

Finally, the Board found that the relevant public looks to the College to stand behind the quality of the educational and certification services associated with the mark. Substantial evidence supports that finding.

Because the College has earned AVMA accreditation, the veterinarians it certifies may hold themselves out as AVMA-approved specialists. Indeed, the AVMA maintains a publicly-available website containing information about all AVMA-recognized organizations, including the College, which allows users of the website to contact the College and to search for specialists by area of medicine and organization. Furthermore, as the Board observed, the College's very name carries the "AVMA's seal of approval" because many AVMA-accredited VSOs, and none that are not AVMA-accredited, have names beginning with the words "American College of Veterinary." Lyons has produced no evidence that she has obtained similar certifications from the AVMA, that she has students enrolled in educational services offered under the mark, or that she offers any certification programs at all. Therefore, substantial evidence supports the Board's finding that members of the public who seek out veterinary sports medicine and rehabilitation services will rely upon the College's certification as evidence of a particular veterinarian's expertise.

III.

In sum, we conclude that the Board's findings were supported by substantial record evidence. One might even say that the lion's share of the evidence supports the Board's decision.

Although Lyons may have been the first to use the mark, the record shows that her use never rose to the level of use *in commerce*. Rather, she initiated efforts to form an AVMA-accredited VSO with the name of the mark, and that endeavor moved forward without her after she was dismissed from the organizing committee. Her involvement with the committee may have been the very reason that the committee adopted the mark; nevertheless, it is clear from the record that the College used the mark in commerce before Lyons, and Lyons cannot in effect appropriate it. The Board's findings to that effect were supported by substantial evidence.

[*Affirmed.*]

NOTES AND QUESTIONS

1. *The McCarthy two-part test.* Does the McCarthy two-part test provide a reliable mechanism for determining ownership in cases involving informal groups? Does it exemplify the tension between a "totality of the circumstances" approach to the use requirement and a bright-line approach? Is it tilted too far toward the totality of the circumstances approach?

2. *Protecting unsophisticated actors.* Do the rules on use and ownership create unnecessary complications for individuals who are not well versed in trademark law? Or should the burden be on those individuals to seek out counsel to forestall future, inefficient ownership disputes (e.g., by appropriate contracts)?

2. Public as "Surrogate" User

COCA-COLA CO. v. BUSCH
44 F. Supp. 405 (E.D. Pa. 1942)

Ganey, District Judge:

. . .

[T]he plaintiff's bill avers that it is engaged and has been for many years in the manufacture of a soft drink syrup under the trademark "Coca-Cola"; that a considerable portion of the public abbreviate the trademark to "koke (coke)," and call for it as "koke (coke)"; that when offered as a soft drink "Koke (coke)" means "Coca-Cola"; that the defendants have adopted a name to be used on a soft drink the words "Koke-Up" . . . that the defendants threaten to manufacture, advertise, offer for sale and sell a soft drink, using the name "Koke-Up"; that unless enjoined by the court the defendants will carry out their threat and put on the market a soft drink named "Koke-Up"; that these threatened acts will constitute unfair competition; that the application of the word "koke" to a soft drink is a representation that it is "Coca-Cola."

. . .

It is generally recognized today that the emphasis on cases concerning trademarks, tradenames and unfair competition is not only the injury occasioned to the innocent parties but equally as much on the injury suffered by the public and it is accordingly becoming increasingly more evident that if defendant's acts result in the confusion and deceit of the public primarily relief will be granted. In other words it seems to me that in the progress of the law of trademark infringement and unfair competition as well, the likelihood of injury to the public which may result from the use of the defendant's product is one of the essentials which the courts consider in granting equitable relief. [cit.]

The purpose of a trademark is to identify the business in connection with which it is used and accordingly it will be protected only when used in connection with a business, for trademarks and the right to their exclusive use are property rights, in the sense that the right to one's trade, and the good will that follows from it, free from unwarranted interference from others is a property right. The trademark is the instrumentality by which this property right is protected and the right grows out of its use in trade not merely out of its adoption. *Hanover Star Milling Co. v. Metcalf*, 240 U.S. 403 [(1916)]; *United Drug Co. v. Theodore Rectanus Co.*, 248 U.S. 90 [(1918)]; [cit.]. Accordingly, here the plaintiff company did not use the word "koke (coke)" or identify its product with the word by sale, advertisement or otherwise and so a strict construction of the authorities on common law trade infringement would seem to hold that there could be no infringement, and accordingly it is to the broader field of unfair competition that we must look to for redress, if any. . . .

The word "koke (coke)" is simply an abbreviation which the public has made of the trademark "Coca-Cola" since it is commonplace in our daily endeavor to shorten and abbreviate anything which is capable of being shortened or abbreviated, and I think it is also common knowledge that there is a marked tendency among American youth, usually to shorten and abbreviate, and it is therefore quite natural, that the purchasing public rather than use the full trade-mark, "Coca-Cola," make resort to the more abbreviated form "koke (coke)." Further the testimony shows conclusively that soft drinks such as "Coca-Cola" are purchased by spoken word in a vast number of instances and when a "Coca-Cola" is wanted, resort is made to the abbreviation "koke (coke)" which has come to be the nickname for "Coca-Cola."

The cases with respect to abbreviations or nicknames in the law of unfair competition are rather few and on the whole not altogether satisfactory. A review of the leading English cases show that the courts grant redress where there is a use of nicknames or an abbreviation of a trademark which have a likelihood of resulting in confusion.

. . .

The American cases are few in number and some while seemingly opposed to the view here adopted, upon careful examination, reveal no inconsistency with the position here taken. In *Bayuk Cigars, Inc. v. Schwartz*, 1 F. Supp. 283, 286 [(D.N.J. 1932)] the court held that the term "Phillies" as applied to the plaintiff's cigars by the purchasing public, though never attached to or used by way of advertising in connection with the sale of the product, was not subject to the protection of a court of equity as against the defendant who later used the term "Phillies" in connection with his brand of cigars. However, the court says: "This result is partly based upon the idea of the court that the plaintiff has not established, by a preponderance of evidence, such a use of the word as would entitle it to the exclusive use of the same, as against the defendant who registered this word and marketed products thereunder prior to the time the word in question was actually applied to the packages containing the plaintiff's cigars." In the instant case there can be no question of the fact that the plaintiff has established by a preponderance of evidence that the word coke is used solely in designation of the plaintiff's product, as the record will show that almost every witness so testified.

. . .

I feel that the abbreviation of the trademark which the public has used and adopted as designating the product of the complainant is equally as much to be protected as the trademark itself and while the name of the defendant's product is "Koke-Up" it is not to be doubted from the evidence in the case that "Koke" is the dominant word which is attempted to be impressed upon the public, since the word "Koke" on the label of the bottle of the product is much larger in size than the other lettering.

. . .

NOTES AND QUESTIONS

1. *A case about the public as surrogate user?* Does the concept of the public as "surrogate" user for the trademark owner make policy sense? If the public is responsible for undertaking the use, perhaps the public should reap the benefit. On the other hand, isn't the public always partially "responsible" for the creation of trademark rights, given that the rules for distinctiveness rest on public perception?

2. *Merely a nickname case?* Perhaps the *Coke* decision stands for the relatively modest proposition that trademark owners are entitled to rights in shortened versions of their marks. Although the *Coke* decision predates the Lanham Act, courts have reached similar results under the Lanham Act. For example, in *Nat'l Cable Television Ass'n, Inc. v. Am. Cinema Editors, Inc.*, 937 F.2d 1572, 1577-78 (Fed. Cir. 1991), the court invoked the principle that even without a use by the alleged trademark owner,

> abbreviations and nicknames of trademarks or names used *only* by the public give rise to protectable rights in the owners of the trade name or mark which the public modified. Such public use by others inures to the claimant's benefit and, where this occurs, public use can reasonably be deemed use "by" that party in the sense of a use on its behalf.

Id. at 434. *See also Johnny Blastoff, Inc. v. Los Angeles Rams Football Co.*, 188 F.3d 427 (7th Cir. 1999) (same). Suppose that a mark owner's mark is LCR for a dice game, and the public expands the mark to "LEFT CENTER RIGHT." Should the public's use inure to the benefit of the mark owner? Should the nickname principle not apply because the public's use isn't a contraction of the trademark? Or does that suggest that a nickname principle is silly? *See George & Co., LLC v. Imagination Entm't Ltd.*, 575 F.3d 383 (4th Cir. 2009) (addressing the issue).

3. *Producer resistance to unwelcome surrogate uses.* In the *Coke* case, suppose that the Coca-Cola Company actually resisted the public's practice of abbreviating the COCA-COLA mark. (The Coca-Cola poster reprinted on page 318 includes language encouraging consumers to "Demand the genuine by full name" because "nicknames encourage substitution.") What are the trademark consequences when a producer resists the public's surrogate use? Consider a similar fact pattern involving rights in the term "hog." Beginning around the early 1970s and into the early 1980s, motorcycle enthusiasts came to use the word "hog" when referring to large motorcycles, particularly large Harley-Davidson motorcycles. Initially, Harley-Davidson resisted the association. By the late 1980s, however, Harley-Davidson embraced the usage, eventually applying for a federal registration. Were the public uses sufficient to establish trademark rights for Harley-Davidson during the 1970s and early 1980s? In the late 1980s? *See Harley-Davidson, Inc. v. Grottanelli*, 164 F.3d 806 (2d Cir. 1999). *Cf. Cont'l Corrugated Container Corp. v. Cont'l Grp., Inc.*, 462 F. Supp. 200, 203 U.S.P.Q. (BNA) 993 (S.D.N.Y. 1978) (deeming a variant on a seller's mark to be protectable when the seller has encouraged such usage through advertising, but questioning whether the same result would follow where the variant has been the subject of mere informal use by customers, without the seller's encouragement).

4. *Surrogate uses and the origin of collegiate marks.* In 1940, Brown's, a local retailer in Madison, Wisconsin, home of the University of Wisconsin, commissioned a company to create a mascot for use in connection with Brown's retail sales of clothing and other

promotional items. The company proceeded to create a "Bucky Badger" logo, perhaps believing that a large, hairy relative of the skunk that digs in the ground appropriately symbolized the University of Wisconsin's athletic teams. Surely enough, the badger logo gradually came into use in connection with the University of Wisconsin's athletic teams (which doesn't surprise us given other probable alternatives, such as dairy cow or cheese-head logos). Many years later, the university began to take the position that it owned exclusive trademark rights in the Bucky Badger logo, and sought a federal registration. Brown's, and others, opposed on the ground that the University had not created the logo and thus could not have properly acquired rights through use. The TTAB dismissed the argument:

> Opposers also assert . . . that because applicant did not create any of the marks it seeks to register and thus was not the first to adopt and use them, applicant is not the "owner" of the marks within the meaning of Section 1(a) of the Trademark Act and therefore is not entitled to register them. However, . . . a claim that applicant is not the owner of the marks would not be well taken. As pointed out in *American Stock Exchange, Inc. v. American Express Co.*, 207 U.S.P.Q. 356, 364 (TTAB 1980), an entity may have "a protectable property right in [a] term even if the company itself has made no use of the term" provided that the public has come to associate the term with the entity or its goods or services. Here, there is no genuine issue that the public, as well as applicant itself and even opposers UBS [University Book Store] and Brown's, have used the marks at issue to refer to applicant and the particular goods and services for which registration is sought. There is accordingly no question as to applicant being the owner of the marks, even if others first adopted and used the marks, since such uses were not as marks to identify and distinguish their own products and services, but were instead references to applicant.

Univ. Bookstore v. Univ. of Wis. Bd. of Regents, 33 U.S.P.Q.2d (BNA) 1385, 1392 n.21 (TTAB 1994). For a full discussion of the abandonment issues in the case, *see infra* section F.

5. *Surrogate uses of previously adopted marks.* In the *Coke* case, at the time when the public "adopted" COKE as a reference to the products of the Coca-Cola Company, there was no evidence that any other producer had previously adopted that mark for similar products. What if the record had shown that a small producer of bottled juices had used COKE in connection with its products long before the public adopted COKE as an indicator of Coca-Cola's products? Should a court still hold that the public's uses of COKE to refer to Coca-Cola products inure to the benefit of the Coca-Cola Company?

A similar case arose in connection with the mark MARCH MADNESS for basketball tournaments. The Illinois High School Association (IHSA) had used the mark MARCH MADNESS in connection with the annual Illinois high school state basketball tournament since the 1940s. In 1982, CBS Sports broadcaster Brent Musburger first used the phrase "March madness" in CBS telecasts of the National Collegiate Athletic Association (NCAA) men's basketball championship tournament. Rapidly, the public and media adopted the phrase as a reference to the NCAA basketball tournament. Consider some of the issues raised by this complex fact situation:

(1) Should the NCAA own trademark rights in MARCH MADNESS used in connection with the NCAA tournament? Do the facts justify application of the surrogate use analysis? If they do, would that analysis suggest that the uncoordinated public uses of MARCH MADNESS in reference to the NCAA tournament inure to the NCAA's benefit? To CBS's benefit? To Brent Musburger's benefit?

(2) If the NCAA does own rights to MARCH MADNESS, should it take those rights subject to the trademark rights of the IHSA in MARCH MADNESS for the Illinois high school tournament? That is, should the court recognize a "dual use" trademark, in which the NCAA owns some rights in the mark and the IHSA owns some rights in the mark? Or should the court rule that the public's use of MARCH MADNESS to refer to the NCAA is an uncoordinated third-party use that has destroyed the IHSA's rights?

If you find the "dual use" solution attractive, consider carefully the scope of rights that the NCAA and the IHSA, respectively, would enjoy. If the NCAA wanted to grant an exclusive license to a video game manufacturer to create a MARCH MADNESS college basketball video game, could the NCAA do so? If the IHSA wanted to enjoin the high school athletic association in the state of Missouri from using MARCH MADNESS in connection with the Missouri high school basketball tournament, could the IHSA do so, or is the IHSA limited to trademark rights in Illinois? *See* Chapter 6 for a discussion of geographic limitations on trademark rights.

PROBLEM 4-6:   OFFICE SPACE

The movie *Office Space* ("a dark, low-profile 1999 comedy about a fictitious Texas software company and the everyday weirdos who work there") has become a cult classic. In the movie, a candy-apple-red–colored SWINGLINE brand stapler figures prominently in the plot. (Because of your inherent hipness, you probably already know this. In case you need a refresher, *see http://www.virtualstapler.com/office_space/* (screen shots of every appearance of said stapler in said movie and explanations of how said stapler figures in said plot).) Although many trademark owners enter into product placement deals with moviemakers to have their products depicted in movies, the use of the stapler in "Office Space" was apparently not such a case. In fact, as of 1999, Swingline did not make candy-apple-red staplers. A movie prop designer created the red stapler used in the movie.

The release of the movie created a sudden demand for candy-apple-red SWINGLINE staplers. Periodically, from 1999 through 2002, individuals began spray-painting their SWINGLINE staplers red and selling them on the Internet. In 2002, Swingline began selling a candy-apple-red stapler labeled with the traditional SWINGLINE word mark. *See http:// www.swingline.com/swingline/us/us/s/2425/iconic-red-stapler.aspx* (advertising said stapler).

Assume that Swingline seeks to register (1) the color "candy-apple-red" used in connection with a stapler and (2) the color "candy-apple-red" combined with the word mark SWINGLINE used on a stapler. Assume that Swingline claims priority of use back to the 1999 use in the movie. Should the movie use inure to Swingline's benefit? Should the uses by individuals from 1999 to 2002 inure to Swingline's benefit? Do you arrive at the same result for both applications? *See generally Viacom Int'l v. IJR Cap. Invstmts, L.L.C.,* 891 F.3d 178 (5th Cir. 2018) (fictional "KRUSTY KRAB" restaurant used in cartoon).

F.   Loss of Rights Through Non-Use or Uncontrolled Uses

We have now seen that U.S. trademark rights arise when a firm adopts and uses a mark. This link between trademark rights and trademark use is not confined to the initial acquisition of rights. Having acquired rights through use, a trademark owner must continue to demonstrate use—or at least control over use—in order to maintain trademark rights. Lanham Act §45 defines trademark abandonment as follows:

§45. (15 U.S.C. §1127) DEFINITIONS

A mark shall be deemed to be "abandoned" if either of the following occurs:
    (1) When its use has been discontinued with intent not to resume such use. Intent not to resume may be inferred from circumstances. Nonuse for 3 consecutive years shall be prima facie evidence of abandonment. "Use" of a mark means the bona fide use of such mark made in the ordinary course of trade, and not made merely to reserve a right in a mark.

(2) When any course of conduct of the owner, including acts of omission as well as commission, causes the mark to become the generic name for the goods or services on or in connection with which it is used or otherwise to lose its significance as a mark. Purchaser motivation shall not be a test for determining abandonment under this paragraph.

1. Abandonment Through Non-Use

EMERGENCY ONE, INC. v. AMERICAN FIREEAGLE, LTD.

228 F.3d 531 (4th Cir. 2000)

MICHAEL, Circuit Judge:

[At the time of the lawsuit, both parties were using marks stipulated to be confusingly similar. Defendant American FireEagle, Ltd. (AFE) sold fire trucks using the mark AMERICAN FIREEAGLE accompanied by a bald eagle superimposed over an American flag. Plaintiff Emergency One, Inc. (E-One) sold fire trucks under the mark AMERICAN EAGLE, also accompanied by a bald eagle superimposed over an American flag. AFE conceded that E-One had acquired rights to the AMERICAN EAGLE mark in a 1989 transaction, several years before AFE adopted and began to use its mark. But E-One had abandoned rights to its mark, according to AFE.]

I

E-One is a fire and rescue truck manufacturer located in Ocala, Florida. In 1989 E-One bought American Eagle Fire Apparatus Co. (American Eagle), a Gainesville, Florida, fire truck manufacturer started by former E-One employees in 1985. The purchase price for American Eagle was $6.5 million, though only $1.6 million was attributed to the company's tangible assets. The balance was attributed to good will, including the value of the AMERICAN EAGLE trademark. Company officials at E-One believed that American Eagle's excellent reputation in rural markets, combined with the inherent patriotic appeal of its bald eagle and American flag trademark, would enable E-One to increase its sales to rural fire departments.

Shortly after the purchase, E-One's president, Ted Fries, spoke to American Eagle's employees in Gainesville, Florida. Among other things, Fries said that E-One intended to continue building American Eagle fire trucks to satisfy existing orders, but that the company ultimately intended to build E-One products in Gainesville. Fries also said that E-One "wouldn't be building American Eagle branded products forever out of Gainesville." Between 1989 and June 1992 E-One built about thirty-five to forty fire trucks to satisfy American Eagle's back orders as well as some new orders that E-One accepted after the purchase. Although the trucks were built according to American Eagle blueprints and in keeping with American Eagle style, some left the factory bearing the E-ONE trademark, while others bore the AMERICAN EAGLE logo and nameplate.

The Gainesville plant was closed shortly after June 1992, ending the manufacture of fire trucks at that facility. However, E-One continued to provide exclusive warranty and repair services on American Eagle trucks. In 1993 and 1994 E-One also refurbished or substantially rebuilt old and damaged American Eagle trucks in a process known as "recycling." E-One would remove the engine, rear axle, transmission, and water pump from a used fire truck. Those components (assuming they were serviceable) would be installed on a new or rebuilt chassis. E-One would then construct a new American Eagle style body for that chassis. As with the brand-new trucks, most left the factory with the E-ONE nameplate. However, one recycled American Eagle truck left the factory in 1994 bearing the AMERICAN EAGLE nameplate and logo. Regardless of what mark appeared on the truck itself, all invoices after the acquisition carried only E-One's name.

By mid-1992 E-One was no longer manufacturing any new fire trucks under the AMERICAN EAGLE brand. However, it promoted the mark in various ways: by selling T-shirts, hats, tote bags, and nameplates bearing the AMERICAN EAGLE logo in "The Fire Locker" (a gift store at the factory), by distributing that merchandise at trade shows, and by requiring that its security guards wear AMERICAN EAGLE badges on their uniforms.

Despite its professed enthusiasm for the AMERICAN EAGLE brand, E-One had no specific plans for use of the mark when it bought the American Eagle company in 1989. E-One first considered using the AMERICAN EAGLE brand on its rescue trucks, but decided that the rescue and fire trucks were already so similar that no advantage would be gained by developing a separate brand. Eventually, E-One decided that the AMERICAN EAGLE mark would best be used to represent a separate product line. It appears that E-One's caution in deciding how to use the AMERICAN EAGLE mark stemmed from a disastrous product launch several years earlier. The company was wary of introducing a new line of trucks and particularly wary of tarnishing a valuable name by associating it with an inferior product.

In 1991 E-One introduced a low cost, limited option fire truck under the E-ONE mark. Around mid-1993 the company considered using the name AMERICAN EAGLE on those trucks, but instead marketed them using the E-One name and descriptive slogans such as "Budget Busters" and "Value and More."

In 1994 Michael Carter founded the defendant corporation, AFE. Carter had worked for American Eagle as a draftsman but left a few months after the company was sold to E-One in 1989. Apparently believing that E-One had abandoned its rights to the AMERICAN EAGLE mark, Carter designed a highly similar mark for AFE, a bald eagle superimposed over an American flag. In February 1994 AFE began using the eagle and flag mark in pre-manufacturing marketing of its fire trucks. In the summer of that same year fire truck dealers began to call both E-One and AFE with questions about the new company, asking whether E-One had started a new company or distribution arm. E-One complained to AFE that its mark was confusingly similar to the AMERICAN EAGLE mark.

[AFE continued to use its AMERICAN FIREEAGLE mark notwithstanding E-One's allegations. E-One announced in September 1995 that it would begin selling its low-cost fire trucks under the AMERICAN EAGLE mark. A year later, E-One sued AFE over AFE's continued use of the AMERICAN FIREEAGLE mark. The only contested issue at trial was whether E-One had abandoned rights to the AMERICAN EAGLE mark. The jury found in favor of E-One, and AFE appealed.]

II

. . .

A

AFE begins by arguing that it was entitled to judgment as a matter of law on the issue of abandonment. AFE contends that E-One's own evidence proved that it had discontinued use of the AMERICAN EAGLE mark for at least three years before it introduced its own line of AMERICAN EAGLE trucks. According to AFE, three years of non-use results in a statutory presumption of abandonment, and E-One failed to rebut that presumption. The district court concluded that E-One only had to produce evidence of its continued use of the mark or its intent to resume such use in order to rebut the presumption. According to the district court, E-One rebutted the presumption by producing evidence that it had continued to use the mark on clothing and promotional merchandise, in the recycling and repairing of American Eagle fire trucks, and on the uniforms of its security personnel.

We hold that promotional use of this type or incidental use in recycling and repair is not the "use" required to preserve trademark rights under the Lanham Act. Nonetheless, we conclude that E-One rebutted the statutory presumption by producing evidence that it intended to resume use of the mark on fire trucks. Consequently, AFE was not entitled to judgment as a matter of law.

Under the Lanham Act a trademark is abandoned when "its use has been discontinued with intent not to resume such use." 15 U.S.C. §1127. Thus, a party claiming that a mark has been abandoned must show "non-use of the name by the legal owner and no intent by that person or entity to resume use in the reasonably foreseeable future." *Stetson v. Howard D. Wolf & Assocs.*, 955 F.2d 847, 850 (2d Cir. 1992). Non-use for three consecutive years alone, however, constitutes prima facie evidence of abandonment. *See* 15 U.S.C. §1127. Proof of three consecutive years of non-use thus creates a presumption—a mandatory inference of intent not to resume use. [cit.] Once the presumption is triggered, the legal owner of the mark has the burden of producing evidence of either actual use during the relevant period or intent to resume use. [cit.] The ultimate burden of proof (by a preponderance of the evidence) remains always on the challenger. [cit.][1]

. . .

Here, the testimony of E-One's own witnesses at trial established that the company discontinued use of the AMERICAN EAGLE mark by mid-1992 when it ceased production of new AMERICAN EAGLE fire trucks. E-One's uses of the mark in the succeeding three-and-one-half years on products other than fire trucks failed to satisfy the statutory requirement of "bona fide use of [the] mark in the ordinary course of trade, and not made merely to reserve a right in [the] mark." 15 U.S.C. §1127. *See also* [*Imperial Tobacco, Ltd. v. Philip Morris, Inc.*, 899 F.2d 1575 (Fed. Cir. 1990)] at 1582-83. Exclusive repair and recycling services like those offered by E-One might be sufficient commercial use of the mark to prevent abandonment, but only if E-One used the mark on the repaired or remanufactured goods or "on documents associated with the goods or their sale." 15 U.S.C. §1127. *Cf. Coup v. Vornado, Inc.*, 9 U.S.P.Q.2d 1824, 1825-26 (T.T.A.B. 1988). The evidence at trial was that only one recycled American Eagle truck left the factory with an AMERICAN EAGLE mark attached, and invoices for all repair and recycling services bore only the E-ONE mark. One recycled American Eagle truck with an AMERICAN EAGLE nameplate over the course of three years is no more than a token use which, standing alone, is legally insufficient to disprove abandonment. *See* [*Exxon Corp. v. Humble Exploration*, 695 F.2d 96 (5th Cir. 1983)] at 99-102.

We therefore conclude that AFE demonstrated that E-One had discontinued use of the AMERICAN EAGLE mark for three years and that E-One failed to rebut that presumption by producing any evidence of the use required by the Lanham Act. However, the case does not end there because E-One did produce evidence that it intended to resume use of the mark on fire trucks. E-One's continuous promotion of the brand by using it on hats, T-shirts, tote bags, and souvenir nameplates is evidence of some intent to resume use of the mark. In addition, E-One executives testified that they actively considered using the AMERICAN EAGLE mark on fire trucks between 1992 and 1995. That testimony was corroborated by an E-One business plan from 1993, which identified the AMERICAN EAGLE mark as one of four possible brand names for a new line of trucks. This evidence of intent to resume use was sufficient to satisfy E-One's burden of production. The evidence also created a triable issue of fact, precluding judgment as a matter of law.

---

1. Effective January 1, 1996, Congress amended §1127, changing the period of non-use that establishes a prima facie case of abandonment from two years to the present standard of three years. *See* Uruguay Round Agreements Act §521, Pub. L. No. 103-465, 108 Stat. 4809 (1994). . . .

AFE contends, however, that E-One's own representatives admitted that their plans to resume use of the mark were indeterminate. At the time of acquisition and at all times up until 1995, E-One had no specific plan to use the AMERICAN EAGLE mark. It is true that the owner of a trademark cannot defeat an abandonment claim, as well as the purposes of the Lanham Act, by simply asserting a vague, subjective intent to resume use of a mark at some unspecified future date. *See Silverman*, 870 F.2d at 46-47. Once the challenger shows discontinued use, the owner must produce evidence of intent to resume use "within the reasonably foreseeable future." *Id.* at 46. [cit.] Requiring the owner to have an intent to use the mark in the reasonably foreseeable future ensures that valuable trademarks are in fact used in commerce as the Lanham Act intends, rather than simply hoarded or warehoused. [cit.]

Of course, what is meant by the "reasonably foreseeable future" will vary depending on the industry and the particular circumstances of the case. *Cf. Defiance Button Mach. Co. v. C & C Metal Prods. Corp.*, 759 F.2d 1053, 1060-61 (2d Cir. 1985). Because fire trucks have very long lives (often twenty to thirty years), the mark stays visible, and the good will value of the mark persists long after production of trucks with that mark has ceased. Thus, it might be reasonable for a fire truck manufacturer to spend five or six years considering the reintroduction of a brand, even though the same passage of time would be unreasonable for a maker of a more ephemeral product, say potato chips. E-One produced evidence that because American Eagle had made a product very similar to E-One's, it was necessary for E-One to develop a new product line to avoid duplication. E-One also produced evidence that its delay in reintroducing the mark was attributable to its skittishness after an embarrassing experience introducing another brand. Finally, E-One produced evidence that it had paid a substantial sum of money for the AMERICAN EAGLE mark only a few years earlier. Under these circumstances, we cannot say as a matter of law that E-One had no intent to reintroduce the mark within the reasonably foreseeable future. That question was a proper one for the jury. AFE thus was not entitled to judgment as a matter of law on the question of abandonment.

[The court proceeded to conclude that AFE was nevertheless entitled to a new trial because the district court failed to instruct the jury that "intent to resume use" for purposes of abandonment analysis must be intent to resume use in the reasonably foreseeable future. Failure to give the instruction was prejudicial error requiring a new trial.]

NOTES AND QUESTIONS

1. *Overcoming abandonment by proving actual use: timing.*   In *Emergency One*, the court notes that a prima facie case of abandonment through three years of non-use can be rebutted by either a showing of actual use or a showing of intent to resume use. Regarding the former, the court calls for the trademark owner to produce evidence of actual use occurring "during the relevant period." Does this reference to the "relevant period" mean the three-year hiatus? That is, must the trademark owner show that the prima facie case was not correctly made out, because during the apparent three-year hiatus the trademark owner actually was engaging in use? What if the trademark owner fails to use the mark for four years but can show actual use beginning in year 4? Might this be acceptable as evidence that could potentially rebut the prima facie case of abandonment, even though the actual use occurred after the "relevant period"?

2. *Overcoming abandonment by proving actual use: nature of use.*   In 1995, Mallett, a salesman, began selling backpacks bearing the PELICAN mark. Anticipating substantial demand, Mallett ordered a large inventory. However, Mallett subsequently suffered a

series of business and personal setbacks. As a result, from about 1999 to 2002, Mallett's sales activity consisted of two trips per year to a trade show and sporadic sales from the trunk of his car. In August 2002, Mallett assigned the mark and business goodwill to Electro-Source. In December 2002, Electro-Source sued a manufacturer named Pelican Products for trademark infringement. Pelican argued that Mallett had abandoned the mark. If the evidence shows that Mallett's sales were made in a good faith effort to continue the business, but were nonetheless minimal and merely amounted to depleting his existing inventory, has Mallett "discontinued" use within the meaning of the Lanham Act §45 abandonment definition? Are his uses "bona fide" and "in the ordinary course of trade" as required under that provision? *See Electro Source, LLC v. Brandess-Kalt-Aetna Grp., Inc.*, 458 F.3d 931 (9th Cir. 2006).

Consider the following three cases. First, consider *Herb Reed Enterprises, LLC v. Florida Entertainment Mgmt., Inc.*, 736 F.3d 1239 (9th Cir. 2013), one of many lawsuits involving rights to the mark THE PLATTERS for a musical group. Herb Reed, one of the original band members, had signed an employment agreement in 1956 with Five Platters, Inc. (FPI), in which he assigned to FPI any rights in the name THE PLATTERS in exchange for shares of FPI stock. Eventually, Reed left the group, and, in 1984, FPI sued Reed for trademark infringement over use of the name. In 1987, Reed and FPI settled. Under the terms of the settlement agreement, Reed retained the right to perform as "Herb Reed and the Platters" but agreed not to perform under the name "The Platters." Apparently, the agreement did not address rights in any commercial recordings, and from 1987 forward, Reed continued to receive copyright royalties from previously-recorded PLATTERS songs. In 2012, Reed (through his company) sued Florida Entertainment Management ("FEM," successor to FPI) for trademark infringement. Reed's company apparently claimed trademark rights in HERB REED AND THE PLATTERS, and asserted that FEM's use of THE PLATTERS infringed. FEM argued abandonment. The court analyzed the issue by addressing uses of THE PLATTERS mark. According to the court

> [t]he receipt of royalties is a genuine but limited usage of the mark that satisfies the "use" requirement, especially when viewed within the totality of the circumstances—namely, that Reed was constrained by the settlement. . . . Receipt of royalties certainly qualifies as placement of "The Platters" mark on goods sold, and supports the finding that there was no abandonment.

Id. at 1248. Does the court's analysis reflect an appropriate use of the totality of the- circumstances test? Or does it suggest that the test could be largely pretextual? In any event, should the court have reframed its analysis, asking whether the mark HERB REED AND THE PLATTERS had been abandoned?

Second, consider the following. Assume that a firm called Action Ink held a registration for the mark ULTIMATE FAN for "promoting the goods and/or services of others by conducting a contest at sporting events." Action Ink last held a contest in 1995. Thereafter, until the time of suit (2012), Action Ink had solicited clients, sent out various infringement threat letters, but had held no contests. After initiating the suit, Action Ink had signed a licensing agreement with Tulane University under which Tulane took a license in exchange for donating 300 tickets (football tickets, we assume) to a charity of Tulane's choice. Do Action Ink's activities after 1995 constitute actual use? Establish evidence of an intent to resume use?

Third, consider how you might apply the totality of the circumstances test to the following facts. Specht formed a start-up company in 1998 called Android Data Company (ADC) to distribute software and engage in various web-based services. ADC registered ANDROID DATA for these services in 2002, but by that time, ADC had stopped its major operations. Assume that ADC discontinued the use of the mark at that time, and consider whether the following activities establish an intent to resume use:

- ADC maintained its website for some time, but by 2005 had allowed the URL *androiddata.com* to lapse.
- Specht passed out some business cards bearing the ANDROID DATA mark in 2005.
- Specht delivered a mass mailing to potential customers in December 2007, but generated no sales for ADC.
- ADC revived the website in 2009 under a new URL, *android-data.com*.

See Specht v. Google Inc., 747 F.3d 929 (2014). How, if at all, is your analysis affected by the fact that another start-up (Android, Inc.) was formed in 2005 to develop an operating system for a smartphone; the start-up was subsequently bought out by Google; and, in November 2007, Google released a beta version of the ANDROID operating system software? *See also S.C. Johnson & Son, Inc. v. Nutraceutical Corp.*, 835 F.3d 660 (7th Cir. 2016) (discussing whether evidence of sales through mark owner's website, and testimony that mark owner's products were sold at retail shops "around the country," sufficed to show mark owner's continued, national use, and also discussing whether the fact that the mark owner's sales appeared to be declining should undermine the conclusion of continued use).

3.   *Overcoming abandonment by proving intent to resume use: timing.*   When a mark owner seeks to overcome abandonment by proving intent to resume use, the mark owner must prove facts from which the requisite intent can be inferred, but must the mark owner also establish that he or she formulated that intent during the three-year period? If the evidence postdates the three-year period, would you conclude that the evidence can never be relevant to assessing abandonment? Can it be relevant under some circumstances? *See Crash Dummy Movie, LLC v. Mattel, Inc.*, 601 F.3d 1387 (Fed. Cir. 2010); *ITC Ltd. v. Punchgini, Inc.*, 482 F.3d 135, 149 n.9 (2d Cir. 2007).

4.   *Intent to resume use "in the reasonably foreseeable future."*   According to the court in *Emergency One*, when a trademark owner seeks to overcome abandonment by a showing of intent to resume use, the evidence must show that the trademark owner contemplates resumption "in the reasonably foreseeable future." One prominent decision credited with establishing this bit of judicial gloss is *Silverman v. CBS Inc.*, 870 F.2d 40 (2d Cir. 1989). Starting in the late 1920s, CBS had broadcast programs featuring the characters "Amos 'n Andy," first on the radio and then on television. In response to complaints from civil rights organizations, CBS ceased "Amos 'n Andy" broadcasts in 1966. In the late 1980s, Silverman wrote a script for a musical that was to feature the Amos 'n Andy characters. When CBS refused to license the characters, Silverman sued for a declaratory judgment that the script and proposed production would not violate CBS's intellectual property rights, and CBS counterclaimed for copyright and trademark infringement/unfair competition. On the trademark issue, Silverman cited CBS's twenty-one years of non-use of "Amos 'n Andy" as evidence of abandonment. CBS attempted to rebut by asserting that it had always intended to resume use at some undefined point in the future. The court found CBS's showing insufficient. To be consistent with the policy goal of preventing the warehousing of marks, intent to resume use had to be construed to mean intent to resume use within the reasonably foreseeable future.

5.   *Intent not to abandon versus intent to resume use.*   In *Exxon Corp. v. Humble Exploration Co.*, 695 F.2d 96, 102-03 (5th Cir. 1983), the Fifth Circuit concluded that a mere showing that the mark owner did not intend to abandon the mark was insufficient because it might permit "hoarding" of marks. According to the Fifth Circuit, the statute calls for an intent to resume use, which "requires the trademark owner to have plans to resume commercial use of the mark." Is the Fifth Circuit's distinction sound as a matter of trademark policy?

6.   *Subjective intent to resume use?*   When a trademark owner seeks to rely on a showing of intent to resume use to overcome a prima facie case of abandonment through non-use, should evidence of the trademark owner's *subjective* intent to resume use (or, more precisely, a trademark owner's disclaimer of any subjective intent *not* to resume use) suffice? *See Natural Answers, Inc. v. SmithKline Beecham Corp.*, 529 F.3d 1325, 1330 (11th Cir. 2008); *Vais Arms, Inc. v. Vais*, 383 F.3d 287, 294 (5th Cir. 2004); *Rivard v. Linville*, 133 F.3d 1446 (Fed. Cir. 1998). Consider whether the intent requirement is actually just a proxy for public perceptions about whether the mark continues to indicate source. If it is, then, irrespective of the mark owner's subjective intentions, if the mark owner objectively manifests an intent to abandon a mark, should the mark owner afterwards be estopped from arguing a contrary intent? Only if there is evidence that the defendant actually relied on the initial statement of intent to abandon?

Suppose that in 2008, a firm states that it plans to rebrand one of its subsidiaries. Assume that the firm adopts the new mark in 2008 but continues to display the old mark in some customer presentations, maintains a website with a domain name corresponding to the old mark, and accepts customer payments made in reference to the old mark. Should the firm's apparent prospective intent to abandon the old mark, articulated in 2008, affect the analysis as to whether the mark owner had discontinued use of the old mark? In particular, should it affect whether the firm's post-2008 uses of the old mark are deemed to be bona fide uses that would negate a finding that the mark owner had discontinued use? *See Wells Fargo & Co. v. ABD Ins. & Fin. Services, Inc.*, 758 F.3d 1069 (9th Cir. 2014).

7. *Intent to resume and a justification based on impossibility.* Suppose that a mark owner has an intent to resume use, but exceptional circumstances make it impossible (or at least impracticable) for the mark owner to act on that intent. In *Continental Distilling Corp. v. Old Charter Distillery Co.*, 188 F.2d 614 (D.C. Cir. 1950), Old Charter and its predecessors had been using OLD CHARTER in connection with whiskey starting in the 1870s. With the onset of Prohibition (in 1920), the trademark owner found itself left with a large inventory of whiskey that could be sold (legally) only to "druggists" for "medicinal purposes." Apparently, some limited amount of OLD CHARTER whiskey was sold through these channels. When Prohibition ended in 1933, another distillery, Continental, registered the trademark CHARTER OAK for whiskey, taking the position that OLD CHARTER had been abandoned and had become "the subject of reappropriation and the property of the first taker." The court rejected the argument "that the slightest cessation of use causes a trademark to roll free, like a fumbled football, so it may be pounced upon by any alert opponent." *Id.* at 619 (footnote omitted). For another famous example, relied on heavily by the court in the OLD CHARTER case, *see Beech-Nut Packing Co. v. P. Lorillard Co.*, 273 U.S. 629 (1927) (Holmes, J.) (excusing Lorillard's four-year lapse in use of the mark BEECH NUT for chewing tobacco; Lorillard had come into ownership of the mark as a result of an antitrust decree and had spent the time ramping up to distribute an updated product under the BEECH NUT mark). Where in the Lanham Act definition of abandonment did Congress afford room to justify non-use? The South African courts have also confronted the issue. *See McDonald's Corp. v. Joburgers Drive-In Rest.* 1997 (1) SA 1 (A) (Supreme Court of South Africa) (explaining non-use as a result of compliance with international sanctions aimed at ending apartheid). What circumstances should justify non-use? *See* TRIPS art. 19(1).

8. *Emergency One after new trial.* The new trial in the *Emergency One* case resulted in a determination that E-One failed to overcome the prima facie case of abandonment. If you were advising American FireEagle, how would you advise your client to proceed? Walk away from the litigation claiming victory? Can American FireEagle do anything about E-One's plans to use the AMERICAN EAGLE mark on a future line of fire trucks? *See Emergency One, Inc. v. American Fire Eagle Co.*, 332 F.3d 264 (4th Cir. 2003), for the second round of the dispute.

9.   *Is abandonment permanent?*   Suppose that *A* first adopts and uses a mark in 1990 and discontinues use of the mark in 1995. Suppose further that by 1998, *A* has engaged in no actual use, which triggers the presumption of abandonment. Suppose further that, as of 1998, *A* has no evidence that would overcome the prima facie case, so that anyone challenging *A*'s rights in the mark would prevail and the mark would be deemed abandoned. What exactly does it mean for a mark to be abandoned? Does it mean that *A* is estopped from ever again claiming exclusive rights? Does it merely mean that *A* loses the benefit of the early period of use?

The distinction becomes important if *A* has a sudden change of heart in 2000, for example, and newly adopts and begins using the mark. What are *A*'s rights as against a junior user, *B*, who begins using the mark on identical goods in 2003? Should the court rule that *A* has permanently ceded any claim of exclusive rights in the mark, and thus cannot enjoin *B*'s use? Or should the court rule simply that *A* can claim priority of use back to 2000—that, in effect, the 1990-95 uses, and the 1995-2000 abandonment, are irrelevant? *See, e.g., Gen. Cigar Co. v. G.D.M. Inc.*, 988 F. Supp. 647 (S.D.N.Y. 1997); *Indianapolis Colts, Inc. v. Metro. Balt. Football Club L.P.*, 34 F.3d 410, 412-13 (7th Cir. 1994).

Similarly, what are *A*'s rights as against intermediate user *C*, who adopts and uses the mark in 1999? Should a court rule that *A*'s change of heart in 2000 has "cured" the abandonment, such that *A* can reclaim the benefit of the 1990-95 uses and thereby establish priority over *C*? *See Cerveceria Centroamericana, S.A. v. Cerveceria India, Inc.*, 892 F.2d 1021 (Fed. Cir. 1989); *AmBrit, Inc. v. Kraft, Inc.*, 812 F.2d 1531 (11th Cir. 1986).

10.   *Is abandonment only a defense?*   Consider the following statement:

> [Abandonment] is not simply an equitable principle like acquiescence or unclean hands that can only be used defensively against a specific party. . . . Instead, abandonment is definitional in nature, setting limits on the scope of the trademark right.

Yellowbook Inc. v. Brandeberry, 708 F.3d 837, 847-48 (6th Cir. 2013). Do you agree? In the case, the mark owner Yellowbook argued that even if Brandeberry, alleged infringer, had previously held some rights in the mark, those rights had long ago been abandoned.

11.   *Actual use and maintenance of registered rights.*   Actual use is also required in order to maintain rights in a registration. For marks registered on the Principal Register, the Lanham Act includes other mechanisms to elicit evidence of the mark owner's actual use at predetermined times, even in the absence of any charge of abandonment. As we discuss in more detail in Chapter 5, the holder of a federal trademark registration on the Principal Register must make a series of filings in order to keep the registration in force. For example, Lanham Act §8 requires registrants on the Principal Register to file an affidavit of continued "use in commerce" during the sixth year of the U.S. registration. If the registrant fails to file a Section 8-compliant affidavit within the prescribed time, the PTO automatically cancels the registration. Similarly, a registration owner must file a renewal application, along with a Section 8 affidavit of continuing use, every ten years in order to renew the registration. Lanham Act §9(a).

12.   *Partial abandonment?*   Suppose that the Ritz Hotel, Ltd. ("Ritz") registers the mark RITZ PARIS for the following goods: "cutlery . . . ; forks and spoons; table knives; fish forks; cake forks; dessert forks; serving forks; table spoons; coffee spoons; serving spoons; mocha spoons; ladles; pie slicers; salad servers; sugar tongs; grape scissors; crab clippers; nut crackers." Six years later, when Ritz sues to enforce the mark against another firm (Shen), Shen argues that Ritz has abandoned rights in the mark because Ritz has made no use of the mark in connection with sugar tongs, grape scissors, crab clippers, or nut crackers for at least five years, and there is no evidence of intent to resume use. Should the court void the registration altogether? Or may the court uphold the registration but delete the unused goods from the registration? The facts are adapted from *Shen Mfg. Co., Inc. v. Ritz Hotel, Ltd.*, 393 F.3d 1238 (Fed. Cir. 2004). *See also Levi Strauss & Co. v. GTFM, Inc.*, 196 F. Supp. 2d 971, 976-77 (N.D. Cal. 2002). If Shen succeeds in persuading the court to delete the unused goods from the registration, what exactly has Shen accomplished? If Shen wants to begin using the mark in connection with soup spoons and sugar tongs, can Shen be assured of proceeding without Lanham Act liability? For sugar tongs but not soup spoons? What are the implications for the drafting of specifications of goods and services in registration documents? Note that if a trademark applicant makes intentional misrepresentations in the specification of goods and services, the applicant may risk losing the registration on the ground that it was fraudulently procured. *See* Chapter 5, section A, for a discussion of the standards for assessing fraudulent procurement in the registration process.

13. *Actual use in registration-based systems.* Although registration-based systems do not require applicants to undertake use in order to *acquire* trademark rights, use is typically required in order to *maintain* and thus to *enforce* those rights against a junior user. Under the EU Trademark Directive, a registration may be canceled ("revoked") for non-use if the owner has not made genuine use of the mark on the goods for five consecutive years without justifiable reason. *See* 2015 Recast Trademark Directive arts. 16 and 19. However, if during the interval between expiry of the five-year period and the filing of an application for revocation, genuine use is started or resumed, the mark will not be revoked.

PROBLEM 4-7: RESIDUAL GOODWILL

Are there other strategies for overcoming a prima facie case of abandonment by non-use? Would a showing of "residual goodwill" suffice? Consider the following problem.

Problem Statement

Dinwoodie and Janis, now respected trademark law professors, formerly performed as members of the band OUTRAGEOUS WAILING FUNK BROTHERS. Sadly, after enjoying moderate success through the mid-1980s, the band split up in 1989, vowing "never to be seen on stage together again" and promising "to give up the funk," which may be understood to mean "henceforth to lead respectable and mundane lives." Today, BROTHERS CDs are still available for purchase at various secondhand music stores, and Web users may access an unauthorized BROTHERS fan website, where BROTHERS music, stickers, and T-shirts are offered for sale.

Analyze whether as of today the band has abandoned the mark OUTRAGEOUS WAILING FUNK BROTHERS, in view of the *Ferrari* and *Stickley* cases discussed in the background readings below.

Background Readings

In *Ferrari S.p.A. Esercizio Fabbricheautomobiliecorse v. McBurnie*, 11 U.S.P.Q.2d (BNA) 1843 (S.D. Cal. 1989), Ferrari produced a limited number of 365 GTB/4 DAYTONA SPYDER vehicles between 1969 and 1974. Sometime after 1974, a California firm, McBurnie, began selling "kit" cars that closely resembled the Ferrari DAYTONA SPYDER. McBurnie argued that Ferrari had abandoned trade dress rights in the vehicles. The court rejected the abandonment argument. First, Ferrari had engaged in extensive parts supply and repair activities:

At trial, the plaintiff produced extensive evidence that since 1974 when it ceased the manufacture of its 365 GTB/4 DAYTONA SPYDER, it has continuously and extensively manufactured mechanical and body parts for the repair and servicing of its DAYTONA automobiles. The evidence indicated without dispute that Ferrari has manufactured and sold to an exclusive licensee an average of 5 or 6 entire front end body parts (everything but the hood, including bumpers), as well as 5 or 6 entire rear end body parts per year since 1974. The evidence clearly showed without dispute, that Ferrari has maintained, used, or replaced all of its original tooling for 365 GTB/4 DAYTONA, and has provided same to its exclusive authorized licensee to manufacture parts as they are needed by DAYTONA owners. There was unrebutted testimony that Ferrari would manufacture original replacement parts for all its cars, including the 365 GTB/4 DAYTONA, so long as these cars continue to be owned and driven.

. . .

The evidence also shows that the Ferrari DAYTONA SPYDERS are still driven extensively. Unrebutted testimony was given by personnel from Ferrari of North America and Ferrari's exclusive parts licensee that they continuously service DAYTONA SPYDERS, including the recommended 3,000 mile check-ups.

Second, the existence of residual goodwill also cut against any conclusion of abandonment:

Even independent of such activities by Ferrari, the DAYTONA SPYDER design is strongly associated with Ferrari, and such association is extremely positive. In essence, Ferrari has not only achieved a strong existing goodwill but continues to maintain a residual goodwill in the unique design of the DAYTONA SPYDER.

In *L. & J.G. Stickley, Inc. v. Canal Dover Furniture Co.*, 79 F.3d 258 (2d Cir. 1996), Gustav Stickley, and later L. & J.G. Stickley, Inc., manufactured "mission"-style furniture in the early twentieth century. The furniture was not commercially successful, and the firm ceased production in the 1920s, although the firm did continue producing other products. In 1989, in response to the renewed popularity of mission-style furniture, the firm began producing reproductions of certain Gustav Stickley designs. In 1993 another producer, Canal Dover, began selling mission-style furniture. Some of Canal Dover's products were similar to original Gustav Stickley designs, and the Stickley firm sued for trade dress infringement.

On the issue of whether the Stickley firm had abandoned trade dress rights, the Second Circuit opined:

Once a registered trademark has been abandoned, any subsequent user of the mark must measure its rights from the time the subsequent use begins, and cannot rely upon any residual secondary meaning in the mark from the original period of use. This is true even if it is the original mark holder that resumes use of the abandoned trademark. [cit.]

Here, the designs of Gustav Stickley were not produced from the early 1920s until 1989. In the parlance of registered trademark cancellation law, L. & J.G. Stickley abandoned its trade dress during this period of time. The over sixty years of non-use of the trade dress, during which time L. & J.G. Stickley manufactured boat hulls and early American reproductions, extinguished any rights L. & J.G. Stickley had in the Gustav Stickley designs. Although L. & J.G. Stickley resumed use of the trade dress in 1989 when it began to "reissue" the Gustav Stickley furniture designs, L. & J.G. Stickley was not entitled to benefit from any use of the trade dress prior to 1989.

The court distinguished the *Ferrari* kit car cases:

In this respect, our case is different from *Ferrari S.P.A. Esercizio v. Roberts*, 944 F.2d 1235 (6th Cir. 1991), *cert. denied*, 505 U.S. 1219 (1992). There, the court found that even though Ferrari had ceased production of its 365 GTB/4 Daytona in 1974, the car design maintained secondary meaning in the eyes of the public because Ferrari continued to design cars with a very similar appearance and continued to manufacture parts for 365 GTB/4 Daytona owners.

PROBLEM 4-8:   TRADEMARK MAINTENANCE PROGRAMS

You represent a large firm that manufactures a wide array of consumer personal care goods, including soaps, shampoos, toothpaste, paper goods, mouthwash, and so forth. The firm's management seeks your advice on a proposal to create a Trademark Maintenance Program for its registered marks. Management explains to you that, in response to shifting consumer preferences, the firm's advertising budget for promoting a given brand may vary widely over time. For example, some of its brands enjoy about a two- to five-year life cycle, after which sales tend to fall off and substantial advertising expenditures can no longer be justified, while other brands have a much longer life cycle. In addition, the firm has found that for many brands having a relatively short life cycle, the firm can often reinvigorate the brand for a "second life" after a two- or three-year hiatus.

The Trademark Maintenance Program would facilitate these variable needs by ensuring that the firm continues, albeit at a minimal level, sales and promotion with respect to brands that have been "retired" at the ends of their life cycles. One purpose for the program is to ensure that the firm will retain rights if it decides to "reinvigorate" the brand. Another is to preclude other entrants from appropriating one of the firm's retired brands. Yet another purpose is for the program to serve as a parking ground for experimental brands that might in the future become major brands for the company.

Is the program likely to succeed in preserving trademark rights for the company under current rules regarding trademark use? If not, what modifications might you suggest for enhancing the prospects that the program will satisfy trademark rules?

PROBLEM 4-9:   TRADEMARKS AND THE RELOCATION OF SPORTS FRANCHISES

Problem Statement

One dark night in 1984, several moving vans showed up in Baltimore, loaded the entire inventory of equipment of the Baltimore Colts (a National Football League (NFL) franchise), and vanished. The next morning, the vans appeared in Indianapolis and unloaded, whereupon the owner announced that he had relocated the franchise to Indianapolis. By all accounts, some Baltimoreans thought the move was a good riddance, while others regretted the blow to civic pride, not to mention the possible erosion of hotel and restaurant revenues.

In either event, the Colts retained their logos and trade dress but renamed the team the Indianapolis Colts. A few years later, in the early 1990s, another professional football league, the Canadian Football League (CFL), started a professional football franchise in Baltimore and named it the Baltimore Colts. Consider the numerous trademark "use" issues arising from this set of facts, as detailed below. To simplify the analysis, assume that the franchises individually own the relevant trademarks, rather than holding them as licensees from the respective leagues.

(1) Suppose that three months elapse between the day of the Colts' relocation and the actual appearance of promotional merchandise bearing the mark INDIANAPOLIS COLTS. Suppose that another three months elapse before the Colts franchise actually plays in an NFL pre-season game as the INDIANAPOLIS COLTS. The following day, the Colts franchise files a federal trademark application for INDIANAPOLIS COLTS for entertainment services in the nature of professional football games.

Suppose that before the first official INDIANAPOLIS COLTS merchandise appears, several enterprising individuals set up temporary stands near the Colts' stadium and began selling clothing and other merchandise imprinted with the name INDIANAPOLIS COLTS. Suppose that one of these individuals, Professor Janis' Brother Billy, actually files a federal registration on INDIANAPOLIS COLTS for promotional goods. Has Brother Billy established priority of use? Would it matter whether the media, and the citizens of Indianapolis, routinely used the designation INDIANAPOLIS COLTS to refer to the NFL football franchise starting on the day of the relocation? For a similar case involving the relocation of the Los Angeles Rams NFL franchise to St. Louis, *see Johnny Blastoff, Inc. v. L.A. Rams Football Co.*, 188 F.3d 427 (7th Cir. 1999).

(2) Suppose that the NFL franchise now known as the Indianapolis Colts sues the Baltimore CFL franchise, seeking to enjoin them from using the mark BALTIMORE COLTS. Assume that the NFL franchise has not engaged in any actual uses of the BALTIMORE COLTS mark since moving to Indianapolis, but has continuously used INDIANAPOLIS COLTS since at least the start of the 1984 season. Should the CFL franchise prevail on an argument of abandonment through non-use? If the CFL franchise does prevail, is the franchise free to use the BALTIMORE COLTS mark in connection with the CFL franchise? If not, why not? These questions were litigated in *Indianapolis Colts, Inc. v. Metropolitan Baltimore Football Club L.P.*, 34 F.3d 410 (7th Cir. 1994). *See also Rust Env't & Infrastructure, Inc. v. Teunissen*, 131 F.3d 1210 (7th Cir. 1997) (characterizing *Indianapolis Colts* as a "one-of-a-kind" case).

(3) Sports franchises have continued to relocate. In 2002, the Colts threatened to move to Los Angeles, which was without an NFL franchise because the Los Angeles Rams had moved to St. Louis (whose St. Louis Cardinals had moved to Arizona) and the Los Angeles Raiders had moved to Oakland (whence they had originally come and surely should stay). When the Cleveland Browns threatened to move to Baltimore (which was without an NFL franchise because the Colts had moved to Indianapolis), John Glenn (who had been with NASA but had relocated to the U.S. Senate) rose in that august chamber to plead for an end to the madness. His legislative proposal—the Sports Heritage Act—would have allowed a "community" to "keep a professional team's name and colors in the event of a relocation," if the franchise had been located in that community for at least ten years. *See* 142 Cong. Rec. S. 1649-02, S1652 (104th Cong. 2d Sess.) (March 7, 1996). Does the Act fit with existing notions of trademark use developed in this chapter? If not, should those concepts of use change to accommodate the Act? (Before you read further, be warned that Senator Glenn makes a graphic reference to the prospect of the Chicago Cubs departing Chicago—a prospect that readers (and especially the co-authors of this casebook) may find highly disturbing.)

For an arguably similar scenario occurring outside the context of sports franchises, consider the following. Suppose that a party registers the following mark for clothing:

Suppose that after some time, the party ceases using the mark in the form shown above, and instead uses the mark as shown below:

Assume that more than three years have passed since the party began using the newer mark. Has the party abandoned rights in the registered mark? Would it be appropriate to borrow the "same continuing commercial impression" test from the tacking cases to determine whether the party's use of the newer mark should be treated as a continuation of the use of the older mark? *See Jack Wolfskin Ausrustung Fur Draussen GmbH & Co. KGAA v. New Millenium Sports, S.L.U.*, 797 F.3d 1363 (Fed. Cir. 2015).

2. Abandonment Through Failure to Control Use

Recall that under the second prong of the Lanham Act definition, abandonment occurs

> [w]hen any course of conduct of the owner, including acts of omission as well as commission, causes the mark to become the generic name for the goods or services on or in connection with which it is used or otherwise to lose its significance as a mark.

Lanham Act §45.

The "course of conduct" most frequently alleged to give rise to abandonment under this prong of the definition is the trademark owner's failure to control uses of the trademark by franchisees or licensees. Similarly, where a mark owner purports to assign rights in a mark to an assignee, but the assignment is later determined to be invalid, abandonment may result. We begin with cases and materials involving licensing relationships and the doctrine forbidding "naked" licensing, and then turn to assignments, and the doctrine prohibiting assignments "in gross."

RESTATEMENT (THIRD) OF UNFAIR COMPETITION (1995)

Section 33, Cmts. A-C*

A. HISTORICAL DEVELOPMENT

. . .

Trademarks were initially used to identify goods that had been manufactured by a particular person or business. The historical conception of trademarks as symbols indicating the physical source of the goods led a number of early courts to conclude that the owner of a trademark could not license others to use the mark without destroying the significance of the designation as an indication of source. Licenses were sometimes declared invalid as a fraud on the public, and licensors risked forfeiture of their rights in the mark through a finding of abandonment.

---

* Copyright 1995 by The American Law Institute.

The narrow conception of trademarks as indications of physical source was eventually replaced by a recognition that trademarks may signify other connections between goods bearing the mark and the trademark owner, including the trademark owner's approval or sponsorship of the goods. The "source" identified by a trademark may now be a distributor, retailer, or other entity that selects the goods on which the mark appears. Trademarks thus came to be understood as indications of consistent and predictable quality assured through the trademark owner's control over the use of the designation. Emphasis on the quality assurance function of trademarks led modern courts to uphold the validity of trademark licenses when the control retained by the licensor was sufficient under the circumstances to insure that the licensee's goods or services would meet the expectations created by the presence of the trademark. Early cases found sufficient control when the licensor provided the principal ingredient for the product, enforced the use of a specific product formula, or controlled the licensee through stock ownership or other business relationship.

The right of a trademark owner to license the use of its mark by others was confirmed in 1946 by the enactment of the Lanham Act. Section 5 of the Act provides that the use of a mark by "related companies" inures to the benefit of the registrant or applicant for registration. A "related company" is one "whose use of a mark is controlled by the owner of the mark with respect to the nature and quality of the goods or services on or in connection with which the mark is used." The common law now recognizes the licensing of trademarks under similar principles.

B.   EFFECT OF A TRADEMARK LICENSE

If the trademark owner exercises reasonable control over the nature and quality of the licensee's goods or services, the benefits of the licensee's use accrue to the trademark owner. The owner may thus rely on use by controlled licensees to prove secondary meaning, the extent of the owner's geographic priority, or the fact of continuing use of the mark. If the license authorizes use on goods or services other than those previously marketed by the trademark owner, the licensee's use can also extend the trademark owner's rights into additional product markets.

An uncontrolled or "naked" license allows use of the trademark on goods or services for which the trademark owner cannot offer a meaningful assurance of quality. When a trademark owner fails to exercise reasonable control over the use of the mark by a licensee, the presence of the mark on the licensee's goods or services misrepresents their connection with the trademark owner since the mark no longer identifies goods or services that are under the control of the owner of the mark. Although prospective purchasers may continue to perceive the designation as a trademark, the courts have traditionally treated an erosion of the designation's capacity for accurate identification resulting from uncontrolled licensing as a loss of trademark significance, thus subjecting the owner of the mark to a claim of abandonment. . . .

C.   REQUIREMENT OF REASONABLE CONTROL

The presence of a trademark on goods or services does not guarantee any specific level of quality. Just as the trademark owner is free to choose the quality of its own goods or services, it is free to choose the quality of the goods or services marketed under the designation by its licensees. However, the presence of a trademark ordinarily indicates to prospective purchasers that the trademark owner has concluded that the goods or services are of sufficient quality to be marketed under its designation. The requirement of reasonable control is intended to maintain consistency in the quality of the goods or services marketed under the trademark by the licensor and its licensees by insuring that decision-making authority over quality remains with the owner of the mark.

The Lanham Act does not define the extent or manner of supervision necessary to satisfy the requirement of reasonable control. Cases both under the Act and at common law apply a flexible standard responsive to the particular facts of each case. The ultimate issue is whether the control exercised by the licensor is sufficient under the circumstances to satisfy the public's expectation of quality assurance arising from the presence of the trademark on the licensee's goods or services. Any evidence relating to the likelihood that the quality of the licensee's goods or services will depart from the standards imposed or anticipated by the owner of the trademark is relevant in determining the adequacy of the licensor's control.

. . .

Contractual provisions requiring the use of ingredients or parts supplied by the licensor or other approved source may in some cases constitute sufficient quality control. Under some circumstances the licensor may reasonably adopt and rely on the standards, inspections, or enforcement procedures of third persons such as independent testing organizations or government agencies. Similarly, supervision exercised by a controlled licensee over the use of the designation by sublicensees can be sufficient to protect the continued validity of the mark. Legal or practical control by the licensor over the operations of a licensee arising from stock ownership, common management, or family relationships can also contribute to a finding of reasonable quality control.

The law of trademarks relies primarily on the self-interest of the trademark owner to insure adequate control over the use of the mark by licensees. Because a finding of inadequate control can result in a forfeiture of trademark rights, courts impose a heavy burden on the person asserting a lack of reasonable control by a licensor. As a general matter, courts are reluctant to interfere with the marketing arrangements adopted by trademark owners, and minimal control over the quality of a licensee's goods or services is often sufficient to satisfy the requirement imposed under this Section.

STANFIELD v. OSBORNE INDUSTRIES, INC.

52 F.3d 867 (10th Cir.), cert. denied, 516 U.S. 920 (1995)

TACHA, Circuit Judge:

I.   BACKGROUND

In 1972, plaintiff developed several agricultural products including a fiberglass heating pad for newborn hogs. He presented these ideas in a letter to the president of First State Bank in Osborne, Kansas. Although plaintiff was not in the business of manufacturing these products at the time of his letter, he indicated that he would call his business "Stanfield Products" if he went into business. Osborne community leaders subsequently created defendant OII to manufacture plaintiff's products. OII was incorporated in May 1973.

The organizers of OII approached defendant Stanley M. Thibault in March 1973 about becoming involved with OII. Stanley Thibault moved to Osborne in September 1973 to become president of OII. In that same month, plaintiff agreed to allow OII to manufacture the products he had developed in exchange for royalties on sales (the 1973 agreement). Plaintiff simultaneously became an employee of OII.

In April 1974, defendant Ronald Thibault, Stanley's brother, undertook several special design projects for OII. Ronald became a full-time employee of OII in April 1975 when he took the position of vice president in charge of marketing and engineering. Ronald decided that OII needed to reduce its dependence on the company that distributed OII's products and develop its own markets. He concluded that OII would need its own trademark to foster its independence. When plaintiff learned of OII's plan to develop a trademark, he insisted that OII use the word "Stanfield" in its mark. OII agreed, and the parties entered into the following agreement (the 1975 agreement):

LICENSE AGREEMENT

THIS AGREEMENT, made and entered into as of this 5th day of July, 1975, by and between Phillip W. Stanfield, of the County of Osborne, State of Kansas, hereinafter referred to as First Party, and Osborne Industries, Inc., hereinafter referred to as Second Party:

WITNESSETH THAT:

WHEREAS, Second Party is manufacturing certain products of which First Party is the inventor as enumerated in a certain License Agreement by and between said parties dated the 3rd day of October, 1973, and
WHEREAS, Second Party is manufacturing certain products other than invented by First Party, and

WHEREAS, Second Party desires to use the name "Stanfield" on all or part of the products manufactured by Second Party whether or not the same be invented by First Party, as a distinctive mark on said products in conjunction with the name of said products, and

WHEREAS, Second Party desires to use the name "Stanfield" as a distinctive mark on all or part of its products manufactured, at its discretion for a period of Fifteen (15) years from the date of this agreement and that said design of the distinctive mark bearing the name "Stanfield" shall be at the sole discretion of said party of the Second Part as to the design of the same, and

WHEREAS, both parties agree that all products manufactured by Second Party shall bear a distinctive mark and shall bear all marks required by the patent laws pertaining to and in conjunction with a License Agreement between the parties entered into on the 3rd day of October, 1973, and in the event that any of those distinctive marks referring specifically to "Stanfield" products or used in connection with "Stanfield" products shall be registered as a trademark, Second Party will be entitled to use said trademark in connection with the License Agreement dated the 3rd day of October, 1973 by and between the parties and shall use said mark in accordance with the trademark laws.

WHEREAS, in consideration of the use of the name "Stanfield" as above described in this Agreement in regard to any or all products manufactured by Second Party, the sum of $75.00 shall be paid to First Party by Second Party for the use of said name as above described.

This Agreement shall inure to the benefit of and be binding upon the Parties hereto, their respective heirs, legal representatives, successors and assigns.

IN WITNESS WHEREOF, the parties have hereunto executed this Agreement as of the day and year first above written.

OII commissioned an artist to design two trademarks. One mark consisted of the word "Stanfield"; the other mark was a circle design incorporating the word "Stanfield." By September 1976 OII was using both trademarks. OII applied for registration of these trademarks in March 1977. The United States Patent and Trademark Office registered the circle design mark on the principal register of trademarks on January 24, 1978.

Meanwhile, plaintiff had become ill and grown disenchanted with OII. He resigned from OII on September 23, 1975. Since his resignation, plaintiff has had no involvement with OII. In February 1976, the Patent and Trademark Office rejected plaintiff's application for a patent on the hog heating pad. OII stopped paying royalties to plaintiff on the sale of heating pads in December 1976.

Plaintiff filed his first lawsuit against OII in Kansas state court in February 1977, claiming that OII had breached the 1973 agreement by discontinuing the payment of royalties. In that lawsuit, plaintiff alleged that OII's use of the word "Stanfield" was conditioned upon the payment of royalties. Although the jury returned a verdict in plaintiff's favor, the Kansas Supreme Court ultimately overturned that verdict. [cit.] The court held that, under the terms of the parties' contract, OII was not obligated to pay royalties to plaintiff after the Patent and Trademark Office denied plaintiff's patent application. [cit.]

In connection with the state court case, defendant informed plaintiff that OII considered the July 1975 agreement a release of plaintiff's rights in the word "Stanfield," and that OII had registered its "Stanfield" trademark. OII has continuously used its trademarks in commerce since 1976. In 1983, OII filed declarations with the Patent and Trademark Office to obtain incontestability status.

In September 1991, plaintiff requested that OII discontinue use of the Stanfield trademark, basing his request on his understanding that the 1975 license agreement had expired. OII continued using the trademark, and plaintiff filed this action alleging . . . that defendant's use of the Stanfield trademark violated 15 U.S.C. §1125. . . .

II. DISCUSSION

. . .

B. THE 1975 AGREEMENT

As a preliminary matter, we must determine the nature of the parties' 1975 agreement, which is at the core of their dispute. Plaintiff contends that the 1975 agreement was a limited license permitting OII to use the "Stanfield" marks for fifteen years. Defendants argue, and the district court agreed, that the 1975 agreement was a naked license, meaning that plaintiff abandoned any rights in the trademark.

Naked (or uncontrolled) licensing of a mark occurs when a licensor allows a licensee to use the mark on any quality or type of good the licensee chooses. 2 J. Thomas McCarthy, *McCarthy on Trademarks and Unfair Competition* §18.15, at 69 (3d ed. 1992) [hereinafter *McCarthy on Trademarks*]. Such uncontrolled licensing can cause the mark to lose its significance. *Id.* When "a trademark owner engages in naked licensing, without any control over the quality of goods produced by the licensee, such a practice is inherently deceptive and constitutes abandonment of any rights to the trademark by the licensor." *First Interstate Bancorp v. Stenquist*, 16 U.S.P.Q.2d (BNA) 1704, 1706 (N.D. Cal. 1990). Thus, the licensor must "take some reasonable steps to prevent misuses of his trademark in the hands of others." *Dawn Donut Co. v. Hart's Food Stores, Inc.*, 267 F.2d 358, 367 (2d Cir. 1959). "The critical question . . . is whether the plaintiff sufficiently policed and inspected its licensee['s] operations to guarantee the quality of the products [the licensee] sold." *Id.* Because a finding of insufficient control results in the forfeiture of a mark,[2] a party asserting insufficient control by a licensor must meet a high burden of proof. *Transgo, Inc. v. Ajac Transmission Parts Corp.*, 768 F.2d 1001, 1017 (9th Cir. 1985), *cert. denied*, 474 U.S. 1059 (1986).

We first review the agreement between the parties for evidence of control. *See Dawn Donut*, 267 F.2d at 368. The 1975 agreement did not give plaintiff an express contractual right to inspect or supervise OII's operations in any way. OII had the right to use the "Stanfield" marks on any of the products it manufactured, including products not developed by plaintiff. Moreover, OII had the "sole discretion" to design the mark. The agreement, then, did not contemplate that plaintiff would have any control of OII's use of the "Stanfield" marks.

---

2. The parties dispute whether plaintiff ever had any rights in the "Stanfield" trademark. Because this case is an appeal from summary judgment, we accept plaintiff's contention that he had rights in the mark.

The absence of an express contractual right of control does not necessarily result in abandonment of a mark, as long as the licensor in fact exercised sufficient control over its licensee. *Id.*; *see also First Interstate Bancorp*, 16 U.S.P.Q.2d (BNA) at 1705-06. In the instant case, it is undisputed that plaintiff had no contact whatsoever with OII after his employment terminated. Plaintiff contends that he exercised control over OII's use of the "Stanfield" marks by examining one swine heating pad produced by OII,[4] by looking at several pet pads, and by occasionally reviewing OII's promotional materials and advertising. He also contends that his lack of knowledge of any quality control problems is evidence of his control. None of this, however, is evidence that plaintiff actually exercised control *over* OII.

Plaintiff next maintains that he relied on OII for quality control and argues that his reliance on the licensee's quality control is sufficient for him to avoid a finding of a naked license. We disagree.

In cases in which courts have found that a licensor justifiably relied on a licensee for quality control, some special relationship existed between the parties. *See, e.g., Taco Cabana Int'l, Inc. v. Two Pesos, Inc.*, 932 F.2d 1113, 1121 (5th Cir. 1991), *aff'd on other grounds*, 505 U.S. 763 (1992); *Transgo*, 768 F.2d at 1017-18; *Land O' Lakes Creameries, Inc. v. Oconomowoc Canning Co.*, 330 F.2d 667, 670 (7th Cir. 1964). In *Taco Cabana*, the court examined a cross-license between two brothers who had run a chain of restaurants together for a number of years. When the brothers decided to divide the business, they agreed that both would continue to use the same trade dress in their respective restaurants. Because the parties had maintained a close, long-term working relationship, the court held that they could justifiably rely on each other to maintain quality. *Taco Cabana*, 932 F.2d at 1121. In *Transgo*, the licensor itself manufactured at least ninety percent of the goods sold by its licensee, utilizing its own procedures to maintain quality. [cit.] And in *Land O' Lakes*, the court found that the licensor reasonably relied on the licensee to maintain quality because the parties had maintained a successful association with no consumer complaints for over forty years. [cit.]

In contrast, the relationship between plaintiff and defendant here was neither close nor successful. Since 1975, the parties have had no contact with each other except as adversaries in litigation. Under these circumstances, plaintiff could not rely on OII's quality control as a substitute for his own control as a licensor.

. . .

The terms of the parties' agreement, and their subsequent actions, compel us to hold that the 1975 agreement between plaintiff and OII was a naked license, by which plaintiff abandoned all his rights in the "Stanfield" marks.

. . .

---

4. The district court noted that plaintiff stated in a deposition that he examined one swine heating pad sent to him by his son. *Stanfield*, 839 F. Supp. at 1505 n.2. Plaintiff subsequently filed an affidavit contending that he examined additional pads "from time to time." We agree with the district court that plaintiff cannot create a genuine issue of material fact by contradicting his earlier statement. *See Bank Leumi Le-Israel, B.M. v. Lee*, 928 F.2d 232, 237 (7th Cir. 1991) ("[A] genuine issue of material fact cannot be established by a party contradicting his own earlier statements unless there is a plausible explanation for the incongruity.").

NOTES AND QUESTIONS

1. *Control over the consistency of quality.* The point of the quality control requirement is to ensure that goods or services sold under the mark are *consistent* in quality. This
is not the same as requiring "high" quality, nor does it mean that mark owners who deal in
high quality goods are excused from the quality control requirement, as Judge Easterbrook
pointed out:

> This argument that licensors may relinquish all control of licensees that operate "high qual-
> ity" businesses misunderstands what judicial decisions and the *Restatement* mean when they
> speak about "quality." There is no rule that trademark proprietors must ensure "high quality"
> goods—or that "high quality" permits unsupervised licensing. "Kentucky Fried Chicken" is
> a valid mark, see *Kentucky Fried Chicken Corp. v. Diversified Packaging Corp.*, 549 F.2d 368
> (5th Cir. 1977), though neither that chain nor any other fast-food franchise receives a star
> (or even a mention) in the *Guide Michelin*. The sort of supervision required for a trademark
> license is the sort that produces *consistent* quality. "Trademarks [are] indications of consistent
> and predictable quality assured through the trademark owner's control over the use of the
> designation." *Restatement [(Third) of Unfair Competition]* §33 comment b. See also William
> M. Landes & Richard A. Posner, *The Economic Structure of Intellectual Property Law* 166-68,
> 184-86 (2003).
>
> A person who visits one Kentucky Fried Chicken outlet finds that it has much the same
> ambiance and menu as any other. A visitor to any Burger King likewise enjoys a comforting
> familiarity and knows that the place will not be remotely like a Kentucky Fried Chicken outlet
> (and is sure to differ from Hardee's, Wendy's, and Applebee's too). The trademark's function is
> to tell shoppers what to expect—and whom to blame if a given outlet falls short. The licensor's
> reputation is at stake in every outlet, so it invests to the extent required to keep the consumer
> satisfied by ensuring a repeatable experience. See generally *Two Pesos, Inc. v. Taco Cabana, Inc.*,
> 505 U.S. 763 (1992).

Eva's Bridal Ltd. v. Halanick Enters., Inc., 639 F.3d 788, 790 (7th Cir. 2011).

2. *Naked licensing in the franchising context.* The *Stanfield* case involves a licensor-
licensee relationship. Allegations of naked licensing frequently arise in disputes following the
breakdown of a franchisor-franchisee relationship. In the typical case, a franchisor has terminated a franchisee on the ground that the franchisee has breached the franchise agreement.
The franchisee continues to operate the franchise under the franchisor's trademarks, and
the franchisor sues for trademark infringement. In defense, the franchisee argues that the
franchisor has not exercised sufficient control over the quality of goods or services provided
by franchisees, and therefore the franchisor has abandoned the marks. Although franchi-
sors typically prevail as against such challenges, courts are not uniform in their approaches
to examining the sufficiency of quality control provisions in franchise agreements. In some
cases, courts engage in a fairly searching review. The *Stanfield* case, though not a classic
franchisor-franchisee case, is indicative of the more searching review.

In other cases, courts emphasize that franchisees bear a very heavy burden of dem-
onstrating abandonment through uncontrolled licensing. For example, in *Kentucky Fried
Chicken Corp. v. Diversified Packaging Corp.*, 549 F.2d 368 (5th Cir. 1977), defendant
Diversified allegedly was selling supplies bearing Kentucky Fried Chicken (KFC) marks to
KFC franchisees without KFC's authorization. Diversified argued that KFC had abandoned
the mark by failing to control the quality of goods and services offered by KFC franchisees.
The court acknowledged the important public policy rationale underlying the quality con-
trol requirement:

> Courts have long imposed upon trademark licensors a duty to oversee the quality of licensees'
> products. *See, e.g., Denison Mattress Factory v. Spring-Air Co.*, 308 F.2d 403, 409 (5th Cir. 1962).

> The rationale for this requirement is that marks are treated by purchasers as an indication that the trademark owner is associated with the product. Customers rely upon the owner's reputation when they select the trademarked goods. If a trademark owner allows licensees to depart from its quality standards, the public will be misled, and the trademark will cease to have utility as an informational device. A trademark owner who allows this to occur loses its right to use the mark.

Id. at 387. Nonetheless, the court emphasized that challengers bear a "heavy burden":

> Retention of a trademark requires only minimal quality control, for in this context we do not sit to assess the quality of products sold on the open market. We must determine whether Kentucky Fried has abandoned quality control; the consuming public must be the judge of whether the quality control efforts have been ineffectual. We find that Kentucky Fried has sufficiently overseen the operations of its franchisees. Container has failed to carry the heavy burden placed on a party seeking to establish a forfeiture.

Id.

Which view of the quality control requirement—the more deferential view of *Kentucky Fried Chicken* or the more searching view of *Stanfield*—better serves the purposes of the trademark system?

3. *Naked licensing outside the franchising context—examples.* In *Eva's Bridal*, various family members operated a set of bridal shops under the EVA'S BRIDAL mark. One family member had licensed the use of the mark to another using a license agreement that contained no quality control provisions, and the licensor admitted having made no attempt to exercise control over any aspect of the licensee's business. Faced with a claim that this constituted naked licensing, the licensor argued that it never had any reason to doubt that the licensee adhered to high standards. Analyzing the naked licensing issue, Judge Easterbrook asserted that there was no general rule for determining how much quality control sufficed. Instead, the nature of the business and consumers' particular expectations needed to be taken into account. *Eva's Bridal Ltd. v. Halanick Enters., Inc.*, 639 F.3d 788, 790, 791 (7th Cir. 2011). Applying those considerations to the case at hand, Judge Easterbrook concluded that this case was "the extreme case: plaintiffs had, and exercised, *no* authority over the appearance and operations of defendants' business, or even over what inventory to carry or avoid. That is the paradigm of a naked license." Do you agree that this is the paradigmatic case? If it was reasonable for the mark owner to rely on the licensee to maintain consistent quality, and there was no evidence of inconsistencies, is there a reason to invoke the naked licensing rule? Or should there be a no-harm, no-foul exception to that rule? Should the court's contextual analysis include consideration of the fact that the business was not a formal franchising system, but was instead a less formal set of arrangements among family? If it should, which way should those considerations cut? Is *Eva's Bridal* consistent with the cases cited at the end of the *Stanfield* opinion?

In *Tumblebus Inc. v. Cranmer*, 399 F.3d 754 (6th Cir. 2005), plaintiff had retrofitted school buses with gymnastics equipment and had operated the buses in the Louisville area, taking them to birthday parties, day care centers, and the like. Plaintiff used the mark TUMBLEBUS in connection with the buses and the associated services. Later, plaintiff also began selling buses to others around the country who provided similar services, often using the TUMBLEBUS mark. Plaintiff did not set up a formal franchising operation, and its agreements with bus purchasers were generally informal and apparently included no formal quality control mechanisms. Eventually, a competitor, Cranmer, began using TUMBLEBUS for identical services in the Louisville area, and plaintiff sued. Cranmer argued that the plaintiff had abandoned the mark through naked licensing. Consider a pair of questions. First, should the court apply *KFC*'s more deferential approach to naked licensing (i.e., requiring the trademark challenger to make a strong showing of naked licensing) or the approach exemplified by *Stanfield*—or neither? Second, what of the argument that there can be no naked licensing because there is no license? A license requires quality control provisions because it authorizes junior users to engage in acts that would otherwise give rise to confusion. If junior users aren't engaging in any such acts, then any agreement between trademark owner and junior user shouldn't be construed as a license, and therefore need not include quality control provisions. Assume here that uses of the mark by junior users who are geographically remote from Louisville would not require a license, a topic that we explore in more detail in Chapter 6. Should the court reject defendant's naked licensing argument? *See also Freecycle Sunnyvale v. Freecycle Network*, 626 F.3d 509 (9th Cir. 2010) (quality control issue involving a non-profit corporation that operated through local volunteer member groups interested in "freecycling"—meaning giving stuff away rather than throwing it away).

   4.   *Consent as a substitute for the quality control requirement?*   During consideration of the Revised Trademark Law Treaty in 2003 by the WIPO Standing Committee on Trademarks, some participants proposed that countries should be required to treat licensed uses as inuring to the benefit of the licensor as long as the licensee's use occurred with the consent of the licensor. Draft Revised Trademark Law Treaty, WIPO Doc. SCT 11/2 Art. 20 (June 12, 2003) (specifying that "use of a mark by natural persons or legal entities other than the holder shall be deemed to constitute use by the holder himself if such use is made with the holder's consent"). National statutory requirements of control would have been prohibited, according to the notes accompanying the draft. *See* WIPO Doc. SCT/11/4 at 20.03. Would such an approach have served the purposes of trademark law? Is the consent approach instructive in deciding cases like *Tumblebus* and *Eva's Bridal*, for example? The final text of the treaty (called the Singapore Treaty on the Law of Trademarks, adopted in 2006), omitted the relevant consent language, largely at the behest of the United States. *See* Singapore Treaty on the Law of Trademarks Art. 19(3) (successor to draft Art. 20), *http:// www.wipo.int/treaties/en/ip/singapore/*.

   5.   *Intersection between abandonment and genericness.*   The second prong of the abandonment definition incorporates the concept of genericness. Genericness refers to a situation in which parties use a mark in connection with an entire class of goods, perhaps as a consequence of a mark owner's failure to control usage. Paragraph (2) of the Lanham Act definition of abandonment also specifies that "[p]urchaser motivation shall not be a test for determining abandonment under this paragraph." Congress added this language in the Trademark Clarification Act of 1984, Pub. L. No. 98-620, 98 Stat. 3335 (Nov. 1984), to repudiate a passage in a Ninth Circuit decision, *Anti-Monopoly, Inc. v. General Mills Fun Group, Inc.*, 684 F.2d 1316 (9th Cir. 1982), *cert. denied*, 459 U.S. 1227 (1983). We discussed the *Anti-Monopoly* decision in Chapter 2.

   6.   *Licensee challenges to validity.*   Suppose that the party alleging that a mark owner abandoned through naked licensing is the former licensee. Should a licensee be able to challenge the validity of the mark that it has licensed? Should courts uphold license clauses that prohibit the licensee from making such challenges? *See Seven-Up Bottling Co. v. Seven-Up Co.*, 561 F.2d 1275, 1279 (8th Cir. 1977); *cf. Lear, Inc. v. Adkins*, 395 U.S. 653, 673-74 (1969); *see also MedImmune, Inc. v. Genentech, Inc.*, 549 U.S. 118 (2007).

PROBLEM 4-10:   QUALITY CONTROL AND DIFFERENTIATED PRODUCT LINES

   Oxford Beauty Salon uses the mark LIVE HIGH in connection with high-end beauty salon services attractive to urban sophisticates. Oxford licenses the use of its mark for salon services to its licensee Hoosier Hair Parlor, with all necessary quality control provisions in the license, and takes all legally sufficient steps to control the quality of services provided by Hoosier under the mark (regular documented visits, inspections, etc.). But in fact, Hoosier's salon is not of the same caliber as Oxford's high-end salon, with a different physical appearance and offering a different range of salon services. Indeed, a consumer visiting Hoosier's salon who was familiar with the Oxford salon would perceive a noticeable difference, to put it mildly. Is this naked licensing?

UNIVERSITY BOOK STORE v. UNIVERSITY OF WISCONSIN BOARD OF REGENTS

33 U.S.P.Q.2d (BNA) 1385 (TTAB 1994)

HOHEIN, Administrative Trademark Judge:

[The Board of Regents of the University of Wisconsin System applied to register the "Bucky Badger" logo, the "Bucky on W" logo (reproduced below), and the word mark WISCONSIN BADGERS for various clothing items, educational services, and entertainment-related services, including sporting events. The University Book Store (UBS), Brown's, and other Madison, Wisconsin, retailers opposed, arguing that the university had abandoned rights in the marks. According to opposers, numerous third parties unaffiliated with the university had used the marks for many years, and the university had admitted in internal correspondence that it lacked exclusive rights in the marks.]

ABANDONMENT

Turning first to the claim of abandonment, since it is the ground common to all six oppositions, opposers essentially contend that whatever ownership interests, if any, applicant may be said to have had in the "Bucky Badger," "Bucky on W" and "WISCONSIN BADGERS" marks, such rights have been lost by applicant's failure over many years prior to January 1988 to control the nature and quality of numerous third-party uses of the marks. Applicant, while not disputing opposers' assertion that it did not actually create the marks in issue, argues that the purchasing public regards the marks as having originated with applicant inasmuch as it has adopted and continuously used them as indicia of source or origin for its goods and services. . . .

Section 45 of the Trademark Act provides in relevant part that "[a] mark shall be deemed to be 'abandoned' when," among other things, "the following occurs":

(2) When any course of conduct of the owner, including acts of omission as well as commission, causes the mark to become the generic name for the goods or services on or in connection with which it is used or otherwise to lose its significance as a mark. Purchaser motivation shall not be a test for determining abandonment under this paragraph.

As explained by Judge Nies in *Wallpaper Manufacturers, Ltd. v. Crown Wallcovering Corp.*, 680 F.2d 755 (C.C.P.A. 1982), maintenance of exclusivity of rights in a mark is not required in order to avoid a finding of abandonment, since "[f]ew longstanding trademarks could survive so rigid a standard." Instead, so long as at least some members of the purchasing public identify applicant with each of the marks at issue, it cannot be said that applicant's course of conduct has caused any of such marks to lose its significance as a mark. [680 F.2d at 765.] In this case, as in *Crown*, it is necessary to remember that (emphasis by the court):

[There is a] distinction between conduct of a trademark owner which results in a loss of right to enjoin a particular use because of an affirmative *defense* available to that user and conduct which results in the loss of *all* rights of protection as a mark against use by anyone. Only when all rights of protection are extinguished is there abandonment. E. Vandenburgh, Trademark Law and Procedure 267-68 (2d ed. 1968). While this states only a conclusion without any guides as to when all rights are deemed to have been lost, it is helpful, nevertheless, to keep the distinction in mind.

Id. Thus, under *Crown*, whether any of the opposers has a right to continue to use any of the marks applicant seeks to register is not determinative of the question of abandonment; rather, the focus must be on what rights, if any, applicant has in the marks. *Id.* Moreover . . . abandonment occurs only when a mark loses its significance as a mark. The court recognized, however, with respect to the obligation to police a mark, that (footnotes omitted):

Without question, distinctiveness can be lost by failing to take action against infringers. If there are numerous products in the marketplace bearing the alleged mark, purchasers may learn to ignore the "mark" as a source indication. When that occurs, the conduct of the former owner, by failing to police its mark, can be said to have caused the mark to lose its significance as a mark. However, an owner is not required to act immediately against every possibly infringing use to avoid a holding of abandonment. *United States Jaycees v. Philadelphia Jaycees*, 639 F.2d 134 (3d Cir. 1981). Such a requirement would unnecessarily clutter the courts. Some infringements are short-lived and will disappear without action by the trademark owner. . . . Other infringements may be characterized as "creeping," starting as a business name, and only become serious when later use is as a trademark. . . .

[680 F.2d at 766.]

. . .

Accordingly, applying the relevant law to the material facts not genuinely in dispute, we find that applicant has not abandoned the marks which it seeks to register. By way of background, it is clear that the "Bucky Badger" figure was created in 1940 by Arthur C. Evans, an artist with the firm then known as the Anson W. Thompson Company, which was requested by Brown's to produce, for sale by Brown's, a sheet of decals which included mascots designed and intended to represent applicant. . . .

Brown's has continuously sold decals depicting "Bucky" since 1940 and, later on, UBS likewise sold a version of such decals. Applicant's earliest use of the "Bucky Badger" figure it seeks to register occurred in 1948, when "Bucky" appeared on the front cover of the University's 1948 FOOTBALL FACTS AND CENTENNIAL SPORTS REVIEW. Although the "Bucky Badger" figure also eventually came to signify applicant's educational services, the earliest documented use of "Bucky" in such capacity is an appearance on the front cover of a 1957-58 *Freshman Course Guide*. . . . Insofar as use of the "Bucky Badger" mascot on clothing is concerned, both UBS and Brown's were selling apparel which was so imprinted by the early 1950s and have continued to do so. . . . Marketing of such clothing by applicant did not occur until, at the earliest, sometime in 1983.

[The TTAB found similar facts regarding uses of the "Bucky on W" logo.]

As to the "WISCONSIN BADGERS" mark, it is plain from the record that the words "BADGER" and "BADGERS" have long been associated with applicant. For example, the former word has been continuously used as the title of the University's yearbook since about 1889 and the latter term has been continuously used, first in reference to applicant's football team and later to refer as well to its other athletic teams, since 1893. While the phrase "WISCONSIN BADGERS" has long been used as a nickname for applicant's athletic teams and their fans, including members of the student body and faculty involved with the University's educational services, the earliest documented reference to applicant's athletic teams as the "WISCONSIN BADGERS" appears in a 1945 newspaper article. By the late 1980s such usage was quite prevalent. The record further discloses that Brown's, since as early as 1955, and UBS, since the early 1960s, have continuously sold clothing bearing the mark "WISCONSIN BADGERS" and that third parties, including certain other members of [the Wisconsin Merchants Federation (WMF), one of the opposers], have sold and/or continue to sell such imprinted apparel during the period from 1945 to the present. By contrast, it was not until the early 1980s that applicant itself first made actual use of the "WISCONSIN BADGERS" mark on imprinted clothing.

While opposers are consequently correct that in most instances, applicant has not been the first user of the subject marks for the goods and services for which registration is sought, it is critical to keep in mind that none of the opposers, or any third party, has ever used such marks as its own mark to identify and distinguish the particular goods and services involved in these proceedings. Opposers have admitted, in their responses to applicant's requests for admissions, that they have never made use of the marks applicant seeks to register as their marks. Instead, it is manifest from the record that opposers, and third parties alike, have merely sold and occasionally advertised items of apparel and other merchandise which have been imprinted with the marks.

Such sales and advertising by opposers and various third parties for many years prior to applicant's institution of a formal licensing program in January 1988 simply reflect the fact that applicant, over the years, tolerated sales and advertising of goods, including clothing, bearing the marks it presently seeks to register. Applicant, like numerous other colleges and universities, permitted others to sell imprinted merchandise as expressions of community support and goodwill. Advertising of merchandise featuring various indicia associated with applicant, including the marks at issue herein, frequently coincided with events sponsored by applicant, such as athletic events and alumni gatherings.

Thus, rather than constituting uncontrolled use by opposers and third parties which resulted in the marks losing all source indicating significance, the reality of the situation which existed for many years may best be characterized as that of a royalty-free, nonexclusive, implied license to use marks which, particularly in and around the University's Madison campus, principally signified applicant in the mind of the consuming public and have continued to do so. . . . While it is also the case that, by and large, applicant had no formal system of quality control over the subject marks before January 1988, it must be remembered that "the inference of abandonment is not drawn . . . [where] satisfactory quality was maintained, and, hence, no deception of purchasers occurred." *Stockpot, Inc. v. Stock Pot Restaurant, Inc.*, 220 USPQ 52, 59 (T.T.A.B. 1983), *aff'd*, 737 F.2d 1576 (Fed. Cir. 1984). Therefore, even without, essentially, a formal system of quality control over the clothing and other imprinted merchandise sold by opposers and numerous third parties, the subject marks were not abandoned by applicant since the quality of the apparel imprinted with such marks remained at an acceptable level in virtually all instances.

Furthermore, while it is true that, as to the "Bucky Badger" figure and the terms "BADGER" and/or "BADGERS," "Bucky" and such words are in a sense ubiquitous, especially in and around the State of Wisconsin, due in large part to the facts that the badger (*taxidea taxus*) is the Wisconsin state animal and that Wisconsin is nicknamed the "Badger State," the third-party uses of "Bucky" and the terms "BADGER" and/or "BADGERS" shown on the record with respect to various diverse and distinctly different businesses located in Madison and other localities in the State of Wisconsin simply do not demonstrate that applicant has abandoned the marks it desires to register. Rather, and not surprisingly, that certain third parties, particularly those operating in and around Madison, are using the "Bucky Badger" image and/or the designation "BADGER" in connection with such disparate businesses as a laundromat, a bowling alley, a dental practice, and a restaurant/bar and social club clearly reflect an effort by those establishments to appeal to students at the University and thereby solicit their patronage. Use by other third parties of the "Bucky Badger" figure and/or the term "BADGER," in conjunction with such vastly different commercial enterprises as a fence company, a trucking firm, a bus company, a locksmith and security business, an automobile parts wholesaler, an industrial sand and limestone producer, a radiator repair shop, a snack food wholesaler, a food canning company, a medical supply firm, a self-storage facility, a balloon delivery service, a wholesale food distributor and a moving company, is plainly meant to emphasize or underscore that those firms are based in Madison or otherwise are located in the State of Wisconsin.

Opposers, in stressing that such uncontrolled uses by third parties amount to a forfeiture of any rights applicant may have had in the subject marks, are basically contending that applicant must maintain a right in gross in each mark. However, as noted previously, exclusivity of rights is not required as a matter of law in order for applicant to avoid a finding of abandonment. Even in instances where, arguably, applicant and others are each using the "Bucky Badger" figure and/or the words "BADGER" and "BADGERS," such as the use thereof by the Badger Conference and Niagara High School and the use of "Bucky" by groups of cross-country runners, Vietnam veterans and firefighters, the activities of these third parties are sufficiently different and distinct in nature from the university level educational and entertainment services rendered by applicant so as to preclude any inference of abandonment of the subject marks by applicant. Consequently, while a number of third parties, as well as applicant, use the image of "Bucky Badger" and/or the words "BADGER" or "BADGERS" in connection with their activities and the promotion thereof, the fact that such indicia have been diluted and are accordingly weak in terms of the scope of protection to which they would be entitled does not mean, in the case of both the uses thereof made by applicant, and those by its nonexclusive, implied licensees which inured to applicant's benefit, that the marks applicant seeks to register have lost their significance as marks. *See* 2 J. McCarthy, *McCarthy on Trademarks & Unfair Competition*, Section 17.05 (3d ed. 1994).

Opposers also assert that until January 1988, applicant not only failed to object to any uses of the subject marks by others, but conceded that such marks were in the public domain and thus could be used by anyone. Specifically, opposers place heavy emphasis on their contention that in the early- and mid-1980s, applicant disclaimed any protectable trademark interest in marks it now seeks to register by affirmatively stating, both in letters to third parties which had inquired as to whether permission to use the marks was necessary and in an internal memo, that the subject marks were in the public domain. For example, a November 5, 1982, letter signed by Michael A. Liethen, who was then the director of the University's Office of Administrative Legal Services, replied as follows to an inquiry received by applicant from Northern Cap Manufacturing Company:

This is in response to your October 12, 1982, letter inquiring about using University of Wisconsin–Madison logos on a line of headwear you plan to manufacture and sell.

With one exception, University of Wisconsin–Madison logos are in the public domain. They may therefore be used without a license or royalty arrangement with the University. The exception is the [athletic department] image of Bucky Badger superimposed over a large W. This particular logo is trademarked in the name of the Board of Regents of the University of Wisconsin System.

As for the logos which are in the public domain, they may be used without any prior arrangement with the University. Of course, your products using these logos may not be marketed in any way which states or implies that the product or product-line is endorsed by the University. The University would consider legal action under those circumstances.

[The Board proceeded to quote from other letters and internal memoranda.]

Opposers nevertheless acknowledge that, during this time frame, applicant modified the basic form letters it sent in response to third-party requests for permission to use the marks at issue. In particular, beginning in 1983 and continuing until the commencement of its formal licensing program in conjunction with CCI/ICE, letters written by Gail Snowden, who as an attorney with the University's Office of Administrative Legal Services was principally assigned the duty of responding to third-party inquiries regarding use of the subject marks and reviewing (along with Mr. Hove and Ms. Robinson) the nature and quality of any licenses granted, make no mention of the marks as being in the public domain. Instead, if the uses proposed were considered to be in "good taste" and otherwise did not imply University endorsement or expose the University to potential product liability problems, applicant granted the requests it received to use the marks on a royalty-free, nonexclusive basis. . . .

. . .

Moreover, uncertainties created by the litigation leading to *Pitt III*, including the prior decision by the court of appeals in *University of Pittsburgh v. Champion Products Inc.*, 686 F.2d 1040 (3d Cir. 1982), led applicant, as expressed by Mr. Hove in a December 17, 1982, memo to Mr. Liethen, to question its stance:

Earlier this week I was in Chicago at a meeting with my counterparts from around the Big Ten. The Michigan State representative was talking about their recent move into licensing their university name, seal, athletic mascot, etc. I asked him how they could do this since what they were suddenly protecting had been in the public domain for such a long time. He claimed that a recent reversal of the lower court opinion in the Champion vs. Pitt case has thrown out the public domain argument. According to him, it is now possible to control everything—including permission to use the *name* of your school on commercial items.

If this is the case, I feel we should rethink our position on this whole matter. There is a considerable amount of potential revenue to be realized from a licensing program. . . .

What is important for present purposes is not whether applicant was correct in its belief that the subject marks were in the public domain and therefore could be used by anyone, but whether such position had the effect on the relevant purchasing public, including not just the ultimate consumers but also UBS, Brown's, certain additional WMF members and other retailers which have marketed apparel imprinted with the marks, of causing the marks to lose their significance as marks. . . .

Opposers additionally fault applicant for failing to act against third-party users, including asserted infringers, and for a lack of effective quality control. In particular, opposers accuse applicant of failing to seek out and object to uses of the marks at issue or to take meaningful action with respect to instances of third-party use known to applicant. Opposers' contentions, however, ignore the reality of the symbiotic relationship which existed between the University and various businesses located in and around its

Madison, Wisconsin campus. As mentioned earlier, the record is clear that applicant tolerated various uses by others of the marks it seeks to register as expressions in the business community of goodwill and support for the educational and entertainment services provided by applicant. The presence of the University, with its faculty, support personnel and large student population, provided in turn a significant source of customers for local businesses, including the bookstores run by UBS and Brown's as well as other firms which in large measure have catered to the various needs of persons at the University.

Moreover, as previously pointed out, with but a single insignificant exception, there is no evidence that the nature and quality of imprinted apparel displaying the subject marks has been anything other than, at a minimum, that which meets the standard of merchantable quality, even in the absence of a formal licensing program by applicant. While the record also reveals a few sporadic and short-lived instances of uses of the "Bucky Badger" image and/or name in ways which applicant and some members of the purchasing public found offensive or indecent,[37] a standard of tastefulness, even if somewhat subjectively and at times haphazardly maintained, was effectively the norm.

. . .

Finally, opposers urge that there has been no fundamental change in the market for merchandise imprinted with the marks at issue which would justify applicant's adoption of its formal licensing program and excuse its asserted delay in claiming enforceable rights after many years of essentially regarding the marks as public property. Aside from the fact that, as discussed above, the supposition concerning applicant's alleged delay and its belief that the marks were in the public domain do not entitle opposers to relief on their theory of abandonment, the record is clear that applicant had legitimate reasons for adopting a formal licensing program and including therein the subject marks. Not only was applicant increasingly concerned with the prospect of additional embarrassing, obscene or other inappropriate uses of the marks and potential product liability problems if the marks were used in connection with dangerous, unsafe or unauthorized products or events, but the entire nature of the market for merchandise imprinted with college and university indicia underwent a major change starting at about the end of the 1970s. While it is undisputed that . . . applicant has experienced only a steady rather than a sudden or sharp increase in the growth of sales of merchandise imprinted with indicia of the University,[40] the market as a whole for merchandise, including apparel, bearing major college and university insignia

---

37. The chief example thereof concerns the sale during the mid-1980s of a T-shirt featuring "Bucky" "giving the finger" and bearing a correspondingly vulgar slogan. Sales thereof, by vendors unconnected with applicants, principally occurred in the fall outside the university's Camp Randall football stadium, although some of the shirts were also available in stores. Such sales provoked complaints to applicant primarily from alumni and parents of young children, who thought that applicant sponsored, endorsed or otherwise condoned the shirts and that the message conveyed thereby was inappropriate. Unlike the case of sales by an enterprising student at the University of "GET LUCKY, BUCKY" condoms, which ended shortly after a dean had a heart-to-heart chat with the entrepreneur and expressed applicant's objection to the use of "Bucky" in such a manner, applicant unsuccessfully tried various means to stop sales of the offending T-shirts, including imploring the district attorney (who declined out of First Amendment concerns) to take action against infringing vendors. Nevertheless, after a while, sales thereof quickly decreased and eventually ceased once the novelty of such shirts among the profane wore off.

40. The reason therefor is explained by the fact that applicant, during such period, was neither a prominent athletic power with many nationally ranked teams nor was its general reputation or following, despite a large number of graduates, truly national in scope.

increased dramatically during the late 1970s and continued to grow appreciably throughout the 1980s. The substantial growth in the popularity of such items, and the resultant need by the colleges and universities affected thereby for tighter control over their names and other identifying symbols, caused applicant and other similarly situated institutions of higher learning to recognize that the protection and enforcement mechanisms offered by formal licensing programs were necessary in order to avoid the problems brought about by the fundamental change in the market for imprinted collegiate merchandise. . . .

In summary, not only is it the case that none of the opposers, or any third party, has ever used the marks at issue as its own mark for the particular goods and services set forth in the applications involved in these proceedings, but the use thereby was tantamount to a royalty-free, nonexclusive, implied license from applicant which inured to applicant's benefit. Applicant tolerated uses of the marks, when their use in advertising and on clothing and other types of imprinted merchandise were plainly in reference to the University, as expressions of support for its athletic and academic programs by the business community. . . .

Consequently, while many third parties use or have used the "Bucky Badger" image and the words "BADGER" and/or "BADGERS" in connection with a wide variety of diverse businesses and activities which are distinctly different from the goods and services for which applicant seeks registration, such evidence demonstrates only that the marks are diluted and therefore weak. . . . Plainly, in these circumstances, the marks have not lost all significance as marks for applicant's goods and services and therefore, as a matter of law, have not been abandoned. . . .

NOTES AND QUESTIONS

1. *Special treatment for universities?* Did the TTAB treat the university more generously than it would have treated a for-profit corporate trademark owner? If so, is this treatment nonetheless justifiable, at least on the facts presented in *University of Wisconsin?* University trademark licensing has become a significant source of revenue for a number of colleges and universities around the country. *See, e.g.,* Jack Revoyr, *Non-Definitive History of Collegiate Licensing,* 88 TRADEMARK REP. 370 (1998); Robert Lattinville, *Logo Cops: The Law and Business of Collegiate Licensing,* 5 KAN. J.L. & PUB. POL'Y 81 (Spring 1996).

What are the practical implications of the TTAB's ruling for competition among universities located in the same state? For example, suppose that an operator of for-profit colleges sought to start the "Wisconsin A&M University." What is the risk that the scope of the University of Wisconsin's marks would encompass Wisconsin A&M—that is, what is the likelihood that consumers would be confused between the two? You should be able to provide a more doctrinally detailed analysis after you have studied the likelihood-of-confusion cases in Chapter 7. *See Florida Int'l Univ. Bd. of Trustees v. Florida Nat'l Univ., Inc.,* 830 F.3d 1242, 1265 (11th Cir. 2016), which concludes, among other things, that "potential college students are relatively sophisticated consumers who are unlikely to be easily or meaningfully confused by similar-sounding university names." We assume that you already knew that.

2. *Abandonment versus laches.* Having prevailed in the opposition proceeding, the University of Wisconsin is free to enforce its registered rights. It might be expected to act against future purveyors of unauthorized Badger apparel, "Get Lucky, Bucky" items, and the like. Suppose, however, that the university sues one of the local Madison bookstores that began selling BUCKY BADGER apparel in the 1940s. Should the university be entitled to enjoin the bookstore? The question points up the differences between laches and abandonment. The TTAB in *University of Wisconsin* held only that the university had

not abandoned rights in the marks. Whether a particular party would have a laches defense against enforcement of those rights is a separate issue. As the Court of Customs and Patent Appeals noted, there is a "distinction between conduct of a trademark owner which results in a loss of right to enjoin a particular use because of an affirmative defense available to that user and conduct which results in the loss of all rights of protection as a mark against use by anyone." *Wallpaper Mfrs., Ltd. v. Crown Wallcovering Corp.*, 680 F.2d 755, 765 (C.C.P.A. 1982). A decision of no abandonment merely signifies that *some* rights remain with the registrant. *See id.* ("Only when all rights of protection are extinguished is there abandonment.").

Cases like *Stanfield* and the *University of Wisconsin* involve trademark licensing arrangements. Essentially, a license provides a limited right for an individual to use the licensed mark. As we have seen, any use by the licensee inures to the benefit of the licensor if there is control of quality of the products prepared under license—i.e., if the license is not "naked." Naked licensing is one course of conduct that can trigger abandonment.

The cases that follow deal with assignments. An assignment is the outright sale and transfer of a mark. An assignee acquires the rights, including the priority, of the assignor. Because trademarks do not exist apart from the goodwill they symbolize, marks cannot be assigned unless accompanied by that goodwill. Efforts to make such assignments without the accompanying goodwill—designated as assignments "in gross"—are ineffective in transferring the assignor's rights (most particularly, the assignor's priority), as Lanham Act §10(a)(1) specifies:

> (a)(1) A registered mark or a mark for which application to register has been filed shall be assignable with the goodwill of the business in which the mark is used, or with that part of the goodwill of the business connected with the use of and symbolized by the mark. [However, no intent-to-use] application . . . shall be assignable prior to . . . the filing of the verified statement of use under section 1(d), except for an assignment to a successor to the business of the applicant, or portion thereof, to which the mark pertains, if that business is ongoing and existing.

An assignment that is in gross (and therefore fails to comply with Section 10) is another example of conduct that can lead to abandonment. If Dinwoodie purports to assign a mark to Janis with no accompanying transfer of goodwill, and Dinwoodie thereafter stops using the assigned mark, then (1) the Dinwoodie-to-Janis assignment will be nullified, such that Dinwoodie will have (unwittingly) retained rights in the mark, but (2) Dinwoodie's failure to use the mark may result in abandonment by Dinwoodie, leaving Janis to rely on his own adoption and use to establish priority. The cases and materials that follow discuss such scenarios, and explore what is needed in order for an assignment to transfer goodwill along with rights in the mark.

E. & J. GALLO WINERY v. GALLO CATTLE COMPANY
967 F.2d 1280 (9th Cir. 1992)

FLETCHER, Circuit Judge:

Defendant/Counterclaimant Joseph E. Gallo ("Joseph") appeals. Plaintiff/Counterdefendant E. & J. Gallo Winery ("the Winery"), owned by Joseph's older brothers Ernest and Julio Gallo, initially brought a trademark infringement action against Joseph for the use of the name GALLO on retail packages of cheese. Joseph counterclaimed against the Winery and Ernest and Julio, asserting that he had inherited a one-third ownership interest in the Winery (and thus its trademarks) from their parents, who died in 1933. The district court granted summary judgment in favor of Ernest and Julio on the counterclaims, granted judgment following a bench trial in favor of the Winery on the trademark claims, and permanently enjoined Joseph from using the GALLO name as a trademark on retail packages of cheese and in advertisements.

. . .

FACTS

This lawsuit arises out of a tortuous family history apparently involving sibling rivalry on a grand scale. Because Joseph's counterclaims concern his parents' estates, the relevant facts date back nearly a century. [The individual parties to the action, Ernest, Julio, and Joseph, are the children of Joseph Gallo ("Joseph Sr.") and Assunto ("Susie") Bianco, immigrants to Northern California from Italy in the early 1900s. Joseph Sr. and Susie married in 1908. Throughout the 1920s, the family purchased a series of vineyards, where they grew their own wine grapes, bought wine grapes from other local growers, and shipped the grapes to the Midwest and the East Coast, where customers made wine with them for their home use under an exception to Prohibition. Ernest and Julio became involved in this shipping business during the mid- to late-1920s. The Great Depression caused the grape business to suffer. Prices dropped; the 1932 season was a financial disaster for Joseph Sr. and Susie. On June 21, 1933, Joseph Sr. took Susie's life and his own. Joseph Sr. died intestate. Ernest obtained a court order authorizing him to continue Joseph Sr.'s business, described as "that of raising grapes and other crops and farming and selling produce." On April 29, 1935, the probate court approved Ernest's second and final account of Joseph Sr.'s estate, and entered a decree distributing a one-third interest in the remaining assets of the estate to each son. The account did not list any wine business or assets of a wine business, but it did list "E. & J. Gallo Winery" as a creditor of the estate. "E. & J. Gallo Winery" refers to the partnership Ernest and Julio formed after their parents' deaths.]

. . .

II.   THE GALLO BROTHERS DEVELOP THEIR BUSINESSES

Ernest and Julio continued to develop their wine business through the 1930s, selling the wine in barrels and tank cars to regional bottlers, who in turn sold the wine under their own trademarks. It was not until 1940, when the Winery began its own bottling operations, that the GALLO label was seen by the consuming public. In 1942, the Winery obtained its first registered trademark including the word GALLO. The following year Ernest and Julio moved the bottling operations to Modesto, and by the early 1960s, they had established distribution of the Gallo brand in all major U.S. markets. Today, following several decades of extensive advertising and promotion, GALLO wine has become the best-selling brand in the country.

Including its first trademark in 1942, the Winery has acquired eleven different registered trademarks containing GALLO. Ernest and Julio themselves registered all but one of the eleven. The exception is a trademark initially obtained by a company called Gallo Salame that developed in the late 1940s independently from the Gallo family—nobody in the company bore the name of Gallo. Gallo Salame initially sold salami and other prepared meat products to the service delicatessen trade, but in 1959 it began selling its products directly to consumers. By 1970 Gallo Salame was selling combination packs of sliced cheese and salami or pepperoni, and that year it obtained a registered trademark consisting of a shield with the word "Gallo" in script, together with a depiction of the Golden Gate Bridge and a cable car. In 1979, the Winery sued Gallo Salame for trademark infringement and dilution, and in 1983 the parties settled, with Gallo Salame assigning its registered trademark to the Winery as part of the settlement. The settlement also licensed the GALLO SALAME mark back to Gallo Salame, which continues to manufacture and sell its products under the mark.

. . .

Joseph managed the Winery's ranches until 1967, during which time he purchased and farmed several pieces of land, including vineyards and a dairy. In many of these ventures he used his name, "Joseph Gallo," as a trade name. He sold grapes from his vineyards—many to the Winery—under the trade name "Joseph Gallo Vineyards," and he operated his ranches under similar trade names incorporating his own name. In 1955, he established the "Gallo Cattle Company," a partnership, and he proceeded to raise and sell dairy cattle on the land not dedicated to the vineyards. In the late 1970s, the Gallo Cattle Company established a large dairy, and in 1983, it entered the cheese business.

Joseph's original intention in entering the cheese business was to sell cheese in large blocks to commercial purchasers, who would then repackage the cheese for consumer distribution. However, in 1984, Joseph began distributing consumer size packages of cheese for the retail market, labeled with a trademark consisting of his name, "Joseph Gallo," and a pastoral scene of cows and a dairy barn.

Later that year, Ernest and Julio learned that Joseph was selling retail cheese labeled JOSEPH GALLO, and Ernest told him that this infringed the Winery's trademarks and violated a prior oral commitment Joseph had given not to use the GALLO name on his products. The Winery also notified Gallo Salame, which insisted that the Winery either stop Joseph from using the mark or get him to enter into a licensing agreement with the Winery. For two years, the Gallo brothers negotiated unsuccessfully. Finally, on April 17, 1986, the Winery filed its complaint against Joseph, the Gallo Cattle Company, and Michael D. Gallo, Joseph's son and general partner of Gallo Cattle (collectively, "Joseph" or "defendants").

III. THE LITIGATION

The Winery's complaint included claims for trademark infringement, trademark dilution, and unfair competition, and sought an injunction preventing Joseph from marketing, advertising, selling, or distributing cheese bearing any trademark containing the word GALLO. In his answer, Joseph raised twelve affirmative defenses and brought several counterclaims against the Winery and Ernest and Julio. . . .

. . .

Following a seventeen-day bench trial on the Winery's claims from November 22 through December 28, 1988, Judge Coyle ruled for the Winery and issued an order on June 19, 1989 permanently enjoining Joseph from using the GALLO mark on retail cheese packages and from using the GALLO name in advertising. . . .

. . .

DISCUSSION

. . .

II. JUDGMENT FOR THE WINERY ON ITS TRADEMARK CLAIMS

The district court held that Joseph's use of his name on retail packages of cheese infringed the Winery's trademarks and constituted unfair competition under the Lanham Act, 15 U.S.C. §§1114, 1125(a). The court also held for the Winery on its state claim of trademark dilution, Cal. Bus. & Prof. Code §14330. Joseph challenges the district court's judgment on several grounds. . . .

. . .

B.   The GALLO SALAME Trademark

Joseph claims that the Winery lacks a valid ownership interest in the GALLO SALAME trademark because the agreement settling the Winery's infringement suit against Gallo Salame represented an invalid assignment of the mark. Without valid ownership of the GALLO SALAME mark, Joseph further contends, the Winery's wine marks alone cannot support the district court's judgment, because wine and cheese are different products.

Under its settlement with Gallo Salame in 1983, the Winery received an assignment of the GALLO SALAME mark, which it then licensed back to Gallo Salame for its continued use on combination meat and cheese packages. Joseph argues that this constituted an invalid assignment in gross, because the assignment did not transfer the goodwill or tangible assets of Gallo Salame. Assignments of trademarks in gross are traditionally invalid. "[T]he law is well settled that there are no rights in a trademark alone and that no rights can be transferred apart from the business with which the mark has been associated." *Mister Donut of America, Inc. v. Mr. Donut, Inc.*, 418 F.2d 838, 842 (9th Cir. 1969), *criticized on other grounds, Golden Door, Inc. v. Odisho*, 646 F.2d 347 (9th Cir. 1980). It is not necessary that the entire business or its tangible assets be transferred; it is the goodwill of the business that must accompany the mark. *Money Store v. Harriscorp Fin., Inc.*, 689 F.2d 666, 676 (7th Cir. 1982). As the Lanham Act states the principle, a mark is "assignable with the goodwill of the business in which the mark is used, or with that part of the goodwill of the business connected with the use of and symbolized by the mark." 15 U.S.C. §1060. The purpose behind requiring that goodwill accompany the assigned mark is to maintain the continuity of the product or service symbolized by the mark and thereby avoid deceiving or confusing consumers. 1 J. McCarthy, Trademarks and Unfair Competition §18:1(C) (2d ed. 1984).

The district court made a factual finding that goodwill had been assigned along with the mark GALLO SALAME. This finding rested on two facts. First, Gallo Salame gave to the Winery information "sufficient to enable [it] to continue the lure of business Gallo Salame had been conducting under the Gallo mark." This established the continuity that trademark law seeks to extend to the public. Second, the mark was transferred as part of the settlement of a *bona fide* infringement suit. It may not be immediately apparent why the settlement context implies transfer of goodwill. It does so because a *bona fide* infringement suit is predicated on the plaintiff's belief that the defendant has unfairly capitalized on plaintiff's goodwill; in other words, defendant wrongfully took goodwill from plaintiff. The district court found that prior to the assignment many consumers believed that Gallo Salame's products "were put out by the same company that put out Gallo wine. Since the Gallo brand had become equated with wine in the public mind, Plaintiff's goodwill rubbed off on Gallo Salame." It is this goodwill, the subject of the lawsuit, that was returned to the Winery.

That the transfer of the GALLO SALAME mark served the goal of minimizing consumer confusion becomes most clear when we view the assignment/lease-back transaction as a whole. In approving it, the district court adopted the reasoning of the federal circuit in *VISA, U.S.A., Inc. v. Birmingham Trust Nat'l Bank*, 696 F.2d 1371 (Fed. Cir. 1982), *cert. denied sub nom. South Trust Bank of Alabama v. VISA, U.S.A., Inc.*, 464 U.S. 826 (1983). In *Visa*, the court upheld an assignment/license-back of the mark CHECK-O.K., used in connection with check cashing services. The court found the arrangement to be valid as long as it satisfied the principal requirement applicable to all trademark licenses: that the licensor "provide[] for adequate control . . . over the quality of goods or services produced under the mark." 696 F.2d at 1377; *see also Star-Kist Foods, Inc. v. P.J. Rhodes & Co.*, 769 F.2d 1393, 1396 (9th Cir. 1985) (noting same requirement for valid license). The district court specifically found that the settlement agreement sets out, and that the Winery is maintaining, a quality control program under which the Winery actively monitors Gallo Salame's practices.

We agree with the federal circuit that a simultaneous assignment and license-back of a mark is valid, where, as in this case, it does not disrupt continuity of the products or services associated with a given mark. Here, consumers of Gallo Salame's products who mistakenly believed they were purchasing a product of the Winery were identifying the product with the Winery's goodwill. The assignment/lease-back had the beneficial effect of bringing "commercial reality into congruence with customer perception that [the Winery] was controlling [Gallo Salame's] use." 1 J. McCarthy, *supra* §18:1(I). The assignment/license-back is a "well-settled commercial practice." *VISA*, 696 F.2d at 1377; *see also Syntex Laboratories, Inc. v. Norwich Pharmacal Co.*, 315 F. Supp. 45, 55-56 (S.D.N.Y. 1970), *aff'd on other grounds*, 437 F.2d 566 (2d Cir. 1971); *Raufast S.A. v. Kicker's Pizzazz, Ltd.*, 208 U.S.P.Q. 699 (E.D.N.Y. 1980). We see no reason to invalidate it where it maintains the public's expectations of continuity.

[The court concluded that the district court did not commit clear error in making the ultimate finding that Joseph's mark created a likelihood of confusion.]

NOTES AND QUESTIONS

1. *What must be transferred in order to transfer goodwill?* Early U.S. case law on in-gross assignments required transfer of assets along with the mark (such as production equipment, manufacturing formulas, etc.) in order for goodwill to be transferred. While the accompanying transfer of the means of production remains relevant, more recently courts have performed a case-by-case analysis of whether the assignee is able to provide the product or service in question to consumers in a manner that preserves continuity of consumers' expectations. For example, a retail store selling supplies to diabetic patients under the mark SUGARBUSTERS purported to transfer the mark via a "servicemark purchase agreement" reciting the transfer of "the goodwill of the business connected with" the mark. The assignee was a limited liability corporation (Sugar Busters L.L.C.) that had been set up by a group of doctors and a former CEO who had co-authored a best-selling diet book that included "SUGAR BUSTERS!" as part of the title. The assignee did not succeed to any of the assignor's physical assets, but this alone did not make the assignment an improper in-gross transfer. Instead, it was necessary to consider whether the assignee's sales of the book would be sufficiently similar to the assignor's past retail sales of supplies to prevent consumer deception. *Sugar Busters L.L.C. v. Brennan*, 177 F.3d 258 (5th Cir. 1999) (finding a lack of sufficient similarity; vacating an injunction and remanding to the lower court for consideration of other trademark issues).

This movement is consistent with international trends toward liberalization of assignment rules. *See, e.g.*, Section 48(1) of the Canadian Trademarks Act; Michael Fammler, *The New German Act on Marks: EC Harmonisation and Comprehensive Reform*, 17 Eur. Intell. Prop. Rev. 22, 26 (1995) (noting that German law no longer requires the accompanying transfer of the business but that assignments are required to be recorded if they are to be relied upon by the assignee). Which approach is preferable for this inquiry: a relatively rigid rule that is relatively inexpensive to administer, or a flexible (but perhaps more fair) rule that is more expensive to administer?

2. *Proving that goodwill was transferred.* In considering whether the assignee is able to provide the product or service in question to consumers in a manner that preserves continuity of consumers' expectations, what factors should courts consider? *See* Restatement (Third) of Unfair Competition §34, cmts. b-c (1995).

3. *Implicit transfers of goodwill.* Under U.S. law, trademarks may be transferred by the sale of the business in connection with which they are used. "A sale of a business

and of its goodwill carries with it the sale of the trade-mark used in connection with the business, although not expressly mentioned in the instrument of sale." *President Suspender Co. v. MacWilliam*, 238 F. 159, 162 (2d Cir. 1916), *cert. denied*, 243 U.S. 636 (1917). Indeed, the transfer of the marks can occur even without express recitation of the transfer of corporate goodwill if the assets of the former company have been wholly transferred to a successor. *See, e.g., Dial-A-Mattress Operating Corp. v. Mattress Madness, Inc.*, 841 F. Supp. 1339, 1350 (E.D.N.Y. 1994), *reconsideration denied*, 847 F. Supp. 18 (1994). Do you agree with this approach? Does it suggest a lack of loyalty to the general concept of prohibiting in-gross assignments?

4. *Prohibition against assignment of ITUs.* Section 10 of the Lanham Act, 15 U.S.C. §1060(a)(1), states, in part, "[N]o application to register a mark under Section 1(b) . . . shall be assignable prior . . . to the filing of the verified statement of use under Section 1(d), . . . except for an assignment to a successor to the business of the applicant, or portion thereof, to which the mark pertains, if that business is ongoing and existing." This section of the Lanham Act was included by Congress in 1988 as a result of its concern about the potential for trafficking in intent-to-use applications before the use in commerce of the marks in question. S. Rep. No. 100-5115, 100th Cong., 2d Sess. 25 (1988). *See also Clorox Co. v. Chemical Bank*, 40 U.S.P.Q.2d (BNA) 1098 (TTAB 1996) (purported assignment of ITU prior to filing of verified statement of use was invalid under Lanham Act §10, and the registration that matured from the ITU was rendered void).

Suppose that *A* files an ITU application. While the application is pending, and before any statement verifying use is filed, *A* assigns the application to *C*. *A* is a wholly-owned subsidiary of *C*, and *C* takes the position that the transfer is a mere housekeeping matter. The assignment is recorded at the PTO and recites that the goodwill appurtenant to the mark is being transferred. What is the best argument that, notwithstanding the apparently innocuous nature of the transfer, it nonetheless violates the rule against assigning ITU applications in Lanham Act Section 10(a)(1)? *Central Garden & Pet Company v. Doskocil Manufacturing Company, Inc.*, 108 U.S.P.Q.2d (BNA) 1134 (TTAB 2013).

Should an intent-to-use application be assignable by the applicant prior to actual use of the mark and the corresponding issuance of a registration? *Compare* Section 10 of the Lanham Act *with* Daniel R. Bereskin, *Intent-to-Use in Canada After Three Decades*, 79 TRADEMARK REP. 379, 387-88 (1989) (arguing that under the Canadian system "the right to obtain a registration from an application based on intent-to-use can be assigned prior to the issuance of the registration, regardless of whether there has been any use of the trademark prior to the assignment [because] . . . the Registrar is required to register the trademark upon [proof of use] . . . by the applicant [or] the successor in title"). Which answer comports best with the philosophy underlying the protection of trademarks? What about a contract in which an ITU applicant agrees to assign an ITU application (and accompanying goodwill) to an assignee after the applicant files the verified statement of use? *See* TMEP §501.01(a).

5. *Recordation of assignments.* Section 10(a)(4) of the Lanham Act provides for the recordation of assignments, but recordation is not mandatory. It merely protects the assignee against subsequent fraudulent sales of the same trademark. Might there be any reason to require recordation as a prerequisite to assignment? If the assignee fails to timely record, and the assignor sells the same trademark to a third party, which party should own the trademark? What relief will be available to the "losing" assignee, who does not obtain the trademark?

6. *Transfers of domain names.* Domain names can be transferred, subject to constraints such as anticybersquatting statutes, far more easily than trademarks. Why might this be so? Which set of rules regulating assignments is preferable?

5

REGISTRATION

In this chapter, we consider issues that arise when an applicant seeks to register a mark under the Lanham Act. In contrast with most of the chapters of this book, in which we treat registered marks together with common law marks, this chapter focuses solely on procedural and substantive aspects of mark registration. We first provide an overview of the registration process and a discussion of post-registration actions and incontestability (section A). We next turn to a set of substantive rules on registrability—the Lanham Act §2 exclusions to registration (section B). The rules that we study in that section extend and refine our previous study of the standard rules on distinctiveness (Chapter 2).

A. THE REGISTRATION PROCESS, POST-REGISTRATION ACTIONS, AND INCONTESTABILITY

1. Overview of Relevant Provisions

The law of distinctiveness, functionality, and use derive primarily from case law, as the preceding chapters have demonstrated. By contrast, the law of the trademark registration process is embodied largely in Lanham Act provisions, as supplemented by the regulations of the United States Patent and Trademark Office (PTO) and the PTO's Trademark Manual of Examining Procedure (TMEP). The narrative in this section introduces and summarizes some of the important Lanham Act provisions for your convenience. Figure 5-1 lists the pertinent provisions.

FIGURE 5-1

15 U.S.C. §1051 (L.A. §1)	"Use" and "intent to use" applications for registration on the Principal Register
15 U.S.C. §§1057-1059 (L.A. §§7-9)	Issuance of registration; duration; renewal
15 U.S.C. §§1062-1064 (L.A. §§12-14)	Examination and publication of pending applications; opposition and cancellation proceedings
15 U.S.C. §§1072 and 1115(a) (L.A. §§22 and 33(a))	Effects of registration on the Principal Register
15 U.S.C. §§1065 and 1115(b) (L.A. §§15 and 33(b))	Incontestability of Principal Register registration and defenses to incontestability
15 U.S.C. §§1091-1095 (L.A. §§23-27)	Registration on the Supplemental Register
15 U.S.C. §§1111-1112 (L.A. §§29-30)	Notice; classification
15 U.S.C. §1126 (L.A. §44)	International conventions
15 U.S.C. §§1141-1141n (L.A. §§60-74)	Madrid Protocol

Consider the following fact pattern as you read this section's narrative on the registration process. Your client, JC, Inc., manufactures apparel for softball players at its facility in Bargersville, Indiana. JC, Inc. is a medium-sized company whose customers are high schools and competitive softball organizations in Indiana, Illinois, and Iowa. JC advertises regionally and sells its product from its headquarters in Bargersville and through its website. Two years ago, JC began manufacturing a new line of uniforms under the name JAGUAR. The JAGUAR line is JC's most expensive uniform, and sales have been strong.

JC's new general counsel, Aimee Kyle, has contacted you for advice on trademark protection for the JAGUAR name. Kyle asks a number of questions:

(1) Has the company lost the opportunity to claim trademark protection by failing to register prior to adopting the trademark? If the company does not need to register in order to acquire rights, what is the point of registering? If the company tries to get a registration, but fails, does the company have to stop using the JAGUAR name?

(2) Is state trademark protection a better option than federal trademark protection? (Kyle has heard that state trademark protection is cheaper.)

(3) Is the company obligated to search for similar trademarks before applying for registration? Even if it is not obligated to do so, would a search be desirable?

(4) If a registration is issued, how long will it last? Will the company need to take any steps to keep the registration in force?

(5) Is it a problem that the company has never used the TM or ® notice on its JAGUAR products? Should the company start using a notice? Which one?

(6) If the company succeeds in getting a registration, is it "bullet-proof," or might one of the company's competitors try to invalidate the registration through proceedings at the PTO? Through proceedings in court?

(7) If approximately a year from now JC plans to introduce a companion line of sweatshirts and jackets under the name BIG CAT, is it too early to file for a trademark registration?

(8) If JC hopes to market its products to customers in Mexico and Canada, must JC file separate applications to register JAGUAR in those countries?

(9) How much money will the company need to devote to these endeavors?

The following narrative addresses many of these questions.

"Examination" versus "Registration." Most trademark "registration" systems can be located somewhere along a spectrum between a pure examination system and a pure registration system. In systems falling closer to the pure registration model (such as the systems in place in many civil law countries), the trademark office reviews applications primarily for compliance with formal requirements, leaving the issue of compliance with substantive prerequisites largely to later proceedings (either in court or before an administrative tribunal). In such a system, the up-front investment in administrative apparatus is relatively low, the costs being shifted to the judicial system, where they are borne primarily by private litigants.

By contrast, in systems located closer to the pure "examination" paradigm, the trademark office examines applications in some detail for compliance with both formal and substantive requirements. Registered rights carry a presumption of validity, although evidence overcoming this presumption may be considered by courts in litigation. A well-functioning examination system requires a relatively large up-front investment in administrative resources, although applicant fees may constitute the funding source.

The U.S. "registration" system is closer conceptually in character to an examination system. Trademark examiners review applications for compliance with both formal requirements (many of which can be found in Lanham Act §1) and substantive requirements (largely the domain of Lanham Act §2 for common types of marks). The initial examination is ex parte, although the Lanham Act also provides for public participation in later stages of the examination process: after an application has been found allowable and is published, interested members of the public—such as JC's competitors—may initiate an administrative "opposition" procedure before the PTO during a limited time period, as detailed below. After the opposition period has expired and the registration issues, the public may initiate an administrative proceeding before the PTO to cancel the registration. Additionally, in keeping with an examination model, the Lanham Act provides that registrants on the Principal Register enjoy a presumption of validity, which may become conclusive to the extent that the registration qualifies for incontestable status. We discuss incontestability at the end of this section.

Ex parte adjudication schemes are, unfortunately, subject to abuse. There is no "opposing litigant" to challenge the applicant's assertions or, in extreme cases, to uncover the applicant's fraud. Where fraud is revealed (usually later, in an opposition or cancellation proceeding or in litigation), the registration is canceled.

Is the U.S. trademark system well served by an examination scheme? Should the United States create a scheme that is even more substantive (in that it is deemed to create rights that are hard to obtain but also hard to defeat with respect to the registered goods or services)? *See* Rebecca Tushnet, *Registering Disagreement: Registration in Modern American Trademark Law*, 130 HARV. L. REV. 867 (2017) (laying out a proposal for a more substantive registration system).

Why not dispense with examination on the merits and employ a true registration scheme instead? To what extent is it preferable to invest up front in thorough administrative procedures to minimize erroneous grants of rights? To what extent is it preferable to leave the difficult merits determinations for the courts, on the theory that the market will decide which registrations are sufficiently valuable to justify the "purchase" of an elaborate merits determination by a court?

How might the choices between examination and registration systems affect JC, Inc.'s business practices? Under an examination system, the examination of an application includes a search for prior registered marks that may be confusingly similar to the mark at issue in the application. (In ex parte examination in the United States, examiners do not search for unregistered marks in view of the practical difficulties involved in doing so. *See* TMEP §1207.03.) The applicant bears no obligation to conduct a search, although many applicants do so anyway prior to adopting a mark (to gauge the likelihood of receiving a registration and to assess the possibility that use of the mark may constitute infringement). *See infra* Chapter 12 for a further discussion of the relevance of trademark searches to trademark infringement remedies. By contrast, under a registration system, it is common for a trademark authority to conduct no search at all, or little more than a cursory search. Under which system is JC, Inc. better served? Based on what you know of the facts of JC, Inc.'s case, would you recommend that JC, Inc. do a pre-filing search? If you were conducting the search, where would you search? Note that many trademark lawyers use commercial search services rather than conducting searches themselves.

We have discussed how domain names are different from trademarks. However, producers now frequently wish to acquire the domain name corresponding to the trademark they wish to use. Thus, acquiring that domain name is frequently an important part of a marketing strategy. For example, suppose that JC, Inc. wants to set up a web page devoted to the Jaguar line at jaguar.com. Names in the most popular generic top-level domains such as .com, .net, and

.org are acquired on a quite different basis than trademarks. In particular, domain name rights are dependent on registration of the domain name with a domain name registrar accredited by ICANN. The domain name system can thus be regarded as a first-to-file system. Moreover, for the most common generic top-level domain names, the registrar undertakes only a very cursory review of the domain name application; as long as there is no identical name registered in that domain, the registration is granted. For example, prior domain name registrations of jacksonvillejaguars.com by the NFL football club or jaguarcars.com by the auto manufacturer would not preclude JC, Inc. from registering jaguar.com, because the registrar would check to ensure only that *that precise domain name* had not previously been registered.

Why was this system for the acquisition of domain names preferred over the alternatives? What are the alternatives? What are the costs and benefits of this approach? Can one defend the use of an examination system for trademarks and a registration system for domain names?

In 2002, ICANN authorized the creation of a variety of new generic top-level domains, such as .biz, .museum, and .info. Since then, there has been a proliferation of new generic top-level domains. The system for acquiring names in some of these domains is a modified registration system. For example, names can be obtained in the .biz domain (which is an unrestricted domain, meaning that ownership of names in that domain is not limited to particular types of businesses or persons) on a first-to-register basis. But before registration applications were accepted, there was a "sunrise" period during which trademark owners could assert a claim to the name in that domain corresponding to their trademark. What objectives underlie the use of sunrise periods? What does this tell you about the allocation of costs associated with a pure first-to-register system?

Advantages of Principal Register Registration.   Why should JC bother filing an application for registration in the first place? As we have learned, U.S. trademark rights are acquired through use, and unregistered rights can be enforced in federal court via a Lanham Act §43(a) action. Trademark registration, then, does not create rights; it only confirms the existence of rights. JC appears to have acquired federal trademark rights in JAGUAR for uniforms through JC's adoption of the mark in interstate commerce, subject to the possibility that others have acquired prior rights.

However, trademark registration does serve an important purpose: It provides notice to the public of the existence and nature of the claim of rights. In theory, this benefits the public by reducing the cost of avoiding infringement. For example, in deciding whether to adopt the mark BIG CAT for sweatshirts and jackets, JC could order a search of the trademark register to determine if the mark is the subject of a registration before investing in signage, advertisements, menus, and so forth. Of course, JC must be advised that there may be many holders of unregistered rights, and the existence of these rights could also affect JC's freedom to use the mark.

In recognition of the public benefits of having a trademark register, the Lanham Act provides significant inducements to persuade parties to register their marks on the Principal Register. As a consequence, trademark registration is routine, especially in large consumer-oriented businesses, though it is by no means ubiquitous. Sections 33(a) and 7(b) of the Lanham Act lay out the major benefits of Principal Register registration. Under these sections, Principal Register registrations constitute prima facie evidence of:

(1)   The validity of the registered mark and the validity of the registration;
(2)   The registrant's ownership of the mark; and,
(3)   The registrant's exclusive right to use the registered mark in commerce on or in connection with the goods or services specified in the registration.

In addition, owners of registered trade dress do not bear the burden of establishing non-functionality. *Cf.* Lanham Act §43(a)(3) (imposing such a burden on owners of unregistered trade dress).

In a number of courts, if a registration has not yet received incontestability, the presumption of validity is "easily rebuttable." *Custom Vehicles, Inc. v. Forest River, Inc.*, 476 F.3d 481, 486 (7th Cir. 2007). Courts have generally held that only a preponderance of the evidence is needed to overcome the Section 33(a) and Section 7(b) presumptions. *See Vuitton et Fils S.A. v. J. Young Enters., Inc.*, 644 F.2d 769, 775-76 (9th Cir. 1981) (the presumption of validity need not be rebutted by "clear and convincing" evidence; only a preponderance of the evidence is required); *Keebler Co. v. Rovira Biscuit Corp.*, 624 F.2d 366, 373 (1st Cir. 1980) (same). The presumption only shifts the burden of production to the trademark challenger. *See Liquid Controls Corp. v. Liquid Control Corp.*, 802 F.2d 934 (7th Cir. 1986); *but cf. Zobmondo Entm't, LLC v. Falls Media, LLC*, 602 F.3d 1108 (9th Cir. 2010) (shifting burden of proof, not just production, to defendant). Also, some courts have held that the presumptions are of the "bursting bubble" variety: Where the trademark challenger has met the burden of producing rebuttal evidence, the presumptions disappear. *See Igloo Prods. Corp. v. Brantex, Inc.*, 202 F.3d 814 (5th Cir. 2000); *Lane Capital Mgmt., Inc. v. Lane Capital Mgmt., Inc.*, 192 F.3d 337 (2d Cir. 1999); *Door Sys., Inc. v. Pro-line Door Sys., Inc.*, 83 F.3d 169 (7th Cir. 1996); *see also Tie-Tech, Inc. v. Kinedyne Corp.*, 296 F.3d 778, 783 (9th Cir. 2002) ("Once the presumption of validity is overcome . . . the mark's registration is merely evidence 'of registration,' nothing more.").

Other courts seem to take the presumption of validity more seriously. In one case, the First Circuit asserted that the trademark challenger must offer "significantly probative evidence" of invalidity to overcome the presumption. Only then would the registrant be required to "assume the devoir of persuasion on the issue of whether its mark has acquired secondary meaning." *Borinquen Biscuit Corp. v. M.V. Trading Corp.*, 443 F.3d 112, 118 (1st Cir. 2006). *See also Americana Trading, Inc. v. Russ Berrie & Co.*, 966 F.2d 1284 (9th Cir. 1992) (calling for district court to give greater weight to the presumptive effect of registration).

The Lanham Act §33(a)/§7(b) presumptions of validity, ownership, and exclusive right to use become *conclusive* if the registration attains incontestable status, as we will discuss below. In addition, Lanham Act §7(c) provides that registrations are accorded nationwide constructive priority of use as of their application dates. We will discuss the importance of nationwide priority of use in Chapter 6.

While the benefits of Principal Registration are significant, there are mitigating considerations. Registrations that have *not* become incontestable remain subject to "any legal or equitable defense or defect . . . which might have been asserted if such mark had not been registered." Lanham Act §33(a). Furthermore, even incontestable registrations are subject to a series of defenses. *See* Lanham Act §33(b), discussed below (in section A.3).

Principal Register versus Supplemental Register.   Certain marks that do not meet the standards set out in Lanham Act §2 but are nevertheless *capable* of distinguishing the applicant's goods or services from those of competitors, may be registered on the Supplemental Register in accordance with Lanham Act §§23-28. The Supplemental Register has been used primarily as a mechanism to assist U.S. applicants in acquiring foreign trademark registrations. A trademark applicant seeking to receive a registration outside its country of origin under the so-called *telle quelle* procedure of the Paris Convention must show that it has first acquired *registered* rights in its home jurisdiction. (The Paris Convention prohibits countries from requiring home country registration as a precondition to a direct application. *See* Paris Convention art. 6(2).) The Supplemental Register was developed to provide a means for U.S. applicants to show evidence of a home registration.

The Supplemental Register does also serve the additional function that its name implies: a parking place for applications that do not meet Lanham Act protectability standards, perhaps because the applicant is still in the process of attempting to establish secondary meaning, or perhaps because the applicant never really expects to establish it. Review the Lanham Act. Are there any substantial benefits to registering on the Supplemental Register? *See ERBE Electromedizin GmbH v. Canady Tech. LLC*, 629 F.3d 1278, 1288 (Fed. Cir. 2010) (noting that registration on the Supplemental Register does not confer a presumption of validity); *see also Innovation Ventures, LLC v. N.V.E., Inc.*, 747 F. Supp. 2d 853, 858-59 (E.D. Mich. 2010) (noting the argument that a supplemental registration confers no substantive rights and therefore cannot, as a matter of law, cause damages to a competitor).

Key Parts of the Application.   The application for registration of a U.S. trademark is a relatively straightforward document. *See* Lanham Act §1(a) (basic requirements for contents of use-based application), Lanham Act §1(b) (same, for intent-to-use application), TMEP Chapter 800 (providing a detailed recitation of the required contents of the application). Applications can be filed electronically. *See http://www.uspto.gov/teas/eTEAStutorial. htm* for a tutorial explaining the relevant forms and details for electronic filing. The majority of applications in the United States are now filed electronically. All applications seeking to use the benefits of the Madrid system must be filed electronically. *See In re Borlind GmbH*, 73 U.S.P.Q.2d (BNA) 2019 (TTAB 2005) (refusing to accept a filing that had been submitted in hard copy by mail).

Applicants cannot seek a single registration for multiple marks. An application for a "phantom" trademark (for example, *XXXX* FLAVORS, where *XXXX* is a placeholder for a term or symbol that may vary from mark to mark) would be rejected as violating the requirement for one mark per registration. *See In re Int'l Flavors & Fragrances Inc.*, 183 F.3d 1361 (Fed. Cir. 1999) (affirming the refusal to register "phantom" marks); *Cineplex Odeon Corp. v. Fred Wehrenberg Circuit of Theatres, Inc.*, 56 U.S.P.Q.2d (BNA) 1538 (TTAB 2000) (sustaining examiner's rejection of phantom mark).

A few key parts of the application bear mentioning here. Applications must contain:

- A list of the particular goods or services on or in connection with which the applicant uses or intends to use the mark, TMEP §805, §§1402 *et seq.*; 37 C.F.R. §2.32(a)(6), and a designation of the international class number(s) that are appropriate for the identified goods or services, if this information is known. TMEP §805, §§1401 *et seq.*; 37 C.F.R. §2.32(a)(7).
- A drawing of the mark, except for registrations of sound, scent, or other nonvisual marks. TMEP §807. For word marks, a typed rendition of the word suffices. TMEP §807.06; 37 C.F.R. §2.52(a)(1).
- A *filing basis* (specified either in the application as filed or in amendments to the application), discussed in more detail below.
- A specimen showing the use of the mark in connection with the goods or services. A Section 1(a) (use-based) application must include a specimen, whereas a Section 1(b) application need not include a specimen at the time of filing, but must include one in the statement of use. A specimen should be "a label, tag, or container for the goods, or a display associated with the goods"—that is, evidence of the manner in which the mark is presented to consumers, and verification that the mark is in use. 37 C.F.R. §2.56(b)(1); TMEP §904.04. If the applicant files electronically, the specimen should take the form of a digitized image. 37 C.F.R.

§2.56(c). Responding to concerns about the accuracy of registrants' allegations of use, the PTO has amended its regulations to clarify that the PTO has the authority to require, upon request, information about the identified goods or services with which the mark is used. The information may include additional specimens, affidavits, or other exhibits. *See Changes in Requirements for Specimens and for Affidavits or Declarations of Continued Use or Excusable Nonuse in Trademark Cases,* 77 Fed. Reg. 30197 (May 22, 2012). Such requests might be made in a variety of settings—for example, in connection with an applicant's statement of use to perfect an ITU application, or in a registrant's declaration of continued use under Lanham Act §8.

As we discussed in Chapter 4, U.S. law provided five filing bases: (1) actual use of a mark in commerce under Lanham Act §1(a); (2) bona fide intention to use a mark in commerce under Lanham Act §1(b); (3) a claim of priority, based on an earlier-filed foreign application under Lanham Act §44(d); (4) registration of a mark in the applicant's country of origin under Lanham Act §44(e); and (5) a request for extension of protection based on an international filing under the Madrid Protocol (also known as a Lanham Act §66(a) filing). *See* 37 C.F.R. §2.34 and TMEP §§806.01 *et seq.* for a list of the requirements for each basis.

Most U.S. applications are now filed under the intent-to-use filing basis, which we discussed along with actual use in Chapter 4 (section B). A much smaller number of applications involve the Section 44 filing bases. Foreign companies may make requests for extensions of protection into the United States under Section 66 (which implements the Madrid Protocol). We introduced Section 44 and the Madrid Protocol in Chapter 4, but the Protocol warrants some additional attention here.

From the perspective of U.S.-based applicants, United States membership in the Madrid system facilitates the acquisition of rights on a multinational basis. Applicants seeking registration with the PTO may seek an extension of protection in other countries of the Madrid system by so indicating when they file with the PTO. Those requests for extension of protection in foreign countries are assessed under the laws of the countries in question, just as requests for extensions of protection in the United States are assessed under U.S. trademark law.

Under the Madrid Protocol, if a "home" registration is canceled, any extensions of protections are canceled. *See* Madrid Protocol, arts. 6(3), 6(4); 15 U.S.C. §1141j(a). But, unlike the rule that applied under the 1891 Madrid Agreement, the trademark owner may, by filing with the national office in question within three months of the cancellation of the International Registration, transform its Madrid-based International Registration into a national filing (under Lanham Act §1 or §44) and retain the same priority date as was afforded the International Registration. *See* Madrid Protocol, art. 9 *quinquies.* The transformation procedure in U.S. law is contained in Section 70(c) of the Lanham Act. *See* 15 U.S.C. §1141j(c). As of May 2018, the Madrid Union had one hundred and one members covering 117 countries. Almost all now operate under the Protocol.

Disclaimer Practice.   Lanham Act §6 authorizes the PTO to require applicants to disclaim unregistrable components of otherwise registrable marks. The point of disclaimer practice is to allow the registration of composite marks having nonregistrable components, without creating the false impression that the applicant is claiming exclusive rights in any of the nonregistrable components in isolation. *See In re Stereotaxis, Inc.,* 429 F.3d 1039 (Fed. Cir. 2005) (upholding PTO's requirement that applicant disclaim the word STEREOTAXIS in a logo for twelve specified goods and services, including magnetic medical devices, on the ground that the term was descriptive of at least one of the products or services).

For example, consider the mark TOILET DUCK for a toilet cleaner. The mark is a "composite" mark (meaning that it can readily be divided into separate components), one component of which (TOILET) is descriptive or generic for the goods in question. In such a case, the applicant might disclaim protection for TOILET apart from the TOILET DUCK mark as a whole in order to secure registration of the entire composite mark. The disclaimer does *not* result in erasing the disclaimed component from the mark. In an infringement case, the court would consider the TOILET DUCK mark as a whole (not just the DUCK component) in determining infringement. *Cf. M2 Software Inc. v. M2 Commc'ns Inc.*, 450 F.3d 1378, 1384 (Fed. Cir. 2006) ("When comparing the similarity of marks, a disclaimed term . . . may be given little weight, but it may not be ignored.").

Publication.   If the PTO determines that the mark is entitled to registration, it publishes the mark in the *Official Gazette* of the United States Patent and Trademark Office for opposition. 15 U.S.C. §1062; 37 C.F.R. §2.80; TMEP §1502. Interested parties may monitor the *Gazette* and initiate opposition proceedings where warranted, as described below.

Opposition.   A trademark opposition is an inter partes administrative proceeding before the Trademark Trial and Appeal Board (TTAB), in which interested members of the public may challenge the PTO's decision to register a mark. More particularly:

> Any person who believes that he or she would be damaged by the registration of a mark on the Principal Register may oppose registration by filing a notice of opposition with the Trademark Trial and Appeal Board, and paying the required fee within thirty days after the date of publication or within an extension period granted by the Board for filing an opposition. *See* 15 U.S.C. §1063; 37 C.F.R. §§2.101 through 2.107.
>
> The notice of opposition must include a concise statement of the reasons for the opposer's belief that the opposer would be damaged by the registration of the opposed mark, and must state the grounds for opposition.

TMEP §1503.01. Note that the standing requirement—"any person who believes that he or she would be damaged by the registration"—is generous, as discussed in more detail below.

Opposers may assert a variety of grounds for opposition. Ordinarily, opposers assert that a registration would run afoul of one or more of the Section 2 prohibitions. Recall, for example, the oppositions grounded in Section 2(d) in our discussion of the priority of use issues in Chapter 4. Opposers may also assert that registration of a mark would cause damage as a result of trademark dilution, *see* Lanham Act §13(a), a ground of rejection that is not available to examiners in ex parte examination. *See* Lanham Act §2(f). The dilution concept is defined in Lanham Act §43(c). *See infra* Chapter 8 for a discussion.

One court elaborated on the procedural aspects of oppositions (and other inter partes proceedings) as follows:

> The TTAB is an administrative tribunal of the PTO with jurisdiction over inter partes challenges to the registration of trademarks. See 15 U.S.C.A. §1067(a). Procedure in inter partes matters diverges from that in district court at the trial stage, in that the taking of testimony does not occur in the presence of the TTAB. Instead, testimony is taken by deposition during set testimony periods, and the TTAB resolves all factual issues based on the written record submitted by the parties. See 37 C.F.R. §§2.121, 2.123, 2.125 (2006).
>
> Inter partes proceedings before the TTAB are governed by the Rules of Practice in Trademark Cases adopted by the PTO and set forth in Part 2 of Title 37 of the Code of Federal Regulations. See 35 U.S.C.A. §23 (granting the Director of the PTO the authority to "establish rules for taking affidavits and depositions required in cases in the [PTO]"). The PTO's

rules were "adapted from the Federal Rules [of Civil Procedure], with modifications appropriate to the administrative process." [cit.] Under the PTO's rules, the Federal Rules of Civil Procedure generally apply to all phases of inter partes proceedings, see 37 C.F.R. §2.116(a), including discovery and the taking of depositions, see 37 C.F.R. §2.120(a).

As an administrative tribunal of limited jurisdiction, the TTAB is empowered only to decide whether a given trademark is registrable. See 15 U.S.C.A. §§1067, 1068; 15 U.S.C.A. §1070; [cit.]. Although the TTAB has the authority to impose limited sanctions upon parties that fail to cooperate during discovery, see 37 C.F.R. §§2.120(e), (g), the TTAB lacks the authority to compel witnesses through the subpoena power to appear for testimony in inter partes proceedings. See 37 C.F.R. §2.120(b); [cit.].

Accordingly, Congress granted district courts subpoena authority under 35 U.S.C.A. §24 to command the appearance of witnesses in administrative proceedings before the PTO. See Frilette v. Kimberlin, 508 F.2d 205, 207 (3d Cir. 1975) (en banc); [cit.]. Under this statute, district courts have "jurisdiction to . . . issu[e] . . . subpoenas" in PTO proceedings. Frilette, 508 F.2d at 207. This narrow jurisdictional grant assigns district courts the limited function in contested PTO matters of "issu[ing] and enforc[ing] subpoenas in connection with the preparation of evidence for submission" to the administrative tribunal. Id. at 209. Thus, §24 assigns a supportive role to the district courts to ensure the smooth functioning of the procedures adopted by the PTO. See id. at 210 (describing the function of the district court as "cooperatively complementing" the PTO) (internal quotation marks omitted).

Rosenruist-Gestao e Servicos LDA v. Virgin Enters. Ltd., 511 F.3d 437, 443-44 (4th Cir. 2007).

Lanham Act §13 governs standing in opposition proceedings. The Federal Circuit has interpreted Section 13 to confer standing where the opposer has (1) a "real interest" in the outcome of the proceedings and (2) a "reasonable belief" basis for believing that damages will accrue. See Ritchie v. Simpson, 170 F.3d 1092 (Fed. Cir. 1999). According to the court, in order to satisfy the "real interest" requirement, the opposer must plead "a direct and personal stake in the outcome of the opposition," but this does *not* mean that the opposer must show "a specific commercial interest, not shared by the general public." Id. at 1095, 1096. As to the reasonableness prong, the court contemplated that the opposer might demonstrate reasonableness by alleging that he or she possesses a trait or characteristic that is "clearly and directly implicated by the proposed trademark," or by alleging that others share the same belief of harm from the proposed trademark. Id. at 1098. See also Empresa Cubana Del Tabaco v. General Cigar Co., Inc., 753 F.3d 1270 (Fed. Cir. 2014) (discussing these requirements).

Fraudulent Procurement.   In stating a filing basis, and in any other dealings with the PTO, the applicant owes the Office a duty of candor. An applicant who breaches this duty may be guilty of fraudulent procurement, a ground for canceling the registration. See Lanham Act §14(3) (fraudulent procurement is a basis for cancellation); Lanham Act §33(b)(1) (fraudulent procurement is a preserved defense against incontestable registrations). Prior to 2009, the Federal Circuit had held that an applicant engaged in fraudulent procurement when the applicant made statements which were (1) false; (2) made with knowledge of the falsity; and (3) material to the examiner's decision to approve the application. See L.D. Kichler Co., Inc. v. Davoil, Inc., 192 F.3d 1349, 1351 (Fed. Cir. 1999); Metro Traffic Control, Inc. v. Shadow Network, Inc., 104 F.3d 336, 340 (Fed. Cir. 1997). In a series of cases, the TTAB had held that the "knowledge of the falsity" prong could be satisfied by a showing that the applicant knew or should have known of the falsity of the statement. See, e.g., Medinol Ltd. v. Neuro Vasx, Inc., 67 U.S.P.Q.2d (BNA) 1205, 1209 (TTAB 2003). In 2009, the Federal Circuit rejected this interpretation. In re Bose Corp., 580 F.3d 1240, 1244 (Fed. Cir. 2009) ("By equating 'should have known' of the falsity with a subjective intent, the Board erroneously lowered the fraud standard to a simple negligence standard"). *MPC Franchise, LLC v. Tarntino*, 826 F.3d 653 (2d Cir. 2016) (clarifying that the Second Circuit standard for fraudulent procurement is consistent with *Bose*, and ruling that the mark owner knew that others had rights to use the mark and intended to mislead the PTO by attesting otherwise in his trademark application); *cf. Lorenaza v. South Am. Rest. Corp.*, 799 F.3d 31 (1st Cir. 2015) (ruling that the proponent of the fraudulent procurement allegation failed to allege any false statement).

TTAB decisions applying *Bose* treat it as having adopted an intent standard, and some have restated the fraudulent procurement test as follows: (1) applicant/registrant made a false representation to the USPTO; (2) the false representation is material to the registrability of a mark; (3) applicant/registrant had knowledge of the falsity of the representation; and (4) applicant/registrant made the representation with intent to deceive the USPTO. *See ShutEmDown Sports, Inc. v. Lacy*, 102 U.S.P.Q.2d (BNA) 1036 (TTAB 2012). The Eleventh Circuit rejected the argument that evidence of willful blindness should suffice to establish fraudulent intent. *Sovereign Military Hospitaller Order of Saint John of Jerusalem of Rhodes and of Malta v. Florida Priory of the Knights Hospitallers of the Sovereign Order of Saint John of Jerusalem, Knights of Malta*, 628 F.3d 1330 (11th Cir. 2012).

The *Bose* decision did not specify how to assess materiality for fraudulent procurement. The Federal Circuit's jurisprudence on inequitable conduct in the patent area (an analog to fraudulent procurement in trademarks) specifies that a showing of inequitable conduct also requires evidence of intent and materiality. In a critical en banc ruling, the Federal Circuit decided that materiality for inequitable conduct in patent matters is to be assessed under a but-for analysis: The misrepresentation or omission at issue is material if a patent would not have issued but for the misrepresentation or omission. *See Therasense, Inc. v. Becton, Dickinson & Co.*, 649 F.3d 1276 (Fed. Cir. 2011) (en banc). The court rejected a more relaxed standard of materiality on the ground that the use of that standard had led to a proliferation of dubious inequitable conduct charges. For example, the court rejected the "reasonable examiner" standard, under which materiality is satisfied simply by a showing that a reasonable examiner would have considered the information at issue to be important in deciding patentability. Should courts follow the *Therasense* ruling on materiality when assessing materiality in the context of fraudulent procurement of trademarks? For one approach, see *Fair Isaac Corp. v. Experian Information Solutions, Inc.*, 650 F.3d 1139, 1149-50 (8th Cir. 2011) (implicitly endorsing a "reasonable examiner" standard without discussing *Therasense* or the prospect of alternative standards).

Even under the stringent standard of the *Bose* case, fraud contentions may succeed, at least where the facts are extreme. In *Nationstar Mortgage LLC v. Ahmad*, 112 U.S.P.Q.2d (BNA) 1361 (TTAB 2014), Nationstar asserted that Ahmad had filed an application under Section 1(a) claiming use of NATIONSTAR in connection with various services, but knew that he had not used the mark for any of those services at the time of filing. The TTAB concluded that the opposition should be sustained on the fraud argument. The Board declined to credit Ahmad's testimony purporting to show use. The Board expressed skepticism about Ahmad's credibility, and noted that he was either unwilling or unable to provide information that would have helped authenticate the business cards, flyers, and letters that he offered in an attempt to corroborate his assertions of use. The Board inferred that Ahmad had made false representations with an intent to deceive the PTO. That Ahmad had filed the application *pro se* did not spare him from the fraud finding under these circumstances, the Board decided.

The Lanham Act establishes liability for applicants who procure registrations by fraud. Lanham Act §38 specifies that

Any person who shall procure registration in the Patent and Trademark Office of a mark by a false or fraudulent declaration or representation, oral or in writing, or by any false means, shall be liable in a civil action by any person injured thereby for any damages sustained in consequence thereof.

Under what circumstances would anyone be injured sufficiently to establish standing to bring a civil action invoking Section 38? Is the mere presence of a fraudulent registration on the register injury enough? The Supreme Court's decisions in *Nike, Inc. v. Already, LLC*, 568 U.S. 85 (2014) (cited in Chapter 2) and *Lexmark Int'l, Inc. v. Static Control Components, Inc.*, 134 S. Ct. 1377 (2014) (see Chapter 10) may assist you in your analysis. *See East Iowa Plastics, Inc. v. PI, Inc.*, 832 F.3d 899 (8th Cir. 2016).

2.   Post-Registration Actions

Notice.   Lanham Act §22 provides that registrants *may* display the registered mark with the ® ("R in a circle") notice or equivalent words. Technically, then, the use of the notice is permissive. However, registrants who fail to give notice in the form of such a marking cannot collect profits or damages for infringement unless the infringement defendant had actual notice of the registration, Lanham Act §22, or unless the mark owner prevails on a parallel claim for damages under Lanham Act §43(a). Accordingly, the use of the notice is ubiquitous among registrants, and JC, Inc. should be so advised.

Those who assert ownership of common law rights in a mark frequently choose to display the mark with a "TM" notice (or "SM" for service mark), to signal the marketplace informally that common law rights are claimed.

Maintenance and Renewal.   A trademark registration may remain in force indefinitely, but only if the registrant makes timely filings to maintain and renew the registration. In particular, Lanham Act §8(a) and (b) specifies that within the year following five years after registration, or within the six-month grace period after expiration of that period, registrants must file an affidavit attesting to the continued use of the mark in connection with the goods and services recited in the registration, or provide an excuse for nonuse. The Section 8 affidavit requirement operates to clear the register of deadwood—marks no longer in use or no longer of interest to the registrants.

Lanham Act §8(a) also provides that a trademark registration for which a proper Section 8 affidavit has been timely filed remains in force for ten years. However, a registration may be renewed for successive ten-year periods without limitation if the registrant timely files a renewal application. *See* Lanham Act §9(a) (specifying that the renewal application must be filed within one year before the expiration of the registration, or within the six-month grace period after the expiration of the registration upon payment of a grace period surcharge); *see also* 37 C.F.R. §2.182. Along with the renewal application, the registrant must also file a Section 8 affidavit of continued use. *See* Lanham Act §8(a)(3); TMEP §1604.01 (specifying that registrants must file a Section 8 affidavit or declaration of continued use or excusable nonuse at the end of each successive ten-year period following the date of registration, or within the six-month grace period after the end of the ten-year period). If JC's registration issues on August 15, 2007, when will JC need to make filings under Sections 8 and 15 during the following twenty-five years?

These provisions impose long-term, continuing obligations on trademark owners—and their lawyers. JC, Inc. must recognize the need to take affirmative steps to maintain its registration in force. If JC, Inc. develops a trademark portfolio of even modest size, it will need to budget resources for managing the required filings, perhaps through arrangements with outside counsel.

A particular concern is whether the affidavit of continued use accurately reflects the registrant's actual activities in the marketplace. A USPTO study released in July 2014 suggests that there is a reasonable basis for this concern. In nearly half of five hundred randomly-selected registrations, the registrant failed to meet the USPTO's request to verify the previously claimed use on particular goods and/or services. In May 2017, the USPTO sought public comments on a proposal for a streamlined cancellation proceeding limited to the grounds of either abandonment or nonuse. *Improving the Accuracy of the Trademark Register: Request for Comments on Possible Streamlined Version of Cancellation Proceedings on Grounds of Abandonment and Nonuse*, 82 Fed. Reg. 22517 (May 16, 2017), *https:// www.gpo.gov/fdsys/pkg/FR-2017-05-16/html/2017-09856.htm*. Do you think that the proposed changes would improve the utility of the register as a form of public notice?

Cancellation. The cancellation proceeding is a counterpart to the opposition proceeding. By way of the opposition proceeding, the Lanham Act provides for interested members of the public to challenge the PTO's decision to register in an inter partes administrative proceeding before registration actually occurs. The cancellation proceeding provides a similar opportunity for challenge after the registration has been issued. Like oppositions, cancellations are heard before the TTAB.

Lanham Act §14 provides that any person who believes he is or will be damaged by a registration, including as a result of dilution, may petition to cancel a registration. According to Section 14(3), a cancellation petition may be filed at any time after registration, if the cancellation is based on one or more of the following grounds:

- genericness
- functionality
- abandonment
- use of the mark by the registrant to misrepresent the source of the goods or services
- violation of Section 4 (relating to collective marks and certification marks)
- violation of Section 2(a), (b), or (c)

A petition for cancellation based on any other grounds must be filed within five years from the date of registration. *See* Lanham Act §14(1). This is a significant limitation. A cancellation based on the prior use of a confusingly similar mark (Section 2(d)), or based on any of the grounds specified in Section 2(e) (including descriptiveness), cannot be initiated after expiration of the five-year period. Importantly, these limitations operate independently of the incontestability provisions of Lanham Act §15. That is, even if a registrant fails to follow the procedures for attaining incontestable status under Section 15, the Section 14 limitations on the grounds for cancellation procedures after five years still apply. *See* TMEP §1605.06.

Appeals from the TTAB. As we previously noted (Chapter 1), while TTAB determinations are usually appealed to the Court of Appeals for the Federal Circuit (as authorized by Lanham Act §21(a)), the Lanham Act alternatively permits an applicant, or a party to an inter partes proceeding, to initiate a civil action in the place of an appeal to the Federal Circuit. 15 U.S.C. §1071(b)(1). As the Fourth Circuit has explained:

> In a §1071(b) action, the district court reviews the record de novo and acts as the finder of fact. *Durox Co. v. Duron Paint Mfg. Co.*, 320 F.2d 882, 883-84 (4th Cir. 1963). The district court has authority independent of the PTO to grant or cancel registrations and to decide any related matters such as infringement and unfair competition claims. 15 U.S.C. §1071(b)(1). The district court must admit the PTO record if a party so moves, and if admitted, the record

"shall have the same effect as if originally taken and produced in the suit." *Id.* at §1071(b)(3). Whether or not the record is admitted, the parties have an unrestricted right to submit further evidence as long as it is admissible under the Federal Rules of Evidence and Civil Procedure. *Id.; see also Kappos v. Hyatt,* 132 S. Ct. 1690, 1700 (2012) (interpreting §1071(b)'s patent parallel, 35 U.S.C. §145).

Kappos is the primary case interpreting the patent and trademark civil action statutes. In *Kappos,* the PTO argued that in a §145 proceeding where new evidence is admitted, the district court should defer to its findings, and "should overturn the PTO's factual findings only if the new evidence clearly establishes that the agency erred." 132 S. Ct. 1690, 1695-96 (2012). The Supreme Court rejected the PTO's premise that a §145 suit "creates a special proceeding that is distinct from a typical civil suit filed in federal district court," *id.* at 1696, and adopted the Federal Circuit's position that "where new evidence is presented to the district court on a disputed fact question, a de novo finding will be necessary to take such evidence into account together with the evidence before the board." *Id.* at 1700 (quoting *Fregeau v. Mossinghoff,* 776 F.2d 1034, 1038 (Fed. Cir. 1985)). It held that the district court "does not act as the 'reviewing court' envisioned by the APA," because the court must determine, among other things, "how the new evidence comports with the existing administrative record," and "as a logical matter [it] can only make [this] determination[ ] de novo because it is the first tribunal to hear the evidence." *Id.* at 1696, 1700.

Kappos also explicitly defines the only situation where consideration of the TTAB decision is permitted. The Court adopted the Federal Circuit's rule that "the district court may, in its discretion, 'consider the proceedings before and findings of the Patent Office in deciding what weight to afford an applicant's newly-admitted evidence.'" *Id.* at 1700 (quoting *Hyatt v. Kappos,* 625 F.3d 1320, 1335 (Fed. Cir. 2010)). In sum, where new evidence is submitted, de novo review of the entire record is required because the district court "cannot meaningfully defer to the PTO's factual findings if the PTO considered a different set of facts." *Id.*

Swatch AG v. Beehive Wholesale, LLC, 739 F.3d 150, 155-56 (4th Cir. 2014). Where the facts show that an applicant had failed to provide the newly-admitted evidence to the PTO, district courts are permitted to give less weight to that evidence. *Hyatt,* 625 F.3d at 1335.

In *Bd. of Trustees of the Univ. of Alabama v. Houndstooth Mafia Ent. LLC,* 163 F. Supp. 3d 1150 (N.D. Ala. 2016), the court dealt with the question of the relationship between district courts and the TTAB in the context of actions under Lanham Act §21(b). The University of Alabama had filed a Section 21(b) civil action challenging a TTAB decision dismissing the University's opposition to Houndstooth's registration of HOUNDSTOOTH MAFIA for various goods. The parties decided to settle the civil action. The terms of the settlement agreement provided that Houndstooth would assign rights in the mark to the University, and that the TTAB decision would be vacated. The court approved the settlement and entered a consent judgment ordering that the TTAB decision be vacated. The PTO resisted, asserting that private parties should not have the ability to undo a precedential decision of the TTAB by agreeing to have it vacated. Does (or should) the PTO have authority to resist the court's order? Is the district court in a Section 21(b) action acting, in effect, as a reviewing court akin to an appellate tribunal? Or is the relationship better characterized in some different way?

A legislative proposal advanced in 2015-2016 would have given the Court of Appeals for the Federal Circuit exclusive appellate jurisdiction over all appeals from Section 21(b) district court actions. H.R. 9, Innovation Act, 114th Cong. (2015-16) (proposed Section 9(h)(10), one of a set of so-called technical corrections).

Orders to Cancel. Recall that Lanham Act §37 empowers courts to order that a registration be cancelled in whole or in part. (We previously discussed Section 37 in Chapter 2 (after *Zatarains*), and in Chapter 3 (where we saw the Second Circuit exercising that power in *Louboutin*).) Section 37 does not create an independent basis for federal court jurisdiction. Rather, it may be asserted as a defense in a trademark infringement action. *Airs Aromatics, LLS v. Opinion Victoria's Secret Stores Brand Mgmt., Inc.,* 744 F.3d 595 (9th Cir. 2014).

3. Incontestability

As discussed above, Section 33(a) provides a set of evidentiary benefits to registrants on the Principal Register, and, in addition, the Lanham Act offers the benefit of "incontestability" to qualifying registrations. The key prerequisite is that the registered mark has been in "continuous use" for five years from the date of registration, and that it remains in use at the time when incontestability is claimed.

When it crafted the Lanham Act, Congress sought to provide a "quiet title" mechanism for trademark registrations. Eminent trademark lawyer Edward Rogers testified before Congress that

> the purpose of this incontestable business is to clean house. The existing law is that a trademark of the registrant may be canceled at any time, and the courts interpret "at any time" to mean just that. The result is that old marks that have been registered under the act of 1881 and that have been renewed from time to time are always subject to cancellation, which tends to a feeling of insecurity in trade-mark property.
>
>   Then there is the second [reason], that small users . . . frequently are out to get what they can. They will conserve a small use and wait and hide behind the bush until a man who has spent a lot of money in a trademark begins to get to the point where he cannot abandon it without enormous loss, and then our small user hops out from behind the bush and barks and says "All right, you can have it if you pay me so much." And that is bad. Something ought to be done to stop that kind of thing, and it seems to me, and it seemed to the committee last year, . . . that after a mark had been on the register for 5 years, and registration being made notice, if anyone had any objection he ought to come in with it in 5 years and state his objection, and if he does not do it, he ought to be foreclosed.

Hearings on H.R. 4744 Before the Subcomm. on Trade-marks of the House Comm. on Patents, 76th Cong., 1st Sess. 106-07 (1939) (statement of Edward S. Rogers). As eventually enacted, the Lanham Act contained two related provisions responding to Rogers' concerns: the Section 14 time limit on cancellations and the Section 15 (and 33) incontestability concept.

In Lanham Act §14, Congress provided a five-year time limit for initiating cancellation proceedings, subject to exceptions specified in Lanham Act §14(3)-(5). *See, e.g., Consorzio del Prosciutto di Parma v. Parma Sausage Prods. Inc.*, 23 U.S.P.Q.2d (BNA) 1894, 1899 (TTAB 1992) (under Section 14, "once a trademark owner has had a registration for five years, his property interests come to the fore, and his registration will thenceforth be safe from attack unless he makes the registration vulnerable through his own actions, or unless he was never entitled to the registration to begin with"). One commentator has described Section 14's time limit as a "defensive measure addressing the validity of the registration itself," in contrast to incontestability, which is a matter of "the validity of [the registration's] evidentiary significance as an offensive weapon in litigation." Theodore H. Davis Jr., *Of "Ugly Stiks" and Uglier Case Law. A Comment on the Federal Registration of Functional Designs after* Shakespeare Co. v. Silstar Corp. of America, 51 WASH. & LEE L. REV. 1257, 1282-83 (1994) (some footnotes omitted). Accordingly, after Section 14's time limit has run, a registration is subject to challenge in a cancellation proceeding only on the grounds specified in Sections 14(3)-(5), irrespective of whether the registrant has followed the procedures for achieving incontestability under Section 15. *See, e.g., Strang Corp. v. The Stouffer Corp.*, 16 U.S.P.Q.2d (BNA) 1309, 1311 (TTAB 1990) (observing that Sections 14 and 15 "speak to different purposes" and that "the concept of incontestability is irrelevant to a cancellation proceeding" in that Section 14's limitations apply even if Section 15 incontestability has not been invoked).

In Lanham Act §§15 and 33(b), Congress provided that the registrant's exclusive right to use would become incontestable after five years' continuous use, under the conditions specified in Lanham Act §15, and that for an incontestable registration, the Section 33 registration presumption would be "conclusive," though still subject to a set of preserved defenses set forth in Section 33(b). More particularly, Lanham Act §15 lists four prerequisites for obtaining incontestability status for a Principal Register registration and, in the preamble, carves out a number of exceptions (including the Section 14(3) and (5) exceptions). If the registrant satisfies the requirements of Section 15, and no exception applies, the registrant's *right to use* the registered mark in connection with those goods and services for which five years' use has been demonstrated becomes incontestable.

Lanham Act §33(b) sets out rules concerning the scope and evidentiary significance of incontestable status. Section 33(b)'s preamble specifies that the ordinary registration presumption that applies to registered marks (as set out in Section 33(a)) is converted to a "conclusive" presumption for incontestable registrations. However, Section 33(b) also lists nine preserved defenses—i.e., defenses that can be raised even as to incontestable registrations. The existence of the list of preserved defenses serves as a reminder that "incontestable" is by no means synonymous with "bulletproof." Indeed, the list is lengthy, and Congress has twice added to it. Moreover, because Section 33(b) specifies that the conclusive evidentiary presumptions arise only "to the extent that" the right to use properly becomes incontestable under Section 15, the provisos and exceptions of Section 15 (which, in turn, incorporate by reference Section 14) also operate as preserved defenses.

The following case is the sole Supreme Court case on the doctrine and policy of incontestability.

PARK 'N FLY, INC. v. DOLLAR PARK & FLY, INC.

469 U.S. 189 (1985)

Justice O'CONNOR delivered the opinion of the Court:

I

Petitioner operates long-term parking lots near airports. After starting business in St. Louis in 1967, petitioner subsequently opened facilities in Cleveland, Houston, Boston, Memphis, and San Francisco. Petitioner applied in 1969 to the United States Patent and Trademark Office (Patent Office) to register a service mark consisting of the logo of an airplane and the words "Park 'N Fly." The registration issued in August 1971. Nearly six years later, petitioner filed an affidavit with the Patent Office to establish the incontestable status of the mark. As required by §15 of the Trademark Act of 1946 (Lanham Act), 60 Stat. 433, as amended, 15 U.S.C. §1065, the affidavit stated that the mark had been registered and in continuous use for five consecutive years, that there had been no final adverse decision to petitioner's claim of ownership or right to registration, and that no proceedings involving such rights were pending. Incontestable status provides, subject to the provisions of §15 and §33(b) of the Lanham Act, "conclusive evidence of the registrant's exclusive right to use the registered mark. . . ." §33(b), 15 U.S.C. §1115(b).

Respondent also provides long-term airport parking services, but only has operations in Portland, Oregon. Respondent calls its business "Dollar Park and Fly." Petitioner filed this infringement action in 1978 in the United States District Court for the District of Oregon and requested the court permanently to enjoin respondent from using the words "Park and Fly" in connection with its business. Respondent counterclaimed and sought cancellation of petitioner's mark on the grounds that it is a generic term. See §14(c), 15

U.S.C. §1064(c). Respondent also argued that petitioner's mark is unenforceable because it is merely descriptive. See §2(e), 15 U.S.C. §1052(e). . . .

After a bench trial, the District Court found that petitioner's mark is not generic and observed that an incontestable mark cannot be challenged on the grounds that it is merely descriptive. . . . Finally, the District Court found sufficient evidence of likelihood of confusion. The District Court permanently enjoined respondent from using the words "Park and Fly" and any other mark confusingly similar to "Park 'N Fly."

The Court of Appeals for the Ninth Circuit reversed. 718 F.2d 327 (1983). The District Court did not err, the Court of Appeals held, in refusing to invalidate petitioner's mark. *Id*. at 331. The Court of Appeals noted, however, that it previously had held that incontestability provides a defense against the cancellation of a mark, but it may not be used offensively to enjoin another's use. *Ibid*. Petitioner, under this analysis, could obtain an injunction only if its mark would be entitled to continued registration without regard to its incontestable status. Thus, respondent could defend the infringement action by showing that the mark was merely descriptive. Based on its own examination of the record, the Court of Appeals then determined that petitioner's mark is in fact merely descriptive, and therefore respondent should not be enjoined from using the name "Park and Fly." *Ibid*.

The decision below is in direct conflict with the decision of the Court of Appeals for the Seventh Circuit in *Union Carbide Corp. v. Ever-Ready Inc.*, 531 F.2d 366, *cert. denied*, 429 U.S. 830 (1976). We granted certiorari to resolve this conflict, 465 U.S. 1078 (1984), and we now reverse.

II

. . .

This case requires us to consider the effect of the incontestability provisions of the Lanham Act in the context of an infringement action defended on the grounds that the mark is merely descriptive. With respect to incontestable trade or service marks, §33(b) of the Lanham Act states that "registration shall be conclusive evidence of the registrant's exclusive right to use the registered mark" subject to the conditions of §15 and certain enumerated defenses. Section 15 incorporates by reference subsections (c) and (e) of §14, 15 U.S.C. §1064. An incontestable mark that becomes generic may be canceled at any time pursuant to §14(c). That section also allows cancellation of an incontestable mark at any time if it has been abandoned, if it is being used to misrepresent the source of the goods or services in connection with which it is used, or if it was obtained fraudulently or contrary to the provisions of §4, 15 U.S.C. §1054, or §2(a)-(c), 15 U.S.C. §1052(a)-(c).

One searches the language of the Lanham Act in vain to find any support for the offensive/defensive distinction applied by the Court of Appeals. The statute nowhere distinguishes between a registrant's offensive and defensive use of an incontestable mark. On the contrary, §33(b)'s declaration that the registrant has an "exclusive right" to use the mark indicates that incontestable status may be used to enjoin infringement by others. A conclusion that such infringement cannot be enjoined renders meaningless the "exclusive right" recognized by the statute. Moreover, the language in three of the defenses enumerated in §33(b) clearly contemplates the use of incontestability in infringement actions by plaintiffs. See §33(b)(4)-(6), 15 U.S.C. §1115(b)(4)-(6).

The language of the Lanham Act also refutes any conclusion that an incontestable mark may be challenged as merely descriptive. A mark that is merely descriptive of an applicant's goods or services is not registrable unless the mark has secondary meaning. Before a mark achieves incontestable status, registration provides prima facie evidence of the registrant's exclusive right to use the mark in commerce. §33(a), 15 U.S.C. §1115(a). The

Lanham Act expressly provides that before a mark becomes incontestable an opposing party may prove any legal or equitable defense which might have been asserted if the mark had not been registered. *Ibid.* Thus, §33(a) would have allowed respondent to challenge petitioner's mark as merely descriptive if the mark had not become incontestable. With respect to incontestable marks, however, §33(b) provides that registration is conclusive evidence of the registrant's exclusive right to use the mark, subject to the conditions of §15 and the seven defenses enumerated in §33(b) itself. Mere descriptiveness is not recognized by either §15 or §33(b) as a basis for challenging an incontestable mark.

The statutory provisions that prohibit registration of a merely descriptive mark but do not allow an incontestable mark to be challenged on this ground cannot be attributed to inadvertence by Congress. The Conference Committee rejected an amendment that would have denied registration to any descriptive mark, and instead retained the provisions allowing registration of a merely descriptive mark that has acquired secondary meaning. See H.R. Conf. Rep. No. 2322, 79th Cong., 2d Sess., 4 (1946) (explanatory statement of House managers). The Conference Committee agreed to an amendment providing that no incontestable right can be acquired in a mark that is a common descriptive, i.e., generic, term. *Id.* at 5. Congress could easily have denied incontestability to merely descriptive marks as well as to generic marks had that been its intention.

The Court of Appeals in discussing the offensive/defensive distinction observed that incontestability protects a registrant against cancellation of his mark. 718 F.2d at 331. This observation is incorrect with respect to marks that become generic or which otherwise may be canceled at any time pursuant to §14(c) and (e). Moreover, as applied to marks that are merely descriptive, the approach of the Court of Appeals makes incontestable status superfluous. Without regard to its incontestable status, a mark that has been registered five years is protected from cancellation except on the grounds stated in §14(c) and (e). Pursuant to §14, a mark maybe canceled on the grounds that it is merely descriptive only if the petition to cancel is filed within five years of the date of registration. §14(a), 15 U.S.C. §1064(a). The approach adopted by the Court of Appeals implies that incontestability adds nothing to the protections against cancellation already provided in §14. The decision below not only lacks support in the words of the statute; it effectively emasculates §33(b) under the circumstances of this case.

III

Nothing in the legislative history of the Lanham Act supports a departure from the plain language of the statutory provisions concerning incontestability. Indeed, a conclusion that incontestable status can provide the basis for enforcement of the registrant's exclusive right to use a trade or service mark promotes the goals of the statute. The Lanham Act provides national protection of trademarks in order to secure to the owner of the mark the goodwill of his business and to protect the ability of consumers to distinguish among competing producers. See S. Rep. No. 1333, at 3, 5. National protection of trademarks is desirable, Congress concluded, because trademarks foster competition and the maintenance of quality by securing to the producer the benefits of good reputation. *Id.* at 4. The incontestability provisions, as the proponents of the Lanham Act emphasized, provide a means for the registrant to quiet title in the ownership of his mark. See *Hearings on H.R. 82 Before the Subcommittee of the Senate Committee on Patents*, 78th Cong., 2d Sess., 21 (1944) (remarks of Rep. Lanham); *id.* at 21, 113 (testimony of Daphne Robert, ABA Committee on Trade Mark Legislation); *Hearings on H.R. 102 et al. before the Subcommittee on Trade-Marks of the House Committee on Patents*, 77th Cong., 1st Sess., 73 (1941) (remarks of Rep. Lanham). The opportunity to obtain incontestable status by satisfying the requirements of §15 thus encourages producers to cultivate the goodwill associated with a particular mark.

This function of the incontestability provisions would be utterly frustrated if the holder of an incontestable mark could not enjoin infringement by others so long as they established that the mark would not be registrable but for its incontestable status.

Respondent argues, however, that enforcing petitioner's mark would conflict with the goals of the Lanham Act because the mark is merely descriptive and should never have been registered in the first place.[5] Representative Lanham, respondent notes, explained that the defenses enumerated in §33(b) were "not intended to enlarge, restrict, amend, or modify the substantive law of trademarks either as set out in other sections of the act or as heretofore applied by the courts under prior laws." 92 Cong. Rec. 7524 (1946). Respondent reasons that because the Lanham Act did not alter the substantive law of trademarks, the incontestability provisions cannot protect petitioner's use of the mark if it were not originally registrable. Moreover, inasmuch as petitioner's mark is merely descriptive, respondent contends that enjoining others from using the mark will not encourage competition by assisting consumers in their ability to distinguish among competing producers.

These arguments are unpersuasive. Representative Lanham's remarks, if read in context, clearly refer to the effect of the defenses enumerated in §33(b). There is no question that the Lanham Act altered existing law concerning trademark rights in several respects. . . . Most significantly, Representative Lanham himself observed that incontestability was one of "the valuable new rights created by the act." 92 Cong. Rec. 7524 (1946).

Respondent's argument that enforcing petitioner's mark will not promote the goals of the Lanham Act is misdirected. Arguments similar to those now urged by respondent were in fact considered by Congress in hearings on the Lanham Act. For example, the United States Department of Justice opposed the incontestability provisions and expressly noted that a merely descriptive mark might become incontestable. *Hearings on H.R. 82*, at 59-60 (statement of the U.S. Dept. of Justice). This result, the Department of Justice observed, would "go beyond existing law in conferring unprecedented rights on trade-mark owners," and would undesirably create an exclusive right to use language that is descriptive of a product. *Id.* at 60; see also *Hearings on H.R. 102*, at 106-107, 109-110 (testimony of Prof. Milton Handler); *id.* at 107, 175 (testimony of attorney Louis Robertson). These concerns were answered by proponents of the Lanham Act, who noted that a merely descriptive mark cannot be registered unless the Commissioner finds that it has secondary meaning. *Id.* at 108, 113 (testimony of Karl Pohl, U.S. Trade Mark Assn.). Moreover, a mark can be challenged for five years prior to its attaining incontestable status. *Id.* at 114 (remarks of Rep. Lanham). The supporters of the incontestability provisions further observed that a generic mark cannot become incontestable and that §33(b)(4) allows the nontrademark use of descriptive terms used in an incontestable mark. *Id.* at 110-111 (testimony of Wallace Martin, chairman, ABA Committee on Trade Mark Legislation).

---

5. The dissent similarly takes the position that the mark was improperly issued because it was descriptive and petitioner failed to prove that it had secondary meaning. Neither the District Court nor the Court of Appeals made any finding whether the mark was properly issued in 1971. After the Patent Office denied the initial application for registration in 1970, petitioner filed a request for reconsideration arguing that the mark was not descriptive. The Patent Office subsequently granted registration without specifying whether the mark had secondary meaning or instead was not descriptive. Unlike the dissent, we decline to determine in the first instance whether the mark improperly issued. Our holding is not affected by the possibility that the mark was or has become merely descriptive.

The alternative of refusing to provide incontestable status for descriptive marks with secondary meaning was expressly noted in the hearings on the Lanham Act. *Id.* at 64, 69 (testimony of Robert Byerley, New York Patent Law Assn.); *Hearings on S. 895 Before the Subcommittee of the Senate Committee on Patents,* 77th Cong., 2d Sess., 42 (1942) (testimony of Elliot Moyer, Special Assistant to the Attorney General). Also mentioned was the possibility of including as a defense to infringement of an incontestable mark the "fact that a mark is a descriptive, generic, or geographical term or device." *Id.* at 45, 47. Congress, however, did not adopt either of these alternatives. Instead, Congress expressly provided in §§33(b) and 15 that an incontestable mark could be challenged on specified grounds, and the grounds identified by Congress do not include mere descriptiveness.

The dissent echoes arguments made by opponents of the Lanham Act that the incontestable status of a descriptive mark might take from the public domain language that is merely descriptive. *Post,* at 672-673. As we have explained, Congress has already addressed concerns to prevent the "commercial monopolization," *Post,* at 672, of descriptive language. The Lanham Act allows a mark to be challenged at any time if it becomes generic, and, under certain circumstances, permits the nontrademark use of descriptive terms contained in an incontestable mark. Finally, if "monopolization" of an incontestable mark threatens economic competition, §33(b)(7), 15 U.S.C. §1115(b)(7), provides a defense on the grounds that the mark is being used to violate federal antitrust laws. At bottom, the dissent simply disagrees with the balance struck by Congress in determining the protection to be given to incontestable marks.

IV

Respondent argues that the decision by the Court of Appeals should be upheld because trademark registrations are issued by the Patent Office after an ex parte proceeding and generally without inquiry into the merits of an application. This argument also unravels upon close examination. The facts of this case belie the suggestion that registration is virtually automatic. The Patent Office initially denied petitioner's application because the examiner considered the mark to be merely descriptive. Petitioner sought reconsideration and successfully persuaded the Patent Office that its mark was registrable.

More generally, respondent is simply wrong to suggest that third parties do not have an opportunity to challenge applications for trademark registration. If the Patent Office examiner determines that an applicant appears to be entitled to registration, the mark is published in the Official Gazette. §12(a), 15 U.S.C. §1062(a). Within 30 days of publication, any person who believes that he would be damaged by registration of the mark may file an opposition. §13, 15 U.S.C. §1063. Registration of a mark provides constructive notice throughout the United States of the registrant's claim to ownership. §22, 15 U.S.C. §1072. Within five years of registration, any person who believes that he is or will be damaged by registration may seek to cancel a mark. §14(a), 15 U.S.C. §1064(a). A mark may be canceled at any time for certain specified grounds, including that it was obtained fraudulently or has become generic. §14(c), 15 U.S.C. §1064(c).

The Lanham Act, as the dissent notes, authorizes courts to grant injunctions "according to principles of equity." §34, 15 U.S.C. §1116. Neither respondent nor the opinion of the Court of Appeals relies on this provision to support the holding below. Whatever the precise boundaries of the courts' equitable power, we do not believe that it encompasses a substantive challenge to the validity of an incontestable mark on the grounds that it lacks secondary meaning. To conclude otherwise would expand the meaning of "equity" to the point of vitiating the more specific provisions of the Lanham Act. Similarly, the power of the courts to cancel registrations and "to otherwise rectify the register," §37, 15 U.S.C. §1119, must be subject to the specific provisions concerning incontestability. In effect, both respondent and the dissent argue that these provisions offer insufficient protection against improper registration of a merely descriptive mark, and therefore the validity of petitioner's mark may be challenged notwithstanding its incontestable status. Our responsibility, however, is not to evaluate the wisdom of the legislative determinations reflected in the statute, but instead to construe and apply the provisions that Congress enacted. . . .

VI

We conclude that the holder of a registered mark may rely on incontestability to enjoin infringement and that such an action may not be defended on the grounds that the mark is merely descriptive. . . .

Justice STEVENS, dissenting:

. . .

The mark "Park 'N Fly" is at best merely descriptive in the context of airport parking. Section 2 of the Lanham Act plainly prohibits the registration of such a mark unless the applicant proves to the Commissioner of the Patent and Trademark Office that the mark "has become distinctive of the applicant's goods in commerce," or to use the accepted shorthand, that it has acquired a "secondary meaning." See 15 U.S.C. §1052(e), (f). Petitioner never submitted any such proof to the Commissioner, or indeed to the District Court in this case. Thus, the registration plainly violated the Act. . . .

If the registrant of a merely descriptive mark complies with the statutory requirement that prima facie evidence of secondary meaning must be submitted to the Patent and Trademark Office, it is entirely consistent with the policy of the Act to accord the mark incontestable status after an additional five years of continued use. For if no rival contests the registration in that period, it is reasonable to presume that the initial prima facie showing of distinctiveness could not be rebutted. But if no proof of secondary meaning is ever presented, either to the Patent and Trademark Office or to a court, there is simply no rational basis for leaping to the conclusion that the passage of time has transformed an inherently defective mark into an incontestable mark. . . .

NOTES AND QUESTIONS

1. *Extratextual defenses.*   Does *Park 'N Fly* establish an absolute rule against recognizing "extratextual" defenses (i.e., defenses not specifically listed in Section 33(b))? The issue arose in connection with the functionality defense, which was not among the listed defenses in Section 33(b) in a pre-1999 version of the Lanham Act. *See generally* Theodore H. Davis Jr., *Of "Ugly Stiks" and Uglier Case Law. A Comment on the Federal Registration of Functional Designs after* Shakespeare Co. v. Silstar Corp. of America, 51 WASH. & LEE L. REV. 1257 (1994). In 1999 Congress amended Section 33(b) to add functionality to the list of preserved defenses, obviating the immediate issue but leaving the larger question of extratextual defenses unanswered. *Cf. John R. Thompson Co. v. Holloway*, 366 F.2d 108, 113 (5th Cir. 1966) (incontestable registration cannot be challenged on the ground that the mark is primarily merely a surname).

2. *Effect of establishing Section 33(b) defense.*   If a trademark challenger establishes one of the "defenses or defects" under Section 33(b), what is the result? Is the registration rendered invalid, or does the registrant merely lose the "conclusive" evidentiary presumptions and instead be accorded only treatment under Section 33(a), which states that the registration receives "prima facie" presumptions and is subject to "any legal or equitable defense or defect . . . which might have been asserted if such mark had not been registered"? In a footnote in the *Park 'N Fly* opinion, the Court adopted the latter approach, citing support in the legislative history:

> Representative Lanham made his remarks to clarify that the seven defenses enumerated in §33(b) are not substantive rules of law which go to the validity or enforceability of an incontestable mark. 92 Cong. Rec. 7524 (1946). Instead, the defenses affect the evidentiary status of registration where the owner claims the benefit of a mark's incontestable status. If one of these defenses is established, registration constitutes only prima facie and not conclusive evidence of the owner's right to exclusive use of the mark.

Park 'N Fly, 469 U.S. at 200 n.6. Does this approach help to explain the difference between exceptions to incontestability (as codified in Section 15) and defenses to incontestability (as codified in Section 33(b))?

3. *Incontestability versus strength.* A registrant who successfully invokes incontestable status must still prove liability. Suppose that the theory of liability is trademark infringement. The registrant would be required to prove likelihood of confusion, under a multi-factor standard that would include consideration of mark "strength." *See* Chapter 7 for a discussion of mark strength. Is incontestable status equivalent to substantial mark strength? *See Oreck Corp. v. U.S. Floor Sys., Inc.*, 803 F.2d 166, 171 (5th Cir. 1986) ("Incontestable status does not make a weak mark strong"). *But cf. Dieter v. B & H Indus.*, 880 F.2d 322, 329 (11th Cir. 1989), *cert. denied*, 498 U.S. 950 (1990) ("Because [plaintiff's] mark is incontestable, then it is presumed to be . . . a relatively strong mark.").

More recently, an Eleventh Circuit panel opined that *Dieter* was "almost certainly incorrect" because (1) the fact that a mark attained incontestable status at some point in the past is not probative of its current strength in the marketplace; and (2) because the 1988 amendments to the Lanham Act added the phrase "subject to proof of infringement" to Lanham Act §15, thus decoupling incontestability from the infringement analysis. *See Sovereign Military Hospitaller Order of St. John of Jerusalem of Rhodes and of Malta v. Florida Priory of the Knights Hospitallers of the Sovereign Order of St. John of Jerusalem, Knights of Malta, the Ecumenical Order*, 809 F.3d 1171 (11th Cir. 2015) (reluctantly following *Dieter* on the ground that it remains binding in the absence of a contrary en banc ruling).

4. *Illegitimacy.* One scholar has argued that the concept of trademark incontestability is "illegitimate," on two grounds:

> First, the Lanham Act's primary, express purpose was to codify the existing common law of trademarks and not to create any new trademark rights. The incontestability provisions of the Lanham Act, however, created new rights never before recognized at common law. To that extent, the incontestability provisions are contrary to the express purpose of the statute and therefore insupportable.
>
> Incontestability also attempts to make a trademark itself the subject of property ownership, another concept that the common law has rejected both before and after the passage of the Lanham Act. Trademark rights are traditionally defined at common law as the right to use a certain mark on certain goods and the right to exclude others from using similar marks on similar goods in a way that would be likely to confuse or deceive the public. This is not the same as saying trademarks themselves are property. To the extent incontestability makes (or attempts to make) trademarks property, it is completely inconsistent with the common law of trademarks.

Kenneth L. Port, *The Illegitimacy of Trademark Incontestability*, 26 IND. L. REV. 519, 520 (1993) (footnote omitted). Do you agree? *Cf.* Rebecca Tushnet, *Fixing Incontestability: The Next Frontier?*, 23 B.U. J. SCI. & TECH. L. 434 (2017) (agnostic as to whether incontestability should be retained, but arguing that the procedures for claiming incontestable status should be improved to cut down on improper claims).

5.   *A doctrine of salience?* The incontestable registration at issue in *Park 'N Fly* was *not* the word mark PARK 'N FLY for airport parking services. Rather, as the Court notes, the registration was for a logo mark including the words "Park 'N Fly," as shown.

Indeed, the mark owner held a separate registration for the word mark PARK 'N FLY for airport parking services, and it had not yet become incontestable. Strictly speaking, the Supreme Court had no need to ponder the distinction between the registrations, because the Court was dealing with a broad legal question: whether *any* incontestable registration could be challenged for descriptiveness. Yet it may seem curious that in Justice Stevens' dissent, and in responsive parts of the Court's opinion, the discussion about descriptiveness seems to focus on whether the words "Park 'N Fly" are descriptive for the specified services, rather than focusing on the registered logo mark actually at issue.

At least one court explained away this apparent anomaly by invoking "salience." *KP Permanent Make-up, Inc. v. Lasting Impression I, Inc.*, 408 F.3d 596, 603-04 (9th Cir. 2005). That is, in *Park 'N Fly*, the most salient feature of the logo mark was the phrase "Park 'N Fly," so that the logo mark registration could be treated as the essential equivalent of the word mark registration. Judge (later Justice) Kennedy had relied on salience in treating the two registrations as equivalent in the Ninth Circuit's *Park 'N Fly* decision. 718 F.2d 327, 331 n.3 (9th Cir. 1983). Is salience a legitimate doctrine—flowing, perhaps, from empirical evidence of consumers' actual reactions to a given mark? Or is salience a convenient excuse for simplifying the analysis? Consider to what extent the notion of salience duplicates doctrines already in place in the analysis of likelihood of confusion and distinctiveness. In *KP Permanent*, the Ninth Circuit deemed the words "Micro Colors" to be the most salient part of the logo mark at issue (reproduced here).

Note that we will encounter the *KP Permanent* litigation again; the Ninth Circuit's 2005 decision followed a remand from the Supreme Court, which had addressed the standard for the fair use defense. We discuss that defense in Chapter 9.

B.   EXCLUSIONS FROM REGISTRATION

1.   Overview

The cases that follow explore the prohibitions of Lanham Act §2. That section expresses the major substantive obstacles to trademark registration on the Principal Register. As such, applying Section 2 is paramount in the day-to-day operations of the PTO.

Some aspects of Section 2 should be familiar to you. We have already discussed distinctiveness, nonfunctionality, and use as the principal substantive criteria for obtaining trademark rights. Some of the concepts that we have discussed are codified in Section 2, albeit in a very general way. For example, Section 2's preamble effectively codifies the prohibition against protecting generic marks (by referring to marks "by which the goods of the applicant may be distinguished from the goods of others"). Section 2(e)(1), together with Section 2(f), codifies the basic rule that merely descriptive marks are not protectable unless secondary meaning is shown. Similarly, Section 2(e)(5) provides that functional matter is not protectable. Finally, we have already seen the role of Section 2(d) in priority of use. *See* Chapter 4. In practice, exclusions based on these provisions comprise the bulk of Section 2 rejections. Of course, there are several other exclusions in Section 2, many of which augment or even extend common law rules. As you study these materials, consider the following general question: To what extent are each of the Section 2 exclusions related to the internal logic of trademark law, and to what extent are they attributable to external concerns (morality, for example)?

The structure of Section 2 is challenging, to put it charitably. Section 2(a)-(e) lists a wide variety of substantive bars to registration. Section 2(f) specifies that some of the bars can be overcome by a showing of secondary meaning, while others are absolute bars. You may find it convenient to rearrange Section 2 into two lists of prohibitions: those that impose absolute bars, and those that can be overcome with a secondary meaning showing. You will discover that Section 2 requires some extremely fine line drawing.

In general, Section 2's provisions may come into play in ex parte examination, opposition, cancellation, or infringement litigation, but there are idiosyncrasies here, too, depending on the procedural context. Section 2(f) dilution is not a ground of objection available in ex parte examination. All Section 2 grounds of objection may be invoked in opposition proceedings. In cancellation proceedings, all Section 2 grounds may be invoked for five years after the registration date, after which the grounds are restricted as specified in Lanham Act §14.

2.   Scandalous, Disparaging, Deceptive, and Deceptively Misdecriptive Marks Under Section 2(a) and 2(e)(1)

Lanham Act §2 provides:

> No trademark by which the goods of the applicant may be distinguished from the goods of others shall be refused registration on the principal register on account of its nature unless it—
> (a) Consists of or comprises immoral, deceptive, or scandalous matter; or matter which may disparage or falsely suggest a connection with persons, living or dead, institutions, beliefs, or national symbols, or bring them into contempt, or disrepute. . . .

For several decades, the USPTO invoked Section 2(a)'s immoral/scandalous/disparaging prohibitions primarily against a narrow band of applications deemed to contain profane subject matter. In the 1990s, that practice expanded when a group of Native Americans petitioned to cancel various registrations owned by the Washington Redskins franchise of the National Football League, arguing that the marks had racial overtones that were disparaging to Native Americans. *Harjo v. Pro-Football, Inc.*, 50 U.S.P.Q.2d (BNA) 1705 (TTAB 1999), *rev'd*, 284 F. Supp. 96 (D.D.C. 2003); Stephen R. Baird, *Moral Intervention in the Trademark Arena: Banning the Registration of Scandalous and Immoral Trademarks*, 83 Trademark Rep. 661 (1993) (arguing for an expanded role for Section 2(a) scandalous/immoral bars).

Although the petition was eventually dismissed on the ground of laches, *Pro-Football, Inc. v. Harjo*, 565 F.3d 880 (D.C. Cir. 2009), a new group of petitioners prevailed in the TTAB, and a lower court upheld the TTAB's ruling. *Pro-Football, Inc. v. Blackhorse*, 112 F. Supp. 3d 439 (E.D. Va. 2015). The mark owner appealed to the Court of Appeals for the Fourth Circuit.

Meanwhile, an Asian-American band had sought to register the mark THE SLANTS, received a Section 2(a) rejection (on the ground that the subject matter was disparaging to Asian-Americans), and had appealed the rejection to the Court of Appeals for the Federal Circuit. There, the band successfully challenged the Section 2(a) disparagement bar as a facial violation of the First Amendment's Free Speech Clause. The Supreme Court granted *certioriari*, and rendered the following decision in *Matal v. Tam* upholding the Federal Circuit's ruling. In view of *Tam*, the *Blackhorse* petitioners conceded that they could not prevail in their case. *Tam* thus signaled the end of the use of Section 2(a)'s disparagement clause to challenge applications to register racially-insensitive marks.

MATAL v. TAM
137 S. Ct. 1744 (2017)

Justice ALITO announced the judgment of the Court and delivered the opinion of the Court with respect to Parts I, II, and III-A, and an opinion with respect to Parts III-B, III-C, and IV, in which THE CHIEF JUSTICE, Justice THOMAS, and Justice BREYER join.

This case concerns a dance-rock band's application for federal trademark registration of the band's name, "The Slants." "Slants" is a derogatory term for persons of Asian descent, and members of the band are Asian-Americans. But the band members believe that by taking that slur as the name of their group, they will help to "reclaim" the term and drain its denigrating force.

The Patent and Trademark Office (PTO) denied the application based on a provision of federal law prohibiting the registration of trademarks that may "disparage . . . or bring . . . into contemp[t] or disrepute" any "persons, living or dead." 15 U.S.C. §1052(a). We now hold that this provision violates the Free Speech Clause of the First Amendment. It offends a bedrock First Amendment principle: Speech may not be banned on the ground that it expresses ideas that offend.

I

A

"The principle underlying trademark protection is that distinctive marks—words, names, symbols, and the like—can help distinguish a particular artisan's goods from those of others." . . . It helps consumers identify goods and services that they wish to purchase, as well as those they want to avoid. [cit.]

"[F]ederal law does not create trademarks." [*B & B Hardware, Inc. v. Hargis Industries, Inc.*, 135 S. Ct. 1293, 1299 (2015).] Trademarks and their precursors have ancient origins, and trademarks were protected at common law and in equity at the time of the founding of our country. [*Trade-Mark Cases*, 100 U.S. 82, 92 (1879).] . . . There are now more than two million marks that have active federal certificates of registration. [cit.] This system of federal registration helps to ensure that trademarks are fully protected and supports the free flow of commerce. "[N]ational protection of trademarks is desirable," we have explained, "because trademarks foster competition and the maintenance of quality by securing to the producer the benefits of good reputation." *San Francisco Arts & Athletics,*

Inc. v. United States Olympic Comm., 483 U.S. 522, 531 (1987) (internal quotation marks omitted). . . .

B

Without federal registration, a valid trademark may still be used in commerce. [cit.] And an unregistered trademark can be enforced against would-be infringers in several ways. Most important, even if a trademark is not federally registered, it may still be enforceable under §43(a) of the Lanham Act, which creates a federal cause of action for trademark infringement. See *Two Pesos, supra*, at 768 ("Section 43(a) prohibits a broader range of practices than does §32, which applies to registered marks, but it is common ground that §43(a) protects qualifying unregistered trademarks" (internal quotation marks and citation omitted)).[1] Unregistered trademarks may also be entitled to protection under other federal statutes, such as the Anticybersquatting Consumer Protection Act, 15 U.S.C. §1125(d); [cit.]. And an unregistered trademark can be enforced under state common law, or if it has been registered in a State, under that State's registration system. [cit.]

Federal registration, however, "confers important legal rights and benefits on trademark owners who register their marks." *B & B Hardware*, 135 S. Ct., at 1317 (internal quotation marks omitted). Registration on the principal register (1) "serves as 'constructive notice of the registrant's claim of ownership' of the mark," *ibid.* (quoting 15 U.S.C. §1072); (2) "is 'prima facie evidence of the validity of the registered mark and of the registration of the mark, of the owner's ownership of the mark, and of the owner's exclusive right to use the registered mark in commerce on or in connection with the goods or services specified in the certificate,'" *B & B Hardware*, 135 S. Ct., at 1300 (quoting §1057(b)); and (3) can make a mark "'incontestable'" once a mark has been registered for five years," *ibid.* (quoting §§1065, 1115(b)); see *Park 'N Fly*, 469 U.S., at 193. Registration also enables the trademark holder "to stop the importation into the United States of articles bearing an infringing mark." 3 McCarthy §19:9, at 19-38; see 15 U.S.C. §1124.

C

The Lanham Act contains provisions that bar certain trademarks from the principal register. For example, a trademark cannot be registered if it is "merely descriptive or deceptively misdescriptive" of goods, §1052(e)(1), or if it is so similar to an already registered trademark or trade name that it is "likely . . . to cause confusion, or to cause mistake, or to deceive," §1052(d).

At issue in this case is one such provision, which we will call "the disparagement clause." This provision prohibits the registration of a trademark "which may disparage . . . persons, living or dead, institutions, beliefs, or national symbols, or bring them into

---

1. In the opinion below, the Federal Circuit opined that although "Section 43(a) allows for a federal suit to protect an unregistered trademark," "it is not at all clear" that respondent could bring suit under §43(a) because "there is no authority extending §43(a) to marks denied under §2(a)'s disparagement provision." *In re Tam*, 808 F.3d 1321, 1344-1345, n. 11 (en banc), as corrected (Feb. 11, 2016). When drawing this conclusion, the Federal Circuit relied in part on our statement in *Two Pesos* that "the general principles qualifying a mark for registration under §2 of the Lanham Act are for the most part applicable in determining whether an unregistered mark is entitled to protection under §43(a)." 505 U.S., at 768. We need not decide today whether respondent could bring suit under §43(a) if his application for federal registration had been lawfully denied under the disparagement clause.

contempt, or disrepute." §1052(a). This clause appeared in the original Lanham Act and has remained the same to this day. See §2(a), 60 Stat. 428.

When deciding whether a trademark is disparaging, an examiner at the PTO generally applies a "two-part test." The examiner first considers "the likely meaning of the matter in question, taking into account not only dictionary definitions, but also the relationship of the matter to the other elements in the mark, the nature of the goods or services, and the manner in which the mark is used in the marketplace in connection with the goods or services." Trademark Manual of Examining Procedure §1203.03(b)(i) (Apr. 2017), p. 1200-150, *http://tmep.uspto.gov.* "If that meaning is found to refer to identifiable persons, institutions, beliefs or national symbols," the examiner moves to the second step, asking "whether that meaning may be disparaging to a substantial composite of the referenced group." *Ibid.* If the examiner finds that a "substantial composite, although not necessarily a majority, of the referenced group would find the proposed mark . . . to be disparaging in the context of contemporary attitudes," a prima facie case of disparagement is made out, and the burden shifts to the applicant to prove that the trademark is not disparaging. *Ibid.* What is more, the PTO has specified that "[t]he fact that an applicant may be a member of that group or has good intentions underlying its use of a term does not obviate the fact that a substantial composite of the referenced group would find the term objectionable." *Ibid.*

D

Simon Tam is the lead singer of "The Slants." He chose this moniker in order to "reclaim" and "take ownership" of stereotypes about people of Asian ethnicity. The group "draws inspiration for its lyrics from childhood slurs and mocking nursery rhymes" and has given its albums names such as "The Yellow Album" and "Slanted Eyes, Slanted Hearts."

Tam sought federal registration of "THE SLANTS," on the principal register, but an examining attorney at the PTO rejected the request, applying the PTO's two-part framework and finding that "there is . . . a substantial composite of persons who find the term in the applied-for mark offensive." The examining attorney relied in part on the fact that "numerous dictionaries define 'slants' or 'slant-eyes' as a derogatory or offensive term." The examining attorney also relied on a finding that "the band's name has been found offensive numerous times" — citing a performance that was canceled because of the band's moniker and the fact that "several bloggers and commenters to articles on the band have indicated that they find the term and the applied-for mark offensive."

Tam contested the denial of registration before the examining attorney and before the PTO's Trademark Trial and Appeal Board (TTAB) but to no avail. Eventually, he took the case to federal court, where the en banc Federal Circuit ultimately found the disparagement clause facially unconstitutional under the First Amendment's Free Speech Clause. The majority found that the clause engages in viewpoint-based discrimination, that the clause regulates the expressive component of trademarks and consequently cannot be treated as commercial speech, and that the clause is subject to and cannot satisfy strict scrutiny. The majority also rejected the Government's argument that registered trademarks constitute government speech, as well as the Government's contention that federal registration is a form of government subsidy. And the majority opined that even if the disparagement clause were analyzed under this Court's commercial speech cases, the clause would fail the "intermediate scrutiny" that those cases prescribe.

. . .

The Government filed a petition for certiorari, which we granted in order to decide whether the disparagement clause "is facially invalid under the Free Speech Clause of the First Amendment." . . .

III

Because the disparagement clause applies to marks that disparage the members of a racial or ethnic group, we must decide whether the clause violates the Free Speech Clause of the First Amendment. And at the outset, we must consider three arguments that would either eliminate any First Amendment protection or result in highly permissive rational-basis review. Specifically, the Government contends (1) that trademarks are government speech, not private speech, (2) that trademarks are a form of government subsidy, and (3) that the constitutionality of the disparagement clause should be tested under a new "government-program" doctrine. We address each of these arguments below.

A

The First Amendment prohibits Congress and other government entities and actors from "abridging the freedom of speech"; the First Amendment does not say that Congress and other government entities must abridge their own ability to speak freely. And our cases recognize that "[t]he Free Speech Clause . . . does not regulate government speech." *Pleasant Grove City v. Summum*, 555 U.S. 460, 467 (2009); see *Johanns v. Livestock Marketing Assn.*, 544 U.S. 550, 553 (2005) ("[T]he Government's own speech . . . is exempt from First Amendment scrutiny"); *Board of Regents of Univ. of Wis. System v. Southworth*, 529 U.S. 217, 235 (2000).

As we have said, "it is not easy to imagine how government could function" if it were subject to the restrictions that the First Amendment imposes on private speech. *Summum, supra*, at 468; see *Walker v. Texas Div., Sons of Confederate Veterans, Inc.*, 135 S. Ct. 2239, 2245-2247 (2015). "'[T]he First Amendment forbids the government to regulate speech in ways that favor some viewpoints or ideas at the expense of others,'" *Lamb's Chapel v. Center Moriches Union Free School Dist.*, 508 U.S. 384, 394 (1993), but imposing a require-ment of viewpoint-neutrality on government speech would be paralyzing. When a govern-ment entity embarks on a course of action, it necessarily takes a particular viewpoint and rejects others. The Free Speech Clause does not require government to maintain viewpoint neutrality when its officers and employees speak about that venture.

Here is a simple example. During the Second World War, the Federal Government produced and distributed millions of posters to promote the war effort. There were posters urging enlistment, the purchase of war bonds, and the conservation of scarce resources. These posters expressed a viewpoint, but the First Amendment did not demand that the Government balance the message of these posters by producing and distributing posters encouraging Americans to refrain from engaging in these activities.

But while the government-speech doctrine is important—indeed, essential—it is a doctrine that is susceptible to dangerous misuse. If private speech could be passed off as government speech by simply affixing a government seal of approval, government could silence or muffle the expression of disfavored viewpoints. For this reason, we must exercise great caution before extending our government-speech precedents.

At issue here is the content of trademarks that are registered by the PTO, an arm of the Federal Government. The Federal Government does not dream up these marks, and it does not edit marks submitted for registration. Except as required by the statute involved here, 15 U.S.C. §1052(a), an examiner may not reject a mark based on the viewpoint that it appears to express. Thus, unless that section is thought to apply, an examiner does not inquire whether any viewpoint conveyed by a mark is consistent with Government policy or whether any such viewpoint is consistent with that expressed by other marks already on the principal register. Instead, if the mark meets the Lanham Act's viewpoint-neutral requirements, registration is mandatory. *Ibid.* (requiring that "[n]o trademark . . . shall be refused registration on the principal register on account of its nature unless" it falls within an enumerated statutory exception). And if an examiner finds that a mark is eligible for placement on the principal register, that decision is not reviewed by any higher official unless the registration is challenged. See §§1062(a), 1071; 37 C.F.R §41.31(a) (2016). Moreover, once a mark is registered, the PTO is not authorized to remove it from the register unless a party moves for cancellation, the registration expires, or the Federal Trade Commission initiates proceedings based on certain grounds. See 15 U.S.C. §§1058(a), 1059, 1064; 37 C.F.R. §§2.111(b), 2.160.

In light of all this, it is far-fetched to suggest that the content of a registered mark is government speech. If the federal registration of a trademark makes the mark government speech, the Federal Government is babbling prodigiously and incoherently. It is saying many unseemly things. It is expressing contradictory views.[9] It is unashamedly endorsing a vast array of commercial products and services. And it is providing Delphic advice to the consuming public.

For example, if trademarks represent government speech, what does the Government have in mind when it advises Americans to "make.believe" (Sony), "Think different" (Apple), "Just do it" (Nike), or "Have it your way" (Burger King)? Was the Government warning about a coming disaster when it registered the mark "EndTime Ministries"?

The PTO has made it clear that registration does not constitute approval of a mark. See *In re Old Glory Condom Corp.*, 26 USPQ 2d 1216, 1220, n. 3 (T.T.A.B. 1993) ("[I]ssuance of a trademark registration . . . is not a government imprimatur"). And it is unlikely that more than a tiny fraction of the public has any idea what federal registration of a trademark means. See *Application of National Distillers & Chemical Corp.*, 49 C.C.P.A. (Pat.) 854, 863, 297 F.2d 941, 949 (1962) (Rich, J., concurring) ("The purchasing public knows no more about trademark registrations than a man walking down the street in a strange city knows about legal title to the land and buildings he passes" (emphasis deleted)).

None of our government speech cases even remotely supports the idea that registered trademarks are government speech. In *Johanns*, we considered advertisements promoting the sale of beef products. A federal statute called for the creation of a program of paid advertising "'to advance the image and desirability of beef and beef products.'" 544 U.S., at 561 (quoting 7 U.S.C. §2902(13)). Congress and the Secretary of Agriculture provided guidelines for the content of the ads, Department of Agriculture officials attended the meetings at which the content of specific ads was discussed, and the Secretary could edit or reject any proposed ad. 544 U.S., at 561. Noting that "[t]he message set out in the beef promotions [was] from beginning to end the message established by the Federal Government," we held that the ads were government speech. *Id.*, at 560. The Government's involvement in the creation of these beef ads bears no resemblance to anything that occurs when a trademark is registered.

Our decision in *Summum* is similarly far afield. A small city park contained 15 monuments. Eleven had been donated by private groups, and one of these displayed the Ten

---

9. Compare "Abolish Abortion," Registration No. 4,935,774 (Apr. 12, 2016), with "I Stand With Planned Parenthood," Registration No. 5,073,573 (Nov. 1, 2016); compare "Capitalism Is Not Moral, Not Fair, Not Freedom," Registration No. 4,696,419 (Mar. 3, 2015), with "Capitalism Ensuring Innovation," Registration No. 3,966,092 (May 24, 2011); compare "Global Warming Is Good," Registration No. 4,776,235 (July 21, 2015), with "A Solution to Global Warming," Registration No. 3,875,271 (Nov. 10, 2010).

Commandments. A religious group claimed that the city, by accepting donated monuments, had created a limited public forum for private speech and was therefore obligated to place in the park a monument expressing the group's religious beliefs.

Holding that the monuments in the park represented government speech, we cited many factors. Governments have used monuments to speak to the public since ancient times; parks have traditionally been selective in accepting and displaying donated monuments; parks would be overrun if they were obligated to accept all monuments offered by private groups; "[p]ublic parks are often closely identified in the public mind with the government unit that owns the land"; and "[t]he monuments that are accepted . . . are meant to convey and have the effect of conveying a government message." *Id.*, at 472.

Trademarks share none of these characteristics. Trademarks have not traditionally been used to convey a Government message. With the exception of the enforcement of 15 U.S.C. §1052(a), the viewpoint expressed by a mark has not played a role in the decision whether to place it on the principal register. And there is no evidence that the public associates the contents of trademarks with the Federal Government.

This brings us to the case on which the Government relies most heavily, *Walker*, which likely marks the outer bounds of the government-speech doctrine. Holding that the messages on Texas specialty license plates are government speech, the *Walker* Court cited three factors distilled from *Summum*. First, license plates have long been used by the States to convey state messages. Second, license plates "are often closely identified in the public mind" with the State, since they are manufactured and owned by the State, generally designed by the State, and serve as a form of "government ID." Third, Texas "maintain[ed] direct control over the messages conveyed on its specialty plates." As explained above, none of these factors are present in this case.

In sum, the federal registration of trademarks is vastly different from the beef ads in *Johanns*, the monuments in *Summum*, and even the specialty license plates in *Walker*. Holding that the registration of a trademark converts the mark into government speech would constitute a huge and dangerous extension of the government-speech doctrine. For if the registration of trademarks constituted government speech, other systems of government registration could easily be characterized in the same way.

Perhaps the most worrisome implication of the Government's argument concerns the system of copyright registration. If federal registration makes a trademark government speech and thus eliminates all First Amendment protection, would the registration of the copyright for a book produce a similar transformation? See [*Tam*], 808 F.3d, at 1346 (explaining that if trademark registration amounts to government speech, "then copyright registration" which "has identical accoutrements" would "likewise amount to government speech").

The Government attempts to distinguish copyright on the ground that it is "'the engine of free expression,'" but as this case illustrates, trademarks often have an expressive content. Companies spend huge amounts to create and publicize trademarks that convey a message. It is true that the necessary brevity of trademarks limits what they can say. But powerful messages can sometimes be conveyed in just a few words.

Trademarks are private, not government, speech.

B

We next address the Government's argument that this case is governed by cases in which this Court has upheld the constitutionality of government programs that subsidized speech expressing a particular viewpoint. These cases implicate a notoriously tricky question of constitutional law. "[W]e have held that the Government 'may not deny a benefit to a person on a basis that infringes his constitutionally protected . . . freedom of speech even if he has no entitlement to that benefit.'" *Agency for Int'l Development v. Alliance for Open*

Society Int'l, Inc., 133 S. Ct. 2321, 2328 (2013) (some internal quotation marks omitted). But at the same time, government is not required to subsidize activities that it does not wish to promote. *Ibid.* Determining which of these principles applies in a particular case "is not always self-evident," 133 S. Ct., at 2330, but no difficult question is presented here.

Unlike the present case, the decisions on which the Government relies all involved cash subsidies or their equivalent. In *Rust v. Sullivan*, 500 U.S. 173 (1991), a federal law provided funds to private parties for family planning services. In *National Endowment for Arts v. Finley*, 524 U.S. 569 (1998), cash grants were awarded to artists. And federal funding for public libraries was at issue in *United States v. American Library Assn., Inc.*, 539 U.S. 194 (2003). In other cases, we have regarded tax benefits as comparable to cash subsidies. See *Regan v. Taxation With Representation of Wash.*, 461 U.S. 540 (1983); *Cammarano v. United States*, 358 U.S. 498 (1959).

The federal registration of a trademark is nothing like the programs at issue in these cases. The PTO does not pay money to parties seeking registration of a mark. Quite the contrary is true: An applicant for registration must pay the PTO a filing fee of $225-$600. 37 C.F.R. §2.6(a)(1). (Tam submitted a fee of $275 as part of his application to register THE SLANTS.) And to maintain federal registration, the holder of a mark must pay a fee of $300-$500 every 10 years. §2.6(a)(5); see also 15 U.S.C. §1059(a). The Federal Circuit concluded that these fees have fully supported the registration system for the past 27 years.

The Government responds that registration provides valuable non-monetary benefits that "are directly traceable to the resources devoted by the federal government to examining, publishing, and issuing certificates of registration for those marks." But just about every government service requires the expenditure of government funds. This is true of services that benefit everyone, like police and fire protection, as well as services that are utilized by only some, *e.g.*, the adjudication of private lawsuits and the use of public parks and highways.

Trademark registration is not the only government registration scheme. For example, the Federal Government registers copyrights and patents. State governments and their subdivisions register the title to real property and security interests; they issue driver's licenses, motor vehicle registrations, and hunting, fishing, and boating licenses or permits.

Cases like *Rust* and *Finley* are not instructive in analyzing the constitutionality of restrictions on speech imposed in connection with such services.

C

Finally, the Government urges us to sustain the disparagement clause under a new doctrine that would apply to "government-program" cases. For the most part, this argument simply merges our government-speech cases and the previously discussed subsidy cases in an attempt to construct a broader doctrine that can be applied to the registration of trademarks. The only new element in this construct consists of two cases involving a public employer's collection of union dues from its employees. But those cases occupy a special area of First Amendment case law, and they are far removed from the registration of trademarks.

In *Davenport v. Washington Ed. Assn.*, 551 U.S. 177, 181-182 (2007), a Washington law permitted a public employer automatically to deduct from the wages of employees who chose not to join the union the portion of union dues used for activities related to collective bargaining. But unless these employees affirmatively consented, the law did not allow the employer to collect the portion of union dues that would be used in election activities. A public employee union argued that this law unconstitutionally restricted its speech based on its content; that is, the law permitted the employer to assist union speech on matters relating to collective bargaining but made it harder for the union to collect money to support its election activities. Upholding this law, we characterized it as imposing a "modest limitation" on an "extraordinary benefit," namely, taking money from the wages of non-union members and turning it over to the union free of charge. Refusing to confer an even greater benefit, we held, did not upset the marketplace of ideas and did not abridge the union's free speech rights.

Ysursa v. Pocatello Ed. Assn., 555 U.S. 353 (2009), is similar. There, we considered an Idaho law that allowed public employees to elect to have union dues deducted from their wages but did not allow such a deduction for money remitted to the union's political action committee. . . .

Davenport and *Ysursa* are akin to our subsidy cases. Although the laws at issue in *Davenport* and *Ysursa* did not provide cash subsidies to the unions, they conferred a very valuable benefit—the right to negotiate a collective-bargaining agreement under which non-members would be obligated to pay an agency fee that the public employer would collect and turn over to the union free of charge. As in the cash subsidy cases, the laws conferred this benefit because it was thought that this arrangement served important government interests. See *Abood v. Detroit Bd. of Ed.*, 431 U.S. 209, 224-226 (1977). But the challenged laws did not go further and provide convenient collection mechanisms for money to be used in political activities. In essence, the Washington and Idaho lawmakers chose to confer a substantial non-cash benefit for the purpose of furthering activities that they particularly desired to promote but not to provide a similar benefit for the purpose of furthering other activities. Thus, *Davenport* and *Ysursa* are no more relevant for present purposes than the subsidy cases previously discussed.

Potentially more analogous are cases in which a unit of government creates a limited public forum for private speech. See, *e.g., Good News Club v. Milford Central School*, 533 U.S. 98, 106-107 (2001); *Rosenberger v. Rector and Visitors of Univ. of Va.*, 515 U.S. 819, 831 (1995); *Lamb's Chapel*, 508 U.S., at 392-393. See also *Legal Services Corporation v. Velazquez*, 531 U.S. 533, 541-544 (2001). When government creates such a forum, in either a literal or "metaphysical" sense, see *Rosenberger*, 515 U.S., at 830 some content- and speaker-based restrictions may be allowed, see *id.*, at 830-831. However, even in such cases, what we have termed "viewpoint discrimination" is forbidden. *Id.*, at 831.

Our cases use the term "viewpoint" discrimination in a broad sense, and in that sense, the disparagement clause discriminates on the bases of "viewpoint." To be sure, the clause evenhandedly prohibits disparagement of all groups. It applies equally to marks that damn Democrats and Republicans, capitalists and socialists, and those arrayed on both sides of every possible issue. It denies registration to any mark that is offensive to a substantial percentage of the members of any group. But in the sense relevant here, that is viewpoint discrimination: Giving offense is a viewpoint.

We have said time and again that "the public expression of ideas may not be prohibited merely because the ideas are themselves offensive to some of their hearers." *Street v. New York*, 394 U.S. 576, 592 (1969). [cit.]

For this reason, the disparagement clause cannot be saved by analyzing it as a type of government program in which some content- and speaker-based restrictions are permitted.[16]

IV

Having concluded that the disparagement clause cannot be sustained under our government-speech or subsidy cases or under the Government's proposed "government-program"

---

16. We leave open the question whether this is the appropriate framework for analyzing free speech challenges to provisions of the Lanham Act.

doctrine, we must confront a dispute between the parties on the question whether trademarks are commercial speech and are thus subject to the relaxed scrutiny outlined in *Central Hudson Gas & Elec. Corp. v. Public Serv. Comm'n of N. Y.*, 447 U.S. 557 (1980). The Government and *amici* supporting its position argue that all trademarks are commercial speech. They note that the central purposes of trademarks are commercial and that federal law regulates trademarks to promote fair and orderly interstate commerce. Tam and his *amici*, on the other hand, contend that many, if not all, trademarks have an expressive component. In other words, these trademarks do not simply identify the source of a product or service but go on to say something more, either about the product or service or some broader issue. The trademark in this case illustrates this point. The name "The Slants" not only identifies the band but expresses a view about social issues.

We need not resolve this debate between the parties because the disparagement clause cannot withstand even *Central Hudson* review.[17] Under *Central Hudson*, a restriction of speech must serve "a substantial interest," and it must be "narrowly drawn." *Id.*, at 564-565 (internal quotation marks omitted). This means, among other things, that "[t]he regulatory technique may extend only as far as the interest it serves." *Id.*, at 565. The disparagement clause fails this requirement.

It is claimed that the disparagement clause serves two interests. The first is phrased in a variety of ways in the briefs. Echoing language in one of the opinions below, the Government asserts an interest in preventing "'underrepresented groups'" from being "'bombarded with demeaning messages in commercial advertising.'" An *amicus* supporting the Government refers to "encouraging racial tolerance and protecting the privacy and welfare of individuals." But no matter how the point is phrased, its unmistakable thrust is this: The Government has an interest in preventing speech expressing ideas that offend. And, as we have explained, that idea strikes at the heart of the First Amendment. Speech that demeans on the basis of race, ethnicity, gender, religion, age, disability, or any other similar ground is hateful; but the proudest boast of our free speech jurisprudence is that we protect the freedom to express "the thought that we hate." *United States v. Schwimmer*, 279 U.S. 644, 655 (1929) (Holmes, J., dissenting).

The second interest asserted is protecting the orderly flow of commerce. Commerce, we are told, is disrupted by trademarks that "involv[e] disparagement of race, gender, ethnicity, national origin, religion, sexual orientation, and similar demographic classification." 808 F.3d, at 1380-1381 (opinion of Reyna, J.). Such trademarks are analogized to discriminatory conduct, which has been recognized to have an adverse effect on commerce. See *ibid.*

A simple answer to this argument is that the disparagement clause is not "narrowly drawn" to drive out trademarks that support invidious discrimination. The clause reaches any trademark that disparages *any person, group, or institution*. It applies to trademarks like the following: "Down with racists," "Down with sexists," "Down with homophobes." It is not an anti-discrimination clause; it is a happy-talk clause. In this way, it goes much further than is necessary to serve the interest asserted.

The clause is far too broad in other ways as well. The clause protects every person living or dead as well as every institution. Is it conceivable that commerce would be disrupted

---

17. As with the framework discussed in Part III-C of this opinion, we leave open the question whether *Central Hudson* provides the appropriate test for deciding free speech challenges to provisions of the Lanham Act. And nothing in our decision should be read to speak to the validity of state unfair competition provisions or product libel laws that are not before us and differ from §1052(d)'s disparagement clause.

by a trademark saying: "James Buchanan was a disastrous president" or "Slavery is an evil institution"?

There is also a deeper problem with the argument that commercial speech may be cleansed of any expression likely to cause offense. The commercial market is well stocked with merchandise that disparages prominent figures and groups, and the line between commercial and non-commercial speech is not always clear, as this case illustrates. If affixing the commercial label permits the suppression of any speech that may lead to political or social "volatility," free speech would be endangered.

. . .

[Affirmed.]

Justice KENNEDY, with whom Justice GINSBURG, Justice SOTOMAYOR, and Justice KAGAN join, concurring in part and concurring in the judgment.

. . .

The Court is correct in its judgment, and I join Parts I, II, and III-A of its opinion. This separate writing explains in greater detail why the First Amendment's protections against viewpoint discrimination apply to the trademark here. It submits further that the viewpoint discrimination rationale renders unnecessary any extended treatment of other questions raised by the parties.

I

Those few categories of speech that the government can regulate or punish—for instance, fraud, defamation, or incitement—are well established within our constitutional tradition. [cit.] Aside from these and a few other narrow exceptions, it is a fundamental principle of the First Amendment that the government may not punish or suppress speech based on disapproval of the ideas or perspectives the speech conveys. See *Rosenberger v. Rector and Visitors of Univ. of Va.*, 515 U.S. 819, 828-829 (1995).

The First Amendment guards against laws "targeted at specific subject matter," a form of speech suppression known as content based discrimination. *Reed v. Town of Gilbert*, 135 S. Ct. 2218, 2230 (2015). This category includes a subtype of laws that go further, aimed at the suppression of "particular views . . . on a subject." *Rosenberger*, 515 U.S., at 829. A law found to discriminate based on viewpoint is an "egregious form of content discrimination," which is "presumptively unconstitutional." *Id.*, at 829-830.

At its most basic, the test for viewpoint discrimination is whether—within the relevant subject category—the government has singled out a subset of messages for disfavor based on the views expressed. See *Cornelius v. NAACP Legal Defense & Ed. Fund, Inc.*, 473 U.S. 788, 806 (1985) ("[T]he government violates the First Amendment when it denies access to a speaker solely to suppress the point of view he espouses on an otherwise includible subject"). In the instant case, the disparagement clause the Government now seeks to implement and enforce identifies the relevant subject as "persons, living or dead, institutions, beliefs, or national symbols." 15 U.S.C. §1052(a). Within that category, an applicant may register a positive or benign mark but not a derogatory one. The law thus reflects the Government's disapproval of a subset of messages it finds offensive. This is the essence of viewpoint discrimination.

The Government disputes this conclusion. It argues, to begin with, that the law is viewpoint neutral because it applies in equal measure to any trademark that demeans or offends. This misses the point. A subject that is first defined by content and then regulated or censored by mandating only one sort of comment is not viewpoint neutral. To prohibit all sides from criticizing their opponents makes a law more viewpoint based, not less so. Cf.

Rosenberger, supra, at 831-832 ("The . . . declaration that debate is not skewed so long as multiple voices are silenced is simply wrong; the debate is skewed in multiple ways"). The logic of the Government's rule is that a law would be viewpoint neutral even if it provided that public officials could be praised but not condemned. The First Amendment's viewpoint neutrality principle protects more than the right to identify with a particular side. It protects the right to create and present arguments for particular positions in particular ways, as the speaker chooses. By mandating positivity, the law here might silence dissent and distort the marketplace of ideas.

The Government next suggests that the statute is viewpoint neutral because the disparagement clause applies to trademarks regardless of the applicant's personal views or reasons for using the mark. Instead, registration is denied based on the expected reaction of the applicant's audience. In this way, the argument goes, it cannot be said that Government is acting with hostility toward a particular point of view. For example, the Government does not dispute that respondent seeks to use his mark in a positive way. Indeed, respondent endeavors to use The Slants to supplant a racial epithet, using new insights, musical talents, and wry humor to make it a badge of pride. Respondent's application was denied not because the Government thought his object was to demean or offend but because the Government thought his trademark would have that effect on at least some Asian-Americans.

The Government may not insulate a law from charges of viewpoint discrimination by tying censorship to the reaction of the speaker's audience. The Court has suggested that viewpoint discrimination occurs when the government intends to suppress a speaker's beliefs, *Reed, supra*, at 135 S. Ct., at 2229-2230, but viewpoint discrimination need not take that form in every instance. The danger of viewpoint discrimination is that the government is attempting to remove certain ideas or perspectives from a broader debate. That danger is all the greater if the ideas or perspectives are ones a particular audience might think offensive, at least at first hearing. An initial reaction may prompt further reflection, leading to a more reasoned, more tolerant position.

Indeed, a speech burden based on audience reactions is simply government hostility and intervention in a different guise. The speech is targeted, after all, based on the government's disapproval of the speaker's choice of message. And it is the government itself that is attempting in this case to decide whether the relevant audience would find the speech offensive. For reasons like these, the Court's cases have long prohibited the government from justifying a First Amendment burden by pointing to the offensiveness of the speech to be suppressed.

The Government's argument in defense of the statute assumes that respondent's mark is a negative comment. In addressing that argument on its own terms, this opinion is not intended to imply that the Government's interpretation is accurate. From respondent's submissions, it is evident he would disagree that his mark means what the Government says it does. The trademark will have the effect, respondent urges, of reclaiming an offensive term for the positive purpose of celebrating all that Asian-Americans can and do contribute to our diverse Nation. While thoughtful persons can agree or disagree with this approach, the dissonance between the trademark's potential to teach and the Government's insistence on its own, opposite, and negative interpretation confirms the constitutional vice of the statute.

II

The parties dispute whether trademarks are commercial speech and whether trademark registration should be considered a federal subsidy. The former issue may turn on whether certain commercial concerns for the protection of trademarks might, as a general matter, be the basis for regulation. However that issue is resolved, the viewpoint based discrimination at issue here necessarily invokes heightened scrutiny.

"Commercial speech is no exception," the Court has explained, to the principle that the First Amendment "requires heightened scrutiny whenever the government creates a regulation of speech because of disagreement with the message it conveys." *Sorrell v. IMS Health Inc.*, 564 U.S. 552, 566 (2011) (internal quotation marks omitted). Unlike content based discrimination, discrimination based on viewpoint, including a regulation that targets speech for its offensiveness, remains of serious concern in the commercial context. See *Bolger v. Youngs Drug Products Corp.*, 463 U.S. 60, 65, 71-72 (1983).

To the extent trademarks qualify as commercial speech, they are an example of why that term or category does not serve as a blanket exemption from the First Amendment's requirement of viewpoint neutrality. Justice Holmes' reference to the "free trade in ideas" and the "power of . . . thought to get itself accepted in the competition of the market," *Abrams v. United States*, 250 U.S. 616, 630 (1919) (dissenting opinion), was a metaphor. In the realm of trademarks, the metaphorical marketplace of ideas becomes a tangible, powerful reality. Here that real marketplace exists as a matter of state law and our common-law tradition, quite without regard to the Federal Government. See *ante*. These marks make up part of the expression of everyday life, as with the names of entertainment groups, broadcast networks, designer clothing, newspapers, automobiles, candy bars, toys, and so on. Nonprofit organizations—ranging from medical-research charities and other humanitarian causes to political advocacy groups—also have trademarks, which they use to compete in a real economic sense for funding and other resources as they seek to persuade others to join their cause. To permit viewpoint discrimination in this context is to permit Government censorship.

This case does not present the question of how other provisions of the Lanham Act should be analyzed under the First Amendment. It is well settled, for instance, that to the extent a trademark is confusing or misleading the law can protect consumers and trademark owners. See, *e.g.*, *FTC v. Winsted Hosiery Co.*, 258 U.S. 483, 493 (1922) ("The labels in question are literally false, and . . . palpably so. All are, as the Commission found, calculated to deceive and do in fact deceive a substantial portion of the purchasing public"). This case also does not involve laws related to product labeling or otherwise designed to protect consumers. See *Sorrell, supra*, at 579 ("[T]he government's legitimate interest in protecting consumers from commercial harms explains why commercial speech can be subject to greater governmental regulation than noncommercial speech" (internal quotation marks omitted)). These considerations, however, do not alter the speech principles that bar the viewpoint discrimination embodied in the statutory provision at issue here.

It is telling that the Court's precedents have recognized just one narrow situation in which viewpoint discrimination is permissible: where the government itself is speaking or recruiting others to communicate a message on its behalf. [cit.] The exception is necessary to allow the government to stake out positions and pursue policies. [cit.] But it is also narrow, to prevent the government from claiming that every government program is exempt from the First Amendment. These cases have identified a number of factors that, if present, suggest the government is speaking on its own behalf; but none are present here. See *ante*.

There may be situations where private speakers are selected for a government program to assist the government in advancing a particular message. That is not this case either. The central purpose of trademark registration is to facilitate source identification. To serve that broad purpose, the Government has provided the benefits of federal registration to millions of marks identifying every type of product and cause. Registered trademarks do so by means of a wide diversity of words, symbols, and messages. Whether a mark is disparaging bears no plausible relation to that goal. While defining the purpose and scope of a federal program for these purposes can be complex, see, *e.g., Agency for Int'l Development v. Alliance for Open Society Int'l, Inc.*, 133 S. Ct. 2321, 2328 (2013), our cases are clear that viewpoint discrimination is not permitted where, as here, the Government "expends funds to encourage a diversity of views from private speakers," *Velazquez, supra*, at 542 (internal quotation marks omitted).

A law that can be directed against speech found offensive to some portion of the public can be turned against minority and dissenting views to the detriment of all. The First Amendment does not entrust that power to the government's benevolence. Instead, our reliance must be on the substantial safeguards of free and open discussion in a democratic society.

For these reasons, I join the Court's opinion in part and concur in the judgment.

[Justice Thomas' concurring opinion is omitted.]

IN RE BRUNETTI

877 F.3d 1330 (Fed. Cir. 2017)

Moore, Circuit Judge:

Erik Brunetti appeals from the decision of the Trademark Trial and Appeal Board ("Board") affirming the examining attorney's refusal to register the mark FUCT [for various items of apparel] because it comprises immoral or scandalous matter under 15 U.S.C. §1052(a) ("§2(a)"). We hold substantial evidence supports the Board's findings and it did not err concluding the mark comprises immoral or scandalous matter. We conclude, however, that §2(a)'s bar on registering immoral or scandalous marks is an unconstitutional restriction of free speech. We therefore reverse the Board's holding that Mr. Brunetti's mark is unregistrable.

BACKGROUND

I.　Section 2(a)'s Bar on Registration of Immoral or Scandalous Marks

[W]hile §2(a) identifies "immoral" and "scandalous" subject matter as separate bases to refuse to register a trademark—and are provisions separated by the "deceptive" provision—the PTO generally applies the bar on immoral or scandalous marks as a unitary provision ("the immoral or scandalous provision"). . . .

To determine whether a mark should be disqualified under §2(a), the PTO asks whether a "substantial composite of the general public" would find the mark scandalous, defined as "shocking to the sense of truth, decency, or propriety; disgraceful; offensive; disreputable; . . . giving offense to the conscience or moral feelings; . . . or calling out for condemnation." [cit.] Alternatively, "the PTO may prove scandalousness by establishing that a mark is 'vulgar.'" [cit.] The PTO makes a determination as to whether a mark is scandalous "in the context of contemporary attitudes" and "in the context of the marketplace as applied to only the goods described in the application." [cit.]

Because the scandalousness determination is made in the context of contemporary attitudes, the concept of what is actually immoral or scandalous changes over time. Early cases often, but not always, focused on religious words or symbols. See, e.g., *In re Riverbank Canning Co.*, 95 F.2d 327, 329 (CCPA 1938) (MADONNA for wine); . . . *In re Reemtsma Cigarettenfab-riken G.M.B.H.*, 122 U.S.P.Q. 339 (T.T.A.B. 1959) (SENUSSI (a Muslim sect that forbids smoking) for cigarettes); *In re Sociedade Agricola E. Comerical Dos Vinhos Messias, S.A.R.L.*, 159 U.S.P.Q. 275 (T.T.A.B. 1968) (MESSIAS for wine and brandy). In later cases, the PTO rejected a wider variety of marks as scandalous. See, e.g., *Runsdorf*, 171 U.S.P.Q. at 443 (BUBBY TRAP for brassieres); *McGinley*, 660 F.2d at 482 (mark consisting of "a photograph of a nude man and woman kissing and embracing in a manner appearing to expose the male genitalia" for a swingers newsletter); *In re Tinseltown, Inc.*, 212 U.S.P.Q. 863 (T.T.A.B. 1981) (BULLSHIT on handbags, purses, and other personal accessories); *Greyhound Corp. v. Both Worlds, Inc.*, 6 U.S.P.Q.2d 1635 (T.T.A.B. 1988) (mark depicting a defecating dog); *Mavety*, 33 F.3d 1367 (BLACK TAIL for adult entertainment magazines).

. . .

DISCUSSION

Mr. Brunetti argues substantial evidence does not support the Board's finding the mark FUCT is vulgar under §2(a) of the Lanham Act. He argues even if the mark is vulgar, §2(a) does not expressly prohibit the registration of vulgar marks and a mark should be approved for registration when there is doubt as to its meaning, as he alleges there is here. Alternatively, Mr. Brunetti challenges the constitutionality of §2(a)'s bar on immoral or scandalous marks.

I.   THE MARK FUCT IS VULGAR AND THEREFORE SCANDALOUS

[The court determined that it was "undisputed that the word 'fuck' is vulgar" and that substantial evidence supported the Board's finding that "'fuct' is a 'phonetic twin' of 'fucked,' the past tense of the word 'fuck.'" The court also concluded that vulgar terms fell within the scope of the term "scandalous" as used in Section 2(a), in view of the court's precedent and the meaning of "scandalous" at the time the Lanham Act was adopted.]

II.   SECTION 2(A)'S BAR ON IMMORAL OR SCANDALOUS MARKS IS UNCONSTITUTIONAL UNDER THE FIRST AMENDMENT

When Mr. Brunetti filed his appeal, his constitutional argument was foreclosed by binding [Federal Circuit] precedent. . . .

Following the issuance of the Supreme Court's decision in *Tam*, we requested additional briefing from the parties regarding the impact of the Supreme Court's decision. . . . The government contends *Tam* does not resolve the constitutionality of §2(a)'s bar on registering immoral or scandalous marks because the disparagement provision implicates viewpoint discrimination, whereas the immoral or scandalous provision is viewpoint neutral.

While we question the viewpoint neutrality of the immoral or scandalous provision, we need not resolve that issue. Independent of whether the immoral or scandalous provision is viewpoint discriminatory, we conclude the provision impermissibly discriminates based on content in violation of the First Amendment.

A.   *Section 2(a)'s Bar on Registering Immoral or Scandalous Marks Is an Unconstitutional Content-Based Restriction on Speech*

The government restricts speech based on content when "a law applies to particular speech because of the topic discussed or the idea or message expressed." [cit.] Content-based statutes are presumptively invalid. [cit.] To survive, such statutes must withstand strict scrutiny review, which requires the government to "prove that the restriction furthers a compelling interest and is narrowly tailored to achieve that interest." [cit.] *States v. Playboy Entm't Grp., Inc.*, 529 U.S. 803, 813 (2000) ("If a statute regulates speech based on its content, it must be narrowly tailored to promote a compelling Government interest. If a less restrictive alternative would serve the Government's purpose, the legislature must use that alternative."). Strict scrutiny applies whether a government statute bans or merely burdens protected speech. See *Playboy*, 529 U.S. at 812 ("The Government's content-based burdens must satisfy the same rigorous scrutiny as its content-based bans.").

The government concedes that §2(a)'s bar on registering immoral or scandalous marks is a content-based restriction on speech. And the government does not assert that the immoral or scandalous provision survives strict scrutiny review. Instead, the government contends §2(a)'s content-based bar on registering immoral or scandalous marks does not implicate the First Amendment because trademark registration is either a government subsidy program or limited public forum. Alternatively, the government argues trademarks are commercial speech implicating only the intermediate level of scrutiny set forth in *Central Hudson*. Under a less exacting degree of scrutiny, the government argues the immoral or scandalous provision is an appropriate content-based restriction tailored to substantial government interests. We consider these arguments in turn.

1.   Trademark Registration Is Not a Government Subsidy Program

. . .

The government argues . . . that §2(a)'s bar on registering immoral or scandalous marks is simply a reasonable exercise of its spending power, in which the bar on registration is a constitutional condition defining the limits of trademark registration. Our court rejected the applicability of this analysis to trademark registration, 9-3, in our en banc decision in *Tam*. The four Justices who reached the issue in *Tam* likewise held the government subsidy framework does not apply to trademark registration. 137 S. Ct. at 1761 (Alito, J.). . . .

Unlike trademark registration, the programs at issue in the Supreme Court's cases upholding the constitutionality of conditions under the Spending Clause necessarily and directly implicate Congress' power to spend or control government property. For example, *Rust* addressed a condition on the distribution of federal funds for family planning services. The Supreme Court's plurality opinion in *United States v. American Library Association, Inc.* upheld a condition on federal funding for Internet access to public libraries. 539 U.S. 194, 212 (2003). . . . "The federal registration of a trademark is nothing like the programs at issue in these cases." *Tam*, 137 S. Ct. at 1761 (Alito, J.).

Trademark registration does not implicate Congress' power to spend funds. [The court noted that an applicant does not receive federal funds upon the PTO's consideration of, or grant of, a trademark. And the fact that the government must expend certain federal funds such as PTO employee benefits trademarks did not transform trademark registration into a government subsidy because just about every government service requires the expenditure of some government funds.]

Nor is the grant of trademark registration a subsidy equivalent. [The court acknowledged the benefits of registration including, in addition to those mentioned by Alito, J., in *Tam*, "the right to sue in federal court, id. §1121, the right to recover treble damages for willful infringement, id. §1117, a complete defense to state or common law claims of trademark dilution, id. §1125(c)(6), . . . the right to prevent 'cybersquatters' from misappropriating a domain name, 15 U.S.C. §1125(d), and qualification for a simplified process for obtaining recognition and protection of a mark in countries that have signed the Paris Convention, see id. §1141b (Madrid Protocol)."] While these benefits are valuable, they are not analogous to Congress' grant of federal funds. The benefits of trademark registration arise from the statutory framework of the Lanham Act, and the Lanham Act in turn derives from the Commerce Clause. [The court held that when government registration does not implicate Congress' authority under the Spending Clause, the government subsidy line of case law does not govern the constitutionality of §2(a)'s bar on registering immoral or scandalous marks.]

2. Trademark Registration Is Not a Limited Public Forum

The constitutionality of speech restrictions on government property are analyzed under the Supreme Court's "forum analysis," which "determine[s] when a governmental entity, in regulating property in its charge, may place limitations on speech." [cit.] . . . To determine the constitutional bounds of speech restrictions on government property, the forum analysis instructs us to first classify the government's property as one of three forums.

[The first two forums are traditional public forums and designated public forums, in which "the government's ability to permissibly restrict expressive conduct is very limited." Content-based restrictions on speech "must be narrowly tailored to serve a compelling government interest, and restrictions based on viewpoint are prohibited."]

The remaining forum category is the limited public forum, at times referred to as a non-public forum. Limited public forums are places the government has "limited to use by certain groups or dedicated solely to the discussion of certain subjects." As with traditional and designated public forums, regulations that discriminate based on viewpoint in limited public forums are presumed unconstitutional. *Rosenberger v. Rector & Visitors of Univ. of Va.*, 515 U.S. 819, 830 (1995). Content-based restrictions on speech are subject to a lesser degree of scrutiny and remain constitutional "so long as the distinctions drawn are reasonable in light of the purpose served by the forum." *Cornelius v. NAACP Legal Def. & Educ. Fund, Inc.*, 473 U.S. 788, 806 (1985). Thus, where the government has opened its property for a limited purpose, it can constitutionally restrict speech consistent with that purpose as long as "the regulation on speech is reasonable and not an effort to suppress expression merely because officials oppose the speaker's view." [cit.]

The government argues that the federal trademark registration program is a limited public forum, subjecting §2(a)'s content-based restriction on marks comprising immoral or scandalous subject matter to a less demanding degree of scrutiny. Without articulating why the federal trademark registration program is a limited public forum, the government's letter brief analogizes trademark registration to city buses and a military cemetery. At oral argument, the government identified the principal register as the limited public forum, which it contended is a metaphysical forum much like the forum at issue in *Rosenberger*.

The Supreme Court has found the existence of a limited public forum only when the government restricts speech on its own property. At one end of that spectrum are venues that are owned and controlled by government entities. See, e.g., *Greer v. Spock*, 424 U.S. 828, 838 (1976) (military base); *Jones v. N.C. Prisoners' Labor Union, Inc.*, 433 U.S. 119, 134 (1977) (prison facilities); *Int'l Soc. for Krishna Consciousness*, 505 U.S. at 680-83 (Port Authority airport terminal). These cases unquestionably concern "a governmental entity, . . . regulating property in its charge." [cit.] Other cases involve property that is clearly government owned, although present in public locations. See, e.g., *United States v. Kokinda*, 497 U.S. 720, 727-30 (1990) (sidewalk outside of Postal Service); *Members of City Council of L.A. v. Taxpayers for Vincent*, 466 U.S. 789, 814 (1984) (public utility poles). Several of the Court's remaining limited public forum cases involve speech restrictions that occur on public school property. [cit.]

While some of the Supreme Court's limited public forum cases have involved forums that exist "more in a metaphysical than in a spatial or geographic sense," these forums have nonetheless been tethered to government properties. [In *Rosenberger*, the Supreme Court concluded that a public university's Student Activities Fund ("SAF") intended to support a broad range of extracurricular student activities related to the educational purpose of the university was a limited public forum.]

Because trademarks are by definition used in commerce, the trademark registration program bears no resemblance to these limited public forums. The speech that flows from trademark registration is not tethered to a public school, federal workplace, or any other government property. A principal feature of trademarks is that they help "consumers identify goods and services that they wish to purchase, as well as those they want to avoid." *Tam*, 137 S. Ct. at 1751. "These marks make up part of the expression of everyday life, as with the names of entertainment groups, broadcast networks, designer clothing, newspapers, automobiles, candy bars, toys, and so on." Id. at 1768 (Kennedy, J.). By their very purpose, trademarks exist to convey messages throughout commerce. It is difficult to analogize the Nike swoosh or the Nike JUST DO IT mark located on a Nike shirt in a Nike store as somehow a government created limited public forum. The registration and use of registered trademarks simply does not fit within the rubric of public or limited public forum cases. "[T]he forum analysis requires consideration not only of whether government property has been opened to the public, but also of the nature and purpose of the property at issue." *Preminger*, 517 F.3d 1299 (internal citations omitted). [cit.]

A snapshot of marks recently rejected under the immoral or scandalous provision reveals the breadth of goods and services impacted by §2(a)'s bar on such marks, including speech occurring on clothing, books, websites, beverages, mechanical contraptions, and live entertainment. These refusals chill speech anywhere from the Internet to the grocery store. And none of them involve government property over which the government can assert a right to "legally preserve the property under its control for the use to which it is dedicated." *Lamb's Chapel*, 508 U.S. at 390.

That registered marks also appear on the government's principal register does not transform trademark registration into a limited public forum. The government does not open the principal register to any exchange of ideas—it is ancillary to trademark registration. The principal register is simply a database identifying the marks approved for use in commerce. . . . If the government can constitutionally restrain the expression of private speech in commerce because such speech is identified in a government database, so too could the government restrain speech occurring on private land or in connection with privately-owned vehicles, simply because those private properties are listed in a database. . . . As the government recognized, such a suppression of speech would raise serious concerns under the unconstitutional conditions doctrine. . . . We thus conclude that government registration of trademarks does not create a limited public forum in which the government can more freely restrict speech.

> 3. The Prohibition on the Registration of Immoral or Scandalous Trademarks Targets the Expressive Content of Speech and Therefore Strict Scrutiny Should Be Applied

Commercial speech is speech which does "no more than propose a commercial transaction." *Va. State Bd. of Pharmacy v. Va. Citizens Consumer Council, Inc.*, 425 U.S. 748, 762 (1976) (citation omitted). Trademarks certainly convey a commercial message, but not exclusively so. There is no doubt that trademarks "identify the source of a product or service, and therefore play a role in the 'dissemination of information as to who is producing and selling what product, for what reason, and at what price.'" [cit.] However, trademarks—including immoral or scandalous trademarks—also "often have an expressive content." *Tam*, 137 S. Ct. at 1760. For immoral or scandalous marks, this message is often uncouth. But it can espouse a powerful cause. See, e.g., FUCK HEROIN, Appl. No. 86,361,326; FUCK CANCER, Appl. No. 86,290,011; FUCK RACISM, Appl. No. 85,608,559. It can put forth a political view, see DEMOCRAT.BS, Appl. No. 77,042,069, or REPUBLICAN.BS, Appl. No. 77,042,071. While the speech expressed in trademarks is brief, "powerful messages can sometimes be conveyed in just a few words." *Tam*, 137 S. Ct. at 1760.

[T]here can be no question that the immoral or scandalous prohibition targets the expressive components of the speech. As in this case, the agency often justifies its rejection of marks on the grounds that they convey offensive ideas. [Joint Appendix] at 8-9 (explaining that Mr. Brunetti's use of his trademark is scandalous because his mark "objectifies women and offers degrading examples of extreme misogyny" and contains a theme "of extreme nihilism" with "anti-social imagery" and is "lacking in taste"). These are each value judgments about the expressive message behind the trademark. Whether marks comprise immoral or scandalous subject matter hinges on the expressive, not source-identifying, nature of trademarks.

While different provisions of the Lanham Act may appropriately be classified as targeting a mark's source-identifying information—for example, §2(e)'s bar on registering marks that are "merely descriptive" or "geographically descriptive"—the immoral or scandalous provision targets a mark's expressive message, which is separate and distinct from the commercial purpose of a mark as a source identifier. Justice Kennedy explained in his concurrence: "The central purpose of trademark registration is to facilitate source identification. . . . Whether a mark is disparaging bears no plausible relation to that goal." 137 S. Ct. at 1768 (Kennedy, J.). We find the same logic applies to the immoral or scandalous prohibition. As in the case of disparaging marks, the PTO's rejections under §2(a)'s bar on immoral or scandalous marks are necessarily based in the government's belief that the rejected mark conveys an expressive message—namely, a message that is scandalous or offensive to a substantial composite of the general population. See *Tam*, 808 F.3d at 1338. Section 2(a) regulates the expressive components of speech, not the commercial components of speech, and as such it should be subject to strict scrutiny. See *Sorrell v. IMS Health Inc.*, 564 U.S. 552, 565 (2011). There is no dispute that §2(a)'s bar on the registration of immoral or scandalous marks is unconstitutional if strict scrutiny applies.

4. Section 2(a)'s Bar on Immoral or Scandalous Marks Does Not Survive Intermediate Scrutiny

Section 2(a)'s bar on the registration of immoral or scandalous marks is unconstitutional even if treated as a regulation of purely commercial speech reviewed according to the intermediate scrutiny framework established in *Central Hudson*, 447 U.S. at 566. Intermediate scrutiny requires that "the State must show at least that the statute directly advances a substantial governmental interest and that the measure is drawn to achieve that interest." *Sorrell*, 564 U.S. at 572.

Commercial speech is subject to a four-part test which asks whether (1) the speech concerns lawful activity and is not misleading; (2) the asserted government interest is substantial; (3) the regulation directly advances that government interest; and (4) whether the regulation is "not more extensive than necessary to serve that interest." *Central Hudson*, 447 U.S. at 566; see also *Bd. of Tr. of State Univ. of N.Y. v. Fox*, 492 U.S. 469, 479-80 (1989) (explaining the fourth prong of *Central Hudson* requires "not necessarily the least restrictive means but . . . a means narrowly tailored to achieve the desired objective").

"Under a commercial speech inquiry, it is the State's burden to justify its content-based law as consistent with the First Amendment." *Sorrell*, 564 U.S. at 565.

The immoral or scandalous provision clearly meets the first prong of the *Central Hudson* test, which requires we first confirm the speech "concern lawful activity and not be misleading." . . .

Central Hudson's second prong, requiring a substantial government interest, is not met. The only government interest related to the immoral or scandalous provision that we can discern from the government's briefing is its interest in "protecting public order and morality." At oral argument, the government struggled to identify the substantial interest in barring registration of trademarks comprising immoral or scandalous subject matter. The government framed its interest based on the government's own perception of proposed marks, including what types of marks the government would "want to promote" or "has deemed to be most suitable." At another point, the government indicated its interest is to shield its examiners from immoral or scandalous marks: "whether or not its examiners are forced to decide whether one drawing of genitalia is confusingly similar to another drawing of genitalia." Ultimately, the government stated, "Congress' primary interest is the promotion of the use of non-scandalous marks in commerce." . . . Whichever articulation of the government's interest we choose, the government has failed to identify a substantial interest justifying its suppression of immoral or scandalous trademarks.

First, the government does not have a substantial interest in promoting certain trademarks over others. The Supreme Court [in *Tam*] rejected the government's claim that trademarks are government speech. Our conclusion that trademark registration is neither a government subsidy nor a limited public forum forecloses any remaining interest the government may have in approving only marks it "has deemed to be most suitable." Oral Arg. at 22:56-23:00; see also *Tam*, 137 S. Ct. at 1760-63 (plurality rejecting the government subsidy argument) (Alito, J.).

Second, Supreme Court precedent makes clear that the government's general interest in protecting the public from marks it deems "off-putting," whether to protect the general public or the government itself, is not a substantial interest justifying broad suppression of speech. "[T]he fact that society may find speech offensive is not a sufficient reason for suppressing it." *Hustler Magazine, Inc. v. Falwell*, 485 U.S. 46, 55 (1988); *Bolger v. Youngs Drug Prods. Corp.*, 463 U.S. 60, 71 (1983) ("At least where obscenity is not involved, we have consistently held that the fact that protected speech may be offensive to some does not justify its suppression." (citation omitted)); [cit.]. "Where the designed benefit of a content-based speech restriction is to shield the sensibilities of listeners, the general rule is that the right of expression prevails, even where no less restrictive alternative exists." *Playboy*, 529 U.S. at 813.

The Supreme Court's decision in *Tam* supports our conclusion that the government's interest in protecting the public from off-putting marks is an inadequate government interest for First Amendment purposes. See, e.g., 137 S. Ct. at 1764 (applying *Central Hudson* and rejecting the government's "interest in preventing speech expressing ideas that offend" because "that idea strikes at the heart of the First Amendment") (Alito, J.). In *Tam*, the Court acknowledged that it is a "bedrock First Amendment principle" that "Speech may not be banned on the ground that it expresses ideas that offend." *Tam*, 137 S. Ct. at 1751 (Alito, J.); see also id. at 1767 ("[T]he Court's cases have long prohibited the government from justifying a First Amendment burden by pointing to the offensiveness of the speech to be suppressed.") (Kennedy, J.). Both Justice Alito's and Justice Kennedy's opinions support their conclusions that the disparagement provision is unconstitutional citing cases holding "the public expression of ideas may not be prohibited merely because the ideas are themselves offensive to some of their hearers." [cit.] The government's interest in suppressing speech because it is off-putting is unavailing.

While the government's interest in *Tam* related to a viewpoint-based restriction on speech, we note the cases on which the Supreme Court relied are not so limited. The cases cited in *Tam* are directed to speech that may be offensive, but not all involve speech that is disparaging or viewpoint discriminatory. Many involve speech that, rather than disparaging others, involved peaceful demonstrations. See, e.g., *Bachellar v. Maryland*, 397 U.S. 564, 566-67 (1970) (peaceful Vietnam war protest carrying signs such as "Make Love not War"); [cit.] Other cases do not appear to involve viewpoint discrimination at all. For example, *Hustler Magazine* concerned a parody interview of Jerry Falwell in which the actor playing him stated his "'first time' was during a drunken incestuous rendezvous with his mother in an outhouse." 485 U.S. at 48. While such a parody interview is offensive, its function as a parody does not clearly involve the expression of beliefs, ideas, or perspectives. . . . The Supreme Court's narrative that the government cannot justify restricting speech because it offends, together with its reliance on cases involving a variety of different speech restrictions, reinforce our conclusion that the government's interest in protecting the public from off-putting marks is not substantial.

Finally, the government does not have a substantial interest in protecting the public from scandalousness and profanities. The government attempts to justify this interest by pointing to the Supreme Court's decision in *FCC v. Pacifica Foundation*, 438 U.S. 726 (1978). . . .

The government's interest in protecting the public from profane and scandalous marks is not akin to the government's interest in protecting children and other unsuspecting listeners from a barrage of swear words over the radio in *Pacifica*. A trademark is not foisted upon listeners by virtue of its being registered. Nor does registration make a scandalous mark more accessible to children. Absent any concerns that trademark registration invades a substantial privacy interest in an intolerable manner, the government's interest amounts to protecting everyone, including adults, from scandalous content. But even when "many adults themselves would find the material highly offensive," adults have a First Amendment right to view and hear speech that is profane and scandalous. *Playboy*, 529 U.S. at 811 (First Amendment right to view "sexually explicit adult programming or other programming that is indecent"). . . .

Even if we were to hold that the government has a substantial interest in protecting the public from scandalous or immoral marks, the government could not meet the third prong of *Central Hudson*, which requires the regulation directly advance the government's asserted interest. As the government has repeatedly exhorted, §2(a) does not directly prevent applicants from using their marks. . . . In this electronic/Internet age, to the extent that the government seeks to protect the general population from scandalous material, with all due respect, it has completely failed.

Finally, no matter the government's interest, it cannot meet the fourth prong of *Central Hudson*. The PTO's inconsistent application of the immoral or scandalous provision creates an "uncertainty [that] undermines the likelihood that the [provision] has been carefully tailored." See *Reno*, 521 U.S. at 871. Nearly identical marks have been approved by one examining attorney and rejected as scandalous or immoral by another. [The court noted various academic studies showing these inconsistencies; illustrated the point by examples referencing the indisputably vulgar term "fuck," which are not always rejected as a matter of course; and quoted the Board on the vague and subjective nature of determining public perceptions of a trademark's morality or immorality, offensiveness, or even vulgarity.] [T]he subjectivity in the determination of what is immoral or scandalous and the disparate and unpredictable application of these principles cause us to conclude that the prohibition at issue in this case would also fail the fourth prong of the *Central Hudson* analysis.

We conclude that the government has not presented us with a substantial government interest justifying the §2(a) bar on immoral or scandalous marks. As we concluded in *Tam*, "All of the government's proffered interests boil down to permitting the government to burden speech it finds offensive." *Tam*, 808 F.3d at 1357. We also conclude that the government has failed to demonstrate that its restriction will advance the interests it asserts and that it is narrowly tailored to achieve that objective. Section 2(a)'s bar on immoral or scandalous marks does not survive intermediate scrutiny under *Central Hudson*.

5.   There Is No Reasonable Definition of the Statutory Terms Scandalous and Immoral Which Would Preserve Their Constitutionality

We construe statutes narrowly to preserve their constitutionality, when possible. [cit.] However [it is] permissible to construe a statute in a manner that preserves its constitutionality only where the construction is reasonable.

The concurrence agrees that the scandalous and immoral prohibitions as construed by the government, this court, and our predecessor court are unconstitutional. . . . The concurrence proposes that we "narrow the immoral-scandalous provision's scope to obscene marks in order to preserve its constitutionality." While the legislature could rewrite the statute to adopt such a standard, we cannot.

It is not reasonable to construe the words immoral and scandalous as confined to obscene material. There is no dispute that an obscene mark would be scandalous or immoral; however, not all scandalous or immoral marks are obscene. . . . The PTO has for a century rejected marks as scandalous or immoral that are clearly not obscene. As set forth above, many of the early cases applying the immoral or scandalous provision involved blasphemous marks touching on religion, which were not obscene.

The Supreme Court has made clear that the definition of obscenity for purposes of the First Amendment is "material which deals with sex in a manner appealing to prurient interest," i.e., "material having a tendency to excite lustful thoughts." *Roth v. United States*, 354 U.S. 476, 487 & n.20 (1957). This "definition does not reflect the precise meaning of 'obscene' as traditionally used in the English language," and instead is limited to "obscene material '*which deals with sex.*'" *Miller v. California*, 413 U.S. 15, 20 n.2 (1973) (emphasis added).

Despite the concurrence's suggestion to the contrary, none of the dictionary definitions cited define "immoral" or "scandalous" in sexual terms. . . .

Unlike the terms "immoral" and "scandalous," the statutory terms at issue in the cases cited in the concurrence are by their nature limited to material "which deals with sex." [cit.] We do not see how the words "immoral" and "scandalous" could reasonably be read to be limited to material of a sexual nature. We cannot stand in the shoes of the legislature and rewrite a statute.

CONCLUSION

The trademark at issue is vulgar. . . . Many of the marks rejected under §2(a)'s bar on immoral or scandalous marks, including the marks discussed in this opinion, are lewd, crass, or even disturbing. We find the use of such marks in commerce discomforting, and are not eager to see a proliferation of such marks in the marketplace. There are, however, a cadre of similarly offensive images and words that have secured copyright registration by the government. There are countless songs with vulgar lyrics, blasphemous images, scandalous books and paintings, all of which are protected under federal law. No doubt many works registered with the Copyright Office offend a substantial composite of the general public. There are words and images that we do not wish to be confronted with, not as art, nor in the marketplace. The First Amendment, however, protects private expression, even private expression which is offensive to a substantial composite of the general public. The government has offered no substantial government interest for policing offensive speech in the context of a registration program such as the one at issue in this case.

We hold that the bar in §2(a) against immoral or scandalous marks is unconstitutional because it violates the First Amendment. We reverse the Board's holding that Mr. Brunetti's mark is unregistrable under §2(a).

Reversed.

DYK, Circuit Judge, concurring in the judgment:

As an initial matter, I agree with the majority that the Supreme Court's recent decision in *Matal v. Tam*, 137 S. Ct. 1744 (2017), does not dictate the facial invalidity of the immoral-scandalous provision. . . . Nonetheless, I also agree that the immoral-scandalous provision raises some serious First Amendment questions, as the majority opinion concludes.

I think that we are obligated to construe the statute to avoid these constitutional questions. Courts must, "where possible, construe federal statutes so as 'to avoid serious doubt of their constitutionality.'" [cit.] A saving construction of a statute need only be "fairly possible," and "every reasonable construction must be resorted to." [cit.]

One such fairly possible reading is available to us here by limiting the clause's reach to obscene marks, which are not protected by the First Amendment. . . .

As the Supreme Court has done with the obscenity statutes, here when faced with constitutional doubt as to the immoral-scandalous provision, we should adopt a narrowing construction and limit the statute to obscenity. . . .

Under these circumstances, we can appropriately narrow the immoral-scandalous provision's scope to obscene marks in order to preserve its constitutionality, and we are obligated to do so.

Because there is no suggestion that Mr. Brunetti's mark is obscene, however, I agree that the decision of the Trademark Trial and Appeal Board must be reversed. For these reasons, I concur in the judgment.

NOTES AND QUESTIONS

1. *What governmental interest?* Why did the Lanham Act bar scandalous or disparaging marks from registration? To avoid the impression that the government endorses such marks? To avoid consuming PTO time in examining such marks? To protect consumers from being exposed to such marks? To discourage producers from investing in goodwill associated with such marks? Could a registration bar ever accomplish any of these goals? If not, then was such a bar good trademark policy, quite apart from First Amendment considerations?

2. *What speech is restricted?* What exactly does a registration bar preclude? For example, if Tam were barred from registering THE SLANTS for his band, would Tam have to change the band's name? Would Tam be barred from asserting unregistered rights under Section 43(a) to exclude others from selling unauthorized SLANTS merchandise? Or does the bar merely deny Tam the benefits of registration? If only the last of these is true, does the bar amount to a substantial burden on speech? Both *Tam* and *Brunetti* discuss registration benefits in rather glowing terms. Does that surprise you? In the cases that you have

read thus far in this casebook, to what extent do courts focus on the existence and benefits of registration in fashioning rules?

3.   *Trademark registration as government speech, a government subsidy, or a government program.* In *Tam*, the Court concludes that the act of registering a trademark is not government speech, because trademarks are not traditionally used to convey government messages; trademark registrations are not closely identified in the public mind with the government; and the government does not maintain direct control of the messages conveyed via registered trademarks. Does the Court correctly characterize the trademark registration scheme? Are you persuaded by the Court's distinction between trademark registration and specialty license plates (which were at issue in the *Walker* case, and deemed to be government speech)? The Court also rules that trademark registration is not a form of government subsidy, nor is it akin to a government program in which some content-based restrictions are allowed. Had the Court ruled otherwise on any of these arguments, the disparagement bar would have received no First Amendment scrutiny or only rational basis review. If you think, based on the preceding notes, that the government interest here is not especially strong and the restriction on speech is something more than trivial, you may understand why part of the PTO's strategy involved pressing the government speech/government subsidy/government program arguments.

4.   *Trademark registration as commercial speech?* The Court in *Tam* avoids determining whether trademark registration is commercial speech (triggering relaxed First Amendment scrutiny in which a speech restriction must be "narrowly drawn" to serve a "substantial interest" under the *Central Hudson* test) or expressive speech (triggering heightened First Amendment scrutiny to the extent that the government seeks to regulate the content of that expression to suppress particular viewpoints). The Court concludes that the disparagement restriction would not survive even relaxed scrutiny. Do you agree with the Court's assessment of the interests being served and the scope of the restriction on speech? Or should the Court have applied its framework for viewpoint discriminatory speech?

5.   *Brunetti as the echo of* Tam? Is *Brunetti* anything more than the echo of *Tam*? What is your view of Judge Dyk's concurring opinion that the court could have avoided the constitutional question by narrowly construing the scandalousness bar as confined to obscenity as understood in First Amendment jurisprudence?

6.   *Effect on other Lanham Act provisions.* Are any of the other Section 2 bars arguably unconstitutional in view of *Tam* and *Brunetti*? For example, if a mark is denied registration because it is merely descriptive, is that a restriction on expressive content raising First Amendment speech implications? Or is it a restriction that targets whether the mark is a source identifier, and therefore "separate and distinct" from content-based restrictions, as the Federal Circuit asserts in *Brunetti* (and Justice Kennedy asserts in his concurrence in *Tam*)? We will discuss the possible effect of *Tam* on other non-registration provisions of the Lanham Act in Chapters 8 and 9.

7.   *Effect on unregistered rights.* In footnote 1 of the *Tam* opinion, the Court declined to decide whether the Section 2 bars would also apply to assertions of unregistered rights under Section 43(a). But the Federal Circuit in *Tam* did take a view, suggesting in dicta (especially in the panel opinion) that if there could be no trademark *registration* of the SLANTS mark because it disparaged Asian-Americans, then there could be no common law rights either. To similar effect, a lower court ruled explicitly that the Section 2 bars does extend to actions to enforce unregistered rights under Section 43(a). *Renna v. County of Union, N.J.*, 88 F. Supp. 3d 310 (D.N.J. 2014) (Section 2(b) bar against registering official seals should be extended to Section 43(a) action). And dicta in *Two Pesos* suggested that the Section 2 bars are "for the most part applicable" in Section 43(a) actions, as the Court pointed out in *Tam* footnote 1. This position is probably inconsistent with conventional trademark thought. Should courts adopt the *Two Pesos* dictum? Should it extend to all of the Section 2 bars?

8. Tam *and* Brunetti *from the perspective of trademark policy.* Would it be wise trademark policy to deny registrations for disparaging or scandalous matter (if it could be done constitutionally)? Is the PTO equipped to administer such prohibitions? Is the cost of administration worth the benefit?

9. *A registry of non-marks?* Scholars overseas have proposed creating a registry for terms and symbols that should be per se denied protection as marks. Such "non-marks" could include those having a "potential for commercial exploitation as an icon of hatred, genocide or other consensually identified destructive social value." *See* Jeremy Phillips & Ilanah Simon, *No Marks for Hitler: A Radical Reappraisal of Trade Mark Use and Political Sensitivity*, [2004] EUR. INTELL. PROP. REV. 327 (setting forth the proposal); Caspar P.L. van Woensel, *Fuhrer Wines at Your Local Store: Legal Means Against Commercial Exploitation of Intolerable Portrayals*, [2005] EUR. INTELL. PROP. REV. 37 (criticizing the proposal and offering other avenues of relief). The debate was sparked by Italian vintner Lunardelli's sales of FUHRER wine (depicting Adolph Hitler and including phrases associated with Nazism, like SIEG HEIL). Is there a way to structure a registry of non-marks in the United States that would survive First Amendment scrutiny after *Tam* and *Brunetti*?

IN RE BUDGE MFG. CO., INC.

857 F.2d 773 (Fed. Cir. 1988)

NIES, Circuit Judge:

Budge Manufacturing Co., Inc., appeals from the final decision of the United States Trademark Trial and Appeal Board refusing registration of LOVEE LAMB for "automotive seat covers," application Serial No. 507,974 filed November 9, 1984. The basis for rejection is that the term LAMB is deceptive matter within the meaning of section 2(a) of the Lanham Act, 15 U.S.C. §1052(a) (1982), as applied to Budge's goods which are made wholly from synthetic fibers. We affirm.

OPINION

Section 2(a) of the Lanham Act bars registration of a mark which: "Consists of or comprises . . . deceptive . . . matter. . . ." As stated in *In re Automatic Radio Mfg. Co.*, 404 F.2d 1391, 1396 (C.C.P.A. 1969): "The proscription [of Section 2(a)] is not against misdescriptive terms unless they are also deceptive." Thus, that a mark or part of a mark may be inapt or misdescriptive as applied to an applicant's goods does not make it "deceptive." *Id.* (AUTOMATIC RADIO not a deceptive mark for air conditioners, ignition systems, and antennas.) Recognizing that premise, the Trademark Trial and Appeal Board has sought to articulate a standard by which "deceptive matter" under section 2(a) can be judged. . . .

[After reviewing TTAB precedent, the Federal Circuit adopted the following standard for Section 2(a) deceptiveness.]

(1) Is the term misdescriptive of the character, quality, function, composition or use of the goods?

(2) If so, are prospective purchasers likely to believe that the misdescription actually describes the goods?

(3) If so, is the misdescription likely to affect the decision to purchase?

In *ex parte* prosecution, the burden is initially on the Patent and Trademark Office (PTO) to put forth sufficient evidence that the mark for which registration is sought meets the above criteria of unregistrability. Mindful that the PTO has limited facilities for acquiring evidence—it cannot, for example, be expected to conduct a survey of the marketplace or obtain consumer affidavits—we conclude that the evidence of record here is sufficient to establish a *prima facie* case of deceptiveness.

That evidence shows with respect to the three-pronged test:

(1)   Budge admits that its seat covers are not made from lamb or sheep products. Thus, the term LAMB is misdescriptive of its goods.

(2)   Seat covers for various vehicles can be and are made from natural lambskin and sheepskin. Applicant itself makes automobile seat covers of natural sheepskin. Lambskin is defined, *inter alia*, as fine-grade sheep skin. *See Webster's Third New International Dictionary* 639 (unabr. 1976). The board's factual inference is reasonable that purchasers are likely to believe automobile seat covers denominated by the term LAMB or SHEEP are actually made from natural sheep or lamb skins.

(3)   Evidence of record shows that natural sheepskin and lambskin is more expensive than simulated skins and that natural and synthetic skins have different characteristics. Thus, the misrepresentation is likely to affect the decision to purchase.

Faced with this *prima facie* case against registration, Budge had the burden to come forward with countering evidence to overcome the rejection. It wholly failed to do so.

Budge argues that its use of LAMB as part of its mark is not misdescriptive when considered in connection with the text in its advertising, which states that the cover is of "simulated sheepskin." Some, but not all, of Budge's specimen labels also have this text. This evidence is unpersuasive. . . .

. . . Misdescriptiveness of a term may be negated by its meaning in the context of the whole mark inasmuch as the combination is seen together and makes a unitary impression. *A.F. Gallun & Sons Corp. v. Aristocrat Leather Prods., Inc.*, 135 U.S.P.Q. 459, 460 (TTAB 1962) (COPY CALF not misdescriptive, but rather suggests *imitation* of calf skin). The same is not true with respect to explanatory statements in advertising or on labels which purchasers may or may not note and which may or may not always be provided. The statutory provision bars registration of *a mark* comprising deceptive matter. Congress has said that the advantages of registration may not be extended to a mark which deceives the public. Thus, the mark standing alone must pass muster, for that is what the applicant seeks to register, not extraneous explanatory statements. . . .

Finally, we note the evidence of Budge's extensive sales since 1974 under the mark. However, it is too well established for argument that a mark which includes deceptive matter is barred from registration and cannot acquire distinctiveness.

[*Affirmed.*]

NOTES AND QUESTIONS

1.   *Policy underlying Section 2(a)'s deceptiveness bar.*   Why should the Lanham Act bar the registration of deceptive marks? Does your answer reflect traditional trademark policy concerns—like those justifying the distinctiveness rules? If so, does the deceptiveness bar rest on firm constitutional grounds, notwithstanding *Tam* and *Brunetti*?

2. *Section 2(a) deceptiveness in Section 43(a) cases?* The *Budge* court notes that "Congress has said that the *advantages of registration* may not be extended to a mark which deceives the public" (emphasis supplied). Is this meant to imply that the policies underlying Section 2(a) apply only in the context of registration, and that the Section 2(a) deceptiveness bar therefore would not extend to assertions of unregistered rights?

3. *Using deceptive marks.* The Section 2(a) deceptiveness bar does not bar a mark owner from *using* a deceptive mark. However, the use of deceptive marks may also violate other federal or state laws. *See, e.g., Community State Bank N.A. v. Community State Bank*, 758 N.W.2d 520 (Iowa 2008) (discussing whether a bank's use of a name and logo violated an Iowa Code provision prohibiting nationally chartered banks from using the term "state" in their "legally chartered" names); *see also* 15 U.S.C. §45 (declaring "unfair or deceptive acts or practices in or affecting commerce" to be unlawful and empowering the Federal Trade Commission to institute proceedings against violators). Such a use might also violate the Lanham Act's false advertising provision. *See* Chapter 10.

4. *"Deceptive" under Section 2(a) versus "deceptively misdescriptive" under Section 2(e)(1).* The Lanham Act attempts to draw a sharp distinction between marks that are "deceptive" and those that are "deceptively misdescriptive." Deceptive marks are absolutely barred from protection, while deceptively misdescriptive marks can be protected if secondary meaning can be shown. *See* Lanham Act §2(f). In *Budge*, the Federal Circuit articulated a three-pronged test for determining whether a mark is deceptive under Section 2(a). The PTO has suggested that a term that satisfies to the first two prongs of the *Budge* test will be deemed deceptively misdescriptive under Section 2(e)(1). That is, if a mark is (1) misdescriptive of the goods/services, and (2) prospective purchasers are likely to believe the misdescription, the mark is deceptively misdescriptive within Section 2(e)(1). *See* TMEP §1203.02(a). Put another way, if the misrepresentation is merely a *relevant factor* in the consumer's purchase decision, as opposed to being *material* to the consumer's purchase decision, the mark is deceptively misdescriptive under Section 2(e)(1), not deceptive under Section 2(a). *See In re Shniberg*, 79 U.S.P.Q.2d (BNA) 1309 (TTAB 2006) (endorsing this distinction).

PROBLEM 5-1: SECTION 2(a) DECEPTIVENESS VERSUS SECTION 2(e)(1) DECEPTIVE MISDESCRIPTIVENESS

Analyze the following and check your analysis against the holdings that we provide.

(1) ORGANIK for cotton textiles that are not from organically grown plants.
   Held: deceptive under Section 2(a). *See In re Organik Techs. Inc.*, 41 U.S.P.Q.2d (BNA) 1690 (TTAB 1997).
(2) GLASS WAX for glass polish that does not contain wax.
   Held: deceptively misdescriptive under Section 2(e)(1).
(3) COTTON COLA for a carbonated beverage (that does not contain cotton — or cola).
   Held: neither deceptive under Section 2(a) nor deceptively misdescriptive under Section 2(e)(1); inherently distinctive.

PROBLEM 5-2:   TEMPORARY DECEPTION AND THE SECTION 2(a) DECEPTIVENESS INQUIRY

Suppose that Dinwoodie and Janis open a restaurant named CAFETERIA. The restaurant serves comfort food that would often be associated with cafeteria-style restaurants, but in a modern, elegant setting where waiters serve food at the table and prices are considerably higher than they would be at the typical cafeteria. Assume that the evidence shows that consumers are initially deceived by the name and exterior appearance of the restaurant, but that when customers enter the restaurant and are seated, the deception diminishes. Should our application to register CAFETERIA for "a restaurant providing full service to sit-down patrons, excluding a cafeteria-style restaurant" be rejected as deceptive under Section 2(a)? *See In re ALP of South Beach, Inc.*, 79 U.S.P.Q.2d (BNA) 1009 (TTAB 2006). The timing question is also important in assessing the likelihood-of-confusion issue. *See* Chapter 7, section E, concerning confusion away from the point of sale, including a theory dubbed "initial interest" confusion.

PROBLEM 5-3: GOVERNMENT SYMBOLS

The great city of Terre Haute, Indiana, is notorious for many things. Seeking to take advantage of this notoriety, suppose that the city authorities apply to register the city's official seal (shown below) as a trademark on the Principal Register. City authorities file two applications, one for the use of the seal in connection with "government services," and another for the use of the seal on "goods in the nature of t-shirts, caps, pens, mugs, and other promotional items." Does Lanham Act §2(b) bar registration given that the applicant is the City of Terre Haute? If Section 2(b) does bar registration, does the bar apply to both applications? *See In re City of Houston*, 731 F.3d 1326 (Fed. Cir. 2013).

Lanham Act §2(b) bars the registration of any mark that "[c]onsists of or comprises the flag or coat of arms or other insignia of the United States, of any State or municipality, or of any foreign nation, or any simulation thereof." Like the Section 2(a) deceptiveness bar, the Section 2(b) bar cannot be overcome by evidence of secondary meaning. Consider whether the policy rationale for Section 2(b) is analogous to the rationale supporting the Section 2(a) deceptiveness bar.

Under Paris Convention, art. *6ter*, "countries . . . agree to refuse . . . registration and to prohibit by appropriate measures the use, without authorization by the competent authorities, as trademarks . . . armorial bearings, flags and other state emblems. . . ." Does Section 2(b) fully implement the United States' obligations under Article *6ter*?

3.   Geographic Marks

Trademarks that evoke connections with geographic regions can be powerful marketing tools. The Lanham Act calls for careful scrutiny of applications to register marks that have geographic components, as the materials in this section illustrate.

§1052. (§2) TRADEMARKS REGISTRABLE ON THE PRINCIPAL REGISTER

No trademark by which the goods of the applicant may be distinguished from the goods of others shall be refused registration on the principal register on account of its nature unless it . . .

(e) Consists of a mark which . . . (2) when used on or in connection with the goods of the applicant is primarily geographically descriptive of them, except as indications of regional origin may be registrable under section 4 [15 U.S.C. §1054] . . . (3) when used on or in connection with the goods of the applicant is primarily geographically deceptively misdescriptive of them. . . .

(f) Except as expressly excluded in subsections (a), (b), (c), (d), (e)(3), and (e)(5) of this section, nothing herein shall prevent the registration of a mark used by the applicant which has become distinctive of the applicant's goods in commerce. . . . Nothing in this section shall prevent the registration of a mark which, when used on or in connection with the goods of the applicant, is primarily geographically deceptively misdescriptive of them, and which became distinctive of the applicant's goods in commerce before the date of the enactment of the North American Free Trade Agreement Implementation Act [Dec. 8, 1993].

IN RE THE NEWBRIDGE CUTLERY CO.

776 F.3d 854 (Fed. Cir. 2015)

LINN, Circuit Judge:

BACKGROUND

Applicant is an Irish company headquartered in Newbridge, Ireland, that designs, manufactures and sells housewares, kitchen ware and silverware in the United States and elsewhere around the world under the mark NEWBRIDGE HOME. Applicant designs its products in Newbridge, Ireland, and manufactures some, but not all, of its products there. In the United States, its products are available for sale through its website and through retail outlets that feature products from Ireland.

. . .

The Trademark Examiner refused to register the mark as being primarily geographically descriptive when applied to applicant's goods under 15 U.S.C. §1052(e)(2) (2012). The Board affirmed, concluding that Newbridge, Ireland, is a generally known geographic place and the relevant American public would make an association between applicant's goods and Newbridge, Ireland.

The Newbridge Cutlery Company appeals. . . .

ANALYSIS

. . .

II.   15 U.S.C. §1052(E)

There have been few decisions by this court dealing with primarily geographically descriptive marks. We last discussed such marks in detail nearly thirty years ago. *See In re Societe Generale Des Eaux Minerales De Vittel S.A.*, 824 F.2d 957 (Fed. Cir. 1987). To give context to our analysis, we begin with a discussion of the evolution of the current statutory framework.

A.

In various circumstances, geographical names have long been refused trademark protection in the United States. *See, e.g., Delaware & Hudson Canal Co. v. Clark*, 80 U.S. 311, 324, 13 Wall. 311, 20 L. Ed. 581 (1871). The Trademark Act enacted in 1905 prohibited registering any mark that was "merely a geographical name or term." Act of Feb. 20, 1905, ch. 592, 33 Stat. 724, 726 (repealed 1946); 15 U.S.C. §85 (1940).

In interpreting this phrase, the Patent Office (now the PTO), with the blessing of the courts, would reject applications upon a showing that a mark was a geographical name, independent of any consumer recognition of the name. For instance, in *In re Kraft–Phenix Cheese Corp.*, the Court of Customs and Patent Appeals affirmed a rejection of CHANTELLE, a town in France, for cheese stating:

> [T]he fact that the town is little known in this country does not change the situation. The statute, in prohibiting the registration of geographical terms made no exemption in favor of those which lacked importance or of those which were not well known by the people in this country. The Patent Office and the courts are not privileged to read unwarranted exemptions into the act.

28 CCPA 1153, 120 F.2d 391, 392 (1941) (citing cases); *see also In re Nisley Shoe Co.*, 19 CCPA 1211, 58 F.2d 426, 427 (1932) (explaining that the analogous provision preventing registration of a mark "which consists merely in the name of an individual," 15 U.S.C. §85 (1940), "makes no exception in the case of uncommon or rare names"). *See generally* 2 J.T. McCarthy, Trademarks & Unfair Competition §14:27 (4th ed. 2014) ("McCarthy"). The policy rationale for refusing to register such marks was that allowing such registration would preempt other merchants from the named location from identifying the origin of their own goods. *See, e.g., In re Plymouth Motor Corp.*, 18 CCPA 838, 46 F.2d 211, 213 (1931) ("a geographical name or term, by which is meant a term denoting locality, cannot be exclusively appropriated as a trade-mark because such a term is generic or descriptive, and any one who can do so truthfully is entitled to use it" (internal quotations omitted)), *overruled on other grounds by In re Canada Dry Ginger Ale*, 24 CCPA 804, 86 F.2d 830, 833 (1936); *accord Canada Dry*, 86 F.2d at 831 (quoting *Delaware & Hudson Canal*, 80 U.S. at 324).

In 1938, Congressman Lanham proposed major amendments to the Trademark Act. *See* H.R. 9041, 75th Cong. (3rd Sess.) (Jan. 19, 1938). With regard to geographical marks, he originally proposed prohibiting the registration of any mark that "has merely a descriptive or geographical meaning," *id.* §3(e), thus keeping the law of geographic marks essentially unchanged. In discussing this section, Mr. Edward S. Rogers, "who played a significant role in drafting the Lanham Act," [cit.], claimed that the 1905 statute, preventing registration on "merely geographical names," was "very troublesome." Hearings on H.R. 9041 Before the Subcomm. On Trade-marks of the House Comm. on Patents, 75th Cong., 3rd Sess. at 71 (1938). According to Mr. Rogers:

> The present construction of the Patent Office of that language is that they take a word without reference to its connotation, and if it appears in the atlas anywhere as the name of a place, or if it appears in the Postal Guide they say that is a geographical name or term, and hence is not registrable.

Id. at 71-72.

The next year, Congressman Lanham proposed an amended bill that would prevent registration for "a mark which, when applied to the goods of the applicant, has merely a descriptive or geographical, *and no other, meaning.*" H.R. 4744, 76th Cong. (1st Sess.)

§2(e) (Mar. 3, 1939) (emphasis added). In discussing this language, Mr. Rogers reiterated the problem of where to draw the line on the registrability of geographical names, and suggested amending the statute to prevent registration of marks, which, "when applied to the goods of the applicant, [are] primarily geographical *and* descriptive of them." Hearings on H.R. 4744 before the Subcomm. on Trade-Marks of the House Comm. on Patents, 76th Cong., 1st Sess. 19 (Mar. 28, 1939) (emphasis added). The next day, at the behest of Congressman Lanham, Mr. Rogers read into the record an amended version of this section, which, *inter alia*, would prevent registration of a mark which, "[w]hen applied to the goods of the applicant is primarily geographically descriptive of them." *See id*. at 39 (Mar. 29, 1939). When Congressman Lanham reintroduced the bill later that year, he used this language, *see* H.R. 6618, 76th Cong. (1st Sess.) §2(e) (June 1, 1939), and this language survived in the statute as enacted. In addition, the statute was subsequently amended to also refuse registration for primarily geographically deceptively misdescriptive marks. *See* [*In re Nantucket, Inc.,*] 677 F.2d 95, 108-11 (C.C.P.A. 1982) (Nies, J., concurring) (describing this legislative history).

Thus, in the Lanham Act, section 1052(e) instructed the PTO to refuse to register a mark if, "when applied to the goods of the applicant it is primarily geographically descriptive or deceptively misdescriptive of them." §1052(e)(2) (1946). Both primarily geographically descriptive and deceptively misdescriptive marks could be registered, however, if they acquired distinctiveness. *See id*. §1052(f). In sum:

> "The 1946 Lanham Act steered away from the prior practice of looking a word up in an atlas or gazetteer and then refusing registration if there was any place on earth called by that word."

In re Jacques Bernier, Inc., 894 F.2d 389, 391 (Fed. Cir. 1990) (quoting 1 McCarthy §14:10, at 647 (2d ed. 1984)) (internal ellipses removed). Thus, while the genesis of the refusal to register geographical names was to prevent a first registrant from preempting all other merchants from identifying the source of their goods, the focus of the 1946 Lanham Act moved to a more nuanced restriction that considered the primary significance of the mark when applied to the goods.

Congress later replaced the phrase "when applied to the goods of the applicant" with "when used on or in connection with the goods of the applicant." 15 U.S.C. §1052(e)(2) (1988). The legislative history of these revisions explains that these changes were "not substantive and [were] not intended to change the law." S. Rep. No. 100-515, at 22, *reprinted in* 1988 U.S.C.C.A.N. 5577, 5584 (discussing the identical amendments in §1051); *id*. at 27, 1988 U.S.C.C.A.N. at 5590 (analogizing the §1051 and §1052(e) amendments).

Finally, in 1993, following the United States' entry into the North American Free Trade Agreement, Dec. 17, 1992, art. 1712, 32 I.L.M. 605 (hereinafter "NAFTA"), §1052(e) was amended to essentially its current form, in which primarily geographically descriptive marks and primarily geographically deceptively misdescriptive marks are divided into two subsections, (e)(2) and (e)(3), respectively, with the latter now foreclosed from registration even if acquired distinctiveness is shown. *See* 15 U.S.C. §1052(f) (2012). The legislative history of the 1993 NAFTA amendments explains that "[t]he law as it relates to 'primarily geographically descriptive' marks would remain unchanged." 139 Cong. Rec. 30,237 (1993), *quoted in Cal. Innovations*, 329 F.3d at 1339-40.

While the 1993 amendments have now foreclosed registration of geographically deceptively misdescriptive marks, they made no distinction, in geographical significance, between geographically descriptive marks and geographically deceptively misdescriptive marks. Under the statute, it is clear that refusal to register extends under both subsections (e)(2) and (e)(3) only to those marks for which the geographical meaning is perceived by the relevant public as the *primary* meaning and that the geographical significance of the mark is to be assessed as it is used *on or in connection with the goods.*

B.

This court's predecessor provided considerable guidance in interpreting the statutory language relating to primarily geographical marks in *Nantucket*, a pre-NAFTA case dealing with primarily geographically deceptively misdescriptive marks. The PTO rejected the mark NANTUCKET for shirts because it considered the mark primarily geographically deceptively misdescriptive, as the "term NANTUCKET has a readily recognizable geographic meaning, and no alternative non-geographic significance." *Id.* at 97. The Court of Customs and Patent Appeals reversed, concluding that there was no showing of an association in the public's mind between the place, i.e., Nantucket, and the marked goods, i.e., the shirts. *See id.* at 101. The court explained:

> "The wording of [§1052(e)] makes it plain that not all terms which are geographically suggestive are unregistrable. Indeed, the statutory language declares nonregistrable only those words which are 'primarily geographically descriptive.' The word 'primarily' should not be overlooked, for it is not the intent of the federal statute to refuse registration of a mark where the geographic meaning is minor, obscure, remote, or unconnected with the goods. Thus, if there be no connection of the geographical meaning of the mark with the goods in the public mind, that is, if the mark is arbitrary when applied to the goods, registration should not be refused under §2(e)(2)."

Id. at 99. . . .

Nantucket's requirement that the mark be "connected" with the goods flowed, in part, from the statutory requirement that the mark has to be primarily geographically descriptive or deceptively misdescriptive "when applied to the goods of the applicant." *Id.* at 98; *In re Loew's Theatres, Inc.*, 769 F.2d 764, 767 (Fed. Cir. 1985). The rationale for allowing registration of marks that relevant consumers do not view as primarily geographic is that the consumer would consider such marks "arbitrary." *Nantucket*, 677 F.2d at 100 n. 8 (quoting Restatement (First) of Torts §720 cmt. d). *See also* Restatement (First) of Torts §720 cmt. c (expounding on the rationale). [The fact that] the phrase "when applied to the goods of the applicant" was replaced, in 1988, with the phrase "when used on or in connection with," did not change the law. *Nantucket*'s interpretation of §1052(e) is bolstered by the legislative history, which indicates that this section was introduced to eliminate rejections of geographical trademarks made without reference to their connotations to consumers in association with the goods or services for which the marks are used.

Since *Nantucket*, this court has set out specific requirements for determining whether a mark is primarily geographically descriptive or primarily geographically deceptively misdescriptive. As the statute uses the phrase "primarily geographically" in both the descriptive and deceptively misdescriptive subsections, this court's decisions relating to one subsection inform the meaning of the other and make clear that to refuse registration under either subsection the Trademark Examiner must show that: (1) "the mark sought to be registered is the name of a place known generally to the public," *Vittel*, 824 F.2d at 959, and (2) "the public would make a goods/place association, i.e., believe that the goods for which the mark is sought to be registered originate in that place." *Id. Accord In re Miracle Tuesday, LLC*, 695 F.3d 1339, 1343 (Fed. Cir. 2012) (describing analogous factors for primarily geographically deceptively misdescriptive marks) (citing *Cal. Innovations*, 329 F.3d at 1341).

To refuse registration of a mark as being primarily geographically descriptive, the PTO must also show that (3) "the source of the goods is the geographic region named in the mark." *Bernier*, 894 F.2d at 391. *Accord* Trademark Manual of Examining Procedure ("TMEP") §1210.01(a). In applying prongs (1) and (2) of this test, our precedent establishes that the relevant public is the purchasing public in the United States of these types of goods. As we made clear in *Vittel*, "we are not concerned with the public in other countries." *Vittel*, 824 F.2d at 960; [cit.]

Regarding the first prong of the test, that the population of the location is sizable and/or that members of the consuming public have ties to the location (to use the example in *Loew's*: that Durango, Mexico, would be recognized by "the Mexican population of this country") is evidence that a location is generally known. *See Loew's*, 769 F.2d at 766, 768. By contrast, that the geographic meaning of a location is "minor, obscure [or] remote" indicates that the location is not generally known. *See Nantucket*, 677 F.2d at 99 (internal quotations omitted). Of course, there are many probative factors to the question of whether a location is generally known, and these are just a few examples.

In establishing the goods/place association required by the second prong of the test, we have explained that the PTO only needs to show "a *reasonable predicate* for its conclusion that the public would be *likely* to make the particular goods/place association on which it relies." *Miracle Tuesday*, 695 F.3d at 1344 (quoting *In re Pacer Tech.*, 338 F.3d 1348, 1351 (Fed. Cir. 2003) (itself quoting *Loew's*, 769 F.2d at 768)) (emphasis in *Pacer*). It need not show an "actual" association in consumers' minds. *Id.* (citing *Pacer*, 338 F.3d at 1351). A goods/place association can be shown even where the location is not "'well-known'" or "'noted'" for the relevant goods. *Cal. Innovations*, 329 F.3d at 1338 (quoting *Loew's*, 769 F.2d at 767). If the Trademark Examiner establishes such a *prima facie* case, an applicant may rebut this showing with evidence "that the public would not actually believe the goods derive from the geographic location identified by the mark." *In re Save Venice New York, Inc.*, 259 F.3d 1346, 1354 (Fed. Cir. 2001).

The PTO has long held that where: (1) a location is generally known; (2) the term's geographic significance is its primary significance; and (3) the goods do, in fact, originate from the named location, a goods/place association can be presumed. *See, e.g., In re Handler Fenton Westerns, Inc.*, 214 U.S.P.Q. 848, 849 (T.T.A.B. 1982); *Board's Decision* at *3 (citing cases); TMEP §1210.04 (citing cases); *see also Nantucket*, 677 F.2d at 102 (Nies, J., concurring) ("[W]e must start with the concept that a geographic name of a place of business is a descriptive term when used on the goods of that business. There is a public goods/place association, in effect, presumed." (internal footnote removed)). This presumption may well be proper, but, as this case can be decided on other grounds, we do not address its propriety and leave it for another day.

III. THE EXAMINER'S REFUSAL

The Examiner found that the primary significance of the word "Newbridge" is a "generally known geographic place," i.e., Newbridge, Ireland, and that the goods originated there. The Examiner then applied the TMEP's presumption that a goods/place association existed. The word "home," according to the Examiner, was "generic or highly descriptive" and, therefore, did not affect the geographic significance of the term. Accordingly, the Examiner rejected the mark under §1052(e)(2).

There is no dispute that applicant's goods are made in Newbridge, Ireland. Additionally, applicant does not contend that the presence of the term "home" in the mark affects whether the mark is primarily geographically descriptive. Accordingly, the question before us is whether "Newbridge" is primarily geographically descriptive when used on or in connection with applicant's goods.

A.   Primary Significance of Newbridge

The Board concluded that Newbridge, Ireland, is a place known generally to the public because it is (1) the second largest town in County Kildare and the seventeenth largest in the Republic of Ireland; (2) it is listed in the *Columbia Gazetteer of the World*; and (3) it appears on a number of websites including Wikipedia and tourism websites that advertise the location as "a large commercial town" with a "silverware visitor centre" in addition to museums, gardens, historical and battle sites, and a famous horse racing track.

Applicant argues that the relevant purchasing public would not be aware of the sources cited by the Board. Applicant also claims that Newbridge, Ireland, is not generally known to the relevant public as the name of a place based on the fact that the word "newbridge" has other, non-geographic meanings that would be more significant to an American consumer and that there are "several geographic locations called 'Newbridge.'" Applicant also claims that Newbridge, Ireland, "is not found in commonly available political maps of Ireland on the internet" and that the PTO has registered other marks with the term "Newbridge." The PTO responds that Newbridge is a town in Ireland from which applicant takes its name and from which applicant's products actually originate. According to the PTO, this (1) distinguishes applicant's situation from those in which others have registered the mark and (2) indicates the mark's geographic significance irrespective of what other meanings and connotations the mark might have in the abstract. Finally, at oral argument, the solicitor implied that in this day and age, where the average American consumer has instant internet access, a location is generally known if the existence of the location can be reasonably found on the internet.

The conclusion that Newbridge, Ireland, a town of less than twenty thousand people, is a place known generally to the relevant American public is not supported by substantial evidence. That Newbridge is the second largest town in County Kildare and the seventeenth largest in the Republic of Ireland reveals nothing about what the relevant American purchaser might perceive the word "Newbridge" to mean and is too insignificant to show that Newbridge is a place known generally to the American purchasing public. Similarly, while the Board relied on the *Columbia Gazetteer of the World* listing, what is missing is any evidence to show the extent to which the relevant American consumer would be familiar with the locations listed in this gazetteer.

Likewise, the fact that Newbridge, Ireland, is mentioned on some internet websites does not show that it is a generally known location. The internet (and websites such as Wikipedia) contains enormous amounts of information: some of it is generally known, and some of it is not. *Cf. In re Bavaria St. Pauli Brauerie AG*, 222 U.S.P.Q. 926, 928 (T.T.A.B. 1984) ("there are dozens of other place names on the same page of the gazetteer that are likewise devoid of significance as places which any substantial quantity of American purchasers would associate with any particular products"). There is simply no evidence that the relevant American consumer would have any meaningful knowledge of all of the locations mentioned in the websites cited by the PTO.

Further, it is simply untenable that any information available on the internet should be considered known to the relevant public. The fact that potential purchasers have enormous amounts of information instantly available through the internet does not evidence the extent to which consumers of certain goods or services in the United States might use this information to discern the primary significance of any particular term. Neither is a place necessarily "generally known" just because a purchaser is informed that the name of the mark is the name of the place. In *Vittel*, we approvingly cited a Board decision that allowed registration of the mark AYINGER BIER for beer, even though the mark was present on the label and "in picture and words, show[ed] the brewery to be located in Aying." *Vittel*, 824 F.2d at 960 (citing *In re Brauerei Aying Franz Inselkammer KG*, 217 U.S.P.Q. 73 (T.T.A.B. 1983)). Of course, a potential purchaser of this beer would, seeing the label, learn of the existence of Aying (and learn that this was the origin of the beer). Nevertheless, Aying, Germany, was considered obscure for the purposes of §1052(e)(2).

To be clear, we do not foreclose the PTO from using gazetteer entries or internet websites to identify whether a location is generally known. *See In re Bayer Aktiengesellschaft*, 488 F.3d 960, 969 (Fed. Cir. 2007). For example, we have credited gazetteer entries as part of the evidence used to establish that Durango, Mexico, was generally known. *See Loew's*, 769 F.2d at 766 n. 3. But the gazetteer showing was just one piece of evidence that together with other evidence was sufficient to establish a *prima facie* case that Durango is known generally to the relevant public. *See id.* at 768. Gazetteer entries and internet websites are valuable for the information they provide. But the mere entry in a gazetteer or the fact that a location is described on the internet does not necessarily evidence that a place is known generally to the relevant public. *See Vittel*, 824 F.2d at 959 ("In dealing with all of these questions of the public's response to word symbols, we are dealing with the supposed reactions of a segment of the American public, in this case the mill-run of cosmetics purchasers, not with the unusually well-travelled, the aficionados of European watering places, or with computer operators checking out the meaning of strange words on NEXIS.").

We have also considered the PTO's evidence in toto and find that it likewise is not substantial evidence for the proposition that, to the relevant public, Newbridge, Ireland, is generally known. That Newbridge, Ireland, is not generally known is supported by the fact that certain maps and atlases do not include it. That "Newbridge" has other meanings, both geographical and non-geographical, also makes it less likely that Newbridge, Ireland, is generally known as the name of a place. On the other hand, the fact that the PTO has registered "newbridge" in contexts where the goods did not originate from Newbridge is not particularly probative since the PTO may have found no goods/place association in those contexts and, in any event, "decisions regarding other registrations do not bind either the agency or this court." *In re Boulevard Entm't, Inc.*, 334 F.3d 1336, 1343 (Fed. Cir. 2003) (citing *In re Nett Designs*, 236 F.3d 1339, 1342 (Fed. Cir. 2001)).

In sum, the facts here are similar to those of the Board's decision in *Bavaria*, which we cited approvingly in *Vittel*, which held that Jever, West Germany, a town of 10,342, was not generally known, despite being mentioned in a geographical index. *Vittel*, 824 F.2d at 960 (citing *Bavaria*, 222 U.S.P.Q. 926). Here, as in *Bavaria*, the evidence as a whole suggests that Newbridge, Ireland, is not generally known. Thus, to the relevant public the mark NEWBRIDGE is not *primarily* geographically descriptive of the goods, which is what matters. *See, e.g., Nantucket*, 677 F.2d at 100 n. 8 ("public association is determinative of arbitrariness"). Prong one of the test for primarily geographically descriptive marks is therefore not met. Accordingly, we need not and do not separately consider whether a goods/place association exists.

[*Reversed and remanded.*]

NOTES AND QUESTIONS

1.   *Evolution of the rules for geographic marks.*   As the *Newbridge* court explains, prior to the Lanham Act, the PTO barred registration of any mark that named a geographic location. This led to some results that might seem silly. *See, e.g., Companhia Antarctica Paulista v. Coe*, 146 F.2d 669 (D.C. Cir.), *cert. denied*, 324 U.S. 880 (1945) (upholding

the Office's refusal to register ANTARCTICA for soft drinks). On the other hand, courts recognized the principle that geographic terms that had attained secondary meaning might be protected in an unfair competition action. *La Republique Francais v. Saratoga Vichy Spring Co.*, 191 U.S. 427, 435 (1903); *Elgin Nat'l Watch Co. v. Illinois Watch Case Co.*, 179 U.S. 665, 673-74 (1901), *abrogated on other grounds, Hurn v. Oursler*, 289 U.S. 238 (1933). The Lanham Act rejected the PTO's practice, substituting the current rule: Marks that are "primarily geographically descriptive" receive a rejection, but the rejection can be overcome by a showing of secondary meaning. Do you agree with the current approach? Or is unfettered access to geographic terms sufficiently important to justify the pre–Lanham Act approach, even if that approach sometimes generates silly results?

2.   *A three-part test for Section 2(e)(2).*   The PTO uses a three-part test for analyzing a mark under Section 2(e)(2):

(1)   the primary significance of the mark is a generally known geographic location;
(2)   the goods or services originate in the place identified in the mark; and
(3)   purchasers would be likely to believe that the goods or services originate in the geographic place identified in the mark [i.e., goods/place or services/place association].

TMEP §1210.01(a) (Oct. 2017) (internal citations omitted). The *Newbridge* court adopts this same three-part inquiry (although it recites the inquiries in a different order). When you address geographic marks, you may find it helpful to start by asking whether the goods or services originate in the place allegedly identified in the mark. If they do, then there may be a geographic descriptiveness issue under Section 2(e)(2), and you should proceed to determine whether the other elements of the test are met. If they do not, the mark cannot be primarily geographically descriptive, but it might be primarily geographically deceptively misdescriptive under Section 2(e)(3), the subject of the next main case.

3.   *Analyzing whether goods or services originate in the place identified in the mark.* What does it mean for goods to "originate" from a place, as specified in part (2) of the PTO's test? Must they be manufactured there (or, in the case of services, actually rendered there)? What if the goods are designed in that place, but manufactured elsewhere? What if an ingredient of the product originates from the place, but the product is made somewhere else? In the case of services, what if they are rendered online? What if the applicant has its headquarters or its research and development facility at the named place? *In re Miracle Tuesday, LLC*, 695 F.3d 1339, 1344-45 (Fed. Cir. 2012) (discussing the point). What is the time frame for the inquiry? Suppose that a product is originally made in Indiana by a small company, but later the company grows and moves its manufacturing operations to Kentucky and Ohio. Must the analysis for geographic origin change?

4.   *Analyzing whether the primary significance of a mark is a generally known geographic location.* According to the *Newbridge* court, to show that the primary significance of a mark is a generally known geographic location, one might look for evidence that "the population of the location is sizable and/or that members of the consuming public have ties to the location," and one might also consider many other "probative factors," such as:

Online evidence: The court rejected the argument that any geographic location mentioned online is "generally known." Do you agree? What additional facts would be relevant?

Factors beyond population size: Do you agree that inquiring into population alone is unsatisfactory? Consider the mark MOAB for mountain bikes made in Moab, Utah. Moab has a population of around 5,000 people, but draws well over 1 million visitors per year, thanks to its proximity to national parks and its famous slickrock trails, well known in the mountain biking community. Is the primary significance of "Moab" therefore a generally known geographic location, at least among mountain bike purchasers? In arriving at such a conclusion, based primarily on factors such as the consumer's ties to the location, does your analysis for primary geographic significance collapse into the supposedly separate analysis for goods/place association? Is that a problem?

Composite marks. Is the primary significance of THE AMERICAN GIRL for shoes geographic because the phrase contains a single geographic term? *See Hamilton-Brown Shoe Co. v. Wolf Bros. & Co.*, 240 U.S. 251 (1916); *see also Forschner Grp., Inc. v. Arrow Trading Co. Inc.*, 30 F.3d 348 (2d Cir. 1994) (SWISS ARMY KNIFE for a multi-function knife). What about the composite mark below, used for fast-food products?

See In re International Taste Inc., 53 U.S.P.Q.2d (BNA) 1604 (TTAB 2000).

5.   *Analyzing the goods/place and services/place association: the PTO's presumption.*   The PTO presumes a goods/place or services/place association where the other elements of the geographic descriptiveness test have been met. *See, e.g., In re Trans Continental Records, Inc.*, 62 U.S.P.Q.2d (BNA) 1541, 1542 (TTAB 2002). In *Newbridge*, the Federal Circuit acknowledges the PTO's practice but declines to rule on its propriety. Should the Federal Circuit adopt the presumption if an appropriate case presents the issue?

6.   *Generic geographic terms.*   Suppose that a term had primary geographic significance at one time when used as part of a mark, and also indicated where the goods were made, but since then has ceased to have a primary geographic connotation in the context of the mark, and has instead come to signify a class of goods, irrespective of where they are made. Should the mark be deemed generic? Might the mark then be deemed generic? *See, e.g., Schweizerishe Kaeseunion Bern v. Saul Starck, Inc.*, 293 N.Y.S. 816 (1937) (SWISS CHEESE); *Lea v. Deakin*, 15 F. Cas. 95 (C.C.N.D. Ill. 1879) (WORCESTERSHIRE SAUCE).

7.   *Fair use of geographic designations.*   Do producers have a "right" to indicate truthfully the geographic origin of their products? The answer might be easier to reach if we ask whether a producer has the freedom to use a truthful geographic designation in a descriptive sense, even if that designation is the subject of trademark protection. The doctrine of fair use, a defense to an allegation of trademark infringement, supplies the relevant framework for answering this question in many cases. We will study the fair use doctrine in Chapter 9.

8.   *Geographic certification marks—exception from Section 2(e)(2).* Section 2(e)(2) carves out an exception for "indications of regional origin" that "may be registrable under section 4," the certification marks provision. For example, the designation IDAHO for potatoes grown in Idaho is registered under Section 4 as a geographic certification mark even though it is presumably not registrable as a trademark (because it is primarily geographically descriptive, and an effort to show secondary meaning would presumably fail, because the designation does not point to any particular Idaho potato grower). *See* TMEP 1306.05(j) (Oct. 2017) (providing examples of registered geographic certification marks). A designation functions as a geographic certification mark if its use is controlled by the certifier and limited to products that meet the certifier's standards of geographic origin, and if purchasers understand the designation to refer only to products produced in the specified geographic location. *See, e.g., Institut National des Appellations d'Origine v. Brown-Forman Corp.*, 47 U.S.P.Q.2d (BNA) 1875 (TTAB 1998). Certification mark status is also available to regional indications under common law. *Id.* at 1885 (recognizing COGNAC as a common law regional certification mark for brandy from the Cognac region of France); *State of Florida v. Real Juices Inc.*, 330 F. Supp. 428 (M.D. Fla. 1971) (SUNSHINE TREE for citrus from Florida).

   9. *Appellations of origin.* While U.S. law protects geographic certification marks, it does not recognize, as such, a form of intellectual property right known as geographical indications of origin or appellations of origin. International agreements require certain protection for geographical indications of origin, *see, e.g.*, TRIPS Agreement arts. 22-24, and U.S. law complies with those obligations partly through the availability of geographic certification marks, partly through regulations of the BATF, and partly through prohibitions on the registration of certain terms as trademarks. *See, e.g.*, Lanham Act §2(a) (prohibiting the registration of certain geographical indications used in connection with wine and spirits); TMEP §1210.08 (Oct. 2017) (offering guidance on applying the wine and spirits provision in Section 2(a)). In contrast, other countries have long featured systems that allow for the registration and protection of geographical indications as such. Most notable in this regard is the European Union, which permits registration of both EU and non-EU geographical indications under Regulation (EU) No 1151/2012 of 21 November 2012. There are some indications that the scope of protection for geographic certification marks is more restrictive than protection as a geographical indication, perhaps reflecting the certification mark's closer ties to trademark and unfair competition principles. *See Institut National des Appellations d'Origine v. Brown-Forman Corp.*, 47 U.S.P.Q.2d (BNA) 1875, 1885 (TTAB 1998) (holding that in cases involving geographic certification marks, the offending mark must "point uniquely and unmistakably" to the certification mark owner to sustain an opposition under Section 2(a)'s "false suggestion of connection" bar, or give rise to a likelihood of confusion under Section 2(d)).

IN RE CALIFORNIA INNOVATIONS, INC.
329 F.3d 1334 (Fed. Cir. 2003)

RADER, Circuit Judge:

   [Applicant California Innovations had filed an ITU trademark application for a composite mark including the words CALIFORNIA INNOVATIONS and a design, for various products, such as insulated bags and wraps. The products did not originate in California. After the PTO examiner refused registration on the ground that the mark was primarily geographically deceptively misdescriptive under 15 U.S.C. §1052(e)(3), and the TTAB upheld the examiner, the applicant appealed to the Federal Circuit.]

II

   The Lanham Act addresses geographical marks in three categories. The first category, §1052(a), identifies geographically deceptive marks:

> No trademark by which the goods of the applicant may be distinguished from the goods of others shall be refused registration on the principal register on account of its nature unless it—(a) Consists of or comprises immoral, *deceptive*, or scandalous matter; or matter which may disparage or falsely suggest a connection with persons, living or dead, institutions, beliefs, or national symbols, or bring them into contempt, or disrepute.

15 U.S.C. §1052(a) (2000) (emphasis added). Although not expressly addressing geographical marks, §1052(a) has traditionally been used to reject geographic marks that materially deceive the public. A mark found to be deceptive under §1052(a) cannot receive protection under the Lanham Act. To deny a geographic mark protection under §1052(a), the PTO must establish that (1) the mark misrepresents or misdescribes the goods, (2) the

public would likely believe the misrepresentation, and (3) the misrepresentation would materially affect the public's decision to purchase the goods. *See In re Budge Mfg. Co.*, 857 F.2d 773, 775 (Fed. Cir. 1988). This test's central point of analysis is materiality because that finding shows that the misdescription deceived the consumer. *See In re House of Windsor*, 221 USPQ 53, 56-57 (T.T.A.B. 1983).

The other two categories of geographic marks are (1) "primarily geographically descriptive" marks and (2) "primarily geographically deceptively misdescriptive" marks under §1052(e). The North American Free Trade Agreement, *see* North American Free Trade Agreement, Dec. 17, 1992, art. 1712, 32 I.L.M. 605, 698 [hereinafter NAFTA], as implemented by the NAFTA Implementation Act in 1993, *see* NAFTA Implementation Act, Pub. L. No. 103-182, 107 Stat. 2057 (1993), has recently changed these two categories. Before the NAFTA changes, §1052(e) and (f) stated:

> No trademark by which the goods of the applicant may be distinguished from the goods of others shall be refused registration on the principal register on account of its nature unless it—
>   (e) Consists of a mark which . . .
>   (2) when used on or in connection with the goods of the applicant is primarily geographically descriptive or deceptively misdescriptive of them. . . .
>   (f) Except as expressly excluded in paragraphs (a)-(d) of this section, nothing in this chapter shall prevent the registration of a mark used by the applicant which has become distinctive of the applicant's goods in commerce.

15 U.S.C. §1052(e)(2) and (f) (1988). The law treated these two categories of geographic marks identically. Specifically, the PTO generally placed a "primarily geographically descriptive" or "deceptively misdescriptive" mark on the supplemental register. Upon a showing of acquired distinctiveness, these marks could qualify for the principal register.

Thus, in contrast to the permanent loss of registration rights imposed on deceptive marks under §1052(a), pre-NAFTA §1052(e)(2) only required a temporary denial of registration on the principal register. Upon a showing of distinctiveness, these marks could acquire a place on the principal register. . . .

In the pre-NAFTA era, the focus on distinctiveness overshadowed the deceptiveness aspect of §1052(e) (2) and made it quite easy for the PTO to deny registration on the principal register to geographically deceptively misdescriptive marks under §1052(e)(2). On the other hand, the deception requirement of §1052(a) protected against fraud and could not be overlooked. Therefore, the PTO had significantly more difficulty denying registration based on that higher standard. *See generally* Andrew P. Vance, *Can't Get There from Here: How NAFTA and GATT Have Reduced Protection for Geographical Trademarks*, 26 Brook. J. Int'l L. 1097 (2001).

Before NAFTA, in *In re Nantucket*, 209 USPQ 868, 870 (T.T.A.B. 1981), the Board used a three-prong test to detect either primarily geographically descriptive or deceptively misdescriptive marks. Under the Board's test, the only substantive inquiry was whether the mark conveyed primarily a geographical connotation. On appeal in *In re Nantucket*, this court's predecessor rejected that test. . . . *In re Nantucket, Inc.*, 677 F.2d 95, 97-98 (CCPA 1982). Thus *In re Nantucket*, for the first time, set forth a goods-place association requirement. *Id.* at 99-100. In other words, this court required a geographically deceptively misdescriptive mark to have more than merely a primary geographic connotation. Specifically, the public must also associate the goods in question with the place identified by the mark—the goods-place association requirement. However, this court did not require a showing that the goods-place association was material to the consumer's decision before rejection under §1052(e).

        . . .

As noted, the Lanham Act itself does not expressly require different tests for geographically misleading marks. In order to implement the Lanham Act prior to the NAFTA amendments, the PTO used a low standard to reject marks for geographically deceptive misdescriptiveness under pre-NAFTA §1052(e), which was relatively simple to meet. In contrast, the PTO required a much more demanding finding to reject for geographical deception under §1052(a). This distinction was justified because rejection under subsection (a) was final, while rejection under pre-NAFTA subsection (e)(2) was only temporary, until the applicant could show that the mark had become distinctive. The more drastic consequence establishes the propriety of the elevated materiality test in the context of a permanent ban on registration under §1052(a).

NAFTA and its implementing legislation obliterated the distinction between geographically deceptive marks and primarily geographically deceptively misdescriptive marks. Article 1712 of NAFTA provides:

> 1. Each party [United States, Mexico, Canada] shall provide, in respect of geographical indications, the legal means for interested persons to prevent:
>> (a) the use of any means in the designation or presentation of a good that indicates or suggests that the good in question originates in a territory, region or locality other than the true place of origin, in a manner that misleads the public as to the geographical origin of the good. . . .

See NAFTA, Dec. 17, 1992, art. 1712, 32 I.L.M. 605, 698. This treaty shifts the emphasis for geographically descriptive marks to prevention of any public deception. Accordingly, the NAFTA Act amended §1052(e) to read:

> No trademark by which the goods of the applicant may be distinguished from the goods of others shall be refused registration on the principal register on account of its nature unless it—
>> (e) Consists of a mark which (1) when used on or in connection with the goods of the applicant is merely descriptive or deceptively misdescriptive of them, (2) when used on or in connection with the goods of the applicant is primarily geographically descriptive of them, except as indications of regional origin may be registrable under section 4 [15 U.S.C.S. §1054], (3) when used on or in connection with the goods of the applicant is primarily geographically deceptively misdescriptive of them, (4) is primarily merely a surname, or (5) comprises any matter that, as a whole, is functional.
>> (f) Except as expressly excluded in subsections (a), (b), (c), (d), (e)(3), and (e)(5) of this section, nothing herein shall prevent the registration of a mark used by the applicant which has become distinctive of the applicant's goods in commerce.

15 U.S.C. §1052(e)-(f) (2000).

Recognizing the new emphasis on prevention of public deception, the NAFTA amendments split the categories of geographically descriptive and geographically deceptively misdescriptive into two subsections (subsections (e)(2) and (e)(3), respectively). Under the amended Lanham Act, subsection (e)(3)—geographically deceptive misdescription—could no longer acquire distinctiveness under subsection (f). Accordingly, marks determined to be primarily geographically deceptively misdescriptive are permanently denied registration, as are deceptive marks under §1052(a).

Thus, §1052 no longer treats geographically deceptively misdescriptive marks differently from geographically deceptive marks. Like geographically deceptive marks, the analysis for primarily geographically deceptively misdescriptive marks under §1052(e)(3) focuses on deception of, or fraud on, the consumer. The classifications under the new §1052 clarify that these two deceptive categories both receive permanent rejection. Accordingly, the test for rejecting a deceptively misdescriptive mark is no longer simple lack of distinctiveness, but the higher showing of deceptiveness.

The legislative history of the NAFTA Act confirms the change in standard for geographically deceptively misdescriptive marks. In a congressional record statement, which appears to be the equivalent of a committee report, the Senate Judiciary Committee acknowledges the new standard for these marks:

> [T]he bill creates a distinction in subsection 2(e) of the Trademark Act between geographically "descriptive" and "misdescriptive marks and amends subsections 2(f) and 23(a) of the Act to preclude registration of" primarily geographically deceptively misdescriptive marks on the principal and supplemental registers, respectively. The law as it relates to "primarily geographically descriptive" marks would remain unchanged.

139 Cong. Rec. S16,092 (1993).

The amended Lanham Act gives geographically deceptively misdescriptive marks the same treatment as geographically deceptive marks under §1052(a). Because both of these categories are subject to permanent denial of registration, the PTO may not simply rely on lack of distinctiveness to deny registration, but must make the more difficult showing of public deception. In other words, by placing geographically deceptively misdescriptive marks under subsection (e)(3) in the same fatal circumstances as deceptive marks under subsection (a), the NAFTA Act also elevated the standards for identifying those deceptive marks.

Before NAFTA, the PTO identified and denied registration to a primarily geographically deceptively misdescriptive mark with a showing that (1) the primary significance of the mark was a generally known geographic location, and (2) "the public was likely to believe the mark identified the place from which the goods originate and that the goods did not come from there." [*In re Loew's Theatres, Inc.*, 769 F.2d 764, 768 (Fed. Cir. 1985).] The second prong of the test represents the "goods-place association" between the mark and the goods at issue. This test raised an inference of deception based on the likelihood of a goods-place association that did not reflect the actual origin of the goods. A mere inference, however, is not enough to establish the deceptiveness that brings the harsh consequence of non-registrability under the amended Lanham Act. As noted, NAFTA and the amended Lanham Act place an emphasis on actual misleading of the public.

Therefore, the relatively easy burden of showing a naked goods-place association without proof that the association is material to the consumer's decision is no longer justified, because marks rejected under §1052(e)(3) can no longer obtain registration through acquired distinctiveness under §1052(f). To ensure a showing of deceptiveness and misleading before imposing the penalty of non-registrability, the PTO may not deny registration without a showing that the goods-place association made by the consumer is material to the consumer's decision to purchase those goods. This addition of a materiality inquiry equates this test with the elevated standard applied under §1052(a). *See House of Windsor*, 221 USPQ at 56-57 (establishing "a 'materiality' test to distinguish marks that fall within the proscription of Section 2(e)(2) from those that fall also within the proscription of Section 2(a)"). This also properly reflects the presence of the deceptiveness criterion often overlooked in the "primarily geographically *deceptively* misdescriptive" provision of the statute.

The shift in emphasis in the standard to identify primarily geographically deceptively misdescriptive marks under §1052(e)(3) will bring that section into harmony with §1052(a). Both sections involve proof of deception with the consequence of non-registrability. The adherence to the pre-NAFTA standard designed to focus on distinctiveness would almost read the term "deceptively" out of §1052(e)(3), which is the term that the NAFTA amendments to the Lanham Act have reemphasized. Accordingly, under the amended Lanham Act, both subsection (a) and subsection (e)(3) share a similar legal standard.

Since the NAFTA amendments, this court has dealt with two cases involving §1052(e)(3). *Wada*, 194 F.3d 1297; *In re Save Venice New York, Inc.*, 259 F.3d 1346, 59 USPQ.2d 1778 (Fed. Cir. 2001). Although neither of those cases explores the effect of the NAFTA Act on the test for determining geographically deceptive misdescription, both cases satisfy the new NAFTA standard. "[I]f there is evidence that goods like applicant's or goods related to applicant's are a principal product of the geographical area named by the mark, then the deception will most likely be found material and the mark, therefore, deceptive." *House of Windsor*, 221 USPQ at 57. "[I]f the place is noted for the particular goods, a mark for such goods which do not originate there is likely to be deceptive under §2(a) and not registrable under any circumstances." *Loew's Theatres*, 769 F.2d at 768, n.6.

In *Save Venice*, this court affirmed the Board's refusal to register applicant's marks "THE VENICE COLLECTION" and "SAVE VENICE, INC." because of the "substantial evidence available showing that Venice, Italy is *known for* glass, lace, art objects, jewelry, cotton and silk textiles, printing and publishing." 259 F.3d at 1354 (emphasis added). Although the court in *Save Venice* did not expressly address the materiality issue, because it was not officially recognized in this context, the court emphasized that "all of the applicant's goods are associated with *traditional Venetian products.*" *Id.* at 1350 (emphasis added). The court in *Save Venice* concluded that the public would mistakenly believe they were purchasing "traditional Venetian products" because the applicant's products were "indistinguishable" from the products traditionally originating in Venice. *Id.* at 1350-54. Thus, the record in *Save Venice* satisfies the test for deception.

Similarly, in *Wada*, this court affirmed the Board's refusal to register applicant's mark "NEW YORK WAYS GALLERY" because there was "evidence that showed . . . New York is *well-known* as a place where leather goods and handbags are designed and manufactured." *Wada*, 194 F.3d at 1299-1300 (emphasis added).* Again, the court in *Wada* did not expressly make a finding that the goods-place association would materially influence the consumer. However, this court noted that the public, "upon encountering goods bearing the mark NEW YORK WAYS GALLERY, would believe that the goods" originate in New York, "a world-renown fashion center . . . well-known as a place where goods of this kind are designed, manufactured, or sold." *Id.* This showing that the place was not only well-known, but renowned for the products at issue supports a finding of materiality. *See House of Windsor*, 221 USPQ at 57.

Thus, due to the NAFTA changes in the Lanham Act, the PTO must deny registration under §1052(e)(3) if (1) the primary significance of the mark is a generally known geographic location, (2) the consuming public is likely to believe the place identified by the mark indicates the origin of the goods bearing the mark, when in fact the goods do not come from that place, and (3) the misrepresentation was a material factor in the consumer's decision.

As a result of the NAFTA changes to the Lanham Act, geographic deception is specifically dealt with in subsection (e)(3), while deception in general continues to be addressed under subsection (a). Consequently, this court anticipates that the PTO will usually address

---

* The court in *Wada* discussed the NAFTA amendments in the context of whether an applicant could disclaim the geographic element of a mark to avoid rejection. The court affirmed the PTO's policy that a disclaimer of the geographic element of a mark will not render a geographically deceptively misdescriptive mark registrable. The court stated that such a policy "complies with Article 1712 of NAFTA." *Wada*, 194 F.3d at 1300-1301.

geographically deceptive marks under subsection (e)(3) of the amended Lanham Act rather than subsection (a). While there are identical legal standards for deception in each section, subsection (e)(3) specifically involves deception involving geographic marks.

[The court remanded to allow the PTO to apply the new test.]

NOTES AND QUESTIONS

1. *Adding a materiality element to Section 2(e)(3).* The *California Innovations* court holds that the test for the post-NAFTA Section 2(e)(3) must include a materiality element. An interpretation that omitted a materiality element, according to the court, "would almost read the term 'deceptively' out of" Section 2(e)(3). Do you agree? Does the inclusion of "deceptively" in a Section 2 provision always signal Congress' intent to impose a materiality criterion? Consider the test for "Section 2(e)(1) deceptively misdescriptive" marks, discussed *supra* in the notes following *Budge*. No requirement of materiality is imposed under Section 2(e)(1). Why not? Is it really the consequences of these various rejections, rather than the inclusion of the "deceptiveness" language, that explain when courts impose a materiality criterion? Contrast the consequences to the applicant of a Section 2(a) deceptiveness or Section 2(e)(3) rejection, with the consequences of a Section 2(e)(1) deceptively misdescriptive rejection. For the sake of symmetry, should Congress amend the Lanham Act to delete the word "deceptively" from Section 2(e)(1), so that "deceptively" always would be a signal for applying a materiality criterion? Alternatively, would Congress be better off eliminating all references to "deceptiveness" and inserting express materiality requirements into those subsections where they are deemed appropriate?

2. *Significance of materiality requirement in Section 2(e)(3).* Does the addition of the materiality requirement substantially limit the scope of the Section 2(e)(3) bar? Consider the mark PHILADELPHIA CREAM CHEESE for a cream cheese product that does not originate in Philadelphia. Suppose the mark is primarily geographic, and that consumers would associate the product with Philadelphia, but that consumers do not place weight on the geographic association in deciding whether to purchase the product. The addition of the materiality requirement is dispositive; in the absence of such a requirement, a Section 2(e)(3) objection might be proper, but with the addition of such a requirement, a Section 2(e)(3) rejection would fail. Which result is preferable as a policy matter?

Consider another example: ALASKA BANANAS for bananas not grown in Alaska. Would the presence of the materiality requirement affect the outcome here? Or would a Section 2(e)(3) rejection have failed anyway on the goods-place association prong? Will, in fact, the goods-place association requirement, rather than the materiality requirement, be the critical issue in many cases?

3. *Comparing Section 2(e)(3) "primarily geographically deceptively misdescriptive" and Section 2(a) "deceptive" marks.* The court in *California Innovations* recognizes that by requiring materiality for a showing under Section 2(e)(3), the analysis of a geographic mark under Section 2(e)(3) would be identical to the analysis of that mark under the Section 2(a) deceptiveness bar. From the perspective of protecting consumers, does this result make sense? Or are "deceptive" marks more insidious than geographically deceptively misdescriptive ones? Or is the preservation of symmetry in the statute (as discussed above in note 1) more important?

4. *An alternative interpretation of Section 2(e)(3).* Consider the following critique of *California Innovations:*

There is a simpler and more logical way to interpret the NAFTA amendments to section 2: Congress simply retained the familiar two-part test for identifying primarily geographically deceptively misdescriptive marks, but chose to impose a conclusive ban on registration of such marks, just as it imposes a conclusive ban on, inter alia, deceptive, scandalous, immoral, disparaging, or functional marks. In so doing, rather than upset settled pre-NAFTA expectations, it grandfathered any primarily geographically deceptively misdescriptive marks (unless also deceptive under section 2(a)) that had already achieved distinctiveness under the pre-NAFTA trademark regime, which for several decades had permitted such marks to be registered once they acquired distinctiveness. Moreover, Congress retained the older, more flexible standard (i.e., the presumptive registration ban, defeasible under section 2(f) through acquired distinctiveness) for deceptively misdescriptive non-geographic marks, because it intended to subject inaccurate geographic marks to more rigorous standards than inaccurate non-geographic marks, which were not a concern of NAFTA. This interpretation . . . is the only interpretation under which section 2(e)(3) and section 2(f) are fully operative provisions.

Mary LaFrance, *Innovations Palpitations: The Confusing Status of Geographically Misdescriptive Trademarks*, 12 J. INTELL. PROP. L. 125, 148 (2004). Do you agree with Professor LaFrance's approach to the statute? Professor LaFrance proceeds to suggest that under this interpretation, "it would indeed be more difficult to register a false geographic mark in the post-NAFTA regime," a policy choice that should be left to Congress, even if Congress' choice is premised on an incorrect understanding of NAFTA's requirements. She also argues that under the Federal Circuit's reading of the statute, ironically, it may be "easier to register geographically confusing marks than other types of confusing marks." *Id*. For additional commentary, *see, e.g.*, Robert Brauneis & Roger E. Schechter, *Geographic Trademarks and the Protection of Competitor Communication*, 96 TRADEMARK REP. 782 (2006).

   5. *Proving materiality.*   The Federal Circuit has ruled that to prove materiality under the *California Innovations* formulation, one must prove that a *substantial portion* of relevant consumers are likely to be deceived, the relevant consumer group being "the entire U.S. population interested in purchasing the product or service." *In re Spirits Int'l N.V.*, 563 F.3d 1347, 1356 (Fed. Cir. 2009) (involving the mark MOSKOVSKAYA for vodka not made in Moscow; MOSKOVSKAYA, translated from Russian, means "of or from Moscow"). Suppose the evidence shows that Moscow is widely known for high-quality vodka; Russian is a common, modern language understood by an appreciable number of U.S. consumers; and over 700,000 Russian speakers live in the United States. Does the evidence suffice to show materiality? What is the relevant consumer base, the vodka-consuming subset of the U.S. population? Only those U.S. vodka consumers who speak Russian? Are there clear objective criteria for establishing the relevant consumer base—or is that determination relatively flexible and subject to value judgments? *See Corporacion Habanos, S.A. v. Guantanamera Cigars Co.*, 102 U.S.P.Q.2d (BNA) 1085 (TTAB 2012) (substantial portion of cigar consumers would be influenced in their purchase decision by the misdescriptive geographic connotation of GUANTANAMERA for cigars not made in Guantanamo province, Cuba). The TTAB noted that it was rejecting the proposition that direct evidence (presumably including survey or consumer testimony) is necessary to establish materiality. Indirect evidence such as "website evidence, and even expert testimony" may be used. *Id*. at 1099.

   6. *Presuming materiality.* The Federal Circuit and the TTAB have presumed materiality in Section 2(e)(3) cases under certain circumstances. *In re Miracle Tuesday, LLC*, 695 F.3d 1339, 1346-47 (Fed. Cir. 2012) (in cases involving goods, inferring materiality based on evidence that the named place is famous as a source of the goods); *In re Les Halles de Paris, J.V*, 334 F.3d 1371 (Fed. Cir. 2003) (inferring materiality from evidence of a "very strong services-place association"). Is the presumption good policy? Should it be limited to administrative proceedings before the PTO, or should it also apply in litigation?

7. *Proving a goods-place or services-place association.*   Recall that in *Newbridge*, the Federal Circuit specified that evidence of a goods-place association must simply establish a "reasonable predicate" for the conclusion that the public would be "likely" to make the association, and that there is no requirement that the location be "well-known" or "noted" for the goods. The Federal Circuit appears to impose a heightened standard for proving a services-place association. In *In re Les Halles de Paris, J.V*, 334 F.3d 1371 (Fed. Cir. 2003), applicant sought to register LE MARAIS for restaurant services for a restaurant located in New York serving French kosher cuisine. The PTO had refused registration on Section 2(e)(3) grounds, concluding that the mark might misleadingly invoke a connection to the Jewish quarter of Paris, known as Le Marais. Reversing the rejection, the Federal Circuit took the view that the evidence showed merely that LE MARAIS "conjures up memories or images of the Le Marais area of Paris." *Id.* at 1375. That was insufficient to support the Section 2(e)(3) rejection. The record instead needed to show that "patrons, though sitting in New York, would believe the food served by the restaurant was imported from Paris, or that the chefs in New York received specialized training in the region in Paris, or that the New York menu is identical to a known Parisian menu, or some other heightened association between the services and the relevant place." *Id.* at 1374. Is this a sound rule?

8. *Liability for using misdescriptive or deceptive geographic designations.*   As we saw in connection with cases on Section 2(a) deceptiveness (*e.g., Budge*), Section 2 speaks to the propriety of *registering* deceptive marks. It does not tell us whether *using* those marks would be permissible. That latter question implicates Lanham Act §43(a) and other bodies of law outside the Lanham Act. *See, e.g., Scotch Whisky Ass'n v. Consolidated Distilled Prods., Inc.*, 210 U.S.P.Q. (BNA) 639 (N.D. Ill. 1981) (finding violation of Section 43(a) where mark LOCH-A-MOOR used on liqueur produced in the United States and not Scotland).

4.   Name Marks

IN RE UNITED DISTILLERS, PLC
56 U.S.P.Q.2d (BNA) 1220 (TTAB 2000)

CHAPMAN, J.:

On December 16, 1996, United Distillers plc filed an intent-to-use application to register the mark HACKLER on the Principal Register for "alcoholic beverages, namely, distilled spirits, except Scotch whisky, and liqueurs." . . . Registration has been finally refused under Section 2(e)(4) of the Trademark Act, 15 U.S.C. §1052(e)(4), on the basis that the term HACKLER is primarily merely a surname.

Applicant has appealed. . . .

Clearly, the issue presented to the Board is whether the term "HACKLER" is primarily merely a surname, in terms of what the word means to the relevant purchasers of applicant's goods. A term is primarily merely a surname if, when applied to a particular product (or used in connection with a particular service), its primary significance to the purchasing public is that of a surname. The burden is on the Patent and Trademark Office to establish a prima facie case that the involved term is primarily merely a surname. [cit.] Further, the question of whether the term sought to be registered is primarily merely a surname can be resolved only on a case by case basis. [cit.]

Among the factors to be considered in determining whether a term is primarily merely a surname are the following: (i) whether the surname is rare; (ii) whether anyone connected with applicant has the involved term as a surname; (iii) whether the term has any other recognized meaning; and (iv) whether the term has the "look and feel" of a surname. *See In re Benthin Management GmbH*, 37 U.S.P.Q.2d 1332 (T.T.A.B. 1995).

Based on this record, we find that the term HACKLER is a rare surname with only one listing in the Manhattan telephone directory and four total listings (one of which appears to be a repeat) in the Washington, D.C., and the Northern Virginia telephone directories. As we have noted before, when considering Phonedisc evidence, we recognize the massive scope of that database. (According to the Phonedisc prefatory comment appearing in the submission from the Examining Attorney, there are approximately 80 million entries in the database.) *See In re Benthin Management GmbH, supra*, at 1333.

Applicant submitted Webster's Third New International Dictionary (1993) definition of "hackler" as "one that hackles; esp.: a worker who hackles hemp, flax or broomcorn"; and, in the same dictionary, "hackle" has several definitions, including "n. 1. A comb or board with long metal teeth for dressing flax, hemp, or jute"; and "hackle" or "hackles" as "v. To separate the long fibers of (flax, hemp, or jute) from waste material and from each other by combing with a hackle."

In addition, applicant submitted (i) a copy of the poem "The Hackler from Grousehall," in which the opening line is "I am a roving hackler that loves the Shamrock shore, ..."; and (ii) some of applicant's own promotional materials, used in connection with the involved goods, which include the following statements:

> The Hackler was a distiller of high quality Irish Poitin in 19th century Ireland; and
> What or Who is the HACKLER?
> The HACKLER brand name is based on a real person—The HACKLER of Grouse Hall, who lived in 19th Century Ireland and was a weaver and distiller of highest quality Poitin.[1]

While the term HACKLER certainly can be a surname, nonetheless, the word has another significance or meaning. "Hackler" is defined in a 1993 edition of Webster's dictionary as a person who hackles (separates the long fibers of flax, hemp or jute from waste materials and each other). Moreover, the record shows that applicant promotes the term HACKLER for its goods (distilled spirits) as relating to "The Hackler of Grouse Hall," a person who was a hackler by trade in the 19th century.

Further, there is no evidence that HACKLER is the surname of anyone connected with applicant.

We next consider the question of whether the word HACKLER has the "look and feel" of a surname. Obviously, surnames are sometimes derived from occupation names, e.g., "Weaver." This factor is a close question in this case because we cannot stay [*sic*, say] that HACKLER has a clear "look and feel" as either that of a surname, or an arbitrary term. Thus, this factor is neutral.

In light of the dictionary meaning of the word "hackler," and applicant's promotion of its products making an association with the word used in connection with a person who was a "hackler," we find that this relatively rare surname will not be perceived as primarily merely a surname. That is, it cannot be said that the primary significance to the relevant purchasing public, i.e., purchasers and prospective purchasers of applicant's distilled spirits, would be solely that of a surname. [cit.]

To the extent there is any doubt on the question of whether the mark would be perceived as primarily merely a surname, we resolve such doubt in favor of the applicant. [cit.]

---

1. Also in these promotional materials, it states "Poitin (pronounced potcheen) is Ireland's infamous white spirit which has been banned since 1661."

Decision: The refusal to register under Section 2(e)(4) is *reversed*.

NOTES AND QUESTIONS

1.   *Rationale for secondary meaning requirement.*   According to the Restatement (Third) of Unfair Competition:

> The rationale for requiring proof of secondary meaning for personal names is somewhat analogous to that applicable to descriptive terms. The known multiplicity of similar personal names may make consumers hesitant to assume a common source for products bearing a particular name. . . . Because trademark rights in personal names limit the opportunity for similarly named persons to exploit their name in business, protection is extended to a prior user only upon proof that the recognition of trademark rights is necessary to prevent the misappropriation of good will and the deception of consumers.

Restatement (Third) of Unfair Competition §14 cmt. e (1995). Early cases reciting this general principle include *Elgin Nat'l Watch Co. v. Illinois Watch Case Co.*, 179 U.S. 665 (1901); *Herring-Hall-Marvin Safe Co. v. Hall's Safe Co.*, 208 U.S. 554 (1908); *L. E. Waterman Co. v. Modern Pen Co.*, 235 U.S. 88 (1914). Under this rationale, would an engineer's curriculum vitae reflecting her expertise in robotics suffice to establish that her surname would have secondary meaning in connection with a robotics text? *See, e.g., Flynn v. AK Peters Ltd.*, 377 F.3d 13 (1st Cir. 2004). If not, what additional evidence would suffice?

2.   *Factors approach for determining whether a term is "primarily merely a surname" under Section 2(e)(4).* Applicant Beds & Bars Ltd. sought to register BELUSHI'S for travel and tourism services. How should the PTO analyze whether the purchasing public would perceive the mark to be primarily merely a surname? In *United Distillers*, the TTAB invokes factors from the *Benthin* case. Are there additional factors that the TTAB may consider in a given case? Suppose that the evidence shows that "Belushi" is a very rare surname, but on the other hand is widely known due to the fame of comedian John Belushi. Would you uphold the Section 2(e)(4) rejection? Is there another viable ground of rejection? *In re Beds & Bars Ltd.*, 122 U.S.P.Q.2d (BNA) 1546 (TTAB 2017).

3.   *Generic name marks?*   Can a name mark become generic? A few examples do exist. *See, e.g., Singer Mfg. Co. v. June Mfg. Co.*, 163 U.S. 169 (1896) (SINGER for sewing machines); *Murphy Door Bed Co. v. Interior Sleep Sys., Inc.*, 874 F.2d 95 (2d Cir. 1989) (MURPHY BED for a foldaway bed).

4.   *Surnames in domain names.*   If a man named Willard Boyd seeks to register BOYD.COM for online services relating to the law of cultural artifacts, should the examiner impose a Section 2(e)(4) rejection? *See* TMEP §1215.03 (rev. Apr. 2013).

5.   *Surnames versus first names under Section 2(e)(4).*   Suppose that your client seeks to register MICKY'S for a pub in Iowa City, Iowa. Should the examiner impose a Section 2(e)(4) rejection? Presumably, the mark would be widely perceived as the possessive form of a first name—but not a surname. Should this distinction matter? *See, e.g., 815 Tonawanda Street Corp. v. Fay's Drug Co., Inc.*, 842 F.2d 643 (2d Cir. 1988) (assertion of common law rights in the mark FAY'S for a drug store); *Brooks v. Creative Arts by Calloway, LLC*, 93 U.S.P.Q.2d (BNA) 1823 (TTAB 2010) (opposition involving mark CAB CALLOWAY for music sales); *In re Gregory*, 70 U.S.P.Q.2d (BNA) 1792 (TTAB 2004) (application to register ROGAN for jewelry and handbags, filed by Rogan Gregory). The 1905 Act prohibited the registration of the name of an individual, and this prohibition was not limited to surnames. *See Ex parte Dallioux*, 83 U.S.P.Q. (BNA) 262 (Comm'r 1949) (discussing the 1905 Act practice).

6.   *"Merely" versus "primarily merely."*   Prior to the Lanham Act, U.S. trademark law prohibited the registration of any word mark that consisted "merely in the name of an individual." Trade-Mark Act of 1905, 33 Stat. 726 (1905), as amended 43 Stat. 647 (1924). In hearings prior to the passage of the Lanham Act, commentators pointed out that this language could be applied to achieve the absurd result of eliminating registration for all word marks altogether, given that "[t]here is somewhere on the earth's surface some person who has any name that you can possibly think of." *Hearings on H.R. 4744*, 76th Cong., 1st Sess. 40 (1939). The addition of the term "primarily" to the provision was intended to signal that even if a term could be found somewhere in use as a name, this did not automatically preclude registration; instead, the PTO would need to provide evidence that the term would be understood "primarily" as a name. *See Sears, Roebuck & Co. v. Watson*, 204 F.2d 32 (D.C. Cir.), *cert. denied sub nom. Sears, Roebuck & Co. v. Marzall*, 346 U.S. 829 (1953).

7.   *Surnames and the doctrine of foreign equivalents.*   Some terms that arguably have the appearance of surnames in English also have non-surname meanings when translated into another language. The term "Fiore" has no English meaning—and therefore might be taken as a surname—but translates to "flower" in Italian. Suppose that an applicant seeks to register FIORE for athletic bags. Should the examiner analyze the word in English and reject the application under Section 2(e)(4)? Or should the examiner invoke the doctrine of foreign equivalents, translate the term into Italian, and give weight to the non-surname meaning? In deciding whether to invoke the doctrine of foreign equivalents, should the examiner determine whether U.S. consumers would be likely to translate the term FIORE when confronted with the goods? If the applicant is Isabella Fiore LLC, does this affect your analysis? *See In re Isabella Fiore LLC*, 75 U.S.P.Q.2d (BNA) 1564 (TTAB 2007).

8.   *Statutory numbering.*   Former Section 2(e)(3) of the Lanham Act became current Section 2(e)(4) when the North American Free Trade Agreement Implementation Act, Pub. L. No. 103-182, took effect on January 1, 1994.

IN RE SAUER

27 U.S.P.Q.2d (BNA) 1073 (TTAB 1993)

CISSEL, Member:

On August 30, 1989 Debbie Sauer applied to register the mark shown below on the Principal Register for "an oblong shaped ball made of white leather with red stitching at the seams."

At the request of the Examining Attorney, applicant disclaimed the word "BALL" and the configuration of the goods apart from the mark as shown.

Registration has been finally refused under Sections 2(a) and 2(c) of the Lanham Act. Applicant has appealed. . . .

The refusal under Section 2(a) of the Act is based on the contention that the mark falsely suggests a connection with Bo Jackson, a well-known professional athlete. The refusal under Section 2(c) is based on the contention that the mark consists of the name identifying Mr. Jackson, and thus cannot be registered by applicant without Mr. Jackson's written consent to registration. . . .

As the Examining Attorney correctly points out, the test for determining the propriety of a refusal to register based on Section 2(a) has four parts. The mark must be shown to be the same as or a close approximation of the person's previously used name or identity. It must be established that the mark (or part of it) would be recognized as such. It must be shown that the person in question is not connected with the goods or services of the applicant, and finally, the person's name or identity must be of sufficient fame that when it is used as part or all of the mark on applicant's goods, a connection with that person is likely to be made by someone considering purchasing the goods. *Buffett v. Chi-Chi's, Inc.*, 226 U.S.P.Q. 428 (T.T.A.B. 1985).

The evidence submitted by the Examining Attorney establishes that Bo Jackson is a famous athlete who has played both professional football and baseball. Included in these materials are Bo Jackson baseball cards; Bo Jackson football cards; advertisements for Bo Jackson figurines and toys; a copy of a tag from a Bo Jackson model baseball glove; a copy of a Cheerios cereal box referring to Bo Jackson; and copies of magazines with articles about and cover references to Bo Jackson. These materials show that Bo Jackson is well known and has been a highly regarded collegiate and professional athlete in both baseball and football. The aforementioned evidence establishes that "Bo" is widely recognized and used as Bo Jackson's nickname, which he has had since childhood. He is frequently referred to by "Bo" alone, without any reference at all to his surname.

Applicant argues that "Bo" is also the given name of several other widely recognized celebrities, such as Bo Diaz, Bo Belinsky, Bo Bo Osborne and Bo Schembechler, and that therefore "Bo" would not necessarily be understood to refer to Bo Jackson. While these other people named "Bo" have been in the public eye to varying degrees, the record does not show that any of them is famous to nearly the same degree as Bo Jackson is, or that any of them is famous as both a baseball and football star like Bo Jackson is. Further, there is no evidentiary support for the proposition that any of the other people named by applicant has ever commercially exploited his or her nickname in connection with the sale of products as Bo Jackson has.

The mark uses Bo Jackson's famous nickname in combination with the generic term "Ball" and the design of a ball which appears to be a combination of a baseball and a football (oblong like a football, but with exposed stitching like a baseball). Applicant's press release confirms this dual nature of the ball. The evidence also confirms the dual nature of Bo Jackson's notoriety as both a baseball player and a football player. The use of his name "Bo" as part of a mark which suggests both kinds of balls on goods like these plainly would be recognized by prospective purchasers of such goods as a reference to Bo Jackson.

As to the third part of the test, the record does not reflect any connection between applicant and Bo Jackson, nor has applicant claimed that any such connection exists.

The record is clear that Bo Jackson has achieved great fame and notoriety, so that when his nickname is used as part of the "Bo Ball" and design mark on applicant's goods, purchasers will likely make a connection between him and applicant's products. In that all four parts of the test for refusal under Section 2(a) are met, the refusal is affirmed.

The refusal based on Section 2(c) of the Act is also well taken. That section prohibits registration of a mark which "consists of or comprises a name . . . identifying a particular living individual except by his written consent. . . ." The section operates to bar the registration of marks containing not only full names, but also surnames, shortened names, nicknames, etc., so long as the name in question does, in fact, "identify" a particular living individual. [cit.] A name is deemed to "identify" a particular living individual, for purposes of Section 2(c), only if the "individual bearing the name in question will be associated with the mark as used on the goods, either because that person is so well known that the public would reasonably assume the connection, or because the individual is publicly connected with the business in which the mark is used." *See Martin v. Carter Hawley Hale Stores, Inc.*, 206 U.S.P.Q. 931 (T.T.A.B. 1979). *See also* 1 J. McCarthy, Trademarks and Unfair Competition, Section 13.12, at 618 (2d ed. 1984).

In the case at hand this test is met. The record establishes that Bo Jackson is widely known by his nickname, and that when his nickname is used without his surname in connection with the goods of applicant, an association between him and the goods or with applicant's business would be assumed by purchasers of such products. His fame as both a baseball player and a football player, and the fact that he has commercially endorsed other products support this conclusion. He has not given applicant his written consent to use and register his name.

Decision: The refusal under Section 2(c) is therefore affirmed as well as the refusal under Section 2(a).

NOTES AND QUESTIONS

1. *Connection to privacy and publicity rights.* The rationale for the Section 2(c) and 2(a) bars at issue in the BO BALL case is to protect individuals' rights of privacy and publicity. *In re Hoefflin*, 97 U.S.P.Q.2d (BNA) 1174, 1176 (TTAB 2010). As we discuss in Chapter 11, rights of publicity allow individuals to enjoin unauthorized uses of their personal identities under specified circumstances. The Section 2(c) and 2(a) bars augment these rights by precluding third parties from *registering* aspects of an individual's personal identity as a mark. But publicity rights are a matter of state law, so should the PTO look to determine the scope of the 2(c) and 2(a) bars? Which state's law? Note that Section 2(a) encompasses not only "persons," but also "institutions," whereas state publicity rights generally are limited to natural persons. How should the PTO deal with this issue in a case such as *In re White*, 73 U.S.P.Q.2d (BNA) 1713 (TTAB 2004), involving a Section 2(a) rejection of APACHE for cigarettes, in an application filed by the St. Regis Band of Mohawk Indians of New York?

2. *Scope of the Section 2(a) inquiry—historical names.* The Section 2(c) bar extends only to living individuals (with a limited exception for U.S. presidents), but the Section 2(a) bar extends to persons "living or dead." Does this mean that Section 2(a) erects essentially a permanent bar against registering the names of historical figures for any products or services? For example, suppose that an applicant seeks to register OLIVER WENDELL HOLMES in connection with beer. Justice Holmes died in 1935, and suppose that there is no evidence that any relevant privacy or publicity rights still exist. (As we will learn in Chapter 11, this is a real possibility under the publicity laws of many states. Some refuse to recognize a post-mortem right of publicity altogether, while others recognize it, but impose a time limit.) Should the PTO read the language of Section 2(a) in view of its rationale and decline to impose a Section 2(a) bar? *See Lucien Piccard Watch Corp. v. Since 1868 Crescent Corp.*, 314 F. Supp. 329, 165 U.S.P.Q. 459 (S.D.N.Y. 1970) (DA VINCI); *In re MC MC S.r.l.*, 88 U.S.P.Q.2d 1378 (TTAB 2008) (MARIA CALLAS). *See also* Kruti Trevedi, *The Selling of Renoir*, WALL ST. J., Sept. 2, 1999, at B1 (describing a dispute among descendants of the French painter Renoir over the use of RENOIR for various goods).

3. *Time frame for the Section 2(c) inquiry.* In the BO BALL case, the TTAB concludes that a mark identifies an individual in the sense of Section 2(c) only when "that person is so well known that the public would reasonably assume the connection," or when an individual "is publicly connected with the business in which the mark is used." Well known or publicly connected as of when? Consider how the TTAB might have dealt with this issue had the issue arisen today, many years after Bo Jackson's 1994 retirement from professional athletics. *See also Ross v. Analytical Techs., Inc.*, 51 U.S.P.Q.2d (BNA) 1269 (TTAB 1999), finding that the name Ross was publicly connected to the business of electrochemical analysis as of the time of the registration (mid-1990s) even though Mr. Ross was no longer active in the field at the time. It was sufficient that Mr. Ross had been widely known in the field from the 1960s through the late 1980s.

4. *How well known is "well known" for Section 2(c) purposes?* Fame is difficult to gauge in the trademark context. In the BO BALL case, the TTAB seemed to have little difficulty deciding that Bo Jackson was sufficiently well known by the general public to justify a Section 2(c) rejection. Contrast that case with *Martin v. Carter Hawley Hale Stores, Inc.*, 206 U.S.P.Q. (BNA) 931 (TTAB 1979). Carter Hawley Hale sought to register NEIL MARTIN for men's shirts, and Neil Martin opposed. Neil Martin was apparently well known within certain limited professional and social circles but was not well known to the general public, nor was he ever publicly connected with the clothing field. The TTAB rejected the opposition.

The analysis for trademark dilution under Lanham Act §43(c) also requires a threshold determination as to fame, although the dilution inquiry rests on the fame of a given *mark*, not the fame of any individual. *See* Chapter 8.

5. *Should Section 2(c) consent be revocable?* Dale Earnhardt Jr. is a famous NASCAR driver and son of likewise famous Dale Earnhardt Sr. Near the beginning of his professional racing career, Dale Jr. consented to allow his father's company, Dale Earnhardt Inc., to register DALE EARNHARDT JR., apparently for various goods and/or services. Subsequently, Dale Sr. was killed in a crash at the Daytona 500, and the rights in the trademark registration passed, through a series of transactions, to the deceased's wife, Teresa (Dale Jr.'s stepmother). Suppose Dale Jr. now wishes to regain control over the trademark registration. If Dale Jr. files a "revocation" of his Section 2(c) consent with the PTO, does the PTO have the authority to accept it? Set aside questions that you may have about whether Dale Jr.'s attempted revocation would breach any contract that he may have signed with Dale Earnhardt Inc.

6. *Fair use of one's name.* Is there a "right" to use one's own name in connection with commercial activities? Section 2 limits the circumstances under which one may obtain a federal registration for a name mark. That section does not, of course, determine whether any party is free to use the mark, as we noted in connection with the *Tam* case. In modern cases, the question of one's freedom to use a name in connection with goods or services ordinarily arises when that person asserts a defense of "fair use" in response to an allegation of trademark infringement. There are a large number of fair use cases involving name marks, as we shall see when we discuss the fair use defense in Chapter 9.

PROBLEM 5-4: CELEBRITY NAMES

Suppose that the celebrity recording artists Beyonce and Jay-Z are your clients. They inform you that they expect to become parents. (Actually, their people inform you of that. You wouldn't expect them to show up in person in your office, would you?) The blessed event is expected to occur in about three months. They intend to name the child Blue Ivy Carter and have spoken with their marketing people about launching a line of baby clothes under the BLUE IVY CARTER name. Their people tell you that Beyonce and Jay-Z insist on doing whatever they need to do to protect the baby's name from "exploitation by unscrupulous third parties." What is your advice? You might wish to consider a few of the following questions: (1) who owns the trademark rights in the baby's name? The parents? Beyonce alone? The baby? (2) Could the parents file an application now to register BLUE

IVY CARTER for baby clothes? (3) If, as expected, others file applications for registration soon after the baby is born (and the name is publicly announced), what is the likely disposition of those other applications? (4) Suppose that a member of Beyonce's entourage hears about the baby's name long before the baby is born, and files an application to register BLUE IVY CARTER for fragrances, two months before Beyonce and Jay Z file their application. What effect would this have on Beyonce and Jay-Z's application?

PROBLEM 5-5:   REVIEW EXERCISES—APPLYING SECTION 2

Applicants seek to register the following on the Principal Register. Analyze whether registration on the Principal Register would be barred under any of the provisions of Section 2.

(1) **GEORGE WASHINGTON ATE HERE** for restaurant services in Indiana.

(2) **LADY SALE** for a vineyard operated by Ms. Hillary Sale. Would your answer be different if the mark were H. SALE? If the mark were SALE?

(3) **BENJAMIN'S** for a cafe in the town of Franklin, Indiana, near the campus of Franklin College, which features a statue of Ben Franklin.

(4) **JAPAN LANDSCAPING** for landscaping services offered in and around the Los Angeles metro area. Assume that the applicant is a California corporation with its sole office in Los Angeles, California, and that the applicant is not affiliated with any Japanese company. The company name is listed in several standard telephone directories, as well as one directory that specializes in businesses that cater to Japanese-speaking customers.

(5) **U.S. HEALTH CLUB** for vitamins.

(6) **UNION JACK** for fish.

(7) **PRINCE CHARLES** for a meat product.

(8) **WORLD BOOK** for encyclopedias.

(9) **'BAMA** for food products, some of which use ingredients from Chilton County, Alabama.

(10) **MAID IN PARIS** for perfumes not made in Paris, France.

(11) **NORTHERN** for wire and cable.

(12) **ATLANTIC** for magazines and books.

(13) **BULLSHIT** for various alcoholic beverages. The applicant is Red Bull GmBH, known as the maker of the RED BULL non-alcoholic energy drink.

(14) **SWISSGOLD** for wristwatches made in China. The packaging, though not the watches, indicates that the watches are "made in China." The watches have some gold and some non-gold parts.

(15) **BAIKALSKAYA** for Russian vodka made in the Lake Baikal region. Assume that BAIKALSKAYA translates to "from Baikal." Also assume that only a small percentage of the general American public is familiar with Lake Baikal, but that 15 percent of American consumers who purchase vodka are familiar with Lake Baikal.

(16) **SHINNECOCK BRAND LIGHTS** for cigarettes, filed by an individual who is a member of the Shinnecock Indian Nation but was not acting on behalf of the Nation.

(17) **EARNHARDT COLLECTION** for home designs and furniture. The applicants are the son (Kerry) and daughter-in-law of famous NASCAR driver Dale Earnhardt, now deceased. *See Earnhardt v. Kerry Earnhardt, Inc.*, 864 F.3d 1374 (Fed. Cir. 2017); Bob Pockrass, *Kerry Earnhardt in battle with Teresa Earnhardt over name*, *http://www.espn.com/racing/nascar/story/_/id/15474534/kerry-earnhardt-battle-teresa-earnhardt-name* (May 6, 2016) (explaining that it was Teresa Earnhardt—Dale's widow and Kerry's step-mother—who opposed the application).

III

SCOPE AND ENFORCEMENT OF TRADEMARK RIGHTS

6

GEOGRAPHIC LIMITS ON TRADEMARK RIGHTS

A. GEOGRAPHIC LIMITS ON COMMON LAW RIGHTS: *TEA ROSE* DOCTRINE

UNITED DRUG CO. v. THEODORE RECTANUS CO.

248 U.S. 90 (1918)

Mr. Justice PITNEY delivered the opinion of the Court:

The essential facts are as follows: About the year 1877 Ellen M. Regis, a resident of Haverhill, Mass., began to compound and distribute in a small way a preparation for medicinal use in cases of dyspepsia and some other ailments, to which she applied as a distinguishing name the word "Rex"—derived from her surname. The word was put upon the boxes and packages in which the medicine was placed upon the market, after the usual manner of a trade-mark. At first alone, and afterwards in partnership with her son under the firm name of "E. M. Regis & Co.," she continued the business on a modest scale; . . . and subsequently, in the year 1911, petitioner purchased the business with the trade-mark right, and has carried it on in connection with its other business, which consists in the manufacture of medicinal preparations, and their distribution and sale through retail drug stores, known as "Rexall stores," situate in the different States of the Union, four of them being in Louisville, Ky.

Meanwhile, about the year 1883, Theodore Rectanus, a druggist in Louisville, familiarly known as "Rex," employed this word as a trade-mark for a medicinal preparation known as a "blood purifier." He continued this use to a considerable extent in Louisville and vicinity, spending money in advertising and building up a trade, so that—except for whatever effect might flow from Mrs. Regis' prior adoption of the word in Massachusetts, of which he was entirely ignorant—he was entitled to use the word as his trade-mark. In the year 1906 he sold his business, including the right to the use of the word, to respondent; and the use of the mark by him and afterwards by respondent was continuous from about the year 1883 until the filing of the bill in the year 1912.

Petitioner's first use of the word "Rex" in connection with the sale of drugs in Louisville or vicinity was in April, 1912, when two shipments of "Rex Dyspepsia Tablets," aggregating 150 boxes and valued at $22.50, were sent to one of the "Rexall" stores in that city. Shortly after this the remedy was mentioned by name in local newspaper advertisements published by those stores. In the previous September, petitioner shipped a trifling amount—5 boxes—to a drug store in Franklin, Ky., approximately 120 miles distant from Louisville. There is nothing to show that before this any customer in or near Kentucky had heard of the Regis remedy, with or without the description "Rex," or that this word ever possessed any meaning to the purchasing public in that State except as pointing to Rectanus and the Rectanus Company and their "blood purifier." That it did and does convey the latter meaning in Louisville and vicinity is proved without dispute. Months before petitioner's first shipment of its remedy to Kentucky, petitioner was distinctly notified (in June, 1911) by one of its Louisville distributors that respondent was using the word "Rex" to designate its medicinal preparations, and that such use had been commenced by Mr. Rectanus as much as 16 or 17 years before that time.

There was nothing to sustain the allegation of unfair competition, aside from the question of trade-mark infringement. As to this, both courts found, in substance, that the use of the same mark upon different but somewhat related preparations was carried on by the parties and their respective predecessors contemporaneously, but in widely separated localities, during the period in question—between 25 and 30 years—in perfect good faith, neither side having any knowledge or notice of what was being done by the other. The District Court held that because the adoption of the mark by Mrs. Regis antedated its adoption by Rectanus, petitioner's right to the exclusive use of the word in connection with medicinal preparations intended for dyspepsia and kindred diseases of the stomach and digestive organs must be sustained, but without accounting for profits or assessment of damages for unfair trade. [cit.] The Circuit Court of Appeals held that in view of the fact that Rectanus had used the mark for a long period of years in entire ignorance of Mrs. Regis' remedy or of her trade-mark, had expended money in making his mark well known, and had established a considerable though local business under it in Louisville and vicinity, while on the other hand during the same long period Mrs. Regis had done nothing, either by sales agencies or by advertising, to make her medicine or its mark known outside of the New England States, saving sporadic sales in territory adjacent to those States, and had made no effort whatever to extend the trade to Kentucky, she and her successors were bound to know that, misled by their silence and inaction, others might act, as Rectanus and his successors did act, upon the assumption that the field was open, and therefore were estopped to ask for an injunction against the continued use of the mark in Louisville and vicinity by the Rectanus Company.

The entire argument for the petitioner is summed up in the contention that whenever the first user of a trade-mark has been reasonably diligent in extending the territory of his trade, and as a result of such extension has in good faith come into competition with a later user of the same mark who in equal good faith has extended his trade locally before invasion of his field by the first user, so that finally it comes to pass that the rival traders are offering competitive merchandise in a common market under the same trade-mark, the later user should be enjoined at the suit of the prior adopter, even though the latter be the last to enter the competitive field and the former have already established a trade there. Its application to the case is based upon the hypothesis that the record shows that Mrs. Regis and her firm, during the entire period of limited and local trade in her medicine under the Rex mark, were making efforts to extend their trade so far as they were able to do with the means at their disposal. There is little in the record to support this hypothesis; but, waiving this, we will pass upon the principal contention.

The asserted doctrine is based upon the fundamental error of supposing that a trade-mark right is a right in gross or at large, like a statutory copyright or a patent for an invention, to either of which, in truth, it has little or no analogy. *Canal Co. v. Clark*, 13 Wall. 311; *McLean v. Fleming*, 96 U.S. 245, 254. There is no such thing as property in a trade-mark except as a right appurtenant to an established business or trade in connection with which the mark is employed. The law of trade-marks is but a part of the broader law of unfair competition; the right to a particular mark grows out of its use, not its mere adoption; its function is simply to designate the goods as the product of a particular trader and to protect his good will against the sale of another's product as his; and it is not the subject of property except in connection with an existing business. *Hanover Milling Co. v. Metcalf*, 240 U.S. 403, 412-414.

The owner of a trade-mark may not, like the proprietor of a patented invention, make a negative and merely prohibitive use of it as a monopoly. [cit.]

In truth, a trade-mark confers no monopoly whatever in a proper sense, but is merely a convenient means for facilitating the protection of one's good-will in trade by placing a distinguishing mark or symbol—a commercial signature—upon the merchandise or the package in which it is sold.

It results that the adoption of a trade-mark does not, at least in the absence of some valid legislation enacted for the purpose, project the right of protection in advance of the extension of the trade, or operate as a claim of territorial rights over areas into which it thereafter may be deemed desirable to extend the trade. And the expression, sometimes met with, that a trade-mark right is not limited in its enjoyment by territorial bounds, is true only in the sense that wherever the trade goes, attended by the use of the mark, the right of the trader to be protected against the sale by others of their wares in the place of his wares will be sustained.

. . .

Conceding everything that is claimed in behalf of the petitioner, the entire business conducted by Mrs. Regis and her firm prior to April, 1911, when petitioner acquired it, was confined to the New England States with inconsiderable sales in New York, New Jersey, Canada, and Nova Scotia. There was nothing in all of this to give her any rights in Kentucky, where the principles of the common law obtain. [cit.] . . .

Undoubtedly, the general rule is that, as between conflicting claimants to the right to use the same mark, priority of appropriation determines the question. [cit.] But the reason is that purchasers have come to understand the mark as indicating the origin of the wares, so that its use by a second producer amounts to an attempt to sell his goods as those of his competitor. The reason for the rule does not extend to a case where the same trade-mark happens to be employed simultaneously by two manufacturers in different markets separate and remote from each other, so that the mark means one thing in one market, an entirely different thing in another. It would be a perversion of the rule of priority to give it such an application in our broadly extended country that an innocent party who had in good faith employed a trade-mark in one State, and by the use of it had built up a trade there, being the first appropriator in that jurisdiction, might afterwards be prevented from using it, with consequent injury to his trade and good will, at the instance of one who theretofore had employed the same mark but only in other and remote jurisdictions, upon the ground that its first employment happened to antedate that of the first-mentioned trader.

. . .

The same point was involved in *Hanover Milling Co. v. Metcalf*, 240 U.S. 403, 415, where we said:

> In the ordinary case of parties competing under the same mark in the same market, it is correct to say that prior appropriation settles the question. But where two parties independently are employing the same mark upon goods of the same class, but in separate markets wholly remote the one from the other, the question of prior appropriation is legally insignificant, unless at least it appear that the second adopter has selected the mark with some design inimical to the interests of the first user, such as to take the benefit of the reputation of his goods, to forestall the extension of his trade, or the like.

In this case, as already remarked, there is no suggestion of a sinister purpose on the part of Rectanus or the Rectanus Company; hence the passage quoted correctly defines the status of the parties prior to the time when they came into competition in the Kentucky market. And it results, as a necessary inference from what we have said, that petitioner, being the newcomer in that market, must enter it subject to whatever rights had previously been acquired there in good faith by the Rectanus Company and its predecessor. To hold otherwise—to require Rectanus to retire from the field upon the entry of Mrs. Regis' successor—would be to establish the right of the latter as a right in gross, and to extend it to territory wholly remote from the furthest reach of the trade to which it was annexed, with the effect not merely of depriving Rectanus of the benefit of the good will resulting from his long-continued use of the mark in Louisville and vicinity, and his substantial expenditures in building up his trade, but of enabling petitioner to reap substantial benefit from the publicity that Rectanus has thus given to the mark in that locality, and of confusing if not misleading the public as to the origin of goods thereafter sold in Louisville under the Rex mark, for, in that market, until petitioner entered it, "Rex" meant the Rectanus product, not that of Regis.

. . .

Here the essential facts are so closely parallel to those that furnished the basis of decision in the *Allen & Wheeler Case*, reported *sub nom. Hanover Milling Co. v. Metcalf*, 240 U.S. 403, 419-420, as to render further discussion unnecessary. Mrs. Regis and her firm, having during a long period of years confined their use of the "Rex" mark to a limited territory wholly remote from that in controversy, must be held to have taken the risk that some innocent party might in the meantime hit upon the same mark, apply it to goods of similar character, and expend money and effort in building up a trade under it; and since it appears that Rectanus in good faith, and without notice of any prior use by others, selected and used the "Rex" mark, and by the expenditure of money and effort succeeded in building up a local but valuable trade under it in Louisville and vicinity before petitioner entered that field, so that "Rex" had come to be recognized there as the "trade signature" of Rectanus and of respondent as his successor, petitioner is estopped to set up their continued use of the mark in that territory as an infringement of the Regis trade-mark. Whatever confusion may have arisen from conflicting use of the mark is attributable to petitioner's entry into the field with notice of the situation; and petitioner cannot complain of this. As already stated, respondent is not complaining of it.

Decree affirmed.

NOTES AND QUESTIONS

1. *Restating the rule of priority.* In Chapter 4, we discussed the rule for priority of trademark rights in the United States: The first to use a mark in commerce is the owner of the trademark rights therein. In light of the geographic limits on trademark rights discussed in *United Drug*, how might you restate that proposition? How would the rule change if the terms that were being used as marks by both parties were initially descriptive?

2. *Rationale for geographic limits on trademark rights.* What was the rationale for the Court's decision in *United Drug*? Was the inability of the petitioner to prevent the use by the respondent of the mark in the area in question based on its failure to expand timely into the Louisville area? Was the petitioner estopped from suit by virtue of having allowed the respondent to use the mark in that area without objection? Or was there some other, more affirmative reason the respondent should be entitled to use the mark in that geographic area?

3. *Consequences of the common law rule.* What purposes are served by affording rights to a "good faith remote junior user"? To what extent do such rights interfere with the basic purposes of trademark law? To what extent are they consistent with those purposes? What behavior or practices, if any, does the rule incentivize on the part of trademark owners or prospective users of trademarks? In what circumstances can a trademark owner obtain a nationwide injunction based on unregistered rights? *See Emergency One, Inc. v. Am. Fire Eagle Engine Co.*, 332 F.3d 264 (4th Cir. 2003).

   4.   *Good faith.* What is required for a junior user to show that it is acting in good faith? Is it sufficient that it not have actual notice of the senior user's mark? What if the junior user had conducted a search of various trade directories and state trademark registries (in which the senior user was listed) but had not noticed the plaintiff's entry? What if the junior user is aware of the senior user's use but does not believe that the senior user will expand into the junior user's territory? *See C.P. Interests, Inc. v. California Pools, Inc.*, 238 F.3d 690 (5th Cir. 2001) (remote junior user's "knowledge of use is but one factor in the good faith inquiry"). Is there language in *United Drug* that supports the Fifth Circuit's reading of the standard of good faith? *See* Restatement (Third) of Unfair Competition §19, cmt. (d) (1995) (a junior user does not act in "good faith" if the junior user intends or expects that its use will "create, either immediately or in the future, a likelihood of confusion with the goods, services, or business of the prior user"). What about the role of trademark counsel? Should a junior user be required to show that it had retained competent trademark counsel to conduct a trademark search and had relied on the results of that search?

   5.   *Area of use.* The Restatement notes that "the geographic scope of priority extends beyond the area in which the prior user has actually used the mark if the user's association with the mark is known to prospective purchasers in other areas." Restatement (Third) of Unfair Competition §19, cmt. (b) (1995). What might carry the user's association with the mark beyond the area of actual use, and thus potentially expand the geographic scope of rights? To what extent could case law on "use" sufficient to acquire rights, *see supra* Chapter 4, helpfully inform an analysis of this question?

   6.   *Modification of the common law rule: the zone of natural expansion.* Should it matter for the purposes of the good faith remote junior user rule that the senior user was engaged in a business that was likely to expand in geographic reach (e.g., a manufacturer of widgets for use on any number of industrial items) rather than a business that might seem inherently local (e.g., a local restaurant)? The *United Drug* court left open, and some lower courts developed, the possible existence of a zone of natural expansion permitting the senior trademark owner to exercise rights both in the area in which it used the mark and in the zone of natural expansion. *See* 1 J. Thomas McCarthy, Trademark and Unfair Competition Law §26:2. What motivated this evolution? How should this zone be defined? *See Tally-Ho, Inc. v. Coast Cmty. Coll. Dist.*, 889 F.2d 1018 (11th Cir. 1989) (suggesting criteria). What are the consequences of interpreting the scope of that zone broadly? Narrowly? In recent years, some courts have rejected this concept, *see, e.g., Raxton Corp. v. Anania Assocs.*, 668 F.2d 622 (1st Cir. 1982), and the Restatement (Third) of Unfair Competition looks upon the concept with disfavor. *See* Restatement (Third) of Unfair Competition §19, cmt. (c) (1995). Could a court achieve the same objectives as the concept of the zone of natural expansion through other doctrinal devices? *See id.*

   7.   *Remedy in* United Drug. What is the precise holding of the *United Drug* case? That the senior user cannot enjoin the good faith junior user? Or does the opinion also address the junior user's rights? For example, does the *United Drug* case also hold that the junior user can enjoin the senior user from using the mark in Louisville? Or does the *United Drug* case contemplate the possibility of concurrent use by the senior and junior users in Louisville? We consider a similar question in the notes following the CARELINK case (*see infra* page 442).

8. *Partial geographic abandonment.* In *Tumblebus Inc. v. Cranmer*, 399 F.3d 754 (6th Cir. 2005), the plaintiff used the TUMBLEBUS mark itself in Louisville, Kentucky, and arguably engaged in naked licensing (causing abandonment) in various other parts of the United States. The defendant (Cranmer) began using TUMBLEBUS for identical services in the Louisville area, and plaintiff sued. The defendant argued abandonment, relying on the alleged naked licensing elsewhere in the United States. The Sixth Circuit rejected the defendant's argument.

> Moreover, Cranmer's abandonment defense lacks force because it relies on abandonment of the TUMBLEBUS mark in other parts of the United States to effectuate a forfeiture of Tumblebus Inc.'s rights to the mark in the greater Louisville area. In support of her abandonment defense, Cranmer asserts that, in creating the Lanham Act, Congress recognized the need for nationalization of trademark law in light of the increasing nationalization of trade and commerce. Arguably, some of our prior decisions have suggested that a junior mark-user's operation in a different geographic region from the senior mark-user might not, by itself, foreclose the senior mark-user's claim for infringement against the junior user. [cit.] These cases would be turned on their heads, however, if we were to conclude that, because trademark rights may extend beyond the particular geographic area in which a business operates, a trademark holder may also lose any rights it has in a mark anywhere in the United States by abandoning the mark in one part of the country or by failing to establish a mark with national significance.
>
> Indeed, contrary to Cranmer's suggestion otherwise, there is considerable support for the concept that rights in a mark may be abandoned in certain geographic areas but not others (i.e., "partial geographic abandonment"). *See Sheila's Shine Prods., Inc. v. Sheila Shine, Inc.*, 486 F.2d 114, 124-25 (5th Cir. 1973); [cit.]; Restatement (Third) of Unfair Competition §33 cmt. b ("If substantial uncontrolled use is confined to a particular geographic or product market, a court may conclude that the mark has been abandoned only in that geographic area or in connection with use on that product. The trademark owner then retains its priority in the use of the mark in other areas or on other products.").
>
> In the end, we must return to the statutory mandate of §1127, which provides that abandonment occurs when a term "lose[s] its significance as a mark." So long as the TUMBLEBUS mark retains its significance in the greater Louisville area, we fail to see why Tumblebus Inc. should be foreclosed from asserting its rights in the TUMBLEBUS mark in that market. *See Exxon*, 109 F.3d at 1079-80 ("[I]f a trademark has not ceased to function as an indicator of origin there is no reason to believe that the public will be misled; under these circumstances, neither the express declaration of Congress's intent in subsection 1127(2) nor the corollary policy considerations which underlie the doctrine of naked licensing warrant a finding that the trademark owner has forfeited his rights in the mark."). Given the lack of evidence in the record suggesting that the TUMBLEBUS mark has in fact lost its significance in the greater Louisville area, we conclude that the district court did not err in determining that Tumblebus Inc. is likely to succeed on its mark infringement claim notwithstanding Cranmer's asserted defense of abandonment.

Does this argument make sense as a matter of common law analysis?

In a complex dispute between the respective operators of Patsy's Italian Restaurant and Patsy's Pizzeria, there was evidence of naked licensing of the PATSY'S PIZZERIA mark. Specifically, of the nine restaurants operating under the PATSY'S PIZZERIA name, there was evidence of inadequate quality control in connection with two—a restaurant located on Staten Island, and another located in Syosset. On appeal, the following question arose: Did the finding of naked licensing result in the abandonment of all rights in the PATSY'S PIZZERIA mark, or only an abandonment in Staten Island and Syosset? In *Patsy's Italian Restaurant, Inc. v. Banas*, 658 F.3d 254 (2d Cir. 2011), the court endorsed a concept of geographically-limited abandonment:

> Appellants first argue that any finding of naked licensing necessarily acted as a total abandonment of all rights. We disagree. Although some forms of trademark abandonment may result in a loss of all rights in the mark, *see e.g., Feathercombs, Inc. v. Solo Prods. Co.*, 306 F.2d 251, 256

(2d Cir. 1962), abandonment of a mark through naked licensing has different effects on the validity of the mark in different markets. *See Dawn Donut Co. v. Hart's Food Stores, Inc.*, 267 F.2d 358, 369 (2d Cir. 1959) (a finding of naked licensing in the retail market would not result in the loss of trademark rights in the wholesale market). For example, if a restaurant operates in both New York and California, but engages in naked licensing only in California, the restaurant's registered mark may lose its significance in California while retaining its significance in New York. Thus, naked licensing will lead to an abandonment of a mark only where the mark loses its significance. 15 U.S.C. §1127.

As a result, we agree with the district court that a mark owner can abandon a mark through naked licensing in a particular geographic area without abandoning its rights throughout the entire United States. *See also Tumblebus Inc. v. Cranmer*, 399 F.3d 754, 765-66 (6th Cir. 2005) (recognizing that "there is considerable support for the concept that rights in a mark may be abandoned in certain geographic areas but not others"); [cit.].

Id. at 264-65. Do you agree with the proposition that the geographic scope of the loss of rights should match the geographic scope of the naked licensing activity?

B.   GEOGRAPHIC LIMITS AND REGISTERED RIGHTS

DAWN DONUT CO., INC. v. HART'S FOOD STORES, INC.

267 F.2d 358 (2d Cir. 1959)

LUMBARD, Circuit Judge:

The principal question is whether the plaintiff, a wholesale distributor of doughnuts and other baked goods under its federally registered trademarks "Dawn" and "Dawn Donut," is entitled under the provisions of the Lanham Trade-Mark Act to enjoin the defendant from using the mark "Dawn" in connection with the retail sale of doughnuts and baked goods entirely within a six county area of New York State surrounding the city of Rochester. The primary difficulty arises from the fact that although plaintiff licenses purchasers of its mixes to use its trademarks in connection with the retail sales of food products made from the mixes, it has not licensed or otherwise exploited the mark at the retail level in defendant's market area for some thirty years.

. . .

Plaintiff, Dawn Donut Co., Inc., of Jackson, Michigan since June 1, 1922 has continuously used the trademark "Dawn" upon 25 to 100 pound bags of doughnut mix which it sells to bakers in various states, including New York, and since 1935 it has similarly marketed a line of sweet dough mixes for use in the baking of coffee cakes, cinnamon rolls and oven goods in general under that mark. In 1950 cake mixes were added to the company's line of products. Dawn's sales representatives call upon bakers to solicit orders for mixes and the orders obtained are filled by shipment to the purchaser either directly from plaintiff's Jackson, Michigan plant, where the mixes are manufactured, or from a local warehouse within the customer's state. For some years plaintiff maintained a warehouse in Jamestown, New York, from which shipments were made, but sometime prior to the commencement of this suit in 1954 it discontinued this warehouse and has since then shipped its mixes to its New York customers directly from Michigan.

Plaintiff furnishes certain buyers of its mixes, principally those who agree to become exclusive Dawn Donut Shops, with advertising and packaging material bearing the trademark "Dawn" and permits these bakers to sell goods made from the mixes to the consuming public under that trademark. These display materials are supplied either as a courtesy or at a moderate price apparently to stimulate and promote the sale of plaintiff's mixes.

The district court found that with the exception of one Dawn Donut Shop operated in the city of Rochester, New York during 1926-27, plaintiff's licensing of its mark in connection with the retail sale of doughnuts in the state of New York has been confined to areas not less than 60 miles from defendant's trading area. The court also found that for the past eighteen years plaintiff's present New York state representative has, without interruption, made regular calls upon bakers in the city of Rochester, N.Y., and in neighboring towns and cities, soliciting orders for plaintiff's mixes and that throughout this period orders have been filled and shipments made of plaintiff's mixes from Jackson, Michigan into the city of Rochester. But it does not appear that any of these purchasers of plaintiff's mixes employed the plaintiff's mark in connection with retail sales.

The defendant, Hart Food Stores, Inc., owns and operates a retail grocery chain within the New York counties of Monroe, Wayne, Livingston, Genesee, Ontario and Wyoming. The products of defendant's bakery, Starhart Bakeries, Inc., a New York corporation of which it is the sole stockholder, are distributed through these stores, thus confining the distribution of defendant's product to an area within a 45 mile radius of Rochester. Its advertising of doughnuts and other baked products over television and radio and in newspapers is also limited to this area. Defendant's bakery corporation was formed on April 13, 1951 and first used the imprint "Dawn" in packaging its products on August 30, 1951. The district court found that the defendant adopted the mark "Dawn" without any actual knowledge of plaintiff's use or federal registration of the mark, selecting it largely because of a slogan "Baked at midnight, delivered at Dawn" which was originated by defendant's president and used by defendant in its bakery operations from 1929 to 1935. Defendant's president testified, however, that no investigation was made prior to the adoption of the mark to see if anyone else was employing it. Plaintiff's marks were registered federally in 1927, and their registration was renewed in 1947. Therefore by virtue of the Lanham Act, 15 U.S.C.A. §1072, the defendant had constructive notice of plaintiff's marks as of July 5, 1947, the effective date of the Act.

Defendant's principal contention is that because plaintiff has failed to exploit the mark "Dawn" for some thirty years at the retail level in the Rochester trading area, plaintiff should not be accorded the exclusive right to use the mark in this area.

We reject this contention as inconsistent with the scope of protection afforded a federal registrant by the Lanham Act.

Prior to the passage of the Lanham Act courts generally held that the owner of a registered trademark could not sustain an action for infringement against another who, without knowledge of the registration, used the mark in a different trading area from that exploited by the registrant so that public confusion was unlikely. *Hanover Star Milling Co. v. Metcalf*, 1916, 240 U.S. 403; [cit.]. By being the first to adopt a mark in an area without knowledge of its prior registration, a junior user of a mark could gain the right to exploit the mark exclusively in that market.

But the Lanham Act, 15 U.S.C.A. §1072, provides that registration of a trademark on the principal register is constructive notice of the registrant's claim of ownership. Thus, by eliminating the defense of good faith and lack of knowledge, §1072 affords nationwide protection to registered marks, regardless of the areas in which the registrant actually uses the mark. [cit.]

That such is the purpose of Congress is further evidenced by 15 U.S.C.A. §1115(a) and (b) which make the certificate of registration evidence of the registrant's "exclusive right to use the . . . mark in commerce." "Commerce" is defined in 15 U.S.C.A. §1127 to include all the commerce which may lawfully be regulated by Congress. These two provisions of the Lanham Act make it plain that the fact that the defendant employed the mark "Dawn," without actual knowledge of plaintiff's registration, at the retail level in a limited geographical area of New York state before the plaintiff used the mark in that market, does not entitle it either to exclude the plaintiff from using the mark in that area or to use the mark concurrently once the plaintiff licenses the mark or otherwise exploits it in connection with retail sales in the area.

Plaintiff's failure to license its trademarks in defendant's trading area during the thirty odd years that have elapsed since it licensed them to a Rochester baker does not work an abandonment of the rights in that area. We hold that 15 U.S.C.A. §1127, which provides for abandonment in certain cases of non-use, applies only when the registrant fails to use his mark, within the meaning of §1127, anywhere in the nation. Since the Lanham Act affords a registrant nationwide protection, a contrary holding would create an insoluble problem of measuring the geographical extent of the abandonment. Even prior to the passage of the Lanham Act, when trademark protection flowed from state law and therefore depended on use within the state, no case, as far as we have been able to ascertain, held that a trademark owner abandoned his rights within only part of a state because of his failure to use the mark in that part of the state. [cit.]

Accordingly, since plaintiff has used its trademark continuously at the retail level, it has not abandoned its federal registration rights even in defendant's trading area.

. . .

[W]e turn to the question of whether on this record plaintiff has made a sufficient showing to warrant the issuance of an injunction against defendant's use of the mark "Dawn" in a trading area in which the plaintiff has for thirty years failed to employ its registered mark.

The Lanham Act, 15 U.S.C.A. §1114, sets out the standard for awarding a registrant relief against the unauthorized use of his mark by another. It provides that the registrant may enjoin only that concurrent use which creates a likelihood of public confusion as to the origin of the products in connection with which the marks are used. Therefore if the use of the marks by the registrant and the unauthorized user are confined to two sufficiently distinct and geographically separate markets, with no likelihood that the registrant will expand his use into defendant's market,[4] so that no public confusion is possible, then the registrant is not entitled to enjoin the junior user's use of the mark. [cit.]

As long as plaintiff and defendant confine their use of the mark "Dawn" in connection with the retail sale of baked goods to their present separate trading areas it is clear that no public confusion is likely.

The district court took note of what it deemed common knowledge, that "retail purchasers of baked goods, because of the perishable nature of such goods, usually make such purchases reasonably close to their homes, say within about 25 miles, and retail purchases of such goods beyond that distance are for all practical considerations negligible." No objection is made to this finding and nothing appears in the record which contradicts it as applied to this case.

Moreover, we note that it took plaintiff three years to learn of defendant's use of the mark and bring this suit, even though the plaintiff was doing some wholesale business in the Rochester area. This is a strong indication that no confusion arose or is likely to arise

---

4. To sustain a claim for injunctive relief, the plaintiff need not show that the marks are actually being used concurrently in the same trading area. Since the statutory standard for the invocation of injunctive relief is the likelihood of confusion, it is enough that expansion by the registrant into the defendant's market is likely in the normal course of its business. Even prior to the passage of the Lanham Act the courts held that the second user of a mark was not entitled to exclude the registered owner of the mark from using it in a territory which the latter would probably reach in the normal expansion of his business. See *Hanover Star Milling Co. v. Metcalf*, 1916, 240 U.S. 403; [cit.]. Certainly, under the Lanham Act, evincing a congressional purpose to afford a registrant nationwide protection, the subsequent user is not entitled to any greater immunity.

either from concurrent use of the marks at the retail level in geographically separate trading areas or from its concurrent use at different market levels, viz. retail and wholesale in the same area.

The decisive question then is whether plaintiff's use of the mark "Dawn" at the retail level is likely to be confined to its current area of use or whether in the normal course of its business, it is likely to expand the retail use of the mark into defendant's trading area. If such expansion were probable, then the concurrent use of the marks would give rise to the conclusion that there was a likelihood of confusion.

The district court found that in view of the plaintiff's inactivity for about thirty years in exploiting its trademarks in defendant's trading area at the retail level either by advertising directed at retail purchasers or by retail sales through authorized licensed users, there was no reasonable expectation that plaintiff would extend its retail operations into defendant's trading area. There is ample evidence in the record to support this conclusion and we cannot say that it is clearly erroneous.

We note not only that plaintiff has failed to license its mark at the retail level in defendant's trading area for a substantial period of time, but also that the trend of plaintiff's business manifests a striking decrease in the number of licensees employing its mark at the retail level in New York state and throughout the country. In the 1922-30 period plaintiff had 75 to 80 licensees across the country with 11 located in New York. At the time of the trial plaintiff listed only 16 active licensees not one of which was located in New York.

The normal likelihood that plaintiff's wholesale operations in the Rochester area would expand to the retail level is fully rebutted and overcome by the decisive fact that plaintiff has in fact not licensed or otherwise exploited its mark at retail in the area for some thirty years.

Accordingly, because plaintiff and defendant use the mark in connection with retail sales in distinct and separate markets and because there is no present prospect that plaintiff will expand its use of the mark at the retail level into defendant's trading area, we conclude that there is no likelihood of public confusion arising from the concurrent use of the marks and therefore the issuance of an injunction is not warranted. *A fortiori* plaintiff is not entitled to any accounting or damages. However, because of the effect we have attributed to the constructive notice provision of the Lanham Act, the plaintiff may later, upon a proper showing of an intent to use the mark at the retail level in defendant's market area, be entitled to enjoin defendant's use of the mark.

. . .

NATIONAL ASS'N FOR HEALTHCARE COMMUNICATIONS, INC. v. CENTRAL ARKANSAS AREA AGENCY ON AGING, INC.

257 F.3d 732 (8th Cir. 2001)

LOKEN, Circuit Judge:

This is an action under the Lanham Act and state law to determine which party has the superior right to use the service mark "CareLink" in Arkansas. The National Association for Healthcare Communications, Inc. ("Healthcom") was the first to use the mark nationally. It has a federal service mark registration pending but must rely in this case on its common law trademark rights as enforced under the Lanham Act. *See* 15 U.S.C. §1125(a). The Central Arkansas Area Agency on Aging, Inc. ("CA") was the first to use the mark in six counties in central Arkansas and has registered its mark under the Arkansas trademark statutes. *See* Ark. Code Ann. Tit. 4, Ch. 71 (Michie Supp. 1999). The district court held that

CA as first user prevailed in its six-county trade area and that CA's state registration entitled it to statewide relief. Accordingly, the court enjoined Healthcom from using the CareLink mark anywhere in Arkansas. Healthcom appeals. Agreeing that CA is entitled to injunctive relief, but limited to the six Arkansas counties where it has used the mark, we remand to the district court with instructions to modify the injunction.

I

The Parties' Use of the CareLink Mark. Healthcom is an Illinois corporation that provides remote electronic monitoring devices and emergency response services for at-home clients in twenty-five States, including Arkansas. Healthcom solicits local hospitals and home health care agencies to become members of Healthcom's National Association for Emergency Response, Inc. Each member's subscribers (individual clients or patients) are then offered a variety of CareLink at-home emergency [medical] response services. . . . Each provider-member markets CareLink programs and equipment to its patients, bills the patients, and pays Healthcom a monthly fee for each patient using CareLink services.

CA is a private, nonprofit Arkansas corporation organized in 1979 to provide a broad range of support services to elderly and disabled persons in a six-county region in central Arkansas. CA's mission is to provide cost-effective, community-based alternatives to nursing home care. CA has 750 employees and 300 volunteers who assist some 10,000 elderly persons in the region. CA has never provided personal emergency response services, but it has occasionally paid for such services being provided to CA clients. In January 1995, CA adopted the trade name "CareLink" to use in lieu of its corporate name, which had proved awkward and hard to remember, and which created the mis-impression that CA is a government agency.

Facts Relating to First Usage. Healthcom began marketing emergency response services under the CareLink service mark in 1991 or early 1992. From 1992 to 1995, Healthcom spent an estimated $50,000 attempting to sell its services in Arkansas. Despite these efforts, during this period Healthcom made only one $385 sale in Arkansas, to an end user who stopped using its CareLink service in April 1994. Healthcom had no Arkansas customers from April 1994 to September 1995, when it entered into a contract with North Arkansas Regional Medical Center in Harrison. By July 1999, Healthcom had contracts with seven Arkansas health care providers and served 350 individual subscribers. Healthcom estimated that its total Arkansas revenues in 1999 would be just over $82,000. Healthcom has *never* had a customer for its CareLink services located within the six-county region served by CA. Healthcom applied for federal trademark registration on May 4, 1999, and its application is pending.

CA adopted the CareLink trade name and logo in early 1995 and has prominently displayed the logo on stationery, business cards, client information materials, and other publicity materials. CA registered its CareLink mark with the Arkansas Secretary of State on March 23, 1995, and has used the mark in promoting all of its services, except hospice care. CA's annual revenues grew from $5,000,000 to $12,000,000 from early 1995 to mid-1999. Although CA derives most of its revenues from government grants, in 1999 it received approximately $138,000 in private donations and an estimated $250,000 from clients able to pay for its services. All of CA's clients reside in its six-county region, but its activities are publicized beyond central Arkansas through news coverage, telephone listings, advertisements, and a monthly column in an Arkansas newspaper for the elderly.

The Dispute Unfolds. CA did not know of Healthcom's prior usage when it adopted the CareLink name and logo and received a state registration in early 1995. When CA learned that the North Arkansas Regional Medical Center was using Healthcom's CareLink mark for emergency response services in northern Arkansas, CA sent a cease-and-desist letter to that provider. The parties were unable to resolve the resulting dispute. Healthcom then commenced this action, alleging common law trademark infringement and unfair competition in violation of the Lanham Act, 15 U.S.C. §1125(a), and seeking an injunction barring CA from using the mark and cancellation of CA's state registration. CA counterclaimed, alleging unfair competition under the Lanham Act and trademark infringement under Ark. Code Ann. §4-71-212, and seeking an injunction prohibiting Healthcom from using its CareLink mark in Arkansas or, alternatively, in CA's six-county region.

Deciding the case on cross motions for summary judgment, the district court dismissed Healthcom's claims because its use of the CareLink mark in Arkansas prior to CA's state registration was *de minimis*. The court granted CA a permanent injunction prohibiting Healthcom from using the mark anywhere in Arkansas because CA's use of the mark has been substantial, because a statewide injunction is necessary "to prevent confusion among consumers and to prevent Healthcom from passing off its services as those of [CA]," and because CA's state registration entitles it to a statewide injunction. Healthcom appeals, arguing that its common law trademark is entitled to priority because it first used the mark in Arkansas. Alternatively, Healthcare argues the district court abused its discretion in granting CA an overly broad injunction.

II

Nearly a century ago, the Supreme Court established what is now called the *Tea Rose/Rectanus* doctrine—the first user of a common law trademark may not oust a later user's good faith use of an infringing mark in a market where the first user's products or services are not sold. *See United Drug Co. v. Theodore Rectanus Co.*, 248 U.S. 90, 100-01 (1918); *Hanover Star Milling Co. v. Metcalf*, 240 U.S. 403, 415 (1916). The rationale is a core principle of trademark law: the owner of a mark may not "monopolize markets that his trade has never reached and where the mark signifies not his goods but those of another." *Hanover Star Milling*, 240 U.S. at 416. That essential principle applies even when the first user has federally registered its mark under the Lanham Act, with one important modification: the owner of a *registered* mark has the right to expand its use into a new market unless an infringing user had penetrated that market *prior to registration*. [cit.]

In this case we must apply the *Tea Rose/Rectanus* doctrine in resolving two distinct inquiries. First, we must determine whether Healthcom, as the first user of a CareLink common law mark elsewhere in the country, is entitled by reason of its own market penetration to oust CA from any area in Arkansas. Second, to the extent Healthcom failed to prove first use in Arkansas, we must determine whether CA, as owner of a state-registered mark used only in six counties, is entitled to statewide injunctive relief against Healthcom's present use of its mark.

A

It is undisputed that, in early 1995, CA adopted the CareLink mark in good faith, without knowledge of Healthcom's prior use. To be entitled to injunctive relief against CA's subsequent good faith use, Healthcom must prove that its prior use of the mark penetrated the geographic market in question. In determining whether Healthcom achieved the necessary market penetration, we apply the factors identified in our often-cited *Sweetarts* cases:

> [Healthcom's] dollar value of sales at the time [CA] entered the market, number of customers compared to the population of the state, relative and potential growth of sales, and length of time since significant sales. Though the market penetration need not be large to entitle [Healthcom] to protection, it must be significant enough to pose the real likelihood of confusion among the consumers in that area.

Sweetarts v. Sunline, Inc., 380 F.2d 923, 929 (8th Cir. 1967); *Sweetarts v. Sunline, Inc.*, 436 F.2d 705, 708 (8th Cir. 1971) (citation omitted). Where the first user's activities in a remote area are "so small, sporadic, and inconsequential" that its market penetration is *de minimis*, the first user is not entitled to protection against a later user's good faith adoption of the mark in that area. *Sweetarts*, 380 F.2d at 929.

Healthcom argues that it penetrated the Arkansas market through its one sale to an end user in 1992, its seven provider-member contracts and 350 subscribers since the fall of 1995, and its continuous advertising and marketing efforts beginning in 1992. Healthcom errs in assuming without proof that the entire State of Arkansas is a single geographic market for these purposes. CA adopted its CareLink mark for use in six counties in central Arkansas, not the entire State. Healthcom has *never* made a sale in that area, nor has it even attempted to prove that CA's use of the mark in its region is causing a likelihood of confusion elsewhere in the State. For this reason alone, Healthcom has not penetrated CA's six-county trade area, and the district court properly denied Healthcom injunctive relief against CA's use in that area.

This leaves the question whether Healthcom is entitled to injunctive relief as a prior user with market penetration in any other part of Arkansas. We agree with the district court that Healthcom's one $385 sale long before CA's adoption of its mark was *de minimis* market penetration. That leaves Healthcom's reliance on later sales and continuous advertising. CA argues that sales in Arkansas after CA began using the mark are irrelevant, and that Healthcom's prior advertising may not be used to satisfy the *Sweetarts* market penetration test. Those are strong arguments. The issue is whether they warrant summary judgment.

Sweetarts expressly recognized that the market penetration issue is focused on the time when the later user entered the market. However, subsequent sales by the first user *may* establish a trend of increased sales justifying a finding of market penetration. *See Natural Footwear*, [*Ltd. v. Hart, Schaffer & Marx*, 760 F.2d 1383, 1401 (3d Cir. 1985)]. Likewise, while "advertising alone is not sufficient to satisfy the significant market penetration test of *Sweetarts*," *Flavor Corp. of Am. v. Kemin Indus., Inc.*, 493 F.2d 275, 284 (8th Cir. 1974), we are not prepared to say as a matter of law that a first user's highly focused local advertising, followed by initial sales shortly after a later user enters the market, may never satisfy the *Sweetarts* test. [cit.] Nevertheless, we need not decide whether CA is entitled to summary judgment on the market penetration issue statewide because Healthcom presented no evidence that CA is presently likely to enter areas of Arkansas beyond its six-county region, and no evidence that any customers or potential customers of Healthcom are actually confused, or likely to be confused, by CA's use of its CareLink mark in serving a six-county region where Healthcom does no business. In these circumstances, the district court properly dismissed all of Healthcom's claims for relief. [cit.]

B

Having concluded that Healthcom is not entitled to injunctive relief, we turn to CA's counterclaim for injunctive relief and the district court's grant of a statewide injunction. As we have explained, CA has superior common law rights in its six-county region, and it is a state-registered user of the CareLink mark. Therefore, under both the Lanham Act and the Arkansas trademark statute, CA is entitled to an injunction against an infringing use that is likely to cause confusion as to origin. *See* 15 U.S.C. §1125(a)(1)(A); Ark. Code Ann. §4-71-212(1). In 1997, Healthcom attempted to sell its CareLink emergency response services to a health care provider in Little Rock, within CA's six-county territory. Healthcom concedes that the CareLink mark is entitled to trademark protection and that this kind of overlapping use of the parties' CareLink marks would create a likelihood of confusion among health care providers and end users. Therefore, the district court did not abuse its discretion in enjoining Healthcom from using a CareLink mark in CA's six-county region. [cit.]

The question whether CA is entitled to a statewide injunction is far more difficult. The Arkansas trademark statute "provide[s] a system of state trademark registration and protection substantially consistent with the federal system of trademark registration and protection under the [Lanham Act]." Ark. Code Ann. §4-71-218(b). State registration confers the statewide right to use a service mark in connection with the registered services, subject to defenses such as good faith prior use in a particular local market. Under the Lanham Act:

> [T]he nationwide right conferred by registration does not entitle the owner to injunctive relief unless there is a present likelihood of confusion. Therefore, to enjoin a geographically remote infringer, the registered owner must prove that its trademarked products and the infringing products are being sold in the same geographic area, or that the owner has concrete plans to expand into the infringer's trade area.

Minnesota Pet Breeders, Inc. v. Schell & Kampeter, Inc., 41 F.3d 1242, 1246 (8th Cir. 1994); *see Dawn Donut Co. v. Hart's Food Stores, Inc.*, 267 F.2d 358 (2d Cir. 1959). Here, CA serves only the six-county region and presented no evidence of "concrete plans" to expand elsewhere in the State. Although both parties alleged there would be a likelihood of confusion if they used the CareLink mark in the same local area, neither presented evidence that the entire State is a single market for these kinds of services, or that health care providers or end users are confused by the use of two CareLink marks in different parts of the State. In these circumstances, CA did not establish its right to a statewide remedy under the *Pet Breeders* standard.

Alternatively, CA argues that it is entitled to a statewide injunction because its publicity and solicitations reach potential donors outside the six-county region who are likely to be confused by Healthcom's use of a similar mark. But CA offered no evidence of actual or likely confusion among its potential out-state donors. . . . Thus, the unproved possibility of donor confusion does not justify a statewide injunction.

In summary, the absence of concrete evidence of likelihood of confusion outside of CA's six-county region makes it improvident to grant a statewide injunction on this record. Healthcom is now enjoined from using its CareLink mark in CA's trade area. If CA never expands beyond that area, this injunction may be all the judicial action that is required. If CA does decide to expand, its statewide registration puts Healthcom at risk of being ousted. But any future prayer by CA for a broader injunction may raise issues that would be better resolved on a fuller fact record, such as whether Healthcom was the first user in any local market; whether the CareLink mark is descriptive and, if so, whether CA's mark has become incontestable or has acquired secondary meaning; precisely what services CA claims its registration covers; and whether there is likelihood of confusion between users of those services and users of Healthcom's emergency response services. [cit.] Additional issues would be raised if Healthcom's mark is granted federal registration. *See Spartan Food Sys., Inc. v. HFS Corp.*, 813 F.2d 1279, 1284 (4th Cir. 1987); *Burger King of Fla., Inc. v. Hoots*, 403 F.2d 904, 906-07 (7th Cir. 1968).

We affirm the dismissal of Healthcom's claims and the grant of a permanent injunction barring Healthcom's use of its CareLink mark in CA's six-county trade area. We reverse the grant of a statewide injunction and remand to the district court for an appropriate modification of its Judgment dated January 31, 2000.

GUTHRIE HEALTHCARE SYSTEM v. CONTEXTMEDIA, INC.

826 F.3d 27 (2d Cir. 2016)

LEVAL, Circuit Judge:

Plaintiff and Defendant each appeal from the judgment of the United States District Court for the Southern District of New York (Forrest, J.), which, following a bench trial, imposed on Defendant a limited injunction. Defendant contests the finding of liability, and Plaintiff contests the limited scope of the injunction. The complaint alleged trademark infringement in violation of the Lanham Act, 15 U.S.C. §1114, unfair competition, and a number of related claims, on the basis that Defendant's trademark logo was confusingly similar to Plaintiff's trademark. The court ruled in Plaintiff's favor, finding that a likelihood of confusion resulted from Defendant's use of trademarks similar to Plaintiff's. The court accordingly granted permanent injunctive relief, prohibiting Defendant from using its marks within Plaintiff's geographic service area ("Guthrie Service Area") (covering the "Twin Tiers" region of Northern Pennsylvania and Southern New York), but held that Defendant may continue to use its marks everywhere outside the Guthrie Service Area, as well as without restriction in Internet transmissions, on Defendant's websites and on social media.

We agree with the district court's liability determination that there is a likelihood of confusion between Plaintiff's and Defendant's trademarks. We conclude, however, that, in restricting the scope of the injunction, the court misapplied the law, and failed to adequately protect the interests of Plaintiff and the public from likely confusion. We therefore affirm the judgment in part, vacate in part, expand the scope of the injunction, and remand for further consideration of the scope of the injunction.

BACKGROUND

I. PLAINTIFF

Plaintiff Guthrie Healthcare System is a Pennsylvania non-profit corporation composed of Guthrie Healthcare, the Guthrie Clinic, and the Guthrie Foundation. Operating primarily in the Twin Tiers region of New York and Pennsylvania, Plaintiff has 32 medical facilities, including three hospitals and 29 clinics, as well as a number of specialized healthcare facilities such as a cardiology center and a cancer center. Plaintiff also operates home healthcare services, hospice services, and a durable medical equipment company. It has a multi-disciplinary medical group practice that includes more than 280 physicians and 130 mid-level providers (physician assistants and nurse practitioners) who practice in New York and Pennsylvania. It also operates a pharmacy, and several medical supply stores, which sell directly to the public.

Plaintiff recruits doctors and residents nationwide. It provides educational programs for its physicians, nurses, and medical technicians. Additionally, it operates the Guthrie School of Nursing, which recruits students nationwide. The Guthrie Foundation conducts medical research and fundraising beyond the Guthrie Service Area, and disseminates medical information over the Internet, as well as in symposia and seminars. It requires that such information meet evidence-based medicine guidelines.

Plaintiff refuses to endorse third-party products or services or to host advertisements, in order to accommodate research funders' sensitivities, preserve its eligibility for clinical trials, and avoid the fact or appearance of conflict of interest, bias, or partiality.

Plaintiff derives a substantial portion of its patient-care revenue from referrals from physicians and medical professionals. Around 20% of the approximately $300 million annually paid to Plaintiff for specialized medical care comes from referrals by other doctors and medical professionals who are not affiliated with Plaintiff. Plaintiff focuses considerable marketing efforts on these referring doctors and medical professionals, inviting them to classes, seminars, and symposia, and assuring them that Guthrie will not seek to provide medical services to the referred patients beyond those for which they were referred.

II. DEFENDANT CMI

Defendant ContextMedia ("CMI"), founded in 2006, has offices in Chicago and New York City, and employs 42 people. Rishi Shah is CMI's president and one of its directors. Defendant serves approximately 2,600 physician practices, and operates in all 50 states.

Defendant's business is to deliver health-related content to physician practices. Defendant installs digital screens in waiting areas, examination rooms, and infusion rooms in physician practices which play short videos and clips about health and wellness to patients at those facilities. In the vast majority of instances, Defendant's revenue comes from advertising displayed with its content; a small number of physicians who subscribe to its service pay a fee in order to avoid advertisements. The advertisers whose ads appear together with Defendant's content, its "sponsors," are mostly large pharmaceutical companies; their ads are displayed in between the segments of educational health-related programming.

The material Defendant displays on its screens is primarily educational digital content related to health and wellness, such as short segments on nutrition and exercise tips. Much of this material is created by organizations such as the American Heart Association, the American Dietetic Association, the Academy of Nutrition and Dietetics, the Juvenile Diabetes Research Foundation, Health Day TV, and D Life, among others, from which Defendant obtains licenses to broadcast their materials.

Medical offices that wish to display CMI's programming in their practices enroll as Defendant's "members." Defendant then installs flat panel display units, media players, and necessary hardware in their waiting rooms. Defendant recruits new members by placing cold calls to physician practices.

Defendant has two websites: *www.contextmediahealth.com*, which serves primarily members, and *www.contextmediainc.com*, which is directed primarily to potential sponsors, prospective employees, and media.

The CMI screen is divided into three sections. A sidebar on the left side of the screen displays CMI's marks. There is also a main content window, and a news ticker at the bottom of the screen. The main content window also occasionally displays the CMI marks.

III.   THE TRADEMARKS

a.   *Plaintiff's Trademark*

Plaintiff launched the Guthrie Trademark and a new brand identity in September 2001. The mark was developed by Monigle Associates, a consulting firm that works in corporate branding and identity. Soon after, every aspect of Plaintiff's business bore the Guthrie Trademark. Plaintiff applied to register the Guthrie Trademark with the United States Patent and Trademark Office ("PTO") in 2006, and the mark became a Registered Trademark on January 22, 2008. Plaintiff's mark is pictured below:

The Guthrie Trademark has two elements—a logo on the left and the Guthrie name, which appears in bold, capital letters to the right of the logo. This litigation concerns primarily the logo. . . . The word "Guthrie" is always presented in large, bold, capital letters to the right of the logo.

The Guthrie Trademark is prominently featured on both the primary Guthrie website (*www.guthrie.org*) and the website focused on personnel recruitment and business development (*www.ichoseguthrie.org*). The Trademark appears on Guthrie facilities, personnel badges, business cards, stationery, brochures, reports, publications, billboards, buses, and in print and television advertisements.

Beginning in 2001, Plaintiff ran television advertising that prominently displayed the Guthrie Trademark in New York and Pennsylvania. Plaintiff has also partnered with television stations to produce health-related features that have been broadcast to wide audiences, also featuring the Guthrie Trademark. From July 1, 2008 to June 30, 2013, Plaintiff spent $7.25 million promoting the Guthrie Mark and brand.

Starting in 2010, Plaintiff began a new program called digital signage, designed to "push" health-related content out to video screens at Guthrie facilities. Only two such screens are now in place, but according to Joseph Scopelliti, the President and CEO of Guthrie, "many more" are planned. The project was included in the 2013 and 2014 Fiscal Year budgets. However, the two screens that are in place have been there since 2011 (or 2010), and no more have gone up. There has been no development or implementation of content for the screens.

b.   Defendant's Trademarks

In late 2007, Defendant hired Anthony Bonilla, a graphic designer, to develop a logo. Defendant began using Bonilla's designs as its logos in March 2008.

Defendant's eight marks at issue in this litigation contain the same graphic element, although the colors of the background elements differ. Defendant's Mark 1 is pictured below:

Like the Guthrie logo, Defendant's logo consists of a shield containing a stylized human figure composed of crescent moon segments, topped by a detached oval head. . . .

[The defendant] uses the logo in eight different marks, the differences lying primarily in the different text and in the varying colors of the background shield. . . .

The PTO originally refused to register three of Defendant's marks because of likelihood of confusion with Plaintiff's mark. Defendant responded to the PTO and made many of the same arguments it made in this case. The PTO ultimately approved the marks for registration, and registered Defendant's first seven marks between 2009 and 2013. . . .

Defendant has rebranded itself as ContextMedia Health. . . .

. . .

V.   Proceedings Below

Plaintiff filed this action on October 26, 2012. The amended complaint asserts [*inter alia*] eight counts of trademark infringement under 15 U.S.C. §1114; a claim of unfair competition under 15 U.S.C. §1125(a); [and a] a claim of false designation of origin under 15 U.S.C. §1125(a) . . . .

Defendants moved for summary judgment on all counts, and the district court granted it in part. The court found that there was no triable issue of material fact as to actual consumer confusion, bad faith, or willful deception for Marks 1-7; as a result, monetary relief was not available under the Lanham Act. . . .

[The district court held a bench trial and found] that there was a "likelihood of confusion" as between Plaintiff's and Defendant's trademarks in the Guthrie Service Area. However, the court ruled that there was no such likelihood of confusion outside of the Guthrie Service Area.

The court enjoined Defendant from using its marks within the Guthrie Service Area, but expressly authorized Defendant to "continue to use its marks on its websites, in social media, and in other online content that is made available to the public at large through the Internet." The court also denied an injunction for local use by Defendant in two New York counties (Tompkins and Schuyler) where Plaintiff maintains patient treatment facilities.

Plaintiff appeals from the limited scope of the injunction, and Defendant appeals from the finding of infringement.

DISCUSSION

. . .

B.   Applying the Polaroid Factors

[The court noted that "in addressing likelihood of confusion and the appropriate remedy, we generally examine the non-exclusive list of eight factors suggested by Judge Friendly in his landmark opinion in *Polaroid Corp. v. Polarad Electronics Corp.*, 287 F.2d 492, 495 (2d Cir. 1961)" (*see infra* Chapter 7).]

In this case, as is often true, the factors that have the greatest pertinence are the degree of similarity between the two marks, and the proximity of Defendant's area of commerce to Plaintiff's. . . .

a.   *Similarity of the Marks*

The logos employed in Plaintiff's and Defendant's marks are jaw-droppingly similar— nearly identical not only in conception but also, as described above, in the great majority of the fine details of execution. . . . [The court's conclusion that there was a likelihood of confusion was not altered by the presence of wording in either party's marks, including the Defendant's new ContextMedia brand.]

In short, given the degree of similarity between Plaintiff's and Defendant's marks, together with the distinctiveness of the logos and the proximity of Plaintiff's and Defendant's areas of commerce, which we discuss below, it would be surprising if ordinary viewers familiar with Plaintiff's mark did not draw the mistaken inference, on seeing Defendant's mark and message, that the message they were seeing came from Plaintiff or its affiliate. Confusion resulting from the similarity is not only likely, it is highly probable; indeed in our view it is virtually unavoidable. . . .

b.   *Proximity of Areas of Commerce*

The proximity factor can apply to both the subject matter of the commerce in which the two parties engage and the geographic areas in which they operate. Its pertinence depends on the logical proposition that the public is less likely to draw an inference of relatedness from similar marks when the marks' users are in dissimilar areas of commerce, or, depending on circumstances, are involved in localized commerce in geographic areas widely distant from one another. . . .

[The court concluded that the Plaintiff and Defendant operate in closely-related fields, a factor discussed below at length in Chapter 7, making confusion likely. The court continued:]

Proximity in a geographic sense also supports a likelihood of confusion. In the first place, Defendant's communications reach into the Guthrie Service Area. Defendant places screens in doctor's offices in the areas of New York and Pennsylvania where Plaintiff's care facilities are located; its Internet communications reach medical professionals operating in Plaintiff's area of operations; furthermore, its communications seeking sponsorship from pharmaceutical companies that operate nationwide are affecting business entities that operate in Plaintiff's area of commerce. Those who see Defendant's trademark-identified communications in Plaintiff's geographic area have every reason to believe they are affiliated with Plaintiff. The fact that Defendant's communications focus on such subjects as cardiology, rheumatology, diabetes, and dermatology, increases the likelihood that persons familiar with Plaintiff's health care network would infer affiliation from the similarity of the marks.

Furthermore, Plaintiff's activities are not confined to the Guthrie Service Area where most of its care facilities are located. Plaintiff recruits doctors, nurses, and other personnel throughout the country; it receives referrals from doctors who may be anywhere in the United States; and it distributes medical content through the Internet. While the number of instances of confusion occurring outside the Guthrie Service Area is likely to be smaller than within, reasonable persons outside that area will encounter the two marks in connection with medicine-related commerce and will predictably mistakenly assume a relationship.

The district court found that the proximity factor favored Plaintiff as to Defendant's activity within Plaintiff's area of commerce. Defendant contests this finding. In our view there can be little doubt the district court was correct.

[The court also found that the strength of the mark and the buyer sophistication factors favored the Plaintiff and that the other factors did not bear on the ultimate conclusion. In considering the so-called bridging the gap factor, *see infra* Chapter 7, the court noted that this factor, which focuses on "the likelihood that the prior owner will bridge the gap," *Polaroid Corp.*, 287 F.2d at 495, becomes pertinent primarily when the junior user makes a credible case that there is little or no likelihood of consumer confusion because the senior user operates in a different field of enterprise or a different geographic area. In such circumstances, the senior user can undercut the force of the junior user's argument by showing a likelihood that it will expand geographically or into other areas of commerce so that the likelihood of confusion will increase. The senior user of the mark is the entitled user and should not be confined within the present scope of its commerce by the risk of confusion that will result from a reasonably plausible expansion of its business. In our case, because Defendant is already using its marks in both the subject matter area and the geographic area of Plaintiff's commerce, there is no gap. Defendant's use of its marks already causes an actionable likelihood of confusion.]

[Thus, the court concluded that "the extraordinary similarity of the marks, the proximity of commerce both as to subject matter and geographic area, the strength of Plaintiff's mark, and the absence among consumers of sufficient sophistication to protect against confusion, all work together to make a powerful showing of likelihood of confusion. . . . On the other hand, the district court appeared to conclude that, because under present circumstances it found no probability of confusion resulting from Defendant's use of its marks outside Guthrie's Service Area, Plaintiff was not entitled to an injunction outside that area. This was a misunderstanding of the law. We discuss this issue further in the next section dealing with the scope of the injunction."]

C.   Scope of the Injunction

Plaintiff contends the district court misapplied the governing law in fashioning a narrowly limited injunction, which failed to give Plaintiff adequate protection from Defendant's use of virtually identical marks. We agree.

It appears the district court reasoned that, because a senior user must show not only a possibility but a probability of confusion in order to win entitlement to an injunction, a senior user that shows such a probability of confusion in one geographic area and thus wins an injunction, is not entitled to have the injunction apply to additional areas, unless the senior user proves a probability of confusion in those additional areas as well. The court credited Plaintiff with having proven a probability of confusion in the Guthrie Service Area and accordingly awarded an injunction covering that area. But as for additional areas, the court found that Plaintiff had failed to satisfy the probability standard, and accordingly concluded it was not entitled to an injunction going beyond the Service Area.

This misinterpreted the law. It is correct that a senior user must prove a probability of confusion in order to win an injunction. But it does not follow that the injunction may extend only into areas for which the senior user has shown probability of confusion. It is not as if the senior user must prove a new claim of infringement for each geographic area in which it seeks injunctive relief. Once the senior user has proven entitlement to an injunction, the scope of the injunction should be governed by a variety of equitable factors—the principal concern ordinarily being providing the injured senior user with reasonable protection from the junior user's infringement. Of course, if the junior user demonstrates that in a particular geographic area there is no likelihood of confusion, ordinarily no useful purpose would be served by extending the injunction into that area, potentially inflicting great harm on the junior user without meaningful justification. See *Dawn Donut Co. v. Hart's Food Stores, Inc.*, 267 F.2d 358, 364-65 (2d Cir. 1959) (upholding the district court's finding that, "in view of the plaintiff's inactivity for about thirty years in exploiting its trademarks in defendant's trading area at the retail level . . . there was no reasonable expectation that plaintiff would extend its retail operations into defendant's trading area").

Plaintiff complains particularly that the court's order (i) expressly allows Defendant to use what is essentially Plaintiff's logo on the Internet, notwithstanding that these uses unquestionably enter the Guthrie Service Area and will predictably cause confusion there, (ii) does not even prohibit Defendant from making local use of the infringing marks in two counties where Plaintiff operates facilities, and (iii) leaves Defendant free to use what is essentially Plaintiff's mark throughout the nation, beyond the counties where Plaintiff operates facilities, despite Plaintiff's showing of some likelihood of confusion beyond its Service Area.

All three of these arguments have merit. The first problem with the injunction is that it allows Defendant to make substantial use of the marks within the Guthrie Service Area. The court's ruling leaves Defendant free to use the marks on the Internet, notwithstanding that Defendant's webpages are accessible in Plaintiff's Service Area, and are likely to cause confusion there. Secondly, the district court also expressly allowed Defendant unrestricted use of the marks in two counties (Tompkins and Schuyler) where Plaintiff maintained healthcare facilities, explaining that Plaintiff had "presented no evidence regarding the setup of these locations, in particular the patient waiting-room experience there . . . [and] [a]ccordingly . . . ha[d] not proven that any patient exposure to [Defendant's] content in waiting rooms in those counties would occur or would be similar to exposure in the 11 counties discussed at trial." The court's explanation for excluding these counties where Plaintiff maintains patient care facilities from the scope of the injunction seems to us unpersuasive.

Regarding Plaintiff's argument that the district court erred by allowing Defendant to continue to use its marks throughout the nation, Defendant responds by citing and misreading circuit precedent, in particular *Dawn Donut Co.*, 267 F.2d 358; [and] *Starter Corp. v. Converse, Inc.*, 170 F.3d 286 (2d Cir. 1999). We agree with Plaintiff that the district court did not correctly apply the law and the equities in so limiting the injunction.

The district court relied primarily on the proposition asserted in *Starter Corp.* that a permanent injunction must be "narrowly tailored to fit specific legal violations" and that a court "should not impose unnecessary burdens on lawful activity." *Starter Corp.*, 170 F.3d at 299. This proposition is without question a correct statement of the law. However, it does not follow from it that a senior user who has proven entitlement to an injunction affecting one geographic area by reason of the junior user's infringement must show the same high degree of probability of harm in every further area into which the injunction might extend, thus allowing the infringer free use of the infringing mark in all areas as to which the senior user has not shown a substantial probability of confusion. "[A] party who has once infringed a trademark may be required to suffer a position less advantageous than that of an innocent party . . . and a court can frame an injunction which will keep a proven infringer safely away from the perimeter of future infringement." *Patsy's Brand, Inc.*, 317 F.3d at 220 (internal citations and quotation marks omitted).

Defendant's reliance on *Dawn Donut* is misplaced for several reasons. In that case, the absence of likelihood of confusion was proven by the defendant by showing that in 30 years of operation the plaintiff had never sought to use its mark in the defendant's area. The court noted that there was "ample evidence" supporting the absence of likelihood of confusion. *Dawn Donut Co.*, 267 F.2d at 365. Furthermore, the court ruled that, if the plaintiff later made a showing of intent to use the mark in the defendant's market area, then the plaintiff "may later . . . be entitled to enjoin defendant's use of the mark." Id. Finally, *Dawn Donuts* did not present the problem, like this case, of a plaintiff who has shown entitlement to an injunction in one geographic area and seeks to have the injunction extend beyond as well. It therefore has no pertinence to the question at issue here. . . .

Nor does *Starter Corp.* support the district court's approach. While that case did involve the scope of the injunction awarded against a proven infringer, the reasons that justified the Court of Appeals in concluding that the injunction was too broad were very different. At the trial, the plaintiff's own witnesses had testified that the particular use by the defendant that was ultimately found to have been wrongly enjoined "was not at issue in [the] litigation and its attorneys so agreed." *Starter Corp.*, 170 F.3d at 300. Furthermore, the plaintiff had "virtually conceded that there would be no 'likelihood that purchasers of the product may be misled in the future.'" Id. (citation omitted).

In our case, in addition to proving that Defendant was infringing Plaintiff's mark, subjecting Plaintiff to a high probability of confusion in its main Service Area, Plaintiff has also shown that its activities and commercial relationships extended beyond that area, rendering it vulnerable to plausibly foreseeable confusions and harms resulting from Defendant's use of the marks outside the Guthrie Service Area.

Plaintiff recruits doctors, residents, and nursing students nationwide; it disseminates medical information over the Internet; it receives referrals from other physicians and medical professionals, who may be anywhere in the country; and, with respect to its medical research and clinical trials, it solicits funding beyond its Service Area. In all of these activities, Plaintiff is exposed to the risk of confusion and harm resulting from Defendant's use of the marks outside that area. For example, in order to avoid the fact or appearance of conflict of interest, which might harm its reputation with funders of its medical research or cause it to be disqualified by U.S. Government agencies from clinical trials, Plaintiff takes care not to endorse products or host advertisements for third-party products or services. If Defendant's transmissions were to display advertising of pharmaceutical products or endorsements, and this were observed outside the Guthrie Service Area by Plaintiff's potential funders or by government agencies, who would predictably believe that what they saw came from Plaintiff, Plaintiff could suffer serious harm to its reputation, impacting its receipt of funding grants or its eligibility to conduct clinical trials. Furthermore, potential doctors and nurses around the country whom Plaintiff seeks to recruit might well be affected in their employment decisions by what they see on Defendant's screens or transmissions. The same might apply to referrals of patients.

The district court's limitation on the geographic scope of the injunction also could cause Plaintiff substantial harm in another manner. Because the district court authorized Defendant to use what is in effect Plaintiff's mark as Defendant's mark outside the Service

Area, Plaintiff, which now operates over 100 facilities in the Twin Tiers region, cannot expand beyond those borders without subjecting itself to a high risk of consumer confusion. This cloud affecting Plaintiff's mark beyond the counties where it presently maintains facilities might substantially impair its opportunity for growth and its eligibility as a prospective merger partner with entities operating outside its Service Area, diminishing its value as a commercial entity. See *Savin Corp.*, 391 F.3d at 459-60 (discussing the need to "protect the senior user's interest in being able to enter a related field at some future time").

No doubt, an injured senior user must show evidence of plausibly foreseeable confusion beyond its main area of injury before the trial court is required even to consider extending the injunction into such additional areas. In the evidence summarized above Plaintiff easily satisfied that requirement.

In so ruling, we do not imply that senior users who prove likely confusion and infringement by a junior user's use of their marks in their area of operation are necessarily entitled to injunctions extending beyond their geographic area of operation. Every case turns on its particular facts, and in many instances it will be clear, for a variety of reasons, that an injunction of narrow geographic scope will grant the senior user completely adequate protection, and that an injunction going further would be not only unnecessary but unjust. Trademark cases vary enormously depending on highly specific factual differences, so that it is perilous to generalize in asserting rules. Plaintiff in our case made a showing of plausibly foreseeable confusion and harm resulting from Defendant's use of its marks beyond the area where confusion was probable. Even assuming it failed to show probability of confusion beyond its Service Area, that is not the governing standard in such circumstances. Plaintiff was entitled to have the district court consider extending the injunction beyond the area where confusion was probable upon proper consideration of all the equities.[10]

We recognize further that the competing equities do not always favor a senior user that has shown infringement. Cases frequently arise in which imposition of a broad injunction on an innocent infringer, which had no realistic way of knowing that its mark was subject to a prior claim, would cause the junior user a catastrophic loss of goodwill acquired through investment of years of toil and large amounts of money. In such cases, notwithstanding that the legal right unquestionably belongs to the senior user, competing equities can complicate the issue of the breadth of injunctive relief. In our case, in contrast, a number of equitable considerations appear to favor Plaintiff.

Although Defendant did not act with bad faith in the sense of deliberately sowing confusion between its marks and Plaintiff's, Defendant could easily have avoided the problem that arose from its adoption of marks already reserved by another user. Precisely for the purpose of giving notice of its mark to the world, Plaintiff had registered its mark with the PTO. Had Defendant exercised the precaution of running a trademark search before launching its marks, it would have learned that they were unavailable and would surely have had the good sense not to proceed with a logo so nearly identical to one for which trademark rights were already established. Defendant did not conduct a trademark search until it sought to register its marks and was notified by the PTO on February 28, 2012, that the

---

10. Nor do we imply that a prevailing plaintiff operating within a narrow service area is necessarily entitled to an injunction barring the infringing defendant from using its mark on the Internet because of the availability of material on the Internet within the plaintiff's service area. The proper scope of the injunction depends on likelihood of confusion, which in turn depends on innumerable variable factors. The particular facts of this case lead us to conclude that Defendant's use of the logo on the Internet will cause sufficient likelihood of confusion to justify barring Defendant from Internet use. In other infringing circumstances, whether because of differences in the marks, geographic separation, differences between plaintiff's and defendant's commerce, or other reasons, a defendant's use of its mark on the Internet would cause little or no likelihood of confusion, and need not be enjoined.

marks it sought to register were "striking[ly] similar" to Plaintiff's already registered mark. Accordingly, while Defendant is not a "bad faith" infringer, nor is it an entirely innocent infringer. The government had placed a convenient tool at its disposition, which it could have used to avoid this infringement, and it failed to utilize that tool.

Furthermore, this is not a case in which an injunction would have catastrophic effects on the infringer's business. In some cases, an innocently infringing junior user has invested many years of toil and large sums of money in the development of goodwill in its mark before learning of the prior reservation of rights. Defendant here had only recently begun using the logo. Nor is this a case in which the junior user is compelled to give up the name of its business. What is at stake is only the use of a decorative logo. No reason appears why Defendant cannot change its logo to one that is not confusingly similar to Plaintiff's without suffering major harm to its business.[11] Finally, Plaintiff is the injured party, and so far as we can see was without fault in the matter.

Finally, the equitable interests to be considered in fashioning an injunction are not only those of the parties to the litigation. An important beneficiary of the trademark system is the public. The public has a great interest in administration of the trademark law in a manner that protects against confusion. By perpetuating a highly confusing circumstance, the court's injunctive order harmed that public interest. The public interest would undoubtedly be better served by the elimination of this confusion.

For the reasons explained above, we affirm the district court's finding of liability to the extent it found that Defendant infringes Plaintiff's mark. However, to the extent the court ruled that Defendant has not infringed Plaintiff's mark by using its marks outside Plaintiff's main Service Area, its judgment is vacated. The injunction ordered by the district court is affirmed to the extent that it enjoined Defendant from use of its marks. The scope of the injunction is hereby expanded to include Tompkins and Schuyler counties. We vacate the district court's order to the extent it leaves Defendant free to use its marks outside Plaintiff's Service Area, and in online applications. We leave it to the district court to determine whether the injunction can be tailored to allow Defendant some limited use of its marks outside Plaintiff's Service Area (expanded to include Tompkins and Schuyler counties) and on the Internet, giving due weight to Plaintiff's interest in protection from the risk of confusion in the marketplace and to all other appropriate equitable considerations. The matter is remanded for further proceedings in accordance with this ruling.

NOTES AND QUESTIONS

1. *The common law rule in light of federal registration.* United Drug caused us to refine the rule for priority of trademark rights in the United States that we articulated in Chapter 4. Does the availability of federal registration, as seen in operation in *Dawn Donut*, require our further refinement of the rule? What is the precise effect of federal registration on the rights of the different users? *See* 15 U.S.C. §1072; *see also Thrifty Rent-A-Car Sys., Inc. v. Thrift Cars, Inc.*, 831 F.2d 1177 (1st Cir. 1987).

2. *The effect of federal registration in* Healthcare Communications. The *National Ass'n for Healthcare Communications* court noted that if CA decided to expand and seek a broader injunction, many other issues might be raised and that "additional issues would

---

11. The district court might contemplate diminishing any harm to Defendant caused by a mandatory logo change by allowing the change to be made in stages, perhaps beginning with the addition of a reasonably prominent disclaimer of connection to Plaintiff.

be raised if Healthcom's mark is granted federal registration." What issues would be raised if the PTO granted Healthcom's pending application for a federal registration? If you were counsel for CA, what arguments would you make (both in any proceeding before the PTO and in any infringement proceedings) to preserve the broadest rights for your client? Indeed, if federal registration is of potential significance, several variations on the facts might have been presented to the court:

- Both Healthcom and CA have rights only at common law.
- Healthcom's application for federal registration is granted, and CA relies on common law rights.
- CA's application for a federal registration is granted, and Healthcom's application is denied, forcing Healthcom to rely on common law rights.

How should a court allocate rights in each of these three situations?

3. *Federal registration and local rights.* The Second Circuit in *Patsy's Italian Restaurant, Inc. v. Banas,* 658 F.3d 254 (2d Cir. 2011), emphasized that "local rights owned by another have been consistently viewed as sufficient to prevent a party from obtaining registration of a federal mark." *Id.* at 266. Why is this so? (Consider the scope of rights granted by federal registration.) How local can those prior rights be and still constitute an impediment to federal registration? *See id.* at 266-68. Review Section 2(d) of the Lanham Act: Does it impose any restriction on the type of use that might preclude federal registration?

4. *The effect of (incontestable) federal registrations on good faith remote junior users.* Section 33(b)(5) of the Lanham Act provides that even where a registration has become incontestable, it shall be a defense to an infringement action that "the mark whose use . . . is alleged to be an infringement was adopted without knowledge of the registrant's prior use and has been continuously used by [the allegedly infringing] party" from a date prior to the date of constructive use under Section 7(c), or the federal registration of the mark if the application for registration was filed before the effective date of the Trademark Law Revision Act of 1988. Does Section 33(b)(5) codify the good faith remote junior user defense? Is the statutory defense different from the common law defense? *See Quiksilver, Inc. v. Kymsta Corp.,* 466 F.3d 749 (9th Cir. 2006) (holding that there is no element of remoteness in Section 33(b)(5)); *Champions Golf Club, Inc. v. The Champions Golf Club, Inc.,* 78 F.3d 1111, 1124 (6th Cir. 1996) (incorporating remoteness element). Should it be? (Note that under Section 33(a), the defenses listed in Section 33(b) are available in any action for infringement of a registered mark.) Section 33(b)(5) makes clear that the subsequent user's defense under this provision is limited to "the area of its continuous use" prior to the registrant's filing or registration date. How would you assess whether the junior user has engaged in "continuous use"? *See Quiksilver, Inc. v. Kymsta Corp.,* 466 F.3d 749 (9th Cir. 2006) (in dispute over ROXY mark, defendant had over time changed its product label from "ROXYWEAR BY ROXANNE HEPTNER" to "ROXYWEAR BY ROXX" and ultimately largely distributed its merchandise as private-label apparel). If a defendant has used the mark without knowledge of the plaintiff's mark prior to the date of the plaintiff's registration, thus potentially coming within the scope of Section 33(b)(5), would the defendant automatically be immune from liability for trademark infringement? What more might you want to know to answer this question? *Cf. Sinhdarella v. Vu,* 85 U.S.P.Q.2d (BNA) 2007, 2014 (N.D. Cal. 2008).

5. *Concurrent use registrations.* The common law rule that users who in good faith make concurrent use of a trademark in remote locations may continue to use in their respective territories of use is reflected in trademark registration practice. The PTO will issue

concurrent use registrations, granting federal registration of the mark of each concurrent user in their territory. *See* 15 U.S.C. §1052(d); *see also Woman's World Shops, Inc. v. Lane Bryant Inc.*, 5 U.S.P.Q.2d (BNA) 1985 (TTAB 1988) (junior user must act in good faith); *see generally* TMEP §1207.04. But obviously, no single producer will get nationwide rights that would normally flow from a federal registration; that is to say, more than one registrant may obtain registration of the same or a similar mark, but for different parts of the United States. If the senior user used in California and a junior used in good faith in New York, who should obtain rights in the other forty-eight states? The senior user nationally? If not, what variables should affect that question? *See Weiner King, Inc. v. Weiner King Corp.*, 201 U.S.P.Q. (BNA) 894, 910 (TTAB 1979), *aff'd in part, rev'd in part, Weiner King, Inc. v. Weiner King Corp.*, 615 F.2d 512 (C.C.P.A. 1980). Section 2(d) requires that such concurrent registration not be likely to cause confusion of buyers or others. To what extent does the rule in Section 2(d) codify (in the registration context) the good faith remote junior user rule? To what extent should there be differences in the conditions under which a good faith remote junior user can continue to use and under which it can obtain a concurrent use registration under Section 2(d)? Should concurrent registrations issue when one or more of the parties to a concurrent use proceeding does business on the Internet? *See CDS, Inc. v. I.C.E.D. Mgmt., Inc.*, 80 U.S.P.Q.2d (BNA) 1572 (TTAB 2006). The TTAB has stressed that the advent of the Internet has not undermined the vitality of the concurrent use principle. *See America's Best Franchising, Inc. v. Abbott*, 2013 WL 3168104 (TTAB Mar. 20, 2013). Should it? Or does it make it even more important? What does *Guthrie Healthcare* suggest (if anything) on the relevance of the Internet?

6.   *Concurrent use agreements.* Beatrice commenced use of the HOMESTEAD mark for food products in 1953. Fairway was the junior user, having started use of the same mark in 1956. By the time that the parties each sought federal registrations, Beatrice was using the mark in twenty-three states, and Fairway was using the mark HOMESTEAD in five states. A concurrent use proceeding was instituted. Pursuant to an agreement between Beatrice and Fairway, the junior user Fairway restricted its application to its five-state area and the portions of two states where it had impending entry. The senior user Beatrice claimed the area comprising the remainder of the United States. Should the Trademark Office recognize the division of the country made in the agreement between the parties? Which party should be granted registered rights with respect to the states that had not yet been entered by either party, if that allocation is not made according to the parties' agreement? Should the PTO leave those areas subject to no registration? *See In re Beatrice Foods Co.*, 429 F.2d 466 (C.C.P.A. 1970); *Amalgamated Bank of New York v. Amalgamated Trust & Sav. Bank*, 842 F.2d 1270 (Fed. Cir. 1988).

7.   *The effect of constructive use.* As we saw in Chapter 5, Section 7(c) of the Lanham Act now provides that, contingent upon ultimate registration, the filing of an application for registration on the Principal Register (whether an ITU or a use-based application) constitutes "constructive use of the mark, conferring a right of priority, nationwide in effect," against others who have not previously used the mark or filed an application for its registration. The Restatement suggests that this still does not enable an injunction to be granted against use in remote areas absent a likelihood of confusion. *See* Restatement (Third) of Unfair Competition §19, cmt. (e) (1995) (suggesting that Section 7(c) does not alter the *Dawn Donut* rule). If not, what is the practical effect of Section 7(c)? What advantages does Section 7(c) provide an applicant not already offered by Section 22?

8.   *Applying the* Dawn Donut *rule.* What must a trademark registrant show under *Dawn Donut* to satisfy a court that an area is one in which there is a likelihood that the registrant will expand its use? Was the analysis by the *Guthrie* court consistent with *Dawn Donut*?

What considerations should a court take into account in assessing the question of "likely expansion"? What incentives does this rule create for trademark owners?

9. *Clarifying some terminology.* Is the area of "likely expansion" relevant to the *Dawn Donut* rule the same concept as the "zone of natural expansion" discussed *supra* in note 6 after the *United Drug* opinion? Is the concept captured by the test of "market penetration" in *National Ass'n for Healthcare Communications* the same as either, both, or neither of the concepts of "area of likely expansion" and the "zone of natural expansion"? To answer these questions, consider the consequences of an area being found to be, respectively, a "zone of natural expansion," "an area of likely expansion," and an "area in which there is market penetration."

10. *State boundaries.* Measuring the reach of a producer's use is an extremely difficult task. In light of that, is it not sensible to work from the default position that state political boundaries define the geographic reach of rights? Why does the Eighth Circuit reject that approach? What if Arkansas state law expressly conferred automatic statewide rights on holders of state registrations? *Cf.* Restatement (Third) of Unfair Competition §19, cmt. (e) (1995); *see also Spartan Food Sys., Inc. v. HFS Corp.*, 813 F.2d 1279 (4th Cir. 1987).

11. *Critiquing* Dawn Donut. One judge in a Sixth Circuit case has expressed the following dissatisfaction with the *Dawn Donut* rule:

> The Dawn Donut Rule [declining to enter an injunction in the absence of a showing that the senior user had imminent likelihood of entry into the infringer's territory] was enunciated in 1959. Entering the new millennium, our society is far more mobile than it was four decades ago. For this reason, and given that recent technological innovations such as the Internet are increasingly deconstructing geographical barriers for marketing purposes, it appears . . . that a re-examination of precedents would be timely to determine whether the Dawn Donut Rule [as to likelihood of entry] has outlived its usefulness.

Circuit City Stores, Inc. v. Carmax, Inc., 165 F.3d 1047, 1057 (6th Cir. 1999) (Jones J., concurring). Do you agree with this critique? Alternatively, does the ease with which marks cross borders mean that trademark law will have to adopt a greater range of doctrines that accommodate co-existence?

12. *Critiquing the "zone of natural expansion."* To what extent is the doctrine of the zone of natural expansion relevant to the availability of federal registration? *See* Restatement (Third) of Unfair Competition §19, cmt. (c) (1995).

13. *Partial geographic abandonment and federal registration.* How would the partial geographic abandonment argument discussed above in *Tumblebus* be affected by the existence of a federal registration owned by the plaintiff?

C.   THE TERRITORIAL NATURE OF U.S. TRADEMARK RIGHTS

PERSON'S CO., LTD. v. CHRISTMAN
900 F.2d 1565 (Fed. Cir. 1990)

EDWARD S. SMITH, Senior Circuit Judge:

BACKGROUND

The facts pertinent to this appeal are as follows: In 1977, Takaya Iwasaki first applied a stylized logo bearing the name "PERSON'S" to clothing in his native Japan. Two years later Iwasaki formed Person's Co., Ltd., a Japanese corporation, to market and distribute the clothing items in retail stores located in Japan.

In 1981, Larry Christman, a U.S. citizen and employee of a sportswear wholesaler, visited a Person's Co. retail store while on a business trip to Japan. Christman purchased several clothing items bearing the "PERSON'S" logo and returned with them to the United States. After consulting with legal counsel and being advised that no one had yet established a claim to the logo in the United States, Christman developed designs for his own "PERSON'S" brand sportswear line based on appellant's products he had purchased in Japan. In February 1982, Christman contracted with a clothing manufacturer to produce clothing articles with the "PERSON'S" logo attached. These clothing items were sold, beginning in April 1982, to sportswear retailers in the northwestern United States. Christman formed Team Concepts, Ltd., a Washington corporation, in May 1983 to continue merchandising his sportswear line, which had expanded to include additional articles such as shoulder bags. All the sportswear marketed by Team Concepts bore either the mark "PERSON'S" or a copy of appellant's globe logo; many of the clothing styles were apparently copied directly from appellant's designs.

In April 1983, Christman filed an application for U.S. trademark registration in an effort to protect the "PERSON'S" mark. Christman believed himself to be the exclusive owner of the right to use and register the mark in the United States and apparently had no knowledge that appellant soon intended to introduce its similar sportswear line under the identical mark in the U.S. market. Christman's registration issued in September 1984 for use on wearing apparel.

In the interim between Christman's first sale and the issuance of his registration, Person's Co., Ltd. became a well known and highly respected force in the Japanese fashion industry. The company, which had previously sold garments under the "PERSON'S" mark only in Japan, began implementing its plan to sell goods under this mark in the United States. According to Mr. Iwasaki, purchases by buyers for resale in the United States occurred as early as November 1982. This was some seven months subsequent to Christman's first sales in the United States. Person's Co. filed an application for U.S. trademark registration in the following year, and, in 1985, engaged an export trading company to introduce its goods into the U.S. market. The registration for the mark "PERSON'S" issued in August 1985 for use on luggage, clothing and accessories. After recording U.S. sales near 4 million dollars in 1985, Person's Co. granted California distributor Zip Zone International a license to manufacture and sell goods under the "PERSON'S" mark in the United States.

In early 1986, appellant's advertising in the U.S. became known to Christman and both parties became aware of confusion in the marketplace. Person's Co. initiated an action to cancel Christman's registration on the following grounds: (1) likelihood of confusion; (2) abandonment; and (3) unfair competition within the meaning of the Paris Convention. Christman counterclaimed and asserted prior use and likelihood of confusion as grounds for cancellation of the Person's Co. registration.

After some discovery, Christman filed a motion with the Board for summary judgment on all counts. In a well reasoned decision, the Board held for Christman on the grounds that Person's use of the mark in Japan could not be used to establish priority against a "good faith" senior user in U.S. commerce. The Board found no evidence to suggest that the "PERSON'S" mark had acquired any notoriety in this country at the time of its adoption by Christman. Therefore, appellant had no reputation or goodwill upon which Christman could have intended to trade, rendering the unfair competition provisions of the Paris Convention inapplicable. The Board also found that Christman had not abandoned the mark, although sales of articles bearing the mark were often intermittent. The Board granted summary judgment to Christman and ordered appellant's registration cancelled.

The Board held in its opinion on reconsideration that Christman had not adopted the mark in bad faith despite his appropriation of a mark in use by appellant in a foreign country. The Board adopted the view that copying a mark in use in a foreign country is not in bad faith unless the foreign mark is famous in the United States or the copying is undertaken for the purpose of interfering with the prior user's planned expansion into the United States. Person's Co. appeals and requests that this court direct the Board to enter summary judgment in its favor.

. . .

PRIORITY

The first ground asserted for cancellation in the present action is §2(d) of the Lanham Act; each party claims prior use of registered marks which unquestionably are confusingly similar and affixed to similar goods.

. . .

In the present case, appellant Person's Co. relies on its use of the mark in Japan in an attempt to support its claim for priority in the United States. Such foreign use has no effect on U.S. commerce and cannot form the basis for a holding that appellant has priority here. The concept of territoriality is basic to trademark law; trademark rights exist in each country solely according to that country's statutory scheme. Christman was the first to use the mark in United States commerce and the first to obtain a federal registration thereon. Appellant has no basis upon which to claim priority and is the junior user under these facts.[16]

BAD FAITH

Appellant vigorously asserts that Christman's adoption and use of the mark in the United States subsequent to Person's Co.'s adoption in Japan is tainted with "bad faith" and that the priority in the United States obtained thereby is insufficient to establish rights superior to those arising from Person's Co.'s prior adoption in a foreign country. Relying on *Woman's World Shops, Inc. v. Lane Bryant, Inc.*, Person's Co. argues that a "remote junior user" of a mark obtains no right superior to the "senior user" if the "junior user" has adopted the mark with knowledge of the "senior user's" prior use.[18] In *Woman's World*, the senior user utilized the mark within a limited geographical area. A junior user from a different geographical area of the United States sought unrestricted federal registration for a nearly identical mark, with the exception to its virtually exclusive rights being those of the known senior user. The Board held that such an appropriation with knowledge failed to satisfy the good faith requirements of the Lanham Act and denied the concurrent use rights sought by the junior user. Person's Co. cites *Woman's World* for the proposition that a junior user's adoption and use of a mark with knowledge of another's prior use constitutes bad faith. It is urged that this principle is equitable in nature and should not be limited to knowledge of use within the territory of the United States.

---

16. Section 44 of the Lanham Act, 15 U.S.C. §1126 (1982), permits qualified foreign applicants who own a registered mark in their country of origin to obtain a U.S. trademark registration without alleging actual use in U.S. commerce. If a U.S. application is filed within six months of the filing of the foreign application, such U.S. registration will be accorded the same force and effect as if filed in the United States on the same date on which the application was first filed in the foreign country. The statutory scheme set forth in §44 is in place to lower barriers to entry and assist foreign applicants in establishing business goodwill in the United States. Person's Co. does not assert rights under §44, which if properly applied, might have been used to secure priority over Christman.

18. Appellant repeatedly makes reference to a "world economy" and considers Christman to be the remote junior user of the mark. Although Person's did adopt the mark in Japan prior to Christman's use in United States commerce, the use in Japan cannot be relied upon to acquire U.S. trademark rights. Christman is the senior user as that term is defined under U.S. trademark law.

While the facts of the present case are analogous to those in *Woman's World*, the case is distinguishable in one significant respect. In *Woman's World*, the first use of the mark by both the junior and senior users was in United States commerce. In the case at bar, appellant Person's Co., while first to adopt the mark, was not the first user in the United States. Christman is the senior user, and we are aware of no case where a senior user has been charged with bad faith. The concept of bad faith adoption applies to remote junior users seeking concurrent use registrations; in such cases, the likelihood of customer confusion in the remote area may be presumed from proof of the junior user's knowledge. In the present case, when Christman initiated use of the mark, Person's Co. had not yet entered U.S. commerce. The Person's Co. had no goodwill in the United States and the "PERSON'S" mark had no reputation here. Appellant's argument ignores the territorial nature of trademark rights.

The Board found that, at the time of registration, Christman was not aware of appellant's intention to enter the U.S. clothing and accessories market in the future. Christman obtained a trademark search on the "PERSON'S" mark and an opinion of competent counsel that the mark was "available" in the United States. Since Appellant had taken no steps to secure registration of the mark in the United States, Christman was aware of no basis for Person's Co. to assert superior rights to use and registration here. Appellant would have us infer bad faith adoption because of Christman's awareness of its use of the mark in Japan, but an inference of bad faith requires something more than mere knowledge of prior use of a similar mark in a foreign country.

As the Board noted . . . , Christman's prior use in U.S. commerce cannot be discounted solely because he was aware of appellant's use of the mark in Japan. While adoption of a mark with knowledge of a prior actual *user* in U.S. commerce may give rise to cognizable equities as between the parties, no such equities may be based upon knowledge of a similar mark's existence or on a problematical intent to use such a similar mark in the future. Knowledge of a foreign use does not preclude good faith adoption and use in the United States. While there is some case law supporting a finding of bad faith where (1) the foreign mark is famous here or (2) the use is a nominal one made solely to block the prior foreign user's planned expansion into the United States, as the Board correctly found, neither of these circumstances is present in this case.

We agree with the Board's conclusion that Christman's adoption and use of the mark were in good faith. Christman's adoption of the mark occurred at a time when appellant had not yet entered U.S. commerce; therefore, no prior user was in place to give Christman notice of appellant's potential U.S. rights. Christman's conduct in appropriating and using appellant's mark in a market where he believed the Japanese manufacturer did not compete can hardly be considered unscrupulous commercial conduct. Christman adopted the trademark being used by appellant in Japan, but appellant has not identified any aspect of U.S. trademark law violated by such action. Trademark rights under the Lanham Act arise solely out of use of the mark in U.S. commerce or from ownership of a foreign registration thereon; "[t]he law pertaining to registration of trademarks does not regulate all aspects of business morality." When the law has been crafted with the clarity of crystal, it also has the qualities of a glass slipper: it cannot be shoe-horned onto facts it does not fit, no matter how appealing they might appear.

. . .

CONCLUSION

In *United Drug Co. v. Rectanus Co.*, the Supreme Court of the United States determined that "[t]here is no such thing as property in a trademark except as a right appurtenant to an established business or trade in connection with which the mark is employed. . . .

[I]ts function is simply to designate the goods as the product of a particular trader and to protect his goodwill against the sale of another's product as his; and it is not the subject of property except in connection with an existing business."[36] In the present case, appellant failed to secure protection for its mark through use in U.S. commerce; therefore, no established business or product line was in place from which trademark rights could arise. Christman was the first to use the mark in U.S. commerce. This first use was not tainted with bad faith by Christman's mere knowledge of appellant's prior foreign use, so the Board's conclusion on the issue of priority was correct. Appellant also raises no factual dispute which is material to the resolution of the issue of abandonment. Accordingly, the grant of summary judgment was entirely in order, and the Board's decision is affirmed.

Affirmed.

GRUPO GIGANTE v. DALLO & CO., INC.

391 F.3d 1088 (9th Cir. 2004)

KLEINFELD, Circuit Judge:

This is a trademark case. The contest is between a large Mexican grocery chain that has long used the mark, but not in the United States, and a small American chain that was the first to use the mark in the United States, but did so, long after the Mexican chain began using it, in a locality where shoppers were familiar with the Mexican mark.

FACTS

Grupo Gigante S.A. de C.V. ("Grupo Gigante") operates a large chain of grocery stores in Mexico, called "Gigante," meaning "Giant" in Spanish. Grupo Gigante first called a store "Gigante" in Mexico City in 1962. In 1963, Grupo Gigante registered the "Gigante" mark as a trade name in Mexico, and has kept its registration current ever since. The chain was quite successful, and it had expanded into Baja California, Mexico, by 1987. By 1991, Grupo Gigante had almost 100 stores in Mexico, including six in Baja, all using the mark "Gigante." Two of the Baja stores were in Tijuana, a city on the U.S.-Mexican border, just south of San Diego.

As of August 1991, Grupo Gigante had not opened any stores in the United States. That month, Michael Dallo began operating a grocery store in San Diego, using the name "Gigante Market." In October 1996, Dallo and one of his brothers, Chris Dallo, opened a second store in San Diego, also under the name Gigante Market. The Dallo brothers—who include Michael, Chris, and their two other brothers, Douray and Rafid—have since controlled the two stores through various limited liability corporations.

In 1995, which was after the opening of the Dallos' first store and before the opening of their second, Grupo Gigante began exploring the possibility of expanding into Southern California. It learned of the Dallos' Gigante Market in San Diego. Grupo Gigante decided against entering the California market at that time. It did nothing about the Dallos' store despite Grupo Gigante's knowledge that the Dallos were using "Gigante" in the store's name.

In 1998, Grupo Gigante decided that the time had come to enter the Southern California market. It arranged a meeting with Michael Dallo in June 1998 to discuss the

---

36. 248 U.S. at 97. It goes without saying that the underlying policy upon which this function is grounded is the protection of the public in its purchase of a service or product. *See, e.g., In re Canadian Pacific Ltd.*, 754 F.2d 992, 994 (Fed. Cir. 1985).

Dallos' use of the name "Gigante." Grupo Gigante was unsuccessful at this meeting in its attempt to convince Dallo to stop using the "Gigante" mark. Also in June 1998, Grupo Gigante registered the "Gigante" mark with the state of California. The Dallos did likewise in July 1998. Neither has registered the mark federally.

About one year later, in May 1999, Grupo Gigante opened its first U.S. store. That store was followed by a second later that year, and then by a third in 2000. All three stores were in the Los Angeles area. All were called "Gigante," like Grupo Gigante's Mexican stores.

. . .

The district court disposed of the case in a published decision on cross motions for summary judgment. The court recognized that under the "territoriality principle," use of a mark in another country generally does not serve to give the user trademark rights in the United States. Thus, the territoriality principle suggests that the Dallos' use of the mark, which was the first in the United States, would entitle them to claim the mark. But it held that because Grupo Gigante had already made Gigante a well-known mark in Southern California by the time the Dallos began using it, an exception to the territoriality principle applied. As the district court interpreted what is known as the "famous-mark" or "well-known mark" exception to the territoriality principle, Grupo Gigante's earlier use in Mexico was sufficient to give it the superior claim to the mark in Southern California. The court held, therefore, that Grupo Gigante was entitled to a declaratory judgment that it had a valid, protectable interest in the Gigante name. Nevertheless, the court held that laches barred Grupo Gigante from enjoining the Dallos from using the mark at their two existing stores. The Dallos appeal the holding that Grupo Gigante has a protectable right to use the mark in Southern California. Grupo Gigante appeals the laches holding. We agree in large part with the district court's excellent opinion, but some necessary qualifications to it require a remand.

ANALYSIS

THE EXCEPTION FOR FAMOUS AND WELL-KNOWN FOREIGN MARKS

. . .

A fundamental principle of trademark law is first in time equals first in right. But things get more complicated when to time we add considerations of place, as when one user is first in time in one place while another is first in time in a different place. The complexity swells when the two places are two different countries, as in the case at bar.

Under the principle of first in time equals first in right, priority ordinarily comes with earlier *use* of a mark in commerce. It is "not enough to have invented the mark first or even to have registered it first." If the first-in-time principle were all that mattered, this case would end there. It is undisputed that Grupo Gigante used the mark in commerce for decades before the Dallos did. But the facts of this case implicate another well-established principle of trademark law, the "territoriality principle." The territoriality principle, as stated in a treatise, says that "[p]riority of trademark rights in the United States depends solely upon priority of use in the United States, not on priority of use anywhere in the world." Earlier use in another country usually just does not count.[10] Although we have not had occasion to address this principle, it has been described by our sister circuits as "basic to

---

10. See *Person's Co., Ltd. v. Christman*, 900 F.2d 1565, 1569-70 (Fed. Cir. 1990); *Buti v. Perosa, S.R.L.*, 139 F.3d 98, 103-05 (2d Cir. 1998); *Fuji Photo Film Co., Inc. v. Shinohara Shoji Kabushiki Kaisha*, 754 F.2d 591, 599 (5th Cir. 1985).

trademark law," in large part because "trademark rights exist in each country solely according to that country's statutory scheme." While Grupo Gigante used the mark for decades before the Dallos used it, Grupo Gigante's use was in Mexico, not in the United States. Within the San Diego area, on the northern side of the border, the Dallos were the first users of the "Gigante" mark. Thus, according to the territoriality principle, the Dallos' rights to use the mark would trump Grupo Gigante's.

Grupo Gigante does not contest the existence of the territoriality principle. But like the first-in-time, first-in-right principle, it is not absolute. The exception, as Grupo Gigante presents it, is that when foreign use of a mark achieves a certain level of fame for that mark within the United States, the territoriality principle no longer serves to deny priority to the earlier foreign user. The Dallos concede that there is such an exception, but dispute what it takes for a mark to qualify for it. Grupo Gigante would interpret the exception broadly, while the Dallos would interpret it narrowly.

. . .

There is no circuit-court authority—from this or any other circuit—applying a famous-mark exception to the territoriality principle. At least one circuit judge has, in a dissent, called into question whether there actually is any meaningful famous-mark exception. We hold, however, that there is a famous-mark exception to the territoriality principle. While the territoriality principle is a long-standing and important doctrine within trademark law, it cannot be absolute. An absolute territoriality rule without a famous-mark exception would promote consumer confusion and fraud. Commerce crosses borders. In this nation of immigrants, so do people. Trademark is, at its core, about protecting against consumer confusion and "palming off." There can be no justification for using trademark law to fool immigrants into thinking that they are buying from the store they liked back home.

It might not matter if someone visiting Fairbanks, Alaska from Wellington, New Zealand saw a cute hair-salon name—"Hair Today, Gone Tomorrow," "Mane Place," "Hair on Earth," "Mary's Hair'em," or "Shear Heaven"—and decided to use the name on her own salon back home in New Zealand. The ladies in New Zealand would not likely think they were going to a branch of a Fairbanks hair salon. But if someone opened a high-end salon with a red door in Wellington and called it Elizabeth Arden's, women might very well go there because they thought they were going to an affiliate of the Elizabeth Arden chain, even if there had not been any other Elizabeth Ardens in New Zealand prior to the salon's opening. If it was not an affiliate, just a local store with no connection, customers would be fooled. The real Elizabeth Arden chain might lose business if word spread that the Wellington salon was nothing special.

The most cited case for the famous-mark exception is *Vaudable v. Montmartre, Inc.*, a 1959 trial court decision from [the state courts of] New York. A New York restaurant had opened under the name "Maxim's," the same name as the well-known Parisian restaurant in operation since 1893, and still in operation today. The New York Maxim's used similar typography for its sign, as well as other features likely to evoke the Paris Maxim's—particularly among what the court called "the class of people residing in the cosmopolitan city of New York who dine out" (by which it apparently meant the sort of people who spend for dinner what some people spend for a month's rent). The court enjoined the New York use, even though the Paris restaurant did not operate in New York, or in the United States, because the Maxim's mark was "famous."

While *Vaudable* stands for the principle that even those who use marks in other countries can sometimes—when their marks are famous enough—gain exclusive rights to the marks in this country, the case itself tells us little about just how famous or well-known the foreign mark must be. The opinion states in rather conclusory terms that the Paris Maxim's "is, of course, well known in this country," and that "[t]here is *no doubt* as to its unique and eminent position as a restaurant of international fame and prestige." This language suggests that Maxim's had achieved quite a high degree of fame here, and certainly enough to qualify for the exception to the territoriality principle, but it suggests nothing about just how much fame was necessary. It does not suggest where the line is between "Shear Heaven" and Maxim's. . . .

Grupo Gigante urges us to adopt the approach the district court took. The district court held that the correct inquiry was to determine whether the mark had attained secondary meaning in the San Diego area. . . .

Applying its interpretation of the famous-mark exception, the district court concluded that Grupo Gigante's use of the mark had achieved secondary meaning in the San Diego area by the time the Dallos opened their first store, and thus the court held that Grupo Gigante's use was eligible for the exception to the territoriality principle. Grupo Gigante asserts that we, too, should adopt secondary meaning as the definition of the exception. We decline to go quite this far, however, because following the district court's lead would effectively cause the exception to eclipse the territoriality rule entirely.

Secondary meaning has two functions. First, it serves to determine whether certain marks are distinctive enough to warrant protection. . . .

Second, and most relevant to this case, secondary meaning defines the geographic area in which a user has priority, regardless of who uses the mark first. Under what has become known as the *Tea Rose–Rectanus* doctrine, priority of use in one geographic area within the United States does not necessarily suffice to establish priority in another area. . . . The practical effect is that one user may have priority in one area, while another user has priority over the very same mark in a different area. . . . Secondary meaning comes into play in determining just how far each user's priority extends. Courts ask whether the first, geographically limited use of the mark is well-known enough that it has gained secondary meaning not just within the area where it has been used, but also within the remote area, which is usually the area where a subsequent user is claiming the right to use the mark.

[Assume, for example, that Grupo Gigante had been using the mark in Arizona as well as in various parts of Mexico. If that were the case,] we would analyze, under the *Tea Rose–Rectanus* doctrine, whether Grupo Gigante's use of the mark had achieved secondary meaning in San Diego. This is how the district court analyzed the actual dispute, as a result of having defined the exception to the territoriality principle in terms of secondary meaning. In other words, the district court treated Grupo Gigante's use of the mark exactly as it would have had Grupo Gigante used the mark not only in Mexico, but also in another part of the United States. Under the district court's interpretation of the exception to the territoriality principle, the fact that Grupo Gigante's earlier use of the mark was entirely outside of the United States becomes irrelevant.

The problem with this is that treating international use differently is what the territoriality principle does. This interpretation of the exception would effectively eliminate the territoriality principle by eliminating any effect of international borders on protectability. We would end up treating foreign uses of the mark just as we treat domestic uses under the *Tea Rose–Rectanus* doctrine, asking in both cases whether the use elsewhere resulted in secondary meaning in the local market.

We would go too far if we did away with the territoriality principle altogether by expanding the famous-mark exception this much. The territoriality principle has a long history in the common law,[30] and at least two circuits have described it as "basic to trademark law."[31] That status reflects the lack of a uniform trademark regime across international borders. What one must do to acquire trademark rights in one country will not always be the same as what one must do in another. And once acquired, trademark rights gained in other countries are governed by each country's own set of laws. Furthermore, we are arguably required by the Paris Convention, of which the United States is a signatory, to preserve the territoriality principle in some form.[33] Thus, we reject Grupo Gigante's argument that we should define the well-known mark exception as merely an inquiry into whether the mark has achieved secondary meaning in the area where the foreign user wishes to assert protection.

To determine whether the famous-mark exception to the territoriality rule applies, the district court must determine whether the mark satisfies the secondary-meaning test. The district court determined that it did in this case, and we agree with its persuasive analysis. But secondary meaning is not enough.

In addition, where the mark has not before been used in the American market, the court must be satisfied, by a preponderance of the evidence, that a *substantial* percentage of consumers in the relevant American market is familiar with the foreign mark. The relevant American market is the geographic area where the defendant uses the alleged infringing mark. In making this determination, the court should consider such factors as the intentional copying of the mark by the defendant, and whether customers of the American firm are likely to think they are patronizing the same firm that uses the mark in another country. While these factors are not necessarily determinative, they are particularly relevant because they bear heavily on the risks of consumer confusion and fraud, which are the reasons for having a famous-mark exception.

Because the district court did not have the benefit of this additional test, we vacate and remand so that it may be applied. . . . The concurring opinion is incorrect in its suggestion that the case necessarily must go to trial because distinctiveness of a mark is a question of fact and defendants have contested the reliability of plaintiffs' survey evidence. That conclusion flies in the face of the 1986 triumvirate of summary judgment cases. . . .

Paris Convention Claims

The district court properly held that Grupo Gigante's claim for "use of a well-known mark" under Article 6 *bis* of the Paris Convention is duplicative of its claim that, because the Gigante mark is well-known, that mark is entitled to protection under the Lanham Act. The district court also properly rejected Grupo Gigante's claim for unfair competition under Article 10 *bis* of the Paris Convention.

---

30. As McCarthy has noted, traces of the territoriality principle appear in Justice Holmes's opinion for the U.S. Supreme Court in *A. Bourjois & Co. v. Katzel*, 260 U.S. 689, 692 (1923). McCarthy, *supra*, at §29:1, p. 29-4; *see also Philip Morris Inc. v. Allen Distribs., Inc.*, 48 F. Supp. 2d 844, 850 (S.D. Ind. 1999) (identifying *Bourjois* as marking the shift from "the 'universality' principle [to] a 'territoriality principle' that recognizes a separate legal existence for a trademark in each country whose laws afford protection to the mark").

31. *Fuji Photo*, 754 F.2d at 599; *Person's*, 900 F.2d at 1569.

33. *Paris Convention for the Protection of Industrial Property*, Mar. 20, 1883, as revised at Stockholm, July 14, 1967, art. 6(3), 21 U.S.T. 1583, §6(3) ("A mark duly registered in a country of the Union shall be regarded as independent of marks registered in the other countries of the Union, including the country of origin.").

There has been some understandable confusion among the district courts with respect to whether the Paris Convention, implemented in §44 of the Lanham Act, creates substantive law or a right of action applicable to international trademark disputes. *Compare Mattel, Inc. v. MCA Records, Inc.*, 28 F. Supp. 2d 1120, 1158 (C.D. Cal. 1998) (holding that the Paris Convention does not create a right of action separate and distinct from those available under the Lanham Act), *with Maison Lazard et Compagnie v. Manfra, Tordella & Brooks, Inc.*, 585 F. Supp. 1286, 1289 (S.D.N.Y. 1984) (holding that the Paris Convention creates a distinct cause of action for unfair competition). That confusion results from the interplay between Article 10*bis* and §44 of the Lanham Act. [A]rticle 10*bis* requires member countries "to assure to nationals of [other member countries] effective protection against unfair competition." [cit.] Section 44 of the Lanham Act implements Article 10*bis* by extending Lanham Act protection to foreign nationals to the extent necessary to satisfy the United States' treaty obligations:

> Any person whose country of origin is a party to any convention or treaty relating to trademarks, trade or commercial names, or the repression of unfair competition, to which the United States is also a party, or extends reciprocal rights to nationals of the United States by law, shall be entitled to the benefits of this section under the conditions expressed herein to the extent necessary to give effect to any provision of such convention, treaty or reciprocal law, in addition to the rights to which any owner of a mark is otherwise entitled by this chapter.

15 U.S.C. §1126(b).[35]

Grupo Gigante uses the phrase "in addition to the rights to which any owner of a mark is otherwise entitled to by this chapter" to argue that §44 of the Lanham Act implements certain additional substantive rights created by international treaties. Although that may be true as a general matter, Article 10*bis* itself does not create additional substantive rights. . . .

As we held in *Kemart Corp. v. Printing Arts Research Laboratories, Inc.*, 269 F.2d 375, 389 (9th Cir. 1959), "the Paris Convention was not intended to define the substantive law in the area of 'unfair competition' of the signatory countries." More recently, we concluded that the interaction between §44 of the Lanham Act and Article 10*bis* of the Paris Convention simply results in equal treatment of foreign and domestic parties in trademark disputes:

> A foreign national is entitled to the same "effective protection against unfair competition" to which an American is entitled, Paris Convention, art. 10bis, and in turn, the American gets the same right that the foreign national gets. . . . But [a party] has no claim to a nonexistent federal cause of action for unfair competition. As said, the Paris Convention provides for national treatment, and does not define the substantive law of unfair competition.

Mattel, 296 F.3d at 908. *See also Int'l Café*, 252 F.3d at 1278 (holding that the Paris Convention "only requires 'national treatment'").

Because the Paris Convention creates neither a federal cause of action nor additional substantive rights, the district court properly dismissed Grupo Gigante's Paris Convention claims.

---

35. Section 44(h) of the Lanham Act [which provides that a national of a Paris Union country "shall be entitled to effective protection against unfair competition"] similarly "creates a federal right that is coextensive with the substantive provisions of the treaty involved." *Mattel*, 296 F.3d at 907.

PRIORITY BASED ON CALIFORNIA LAW

[The court also dismissed claims by Grupo Gigante that even if it failed to establish that the Gigante mark is famous and well known, it has established priority under California law because California does not recognize the territoriality principle and, consequently, use anywhere in the world suffices to establish priority in California. It held that as a general matter, trademark claims under California law are "substantially congruent" with federal claims and thus lend themselves to the same analysis.]

. . .

Vacated and Remanded.

GRABER, Circuit Judge, concurring:

I concur in the majority's opinion because I agree that a foreign owner of a supposedly famous or well-known foreign trademark must show a higher level of "fame" or recognition than that required to establish secondary meaning. Ultimately, the standard for famous or well-known marks is an intermediate one. To enjoy extraterritorial trademark protection, the owner of a foreign trademark need not show the level of recognition necessary to receive nation-wide protection against trademark dilution. On the other hand, the foreign trademark owner who does not use a mark in the United States must show more than the level of recognition that is necessary in a domestic trademark infringement case.

Nonetheless, I write separately to express my view that the evidence that Plaintiffs have presented thus far is insufficient as a matter of law to establish that their mark is famous or well-known. . . .

The [plaintiff's survey] evidence is insufficient in two important respects. First, the survey result is highly questionable in view of its narrowly defined survey population. . . .

Because Plaintiffs sell widely available, non-specialized goods to the general public, it is uninformative to focus exclusively on Mexican-Americans living in San Diego County. The district court's reliance on Plaintiffs' survey is especially problematic because its population was limited to Mexican-Americans who had recently purchased Mexican-style food at a supermarket or grocery store. . . .

Because a conclusion that Plaintiffs have a protectable interest would prohibit Defendants from selling groceries under that mark to *any* residents of San Diego County— not just to Mexican-Americans—it makes little sense to define the relevant public so narrowly. Comprised of all grocery shoppers, the "relevant sector of the public" in this case is the very antithesis of a specialized market; because everyone eats, the relevant sector of the public consists of all residents of San Diego County, without qualification.

Second, in view of the standard we announce today, I do not believe that a showing that 20 to 22 percent of the relevant market is familiar with the foreign mark establishes that a "significant" or "substantial" percentage of that market is familiar with the foreign mark. On that ground alone, I would conclude that Plaintiffs have failed, so far, to show that their mark is famous or well-known.

. . .

When a foreign mark has not been used in the United States, I would require the owner of the foreign mark to show, through surveys and other evidence, that a majority of the defendant's customers and potential customers, on aggregate, were familiar with the foreign mark when the defendant began its allegedly infringing use. Admittedly, that is a high standard. However, I believe that a stringent standard is required when conferring trademark protection to a mark that has never been, and perhaps never may be, used in this country. A conclusion that Plaintiffs' mark is well-known in the relevant sector brings with it the right to oust Defendants from their own market, notwithstanding the fact that they have established priority of use. A bare showing of acquired distinctiveness should not suffice to invert the ordinary allocation of trademark rights.

. . .

ITC LIMITED v. PUNCHGINI, INC.

482 F.3d 135 (2d Cir. 2007)

RAGGI, Circuit Judge:

[Plaintiff ITC Limited (ITC) is an Indian corporation. Through its subsidiary, ITC Hotels Limited, it owns and operates a five-star hotel in New Delhi, India, that contains the BUKHARA restaurant. The New Delhi BUKHARA opened in 1977, has remained in continuous operation, and has acquired a measure of international renown. In 2002 and 2003, it was named one of the world's fifty best restaurants by London-based *Restaurant* magazine. ITC has sought to extend the international reach of the Bukhara brand, opening Bukhara restaurants in Hong Kong, Bangkok, Bahrain, Montreal, Bangladesh, Singapore, Kathmandu, Ajman, New York (for five years), and Chicago (for ten years). In 1987, plaintiff ITC Limited (ITC) obtained a federal U.S. trademark registration for BUKHARA for restaurant services. However, the New York restaurant closed on December 17, 1991, and on August 28, 1997, ITC cancelled its Chicago franchise. ITC has not owned, operated, or licensed any restaurant in the United States using the BUKHARA mark since terminating the Chicago restaurant franchise. As of May 2004, ITC-owned or -authorized Bukhara restaurants were in operation only in New Delhi, Singapore, Kathmandu, and Ajman.

In 1999, the defendants, who had worked either in the New Delhi restaurant or the New York BUKHARA restaurant, formed a company with the goal of opening a restaurant in New York. They considered naming the restaurant "Far Pavilions" and "Passage to India" before settling on BUKHARA GRILL. As one of the defendants candidly acknowledged, there was then "no restaurant Bukhara in New York, and we just thought we will take the name." In addition to the name, the defendants' restaurant mimicked the logos, decor, staff uniforms, wood-slab menus, and red-checkered customer bibs of the plaintiff's restaurants. In 2003, ITC sued defendants in federal court in New York claiming that defendants' use of a similar mark for a restaurant in New York constituted trademark infringement, unfair competition, and false advertising in violation of federal and state law. As an affirmative defense, defendants charged ITC with abandonment of its United States rights to the BUKHARA mark and, on that ground, they filed a counterclaim seeking cancellation of the ITC registration. The district court awarded summary judgment in favor of defendants on all claims, and ITC appealed.]

. . .

B.   TRADEMARK INFRINGEMENT

. . .

[D]efendants submit that ITC's infringement claim [under both federal and state law] is necessarily defeated as a matter of law by proof that, by the time they opened their Bukhara Grill restaurants in New York, ITC had effectively abandoned the Bukhara mark in the United States. Like the district court, we conclude that defendants successfully established abandonment as a matter of law, warranting both summary judgment in their favor and cancellation of ITC's registered mark.

[ITC conceded that defendants had proved that ITC had not used the BUKHARA mark for restaurant services in the United States since August 28, 1997, giving rise to a presumption of abandonment. Nevertheless, ITC insisted that a triable issue of fact exists with respect to its intent to resume use of the service mark in the United States.]

ITC argues that four facts would allow a reasonable factfinder to infer its intent to resume use of the Bukhara mark for restaurants in the United States: (1) the reasonable grounds for its suspension of use of the mark, (2) its efforts to develop and market a Dal Bukhara line of packaged food, (3) its attempts to identify potential United States restaurant franchisees, and (4) its continued use of the Bukhara mark for restaurants outside the United States. We are not persuaded.

* Grounds for Suspending Use

ITC advances two reasons for suspending use of the Bukhara mark in the United States from 1997 to 2000: (a) Indian regulations requiring it to return profits earned abroad severely hindered its ability to open and operate profitable Bukhara restaurants in the United States, and (b) depressed market conditions in the hospitality industry from 1988 to 2003 inhibited its development of franchise partnerships in the United States. Because these reasons are unsupported by record evidence, they plainly cannot demonstrate the requisite intent.[11]

. . .

* Marketing Dal Bukhara Food Products

ITC points to only one piece of evidence during the relevant 1997-2000 period indicating its intent to use the name Bukhara in connection with packaged foods: the minutes from a July 27, 2000 corporate management committee meeting in India, which approved an initiative to market food products under the name "Bukhara Dal." Significantly, the minutes nowhere indicate ITC's intent to market this product in the United States, much less ITC's intent to resume use of the Bukhara mark for restaurants in this country. Accordingly, we conclude that the minutes, by themselves, are insufficient to create a genuine issue of material fact as to ITC's intent to resume use of its registered service mark in the United States.

The remaining evidence adduced by ITC all post-dates the relevant 1997-2000 period of non-use. . . . These acts, all occurring well after 2000 and suggesting future use of the Bukhara mark for a product other than restaurants, are insufficient to support the necessary inference that, *in the* non-use period, ITC maintained an intent to resume use of the mark for restaurants in the United States in the reasonably foreseeable future.

* Identifying Bukhara Franchisees

ITC argues that evidence of its discussions with various persons about expanding the Bukhara restaurant franchise to New York, California, and Texas creates a jury issue as to its intent to resume use of its registered mark within a reasonably foreseeable time. . . . [However, this evidence post-dated the 1997-2000 period of non-use that gives rise to the presumption of abandonment and makes no mention of any intent to resume use arising during this critical time frame. Accordingly, this evidence is insufficient to raise a material issue of fact.]

---

11. We do not decide whether such allegations, if supported by evidence, would permit any inference of ITC's intent to resume use of the Bukhara mark for restaurants in the foreseeable future. We note only that the conclusion is by no means obvious.

* Bukhara Restaurants Outside the United States

Finally, ITC cites *La Societe Anonyme des Parfums le Galion v. Jean Patou, Inc.* to support its argument that the continued operation of its Bukhara restaurants outside the United States demonstrates "an ongoing program to exploit the mark commercially," giving rise to an inference of an intent to resume the mark's use in this country. [cit.]. . . . Nothing in that case suggests that ongoing foreign use of a mark, by itself, supports an inference that the owner intends to re-employ a presumptively abandoned mark in the United States. Indeed, we identify no authority supporting that conclusion.

. . .

C.   Unfair Competition

1.   *Federal Claim Under Section 43(a)(1)(A) of the Lanham Act*

ITC claims that defendants violated section 43(a)(1)(A) of the Lanham Act by engaging in unfair competition in the use of its Bukhara mark and its related trade dress.[13] . . .

In light of our conclusion that, as a matter of law, ITC abandoned its registered Bukhara mark as of August 28, 2000, ITC confronts a high hurdle in demonstrating that, at the time of defendants' challenged actions, it possessed a priority right to the use of the Bukhara mark and related trade dress for restaurants in the United States. [cit.]; *Emergency One, Inc. v. American Fire Eagle Engine Co.*, 332 F.3d 264, 268 (4th Cir. 2003) ("The priority to use a mark . . . can be lost through abandonment."); *see also Exxon Corp. v. Humble Exploration Co.*, 695 F.2d at 103-04 (observing that it would be "incongruous" to allow plaintiff who had abandoned mark to successfully sue defendant for false designation or representation of origin). To clear this hurdle, ITC invokes the famous marks doctrine. It submits that, because (1) since 1977, it has continuously used its Bukhara mark and trade dress outside the United States; and (2) that mark was renowned in the United States before defendants opened their first Bukhara Grill restaurant in New York in 1999, it has a priority right to the mark sufficient to claim section 43(a)(1)(A) protection in this country. . . .

a.   The Territoriality Principle

The principle of territoriality is basic to American trademark law. . . . Precisely because a trademark has a separate legal existence under each country's laws, ownership of a mark in one country does not automatically confer upon the owner the exclusive right to use that mark in another country. Rather, a mark owner must take the proper steps to ensure that its rights to that mark are recognized in any country in which it seeks to assert them. *Cf. Barcelona.com, Inc. v. Excelentisimo Ayuntamiento de Barcelona*, 330 F.3d 617, 628 (4th Cir. 2003) ("United States courts do not entertain actions seeking to enforce trademark rights that exist only under foreign law."); [cit.].

As we have already noted, United States trademark rights are acquired by, and dependent upon, priority of use. [cit.] The territoriality principle requires the use to be in the United States for the owner to assert priority rights to the mark under the Lanham Act. [cit.] Thus, absent some use of its mark in the United States, a foreign mark holder

---

13. In its amended complaint, ITC also asserted an unfair competition claim under section 44(h) of the Lanham Act. [cit.] The district court did not explicitly pass on this claim in dismissing the entirety of ITC's complaint, and ITC does not press it on this appeal. Accordingly, we deem any such claim waived, [cit.], and we treat ITC's unfair competition claim as having been brought solely under section 43(a).

generally may not assert priority rights under federal law, even if a United States competitor has knowingly appropriated that mark for his own use. *See Person's Co. v. Christman*, 900 F.2d at 1569-70 (holding that foreign use is not sufficient to establish priority rights even over a United States competitor who took mark in bad faith).

b.   The Famous Marks Doctrine as an Exception to the Territoriality Principle

ITC urges us to recognize an exception to the territoriality principle for those foreign marks that, even if not used in the United States by their owners, have achieved a certain measure of fame within this country.

(1)   ORIGIN OF THE FAMOUS MARKS DOCTRINE

The famous marks doctrine is no new concept. It originated in the 1925 addition of Article 6*bis* to the Paris Convention. Article 6*bis*, which by its terms applies only to trademarks, requires member states

> ex officio if their legislation so permits, or at the request of an interested party, to refuse or to cancel the registration, and to prohibit the use, of a trademark which constitutes a reproduction, an imitation, or a translation, liable to create confusion, of a mark considered by the competent authority of the country of registration or use to be well known in that country as being already the mark of a person entitled to the benefits of this Convention and used for identical or similar goods. These provisions shall also apply when the essential part of the mark constitutes a reproduction of any such well-known mark or an imitation liable to create confusion therewith.

One commentator has observed that the "purpose" of Article 6*bis* "is to avoid the registration and use of a trademark, liable to create confusion with another mark already well known in the country of such registration or use, although the latter well-known mark is not, or not yet, protected in that country by a registration which would normally prevent the registration or use of the conflicting mark." G.H.C. Bodenhausen, *Guide to the Application of the Paris Convention for the Protection of Industrial Property* 90 (1968).

(2)   THE FAMOUS MARKS DOCTRINE IN THE UNITED STATES

(a)   State Common Law

The famous marks doctrine appears first to have been recognized in the United States by a New York trial court in a common law action for unfair competition in the use of a trademark. *See Maison Prunier v. Prunier's Rest. & Café*, 159 Misc. 551, 557-58 (N.Y. Sup. Ct. 1936). The owner of "Maison Prunier," a Paris restaurant with a branch in London, sought to enjoin defendants' operation of a New York City restaurant named "Prunier's Restaurant and Café." The New York restaurant had apparently adopted both the Paris restaurant's name and slogan ("*Tout ce qui vient de la mer*") and boldly advertised itself as "The Famous French Sea Food Restaurant." While the French plaintiff conceded that it had never operated a restaurant in the United States, it nevertheless sought relief for the unauthorized use of its name and mark under the common law of unfair competition.

In ruling in favor of the plaintiff, the trial court first observed that "the right of a French corporation to sue here for protection against unfair competition was expressly granted in [Article 10*bis* of] the [Paris] convention between the United States and various other powers for the protection of industrial property." [cit.] It then ruled that "actual competition in a product is not essential to relief under the doctrine of unfair competition." [cit.] The plaintiff was entitled to protection from "'any injury which might result to it from the deception of the public through the unauthorized use of its trade name, or a trade name which would lead the public to believe that it was in some way connected with the plaintiff.'" *Id.* at 556, 288 N.Y.S. at 534 (quoting *Long's Hat Stores Corp. v. Long's Clothes, Inc.*, 224 A.D. 497, 498 (1st Dep't 1928)). Although the court acknowledged the general rule of territoriality, [cit.] it recognized an exception to the rule where the second user was guilty of bad faith, [cit.]. The court identified the fame of the mark as a factor relevant to deciding whether the second user had, in good faith, made use of a mark without knowing of its prior use by another party. [cit.] The *Prunier* court concluded that the French plaintiff was entitled to protection against unfair competition because its trademark enjoyed "wide repute" and the facts of the case indicated a total lack of good faith on the part of the defendants. The basis of this holding, it should be noted, was not Article 6*bis* of the Paris Convention. Instead, the holding was based entirely on New York common law principles of unfair competition.

[The court also noted the decision of another New York trial court twenty years later in *Vaudable v. Montmartre, Inc.*, discussed in *Grupo Gigante, supra*, and emphasized that in granting the requested injunction the *Vaudable* "court concluded that the lack of direct competition between the two restaurants was 'immaterial' to a common law claim for unfair competition."]

(b) Federal Actions

(i) Trademark Board Rulings

A quarter century later, the federal Trademark Trial and Appeal Board (the "Trademark Board") invoked *Vaudable*'s recognition of the famous marks doctrine in several *inter partes* proceedings. . . .

. . . In applying this principle to this case, however, we identify a significant concern: nowhere in the three cited rulings does the Trademark Board state that its recognition of the famous marks doctrine derives from any provision of the Lanham Act or other federal law. Indeed, the federal basis for the Trademark Board's recognition of the famous marks doctrine is never expressly stated. Its reliance on *Vaudable* suggests that recognition derives from state common law. At least one Trademark Board member, however, has questioned whether state common law can support recognition of the famous marks doctrine as a matter of federal law:

> [I]t seems to me that the *Vaudable* decision according protection to the famous Maxim's restaurant in the United States . . . is inapplicable in this case since that decision was based on a theory of unfair competition, namely misappropriation, under the law of the State of New York. Under Federal law, it seems to me that application of the well-known marks doctrine depends on whether the applicable text of the Paris Convention . . . and, in particular, Article 6*bis* of that Convention, is self-executing [so as to become part of federal law].

Mother's Rests., Inc. v. Mother's Other Kitchen, Inc., 218 U.S.P.Q. 1046, *21 (Allen, concurring in part, dissenting in part) (internal citations omitted). Because we conclude that the Trademark Board's reliance on state law to recognize the famous marks doctrine falls outside the sphere to which we owe deference [an agency's interpretation of the statute it administers], we consider *de novo* the question of that doctrine's existence within federal trademark law.

(ii) Federal Case Law

To date, the Ninth Circuit Court of Appeals is the only federal appeals court to have recognized the famous marks doctrine as a matter of federal law. *See Grupo Gigante S.A. de C.V. v. Dallo & Co.*, 391 F.3d at 1088. . . .

In *Grupo Gigante*, the Ninth Circuit did not reference either the language of the Lanham Act nor Article 6*bis* of the Paris Convention to support recognition of the famous marks doctrine. Indeed, elsewhere in its opinion, the court specifically stated that the Paris Convention creates no "additional substantive rights" to those provided by the Lanham Act. . . . Thus, it appears that the Ninth Circuit recognized the famous marks doctrine as a matter of sound policy: "An absolute territoriality rule without a famous marks exception would promote customer confusion and fraud." Id. at 1094.

This court has twice referenced the famous marks doctrine, but on neither occasion were we required to decide whether it does, in fact, provide a legal basis for acquiring priority rights in the United States for a foreign mark not used in this country. *See Buti v. Impressa Perosa, S.R.L.*, 139 F.3d at 104 n.2 (referencing *Mother's Restaurants* and *Vaudable* but, in the end, concluding that famous marks doctrine "has no application here given that Impressa has made no claim under that doctrine"); *see also Empresa Cubana del Tabaco v. Culbro Corp.*, 399 F.3d at 481 (declining to decide whether famous marks doctrine should be recognized . . .).[19]

District courts in this Circuit have reached varying conclusions about the applicability of the famous marks doctrine to Lanham Act claims. In *Empresa Cubana del Tabaco v. Culbro Corp.*, 213 F. Supp. 2d at 283-84, Judge Sweet concluded that the rights identified in Article 6*bis* of the Paris Convention could not be pursued in a section 44(h) claim, but could be pursued under section 44(b); [*see also De Beers LV Trademark Ltd. v. DeBeers Diamond Syndicate Inc.*, 440 F. Supp. 2d 249 (S.D.N.Y. 2006) (supporting well-known mark claim under Section 43(a)].

[In 2005,] in *Almacenes Exito S.A. v. El Gallo Meat Market, Inc.*, Judge Rakoff reached a different conclusion, ruling that "[t]o the extent the famous marks doctrine is a creature of common law it may support state causes of action, but it has no place in federal law where Congress has enacted a statute, the Lanham Act, that carefully prescribes the bases for federal trademark claims," 381 F. Supp. 2d 324, 326-27 (S.D.N.Y. 2005) (internal citation omitted). Identifying the territoriality principle as a "bedrock principle of federal trademark law," [cit.], Judge Rakoff concluded that recognition of a famous marks exception represented "such a radical change in basic federal trademark law" that it could "only be made by Congress, not by the courts," [cit.]. He specifically rejected the argument advanced here by ITC, i.e., that the Lanham Act itself recognizes a famous marks exception by providing a foreign plaintiff with substantive rights identified in Article 6*bis*. He observed that "the Paris Convention, as incorporated by the Lanham Act, only requires 'national treatment.'" [cit.] We agree with this analysis for reasons discussed in the next two lettered subsections of this opinion.

(c)   Treaties Protecting Famous Marks and United States Implementing Legislation

ITC insists that Article 6*bis* of the Paris Convention, together with Article 16(2) [of TRIPS,] provides legal support for its claim to famous marks protection. . . . TRIPS Article 16(2) extends Article 6*bis* to service marks. [cit.]

At the outset, we observe that ITC does not specifically contend that these two treaty articles are self-executing. While *Vanity Fair Mills v. T. Eaton Co.*, 234 F.2d 633 (2d Cir. 1956), might support such an argument with respect to Article 6*bis* protection

---

19. In *Empresa Cubana*, however, we did observe, in *dictum*, that "[t]o the extent that a foreign entity attempts to utilize the famous marks doctrine as [a] basis for its right to a U.S. trademark and seeks to prevent another entity from using the mark in the United States, the claim should be brought under Section 43(a)." [cit.]

of trademarks, *see id.* at 640 (observing in *dictum* that, upon ratification by Congress, the Paris Convention required "no special legislation in the United States . . . to make [it] effective here"),[22] no similar conclusion can extend to Article 16(2) protection of service marks because TRIPS is plainly not a self-executing treaty. [cit.] While Congress has amended numerous federal statutes to implement specific provisions of the TRIPS agreement, it appears to have enacted no legislation aimed directly at Article 16(2).[23]

ITC nevertheless submits that Lanham Act sections 44(b) and (h) effectively incorporate the protections afforded famous marks by the Paris Convention and TRIPS. [cit.] ITC's argument is, however, at odds with this court's 2005 ruling in *Empresa Cubana del Tabaco v. Culbro Corporation*, 399 F.3d 462. In that case, we expressly held that the Paris Convention creates no substantive United States rights beyond those independently provided in the Lanham Act. [The court cited a number of cases holding that the Paris Convention simply guaranteed national treatment.] Although this statement was made in the context of a claim asserting substantive rights under Article 10*bis* of the Paris Convention, the reasoning applies with equal force to claimed famous marks protection under Article 6*bis* and TRIPS Article 16(2) because no famous marks rights are independently afforded by the Lanham Act. *See Almacenes Exito S.A. v. El Gallo Meat Mkt.*, 381 F. Supp. 2d at 327-28.

In reaching this conclusion, we are mindful that one leading commentator urges otherwise. [cit.] McCarthy concludes that "both the TRIPS Agreement and the Paris Convention Article 6*bis* require the United States to recognize rights" in famous foreign marks, even if they have not been registered or used in the United States. *See* 4 McCarthy, supra, §29:62, at 29-167. "In the author's view, this international obligation is enforced in the United States by Lanham Act §44(b) and §44(h)." [cit.] McCarthy appears to construe the statutory "entitle[ment] to effective protection against unfair competition," conferred by section 44(h), to create a federal right to famous marks protection "'coextensive with the substantive provisions'" of Articles 6*bis* and 16(2). [cit.] We cannot agree.

. . .

[W]e do not ourselves discern in the plain language of sections 44(b) and (h) a clear congressional intent to incorporate a famous marks exception into federal unfair competition law. Section 44(b) guarantees foreign mark holders only "the benefits of this section . . . to the extent necessary to give effect to any . . . convention, treaty or reciprocal law," as well as the "rights to which any owner of a mark is otherwise entitled by this chapter." 15 U.S.C. §1126(b). In short, whatever protections Article 6*bis* and Article 16(2) might contemplate for famous marks, section 44(b) grants foreign mark holders covered by these treaties only those protections of United States law already specified in the Lanham Act. [cit.] The Lanham Act's unfair competition protections, as we have already explained, are cabined by the long-established principle of territoriality. [cit.]

To the extent Section 44(h) references an "entitle[ment] to effective protection against unfair competition," 15 U.S.C. §1126(h), our precedent precludes us from construing this

---

22. *But see International Café, S.A.L. v. Hard Rock Café Int'l, Inc.*, 252 F.3d 1274, 1277 n.5 (11th Cir. 2001) (concluding that the Paris Convention is not self-executing because, on its face, it provides for effectiveness through domestic implementing legislation).

23. . . . Significantly, Congress has enacted legislation to implement TRIPs Article 16(3), which contemplates the extension of anti-dilution protection to certain famous marks. *See* Federal Trademark Dilution Act of 1995, Pub. L. No. 104-98, 109 Stat. 985 (1995) (codified at 15 U.S.C. §1125(c)); *see* H. Rep. 104-374, reprinted in 1995 U.S.C.C.A.N. 1029 (indicating that anti-dilution act was intended to make United States law consistent with terms of TRIPs and Paris Convention). No comparable legislation exists with respect to Article 16(2).

phrase to afford foreign mark holders any rights beyond those specified in section 44(b). *See Havana Club Holding, S.A. v. Galleon S.A.*, 203 F.3d 116, 134 (2d Cir. 2000) (characterizing the "[r]ights under section 44(h)" as "co-extensive with treaty rights under section 44(b), including treaty rights relating to . . . the repression of unfair competition" (internal quotation marks omitted)); [cit.].

We further note that, in section 44(d) of the Lanham Act, Congress detailed circumstances under which the holders of foreign *registered* marks can claim priority rights in the United States, notably including among those circumstances actual or intended use in the United States within a specified time. [cit.] Congress's specificity in dealing with registered marks cautions against reading a famous marks exception into sections 44(b) and (h), which nowhere reference the doctrine, much less the circumstances under which it would appropriately apply despite the fact that the foreign mark was not used in this country. . . . Before we construe the Lanham Act to include such a significant departure from the principle of territoriality, we will wait for Congress to express its intent more clearly.

(d)   Policy Rationales Cannot, by Themselves, Support Judicial Recognition of the Famous Marks Doctrine Under Federal Law

Even if the Lanham Act does not specifically incorporate Article 6*bis* and Article 16(2) protections for famous foreign marks, ITC urges this court to follow the Ninth Circuit's lead and to recognize the famous marks doctrine as a matter of sound policy. [cit.] ITC argues that the United States cannot expect other nations to protect famous American trademarks if United States courts decline to afford reciprocal protection to famous foreign marks.

We acknowledge that a persuasive policy argument can be advanced in support of the famous marks doctrine. [cit.] The fact that a doctrine may promote sound policy, however, is not a sufficient ground for its judicial recognition, particularly in an area regulated by statute. [cit.] In light of the comprehensive and frequently modified federal statutory scheme for trademark protection set forth in the Lanham Act, we conclude that any policy arguments in favor of the famous marks doctrine must be submitted to Congress for it to determine whether and under what circumstances to accord federal recognition to such an exception to the basic principle of territoriality. [cit.] Absent such congressional recognition, we must decline ITC's invitation to grant judicial recognition to the famous marks doctrine simply as a matter of sound policy.

For all these reasons, we affirm the district court's award of summary judgment in favor of defendants on ITC's federal unfair competition claim.

2.   State Common Law Claim for Unfair Competition

a.   ITC's Reliance on the Famous Marks Doctrine to Sue for Unfair Competition Under New York Law

ITC submits that, even if we affirm the district court's dismissal of its federal unfair competition claim, we must reverse the dismissal of its parallel state law claim. As it correctly observes, New York common law allows a plaintiff to sue for unfair competition where a "property right or a commercial advantage" has been "misappropriated." *Flexitized, Inc. v. National Flexitized Corp.*, 335 F.2d 774, 781-82 (2d Cir. 1964). Nevertheless, in light of ITC's abandonment of the Bukhara mark and dress for restaurants in the United States, its common law assertion of a "property right or a commercial advantage" in these designations based on their foreign use depends on whether New York recognizes the famous marks doctrine in the circumstances here at issue.

As we have already noted, at least two New York cases indicate such recognition as a general matter: *Vaudable v. Montmartre, Inc.*, 20 Misc. 2d 757, and *Maison Prunier v. Prunier's Rest. & Café*, 159 Misc. 551. Neither the New York Court of Appeals nor any intermediate New York appellate court, however, has ever specifically adopted the views expressed in *Prunier* and *Vaudable* to accord common law protection to the owners of famous marks. [The court thus decided to certify the question to the New York Court of Appeals for a definitive resolution.]

b. Certifying the Question of New York's Common Law Recognition of the Famous Marks Doctrine

[The court certified the following questions to the New York Court of Appeals: First, "[d]oes New York common law permit the owner of a famous mark or trade dress to assert property rights therein by virtue of the owner's prior use of the mark or dress in a foreign country?" If the New York Court of Appeals were to answer that question in the affirmative, the Second Circuit asked the New York Court to consider a second query: "How famous must a foreign mark or trade dress be to permit its owner to sue for unfair competition?"

Although the Second Circuit had not had any prior occasion to address this question, it noted for the New York court a number of possible standards. These standards included (a) secondary meaning in New York; (b) the "Ninth Circuit's compromise standard," which can be described as "secondary meaning plus"; and (c) "the high standard of recognition established by section 43(c) of the Lanham Act, the federal anti-dilution statute." The Second Circuit also noted that "should the Court of Appeals decide to articulate an entirely new and different standard of recognition for the application of the famous marks doctrine, among the factors it might consider are those identified as relevant in the non-binding 'Joint Recommendation Concerning Provisions on the Protection of Well-Known Marks,' adopted by the World Intellectual Property Organization in 1999:

[1] the degree of knowledge or recognition of the mark in the relevant sector of the public;

[2] the duration, extent and geographical area of any use of the mark;

[3] the duration, extent and geographical area of any promotion of the mark, including advertising or publicity and the presentation, at fairs or exhibitions, of the goods and/or services to which the mark applies;

[4] the duration and geographical area of any registrations, and/or any application for registration, of the mark, to the extent that they reflect use or recognition of the mark;

[5] the record of successful enforcement of rights in the mark, in particular, the extent to which the mark was recognized as well known by competent authorities; [and]

[6] the value associated with the mark.

World Intellectual Property Organization, Joint Recommendation Concerning Provisions on the Protection of Well-Known Marks (Sept. 1999), *available at http://www.wipo.int/ about-ip/en/development iplaw/pub 833.htm*."]

We express no view as to how New York should define its state common law. We simply reserve decision on ITC's challenge to the district court's dismissal of its state common law claim for unfair competition pending the New York Court of Appeals response to our certified questions.

. . .

BELMORA LLC v. BAYER CONSUMER CARE AG

819 F.3d 697 (4th Cir. 2016)

AGEE, Circuit Judge:

I.   BACKGROUND

A.   THE FLANAX MARK

[Bayer Consumer Care AG ("BCC")] registered the trademark FLANAX in Mexico for pharmaceutical products, analgesics, and anti-inflammatories. It has sold naproxen sodium tablets under the FLANAX brand in Mexico since 1976. FLANAX sales by BCC have totaled hundreds of millions of dollars, with a portion of the sales occurring in Mexican cities near the United States border. BCC's FLANAX brand is well-known in Mexico and other Latin American countries, as well as to Mexican-Americans and other Hispanics in the United States, but BCC has never marketed or sold its FLANAX in the United States. Instead, BCC's sister company, [Bayer Healthcare LLC ("BHC," and collectively with BCC, "Bayer")], sells naproxen sodium pain relievers under the brand ALEVE in the United States market.

Belmora LLC began selling naproxen sodium tablets in the United States as FLANAX in 2004. The following year, Belmora registered the FLANAX mark in the United States. Belmora's early FLANAX packaging (below, left) closely mimicked BCC's Mexican FLANAX packaging (right), displaying a similar color scheme, font size, and typeface.

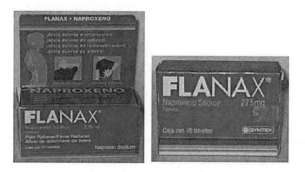

Belmora later modified its packaging (below), but the color scheme, font size, and typeface remain similar to that of BCC's FLANAX packaging.

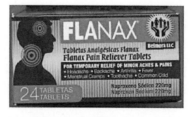

In addition to using similar packaging, Belmora made statements implying that its FLANAX brand was the same FLANAX product sold by BCC in Mexico. For example, Belmora circulated a brochure to prospective distributors that stated,

> For generations, Flanax has been a brand that Latinos have turned to for various common ailments. Now you too can profit from this highly recognized topselling brand among Latinos. Flanax is now made in the U.S. and continues to show record sales growth everywhere it is sold. Flanax acts as a powerful attraction for Latinos by providing them with products they know, trust and prefer.

Belmora also employed telemarketers and provided them with a script containing similar statements. This sales script stated that Belmora was "the direct producers of FLANAX in the US" and that "FLANAX is a very well known medical product in the Latino American market, for FLANAX is sold successfully in Mexico." Belmora's "sell sheet," used to solicit orders from retailers, likewise claimed that "Flanax products have been used [for] many, many years in Mexico" and are "now being produced in the United States by Belmora LLC."

Bayer points to evidence that these and similar materials resulted in Belmora's distributors, vendors, and marketers believing that its FLANAX was the same as or affiliated with BCC's FLANAX. For instance, Belmora received questions regarding whether it was legal for FLANAX to have been imported from Mexico. And an investigation of stores selling Belmora's FLANAX "identified at least 30 [purchasers] who believed that the Flanax products . . . were the same as, or affiliated with, the Flanax products they knew from Mexico."

B.   PROCEEDINGS BELOW

1.

In 2007, BCC petitioned the TTAB to cancel Belmora's registration for the FLANAX mark, arguing that Belmora's use and registration of the FLANAX mark violated Article 6bis of the Paris Convention "as made applicable by Sections 44(b) and (h) of the Lanham Act." BCC also sought cancellation of Belmora's registration under §14(3) of the Lanham Act because Belmora had used the FLANAX mark "to misrepresent the source of the goods . . . [on] which the mark is used."

The TTAB dismissed BCC's Article 6bis claim, concluding that Article 6bis "is not self-executing" and that §44 of the Lanham Act did not provide "an independent basis for cancellation." However, the TTAB allowed Bayer's §14(3) claim to proceed. In 2014 . . . the TTAB ordered cancellation of Belmora's FLANAX registration, concluding that Belmora had misrepresented the source of the FLANAX goods and that the facts "d[id] not present a close case." The TTAB noted that Belmora 1) knew the favorable reputation of Bayer's FLANAX product, 2) "copied" Bayer's packaging, and 3) "repeatedly invoked" that reputation when marketing its product in the United States.

2.

Shortly after the TTAB's ruling, Bayer filed suit in the Southern District of California, alleging that 1) BCC was injured by Belmora's false association with its FLANAX product in violation of Lanham Act §43(a)(1)(A), and 2) BCC and BHC were both injured by Belmora's false advertising of FLANAX under §43(a)(1)(B). The complaint also alleged three claims under California state law.

Belmora meanwhile appealed the TTAB's cancellation order and elected to proceed with the appeal as a civil action in the Eastern District of Virginia. It argued that the TTAB erred in concluding that Bayer "had standing and/or a cause of action" under §14(3) and in finding that Belmora had misrepresented the source of its goods. Belmora also sought a declaration that its actions had not violated the false association and false advertising provisions of Lanham Act §43(a), as Bayer had alleged in the California district court proceeding. Bayer filed a counterclaim challenging the TTAB's dismissal of its Paris Convention treaty claims.

The California case was transferred to the Eastern District of Virginia and consolidated with Belmora's pending action. Belmora then moved the district court to dismiss Bayer's §43(a) claims under Rule 12(b)(6) and for judgment on the pleadings under Rule 12(c) on the §14(3) claim. On February 6, 2015 . . . the district court issued a memorandum opinion and order ruling in favor of Belmora across the board.

The district court acknowledged that "Belmora's FLANAX . . . has a similar trade dress to Bayer's FLANAX and is marketed in such a way that capitalizes on the goodwill of Bayer's FLANAX." It nonetheless "distilled" the case "into one single question":

> Does the Lanham Act allow the owner of a foreign mark that is not registered in the United States and further has never used the mark in United States commerce to assert priority rights over a mark that is registered in the United States by another party and used in United States commerce?

The district court concluded that "[t]he answer is no" based on its reading of the Supreme Court's decision in *Lexmark International, Inc. v. Static Control Components, Inc.*, 134 S. Ct. 1377. Accordingly, the district court dismissed Bayer's false association and false advertising claims for lack of standing. At the same time, it reversed the TTAB's §14(3) cancellation order.

Bayer filed a timely notice of appeal, and we have jurisdiction under 28 U.S.C. §1291. The U.S. Patent and Trademark Office ("USPTO") intervened to defend the TTAB's decision to cancel Belmora's registration and to argue that the Lanham Act conforms to the United States' commitments in Article 6bis of the Paris Convention.[3]

II. DISCUSSION

. . .

A.   False Association and False Advertising Under Section 43(a)

The district court dismissed Bayer's false association[4] and false advertising claims because, in its view, the claims failed to satisfy the standards set forth by the Supreme Court in *Lexmark*. At the core of the district court's decision was its conclusion that 1) Bayer's claims fell outside the Lanham Act's "zone of interests"—and are not cognizable— "because Bayer does not possess a protectable interest in the FLANAX mark in the United States," and 2) that a "cognizable economic loss under the Lanham Act" cannot exist as to a "mark that was not used in United States commerce."

On appeal, Bayer contends these conclusions are erroneous as a matter of law because they conflict with the plain language of §43(a) and misread *Lexmark*.

---

3. The district court had agreed with the TTAB that Article [6*bis*] does not create an independent cause of action for the cancellation of Belmora's FLANAX registration. Because Bayer appears to have abandoned its treaty claims on appeal and their resolution is not necessary to our decision, we do not address any issue regarding the Paris Convention arguments.

4. As the district court pointed out, we have sometimes denominated Lanham Act §43(a)(1)(A) claims as "false designation" claims. We think it preferable to follow the Supreme Court's terminology in *Lexmark* and instead refer to such claims as those of "false association," although the terms can often be used interchangeably.

1.

"While much of the Lanham Act addresses the registration, use, and infringement of trademarks and related marks, §43(a) . . . goes beyond trademark protection." *Dastar Corp. v. Twentieth Century Fox Film Corp.*, 539 U.S. 23, 28-29 (2003). . . .

Subsection A, which creates liability for statements as to "affiliation, connection, or association" of goods, describes the cause of action known as "false association." Subsection B, which creates liability for "misrepresent[ing] the nature, characteristics, qualities, or geographic origin" of goods, defines the cause of action for "false advertising."

Significantly, the plain language of §43(a) does not require that a plaintiff possess or have used a trademark in U.S. commerce as an element of the cause of action. Section 43(a) stands in sharp contrast to Lanham Act §32, which is titled as and expressly addresses "infringement." 15 U.S.C. §1114 (requiring for liability the "use in commerce" of "any reproduction, counterfeit, copy, or colorable imitation *of a registered mark*" (emphasis added)). Under §43(a), it is the defendant's use in commerce—whether of an offending "word, term, name, symbol, or device" or of a "false or misleading description [or representation] of fact"—that creates the injury under the terms of the statute. And here the alleged offending "word, term, name, symbol, or device" is Belmora's FLANAX mark.

What §43(a) does require is that Bayer was "likely to be damaged" by Belmora's "use[] in commerce" of its FLANAX mark and related advertisements. The Supreme Court recently considered the breadth of this "likely to be damaged" language in *Lexmark*, a false advertising case arising from a dispute in the used-printer-cartridge market. 134 S. Ct. at 1383, 1388. The lower courts in *Lexmark* had analyzed the case in terms of "prudential standing"—that is, on grounds that are "prudential" rather than constitutional. Id. at 1386. The Supreme Court, however, observed that the real question in *Lexmark* was "whether Static Control has a cause of action under the statute." Id. at 1387. This query, in turn, hinged on "a straightforward question of statutory interpretation" to which it applied "traditional principles" of interpretation. Id. at 1388. As a threshold matter, the Supreme Court noted that courts must be careful not to import requirements into this analysis that Congress has not included in the statute:

> We do not ask whether in our judgment Congress should have authorized Static Control's suit, but whether Congress in fact did so. Just as a court cannot apply its independent policy judgment to recognize a cause of action that Congress has denied, it cannot limit a cause of action that Congress has created merely because "prudence" dictates.

Id.

The Court concluded that §43(a)'s broad authorization—permitting suit by "any person who believes that he or she is or is likely to be damaged"—should not be taken "literally" to reach the limits of Article III standing, but is framed by two "background principles," which may overlap. Id.

First, a plaintiff's claim must fall within the "zone of interests" protected by the statute. Id. The scope of the zone of interests is not "especially demanding," and the plaintiff receives the "benefit of any doubt." Id. at 1389. Because the Lanham Act contains an "unusual, and extraordinarily helpful" purpose statement in §45, identifying the statute's zone of interests "requires no guesswork." Id. Section 45 provides:

> The intent of this chapter is to regulate commerce within the control of Congress by making actionable the deceptive and misleading use of marks in such commerce; to protect registered marks used in such commerce from interference by State, or territorial legislation; to protect persons engaged in such commerce against unfair competition; to prevent fraud and deception

in such commerce by the use of reproductions, copies, counterfeits, or colorable imitations of registered marks; and to provide rights and remedies stipulated by treaties and conventions respecting trademarks, trade names, and unfair competition entered into between the United States and foreign nations.

Lanham Act §45, 15 U.S.C. §1127.[5]

The Supreme Court observed that "[m]ost of the enumerated purposes are relevant to a false-association case," while "a typical false-advertising case will implicate only the Act's goal of 'protecting persons engaged in commerce within the control of Congress against unfair competition.'" *Lexmark*, 134 S. Ct. at 1389. The Court concluded "that to come within the zone of interests in a suit for false advertising under [§43(a)], a plaintiff must allege an injury to a commercial interest in reputation or sales." Id. at 1390.

The second *Lexmark* background principle is that "a statutory cause of action is limited to plaintiffs whose injuries are proximately caused by violations of the statute." Id. The injury must have a "sufficiently close connection to the conduct the statute prohibits." Id. In the §43(a) context, this means "show[ing] economic or reputational injury flowing directly from the deception wrought by the defendant's advertising; and that that occurs when deception of consumers causes them to withhold trade from the plaintiff." Id. at 1391.

The primary lesson from *Lexmark* is clear: courts must interpret the Lanham Act according to what the statute says. To determine whether a plaintiff "falls within the class of plaintiffs whom Congress has authorized to sue," we "apply traditional principles of statutory interpretation." Id. at 1387. The outcome will rise and fall on the "meaning of the congressionally enacted provision creating a cause of action." Id. at 1388.

We now turn to apply these principles to the case before us.

2.

a.

We first address the position, pressed by Belmora and adopted by the district court, that a plaintiff must have initially used its own mark in commerce within the United States as a condition precedent to a §43(a) claim. In dismissing BCC's §43(a) claims, the district court found dispositive that "Bayer failed to plead facts showing that it used the FLANAX mark in commerce in [the] United States." Upon that ground, the district court held "that Bayer does not possess a protectable interest in the [FLANAX] mark."

As noted earlier, such a requirement is absent from §43(a)'s plain language and its application in *Lexmark*. Under the statute, the defendant must have "use[d] in commerce" the offending "word, term, name, [or] symbol," but the plaintiff need only "believe[ ] that he or she is or is likely to be damaged by such act."

It is important to emphasize that this is an unfair competition case, not a trademark infringement case. Belmora and the district court conflated the Lanham Act's infringement provision in §32 (which authorizes suit only "by the registrant," and thereby requires the

---

5. In the same section, the Lanham Act defines "commerce" as "all commerce which may lawfully be regulated by Congress." Lanham Act §45, 15 U.S.C. §1127. We have previously construed this phrase to mean that the term is "coterminous with that commerce that Congress may regulate under the Commerce Clause of the United States Constitution." *Int'l Bancorp, LLC v. Societe des Bains de Mer et du Cercle des Etrangers a Monaco*, 329 F.3d 359, 363-64 (4th Cir. 2003). "Commerce" in Lanham Act context is therefore an expansive concept that "necessarily includes all the explicitly identified variants of interstate commerce, foreign trade, and Indian commerce." Id. at 364 (citing U.S. Const. art. I, §8, cl. 3); see also infra n. 6.

plaintiff to have used its own mark in commerce) with unfair competition claims pled in this case under §43(a). Section 32 makes clear that Congress knew how to write a precondition of trademark possession and use into a Lanham Act cause of action when it chose to do so. It has not done so in §43(a).

Given that *Lexmark* advises courts to adhere to the statutory language, "apply[ing] traditional principles of statutory interpretation," *Lexmark*, 134 S. Ct. at 1388, we lack authority to introduce a requirement into §43(a) that Congress plainly omitted. Nothing in *Lexmark* can be read to suggest that §43(a) claims have an unstated requirement that the plaintiff have first used its own mark (word, term, name, symbol, or device) in U.S. commerce before a cause of action will lie against a defendant who is breaching the statute.

The district court thus erred in requiring Bayer, as the plaintiff, to have pled its prior use of its own mark in U.S. commerce when it is the defendant's use of a mark or misrepresentation that underlies the §43(a) unfair competition cause of action. Having made this foundational error, the district court's resolution of the issues requires reversal.[6]

Admittedly, some of our prior cases appear to have treated a plaintiff's use of a mark in United States commerce as a prerequisite for a false association claim. See *Lamparello v. Falwell*, 420 F.3d 309, 313 (4th Cir. 2005) ("Both infringement [under §32] and false designation of origin [under §43(a)] have [the same] five elements."); [cit.]. However, none of these cases made that consideration the ratio decidendi of its holding or analyzed whether the statute in fact contains such a requirement. [cit.] Moreover, all of these cases predate *Lexmark*, which provides the applicable Supreme Court precedent interpreting §43(a). [cit.]

Although the plaintiffs' use of a mark in U.S. commerce was a fact in common in [*Lamparello* and other cases cited by the court], substantial precedent reflects that §43(a) unfair competition claims come within the statute's protectable zone of interests without the preconditions adopted by the district court and advanced by Belmora. As the Supreme Court has pointed out, §43(a) "goes beyond trademark protection." *Dastar Corp.*, 539 U.S. at 29. For example, a plaintiff whose mark has become generic—and therefore not protectable—may plead an unfair competition claim against a competitor that uses that generic name and "fail[s] adequately to identify itself as distinct from the first organization" such that the name causes "confusion or a likelihood of confusion." *Blinded Veterans Ass'n v. Blinded Am. Veterans Found.*, 872 F.2d 1035, 1043 (D.C. Cir. 1989); see also *Kellogg Co. v. Nat'l Biscuit Co.*, 305 U.S. 111, 118-19 (1938) (requiring the defendant to "use reasonable care to inform the public of the source of its product" even though the plaintiff's "shredded wheat" mark was generic and therefore unprotectable); *Singer Mfg. Co. v. June Mfg. Co.*, 163 U.S. 169, 203-04 (1896) (same, for "Singer" sewing machines).

---

6. Even though the district court's error in transposing §43(a)'s requirements for a defendant's actions upon the plaintiff skews the entire analysis, the district court also confused the issues by ill-defining the economic location of the requisite unfair competition acts. As noted earlier, supra n. 5, a defendant's false association or false advertising conduct under §43(a) must occur in "commerce within the control of Congress." Such commerce is not limited to purchases and sales within the territorial limits of the United States as the district court seems to imply at times with regard to §43(a) and §14(3) claims. . . . Instead, as we explained in *International Bancorp*, Lanham Act "commerce" includes, among other things, "foreign trade" and is not limited to transactions solely within the borders of the United States. *Int'l Bancorp*, 329 F.3d at 364. Of course, any such "foreign trade" must satisfy the Lexmark "zone of interests" and "proximate cause" requirements to be cognizable for Lanham Act purposes.

Likewise, in a "reverse passing off" case, the plaintiff need not have used a mark in commerce to bring a §43(a) action. A reverse-passing-off plaintiff must prove four elements: "(1) that the work at issue originated with the plaintiff; (2) that origin of the work was falsely designated by the defendant; (3) that the false designation of origin was likely to cause consumer confusion; and (4) that the plaintiff was harmed by the defendant's false designation of origin." *Universal Furniture Int'l, Inc. v. Collezione Europa USA, Inc.*, 618 F.3d 417, 438 (4th Cir. 2010). Thus, the plaintiff in a reverse passing off case must plead and prove only that the work "originated with" him—not that he used the work (which may or may not be associated with a mark) in U.S. commerce. Id.

The generic mark and reverse passing off cases illustrate that §43(a) actions do not require, implicitly or otherwise, that a plaintiff have first used its own mark in United States commerce. If such a use were a condition precedent to bringing a §43(a) action, the generic mark and reverse passing off cases could not exist.

In sum, the Lanham Act's plain language contains no unstated requirement that a §43(a) plaintiff have used a U.S. trademark in U.S. commerce to bring a Lanham Act unfair competition claim. The Supreme Court's guidance in *Lexmark* does not allude to one, and our prior cases either only assumed or articulated as dicta that such a requirement existed. Thus, the district court erred in imposing such a condition precedent upon Bayer's claims.[8]

As Bayer is not barred from making a §43(a) claim, the proper *Lexmark* inquiry is twofold. Did the alleged acts of unfair competition fall within the Lanham Act's protected zone of interests? And if so, did Bayer plead proximate causation of a cognizable injury? We examine the false association and false advertising claims in turn.

b.

I.

As to the zone of interests, *Lexmark* advises that "[m]ost of the [Lanham Act's] enumerated purposes are relevant to false-association cases." One such enumerated purpose is "making actionable the deceptive and misleading use of marks" in "commerce within the control of Congress." Lanham Act §45, 15 U.S.C. §1127. . . . As pled, BCC's false association claim advances that purpose.

The complaint alleges Belmora's misleading association with BCC's FLANAX has caused BCC customers to buy the Belmora FLANAX in the United States instead of purchasing BCC's FLANAX in Mexico. For example, the complaint alleges that BCC invested heavily in promoting its FLANAX to Mexican citizens or Mexican-Americans in border areas. Those consumers cross into the United States and may purchase Belmora FLANAX

---

8. A plaintiff who relies only on foreign commercial activity may face difficulty proving a cognizable false association injury under §43(a). A few isolated consumers who confuse a mark with one seen abroad, based only on the presence of the mark on a product in this country and not other misleading conduct by the mark holder, would rarely seem to have a viable §43(a) claim. The story is different when a defendant, as alleged here, has—as a cornerstone of its business—intentionally passed off its goods in the United States as the same product commercially available in foreign markets in order to influence purchases by American consumers. See M. Kramer Mfg. Co. v. Andrews, 783 F.2d 421, 448 (4th Cir. 1986) ("[E]vidence of intentional, direct copying establishes a prima facie case of secondary meaning sufficient to shift the burden of persuasion to the defendant on that issue."). Such an intentional deception can go a long way toward establishing likelihood of confusion. See *Blinded Veterans*, 872 F.2d at 1045 ("Intent to deceive . . . retains potency; when present, it is probative evidence of a likelihood of confusion.").

here before returning to Mexico. And Mexican-Americans may forego purchasing the FLANAX they know when they cross the border to visit Mexico because Belmora's alleged deception led them to purchase the Belmora product in the United States.

In either circumstance, BCC loses sales revenue because Belmora's deceptive and misleading use of FLANAX conveys to consumers a false association with BCC's product. Further, by also deceiving distributors and vendors, Belmora makes its FLANAX more available to consumers, which would exacerbate BCC's losses. . . . In each scenario, the economic activity would be "within the control of Congress" to regulate. Lanham Act §45, 15 U.S.C. §1127.

We thus conclude that BCC has adequately pled a §43(a) false association claim for purposes of the zone of interests prong. Its allegations reflect the claim furthers the §45 purpose of preventing "the deceptive and misleading use of marks" in "commerce within the control of Congress."

II.

Turning to *Lexmark*'s second prong, proximate cause, BCC has also alleged injuries that "are proximately caused by [Belmora's] violations of the [false association] statute." The complaint can fairly be read to allege "economic or reputational injury flowing directly from the deception wrought by the defendant's" conduct. As previously noted, BCC alleges "substantial sales in major cities near the U.S.-Mexico border" and "millions of dollars promoting and advertising" its FLANAX brand in that region. Thus, BCC may plausibly have been damaged by Belmora's alleged deceptive use of the FLANAX mark in at least two ways. As reflected in the zone of interests discussion, BCC FLANAX customers in Mexico near the border may be deceived into foregoing a FLANAX purchase in Mexico as they cross the border to shop and buy the Belmora product in the United States. Second, Belmora is alleged to have targeted Mexican-Americans in the United States who were already familiar with the FLANAX mark from their purchases from BCC in Mexico. We can reasonably infer that some subset of those customers would buy BCC's FLANAX upon their return travels to Mexico if not for the alleged deception by Belmora. Consequently, BCC meets the *Lexmark* pleading requirement as to proximate cause.

BCC may ultimately be unable to prove that Belmora's deception "cause[d] [these consumers] to withhold trade from [BCC]" in either circumstance, *Lexmark*, 134 S. Ct. at 1391, but at the initial pleading stage we must draw all reasonable factual inferences in BCC's favor. Having done so, we hold BCC has sufficiently pled a §43(a) false association claim to survive Belmora's Rule 12(b)(6) motion. The district court erred in holding otherwise.

[The court was also satisfied that BCC and BCH's false advertising claim satisfied *Lexmark*.] . . .

d.

We thus conclude that the Lanham Act permits Bayer to proceed with its claims under §43(a)—BCC with its false association claim and both BCC and BHC with false advertising claims. It is worth noting, as the Supreme Court did in *Lexmark*, that "[a]lthough we conclude that [Bayer] has alleged an adequate basis to proceed under [§43(a)], it cannot obtain relief without evidence of injury proximately caused by [Belmora's alleged misconduct]. We hold only that [Bayer] is entitled to a chance to prove its case."

In granting Bayer that chance, we are not concluding that BCC has any specific trademark rights to the FLANAX mark in the United States. Belmora owns that mark. But trademark rights do not include using the mark to deceive customers as a form of unfair competition, as is alleged here. Should Bayer prevail and prove its §43(a) claims, an appropriate remedy might include directing Belmora to use the mark in a way that does not sow confusion. See Lanham Act §34(a), 15 U.S.C. §1116(a) (authorizing injunctions based on "principles of equity"). Of course, the precise remedy would be a determination to be made by the district court in the first instance upon proper evidence.[11] We leave any potential remedy to the district court's discretion should this case reach that point. We only note that any remedy should take into account traditional trademark principles relating to Belmora's ownership of the mark.

B.   Cancellation Under Section 14(3)

The TTAB ordered the cancellation of Belmora's FLANAX trademark under §14(3), finding that the preponderance of the evidence "readily establishe[d] blatant misuse of the FLANAX mark in a manner calculated to trade in the United States on the reputation and goodwill of petitioner's mark created by its use in Mexico." In reversing that decision and granting Belmora's motion for judgment on the pleadings, the district court found that BCC, as the §14(3) complainant, "lack[ed] standing to sue pursuant to *Lexmark*" under both the zone of interests and the proximate cause prongs. The district court also reversed the TTAB's holding that Belmora was using FLANAX to misrepresent the source of its goods "because Section 14(3) requires use of the mark in United States commerce and Bayer did not use the FLANAX mark in the United States."

On appeal, Bayer argues that the district court erred in overturning the TTAB's §14(3) decision because it "read a use requirement into the section that is simply not there." For reasons that largely overlap with the preceding §43(a) analysis, we agree with Bayer.

1.

Section 14(3) of the Lanham Act creates a procedure for petitioning to cancel the federal registration of a mark that the owner has used to misrepresent the source of goods. . . . The petitioner must establish that the "registrant deliberately sought to pass off its goods as those of petitioner." See 3 McCarthy, §20:30 (4th ed. 2002).

If successful, the result of a §14(3) petition "is the cancellation of a registration, not the cancellation of a trademark." Id. §20:40. Cancellation of registration strips an owner of "important legal rights and benefits" that accompany federal registration, but it "does not invalidate underlying common law rights in the trademark." Id. §20:68; see also *B & B Hardware Inc. v. Hargis Indus., Inc.*, ___ U.S. ___, 135 S. Ct. 1293, 1300 (2015).

To determine what parties §14(3) authorizes to petition for cancellation, we again apply the *Lexmark* framework. The relevant language in §14(3) closely tracks similar language from §43(a) that the Supreme Court considered in *Lexmark*: "[A]ny person who believes that he is or will be damaged" by the mark's registration may petition for cancellation under §14(3), just as "any person who believes that he or she is or is likely to be damaged" may bring an unfair competition action under §43(a). The same two-prong inquiry from *Lexmark* provides the mode of analysis.

---

11. For example, a remedy might include altering the font and color of the packaging or the "ready remedy" of attaching the manufacturer's name to the brand name. *Blinded Veterans*, 872 F.2d at 1047. Another option could be for the packaging to display a disclaimer—to correct for any deliberately created actual confusion. See id. ("The district court could, however, require [Blinded American Veterans Foundation] to attach a prominent disclaimer to its name alerting the public that it is not the same organization as, and is not associated with, the Blinded Veterans Association.").

To determine if a petitioner falls within the protected zone of interests, we note that §14(3) pertains to the same conduct targeted by §43(a) false association actions—using marks so as to misrepresent the source of goods. Therefore, "[m]ost of the [Lanham Act's] enumerated purposes are relevant" to §14(3) claims as well. See *Lexmark*, 134 S. Ct. at 1389. As for proximate cause, we once again consider whether the plaintiff has "show[n] economic or reputational injury flowing directly from the deception wrought by the defendant's [conduct]."[12] Id. at 1391. As with §43(a), neither §14(3) nor *Lexmark* mandate that the plaintiff have used the challenged mark in United States commerce as a condition precedent to its claim. See *Empresa Cubana Del Tabaco v. Gen. Cigar Co.*, 753 F.3d 1270, 1278 (Fed. Cir. 2014) ("In the proceedings before the Board, however, Cubatabaco need not own the mark to cancel the Registrations under [Section 14(3)].").

2.

Applying the framework from *Lexmark*, we conclude that the Lanham Act authorizes BCC to bring its §14(3) action against Belmora. BCC's cancellation claim falls within the Lanham Act's zone of interests because it confronts the "deceptive and misleading use of marks." Lanham Act §45, 15 U.S.C. §1127. And BCC has also adequately pled a proximately caused injury to survive Belmora's Rule 12(c) motion for the same reasons previously discussed for the false association and false advertising claims. The district court thus erred in reversing the TTAB's decision cancelling the registration of Belmora's FLANAX mark.

Vacated and Remanded.

NOTES AND QUESTIONS

1.   *The international dimension.* In what ways is the doctrine articulated in *Person's* different from the doctrinal rules governing geographically separate use articulated in the purely domestic context by the *United Drug* and other courts? To what extent are the different results a product of the same trademark theories? What justifies the differences in treatment of the national and international settings? The Ninth Circuit notes that if the dispute had been between an "Arizonan Grupo Gigante" and the Dallos brothers, a different "territoriality" rule (*Tea Rose–Rectanus*) would have applied. Why? See Graeme B. Dinwoodie, *Trademarks and Territory: Detaching Trademark Law from the Nation-State*, 41 Hous. L. Rev. 885 (2004) (suggesting a distinction between "intrinsic" territoriality and "political" territoriality, which gives rise to a different result in domestic and international cases).

2.   *Exceptions to the rule of territoriality.* The *Person's* court recognizes two exceptions to the general principle of territoriality. What are they, and why does the court recognize these exceptions?

3.   *The "famous" or "well-known marks" doctrine.* Why does the Paris Convention contain Article 6*bis*? Until a flurry of case law after the turn of the century, U.S. courts had

---

12. The USPTO suggests that §14(3) might require a lesser showing of causation because it sets forth an administrative remedy, whereas the Supreme Court based its *Lexmark* analysis on common law requirements for judicial remedies. See *Empresa Cubana Del Tabaco v. Gen. Cigar Co.*, 753 F.3d 1270, 1275 (Fed. Cir. 2014) ("A petitioner is authorized by statute to seek cancellation of a mark where it has both a real interest in the proceedings as well as a reasonable basis for its belief of damage."). We need not resolve this issue for purposes of the current decision.

rarely tackled the well-known marks doctrine. Why might that be? (Reread Article 6*bis* and consider how the United States might best be said to comply with the obligation to protect well-known marks.) *See* Dinwoodie, *Trademarks and Territory, supra* at 913. Which of the *Grupo Gigante* and *ITC* courts has the better of the argument regarding the existence of the well-known marks doctrine in federal law? On what provision of the Lanham Act (or any other source) would you rest a claim to protect a well-known mark that had not been used in the United States? To what extent is the result in *Belmora* different from that which might have pertained after a claim that Flanax was a well-known mark?

4.   *The well-known mark doctrine before the TTAB.* As the Federal Circuit recognized in *Person's*, the Trademark Trial and Appeal Board had for many years recognized the well-known mark doctrine. *See, e.g., The All England Lawn Tennis Club (Wimbledon) Ltd. v. Creations Aromatiques, Inc.*, 220 U.S.P.Q. 1069, 1072 (T.T.A.B. 1983); *Mother's Rests, Inc. v. Mother's Other Kitchen, Inc.*, 218 U.S.P.Q. 1046, 1048 (T.T.A.B. 1983); *Franpovi SA v. Wessin*, 89 U.S.P.Q.2d (BNA) 1637 (TTAB 2009) (allowing opposition to proceed on basis of the well-known mark doctrine). But, as reflected in *Belmora*, the Board has in recent years retrenched in light of the language of Section 2(d). *See also In Sun Hee Jung v. Magic Snow, LLC*, 2017 WL 4174422 (TTAB Sept. 20, 2017) (holding that "the 'well known mark' doctrine provides no basis for a Section 2(d) ground for opposition because it does not establish use of the mark in the United States as required by the statutory language of that section"). Is the United States thus in violation of Article 6bis of the Paris Convention? *See id.* (noting that this holding was not altered by the United States–Korea Free Trade Agreement, which incorporates the Paris Convention, because that agreement was not self-executing). In *Belmora*, the losing registrant, rather than appealing to the Federal Circuit, filed a notice of election to have review of the TTAB cancellation order by a district court in the Fourth Circuit under Section 21 of the Lanham Act. Assume that the Fourth Circuit and the Federal Circuit disagree on the existence of a well-known mark doctrine; which case law should the court apply?

5.   *Defining a well-known mark under U.S. law.* The Ninth Circuit decision in *Grupo Gigante* is the only federal appellate analysis of the precise level of fame or distinctiveness required to show that a mark is well known or famous for the purposes of this Article 6*bis*–related doctrine. *See also Empresa Cubana del Tabaco v. Culboro Corp.*, 70 U.S.P.Q.2d (BNA) 1650 (S.D.N.Y. 2004), *rev'd on other grounds, Empresa Cubana del Tabaco v. Culboro Corp.*, 399 F.3d 462 (2d Cir. 2005). Do you agree with the standard articulated by the majority? Would the statutory basis for the doctrine (if one exists) affect your analysis? Judge Graber formally writes only to question whether the plaintiffs' evidence was sufficient as a matter of law to meet the standard announced by the court. To support her argument that it was not, Judge Graber is required to elaborate on the application of the court's "heightened" standard. Do you agree with this "elaboration," and is it fully consistent with the standard articulated in Judge Kleinfeld's opinion? Is the standard of "fame" required for a mark to receive protection under the doctrine discussed in *Grupo Gigante* and *Person's* the same as the standard required for a showing of "fame" for the purposes of dilution protection? *See infra* Chapter 8. Should the number of foreign registrations matter? *Cf. In re Bayer AG*, 488 F.3d 960 (Fed. Cir. 2007). If not, perhaps we need to refer to a standard of fame *for the purposes of dilution protection* and a separate standard of fame *for the purposes of the well-known marks doctrine*. Alternatively, and perhaps preferably, we could simply start referring to the doctrine discussed in these cases as the "well-known marks doctrine," as the Paris Convention would suggest. For a critique of the standard required to show "well-known" status, *see* Graeme B. Dinwoodie, *Trademarks and Territory: Detaching Trademark Law from the Nation-State*, 41 Hous. L. Rev. 885 (2004). Should the intent of the foreign mark owner to use its mark in the

United States be relevant to whether that mark should be protected in the United States under the well-known marks doctrine? *See Fiat Group Automobiles S.p.A. v. ISM, Inc.*, 94 U.S.P.Q.2d (BNA) 1111, 1114-16 (TTAB 2010) (allowing understanding of what is a "famous" mark for purposes of opposition based on alleged dilution of well-known mark used only abroad to be informed by the statutory definition of "mark" including the "intent to use coupled with the filing of an application"). The *Grupo Gigante* court talks of the mark being well known in the relevant American market. In what circumstances would it be appropriate to regard the relevant market as comprising the entire United States? *See Paleteria La Michoacana v. Productos Lacteos Tocumbo S.A.*, 69 F. Supp. 2d 175 (D.D.C. 2014).

6. *Scope of protection for well-known marks.* If a mark is well known in the United States, what should be the scope of protection it receives? Protection against confusion? Protection against dilution (as you will discover in Chapter 8, only "famous" marks receive protection against dilution under Section 43(c)). *See Fiat Group Automobiles S.p.A. v. ISM, Inc.*, 94 U.S.P.Q.2d (BNA) 1111 (TTAB 2010). As a matter of international law, compare Article 6*bis* of the Paris Convention, Article 16(3) of TRIPS, and Article 4 of WIPO's Joint Recommendation Concerning Provisions on the Protection of Well-Known Marks (Sept. 1999).

7. *International definition of "well-known marks."* Article 16(2) of the TRIPS Agreement offers guidance as to the meaning of "well-known marks" under international law. It states that "[i]n determining whether a trade mark is well-known, members shall take account of the knowledge of the trade mark in the relevant sector of the public, including knowledge in the member concerned which has been obtained as a result of the promotion of the trademark." As the *ITC* court notes, even more detailed provision is found in a joint nonbinding recommendation of the WIPO and Paris Union assemblies. In addition to the provisions quoted by the Second Circuit, the WIPO Joint Recommendation, art. 2(3)(i), prohibits member states from requiring that a mark be used in a member state as a condition for protection as "well known." If the Second Circuit is correct in its interpretation of federal law, is the United States in violation of international obligations? *See* Free Trade Agreement, May 6, 2003, U.S.-Sing., art. 16.2(b)(1) (providing that each party shall give effect to the Joint Recommendation on Well-Known Marks); *see generally* Dinwoodie, *Trademark and Territory, supra* at 924.

8. *Further proceedings in* Punchgini. The New York Court of Appeals answered (somewhat obliquely) the questions certified to it by the Second Circuit. *See ITC Ltd. v. Punchgini, Inc.*, 880 N.E.2d 852 (2007). Noting that New York had "long recognized two theories of common-law unfair competition, palming off and misappropriation," the Court held that

> the New York cases cited by the District Court and the Second Circuit as embodying the famous or well-known marks doctrine in New York common law—*Prunier* and *Vaudable*—were, in fact, decided wholly on misappropriation theories. . . . What *Prunier* and *Vaudable* stand for then, is the proposition that for certain kinds of businesses (particularly cachet goods/services with highly mobile clienteles), goodwill can, and does, cross state and national boundary lines. Accordingly, while we answer "Yes" to the first certified question, we are not thereby recognizing the famous or well-known marks doctrine, or any other new theory of liability under the New York law of unfair competition. Instead, we simply reaffirm that when a business, through renown in New York, possesses goodwill constituting property or a commercial advantage in this state, that goodwill is protected from misappropriation under New York unfair competition law. This is so whether the business is domestic or foreign.

The Court then elaborated on the elements of such a claim. It required: (1) "actual goodwill" in New York"; and (2) appropriation (i.e., deliberate copying) of that goodwill.

Although the Court did not provide an exhaustive list of the factors relevant to whether goodwill existed, it listed as relevant "evidence that the defendant intentionally associated its goods with those of the foreign plaintiff in the minds of the public, such as public statements or advertising stating or implying a connection with the foreign plaintiff; direct evidence, such as consumer surveys, indicating that consumers of defendant's goods or services believe them to be associated with the plaintiff; and evidence of actual overlap between customers of the New York defendant and the foreign plaintiff."

When the *Punchgini* case returned to the federal courts, the Court of Appeals for the Second Circuit affirmed the summary dismissal of the plaintiff's claims under New York law. *See ITC Ltd. v. Punchgini, Inc.*, 518 F.3d 159 (2d Cir. 2008). The court held that although ITC adduced sufficient evidence of deliberate copying, the test articulated by the New York Court of Appeals required that the plaintiff also show that "the BUKHARA mark, when used in New York, calls to mind for defendant's potential customers ITC's goodwill, or that defendant's customers primarily associate the BUKHARA mark with ITC," and ITC had failed to offer proof on this secondary meaning issue. The Second Circuit explained:

> [W]e observe that ITC's proffered evidence of goodwill derived entirely from foreign media reports and sources and was unaccompanied by any evidence that would permit an inference that such reports or sources reach the relevant consumer market in New York. ITC proffered no evidence that it had "directly targeted advertising of its Indian or other foreign 'Bukhara' restaurants to the United States." It made no attempt to prove its goodwill in the relevant market through consumer study evidence linking the Bukhara mark to itself, and it presented no research reports demonstrating strong brand name recognition for the Bukhara mark anywhere in the United States. Moreover, the record is devoid of any evidence of actual overlap between customers of defendants' restaurant and ITC's Bukhara. . . .

Nor would the Second Circuit allow the plaintiff to rely on the one element of the New York Court of Appeals' test (deliberate copying) to prove the other (consumer association).

9. *Federal and state comparisons.* How does the cause of action endorsed by the New York Court of Appeals differ from the protection offered well-known marks by the *Grupo Gigante* court? How does the standard of "actual goodwill" in the second element of the New York test differ from the distinctiveness that a trademark plaintiff must show to make out an infringement case? How does it differ from the standard of fame required to make out a dilution claim under federal law? From the "secondary meaning plus" standard of *Grupo Gigante*?

INTERNATIONAL BANCORP, LLC v. SOCIETE DES BAINS DE MER ET DU CERCLE DES ETRANGERS A MONACO

329 F.3d 359 (4th Cir. 2003), cert. denied, 540 U.S. 1106 (2004)

LUTTIG, Circuit Judge:

Plaintiff companies appeal from the district court's summary judgment that their registration and use of forty-three domain addresses infringe a foreign corporation's rights under the Lanham Act . . . where the foreign corporation advertised its trademark domestically, but only rendered services under it abroad. We conclude that the district court's judgment, although not its reasoning, was correct, and therefore affirm.

I

Appellee, Societe des Bains de Mer et du Cercle des Etrangers a Monaco ("SBM"), owns and operates historic properties in Monte Carlo, Monaco, including resort and casino facilities. One of its properties, a casino, has operated under the "Casino de Monte Carlo" trademark since 1863. The mark is registered in Monaco, but not in the United States. SBM promotes this casino, along with its other properties, around the world. For 18 years, SBM has promoted its properties from a New York office staffed with four employees. SBM's promotions within the United States, funded with $1 million annually, include trade show participation, advertising campaigns, charity partnerships, direct mail solicitation, telephone marketing, and solicitation of media coverage.

Appellants, the plaintiff companies, are five companies [domiciled in the United Kingdom, and] formed and controlled by a French national, which operate more than 150 web sites devoted to online gambling. Included in this roster are 53 web sites whose domain addresses incorporate some portion of the term "Casino de Monte Carlo."[1] These web sites, along with the gambling software they employ, also exhibit pictures of *the* Casino de Monte Carlo's exterior and interior, contain renderings that are strikingly similar to the Casino de Monte Carlo's interior, and make allusion to the geographic location of Monte Carlo, implying that they offer online gambling as an alternative to *their* Monaco-based casino, though they operate no such facility.

[After the development of a dispute between the parties regarding the ownership of the domain names,] the plaintiff companies brought suit in federal court against SBM seeking declaratory judgment . . . that they are entitled to the disputed domain names. SBM counterclaimed under the Lanham Act for trademark infringement under section 1125(a); trademark dilution under section 1125(c); cybersquatting under section 1125(d)(1); and unfair competition in violation of section 1126(h). The district court ruled against SBM on its section 1125(c) trademark dilution claim . . . and on its section 1126(h) unfair competition claim. But the court ruled in favor of SBM on its trademark infringement claim. . . . The plaintiff companies now appeal from that adverse judgment.

. . .

III

[The plaintiff companies claimed that SBM did not have a protectable interest in the "Casino de Monte Carlo" mark because the mark was neither used in commerce, nor was it distinctive.]

A

[The court and parties agreed that the critical question in assessing whether SBM "used its mark in commerce" is whether the *services* SBM provided under the "Casino de Monte Carlo" mark were rendered in commerce. The majority noted that the Lanham Act defined the term "commerce" as "all commerce which may lawfully be regulated by Congress."]

Understanding commerce under the Act to be coterminous with that commerce Congress may regulate under the Commerce Clause, we turn next to the determination of what constitutes "*use in* commerce" under the Act. Again we rely on section 1127, which provides, of particular relevance here, a specific definition of that term as it relates to servicemarks, which the "Casino de Monte Carlo" mark unquestionably is:

> The term "use in commerce" means the *bona fide use of a mark in the ordinary course of trade, and not made merely to reserve a right in a mark.* For purposes of this chapter, a mark shall be deemed to be used in commerce—

---

1. *E.g.*, casinodemontecarlo.com, casinodemontecarlo.net, casinomontecarlo.com, casino-monte carlo.net, casinomontecarlo.org, and casinomontecarlo.net.

. . .

> (2) *on services* when it is used or displayed in the sale or advertising of services *and the services are rendered in commerce,* or the services are rendered in more than one State or in the United States and a foreign country and the person rendering the services is engaged in commerce in connection with the services.

15 U.S.C. §1127 (emphasis added).

Consistent with this definition of the statutory "use in commerce" requirement, the Supreme Court has said that "[t]here is no such thing as property in a trade-mark except as a right appurtenant to an established business or trade in connection with which the mark is employed. . . . [T]he right to a particular mark grows out of its use, not its mere adoption"; *United Drug Co. v. Theodore Rectanus, Co.,* 248 U.S. 90, 97 (1918). Because a mark is used in commerce only if it accompanies services rendered in commerce, *i.e.,* it is employed appurtenant to an established business or trade that is in commerce, "mere advertising" of that mark does not establish its protectability though advertising is itself commerce that Congress may regulate.

With these principles in clear view, we proceed to address whether the "Casino de Monte Carlo" mark was used in commerce. [The court concluded that there was no evidence that the SBM New York office booked reservations to the casino (as opposed to various SBM resorts) and that the operations of the New York office insofar as they pertained to the casino were merely promotional in nature.]

The Lanham Act and the Supreme Court . . . make clear that a mark's protection may not be based on "mere advertising."

Because SBM presented no record evidence that the New York office did anything other than advertise the "Casino de Monte Carlo" mark, if its case rested on this alone, the plaintiff companies would have the better of the argument. When they appeared before the court, however, we asked the parties to address . . . whether the casino services at issue were rendered in foreign trade, and the plaintiff companies conceded that the record contained evidence that United States citizens went to and gambled at the casino. This concession, when taken together with the undisputed fact that the Casino de Monte Carlo is a subject of a foreign nation, makes unavoidable the legal conclusion that foreign trade was present here, and that as such, so also was "commerce" under the Lanham Act.

Since the nineteenth century, it has been well established that the Commerce Clause reaches to foreign trade. And, for the same length of time, the Supreme Court has defined foreign trade as trade between subjects of the United States and subjects of a foreign nation. *See In re: Trade-Mark Cases,* 100 U.S. 82, 96 (1879). . . . [W]hile SBM's promotions within the United States do not on their own constitute a use in commerce of the "Casino de Monte Carlo" mark, the mark is nonetheless used in commerce because United States citizens purchase casino services sold by a subject of a foreign nation, which purchases constitute trade with a foreign nation that Congress may regulate under the Commerce Clause. And SBM's promotions "use[] or display[] [the mark] in the sale or advertising of [these] services . . . rendered in commerce."

. . .

Because SBM used its mark in the sale and advertising of its gambling services to United States citizens; because its rendering of gambling services to United States citizens constitutes foreign trade; because foreign trade is commerce Congress may lawfully regulate; and because commerce under the Lanham Act comprises all commerce that Congress may lawfully regulate, the services SBM renders under the "Casino de Monte Carlo" mark to citizens of the United States are services rendered in commerce, and the "use in commerce" requirement that the Lanham Act sets forth for the mark's protectability is satisfied.

B

The use of an unregistered mark in foreign trade does not in any way assure its owner that the mark will merit Lanham Act protection; it only makes such protection possible. For an unregistered mark that is used in foreign trade to merit Lanham Act protection, that mark must be distinctive among United States consumers. The plaintiff companies argue that even if the "Casino de Monte Carlo" mark is used in commerce, it is not distinctive because it is merely geographically descriptive, and that since it is not distinctive, it is not protectable.

[The court held that, although geographically descriptive, the mark possessed secondary meaning and could thus be protected. The court relied on the typical factors relevant to a secondary meaning inquiry (including substantial advertising and sales success in the United States), and noted also that under the Fourth Circuit case law of *Larsen v. Terk Technologies*, 151 F.3d 140 (4th Cir. 1998), SBM could meet its burden of proving secondary meaning because it had established that the plaintiff companies *directly* and *intentionally* copied the "Casino de Monte Carlo" mark. Under *Larsen*, a trademark plaintiff that proves that the defendant directly and intentionally copied its mark is presumed to have proved that mark's secondary meaning, and the defendant must then disprove that presumption.]

D

. . .

As to the dissent's failings, as we imagine them, first the dissent conflates the two distinct aspects of the statutory "use in commerce" requirement. The distinct elements of the analysis are set out above. [cit.] But in short, section 1127 defines the term "use in commerce" with respect to services as being when a mark is "used or displayed in the sale or advertising of services *and* the services are rendered in commerce." As a consequence of the *conjunctive* command, it is not enough for a mark owner simply to render services in foreign commerce for it to be eligible for trademark protection. Nor is it enough for a mark owner simply to use or display a mark in the sale or advertising of services to United States consumers. *Both* elements are required, and *both* elements must be distinctly analyzed.

. . .

The dissent's different understanding of the statute and of the two elements it sets out for establishing "use in commerce" is that *both* elements of "use in commerce" must occur within the geographic borders of the United States, a merging of the contents of the two elements that is not provided for by the statute. The dissent believes it can defend this proposition on the basis that many courts over the years have said that "use" must occur in the United States in order for a mark to merit Lanham Act protection. But, a "use in commerce" whose elements occur, as here, both in the United States and abroad is not exclusive foreign use, and is not controlled by the principles of law upon which the dissent relies. Indeed, that the statute's definition of the term "commerce" encompasses foreign commerce (thus naturally including some services rendered outside the United States borders) points, in fact, in the opposite direction from the dissent's conclusion.

[Moreover, while] the authorities to which the dissent cites . . . support the general contention that "use" must be in the United States, they do not support the very different conclusion that *both* distinct elements of the statutory "use in commerce" definition for servicemarks must occur within the United States. . . .

The dissent suggests that the Federal Circuit opposes our rule. In particular, it points to *Person's Co. Ltd. v. Christman*, 900 F.2d 1565 (Fed. Cir. 1990). In *Person's*, [while] the record did disclose a single occurrence when a United States citizen purchased goods in

Japan from the company, thus arguably meeting the commerce requirement, no evidence whatsoever was proffered that the company had in any way used or displayed its mark to advertise or sell its product to United States consumers. Thus it was that only "foreign use" (*i.e.*, the foreign advertising of its product to foreign consumers) of the mark existed. Of course, the court's rejection of *such* foreign use in no way reflects upon the case before us today where SBM did use and display its mark to advertise or sell its services in the United States to United States consumers.[8]

. . .

As to the dissent's last principal basis for its objection to our holding today, it is one of policy. The dissent fears that we are undoing all of the good of our country's trademark laws. [cit.] We do concede that policy is not our forte. But, we cannot help but note that since avoidance of consumer confusion is the ultimate end of all trademark law, this case presents a paradigmatic situation in which we may see our laws working, as intended, to reduce consumer confusion.

Indeed, the very fact that the Board [has] acknowledge[d] that foreign trademarks deemed "famous" can, with neither a demonstrated connection to qualifying commerce nor a demonstrated use or display of the mark in order to advertise or sell services in such qualifying commerce, enjoy Lanham Act protection, [cit.], illustrates the very real interest that our trademark laws have in minimizing consumer confusion, so that our economy may enjoy the greatest possible of efficiencies and confirms that trademarks developed overseas can themselves lead to such undesirable and inefficient consumer confusion here at home.

Ultimately, though, if SBM's mark merits protection under the statute, we must provide it to them.[14] We do not know that this is "reverse imperialism," *see post* at 389, but we do know that the law requires that we permit mark owners like SBM to petition our courts for protection. And we know as well that if such owners, upon their petition, can demonstrate that they meet the requirements of the statute, that they are then *entitled* to protection, and that it is beyond us to refuse it to them.

[The majority found that it could not conclude that the district court committed clear error in determining that the plaintiff companies' use of the mark would cause consumer confusion and thus affirmed the district court's grant of summary judgment to SBM.]

Diana Gribbon Motz, Circuit Judge, dissenting:

The majority reaches the unprecedented conclusion that an entity's use of its foreign trademark solely to sell services in a foreign country entitles it to trademark protection

---

8. The dissent suggests that our distinguishing of *Person's* must be wrong because application of our rule to the facts of the *Person's* case would result in a different outcome than the Federal Circuit reached in that case. [cit.] That is not correct. The statutory provision we apply today is directed solely and specifically to *services* and to evaluating what constitutes use in commerce for servicemarks. We would not apply our interpretation of the statutory provisions addressing services to a case involving goods. . . .

14. The dissent also implies that since SBM could register its mark in the United States, we should not be overly concerned with providing them the right of Lanham Act protection we today provide them. [cit.] That fact is, in our minds, as irrelevant here as it would be in a case involving a domestic manufacturer who, having sold products in interstate commerce under an unregistered mark, sought the protection of the Lanham Act from an infringer. It is inconceivable that courts would interpret the Lanham Act to punish such mark owners for failing to register their mark where their mark otherwise meets the statutory requirements for protection. Here, as much, it is inconceivable that SBM's registration status should affect our analysis of whether or not its mark qualifies for protection under the plain text of the statute.

under United States law, even though the foreign mark holder has never used or registered its mark in the United States. In my view, the majority errs in holding that the protection of United States trademark law extends to a mark used exclusively in Monaco by a company incorporated there. For this reason and others set forth within, I respectfully dissent.

I

[Under 15 U.S.C. §1127], there are two essential elements that must be present to constitute "use in commerce" for Lanham Act purposes: (1) advertising that employs the mark and (2) the rendering of services to which the mark attaches. Neither alone is sufficient. This two-pronged statutory meaning of "use in commerce" is what I refer to when I say that SBM did not "use" its mark in commerce because it did not "use" the mark in the United States.[1] Prior to today's holding, all existing authority, employing precisely this same two-pronged understanding of use, has similarly concluded that use in the United States is necessary to meet the Lanham Act's use in commerce requirement. None of this authority has ever suggested that if one element of the use in commerce requirement—advertising—takes place in the United States while the other—the rendering of services—occurs outside the United States, there has been use in the United States. Both elements must occur in the United States in order to satisfy the use in commerce requirement.

[B]ecause SBM has not rendered its casino services in the United States, it has not satisfied the statutory use in commerce requirement in a manner sufficient to merit protection under the Lanham Act. . . .

[I]t has long been recognized that use of a foreign mark in a foreign country creates no trademark rights under United States law. . . . 3 Rudolf Callman, The Law of Unfair Competition, Trademarks and Monopolies §19.24 (4th ed. 1998) ("Callman") ("It is well settled that foreign use creates no trademark rights in the United States.").[3]

Until today, every court to address this issue has held that use of *a foreign trademark* in connection with goods and services sold *only* in a foreign country by a foreign entity does not constitute "use of the mark" in United States commerce sufficient to merit protection under the Lanham Act. [The dissent cited, *inter alia*, *Person's Co., Ltd. v. Christman*, and *Buti v. Perosa*, 139 F.3d 98, 103 (2d Cir. 1998).] . . .

I recognize that, consistent with the Paris Convention and other international agreements, owners of foreign trademarks can obtain United States trademark protection by *registering* their marks in the United States without having to show actual prior use in this country. *See* 15 U.S.C.A. §1126(e) (West Supp. 2002). . . . But, as the majority acknowledges, SBM has not registered its mark in the United States. [cit.]

---

1. This two-pronged meaning of "use" originated in the pre–Lanham Act trademark cases. *See, e.g., Trade-Mark Cases*, 100 U.S. 82, 94-95 (1879). The Lanham Act's "use in commerce" requirement draws directly on this earlier understanding. [cit.] . . .

3. This principle, that use in the United States provides the foundation for U.S. trademark rights, is a corollary of the well-established principle that trademark rights exist in each country solely as determined by that country's law. [cit.] The United States has long committed itself to this territoriality principle by joining international agreements based on it. *See, e.g.*, Paris Convention for the Protection of Industrial Property, March 20, 1883, art. 6(3)—a convention that the United States joined in 1883. The majority builds its contrary thesis on the unremarkable proposition that for Lanham Act purposes "commerce" is defined as "all commerce which may lawfully be regulated by Congress." 15 U.S.C.A. §1127 (West 1998 and Supp. 2002). What the majority overlooks is that to the extent Congress can regulate sales of goods and services by foreigners, bearing foreign marks, in foreign nations, it has chosen to do so by providing in the Lanham Act for compliance with international agreements based on the territoriality principle. *See, e.g.*, 15 U.S.C. §1126(b) (West 1998).

Moreover, when the owner of a foreign trademark, like SBM, has properly registered its foreign mark under the Lanham Act, . . . the holder of the mark can maintain United States protection of the mark *only* if it complies with the requirements of United States law. . . .

Thus, even when the owner of a foreign mark has registered its mark in the United States, it will be presumed to have abandoned the mark if it does not use the mark for the statutorily required period of time *in the United States.* Use, no matter how extensive, of the mark in a foreign country during this period, does not rebut the presumption of abandonment. . . .

Before concluding, I must note the potential consequences of adoption of the majority's rule. The rule announced by the majority today would mean that any entity that uses a foreign mark to advertise and sell its goods or services to United States citizens in a foreign country would be eligible for trademark protection under United States law. Such a rule threatens to wreak havoc over this country's trademark law and would have a stifling effect on United States commercial interests generally. Before investing in a mark, firms and individuals would be forced to scour the globe to determine when and where American citizens had purchased goods or services from foreign subjects to determine whether there were trademarks involved that might be used against them in a priority contest or in an infringement action in the United States.[8] On the other hand, SBM and companies like it would, under the majority's rule, suddenly acquire a windfall of potential United States trademark rights for all of the goods and services advertised to and purchased by United States citizens while traveling in their countries. Like some sort of foreign influenza, these new entitlements would accompany American travelers on their return home, creating a vast array of new duties for individuals in the United States seeking to use the same or similar marks on goods or services sold in the United States.

Of course, if the law required us to permit this sort of reverse imperialism, whereby foreign subjects would be allowed to colonize American markets with their foreign trademarks based on sales conducted exclusively abroad, we would have no choice but to allow it. But the law does not compel this. Rather, the majority's new theory is contrary to all extant authority. Applying this authority here leads to only one conclusion: SBM's use in Monaco of its "Casino de Monte Carlo" mark does not constitute "use in commerce" of the United States sufficient to gain protection under the Lanham Act. Therefore, the grant of summary judgment to SBM should be reversed.[9] On this ground, the plaintiff companies were entitled to judgment as a matter of law.

. . .

---

8. Although I appreciate the majority's concern with the policy objective of avoiding consumer confusion, [cit.], I do not see how its rule would enhance the ability of trademark law to achieve this objective. Indeed, by allowing foreign mark holders to acquire trademark protection in the United States for goods and services sold exclusively abroad, the majority's rule would likely generate a whole new set of trademark disputes in the United States, exacerbating consumer confusion in the process. Moreover, for the reasons mentioned in the text, the "notice" function of trademarks vis-a-vis other firms would be severely undermined by the majority's rule. [cit.]

9. Nor does the "famous marks" doctrine provide SBM any refuge. That doctrine has been applied so seldom (never by a federal appellate court and only by a handful of district courts) that its viability is uncertain. Perhaps for this reason, SBM conceded in the district court that it could not prevail on a famous marks argument without showing "some use" of its mark in the United States. [cit.] Since SBM has shown *no* use of its mark in the United States, this concession forecloses appellate pursuit of this argument.

NOTES AND QUESTIONS

1.   *"Use in commerce."* Which interpretation of "use in commerce" is consistent with the statutory definition? Is the majority correct that the dissent has improperly conflated two elements of the definition? Which approach makes the most sense as a matter of trademark policy? To what extent has the majority discarded the principle of territoriality? Is the dissent's accusation of "reverse imperialism" persuasive? *See* Graeme B. Dinwoodie, *Trademarks and Territory: Detaching Trademark Law from the Nation-State*, 41 Hous. L. Rev. 885 (2004) (criticizing *International Bancorp*). How else might SBM have sought to establish its claim against the defendant domain name owners?

2.   *Reaction to* International Bancorp. The Trademark Trial Appeal Board has continued to apply the doctrine announced in *Person's* and as a result has effectively declined to follow *International Bancorp. See First Niagara Ins. Brokers Inc. v. First Niagara Fin. Grp. Inc.*, 77 U.S.P.Q.2d (BNA) 1334 (TTAB 2005) (reaffirming that "advertising and promotion of a mark in connection with goods and services marketed in a foreign country (whether the advertising occurs inside or outside the United States) creates no priority rights in said mark in the United States" unless the mark is famous or the domestic applicant acted in bad faith), *rev'd on other grounds*, 476 F.3d 867 (Fed. Cir. 2007). Formally, the Board in *First Niagara* distinguished *International Bancorp*, noting that in the case before it, the foreign (Canadian) party's activities in the United States were "minimal and incidental" and its advertising was directed to Canadian purchasers. Moreover, the offering of the services at issue (insurance brokerage services) in the United States required licensing under state law, and the Canadian opposer had not obtained any such license. The Court of Appeals for the Federal Circuit reversed the Board on the ground that it had applied the wrong test. Opposition under Section 2(d), as opposed to the establishment of U.S. trademark rights by an opposer, requires that the opposer's mark has been "used in the United States" rather than "used in commerce." *See* 15 U.S.C. §1052(d). The Federal Circuit remanded for the Board to apply that test, but did not comment on the Board's reading of "use in commerce."

3.   *The effects of the* International Bancorp *rule*. Will the approach of the Fourth Circuit favor any particular type of marks?

4.   *Proving the distinctiveness of a mark used in connection with services rendered in foreign trade*. How should a court assess the distinctiveness (particularly the acquired distinctiveness) of a mark, the protectability of which is dependent on its use in connection with services that are rendered in foreign trade? Which consumers should the court focus on in assessing consumer understanding?

PROBLEM 6-1: SCOTTISH BEER SALES

Joe the Beer Guy owns a pub in the rural community of Hills, Scotland. Through the pub, Joe sells beer under the LONE TREE mark. Locals deem the beer particularly insipid (almost English in taste). However, Joe advertises the beer as a "traditional Highlands brew" in guides prepared by the Scottish Tourist Board for distribution at various travel fairs in the United States. Indeed, the magazine contains coupons offering discounts. The advertising has only some effect: A few American tourists drink in Joe's pub. Has Joe established use "in commerce" for purposes of the U.S. Lanham Act? Would your answer change if Joe's pub was called THE LONE TREE, and he claimed rights in the mark LONE TREE for bar and restaurant services?

D.   EXTRATERRITORIAL ENFORCEMENT OF U.S. TRADEMARK RIGHTS

Conceptually *Person's, Grupo Gigante, ITC, Belmora,* and *International Bancorp* present a similar problem. Each asks whether activity (either wholly or partially) outside the United States might give rise to U.S. trademark rights, such that the putative right owner can restrain the conduct in the United States of another party.* The problems raised by territoriality can, however, be reversed. A party clearly owning U.S. rights might wish to restrain conduct occurring in large part abroad. This implicates the extraterritorial application of the Lanham Act to protect U.S. rights, and we address that issue in this part of the chapter. Notice, however, that many of the same concepts of territoriality and use already discussed in this chapter (and in Chapter 4) might be relevant to a threshold question of whether the use sought to be restrained in fact is occurring in the United States (in which case extraterritorial considerations are not relevant) or abroad (in which case they are).

STEELE v. BULOVA WATCH CO.
344 U.S. 280 (1952)

Mr. Justice CLARK delivered the opinion of the Court:

The issue is whether a United States District Court has jurisdiction to award relief to an American corporation against acts of trade-mark infringement and unfair competition consummated in a foreign country by a citizen and resident of the United States. Bulova Watch Company, Inc., a New York corporation, sued Steele, petitioner here, in the United States District Court for the Western District of Texas. The gist of its complaint charged that BULOVA, a trade-mark properly registered under the laws of the United States, had long designated the watches produced and nationally advertised and sold by the Bulova Watch Company; and that petitioner, a United States citizen residing in San Antonio, Texas, conducted a watch business in Mexico City where, without Bulova's authorization and with the purpose of deceiving the buying public, he stamped the name BULOVA on watches there assembled and sold. Basing its prayer on these asserted violations of the trade-mark laws of the United States, Bulova requested injunctive and monetary relief. Personally served with process in San Antonio, petitioner answered by challenging the court's jurisdiction over the subject matter of the suit and by interposing several defenses, including his due registration in Mexico of the mark BULOVA and the pendency of Mexican legal proceedings thereon, to the merits of Bulova's claim. The trial judge, having initially reserved disposition of the jurisdictional issue until a hearing on the merits, interrupted the presentation of evidence and dismissed the complaint "with prejudice," on the ground that the court lacked jurisdiction over the cause. This decision rested on the court's findings that petitioner had committed no illegal acts within the United States. With one judge dissenting, the Court of Appeals reversed; it held that the pleadings and evidence disclosed a cause of action within the reach of the Lanham Trade-Mark Act of 1946. [cit.] The dissenting judge thought that

---

* The cases are hardly identical fact patterns, of course. For example, the extent of U.S. activity by the domain name owners in *International Bancorp* is not discussed extensively by the court, but (while it did apparently exist) it is not as clear as the (too late) U.S. sales by Person's. And while *International Bancorp* involves a claim of infringement, *Person's* arises in the context of a priority dispute. Thus, the defendant user in the United States in *Person's* was claiming not only the right to use the mark in the United States, but *ownership* of the U.S. registration.

"since the conduct complained of substantially related solely to acts done and trade carried on under full authority of Mexican law, and were confined to and affected only that Nation's internal commerce, (the District Court) was without jurisdiction to enjoin such conduct." We granted certiorari. [cit.]

Petitioner concedes, as he must, that Congress in prescribing standards of conduct for American citizens may project the impact of its laws beyond the territorial boundaries of the United States. [cit.] Resolution of the jurisdictional issue in this case therefore depends on construction of exercised congressional power, not the limitations upon that power itself. And since we do not pass on the merits of Bulova's claim, we need not now explore every facet of this complex and controversial Act.

The Lanham Act, on which Bulova posited its claims to relief, confers broad jurisdictional powers upon the courts of the United States. The statute's expressed intent is [*inter alia*] "to regulate commerce within the control of Congress by making actionable the deceptive and misleading use of marks in such commerce; . . . and to provide rights and remedies stipulated by treaties and conventions respecting trade-marks, trade names, and unfair competition entered into between the United States and foreign nations." [cit.] To that end, section 32(1) holds liable in a civil action by a trade-mark registrant "[a]ny person who shall, in commerce," infringe a registered trade-mark in a manner there detailed. "Commerce" is defined as "all commerce which may lawfully be regulated by Congress." Section 45. The district courts of the United States are granted jurisdiction over all actions "arising under" the Act, [cit.], and can award relief which may include injunctions, "according to the principles of equity," to prevent the violation of any registrant's rights, [cit.].

The record reveals the following significant facts which for purposes of a dismissal must be taken as true: Bulova Watch Company, one of the largest watch manufacturers in the world, advertised and distributed BULOVA watches in the United States and foreign countries. Since 1929, its aural and visual advertising, in Spanish and English, has penetrated Mexico. Petitioner, long a resident of San Antonio, first entered the watch business there in 1922, and in 1926 learned of the trade-mark BULOVA. He subsequently transferred his business to Mexico City and, discovering that BULOVA had not been registered in Mexico, in 1933 procured the Mexican registration of that mark. Assembling Swiss watch movements and dials and cases imported from that country and the United States, petitioner in Mexico City stamped his watches with BULOVA and sold them as such. As a result of the distribution of spurious "Bulovas," Bulova Watch Company's Texas sales representative received numerous complaints from retail jewelers in the Mexican border area whose customers brought in for repair defective "Bulovas" which upon inspection often turned out not to be products of that company. Moreover, subsequent to our grant of certiorari in this case the prolonged litigation in the courts of Mexico has come to an end. On October 6, 1952, the Supreme Court of Mexico rendered a judgment upholding an administrative ruling which had nullified petitioner's Mexican registration of BULOVA.

On the facts in the record we agree with the Court of Appeals that petitioner's activities, when viewed as a whole, fall within the jurisdictional scope of the Lanham Act. This Court has often stated that the legislation of Congress will not extend beyond the boundaries of the United States unless a contrary legislative intent appears. [cit.] The question thus is "whether Congress intended to make the law applicable" to the facts of this case. [cit.] For "the United States is not debarred by any rule of international law from governing the conduct of its own citizens upon the high seas or even in foreign countries when the rights of other nations or their nationals are not infringed. With respect to such an exercise of authority there is no question of international law, but solely of the purport of the municipal law which establishes the duty of the citizen in relation to his own government." [cit.] As Mr. Justice Minton, then sitting on the Court of Appeals, applied the principle in a case involving unfair methods of competition: "Congress has the power to prevent unfair trade practices in foreign commerce by citizens of the United States, although some of the acts are done outside the territorial limits of the United States." [cit.] Nor has this Court in tracing the commerce scope of statutes differentiated between enforcement of legislative policy by the Government itself or by private litigants proceeding under a statutory right. [cit.] The public policy served is the same in each case. In the light of the broad jurisdictional grant in the Lanham Act, we deem its scope to encompass petitioner's activities here. His operations and their effects were not confined within the territorial limits of a foreign nation. He bought component parts of his wares in the United States, and spurious "Bulovas" filtered through the Mexican border into this country; his competing goods could well reflect adversely on Bulova Watch Company's trade reputation in markets cultivated by advertising here as well as abroad. Under similar factual circumstances, courts of the United States have awarded relief to registered trade-mark owners, even prior to the advent of the broadened commerce provisions of the Lanham Act. [cit.] Even when most jealously read, that Act's sweeping reach into "all commerce which may lawfully be regulated by Congress" does not constrict prior law or deprive courts of jurisdiction previously exercised. We do not deem material that petitioner affixed the mark BULOVA in Mexico City rather than here, or that his purchases in the United States when viewed in isolation do not violate any of our laws. They were essential steps in the course of business consummated abroad; acts in themselves legal lose that character when they become part of an unlawful scheme. [cit.] "[I]n such a case it is not material that the source of the forbidden effects upon . . . commerce arises in one phase or another of that program." [cit.] In sum, we do not think that petitioner by so simple a device can evade the thrust of the laws of the United States in a privileged sanctuary beyond our borders.

    . . .

    Nor do we doubt the District Court's jurisdiction to award appropriate injunctive relief if warranted by the facts after trial. [cit.] Mexico's courts have nullified the Mexican registration of BULOVA; there is thus no conflict which might afford petitioner a pretext that such relief would impugn foreign law. The question, therefore, whether a valid foreign registration would affect either the power to enjoin or the propriety of its exercise is not before us. Where, as here, there can be no interference with the sovereignty of another nation, the District Court in exercising its equity powers may command persons properly before it to cease or perform acts outside its territorial jurisdiction. [cit.]
    Affirmed.
    Mr. Justice BLACK took no part in the decision of this case.
    Mr. Justice REED, with whom Mr. Justice DOUGLAS joined, dissented.

VANITY FAIR MILLS, INC. v. T. EATON CO., LTD.

234 F.2d 633 (2d Cir.), cert. denied, 352 U.S. 871 (1956)

WATERMAN, Circuit Judge:
    This case presents interesting and novel questions concerning the extraterritorial application of the Lanham Act, [cit.], and the International Convention for the Protection of Industrial Property (Paris Union), [cit.]. Plaintiff's complaint . . . alleged trade-mark infringement and unfair competition both in the United States and Canada. Defendants moved to dismiss . . . on the grounds that [*inter alia*] . . . the district court lacked jurisdiction over the subject matter of the complaint insofar as it related to defendants' alleged trade-mark infringement and unfair competition in the Dominion of Canada . . . . The district court found that . . . it lacked subject matter jurisdiction over that portion of the

complaint raising Canadian trade-mark issues, and, alternatively, that it was an inconvenient forum for the trial of such issues. That portion of the complaint asserting claims based upon violation of United States trade-marks and unfair competition in this country was recognized by the district court as within its jurisdiction, but because the complaint was thought to inextricably combine the Canadian and American issues, the court dismissed the complaint in its entirety, with leave to file an amended complaint stating separately the American issues. Plaintiff chose to stand on its original complaint, and appealed from the judgment dismissing the complaint.

. . .

Plaintiff, Vanity Fair Mills, Inc., is a Pennsylvania corporation, having its principal place of business at Reading, Pennsylvania. It has been engaged in the manufacture and sale of women's underwear under the trade-mark VANITY FAIR since about the year 1914 in the United States, and has been continuously offering its branded merchandise for sale in Canada since at least 1917. . . .

Beginning in 1914 plaintiff has protected its trade-mark rights by registrations with the United States Patent Office of the trade-mark VANITY FAIR as applying to various types of underwear. . . .

Defendant, The T. Eaton Company, Limited, is a Canadian corporation engaged in the retail merchandising business throughout Canada, with its principal office in Toronto, Ontario. It has a regular and established place of business within the Southern District of New York. On November 3, 1915, defendant filed with the proper Canadian official an application for the registration in Canada of the trade-mark VANITY FAIR, claiming use in connection with [various items of women's clothing]. On November 10, 1915, the proper Canadian official granted defendant's application for the registration of that mark. . . . In 1919 plaintiff sought to register the trade-mark Vanity Fair in Canada for "ready made underwear," but its application was rejected as a matter of course because of the prior registration of defendant. . . .

During the years 1945-1953 the defendant ceased to use its own "Vanity-Fair" trade-mark, purchased branded merchandise from the plaintiff, and sold this merchandise under advertisements indicating that it was of United States origin and of plaintiff's manufacture. These purchases by defendant from plaintiff were made through defendant's New York office. In 1953 defendant resumed the use of its own trade-mark VANITY FAIR and, simultaneously, under the same trade-mark, sold plaintiff's branded merchandise and cheaper merchandise of Canadian manufacture. Defendant at this time objected to plaintiff's sales of its branded merchandise to one of defendant's principal competitors in Canada, the Robert Simpson Company. The Simpson Company discontinued purchases of plaintiff's branded merchandise after being threatened with infringement suits by defendant.

. . .

[P]laintiff asserts that defendant has advertised feminine underwear in the United States under the trade-mark VANITY FAIR, and that it has sold such underwear by mail to customers residing in the United States.

The complaint seeks injunctive relief against the use by defendant of the trade-mark VANITY FAIR in connection with women's underwear both in Canada and the United States, a declaration of the superior rights of the plaintiff in such trade-mark, and an accounting for damages and profits.

The initial question is whether the district court had jurisdiction over all, or only part, of the action. . . .

Plaintiff asserts [*inter alia*] that its claims arise under the laws of the United States and should be governed by those laws. The result sought—extraterritorial application of American law—is contrary to usual conflict-of-laws principles. *First*, the legal status of foreign nationals in the United States is determined solely by our domestic law—foreign law confers no privilege in this country that our courts are bound to recognize. [cit.] And when trade-mark rights within the United States are being litigated in an American court, the decisions of foreign courts concerning the respective trade-mark rights of the parties are irrelevant and inadmissible. *George W. Luft Co. v. Zande Cosmetic Co.*, 2 Cir., 1944, 142 F.2d 536, 539. Similarly, the rights and liabilities of United States citizens who compete with foreign nationals in their home countries are ordinarily to be determined by the appropriate foreign law. [cit.] This fundamental principle, although not without exceptions, is the usual rule, and is based upon practical considerations such as the difficulty of obtaining extraterritorial enforcement of domestic law, as well as on considerations of international comity and respect for national integrity. *Second*, the creation and extent of tort liability is governed, according to the usual rule, by the law of the place where the alleged tort was committed (*lex loci delicti*). The place of the wrong (*locus delicti*) is where the last event necessary to make an actor liable takes place. If the conduct complained of is fraudulent misrepresentation, the place of the wrong is not where the fraudulent statement was made, but where the plaintiff, as a result thereof, suffered a loss. Thus in cases of trade-mark infringement and unfair competition, the wrong takes place not where the deceptive labels are affixed to the goods or where the goods are wrapped in the misleading packages, but where the passing off occurs, *i.e.*, where the deceived customer buys the defendant's product in the belief that he is buying the plaintiff's. In this case, with the exception of defendant's few mail order sales into the United States, the passing-off occurred in Canada, and hence under the usual rule would be governed by Canadian law.

Conflict-of-laws principles, however, are not determinative of the question whether the International Convention and/or the Lanham Act provide relief in American courts and under American law against acts of trade-mark infringement and unfair competition committed in foreign countries by foreign nationals. If the International Convention or the Lanham Act provides such relief, and if the provisions are within constitutional powers, American courts would be required to enforce these provisions. [*See Steele v. Bulova Watch Co.*, 1952, 344 U.S. 280.] It is therefore necessary to determine whether the International Convention or the Lanham Act provides such relief. Only if it is determined that they do not provide such extensive relief. . . .

I. THE INTERNATIONAL CONVENTION

Plaintiff asserts that the International Convention for the Protection of Industrial Property (Paris Union), [cit.], to which both the United States and Canada are parties, is self-executing; that by virtue of Article VI of the Constitution it is a part of the law of this country which is to be enforced by its courts; and that the Convention has created rights available to plaintiff which protect it against trade-mark infringement and unfair competition in foreign countries. Plaintiff would appear to be correct in arguing that no special legislation in the United States was necessary to make the International Convention effective here, but it erroneously maintains that the Convention created private rights *under American law* for acts of unfair competition occurring in foreign countries.

The International Convention is essentially a compact between the various member countries to accord in their own countries to citizens of the other contracting parties trade-mark and other rights comparable to those accorded their own citizens by their domestic law. The underlying principle is that foreign nationals should be given the same treatment in each of the member countries as that country makes available to its own citizens. In addition, the Convention sought to create uniformity in certain respects by obligating each member nation "to assure to nationals of countries of the Union an effective protection against unfair competition."

The Convention is not premised upon the idea that the trade-mark and related laws of each member nation shall be given extraterritorial application, but on exactly the converse principle that each nation's law shall have only territorial application. Thus a foreign national of a member nation using his trade-mark in commerce in the United States is accorded extensive protection here against infringement and other types of unfair competition by virtue of United States membership in the Convention. But that protection has its source in, and is subject to the limitations of, American law, not the law of the foreign national's own country. Likewise, the International Convention provides protection to a United States trade-mark owner such as plaintiff against unfair competition and trade-mark infringement in Canada—but only to the extent that Canadian law recognizes the treaty obligation as creating private rights or has made the Convention operative by implementing legislation. Under Canadian law, unlike United States law, the International Convention was not effective to create any private rights in Canada without legislative implementation. However, the obligations undertaken by the Dominion of Canada under this treaty have been implemented by legislation. . . . If plaintiff has any rights under the International Convention (other than through section 44 of the Lanham Act . . .), they are derived from this Canadian law, and not from the fact that the International Convention may be a self-executing treaty which is a part of the law of this country.

II. THE LANHAM ACT

Plaintiff's primary reliance is on the Lanham Act. . . . Plaintiff advances two alternative arguments, the first one based on the decision of the Supreme Court in *Steele v. Bulova Watch Co.*, [cit.], giving the provisions of the Lanham Act an extraterritorial application against acts committed in Mexico by an American citizen, and the second based specifically on section 44 of the Act, [cit.], which was intended to carry out our obligations under the International Conventions.

A. GENERAL EXTRATERRITORIAL APPLICATION OF THE LANHAM ACT—BULOVA

Section 32(1)(a) of the Lanham Act, [cit.], one of the more important substantive provisions of the Act, protects the owner of a registered mark from use "in commerce" by another that is "likely to cause confusion or mistake or to deceive purchasers as to the source of origin" of the other's good or services. "Commerce" is defined by the Act as "all commerce which may lawfully be regulated by Congress." Section 45. Plaintiff, relying on *Steele v. Bulova Watch Co.*, [cit.], argues that section 32(1)(a) should be given an extraterritorial application, and that this case falls within the literal wording of the section since the defendant's use of the mark VANITY FAIR in Canada had a substantial effect on "commerce which may be lawfully regulated by Congress."

While Congress has no power to regulate commerce in the Dominion of Canada, it does have power to regulate commerce "with foreign Nations, and among the several States." Const. Art. 1, §8, cl. 3. This power is now generally interpreted to extend to all commerce, even intrastate and entirely foreign commerce, which has a substantial effect on commerce between the states or between the United States and foreign countries. . . . Thus it may well be that Congress could constitutionally provide infringement remedies so long as the defendant's use of the mark has a substantial effect on the foreign or interstate commerce of the United States. But we do not reach this constitutional question because we do not think that Congress intended that the infringement remedies provided in section 32(1) (a) and elsewhere should be applied to acts committed by a foreign national in his home country under a presumably valid trademark registration in that country.

The Lanham Act itself gives almost no indication of the extent to which Congress intended to exercise its power in this area. While section 45, [cit.], states a broad definition of the "commerce" subject to the Act, both the statement of Congressional intent in the same section and the provisions of section 44, [cit.], indicate Congressional regard for the basic principle of the International Conventions, *i.e.*, equal application to citizens and foreign nationals alike of the territorial law of the place where the acts occurred. And the Supreme Court, in *Steele v. Bulova Watch Co.*, [cit.], the only other extraterritorial case since the Lanham Act, did not intimate that the Act should be given the extreme interpretation urged upon us here.

In the *Bulova* case, [the Fifth Circuit,] assuming that the defendant had a valid registration under Mexican law, found that the district court had jurisdiction to prevent the defendant's use of the mark in Mexico, on the ground that there was a sufficient effect on United States commerce. Subsequently, the defendant's registration was canceled in Mexican proceedings, and on review of the Fifth Circuit's decision, the Supreme Court noted that the question of the effect of a valid registration in the foreign country was not before it. The Court affirmed the Fifth Circuit, holding that the federal district court had jurisdiction to prevent unfair use of the plaintiff's mark in Mexico. In doing so the Court stressed three factors: (1) the defendant's conduct had a substantial effect on United States commerce; (2) the defendant was a United States citizen and the United States has a broad power to regulate the conduct of its citizens in foreign countries; and (3) there was no conflict with trade-mark rights established under the foreign law, since the defendant's Mexican registration had been canceled by proceedings in Mexico. Only the first factor is present in this case.

We do not think that the *Bulova* case lends support to plaintiff; to the contrary, we think that the rationale of the Court was so thoroughly based on the power of the United States to govern "the conduct of *its own citizens* upon the high seas or even in foreign countries *when the rights of other nations or their nationals are not infringed*," that the absence of one of the above factors might well be determinative and that the absence of both is certainly fatal.[14] . . . [T]he action has only been brought against Canadian citizens. We conclude that the remedies provided by the Lanham Act, other than in section 44, should not be given an extraterritorial application against foreign citizens acting under presumably valid trade-marks in a foreign country.

B.   Section 44 of the Lanham Act

Plaintiff's alternative contention is that section 44 of the Lanham Act, which is entitled "International Conventions," affords to United States citizens all possible remedies against unfair competition by foreigners who are nationals of convention countries, including the relief requested in this case. . . .

Since United States citizens are given by subsection (i) of section 44 only the same benefits which the Act extends to eligible foreign nationals, and since the benefits conferred on those foreign nationals have no extraterritorial application, the benefits accorded to citizens by this section can likewise have no extraterritorial application. . . .

[The court thus affirmed the dismissal of the complaint but gave plaintiff permission to file an amended complaint restricted to the "American issues" if it wished.]

Affirmed as modified.

---

14. At the time the Fifth Circuit decided the *Bulova* case, [cit.], the defendant's Mexican registration had not been canceled. Since the Fifth Circuit assumed that the defendant had a valid Mexican registration, it thought the presence or absence of a foreign trade mark was not a determinative factor. We need not decide that question because of the additional fact that the defendant here is not an American citizen.

STERLING DRUG, INC. v. BAYER AG

14 F.3d 733 (2d Cir. 1994)

NEWMAN, Circuit Judge:

[The defendant, Bayer AG, was a German company that owned rights to the BAYER mark for pharmaceuticals in most countries of the world (including Germany), but not the United States. The U.S. rights were owned by the plaintiff, Sterling Drug. Sterling brought an action to restrain certain uses of the mark BAYER by the defendant, alleging both trademark infringement and violation of agreements between the parties regarding the use of the mark in the United States. The district court found that Bayer violated both Sterling's contract and trademark rights and enjoined Bayer AG and its subsidiaries from using the BAYER mark in the United States or abroad if such foreign use might make its way to the American public (for example, in press releases likely to be reported on in the United States or in advertisements in newspapers with significant U.S. distribution). Bayer appealed, arguing that the injunction's extraterritorial provisions interfered impermissibly with its rights under foreign laws and impaired "the ability of one of Europe's largest corporations to conduct its everyday business in its home country and around the world." The government of Germany appeared as amicus curiae and contended that the extraterritorial prohibitions of the injunction failed to respect its sovereign rights. The Court of Appeals for the Second Circuit vacated the injunction's extraterritorial provisions because the district court had not considered whether the *Vanity Fair* factors supported the extraterritorial aspects of the injunction. The court, however, remanded the case to the district court rather than simply revise the injunction to eliminate its extraterritorial provisions. In so doing, the court indicated some flexibility toward the application of the *Vanity Fair* factors.]

[I]f we applied the *Vanity Fair* test mechanically to the instant case, we would forbid the application of the Lanham Act abroad against a foreign corporation that holds superior rights to the mark under foreign law. But such an unrefined application of that case might mean that we fail to preserve the Lanham Act's goals of protecting American consumers against confusion, and protecting holders of American trademarks against misappropriation of their marks. A more careful application of *Vanity Fair* is necessary because the instant case is not on all fours with *Vanity Fair*. In *Vanity Fair*, the plaintiff sought a *blanket prohibition* against the Canadian retailer's use of "Vanity Fair" in connection with the sale of defendant's products in Canada. Sterling, on the other hand, seeks to enjoin only those uses of the "Bayer" mark abroad that are likely to make their way to American consumers.[7] Sterling is not concerned with Bayer AG's use of the mark abroad so long as that use does not enter the channels of international communication that lead to the United States. While the stringent *Vanity Fair* test is appropriate when the plaintiff seeks an absolute bar against a corporation's use of its mark outside our borders, that test is unnecessarily demanding when the plaintiff seeks the more modest goal of limiting foreign uses that reach the United States. Though Congress did not intend the Lanham Act to be used as a sword to eviscerate

---

7. Sterling seizes upon this distinction to argue that the instant injunction is therefore not an "extraterritorial" application of the Lanham Act at all. [cit.] Sterling conflates the effect of the challenged *conduct* with the effect of the challenged *injunction*. While it is true that the injunction seeks to reach only the *domestic* effects of Bayer's *conduct*, it does so through the mechanism of an *extraterritorial injunction*, i.e., one that prohibits Bayer AG from undertaking certain actions outside U.S. borders. The injunction has provisions that are clearly extraterritorial, including, for example, one that prohibits Bayer AG from advertising in foreign magazines such as *Der Spiegel* because their American circulations exceed 5,000 copies.

completely a foreign corporation's foreign trademark, it did intend the Act to be used as a shield against foreign uses that have significant trademark-impairing effects upon American commerce.

[The court also offered some guidance to the district court.] "In establishing the parameters of injunctive relief in the case of lawful concurrent users, a court must take account of the realities of the marketplace." [cit.] In today's global economy, where a foreign TV advertisement might be available by satellite to U.S. households, not every activity of a foreign corporation with any tendency to create some confusion among American consumers can be prohibited by the extraterritorial reach of a District Court's injunction.

Upon remand, the District Court may grant an extraterritorial injunction carefully crafted to prohibit only those foreign uses of the mark by Bayer AG that are likely to have significant trademark-impairing effects on United States commerce. If the Court finds that Bayer AG's use of the mark abroad carries such significant effects in the United States, the District Court may require Bayer AG to take appropriate precautions against using the mark in international media in ways that might create confusion among United States consumers as to the source of "Bayer" pharmaceutical products in the United States. It might be appropriate, to take examples offered by appellee, to prevent Bayer AG from placing a full-page "Bayer" advertisement in the U.S. edition of a foreign magazine or newspaper, or inviting representatives of the U.S. press to an offshore briefing in which Bayer AG distributed materials describing "Bayer's" analgesics products for publication in the U.S. On the other hand, it might be inappropriate, to take examples offered by the *amicus curiae*, to leave the injunction so broad as to ban the announcement of new medical research in *Lancet*, or an employment notice in *Handelsblatt*, or a press conference in England to publicize a new over-the-counter remedy developed in the United States, or sponsorship of a German soccer team if that team might appear, wearing "Bayer" jerseys, on a television broadcast carried by an American sports cable channel.

In fashioning the injunction, the Court should "balanc[e] . . . the equities to reach an appropriate result protective of the interests of both parties." [cit.] Where, as in the instant case, both parties have legitimate interests, consideration of those interests must receive especially sensitive accommodation in the international context. While Bayer AG suggests that we must accept these conflicts as the unavoidable result of an international community of nations in which each nation exercises the power to grant trademark rights, we prefer to allow the District Court to fashion an appropriately limited injunction with only those extraterritorial provisions reasonably necessary to protect against significant trademark-impairing effects on American commerce.

. . .

McBEE v. DELICA CO.

417 F.3d 107 (1st Cir. 2005)

LYNCH, Circuit Judge:

. . .

The plaintiff, Cecil McBee, an American citizen and resident, seeks to hold the defendant, Delica Co., Ltd. (Delica), responsible for its activities in Japan said to harm McBee's reputation in both Japan and the United States and for Delica's purported activities in the United States. McBee is a well-known American jazz musician; Delica is a Japanese corporation that adopted the name "Cecil McBee" for its adolescent female clothing line. McBee sued for false endorsement and dilution under the Lanham Act. The district court dismissed all of McBee's Lanham Act claims, concluding that it lacked subject matter jurisdiction. [cit.]

We affirm, albeit on different reasoning. . . .

I.

The relevant facts are basically undisputed. McBee, who lives in both Maine and New York, is a jazz bassist with a distinguished career spanning over forty-five years. He has performed in the United States and worldwide, has performed on over 200 albums, and has released six albums under his own name (including in Japan). He won a Grammy Award in 1989, was inducted into the Oklahoma Jazz Hall of Fame in 1991, and teaches at the New England Conservatory of Music in Boston. McBee has toured Japan several times, beginning in the early 1980s, and has performed in many major Japanese cities, including Tokyo. He continues to tour in Japan. McBee has never licensed or authorized the use of his name to anyone, except of course in direct connection with his musical performances, as for example on an album. In his own words, he has sought to "have [his] name associated only with musical excellence."

Delica is a Japanese clothing retailer. In 1984, Delica adopted the trade name "Cecil McBee" for a line of clothing and accessories primarily marketed to teenaged girls. Delica holds a Japanese trademark for "Cecil McBee," in both Japanese and Roman or English characters, for a variety of product types. Delica owns and operates retail shops throughout Japan under the brand name "Cecil McBee"; these are the only stores where "Cecil McBee" products are sold. There are no "Cecil McBee" retail shops outside of Japan. . . .

Delica puts out a "style book" or catalog that includes pictures and descriptions of the products in its "Cecil McBee" line; this style book is written in Japanese with some English words for effect. The style book is available in Japan at the retail stores and in certain other locations; sometimes it is included with shipped packages of "Cecil McBee" products. The style book contains telephone and fax numbers which allow a customer to order "Cecil McBee" merchandise from another company, Opus M. Co., Ltd., and have it shipped directly to the customer. Opus M. Co. buys the goods from Delica for this purpose, and then uses yet another company, Hamasho Co., Ltd., to do the shipping. It is undisputed that Hamasho Co. has never shipped any "Cecil McBee" goods outside of Japan. As described later, Delica's policy generally is to decline orders from the United States.

Delica operates a website, *http://www.cecilmcbee.net*, which contains pictures and descriptions of "Cecil McBee" products, as well as locations and telephone numbers of retail stores selling those products. The website is created and hosted in Japan, and is written almost entirely in Japanese, using Japanese characters (although, like the style book, it contains some English words). . . . [T]he site does not allow purchases of "Cecil McBee" products to be made online. The website can be viewed from anywhere in the Internet-accessible world.

. . .

In 1995, . . . McBee petitioned the Japanese Patent Office to invalidate Delica's English-language trademark on "Cecil McBee."

On February 28, 2002, the Japanese Patent Office ruled Delica's trademark in Japan invalid, [but after appeals in the courts, that registration was reinstated].

In early 2002, Delica formulated a policy not to sell or ship "Cecil McBee" brand products to the United States and informed its managers throughout the company. Delica's admitted reason for this policy was to prevent McBee from being able to sue Delica in the United States.

McBee was beginning to consider just such a strategy. From December 2001 through early 2003, McBee retained three Japanese-speaking investigators to attempt to purchase "Cecil McBee" products from Delica and have them shipped to Maine. They met with mixed success. . . .

[The investigators managed to persuade some stores to ship to an address in Japan from which the investigator would then arrange to have the products forwarded to Maine, and some of the stores, at various times, shipped directly to the investigators in Maine.] The total value of "Cecil McBee" merchandise purchased by these three investigators—including both goods shipped directly to Maine by Delica and goods shipped via the indirect method—was approximately $2,500. As counsel for McBee has conceded, there is no evidence of any other "Cecil McBee" sales by Delica to the United States.

Further, there is virtually no evidence of "Cecil McBee" brand goods entering the United States after being sold by Delica in Japan. . . .

II.

. . .

On appeal, McBee renews his argument that his claims for a domestic injunction, both against Delica's sales into the United States and against its broadcasting of its website in the United States, do not constitute extraterritorial applications of the Lanham Act at all. Further, while McBee concedes that United States courts lack jurisdiction over his Lanham Act claim for an injunction against Delica's sales in Japan, he argues that the district court had extraterritorial jurisdiction over damages claims against those same sales. Delica responds by arguing that United States courts lack extraterritorial jurisdiction over all of McBee's Lanham Act claims. . . .

III.

A.   Framework for Assessing Extraterritorial Use of the Lanham Act

By extraterritorial application of the Lanham Act, we mean application of the Act to activity (such as sales) of a defendant outside of the territorial boundaries of the United States. In addressing extraterritorial application of the Lanham Act, we face issues of Congressional intent to legislate extraterritorially, undergirded by issues of Congressional power to legislate extraterritorially. Usually in addressing questions of extraterritoriality, the Supreme Court has discussed Congressional intent, doing so by employing various presumptions designed to avoid unnecessary international conflict. *See, e.g.,* [cit.]; *EEOC v. Arabian Am. Oil Co.,* 499 U.S. 244, 248 (1991) ("It is a longstanding principle of American law that legislation of Congress, unless a contrary intent appears, is meant to apply only within the territorial jurisdiction of the United States." (internal quotation marks and citation omitted)).

The parties characterize the extraterritoriality issue as, at least in part, one of subject matter jurisdiction under the Act, and it is often viewed that way. [cit.]

The Supreme Court has long since made it clear that the Lanham Act could sometimes be used to reach extraterritorial conduct, but it has never laid down a precise test for when such reach would be appropriate. *Steele v. Bulova Watch Co.,* 344 U.S. 280 (1952); [cit.]. The circuit courts have established a variety of tests for determining when extraterritorial application of the Lanham Act is appropriate, treating different factual contexts as all subject to the same set of criteria. *See Vanity Fair Mills v. T. Eaton Co.,* 234 F.2d 633, 642 (2d Cir. 1956); *see also Int'l Café, S.A.L. v. Hard Rock Café Int'l (U.S.A.), Inc.,* 252 F.3d 1274, 1278-79 (11th Cir. 2001) (applying *Vanity Fair*); *Nintendo of Am., Ltd. v. Aeropower Co.,* 34 F.3d 246, 250-51 (4th Cir. 1994) (adopting the *Vanity Fair* test, although requiring a "significant effect" rather than a "substantial effect" on United States commerce). . . *Am. Rice, Inc. v. Ark. Rice Growers Coop. Ass'n,* 701 F.2d 408, 414 & n.8 (5th Cir. 1983) (modifying *Vanity Fair's* first prong to require only "some effect" on United States commerce). This court has not previously addressed the question.

. . .

The *Steele* Court did not define the outer limits of Congressional power because it was clear that the facts presented a case within those limits. The *Steele* Court explicitly and implicitly relied on two different aspects of Congressional power to reach this conclusion. First, it explicitly relied on the power of Congress to regulate "the conduct of its own citizens," even extraterritorial conduct. [cit.] This doctrine is based on an idea that Congressional power over American citizens is a matter of domestic law that raises no serious international concerns, even when the citizen is located abroad. [cit.]

Second, *Steele* also implicitly appears to rely on Congressional power over foreign commerce, although the Foreign Commerce clause is not cited—the Court noted that the defendant's actions had an impact on the plaintiff's reputation, and thus on commerce within the United States. [cit.] The *Steele* Court concluded that an American citizen could not evade the thrust of the laws of the United States by moving his operations to a "privileged sanctuary" beyond our borders. [cit.]

For purposes of determining subject matter jurisdiction, we think certain distinctions are important at the outset. The reach of the Lanham Act depends on context; the nature of the analysis of the jurisdictional question may vary with that context. *Steele* addressed the pertinent Lanham Act jurisdictional analysis when an American citizen is the defendant. In such cases, the domestic effect of the international activities may be of lesser importance and a lesser showing of domestic effects may be all that is needed. We do not explore this further because our case does not involve an American citizen as the alleged infringer.

When the purported infringer is not an American citizen, and the alleged illegal activities occur outside the United States, then the analysis is different, and appears to rest solely on the foreign commerce power. Yet it is beyond much doubt that the Lanham Act can be applied against foreign corporations or individuals in appropriate cases; no court has ever suggested that the foreign citizenship of a defendant is always fatal. *See, e.g., Sterling Drug, Inc. v. Bayer AG*, 14 F.3d 733, 746 (2d Cir. 1994); *Wells Fargo & Co. v. Wells Fargo Express Co.*, 556 F.2d 406, 429 (9th Cir. 1977). Some academics have criticized treating the Lanham Act differently from patent and copyright law, which generally are not applied extraterritorially. [cit.] Nonetheless, the Supreme Court recently reaffirmed the *Steele* approach to extraterritorial jurisdiction under the Lanham Act by distinguishing it in *Arabian American Oil Co.* [cit.] The question becomes one of articulating a test for Lanham Act jurisdiction over foreign infringing activities by foreign defendants.

The decisions of the Supreme Court in the antitrust context seem useful to us as a guide. The Court has written in this area, on the issue of extraterritorial application, far more recently than it has written on the Lanham Act, and thus the decisions reflect more recent evolutions in terms of legal analysis of extraterritorial activity. As the Court noted in *Steele*, Lanham Act violations abroad often radiate unlawful consequences into the United States. [cit.] One can easily imagine a variety of harms to American commerce arising from wholly foreign activities by foreign defendants. There could be harm caused by false endorsements, passing off, or product disparagement, or confusion over sponsorship affecting American commerce and causing loss of American sales. Further, global piracy of American goods is a major problem for American companies: annual losses from unauthorized use of United States trademarks, according to one commentator, now amount to $200 billion annually. [cit.] In both the antitrust and the Lanham Act areas, there is a risk that absent a certain degree of extraterritorial enforcement, violators will either take advantage of international coordination problems or hide in countries without efficacious antitrust or trademark laws, thereby avoiding legal authority.

In *Hartford Fire Ins. Co. v. California*, 509 U.S. 764 (1993), the Supreme Court addressed the issue of when a United States court could assert jurisdiction over Sherman Act claims brought against foreign defendants for a conspiracy that occurred abroad to raise reinsurance prices. . . .

The framework stated in *Hartford Fire* guides our analysis of the Lanham Act jurisdictional question for foreign activities of foreign defendants. We hold that the Lanham Act grants subject matter jurisdiction over extraterritorial conduct by foreign defendants only where the conduct has a substantial effect on United States commerce.[9] Absent a showing of such a substantial effect, at least as to foreign defendants, the court lacks jurisdiction over the Lanham Act claim. Congress has little reason to assert jurisdiction over foreign defendants who are engaging in activities that have no substantial effect on the United States, and courts, absent an express statement from Congress, have no good reason to go further in such situations. [cit.]

The substantial effects test requires that there be evidence of impacts within the United States, and these impacts must be of a sufficient character and magnitude to give the United States a reasonably strong interest in the litigation. [cit.] The "substantial effects" test must be applied in light of the core purposes of the Lanham Act, which are both to protect the ability of American consumers to avoid confusion and to help assure a trademark's owner that it will reap the financial and reputational rewards associated with having a desirable name or product. [cit.] The goal of the jurisdictional test is to ensure that the United States has a sufficient interest in the litigation, as measured by the interests protected by the Lanham Act, to assert jurisdiction.

Of course, the *Vanity Fair* test includes a "substantial effects" inquiry as part of its three-part test. We differ from the *Vanity Fair* court in that we disaggregate the elements of its test: we first ask whether the defendant is an American citizen, and if he is not, then we use the substantial effects test as the sole touchstone to determine jurisdiction.

If the substantial effects test is met, then the court should proceed, in appropriate cases, to consider comity. We also transplant for Lanham Act purposes *Hartford Fire*'s holding that comity considerations are properly analyzed not as questions of whether there is subject matter jurisdiction, but as prudential questions of whether that jurisdiction should be exercised. [cit.] Our analysis differs again from *Vanity Fair* on this point. *See Vanity Fair*, 234 F.2d at 642. *Vanity Fair* and other cases have considered as part of the basic jurisdictional analysis whether the defendant acted under color of protection of the trademark laws of his own country. We disagree and do not see why the scope of Congressional intent and power to create jurisdiction under the Lanham Act should turn on the existence and meaning of foreign law.

Congress could, of course, preclude the exercise of such Lanham Act jurisdiction by statute or by ratified treaty. Or it could by statute define limits in Lanham Act jurisdiction in such international cases, as it has chosen to do in the antitrust area. *See* 15 U.S.C. §6a. It has not done so.

B. Application of the Framework

. . .

1. *Claim for Injunction Barring Delica's United States Sales*

[The court accepted that the district court had subject-matter jurisdiction over McBee's claim for an injunction against Delica's sales of "Cecil McBee" goods in the

---

9. . . . We need not and do not decide whether a defendant's intent to target United States commerce plays any role in the jurisdictional inquiry for purposes of extraterritorial application of the *Lanham Act*—either, for example, as a requirement in addition to the substantial effect requirement, or instead as a factor that, if present, may reduce the amount of effects on United States commerce that a plaintiff must show. It is evident that Delica, in this case, had no intent to target United States commerce. . . .

United States without having to satisfy the "substantial effect on United States commerce" test. The $2,500 worth of goods sold by Delica to McBee's investigators in the United States were in United States commerce, at least insofar as some of those goods were shipped directly by Delica to the buyers in the United States. However, the court affirmed dismissal of the claims; there was no evidence of existing confusion or dilution, since these few sales were all made to McBee's own investigators, who were brought in to assist in this litigation and therefore fully understood McBee's lack of any relationship with Delica. In a footnote, the court declined to "reach the more complicated question of whether comity concerns would ever allow a court to decline to exercise jurisdiction when an injunction is sought against sales in the United States."]

2.   *Claim for Injunction Barring Access to Internet Website*

McBee next argues that his claim for an injunction against Delica's posting of its Internet website in a way that is visible to United States consumers also does not call for an extraterritorial application of the Lanham Act. Here McBee is incorrect: granting this relief would constitute an extraterritorial application of the Act, and thus subject matter jurisdiction would only be appropriate if McBee could show a substantial effect on United States commerce. McBee has not shown such a substantial effect from Delica's website.

We begin with McBee's argument that his website claim, like his claim for Delica's sales into the United States, is not an extraterritorial application of the Lanham Act. McBee does not seek to reach the website because it is a method, by Delica, for selling "Cecil McBee" goods into the United States. In such a case, if a court had jurisdiction to enjoin sales of goods within the United States, it might have jurisdiction to enjoin the website as well, or at least those parts of the website that are necessary to allow the sales to occur. Rather, the injury McBee complains about from the website is that its mere existence has caused him harm, because United States citizens can view the website and become confused about McBee's relationship with the Japanese clothing company. In particular, McBee argues that he has suffered harm from the fact that Delica's website often comes up on search engines ahead of fan sites about McBee's jazz career.

Delica's website, although hosted from Japan and written in Japanese, happens to be reachable from the United States just as it is reachable from other countries. That is the nature of the Internet. The website is hosted and managed overseas; its visibility within the United States is more in the nature of an effect, which occurs only when someone in the United States decides to visit the website. To hold that any website in a foreign language, wherever hosted, is automatically reachable under the Lanham Act so long as it is visible in the United States would be senseless. The United States often will have no real interest in hearing trademark lawsuits about websites that are written in a foreign language and hosted in other countries. McBee attempts to analogize the existence of Delica's website, which happens to be visible in any country, to the direct mail advertising that the *Vanity Fair* court considered to be domestic conduct and so held outside the scope of the extraterritoriality analysis. [cit.] The analogy is poor for three reasons: first, the advertising in *Vanity Fair* was closely connected with mail-order sales; second, direct mail advertising is a far more targeted act than is the hosting of a website; and third, Delica's website, unlike the advertising in *Vanity Fair*, is in a foreign language.

Our conclusion that McBee's website claim calls for extraterritorial application of the Lanham Act is bolstered by a consideration of the now extensive case law relating to treatment of Internet websites with respect to personal jurisdiction. We recognize that the contexts are distinct, but the extraterritorial application of jurisdiction under the Lanham Act evokes concerns about territorial restraints on sovereigns that are similar to concerns driving personal jurisdiction. To put the principle broadly, the mere existence of a website that is visible in a forum and that gives information about a company and its products is not enough, by itself, to subject a defendant to personal jurisdiction in that forum. [cit.]

Something more is necessary, such as interactive features which allow the successful online ordering of the defendant's products. [cit.] The mere existence of a website does not show that a defendant is directing its business activities towards every forum where the website is visible; as well, given the omnipresence of Internet websites today, allowing personal jurisdiction to be premised on such a contact alone would "eviscerate" the limits on a state's jurisdiction over out-of-state or foreign defendants. [cit.]

Similarly, allowing subject matter jurisdiction under the Lanham Act to automatically attach whenever a website is visible in the United States would eviscerate the territorial curbs on judicial authority that Congress is, quite sensibly, presumed to have imposed in this area.

Our conclusion does not make it impossible for McBee to use the Lanham Act to attack a Japan-based website; it merely requires that McBee first establish that the website has a substantial effect on commerce in the United States before there is subject matter jurisdiction under the Lanham Act. We can imagine many situations in which the presence of a website would ensure (or, at least, help to ensure) that the United States has a sufficient interest. The substantial effects test, however, is not met here.

Delica's website is written almost entirely in Japanese characters; this makes it very unlikely that any real confusion of American consumers, or diminishing of McBee's reputation, would result from the website's existence. In fact, most American consumers are unlikely to be able to understand Delica's website at all. Further, McBee's claim that Americans looking for information about him will be unable to find it is unpersuasive: the Internet searches reproduced in the record all turned up both sites about McBee and sites about Delica's clothing line on their first page of results. The two sets of results are easily distinguishable to any consumer, given that the Delica sites are clearly shown, by the search engines, as being written in Japanese characters. Finally, we stress that McBee has produced no evidence of any American consumers going to the website and then becoming confused about whether McBee had a relationship with Delica.

3.   *Claim for Damages for Delica's Japanese Sales*

McBee's claim for damages due to Delica's sales in Japan fares no better, because these sales as well have no substantial effect on commerce in the United States. . . .

McBee's first argument, that *American* consumers are being confused and/or led to think less of McBee's name because of Delica's Japanese sales, cuts very close to the core purposes of the Lanham Act. [cit.] Such confusion and reputational harm in the eyes of American consumers can often—although not always—be inferred from the fact that American consumers have been exposed to the infringing mark. But no inference of dilution or other harm can be made in situations where American citizens are not exposed at all to the infringing product. The trouble with McBee's argument is that there is virtually no evidence that American consumers are actually seeing Delica's products.

Quite commonly, plaintiffs in these sorts of cases can meet their burden by presenting evidence that while the initial sales of infringing goods may occur in foreign countries, the goods subsequently tend to enter the United States in some way and in substantial quantities. *See, e.g., Steele,* 344 U.S. at 28; [cit.]. McBee has presented essentially no evidence that Delica's products have been brought into the United States after their initial sale in Japan. . . .

McBee's second argument is that Delica's sales have confused Japanese consumers, hindering McBee's record sales and touring career in Japan. Evidence of economic harm to McBee in Japan due to confusion of Japanese consumers is less tightly tied to the interests that the Lanham Act intends to protect, since there is no United States interest in protecting *Japanese consumers*. American courts do, however, arguably have an interest in protecting American commerce by protecting *McBee* from lost income due to the tarnishing of his trademark in Japan. Courts have considered sales diverted from American companies in foreign countries in their analyses. *See Totalplan*, 14 F.3d at 830-31; *see also Am. Rice*, 701 F.2d at 414-15 (considering diverted sales in finding "some effects" test met).

Assuming *arguendo* that evidence of harm to an American plaintiff's economic interests abroad, due to the tarnishing of his reputation there, might sometimes meet the substantial effects test, McBee has presented no evidence of such harm in this case. . . .

McBee has not shown that Delica's Japanese sales have a substantial effect on United States commerce, and thus McBee's claim for damages based on those sales, as well as McBee's claim for an injunction against Delica's website, must be dismissed for lack of subject matter jurisdiction. We need not reach the issue of whether we should decline jurisdiction because of comity.[15] Were we to assert jurisdiction in this case, where there is no evidence of any harm to American commerce beyond the facts that the plaintiff is an American citizen and that the allegedly infringing goods were sold and seen in a foreign country, we would be forced to find jurisdiction in almost all false endorsement or trademark cases involving an American plaintiff and allegedly infringing sales abroad.

. . .

The district court's decision ordering judgment for the defendant Delica is *affirmed*. . . .

TRADER JOE'S CO. v. HALLATT
835 F.3d 690 (9th Cir. 2016)

CHRISTEN, Circuit Judge:

This trademark infringement case turns on the extraterritorial reach of the Lanham Act. It is uncontested that Defendant Michael Norman Hallatt purchases Trader Joe's-branded goods in Washington state, transports them to Canada, and resells them there in a store he designed to mimic a Trader Joe's store. Trader Joe's sued for trademark infringement and unfair competition under the Lanham Act and Washington state law. The district court recognized that the Lanham Act can apply to conduct that occurs abroad, but it dismissed the Lanham Act claims for lack of subject-matter jurisdiction after concluding that Hallatt's allegedly infringing activity takes place in Canada, and that Trader Joe's did not adequately explain how Hallatt's activity impacts American commerce. The district court dismissed Trader Joe's' state law claims for similar reasons.

We affirm in part and reverse in part. . . .

---

15. Were we to reach comity principles, they would most likely counsel for dismissal of McBee's claim seeking damages for Delica's sales in Japan. McBee argues that so long as he seeks only damages and not an injunction, there is no "true conflict" with Japanese law because it would be theoretically possible for Delica to comply with both Japanese and United States law. *See Hartford Fire*, 509 U.S. at 798-99. McBee's argument makes no sense: an injunction would no more create a "true conflict" under this definition than damages, for under either form of relief it would be theoretically possible for Delica to comply with both nations' laws by not using the trademark. There is no meaningful distinction between an injunction and damages for this purpose. The reasoning developed in the antitrust context in *Hartford Fire* is not "automatically transferable" to the trademark context: "It is one thing for the British reinsurers in *Hartford Fire* to be barred under United States law from boycotting activity that they might be free to engage in without violating British law. But it is quite a different thing for the holder of rights in a mark under German law to be ordered to refrain from uses of that mark protected by German law." *Sterling Drug*, 14 F.3d at 746-47.

BACKGROUND

The complaint alleges that Trader Joe's is a well-known American grocery store that sells specialty goods at reasonable prices from its distinctive, South Pacific-themed stores. It is headquartered in Monrovia, California, but it operates hundreds of stores throughout the United States, including more than a dozen stores in Washington. About eighty percent of the goods Trader Joe's sells in its stores are Trader Joe's-branded products that are available only at Trader Joe's. Trader Joe's does not franchise its intellectual property or license others to sell its products. Trader Joe's maintains strict quality control standards when transporting and storing perishable goods to protect the safety of its customers and to ensure that Trader Joe's stores sell only fresh, high-quality goods. Trader Joe's has rejected offers from third parties to enter into franchise agreements, in part because of the difficulty of "ensuring that these third parties will ship, handle, and store food products pursuant to Trader Joe's exacting standards." Trader Joe's does not operate outside of the United States, but Canadian consumers regularly travel across the border to shop at Trader Joe's stores located in northern Washington.

Trader Joe's owns several federally registered and common-law trademarks associated with its stores and products. Its family of marks includes a trademark for the red, stylized "Trader Joe's" text, see Fig. 1, and numerous trademarks for Trader Joe's-branded products. Trader Joe's also alleges that it has trade dress protection for its South Pacific-themed store design. *See Two Pesos, Inc. v. Taco Cabana, Inc.*, 505 U.S. 763, 775-76 (1992). . . . Trader Joe's carefully cultivates its brand through advertising, promotion, and word-of-mouth referrals, and, according to the complaint, its trademarks and trade dress "have come to symbolize extraordinary goodwill and have achieved great fame both within and outside the United States" due to these efforts. This fame and popularity has generated substantial domestic and international demand for Trader Joe's products.

Fig. 1:

In October 2011, staff members at the Bellingham Trader Joe's store noticed something odd about one of their customers: Canadian resident Michael Norman Hallatt visited the store several times per week to buy large quantities of Trader Joe's products. When questioned, Hallatt admitted that he drives the goods he purchases across the Canadian border where he distributes them to Canadian customers. Trader Joe's later learned from one of its Canadian customers that Hallatt opened a store in Canada named Transilvania Trading (which he later renamed "Pirate Joe's") where he resells, at substantially inflated prices, Trader Joe's goods purchased in Washington. Trader Joe's alleges that Hallatt uses its intellectual property to solicit business for Pirate Joe's: He advertises his wares with Trader Joe's trademarks, operates a website accessible from the United States, displays an exterior sign at Pirate Joe's that uses a font similar to the trademarked "Trader Joe's" insignia, Fig. 2, and designed the Pirate Joe's store to mimic Trader Joe's trade dress. Hallatt sells perishable goods at Pirate Joe's that he does not transport or store in a manner consistent with the strict quality control standards used by Trader Joe's. Trader Joe's has received at least one complaint from a consumer who became sick after eating a Trader Joe's-branded product she purchased from Pirate Joe's.

Fig. 2:

Trader Joe's told Hallatt that it does not sanction his activity and demanded that he stop reselling Trader Joe's products from Pirate Joe's. Hallatt refused. Trader Joe's declined to serve Hallatt as a customer, but Hallatt, undeterred, began donning "disguises to shop at Trader Joe's without detection" and driving "to Seattle, Portland, and even California to purchase TRADER JOE'S-branded products and evade Trader Joe's refusal to sell to them." The complaint also alleges that Hallatt pays third parties in Washington to buy Trader Joe's goods on his behalf. On appeal, Trader Joe's contends that Hallatt accomplishes his scheme in part because he is a United States Lawful Permanent Resident (LPR), an immigration status that enables him to live and work legally in the United States. All told, Hallatt has spent more than $350,000 purchasing Trader Joe's products to resell in Canada.

Trader Joe's sued Hallatt (doing business as Pirate Joe's) for trademark infringement in the Western District of Washington, invoking that court's federal question and supplemental jurisdiction. Trader Joe's alleged that Hallatt violated federal and state trademark and unfair competition laws by misleading consumers "into falsely believing that Pirate Joe's and/or Transilvania Trading have been authorized or approved by Trader Joe's," displaying Trader Joe's trademarks and mimicking Trader Joe's trade dress, and reselling Trader Joe's goods without authorization and without adhering to Trader Joe's' strict quality control practices. According to Trader Joe's, this conduct dilutes its trademarks, confuses consumers, and damages Trader Joe's' reputation by associating it with high-cost, reduced-quality goods. The complaint includes six claims for relief, four of which arise under the Lanham Act and two of which arise under Washington law: (1) federal trademark infringement, 15 U.S.C. §1114(1); (2) unfair competition, false endorsement, and false designation of origin, 15 U.S.C. §1125(a)(1)(A); (3) false advertising, 15 U.S.C. §1125(a)(1)(B); (4) federal trademark dilution, 15 U.S.C. §1125(c); (5) state trademark dilution, Wash. Rev. Code §19.77.160; and (6) deceptive business practices in violation of the Washington Consumer Protection Act, Wash. Rev. Code §19.86.020. Trader Joe's asked the district court to award it damages and permanently enjoin Hallatt from reselling its goods or using its trademarks in Canada.

The district court granted Hallatt's motion to dismiss Trader Joe's' federal claims for lack of subject-matter jurisdiction, concluding that the Lanham Act did not apply to Hallatt's conduct in Canada. [The district court also dismissed the state law claims for failure to state a claim.] Trader Joe's timely appealed. We have jurisdiction under 28 U.S.C. §1291.

DISCUSSION

A.   Lanham Act Claims

. . .

We determine whether any statute, including the Lanham Act, reaches foreign conduct by applying a two-step framework. *See RJR Nabisco, Inc. v. European Cmty.*, ___ U.S. ___, 136 S. Ct. 2090, 2101 (2016). At step one we ask "whether the statute gives a clear, affirmative indication that it applies extraterritorially." *Id*. The Supreme Court settled this question with regard to the Lanham Act when it held that the Act's "use in commerce" element and broad definition of "commerce" clearly indicate Congress's intent that the Act should apply extraterritorially. *See Steele v. Bulova Watch Co.*, 344 U.S. 280, 286 (1952). Where, as here, Congress intended a statute to apply extraterritorially, we proceed to step two and consider "the limits Congress has (or has not) imposed on the statute's foreign application." *RJR Nabisco*, 136 S. Ct. at 2101. . . .

1.   Subject-Matter Jurisdiction

Trader Joe's argues on appeal that the extraterritorial reach of the Lanham Act is a non-jurisdictional merits question. . . . We agree with Trader Joe's.

When the district court dismissed the federal claims for lack of subject-matter jurisdiction, it did not have the benefit of our recent decision in *La Quinta Worldwide LLC v. Q.R.T.M., S.A. de C.V.*, 762 F.3d 867 (9th Cir. 2014). There, we held that the Lanham Act's "use in commerce" element (the element that gives the Act extraterritorial reach) is not jurisdictional. In *La Quinta*, an American hotel chain, La Quinta Worldwide, sued a Mexican competitor, Quinta Real, for trademark infringement after Quinta Real expressed an intent to expand its business into the United States. The district court held a bench trial and found in La Quinta's favor. On appeal, Quinta Real asserted for the first time "that there is no federal subject-matter jurisdiction over this case." Quinta Real argued that the Lanham Act's "use in commerce" requirement is jurisdictional; its expressions of intent to open a hotel were not sufficient to show a "use in commerce" under the Lanham Act; and that the Ninth Circuit was required to dismiss the appeal for lack of subject-matter jurisdiction.

Our court rejected those arguments. Citing [*Arbaugh v. Y&H Corp.*, 546 U.S. 500 (2006)], we reasoned that "federal courts have subject-matter jurisdiction over all suits pleading 'a colorable claim "arising under" the Constitution or laws of the United States,' so long as Congress does not clearly indicate otherwise." *La Quinta*, 762 F.3d at 873. Because "the 'use in commerce' element of Lanham Act claims under sections 32 and 43(a) is not connected to the Lanham Act's jurisdictional grant in 15 U.S.C. §1121(a)," the element "is not a jurisdictional requirement, and we have subject-matter jurisdiction under 15 U.S.C. §1121(a)." Id. at 872-73. . . .

But this conclusion does not end our work. The district court dismissed Trader Joe's case at the pleadings stage, but as in *Morrison*, "nothing in [its analysis] turned on" the fact that it dismissed the case under Rule 12(b)(1), rather than under Rule 12(b)(6). . . . [O]ur longstanding *Timberlane* test for the Lanham Act's extraterritorial application applies whether the extraterritorial scope of the statute is a jurisdictional or merits question, so remand to the district court would only "require [it to put] a new Rule 12(b)(6) label [on] the same Rule 12(b)(1) conclusion." [cit.] Rather than asking the district court to engage in this exercise, we consider whether the Lanham Act reaches Hallatt's allegedly infringing conduct under the standards set by Rule 12(b)(6).

2.   The Merits of the Lanham Act

We next consider the limits, if any, Congress imposed on the Act's extraterritorial application. *See RJR Nabisco*, 136 S. Ct. at 2101 (discussing "step two"). In 15 U.S.C. §1127, Congress directed that the Lanham Act applies to "all commerce which may lawfully be regulated by Congress." Whether this provision sweeps foreign activities into the Act's proscriptive reach depends on a three-part test we originally applied to the Sherman Act in *Timberlane Lumber Co. v. Bank of America National Trust & Savings Ass'n*, 549 F.2d 597 (9th Cir. 1976). *See Wells Fargo*, 556 F.2d at 427 (extending *Timberlane* test to the Lanham Act). Under *Timberlane*, the Lanham Act applies extraterritorially if:

(1) the alleged violations . . . create some effect on American foreign commerce; (2) the effect [is] sufficiently great to present a cognizable injury to the plaintiffs under the Lanham Act; and (3) the interests of and links to American foreign commerce [are] sufficiently strong in relation to those of other nations to justify an assertion of extraterritorial authority.

Love, 611 F.3d at 613.[5]

a.   *Timberlane* Prongs One and Two

Timberlane's first two prongs require Trader Joe's to allege that Hallatt infringes its trademarks (1) in a way that affects American foreign commerce, and (2) causes Trader Joe's a cognizable injury under the Lanham Act. A defendant's foreign activities need not have a substantial or even significant effect on American commerce, rather, "some effect" may be sufficient. *Compare Am. Rice, Inc. v. Ark. Rice Growers Coop. Ass'n*, 701 F.2d 408, 414 n.8 (5th Cir. 1983) (joining the Ninth Circuit in requiring "some effect"), with *Vanity Fair Mills v. T. Eaton Co.*, 234 F.2d 633, 642 (2d Cir. 1956) (requiring effect to be substantial); *see also* J. Thomas McCarthy, 5 McCarthy on Trademarks & Unfair Competition §29:58 (4th ed. 2016) (discussing different tests).

Plaintiffs usually satisfy *Timberlane*'s first and second prongs by alleging that infringing goods, though sold initially in a foreign country, flowed into American domestic markets. *See Reebok Int'l, Ltd. v. Marnatech Enters., Inc.*, 970 F.2d 552, 556 (9th Cir. 1992) (prongs one and two met when defendants "knew that their counterfeit shoes went back into the United States with regular frequency"); *McBee v. Delica Co., Ltd.*, 417 F.3d 107, 125 (1st Cir. 2005) ("Quite commonly, plaintiffs . . . meet their burden by presenting evidence that while the initial sales of infringing goods may occur in foreign countries, the goods subsequently tend to enter the United States in some way and in substantial quantities.").[6] Trader Joe's does not allege that the Trader Joe's-brand products Hallatt resells from his Canadian store trickle back into American commerce in a manner likely to confuse American consumers. This fact distinguishes *Steele*, where the Court applied the Lanham Act to a defendant's foreign conduct (his sale of counterfeit watches in Mexico) largely because "spurious 'Bulovas' filtered through the Mexican border into this country." 344 U.S. at 286. It also undermines Trader Joe's' argument that *Steele* controls the outcome here. But, as Trader Joe's alternatively argues, whether infringing goods flow into the United States is not dispositive; plaintiffs may show "some effect" on American commerce in myriad ways. *See, e.g., Am. Rice*, 701 F.2d at 414-15 (applying the Lanham Act to defendant's sale of rice in Saudi Arabia, though the goods did not flow back into United States markets, because defendant's business was located in the United States).

---

5. Trader Joe's argues that *Timberlane* does not apply here because Hallatt executed part of his infringing scheme in the United States. We have applied *Timberlane* in cases where some of the defendant's conduct was domestic, so long as the entire scheme culminated in infringing activity abroad. *See, e.g., Reebok*, 970 F.2d at 557 (applying *Timberlane* where "Reebok's trademark infringement claim [was] based both on actions that occurred in the United States as well as in Mexico"); *Wells Fargo*, 556 F.2d at 429 ("We note, however, that, when faced with both Mexican and United States activities of an American citizen that were part of one infringing scheme, this court adopted an analysis which at least in part was premised on the need to deal with the extraterritorial nature of defendant's activities."). We follow that same tack here.

6. *Timberlane* refers to defendant's impact on "American foreign" commerce, *Love*, 611 F.3d at 613, but, as these cases show, we regularly apply the Lanham Act to foreign conduct that impacts domestic commerce because infringing goods flow into American domestic commerce streams. *See, e.g., Steele*, 344 U.S. at 286.

Trader Joe's alleges that Hallatt's foreign conduct has "some effect" on American commerce because his activities harm its reputation and decrease the value of its American-held trademarks. It argues that Hallatt violates 15 U.S.C. §1114(1)(a), the Lanham Act's general prohibition on trademark infringement, by transporting and selling Trader Joe's goods without using proper quality control measures or established product recall practices. By framing its allegation this way, Trader Joe's seeks to circumvent the first sale doctrine, which establishes that "resale by the first purchaser of the original article under the producer's trademark is generally neither trademark infringement nor unfair competition." *See Enesco Corp. v. Price/Costco Inc.*, 146 F.3d 1083, 1085 (9th Cir. 1998). The quality control theory of infringement is cognizable under the Lanham Act notwithstanding the first sale doctrine: "[d]istribution of a product that does not meet the trademark holder's quality control standards may result in the devaluation of the mark by tarnishing its image." . . .

According to Trader Joe's, Hallatt's poor quality control practices could impact American commerce if consumers who purchase Trader Joe's-brand products that have been transported to Canada become ill, and news of such illness travels across the border. Trader Joe's alleges this may harm its reputation, reduce the value of its trademarks, and cause lost sales. Trader Joe's argues its risk of harm is particularly high because Pirate Joe's displays Trader Joe's trademarks, which leads consumers to believe that it is an authorized Trader Joe's retailer. There is nothing implausible about the concern that Trader Joe's will suffer a tarnished reputation and resultant monetary harm in the United States from contaminated goods sold in Canada. Incidents of food-born illness regularly make international news, and Trader Joe's alleges that it is aware of at least one customer who became sick after consuming food sold by Pirate Joe's. Courts have held that reputational harm to an American plaintiff may constitute "some effect" on American commerce. *Steele*, 344 U.S. at 286 (applying Lanham Act extraterritorially where "competing goods could well reflect adversely on Bulova Watch Company's trade reputation in markets cultivated by advertising here as well as abroad"); *Gucci Am., Inc. v. Guess?, Inc.*, 790 F. Supp. 2d 136, 143 (S.D.N.Y. 2011) ("It is well-settled that a showing of . . . harm to plaintiff's goodwill in the United States is sufficient to demonstrate a 'substantial effect on United States commerce.'" (*quoting Steele*, 344 U.S. at 28)); *see also* 15 U.S.C. §§1114, 1125 (making actionable conduct that is likely to cause future harm).

Hallatt's alleged attempt to pass as an authorized Trader Joe's retailer could similarly harm Trader Joe's' domestic reputation and diminish the value of its American-held marks. The complaint alleges that Hallatt sells Trader Joe's goods at inflated prices, so customers who shop at Pirate Joe's may come to mistakenly associate Trader Joe's with overpriced goods. Trader Joe's also alleges that Pirate Joe's has inferior customer service, something Trader Joe's believes reflects poorly on its brand. False endorsement gives rise to an actionable harm under the Lanham Act, *see* 15 U.S.C. §1125(a)(1)(A), and Trader Joe's contends it will suffer this harm in the United States because it draws international shoppers to its northern-Washington stores, and its trademarks stand to lose value in the United States. *See McBee*, 417 F.3d at 119 ("One can easily imagine a variety of harms to American commerce arising from wholly foreign activities by foreign defendants. There could be harm caused by false endorsements, passing off, or product disparagement, or confusion over sponsorship affecting American commerce and causing loss of American sales.").

Finally, Trader Joe's alleges that Hallatt engages in commercial activity in the United States as part of his infringing scheme. *See Reebok*, 970 F.2d at 554-55 (first two *Timberlane* factors satisfied in part because defendant "organized and directed the manufacture of counterfeit REEBOK shoes from the United States"). According to Trader Joe's, Hallatt sources his inventory entirely from the United States: he purchases thousands of dollars of Trader Joe's goods in the United States and re-sells them in his Canadian store. Hallatt's operation may be assisted in part by his U.S. LPR status, 8 U.S.C. §1101(a)(27)(A). *See A.V. by Versace, Inc. v. Gianni Versace, S.p.A.*, 126 F. Supp. 2d 328, 337 (S.D.N.Y. 2001) (applying Lanham Act to foreign conduct of permanent resident alien who "has resided in and done business in the United States"); *cf. Steele*, 344 U.S. at 285 (explaining that the United States government may regulate American citizens' foreign conduct). The complaint also alleged that Hallatt began hiring third parties in Washington, presumably United States citizens, to purchase Trader Joe's goods on his behalf when Trader Joe's refused to serve him as a customer. This domestic economic activity weighs in favor of applying the Lanham Act to Hallatt's conduct. *See Ocean Garden, Inc. v. Marktrade Co.*, 953 F.2d 500, 503-04 (9th Cir. 1991) (applying Lanham Act to foreign conduct of California-based corporate defendant).

Hallatt's domestic activity also distinguishes this case from *Love*, the case the district court found dispositive. The plaintiff in *Love* (Mike Love, a former member of the Beach Boys) sued several British defendants after they distributed compact discs featuring Love's trademark as cover art. In *Love*, it was undisputed "that all relevant acts occurred abroad" (defendants designed, manufactured, and disseminated the infringing CDs entirely in Europe). Love failed to show that the defendants' conduct directly caused Love "monetary injury in the United States," and we affirmed summary judgment in favor of defendants. Here, unlike in *Love*, Hallatt executes a key part of his allegedly infringing scheme in the United States, so the causal showing found lacking in *Love* is satisfied.[9] *See McBee*, 417 F.3d at 118 ("the domestic effect of the international activities may be of lesser importance and a lesser showing of domestic effects may be all that is needed" when defendant engages a scheme involving domestic and foreign conduct (discussing *Steele*)).

For these reasons, Trader Joe's satisfied its burden under *Timberlane* prongs one and two, at least at this early stage of the proceeding.

b. *Timberlane* Prong Three

The third *Timberlane* prong considers international comity, and gives effect to the "rule that we construe statutes to avoid unreasonable interference with other nations' sovereign authority where possible," *RJR Nabisco*, 136 S. Ct. at 2106-07 & n.9. This prong involves weighing seven factors:

> [1] the degree of conflict with foreign law or policy, [2] the nationality or allegiance of the parties and the locations or principal places of business of corporations, [3] the extent to which enforcement by either state can be expected to achieve compliance, [4] the relative significance of effects on the United States as compared with those elsewhere, [5] the extent to which there is explicit purpose to harm or affect American commerce, [6] the foreseeability of such effect, and [7] the relative importance to the violations charged of conduct within the United States as compared with conduct abroad.

Star-Kist Foods, Inc. v. P.J. Rhodes & Co., 769 F.2d 1393, 1395 (9th Cir. 1985) (*citing Timberlane*). No one factor is dispositive; each factor "is just one consideration to be

---

9. *Love* also involved a summary judgment motion; we dismissed plaintiff's Lanham Act claim because Love's evidence did not raise a triable issue of fact about whether CD sales in England impacted attendance at Love's concerts in the United States. Here, we consider an appeal following a motion to dismiss, and so we accept—without requiring Trader Joe's to prove—that the domestic components of Hallatt's operation impact American commerce. . . .

balanced." *Wells Fargo*, 556 F.2d at 428. Having considered these factors, we conclude that it is appropriate to apply the Lanham Act to Hallatt and Pirate Joe's.

Degree of conflict with foreign laws. Courts typically find a conflict with foreign law or policy when there is an ongoing trademark dispute or other proceeding abroad. *Compare Star-Kist*, 769 F.2d at 1396 (finding conflict when defendant's petition to cancel plaintiffs' Philippine trademark registration was pending in the Philippine Patent Office), *with Am. Rice*, 701 F.2d at 415-16 (finding no conflict when defendant's conduct was lawful under Saudi Arabian trademark law). In 2012, Trader Joe's applied for, and was granted, Canadian recognition for its Trader Joe's trademarks, but there is no pending or ongoing adversarial proceeding between Trader Joe's and Hallatt in Canada. Nor is Trader Joe's engaged in any proceeding (so far as we are aware) relating to its Canadian trademarks. This factor therefore weighs in favor of extraterritorial application.

Nationality of parties and location of businesses. This factor typically weighs in favor of extraterritoriality when both parties are United States citizens, or the parties are foreign citizens who operate domestic businesses. *See Reebok*, 970 F.2d at 556 (defendant operated his business from the United States); *Ocean Garden*, 953 F.2d at 504 (both parties were Californian corporations). Trader Joe's is an American corporation with its principal place of business in Monrovia, California. Although Trader Joe's operates no stores in Canada, its trademarks are well-known there. The complaint alleges that Transilvania Trading and Pirate Joe's are (or were) Canadian entities, and that both have (or had) their principal places of business in Vancouver, Canada. As far as we can tell, Hallatt is a Canadian citizen, but because he maintains LPR status in the United States, he subjects himself to the laws of this country. Hallatt is also the driving force behind Pirate Joe's. This is not, as Trader Joe's argues, simply a dispute between an American plaintiff and an American defendant, because the complaint alleges that Hallatt is a Canadian citizen who domiciles in Vancouver. But Hallatt's admission that he holds LPR status edges this factor into Trader Joe's' column. *See A.V. by Versace*, 126 F. Supp. 2d at 337 (applying Lanham Act to foreign conduct when defendant was permanent resident alien, had "resided in and done business in the United States for over forty years," and was the driving force behind the corporate defendant), at least at this stage in the proceedings.

Remedy and enforcement. The third factor requires us to consider the remedy sought and the extent to which the trial court will be able to enforce its order. Trader Joe's seeks damages, including disgorgement to compensate for losses incurred as a result of the infringement, and a permanent injunction to prevent Hallatt from using Trader Joe's trademarks, offering Trader Joe's goods for resale, or mimicking Trader Joe's trade dress. There is nothing to suggest that the district court would have difficulty enforcing a damages award against Hallatt: Hallatt is an LPR and Trader Joe's argues he holds assets here. *See Reebok*, 970 F.2d at 557 (finding American court to be in a superior enforcement position vis-à-vis its Mexican counterparts because "[e]ach of the defendants, their principal places of business, and the vast majority of their assets are located in the United States"). And there is no doubt that the district court could stop Hallatt's operation with a domestic injunction because Hallatt sources his goods entirely from the United States. *See Ocean Garden*, 953 F.2d at 504 ("The injunction would be effective against Marktrade because it is a U.S. corporation which 'orchestrated [its] infringing activities'" here (alteration in original) (citation omitted)). The district court could likewise enforce an injunction against Hallatt's foreign conduct if that conduct is found to violate the Lanham Act. *See Steele*, 344 U.S. at 289 ("[T]he District Court in exercising its equity powers may command persons properly before it to cease or perform acts outside its territorial jurisdiction."); *Ramirez & Feraud Chili Co. v. Las Palmas Food Co.*, 146 F. Supp. 594 (S.D. Cal. 1956) (same), *aff'd*,

245 F.2d 874 (9th Cir. 1957) (per curiam). Neither the remedies sought nor the district court's ability to enforce its orders weigh against applying the Lanham Act here.

Relative significance of effects. Trademark law has two goals: "[p]rotect property in the trademark and protect consumers from confusion." Hallatt's conduct primarily affects the value of Trader Joe's' trademarks in the United States because Trader Joe's holds most of its intellectual property here. On the other hand, Canadian consumers are the most likely to be deceived by Hallatt's conduct because he displays Trader Joe's marks and sells Trader Joe's goods only in Canada. Federal courts ordinarily do not have an interest in protecting foreign consumers from confusion. *See McBee*, 417 F.3d at 126. But Trader Joe's also alleges that its trademarks are well-known in Canada, and that more than forty percent of the credit card transactions at its Bellingham, Washington store are with non-United States residents. Hallatt's sale of Trader Joe's goods in Canada has the potential to mislead these consumers, so this factor weighs in favor of extraterritorial application.

Purpose to harm American commerce and foreseeability. The pleadings, taken in the light most favorable to Trader Joe's, tend to support the conclusion that Hallatt intended to harm Trader Joe's, or, at a minimum, that such harm was foreseeable. Hallatt chose to name his store "Pirate Joe's," suggesting that he knowingly treads on Trader Joe's' goodwill and pirates Trader Joe's' intellectual property. Indeed, one of Hallatt's employees allegedly admitted that "we're pirating Trader Joe's, sort of." The complaint further alleges that Trader Joe's disapproved of Hallatt's conduct, and Hallatt began engaging in subterfuge (such as donning costumes) to purchase goods at Trader Joe's stores without being identified. These factors therefore weigh in favor of extraterritorial application.

Relative importance of conduct within the United States as compared to conduct abroad. Trader Joe's alleges, and Hallatt admits, that an essential part of his commercial venture takes place in the United States: Hallatt purchases Trader Joe's products in Washington with the purpose of reselling them in Canada. That Hallatt uses American commerce streams to accomplish his allegedly infringing scheme weighs in favor of applying the Lanham Act to his conduct. But arguably the conduct most important to Hallatt's operation happens in Canada: According to Trader Joe's, Hallatt displays Trader Joe's trademarks on his Canadian store in a way that confuses Canadian consumers, and Hallatt resells Trader Joe's goods—including perishable goods not transported according to Trader Joe's quality control standards—in Canada. Because most of Hallatt's infringing activity occurs abroad, this factor weighs against extraterritorial application to some extent. *See Reebok*, 970 F.2d at 557 (reasoning that the factor would weigh against extraterritorial application when "actual consumer sales of [the infringing] products may have occurred only" abroad); *Star-Kist*, 769 F.2d at 1396 ("The effect on United States commerce from the alleged illegal use of the trademarks in trade between the Philippines and other foreign countries is relatively insignificant compared to the effect on Philippine commerce.").

* * *

In sum, *Timberlane*'s three prongs favor extraterritorial application of the Lanham Act here. On prongs one and two, Trader Joe's alleges a nexus between Hallatt's foreign conduct and American commerce sufficient to state a Lanham Act claim: Hallatt's conduct may cause Trader Joe's reputational harm that could decrease the value of its American-held trademarks, and Hallatt operates in American commerce streams when he buys Trader Joe's goods in Washington and hires locals to assist him. On prong three, the seven subfactors we use to evaluate potential "interference with other nations' sovereign authority," taken together, do not counsel against applying the Lanham Act here. We therefore conclude that the Lanham Act reaches Hallatt's allegedly infringing activity, and we reverse the district court's dismissal of Trader Joe's' four Lanham Act claims.

B.   STATE LAW CLAIMS

Trader Joe's next contends the district court erred when it granted Hallatt's motion to dismiss its state trademark dilution and Washington Consumer Protection Act (CPA) claims. We agree with the district court that Trader Joe's failed to state a claim under either statute, and we affirm its order dismissing those claims. [The court held that Trader Joe's failed to state a claim for relief under state dilution law because Trader Joe's did not allege that Hallatt used Trader Joe's trademarks in Washington, and dismissed the claim under the CPA because the deception allegedly occurs only in Canada and therefore harms only Canadian consumers.]

NOTES AND QUESTIONS

1. *The* Vanity Fair *factors.* Courts applying the *Vanity Fair* factors typically recite that "none of these three criteria is dispositive of the analysis concerning the Lanham Act's extraterritorial effect, and a court must employ a balancing test of all three factors to determine whether the statute is properly implicated." *Warnaco Inc. v. VF Corp.*, 844 F. Supp. 940, 950 (S.D.N.Y. 1994); *see also Nintendo of Am., Inc. v. Aeropower Co., Ltd.*, 34 F.3d 246, 251 (4th Cir. 1994) (vacating injunction for failure to consider all factors). However, the Court of Appeals in *Vanity Fair* might have suggested some brighter-line applications of the factors. Which "bright lines" can you detect?

2. *Alternative approaches.* In what ways is the approach of the First Circuit in *McBee* different from that of the Second Circuit in *Vanity Fair*? Which is consistent with the Supreme Court's opinion in *Bulova*?

3. *Alternative "effect" requirements.* The Second Circuit has repeatedly affirmed its "substantial effect" test. *See, e.g., Sterling Drug, Inc. v. Bayer AG*, 14 F.3d 733, 746 (2d Cir. 1994). The Fifth Circuit has (like the Ninth Circuit) also taken a more assertive attitude toward the assertion of jurisdiction over extraterritorial activities and required only "some effect" on U.S. commerce. *See Am. Rice, Inc. v. Ark. Rice Growers Coop. Ass'n*, 701 F.2d 408 (5th Cir. 1983); *see also Nintendo of Am., Inc. v. Aeropower Co.*, 34 F.3d 246, 250-51 (4th Cir. 1994) (requiring "significant effect" on U.S. commerce); *see also Paulsson Geophysical Servs., Inc. v. Sigmar*, 529 F.3d 303 (5th Cir. 2008) (noting Fifth Circuit case law but finding that "there is no need to decide what is the smallest 'effect' on United States commerce that is necessary to sustain a court's jurisdiction over United States citizens committing trademark infringement in a foreign country, because the [defendants'] activities in this case rose to the level of the infringing parties in *Bulova* and *American Rice*").

Although the Ninth Circuit test is regarded as less stringent, this does not mean that courts following it will always apply the Lanham Act extraterritorially, as indicated in *Love v. Associated Newspapers, Ltd.*, 611 F.3d 601 (9th Cir. 2010), discussed and distinguished in *Trader Joe's.* Would the outcome in the non-Ninth Circuit cases you have read been different if litigated under the Ninth Circuit test?

4. *What constitutes "substantial effect"?* Although the term "substantial effect" is routinely cited in cases (especially in the Second Circuit) involving extraterritorial activity, the meaning of that term is far from clear. As a district court in the Second Circuit explained,

> [t]he case law in this Circuit is somewhat unclear as to what sort of substantial effect on U.S. commerce is required for a court to exercise jurisdiction over a U.S. citizen's foreign infringement of a U.S. trademark. U.S. consumer confusion or harm to the plaintiff's goodwill in the U.S. certainly suffices. *See Atl. Richfield*, 150 F.3d at 192-93; *Piccoli A/S*, 19 F. Supp. 2d at

170. Financial harm to an American trademark owner whether from the loss of foreign sales or the damage to the trademark owner's reputation abroad is at the very least, relevant to determining whether foreign infringement has a substantial effect on U.S. commerce. *See Bulova Watch*, 344 U.S. at 287 (citing fact that defendant's "competing goods could well reflect adversely on Bulova Watch Company's trade reputation in markets cultivated by advertising here as well as abroad" as a factor weighing in favor of extraterritorial application of Lanham Act); *Totalplan Corp. of Am. v. Colborne*, 14 F.3d 824, 830-31 (2d Cir. 1994) ("Totalplan has not shown that any foreign sales of Love cameras have been diverted from it by Lure's shipment to Japan."); *Software AG, Inc. v. Consist Software Solutions*, No. 08 Civ. 389(CM), 2008 WL 563449, **14-15 (S.D.N.Y. Feb. 21, 2008) (finding substantial effect of foreign false advertising in violation of the Lanham Act because violation jeopardized valuable contracts that were to be performed in the U.S. by plaintiff); *Aerogroup Int'l v. Marlboro Footworks*, 955 F. Supp. 220, 229 (S.D.N.Y. 1997) ("Courts in this district have also found a substantial effect on commerce where an American plaintiff's foreign sales have been diverted, and where there is danger of irreparable injury to a plaintiff's good will and reputation.") (internal citations omitted); *Warnaco Inc. v. VF Corp.*, 844 F. Supp. 940, 952 (S.D.N.Y. 1994) ("[D]iversion of [foreign] sales and adverse impact on foreign licensees can constitute substantial impact on United States commerce.").

The weight to be given to the domestic commercial activities of American citizens that support foreign infringement is less clear. . . . In *Atlantic Richfield*, the Second Circuit rejected the notion that *Bulova* held that "a defendant's domestic activity, even if 'essential' to infringing activity abroad is alone sufficient to constitute a substantial effect on United States commerce." [cit.] The court then found that "even if *Bulova* is read to indicate that a defendant's infringing extraterritorial conduct has a substantial effect on United States commerce whenever some non-infringing domestic activity is 'essential' to that extraterritorial conduct," none of defendant's domestic activities were "essential." [cit.] Summing up its decision, the Second Circuit observed that the "mere presence of the alleged infringer in the United States" will not constitute a substantial effect on United States commerce where:

(i) an alleged infringer's foreign use of a mark does not mislead American consumers in their purchases or cause them to look less favorably upon the mark;

(ii) the alleged infringer does not physically use the stream of American commerce to compete with the trademark owner by, for example, *manufacturing*, *processing*, or *transporting* the competing product in United States commerce; and

(iii) none of the alleged infringer's American activities materially support the foreign use of the mark.

[*Atlantic Richfield*, 150 F.3d] at 193.

Atlantic Richfield plainly left open the possibility that an American infringer's physical use of the stream of American commerce to compete with the trademark owner could constitute a substantial effect on American commerce, at least where those domestic activities materially support the foreign use of the mark and are in themselves domestic infringements of the mark likely to confuse U.S. consumers. None of those factors were in play in *Atlantic Richfield*, as the plaintiff there had shown, "[a]t best . . . that [defendant] ha[d] a geographic presence in the United States and, by inference from that fact, that some decision-making regarding [defendant's] foreign activities ha[d] taken place on American soil." *Id.* After *Atlantic Richfield* courts in this circuit have closely examined the nature and effect of an infringer's domestic activities in support of foreign trademark infringement. *See World Book, Inc. v. IBM Corp.*, 354 F. Supp. 2d 451, 454 (S.D.N.Y. 2005) (granting defendant's motion on the pleadings where "the only domestic activity plaintiff alleges to have occurred in connection with the unauthorized distribution is the mere authorization of that activity."); *Space Imaging Eur., Ltd. v. Space Imaging L.P.*, No. 98 Civ. 2291 (DC), 1999 WL 511759, **4-5 (S.D.N.Y. July 15, 1999) (granting motion for summary judgment in part on the conclusion that defendant's "alleged misconduct was not related to conduct affecting U.S. commerce"); *Piccoli A/S v. Calvin Klein Jeanswear Co.*, 19 F. Supp. 2d 157, 170-171 (S.D.N.Y. 1998) (finding allegations that "defendants [who were American citizens] engaged in an organized scheme pursuant to which Jeanswear sent promotional materials to prospective purchasers which invited them to come to its U.S. showrooms to view, negotiate for and purchase Calvin Klein jeans for unrestricted international distribution" sufficient to defeat a motion to dismiss). [cit.]

In the present case, there is no question that defendants infringed plaintiff's mark [CHIC for services comprising musical performances] in U.S. commerce by advertising on their website (and those of others) their availability to perform as "First Ladies of Chic." They signed and negotiated contracts to perform as "First Ladies of Chic." They concede that they undercut plaintiff's booking fee by agreeing to perform for less money. [cit.] Whether the eventual performance was in the U.S. or abroad, it is undisputed that defendants directed, coordinated, and operated their "First Ladies of Chic" enterprise from the U.S. That is, save for the actual performance abroad, defendants "conducted [their] business almost exclusively within the United States and used the instrumentalities of American commerce to profit at [plaintiff's] expense without regard to where the [infringing performances] ultimately occurred or whether those [performances] violated American law." *Aerogroup Int'l v. Marlboro Footworks*, 955 F. Supp. 220, 230 (S.D.N.Y. 1997); *cf. World Book, Inc. v. IBM Corp.*, 354 F. Supp. 2d 451, 454 (S.D.N.Y. 2005) (finding that Lanham Act did not apply to alleged foreign infringement where only supporting domestic activity was the "mere authorization" of the foreign infringement). Moreover, defendants materially advanced their foreign infringement with their domestic infringement: as part of their effort to attract bookings and concertgoers, defendants advertised their availability to perform anywhere as "First Ladies of Chic" on their own website, www.ladiesofchic.com, and on the websites of American promoters and talent agencies, thus using plaintiff's mark in American commerce in a way that was likely to confuse domestic as well as foreign consumers. That defendants' support of their foreign infringement was itself likely to confuse U.S. consumers further distinguishes this case from cases like *Totalplan Corp. of Am. v. Colborne*, 14 F.3d 824 (2d Cir. 1994). There, the Second Circuit held that a foreign defendant's packaging and transport of allegedly infringing cameras in U.S. commerce did not constitute a substantial effect on U.S. commerce. *Id.* That use of the instrumentalities of U.S. commerce, however, did not itself result in the likely confusion of American consumers. Likewise in *P & G v. Colgate-Palmolive Co.*, No. 96 Civ. 9123 (RPP), 1998 WL 788802, *68 (S.D.N.Y. Nov. 5, 1998), where the court found that the Lanham Act did not apply to allegedly infringing advertisements broadcast exclusively abroad that were filmed and reviewed in the U.S., there was no evidence to suggest that the American activities were themselves infringing. By contrast, it is well-settled that the Lanham Act applies to an American defendant's foreign infringement where that infringement results in a likelihood of a confusion of American consumers, such as when products bearing the infringing mark make their way back into the U.S. *See Atl. Richfield*, 150 F.3d at 193 (citing *Steele v. Bulova Watch Co.*, 344 U.S at 286-87). The Court sees no reason why the Lanham Act should not also apply where a U.S. citizen's foreign infringement is materially furthered by infringing domestic activities that will likely confuse American consumers.

Rodgers v. Wright, 544 F. Supp. 2d 302, 313-15 (S.D.N.Y. 2008); *see also Tire Engineering and Distribution, LLC v. Shandong Linglong Rubber Co.*, 682 F.3d 292 (4th Cir. 2012) (declining to apply Lantham Act based solely on harm to U.S. company's income from foreign infringement where defendant not a U.S. entity). To what extent should it matter whether the activities in the United States were "essential steps" in the course of the business consummated abroad? *Cf. Paulsson Geophysical Servs., Inc. v. Sigmar*, 529 F.3d 303 (5th Cir. 2008).

5. *Conflicts with non-exclusive foreign rights.* If the defendant has no foreign trademark rights in the term but does have the right to use the term in a foreign country (e.g., because the courts or trademark office in the foreign country have determined that a term is generic, descriptive, or otherwise unprotectable, and thus can be used by any trader), should this affect the *Vanity Fair* analysis? Are *exclusive* rights to use a mark required for this factor to favor the defendant? *Cf. Libbey Glass, Inc. v. Oneida Ltd.*, 61 F. Supp. 2d 720, 723 (N.D. Ohio 1999) ("because [the Turkish defendant] has not shown a registration under Turkish law, there is no evidence to support the proposition that Turkey has an interest in this litigation that conflicts with the application of the Lanham Act"). The *Vanity Fair* court articulated the third *Bulova* factor as whether there was a "conflict with trademark rights established by foreign law." 234 F.2d at 642. Is there a difference between a conflict with foreign trademark *law* and foreign trademark *rights*? *Cf. Love v. Mail on Sunday*, 473

F. Supp. 2d 1052 (C.D. Cal. 2007) (declining to exercise jurisdiction over claim for unauthorized use of persona under Section 43(a) where defendant's conduct might have been legal where it occurred given the more restrictive causes of action available there).

6.   *Once extraterritorial jurisdiction is exercised . . .* Once a court decides that it may, under the applicable test, exercise jurisdiction extraterritorially, what should be the geographic focus of its substantive trademark analysis? For example, in which marketplace should courts examine mark strength? In which marketplace should courts assess likely confusion? *Cf. Am. Rice, Inc. v. Producers Rice Mill Inc.*, 518 F.3d 321, 330-31 (5th Cir. 2008).

PROBLEM 6-2: ITALIAN ONLINE MAGAZINE SALES

Playboy Enterprises, Inc. ("PEI") owns U.S. trademark registrations for the mark PLAYBOY for adult magazines. PEI was denied an equivalent trademark registration in Italy on the grounds that the mark was a weak mark not entitled to protection in that country. Tattilo Editrice, S.p.A. ("Tattilo"), an Italian company, publishes an adult magazine in Italy under the mark PLAYMEN. In 1981, PEI obtained an injunction from a federal court in New York against Tattilo enjoining it from publishing, printing, distributing, or selling in the United States an English-language male sophisticate magazine under the name PLAYMEN or any name confusingly similar to PLAYBOY. (PEI obtained similar injunctions in France, Germany, and England.) Since 1981, Tattilo has continued to publish and distribute its magazine in Italy, but not in the United States. In 1996, Tattilo established a website featuring the PLAYMEN name. This site makes available images of the cover of the Italian magazine, as well as its "Women of the Month" feature and several other sexually explicit photographic images. Users of the Internet site also receive "special discounts" on other Tattilo products, such as CD-ROMs and Photo CDs. Tattilo created this site by uploading these images onto a World Wide Web server located in Italy. These images can be accessed at the Internet address *http://www.playmen.it*. Two distinct services are available on the PLAYMEN Internet site. "PLAYMEN Lite" is available without a paid subscription, allowing users of the Internet to view moderately explicit images via computer. In addition, the PLAYMEN Internet site offers the more sexually explicit service called "PLAYMEN Pro." PLAYMEN Pro is available only to users who have paid the subscription price. To subscribe to PLAYMEN Pro, the prospective user must fill out a form and send it via fax to Tattilo. Within twenty-four hours the user receives by email a unique password and login name that enable the user to browse the PLAYMEN Pro service. The PLAYMEN Internet site is widely available to patrons living in the United States. Has Tattilo violated the terms of the injunction? What relief should a federal court in the United States provide? *See Playboy Enters., Inc. v. Chuckleberry Publ'g, Inc.*, 939 F. Supp. 1032 (S.D.N.Y. 1996).

PROBLEM 6-3:   IRISH FURNITURE SALES

Crate & Barrel owns registered U.S. trademark rights in the term CRATE AND BARREL for retail services in the housewares and furniture sector. In addition to extensive advertising and sales in the United States, Crate & Barrel has developed an interactive website on the Internet with the domain name *www.crateandbarrel.com*. The site contains information about Crate & Barrel products and other business information. Website visitors worldwide may purchase products from Crate & Barrel. If an Irish company opens a furniture store in Dublin using the CRATE AND BARREL mark, has the Irish company infringed upon the rights of the U.S. company? What if the Irish company then creates a website at the domain name *www.crateandbarrel.ie.com*? This website identifies itself as Crate & Barrel and allows visitors worldwide to both view and purchase the same household goods and furniture sold in the retail store. The goods sold are similar to the types of goods offered for sale by U.S. Crate & Barrel and are priced in U.S. dollars. Does your answer change? What if the Irish company adds the warning "Goods Sold Only in the Republic of Ireland" to the opening page of its website? What if, despite this statement, website users who wish to purchase goods are given the opportunity to select the United States as part of both their shipping and billing addresses? *See Euromarket Designs, Inc. v. Crate & Barrel Ltd.*, 96 F. Supp. 2d 824 (N.D. Ill. 2000). *See also* WIPO, Joint Recommendation Concerning Provisions on the Protection of Marks, and Other Industrial Property Rights in Signs, on the Internet (Oct. 2001) Art. 2 ("Use of a sign on the Internet shall constitute use in a Member State . . . only if the use has a commercial effect in that Member State"); *id.* art 3 (listing non-exhaustive factors that courts should take into account in determining "commercial effect", including *inter alia*: level and character of commercial activity of the user in relation to the Member State, such as whether the user is actually serving customers located there or has indicated an intent not to deliver the goods to customers located in the Member State, or the offering of post-sales activities in the Member State, such as warranty or service; whether the prices are indicated in the official currency of the Member State; whether the user has indicated, in conjunction with the use of the sign, an address, telephone number or other means of contact in the Member State; and whether the text used in conjunction with the use of the sign is in a language predominantly used in the Member State").

7

Confusion-Based Trademark Liability Theories

This chapter introduces and analyzes the major confusion-based theories under which trademark owners may enforce registered and unregistered trademark rights. The governing Lanham Act provisions are the following, reproduced in relevant part:

§1114. (§32) Remedies; Infringement . . .

(1) Any person who shall, without the consent of the registrant—
    (a) use in commerce any reproduction, counterfeit, copy, or colorable imitation of a registered mark in connection with the sale, offering for sale, distribution, or advertising of any goods or services on or in connection with which such use is likely to cause confusion, or to cause mistake, or to deceive . . .
    . . . shall be liable in a civil action by the registrant for the remedies hereinafter provided.

§1125. (§43) False Designations of Origin, False Descriptions . . .

(a) Civil action

    (1) Any person who, on or in connection with any goods or services, or any container for goods, uses in commerce any word, term, name, symbol, or device, or any combination thereof, or any false designation of origin, false or misleading description of fact, or false or misleading representation of fact, which—
    (A) is likely to cause confusion, or to cause mistake, or to deceive as to the affiliation, connection, or association of such person with another person, or as to the origin, sponsorship, or approval of his or her goods, services, or commercial activities by another person . . .
    . . . shall be liable in a civil action by any person who believes that he or she is or is likely to be damaged by such act.

As we have previously noted, the Section 32 cause of action applies to registered trademark rights and is often labeled as a "trademark infringement" cause of action. The Section 43(a) cause of action that we will discuss in this chapter is a parallel cause of action that applies to unregistered rights, sometimes labeled as a "false designation of origin" cause of action, but also known as "common law trademark infringement," "unregistered trademark infringement," or even "unfair competition." The same confusion theories apply irrespective of whether the case involves registered rights. Thus, for purposes of the materials in this chapter, whether the case is brought as a Section 32 action or a Section 43(a) action will not be dispositive, even though it will be worth noting. As a practical matter, owners of registered rights frequently plead causes of action under Section 32 and Section 43(a) in the alternative.

Although the cases in this chapter deal only with confusion-based theories of enforcement, keep in mind the inevitable link between enforcement issues and the protectability issues discussed in Chapters 2-5—namely that one can only enforce one's *validly created* rights. Courts recite this principle by rote in trademark cases. *See, e.g., Tie Tech, Inc. v. Kinedyne Corp.*, 296 F.3d 778, 783 (9th Cir. 2002) ("A necessary concomitant to proving infringement is, of course, having a valid trademark; there can be no infringement of an invalid mark."). Frequently, courts incorporate protectability issues into their recitations of the overarching trademark infringement standard. For example, in the Third Circuit, "[t]o prove trademark infringement and unfair competition under the Lanham Act, [the plaintiff] must prove: (1) it owns the [asserted] mark; (2) the mark is valid and legally protectable; and (3) [defendant's] use of the mark to identify goods or services is likely to create confusion." *Checkpoint Sys., Inc. v. Check Point Software Techs., Inc.*, 269 F.3d 270, 279 (3d Cir. 2001). Where the mark is the subject of a registration, the registrant enjoys the benefits of the Section 33(a) presumption, relieving the registrant from the initial burden of producing evidence on ownership and validity, and further benefits accrue according to Section 33(b) when the registration becomes incontestable. *See supra* Chapter 5. Where the mark is unregistered, such that the mark owner is proceeding under Section 43(a), the mark owner must produce evidence establishing ownership and validity as well as likely confusion. *See, e.g., Yarmuth-Dion, Inc. v. D'ion Furs, Inc.*, 835 F.2d 990, 992-93 (2d Cir. 1987) (referring to a "two-step" test, the first step concerning protectability and the second step concerning likelihood of confusion). *But see Belmora v. Bayer*, excerpted in Chapter 6, suggesting that a Section 43(a) action could proceed even in the absence of a valid mark.

This chapter concerns what is labeled above in the *Checkpoint* quote as part (3) of the infringement test—what is in fact the heart of any infringement analysis. We first consider how the likelihood-of-confusion standard evolved, and contrast that standard with other potential confusion-based standards (section A). We then turn to modern legal doctrine, which calls for an understanding of the types of actionable "uses" under the Lanham Act (section B) and the multi-factor test for likelihood of confusion (section C).

After establishing this foundation, we explore theories of confusion away from the point of sale (section D) and the theory of "reverse confusion" (section E). Finally, we address indirect and vicarious theories of infringement liability (section F).

A.   EVOLUTION OF THE CONFUSION STANDARD

BORDEN ICE CREAM CO. v. BORDEN'S CONDENSED MILK CO.

201 F. 510 (7th Cir. 1912)

[Borden's Condensed Milk Co., referred to in the opinion as the "old company," sued to enjoin the Borden Ice Cream Co., the "new company," from marketing ice cream under the BORDEN mark. The District Court granted the injunction, and the new company appealed.]

The word "Borden" in the corporate name of the appellee [old company] was taken from the name of Gail Borden, who founded the business in the year 1857, and since that time it has been and is now a trade-name of great value, identified almost universally with the business of milk and milk products of the appellee and its predecessors. The trade-name "Borden," or the word "Borden," constitutes one of the principal assets of the appellee, and is widely known and identified with the good will and public favor enjoyed by it throughout the United States.

On May 31, 1899, the appellee was incorporated under the laws of the state of New Jersey, with broad corporate powers, and specifically authorized "to manufacture, sell and otherwise deal in condensed, preserved and evaporated milk and all other manufactured forms of milk; to produce, purchase and sell fresh milk, and all products of milk; to manufacture, purchase and sell all food products; to raise, purchase and sell all garden, farm and dairy products; to raise, purchase and sell, and otherwise deal in, cattle and all other live stock; to manufacture, lease, purchase and sell all machinery, tools, implements, apparatus and all other articles and appliances used in connection with all or any of the purposes aforesaid, or with selling and transporting the manufactured or other products of the company; and to do any and all things connected with or incidental to the carrying on of such business, or any branch or part thereof."

It may be stated in this connection that the charter of the company contains no express authority to manufacture or sell what is known commercially as ice cream. . . .

[The old company marketed some thirty-two products under some form of the BORDEN mark, including many condensed or evaporated milk products, some of which were sold to confectioners for manufacturing ice cream. Also, one of the old company's products was a malted milk ice cream previously marketed to hospitals, although the old company planned to begin marketing it to the general population.]

On May 25, 1911, the appellants Charles F. Borden, George W. Brown, and Edgar V. Stanley applied to the Secretary of State of the state of Illinois for a license to incorporate under the name of "Borden Ice Cream Company." On July 31, 1911, the appellee [old company] notified the individual appellants that the term "Borden" had become so firmly established in connection with the products of the appellee the use of that word in connection with any company dealing in milk products would lead to the presumption that they were the products of the appellee, and demanded that the word "Borden" be eliminated from appellants' company name.

On the same day appellee protested to the Secretary of State of the state of Illinois against the issuance of any charter under the name of "Borden Ice Cream Company," but on the 16th of August, 1911, a charter was duly issued to the "Borden Ice Cream Company," by which it was authorized "to manufacture and sell ice cream, ices and similar products."

The appellant Charles F. Borden had never before been engaged in the ice cream business, or in buying or selling milk or milk products, or in any similar business, and is not the principal person connected with the appellant Borden Ice Cream Company. The appellant Lawler is an ice cream manufacturer, and has subscribed to 47 out of a total of 50 shares of stock of the Borden Ice Cream Company. Charles F. Borden has subscribed to one share of stock, and has not paid for that. . . .

[I]t does not appear that the malted milk ice cream manufactured by the old company will in any way come into competition with the commercial ice cream proposed to be put on the market by the new company. . . .

CARPENTER, District Judge (after stating the facts as above):
The only theory upon which the injunction in this case can be sustained is upon that known as unfair competition. Relief against unfair competition is granted solely upon the ground that one who has built up a good will and reputation for his goods or business is entitled to all of the resultant benefits. Good will or business popularity is property, and, like other property, will be protected against fraudulent invasion.

The question to be determined in every case of unfair competition is whether or not, as a matter of fact, the name used by the defendant had come previously to indicate and designate the complainant's goods. Or, to put it in another way, whether the defendant, as a matter of fact, is, by his conduct, passing off his goods as the complainant's goods, or his business as the complainant's business.

It has been said that the universal test question in cases of this class is whether the public is likely to be deceived as to the maker or seller of the goods. This, in our opinion, is not the fundamental question. The deception of the public naturally tends to injure the proprietor of a business by diverting his customers and depriving him of sales which otherwise he might have made. This, rather than the protection of the public against imposition, is the sound and true basis for the private remedy. That the public is deceived may be evidence of the fact that the original proprietor's rights are being invaded. If, however, the rights of the original proprietor are in no wise interfered with, the deception of the public is no concern of a court of chancery. *American Washboard Co. v. Saginaw Mfg. Co.*, 103 Fed. 281.

Doubtless it is morally wrong for a person to proclaim, or even intimate, that his goods are manufactured by some other and well-known concern; but this does not give rise to a private right of action, unless the property rights of that concern are interfered with. The use by the new company of the name "Borden" may have been with fraudulent intent; and, even assuming that it was, the trial court had no right to interfere, unless the property rights of the old company were jeopardized. Nothing else being shown, a court of equity cannot punish an unorthodox or immoral, or even dishonest, trader; it cannot enforce as such the police power of the state.

In the case now under our consideration the old company (the appellee) never has manufactured what is known as commercial ice cream. The new company (the appellant) was incorporated for the sole purpose of manufacturing and putting on the market such an article.

Nonexclusive trade-names are public property in their primary sense, but they may in their secondary sense come to be understood as indicating the goods or business of a particular trader. Such trade-names are acquired by adoption and user, and belong to the one who first used them and gave them value in a specific line of business. It is true that the name of a person may become so associated with his goods or business that another person of the same or a similar name engaging in the same business will not be allowed to use even his own name, without affirmatively distinguishing his goods or business.

The secondary meaning of a name, however, has no legal significance, unless the two persons make or deal in the same kind of goods. Clearly the appellants here could make gloves, or plows, or cutlery, under the name "Borden" without infringing upon any property right of the old company. If that is true, they can make anything under the name "Borden" which the appellee has not already made and offered to the public. *George v. Smith* (C.C.) 52 Fed. 830.

The name "Borden," until appellants came into the field, never had been associated with commercial ice cream. By making commercial ice cream the appellants do not come into competition with the appellee. In the absence of competition, the old company cannot assert the rights accruing from what has been designated as the secondary meaning of the word "Borden." The phrase "unfair competition" presupposes competition of some sort. In the absence of competition the doctrine cannot be invoked.

There being no competition between the appellants and appellee, we are confronted with the proposition that the appellee, in order to succeed on this appeal, has and can enforce a proprietary right to the name "Borden" in any kind of business, to the exclusion of all the world.

It is urged that appellee has power, under its charter, to make commercial ice cream, and that it intends some day to do so. If such intention can be protected at this time, it might well be that appellee, having enjoined appellants from making commercial ice cream, would rest content with selling its evaporated milk to ice cream dealers, and never itself manufacture the finished product. But, as was well stated by Judge Coxe, in *George v. Smith, supra*:

> It is the party who uses it first as a brand for his goods, and builds up a business under it, who is entitled to protection, and not the one who first thought of using it on similar goods, but did not use it. The law deals with acts and not intentions.

Appellee also urges that it makes and sells large quantities of evaporated or condensed milk to manufacturers of ice cream, and that if the appellants are permitted to use the name "Borden" in the ice cream business dealers probably will believe that its ice cream is made by appellee, and will in consequence buy the finished product rather than the component parts, and that appellee's sales of evaporated or condensed milk will fall off, to its manifest damage. Such result would be too speculative and remote to form the basis of an order restraining men from using in their business any personal name, especially their own.

Appellee is in this position: If it bases its right to an injunction upon the doctrine of unfair competition, no competition of any kind has been shown by the record. If it relies upon some supposed damage which may result from appellants' use of the name "Borden" in connection with inferior goods, the action is premature, because the appellants, as yet, have neither sold nor made anything.

The order of the District Court must be *reversed*; and it is so ordered.

FLEISCHMANN DISTILLING CORP. v. MAIER BREWING CO.

314 F.2d 149 (9th Cir.), cert. denied, 374 U.S. 830 (1963)

POPE, Circuit Judge:

[Plaintiff James Buchanan & Company manufactured BLACK & WHITE Scotch whisky; plaintiff Fleischmann Distilling Corporation imported and sold it in the United States. Buchanan had long held a federal registration of BLACK & WHITE for Scotch whisky. Defendant Maier Brewing Company was a Los Angeles–area brewer of "low price" beers. Maier manufactured BLACK & WHITE beer and sold it through a wholesaler to defendant Ralphs Grocery Company, a chain of grocery stores in Los Angeles. Plaintiffs sued for trademark infringement, the trial court held for defendants, and plaintiffs appealed.]

With respect to this Scotch whisky the trial court found as follows: "8. 'Black & White' Scotch whisky is a widely known Scotch whisky. It is the leader among Scotch whiskies. Its sales have exceeded one hundred million bottles during the tenure of Fleischmann and more than five hundred thousand cases have been sold in the six year period between 1951 and 1957, in California, more than half of which were sold in Los Angeles County where Ralphs does business. In the alcoholic beverage industry the name 'Black & White' has come to mean Scotch whisky." During the six year period mentioned, the plaintiffs expended more than five million dollars in advertising their Black & White Scotch whisky. . . .

Among the findings from which the trial court drew its conclusion that plaintiffs had not made a case against the defendants was Finding No. 28 as follows: "28. There is no real competition between plaintiffs' Scotch whisky and defendants' beer. This lack of real competition renders it unlikely that there is, or will be, any confusion as to source in the mind of a buyer." This finding seems to suggest that Buchanan, as owner of a registered trademark, would be foreclosed from recovery if there was no real competition between plaintiffs' Scotch whisky and the beer. We think this finding indicates a misconception of the law here applicable, and of the significance of lack of competition.

The earlier trademark Act, that of 1905 (33 Stat. 724 et seq.), provided that a right of action to suppress an infringement of a registered mark arose only if the infringement was used on "goods of the same descriptive properties" as the registrant's goods. However, the Lanham Act of 1946 (15 U.S.C. §1051 et seq.) made plain that infringement might be found and prohibited, though the use of the registered mark was upon goods having different descriptive properties than those set forth in the registration, and though in consequence there was no actual competition between the parties. This Act prohibits use without the registrant's consent "of any registered mark in connection with the sale, offering for sale, or advertising of any goods or services on or in connection with which such use is likely to cause confusion or mistake or to deceive purchasers as to the source of origin of such goods or services."*

Thus the question to be determined here is whether the use by Maier and Ralphs of the name "Black & White" on their beer "is likely to cause confusion or mistake or to deceive purchasers as to the source of origin of such goods or services." . . .

We proceed then to the inquiry whether under the circumstances here shown the use of the name Black & White on defendants' beer is likely to cause confusion as to the source of origin. . . .

[The court first observed that the fact that Scotch whisky and beer have "distinctly different properties" may have been important to consider under the 1905 Act, but the Lanham Act had eliminated the requirement that the infringer's goods be "of the same descriptive properties" as the mark owner's. The court next noted that BLACK & WHITE was not only a distinctive mark, but also a "strong" one. The court also observed that even though many other firms used BLACK & WHITE for various products and services, most were remote from the liquor business. The court then turned to other factors that it perceived to be relevant to the confusion question.]

It is our view, and we so hold, that the average purchaser, as the courts have described him, would be likely to believe, as he noted the Black & White beer in Ralphs' stores, that the maker of the beer had some connection with the concern which had produced the well known Black & White Scotch whisky. It is not material whether he would think that the makers of the Scotch whisky were actually brewing and bottling this beer, or whether it was being produced under their supervision or pursuant to some other arrangement with them. He would probably not concern himself about any such detail. . . .

As the trial court noted, we are dealing here with operations in the alcoholic beverage industry. It seems to us that necessarily the use on defendants' alcoholic beverage of Buchanan's trademark would be likely to cause confusion or mistake or to deceive purchasers as to the source of origin of such goods. . . .

The manager [one of defendants' personnel] knew that the Black & White Scotch "was one of the most popular brands on the market" and when the wholesaler brought up the question of Black & White also being used for Scotch, the manager told him that he knew there was a Black & White Scotch, "one of the most popular brands." Without seeking any legal advice these officers of Maier simply decided for themselves that there was no relation between Scotch whisky and beer and decided to go ahead.

We cannot conclude but that Maier deliberately adopted the name knowing that Black & White was the name and trademark of Buchanan and they must have done so with some purpose in mind. The only possible purpose could have been to capitalize upon the popularity of the name chosen. This popularity, they must have known, would extend to their product because the public would associate the name Black & White with something old and reliable and meritorious in the way of an alcoholic beverage.

It is well settled that plaintiffs were not obliged in order to make a case against the defendants to prove a wrongful intent. *Safeway Stores Inc. v. Rudner*, 9 Cir., 246 F.2d 826, 829. But when the evidence does show or require the inference that another's name was

---

* *Ed. Note*: This provision has since been amended, as explained in the Notes and Questions following this case.

adopted deliberately with a view to obtain some advantage from the good will, good name, and good trade which another has built up, then the inference of likelihood of confusion is readily drawn, for the very act of the adopter has indicated that he expects confusion and resultant profit. . . .

Furthermore, Maier knew, just as we do, that it had open to it a whole dictionary full of words, an encyclopedia full of proper names, and a world atlas full of place names from which to select a non-offending label. The evidence shows that at the time Maier was using no less than 21 separate names or labels. . . .

When a newcomer takes the name Black & White and makes a use of it on a product which in the mind of the buyer is related to or associated with the product of the original trademark owner, we think it may be said that confusion as to the source of origin is likely to result. The use need not be the same as, nor one in competition with the original use. The question is, are the uses related so that they are likely to be connected in the mind of a prospective purchaser?

This is a test which was early applied by the Second Circuit in a somewhat similar case. That court was one of those which prior to the Lanham Act gave to the 1905 Act a liberal construction which anticipated the changes that were written into the Lanham Act to which we have previously alluded.[14] That case was *Aunt Jemima Co. v. Rigney & Co.*, 2 Cir., 247 F. 407, 409.

We think it must be said here, as in the Aunt Jemima case, *supra*, that beer and Scotch whisky, being both within the alcoholic beverage industry, are "so related as to fall within the mischief which equity should prevent." . . .

It is the general public, the unskilled purchaser, who is entitled to protection; and in determining whether there is a likelihood of confusion we must remember that the members of the purchasing public have only general impressions which must guide them in the selection of products. We think that the purchaser of a carton of beer in Ralphs' grocery store would have no way of pulling from his pocket a precise copy of Buchanan's label to compare with the label on the beer. His general impression relates to the name "Black & White" and that is the extent of his knowledge ordinarily.

We hold therefore that the court below was in error in denying the injunction prayed for.

NOTES AND QUESTIONS

1.   *Consumer confusion as a ground for an unfair competition action?* The *Borden's* court insists that whether defendant's actions are likely to deceive consumers is "not the fundamental question" in an unfair competition matter. Instead, evidence of consumer deception is relevant only insofar as it may prove that the defendant diverted customers away from the trademark owner, resulting in actual lost sales, this diversion of customers being "the sound and true basis for the private remedy."

---

14. *See* Robert, "Commentary on The Lanham Trade-Mark Act," appearing in 15 U.S.C.A. §§81-1113 (1948 ed.) p. 265, at 286: "Under the 1905 Act a right of action to suppress an infringement of a registered mark arose only if the infringement was used on 'goods of the same descriptive properties' as the registrant's goods. In its practical application, the phrase 'goods of the same descriptive properties' was construed strictly by some courts and liberally by others, with the inevitable result that no one knew precisely what it meant. Strict construction required that the goods be the same, and some courts held that there must be actual confusion of goods before relief could be granted. But many courts reasoned that if the goods were unlike but somewhat related, purchasers might mistakenly think that the goods of both parties emanated from the same source."

Borden's reflects one side of a lively debate in early unfair competition law. At the time of the *Borden's* case, there was ample support in the case law for the proposition that unfair competition actions existed to protect the rights of individual trademark owners; consumer deception might stand as evidence that trademark owners' rights were being violated, but would not stand as a separate ground for unfair competition actions. Only a suit brought by a public official could vindicate public rights, it was argued. An equally robust line of authority held that redressing consumer deception was a central purpose of the unfair competition action, even though it was a private right of action. *See, e.g.,* HARRY D. NIMS, THE LAW OF UNFAIR COMPETITION AND TRADE-MARKS §§7-8 (3d ed. 1929) (describing the competing theories and citing U.S. and English authority).

Present U.S. law recognizes that the two theories are not mutually exclusive. That is, under present U.S. law, consumer confusion is definitively the touchstone for unfair competition actions brought under Lanham Act §43(a), though unfair competition also simultaneously serves to vindicate private rights. Is this a sound approach? Or is the *Borden's* formula preferable from a policy standpoint? *See* Mark P. McKenna, *The Normative Foundations of Trademark Law*, 82 NOTRE DAME L. REV. 1839 (2007) (arguing that clearer limits can be derived from the *Borden's* formula than from reliance on consumer confusion).

2. *Consumer confusion as a ground for statutory trademark infringement?* The *Borden's* court decided the case under an unfair competition theory, not a theory of statutory trademark infringement. What if *Borden's* had arisen under the statute—could the court still have argued that consumer deception was not relevant to the plaintiff's claim? The answer is probably yes, at least under one construction of the relevant provision, Section 16 of the Trademark Act of 1905:

> [T]he registration of a trademark under the provisions of this act shall be *prima facie* evidence of ownership. Any person who shall, without the consent of the owner thereof, reproduce, counterfeit, copy, or colorably imitate any such trademark and affix the same to merchandise of substantially the same descriptive properties as those set forth in the registration, or to labels, signs, prints, packages, wrappers, or receptacles intended to be used upon or in connection with the sale of merchandise of substantially the same descriptive properties as those set forth in such registration, and shall use, or shall have used, such reproduction, counterfeit, copy, or colorable imitation in commerce among the several States, or with a foreign nation, or with the Indian tribes, shall be liable to an action for damages therefor at the suit of the owner thereof. . . .

The 1905 statute thus proscribed copying or colorably imitating a registered trademark, and affixing the copy to goods of "substantially the same descriptive properties as those set forth in the registration," but did not expressly lay out a confusion standard or expressly recognize consumer deception as a ground for trademark infringement. Over time, however, courts came to construe the statute as incorporating a concept of consumer confusion, particularly in cases involving arguably related but noncompeting goods. *See, e.g.,* DAPHNE ROBERT, THE NEW TRADE-MARK MANUAL 159 (1947) (asserting that the language of Section 16 of the 1905 statute "has not been too strictly construed," and was extended to cases where "'confusion of source' was likely to result"). Moreover, Section 5(b) of the 1905 statute, the counterpart to modern-day Lanham Act §2(d), did expressly refer to consumer confusion:

> *Provided*, That trademarks which are identical with a registered or known trademark owned and in use by another and appropriated to merchandise of the same descriptive properties, or which so nearly resemble a registered or known trademark owned and in use by another and appropriated to merchandise of the same descriptive properties as to be likely to cause confusion or mistake in the mind of the public or to deceive purchasers shall not be registered. . . .

By 1946, when the Lanham Act was passed, the concept that consumer confusion was critical to trademark infringement liability was already firmly established in the case law.

The Lanham Act's legislative history reflects as much. The Senate Report accompanying the Lanham Act asserted expressly that the purposes of the trademark laws included not only protecting trademark owners' investments in goodwill, but also protecting the public against deception. S. Rep. No. 1333, 79th Cong., 2d Sess. 3 (1946) (quoted *supra* in Chapter 1).

The language of the 1946 Lanham Act infringement provision, the governing provision in the *Fleischmann* case, explicitly incorporated a confusion standard:

> Any person who shall, in commerce, (a) use, without the consent of the registrant, any reproduction, counterfeit, copy, or colorable imitation of any registered mark in connection with the sale, offering for sale, or advertising of any goods or services on or in connection with which such use is likely to cause confusion or mistake or to deceive purchasers as to the source of origin of such goods or services; or (b) reproduce, counterfeit, copy, or colorably imitate any such mark and apply such reproduction, counterfeit, copy, or colorable imitation to labels, signs, prints, packages, wrappers, receptacles, or advertisements intended to be used upon or in connection with the sale in commerce of such goods or services, shall be liable to a civil action by the registrant. . . .

Lanham Act §32(1)(a)-(b) (1946).

The 1946 statute also defined "colorable imitation" with reference to the concept of consumer confusion:

> The term "colorable imitation" includes any mark which so resembles a registered mark as to be likely to cause confusion or mistake or to deceive purchasers.

Lanham Act §45(b) (1946).

Thus, by 1946, the statutory law of trademark infringement had embraced the concept of consumer deception, turning away from the approach to unfair competition expressed in *Borden's*. As the *Fleischmann* case demonstrates, courts now focus on consumer confusion in trademark infringement cases, and the same is true in Section 43(a) unfair competition cases. Indeed, courts deciding trademark infringement and Section 43(a) unfair competition questions now routinely cite the rationale of preventing harm to the public:

> In addition to the harm caused the trademark owner, the consuming public is equally injured by an inadequate judicial response to trademark infringement. Many consumers are willing to pay substantial premiums for particular items which bear famous trademarks based on their belief that such items are of the same high quality as is traditionally associated with the trademark owner. As a result of this trademark infringement the consuming public is denied the benefit of their bargains and the reputation and goodwill of the trademark owner is accordingly harmed. For these reasons, it is essential that the trial courts carefully fashion remedies which will take all the economic incentive out of trademark infringement.

Playboy Enters., Inc. v. Baccarat Clothing Co., Inc., 692 F.2d 1272, 1275 (9th Cir. 1982).

Consider carefully the changes in the statutory language detailed above. Did the 1905 Act infringement provision give the trademark owner greater rights? Something approaching property rights in gross? Or lesser rights compared with the 1946 version of the statute? Courts and commentators have uniformly concluded that the scope of trademark rights has steadily expanded over the course of the twentieth century, as the cases in this chapter reflect.

3.   *Actual confusion versus likely confusion.* Establishing that "confusion" is the governing standard for trademark infringement liability leaves open many questions. This note and the following notes explore some of the important questions: (1) Must a trademark owner provide evidence of actual consumer confusion in order to establish liability for trademark infringement or unfair competition? (2) Must a trademark owner provide evidence that *purchasers* (or *potential purchasers*) were likely confused, or merely that the public was likely confused? (3) Must a trademark owner provide evidence of confusion *as to the source of the goods/services*, or may evidence of more generalized confusion as to affiliation suffice?

As to the first question, both the modern statute (from the 1946 Lanham Act to the present), and the case law (extending back even prior to the enactment of the Lanham Act) firmly reject any requirement for showing actual confusion. The trademark infringement and unfair competition provisions in the original (1946) version of the Lanham Act, and all versions since, have imposed liability where the defendant's unauthorized use of the disputed mark "is likely to cause confusion." *See, e.g.*, Lanham Act §32(1)(a). The case law has been similarly emphatic, starting relatively soon after *Borden's. See, e.g., Gehl v. Hebe Co.*, 276 F. 271, 272-73 (7th Cir. 1921) ("Although there was here no evidence of actual confusion on the part of customers, this is not easily available, nor indeed necessary where the words themselves suggest it."); *Holland Furnace Co. v. New Holland Mach. Co.*, 24 F.2d 751, 754 (E.D. Pa. 1927) ("Evidence of specific cases of confusion or deception is not necessary."); *see also* HARRY D. NIMS, THE LAW OF UNFAIR COMPETITION AND TRADE-MARKS §335 (3d ed. 1929) (collecting authorities).

However, there has always been a lingering sense of the importance of actual confusion:

> It appears that the cases where infringement has been adjudged without proof of actual confusion are exceptions to the general rule. In our opinion, such adjudication should be made only where the mark charged to infringe is so strikingly similar that, on its face, it is calculated to result in confusion.

Rytex Co. v. Ryan, 126 F.2d 952, 954 (7th Cir. 1942). We explore this issue in the context of modern confusion analysis in the *Libman* case, *infra*, in section C of this chapter.

4. *Confusion by whom?* Another major question that must be addressed in connection with any confusion-based standard is whose confusion is relevant to liability. Because the operative standard is a forward-looking, "likelihood of" standard, the target group cannot be limited to past purchasers. Is the group, then, past purchasers and prospective purchasers? On this question, the contours of U.S. trademark legislation have changed over time. Starting with the original (1946) version of the Lanham Act (the first legislation to adopt explicitly a confusion standard, as we have seen), the Section 32(1)(a) infringement provision required that the trademark owner show that the alleged infringer's use "is likely to cause confusion, or to cause mistake, or to deceive *purchasers* as to the source of origin of such goods or services." In 1962, Congress amended Section 32(1)(a) to eliminate the final clause. That is, the modern provision, reproduced at the beginning of this chapter, retains the "likely to" language but no longer limits actionable confusion to "purchasers."

Who is the relevant target group for purposes of the modern statute? Could it include casual passersby who view the allegedly infringing goods? Could it include potential investors in the firm that uses the allegedly infringing mark? As we turn to the modern jurisprudence in the next section, consider critically courts' rhetoric on this question, and the significance that courts place on the 1962 amendment. For a useful discussion of the issue, *see Arrowpoint Capital Corp. v. Arrowpoint Asset Mgmt., LLC*, 793 F.3d 313 (3d Cir. 2015) (analyzing whether confusion among brokers or dealers sufficed even if there was no evidence as to confusion among end consumers of investment services).

5. *Confusion as to what?* Another major question arising in connection with a confusion-based standard is what precisely the relevant target group must be confused about. This is a subtle and difficult question. Must there be a showing that consumers would likely purchase the defendant's goods in place of the plaintiff's? Or is it sufficient to show that consumers would likely believe that defendant's goods actually originated with the plaintiff? Or is it sufficient to show that consumers would likely believe that there is some affiliation or connection between defendant and plaintiff? As you read the cases in this chapter, consider whether you detect any difference of opinion among courts about whether actionable confusion extends to confusion about affiliation.

This issue has arisen most frequently in cases concerning so-called related goods (sometimes called "noncompeting" goods). *Borden's* and *Fleischmann* are both "related goods" cases—i.e., the trademark owner's goods do not necessarily compete with the alleged infringer's goods. In *Borden's*, this fact was central to the court's decision to deny relief. In *Fleischmann*, this fact did not preclude the grant of relief. Indeed, the court pointed to differences between the 1905 infringement provision (requiring goods of "substantially the same descriptive properties") and the 1946 infringement provision (requiring a likelihood of confusion "as to the source of origin of such goods") as justification for a broader approach to infringement liability: even if consumers would not have purchased BLACK & WHITE beer in place of BLACK & WHITE Scotch, they still would likely have believed that the beer originated from the same manufacturer as did the Scotch.

As noted above, in 1962 Congress amended Section 32(1)(a), eliminating not only the reference to "purchasers" but also the phrase "source of origin of such goods or services." The likelihood-of-confusion statutory language is now unadorned, requiring merely a showing of a likelihood "to cause confusion, or to cause mistake, or to deceive." As you read the cases in the following sections exploring the modern confusion analysis, consider the implications of this statutory change for the extension of trademark infringement liability to "noncompeting" goods. The materials in section C on the "similarity of goods/ services" factor of the likelihood-of-confusion analysis take up this question.

6. *Deriving a likelihood-of-confusion test.* In this section, we have noted the law's gravitation to a confusion standard that is forward-looking ("likelihood of"), broader than mere purchaser confusion, and broader than mere source confusion. These are the basic overarching parameters of the modern confusion theory. In the next sections, we explore the tests that courts use when they apply the modern confusion theory.

B. THE ACTIONABLE "USE" PREREQUISITE

Beginning with this section, and continuing through the remaining sections, we turn to modern confusion theories. In this section, however, we focus first on the requirement that the alleged infringer "use" the plaintiff's mark in a particular way. We will refer to this requirement as the "actionable use" requirement. In subsequent sections, we consider many aspects of the modern likelihood-of-confusion analysis, which remains the heart of the infringement inquiry.

For many years, the issue of actionable use was uncontroversial and largely unexplored. Starting in the 1990s, the rise of online advertising practices prompted a surge of interest in defining actionable use more precisely. While the Second Circuit's 2009 decision in *Rescuecom* (excerpted below) seems to have brought this particular debate to a close, broader questions about the scope of actionable use linger.

The statute provides little guidance. Section 32(1)(a) imposes liability on anyone "who shall, without the consent of the registrant . . . *use in commerce* any reproduction . . . of a registered mark *in connection with the sale, offering for sale, distribution, or advertising of any goods and services*" if *such use* is likely to cause confusion. Section 43(a) renders liable anyone "who, *on or in connection with any goods or services . . . uses in commerce* any word, term, name, symbol, or device, or any combination thereof" . . . if *such use* is likely to cause confusion. (Emphasis supplied.) What does the statute require that a defendant have done? Make "use *of*" a plaintiff's mark? Make use of the plaintiff's mark "*as* a mark"? Make "*commercial* use" of the plaintiff's mark? Should the Section 45 definition of "use in commerce" that we discussed in the context of establishing trademark rights be deemed informative in the context of infringement? The cases below attempt to provide some answers to these questions. As you study the materials, consider whether those answers are well supported by the statute, the legislative history, and the case law, and consider whether the answers line up well with the basic policy objectives of the trademark system.

HOLIDAY INNS, INC. v. 800 RESERVATIONS, INC.

86 F.3d 619 (6th Cir. 1996), cert. denied, 519 U.S. 1093 (1997)

DAUGHTREY, Circuit Judge:

Holiday Inns, Inc., filed this Lanham Act suit against the defendants, alleging unfair competition and infringement of its trademark telephone number, 1-800-HOLIDAY, known as a "vanity number." The defendants, Call Management Systems, Inc. (a consulting firm that obtains and services 1-800 telephone numbers for businesses), 800 Reservations, Inc. (an agency that makes reservations for a number of hotel chains, including Holiday Inns), and Earthwinds Travel, Inc. (a travel agency), had secured the use and were engaged in using a telephone number that potential Holiday Inns customers frequently dial by mistake when they unintentionally substitute the number zero for the letter "O." That number, 1-800-405-4329, corresponds to the alphanumeric 1-800-H[zero]LIDAY, known in the trade as a "complementary number." It is referred to in this opinion as "the 405 number" to distinguish it from the Holiday Inns numeric, 1-800-465-4329. The district court, although noting that the defendants were violating only the "spirit" and not the "letter" of the Lanham Act, nevertheless granted Holiday Inns partial summary judgment and permanently enjoined 800 Reservations and Call Management from using the 405 number. . . .

. . .

I.

Since 1952, Holiday Inns has operated an international chain of hotels through both franchise agreements and on its own, utilizing the name "Holiday Inn." The hotel chain has advertised extensively and has offered its products and services throughout the United States. The company owns, operates, and licenses approximately 1,300 hotels in the United States and spends between $20,000,000 and $30,000,000 per year on advertising. As a result of its efforts, the district court found that Holiday Inns has earned favorable recognition and acceptance by the traveling public. Holiday Inns, Inc. owns registration in the United States Patent and Trademark Office for several service marks, including the "Holiday Inn" mark, which was registered in 1954.

Holiday Inns has invested a great deal of time, money, and effort to increase the traveling public's awareness of its 1-800-HOLIDAY phone number, which can be dialed to secure reservations or to obtain information about lodging facilities. According to the vice president of Holiday Inns' marketing, the company's vanity number is included in virtually all of its extensive media, print, and radio advertisements. The telephone number is not, however, officially registered as a trademark.

Call Management operates as a "service bureau," formed to assist business customers in obtaining and processing their 1-800 numbers. Albert H. Montreuil, the 50% owner of Call Management, admitted that through his experience with Call Management and its 1-800 numbers, he became aware of the fact that consumers frequently misdial vanity numbers. The most common mistakes made by consumers occur when they dial the number "0" (zero) for the letter "O" and the number "1" (one) for the letter "I." If the complementary numbers dialed in error are not in active use, callers receive a busy signal or a recorded message that indicates that the number is not in service.

Indeed, the phenomenon of misdialed vanity numbers is apparently so well known that businesses and hotel chains like the Marriott and Red Roof Inns, for example, subscribe to both their vanity and complementary numbers in order to ensure receiving calls from all their potential customers. Holiday Inns, however, neglected to take this precaution and did not reserve any complementary numbers.

When Montreuil discovered that numbers complementing 1-800-HOLIDAY had not been reserved, he decided, in May 1993, to reserve them for Call Management. In fact, Montreuil freely admitted during the preliminary injunction hearing that his "sole purpose" in choosing the 405 number was to intercept calls from misdialed customers who were attempting to reach Holiday Inns, and he acknowledged that his company reaped benefits in direct proportion to Holiday Inns's efforts at marketing 1-800-HOLIDAY for securing reservations.

On June 15, 1993, Call Management entered into a verbal agreement with defendant Earthwinds, by which Earthwinds agreed to process calls from customers on the 405 number in return for 10% of all commissions received for placing hotel bookings. The parties further agreed that Earthwinds would answer calls on this 800 service until defendant 800 Reservations was ready to begin operations on its own.

On August 18, 1993, Call Management terminated its arrangement with Earthwinds. As a result, the 405 number was not operational from August 18 to August 20, 1993, when it was reactivated for use by 800 Reservations. At that time, however, Holiday Inns filed suit and moved for a temporary restraining order to enjoin defendants' use of the 405 number. It also sought to restrain defendants from using the "Holiday Inns" trade name or trademark in connection with the advertising or sale of products or services, from representing themselves to be connected with Holiday Inns, and from injuring Holiday Inns's business reputation.

At the district court level, one of the principal disagreements between the parties was whether a customer who had dialed Holiday Inns's complementary number would always receive defendants' recorded message. Defendants insisted that a caller dialing the 405 number would hear the following recorded message at the beginning of *every* call:

> Hello. You have misdialed and have not reached Holiday Inns or any of its affiliates. You've called 800 Reservations, America's fastest growing independent computerized hotel reservation service. One of our highly trained hotel reservation specialists will be with you momentarily to provide the Holiday Inns number or to assist you in finding the lowest rate at over 19,000 properties worldwide, including such hotel chains as Holiday Inns, Guest Quarters, Hampton Inn, Sheraton, Comfort Inn, and many more. If you are a member of a hotel's frequent guest program, have that number ready. Please stay on the line, assistance is just a moment away.

They further claimed that the phone answering system was equipped with certain safeguards and that customers could not bypass the recorded message.

Holiday Inns nevertheless offered affidavits to support its contention that the above message did not play at the beginning of every call. The district court, however, found it unnecessary to resolve this factual dispute, because it determined that sufficient factors existed to grant a preliminary injunction even if the purported message was heard by every customer who dialed the 405 number. The district court found that, because Holiday Inns and the defendants use different computerized reservations systems, Holiday Inns suffered two adverse consequences from the defendants' use of the 405 number. First, 800 Reservations might inform a customer that a particular Holiday Inn had no rooms available when, in fact, vacancies did exist; and, second, a customer would more likely obtain a favorable room rate by contacting Holiday Inns directly, as opposed to contacting 800 Reservations through Holiday Inns' complementary number.[1] . . .

[The district court granted summary judgment in favor of Holiday Inns; Call Management appealed.]

III.

Holiday Inns claims that the defendants violated the Lanham Act by their "use" of Holiday Inns' trademark. The defendants argue, however, that Call Management never used Holiday Inns' registered mark nor any other variant of Holiday Inns' trademark. They only used the phone number, 1-800-405-4329—that is, a number which is neither phonetically nor visually similar to Holiday Inns' trademark, 1-800-HOLIDAY.[5]

The district court agreed with the defendants' argument and found that Call Management never used "1-800-HOLIDAY" or any of Holiday Inns' marks, and "never advertised or publicized anything to do with Holiday Inns or its telephone number." The district judge, therefore, found that in this unique case the defendants also did not create the consumers' confusion, but that the defendants merely took advantage of confusion already in existence. The district court nevertheless concluded that this behavior was "parasitic" and stated:

> The defendants derive benefit *solely* from Holiday Inns reputation. In fact, defendants have no independent reputation. The consumer is not even aware of defendants' existence until after he has misdialed Holiday Inns' vanity number. If not for Holiday Inns spending millions of dollars on advertising each year, defendants would have no service whatsoever to provide to the consumer. For the defendants to be able to reap profits based solely on the advertising efforts and expenditures of others *seems to be a clear violation of the spirit, if not the letter, of the Lanham Act.*

(Emphasis added.)

The few courts that have addressed similar issues have agreed that telephone numbers may be protected as trademarks and that a competitor's use of a confusingly similar telephone number may be enjoined as both trademark infringement and unfair competition. *See, e.g., Dial-A-Mattress Franchise Corp. v. Page*, 880 F.2d 675, 678 (2d Cir. 1989). In *Dial-A-Mattress*, the plaintiff was the customer of record for the local telephone number 628-8737 in the various area codes of the New York metropolitan region. Dial-A-Mattress Franchise Corp. had advertised extensively its services and its phone number in the area with the phrase "DIAL-A-MATTRESS and drop the last 'S' for savings." *Id.* at 676. The defendant, Page, obtained the right to use 1-800-628-8737 (or 1-800-MATTRES) and

---

1. The defendants emphasize that the price of a given room is the same whether one makes a reservation through Holiday Inns' internal reservation system or through 800 Reservations. The average rate, however, may be lower in cases of direct bookings because Holiday Inns is able to provide group discounts, military reductions, government discounts, and other bargains which travel agencies cannot.

5. The defendants concede that "Holiday Inns has trademark rights in its 1-800-HOLIDAY designation." Thus, we need not address the threshold issue of whether 1-800-HOLIDAY, an unregistered cipher, is, indeed, a trademark entitled to protection from infringement. . . .

promoted his number as 1-800-MATTRESS. *Id.* at 677. Dial-A-Mattress brought suit seeking an injunction and damages on claims of trademark infringement, unfair competition, and unjust enrichment under federal and New York law.

The Second Circuit held that although the term "mattress" is a generic term generally not entitled to protection under trademark law, telephone numbers that correlate with generic terms may be entitled to protection. *Id.* at 678. It further determined:

> [D]efendant's use of the telephone number 1-800-628-8737 was confusingly similar to plaintiff's telephone number 628-8737 in those area code regions in which plaintiff solicited telephone orders, *especially in view of defendant's identification of its number as 1-800-MATTRESS after plaintiff had promoted identification of its number as (area code)-MATTRES.*

Id. at 678 (emphasis added).

Despite Holiday Inns' reliance upon the *Dial-A-Mattress* decision, we find the instant case and the Second Circuit opinion clearly distinguishable. In *Dial-A-Mattress*, for example, the defendant intentionally *promoted* his vanity number and actively *caused* confusion; in our case, the defendants engaged in only minimal advertisement of their travel agency and never promoted a vanity number.

. . .

The defendants, on the other hand, cite cases which suggest that the active *promotion* of a deceptively similar vanity number is necessary before the trial court can conclude that unlawful infringement has occurred. In *American Airlines, Inc. v. A 1-800-A-M-E-R-I-C-A-N Corp.*, 622 F. Supp. 673 (N.D. Ill. 1985), for example, the defendant falsely advertised its airline reservation service as an airline company in the yellow pages and listed its company name as "A 1-800-A-M-E-R-I-C-A-N." In finding a Lanham Act violation, the court clarified that the defendant's "wrongful conduct lies in its misleading *use* of the 'Airline Companies' yellow-pages listing *rather than its mere use of its telephone number [1-800-AMERICAN] . . . as such. . . .*" *Id.* at 682 (emphasis added). In other words, the court issued an injunction because the defendant's publicity efforts misled the public and not because the defendant activated a 1-800 number that appeared confusingly similar to the trademark, "American Airlines." *See also Murrin v. Midco Communications, Inc.*, 726 F. Supp. 1195, 1200-01 (D. Minn. 1989) (granting a limited injunction forbidding the advertisement or use of the vanity number 1-800-LAWYER with "dial" or with any symbols resembling dots or hyphens between the letters "LAWYERS" but explicitly rejecting the argument that *any use* of the phone number 529-9377—which spells "lawyers" on the telephone keypad—constitutes infringement upon Murrin's "Dial L.A.W.Y.E.R.S." service mark).

We conclude that although Holiday Inns owns trademark rights in its vanity number 1-800-HOLIDAY, it cannot claim such rights to the 405 number. It follows that the defendant, Call Management, is the rightful assignee of the telephone number 1-800-405-4329.

The plain language of §32 of the Lanham Act forbids only the "*use* in commerce [of] any reproduction, counterfeit, copy, or colorable imitation of a registered mark . . . which . . . is likely to *cause* confusion." 15 U.S.C. §1114 (emphasis added). Additionally, §43(a) of the Act provides a cause of action only against "[a] person who . . . *uses* in commerce any word, term, name, symbol, or device . . . or any false designation of origin, false or misleading description of fact, or false or misleading representation of fact. . . ." 15 U.S.C. §1125(a) (emphasis added). The defendants in this case never *used* Holiday Inns' trademark nor any facsimile of Holiday Inns' marks. Moreover, the defendants did not *create* any confusion; the confusion already existed among the misdialing public. The defendants forward a plausible argument that the service bureau and its travel agents may have helped dispel the confusion by answering calls that would have gone unanswered and informing the customers of their error. In addition, Holiday Inns neglected to take the simple precaution of reserving its complementary number—a practice which many of its competitors have chosen to take.

Even the district court candidly admitted in its opinion that the defendants did not violate the *letter* of the Lanham Act. Holiday Inns also acknowledges that "[g]iven the creative nature of the scheming mind, the law cannot hope to spell out every forbidden act but must be content with general rules which limit competition to that which is fair and 'stop people from playing dirty tricks.'" Thus, both the district court and Holiday Inns acknowledge that the defendants never used a mark or a deceptively similar copy of a mark owned by Holiday Inns—an essential element of proof of a Lanham Act violation. Despite its failure to make this threshold showing, however, Holiday Inns still argues that a "likelihood of confusion" existed among consumers and that such probable confusion establishes the Lanham Act violation. Holiday Inns, in fact, insists that all eight factors which tend to establish the existence of a "likelihood of confusion" undermine the defendants' position in this case. In particular, Holiday Inns emphasizes that the defendants *intended* to intercept calls meant for 1-800-HOLIDAY and cites *Frisch's Restaurants, Inc. v. Elby's Big Boy, Inc.*, for the proposition that the "intent of defendants in adopting [their mark] is a critical factor, since if the mark was adopted with the intent of deriving benefit from the reputation of [the plaintiff,] *that fact alone may be sufficient to justify the inference that there is confusing similarity*." *Frisch's Restaurants, Inc.*, 670 F.2d at 648 (emphasis added) (quoting *Amstar Corp. v. Domino's Pizza, Inc.*, 615 F.2d 252, 263 (5th Cir. 1980), *cert. denied*, 449 U.S. 899 (1980)).

Nevertheless, the defendants' use of a protected mark or their use of a misleading representation is a *prerequisite* to the finding of a Lanham Act violation. Absent such a finding, the eight-factor test of *Frisch's Restaurants, Inc.* is irrelevant. Holiday Inns does not offer, and our own research has not produced, a case in which the defendant neither *used* the offending mark nor *created* the confusion and yet was deemed to have committed a trademark infringement. We believe that stretching the plain language of the Lanham Act to cover the present dispute is unjustified. As a matter of law, therefore, we hold that Call Management, 800 Reservations, and Earthwinds Travel did not violate §§32 and 43 of the Lanham Act by the use of the 405 number.

[Grant of summary judgment reversed.]

NOTES AND QUESTIONS

1. *Actionable use—a non-issue in the "traditional" trademark case?* The *Holiday Inns* case presents a dispute over actionable use that springs from a quirky fact pattern. In trademark cases involving more traditional fact patterns, actionable use issues did not generally arise. Why not? Consider, for example, the *Fleischmann* case, in which the alleged infringer is selling beer under the name BLACK & WHITE. It was apparently undisputed that this activity qualified as an actionable use under the relevant language of Lanham Act §32(1)(a). Did it qualify because the activity took advantage of the plaintiff's mark in some general sense? Or because the alleged infringer's product also displayed the mark? Or only because the alleged infringer also was using the mark as a brand for its own products? Which of these three formulations best expresses the actionable use requirement?

2. *Relationship between actionable use and confusion requirements.* As the *Holiday Inns* opinion reflects, actionable use is a threshold requirement. By finding that the alleged infringer did not engage in actionable use, the court is able to dispose of the case without ever reaching the likelihood-of-confusion inquiry. Is that a good thing, considering the

complexities of the likelihood-of-confusion inquiry? Or does it simply mean that these same complexities (or different ones) will be shifted into the inquiry for actionable use?

3. *Confusion in* Holiday Inns? In *Holiday Inns*, if the Sixth Circuit had found actionable use, and therefore proceeded to review the trial court's likelihood-of-confusion inquiry, how do you think the Sixth Circuit would have ruled? To answer the question, would it be important for you to know more about how callers interpreted the recorded message that played when callers dialed the defendant's number? Would it affect your analysis of confusion if you discovered that the defendant actually provided no recorded message; or, alternatively, if the defendant's message had explicitly stated that the defendant was "not affiliated, associated, connected with, or sponsored by Holiday Inns, Inc." and that the caller needed to dial the letter "O" rather than the number "zero" to reach Holiday Inns? Would any of this evidence be relevant to an inquiry into actionable use? If not, is this a problem?

In the 1990s and early 2000s, there was extensive litigation over trademark liability for keyword advertising. In some cases, trademark owners sued rivals for purchases of keywords, while in others, including *Rescuecom* (excerpted below), trademark owners sued search engines for sales of keywords. The courts split on whether either keyword purchases or keyword sales constituted actionable use. In *1-800 Contacts, Inc. v. WhenU.com, Inc.*, 414 F.3d 400 (2d Cir. 2005), the Second Circuit found no actionable use, relying in part on the Section 45 definition of "use in commerce" to establish what appeared to be a stringent actionable use requirement. In *N. Am. Med. Corp. v. Axiom Worldwide, Inc.*, 522 F.3d 1211 (11th Cir. 2008) (keyword purchase constitutes actionable use), the court seemed less sympathetic to the *1-800 Contacts* view of actionable use. Likewise, scholarly views were divided. Many scholars favored an approach akin to that espoused in *1-800 Contacts. See, e.g.*, Margreth Barrett, *Internet Trademark Suits and the Demise of "Trademark Use,"* 39 U.C. DAVIS L. REV. 371 (2006); Eric Goldman, *Deregulating Relevancy in Internet Trademark Law*, 54 EMORY L.J. 507 (2005); Stacey L. Dogan & Mark A. Lemley, *Trademark and Consumer Search Costs on the Internet*, 41 HOUS. L. REV. 777 (2004). In contrast, we urged courts to resist imposing such a requirement. Graeme B. Dinwoodie & Mark D. Janis, *Confusion over Use: Contextualism in Trademark Law*, 92 IOWA L. REV. 1597 (2007); Graeme B. Dinwoodie & Mark D. Janis, *Lessons from the Trademark Use Debate*, 92 IOWA L. REV. 1703 (2007).

The *Rescuecom* decision resolved the debate—but perhaps only temporarily.

RESCUECOM CORP. v. GOOGLE INC.

562 F.3d 123 (2d Cir. 2009)

LEVAL, Circuit Judge:

BACKGROUND

Rescuecom is a national computer service franchising company that offers on-site computer services and sales. Rescuecom conducts a substantial amount of business over the Internet and receives between 17,000 to 30,000 visitors to its website each month. It also advertises over the Internet, using many web-based services, including those offered by Google. Since 1998, "Rescuecom" has been a registered federal trademark, and there is no dispute as to its validity.

Google operates a popular Internet search engine, which users access by visiting www. google.com. Using Google's website, a person searching for the website of a particular entity in trade (or simply for information about it) can enter that entity's name or trademark into Google's search engine and launch a search. Google's proprietary system responds to such a search request in two ways. First, Google provides a list of links to websites, ordered in what Google deems to be of descending relevance to the user's search terms based on its proprietary algorithms. Google's search engine assists the public not only in obtaining information about a provider, but also in purchasing products and services. If a prospective purchaser, looking for goods or services of a particular provider, enters the provider's trademark as a search term on Google's website and clicks to activate a search, within seconds, the Google search engine will provide on the searcher's computer screen a link to the webpage maintained by that provider (as well as a host of other links to sites that Google's program determines to be relevant to the search term entered). By clicking on the link of the provider, the searcher will be directed to the provider's website, where the searcher can obtain information supplied by the provider about its products and services and can perhaps also make purchases from the provider by placing orders.

The second way Google responds to a search request is by showing context-based advertising. When a searcher uses Google's search engine by submitting a search term, Google may place advertisements on the user's screen. Google will do so if an advertiser, having determined that its ad is likely to be of interest to a searcher who enters the particular term, has purchased from Google the placement of its ad on the screen of the searcher who entered that search term. What Google places on the searcher's screen is more than simply an advertisement. It is also a link to the advertiser's website, so that in response to such an ad, if the searcher clicks on the link, he will open the advertiser's website, which offers not only additional information about the advertiser, but also perhaps the option to purchase the goods and services of the advertiser over the Internet. Google uses at least two programs to offer such context-based links: AdWords and Keyword Suggestion Tool.

AdWords is Google's program through which advertisers purchase terms (or keywords). When entered as a search term, the keyword triggers the appearance of the advertiser's ad and link. An advertiser's purchase of a particular term causes the advertiser's ad and link to be displayed on the user's screen whenever a searcher launches a Google search based on the purchased search term.[1] Advertisers pay Google based on the number of times Internet users "click" on the advertisement, so as to link to the advertiser's website. For example, using Google's AdWords, Company Y, a company engaged in the business of furnace repair, can cause Google to display its advertisement and link whenever a user of Google launches a search based on the search term, "furnace repair." Company Y can also cause its ad and link to appear whenever a user searches for the term "Company X," a competitor of Company Y in the furnace repair business. Thus, whenever a searcher interested in purchasing furnace repair services from Company X launches a search of the term X (Company X's trademark), an ad and link would appear on the searcher's screen, inviting the searcher to the furnace repair services of X's competitor, Company Y. And if the searcher clicked on Company Y's link, Company Y's website would open on the searcher's screen, and the searcher might be able to order or purchase Company Y's furnace repair services.

In addition to Adwords, Google also employs Keyword Suggestion Tool, a program that recommends keywords to advertisers to be purchased. The program is designed to

---

1. Although we generally refer to a single advertiser, there is no limit on the number of advertisers who can purchase a particular keyword to trigger the appearance of their ads.

improve the effectiveness of advertising by helping advertisers identify keywords related to their area of commerce, resulting in the placement of their ads before users who are likely to be responsive to it. Thus, continuing the example given above, if Company Y employed Google's Keyword Suggestion Tool, the Tool might suggest to Company Y that it purchase not only the term "furnace repair" but also the term "X," its competitor's brand name and trademark, so that Y's ad would appear on the screen of a searcher who searched Company X's trademark, seeking Company X's website.

Once an advertiser buys a particular keyword, Google links the keyword to that advertiser's advertisement. The advertisements consist of a combination of content and a link to the advertiser's webpage. Google displays these advertisements on the search result page either in the right margin or in a horizontal band immediately above the column of relevance-based search results. These advertisements are generally associated with a label, which says "sponsored link." Rescuecom alleges, however, that a user might easily be misled to believe that the advertisements which appear on the screen are in fact part of the relevance-based search result and that the appearance of a competitor's ad and link in response to a searcher's search for Rescuecom is likely to cause trademark confusion as to affiliation, origin, sponsorship, or approval of service. This can occur, according to the Complaint, because Google fails to label the ads in a manner which would clearly identify them as purchased ads rather than search results. The Complaint alleges that when the sponsored links appear in a horizontal bar at the top of the search results, they may appear to the searcher to be the first, and therefore the most relevant, entries responding to the search, as opposed to paid advertisements.

Google's objective in its AdWords and Keyword Suggestion Tool programs is to sell keywords to advertisers. Rescuecom alleges that Google makes 97% of its revenue from selling advertisements through its AdWords program. Google therefore has an economic incentive to increase the number of advertisements and links that appear for every term entered into its search engine.

Many of Rescuecom's competitors advertise on the Internet. Through its Keyword Suggestion Tool, Google has recommended the Rescuecom trademark to Rescuecom's competitors as a search term to be purchased. Rescuecom's competitors, some responding to Google's recommendation, have purchased Rescuecom's trademark as a keyword in Google's AdWords program, so that whenever a user launches a search for the term "Rescuecom," seeking to be connected to Rescuecom's website, the competitors' advertisement and link will appear on the searcher's screen. This practice allegedly allows Rescuecom's competitors to deceive and divert users searching for Rescuecom's website. According to Rescuecom's allegations, when a Google user launches a search for the term "Rescuecom" because the searcher wishes to purchase Rescuecom's services, links to websites of its competitors will appear on the searcher's screen in a manner likely to cause the searcher to believe mistakenly that a competitor's advertisement (and website link) is sponsored by, endorsed by, approved by, or affiliated with Rescuecom.

The District Court granted Google's 12(b)(6) motion and dismissed Rescuecom's claims. The court believed that our *1-800* decision [*1-800 Contacts, Inc. v. Whenu.com, Inc.*, 414 F.3d 400 (2d Cir. 2005)] compels the conclusion that Google's allegedly infringing activity does not involve use of Rescuecom's mark in commerce, which is an essential element of an action under the Lanham Act. The district court explained its decision saying that even if Google employed Rescuecom's mark in a manner likely to cause confusion or deceive searchers into believing that competitors are affiliated with Rescuecom and its mark, so that they believe the services of Rescuecom's competitors are those of Rescuecom, Google's actions are not a "use in commerce" under the Lanham Act because the competitor's advertisements triggered by Google's programs did not exhibit Rescuecom's trademark. The court rejected the argument that Google "used" Rescuecom's mark in recommending and selling it as a keyword to trigger competitor's advertisements because the court read *1-800* to compel the conclusion that this was an internal use and therefore cannot be a "use in commerce" under the Lanham Act.

DISCUSSION

. . .

I. Google's Use of Rescuecom's Mark Was a "Use in Commerce"

Our court ruled in *1-800* that a complaint fails to state a claim under the Lanham Act unless it alleges that the defendant has made "use in commerce" of the plaintiff's trademark as the term "use in commerce" is defined in 15 U.S.C. §1127. The district court believed that this case was on all fours with *1-800*, and that its dismissal was required for the same reasons as given in *1-800*. We believe the cases are materially different. The allegations of Rescuecom's complaint adequately plead a use in commerce.

In *1-800*, the plaintiff alleged that the defendant infringed the plaintiff's trademark through its proprietary software, which the defendant freely distributed to computer users who would download and install the program on their computer. The program provided contextually relevant advertising to the user by generating pop-up advertisements to the user depending on the website or search term the user entered in his browser. *Id.* at 404-405. For example, if a user typed "eye care" into his browser, the defendant's program would randomly display a pop-up advertisement of a company engaged in the field of eye care. Similarly, if the searcher launched a search for a particular company engaged in eye care, the defendant's program would display the pop-up ad of a company associated with eye care. *See id.* at 412. The pop-up ad appeared in a separate browser window from the website the user accessed, and the defendant's brand was displayed in the window frame surrounding the ad, so that there was no confusion as to the nature of the pop-up as an advertisement, nor as to the fact that the defendant, not the trademark owner, was responsible for displaying the ad, in response to the particular term searched. *Id.* at 405.

Sections 32 and 43 of the Act . . . *inter alia*, impose liability for unpermitted "use in commerce" of another's mark which is "likely to cause confusion, or to cause mistake, or to deceive," §1114, "as to the affiliation . . . or as to the origin, sponsorship or approval of his or her goods [or] services . . . by another person." §1125(a)(1)(A). The *1-800* opinion looked to the definition of the term "use in commerce" provided in §45 of the Act, 15 U.S.C. §1127. That definition provides in part that "a mark shall be deemed to be in use in commerce . . . (2) on services when it is used or displayed in the sale or advertising of services and the services are rendered in commerce." 15 U.S.C. §1127.[2] Our court found that the plaintiff failed to show that the defendant made a "use in commerce" of the plaintiff's mark, within that definition.

At the outset, we note two significant aspects of our holding in *1-800*, which distinguish it from the present case. A key element of our court's decision in *1-800* was that under the plaintiff's allegations, the defendant did not use, reproduce, or display the plaintiff's mark *at all*. The search term that was alleged to trigger the pop-up ad was the plaintiff's *website address*. *1-800* noted, notwithstanding the similarities between the website address and the mark, that the website address was not used or claimed by the plaintiff as a

---

2. The Appendix to this opinion discusses the applicability of §1127's definition of "use in commerce" to sections of the Lanham Act proscribing infringement.

trademark. Thus, the transactions alleged to be infringing were not transactions involving use of the plaintiff's trademark. *Id.* at 408-409.[3] *1-800* suggested in dictum that is highly relevant to our case that had the defendant used the plaintiff's *trademark* as the trigger to pop-up an advertisement, such conduct might, depending on other elements, have been actionable. [citing *1-800* at n.11]

Second, as an alternate basis for its decision, *1-800* explained why the defendant's program, which might randomly trigger pop-up advertisements upon a searcher's input of the plaintiff's website address, did not constitute a "use in commerce," as defined in §1127. In explaining why the plaintiff's mark was not "used or displayed in the sale or advertising of services," *1-800* pointed out that, under the defendant's program, advertisers could not request or purchase keywords to trigger their ads. *Id.* at 409, 412. Even if an advertiser wanted to display its advertisement to a searcher using the plaintiff's trademark as a search term, the defendant's program did not offer this possibility. In fact, the defendant "did not disclose the proprietary contents of [its] directory to its advertising clients. . . ." *Id.* at 409. In addition to not selling trademarks of others to its customers to trigger these ads, the defendant did not "otherwise manipulate which category-related advertisement will pop up in response to any particular terms on the internal directory." *Id.* at 411. The display of a particular advertisement was controlled by the category associated with the website or keyword, rather than the website or keyword itself. The defendant's program relied upon categorical associations such as "eye care" to select a pop-up ad randomly from a predefined list of ads appropriate to that category. To the extent that an advertisement for a competitor of the plaintiff was displayed when a user opened the plaintiff's website, the trigger to display the ad was not based on the defendant's sale or recommendation of a particular trademark.

The present case contrasts starkly with those important aspects of the *1-800* decision. First, in contrast to *1-800*, where we emphasized that the defendant made no use whatsoever of the plaintiff's trademark, here what Google is recommending and selling to its advertisers is Rescuecom's trademark. Second, in contrast with the facts of *1-800* where the defendant did not "use or display," much less sell, trademarks as search terms to its advertisers, here Google displays, offers, and sells Rescuecom's mark to Google's advertising customers when selling its advertising services. In addition, Google encourages the purchase of Rescuecom's mark through its Keyword Suggestion Tool. Google's utilization of Rescuecom's mark fits literally within the terms specified by 15 U.S.C. §1127. According to the Complaint, Google uses and sells Rescuecom's mark "in the sale . . . of [Google's advertising] services . . . rendered in commerce." §1127.

Google, supported by amici, argues that *1-800* suggests that the inclusion of a trademark in an internal computer directory cannot constitute trademark use. Several district court decisions in this Circuit appear to have reached this conclusion. *See e.g., S & L Vitamins, Inc. v. Australian Gold, Inc.*, 521 F. Supp. 2d 188, 199-202 (E.D.N.Y. 2007) (holding that use of a trademark in metadata did not constitute trademark use within the

---

3. We did not imply in *1-800* that a website can never be a trademark. In fact, the opposite is true. *See* Trademark Manual of Examining Procedures §1209.03(m) (5th ed. 2007) ("A mark comprised of an Internet domain name is registrable as a trademark or service mark only if it functions as an identifier of the source of goods or services."); *see also Two Pesos, Inc. v. Taco Cabana, Inc.*, 505 U.S. 763, 768 (1992) (Section 43(a) of the Lanham Act protects unregistered trademarks as long as the mark could qualify for registration under the Lanham Act.); [cit.]. The question whether the plaintiff's website address was an unregistered trademark was never properly before the *1-800* court because the plaintiff did not claim that it used its website address as a trademark.

meaning of the Lanham Act because the use "is strictly internal and not communicated to the public"); *Merck & Co., Inc. v. Mediplan Health Consulting, Inc.*, 425 F. Supp. 2d 402, 415 (S.D.N.Y. 2006) (holding that the internal use of a keyword to trigger advertisements did not qualify as trademark use). This over-reads the *1-800* decision. First, regardless of whether Google's use of Rescuecom's mark in its internal search algorithm could constitute an actionable trademark use, Google's recommendation and sale of Rescuecom's mark to its advertising customers are not internal uses. Furthermore, *1-800* did not imply that use of a trademark in a software program's internal directory precludes a finding of trademark use. Rather, influenced by the fact that the defendant was not using the plaintiff's trademark at all, much less using it as the basis of a commercial transaction, the court asserted that the particular use before it did not constitute a use in commerce. *See 1-800*, 414 F.3d at 409-12. We did not imply in *1-800* that an alleged infringer's use of a trademark in an internal software program insulates the alleged infringer from a charge of infringement, no matter how likely the use is to cause confusion in the marketplace. If we were to adopt Google and its amici's argument, the operators of search engines would be free to use trademarks in ways designed to deceive and cause consumer confusion.[4] This is surely neither within the intention nor the letter of the Lanham Act.

Google and its amici contend further that its use of the Rescuecom trademark is no different from that of a retail vendor who uses "product placement" to allow one vender to benefit from a competitors' name recognition. An example of product placement occurs when a store-brand generic product is placed next to a trademarked product to induce a customer who specifically sought out the trademarked product to consider the typically less expensive, generic brand as an alternative. *See 1-800*, 414 F.3d at 411. Google's argument misses the point. From the fact that proper, non-deceptive product placement does not result in liability under the Lanham Act, it does not follow that the label "product placement" is a magic shield against liability, so that even a deceptive plan of product placement designed to confuse consumers would similarly escape liability. It is not by reason of absence of a use of a mark in commerce that benign product placement escapes liability; it escapes liability because it is a benign practice which does not cause a likelihood of consumer confusion. In contrast, if a retail seller were to be paid by an off-brand purveyor to arrange product display and delivery in such a way that customers seeking to purchase a famous brand would receive the off-brand, believing they had gotten the brand they were seeking, we see no reason to believe the practice would escape liability merely because it could claim the mantle of "product placement." The practices attributed to Google by the Complaint, which at this stage we must accept as true, are significantly different from benign product placement that does not violate the Act.

Unlike the practices discussed in *1-800*, the practices here attributed to Google by Rescuecom's complaint are that Google has made use in commerce of Rescuecom's mark. Needless to say, a defendant must do more than use another's mark in commerce to violate the Lanham Act. The gist of a Lanham Act violation is an unauthorized use, which "is likely to cause confusion, or to cause mistake, or to deceive as to the affiliation, . . . or as to the origin, sponsorship, or approval of . . . goods [or] services." *See* 15 U.S.C. §1125(a);

---

4. For example, instead of having a separate "sponsored links" or paid advertisement section, search engines could allow advertisers to pay to appear at the top of the "relevance" list based on a user entering a competitor's trademark—a functionality that would be highly likely to cause consumer confusion. Alternatively, sellers of products or services could pay to have the operators of search engines automatically divert users to their website when the users enter a competitor's trademark as a search term. Such conduct is surely not beyond judicial review merely because it is engineered through the internal workings of a computer program.

[cit.]. We have no idea whether Rescuecom can prove that Google's use of Rescuecom's trademark in its AdWords program causes likelihood of confusion or mistake. Rescuecom has alleged that it does, in that would-be purchasers (or explorers) of its services who search for its website on Google are misleadingly directed to the ads and websites of its competitors in a manner which leads them to believe mistakenly that these ads or websites are sponsored by, or affiliated with Rescuecom. This is particularly so, Rescuecom alleges, when the advertiser's link appears in a horizontal band at the top of the list of search results in a manner which makes it appear to be the most relevant search result and not an advertisement. What Rescuecom alleges is that by the manner of Google's display of sponsored links of competing brands in response to a search for Rescuecom's brand name (which fails adequately to identify the sponsored link as an advertisement, rather than a relevant search result), Google creates a likelihood of consumer confusion as to trademarks. If the searcher sees a different brand name as the top entry in response to the search for "Rescuecom," the searcher is likely to believe mistakenly that the different name which appears is affiliated with the brand name sought in the search and will not suspect, because the fact is not adequately signaled by Google's presentation, that this is not the most relevant response to the search. Whether Google's actual practice is in fact benign or confusing is not for us to judge at this time. We consider at the 12(b)(6) stage only what is alleged in the Complaint.

We conclude that the district court was mistaken in believing that our precedent in *1-800* requires dismissal.

[*Vacated and remanded.*]

APPENDIX

On the Meaning of "Use in Commerce" in Sections 32 and 43 of the Lanham Act[5]

In *1-800 Contacts, Inc. v. WhenU.com, Inc.*, 414 F.3d 400 (2d Cir. 2005) ("*1-800*"), our court followed the reasoning of two district court opinions from other circuits, *U-Haul Int'l, Inc. v. WhenU.com, Inc.*, 279 F. Supp. 2d 723 (E.D. Va. 2003) and *Wells Fargo & Co. v. WhenU.com, Inc.*, 293 F. Supp. 2d 734 (E.D. Mich. 2003), which dismissed suits on virtually identical claims against the same defendant. Those two district courts ruled that the defendant's conduct was not actionable under §§32 & 43(a) of the Lanham Act, 15 U.S.C. §§1114 & 1125(a), even assuming that conduct caused likelihood of trademark confusion, because the defendant had not made a "use in commerce" of the plaintiff's mark, within the definition of that phrase set forth in §45 of the Lanham Act, 15 U.S.C. §1127. In quoting definitional language of §1127 that is crucial to their holdings, however, *U-Haul* and *Wells Fargo* overlooked and omitted portions of the statutory text which make clear that the definition provided in §1127 was not intended by Congress to apply in the manner that the decisions assumed.

Our court's ruling in *1-800* that the Plaintiff had failed to plead a viable claim under §§1114 & 1125(a) was justified by numerous good reasons and was undoubtedly the correct result. In addition to the questionable ground derived from the district court opinions, which had overlooked key statutory text, our court's opinion cited other highly persuasive reasons for dismissing the action—among them that the plaintiff did not claim a trademark in the term that served as the basis for the claim of infringement; nor did the defendant's actions cause any likelihood of confusion, as is crucial for such a claim.

---

5. In this discussion, all iterations of the phrase "use in commerce" whether in the form of a noun (a "use in commerce"), a verb ("to use in commerce"), or adjective ("used in commerce"), are intended without distinction as instances of that phrase.

We proceed to explain how the district courts in *U-Haul* and *Wells Fargo* adopted reasoning which overlooked crucial statutory text that was incompatible with their ultimate conclusion. . . . To determine the meaning of the phrase "uses in commerce," which appears in both sections [32 and 43(a)], the *U-Haul* and *Wells Fargo* courts quite understandably looked to the definition of the term "use in commerce," set forth among the Act's definitions in §45, codified at 15 U.S.C. §1127. That definition, *insofar as quoted by the courts*, stated, with respect to services, that a mark shall be deemed to be "used in commerce only when it is used or displayed in the sale or advertising of services and the services are rendered in commerce." *Wells Fargo*, 293 F. Supp. 2d at 757 (internal quotations omitted); *U-Haul*, 279 F. Supp. 2d at 727 (specifying a similar requirement with respect to goods). Adhering to this portion of the definition, and determining that on the particular facts of the case, the defendant had not used or displayed a mark in the sale or advertising of services, those courts concluded that the defendant's conduct was not within the scope of the Act.

In quoting the §1127 definition, however, those district courts overlooked and omitted two portions of the statutory text, which we believe make clear that the definition provided in §1127 is not intended to apply to §§1114 & 1125(a). First, those courts, no doubt reasonably, assumed that the definition of "use in commerce" set forth in §1127 necessarily applies to all usages of that term throughout the Act. This was, however, not quite accurate. Section 1127 does not state flatly that the defined terms have the assigned meanings when used in the statute. The definition is more guarded and tentative. It states rather that the terms listed shall have the given meanings "unless the contrary is plainly apparent from the context."

The second part of §1127 which those courts overlooked was the opening phrase of the definition of "use in commerce," which makes it "plainly apparent from the context" that the full definition set forth in §1127 cannot apply to the infringement sections. The definition in §1127 begins by saying, "The term 'use in commerce' means the *bona fide* use of a mark in the ordinary course of trade, and not made merely to reserve a right in a mark." 15 U.S.C. §1127 (emphasis added). The requirement that a use be a *bona fide* use in the ordinary course of trade in order to be considered a "use in commerce" makes clear that the particular definition was not intended as a limitation on conduct of an accused infringer that might cause liability. . . .[6]

A more detailed examination of the construction of the Lanham Act, and its historical evolution, demonstrates how this unlikely circumstance came to be. The Act employs the term "use in commerce" in two very different contexts. The first context sets the standards and circumstances under which the owner of a mark can qualify to *register* the mark and to receive the *benefits* and *protection* provided by the Act. For example, 15 U.S.C. §1051 provides that "[t]he owner of a trademark *used in commerce* may request registration of its trademark on the principal register," thereby receiving the benefits of enhanced protection (emphasis added).[7] This part of the statute describes the conduct which the statute seeks to encourage, reward, and protect. The second context in which the term "use in commerce"

---

6. The *Wells Fargo* decision, which followed and cited *U-Haul*, unlike *U-Haul*, did quote the part of §1127 which requires a "bona fide use of a mark in the ordinary course of trade," 293 F. Supp. 2d at 758, but failed to note the incompatibility of that requirement with a section defining prohibited actionable conduct.

7. In addition to §1051, a non-exhaustive list of other sections that employ the term "use in commerce" in the same general way, in defining what is necessary to secure the benefits of the Act, include §1065 (incontestability of a mark); §1058 (renewal of a mark); §1091 (eligibility for the supplemental register); §1112 (registration of a mark in plurality of classes); and §1062 (republication of marks registered under acts prior to the Lanham Act).

appears is at the opposite pole. As exemplified in §§1114 & 1125(a), the term "use in commerce," as quoted above, also appears as part of the Act's definition of reprehensible conduct, *i.e.*, the conduct which the Act identifies as infringing of the rights of the trademark owner, and for which it imposes liability. When one considers the entire definition of "use in commerce" set forth in §1127, it becomes plainly apparent that this definition was intended to apply to the Act's use of that term in defining favored conduct, which qualifies to receive the protection of the Act. The definition makes perfect sense in this context. In order to qualify to register one's mark and receive the enhanced protections that flow from registration (giving the world notice of one's exclusive rights in the mark), the owner must have made "bona fide use of the mark in the ordinary course of trade, and not merely to reserve a right in the mark." *Id.* §1127. The bona fide "use" envisioned is, with respect to "goods, when [the mark] is placed in any manner on the goods or their containers or the displays associated therewith or on the tags or labels affixed thereto . . . and the goods are sold or transported in commerce; and on services when [the mark] is used or displayed in the sale or advertising of services . . . rendered in commerce." *Id.* This definition sensibly insures that one who in good faith places his mark on goods or services in commerce qualifies for the Act's protection. In contrast, it would make no sense whatsoever for Congress to have insisted, in relation to §1114 for example, that one who "without the consent of the registrant . . . use[d] . . . [a] counterfeit . . . of a registered mark in connection with the sale . . . of . . . goods [thereby] caus[ing] confusion" will be liable to the registrant *only if* his use of the counterfeit was a "bona fide use of [the] mark in the ordinary course of trade." *Id.* §§1114 & 1127. Such a statute would perversely penalize only the fools while protecting the knaves, which was surely not what Congress intended.

The question then arises how it came to pass that the sections of the statute identifying conduct giving rise to liability included the phrase "use in commerce" as an essential element of liability. This answer results in part from a rearrangement of this complex statute, which resulted in joining together words which, as originally written, were separated from one another. The first incidence of employment of the phrase "use in commerce" in §1114 occurred in 1962 as the result of a mere "rearrangement" of sections, not intended to have substantive significance, which brought together the jurisdiction-invoking phrase, "in commerce" with the verb "use." Prior to the 1962 rearrangement, the term "use in commerce" appeared as an essential element of a trademark owner's qualification for registration and for the benefits of the Act, but did not appear as an essential element of a defendant's conduct necessary for liability. The Act frequently employs the term "in commerce" for the distinct purpose of invoking Congress's Commerce Clause jurisdiction and staying within its limits.[8] The statute also frequently employs the word "use," either as a noun or verb, because that word so naturally and aptly describes what one does with a trademark. Not surprisingly, in the extensive elaborate course of drafting, revision, and rearrangement which the Act has undergone from time to time, as explained below, the words "use" and "in commerce" came into proximity with each other in circumstances where there was no intent to invoke the specialized restrictive meaning given by §1127. In 1988, when Congress enacted the present form of §1127's definition, which was designed to deny registration to an owner who made merely token use of his mark, the accompanying Congressional report made clear that the definition was understood as applying only to the requirements of qualification for registration and other benefits of the Act, and not to

---

8. Section 1127 defines "commerce" to mean "all commerce which may lawfully be regulated by Congress."

conduct causing liability. We briefly trace the history of this evolution below, to show that the restrictive definition of "use in commerce" set forth in §1127 never was intended as a restriction on the types of conduct that could result in liability.

History of the Phrase "Use in Commerce" in the Lanham Act

[The court offered a detailed historical analysis of the development of the "use in commerce" language in the original Lanham Act and later amendments. The court noted that the 1946 Act did not restrict liability for infringement to those who "used in commerce," as defined in §45's restrictive terms. However, the court acknowledged that "a confusing change in statutory diction occurred in 1962 when Congress amended Section 32. The purpose of the amendment was to broaden liability for infringement . . . by expand[ing] the scope of deceptive, or misleading conduct that could constitute infringement. . . . At the same time as making this broadening substantive change, the 1962 amendment made structural changes to the order of the language in Section 32. . . . One of the changes, which is not described in the House or Senate Reports as having any substantive significance, was a rearrangement of the order of words so that "use" and "in commerce" came to appear side by side in the amended version, rather than in separate clauses. The court concluded, however, that "it would be unreasonable to construe mere 'rearrange[ment]' of language in section 32 as having intended to convert the broad liability-imposing term, 'use' into a restrictive, defined term, which had previously applied only to a trademark owner's qualification for registration of the mark—especially when Congress made no mention beyond describing the change as a rearrangement."]

If there was any doubt prior to 1988 on the question whether the narrowing definition of "use in commerce" set forth in §1127, was intended to apply to the utilization of that phrase in the sections providing for the liability of infringers, the doubt was put to rest by the Trademark Law Revision Act of 1988, which inserted into §1127 the requirement that a "use in commerce" be a "bona fide use of a mark in the ordinary course of trade and not merely made to reserve a right in a mark." This was part of a change intended to bring the federal trademark registration system into harmony with the registration system of other nations by providing the possibility of reserving a trademark for intended future use. . . .

While these amendments provided relief in the form of effective reservation of a mark for a time on the basis of a filing of intent to use, registration of a mark under §1051 continued to be limited to those who have in fact "used [the mark] in commerce." And the definition of "use in commerce" set forth in §1127 was amended to require that the use be a "bona fide use . . . in the ordinary course of trade and not made merely to reserve a right in the mark." 15 U.S.C. §1127. Those wishing to reserve a right in the mark were provided for by the new intent-to-use provisions. Actual registration, however, was reserved to mark owners making bona fide use in commerce. As noted above, this definition of "use in commerce" makes eminent good sense as a prerequisite for a mark owner to register the mark and claim the benefits the Act provides to the owners of marks. It makes no conceivable sense as a limitation shielding bad-faith abusers of the marks of others from liability for causing trademark confusion.

The Senate Report for the 1988 amendment confirms that the definition in §1127 was meant to apply only to registering a mark rather than infringing one. The Senate Report explained that the "revised [use in commerce] definition is intended to apply to all aspects of the trademark registration process," and that "[c]learly, however, use of *any type* will continue to be considered in an infringement action." *See* S. Rep. 100-515 100th Cong. at 45 (1988) (emphasis added). This, of course, is consistent with the Lanham Act's intent to make actionable the deceptive and misleading use of marks in commerce—an intent which has not changed since the Lanham Act was first enacted. *See* Lanham Act, 60 Stat. 427, §45

(1946); 15 U.S.C. §1127. According to the Senate Report, a purpose in amending this section was to add "a reference to make clear that the section applies only to acts or practices which occur in [or] affect commerce." *See* S. Rep. 100-515 100th Cong. at 41 (1988). The amendment left only one reference to commerce in §1125(a), which was the "uses in commerce" language. This term was thus employed in the 1988 revision to make clear that liability would be imposed for acts that occur in or affect commerce, i.e. those within Congress's Commerce Clause power. Thus, the term "uses in commerce" in the current §1125(a) is intended to refer to a use that falls within Congress's commerce power, and not to the restrictive definition of "use in commerce," set forth in §45 to define standards of qualification for an owner to register a mark and receive the benefits and protection of the Act.

It therefore appears that the history of the development of the Lanham Act confirms what is also indicated by a common-sense understanding of the provisions. The definition of the term "use in commerce" provided by §1127, was intended to continue to apply, as it did when the definition was conceived in the 1941 bill, to the sections governing qualification for registration and for the benefits of the Act. In that version, the term "use in commerce" did not appear in §32, which established the elements of liability for infringing upon a federally registered mark. The eventual appearance of that phrase in that section did not represent an intention that the phrase carry the restrictive definition which defined an owner's entitlement to registration. The appearance rather resulted from happenstance pairing of the verb "use" with the term "in commerce," whose purpose is to claim the jurisdictional authority of the Commerce Clause. Section 1127, as noted, does not prescribe that its definitions necessarily apply throughout the Act. They apply "unless the contrary is plainly apparent from the context."

THE INTERPRETATION OF §1127's DEFINITION OF "USE IN COMMERCE" WITH RESPECT TO ALLEGED INFRINGERS

In light of the preceding discussion, how should courts today interpret the definition of "use in commerce" set forth in 15 U.S.C. §1127, with respect to acts of infringement prescribed by §§1114 and 1125(a)? The foregoing review of the evolution of the Act seems to us to make clear that Congress did not intend that this definition apply to the sections of the Lanham Act which define infringing conduct. The definition was rather intended to apply to the sections which used the phrase in prescribing eligibility for registration and for the Act's protections. However, Congress does not enact intentions. It enacts statutes. And the process of enacting legislation is of such complexity that understandably the words of statutes do not always conform perfectly to the motivating intentions. This can create for courts difficult problems of interpretation. Because pertinent amendments were passed in 1962 and in 1988, and because the 1988 amendment did not change the pre-existing parts of the definition in §1127, but merely added a sentence, it seems useful to approach the question of the current meaning in two steps. First, what did this definition mean between 1962 and 1988—prior to the 1988 amendment? Then, how was the meaning changed by the 1988 amendment?

Between 1962 and 1988, notwithstanding the likelihood shown by the legislative history that Congress *intended* the definition to apply only to registration and qualification for benefits and not to infringement, a court addressing the issue nonetheless would probably have concluded that the section applied to alleged infringement, as well. Section 1127 states that its definitions apply "unless the contrary is plainly apparent from the context." One who considered the question at the time might well have wondered why Congress would have provided this restrictive definition for acts of trademark infringement with the consequence that deceptive and confusing uses of another's mark with respect to goods would escape liability if the conduct did not include the placement of the mark on goods or their containers, displays, or sale documents, and with respect to services if the conduct did not include the use or display of the mark in the sale or advertising of the services. It is easy to imagine perniciously confusing conduct involving another's mark which does not involve placement of the mark in the manner specified in the definition. Nonetheless, in spite of those doubts, one could not have said it was "plainly apparent from the context" that those restrictions did not apply to sections defining infringement. In all probability, therefore, a court construing the provision between 1962 and 1988 would have concluded that in order to be actionable under §§1114 or 1125(a) the allegedly infringing conduct needed to include placement of the mark in the manner specified in the definition of "use in commerce" in §1127.

The next question is how the meaning of the §1127 definition was changed by the 1988 amendment, which, as noted, left the preexisting language about placement of the mark unchanged, but added a prior sentence requiring that a "use in commerce" be "a bona fide use in the ordinary course of trade, and not made merely to reserve a right in a mark." While it is "plainly apparent from the context" that the new first sentence cannot reasonably apply to statutory sections defining infringing conduct, the question remains whether the addition of this new sentence changed the meaning of the second sentence of the definition without changing its words.

We see at least two possible answers to the question, neither of which is entirely satisfactory. One interpretation would be that, by adding the new first sentence, Congress changed the meaning of the second sentence of the definition to conform to the new first sentence, without altering the words. The language of the definition, which, prior to the addition of the new first sentence, would have been construed to apply both to sections defining infringement, and to sections specifying eligibility for registration, would change its meaning, despite the absence of any change in its words, so that the entire definition now no longer applied to the sections defining infringement. Change of meaning without change of words is obviously problematic.

The alternative solution would be to interpret the two sentences of the statutory definition as of different scope. The second sentence of the definition, which survived the 1988 amendment unchanged, would retain its prior meaning and continue to apply as before the amendment to sections defining infringement, as well as to sections relating to a mark owner's eligibility for registration and for enjoyment of the protections of the Act. The new first sentence, which plainly was not intended to apply to infringements, would apply only to sections in the latter category — those relating to an owner's eligibility to register its mark and enjoy the Act's protection. Under this interpretation, liability for infringement under §§1114 and 1125(a) would continue, as before 1988, to require a showing of the infringer's placement of another's mark in the manner specified in the second sentence of the §1127 definition. It would not require a showing that the alleged infringer made "bona fide use of the mark in the ordinary course of trade, and not merely to reserve a right in the mark." On the other hand, eligibility of mark owners for registration and for the protections of the Act would depend on their showing compliance with the requirements of both sentences of the definition.

We recognize that neither of the two available solutions is altogether satisfactory. Each has advantages and disadvantages. At least for this Circuit, especially given our prior *1-800* precedent, which applied the second sentence of the definition to infringement, the latter solution, according a different scope of application to the two sentences of the definition, seems to be preferable.[12]

---

12. We express no view which of the alternative available solutions would seem preferable if our Circuit had not previously applied the second sentence to sections of the Act defining infringement.

The judges of the *1-800* panel have read this Appendix and have authorized us to state that they agree with it. At the same time we note that the discussion in this Appendix does not affect the result of this case. We assumed in the body of the opinion, in accordance with the holding of *1-800*, that the requirements of the second sentence of the definition of "use in commerce" in §1127 apply to infringing conduct and found that such use in commerce was adequately pleaded. The discussion in this Appendix is therefore dictum and not a binding opinion of the court. It would be helpful for Congress to study and clear up this ambiguity.

NOTES AND QUESTIONS

1. Rescuecom: *opinion and "appendix."* Why do you think that the *Rescuecom* panel rendered an opinion and added a lengthy "appendix" that (the court says) is "dictum and not a binding opinion of the court" and "does not affect the result of this case"? The *Rescuecom* appendix is the most detailed judicial exposition on the actionable use requirement to date. If you were an appellate judge from another circuit, would you look to the *Rescuecom* appendix as persuasive authority, notwithstanding the court's insistence that it is mere dictum? If you were a judge in the Second Circuit, would you continue to rely on *1-800 Contacts*?

2. Rescuecom's *treatment of precedent.* The *Rescuecom* court distinguished *1-800 Contacts* on at least two grounds: (1) the finding that defendant's inclusion of the website address *www.1800contacts.com* was not the same as including plaintiff's mark 1-800 CONTACTS; and (2) the finding that defendant's program did not permit advertisers to request or purchase keywords, but rather chose pop-up advertisements randomly in response to a user's input of a category. Are you persuaded by the *Rescuecom* court's reasoning?

3. Rescuecom's *approach to the statute: the* Rescuecom *construction of Section 45's "use in commerce" definition.* In the *Rescuecom* appendix, the court concludes that the first sentence of the Section 45 definition of "use in commerce" (or, more particularly, the clause "bona fide use of the mark in the ordinary course of trade, and not merely to reserve a right in the mark") does not apply in the infringement context, but that the remainder of the definition does. Is the court's construction plausible as a matter of statutory construction principles? As a pragmatic response to the statutory language?

4. *Should Congress amend the statute?* At the end of the appendix, the *Rescuecom* court recommends that Congress "study and clear up" the ambiguity in the Section 45 definition of "use in commerce." Should Congress take up the recommendation? If so, how should Congress change the Section 45 definition?

5. *Applying* Rescuecom: *a low bar for "use or display"?* The *Rescuecom* court concluded that Google "displays, offers, and sells Rescuecom's mark to Google's advertising customers when selling its advertising services." In what sense is Google displaying the RESCUECOM mark? Is the court setting a very low bar for actionable use? *See Network Automation, Inc. v. Advanced Sys. Concepts, Inc.*, 638 F.3d 1137 (9th Cir. 2011) (endorsing the *Rescuecom* standard and applying it to a keyword purchase); *Kelly-Brown v. Winfrey*, 717 F.3d 295 (2d Cir. 2013).

6. *Applying* Rescuecom: *product substitution.* Suppose that a hotel places a soft drink dispenser in its lobby. The dispenser bears a COCA COLA trademark and dispenses soft drink directly into the user's cup, free of charge. If the hotel begins to stock the dispenser with some nondescript, low-cost cola, has the hotel engaged in an actionable use of the COCA COLA mark? *See Georgia Pacific Consumer Prods., LP v. Von Drehle Corp.*, 618 F.3d 441, 452 (4th Cir. 2010) (discussing the hypothetical and applying it to a case involving substitution of paper towels in plaintiff's dispensers); *see also Georgia-Pacific Consumer Prods., LP v. Myers Supply, Inc.*, 621 F.3d 771 (8th Cir. 2010) (arising from a fact situation similar to that of the Fourth Circuit litigation).

7. *Applying* Rescuecom: *manipulating the placement of products on store shelves.* In *Rescuecom*, the court recites a hypothetical about product shelving (producer of brand "X" products pays a grocer to place brand "X" products next to brand "Y" products) and concludes that this activity should amount to actionable use. Do you agree? In general, do bricks-and-mortar analogies such as the shelf space hypothetical work well to assist in adjudicating disputes about online advertising practices? *See* Graeme B. Dinwoodie & Mark D. Janis, *Lessons from the Trademark Use Debate*, 92 Iowa L. Rev. 1703, 1719-21 (2007) (critiquing the strength of the product shelving analogy prior to *Rescuecom*).

8. *The relationship between actionable use and confusion (and other doctrines).* As the *Rescuecom* court points out, a decision that an alleged infringer engaged in actionable use is only the first step toward liability; the activity must also be shown to give rise to a likelihood of confusion. In some post-*Rescuecom* keyword cases, courts have found that the defendant had engaged in use within the meaning of the Lanham Act, but ultimately found for the defendant on the ground that there was no likelihood of confusion or the defendant's use was permissible (a topic that we take up in Chapter 9). *See, e.g., 1-800 Contacts, Inc. v. Lens.com, Inc.*, 722 F.3d 1229 (10th Cir. 2013); *Network Automation, Inc. v. Advanced Sys. Concepts, Inc.*, 638 F.3d 1137 (9th Cir. 2011). Do these results surprise you?

9. *Actionable use . . . by whom?* Under the *Rescuecom* court's analysis, is it Google or Google's customers that are engaging in actionable use? Is it both? Independently or jointly? If only Google's customers are engaged in actionable use, then Google could only be liable under a theory of indirect infringement—that is, under a theory of facilitating infringement on the part of its customers. *See* Stacey L. Dogan, *Beyond Trademark Use*, 8 J. Telecomm. & High Tech. L. 135 (2010) (arguing that search engine operators should be liable, if at all, under a theory of indirect infringement). Indirect infringement is often difficult to prove, as we discuss in section F of this chapter.

10. *Does actionable use include a "commerciality" requirement?* Lanham Act §32 requires that an alleged infringer's use be a "use in commerce" and that it be "in connection with the sale, offering for sale, distribution, or advertising of any goods or services. . . ." Should the "in connection with" clause be construed to impose a threshold requirement that the alleged infringer's use be commercial in order to be actionable? *See Bosley Medical Institute, Inc. v. Kremer*, 403 F.3d 672 (9th Cir. 2005) (exploring such a requirement); *see also Utah Lighthouse Ministry v. Found. for Apologetic Info. & Research*, 527 F.3d 1045 (10th Cir. 2008) (invoking *Bosley* and finding no commercial use). *Cf. Radiance Foundation, Inc. v. Nat'l Assoc. for the Advancement of Colored People*, 786 F.3d 316 (4th Cir. 2015) (concluding that the "in connection with" requirement calls for some nexus with commerciality and should be informed by First Amendment commercial speech doctrine).

11. *Keyword advertising in Europe.* A number of courts in Europe referred questions regarding liability for trademark infringement based on keyword advertising to the Court of Justice of the European Union. In 2010, the Court of Justice handed down its judgment in three cases that had been referred to it by the French courts. *See Joined Cases C-236/08 to C-238/08, Google France SARL v. Louis Vuitton Malletier, SA*, [2010] E.T.M.R. 30 (ECJ 2010). The Court held, somewhat in line with the lower courts in New York prior to *Rescuecom*, that a "service provider" (such as the Google search engine) is not involved in the type of use that can give rise to trademark liability simply because it sells keyword advertising that consists of the trademark of another. Only uses by a search engine "in its own commercial communication" would fall within the proscription of trademark law; the Court found that this was not the case with keyword advertising. Although this limits the liability of search engines that *sold* the keyword advertising, the Court did not rule out liability for the advertisers that *purchased* that advertising. Indeed, the Court suggested that the function of a trademark could be affected, and hence liability established, where "the ad does not enable normally informed and reasonably attentive internet users, or enables them only with difficulty, to ascertain whether the goods or services referred to by the ad originate from the proprietor of the trade mark or an undertaking economically connected to it or, on the contrary, originate from a third party." Although the Court formally left the assessment of this question to national courts on a case-by-case basis, it suggested liability in a potentially broad range of circumstances.

Eighteen months later, the Court of Justice issued its judgment in the *Interflora* case. *See Interflora Inc. v. Marks & Spencer PLC* (C-323/09), [2012] E.T.M.R. 1 (CJEU 2011). Unlike *Google France*, this was an action by the mark owner (Interflora) against the *purchaser* of the advertising, a rival online flower delivery service operated by a leading British retailer (Marks & Spencer or "M&S"). The defendant's ad text used its own mark, not that of the plaintiff. Rather, the plaintiff's mark was used only to trigger the defendant's ad. The clarity of the language in the opinion is not helped by the Court being compelled to work within the rubric of recent CJEU judgments, which have set the boundaries of protection by reference to various "functions" of trademarks about which the Court has given little guidance. However, a few basic points are clear from the opinion: (1) despite endorsing the apparently strict standard imposed by *Google France* on purchasers of keyword advertising, the Court appeared to backtrack slightly, noting that because "the relevant public comprises reasonably well-informed and reasonably observant internet users, . . . the fact that some internet users may have had difficulty grasping that the service provided by M&S is independent from that of Interflora is not a sufficient basis for a finding that the function of indicating origin has been adversely affected," *id.* ¶50, and thus a defendant would not be liable; (2) the awareness of consumers that the defendant was not part of the plaintiff's network could be shown either on the basis of general knowledge of the market, or through the defendant's ad, *id.* ¶51; (3) that in light of the fact that "the commercial network of the trade mark proprietor is composed of a large number of retailers which vary greatly in terms of size and commercial profile . . . it may be particularly difficult for the reasonably well-informed and reasonably observant Internet user to determine, in the absence of any indication from the advertiser, whether or not the advertiser . . . is part of that network." *Id.* ¶52. The Court did not explore in as much detail as the Advocate-General the variables that might affect the analysis by the national court on remand. In particular, despite endorsing the relevance of the "network" nature of the plaintiff's online flower business, the Court did not address the Advocate-General's general argument that "if the trade mark is not mentioned in the ad, [liability] depends . . . on the nature of goods and services protected by the trade mark . . ." (AG opinion, ¶43) and that the purchase of keyword advertising would be less likely to attract liability if the goods offered by the advertiser were different (AG opinion, ¶45). In discussing the advertising and investment functions of marks (an effect on which might give rise to liability under EU law), the Court appeared to recognize the social value of rival third-party uses:

> the mere fact that the [third party] use . . . obliges the proprietor of that mark to intensify its advertising in order to maintain or enhance its profile with consumers is not a sufficient basis, in every case, for concluding that the trade mark's advertising function is adversely affected. In that regard, although the trade mark is an essential element in the system of undistorted competition which European law seeks to establish its purpose is not, however, to protect its proprietor against practices inherent in competition. Internet advertising on the basis of keywords corresponding to trade marks constitutes such a practice in that its aim, as a general rule, is merely to offer internet users alternatives to the goods or services of the proprietors of those trade marks.

Id. ¶¶57-58.

The *Google France* Court did not rule out what might be called secondary liability for search engines based upon broader principles of unfair competition law. Unlike trademark law, liability for unfair competition is not harmonized throughout Europe. Instead, safe harbors for online service providers *are* harmonized, creating a Europe-wide zone of immunity. But the Court did not categorically situate search engines in that zone, allowing that a service provider *could* be held liable if, "having obtained knowledge of the unlawful nature of . . . the advertisers' activities, it failed to act expeditiously to remove or to disable access to the data concerned," effectively instituting a notice and takedown system as a guarantee of immunity under national law.

Note that (continental) European unfair competition law is broader than Section 43(a) of the Lanham Act as presently interpreted. Is this an issue that should appropriately be dealt with under principles of unfair competition? The *1-800-Contacts* court noted, without comment, that the plaintiff had itself entered into an agreement to have its own pop-up ads delivered to computer users. Should that matter to the question of trademark use? Should it matter to an analysis of unfair competition?

12. *An international solution?* Because the results in keyword litigation have not been consistent between different countries, online actors such as Google adopted different policies regarding keyword advertising in different countries. What alternative approach might Google have taken to protect itself against liability while avoiding the costs of different policies around the world? Given the nature of the Internet, would you favor an international rule regarding the liability of search engines for such advertising practices? What would it be? What are the arguments for resisting an international approach?

C.   THE FACTORS ANALYSIS FOR LIKELIHOOD OF CONFUSION

1.   Overview; Discussion Questions

In section A of this chapter, we explored the basic parameters of confusion theory. We now turn to the specific test that courts use when they apply the likelihood-of-confusion theory. All circuits today employ a likelihood-of-confusion test, which rests on a balance of multiple factors. A typical recitation of factors can be found in *Polaroid Corp. v. Polarad Electronics Corp.*, 287 F.2d 492, 495 (2d Cir. 1961):

> [Likelihood of confusion] is a function of many variables: the strength of [the] mark, the degree of similarity between the two marks, the proximity of the products, the likelihood that the prior owner will bridge the gap, actual confusion, and the reciprocal of defendant's good faith in adopting its own mark, the quality of the defendant's product, and the sophistication of the buyers. Even this extensive catalogue does not exhaust the possibilities—the court may have to take still other variables into account.

Figure 7-1 lists the multi-factor tests that courts in the respective circuits typically invoke. The names of the tests derive from leading cases in the respective jurisdictions. You may find it useful to refer to the chart as you proceed through the cases. Note that the tests all fit the same general pattern. All include as factors (1) the alleged infringer's intent, (2) actual confusion, and (3) a variety of factors that might be lumped together as "market factors." *See* Restatement (Third) of Unfair Competition §§21-23 (1995) (separately articulating rules for market factors, intent, and actual confusion).

The multi-factor tests for likelihood of confusion trace back to the Restatement of Torts §731 (1938). When courts began extending trademark liability in cases in which the trademark owner's and alleged infringer's goods or services were not identical, courts needed a test that expressed how the similarity between goods or services would weigh relative to other potential indicia of confusion. Gradually, courts developed a multi-factor test for "related goods" cases. Eventually, multi-factor tests in various forms came to be adopted for all trademark infringement cases. For a synopsis of the history, *see* Robert G. Bone, *Taking the Confusion Out of "Likelihood of Confusion": Toward a More Sensible Approach to Trademark Infringement*, 106 Nw. U. L. Rev. 1307 (2012).

FIGURE 7-1
Factor Tests in Likelihood-of-Confusion Analysis

Circuit	Factors
First Circuit *Boston Athletic Ass'n v. Sullivan*, 867 F.2d 22, 29-34 (1st Cir. 1989); *Keds Corp. v. Renee Int'l Trading Corp.*, 888 F.2d 215 (1st Cir. 1989).	1. the similarity of the marks; 2. the similarity of the goods; 3. the relationship between the parties' channels of trade; 4. the relationship between the parties' advertising; 5. the classes of prospective purchasers; 6. evidence of actual confusion; 7. the defendant's intent in adopting the mark; and 8. the strength of the plaintiff's mark.
Second Circuit "Polaroid" Factors *Polaroid Corp. v. Polarad Electronics Corp.*, 287 F.2d 492 (2d Cir. 1961), *cert. denied*, 368 U.S. 820 (1961); *Playtex Products, Inc. v. Georgia-Pacific Corp.*, 390 F.3d 158 (2d Cir. 2004).	1. the strength of the senior user's mark; 2. the degree of similarity between the two marks; 3. the proximity of the products; 4. the likelihood that the prior owner will bridge the gap; 5. actual confusion; 6. the junior user's good faith in adopting its own mark; 7. the quality of defendant's product; and 8. the sophistication of buyers.
Third Circuit "Lapp" Factors *Interpace Corp. v. Lapp, Inc.*, 721 F.2d 460 (3d Cir. 1983); *KOS Pharmaceuticals, Inc. v. Andrx Corp.*, 369 F.3d 700 (3d Cir. 2004).	1. the degree of similarity between the owner's mark and the alleged infringing mark; 2. the strength of the owner's mark; 3. the price of the goods and other factors indicative of the care and attention expected of consumers when making a purchase; 4. the length of time the defendant has used the mark without evidence of actual confusion arising; 5. the intent of the defendant in adopting the mark; 6. the evidence of actual confusion; 7. whether the goods, though not competing, are marketed through the same channels of trade and advertised through the same media; 8. the extent to which the targets of the parties' sales efforts are the same; 9. the relationship of the goods in the minds of consumers because of the similarity of function; and 10. other facts suggesting that the consuming public might expect the prior owner to manufacture a product in the defendant's market, or that he is likely to expand into that market.
Fourth Circuit "Pizzeria Uno" Factors *Pizzeria Uno Corp. v. Temple*, 747 F.2d 1522 (4th Cir. 1984); *CareFirst of Maryland, Inc. v. First Care, P.C.*, 434 F.3d 263 (4th Cir. 2006). *Cf. Sara Lee Corp. v. Kayser-Roth Corp*, 81 F.3d 455 (4th Cir. 1996) (suggesting that courts may supplement the *Pizzeria Uno* test with other factors).	1. the strength or distinctiveness of the mark; 2. the similarity of the two marks; 3. the similarity of the goods/services the marks identify; 4. the similarity of the facilities the two parties use in their businesses; 5. the similarity of the advertising used by the two parties; 6. the defendant's intent; and 7. actual confusion.

FIGURE 7-1
(*Continued*)

Fifth Circuit *Roto-Rooter Corp. v. O'Neal*, 513 F.2d 44, 45 (5th Cir. 1975); *Scott Fetzer Co. v. House of Vacuums Inc.*, 381 F.3d 477 (5th Cir. 2004). *Cf. Oreck Corp. v. U.S. Floor Systems, Inc.*, 803 F.2d 166 (5th Cir. 1986) (advocating an 8-factor test), *cert. denied*, 481 U.S. 1069 (1987).	1. the type of mark allegedly infringed; 2. the similarity between the two marks; 3. the similarity of the products or services;	4. the identity of the retail outlets and purchasers; 5. the identity of the advertising media used; 6. the defendant's intent; and 7. any evidence of actual confusion.
Sixth Circuit "Frisch's" Factors *Frisch's Restaurants v. Elby's Big Boy*, 670 F.2d 642 (6th Cir. 1982), *cert. denied*, 459 U.S. 916 (1982); *AutoZone, Inc. v. Tandy Corp*, 373 F.3d 786 (6th Cir. 2004).	1. the strength of the plaintiff's mark; 2. the relatedness of the goods or services offered by the parties; 3. the similarity of the marks;	4. any evidence of actual confusion; 5. the marketing channels used by the parties; 6. the probable degree of purchaser care and sophistication; 7. the defendant's intent; and 8. the likelihood of either party expanding its product line using the marks.
Seventh Circuit *Helene Curtis Indus., Inc. v. Church & Dwight Co.*, 560 F.2d 1325, 1330 (7th Cir. 1977), *cert. denied*, 434 U.S. 1070 (1978); *Sullivan v. CBS Corp.*, 385 F.3d 772 (7th Cir. 2004).	1. the degree of similarity between the marks in appearance and suggestion; 2. the similarity of the products for which the name is used; 3. the area and manner of concurrent use;	4. the degree of care likely to be exercised by consumers; 5. the strength of the complainant's mark; 6. actual confusion; and 7. an intent on the part of the alleged infringer to palm off his products as those of another.
Eighth Circuit "SquirtCo" Factors *SquirtCo v. Seven-Up Co.*, 628 F.2d 1086 (8th Cir. 1980); *Frosty Treats Inc. v. Sony Computer Entm't Am., Inc.*, 426 F.3d 1001 (8th Cir. 27005).	1. The strength of the owner's mark; 2. the similarity between the owner's mark and the alleged infringer's mark;	3. the degree to which the products compete with each other; 4. the alleged infringer's intent to "pass off" its goods as those of the trademark owner; 5. incidents of actual confusion; and 6. the type of product, its costs, and conditions of purchase.
Ninth Circuit "Sleekcraft" Factors *AMF, Inc. v. Sleekcraft Boats*, 599 F.2d 341 (9th Cir. 1979).	1. the strength of the mark; 2. the proximity of the goods; 3. the similarity of the marks;	4. the evidence of actual confusion; 5. the marketing channels used; 6. the type of goods and the degree of care likely to be exercised by the purchaser; 7. the defendant's intent in selecting the mark; and 8. the likelihood of expansion of the product lines.

FIGURE 7-1
(*Continued*)

Tenth Circuit *Sally Beauty Co. v. Beautyco, Inc.,* 304 F.3d 964 (10th Cir. 2002); *Australian Gold, Inc. v. Hatfield,* 436 F.3d 1228 (10th Cir. 2006).	1. The degree of similarity between the marks; 2. the intent of the alleged infringer in adopting its mark;	3. evidence of actual confusion; 4. the relation in the use and the manner of marketing between the goods or services marketed by the competing parties; 5. the degree of care likely to be exercised by purchasers; and 6. the strength or weakness of the marks.
Eleventh Circuit *AmBrit, Inc. v. Kraft, Inc.,* 812 F.2d 1531 (11th Cir. 1986); *Dippin' Dots, Inc. v. Frosty Bites Distribution, LLC,* 369 F.3d 1197 (11th Cir. 2004).	1. the strength of the marks; 2. the similarity of the marks; 3. the similarity of the products;	4. the similarity of retail outlets and purchasers; 5. the similarity of advertising media used; 6. the defendant's intent; and 7. actual confusion.
D.C. Circuit *Partido Revolucionario Dominicano (PRD) Seccional Metropolitana de Washington-DC, Maryland y Virginia v. Partido Revolucionario Dominicano, Seccional de Maryland y Virginia,* 312 F. Supp. 2d 1 (D.D.C. 2004).	**1.** the strength of the senior user's mark; **2.** the degree of similarity between the two marks; **3.** the proximity of the products;	**4.** the likelihood that the prior owner will bridge the gap; **5.** actual confusion; the sophistication of buyers. 6. the junior user's good faith in adopting its own mark; and 7. the quality of defendant's product.
Federal Circuit "DuPont" Factors *In re E. I. Du Pont de Nemours & Co,* 476 F.2d 1357 (C.C.P.A. 1973); *Palm Bay Imports, Inc. v. Veuve Clicquot Ponsardin Maison Fondee En 1772,* 396 F.3d 1369 (Fed. Cir. 2005).	1. The similarity or dissimilarity of the marks in their entireties as to appearance, sound, connotation and commercial impression; 2. the similarity or dissimilarity and nature of the goods or services as described in an application or registration or in connection with which a prior mark is in use; 3. the similarity or dissimilarity of established, likely-to-continue trade channels; 4. the conditions under which and buyers to whom sales are made, i.e., "impulse" vs. careful, sophisticated purchasing;	5. the fame of the prior mark (sales, advertising, length of use); 6. the number and nature of similar marks in use on similar goods; 7. the nature and extent of any actual confusion; 8. the length of time during and conditions under which there has been concurrent use without evidence of actual confusion; 9. the variety of goods on which a mark is or is not used (house mark, "family" mark, product mark); 10. the market interface between applicant and the owner of a prior mark. . .; 11. the extent to which applicant has a right to exclude others from use of its mark on its goods; 12. the extent of potential confusion, i.e., whether de minimis or substantial; and 13. any other established fact probative of the effect of use.

As you study the factors analysis via the cases, notes, and problems below in subsection 2, you may find it useful to consider the following set of discussion questions. Many of these questions reflect fundamental debates about the confusion test that remain unresolved in the case law.

(1) *Does the multi-factor analysis provide predictable, defensible outcomes?*

Multi-factor tests are flexible but often unpredictable. A lengthy and detailed factors test such as the typical likelihood-of-confusion test may take on a life of its own, its application becoming so routinized and technical that courts expend all their energies on elaborating the factors, leaving little room for questions about whether the analysis really effectuates the goals of protecting consumers against deception and producers against erosion of their investments in goodwill. Watch for this phenomenon as you read the cases. *See Sullivan v. CBS Corp.*, 385 F.3d 772, 778 (7th Cir. 2004) (offering a reminder that the factors "operate only as a heuristic device to assist in determining whether confusion exists"); *see generally* Barton Beebe, *An Empirical Study of the Multifactor Tests for Trademark Infringement*, 94 CAL. L. REV. 1581 (2006) (critiquing the conventional wisdom about the operation of various factors, and proposing a uniform national multi-factor standard); Robert G. Bone, *Taking the Confusion Out of "Likelihood of Confusion": Toward a More Sensible Approach to Trademark Infringement*, 106 Nw. U. L. REV. 1307 (2012) (proposing modifications to the factors analysis).

(2)   *Should courts have discretion to add to or subtract from the factors in any given case?*

Courts routinely assert that they have discretion to modify the factors analysis to fit particular circumstances. *See, e.g., Network Automation, Inc. v. Advanced Systems Concepts, Inc.*, 638 F.3d 1137, 1145, 1149 (9th Cir. 2011) (noting that the factors are "intended as an adaptable proxy for consumer confusion, not a rote checklist" and that in determining likely confusion, "we adhere to two long-standing principles: the . . . factors . . . are non-exhaustive, and . . . should be applied flexibly"); *Rosetta Stone Ltd. v. Google, Inc.*, 676 F.3d 144 (4th Cir. 2012) (noting that "[t]his judicially created list of factors is not intended to be exhaustive or mandatory"). As you read the materials in this section, consider how far that flexibility principle can be pushed. Should courts be permitted to dispense with the factors analysis altogether when the court knows "for sure" that consumers will not be confused? *See Top Tobacco, L.P. v. N. Atl. Operating Co., Inc.*, 509 F.3d 380, 381 (7th Cir. 2007) (discussed below in the notes on the similarity of marks factor). Should a court be permitted to skip the full factors analysis when the defendant uses a mark identical to the plaintiff's mark for the same products or services? *See* TRIPS art. 16; *Paulsson Geophysical Services, Inc. v. Sigmar*, 529 F.3d 303 (5th Cir. 2008). *But cf. Jada Toys, Inc. v. Mattel, Inc.*, 518 F.3d 628 (9th Cir. 2008) (expressing concern that when a judge relies on perceived *dissimilarity* of marks to find *no* likelihood of confusion, there may be a danger that the judge's own subjective impressions dominate the analysis and undermine the multi-factor test).

Would it be consistent with sound trademark policy for courts to bias the factors analysis by systematically giving greater weight to certain factors? *See Suntree Technologies, Inc. v. Ecosense Int'l, Inc.*, 693 F.3d 1338, 1346-47 (11th Cir. 2012) ("we consider the type of mark and the evidence of actual confusion to be the two most important factors"). According to Professor Beebe's empirical study, courts routinely short-circuit the multi-factor tests, deciding cases by relying predominantly on a subset of factors: mark similarity, intent (at least when it cuts in the trademark owner's favor), and relatedness of goods (at least when it cuts in the alleged infringer's favor).

(3) *Is the multi-factor test primarily the domain of the fact finder?*

What do the cases reveal about the proper allocation of adjudicative authority over the factors analysis? Should that task be left primarily to the fact finder, on the ground that the fact finder is in the best position to assess evidence about the marketplace? Or should the factors analysis be deemed a question of law and subjected to de novo review on appeal, on the ground that the analysis is so fundamental to the trademark system that the appellate court must be able to assert maximum control over it? Most circuits recite the clearly erroneous standard of review for likelihood of confusion (the First, Third, Fourth, Fifth, Seventh, Eighth, Ninth, Tenth, and Eleventh Circuits). A minority of circuits (the Second, Sixth, and Federal Circuits) review the underlying evaluation of the factors under a clearly erroneous standard, but treat the weighing and balancing of the factors, and the ultimate conclusion as to confusion, as a question of law subject to de novo review. For citations to the relevant cases, *see* 3 J. Thomas McCarthy, Trademarks and Unfair Competition §23:73. Should the clearly erroneous standard apply only to the ultimate conclusion as to likelihood of confusion, or should it also apply to each of the individual factors? *See Pom Wonderful LLC v. Hubbard*, 775 F.3d 1118 (9th Cir. 2014) (addressing the issue). The issue of obedience to the standard of review was debated in *Libman*, one of the main cases excerpted below. Consider whether you would align with majority or dissent in the debate.

Is it important that the factors analysis be amenable to early resolution? Some courts suggest that summary judgment on the confusion question is "disfavored." *Rearden L.L.C. v. Rearden Commerce, Inc.*, 683 F.3d 1190, 1209 (9th Cir. 2012). *See also JL Bev. Co. v. Jim Beam Brands Co.*, 828 F.3d 1098 (9th Cir. 2016) (reversing grant of summary judgment of no likelihood of confusion). Is this good policy? Other courts are more willing to use mechanisms such as summary judgment or Rule 12(b)(6) dismissal. *See, e.g., Eastland Music Group, L.L.C. v. Lionsgate Entm't, Inc.*, 707 F.3d 869 (7th Cir. 2013) (upholding a motion to dismiss on the pleadings). *See also Kibler v. Hall*, 843 F.3d 1068 (6th Cir. 2016) (upholding a grant of summary judgment of no infringement where the plaintiff was a disc jockey who performed under the name DJ LOGIC and the defendant was a rapper whose stage name was LOGIC); *Hornady Mfg. Co., Inc. v. Doubletap, Inc.*, 746 F.3d 995 (10th Cir. 2014) (same).

(4) *What should be the role for expert testimony in proof of the confusion factors?*

It is common for litigants to offer experts to testify about survey evidence on confusion, as we discuss further in the notes below on the actual confusion factor. The use of expert testimony on the other factors, or on the overall mixing of the factors, is less well accepted. *See, e.g., Betterbox Commc'ns Ltd. v. BB Techns., Inc.*, 300 F.3d 325 (3d Cir. 2002) (upholding admission of expert testimony on factors analysis over strong dissent). Consider whether you would follow this approach, or whether you would give a greater role to expert testimony.

(5) *What should be the role of empirical evidence on consumer behavior in proof of the confusion factors?*

Many of the likelihood-of-confusion factors are, at best, indirect proxies for probable consumer behavior and preferences. Judges and lawyers applying the factors are also consumers and have their own subjective preferences, but their preferences may be entirely irrelevant to a proper confusion analysis. Judge Frank, dissenting in *Triangle Publ'ns, Inc. v. Rohrlich*, 167 F.2d 969, 976 (2d Cir. 1948), worried about this problem in a case in which a trial judge made a "shaky kind of guess" to determine whether teenage girls would be likely to confuse plaintiff's SEVENTEEN for magazines with defendant's MISS SEVENTEEN for girdles, a guess that apparently was not informed by the opinions of any actual teenage girls. As one pair of commentators has colorfully pointed out, the likelihood-of-confusion analysis calls for judges and lawyers to perform a kind of "Vulcan mind meld" with the relevant consumers:

> [A]ttorneys and judges are tempted in many cases to *imagine* one or more of the following: (1) what the relevant consumers' background, knowledge, experience and motivations are; (2) what it would be like to have the same background, knowledge, experience and motivations; (3) what circumstances actually prevail in the marketplace and constitute sources of information available to relevant consumers; (4) what information relevant consumers are likely to absorb and process; (5) what thought processes relevant consumers are likely to undergo; and then (6) what belief relevant consumers are likely to reach (and whether it is a confused one). In this situation, we should be quite cautious about assuming that our own subjective impressions and hypotheses concerning consumer thought processes, in response to some or all of the circumstances seemingly apparent from evidence in litigation, can be predictive of consumers' actual perceptions and thought processes in actual marketplace circumstances, no matter how plausible or appealing the arguments may seem. The proposition that a human being can perform a "Vulcan mind meld" with the relevant consumers in the marketplace is, like the term, fiction. The idea that we can share the same thoughts and impressions as those consumers relevant to our cases is unlikely.

William E. Gallagher & Ronald C. Goodstein, *Inference Versus Speculation in Trademark Infringement Litigation: Abandoning the Fiction of the Vulcan Mind Meld*, 94 TRADEMARK REP. 1229, 1232 (2004). As you study the notes on individual factors, consider which factors are especially prone to the problem of the Vulcan mind meld. Do you conclude that the factor test should be changed to ensure that behavioral evidence is incorporated into the confusion analysis? If so, how? Or, do you conclude that the factor test should remain intact, but courts should develop stricter evidentiary rules for accepting proof under any individual factor? If so, what rules would you favor? To what extent (if at all) should judges formulate conclusions about consumer perception based on judicial notice? For example, suppose that a judge perceives that a certain term in a composite word mark is likely to be ignored by the consuming public. May the court simply take that perception as an established fact based on judicial notice? Given that virtually every dispute over likelihood of confusion involves consumer perceptions to some degree, should courts be particularly cautious about taking such facts on judicial notice? Or should they widely embrace judicial notice, so long as they are explicit about doing so? *See Oriental Financial Group, Inc. v. Cooperativa de Ahorro y Crédito Oriental*, 832 F.3d 15, 27 (1st Cir. 2016) (discussing the issue); *see also* Rule 201(b), Federal Rules of Evidence (permitting courts to take judicial notice of any facts that are "not subject to reasonable dispute" because they are "generally known within the trial court's territorial jurisdiction").

(6) *In cases involving registered marks, what should be the role of the registration document in evaluating the confusion factors?*

The registration document identifies the mark and specifies the underlying goods or services, so the document could presumably be given some weight in analyzing the similarity of marks and similarity of goods factors in a likelihood-of-confusion case involving a registered mark. Should the registration document be accorded such a role? Recall (from Chapter 3) that in *Christian Louboutin S.A. v. Yves Saint Laurent Am. Holding, Inc.*, 696 F.3d 206 (2d Cir. 2012), the court required that the registration document be amended to specify that the mark included only "a red lacquered outsole that contrasts with the color of the adjoining 'upper,'" and the court seemed to take the view that the amendment disposed of the confusion claim. *Id.* at 228. Does this reflect the proper role of the registration document in a likelihood-of-confusion analysis? If not, how would you change the court's analysis?

Consider the potential role of the registration document in the following case. William Adams, professionally known as will.i.am, is the front man for The Black Eyed Peas. Suppose that i.am.symbolic, llc (successor-in-interest to Adams) applied to register the mark I AM used in connection with three classes of goods: cosmetics, sunglasses, and jewelry. For each class of goods, the applicant provided the required statement specifically identifying goods within the relevant class, and the applicant also included the recitation "all associated with William Adams, professionally known as 'will.i.am'." The examining attorney refused registration on the basis of prior registrations of I AM for perfume, sunglasses, and jewelry. Suppose that i.am.symbolic challenges the refusal on the ground that the "will.i.am" recitation must be taken into account in applying the likelihood-of-confusion factors. For example, i.am.symbolic says that the limitation affects the meaning and overall commercial impression of the mark for purposes of the similarity of the marks factor. In general, how (if at all) should the applicant's specification of goods influence the confusion analysis? Does your answer depend on whether the confusion analysis is undertaken in the context of registration (Section 2(d)) as opposed to enforcement (Sections 32(1)(a) or 43(a))? If the limitation is to be taken into account, which factors (in addition to the similarity of marks factor) might it affect? *See In re i.am.symbolic, llc*, 866 F.3d 1315 (Fed. Cir. 2017). Also consider the potential significance of the following considerations: whether will.i.am promotes the goods; whether will.i.am is known as "I am"; whether i.am.symbolic owns registrations of I AM for other goods.

2. Applying the Factors Analysis

The cases that follow illustrate how courts work through the constellation of factors in multi-factor confusion tests. The *Virgin* case provides a good overview. We suggest that you study it to help you orient your thinking about modern confusion analysis. The *McDonald's* and *Libman* cases offer less typical, more challenging illustrations.

VIRGIN ENTERPRISES LTD. v. NAWAB

335 F.3d 141 (2d Cir. 2003)

LEVAL, Circuit Judge:

BACKGROUND

[Plaintiff Virgin Enterprises (VEL) owns incontestable registrations for VIRGIN as applied to "retail store services in the fields of . . . computers and electronic apparatus," for a stylized VIRGIN logo as applied to the same services, and for various other marks. VEL operates various businesses in the United States and worldwide under the trade name VIRGIN, including an airline, large-scale record stores called Virgin Megastores, and an Internet information service. Plaintiff or its affiliates also market a variety of goods branded with the VIRGIN name, including music recordings, computer games, books, and luggage. For example, Virgin Megastores sell video game systems, portable CD players, disposable cameras, and DVD players, but not phones or phone services. The stores advertise in a variety of media, including radio. In addition, press releases from VEL or its U.S. affiliate advertised wireless communications services (though not wireless phones) under the name VIRGIN MOBILE.

Defendants operate a small firm that sells wireless communication products (wireless phones, related accessories, and wireless phone service) through a few retail outlets under the name VIRGIN WIRELESS. Defendants claim that a trademark lawyer advised them that the mark VIRGIN was available for use in the telecommunications field, although the record also contains evidence suggesting that no such advice was ever given. Defendants filed applications to register VIRGIN WIRELESS and other, related word marks for wireless telecommunications and retail telephone sales.

Plaintiff sued defendant and moved for a preliminary injunction. The district court denied relief; plaintiff appealed.]

Noting that a party seeking a preliminary injunction must show the probability of irreparable harm in the absence of relief, and either (1) likelihood of success on the merits or (2) serious questions going to the merits and a balance of hardships tipping decidedly in its favor, the [district] court found that plaintiff had failed to satisfy either standard. Arguing against plaintiff's likelihood of success, the court noted that plaintiff's registrations did not claim use of the VIRGIN mark "in telecommunications services or in the associated retail sale of wireless telephones and accessories." While plaintiff's . . . registrations covered the retail sale of "computers and electronic apparatus," they did not extend to telecommunications services and wireless phones.

The court noted that the defendants were the first to use the VIRGIN mark in telecommunications, and the first to attempt to register VIRGIN for telecommunications and retail telephone sales. The court also observed that the dissimilarity in appearance of plaintiff's and defendants' logos and the differences between plaintiff's huge Virgin Megastores and defendants' small retail outlets in malls diminished likelihood of consumer confusion. Finally, because the defendants had expended substantial resources in pursuing their trademark applications and in establishing their retail presence, the court found that plaintiff could not demonstrate that the balance of hardships tipped in its favor.

The court denied the application for preliminary injunction. The crux of the court's decision lay in the facts that plaintiff's prior use and registration of the VIRGIN mark in connection with the sale of consumer electronic equipment did not include the sale of telephones or telephone services, and that defendants were the first to register and use VIRGIN for telephones and wireless telephone service. This appeal followed.

DISCUSSION

. . .

The landmark case of *Polaroid Corp. v. Polarad Electronics Corp.*, 287 F.2d 492 (2d Cir. 1961) (Friendly, J.), outlined a series of nonexclusive factors likely to be pertinent in addressing the issue of likelihood of confusion, which are routinely followed in such cases. *See, e.g., Streetwise Maps, Inc. v. Vandam, Inc.*, 159 F.3d 739, 743-46 (2d Cir. 1998); *Arrow Fastener Co. v. Stanley Works*, 59 F.3d 384, 391-99 (2d Cir. 1995); [cit.].

Six of the *Polaroid* factors relate directly to the likelihood of consumer confusion. These are the strength of the plaintiff's mark; the similarity of defendants' mark to plaintiff's; the proximity of the products sold under defendants' mark to those sold under plaintiff's; where the products are different, the likelihood that plaintiff will bridge the gap by selling the products being sold by defendants; the existence of actual confusion among consumers; and the sophistication of consumers. Of these six, all but the last (which was found by the district court to be neutral) strongly favor the plaintiff. The remaining two *Polaroid* factors, defendants' good or bad faith and the quality of defendants' products, are more pertinent to issues other than likelihood of confusion, such as harm to plaintiff's reputation and choice of remedy. We conclude that the *Polaroid* factors powerfully support plaintiff's position.

Strength of the mark. The strength of a trademark encompasses two different concepts, both of which relate significantly to likelihood of consumer confusion. The first and most important is inherent strength, also called "inherent distinctiveness." This inquiry distinguishes between, on the one hand, inherently distinctive marks—marks that are arbitrary or fanciful in relation to the products (or services) on which they are used—and, on the other hand, marks that are generic, descriptive or suggestive as to those goods. The former are the strong marks. *Abercrombie & Fitch Co. v. Hunting World, Inc.*, 537 F.2d 4, 9 (2d Cir. 1976). The second sense of the concept of strength of a mark is "acquired distinctiveness," *i.e.*, fame, or the extent to which prominent use of the mark in commerce has resulted in a high degree of consumer recognition. *See TCPIP Holding Co. v. Haar Communications Inc.*, 244 F.3d 88, 100 (2d Cir. 2001) (describing these two concepts of strength). . . .

Considering first *inherent distinctiveness*, the law accords broad, muscular protection to marks that are arbitrary or fanciful in relation to the products on which they are used, and lesser protection, or no protection at all, to marks consisting of words that identify or describe the goods or their attributes. The reasons for the distinction arise from two aspects of market efficiency. The paramount objective of the trademark law is to avoid confusion in the marketplace. The purpose for which the trademark law accords merchants the exclusive right to the use of a name or symbol in their area or commerce is *identification*, so that the merchants can establish goodwill for their goods based on past satisfactory performance, and the consuming public can rely on a mark as a guarantee that the goods or services so marked come from the merchant who has been found to be satisfactory in the past. [cit.] At the same time, efficiency and the public interest require that every merchant trading in a class of goods be permitted to refer to the goods by their name, and to make claims about their quality. Thus, a merchant who sells pencils under the trademark *Pencil* or *Clear Mark*, for example, and seeks to exclude other sellers of pencils from using those words in their trade, is seeking an advantage the trademark law does not intend to offer. To grant such exclusivity would deprive the consuming public of the useful market information it receives where every seller of pencils is free to call them pencils. *Abercrombie*, 537 F.2d at 9; [cit.]. The trademark right does not protect the exclusive right to an advertising message—only the exclusive right to an identifier, to protect against confusion in the marketplace. Thus, as a matter of policy, the trademark law accords broader protection to marks that serve exclusively as identifiers and lesser protection where a grant of exclusiveness would tend to diminish the access of others to the full range of discourse relating to their goods. [cit.]

The second aspect of efficiency that justifies according broader protection to marks that are inherently distinctive relates directly to the likelihood of confusion. If a mark is arbitrary or fanciful, and makes no reference to the nature of the goods it designates, consumers who see the mark on different objects offered in the marketplace will be likely to assume, because of the arbitrariness of the choice of mark, that they all come from the same source. For example, if consumers become familiar with a toothpaste sold under an unusual, arbitrary brand name, such as *ZzaaqQ*, and later see that same inherently distinctive brand name appearing on a different product, they are likely to assume, notwithstanding the product difference, that the second product comes from the same producer as the first. The more unusual, arbitrary, and fanciful a trade name, the more unlikely it is that two independent entities would have chosen it. In contrast, every seller of foods has an interest in calling its product "delicious." Consumers who see the word *delicious* used on two or more different food products are less likely to draw the inference that they must all come from the same producer. *Cf. Streetwise Maps*, 159 F.3d at 744 (noting that several map producers use "street" in product names; thus plaintiff's mark using "street" was not particularly distinctive); [cit.]. In short, the more distinctive the mark, the greater the likelihood that the public, seeing it used a second time, will assume that the second use comes from the same source as the first. The goal of avoiding consumer confusion thus dictates that the inherently distinctive, arbitrary, or fanciful marks, i.e., strong marks, receive broader protection than weak marks, those that are descriptive or suggestive of the products on which they are used. *See Abercrombie*, 537 F.2d at 9-11. . . .

The second sense of trademark strength, fame, or "acquired distinctiveness," also bears on consumer confusion. [cit.] If a mark has been long, prominently and notoriously used in commerce, there is a high likelihood that consumers will recognize it from its prior use. Widespread consumer recognition of a mark previously used in commerce increases the likelihood that consumers will assume it identifies the previously familiar user, and therefore increases the likelihood of consumer confusion if the new user is in fact not related to the first. [cit.] A mark's fame also gives unscrupulous traders an incentive to seek to create consumer confusion by associating themselves in consumers' minds with a famous mark. The added likelihood of consumer confusion resulting from a second user's use of a famous mark gives reason for according such a famous mark a broader scope of protection, at least when it is also inherently distinctive, [cit.]

Plaintiff's VIRGIN mark undoubtedly scored high on both concepts of strength. In relation to the sale of consumer electronic equipment, the VIRGIN mark is inherently distinctive, in that it is arbitrary and fanciful; the word "virgin" has no intrinsic relationship whatsoever to selling such equipment. Because there is no intrinsic reason for a merchant to use the word "virgin" in the sale of consumer electronic equipment, a consumer seeing VIRGIN used in two different stores selling such equipment will likely assume that the stores are related.

Plaintiff's VIRGIN mark was also famous. The mark had been employed with worldwide recognition as the mark of an airline and as the mark for megastores selling music recordings and consumer electronic equipment. The fame of the mark increased the likelihood that consumers seeing defendants' shops selling telephones under the mark VIRGIN would assume incorrectly that defendants' shops were a part of plaintiff's organization. [cit.]

There can be no doubt that plaintiff's VIRGIN mark, as used on consumer electronic equipment, is a strong mark, as the district court found. It is entitled as such to a broad scope of protection, precisely because the use of the mark by others in connection with stores selling reasonably closely related merchandise would inevitably have a high likelihood of causing consumer confusion.

Similarity of marks. When the secondary user's mark is not identical but merely similar to the plaintiff's mark, it is important to assess the degree of similarity between them in assessing the likelihood that consumers will be confused. [cit.] Plaintiff's and defendants' marks were not merely similar; they were identical to the extent that both consisted of the same word, "virgin."

The district court believed this factor did not favor plaintiff because it found some differences in appearance. Defendants' logo used a different typeface and different colors from plaintiff's. While those are indeed differences, they are quite minor in relation to the fact that the name being used as a trademark was the same in each case.

Advertisement and consumer experience of a mark do not necessarily transmit all of the mark's features. Plaintiff, for example, advertised its Virgin Megastores on the radio. A consumer who heard those advertisements and then saw the defendants' installation using the name VIRGIN would have no way of knowing that the two trademarks looked different. [cit.] A consumer who had visited one of plaintiff's Virgin Megastores and remembered the name would not necessarily remember the typeface and color of plaintiff's mark. The reputation of a mark also spreads by word of mouth among consumers. One consumer who hears from others about their experience with Virgin stores and then encounters defendants' Virgin store will have no way [of] knowing of the differences in typeface. [cit.]

In view of the fact that defendants used the same name as plaintiff, we conclude the defendants' mark was sufficiently similar to plaintiff's to increase the likelihood of confusion. This factor favored the plaintiff as a matter of law. We conclude that the district court erred in concluding otherwise on the basis of comparatively trivial and often irrelevant differences.

Proximity of the products and likelihood of bridging the gap. The next factor is the proximity of the products being sold by plaintiff and defendant under identical (or similar) marks. *See Arrow Fastener*, 59 F.3d at 396. This factor has an obvious bearing on the likelihood of confusion. When the two users of a mark are operating in completely different areas of commerce, consumers are less likely to assume that their similarly branded products come from the same source. In contrast, the closer the secondary user's goods are to those the consumer has seen marketed under the prior user's brand, the more likely that the consumer will mistakenly assume a common source. [cit.]

While plaintiff had not sold telephones or telephone service prior to defendants' registration evincing intent to sell those items, plaintiff had sold quite similar items of consumer electronic equipment. These included computer video game systems, portable cassette-tape players, compact disc players, MP3 players, mini-disc players, and disposable cameras. Like telephones, many of these are small consumer electronic gadgets making use of computerized audio communication. They are sold in the same channels of commerce. Consumers would have a high expectation of finding telephones, portable CD players, and computerized video game systems in the same stores. We think the proximity in commerce of telephones to CD players substantially advanced the risk that consumer confusion would occur when both were sold by different merchants under the same trade name, VIRGIN.

Our classic *Polaroid* test further protects a trademark owner by examining the likelihood that, even if the plaintiff's products were not so close to the defendants' when the defendants began to market them, there was already a likelihood that plaintiff would in the reasonably near future begin selling those products. *See Cadbury Beverages, Inc. v. Cott Corp.*, 73 F.3d 474, 482 (2d Cir. 1996). VEL's claim of proximity was further strengthened in this regard because, as the district court expressly found, "plans had been formulated [for VEL] to enter [the market for telecommunications products and services] shortly in the future." VEL had already begun marketing telephone service in England which would operate in the United States, and, as the district court found, had made plans to sell telephones and wireless telephone service under the VIRGIN name from its retail stores.

The district court, nonetheless, found in favor of the defendants with respect to the proximity of products and services. We would ordinarily give considerable deference to a factual finding on this issue. Here, however, we cannot do so because it appears the district court applied the wrong test. The court did not assess the *proximity* of defendants' VIRGIN-branded retail stores selling telephone products to plaintiff's VIRGIN-branded retail stores selling other consumer electronic products. It simply concluded that, because defendants were selling exclusively telephone products and services, and plaintiff's electronic products did not include telephones or related services, the defendants must prevail as to the proximity factor.

This represents a considerable misunderstanding of the *Polaroid* test. The famous list of factors of likely pertinence in assessing likelihood of confusion in *Polaroid* was specially designed for a case like this one, in which the secondary user is not in direct competition with the prior user, but is selling a somewhat different product or service. In *Polaroid*, the plaintiff sold optical and camera equipment, while the defendant sold electronic apparatus. The test the court discussed was expressly addressed to the problem "how far a valid trademark shall be protected with respect to goods *other than those to which its owner has applied it.*" 287 F.2d at 495 (emphasis added); *see also Arrow Fastener*, 59 F.3d at 396 (noting that products need not actually compete with each other). The very fact that the test includes the "proximity" between the defendant's products and the plaintiff's and the likelihood that the plaintiff will "bridge the gap" makes clear that the trademark owner does not lose, as the district court concluded, merely because it has not previously sold the precise good or service sold by the secondary user.

In our view, had the district court employed the proper test of proximity, it could not have failed to find a high degree of proximity as between plaintiff VEL's prior sales of consumer electronic audio equipment and defendants' subsequent sales of telephones and telephone services, which proximity would certainly contribute to likelihood of consumer confusion. And plaintiff was all the more entitled to a finding in its favor in respect of these matters by virtue of the fact, which the district court *did* find, that at the time defendants began using the VIRGIN mark in the retail sale of telephones and telephone services, plaintiff already had plans to bridge the gap by expanding its sales of consumer electronic equipment to include sales of those very goods and services in the near future. Consumer confusion was more than likely; it was virtually inevitable.

Actual confusion. It is self-evident that the existence of actual consumer confusion indicates a likelihood of consumer confusion. [cit.] We have therefore deemed evidence of actual confusion "particularly relevant" to the inquiry. *Streetwise Maps*, 159 F.3d at 745.

Plaintiff submitted to the district court an affidavit of a former employee of defendant Cel-Net, who worked at a mall kiosk branded as Virgin Wireless, which stated that individuals used to ask him if the kiosk was affiliated with plaintiff's VIRGIN stores. The district court correctly concluded that this evidence weighed in plaintiff's favor.

Sophistication of consumers. The degree of sophistication of consumers can have an important bearing on likelihood of confusion. Where the purchasers of a product[] are highly trained professionals, they know the market and are less likely than untrained consumers to be misled or confused by the similarity of different marks. The district court recognized that "[r]etail customers, such as the ones catered to by both the defendants and [plaintiff], are not expected to exercise the same degree of care as professional buyers, who are expected to have greater powers of discrimination." On the other hand, it observed that purchasers of cellular telephones and the service plans were likely to give greater care than self-service customers in a supermarket. Noting that neither side had submitted evidence on the sophistication of consumers, the court made no finding favoring either side. We agree that the sophistication factor is neutral in this case.

Bad faith and the quality of the defendants' services or products. Two factors remain of the conventional *Polaroid* test: the existence of bad faith on the part of the secondary user and the quality of the secondary user's products or services. *Polaroid*, 287 F.2d at 495. Neither factor is of high relevance to the issue of likelihood of confusion. A finding that a party acted in bad faith can affect the court's choice of remedy or can tip the balance where questions are close. It does not bear directly on whether consumers are likely to be confused. [cit.] The district court noted some evidence of bad faith on the defendants' part, but because the evidence on the issue was scant and equivocal, the court concluded that such a finding "at this stage [would be] speculative." The court therefore found that this factor favored neither party.

The issue of the quality of the secondary user's product goes more to the harm that confusion can cause the plaintiff's mark and reputation than to the likelihood of confusion. *See Arrow Fastener*, 59 F.3d at 398 (noting that first user's reputation may be harmed if secondary user's goods are of poor quality). In any event, the district court found this factor to be "neutral" with respect to likelihood of confusion. . . .

In summary we conclude that of the six *Polaroid* factors that pertain directly to the likelihood of consumer confusion, all but one favor the plaintiff, and that one—sophistication of consumers—is neutral. The plaintiff is strongly favored by the strength of its mark, both inherent and acquired; the similarity of the marks; the proximity of the products and services; the likelihood that plaintiff would bridge the gap; and the existence of actual confusion. None of the factors favors the defendants. The remaining factors were found to be neutral. Although we do not suggest that likelihood of confusion may be properly determined simply by the number of factors in one party's favor, the overall assessment in this case in our view admits only of a finding in plaintiff's favor that defendants' sale of telephones and telephone-related services under the VIRGIN mark was likely to cause substantial consumer confusion.

[*Reversed.*]

McDONALD'S CORP. v. DRUCK AND GERNER, D.D.S., P.C., d/b/a McDENTAL

814 F. Supp. 1127 (N.D.N.Y. 1993)

SCULLIN, District Judge:

Plaintiff McDonald's Corporation ("Plaintiff" or "McDonald's") is a Delaware corporation whose principal place of business is in Oak Brook, Illinois. McDonald's and its franchisees operate over 8,000 restaurants in the United States, over 400 of which are located in New York State. McDonald's maintains a regional office in Latham, New York ("the Latham office"), located approximately 150 miles from Plattsburgh, New York.

Defendant Druck and Gerner, D.D.S., P.C., d/b/a McDental ("McDental" or "Defendant") is a New York professional corporation located in Plattsburgh, New York, that provides dental services under the name "McDental." Drs. Druck and Gerner named their corporation "McDental," and have operated under this name since the business opened on March 20, 1981, in the Pyramid Mall in Plattsburgh. At the time that they opened, Drs. Druck and Gerner placed an orange illuminated sign with the name "McDental" above the front of the office, and placed a fee schedule sign in the window. Shortly after opening in 1981, Defendant obtained a state service mark for the name "McDental" from the State of New York.[4]

In 1985, Defendant opened a second "McDental" office in South Burlington, Vermont. As with the Plattsburgh office, Defendant contends that this office was "heavily advertised," and, like the Plattsburgh office, was similarly successful. . . .

[McDonald's sued, *inter alia*, for trademark infringement. Druck & Gerner argued that "in 1981 Plaintiff's family of 'Mc' marks combined with generic words was not substantial enough to entitle it to enjoin the use of 'McDental'; that even if it were, there is no likelihood of confusion between Plaintiff and Defendant. . . ."]

The issues in this case as framed by the parties' positions in their briefs and/or the trial testimony include the following: (1) whether Plaintiff owns trademark rights in a family of marks featuring the prefix "Mc" connected to generic non-food terms, (2) whether there is any likelihood that ordinary consumers are likely to be confused as to the source of Defendant's services. . . .

---

4. According to Mr. John Horwitz, Asst. General Counsel to Plaintiff, whose credentials as a specialist in trademark law were not disputed, an applicant receives a state service mark simply by filing an application and paying a fee. No search is conducted to ascertain those with whom the mark might be confused, nor is it possible for others to oppose such marks. Normally, all applications for federal trademarks are published in the USPTO Official Gazette, but, unlike their federal counterparts, state service marks are not published.

DISCUSSION

I. TRADEMARK INFRINGEMENT CLAIMS

. . .

The first step in resolving this case is determining whether Plaintiff possesses a trademark entitled to protection; if this is established, the court must then determine the "likelihood of confusion" with Plaintiff's marks that will result from Defendant's use of its mark. *See McDonald's Corp., Inc. v. McBagel's, Inc.*, 649 F. Supp. 1268, 1272 (S.D.N.Y. 1986).

A. Family of Marks

McDonald's has used in commerce, and obtained federal registrations for, a number of marks distinguished by the "Mc" formative and is the exclusive owner of numerous registrations issued by the USPTO. These registrations encompass both food-related (e.g., "McDonuts") and non-food/generic ("generic") (e.g., "McD," an all-purpose cleaner) items. Underlying its trademark infringement claims is Plaintiff's contention that it possessed at the time of McDental's inception, and continues to possess, a family of "Mc" marks such that Defendant's use of "McDental" is likely to cause confusion among consumers. This contention has been addressed by other courts in litigation involving this plaintiff. *See, e.g., J & J Snack Foods Corp. v. McDonald's Corporation*, 932 F.2d 1460 (Fed. Cir. 1991) (in affirming USPTO ruling that denied trademark registration to snack foods company, court held that McDonald's possesses a family of marks wherein the prefix "Mc" is used with generic food names); *McDonald's Corp. v. McBagel's Inc.*, 649 F. Supp. 1268, 1272 (S.D.N.Y. 1986) (court held that McDonald's owned a family of marks using "Mc" in combination with a generic food item).

The *McBagel's* court, which granted McDonald's request to enjoin the defendant's use of the name "McBagel's" for its restaurant, stated that, "[w]hile it does not hold a registered mark in 'Mc,' plaintiff may claim protection for this prefix as a common component of a 'family of marks.'" *Id.* at 1272 (reference omitted). And, the *McBagel's* court noted that, "[t]he existence vel non of a family of marks is a question of fact based on the distinctiveness of the common formative component and other factors, including the extent of the family's use, advertising, promotion, and its inclusion in a number of registered and unregistered marks owned by a single party." *Id.* On an appeal from the USPTO, the Federal Circuit Court of Appeals defined a "family of marks" as

> a group of marks having a recognizable common characteristic, wherein the marks are composed and used in such a way that the public associates not only the individual marks, but the common characteristic of the family, with the trademark owner. Simply using a series of similar marks does not of itself establish the existence of a family. There must be a recognition among the purchasing public that the common characteristic is indicative of a common origin of the goods.

J & J Snack Foods at 1462.

Evidence produced at trial and recent caselaw clearly establish that Plaintiff possesses a family of marks comprised of the prefix "Mc" combined with food items. However, in the present case, Plaintiff must show that it has a protectable family of marks using the "Mc" prefix such that the use of "McDental" would be confused with Plaintiff's family of marks. As the *McBagel's* court explained:

> Under the Lanham Act, Section 32(1)(a), 15 USC §1114(1)(a); as well as Section 43(a), 15 USC §1125(a), defendants are liable for infringement if their use of the name [McDental] is likely "to cause confusion, or to cause mistake or to deceive" typical consumers into

believing some sponsorship, association, affiliation, connection or endorsement exists between McDonald's and defendants.

McBagel's, 649 F. Supp. at 1273.

1. Family of Marks

Before the court may assess Plaintiff's family of marks vis-a-vis the name McDental, it must address an apparently somewhat unique problem not present in the other cited cases, *to wit*, resolving a dispute between the parties as to the proper date from which to assess the strength of Plaintiff's family of marks. Defendant argues that the court should assess the strength of Plaintiff's family of "Mc" marks by a 1981 time frame, based on its contention that Plaintiff had constructive and/or actual notice of Defendant's alleged infringement in 1981. Defendant contends that this is significant in that, while recognizing that Plaintiff may *presently* possess a family of marks, McDonald's did not possess a family of marks featuring the "Mc" prefix in combination with generic terms in 1981.[6] [cit.]

McDonald's contends that the court should assess the strength of its "Mc" family from a present standpoint, as confusion is measured in this manner, not retroactively, and that the time frame is only relevant, if at all, to the elements of notice and delay in the laches issue. Regarding the issue of laches, Plaintiff argues that it had no notice of McDental until 1987, as this was when the corporate officers with the responsibility as to trademark matters received notice of Defendant's use of the name. Plaintiff further asserts that it took prompt action to compel Defendant to cease its use of its name. Finally, Plaintiff states that regardless of the date employed, the result is the same, as the family of marks was strong enough to justify an injunction as early as 1981 and has continued to be thereafter.

The court notes that Plaintiff is requesting equitable (injunctive) relief only; Plaintiff is not asking for any damages. As injunctive relief is prospective, it would seem illogical to suggest that the court determine "the likelihood of confusion" retroactively. The more rational approach would be to measure the strength of the "family of marks" and the "likelihood of confusion" from a present standpoint. Defendant has not provided, nor has the court located, any authority to the contrary. . . .

[The court concluded that the strength of McDonald's family of marks should be measured as of the time of the lawsuit.]

As stated, numerous courts have held that Plaintiff possesses a family of marks using the "Mc" formative entitled to trademark protection. *See, e.g.*, *McBagel's*, 649 F. Supp. 1268; *J & J Snack Foods*, 932 F.2d 1460. Defendant, however, while acknowledging that "courts have held that plaintiff has a family of marks comprising [sic] of 'Mc' followed by a generic food-related word," disputes whether Plaintiff possesses a family of marks consisting of "Mc" in combination with all generic terms.

As support for this contention, Defendant cites to *Quality Inns International, Inc. v. McDonald's Corp.*, 695 F. Supp. 198 (D. Md. 1988), wherein, in determining whether to enjoin *Quality Inns* from using the term "McSleep Inn" for a chain of economy hotels, the court stated:

> [T]hat is not to say that the prefix "Mc" coupled with any generic word may be precluded by McDonald's. Each allegedly offending use must be tested against the likelihood of confusion,

---

6. The number of McDonald's non-food marks in 1981 differs considerably from the number in 1992. Defendant alleges that it had constructive notice of McDonald's ownership of only three such marks in 1981. . . .

for the scope of enforceability . . . is measured by the scope of confusion. In this case the only examination that is made, and the only conclusions that are reached, relate to the allegedly infringing use of "McSleep Inn" by Quality International in the lodging business.

Id. at 212.

The *Quality Inns* court determined, nonetheless, that Plaintiff was entitled to enjoin Defendant's use of the term "McSleep Inn," noting "that the name McSleep is so similar to the McDonald's family of marks that in whatever clothing it is dressed, the public will persist in perceiving some connection with McDonald's." *Id*. at 220. In arriving at this determination, the court noted that, "[t]he marks that are owned by McDonald's and that were formulated by combining 'Mc' and a generic word are fanciful and enjoy a meaning that associates the product immediately with McDonald's and its products and service." *Id*. at 212.

2.   Likelihood of Confusion

Whether the family of marks possessed by Plaintiff is entitled to protection from Defendant's use of "McDental" turns on "whether there exists a 'likelihood that an appreciable number of ordinarily prudent purchasers [will] be misled, or indeed simply confused, as to the source of the goods in question.'" *Thompson Medical Co., Inc. v. Pfizer, Inc.*, 753 F.2d 208, 213 (2d Cir. 1985) (citation omitted). The Second Circuit has held that "such an assessment properly turns on the examination of many factors," and that this list is not exhaustive—the court may consider others. . . .

Applying the *Polaroid* factors, the court finds that, as in *Quality Inns*, the following factors are of particular importance in assessing the likelihood of confusion in this case: the strength of the mark; the evidence of confusion; the similarity between the marks (including signage and advertising); the proximity of the markets for the products and services identified for the marks, and the likelihood that Plaintiff will bridge the gap; and the intent of Defendant in choosing its mark and its good faith in doing so. *See Quality Inns*, 695 F. Supp. at 217. The court will discuss each of these *seriatim*.

A.   STRENGTH OF THE MARK

Although the strength of Plaintiff's family of marks has already been discussed at some length, it should be noted that Plaintiff offered at trial numerous exhibits and testimony attesting to the widespread familiarity of the public with Plaintiff's use of the "Mc" language. Based on all of the evidence this court concludes, as others have, that Plaintiff's family of marks is a strong one. *See, e.g., id*. at 211-212; *McBagel's*, 649 F. Supp. at 1274-1275.

B.   EVIDENCE OF CONFUSION

Plaintiff also presented survey evidence through its witness, Philip Johnson. Johnson conducted two surveys, in 1988 and 1991, both of which evidenced a likelihood of confusion resulting from Defendant's name. Among the conclusions drawn from the surveys was a finding that some 30% of the population surveyed associated Defendant's name with Plaintiff, the same percentage that another court found to be "substantial." *Quality Inns* at

---

8. Defendant argued at trial that the survey included leading statements, such as, "Who or what company do you believe owns or operates McDental?" This objection was rejected by the *Quality Inns* court. . .. Although the facts are not exactly the same here, the court finds no justification for discrediting the survey evidence.

218. The court rejects Defendant's bases for disallowing the survey evidence, and credits the survey evidence.[8]

In addition to the survey evidence, Plaintiff introduced into evidence deposition testimony including that of former employees of Defendant. This testimony supports a finding that Defendant's name caused confusion among the public as to whether Defendant was somehow associated with Plaintiff. The court finds simply incredible Dr. Druck's testimony that he never heard anyone, even in a joking manner, associate McDental with McDonald's prior to the commencement of this lawsuit, nor did he himself ever associate the name with that of the Plaintiff.

C.   SIMILARITY BETWEEN THE TWO MARKS

The *Quality Inns* court stated that, "it is not the logo or the word 'sleep' that causes the [infringement] problem; it is the use of the fancifully coined word 'McSleep'." *Id*. at 220. Likewise, the similarity between Defendant's name and Plaintiff's various "Mc" marks is obvious, and Defendant cannot hope to distinguish the two on the basis that it is the "Dental" and not the "Mc" that makes the name "instantly recognized." *See id*.

D.   PROXIMITY OF THE PRODUCTS AND THE LIKELIHOOD THAT PLAINTIFF WILL BRIDGE THE GAP

This factor involves the likelihood "that customers mistakenly will assume either that [the defendant's goods] are somehow associated with [the plaintiff's] or are made by [the plaintiff]." *Centaur Communications, Ltd v. A/S/M Communications, Inc.*, 830 F.2d 1217, 1226 (2d Cir. 1987) (citation omitted). Initially, it would appear that dental services and fast food have nothing in common, except for the obvious connection between eating and dentistry, and that this factor should thus be weighed in Defendant's favor.

There was no showing at trial that the Plaintiff planned to enter the dental business *per se*. However, Dr. Cromie, who works with the Ronald McDonald charity houses, testified that since 1985, Plaintiff has included toothbrushes and other similar products in certain of its "Happy Meals" (a product for children). Dr. Cromie also testified that Plaintiff has sponsored dental cleaning via a mobile van that has travelled to different parts of the country, including parts of northern New York. Finally, Dr. Cromie added that the University of Mississippi, through a grant from Plaintiff, has been devising a dental machine for children. Although Dr. Cromie testified that Plaintiff provided the money for this machine, he could not say for certain whether the Plaintiff's name is on the machine.

The *Quality Inns* court found a connection between fast food and lodging, as one is logically associated with the other. *See Quality Inns*, 695 F. Supp. at 220-221. However, notwithstanding the fact that oral hygiene normally follows the ingestion of fast (or any other) food, this court is disinclined to find that Plaintiff, even if it begins providing dental floss with its french fries, is likely to "bridge the gap" in any appreciable manner in this case. The evidence presented by Plaintiff did not convince the court that the proximity of the products in this case, or the likelihood that Plaintiff will "bridge the gap," i.e., enter the field of dental service, weighs in Plaintiff's favor.

E.   INTENT OF DRS. DRUCK AND GERNER AND GOOD FAITH IN CHOOSING THE NAME "MCDENTAL"

When asked at trial why the name "McDental" was chosen for the business, Dr. Druck testified that the name was chosen because it had a "cute" sound to it, and a "quality of retentiveness." Dr. Druck disavowed any attempt to capitalize on the Plaintiff's well-recognized name and its association with family service and quality. He claimed, in essence, that the name was chosen because a friend of his and Dr. Gerner's, Mr. Josh Patrick, thought it was a name that they could remember—more so than other type names—that he never perceived any association with the two names, nor did he perceive anyone else having any association between the two, even in a social or humorous context.

Dr. Gerner echoed Dr. Druck's testimony in stating that the two had chosen "McDental" because they wanted a short, memorable name; that Mr. Patrick had agreed that this was the best name to use; and that Dr. Gerner never considered that there was any similarity between McDental and McDonald's. Dr. Gerner further testified that, prior to 1987, he never heard of anyone making any association between the business and the Plaintiff. However, Dr. Gerner was quoted in a news article as saying, in essence, that the choice of the name "should have been a compliment to McDonald's."

Interestingly enough, Dr. Druck also testified that a local Plattsburgh newspaper published an article entitled, "McDental Being McHassled Over McTrademark," that he "did not know" how the media learned of the lawsuit, but did admit to framing a copy of one of Plaintiff's protest letters and displaying it at the McDental office.

Contrasting with the testimony of the dentists was the testimony of Paul Pontiff, an attorney who advised Drs. Druck and Gerner regarding their name selection. In or about 1981, he had opined that "McDental" would not conflict with Plaintiff, apparently due to the dissimilar nature of the two services, although he informed Druck and Gerner that this was not a legal opinion, as he was not a patent/trademark attorney. It is difficult not to infer that the reason why the dentists sought Mr. Pontiff's opinion in this regard was that they *had indeed* considered the similarity with McDonald's in selecting their name.

The court need not deliberate long on the question of intent here. In short, the court finds that the explanations and statements of Drs. Druck and Gerner regarding the choice of the name "McDental" defy common sense and credibility; that they were fully cognizant of the name's similarity to McDonald's and chose to capitalize on Plaintiff's popularity. Consequently, the court easily finds that the good faith factor weighs in Plaintiff's favor.

Summarizing the relevant *Polaroid* factors, the court concludes that the strength of Plaintiff's mark, evidence of confusion, similarity of the marks and lack of good faith on the part of the individual defendants in choosing their name together support a finding of trademark infringement that warrants the issuance of an injunction in this case absent a valid defense. . . .

LIBMAN COMPANY v. VINING INDUSTRIES, INC.

69 F.3d 1360 (7th Cir. 1995)

Posner, Chief Judge:

The Libman Company brought suit against Vining Industries for infringement of a federally registered trademark on a broom. After a bench trial, the district judge enjoined Vining from selling the infringing line of brooms and in addition awarded Libman almost $1.2 million in monetary relief, representing Vining's profits from that sale. The main ground of the appeal, and the only one we need discuss, is that the district judge committed clear error in finding that consumers were likely to mistake Vining's broom for Libman's.

A broom has, of course, a head of bristles. In 1993, after being twice turned down, Libman succeeded in registering with the U.S. Patent and Trademark Office a trademark that consists of a color scheme in which one vertical band or segment of bristles is a different color (a "contrasting" color, in the language of the trademark registration) from the remaining bristles. The particular choice of contrasting colors is not part of the trademark, however. The contrasting-color band was sometimes red and sometimes green or black, the rest of the bristles being either a very dark gray, verging on black, with the red band, or a lighter gray with the green or black band. Libman had begun marketing these brooms in 1990. They sold well. In 1993 Vining began marketing its own contrasting-color broom, the contrasting colors being light and medium gray.

The parties agree that Libman cannot prove infringement of its trademark without proving that consumers of brooms are likely to be confused about the source of Vining's brooms—and to think that they are Libman's. 15 U.S.C. §1114(1)(b); *AHP Subsidiary Holding Co. v. Stuart Hale Co.*, 1 F.3d 611, 615 (7th Cir. 1993). A trademark is not a property right, but an identifier; so, provided no one is likely to be confused by the alleged infringer, there is no impairment of the interest that the trademark statute protects. The evidence of likelihood of confusion in this case is vanishingly thin. Vining sold several hundred thousand of the allegedly infringing brooms, yet there is no evidence that any consumer ever made such an error; if confusion were likely, one would expect at least one person out of this vast multitude to be confused, or more precisely one would expect Libman to have been able to find one such confused person. Nor was any survey conducted in an effort to determine the likelihood of confusion. The district court pointed out, moreover, that "from a distance, with the cardboard cover in place, the [Vining] broom doesn't have the appearance of a Libman broom." The head of each broom is sold with a plastic wrapper around it, but the opaque label affixed to Vining's wrapper, unlike the label on Libman's wrapper, is so large that it hides the contrasting colors of the bristles. It does not hide them completely, but, especially since they are merely different shades of gray, you have to peer pretty closely to notice this feature of the broom. The labels are not similar and of course the brand names are different. Consistent with the different style of packaging, Libman's advertising (at least the advertising that is in the record, but that is all we have to go on) shows the undressed broom, its contrasting colors boldly displayed. Vining's does not.

But "with their covers removed," the judge went on to say, "the two brooms are quite similar in appearance." The photographs in the record do not support this characterization, as the only thing the brooms have in common, besides being brooms, is that their bristles are in contrasting color bands rather than being all of one color. But this is an element of similarity and we shall not quibble over the district judge's use of the word "quite." The brooms, however, are sold in their wrappers. There is no evidence that the wrapper is ever removed before a sale to the consumer. (There is evidence that at trade shows the wrapper is sometimes removed, but those are promotions to the trade, not to consumers.) A consumer who is curious about the strength or stiffness or other tactile properties of the bristles can feel them through the plastic wrapper, which is very thin; she would have no occasion to ask the salesman to remove the wrapper.

So why is the undressed state of the broom relevant? Because the consumer might, upon removing the opaque wrapper from the Vining broom when she brought the broom home, think that she had bought a Libman rather than a Vining. Here is how her confusion might hurt Libman: The two brands of broom, though sold through the same *type* of outlet (supermarkets and mass-market retailers), are rarely sold by the same outlet, the reason being that retailers prefer to stock only one brand of broom. It's a cheap but bulky item; they don't want to fill up the store with different brands of it. Because a broom is so cheap (under $10), consumers don't spend a lot of time mulling over their decision whether to buy. If their old broom is wearing out, which usually happens after a year or so, they'll look for a new one the next time they find themselves in a store that sells brooms. Suppose that in 1993 you buy a Libman broom. You like it; you think it's a great broom; and you associate the contrasting color bands with the name "Libman." Eventually the broom wears out and you have to buy a new one. You find yourself in a store that does not stock the Libman broom (you don't know this), but only the Vining broom. If you saw them side to side you would know that the Libman, and not the Vining, broom was the one you had had a good experience with. But you don't see them side to side. All you see is a broom that has contrasting color bands. You think it's a Libman broom, and buy it. Had you known it was not a Libman broom you would have waited to replace your old broom until you found yourself in a store that stocked the Libman broom.

This is a plausible narrative, one consistent not only with the objectives of trademark law but also with a large number of cases which hold that where, as in this case, the public does not encounter the parties' trademarks together, the existence of minor differences that would clearly distinguish them in a side-by-side comparison does not refute an inference of likely confusion. [cit.] As we put it years ago in a case involving an alleged confusion between "Dramamine" and "Bonamine," "we must determine the purchasing public's state of mind when confronted by somewhat similar trade names *singly* presented." *G.D. Searle & Co. v. Chas. Pfizer & Co.*, 265 F.2d 385, 388 (7th Cir. 1959). . . .

It would have been nice had the district judge mentioned this theory of confusion rather than just moving without transition or explanation from the fact that the parties' brooms are *not* confusingly similar when seen side by side to the conclusion that one infringed the trademark of the other. Libman did not object when at argument we judges looked at the brooms side by side and remarked their dissimilar appearance. . . .

[Libman neglected to present evidence to support its] theory that satisfied consumers of its broom might be fooled when they shopped for a replacement in a store that sold only Vining's broom. To insist on evidence might seem to be to commit the error of thinking that proof of actual confusion is required in a trademark-infringement case, and of course it is not unless damages are sought. But our point is only that a finding of likely confusion can no more be based on pure conjecture or a fetching narrative alone than any other finding on an issue on which the proponent bears the burden of proof.

To this Libman might reply that deliberate copying ("bad faith") is one of the factors that courts rely on in determining the likelihood of confusion. It is. But in context, "bad faith" in the district judge's opinion does not appear to mean that Vining was trying to confuse consumers. So far as appears—and it is all that the record supports—Vining noticed that Libman's brooms were selling briskly, inferred that consumers like brooms with contrasting color bands, and decided to climb on the bandwagon. We call that competition, not bad faith, provided there is no intention to confuse, and, so far as appears, there was none. The distinction between copying "features whose value to consumers is intrinsic and not exclusively as a signifier of source" and features whose only significance is in identifying the source of the product is emphasized in *Thomas & Betts Corp. v. Panduit Corp.*, 65 F.3d 654, 663 (7th Cir. 1995). *See also Duraco Products, Inc. v. Joy Plastic Enterprises, Ltd.*, 40 F.3d 1431, 1453 (3d Cir. 1994). The line is a fine one. *W.T. Rogers Co. v. Keene*, 778 F.2d 334, 339-40 (7th Cir. 1985). But there is neither evidence nor a finding (as we read the district judge's opinion) that it was deliberately crossed.

The two brooms are not packaged alike and do not have similar names; while the "undressed" brooms are similar, they are not identical; the appearance of the brooms in advertising was dissimilar; and the trademark is a thin one, since adding a colored stripe is hardly a distinctive way of marking a product. We now know, of course, that a color can be a trademark. *Qualitex Co. v. Jacobson Products Co.*, 514 U.S. 159 (1995). And we do not hold that Libman's contrasting-color trademark was insufficiently distinctive to be registrable. *Cf. Application of Data Packaging Corp.*, 453 F.2d 1300 (C.C.P.A. 1972). (Vining argues this, but we need not and do not reach the issue.) Still, we're in the gray area (pardon the pun) where a rather commonplace design used for a trademark may be taken by consumers as a form of decoration—a way, here, of jazzing up the humblest of utilitarian products. 1

McCarthy, *supra,* ¶7.17, p. 7-77. We pointed out that Vining may have taken it so in deciding to produce a similar broom.

We do not want to make a fetish of testimony, expert or otherwise. Sometimes it is obvious just from comparing the products that consumers are likely to be confused as to their source. But this is not such a case. If the record were limited to the brooms themselves and the advertising for them, no reasonable person would think that there was a substantial danger of confusion. We take the district judge to have acknowledged this in the passage we quoted earlier from his opinion. Libman's narrative of possible confusion cannot be regarded as better than a hypothesis, and a hypothesis that has not been tested. It should not have been very hard for Libman to find some satisfied owners of its brooms and confront them with the Vining broom and see whether they thought it was the same brand of broom. Without such evidence it would be pure speculation to conclude that anyone, let alone a significant fraction of the broom-buying public, could have been misled into believing that the Vining broom and the Libman broom were one and the same brand. Restatement (Third) of Unfair Competition §20, comment g (1995).

Either consumers are confused at the point of sale, or they become confused later and this carries over to the next time they are in the market for the product. The district court rightly disparaged the first theory and failed to discuss the second. The evidence supports neither, and the judgment for the plaintiff must therefore be reversed with instructions to enter judgment for the defendant.

Reversed.

COFFEY, Circuit Judge, dissenting:

I am unable to join in the majority opinion because I believe it is contrary to the law of this circuit regarding "likelihood of confusion" and because I am concerned that my colleagues have disregarded the "clearly erroneous" standard of review that governs a district court's findings in this area. Given the centrality of the "likelihood of confusion" concept in the law of trademark infringement, I must respectfully dissent.

I.   THE ELEMENTS OF "LIKELIHOOD OF CONFUSION"

. . .

The majority's approach to the likelihood-of-confusion issue "sweeps under the rug" our well-established seven-factor test, and instead dwells on Libman's failure to produce evidence of actual confusion:

> Without such evidence [of actual confusion] it would be pure speculation to conclude that anyone, let alone a significant fraction of the broom-buying public, could have been misled into believing that the Vining broom and the Libman broom were one and the same brand.

This fetishizing of actual confusion evidence flatly contradicts this court's oft-stated holding that "the plaintiff need not show actual confusion in order to establish likelihood of confusion." [cit.]

Obviously, evidence of actual confusion can be highly probative of the likelihood of confusion. For this reason, our cases recognize that such evidence, when available, is "entitled to substantial weight." *Helene Curtis Industries, Inc. v. Church & Dwight Co.*, 560 F.2d 1325 (7th Cir. 1977), *cert. denied* 434 U.S. 1070 (1978). Nevertheless, the nature of a particular product can make it unlikely that this kind of evidence will ever surface. Under such circumstances, as one commentator has observed, the absence of actual confusion evidence is not particularly significant:

[C]ourts generally acknowledge that a plaintiff need not prove actual confusion in order to establish trademark infringement. This . . . is especially true where the unavailability of such evidence is expected, *for example, where the competing items are low-priced goods usually purchased on impulse and consumers would not be expected to complain about purchasing the wrong product.* . . . In such instances, courts generally treat the actual confusion factor as a non-factor, with the absence of such evidence having no adverse impact on the plaintiff's ability to prove infringement. It must [also] be remembered that in many instances the fact that a plaintiff has not adduced actual confusion evidence does not necessarily mean that actual confusion has not occurred.

Michael J. Allen, *The Role of Actual Confusion Evidence in Federal Trademark Infringement Litigation*, 16 Campbell L. Rev. 19, 23-25 (Winter 1994) (emphasis added). Libman introduced testimony, apparently undisputed by Vining, that brooms are low-cost items generally purchased on impulse. This testimony is "relevant to the likelihood of confusion because presumably consumers take less time purchasing low-cost items, and haste increases the possibility of confusion." *AHP Subsidiary*, 1 F.3d at 616; *Maxim's Ltd. v. Badonsky*, 772 F.2d 388, 393 (7th Cir. 1985) (risk of confusion is greater with low-cost items because purchasers are unlikely to complain when dissatisfied, thus bringing to light confusion). . . .

II.   "APPELLATE REVIEW OF LIKELIHOOD-OF-CONFUSION DETERMINATIONS"

"Whether or not there is a likelihood of confusion is a question of fact as to the *probable* or actual actions and reactions of prospective purchasers of the goods or services of the parties." *McGraw-Edison v. Walt Disney Productions*, 787 F.2d 1163, 1167 (7th Cir. 1986) (quotation omitted . . .). We must therefore uphold a trial court's likelihood-of-confusion determination unless there has been a showing of clear error. . . .

I am concerned that the majority has not applied the "clearly erroneous" standard of review in this case, but rather has engaged in *de novo* fact finding. In one part of its opinion, the majority paraphrases Libman's argument concerning the likelihood of confusion, namely, that satisfied Libman customers will be confused as to the source of Vining's color-contrasted brooms when they encounter them in stores that carry only the Vining broom. The majority initially characterizes this as a "*plausible* narrative." . . . Elsewhere in the opinion, however, the majority contradicts itself by deriding Libman's likelihood-of-confusion argument as "pure conjecture," "fetching narrative," and "no better than a hypothesis." The majority's ultimate conclusion, which appears to be based largely on its own inspection of the brooms side by side,[2] is that "no reasonable person would think there was a substantial danger of confusion."

In my considered opinion, the majority too easily "brushes aside" the Supreme Court's admonition in *Anderson v. Bessemer City* that a reviewing court may not reverse a factual finding simply because it would have decided the issue differently. . . .

These observations apply with particular force in the area of trademark infringement, which is highly fact-specific. *See* Patricia J. Kaeding, *Clearly Erroneous Review of Mixed Questions of Law and Fact: The Likelihood of Confusion Determination in Trademark Law*, 59 U. Chi. L. Rev. 1291, 1309-1310 (Summer 1992) (deferential review promotes

---

2. The value of such a comparison is questionable. Trademark infringement can exist when, as in this case, the goods or services at issue are not typically seen by consumers side by side. . . .

judicial accuracy and the efficient use of appellate resources because "fact-specific issues . . . can be determined with the same, or nearly the same, degree of consistency at the trial level."). . . .

It seems to me that the majority, contrary to our own precedent, has evaluated the likelihood of confusion afresh and substituted its own judgment for that of the district court. My colleagues are too willing to revisit factual issues: not just the ultimate factual issue in this case (likelihood of confusion), but subsidiary findings on issues such as the strength of Libman's mark and the similarity of the broom designs. The district court found that Libman's use of contrasting colors was the "distinguishing feature" of its trademark and that this mark was, at a minimum, strong enough to be protectable under the trademark law. The majority apparently disagrees, and (oblivious to the large amount of money Libman spent to develop, market, and advertise its color-contrasted brooms) disparages the mark as "a thin one," "a rather commonplace design," and merely "a way . . . of jazzing up the humblest of utilitarian products."

The majority also disagrees with the district court's finding that Vining's adoption of a color-contrasted design made its broom similar to Libman's, *even though Vining used a different pair of contrasting colors*. However, as the majority concedes (at least in one part of its opinion), this is a "plausible" finding. It is not as though the trial judge concluded that Lake Michigan and the Sahara Desert are confusingly similar because they are both large. In other words, although I happen to agree with the trial court's finding, my agreement or disagreement is beside the point. The court's clearly-stated finding of similarity is not so tenuous that it should leave any of the members of this panel with "a definite and firm conviction" that a mistake has been committed. The same is true of the district judge's ultimate determination that ordinary purchasers were likely to be confused as to the source of Vining's brooms. . . .

In my view, the majority opinion is "likely to confuse" the law of trademark infringement in this circuit by giving too much analytical weight to the actual confusion factor and by encroaching on the fact-finding role of the district court. I therefore dissent and state for the record that I would affirm the district court.

INTRODUCTION TO NOTES AND QUESTIONS ON THE FACTORS ANALYSIS

As noted previously, we have presented the *Virgin*, *McDental*, and *Libman* cases as illustrations of modern multi-factor confusion tests. The following materials highlight individual factors, summarizing particular issues that arise in connection with those factors. The notes present quite a large number of cases and fact settings in a fairly compressed fashion, to give you a feel for the relevant case law without overwhelming you with details—we hope. In addition, as you work through the group of notes on each individual factor, you should be able to identify a number of factor-specific rules of law, guidelines, or rules of thumb. Lawyers rely on these rules and guidelines to enrich their arguments concerning each of the factors. You should do the same.

NOTES AND QUESTIONS: SIMILARITY OF MARKS FACTOR

1. *Similarity (or dissimilarity) as dispositive?* Professor Barton Beebe concluded on the basis of his empirical study that the similarity factor is "by far the most influential" in the multi-factor analysis. *See* Barton Beebe, *An Empirical Study of the Multifactor Tests for Trademark Infringement*, 94 CAL. L. REV. 1581, 1600 (2006). Did you detect a bias toward the similarity factor in the cases that you have read? Can you tell whether judicial assessments of similarity *cause* a given outcome in the analysis, as opposed to simply providing an attractive means to *justify* a judge's a priori conclusion about confusion?

In *Jada Toys, Inc. v. Mattel, Inc.*, 518 F.3d 628, 632-34 (9th Cir. 2008), the court warned against giving dispositive significance to the similarity of marks factor (or any one factor):

> To hold otherwise would allow the possibility that persuasive evidence of a particular factor may be considered at the expense of relevant evidence of others. This problem is particularly acute where, as here, a court relies on the dissimilarity of the marks to conclude that no likelihood of confusion exists. In such a case, the potential for a judge to elevate his or her own subjective impressions of the relative dissimilarity of the marks over evidence of, for example, actual confusion, is great. And where the subjective impressions of a particular judge are weighed at the expense of other relevant evidence, the value of the multi-factor approach sanctioned by this Court is undermined.

Do you find the Ninth Circuit's guidance helpful? Why or why not?

Compare the approach in *Jada* to Judge Easterbrook's approach in *Top Tobacco, L.P. v. North Atlantic Operating Co., Inc.*, 509 F.3d 380 (7th Cir. 2007). Plaintiff registered TOP for roll-your-own tobacco products (below, left). Defendant markets a competing product under the name ZIG-ZAG (below, right). The phrase "Fresh-Top Canister" appeared on the front of defendant's product for a few years.

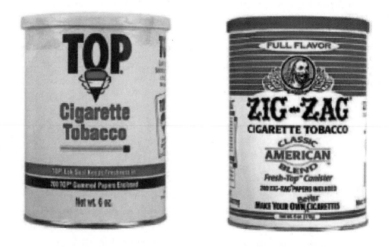

Reviewing a lower court grant of summary judgment of no confusion, Judge Easterbrook concluded that "no one who saw these cans side by side could be confused about who makes which. . . ." *Id.* at 381. The judge expressed no interest in "traips[ing] through the list," *id.* at 383, of likelihood of confusion factors: "A list of factors designed as *proxies* for the likelihood of confusion can't supersede the statutory inquiry. If we know for sure that consumers are not confused about a product's origin, there is no need to consult even a single proxy." *Id.* at 383. Do you agree with this analysis? Should it matter whether judges can articulate a basis for "knowing for sure" that consumers are not confused, or is judicial common sense good enough? Judge Easterbrook also pointed out that there was no evidence of actual confusion and that defendant was using the term "top"

to describe the top of the canister "rather than as the product's brand." *Id. Cf. Facebook, Inc. v. Teachbook.com L.L.C.*, 819 F. Supp. 2d 764, 780-81 (N.D. Ill. 2011) (declining to apply the truncated approach of *Top Tobacco*). The court reasoned that *Top Tobacco* involved "consumer goods sitting next to one another on a store shelf." By contrast, in cases involving websites, the textual and aural similarities between marks will be likely to matter more than the visual similarities because in the online context, consumers are likely to be attracted "through word-of-mouth, hyperlinks, and search engine results." *Id.* at 781. Do you agree?

Whether the ultimate question of likelihood of confusion in any given case can be resolved on summary judgment surely depends in part upon whether the court approaches the similarity of marks factor as suggested by the Ninth Circuit in *Jada*, or as suggested by the Seventh Circuit in *Top Tobacco*. Should summary judgment generally be disfavored in likelihood-of-confusion cases? *See Fortune Dynamic, Inc. v. Victoria's Secret Stores Brand Mgmt., Inc.*, 618 F.3d 1025, 1031 (9th Cir. 2010) ("This case is yet another example of the wisdom of the well-established principle that '[b]ecause of the intensely factual nature of trademark disputes, summary judgment is generally disfavored in the trademark arena.'") (quoting *Entrepreneur Media, Inc. v. Smith*, 279 F.3d 1135, 1140 (9th Cir. 2002)). *But cf. General Conference Corp. of Seventh-Day Adventists v. McGill*, 617 F.3d 402 (6th Cir. 2010) (affirming the grant of summary judgment in favor of plaintiff on likelihood of confusion).

2. *Side-by-side similarity?* The similarity-of-marks factor is probably more complex than it initially seems. Certainly, it calls for a more robust analysis than merely viewing the marks side by side in the courtroom. Instead, the court must attempt to simulate the consumer's encounter with the mark and assess similarity with that real-world context in mind. How exactly might a court do this? How might this shape one's litigation strategies? Consider Judge Posner's comments in *Libman* about the "dressed" and "undressed" brooms, retail practices of broom sellers, and so forth. If modern concepts of confusion under the Lanham Act are not limited to "purchaser" confusion (as we discussed in section A), then does it follow that the similarity assessment should not be limited to similarity as perceived at the point of purchase? Do these comments suggest to you that the similarity analysis is less a technical, matching exercise than a fact-rich inquiry into consumer behavior and marketing practices? If so, is Judge Coffey correct in his *Libman* dissent about the nature of appellate review of the likelihood-of-confusion analysis?

In a trade dress case, Judge Calabresi has warned that side-by-side similarity comparisons in a likelihood-of-confusion analysis could amount to reversible error. In *Malletier v. Burlington Coat Factory Warehouse, Inc.*, 426 F.3d 532 (2d Cir. 2005), plaintiff sold a line of multicolored handbags through its Louis Vuitton stores (and an associated website) and at upscale department stores at prices ranging from $400 to $4,000, while defendant sold a line of multicolored handbags through its discount stores (and an associated website) at about $29.98 per bag. Plaintiff claimed that defendant's trade dress was likely to confuse consumers prior to sale and after sale (theories that we will study in section E of this chapter). Viewing the handbags side by side, the district court had concluded that they were dissimilar, and ultimately denied plaintiff's motion for a preliminary injunction. On appeal, the Second Circuit vacated the denial of the motion for injunctive relief and remanded to the district court:

> While a district court's simultaneous comparison of two products is not an inappropriate heuristic means of investigating similarities and differences in their respective designs on the way to an ultimate conclusion as to whether the products are likely to leave similar impressions on consumers, district courts must be careful to maintain a focus on the ultimate issue of the likelihood of consumer confusion. As a result, the Lanham Act requires a court to analyze the similarity of the products in light of the way in which the marks are actually displayed in their

purchasing context. [cit.] Whether simultaneous viewing by consumers is likely to result in confusion is not relevant when it is serial viewing that is at issue given the market context or the type of confusion claimed. In such a case, a district court must ask not whether differences are easily discernible on simultaneous viewing, but whether they are likely to be memorable enough to dispel confusion on serial viewing.

The need for a contextual analysis, rather than a simple focus on whether simultaneous viewing is likely to cause confusion, is grounded in the purpose of the Lanham Act. That Act seeks to eliminate the confusion that is created in the marketplace by the sale of products bearing highly similar marks. [cit.]

Accordingly, a court that seeks to discern confusion without regard to the marketplace frustrates (however unintentionally) Congress's intent. Though two products may be readily differentiated when carefully viewed simultaneously, those same products may still be confusingly similar in the eyes of ordinary consumers encountering the products individually under typical purchasing conditions, and that "real world" confusion is the confusion that the Act seeks to eliminate. As a result, courts must evaluate the likely effect on consumers of the marks' similar and dissimilar features *with a focus on market conditions*, even if the products appear to be adequately different in a non-marketplace setting.

Id. at 538-39. *Accord Louis Vuitton Malletier v. Dooney & Bourke, Inc.*, 454 F.3d 108, 117 (2d Cir. 2006). In *Burlington Coat Factory*, the parties conceded that the products were not sold side by side, and, in any event, the plaintiff was claiming pre-sale and post-sale confusion, not point-of-sale confusion. Under these circumstances, the district court erred by viewing the handbags simultaneously to assess similarity. *See Burlington Coat Factory*, 426 F.3d at 539.

3. *Sight, sound, and meaning.* Courts may assess mark similarity via a wide variety of comparisons. Frequently, courts recite the triad of "sight, sound, and meaning" to reflect these possible variations. Consider the similarity arguments that might be made in the following cases:

- Alligator graphic for clothing versus dragon graphic for judo uniforms; *see Lacoste Alligator S.A. v. Everlast World's Boxing Headquarters*, 204 U.S.P.Q. (BNA) 945 (TTAB 1979) (marks dissimilar in appearance).
- PEOPLES FEDERAL SAVINGS BANK for a bank versus PEOPLE'S UNITED BANK for a bank. Note that the marks as actually used appear as follows:

Peoples Federal Sav. Bank v. People's United Bank, 672 F.3d 1 (1st Cir. 2012).

- SHOWER TO SHOWER for body powder versus HOUR AFTER HOUR for aerosol deodorant or antiperspirant; *see Johnson & Johnson v. Colgate-Palmolive Co.*, 345 F. Supp. 1216 (D.N.J. 1972) (marks similar in sound and meaning).
- BOY SCOUTS for a youth organization based on the scouting movement and admitting only boys versus YOUTHSCOUTS for a youth organization based on the scouting movement and admitting both boys and girls; *see Wrenn v. Boy Scouts of America*, 89 U.S.P.Q.2d (BNA) 1039 (N.D. Cal. 2008).

- CYCLONE for wire fencing versus TORNADO for wire fencing; *see Hancock v. American Steel & Wire Co.*, 203 F.2d 737 (C.C.P.A. 1953).
- T.G.I. FRIDAY'S for a restaurant versus E.L. SATURDAY'S for a restaurant; *see T.G.I. Friday's, Inc. v. International Restaurant Group, Inc.*, 405 F. Supp. 698 (M.D. La. 1975) (dissimilar visually and phonetically).
- COACH for standardized test preparation materials versus COACH for luxury handbags; *see Coach Services, Inc. v. Triumph Learning LLC*, 668 F.3d 1356 (Fed. Cir. 2012).

The Restatement (Third) of Unfair Competition §21(a) (1995) articulates the similarity factor by calling on courts to consider:

(a) the degree of similarity between the respective designations, including a comparison of:
   (i) the overall impression created by the designations as they are used in marketing the respective goods or services or in identifying the respective businesses;
   (ii) the pronunciation of the designations;
   (iii) the translation of any foreign words contained in the designations;
   (iv) the verbal translation of any pictures, illustrations, or designs contained in the designations;
   (v) the suggestions, connotations, or meanings of the designations.

How would you apply the Restatement standard to the *Virgin*, *Libman*, and *McDental* cases? Where a mark is not a recognized English word, the parties should offer evidence about how consumers would pronounce the word rather than speculating about the general rules of phonetics. *Stoncor Group, Inc. v. Speciality Coatings, Inc.*, 759 F.3d 1327 (Fed. Cir. 2014) (debating whether the mark STONSHIELD for coatings used on concrete floors would be pronounced with a long "o," as in "Stone Shield," or with a short "o," akin to the word "on").

4. *Similarity and online automated corrections.* Suppose that the marks at issue in a confusion factors analysis are BLACKBERRY for mobile communications and CRACKBERRY for, *inter alia*, a website catering to users of BLACKBERRY mobile devices. In assessing the similarity of marks factor, what weight would you give to the fact that the Google search engine auto-corrects "Crackberry" to "Blackberry"?

5. *Anti-dissection rule.* Courts and the PTO routinely declare their aversion to "dissecting" a mark into component parts for purposes of analyzing the similarity factor. However well ingrained the anti-dissection principle may be, courts should not lose sight of the fact that they are undertaking a similarity comparison that attempts to simulate the actual presentation of the marks to the relevant consumers in the relevant commercial context. If it is the case that consumers effectively "dissect" a composite mark—meaning that they focus on certain aspects of the mark and ignore other aspects—then that is the similarity analysis that the court should undertake. This suggests that the anti-dissection principle should be viewed as a starting point only, not an ironclad rule, from which a court should readily depart when the facts indicate that some portion of the mark is dominant in consumers' perceptions. *See, e.g., In re Chatham Int'l, Inc.*, 380 F.3d 1340 (Fed. Cir. 2004) (not error to identify GASPAR as the dominant portion of both applicant's mark JOSE GASPAR GOLD for tequila and prior registered mark GASPAR'S ALE for ale, and to assess similarity by focusing on the dominant portions of the respective marks). Did the court in *McDental* adopt this approach? How would you apply this approach to a case in which plaintiff uses ICE BREAKERS for chewing gum, and defendant uses DENTYNE ICE for chewing gum, DENTYNE being the defendant's house mark? *See Nabisco, Inc. v. Warner-Lambert Co.*, 220 F.3d 43 (2d Cir. 2000). *See also Oakville Hills Cellar, Inc. v. Georgallis Holdings, LLC*, 826 F.3d 1376 (Fed. Cir. 2016) (TTAB was correct to find that MAYARI and MAYA for wine were not similar, declining to dissect MAYARI into MAYA- and -RI).

6. *Family of marks.* The *McDental* case relies on the "family of marks" doctrine. To prove that a mark family exists, a mark owner must show that it owns a group of marks having a recognizable common feature, where (1) the group of marks is used and promoted together in such a way that the public associates the common feature with the mark owner; and (2) the common feature is distinctive. *See J & J Snack Foods Corp. v. McDonald's Corp.*, 932 F.2d 1460 (Fed. Cir. 1991). Does the "family of marks" doctrine square with the anti-dissection principle?

In the *McDental* case, is the relevant family really all marks using the "Mc" formative, or is it all marks using the "McD" formative? Would the case have been decided differently if the dentists had used McCAVITY instead of McDENTAL? The Singapore Court of Appeal resisted McDonald's family of marks theory in *McDonald's Corp. v. Future Enterprises Pte. Ltd.*, [2005] 1 SLR 177. Defendant sought to register MACNOODLES, MACCHOCOLATE, and MACTEA, each appearing with an eagle logo, as illustrated here, in connection with instant noodle, chocolate, and tea mixes, respectively.

McDonald's opposed. The Court of Appeal affirmed the lower court's decision dismissing McDonald's opposition. According to the Court of Appeal, the "Mac" prefix could not be viewed in isolation from the eagle logo for purposes of assessing similarity, the channels of trade were different (defendant's products were sold through grocery stores), and the very fame of the McDonald's mark and the "Golden Arches" logo suggested that a reasonably diligent consumer would not be likely to conclude that defendant was associated with plaintiff. If the case had arisen in the United States, how would you have decided it?

Should courts recognize families of trade dress under these same criteria? *See, e.g., Rose Art Indus. v. Swanson*, 235 F.3d 165 (3d Cir. 2000) (alleged family of trade dress in packaging designs for crayons and colored pencils).

7. *Interrelationship between similarity factor and relatedness of goods factor.* Although courts may initially analyze mark similarity (or any of the other likelihood-of-confusion factors) in isolation, ultimately courts must weigh and balance the factors together. In doing so, many courts recognize a relationship between the similarity factor and the "relatedness of goods/services" factor: "When marks would appear on virtually identical goods or services, the degree of similarity necessary to support a conclusion of likely confusion declines." *Century 21 Real Estate Corp. v. Century Life of America*, 970 F.2d 874, 877 (Fed. Cir. 1992). Some courts characterize this relationship as a "sliding scale" between the similarity and relatedness factors.

As the Federal Circuit has put it:

> In practice, [the] similarity of the marks and relatedness of the goods and services [factors], are often interdependent. [cit.] The parallel treatment of these factors is particularly appropriate when the mark and the product or service combine to form an impression on the consumer as

to the source of the goods. For example, if a consumer encounters two related goods or services within the same market, less similarity between the marks would be required for confusion of that consumer to be likely. On the other hand, even if two marks are identical, if they are encountered in different contexts, the consumer can often easily distinguish between the two products. For these reasons, "[a] diminished standard of similarity is . . . applied when comparing the marks of closely related goods." [cit.] Application of this principle to our case, where the products are essentially identical, leads to the conclusion that the district court was free to accept a lesser showing of similarity between the marks.

Nautilus Group, Inc. v. ICON Health & Fitness, Inc., 372 F.3d 1330, 1345 (Fed. Cir. 2004) (affirming preliminary injunction in favor of plaintiff, owner of BOWFLEX for exercise equipment, against defendant, who used CROSSBOW for exercise equipment).

8. *Expert testimony on similarity.* Should courts draw on the field of linguistics in analyzing similarity of marks? Should trademark litigants employ linguistics experts? The alleged infringer's linguistics expert fared poorly in *Blue Bell Creameries, L.P. v. Denali Co., LLC,* 89 U.S.P.Q.2d (BNA) 1146 (S.D. Tex. 2008). Blue Bell called the expert to testify that MOOO TRACKS for Blue Bell's ice cream was not similar to MOOSE TRACKS for Denali's ice cream. The expert testified that "Mooo" was not a real word, but rather the sound that a cow makes, and proceeded to demonstrate by imitating a cow. The court refused to find that consumers would tend to pronounce "Mooo" with an elongated "o" like a cow—even in Texas, apparently—and rejected the expert's claim that any number of people had been mooing in the courtroom during the trial.

PROBLEM 7-1: PICKLE PROBLEM

Plaintiff Pikle-Rite prepares POLKA pickles principally in Pulaski, and purveys the pickles in packages with pictures of Polish people:

Defendant Chicago Pickle purveys POL-PAK pickles in packages with pickle pictures:

Pikle-Rite promotes its products to the pickle-purchasing public on posters (and also on radio and television broadcasts) and on promotional products such as pencils. Presume that Chicago Pickle presents its pickles to prospective purchasers through similar procedures.

Analyze the similarity factor for purposes of the likelihood-of-confusion test. Is a side-by-side comparison of the labels probative? Does the answer depend upon whether Pikle-Rite has registered the word mark POLKA (as opposed to a logo including the word POLKA), or do we simply look to the manner in which the mark is presented to consumers, regardless of the technicalities of the registration document? If we do compare the labels, do we compare them in toto? Including POLKA's Polish people? POL-PAK's pickle picture?

In point of fact, Pikle-Rite owned a plethora of Principal Register registrations, including the following (three separate registrations):

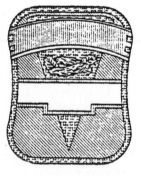

Ponder that.

PROBLEM 7-2:   SIMILARITY FACTOR FOR FOREIGN LANGUAGE WORD MARKS

Assume that Chupa Chups, a manufacturer headquartered in Barcelona, Spain, sells lollipops in the United States under the mark CHUPA CHUPS. Assume further that Dulces Vero, a competitor located in Mexico, also sells lollipops in the U.S. market, under the mark CHUPA GURTS. Chupa Chups sues Dulces Vero on the basis of a trademark infringement theory under the Lanham Act in a U.S. court. Suppose the evidence shows that "chupa" is a form of the Spanish verb "chupar," which translates as "to suck," and that "chupa" is a slang designation in Spanish for lollipops. In analyzing similarity of the marks, is the relevant comparison between CHUPA CHUPS and CHUPA GURTS? Between the English translations of CHUPA CHUPS and CHUPA GURTS? Between CHUPS and GURTS? Between the English translations of CHUPS and GURTS?

PROBLEM 7-3: SIMILARITY ANALYSIS FOR NONVERBAL MARKS

Consider whether the similarity rules of thumb, developed primarily in cases involving word marks, assist you in tackling the following problems, each of which involve marks having nonverbal components. If the rules of thumb do not assist you here, can you articulate additional rules of thumb?

(1) In connection with its FROOT LOOPS cereal, Kellogg uses the word mark TOUCAN SAM and the following toucan logo:

Toucan Golf planned to sell putters under the name TOUCAN GOLD and was using a "Golfbird" logo in connection with its products:

In determining whether the logos are similar for purposes of the likelihood-of-confusion analysis, should the court restrict itself to visual similarity? Or should the court compare all aspects of the TOUCAN SAM character with the GOLFBIRD character? For example, is it relevant that TOUCAN SAM speaks with a British accent while GOLFBIRD, to our knowledge, does not say anything? *See Kellogg Co. v. Toucan Golf, Inc.*, 337 F.3d 616 (6th Cir. 2003) (no similarity, relying on visual characteristics).

(2) Autozone, Inc., uses the following mark in connection with the retail sale of auto parts:

Strick used the following mark for retail automotive services including oil changes:

For purposes of the similarity analysis, should "ZONE" be excised from the mark, or would doing so violate the anti-dissection principle? *See AutoZone, Inc. v. Strick*, 543 F.3d 923 (7th Cir. 2008) (visual similarity when taken as a whole).

(3) ARI sold rice using a girl logo. Suppose that PRM also began selling rice using a girl logo, where PRM's girl was not identical to ARI's girl. For purposes of the similarity analysis, should it matter that customers frequently asked for ARI's product by requesting "girl rice"? Or is this an example of a case in which consumer practices should *not* be accorded weight in a similarity analysis? *See American Rice, Inc. v. Producers Rice Mill, Inc.*, 518 F.3d 321, 331 (5th Cir. 2008).

(4) Hansen makes MONSTER energy drinks, sold in the can shown below left, while National makes FREEK energy drinks, sold in cans depicting a "Freek Man" figure, as shown below right:

How would you evaluate the argument that the FREEK trade dress is similar to the MONSTER trade dress because the picture of the "Freek Man" evokes the word "monster"? *See Hansen Beverage Co. v. Nat'l Beverage Corp.*, 493 F.3d 1074 (9th Cir.), *vacated as moot due to settlement*, 499 F.3d 923 (9th Cir. 2007).

(5) Nora sold bottled water under the NAYA word mark. Perrier sold bottled water under various trademarks. Nora claimed that Perrier was infringing Nora's trade dress in the shape and overall appearance of the bottle. Suppose that the bottles are virtually identical in shape and overall appearance, but that Perrier's word marks and labels are not similar to Nora's NAYA word mark and label. Should Perrier's word marks and label features be taken into account when analyzing similarity? What are the best arguments on behalf of both parties? *See Nora Beverages, Inc. v. Perrier Group of America, Inc.*, 269 F.3d 114 (2d Cir. 2001).

NOTES AND QUESTIONS: STRENGTH FACTOR

1. *Conceptual versus market strength.* Courts have identified two types of mark strength: conceptual strength, referring to the degree of distinctiveness, and market strength, referring to the degree of actual recognition in the marketplace. Should "strength" under the likelihood-of-confusion analysis account for both conceptual and market strength? The *Virgin* court discusses the point, although it uses slightly different labels.

2. *Strength factor as duplicative or dominant?* Does the conceptual strength analysis merely duplicate the distinctiveness analysis? Or is conceptual strength best understood as a measure of the degree of distinctiveness, worth undertaking as part of the likelihood-of-confusion inquiry because it does not simply duplicate the distinctiveness analysis? If the strength analysis were perceived as duplicative, would you expect it to play only a minor role in likelihood-of-confusion analyses? *See* Barton Beebe, *An Empirical Study of the Multifactor Tests for Trademark Infringement*, 94 CAL. L. REV. 1581, 1636-37 (2006) (finding a strong correlation between market strength and the trademark owner's success on likelihood of confusion).

3. *Measuring market strength.* What types of evidence would you expect to use in order to establish (or rebut) market strength? Evidence of secondary meaning? Could that include evidence of copying? Evidence of confusion (or the lack thereof)? *See Vail Assocs., Inc. v. Vend-Tel-Co., Ltd.*, 516 F.3d 853 (10th Cir. 2008). Does it make any sense to use evidence of confusion to assess a confusion factor?

4. *Mark "fame" in the Federal Circuit's likelihood-of-confusion factors analysis.* The Federal Circuit maintains that the mark strength factor is dominant in the likelihood-of-confusion analysis, although the court frequently speaks in terms of mark "fame" rather than mark strength (perhaps an unwise choice of labels given that "fame" is a term of art defined in connection with the Section 43(c) dilution action, discussed *infra* in Chapter 8). *See, e.g., Recot, Inc. v. Becton*, 214 F.3d 1322, 1327 (Fed. Cir. 2000). Why should mark fame be dominant in a confusion analysis? Are stronger (more famous) marks more susceptible to confusion, or more resistant to it? Should mark fame dominate even where the products or services of the respective parties are unrelated? Should mark fame dominate in a Section 2(d) confusion analysis (the context for the Federal Circuit's decisions), even if it does not in a Section 32 or Section 43 confusion analysis? The Federal Circuit's confusion test also includes "the number and nature of similar marks in use on similar goods" as a separate factor. If the number is large (such that the mark is relatively weak and relatively narrow in scope), how should that cut—against the mark applicant (on the ground that a weaker mark is less worthy of registration), or *in favor* of the mark applicant (on the ground that where third-party uses are plentiful, consumers are conditioned to pay close attention to small distinctions)? *See In re Mighty Leaf Tea*, 601 F.3d 1342 (Fed. Cir. 2010) (addressing the issue).

5. *Distinguishing between fame for confusion and fame for dilution.* Should the test for fame for the confusion analysis under Section 2(d) be different from the test for fame for the dilution analysis? The Federal Circuit has differentiated between the two, describing fame in the confusion analysis as a matter of degree and fame in the dilution analysis as binary. *See Coach Servs., Inc. v. Triumph Learning LLC*, 668 F.3d 1356, 1373 (Fed. Cir. 2012) ("While fame for dilution 'is an either/or proposition'—it either exists or does not—fame for likelihood of confusion is a matter of degree along a continuum.") (internal citation omitted). Is this a plausible distinction? The court upheld a determination that the mark COACH for luxury handbags was famous for purposes of a confusion analysis, but not famous for purposes of a dilution analysis. Would it not simply make more sense

to jettison reference to fame in the context of Section 2(d) and use the language of mark strength?

6.   *Strong and famous . . . to whom?* Among consumers who buy high-end champagnes and eat at fine restaurants (we're speaking, of course, about Professor Dinwoodie), VEUVE CLICQUOT is a well-recognized brand of champagne. However, among the less-cultured masses who drink root beer and consider Taco Bell to be an "ethnic" restaurant (we give you Professor Janis), VEUVE CLICQUOT is entirely unknown. For the likelihood-of-confusion analysis, should a showing of fame among customers and potential customers of the goods in question be adequate? Or should one be required to show fame among the general consuming public? *See Palm Bay Imports, Inc. v. Veuve Clicquot Ponsardin Maison Fondee En 1772*, 396 F.3d 1369 (Fed. Cir. 2005).

7.   *Strong and famous . . . as of when?* Is mark strength (or fame, as the Federal Circuit calls it) measured as of the priority date of the mark at issue? Or can it be based on evidence that derives from later activities? *Midwestern Pet Foods, Inc. v. Societe Des Produits Nestle, S.A.*, 685 F.3d 1046, 1052 (Fed. Cir. 2012) (addressing the issue in the context of an opposition). Recall that a similar timing issue arose in connection with the MCDONALDS family of marks in the *McDental* case.

8.   *Analyzing strength of composite marks.* Suppose that a mark owner seeks to show that its mark AUTOZONE for automotive parts is strong, en route to showing that another firm's use of POWERZONE for electronics creates a likelihood of confusion. If the evidence shows that many third parties use marks containing ZONE for various products, does this diminish the market strength of AUTOZONE? Or must the evidence relate to the strength or weakness of the entirety of the mark? *See Autozone, Inc. v. Tandy Corp.*, 373 F.3d 786 (6th Cir. 2004); *see also Boston Duck Tours, LP v. Super Duck Tours, LLC*, 531 F.3d 1 (1st Cir. 2008) (analyzing the strength of the mark BOSTON DUCK TOURS for boat tours). What if the mark at issue always appears alongside a house mark? Does this inevitably diminish the strength of the mark at issue? *See Bridgestone Americas Tire Operations, L.L.C. v. Federal Corp.*, 673 F.3d 1330 (Fed. Cir. 2012).

9.   *Weak—and therefore "thin"—trademarks?* In a dispute between Florida International University (FIU) and Florida National University (FNU) involving the respective universities' names, acronyms, and related designs, the court observed that there was evidence of extensive third-party use of "Florida" and "University" among institutions of higher education in the state of Florida. The court concluded that Florida International's marks were therefore weak, but this finding also seemed to affect the court's views on some of the other likelihood-of-confusion factors. For example, in analyzing the similarity of the respective name marks, the court took the view that consumers would place significant weight on the difference (in meaning) between "International" and "National," because the universities were operating in a crowded field (one that the court had already described as a field having a high degree of commonality among university names). *Florida Int'l Univ. Bd. of Trustees v. Florida Nat'l Univ., Inc.*, 830 F.3d 1242 (11th Cir. 2016). Where there is evidence of widespread third-party use of a mark, should courts deem some trademarks to be "thin," and less likely to be infringed, reasoning that can be found in some copyright cases?

NOTES AND QUESTIONS: INTENT FACTOR

1.   *Intent as a mere factor?* Should intent be a prerequisite for any showing of likelihood of confusion, rather than being merely one of several factors? Should intent be required for some cases and not others—for example, presumed for cases in which defendant is using plaintiff's inherently distinctive mark, but required as an element of plaintiff's case where defendant is using plaintiff's non-inherently distinctive mark that is protected by virtue of secondary meaning? Or, perhaps, presumed for cases where defendant is using plaintiff's registered mark, but required as an element of plaintiff's case where defendant is using plaintiff's unregistered mark? Note that if intent is merely a factor, plaintiff could theoretically prove infringement without any evidence whatsoever of defendant's intent to confuse. Indeed, plaintiff could presumably prove infringement even in the face of defendant's well-evidenced subjective good faith.

2. *Presuming intent.* Intent is always difficult to prove and is ordinarily a matter of inference and/or presumption. In some courts, evidence of mark similarity, along with evidence that defendant had knowledge of the plaintiff's mark, triggers a presumption of bad intent. *See* J. Thomas McCarthy, McCarthy on Trademarks and Unfair Competition §23:115 (collecting authority).

3. *Presuming confusion?* Should courts presume confusion based on evidence of intentional copying? For conflicting views, *see Lois Sportswear, U.S.A., Inc. v. Levi Strauss & Co.*, 799 F.2d 867, 875 (2d Cir. 1986); *Bauer Lamp Co. v. Shaffer*, 941 F.2d 1165, 1172 (11th Cir. 1991).

4. *Intent to do what?* Should courts require something different from simple intent to copy—i.e., proof of intent to trade off the plaintiff's goodwill or to cause confusion, rather than mere intent to copy? What was the nature of the defendant's intent in *McDental?*

5. *Importance of intent.* Professor Beebe's empirical work suggests that "the intent factor, thought by some to be irrelevant, is of decisive importance," and that "survey evidence, thought by many to be highly influential, is in practice of little importance." Barton Beebe, *An Empirical Study of the Multifactor Tests for Trademark Infringement*, 94 Cal. L. Rev. 1581, 1622 (2006). Indeed, Professor Beebe argues that his data show that a finding of bad intent "creates a nearly unrebuttable presumption of a likelihood of confusion." *Id.* at 1628. Can you explain why this might be so?

6. *Rarity of intent-based standards in trademark law.* Intent-based standards do not play a major role in trademark law. The intent factor in the likelihood-of-confusion test, and the concept of the "good faith" junior user in the *Tea Rose* doctrine (Chapter 6), are rare examples of the use of intent-based standards in trademark law. When is intent appropriately made part of a trademark standard? Does this question link to the broader question about whether trademarks are more grounded in property law than in tort law?

7. *Opinion of counsel?* Should second comers have a duty of "due care" to avoid infringing the registered marks of first adopters? That is, suppose that firm *X* plans to begin using a given trademark and receives notice (say, actual notice) that firm *Y* has registered the mark. Should firm *X* have a duty to seek a clearance opinion from counsel, and failing that, be held to have acted with intent to confuse? Or should this evidence be relevant, if at all, only to the question of the appropriate remedy—e.g., enhanced damages and attorney's fees? *See infra* Chapter 12 for a discussion of the law of trademark remedies, including reference to opinions of counsel.

8. *Intent to copy product design.* Lubecore and Groeneveld compete in the market for grease pumps used in commercial trucks. Assume that Lubecore copied the appearance of Groeneveld's grease pump but labeled its pump prominently with its own trademark, and likewise used its own trademark on its sales literature. Suppose that everyone agrees that by copying Groeneveld's trade dress, Lubecore was specifically targeting consumers

who were familiar with Groeneveld's product and offering them another option. Is this the sort of intent evidence that cuts in favor of a likelihood of confusion? Does it cut against a likelihood of confusion? Suppose that customers testified that they assumed that the parties' products operated similarly and that they had a certain "comfort zone" with the Lubecore product because it appeared to be identical to the Groeneveld product. How, if at all, does this evidence affect your analysis of the intent factor? *See Groeneveld Transport Efficiency, Inc. v. Lubecore Int'l, Inc.*, 730 F.3d 994 (6th Cir. 2013).

NOTES AND QUESTIONS: BUYER SOPHISTICATION FACTOR; REASONABLY PRUDENT PURCHASER

1. *Expensive goods versus impulse purchases.* Courts frequently use the price of the goods or services as a proxy for the level of prudence that the reasonably prudent purchaser is attributed in any given case. That is, courts assume a greater level of prudence and care where the goods are expensive, and a lower level of care where the goods are inexpensive and/or are marketed for "impulse" purchases. Does this rule reflect actual consumer behavior? Should courts call for case-specific empirical proof?

2. *Reasonably prudent purchaser and mixed buyer classes.* Suppose that a product is marketed to a range of purchasers, from the sophisticated to the virtually clueless. How should a court construct an appropriate "reasonably prudent purchaser" profile in a "mixed buyer" case? By reference to the least sophisticated consumer? By reference to a weighted average? By some other default rule? *See Brookfield Communications, Inc. v. West Coast Entm't Corp.*, 174 F.3d 1036 (9th Cir. 1999) (discussing the alternatives); *see also McNeil Nutritionals, L.L.C. v. Heartland Sweeteners, L.L.C.*, 511 F.3d 350 (3d Cir. 2007) (looking to the "least sophisticated consumer," but only where the mixed class includes professional buyers). You might review the next two notes on the courts' approaches to separate buyer classes and professional buyers as you consider whether the Third Circuit's approach makes sense.

3. *Reasonably prudent purchaser and separate buyer classes.* Suppose that firm Z uses the mark VELO for professional-grade, concert grand pianos, which sell for $75,000 and up. Firm Υ uses the mark VELO for plastic harmonicas marketed to children at discount stores for $1.75. Who is the relevant "reasonably prudent purchaser"—the purchaser of products of the type sold by defendant (children, parents engaging in impulse buying) or the purchaser of products of the type sold by plaintiff (music professionals)? *See, e.g., Abercrombie & Fitch Co. v. Moose Creek, Inc.*, 486 F.3d 629, 634 n.2 (9th Cir. 2007) (suggesting that the relevant purchasers are those who purchase from the senior user). Many cases discussing the "reasonably prudent purchaser" standard assume a common buyer class, but that assumption does not hold for all cases. Suppose that an investment firm seeks to register "STONE LION CAPITAL" in connection with "financial services, namely investment advisory services, management of investment funds, and fund investment services." The firm markets its services only to high-end investors who invest significant amounts of capital. For purposes of assessing the consumer sophistication factor, is the proper frame of reference the services as specified in the application (which would extend to all potential customers) or the services as actually rendered in practice (high-end customers only)? *See Stone Lion Capital Partners, L.P. v. Lion Capital LLP*, 746 F.3d 1317 (Fed. Cir. 2014).

4. *Professional buyers.* Courts generally assume that professional buyers are more knowledgeable and better able to discriminate among suppliers, thus reducing the likelihood of confusion for any given purchase. *See, e.g., Abercrombie & Fitch Co. v. Moose Creek, Inc.*, 486 F.3d 629, 634 (9th Cir. 2007). Does this assumption strike you as well founded? Suppose that the professional buyer is an engineer buying sophisticated testing equipment. The engineer is undoubtedly knowledgeable about the products, but why should we assume that this knowledge will lead to less confusion? Might the engineer's knowledge actually tend to lead him or her astray (e.g., familiarity with certain testing equipment led the engineer to notice that firm *X*'s equipment is always marketed in a light blue case; consequently, the engineer assumes that testing equipment produced by firm *Y*, but marketed in a light blue case, originates from firm *X*, or assumes that firm *Y* must be affiliated with firm *X*)? It seems to us that this is a plausible scenario (engineers being notorious for their attention to detail — and possible tendency to miss the forest for the trees). In any event, courts should not reflexively assess confusion through the eyes of the general public when the relevant consumers of the goods or services at issue are specialists. *See, e.g., Caliber Auto. Liquidators, Inc. v. Premier Chrysler, Jeep, Dodge, LLC*, 605 F.3d 931 (11th Cir. 2010) (reversing where the lower court considered evidence as to the general public's confusion, and the services at issue were marketed to car retailers, not the general public).

5. *Rhetoric and reality.* Is the concept of the "reasonably prudent purchaser" simply a legal fiction used by courts to set the level at which trademark law will as a matter of policy regulate the marketplace? If so, to what extent should the courts be making an effort to connect this legal fiction to empirical realities about consumer behavior? *See* Graeme B. Dinwoodie, *What Linguistics Can Do for Trademark Law, in* INTERDISCIPLINARY PERSPECTIVES ON TRADE MARKS (Ginsburg, Bently & Davis eds.) (Cambridge Univ. Press 2007). For that matter, could any of the other likelihood-of-confusion factors be better explained as legal fictions or proxies for a variety of policy objectives rather than as direct empirical measures of consumer behavior?

Regardless of whether other policy objectives are at play, courts have found it useful to invoke hypothetical purchaser characteristics as a lens through which to view the confusion analysis. U.S. courts generally refer to the "reasonably prudent purchaser." U.K. courts deciding common law passing off cases have, on occasion, colorfully remonstrated that they are not seeking to be so paternalistic as to protect "a moron in a hurry." *See Morning Star Cooperative Society Ltd. v. Express Newspapers Ltd.*, [1979] F.S.R. 113, 117 (Ch. D. 1978) (UK) (only "a moron in a hurry" would confuse defendant's and plaintiff's products); *see also Mattel, Inc. v. 3894207 Canada, Inc.*, 2006 S.C.C. 22 (2006) (declining to adopt the "moron in a hurry" standard, instead adopting the "ordinary casual consumer somewhat in a hurry" standard). Do these various articulations implicitly confirm that courts are concerned not with empirical reality but with an idealized or normative view of consumer behavior? What if the evidence in a case shows that the products at issue (New York Yankees merchandise comes to our minds) really are purchased by morons in a hurry? Should courts take such reality into account and cast aside their idealized view of consumer behavior? *See Dippin' Dots, Inc. v. Frosty Bites Distribution, LLC*, 369 F.3d 1197, 1209 (11th Cir. 2004) (concluding that the plaintiffs' and defendants' logos "are so different that no reasonable jury could find that even a hurried 8-18 year old impulse shopper could confuse them"); *see also Ty, Inc. v. Softbelly's, Inc.*, 517 F.3d 494 (7th Cir. 2008) (SCREENIE BABIES — for plush bean bag animals used to clean computer monitor screens — likely to cause confusion with BEANIE BABIES for bean bag toys, especially in view of the fact that children who play with BEANIE BABIES toys may also use computers). *See also Atomic Energy of Canada, Ltd. v. Areva NP Canada Ltd.*, 2009 F.C. 980 (Fed. Ct. Canada 2009) (in a case involving logos used in connection with nuclear reactor parts, the level of care and sophistication among relevant consumers was high, and "the fact that Homer Simpson may be confused is insufficient to find confusion").

NOTES AND QUESTIONS: ACTUAL CONFUSION FACTOR

1.   *Likelihood of confusion in the absence of actual confusion?* As we discussed in section A of this chapter, courts have long recited the rule that actual confusion is not a requirement for trademark infringement; only likelihood of confusion need be shown. *See, e.g., Venture Tape Corp. v. McGills Glass Warehouse*, 540 F.3d 56 (1st Cir. 2008) (evidence of actual confusion not required). Are these long-standing recitations mere lip service? Will courts really find a likelihood of confusion in the utter absence of any actual confusion evidence, as the rule implies? *See* Barton Beebe, *An Empirical Study of the Multifactor Tests for Trademark Infringement*, 94 Cal. L. Rev 1581 (2006). What conclusions do you draw from the discussion of this issue in *Libman*? In *Boston Duck Tours, LP v. Super Duck Tours, LLC*, 531 F.3d 1 (1st Cir. 2008), the plaintiff used BOSTON DUCK TOURS and defendant used SUPER DUCK TOURS, both for sightseeing tours in Boston using renovated amphibious army vehicles ("ducks"). The court discounted evidence of actual confusion on the grounds that confusion likely sprang from the plaintiff's "lack of competition in its early years" and its use of a generic phrase (duck tours) for its services. Is this persuasive?

2.   *Actual confusion and damages.* Courts typically hold that a trademark owner who seeks damages must show actual confusion. *See, e.g., Web Printing Controls Co. v. Oxy-Dry Corp.*, 906 F.2d 1202 (7th Cir. 1990) (asserting that a Lanham Act plaintiff seeking damages must show actual confusion resulting in actual injury in the form of lost sales or other injuries); *see also Boosey & Hawkes Music Publishers, Ltd. v. Walt Disney Co.*, 145 F.3d 481, 493 (2d Cir. 1998) (asserting that Second Circuit case law is "well settled" that Lanham Act plaintiffs must prove actual confusion in order to recover damages, or may prove "that the defendant's actions were intentionally deceptive thus giving rise to a rebuttable presumption of consumer confusion"). *But cf. Master's v. UHS of Delaware, Inc.*, 631 F.3d 464 (8th Cir. 2011) (declining to impose a requirement for evidence of actual confusion where the defendant was a former licensee of the plaintiff, the alleged infringement involved uses allegedly outside the scope of the license, and the remedy sought was disgorgement of profits). *See* Chapter 12 for a more detailed treatment of remedies.

3.   *Proving actual confusion: survey evidence.* Trademark owners often present surveys as circumstantial evidence of actual confusion, and generally call experts to testify as to the survey methodology. The law of trademark surveys is a law unto itself. For a discussion of relevant precedent, *see, e.g.,* 5 J. Thomas McCarthy, Trademarks and Unfair Competition, ch. 32 (1996); Shari Seidman Diamond & David J. Franklyn, *Trademark Surveys: An Undulating Path*, 92 Tex. L. Rev. 2029 (2014) (concluding that surveys are especially valuable in trademark litigation in the pre-trial stage, where they may help in shaping trial strategy and in guiding settlement negotiations); *see also* John P. Liefeld, *How Surveys Overestimate the Likelihood of Consumer Confusion*, 93 Trademark Rep. 939 (2003) (identifying two categories of surveys that are allegedly prone to bias against new and lesser-known market entrants); *Smith v. Wal-Mart Stores, Inc.*, 537 F. Supp. 2d 1302 (N.D. Ga. 2008) (identifying two factors deemed particularly important in assessing survey evidence in trademark cases: the selection of the proper universe of prospective purchasers, and proper simulation of actual marketplace conditions in which prospective purchasers would encounter the mark).

The TTAB discussed the format of confusion surveys in *Starbucks U.S. Brands LLC v. Ruben*, 78 U.S.P.Q.2d (BNA) 1741, 1753 (TTAB 2006), a dispute between the owner of the STARBUCKS mark for coffee products and the producer of LESSBUCKS coffee. Starbucks had retained a marketing expert to design "a mall intercept survey involving interviews with two hundred respondents at shopping malls in eight geographically dispersed metropolitan areas." *Id.* The defendant challenged the survey questions as leading, but the TTAB found that the survey questions were consistent with the format accepted in its precedent. In particular, in prior cases, the TTAB had endorsed market surveys that followed the so-called *Ever-Ready* format (originating in *Union Carbide Corp. v. Ever-Ready, Inc.*, 531 F.2d 366 (7th Cir. 1976)). The *Ever-Ready* survey, which sought to establish confusion between defendant's EVER-READY lamps and plaintiff's EVEREADY batteries, flashlights, and bulbs, asked, "Who do you think puts out the lamp shown here? [showing a picture of defendant's EVER-READY lamp and mark]" and "What makes you think so?" *Id.* at 385 n.11.

In *Starbucks*, the survey posed the following questions to respondents who were apparently shown a LESSBUCKS label:

(Question 1a) "This is the name of a retail establishment that serves coffee, tea, and other beverages. Just from knowing this, have you formed an opinion about the name of a company that owns this retail establishment?"

Respondents answering yes to Question 1a were then asked:

(Question 1b) "What is the name of the company?"
(Question 2a) "Do you think the company that owns this retail establishment is connected or affiliated with any other company?"

Respondents answering yes to Question 2a were then asked:

(Question 2b) "What other company?"
(Question 3a) "Do you think the company that owns this retail establishment has authorization, permission or approval from another company to use this name?"

Respondents answering yes to Question 3a were then asked:

(Question 3b) "From what other company?"

The TTAB noted that Question 1a followed the *Ever-Ready* format, and hence was acceptable, and that Questions 2 and 3 "were designed to elicit responses concerning sponsorship, affiliation, permission and approval," consistent with the language of the Lanham Act, and should be deemed appropriate even though they were not explicitly asked in the *Ever-Ready* survey. *Starbucks*, 78 U.S.P.Q.2d (BNA) at 1753. Moreover, each of the three questions included a follow-up question: "What makes you think so?" The TTAB found this question helpful in revealing whether the respondents were "merely guessing" (also, incidentally, a long-standing tactic employed by law professors). *Id.* For other cases discussing the *Ever-Ready* survey format, *see Carl Karcher Enters. Inc. v. Stars Restaurants Corp.*, 35 U.S.P.Q.2d (BNA) 1125, 1132 (TTAB 1995); *Miles Labs. Inc. v. Naturally Vitamin Supplements Inc.*, 1 U.S.P.Q.2d (BNA) 1445 (TTAB 1986).

One commentator observes that the *Ever-Ready* survey format is appropriate for marks that are highly accessible in a consumer's memory—i.e., marks that are strong, at least from a market perspective. *See* Jerre B. Swann, *Likelihood of Confusion Studies and the Straitened Scope of Squirt*, 98 TRADEMARK REP. 739 (2008). Another survey format—the so-called

Squirt survey, from *Squirtco v. Seven-Up Co.*, 628 F.2d 1086 (8th Cir. 1980)—may be more appropriate for weaker marks, because that survey makes the plaintiff's mark available to survey respondents as part of the survey questionnaire. *See* Swann, 98 TRADEMARK REP. at 740 ("Over time, the Squirt format has come to be used in cases where the accessibility of the senior mark in consumers' memory is low to non-existent, so that it must be made *externally available* to respondents as part of the survey design."). Does the *Squirt* survey present the danger that marks that do not ordinarily appear side by side will be presented to survey respondents in that way?

In *Fortune Dynamic, Inc. v. Victoria's Secret Stores Brand Mgmt., Inc.*, 618 F.3d 1025, 1036 (9th Cir. 2010), the Ninth Circuit pointed out that "technical inadequacies" in survey methodology are unlikely to render a survey inadmissible, although they certainly may be taken into account when deciding how much weight to accord the survey results. The district court had excluded a survey from evidence on the grounds that "the survey compared the products side-by-side, failed to replicate real world conditions, failed to properly screen participants, and was 'highly suggestive.'" *Id.* at 1037. The Ninth Circuit agreed that the survey had some shortcomings—it was "conducted over the internet (thereby failing to replicate real world conditions), may have been suggestive, and quite possibly produced counterintuitive results." *Id.* at 1037-38. However, these problems went to the weight to be given to the survey; it was error for the district court to refuse to admit it. *Cf. Water Pik, Inc. v. Med-Systems, Inc.*, 726 F.3d 1136 (10th Cir. 2013) (upholding summary judgment of no infringement; mark owner's survey evidence was admissible, but was deemed to contain numerous methodological flaws and thus did not even raise a triable issue of fact). In *Kraft Foods Group Brands LLC v. Cracker Barrel Old Country Store, Inc.*, 735 F.3d 735 (7th Cir. 2013), Judge Posner thought it clear "that caution is required in the screening of proposed experts on consumer surveys," and reviewed some of the academic literature identifying numerous problems with surveys. Judge Posner's dim view of survey evidence of actual confusion expressed in *Kraft Foods* is worth comparing to the seemingly more enthusiastic view on actual confusion evidence expressed in *Libman*.

4.   *Evidentiary issues concerning trademark surveys.* Confusion surveys may generate difficult evidentiary issues. *See, e.g., Sears, Roebuck and Co. v. Menard Inc.*, 2003 WL 168642 (N.D. Ill. 2003) (excluding confusion survey evidence under *Daubert* standards). *See also* Kenneth A. Plevan, *Daubert's Impact on Survey Experts in Lanham Act Litigation*, 95 TRADEMARK REP. 596 (2005). In *First Nat'l Bank in Sioux Falls v. First Nat'l Bank South Dakota*, 679 F.3d 763, 768 (8th Cir. 2012), the mark owner had kept a "confusion log" on its website, where its employees had collected over 1,500 statements about alleged confusion. The mark owner offered the log as evidence at trial; the alleged infringer objected on the basis of hearsay. How should the court rule? Should the statements in the log fall under a hearsay exception because they reflected the customer's then-existing state of mind?

5.   *Quantity of actual confusion.* Suppose that only 10 percent of survey respondents in a confusion survey indicate actual confusion. Is this a good result for the trademark owner, given that 10 percent of millions of consumers could amount to fairly extensive potential damage? Or is this a terrible result for the trademark owner, given that 90 percent of consumers aren't confused? Courts have considered confusion levels even as low as 8.5 percent to constitute good evidence of confusion, and a number of courts would consider a 15 percent level to be strongly indicative of confusion. *See, e.g., Exxon Corp. v. Texas Motor Exch., Inc.*, 628 F.2d 500 (5th Cir. 1980). What does this suggest to you about the proper role of surveys in trademark infringement litigation?

NOTES AND QUESTIONS: RELATEDNESS OF GOODS/ CHANNELS OF TRADE/BRIDGING THE GAP

1.   *Evolution of the "relatedness of goods" factor.* The evolution of judicial thinking about the "relatedness of goods" factor is one of the more important transitions in the law of trademark infringement over the past century. As we saw in *Borden's* (section A of this chapter), some courts in the early 1900s strictly limited the trademark owner's rights, recognizing a cause of action only when newcomers used the owner's trademark on goods identical to those of the trademark owner. When the newcomer used the mark on goods that did not compete with the trademark owner's goods, the trademark owner was not entitled to redress, even if the trademark owner might later expand, or if the newcomer's goods were closely related to the trademark owner's goods.

The strict approach to noncompeting goods exemplified by *Borden's* began to erode long before the 1946 passage of the Lanham Act. In *Aunt Jemima Mills Co. v. Rigney & Co.*, 247 F. 407 (2d Cir. 1917), *cert. denied*, 245 U.S. 672 (1918), plaintiff used AUNT JEMIMA on pancake batter and defendant sought to use AUNT JEMIMA on pancake syrup. The court refused to be bound by a notion of identical goods:

> [W]e think that the goods, though different, may be so related as to fall within the mischief which equity should prevent. Syrup and flour are both food products, and food products commonly used together. Obviously the public, or a large part of it, seeing this [trademark] on a syrup, would conclude that it was made by the complainant.

Id. at 409-10. The court opined that the public might not draw the same conclusion if, for example, the mark "were used for flatirons." *Id.* at 410. Thus, the court was clearly willing to extend the trademark owner's rights to encompass use of the mark on related goods, but perhaps not beyond that. What is the "mischief" that the court thought that equity should prevent?

Judge Learned Hand arguably went further in *Yale Electric Corp. v. Robertson*, 26 F.2d 972 (2d Cir. 1928). Yale & Towne Mfg. Co. had used the mark YALE for locks and keys; Yale Electric used the mark YALE for flashlights and batteries. On the issue of whether Yale Electric's use created a likelihood of confusion with Yale & Towne's mark, Learned Hand emphasized the threat to Yale & Towne's reputation, even in the absence of actual competition between Yale Electric and Yale & Towne. Accordingly, concluded Learned Hand, a likelihood of confusion could occur, and Yale Electric should be enjoined from use of the mark on flashlights and batteries.

Several courts followed the lead of the *Aunt Jemima* case, extending rights to encompass at least related goods. The *Borden's* case quickly fell out of the mainstream. *See, e.g., Standard Oil Co. of N.M. v. Standard Oil Co. of Cal.*, 56 F.2d 973, 976-77 (10th Cir. 1932) ("Recent, well considered cases upon the law of unfair competition have expanded the narrow rule announced in the Borden Case to an extent that leads us to conclude that the Borden Case is out of harmony with the modern law of unfair competition."). Nims lauded this change as revolutionary:

> In this period [between 1917 and 1929], it has become well settled that actual competition between the parties to [an unfair competition] case, or actual competition between the articles sold by the parties to the action, is not essential. It is now recognized that the important consideration for the court is not competition, but possible deception of the public. It would be difficult indeed to appraise accurately, or perhaps to over-estimate, the extent to which this one change may lessen the use of false pretenses and deceit in the sale of merchandise to the public.

HARRY D. NIMS, UNFAIR COMPETITION AND TRADEMARKS iii (3d ed. 1929).

As Professor McCarthy describes, a reverse trend developed among some judges in the Second Circuit, notably Learned Hand, between the 1940s and the 1960s. *See* 4 J. THOMAS MCCARTHY, TRADEMARKS AND UNFAIR COMPETITION §24:66 (1996). Having authored the *Yale* opinion, Learned Hand seemed to revert to limiting trademark rights to identical goods, while other Second Circuit judges, notably Augustus Hand, invoked the relatedness factor.

However, apart from this reversal, cases from the period show a steady trend toward acceptance of the use of "relatedness of goods" as a factor in adjudicating confusion, rather than imposing an absolute requirement of identity of goods. The *Fleischmann* case (section A of this chapter) exemplifies courts' ready acceptance of the relatedness factor under the 1946 version of the Lanham Act.

The 1962 amendments to the Lanham Act removing the "source of origin" language may have made it even easier for courts to find trademark infringement liability in cases of "related" or even "noncompeting" goods. Consider *Syntex Laboratories, Inc. v. Norwich Pharmacal Co.*, 437 F.2d 566 (2d Cir. 1971). The case involved pharmaceuticals (specifically, Syntex's VAGITROL for an antibacterial cream, and Norwich's VAGESTROL for a suppository). The products were not in any sense interchangeable. Norwich's product was potentially harmful for people with a personal or family history of breast cancer, and Syntex's product was potentially harmful for people who were allergic to sulfa-based drugs. Arguably, the evidence in the case did not show likelihood of confusion among ordinary purchasers as to the *source of origin* of defendant's product. However, the evidence did show that some physicians and pharmacists mistakenly thought that the *products* might be interchangeable—i.e., the evidence showed *product* confusion. The Second Circuit held that this latter evidence of confusion sufficed under post-1962 standards:

> In a case such as the one at bar, where product confusion could have dire effects on public health, looking to such confusion, in addition to source-of-origin confusion, in determining whether there has been trademark infringement, is entirely in accord with public policy, as well as with the Lanham Act.

Id. at 568-69 (footnote omitted).

In addition to *Syntex*, cases such as *Virgin* and *McDental* (in this section) illustrate that courts continue to find liability in noncompeting goods cases where other factors in the likelihood-of-confusion calculus point toward confusion. In 1988, Congress codified the judicial expansion to provide liability in cases of false "affiliation," and "sponsorship," among others. This language is important in disputes over noncompeting goods.

The evolution toward protection of trademarks even as to noncompeting goods reflects not only technical statutory amendments, but also changes in the role of trademarks more broadly, as international standards of trademark protection confirm. *See* TRIPS Agreement art. 16(3). *See also Mattel, Inc. v. 3894207 Canada, Inc.*, 2006 S.C.C. 22 (2006) (confirming that confusion analysis extends to noncompeting goods under Canadian law).

2. *Rights in gross?* We have emphasized throughout this book that trademark rights are not property rights in gross in words and symbols; instead, they are rights to use words and symbols for particular goods and services. Does the multi-factor test for likelihood of confusion upset this model by expanding the trademark owner's rights so that they encompass use of the mark on noncompeting goods (i.e., "related" goods in addition to "identical" goods)? Or can the inclusion of a "relatedness of goods" factor be easily rationalized? For example, what of the argument that a trademark owner enjoys trademark rights not only in particular goods or services that the trademark owner currently sells, but also in goods or services into which the trademark owner might later expand as a natural course of business? Recall that we encountered the concept of a natural zone of expansion in Chapter 6.

Pay close attention to the "rights in gross" argument. It arises again as a response to the "dilution" cause of action (section A of the next chapter), under which liability may be imposed even where the defendant's goods or services are *entirely* unrelated to the plaintiff trademark owner's goods or services.

3. *Unfair competition in the absence of competition?* In the preceding note, we discussed whether the "related goods" factor facilitates the creation of property rights in words. What if we shifted to torts rhetoric? We might start by considering how to characterize the harm that occurs when a defendant usurps a plaintiff's trademark, but does so on goods that are merely "related" and not identical to plaintiff's. What harm does occur? Recall the rhetorical flourish of the *Borden's* case: There could be no "unfair competition," said the court, when there was no "competition." Even though the *Borden's* result has been soundly rejected, as described in note 1 above, isn't this nonetheless a powerful torts-based argument against extending a trademark owner's rights beyond "identical" goods/services? That is, where defendant does not take away sales from plaintiff, how can there be cognizable harm?

4. *Relevance of trademark owner's subjective intent to expand: bridging the gap.* Is the relatedness factor really about the intrinsic nature of the goods/services? Or is relatedness actually a matter of inquiring into the prospect that the trademark owner is likely to expand into the market for the related goods? If the latter, should the focus be on whether the trademark owner intends to so expand, or whether consumers perceive (even mistakenly) that the trademark owner is likely to expand? Consider, for example, *Scarves by Vera, Inc. v. Todo Imports Ltd.*, 544 F.2d 1167 (2d Cir. 1976). Plaintiff (Scarves by Vera) used the mark VERA in connection with women's scarves, apparel, and linens. The evidence showed that in 1969, Scarves by Vera had proposed joint ventures to expand into cosmetics and fragrances, but could not find an appropriate joint venture partner, and took no further steps on the proposal. Defendant Todo was the U.S. distributor for Vera S.A., a Spanish manufacturer of toiletries and cosmetics, and had distributed in the United States a line of men's cologne under the VERA mark. Suppose that many of the leading apparel designers also produced cosmetics and fragrances. What weight would you give that fact? Should the inquiry into gap-bridging give more weight to the producer's intent, or the consumer's perceptions? *See Westchester Media v. PRL USA Holdings, Inc.*, 214 F.3d 658 (5th Cir. 2000) (looking to consumer perception, not merely Polo Ralph Lauren (PRL)'s subjective intent, in assessing likelihood that Polo Ralph Lauren would expand into publishing magazine under POLO name); *Elvis Presley Enterprises Inc. v. Capece*, 141 F.3d 188 (5th Cir. 1998) ("controlling factor" is consumer's perception about likelihood of expansion, not trademark owner's actual intent as to expansion). Do you agree with the approaches taken in these cases?

5. *Consequences of delaying actual expansion.* In the *McDental* case, the court discusses the prospects that McDonald's may expand into the dentistry business, asking whether McDonald's is likely to "bridge the gap" (so to speak). To what extent should we allow trademark owners to reserve future markets for themselves? When we recognize liability in a related-goods case, we may, in effect, be allowing a trademark owner to reserve a future market—the market in the related goods—and it may be a long while before the trademark owner actually enters that market. Is this approach counterproductive?

What should courts do when the evidence shows that a trademark owner could have entered a related-goods market, but declined to do so, until after another had already become established in that market, at which point the trademark owner sued? *See Scarves by Vera, Inc. v. Todo Imports Ltd.*, 544 F.2d 1167 (2d Cir. 1976). For example, since the 1940s, PATSY'S PIZZERIA (a pizza restaurant located in East Harlem) and PATSY'S (an Italian restaurant located in midtown Manhattan) have coexisted, although the pizzeria opened a few years earlier than the Italian restaurant. Suppose that in the 1990s, PATSY'S Italian restaurant decides to begin marketing a pasta sauce under the PATSY'S name. Assume that PATSY'S PIZZERIA sues, alleging a likelihood of confusion and arguing that the Italian restaurant has usurped the pizzeria's opportunity to expand into the pasta sauce market—effectively a "bridging the gap" argument. Should the pizzeria prevail on this argument? *See Patsy's Brand, Inc. v. I.O.B. Realty, Inc.*, 317 F.3d 209 (2d Cir. 2003).

In general, what is the proper time frame for evaluating the relatedness factor? Would you support a rule that looked to the trademark owner's likelihood of expansion as of the time when the newcomer commenced use?

6. *Presumption.* If the defendant is using a mark identical to that of the trademark owner, on goods identical to those of the trademark owner, should a court presume likelihood of confusion? *See* TRIPS Agreement, Art. 16.

7. *Channels of trade.* Kraft sold cheese in grocery stores under the mark CRACKER BARREL. Cracker Barrel Old Country Store (CBOCS), which runs a restaurant chain, sought to sell a variety of food products (such as ham, but not cheese) in grocery stores under its logo, which features the words "Cracker Barrel." CBOCS was already selling these products in small stores adjoining their restaurants, and online, without any objection from Kraft. How important to the overall confusion analysis should it be that CBOCS is seeking to sell through the same distribution channel as Kraft? *Kraft Foods Group Brands LLC v. Cracker Barrel Old Country Store, Inc.*, 735 F.3d 735 (7th Cir. 2013). For another example, *see Kate Spade Saturday LLC v. Saturdays Surf LLC*, 950 F. Supp. 2d 639 (S.D.N.Y. 2013). Saturdays Surf sold men's apparel under the mark SATURDAYS SURF NYC from a website and through department stores such as Bloomingdale's. Kate Spade introduced a line of KATE SPADE SATURDAY clothing for women that it planned to sell from a website and through KATE SPADE SATURDAY retail stores. Are these different channels of trade, cutting against a likelihood of confusion? Is it relevant that the KATE SPADE house mark is very well known for women's clothing?

8. *Relevance of the designation of goods.* Where the mark is registered, the registration indicates the goods or service with which the mark is used. In infringement litigation involving a registered mark, how much attention should courts pay to the identification of goods? In registration proceedings, how much attention should be paid to the identification of goods? For an answer to the latter question, *see, e.g., Centraz Industries Inc. v. Spartan Chemical Co.*, 77 U.S.P.Q.2d (BNA) 1698, 1699 (TTAB 2006):

> With respect to the goods, as often stated, Board proceedings are concerned with registrability and not use of a mark and, thus, the common identification of goods in the registration and application herein frames the issue. *Cunningham v. Laser Golf Corp.*, 222 F.3d 943 (Fed. Cir. 2000); and *Canadian Imperial Bank of Commerce v. Wells Fargo Bank, N.A.*, 811 F.2d 1490 (Fed. Cir. 1987).

The issue may also arise in the context of opposition or cancellation proceedings. In one such case, M2 Communications was applying to register the mark M2 COMMUNICATIONS for goods identified as "interactive multimedia CD-ROMs containing educational information in the fields of pharmaceutical and medical product information, therapies and strategies, and medical, pharmaceutical, and healthcare issues. . . ." Another firm, M2 Software, had previously registered M2 for "computer software featuring business management applications for the film and music industries; and interactive multimedia applications for entertainment, education and information, in the nature of artists' performances and biographical information from the film and music industries." M2 Software initiated an opposition on the basis of its prior registration. In considering the "relatedness of goods" factor, how strictly should the TTAB read the limiting language in M2 Software's registration? That is, should the TTAB conclude that the goods are closely related because both are interactive multimedia products containing educational information? Or should the TTAB conclude that the goods are unrelated because M2 Communications multimedia products are directed to the pharmaceutical and medical industries, while M2 Software's products are directed to the film and music industries? *See M2 Software, Inc. v. M2 Communications, Inc.*, 450 F.3d 1378, 1380 (Fed. Cir. 2006).

In *Applied Info. Sciences Corp. v. eBay, Inc.*, 511 F.3d 966, 970-72 (9th Cir. 2007), the court discussed its approach to the issue:

> A registered trademark holder's protectable interest is limited to those goods or services described in its registration. . . . However, the scope of validity and the scope of relief for infringement are not coextensive. Although the *validity* of a registered mark extends only to the listed goods or services, an owner's *remedies* against confusion with its valid mark are not so circumscribed. The language of the infringement statute, 15 U.S.C. §1114, does not limit remedies for allegedly infringing uses to those goods within the ambit of registration. . . . Thus a trademark owner may seek redress if another's use of the mark on different goods or services is likely to cause confusion with the owner's use of the mark in connection with its registered goods. . . . In sum . . . [h]aving established a protectable interest by proving it is the owner of a registered trademark, the owner does not additionally have to show that the defendant's allegedly confusing use involves the *same* goods or services listed in the registration.

Do you agree with the court's reasoning?

9. *The "something more" standard.* In *In re St. Helena Hospital*, 774 F.3d 747 (Fed. Cir. 2014), the Federal Circuit reversed a Section 2(d) refusal to register TAKETEN for a ten-day residential health improvement program at an in-patient medical facility. The refusal had been based on a prior registration, TAKE10! for "printed manuals, posters, stickers, activity cards and educational worksheets dealing with physical activity and physical fitness." The court concluded that there was not substantial evidence to support the Board's finding that the applicant's services were similar to the goods recited in the prior registration. According to the court, in cases where the relatedness of goods and services is not self-evident, the PTO must show "something more" than the mere fact that the goods and services are used together. *Id.* at 753 (*citing Shen Mfg. Co. v. Ritz Hotel, Ltd.*, 393 F.3d 1238, 1244 (Fed. Cir. 2004)). For example, where an applicant sought to register BLUE MOON for beer, and the PTO asserted a prior registration of BLUE MOON for restaurant services, the PTO was required to show something more than just the fact that some restaurants are known to sell private label beer in order to establish that consumers would assume that the beer served in a restaurant has the same origin as the restaurant services. *In re Coors Brewing Co.*, 343 F.3d 1340 (Fed. Cir. 2003). In *St. Helena*, the Federal Circuit observed that its "something more" rule need not be limited to cases involving the alleged relatedness of restaurant services and certain goods. Instead, the court ruled, the standard applies "whenever the relatedness of the goods and services is not evident, well-known or generally recognized." *St. Helena*, 774 F.3d at 753. Does this suggest that the standard will apply in the majority of contested cases? Is this a good thing?

PROBLEM 7-4: RELATED OR UNRELATED? CONFUSING OR NOT?

Drawing from the rules on relatedness of goods, and your own knowledge of the products and services involved in the cases below, develop arguments for and against likely confusion in the following cases:

(a) GALLO for wine v. GALLO for cheese; *see E&J Gallo Winery v. Gallo Cattle Co.*, 12 U.S.P.Q.2d (BNA) 1657 (E.D. Cal. 1989), *aff'd*, 955 F.2d 1327 (9th Cir. 1992) (goods were related);

(b) V-8 for vegetable juice v. V-8 for vitamins; *see Standard Brands, Inc. v. Smidler*, 151 F.2d 34 (2d Cir. 1945) (goods were related, especially in view of plaintiff's advertising that emphasized that the juice contained vitamins);

(c) BLUE SHIELD for medical health plans v. BLUE SHIELD for mattresses; *see Nat'l Ass'n of Blue Shield Plans v. Standard Mattress Co.*, 478 F.2d 1253 (C.C.P.A. 1973) (mattresses were unrelated to health plan services even though the mattresses were argued to be "healthful" in nature);

(d) RITZ for hotels v. RIT-Z for toilet seats; *see Ritz Hotel Ltd. v. Ritz Closet Seat Corp.*, 17 U.S.P.Q.2d (BNA) 1466 (TTAB 1990);

(e) RITZ for bathroom towels and barbecue mitts v. RITZ for cooking and wine selection classes; *see Shen Mfg. Co. v. The Ritz Hotel Ltd.*, 393 F.3d 1238 (Fed. Cir. 2004). In this case, the court concluded that the relationship between cooking classes and kitchen textiles was akin to the relationship between restaurant services and beer, which is the sort of thing we expect will show up some day as an LSAT question.

(f) IKEA for retail furniture store services, various food items, and various educational seminars (including seminars for "personal development") v. AKEA for nutritional supplements. *Inter Ikea Sys. B.V. v. Akea, LLC*, 110 U.S.P.Q.2d (BNA) 1734 (TTAB 2014).

3.   The Factors Analysis Applied to Private-Label Goods

The following problem explores the question of whether the standard likelihood-of-confusion analysis should apply in disputes between major-brand manufacturers and manufacturers of so-called private-label goods.

PROBLEM 7-5:   LIKELIHOOD OF CONFUSION IN PRIVATE-LABEL GOODS CASES

In the late 1980s Conopco developed a new and improved version of its lotion product (VASELINE Intensive Care Lotion, or VICL) and decided to sell the new version in a new package—a different bottle shape and label from those used previously. Between the fall of 1989 and March 1990, Conopco spent over $37 million to promote the new version of the product and succeeded in placing the product with retailers throughout the country.

Ansehl, a private-label manufacturer, became aware of Conopco's new version of VASELINE and developed a competing private-label product, to be labeled with the diagonally striped black-and-white VENTURE logo and sold through Venture stores. Ansehl previously offered a product that had competed with the old version of Conopco's VICL product for approximately ten years. The illustrations accompanying this problem show the old and new versions, respectively, of both Conopco's and Ansehl's products.

Comparison of Original
Conopco and Ansehl Bottle

Comparison of Revised Conopco
and Ansehl Bottles

Conopco sued Ansehl for trademark infringement under Section 43(a), claiming trade dress protection in the new VICL bottle shape and label. Assume that validity, ownership, and unauthorized use were all properly established, leaving only the likelihood-of-confusion issue.

The evidence on the likelihood-of-confusion factors included the accompanying reproductions, the bottles themselves, and testimony from a variety of witnesses. The back sides of the respective bottles (not shown here) were similar, although the Venture bottle contained language in small print at the bottom of the label stating, "This product is manufactured for VENTURE, and is not associated with any national brand product."

Testimony established that Venture stores carried both the VICL product and the Venture private-label product, and that signage invited consumers to "compare and save." Testimony also established that the diagonally striped Venture logo appeared on store signs, on signs in the store's parking lot, on employees' badges, on other private-label products sold by Venture, and in Venture's advertisements.

A consumer, Mrs. Sickles, testified that she purchased a bottle of the private-label product thinking that it was the VICL product. She also testified that she assumed that brand name manufacturers secretly marketed lower-priced private-label brands. There was no evidence from consumers complaining of confusion between the old version of VICL and the old version of the Venture private-label product.

An employee of Ansehl admitted that he was instructed "to make the revised skin care packaging as close as possible to the VICL packaging." Survey evidence showed that approximately 83 percent of survey respondents taken from a national sample recognized the VICL bottle and label, even with all of the text (except the ingredients list) removed.

Analyze the likelihood of confusion. What are the best arguments for and against the trademark owner? How would you rule? Analyze the general policy implications of private-label marketing practices, drawing on your own experience as a consumer. Should private-label practices be presumed likely to give rise to confusion, such that case outcomes would rest upon private-label manufacturers' ability to rebut the presumption?

The facts are adapted from *Conopco, Inc. v. May Department Stores Co.*, 46 F.3d 1556 (Fed. Cir. 1994). For a more recent opinion applying confusion concepts to private-label goods, *see McNeil Nutritionals, L.L.C. v. Heartland Sweeteners, L.L.C.*, 511 F.3d 350, 367-68 (3d Cir. 2007). In *McNeil*, the Court of Appeals for the Third Circuit referred to the "danger" that producers of private-label products "will be held to a lower standard of infringing behavior" if courts develop a bright line rule that effectively gives private-label producers "per se immunity as long as the store brand's name or logo appears somewhere on the allegedly infringing package, even when the name or logo is tiny." Instead, the Third Circuit emphasized that lower courts should make case-by-case assessments of likely confusion taking into account the precise nature of the store brand label that is applied to the look-alike product. Thus, in the case before it, the court agreed with the district court's denial of an injunction with respect to the trade dress of most (but not all) of the store brand products at issue in the litigation. The court was particularly influenced to find no likely confusion by the prominent display of a well-known store-specific label. Is such an approach too protective of large stores? Is it consistent with approaches to the application of house marks? Alternatively, might there be some benefits (as well as dangers) from adopting a per se rule permitting the sale of store brands if the store brand logo is on the label given that, as the court was informed, "90% of consumers polled were familiar with store brands, and 83% bought them regularly"?

4.   The Factors Analysis Applied to Promotional Goods

BOSTON PROFESSIONAL HOCKEY ASSOCIATION, INC. v. DALLAS CAP & EMBLEM MFG., INC.

510 F.2d 1004 (5th Cir. 1975)

RONEY, Circuit Judge:

Nearly everyone is familiar with the artistic symbols which designate the individual teams in various professional sports. The question in this case of first impression is whether the unauthorized, intentional duplication of a professional hockey team's symbol on an embroidered emblem, to be sold to the public as a patch for attachment to clothing, violates any legal right of the team to the exclusive use of that symbol. . . .

None of the symbols of the various teams have been copyrighted.

[The district court ruled against the trademark owner on the Lanham Act claim.]

THE FACTS

The controlling facts of the case at bar are relatively uncomplicated and uncontested. Plaintiffs play ice hockey professionally. In producing and promoting the sport of ice hockey, plaintiffs have each adopted and widely publicized individual team symbols. During the 1971-72 season, more than eight million fans attended NHL games where they saw the team marks displayed on the jersey fronts of the players and throughout the game programs. For each game on national television, between ten and twenty million hockey enthusiasts saw plaintiffs' marks. Other fans observed the team marks during more than 300 locally televised games a season and on a weekly television series entitled "National Hockey League Action" which is syndicated in over 100 markets. These figures do not include the millions who were exposed to plaintiffs' marks through sporting news coverage in newspapers, magazines and on television.

Plaintiffs have authorized National Hockey League Services, Inc. (NHLS) to act as their exclusive licensing agent. NHLS has licensed various manufacturers to use the team symbols on merchandise and has granted to one manufacturer, Lion Brothers Company, Inc., the exclusive license to manufacture embroidered emblems depicting the marks in question. In the spring of 1972, NHLS authorized the sale of NHL team emblems in connection with the sale of Kraft candies. That promotion alone was advertised on more than five million bags of candy.

Defendant Dallas Cap & Emblem Manufacturing, Inc., is in the business of making and selling embroidered cloth emblems. In August of 1968 and June of 1971, defendant sought to obtain from NHLS an exclusive license to make embroidered emblems representing the team motifs. Although these negotiations were unsuccessful, defendant went ahead and manufactured and sold without authorization emblems which were substantial duplications of the marks. During the month of April 1972, defendant sold approximately 24,603 of these emblems to sporting goods stores in various states. Defendant deliberately reproduced plaintiffs' marks on embroidered emblems and intended the consuming public to recognize the emblems as the symbols of the various hockey teams and to purchase them as such.

THE LAW

The complaint alleged that defendant's manufacture and sale of the team symbols constitutes (1) an infringement of the plaintiffs' registered marks in violation of 15 U.S.C.A. §1114; (2) false designation of origin in violation of 15 U.S.C.A. §1125; and (3) common law unfair competition.

. . .

A cause of action for the infringement of a registered mark in violation of 15 U.S.C.A. §1114 exists where a person uses (1) any reproduction, counterfeit, copy or colorable imitation of a mark; (2) without the registrant's consent; (3) in commerce; (4) in connection with the sale, offering for sale, distribution or advertising of any goods; (5) where such use is likely to cause confusion, or to cause mistake or to deceive. A broadening of the protection afforded by the statute occurred by amendment in 1962 which deleted the previously existing requirement that the confusion or deception must relate to the "source of origin of such goods or service." Pub. L. 87-772, §17, 76 Stat. 773 (1962).

. . .

THE CASE

The difficulty with this case stems from the fact that a reproduction of the trademark itself is being sold, unattached to any other goods or services. The statutory and case law of trademarks is oriented toward the use of such marks to sell something other than the mark itself. The district court thought that to give plaintiffs protection in this case would be tantamount to the creation of a copyright monopoly for designs that were not copyrighted. The copyright laws are based on an entirely different concept than the trademark laws, and contemplate that the copyrighted material, like patented ideas, will eventually pass into the public domain. The trademark laws are based on the needed protection of the public and business interests and there is no reason why trademarks should ever pass into the public domain by the mere passage of time.

Although our decision here may slightly tilt the trademark laws from the purpose of protecting the public to the protection of the business interests of plaintiffs, we think that the two become so intermeshed when viewed against the backdrop of the common law of unfair competition that both the public and plaintiffs are better served by granting the relief sought by plaintiffs.

Underlying our decision are three persuasive points. First, the major commercial value of the emblems is derived from the efforts of plaintiffs. Second, defendant sought and ostensibly would have asserted, if obtained, an exclusive right to make and sell the emblems. Third, the sale of a reproduction of the trademark itself on an emblem is an accepted use of such team symbols in connection with the type of activity in which the business of professional sports is engaged. We need not deal here with the concept of whether every artistic reproduction of the symbol would infringe upon plaintiffs' rights. We restrict ourselves to the emblems sold principally through sporting goods stores for informal use by the public in connection with sports activities and to show public allegiance to or identification with the teams themselves.

AS TO 15 U.S.C.A. §1114

Plaintiffs indisputably have established the first three elements of a §1114 cause of action. Plaintiffs' marks are validly registered and defendant manufactured and sold emblems which were (1) substantial duplications of the marks, (2) without plaintiffs' consent, and (3) in interstate commerce. The issue is whether plaintiffs have proven elements four and five of an action for mark infringement under the Lanham Act, i.e., whether the symbols are used in connection with the sale of goods and whether such use is likely to cause confusion, mistake or deception.

The fourth requisite of a §1114 cause of action is that the infringing use of the registered mark must be in connection with the sale, offering for sale, distribution or advertising of any goods. Although the district court did not expressly find that plaintiffs had failed to establish element four, such a finding was implicit in the court's statement that "in the instant case, the registered trade mark is, in effect, the product itself."

Defendant is in the business of manufacturing and marketing emblems for wearing apparel. These emblems are the products, or goods, which defendant sells. When defendant causes plaintiffs' marks to be embroidered upon emblems which it later markets, defendant uses those marks in connection with the sale of goods as surely as if defendant had embroidered the marks upon knit caps. *See Boston Professional Hockey Association, Inc. v. Reliable Knitting Works, Inc.*, 178 USPQ 274 (E.D. Wis. 1973). The fact that the symbol covers the entire face of defendant's product does not alter the fact that the trademark symbol is used in connection with the sale of the product. The sports fan in his local sporting goods store purchases defendant's fabric and thread emblems because they are embroidered with the symbols of ice hockey teams. Were defendant to embroider the same fabric with the same thread in other designs, the resulting products would still be emblems for wearing apparel but they would not give trademark identification to the customer. The conclusion is inescapable that, without plaintiffs' marks, defendant would not have a market for his particular product among ice hockey fans desiring to purchase emblems embroidered with the symbols of their favorite teams. It becomes clear that defendant's use of plaintiffs' marks is in connection with the sale, offering for sale, distribution, or advertising of goods and that plaintiffs have established the fourth element of a §1114 cause of action.

The fifth element of a cause of action for mark infringement under 15 U.S.C.A. §1114 is that the infringing use is likely to cause confusion, or to cause mistake or to deceive. The district court decided that there was no likelihood of confusion because the usual purchaser, a sports fan in his local sporting goods store, would not be likely to think that defendant's emblems were manufactured by or had some connection with plaintiffs. [cit.] . . . In this case, however, the district court overlooked the fact that the act was amended to eliminate the source of origin as being the only focal point of confusion. The confusion question here is conceptually difficult. It can be said that the public buyer *knew* that the emblems portrayed the teams' symbols. Thus, it can be argued, the buyer is not confused or deceived. This argument misplaces the purpose of the confusion requirement. The confusion or deceit requirement is met by the fact that the defendant duplicated the protected trademarks and sold them to the public knowing that the public would identify them as being the teams' trademarks. The certain knowledge of the buyer that the source and origin of the trademark symbols were in plaintiffs satisfies the requirement of the act. The argument that confusion must be as to the source of the manufacture of the emblem itself is unpersuasive, where the trademark, originated by the team, is the triggering mechanism for the sale of the emblem.

. . .

Reversed and remanded.

NOTES AND QUESTIONS

1.   *A property-rights-in-gross standard?* Consider the following continuum of confusion standards. On one extreme would lie strict standards, such as pre-1962 standards on likelihood of source confusion or even actual confusion. In the middle might lie post-1962 standards encompassing likelihood of confusion as to source, sponsorship, endorsement, or affiliation. *Boston Hockey* would occupy the opposite extreme, under which likelihood of confusion is established merely on a showing of the "use of a mark with the knowledge that the public will be aware of the mark's origin." *See Bd. of Governors of the Univ. of North Carolina v. Helpingstine*, 714 F. Supp. 167, 171 (M.D.N.C. 1989) (identifying *Boston Hockey* as an extreme standard and adopting the intermediate standard). Is this an accurate characterization of *Boston Hockey*?

Some courts have characterized the *Boston Hockey* decision as creating property rights in gross:

> Interpreted expansively, *Boston Hockey* holds that a trademark's owner has a complete monopoly over its use, including its functional use, in commercial merchandising. But our reading of the Lanham Act and its legislative history reveals no congressional design to bestow such broad property rights on trademark owners. Its scope is much narrower: to protect consumers against deceptive designations of the origin of goods and, conversely, to enable producers to differentiate their products from those of others. [cit.] The *Boston Hockey* decision transmogrifies this narrow protection into a broad monopoly. It does so by injecting its evaluation of the equities between the parties and of the desirability of bestowing broad property rights on trademark owners. A trademark is, of course, a form of business property. *See J. McCarthy, Trademarks and Unfair Competition* §§2:6-2:7 (1973). But the "property right" or protection accorded a trademark owner can only be understood in the context of trademark law and its purposes. A trademark owner has a property right only insofar as is necessary to prevent consumer confusion as to who produced the goods and to facilitate differentiation of the trademark owner's goods. *See id.* The *Boston Hockey* court decided that broader protection was desirable. In our view, this extends the protection beyond that intended by Congress and beyond that accorded by any other court. . . .
>
> Indeed, the court in *Boston Hockey* admitted that its decision "may slightly tilt the trademark laws from the purpose of protecting the public to the protection of the business interests of plaintiffs." 510 F.2d at 1011. We think that this tilt was not slight but an extraordinary extension of the protection heretofore afforded trademark owners. It is an extension we cannot endorse.

Int'l Order of Job's Daughters v. Lindeburg & Co., 633 F.2d 912, 918-19 (9th Cir. 1980) (proceeding to acknowledge that an emblem or logo on a promotional product could serve "secondarily" as a trademark if consumers inferred from the logo's presence that the promotional product was sponsored or otherwise endorsed by the trademark owner); *Univ. of Pittsburgh v. Champion Prods., Inc.*, 566 F. Supp. 711, 719 (W.D. Pa. 1983) (citing *Boston Hockey* and concluding that "[w]e believe that it is not the province of the courts to create a property right in gross out of legislation intended solely to protect the consuming public and ethical businessmen from the depredations of manufacturers of counterfeit or deceptive products"). Do you agree with this characterization of *Boston Hockey*?

2. *Retreating from* Boston Hockey. *Boston Hockey* has never been well received. Even the Fifth Circuit has retreated from any broad reading of the case. In *Kentucky Fried Chicken Corp. v. Diversified Packaging Corp.*, 549 F.2d 368 (5th Cir. 1977), the court emphasized that the *Boston Hockey* decision rested on the fact that the relevant consumers there were the buying public, who knew that the *logos* originated with the NHL, even if they did not believe that the *products* originated with the team. That knowledge was central to the finding of confusion in *Boston Hockey*:

> [T]he fact that the buyers knew the symbols originated with Boston Hockey supported the inescapable inference that many would believe that the product itself originated with or was somehow endorsed by Boston Hockey. Buyers may have had no reason to expect Boston Hockey to possess expertise in manufacturing shoulder patches, but to a Bruins fan the club's endorsement would be much more important than the quality of the stitchery. And Boston Hockey had every right to reap the rewards of its trademark's popularity.

Id. at 389. However, the *Kentucky Fried Chicken* court proceeded to say that *Boston Hockey* did not lay down a general principle that the "certain knowledge" of buyers gave rise to this "inescapable inference" of confusion. Where the buyers were not the consuming public, but were Kentucky Fried Chicken franchisees who were presumably familiar with the corporate operation, "the inference is . . . much weaker that the buyers will believe that the source of a trademark-bearing product is the same as the source of the mark itself." *Id.* If this is correct, how would you restate the holding in *Boston Hockey*?

In another important case, *Bd. of Supervisors for Louisiana State Univ. Agric. & Mech. Coll. v. Smack Apparel Co.*, 550 F.3d 465 (5th Cir. 2008), the Fifth Circuit reinforced the point that a confusion analysis was still required in merchandising cases notwithstanding language in *Boston Hockey* that might appear to dispense with it. The court recounted its post-*Boston Hockey* case law:

> [I]n [*Kentucky Fried Chicken*], we recognized that *Boston Hockey* might be read to dispose of the confusion issue when buyers undoubtedly know that the plaintiff is the source and origin of a mark. We reiterated that a showing of likelihood of confusion was still required. But we noted that the circumstances in *Boston Hockey* supported the likelihood of confusion there insofar as the sale of products "universally associated" with the hockey team "supported the inescapable inference that many would believe that the product itself originated with or was somehow endorsed by *Boston Hockey*." In [the district court opinion *Rainbow for Girls v. J.H. Ray Jewelry Co.*, 676 F.2d 1079 (5th Cir. 1982)], which we upheld, also recognized in reference to *Boston Hockey* that "'(i)t is not unreasonable to conclude, given the degree to which sports emblems are used to advertise teams and endorse products, that a consumer seeing the emblem or name of a team on or associated with a good or service would assume some sort of sponsorship or association between the product's seller and the team.'"

Id. at 485 (footnotes omitted). The court conducted a standard likelihood-of-confusion test and found liability. The Eleventh Circuit likewise strained to distance itself from *Boston Hockey* in another merchandising case. *Savannah College of Art and Design, Inc. v. Sportswear, Inc.*, 872 F.3d 1256 (11th Cir. 2017).

    3.   *Legitimizing claims of trademark rights in promotional goods?* Is the promotional goods problem actually just a problem of the trademark system being too formalistic in its notion of "goods"? Or is it a deeper, conceptual problem of the inherent limitations of trademark rights? To approach this question from a practical perspective, consider the following. Suppose that the Johnson County Jaguars girls' softball organization uses a JOHNSON COUNTY JAGUAR logo on its uniforms, just as the NHL teams used logos in *Boston Hockey*. We might say conventionally that the Jaguar organization could assert trademark rights in the JAGUAR logo for services in the nature of a competitive girls' softball team. If the Jaguars organization also sells T-shirts, sweatshirts, and visors imprinted with the JAGUARS logo, could we not simply say that the Jaguars organization could assert trademark rights in the JAGUAR logo for "promotional goods"? Might we also allow the Jaguars organization to register the logo for "promotional goods"? *See, e.g., In re Snap-On Tools Corp.*, 159 U.S.P.Q. (BNA) 254 (TTAB 1968) (tool manufacturer entitled to register SNAP-ON for pencils and ball-point pens, to be used as promotional goods for manufacturer's tools). Would recognition of "promotional goods" as a legitimate classification of goods afford appropriate protection to the scores of trademark owners who sell collateral items to promote their trademarked products? Would recognition of "promotional goods" solve the *Boston Hockey* problem? Or would it simply be an effort to legitimize claims of property rights in gross in a mark?

    The TTAB's approach to the promotional goods issue is explained in *In re WNBA Enterprises LLC*, 70 U.S.P.Q.2d (BNA) 1153 (TTAB 2003). There, the Board allowed the registration of ORLANDO MIRACLE for posters, trading cards, game programs, and many other types of printed goods. The Board noted that the mark was inherently distinctive for the applicant's primary services—women's professional basketball events—and had no difficulty finding the mark inherently distinctive for the applicant's array of goods. Has the TTAB obviated the conceptual problem that promotional goods cases present? Or has the TTAB cleared the way for trademark rights in gross?

    4.   *Promotional goods and the circularity problem.* Suppose that a consumer purchases a sweatshirt bearing the logo of the JOHNSON COUNTY JAGUARS girls' softball team, as described in the preceding note. If the evidence shows that most consumers assume that the use of the logo on the sweatshirt is authorized by the Johnson County Jaguars organization, should that evidence be given weight in an infringement case? That is, if the evidence shows that consumers expect that a sweatshirt manufacturer needed to get permission to use the logo, is this a factor to be taken into account in concluding that the manufacturer did, indeed, need to get permission? Are you bothered by the circularity in the argument? Or are you persuaded that consumer perceptions should rule? What might have caused those perceptions to develop? For other manifestations of the circularity problem, *see, e.g.*, the *Balducci* case in Chapter 9 (circularity problem in the context of assertions of parody defense to trademark infringement).

5. *Aesthetic functionality.* Should the defendants in the *Boston Hockey* case (and in other "promotional goods" cases) have argued that the marks at issue were invalid under a theory of aesthetic functionality? That is, should the defendants have argued that the logos on such items "function" to allow consumers to signal their loyalty, and that third parties should be allowed to compete in the market for loyalty goods given that the logo is the most important ingredient in the commercial success of the product? Or is this an overly robust assertion of aesthetic functionality that would undercut the incentives that the trademark system seeks to provide? *See Au-Tomotive Gold, Inc. v. Volkswagen of Am., Inc.,* 457 F.3d 1062 (9th Cir. 2006) (excerpted in Chapter 3).

6. *Social values of merchandising.* Does the social value of facilitating merchandising generally outweigh its social costs? Does your answer vary depending upon the identity of the mechandiser? For a study that raises questions about whether the conventional economic rationales undergirding trademark law extend well to merchandising, *see* Stacey L. Dogan & Mark A. Lemley, *The Merchandising Right: Fragile Theory or* Fait Accompli?, 54 EMORY L.J. 461 (2005). Now that you have read the case law on which merchandising activity rests, has your view of the social benefits of merchandising changed?

5. The Factors Analysis Applied Under Section 2(d)

LANHAM ACT

Section 2(d) [15 U.S.C. §1052(d)]

No trademark by which the goods of the applicant may be distinguished from the goods of others shall be refused registration on the principal register on account of its nature unless it—

. . .

(d) Consists of or comprises a mark which so resembles a mark registered in the Patent and Trademark Office, or a mark or trade name previously used in the United States by another and not abandoned, as to be likely, when used on or in connection with the goods of the applicant, to cause confusion, or to cause mistake, or to deceive. . . .

Recall that we previously encountered Section 2(d) in Chapter 4 (in disputes concerning priority of use). The PTO applies a multi-factor standard for Section 2(d) likelihood of confusion that does not differ materially from other multi-factor standards. *See* Figure 7-1 (in section C of this chapter), listing the Federal Circuit's *DuPont* factors. As a practical matter, the points of emphasis in a likelihood-of-confusion test applied by an examiner in an ex parte setting may differ from the points of emphasis in a litigation setting. For example, in litigation, the parties might be expected to produce substantial amounts of evidence on actual confusion—perhaps including sophisticated survey evidence, supplemented by expert testimony. This will not likely be the case in an ex parte setting, and the case law under Section 2(d) reflects as much. *See, e.g., In re Majestic Drilling Co., Inc.*, 315 F.3d 1311, 1317 (Fed. Cir. 2003) ("The lack of evidence of actual confusion carries little weight, especially in an *ex parte* context.") (citation omitted).

If an applicant seeks to register a mark in standard characters (e.g., CAPITAL CITY BANK for banking services), how would you assess the similarity of the mark compared to an earlier registered mark that is in a stylized form — for example, CITIBANK as shown below, owned by Citigroup? Suppose that Citigroup argues that the applicant might actually begin to use the mark in any of a number of stylized forms, some of which could conceivably be reminiscent of CITIBANK in its stylized form. Should that be relevant to the similarity analysis? Should this question be answered by assuming that the applicant would adopt only a "reasonable range" of stylized forms? *See Citigroup Inc. v. Capital City Bank Group, Inc.*, 637 F.3d 1344 (Fed. Cir. 2011).

citibank®

Prior to the Federal Circuit's decision in *Citigroup*, the TTAB had used a so-called reasonable manners test for assessing similarity of marks, meaning that if an applicant sought to register a word mark in standard characters, the PTO would consider all reasonable manners in which those words could be depicted. In *Citigroup*, the Federal Circuit rejected the reasonable manners test. The Federal Circuit concluded that "[t]he T.T.A.B. should not first determine whether certain depictions are 'reasonable' and then apply the *DuPont* analysis to only a subset of variations of a standard character mark." *Id.* at 1353. Instead, the TTAB should "simply use the *DuPont* factors to determine the likelihood of confusion between depictions of standard character marks that vary in font style, size and color and the other mark." *Id.* Moreover, "illustrations of the mark as actually used may assist the T.T.A.B. in visualizing other forms in which the mark might appear." *Id. See also In re Viterra Inc.*, 671 F.3d 1358, 1364 (Fed. Cir. 2012) (noting that the *Citigroup* decision "discarded the Board's 'reasonable manners' standard in favor of a standard that allows a broader range of marks to be considered in the *DuPont* analysis when a standard character mark is at issue"). In *Viterra*, the court concluded that its holding in *Citigroup* rejecting the reasonable manners test was not limited to inter partes proceedings (the procedural context in which *Citigroup* arose) but also applied in ex parte examination. *Id.* at 1364-65. The court also refused to limit *Citigroup* to its facts; the *Citigroup* holding applied to cases like this one, in which a standard character mark (XCEED for agricultural seeds) was being rejected under Section 2(d) on the basis of an earlier composite word and design mark:

The *Viterra* court did leave some room for future argument, noting that "[i]n rejecting the 'reasonable manners' test, we are not suggesting that a standard character mark encompasses all possible design elements of the mark. We leave for future cases to determine the appropriate method of comparing design marks with standard character marks." *Id.* at 1365 (proceeding to uphold the rejection).

Suppose that an applicant seeks to register the word mark JUST JESU IT for various clothing items, but actually uses the phrase JUST JESU IT set against a graphic of a "crown of thorns." Should the similarity of marks analysis consider the mark strictly as it appears on the application, or as it appears in actual use? *See Nike Inc. v. Maher*, 100 U.S.P.Q.2d (BNA) 1018 (TTAB 2011). Note that *Nike* was decided before *Viterra*. Would the TTAB have been compelled to change its similarity of marks analysis had the case arisen after *Viterra*? What of the similarity of goods factor: Is the proper comparison between the goods as specified in the parties' respective registrations and applications, or between the goods that the parties actually sell? *See Coach Services, Inc. v. Triumph Learning L.L.C.*, 668 F.3d 1356, 1369 (Fed. Cir. 2012) (declining to take into account the applicant's use on goods beyond those listed in its application, which would have arguably made the parties' goods more similar).

In PTO proceedings, which rely exclusively on documentary submissions in most cases, the likelihood-of-confusion analysis may focus on confusion factors that can readily be analyzed on the documents—factors such as mark similarity. *See, e.g., Bose Corp. v. QSC Audio Products, Inc.*, 293 F.3d 1367, 1371 (Fed. Cir. 2002) (noting the rarity of "[d]irect evidence" of mark fame in PTO proceedings and indicating that fame "may be measured indirectly, among other things, by the volume of sales and advertising expenditures of the goods traveling under the mark, and by the length of time those indicia of commercial awareness have been evident"); *Recot, Inc. v. Becton*, 214 F.3d 1322 (Fed. Cir. 2000) (noted *supra* in section C in the notes on the mark strength factor). In a case in which an applicant's mark is alleged to be confusingly similar to a prior registered mark under Section 2(d), what is the significance (if any) of the strength of the prior registered mark? Suppose that applicant seeks a registration for PEACE LOVE AND JUICE for juice bar services, and the owner of a prior registration of PEACE & LOVE for restaurant services opposes, citing Section 2(d). The evidence shows that many third parties used combinations of "peace" and "love" for restaurants or the like—such as PEACE LOVE AND PIZZA; PEACE LOVE AND BEER; and PEACE LOVE AND CHOCOLATE, to name only a few. Should this evidence be relevant to demonstrate that the opposer's mark is relatively weak, such that the applicant's use of similar terms is less likely to trigger confusion? *See Juice Generation, Inc. v. GS Enterprises LLC*, 794 F.3d 1334 (Fed. Cir. 2015). What other factors would need to be treated differently in the Section 2(d) context?

The following problems explore some special issues that arise in connection with Section 2(d) likelihood-of-confusion matters.

PROBLEM 7-6:   SECTION 2(d) RULE OF DOUBT?

Recall that in examining applications for compliance with Section 2(a), the PTO may apply a "rule of doubt"—i.e., a rule that gives the applicant the benefit of the doubt in close cases regarding Section 2(a), on the ground that the PTO can simply pass the application on for publication and potential opposition by parties who believe that the application does violate Section 2(a). Should the PTO apply the same approach under Section 2(d)? For example, assume that Professor Dinwoodie files an application for registration (of D. MAN for trademark law consulting services), and the PTO is considering rejecting the application under Section 2(d) on the ground that Dinwoodie's mark is confusingly similar to a prior registration of a mark (J. MAN for trademark law consulting services) owned by Professor Janis. If the case is close, should the PTO pass Dinwoodie's application on for publication and simply allow Janis to decide whether to undertake the burden of initiating an opposition?

PROBLEM 7-7: EFFECT OF PTO SECTION 2(d) DETERMINATIONS IN SUBSEQUENT LITIGATION

Professor Dinwoodie filed a Section 1(a) use-based application to register D. MAN for trademark law consulting services. The PTO examiner initially rejected the application on the ground that it was confusingly similar to a prior registration—J. MAN, for trademark law consulting services—owned by Professor Janis. However, after Professor Dinwoodie argued persuasively against the Section 2(d) rejection, the PTO allowed the application, and it was duly published.

(1) Suppose that the opposition period elapses and Professor Dinwoodie's registration issues. Professor Janis then discovers the registration and immediately files a trademark infringement lawsuit in federal district court, alleging that Dinwoodie's use of D. MAN for trademark law consulting services is likely to cause confusion with Janis's registered mark, J. MAN, for trademark law consulting services. Is the district court bound by the PTO's Section 2(d) determination of no likely confusion? If not, what effect should the district court give to the Section 2(d) determination—respectful deference? No deference? *See* Chapter 5.

(2) Suppose that the opposition period elapses and Professor Dinwoodie's registration issues. Professor Janis then discovers the registration and immediately files a cancellation petition with the PTO, arguing that the Section 2(d) rejection was proper. The PTO grants the petition and cancels Professor Dinwoodie's application. Undeterred by this apparent setback, Professor Dinwoodie continues to use D. MAN in connection with his trademark law consulting services. Professor Janis then sues Professor Dinwoodie in federal district court for trademark infringement, arguing that the court should give preclusive effect to the PTO's confusion determination in the inter partes cancellation proceeding. Should it?

In *B&B Hardware, Inc. v. Hargis Indus., Inc.*, 135 S. Ct. 1293, 1312 (2015), in an opinion by Justice Alito, the Court held 7-2 (Justices Thomas and Scalia dissenting) that "[s]o long as the other ordinary elements of issue preclusion are met, when the usages [of a mark] adjudicated by the TTAB are materially the same as those before the district court, issue preclusion should apply." *Id.* But the Court also remarked that "many registrations will not satisfy those ordinary elements," *id.* at 1306, and that therefore "for a great many registration decisions issue preclusion obviously will not apply." *Id.* Elsewhere in the opinion the Court elaborated:

> If a mark owner uses its mark in ways that are materially the same as the usages included in its registration application, then the TTAB is deciding the same likelihood-of-confusion issue as a district court in infringement litigation. By contrast, if a mark owner uses its mark in ways that are materially unlike the usages in its application, then the TTAB is not deciding the same issue. Thus, if the TTAB does not consider the marketplace usage of the parties' marks, the TTAB's decision should "have no later preclusive effect in a suit where actual usage in the marketplace is the paramount issue." [citing 6 McCarthy §32:101, at 32-246.]

Id. at 1308. So was the Court saying that issue preclusion might apply in theory, but rarely would in reality? (Justice Ginsburg filed a concurring opinion that seemed to express that understanding.) Or did the Court leave the door open for routine arguments of preclusion? On remand, the Eighth Circuit determined that "the usages of the marks adjudicated before the TTAB were materially the same as the usages before the district court," and ruled that the requirements for giving preclusive effect to the TTAB's ruling were met. *B&B Hardware, Inc. v. Hargis Indus., Inc.*, 800 F.3d 427 (8th Cir. 2015) (vacating and remanding to the trial court for further proceedings).

(3) Suppose that Juice Generation seeks to register the mark PEACE LOVE & JUICE (with design) for services (juice bars), and GS opposes on the ground that it owns registrations for a family of marks including the phrase PEACE & LOVE (for restaurant services). Yes, we know, it's ironic that owners of peaceful, loving marks would be duking it out with each other—but that's not important right now. When GS was registering its marks, it faced a rejection based on a prior mark, PEECE LUV CHIKIN (used in connection with chicken, we're assuming). If GS had argued that there were many third-party usages of "peace and love" such that consumers tended to distinguish among them even based on minor differences (like spelling "peace" as "peece") should this argument now be available for use against GS in the opposition against Juice Generation—specifically, to indicate that the GS mark must have a relatively narrow scope? *Juice Generation, Inc. v. GS Enterprises LLC*, 794 F.3d 1334, 1340 (Fed. Cir. 2015) (addressing slightly different facts). Patent law might offer an analogy here. It recognizes doctrines of "prosecution disclaimer" and "prosecution history estoppel" that prevent patent applicants from making a representation before the PTO (usually a representation that narrows the scope of patent protection) and then making a contrary representation in litigation. (This exercise of estoppel is different from giving preclusive effect to a PTO determination, of course, but it is worth considering here because, like the issue preclusion problems discussed in this Problem, the estoppel issue treats elements of the PTO administrative proceeding as limiting in later court proceedings.)

PROBLEM 7-8: EFFECT OF LITIGATION DETERMINATIONS IN SUBSEQUENT PTO PROCEEDINGS

(1) Use the facts from Problem 7-7, except assume that the PTO registered Professor Dinwoodie's D. MAN mark without ever discovering Professor Janis's J. MAN registration. Suppose that Professor Janis sues Professor Dinwoodie, alleging that the use of the D. MAN mark infringes the registered J. MAN mark. The court finds no likelihood of confusion, and the judgment becomes final. Then Professor Janis initiates a cancellation proceeding, arguing that Professor Dinwoodie's D. MAN registration should be cancelled on Section 2(d) grounds because it would give rise to a likelihood of confusion in view of Professor Janis's prior registration of J. MAN. Should the PTO dismiss the cancellation proceeding on the rationale that Professor Janis is collaterally estopped from asserting a likelihood of confusion in light of the prior litigation? *See Levi Strauss & Co. v. Abercrombie & Fitch Trading Co.*, 719 F.3d 1367 (Fed. Cir. 2013). For a more complex variation, *see Nasalock Coating Corp. v. Nylock Corp.*, 522 F.3d 1320 (Fed. Cir. 2008).

(2) Suppose that Professor Janis, instead of seeking registration, asserts common law rights in J. MAN for consulting services, suing Professor Dinwoodie under Section 43(a), for his use of D. MAN for consulting services. The court rules for Professor Dinwoodie, finding no likelihood of confusion. Later, Professor Dinwoodie seeks to register D. MAN for consulting services and various promotional items, and Professor Janis opposes, citing his prior use of J. MAN and asserting likelihood of confusion under Section 2(d). What is the preclusive effect of litigation determinations in subsequent opposition or cancellation

proceedings? Should Professor Janis be collaterally estopped from opposing the registration? *See Mayer/Berkshire Corp. v. Berkshire Fashions, Inc.*, 424 F.3d 1229 (Fed. Cir. 2005); *see also DaimlerChrysler Corp. v. Maydak*, 86 U.S.P.Q.2d (BNA) 1945 (TTAB 2008).

PROBLEM 7-9:   SECTION 2(d) AND CONSENT AGREEMENTS

Professor Dinwoodie filed a Section 1(a) use-based application to register D. MAN for trademark law consulting services. The PTO examiner initially rejected the application on the ground that it was confusingly similar to a prior registration, J. MAN for trademark law consulting services, owned by Professor Janis.

Professor Dinwoodie then approached Professor Janis and offered generous cash consideration if Professor Janis would consent to Professor Dinwoodie's registration. When Professor Dinwoodie agreed to throw in Chicago Cubs season tickets and a share of ownership in a Volkswagen Beetle, Professor Janis agreed, and they memorialized the agreement in a signed letter.

Professor Dinwoodie then presented the letter to the PTO as evidence that Janis did not consider Dinwoodie's registration as posing a likelihood of consumer confusion. What effect should the PTO give to the letter of agreement? Would the result be different if the agreement also contained a provision specifying that Professor Dinwoodie would only use the mark in connection with his consulting services in the greater Chicago metropolitan area, while Professor Janis would only use the mark in connection with his consulting services in the greater Iowa City metropolitan area (such as it is)?

D.   CONFUSION AWAY FROM THE POINT OF SALE

Is the Lanham Act concept of confusion confined to confusion occurring at the point of sale? As you read the following cases, consider three dimensions to this question:

(1) Does the language of Lanham Act §§32(1)(a) and 43(a) permit mark owners to assert claims of confusion other than point-of-sale confusion?

(2) Would recognizing claims of confusion away from the point of sale advance the policy goals of the trademark system? In particular, consider how you would explain the harm (if any) that occurs to mark owners as a result of confusion away from the point of sale?

(3) Should the test for claims of confusion away from the point of sale be the same multi-factor test that is used for point-of-sale confusion? If not, what adaptations should be made to the multi-factor test?

1.   Post-Sale Confusion

FERRARI S.P.A. ESERCIZIO v. ROBERTS
944 F.2d 1235 (6th Cir. 1991)

RYAN, Circuit Judge:

I.   THE FACTS

Ferrari is the world famous designer and manufacturer of racing automobiles and upscale sports cars. Between 1969 and 1973, Ferrari produced the 365 GTB/4 Daytona.

Because Ferrari intentionally limits production of its cars in order to create an image of exclusivity, only 1400 Daytonas were built; of these, only 100 were originally built as Spyders, soft-top convertibles. Daytona Spyders currently sell for one to two million dollars. Although Ferrari no longer makes Daytona Spyders, they have continuously produced mechanical parts and body panels, and provided repair service for the cars.

Ferrari began producing a car called the Testarossa in 1984. To date, Ferrari has produced approximately 5000 Testarossas. Production of these cars is also intentionally limited to preserve exclusivity: the entire anticipated production is sold out for the next several years and the waiting period to purchase a Testarossa is approximately five years. A new Testarossa sells for approximately $230,000.

Roberts is engaged in a number of business ventures related to the automobile industry. One enterprise is the manufacture of fiberglass kits that replicate the exterior features of Ferrari's Daytona Spyder and Testarossa automobiles. Roberts' copies are called the Miami Spyder and the Miami Coupe, respectively. The kit is a one-piece body shell molded from reinforced fiberglass. It is usually bolted onto the undercarriage of another automobile such as a Chevrolet Corvette or a Pontiac Fiero, called the donor car. Roberts marketed the Miami Spyder primarily through advertising in kit-car magazines. Most of the replicas were sold as kits for about $8,500, although a fully accessorized "turnkey" version was available for about $50,000.

At the time of trial, Roberts had not yet completed a kit-car version of the Miami Coupe, the replica of Ferrari's Testarossa, although he already has two orders for them. He originally built the Miami Coupe for the producers of the television program "Miami Vice" to be used as a stunt car in place of the more expensive Ferrari Testarossa.

The district court found, and it is not disputed, that Ferrari's automobiles and Roberts' replicas are virtually identical in appearance.

Ferrari brought suit against Roberts in March 1988 alleging trademark infringement, in violation of section 43(a) of the Lanham Act, and obtained a preliminary injunction enjoining Roberts from manufacturing the replica cars.

[Eventually, Ferrari obtained a permanent injunction.]

III.

To prove a violation of section 43(a), Ferrari's burden is to show, [*inter alia*,] that there is a likelihood of confusion based on the similarity of the exterior shape and design of Ferrari's vehicles and Roberts' replicas.

. . .

B. LIKELIHOOD OF CONFUSION

1. District Court's Findings

. . .

Summarized, the district court's findings on the *Frisch* "likelihood of confusion" factors are as follows:

Factor	Favor
1. Strength of the mark	Ferrari
2. Relatedness of the goods	Ferrari
3. Similarity of the marks	Ferrari
4. Evidence of actual confusion	No evidence
5. Marketing channels used	Roberts
6. Likely degree of purchaser care	Roberts
7. Roberts' intent in selecting "mark"	Ferrari
8. Likelihood of expansion of product lines	No evidence

[Reviewing the evidence, the appellate court concluded that Ferrari's mark—the exterior design of the vehicle—was "very strong"; that the similarity of the marks was indisputable because the exteriors were indistinguishable from one another, although Roberts sometimes sold vehicles with an "R" insignia added; and Roberts "conceded that his intent in replicating the exterior design of Ferrari's vehicles was to market a product that looked as much as possible like a Ferrari original," although Roberts also hastened to point out that he never represented to his customers that the vehicles were actually Ferraris. This amounted to "strong evidence that the public is likely to be confused by the similarity of the exterior design of Ferrari's vehicles and Roberts' replicas."]

2.   *Roberts' Objections*

Roberts disagrees with the legal significance of the district court's findings of likelihood of confusion. He argues that for purposes of the Lanham Act, the requisite likelihood of confusion must be confusion at the point of sale—purchaser confusion—and not the confusion of nonpurchasing, casual observers. The evidence is clear that Roberts assured purchasers of his replicas that they were not purchasing Ferraris and that his customers were not confused about what they were buying.

. . .

Roberts argues that his replicas do not violate the Lanham Act because he informed his purchasers that his significantly cheaper cars and kits were not genuine Ferraris and thus there was no confusion at the point of sale. The Lanham Act, however, was intended to do more than protect consumers at the point of sale. When the Lanham Act was enacted in 1946, its protection was limited to the use of marks "likely to cause confusion or mistake or to deceive purchasers as to the source of origin of such goods or services." In 1967 [sic, 1962], Congress deleted this language and broadened the Act's protection to include the use of marks "likely to cause confusion or mistake or to deceive." Thus, Congress intended "to regulate commerce within [its control] by making actionable the deceptive and misleading use of marks in such commerce; [and] . . . to protect persons engaged in such commerce against unfair competition. . . ." 15 U.S.C. §1127. Although, as the dissent points out, Congress rejected an anti-dilution provision when recently amending the Lanham Act, it made no effort to amend or delete this language clearly protecting the confusion of goods *in commerce*. The court in *Rolex Watch* explicitly recognized this concern with regulating commerce:

> The real question before this Court is whether the alleged infringer has placed a product *in commerce* that is "likely to cause confusion, or to cause mistake, or to deceive." . . . The fact that an immediate buyer of a $25 counterfeit watch does not entertain any notions that it is the real thing has no place in this analysis. Once a product is injected into commerce, there is no bar to confusion, mistake, or deception occurring at some future point in time.

Rolex Watch, 645 F. Supp. at 492-93. . . . The *Rolex Watch* court noted that this interpretation was necessary to protect against the cheapening and dilution of the genuine product, and to protect the manufacturer's reputation. *Id.* at 495; *see also Mastercrafters*, 221 F.2d at 466. As the court explained:

> Individuals examining the counterfeits, believing them to be genuine Rolex watches, might find themselves unimpressed with the quality of the item and consequently be inhibited from purchasing the real time piece. Others who see the watches bearing the Rolex trademarks on so many wrists might find themselves discouraged from acquiring a genuine because the items have become too common place and no longer possess the prestige once associated with them.

Rolex Watch, 645 F. Supp. at 495; *see also Mastercrafters*, 221 F.2d at 466. Such is the damage which could occur here. As the district court explained when deciding whether Roberts' former partner's Ferrari replicas would be confused with Ferrari's cars:

> Ferrari has gained a well-earned reputation for making uniquely designed automobiles of quality and rarity. The DAYTONA SPYDER design is well-known among the relevant public and exclusively and positively associated with Ferrari. If the country is populated with hundreds, if not thousands, of replicas of rare, distinct, and unique vintage cars, obviously they are no longer unique. Even if a person seeing one of these replicas driving down the road is not confused, Ferrari's exclusive association with this design has been diluted and eroded. If the replica Daytona looks cheap or in disrepair, Ferrari's reputation for rarity and quality could be damaged. . . .

Ferrari, 11 U.S.P.Q.2d at 1848. The dissent argues that the Lanham Act requires proof of confusion at the point of sale because the eight factor test used to determine likelihood of confusion focuses on the confusion of the purchaser, not the public. The dissent submits that three of the factors, marketing channels used, likely degree of purchaser care and sophistication, and evidence of actual confusion, specifically relate to purchasers. However, evidence of actual confusion is not limited to purchasers. The survey evidence in this case showed that members of the public, but not necessarily purchasers, were actually confused by the similarity of the products. Moreover, the other five factors, strength of the mark, relatedness of the goods, similarity of the marks, defendant's intent in selecting the mark, and likelihood of product expansion, do not limit the likelihood of confusion test to purchasers.

Since Congress intended to protect the reputation of the manufacturer as well as to protect purchasers, the Act's protection is not limited to confusion at the point of sale. Because Ferrari's reputation in the field could be damaged by the marketing of Roberts' replicas, the district court did not err in permitting recovery despite the absence of point of sale confusion.

. . .

[*Affirmed.*]

KENNEDY, Circuit Judge, dissenting:

The majority first misconstrues the scope of protection afforded by the Lanham Act by misapplying the "likelihood of confusion" test and reading an anti-dilution provision into the language of section 43(a). . . .

. . .

The majority never clearly defines the target group that is likely to be confused. Although [case law] counsels that purchasers must be deceived, the majority concludes that the target group is the "public." The majority errs to the extent that its analysis shifts from potential purchasers to the broader more indefinite group of the "public."

The eight-factor test contemplates that the target group is comprised of potential purchasers. For example, the importance of one factor—evidence of actual confusion—is determined by the kinds of persons confused and degree of confusion. "Short-lived confusion or confusion of individuals casually acquainted with a business is worthy of little weight. . . ." *Homeowners Group, Inc. v. Home Marketing Specialists, Inc.*, 931 F.2d 1100, 1110 (6th Cir. 1991) (quoting *Safeway Stores, Inc. v. Safeway Discount Drugs, Inc.*, 675 F.2d 1160, 1167 (11th Cir. 1982)). Two other factors obviously refer to potential purchasers: the marketing channels used and the likely degree of purchaser care and sophistication. Thus, three of the eight factors expressly focus on the likelihood of confusion as to potential purchasers.

. . .

To be sure, some courts have expanded the application of the likelihood of confusion test to include individuals other than point-of-sale purchasers. These courts have included potential purchasers who may contemplate a purchase in the future, reasoning that in the pre-sale context an "observer would identify the [product] with the [original manufac-turer], and the [original manufacturer]'s reputation would suffer damage if the [product] appeared to be of poor quality." *Polo Fashions, Inc. v. Craftex, Inc.*, 816 F.2d 145, 148 (4th Cir. 1987); *see Mastercrafters Clock & Radio Co. v. Vacheron & Constantin-Le Coultre Watches, Inc.*, 221 F.2d 464 (2d Cir.), *cert. denied*, 350 U.S. 832 (1955); *Rolex Watch, U.S.A., Inc. v. Canner*, 645 F. Supp. 484 (S.D. Fla. 1986).

In applying the test in this manner, these courts appear to recognize that the deception of a consumer under these circumstances could dissuade such a consumer from choosing to buy a particular product, thereby foreclosing the possibility of point-of-sale confusion but nevertheless injuring the consumer based on this confusion. The injury stems from the con-sumer's erroneous conclusion that the "original" product is poor quality based on his per-ception of a replica that he thinks is the original. These cases protect a potential purchaser against confusion as to the source of a particular product. Hence, even when expanding the scope of this test, these courts did not lose sight of the focus of section 43(a): the potential purchaser. The majority applies the likelihood of confusion test in a manner which departs from this focus.

The cases which have expanded the scope of the target group are distinguishable from the instant case, however. In *Rolex*, the counterfeit watches were labelled "ROLEX" on their face. Similarly, the *Mastercrafters* court found that the clock was labelled in a man-ner that was not likely to come to the attention of an individual. It is also noteworthy that the Second Circuit has limited *Mastercrafters* "by pointing out that '[i]n that case there was abundant evidence of actual confusion, palming off and an intent to deceive.'" *Bose Corp. v. Linear Design Labs, Inc.*, 467 F.2d 304, 310 n.8 (2d Cir. 1972) (quoting *Norwich Pharmacal Co. v. Sterling Drug, Inc.*, 271 F.2d 569 (2d Cir. 1959), *cert. denied*, 362 U.S. 919 (1960)). No evidence was introduced in the instant case to show actual confusion, palming off or an intent to deceive and, as previously noted, plaintiff does not use any name or logo affiliated with Ferrari on its replicas.

Further, these cases conclude that the proper remedy is to require identification of the source of the replica, not prohibit copying of the product. *See West Point*, 222 F.2d at 589 (stating that under such circumstances "the only obligation of the copier is to identify its product lest the public be mistaken into believing that it was made by the prior patentee"); *see also Coach Leatherware*, 933 F.2d at 173 (Winter, J., dissenting in part) (stating that "[a copier] thus has every right to copy [a product] so long as consumers know they are buy-ing [the copied product]"). Accordingly, even if I were to conclude that plaintiff's copies created confusion in the pre-sale context, I would tailor the remedy to protect only against such confusion; this would best be accomplished through adequate labelling. The major-ity's remedy goes well beyond protection of consumers against confusion as to a product's source. It protects the design itself from being copied. [cit.]

In sum, the relevant focus of the eight-factor test should be upon potential purchasers in the marketplace. Plaintiff's replicas present no likelihood of confusion because plaintiff provides adequate labelling so as to prevent potential purchasers, whether in the pre-sale or point-of-sale context, from confusing its replicas with Ferrari's automobiles. The majority errs by expanding the target group to include the "public," an expansion unsupported by the language and purpose of the Lanham Act. To the extent that the majority expands the target group, the test increasingly protects the design from replication and the producer from dilution, rather than the potential purchaser from confusion.

. . .

I would reverse and remand this case in order that the District Court could properly apply the eight-factor test used to determine the likelihood of confusion vis-à-vis potential purchasers.

NOTES AND QUESTIONS

1. *Statutory basis for post-sale confusion.* The Ferrari court cites the 1962 Lanham Act amendments as confirmation that the statute encompasses claims of post-sale confusion. Do you agree with this interpretation? Courts had recognized post-sale confusion prior to 1962. *See, e.g., Mastercrafters Clock & Radio Co. v. Vacheron & Constatin-Le Coultre Watches, Inc.*, 221 F.2d 464 (2d Cir.), *cert. denied*, 350 U.S. 832 (1955). In *Mastercrafters*, as in some other early cases, the court distinguished between confusion among purchasers and confusion among "secondary" viewers of the mark, which could include members of the public who are potential purchasers. Thus, you may see references in court decisions to "secondary" confusion rather than "post-sale" confusion. *See, e.g., Acad. of Motion Picture Arts & Sciences v. Creative House Promotions, Inc.*, 944 F.2d 1446 (9th Cir. 1991) (statuettes designed to resemble the "Oscar" award; referring to the likelihood that "secondary" viewers might mistake the award for an original even if the purchaser would not).

2. *What's the harm?* What harm, if any, does post-sale confusion cause? *See* Jeremy Sheff, *Veblen Brands*, 96 MINN. L. REV. 769 (2012). According to the *Ferrari* case, how might post-sale confusion harm a trademark owner? The Sixth Circuit supplied a more extensive answer to the question in *General Motors Corp. v. Keystone Automotive Indus., Inc.*, 453 F.3d 351, 358 (6th Cir. 2006):

> Even without point-of-sale confusion, knockoffs can harm the public and the original manufacturer in a number of ways, including: (1) the viewing public, as well as subsequent purchasers, may be deceived if expertise is required to distinguish the original from the counterfeit; (2) the purchaser of an original may be harmed if the widespread existence of knockoffs decreases the original's value by making the previously scarce commonplace; (3) consumers desiring high quality products may be harmed if the original manufacturer decreases its investment in quality in order to compete more economically with less expensive knockoffs; (4) the original manufacturer's reputation for quality may be damaged if individuals mistake an inferior counterfeit for the original; (5) the original manufacturer's reputation for rarity may be harmed by the influx of knockoffs onto the market; and (6) the original manufacturer may be harmed if sales decline due to the public's fear that what they are purchasing may not be the original.

The court also noted the standard countervailing considerations, asserting that "courts should be wary of overprotecting public domain ideas and works whose exploitation can lead to economic efficiency, greater competition, and lower costs for consumers." *Id.* In the case, defendants produced and distributed replacement grilles for plaintiff's automobiles. Defendant's grilles included a recessed area (a "placeholder") shaped to receive the plaintiff's "bow tie" emblem, long used in connection with plaintiff's Chevrolet vehicles. Defendants did not sell the bow-tie emblems. Defendants' packaging included clear markings indicating that the goods were not manufactured by General Motors, and its invoices also included disclaimers. Defendants sold generally to collision shops, which frequently decide which parts to purchase at the direction of insurance companies. On these facts, how would you balance the potential harms of post-sale confusion against the countervailing considerations?

3. *Post-sale confusion of whom?* When we speak of point-of-sale confusion, we are speaking of confusion at the point of sale (of course) *on the part of the purchaser.* When we speak of post-sale confusion, we are speaking of confusion after the point of sale (of course) on the part of . . . whom? Any member of the public who might observe the mark? Any potential purchaser of goods and services of the type who might observe the mark? Does the answer to all of these questions depend on the nature of the goods and services? What if the confused parties are users of the product in a large firm, and under the firm's structure the users have no influence on purchase of the products? Judge Kennedy, dissenting in

Ferrari, is clearly troubled by the problem of expanding the target group beyond prospective purchasers. Formulate arguments for identifying the target group and consider how the identity of the target group may affect the outcome of the post-sale confusion claim in the following three cases: *Lois Sportswear, U.S.A., Inc. v. Levi Strauss & Co.*, 799 F.2d 867 (2d Cir. 1986) (trademarked stitching pattern on the back pocket of jeans); *Hermes Int'l v. Lederer De Paris Fifth Ave., Inc.*, 219 F.3d 104 (2d Cir. 2000) (handbags duplicating the trade dress of high-end Hermès handbags); *Custom Mfg. & Eng'g, Inc. v. Midway Services, Inc.*, 508 F.3d 641 (11th Cir. 2007) (circuit board located inside the housing of a water meter reading system).

4. *What's the test?* To assess post-sale confusion, the *Ferrari* court applied the likelihood-of-confusion factors test. This reveals an important doctrinal point: The post-sale confusion claim is a species of the general group of likelihood-of-confusion claims; it is not a free-standing theory. When courts apply the factors test to assess post-sale confusion, what adaptations (if any) should they make to individual factors to ensure that the inquiry is not focused solely on the point of sale? Consider possible adaptations to the following factors: (1) similarity of marks; (2) intent; (3) actual confusion; (4) consumer sophistication/consumer care. See the following notes for some hints regarding the latter two factors.

5. *Adapting the actual confusion factor.* How would you construct a confusion survey if you did not know in advance whether confusion, if any, existed at the point of sale or away from the point of sale? As a judge assessing likelihood of confusion, what weight would you give a survey that showed a very small percentage of consumers confused at the point of sale and a very small percentage of consumers confused before the sale? Should courts adapt the actual confusion factor to permit the cumulative total confusion to be taken into account?

6. *Adapting the purchaser sophistication/purchaser care factor.* In a post-sale confusion case, how should courts apply the purchaser sophistication/purchaser care factor (or factors)? If the alleged post-sale confusion is being experienced by the general public, is this factor (or factors) relevant at all? In *Ferrari*, the court noted that the sophistication/care factor swung in favor of Roberts, but still found post-sale confusion.

7. Ferrari *revisited.* A more recent "kit car" case involved "body kits" designed to fit on top of a truck chassis to give the truck the appearance of a military vehicle—specifically, according to General Motors, the HUMMER vehicle, in which General Motors claimed trade dress. *Gen. Motors Corp. v. Urban Gorilla, L.L.C.*, 500 F.3d 1222, 1228 (10th Cir. 2007) (reviewing trial court's denial of motion for preliminary injunction); *Gen. Motors Co. v. Urban Gorilla, L.L.C.*, 2010 WL 5395065 (D. Utah Dec. 27, 2010) (judgment after full trial). The court relied on theories of both dilution and likelihood of confusion. As to confusion, the court concluded that the relevant consumer group embraced the "market as a whole," which extended at least to actual and potential HUMMER purchasers (high-income consumers aged 40 and above with families) and actual and potential URBAN GORILLA kit purchasers (described as typically middle to lower income, former military do-it-yourselfers).

2.   Initial Interest Confusion

Courts have recognized claims for initial interest (or "presale") confusion for some time. *See Mobil Oil Corp. v. Pegasus Petroleum Corp.*, 818 F.2d 254, 257 (2d Cir. 1987) (presale confusion allegedly caused by defendant's use of PEGASUS word mark, where plaintiff used flying horse logo mark said to depict Pegasus); *Grotrian, Helfferich, Schulz, Th. Steinweg Nachf. v. Steinway & Sons*, 365 F. Supp. 707, 717 (S.D.N.Y. 1973) (presale confusion allegedly caused by defendant's use of Grotrian-Steinway name for pianos), *modified*, 523 F.2d 1331 (2d Cir. 1975).

Initial interest confusion claims surged briefly to prominence in some early cases addressing online advertising practices, particularly cases involving the use of trademarks as metatags residing in the code behind websites. (Search engine algorithms in use at the time assigned significance to the metatags. If Janis surreptitiously included Dinwoodie's trademark as a metatag in the code for the Janis website, then consumers who used a search engine to search for Dinwoodie's site might receive results that also included the Janis site, and might mistakenly enter the Janis site, although they might quickly recognize their mistake.) In *Brookfield Commc'ns, Inc. v. West Coast Entm't Corp.*, 174 F.3d 1036 (9th Cir. 1999), the court indicated that the unauthorized use of another's trademark as a metatag might support a claim for initial interest confusion. The court analogized metatagging to the hypothetical use of misleading billboards on interstate highways in which one competitor (say, Burger King) puts up a billboard saying (falsely) "Exit here for McDonalds," hoping that consumers will exit, find only the Burger King, and patronize the Burger King. (Remember, this was in the old days, before smartphone apps and GPS.)

In *Playboy Enterprises, Inc. v. Netscape Commc'ns Corp.*, 354 F.3d 1020 (9th Cir. 2004), involving keyword-triggered banner advertisements for adult websites, the court invoked *Brookfield*, reasoning that initial interest confusion could arise when a user clicked on the banner advertisement generated as a result of the user's searches using the term "Playboy" in the mistaken belief that it was an advertisement for a Playboy site, only discovering the mistake after accessing the site. Judge Berzon, concurring in the result, agreed that banner advertisements that were unlabeled (as these were) might give rise to initial interest confusion, but doubted whether practices that merely presented consumers with clearly-labeled choices without actually diverting consumers should be actionable. In *North American Medical Corp. v. Axiom Worldwide, Inc.*, 522 F.3d 1211 (11th Cir. 2008), another metatag case, the court invoked *Brookfield* and *Playboy v. Netscape* and found initial interest confusion, reasoning that the search results were presented in a way that might suggest a connection between the defendant's and plaintiff's products.

More recently, courts have expressed considerable skepticism about initial interest confusion allegations, particularly in the context of online advertising practices. The next case illustrates the current trend.

MULTI TIME MACHINE, INC. v. AMAZON.COM, INC.

804 F.3d 930 (9th Cir. 2015)

SILVERMAN, Circuit Judge:

In the present appeal, we must decide whether the following scenario constitutes trademark infringement: A customer goes online to Amazon.com looking for a certain military-style wristwatch—specifically the "MTM Special Ops"—marketed and manufactured by Plaintiff Multi Time Machine, Inc. The customer types "mtm special ops" in the search box and presses "enter." Because Amazon does not sell the MTM Special Ops watch, what the search produces is a list, with photographs, of several other brands of military style watches that Amazon *does* carry, specifically identified by their brand names—Luminox, Chase-Durer, TAWATEC, and Modus.

MTM brought suit alleging that Amazon's response to a search for the MTM Special Ops watch on its website is trademark infringement in violation of the Lanham Act. MTM contends that Amazon's search results page creates a likelihood of confusion, even though there is no evidence of any actual confusion and even though the other brands are clearly identified by name. The district court granted summary judgment in favor of Amazon, and MTM now appeals.

We affirm. "The core element of trademark infringement" is whether the defendant's conduct "is likely to confuse customers about the source of the products." *E. & J. Gallo Winery v. Gallo Cattle Co.*, 967 F.2d 1280, 1290 (9th Cir. 1992). Because Amazon's search results page clearly labels the name and manufacturer of each product offered for sale and even includes photographs of the items, no reasonably prudent consumer accustomed to shopping online would likely be confused as to the source of the products. Thus, summary judgment of MTM's trademark claims was proper.

I.   FACTUAL AND PROCEDURAL BACKGROUND

MTM manufactures and markets watches under various brand names including MTM, MTM Special Ops, and MTM Military Ops. MTM holds the federally registered trademark "MTM Special Ops" for timepieces. MTM sells its watches directly to its customers and through various retailers. To cultivate and maintain an image as a high-end, exclusive brand, MTM does not sell its watches through Amazon.com. Further, MTM does not authorize its distributors, whose agreements require them to seek MTM's permission to sell MTM's products anywhere but their own retail sites, to sell MTM watches on Amazon.com. Therefore, MTM watches have never been available for sale on Amazon.com.

Amazon is an online retailer that purports to offer "Earth's Biggest Selection of products." Amazon has designed its website to enable millions of unique products to be sold by both Amazon and third party sellers across dozens of product categories.

Consumers who wish to shop for products on Amazon's website can utilize Amazon's search function. The search function enables consumers to navigate Amazon.com's large marketplace by providing consumers with relevant results in response to the consumer's query. In order to provide search results in which the consumer is most likely to be interested, Amazon's search function does not simply match the words in the user's query to words in a document, such as a product description in Amazon.com's catalog. Rather, Amazon's search function—like general purpose web search engines such as Google or Bing—employs a variety of techniques, including some that rely on user behavior, to produce relevant results. By going beyond exactly matching a user's query to text describing a product, Amazon's search function can provide consumers with relevant results that would otherwise be overlooked.

Consumers who go onto Amazon.com and search for the term "mtm special ops" are directed to a search results page. On the search results page, the search query used— here, "mtm special ops"—is displayed twice: in the search query box and directly below the search query box in what is termed a "breadcrumb." The breadcrumb displays the original query, "mtm special ops," in quotation marks to provide a trail for the consumer to follow back to the original search. Directly below the breadcrumb, is a "Related Searches" field, which provides the consumer with alternative search queries in case the consumer is dissatisfied with the results of the original search. Here, the Related Search that is suggested to the consumer is: "mtm special ops watch." Directly below the "Related Searches" field is a gray bar containing the text "Showing 10 Results." Then, directly below the gray bar is Amazon's product listings. The gray bar separates the product listings from the breadcrumb and the "Related Searches" field. The particular search results page at issue is displayed below:

MTM watches are not listed on the page for the simple reason that neither Amazon nor MTM sells MTM watches on Amazon.

MTM filed a complaint against Amazon, alleging that Amazon's search results page infringes MTM's trademarks in violation of the Lanham Act. Amazon filed a motion for summary judgment, arguing that (1) it is not using MTM's mark in commerce and (2) there is no likelihood of consumer confusion. In ruling on Amazon's motion for summary judgment, the district court declined to resolve the issue of whether Amazon is using MTM's mark in commerce, and, instead, addressed the issue of likelihood of confusion. In evaluating likelihood of confusion, the district court utilized the eight-factor test set forth in *AMF Inc. v. Sleekcraft Boats*, 599 F.2d 341 (9th Cir. 1979). Relying on our recent decision in *Network Automation, Inc. v. Advanced Systems Concepts*, 638 F.3d 1137 (9th Cir. 2011), the district court focused in particular on the following factors: (1) the strength of MTM's mark; (2) the evidence of actual confusion and the evidence of no confusion; (3) the type of goods and degree of care likely to be exercised by the purchaser; and (4) the appearance of the product listings and the surrounding context on the screen displaying the results page. Upon reviewing the factors, the district court concluded that the relevant *Sleekcraft* factors established "that there is no likelihood of confusion in Amazon's use of MTM's trademarks in its search engine or display of search results." Therefore, the district court granted Amazon's motion for summary judgment.

> . . .

III. DISCUSSION

To prevail on a claim of trademark infringement under the Lanham Act, "a trademark holder must show that the defendant's use of its trademark 'is likely to cause confusion, or to cause mistake, or to deceive.'" *Fortune Dynamic, Inc. v. Victoria's Secret Stores Brand Mgmt.*, 618 F.3d 1025, 1030 (9th Cir. 2010) (quoting 15 U.S.C. §1125(a)(1)-(a)(1)(A)). "The test for likelihood of confusion is whether a 'reasonably prudent consumer' in the marketplace is likely to be confused as to the origin of the good or service bearing one of the marks." *Dreamwerks Prod. Group v. SKG Studio*, 142 F.3d 1127, 1129 (9th Cir. 1998). "The confusion must 'be probable, not simply a possibility.'" *Murray v. Cable NBC*, 86 F.3d 858, 861 (9th Cir. 1996).

Here, the district court was correct in ruling that there is no likelihood of confusion. Amazon is responding to a customer's inquiry about a brand it does not carry by doing no more than stating clearly (and showing pictures of) what brands it does carry. To whatever extent the *Sleekcraft* factors apply in a case such as this—a merchant responding to a request for a particular brand it does not sell by offering other brands clearly identified as such—the undisputed evidence shows that confusion on the part of the inquiring buyer is not at all likely. Not only are the other brands clearly labeled and accompanied by photographs, there is no evidence of actual confusion by anyone.

To analyze likelihood of confusion, we utilize the eight-factor test set forth in *Sleekcraft*. However, "[w]e have long cautioned that applying the *Sleekcraft* test is not like counting beans." *One Indus.*, 578 F.3d at 1162; *see also Network Automation, Inc. v. Advanced Sys. Concepts*, 638 F.3d 1137, 1145 (9th Cir. 2011) ("The *Sleekcraft* factors are intended as an adaptable proxy for consumer confusion, not a rote checklist."). "Some factors are much more important than others, and the relative importance of each individual factor will be case-specific." *Brookfield Commc'ns v. West Coast Entm't Corp.*, 174 F.3d 1036, 1054 (9th Cir. 1999). Moreover, the *Sleekcraft* factors are not exhaustive and other variables may come into play depending on the particular facts presented. *Network Automation*, 638 F.3d at 1145-46. This is particularly true in the Internet context. *See Brookfield*, 174 F.3d at 1054 ("We must be acutely aware of excessive rigidity when applying the law in the Internet context; emerging technologies require a flexible approach."). Indeed, in evaluating claims of trademark infringement in cases involving Internet search engines, we have found particularly important an additional factor that is outside of the eight-factor *Sleekcraft* test: "the labeling and appearance of the advertisements and the surrounding context on the screen displaying the results page." *Network Automation*, 638 F.3d at 1154.

In the present case, the eight-factor *Sleekcraft* test is not particularly apt. This is not surprising as the *Sleekcraft* test was developed for a different problem—i.e., for analyzing whether two competing brands' *marks* are sufficiently similar to cause consumer confusion. *See Sleekcraft*, 599 F.2d at 348. Although the present case involves *brands* that compete with MTM, such as Luminox, Chase-Durer, TAWATEC, and Modus, MTM does not contend that the *marks* for these competing brands are similar to its trademarks. Rather, MTM argues that the design of Amazon's search results page creates a likelihood of initial interest confusion because when a customer searches for MTM Special Ops watches on Amazon. com, the search results page displays the search term used—here, "mtm special ops"—followed by a display of numerous watches manufactured by MTM's competitors and offered for sale by Amazon, without explicitly informing the customer that Amazon does not carry MTM watches.

Thus, the present case focuses on a different type of confusion than was at issue in *Sleekcraft*. Here, the confusion is not caused by the design of the competitor's mark, but by the design of the web page that is displaying the competing mark and offering the competing products for sale. *Sleekcraft* aside, the ultimate test for determining likelihood of confusion is whether a "reasonably prudent consumer" in the marketplace is likely to be confused as to the origin of the goods. *Dreamwerks*, 142 F.3d at 1129. Our case can be resolved simply by an evaluation of the web page at issue and the relevant consumer. *Cf. Brookfield*, 174 F.3d at 1054 ("[I]t is often possible to reach a conclusion with respect to likelihood of confusion after considering only a subset of the factors."). Indeed, we have previously noted that "[i]n the keyword advertising context [i.e., where a user performs a search on the internet, and based on the keywords contained in the search, the resulting web page displays certain advertisements containing products or services for sale,] the 'likelihood of confusion will ultimately turn on what the consumer saw on the screen and reasonably believed, given the context.'" *Network Automation*, 638 F.3d at 1153. In other words, the case will turn on the answers to the following two questions: (1) Who is the relevant reasonable consumer?; and (2) What would he reasonably believe based on what he saw on the screen?

Turning to the first question, we have explained that "[t]he nature of the goods and the type of consumer is highly relevant to determining the likelihood of confusion in the keyword advertising context." *Network Automation*, 638 F.3d at 1152. "In evaluating this factor, we consider 'the typical buyer exercising ordinary caution.'" *Au-Tomotive Gold, Inc. v. Volkswagen of Am., Inc.*, 457 F.3d 1062, 1076 (9th Cir. 2006) (quoting *Sleekcraft*, 599 F.2d at 353). "Confusion is less likely where buyers exercise care and precision in their purchases, such as for expensive or sophisticated items." *Id*. Moreover, "the default degree of consumer care is becoming more heightened as the novelty of the Internet evaporates and online commerce becomes commonplace." *Network Automation*, 638 F.3d at 1152.

The goods in the present case are expensive. It is undisputed that the watches at issue sell for several hundred dollars. Therefore, the relevant consumer in the present case "is a reasonably prudent consumer accustomed to shopping online." *Toyota Motor Sales, U.S.A., Inc. v. Tabari*, 610 F.3d 1171, 1176 (9th Cir. 2010).

Turning to the second question, as MTM itself asserts, the labeling and appearance of the products for sale on Amazon's web page is the most important factor in this case. This is because we have previously noted that clear labeling can eliminate the likelihood of initial interest confusion in cases involving Internet search terms. *See, e.g., Playboy Enters.*, 354 F.3d at 1030 n.44 (explaining that clear labeling "might eliminate the likelihood of initial interest confusion that exists in this case"); *Network Automation*, 638 F.3d at 1154 (same). Indeed, MTM itself argues: "The common thread of [the Ninth Circuit's decisions in *Brookfield, Playboy,* and *Network Automation*] is that liability under the Lanham Act can only be avoided as a matter of law where there is clear labeling to avoid the possibility of confusion—including initial interest confusion—resulting from the use of another's trademark." Thus, MTM agrees that summary judgment of its trademark claims is appropriate if there is clear labeling that avoids likely confusion.

Here, the products at issue are clearly labeled by Amazon to avoid any likelihood of initial interest confusion by a reasonably prudent consumer accustomed to online shopping. When a shopper goes to Amazon's website and searches for a product using MTM's trademark "mtm special ops," the resulting page displays several products, all of which are clearly labeled with the product's name and manufacturer in large, bright, bold letters and includes a photograph of the item. In fact, the manufacturer's name is listed twice. For example, the first result is "*Luminox Men's 8401 Black Ops Watch* by Luminox." The second result is "*Chase-Durer Men's 246.4BB7-XL-BR Special Forces 1000XL Black Ionic-Plated Underwater Demolition Team Watch* by Chase-Durer." Because Amazon clearly labels each of the products for sale by brand name and model number accompanied by a photograph of the item, it is unreasonable to suppose that the reasonably prudent consumer accustomed to shopping online would be confused about the source of the goods.

MTM argues that initial interest confusion might occur because Amazon lists the search term used—here the trademarked phrase "mtm special ops"—three times at the top of the search page. MTM argues that because Amazon lists the search term "mtm special ops" at the top of the page, a consumer might conclude that the products displayed are types of MTM watches. But, merely looking at Amazon's search results page shows that such consumer confusion is highly unlikely. None of these watches is labeled with the word "MTM" or the phrase "Special Ops," let alone the specific phrase "MTM Special Ops." Further, some of the products listed are not even watches. The sixth result is a book entitled "*Survive!: The Disaster, Crisis and Emergency Handbook* by Jerry Ahem." The tenth result is a book entitled "*The Moses Expedition: A Novel* by Juan Gómez-Jurado." No reasonably prudent consumer, accustomed to shopping online or not, would assume that a book entitled "The Moses Expedition" is a type of MTM watch or is in any way affiliated with MTM watches. Likewise, no reasonably prudent consumer accustomed to shopping online would view Amazon's search results page and conclude that the products offered are MTM watches. It is possible that someone, somewhere might be confused by the search results page. But, "[u]nreasonable, imprudent and inexperienced web-shoppers are not relevant." *Tabari*, 610 F.3d at 1176; *see also Network Automation*, 638 F.3d at 1153 ("[W]e expect consumers searching for expensive products online to be even more sophisticated."). To establish likelihood of confusion, MTM must show that confusion is *likely*, not just *possible*. *See Murray*, 86 F.3d at 861.

MTM argues that in order to eliminate the likelihood of confusion, Amazon must change its search results page so that it explains to customers that it does not offer MTM watches for sale before suggesting alternative watches to the customer. We disagree. The search results page makes clear to anyone who can read English that Amazon carries only the brands that are clearly and explicitly listed on the web page. The search results page is unambiguous—not unlike when someone walks into a diner, asks for a Coke, and is told "No Coke. Pepsi." *See Multi Time Mach., Inc. v. Amazon.com, Inc.*, 792 F.3d 1070, 1080-81 (9th Cir. 2015) (Silverman, J., dissenting).

In light of the clear labeling Amazon uses on its search results page, no reasonable trier of fact could conclude that Amazon's search results page would likely confuse a reasonably prudent consumer accustomed to shopping online as to the source of the goods being offered. *Cf. Playboy*, 354 F.3d at 1030 n. 44 (Clear labeling "might eliminate the likelihood of initial interest confusion that exists in this case."); *Network Automation*, 638 F.3d at 1154 (same). As Judge Berzon put it, "I do not think it is reasonable to find initial interest confusion when a consumer is never confused as to source or affiliation, but instead knows, or should know, from the outset that a product or web link is not related to that of the trademark holder because the list produced by the search engine so informs him." *Playboy*, 354 F.3d at 1034-35 (9th Cir. 2004) (Berzon, J., concurring).

MTM attempts to argue that summary judgment of its claims is inappropriate because there are numerous factual disputes related to Amazon's search results page. But, to the extent there are factual disputes between the parties, none is material to the analysis. MTM cannot dispute the fact that the watches at issue sell for hundreds of dollars. Therefore, as a matter of law, the relevant consumer would be a reasonably prudent consumer accustomed to shopping online. *See Tabari*, 610 F.3d at 1176; *Network Automation*, 638 F.3d at 1152-53. Further, MTM cannot dispute the contents of the web page at issue. A review of Amazon's web page shows that each product listed for sale is clearly labeled with the product's name and manufacturer and a photograph, and no product is labeled with MTM's mark. Thus, the undisputed facts show that it is highly unlikely that a reasonably prudent consumer accustomed to shopping online would be confused as to the source of the goods offered for sale on Amazon's web page.

The likelihood of confusion is often a question of fact, but not always. In a case such as this, where a court can conclude that the consumer confusion alleged by the trademark holder is highly unlikely by simply reviewing the product listing/advertisement at issue, summary judgment is appropriate. *Cf. M2 Software*, 421 F.3d at 1085 (explaining that summary judgment of a trademark claim is appropriate where the plaintiff has failed to present "sufficient evidence to permit a rational trier of fact to find that confusion is 'probable,' not merely 'possible'"). Indeed, in the similar context of evaluating claims of consumer deception when dealing with false advertising claims, we have at least twice concluded—after a review of the label or advertisement at issue—that there was no likelihood of consumer deception as a matter of law because no reasonable consumer could have been deceived by the label/advertisement at issue in the manner alleged by the plaintiff. *See, e.g., Davis v. HSBC Bank*, 691 F.3d 1152, 1162 (9th Cir. 2012); *Freeman v. Time, Inc.*, 68 F.3d 285, 289-90 (9th Cir. 1995).

Further, we are able to conclude that summary judgment is appropriate in the present case without delving into any factors other than: (1) the type of goods and the degree of care likely to be exercised by the purchaser; and (2) the labeling and appearance of the products for sale and the surrounding context on the screen displaying the results page. *Cf. Brookfield*, 174 F.3d at 1054 ("[I]t is often possible to reach a conclusion with respect to likelihood of confusion after considering only a subset of the factors"). However, if we were to evaluate each of the remaining *Sleekcraft factors*, those factors would not change our conclusion, here, because those factors are either neutral or unimportant.

"Actual confusion"—We have held that "[a] showing of actual confusion among significant numbers of consumers provides strong support for the likelihood of confusion." *Playboy*, 354 F.3d at 1026 (noting that a strong showing by the plaintiff in regard to this factor alone can reverse a grant of summary judgment). However, here, there is no evidence of actual confusion. The only "evidence" MTM presented to the district court of actual confusion is the deposition testimony of MTM's president stating that someone named Eric told him, in reference to Amazon's web page, "it's confusing." Hearsay problems aside, this testimony is too speculative to show actual confusion because there is no evidence showing that Eric was a potential consumer. Indeed, at oral argument, MTM conceded that it does not have evidence of actual consumer confusion. Therefore, this factor does not weigh in MTM's favor.

"Defendant's Intent"—We have also held that "[a] defendant's intent to confuse constitutes probative evidence of likely confusion: Courts assume that the defendant's intentions were carried out successfully." *Playboy*, 354 F.3d at 1028 (footnote omitted). MTM argues that the design of Amazon's search results page is evidence of its intent to cause confusion. The design, however, indisputably produces results that are clearly labeled as to the type of product and brand. Amazon has designed its results page to alleviate any possible confusion about the source of the products by clearly labeling each of its products with the product's name and manufacturer. Therefore, this factor also does not weigh in MTM's favor.

"Strength of the Mark"—MTM argues that it has presented sufficient evidence below from which a jury could properly conclude that its trademark is both conceptually strong and commercially strong. However, we find that this factor is unimportant under the circumstances of this case. Even assuming MTM's mark is one of the strongest in the world—on the same level as Apple, Coke, Disney, or McDonald's—there is still no likelihood of confusion because Amazon clearly labels the source of the products it offers for sale.

Further, as we previously found in *Network Automation*, the remaining *Sleekcraft* factors are unimportant in a case, such as this, involving Internet search terms where the competing products are clearly labeled and the relevant consumer would exercise a high degree of care. *See Network Automation*, 638 F.3d at 1150-53 (finding "proximity of goods," "similarity of marks," "marketing channels," and "likelihood of expansion" to be unimportant in a trademark case involving Internet search terms where the advertisements are clearly labeled and the relevant consumers would exercise a high degree of care).

IV. CONCLUSION

In light of Amazon's clear labeling of the products it carries, by brand name and model, accompanied by a photograph of the item, no rational trier of fact could find that a reasonably prudent consumer accustomed to shopping online would likely be confused by the Amazon search results.

[*Affirmed.*]

BEA, Circuit Judge, dissenting:

Today the panel holds that when it comes to internet commerce, judges, not jurors, decide what labeling may confuse shoppers. In so doing, the court departs from our own trademark precedent and from our summary judgment jurisprudence. Because I believe that an Amazon shopper seeking an MTM watch might well initially think that the watches Amazon offers for sale when he searches "MTM Special Ops" are affiliated with MTM, I must dissent.

If her brother mentioned MTM Special Ops watches, a frequent internet shopper might try to purchase one for him through her usual internet retail sites, perhaps Overstock.com, Buy.com, and Amazon.com.[1] At Overstock's site, if she typed "MTM special ops," the site would respond "Sorry, your search: 'mtm special ops' returned no results." Similarly, at Buy.com, she would be informed "0 results found. Sorry. Your search for *mtm special ops* did not return an exact match. Please try your search again."

Things are a little different over at "Earth's most customer-centric company," as Amazon styles itself. There, if she were to enter "MTM Special Ops" as her search request on the Amazon website, Amazon would respond with its page showing (1) MTM Special Ops in the search field (2) "MTM Specials Ops" again—in quotation marks—immediately below the search field and (3) yet again in the phrase "Related Searches: *MTM special ops watch*," (emphasis in original) all before stating "Showing 10 Results." What the website's response will not state is the truth recognized by its competitors: that Amazon does not carry MTM products any more than do Overstock.com or Buy.com. Rather, below the search field, and below the second and third mentions of "MTM Special Ops" noted above,

---

1. MTM sells its products only through its own approved distributors.

the site will display aesthetically similar, multi-function watches manufactured by MTM's competitors. The shopper will see that Luminox and Chase-Durer watches are offered for sale, in response to her MTM query.[2]

MTM asserts the shopper might be confused into thinking a relationship exists between Luminox and MTM; she may think that MTM was acquired by Luminox, or that MTM manufactures component parts of Luminox watches, for instance. As a result of this initial confusion, MTM asserts, she might look into buying a Luminox watch, rather than junk the quest altogether and seek to buy an MTM watch elsewhere. MTM asserts that Amazon's use of MTM's trademarked name is likely to confuse buyers, who may ultimately buy a competitor's goods.

MTM may be mistaken. But whether MTM is mistaken is a question that requires a factual determination, one this court does not have authority to make.

By usurping the jury function, the majority today makes new trademark law. When we allow a jury to determine whether there is a likelihood of confusion, as I would, we do not *make* trademark law, because we announce no new principle by which to adjudicate trademark disputes. Today's brief majority opinion accomplishes a great deal: the majority announces a new rule of law, resolves whether "clear labeling" favors Amazon using its own judgment, and, sub silentio, overrules this court's "initial interest confusion" doctrine.

Capturing initial consumer attention has been recognized by our court to be a grounds for finding of infringement of the Lanham Act since 1997. *Dr. Seuss Enterprises, L.P. v. Penguin Books USA, Inc.*, 109 F.3d 1394, 1405 (9th Cir. 1997) (identifying "initial consumer attention" as a basis for infringement). In 1999, citing *Dr. Seuss*, we expressly adopted the initial interest confusion doctrine in the internet context, and never repudiated it. *Brookfield Communications, Inc. v. West Coast Entertainment Corp.*, 174 F.3d 1036, 1062 (9th Cir. 1999). It may not apply where the competing goods or services are "clearly labeled" such that they cause only mere diversion, but whether such goods or services are clearly labeled so as to prevent a prudent internet shopper's initial confusion depends on the overall function and presentation of the web page. The issue is whether a prudent internet shopper who made the search request and saw the Amazon result—top to bottom—would more likely than not be affected by that "initial interest confusion." That is, an impression—when first shown the results of the requested MTM Special Ops search—that Amazon carries watches that have some connection to MTM, and that those watches are sold under the name Luminox or Chase-Durer. Whether there is likelihood of such initial interest confusion, I submit, is a jury question. Intimations in our case law that initial interest confusion is bad doctrine notwithstanding, it is the law of our circuit, and, I submit, the most fair reading of the Lanham Act.

Tellingly, the majority does not cite to the statutory text, which provides that the nonconsensual use of a registered trademark will infringe where "such use is likely to cause confusion, or cause mistake, or deceive." 15 U.S.C. §1114(1)(a). The majority reads the statute to contain language that it does not, essentially reading the clause "at point of sale"

---

2. As of June 17, 2015, the shopper might be subject to even more confusion if she began her search of Amazon's wares through Google. If she searched Google for "Amazon MTM special ops watch," one of the search results would be a static page on Amazon's website. Amazon's static webpage stated that "At Amazon.com, we not only have a large collection of mtm special ops watch products [which, of course, is flatly untrue], but also a comprehensive set of reviews from our customers. Below we've selected a subset of mtm special ops watch products [a repetition of the untruth] and the corresponding reviews to help you do better research, and choose the product that best suits your needs." Amazon, *http://www.amazon.com/gp/feature.html?ie=UTF8 & docId=1001909381*. Amazon has since removed the page.

into the end of §1114(1)(a). Similarly, the majority reads 15 U.S.C. §1125 to apply only at point of sale — the majority writes that it is unreasonable to suppose that a reasonably prudent consumer accustomed to shopping online would be confused about the source of the goods where Luminox and Chase-Durer watches are labeled as such, but does not address the possibility that a reasonably prudent consumer might initially assume that those brands enjoyed some affiliation with MTM which, in turn, could cause such a shopper to investigate brands which otherwise would not have been of interest to her.

To reach its conclusion, the majority purports to apply this court's precedent in *Network Automation, Inc. v. Advanced Systems Concepts, Inc.*, 638 F.3d 1137, 1145 (9th Cir. 2011). In so doing, the majority ignores the procedural posture of that case. There, plaintiff Network Automation and defendant Advanced Systems Concepts both sold job scheduling and management software. *Id.* at 1142. Network Automation advertised its product by purchasing certain keywords — including registered trademarks belonging to Advanced Systems — which, when typed into various search engines, included Network Automation's website "www.NetworkAutomation.com" as a labeled, sponsored link among the search results. *Id.* Advanced Systems alleged violation of the Lanham Act and moved for a preliminary injunction. *Id.* at 1143. The district court granted a preliminary injunction to Advanced Systems, and Network Automation appealed. *Id.* On appeal, this court reversed and vacated the preliminary injunction.

To do so, this court did *not* find that there was no genuine issue of fact as to likelihood of confusion. Instead, this court properly considered whether the facts, as the court understood them, favored Advanced Systems in *Network Automation* because a preliminary injunction requires "the moving party [there, the plaintiff alleging infringement] demonstrate a fair chance of success on the merits or questions serious enough to require litigation." *Arc of California v. Douglas*, 757 F.3d 975, 993 (9th Cir. 2014). Therefore, the *Network Automation* court properly considered the weight of the evidence to decide whether Advanced Systems had a fair chance of success on the merits. Here, we are not tasked to determine whether MTM is likely to succeed, nor to consider the weight of the evidence. As this is an appeal from a summary judgment, we must decide whether the non-moving party (MTM) tendered a genuine issue of fact. *Network Automation* did not announce a rule that clear labeling is per se a question of law, nor that a judge's determination that products are clearly labeled precludes a triable issue of fact as to trademark infringement.

Indeed, even if *Network Automation* were not so readily distinguishable by its procedural posture, it is factually distinguishable. In *Network Automation*, the "diversionary" goods were clearly labeled on the response page as "Sponsored Links," showing that the producers of those products were the ones advertising for themselves, not for the firm named in the search request. *Network Automation*, 638 F.3d at 1144. Unlike the sponsored links at issue in *Network Automation*, and unlike its competitors Buy.com and Overstock. com, Amazon does not forestall any confusion by informing customers who are searching "MTM Special Ops" that Amazon does not carry any such products. Amazon does just the opposite. It responds by twice naming MTM, and once specifically naming watches.

On this record, a jury could infer that users who are confused by the search results are confused as to why MTM products are not listed. There is a question of fact whether users who are confused by the search result will wonder whether a competitor has acquired MTM or is otherwise affiliated with or approved by MTM. *See Brookfield Communications*, 174 F.3d at 1057. This is especially true as to a brand like MTM, as many luxury brands with distinct marks are produced by manufacturers of lower-priced, better-known brands — just as Honda manufactures Acura automobiles but sells Acura automobiles under a distinct mark that is marketed to wealthier purchasers, and Timex manufactures watches for luxury fashion houses Versace and Salvatore Ferragamo. Like MTM, Luminox manufactures luxury watches, and a customer might think that MTM and Luminox are manufactured by the same parent company. The possibility of initial interest confusion here is likely much higher than if, for instance, a customer using an online grocery website typed "Coke" and only Pepsi products were returned as results. No shopper would think that Pepsi was simply a higher end version of Coke, or that Pepsi had acquired Coke's secret recipe and started selling it under the Pepsi mark.

In any event, even as to expensive goods—for instance, pianos sold under a mark very similar to the famous Steinway and Sons brand's mark—the issue is not that a buyer might buy a piano manufactured by someone other than Steinway thinking that it was a Steinway. The issue is that the defendant's use of the mark would cause initial interest confusion by attracting potential customers' attention to buy the infringing goods because of the trademark holder's hard-won reputation. *Brookfield*, 174 F.3d at 1063 (citing *Grotrian, Helfferich, Schulz, Th. Steinweg Nachf. v. Steinway & Sons*, 523 F.2d 1331, 1341-42 (2d Cir. 1975)).

A jury could infer that the labeling of the search results, and Amazon's failure to notify customers that it does not have results that match MTM's mark, give rise to initial interest confusion. If so, a jury could find that Amazon customers searching for MTM products are subject to more than mere diversion, since MTM is not required to show that customers are likely to be confused at the point of sale. *Playboy Enterprises, Inc. v. Netscape Communications Corp.*, 354 F.3d 1020, 1025 (9th Cir. 2004).

Assuming arguendo that the majority properly found that Amazon's search results are clearly labeled, the majority extends its factual determinations further by determining that in this case, clear labeling outweighs the other eight factors considered in trademark suits, factors that remain the law of this circuit: (1) strength of the mark(s); (2) proximity or relatedness of the goods; (3) similarity of the marks; (4) evidence of actual confusion; (5) marketing channels; (6) degree of consumer care; (7) the defendants' intent; and (8) likelihood of expansion. *Network Automation*, 638 F.3d at 1145 (citing *AMF v. Sleekcraft Boats*, 599 F.2d 341, 348-49 (9th Cir. 1979)). To be sure, courts must be flexible in their application of the factors, as some may not apply in every case. *Playboy*, 354 F.3d at 1026. Here, for instance, the likelihood of expansion does not apply because both MTM and Amazon already sell luxury watches, so whether either is likely to expand its sales into the luxury watch market is not a question. However, where the *Sleekcraft* factors could tip in either direction, there is a jury question. *Fortune Dynamic, Inc. v. Victoria's Secret Stores Brand Management, Inc.*, 618 F.3d 1025, 1039 (9th Cir. 2010). Simply stating that the *Sleekcraft* factors do not favor the plaintiff, or don't bear on the clarity of the labeling, does not resolve the underlying factual question.

Having exercised its own judgment to determine that this presentation is not confusing, the majority purports to consider the *Sleekcraft* factors, though the opinion essentially states that some of the factors are *per se* irrelevant—for instance, as to the *Sleekcraft* factor, "strength of the mark," the majority assert that "under the circumstances of this case," the factor is unimportant because "Amazon clearly labels the source of the products it offers for sale." By reiterating the conclusion at which it had already arrived, the majority ignores the factor and the fact-intensive analysis it entails. A mark's strength is a measure of how uniquely identified it is with a product or service, and therefore how deserving of trademark protection. *Fortune Dynamic*, 618 F.3d at 1032. "A mark's conceptual strength depends largely on the obviousness of its connection to the good or service to which it refers. The less obvious the connection, the stronger the mark, and vice versa." *Id.* at 1032. Conceptual strength is considered along a continuum, and in this circuit, marks may be classified as falling into one of five categories, from conceptually weak to conceptually strong: generic, descriptive, suggestive, arbitrary, or fanciful. *Fortune Dynamic*, 618 F.3d at 1033. Whether a mark is descriptive or suggestive is a question of fact. *Id.* at 1034. In an infringement suit, "the distinction [between a descriptive and suggestive mark] is important because if the mark is suggestive, there is a stronger likelihood that the 'strength of the mark' factor favors the [plaintiff]." *Id.* Here, the phrase "MTM Special Ops" requires "a mental leap from the mark to the product," because the phrase does not expressly refer to watches. *Fortune Dynamic*, 618 F.3d at 1033. Indeed, by evoking elite military forces ("Special Ops"), the goods suggested by the phrase are as likely to be protective gear, binoculars, weapons, or boots as they are watches. A jury could find that the mark is suggestive and conceptually strong because it does not obviously refer to watches, or that it is merely descriptive because the watches are made in a military style. Either way, the weight of the evidence is a question of fact, and there is a genuine issue of fact as to the conceptual strength of the mark. As in *Fortune Dynamic*, "a jury should assess the conceptual strength of [plaintiff's] mark in the first instance." 618 F.3d at 1033. However, the majority simply brushes off the question as irrelevant "under the circumstances." The circumstances surrounding the case are questions of fact, not law, and should be given to a jury to determine.

Similarly, the majority finds that Amazon's intent weighs in favor of Amazon. A defendant's intent is relevant because a "defendant's intent to confuse constitutes probative evidence of likely confusion." *Playboy*, 354 F.3d at 1029. MTM submitted evidence that Amazon vendors and customers had complained to Amazon because they did not understand why they received certain non-responsive search results when they searched for products that are not carried by Amazon. The evidence showed that Amazon employees did not take action to address the complaints by explaining to the public how its search function works.[4] One Amazon employee noted that explaining BBS to the public might draw customers' and vendors' unwanted scrutiny to the matter. Amazon did not disclose to shoppers that its search function responds to customer behavior.

As in *Playboy*, this evidence suggests, "at a minimum, that defendants do nothing to alleviate confusion. . . . Although not definitive, this factor provides some evidence of an intent to confuse on the part of defendants." *Playboy*, 354 F.3d at 1029. From evidence that "Earth's most customer-centric company" took no action on these complaints, a jury could infer that Amazon intended to confuse its customers.

The majority ignores this evidence on the basis of its conclusion that Amazon created a page with clearly labeled wares, and further concludes that Amazon must not have intended to confuse customers, or its page would not be clearly labeled. However, to conclude that there is no triable issue of fact, the majority may not overlook or ignore evidence to the contrary in the record, or assume that a jury would weigh evidence the same way that the panel does.

---

4. Amazon's search algorithm responds to its customers' behavior using a Behavior Based Search ("BBS") technology, which uses data about what customers view and purchase after searching certain terms. Amazon does not program the terms; the function responds solely to customer behavior. If enough customers search for a certain keyword, "X," and then look at or purchase another product "Y," even if X and Y are not obviously related, future customers who search for X may receive search results including Y. But the BBS function is not solely responsible for the search results. The results list also includes matches based on a search of terms on Amazon's pages—for instance, streaming video of a show called Special Ops Mission may be called up. Whether a particular result appears because of BBS or a traditional search of matching terms is not evident from the matches, and the relevant products (which are based on search terms) and recommended products (based on BBS) are mingled together.

Finally, the majority repeatedly states that not only does Amazon clearly label its products, but there is no evidence of actual confusion. Assuming arguendo that there is no evidence from which a jury could infer actual confusion,[5] the absence of actual confusion is not dispositive of whether there is a genuine issue of fact. Where evidence of actual confusion is submitted, it is "strong support for the likelihood of confusion." *Network Automation*, 638 F.3d at 1151. But actual confusion "is not necessary to a finding of likelihood of confusion under the Lanham Act. Indeed, proving actual confusion is difficult and the courts have often discounted such evidence because it was unclear or insubstantial." *Id.* A plaintiff need not show actual confusion to prevail.

Through its cursory review of the *Sleekcraft* factors and conclusory statements about clear labeling, the majority purports to apply this circuit's trademark law, and ignores the doctrine of initial interest confusion. In so doing, the majority today writes new trademark law and blurs the line between innovation and infringement.

More troubling, the majority ignores the role of the jury. Summary judgment law is an aid to judicial economy, but it can be so only to the extent that it comports with the Seventh Amendment. Were we to reverse and remand, MTM might well lose. The likelihood of that outcome is irrelevant to the question whether there is a genuine issue of fact. I respectfully dissent.

NOTES AND QUESTIONS

1.   *Statutory basis for initial interest confusion?* Recall that in *Ferrari*, the court cited the 1962 Lanham Act amendment as statutory support for post-sale confusion claims. Does the 1962 amendment also provide a basis for recognizing initial interest confusion? *See Checkpoint Sys., Inc. v. Check Point Software Technologies, Inc.*, 269 F.3d 270, 295 (3d Cir. 2001) (citing *Ferrari*).

2.   *What's the harm?* How does initial interest confusion harm a trademark owner? Is it a type of "bait-and-switch" tactic? *See AM General Corp. v. DaimlerChrysler Corp.*, 311 F.3d 796 (7th Cir. 2002). In *Australian Gold, Inc. v. Hatfield*, 436 F.3d 1228 (10th Cir. 2006), the court identified three types of harm arising from initial interest confusion:

> Even if the consumer eventually becomes aware of the source's actual identity, or where no actual sale results, there is nonetheless damage to the trademark. This damage can manifest itself in three ways: (1) the original diversion of the prospective customer's interest to a source that he or she erroneously believes is authorized; (2) the potential consequent effect of that diversion on the customer's ultimate decision whether to purchase caused by an erroneous impression that two sources of a product may be associated; and (3) the initial credibility that the would-be buyer may accord to the infringer's products — customer consideration that otherwise may be unwarranted and that may be built on the strength of the protected mark, reputation and goodwill.

---

5. Amazon submitted evidence that purports to show that no customers were confused, because customers who searched for "Luminox" were 21 times as likely to purchase a Luminox watch as were customers who searched for "MTM Special Ops." It isn't surprising that customers who search for an item (Luminox watches) are more likely to buy that item than customers who did not search for it but searched for another product (MTM watches). However, a jury might view this purported evidence of no actual confusion as flawed because a user researching watches might initially be confused about the availability of MTM watches online and so not purchase a Luminox the same day. Further, some users did search for "MTM Special Ops" and purchase a competitor's watch the same day, which a jury could find probative of some confusion.

Id. at 1239. Are these assertions persuasive? Do they describe a phenomenon that is comparable to post-sale confusion? Or more subtle and difficult to measure? Might this explain the *MTM* court's reluctance to accept MTM's initial interest confusion argument? On the other hand, even if the harm from initial interest confusion is ephemeral, perhaps courts should find liability and impose a very limited remedy—for example, in the *MTM* case, a narrowly-drawn injunction requiring Amazon to add a label to its search results instructing consumers that "We don't carry MTM Special Ops Watches." Would this strike an appropriate balance?

3. *Initial interest confusion of whom?* If courts recognize claims of initial interest confusion, should they limit those claims to initial interest confusion among only actual or potential purchasers? *See Elec. Design & Sales, Inc. v. Elec. Data Sys. Corp.*, 954 F.2d 713 (Fed. Cir. 1992); *see also* Jennifer E. Rothman, *Initial Interest Confusion: Standing at the Crossroads of Trademark Law*, 27 Cardozo L. Rev. 105 (2005). If you believe that the harm arising from initial interest confusion is particularly difficult to measure, do you think that limiting initial interest confusion to actual or potential purchasers is an appropriate restrictive strategy?

4. *What's the test?* Courts use the likelihood of confusion factors test to analyze initial interest confusion claims. Should courts adapt the factors for the initial interest confusion context? If so, how? Consider the following possibilities.

> a. *Intent factor—intentional deception as a threshold requirement?* Should initial interest confusion claims be subject to a threshold showing that the alleged infringer has intentionally attempted to divert customers? *See, e.g., CJ Prods. L.L.C. v. Snuggly Plushez L.L.C.*, 809 F. Supp. 2d 127, 158 (E.D.N.Y. 2011); *Designer Skin, L.L.C. v. S&L Vitamins, Inc.*, 560 F. Supp. 2d 811 (D. Ariz. 2008). Would the presence of such a requirement suggest that initial interest confusion is less about consumer harm, and more about harm to competition?
>
> b. *Actual confusion factor—effect of disclaimers.* In a point-of-sale confusion claim, evidence that the alleged infringer disclaimed any affiliation with the mark owner could be used to rebut an allegation of bad intent or actual confusion. What effect (if any) should be given to evidence of a disclaimer in an initial interest confusion case? *See, e.g., New York State Soc'y of Certified Pub. Accountants v. Eric Louis Assocs., Inc.*, 79 F. Supp. 2d 331, 342 (S.D.N.Y. 1999); *see also Australian Gold, Inc. v. Hatfield*, 436 F.3d 1228, 1240 (10th Cir. 2006).
>
> c. *Similarity of goods factor—direct competition requirement?* Should courts insist on *identity* of goods or services as a prerequisite for an initial interest confusion claim? *See Interstellar Starship Services, Ltd. v. Epix, Inc.*, 304 F.3d 936, 945 (9th Cir. 2002); *Lamparello v. Falwell*, 420 F.3d 309 (4th Cir. 2005); *see also* Daniel C. Glazer & Dev R. Dhamija, *Revisiting Initial Interest Confusion on the Internet*, 95 Trademark Rep. 952, 975 (2005).

In *MTM*, the court declares that the conventional multi-factor test for likelihood of confusion is "not particularly apt" in an initial interest confusion case involving online advertising, and endorses the reliance on a subset of those factors, a methodology that it attributes to *Network Automation, Inc. v. Advanced Systems Concepts*, 638 F.3d 1137 (9th Cir. 2011). The *MTM* court (again invoking *Network Automation*) also approves of adding a factor: "the labeling and appearance of the advertisements and the surrounding context on the screen displaying the results page." And it suggests that the inquiry boils down to identifying the relevant consumer and determining what he or she would reasonably believe based on the screen display. Is this methodology a deft adaptation of a flexible confusion analysis, or an example of ill-advised reductionist thinking?

5. *Applying the initial interest confusion test to nonverbal marks.* In *Gibson Guitar Corp. v. Paul Reed Smith Guitars, LP*, 423 F.3d 539 (6th Cir. 2005), Gibson claimed that Paul Reed Smith (PRS) had infringed Gibson's registered rights in the shape of its LES PAUL guitar models. Gibson alleged initial interest confusion, asserting, for example, that a consumer standing on the far side of a guitar store could mistake the shape of the PRS guitar for a Gibson, and (under the spell of this mistaken belief) walk over to examine the PRS guitar. The court seemed to reject as a matter of law the extension of initial interest confusion to product design trade dress, reasoning that "such a theory would prevent competitors from producing even dissimilar product which might appear, from the far end of an aisle in a warehouse store, somewhat similar to a trademarked shape." Do you agree with this reasoning? What is the best response?

6. *Proving initial interest confusion by tracking online behavior.* In *1-800 Contacts, Inc. v. Lens.com, Inc.*, 722 F.3d 1229 (10th Cir. 2013), the court offered a view as to how initial interest confusion might arise on the facts presented:

> a consumer enters a query for "1-800 Contacts" on Google; sees a screen with an ad for Lens.com that is generated because of Lens.com's purchase of one of the nine Challenged Keywords; becomes confused about whether Lens.com is the same source as, or is affiliated with, 1-800; and therefore clicks on the Lens.com ad to view the site.

Id. at 1244. Lens.com's expert evidence (based on Google AdWords data) showed that use of the challenged keywords (corresponding to 1-800 Contacts' marks) had produced advertisements for Lens.com in 1,626 instances, and in only 25 of those instances (1.5%) did the user click on the Lens.com advertisement. On the basis of this evidence, the court concluded that the maximum rate of initial interest confusion was 1.5%. Is this data probative of initial interest confusion? Do we need to know more about the 1,626 instances—for example, do we need to know whether a user typed in "contacts" or "1-800 Contacts" to trigger the ad in any given instance? Do we need to know whether a consumer reviewed the ad and formulated some preliminary conclusions even if he or she never clicked on the ad?

7. *Initial interest confusion under Section 2(d)?* Is there any reason why initial interest confusion (or post-sale confusion) would be an inappropriate basis on which to sustain an opposition under Section 2(d)? *See HRL Assocs., Inc. v. Weiss Assocs., Inc.*, 12 U.S.P.Q.2d (BNA) 1819 (TTAB 1989), *aff'd*, 902 F.2d 1546 (Fed. Cir. 1990).

8. *Flip-flopping in* MTM? The *MTM* decision excerpted above is the second Ninth Circuit panel opinion in the case. In the original opinion, released in July 2015 and reported at 792 F.3d 1070, Circuit Judge Bea and District Judge Quist (sitting by designation) held that there was a triable issue of fact as to initial interest confusion on the record presented in this case, over a dissent by Circuit Judge Silverman. Subsequently, Judges Silverman and Quist voted to grant panel rehearing. (Judge Bea voted against.) The July 2015 opinion was then withdrawn and a second opinion—the one in the casebook—was substituted for it. In the substitute opinion, as you have read, Judges Silverman and Quist found no triable issue of fact on initial interest confusion and granted summary judgment in favor of Amazon.com, over a dissent by Judge Bea.

E.   REVERSE CONFUSION

Consider the following fact pattern as we move to another variation on the traditional confusion theory. Since 1962, the Harlem Wizards have provided "show" basketball performances in the tradition of the Harlem Globetrotters. The Harlem Wizards have appeared at schools, festivals, and the like in various parts of the United States. The Harlem Wizards promote themselves through direct mailings and through their website. In 1996 the National Basketball Association (NBA) franchise known as the Washington Bullets announced that it would change its name to the Washington Wizards beginning in the 1997-98 season.

Consider how the Harlem Wizards might shape a trademark infringement liability theory. In a traditional trademark infringement suit, a senior trademark owner alleges that a junior market entrant is seeking to appropriate the senior's goodwill by engendering source confusion. That is, the junior entrant is using a mark that is confusingly similar to the senior's mark, such that consumers are likely to conclude that the junior's goods or services actually originate with, or are affiliated with, the senior mark owner.

Confusion in this sense—which might be labeled "forward" confusion—seems unlikely to occur in the Harlem Wizards case. Quite the contrary, one might argue that the NBA, with its substantial advertising muscle, could promote its teams so vigorously that consumers might come to assume that the Harlem Wizards is the new market entrant seeking to invoke the Washington Wizards' goodwill. That is, one might argue that consumers are likely to conclude that the *senior's* goods or services actually originate with, or are affiliated with, the *junior* mark user. That theory seems at least facially plausible as applied here: Consumers might come to believe that the Harlem Wizards were a newcomer organization attempting to invoke some connection with an NBA franchise.

If this is confusion at all, it is confusion in reverse. Does the Lanham Act allow for a cause of action for reverse confusion? Should courts recognize such a cause of action? If they do, what should the reverse confusion test be? Consider these questions as you read the next case. Note that, unlike the situation for cases in the preceding section, reverse confusion ordinarily is considered at the point of sale.

For the resolution of the Harlem Wizards saga, *see Harlem Wizards Entm't Basketball, Inc. v. NBA Properties, Inc.*, 952 F. Supp. 1084 (D.N.J. 1997).

A & H SPORTSWEAR, INC. v. VICTORIA'S SECRET STORES, INC.

237 F.3d 198 (3d Cir. 2000)

BECKER, Chief Judge:

FACTS AND PROCEDURAL HISTORY

[A & H uses the mark MIRACLESUIT for "control" swimwear, which reportedly provides the wearer a great deal of "hold-in control" of the hips and waist. Most MIRACLESUIT swimsuits contain underwire bras. A & H secured a federal registration for MIRACLESUIT in 1992.

Victoria's Secret [VS], described by the court as the "lingerie leviathan," sells lingerie and other apparel, including swimwear. VS began selling cleavage-enhancing bras under the name THE MIRACLE BRA in 1993. By 1995, VS had incorporated its bra into swimsuits, using the MIRACLE BRA mark in connection with the swimsuits.

A & H sued, arguing, *inter alia*, reverse confusion, seeking an injunction. The District Court denied the motion; A & H appealed. The following is the Third Circuit's discussion of the appeal on the reverse confusion theory.]

V. THE REVERSE CONFUSION CLAIM

A. INTRODUCTION

We recently recognized the doctrine of "reverse confusion" as a distinct basis for a claim under §43(a) of the Lanham Act. *See Fisons Horticulture, Inc. v. Vigoro Indus., Inc.*, 30 F.3d 366, 475 (3d Cir. 1994). While the essence of a direct confusion claim is that a junior user of a mark is said to free-ride on the "reputation and good will of the senior user by adopting a similar or identical mark," *id.*, reverse confusion occurs when "the junior user saturates the market with a similar trademark and overwhelms the senior user." *Id.* (quoting *Ameritech, Inc. v. American Info. Techs. Corp.*, 811 F.2d 960, 964 (6th Cir. 1987)). The harm flowing from reverse confusion is that

> [t]he public comes to assume the senior user's products are really the junior user's or that the former has become somehow connected to the latter. . . . [T]he senior user loses the value of the trademark—its product identity, corporate identity, control over its goodwill and reputation, and ability to move into new markets.

Ameritech, Inc., 811 F.2d at 964. [cit.] As we explained in *Fisons*, reverse confusion protects "smaller senior users . . . against larger, more powerful companies who want to use identical or confusingly similar trademarks." 30 F.3d at 475. Absent reverse confusion, "a company with a well established trade name and with the economic power to advertise extensively [would be immunized from suit] for a product name taken from a competitor." *Big O Tire Dealers, Inc. v. Goodyear Tire & Rubber Co.*, 561 F.2d 1365, 1372 (10th Cir. 1977).

The doctrine of reverse confusion—or, at least, some of its applications—is not without its critics. *See, e.g.*, Thad G. Long & Alfred M. Marks, *Reverse Confusion: Fundamentals and Limits*, 84 Trademark Rep. 1, 2-3 (1994); Daniel D. Domenico, Note, *Mark Madness: How Brent Musburger and the Miracle Bra May Have Led to a More Equitable and Efficient Understanding of the Reverse Confusion Doctrine in Trademark Law*, 86 VA. L. REV. 597, 613-14, 621-24 (2000).

The chief danger inherent in recognizing reverse confusion claims is that innovative junior users, who have invested heavily in promoting a particular mark, will suddenly find their use of the mark blocked by plaintiffs who have not invested in, or promoted, their own marks. *See Weiner King, Inc. v. Wiener King Corp.*, 615 F.2d 512, 522 (C.C.P.A. 1980). Further, an overly-vigorous use of the doctrine of reverse confusion could potentially inhibit larger companies with established marks from expanding their product lines—for instance, had Victoria's Secret thought, at the outset, that it would not be permitted to carry over its popular The Miracle Bra mark from lingerie to swimwear, it might have chosen not to enter the swimsuit market at all.

This would be an undesirable result; in fact, it is precisely to allow a certain amount of "space" for companies to expand their product lines under established marks that we allow infringement suits against suppliers of non-competing goods. *See Interpace Corp. v. Lapp, Inc.*, 721 F.2d 460, 464 (3d Cir. 1983). This is not to say that the reverse confusion doctrine does not have its proper place; as has been recognized, without the existence of such a claim, smaller business owners might not have any incentive to invest in their marks at all, for fear the mark could be usurped at will by a larger competitor. *See SK & F, Co. v. Premo Pharm. Labs., Inc.*, 625 F.2d 1055, 1067 (3d Cir. 1980) ("[P]ermitting piracy of . . . identifying trade dress can only discourage other manufacturers from making a similar individual promotional effort."). However, these concerns do sensitize us to the potential untoward effects of an overenthusiastic enforcement of reverse confusion claims, although they cannot supersede our judicial recognition of the doctrine.

B.   The Test for Reverse Confusion

As in a direct confusion claim, the ultimate question in a reverse confusion claim is whether there is a likelihood of consumer confusion as to the source or sponsorship of a product. *See Fisons*, 30 F.3d at 475. Although it would seem somewhat counterintuitive to posit that the likelihood of confusion analysis changes from the direct confusion to the reverse confusion context,[19] there are differences between the two situations that bear mentioning. Therefore, to clarify the test for reverse confusion that has developed in our jurisprudence, we will walk through the factors that a district court should consider (where relevant) in assessing such a claim.

1.   The Factors That Are the Same

As an initial matter, there are several factors that should generally be analyzed in the same way for a reverse confusion claim as they are for a direct confusion claim.[20] First, the attentiveness of consumers does not change (factor (3)); in both direct and reverse confusion, the question is whether this is the kind of product that consumers will care enough about to notice the differences, or purchase hastily with only a limited impression. *See Fisons*, 30 F.3d at 476 n.12 (considering this factor in the same manner as it would for direct confusion). Second, and similarly, the degree to which the channels of trade and advertisement overlap (factor (7)) should be analyzed in the same fashion. *See id.* at 475-76 (analyzing the channels of trade in the same manner). Finally, *Lapp* factors (8) and (9), considering the similarity of the targets of the parties' sales efforts and the similarity of products, are also analyzed no differently in the reverse confusion context. *See id.* at 475, 481 (treating these factors in the same way for reverse confusion as they would have been treated for direct confusion).

2.   Similarity of the Marks

Generally speaking, the similarity of the marks themselves is necessarily analyzed in the same way in direct and reverse confusion claims; the court looks to sight, sound, and meaning, and compares whether these elements combine to create a general commercial impression that is the same for the two marks. *See, e.g., Fisons*, 30 F.3d at 478-79 (analyzing the commercial impression of the marks in light of direct confusion principles). Therefore, a district court would not need to examine these in a different manner than it would in a direct confusion claim.

On the other hand, the direct confusion claim in this case was rejected by the District Court in considerable measure because the court felt that the Victoria's Secret housemark, coupled with the disclaimer, alleviated any confusion that might otherwise result. Yet in the reverse confusion context, the presence of housemarks or disclaimers must obviously be treated differently than in the direct confusion context. It is the essence of the reverse confusion claim that, when consumers come across the Miraclesuit in the stream of commerce, they will confuse it with The Miracle Bra and think that it is a Victoria's Secret product. Therefore, the weight of a disclaimer on the Victoria's Secret product is necessarily lessened.

---

19. Indeed, some courts have simply inquired whether there exists a likelihood of confusion between the marks, temporarily putting aside the distinction between "direct" or "reverse" confusion until after such a likelihood has been demonstrated. *See Americana Trading Inc. v. Russ Berrie & Co.*, 966 F.2d 1284, 1290 (9th Cir. 1992) (reversing district court grant of summary judgment to defendants, on the ground that plaintiffs had put forth enough evidence of "confusion"—some direct, some reverse—to create a genuine issue of material fact).

20. We say "generally" only because we recognize that there may be unforeseen circumstances in which these factors actually do apply differently in the reverse confusion context.

Because A & H puts no disclaimer on its product to distinguish it from The Miracle Bra, the consumer considering a purchase of the Miraclesuit will not have the same handy reminder that Miraclesuit is not associated with The Miracle Bra or Victoria's Secret. This is not to say that such a disclaimer may not, in fact, mitigate confusion in some cases; if consumers are faced with the disclaimer every time they flip through the Victoria's Secret catalogue, they are less likely to forget that Miraclesuit is unrelated to The Miracle Bra swimwear.

As to the presence of the housemark on the Victoria's Secret product, not only is there the possibility that consumers will fail to remember the mark when encountering A & H's swimwear, but there is also the possibility that the mark will *aggravate*, rather than mitigate, reverse confusion, by reinforcing the association of the word "miracle" exclusively with Victoria's Secret. *See, e.g., Sands, Taylor & Wood Co. v. Quaker Oats Co.*, 978 F.2d 947, 960 (7th Cir. 1992); *Americana Trading Inc. v. Russ Berrie & Co.*, 966 F.2d 1284, 1288 (9th Cir. 1992). Of course, we do not suggest that this actually occurred in this particular case; after all, the District Court observed that A & H typically includes its own house-mark on Miraclesuits, *see A & H IV*, 57 F. Supp. 2d at 160, but, because the court only conducted a likelihood of confusion analysis for the direct confusion claim, it only briefly addressed the significance of the A & H housemark, *see id.* at 168 n.17.

Clearly, the proper significance to be accorded these facts is a matter best suited for the determination of the trial court. Instead, we merely highlight the questions raised by the use of the housemarks and disclaimers in order to emphasize that a district court must separately examine the similarity factor to determine whether there are any aspects of the analysis that should be different for a reverse confusion claim, and, if so, alter its examination accordingly.

3.   Strength of the Marks

An important difference between reverse and direct confusion manifests in the analysis of the strength of the marks. . . .

a.   Commercial Strength

It has been observed that a consumer first encountering a mark with one set of goods is likely to continue to associate the mark with those goods, and whether any subsequent confusion is "direct" or "reverse" will depend on whether the consumer's first experience was with the junior or the senior user of the mark. *See Banff, Ltd. v. Federated Dep't Stores, Inc.*, 841 F.2d 486, 490 (2d Cir. 1988) (acknowledging such a possibility); Long & Marks, *supra*, at 5. The greater the commercial disparity between the manufacturers, the more likely it is that a consumer's first experience with a mark will be with one particular manufacturer. That is, if one manufacturer—junior or senior—expends tremendous sums in advertising while the other does not, consumers will be more likely to encounter the heavily advertised mark first. Where the greater advertising originates from the senior user, we are more likely to see a case of direct confusion; if the greater advertising originates from the junior user, reverse confusion is more likely. *See* 3 McCarthy, *Trademarks and Unfair Competition* §23:10, at 23-32; *cf. Fisons*, 30 F.3d at 479 (observing that direct confusion involves a junior user "trad[ing] on" a senior user's name and thus expending less on advertising, whereas reverse confusion involves the opposite pattern).

Logically, then, in a direct confusion claim, a plaintiff with a commercially strong mark is more likely to prevail than a plaintiff with a commercially weak mark. Conversely, in a reverse confusion claim, a plaintiff with a commercially weak mark is more likely to prevail than a plaintiff with a stronger mark, and this is particularly true when the plaintiff's weaker mark is pitted against a defendant with a far stronger mark. . . .

Therefore, in a reverse confusion claim, a court should analyze the "commercial strength" factor in terms of (1) the commercial strength of the junior user as compared to the senior user; and (2) any advertising or marketing campaign by the junior user that has resulted in a saturation in the public awareness of the junior user's mark. *See Fisons*, 30 F.3d at 474, 479.

b.   Distinctiveness or Conceptual Strength

. . .

As stated above, in the paradigmatic reverse confusion case, the senior user has a commercially weak mark when compared with the junior user's commercially strong mark. When it comes to conceptual strength, however, we believe that, just as in direct confusion cases, a strong mark should weigh in favor of a senior user. Our decision is supported by the fact that those courts that have clearly distinguished conceptual from commercial strength in the reverse confusion context have weighed a conceptually strong mark in the senior user's favor, in the same manner as they would in direct confusion cases. [cit.]

In *H. Lubovsky, Inc. v. Esprit de Corp.*, 627 F. Supp. 483 (S.D.N.Y. 1986), the court explained that conceptual distinctiveness was relevant in the same way for a reverse confusion claim because "if a customer saw a doll in a toy store bearing a strong familiar trademark like 'Exxon,' he might well assume that the oil company had gone into the toy business; if, on the other hand, he saw a doll bearing a familiar but weak laudatory trademark like Merit, he would be unlikely to assume that it is connected with the similarly named gasoline or cigarettes." *Id*. at 487; *see also* Long & Marks, *supra*, at 22.

The *H. Lubovsky* logic resonates, for it makes more sense to hold that conceptual strength, unlike commercial strength, works in the plaintiff's favor. That is, if we were to apply the rule stated above for commercial strength, i.e., weighing weakness in the plaintiff's favor, we would bring about the perverse result that less imaginative marks would be more likely to win reverse confusion claims than arbitrary or fanciful ones. We therefore hold that, as in direct confusion claims, a district court should weigh a conceptually strong mark in the plaintiff's favor, particularly when the mark is of such a distinctive character that, coupled with the relative similarity of the plaintiff's and defendant's marks, a consumer viewing the plaintiff's product is likely to assume that such a mark would only have been adopted by a single source—i.e., the defendant.

4.   *The Intent of the Defendant*

In the direct confusion context, the intent of the defendant is relevant to the extent that it bears on the likelihood of confusion analysis. . . .

When reverse, rather than direct, confusion is alleged, "intent to confuse," is unlikely to be present. *Cf. Fisons*, 30 F.3d at 480. However, though perhaps unusual, should an intent to confuse exist, it would be relevant to the likelihood of confusion analysis in the same manner as it would for a direct confusion claim. For instance, in *Commerce National Insurance Services, Inc. v. Commerce Insurance Agency, Inc.*, 214 F.3d 432 (3d Cir. 2000), we were confronted with a situation in which the litigants had used very similar marks in noncompetitive industries for a number of years, each fully aware of the other and with no incidents of actual confusion. Eventually, however, the larger company expanded into the smaller company's line of business, deliberately choosing to promote its services under an almost identical mark. In holding that the smaller company could maintain its claim against the larger for reverse confusion, we specifically highlighted the possibility that the larger company had adopted the mark with the deliberate intent of pushing its rival out of the market, and that it was this sort of usurpation of business identity that the reverse confusion doctrine was designed to prevent. *See id.* at 445.

. . .

5. *Factors Relating to Actual Confusion*

As a matter of intuition, one would expect that in a reverse confusion claim, evidence of actual confusion would be as important as in a direct confusion claim, though the nature of the confusion that would be probative would be quite different. *See Lang v. Retirement Living Publ'g Co.*, 949 F.2d 576, 583 (2d Cir. 1991) (holding that evidence of "actual confusion" in which the public thought the senior user was the origin of the junior user's products was irrelevant for a reverse confusion claim). As applied to this case, for example, evidence that consumers thought that The Miracle Bra was an A & H product would be probative on a direct confusion claim, but not on a reverse confusion claim. Conversely, evidence that consumers thought that Miraclesuit was a Victoria's Secret product would support a reverse confusion claim, but not a direct confusion claim. This was apparently the District Court's intuition; although it declined to consider A & H's reverse confusion claim, it did observe that most of the evidence A & H had put forth with regard to "actual confusion" related to direct, rather than reverse, confusion. [cit.]

However, marshalling evidence of actual confusion is often difficult. *See, e.g., Liquid Glass Enters., Inc. v. Dr. Ing. h.c.F. Porsche AG*, 8 F. Supp. 2d 398, 403 (D.N.J. 1998). In our view, if we were to create a rigid division between "direct" and "reverse" confusion evidence, we would run the risk of denying recovery to meritorious plaintiffs. For example, if a plaintiff alleged theories of both direct and reverse confusion and was able to prove a few instances of "actual" confusion in each direction, we might conclude that the plaintiff did not have enough evidence of either type to succeed on either of its claims, even though, taken together, all of the evidence of actual confusion would be probative of a real problem. As we explained in Part V.B.3, *supra*, the manifestation of consumer confusion as "direct" or "reverse" may merely be a function of the context in which the consumer first encountered the mark. Isolated instances of "direct" confusion may occur in a reverse confusion case, and vice versa. *See* Long & Marks, *supra*, at 5. Though we might expect that, in most instances, the consumer's first encounter will be with the mark that has greater commercial strength, this will not invariably be the case.

Given the problems litigants typically encounter in locating evidence of actual confusion, then, we decline to create a strict bar to the use of "direct" confusion evidence in a "reverse" confusion case, or vice versa. However, evidence working in the same direction as the claim is preferred, and "misfitting" evidence must be treated carefully, for large amounts of one type of confusion in a claim for a different type may in fact work against the plaintiff. For instance, the existence of reverse confusion might disprove a plaintiff's claim that its descriptive mark has secondary meaning, thus resulting in no recovery at all. *See Jefferson Home Furniture Co., Inc. v. Jefferson Furniture Co., Inc.*, 549 So. 2d 5, 8 (Ala. 1977).

It follows that the other factor relating to actual confusion, *Lapp* factor (4), examining the time the mark has been used without evidence of actual confusion, should be approached similarly.

. . .

7. *Summary of the Test for Reverse Confusion*

In sum, in the typical case in which there is a claim of reverse confusion, a court should examine the following factors as aids in its determination whether or not there is a likelihood of such confusion:

(1)   the degree of similarity between the owner's mark and the alleged infringing mark;

(2)   the strength of the two marks, weighing both a commercially strong junior user's mark and a conceptually strong senior user's mark in the senior user's favor;

(3)   the price of the goods and other factors indicative of the care and attention expected of consumers when making a purchase;

(4)   the length of time the defendant has used the mark without evidence of actual confusion arising;

(5)   the intent of the defendant in adopting the mark;

(6)   the evidence of actual confusion;

(7)   whether the goods, competing or not competing, are marketed through the same channels of trade and advertised through the same media;

(8)   the extent to which the targets of the parties' sales efforts are the same;

(9)   the relationship of the goods in the minds of consumers, whether because of the near-identity of the products, the similarity of function, or other factors;

(10)   other facts suggesting that the consuming public might expect the larger, more powerful company to manufacture both products, or expect the larger company to manufacture a product in the plaintiff's market, or expect that the larger company is likely to expand into the plaintiff's market.

As with the test for direct confusion, no one factor is dispositive, and in individual cases, particular factors may not be probative on the issue of likelihood of confusion. "The weight given to each factor in the overall picture, as well as its weighing for plaintiff or defendant, must be done on an individual fact-specific basis." *Fisons*, 30 F.3d at 476 n.11. . . .

[The court vacated the district court's judgment as it pertained to reverse confusion and remanded. The district court had erred by requiring a threshold showing of "economic disparity" between plaintiff and defendant before reverse confusion could be considered.]

NOTES AND QUESTIONS

1. *What's the harm?* If you were a judge, would you favor recognizing the reverse confusion theory if the question came to you on first impression? In thinking about this question, consider how you would characterize the harm (if any) that reverse confusion causes. Is it that purchasers are likely to assume that the senior user's product/service actually originates with the junior user, thereby undermining the senior user's investment in goodwill? Or is it that purchasers are likely to assume that the senior user is actually the later comer and potentially an infringer of the junior user's mark? Or is it something else entirely? *See* Anthony L. Fletcher, *The Curious Doctrine of Reverse Confusion — Getting It Right in Reverse*, 95 TRADEMARK REP. 1273, 1306 (2005) (tracing the evolution of the case law and concluding that the "most difficult, and least analyzed, issue in reverse confusion cases is relief"); *Attrezzi, LLC v. Maytag Corp.*, 436 F.3d 32 (1st Cir. 2006) (explaining sources of harm to senior mark owner caused by reverse confusion); *see also Visible Sys. Corp. v. Unisys Corp.*, 551 F.3d 65 (1st Cir. 2008) (upholding finding of reverse confusion). In *Visible Systems*, the alleged harm to Visible Systems was the incorrect perception that it had been acquired by Unisys. Visible Systems was a small software company; Unisys was a large computer manufacturer. There was evidence in the case that Visible Systems' competitors were initially other small software companies, but that over time these companies had been acquired by larger companies such as IBM. Thus, when Unisys used the mark at issue, consumers might think that Unisys had acquired Visible Systems, potentially harming Visible Systems' reputation.

2.   *Alterations to the confusion analysis.* Are you persuaded by the *A & H Sportswear* court's arguments about altering the confusion analysis to make it suitable for reverse confusion cases? For another discussion of potential alterations to the test, *see Dreamwerks Prod. Grp, Inc. v. SKG Studio*, 142 F.3d 1127 (9th Cir. 1998) (noting that the strength of the *junior* user's mark is probative on reverse confusion, and questioning the relevance of the intent factor). For an example of a case in which the court simply followed the factors analysis without alteration, *see Harlem Wizards Entm't Basketball, Inc. v. NBA Properties, Inc.*, 952 F. Supp. 1084 (D.N.J. 1997), discussed in the introduction to this section. *See also Current Commc'ns Group LLC v. Current Media LLC*, 76 U.S.P.Q.2d (BNA) 1686, 1692 (S.D. Ohio 2005) (stating that "just labeling a case a 'reverse confusion case' does not alter the analysis significantly"). Which of these approaches best fits the reverse confusion theory?

3.   *Reverse confusion and the intent factor.* In a reverse confusion case, the relevant intent is not whether the junior user intended to trade off the senior user's goodwill, but rather whether the junior user intended to overwhelm the senior user. How might a mark owner prove intent in a reverse confusion case? With the same type of evidence that would be used in a forward confusion case? In a reverse confusion case, what weight should be placed on the junior user's failure to conduct a trademark search (or to follow up on a trademark search when it identifies a senior user)? *See Fisons Horticulture, Inc. v. Vigoro Indus., Inc.*, 30 F.3d 466, 480 (3d Cir. 1994) ("The questions the district court should consider here are whether [the junior user] conducted an adequate name search for other companies marketing similar goods under trademarks including the name 'Fairway,' and whether it followed through with its investigation when it found there were such companies" as opposed to exhibiting carelessness); *cf. Star Indus., Inc. v. Bacardi & Co. Ltd.*, 412 F.3d 373, 388 n.3 (2d Cir. 2005) (the approach to intent in *Fisons* "is at odds with this circuit's precedents, which preclude finding bad faith on the basis of an inadequate trademark search, at least in the absence of evidence that the inadequate design or the failure to correct inadequacies in the search was motivated by an intent to sow consumer confusion or to exploit the good will or reputation of the senior user"), *cert. denied*, 547 U.S. 1019 (2006).

4.   *Reverse confusion and the strength factor.* The *A & H* court recommends that the mark strength factor in reverse confusion analysis operate on the basis that (1) the commercial strength of the junior user's mark favors reverse confusion, and that (2) the relative conceptual strength of the senior user's mark favors reverse confusion. Do you agree with both propositions? Some cases appear to follow the *A & H* mark strength analysis. *See Attrezzi, LLC v. Maytag Corp.*, 436 F.3d 32 (1st Cir. 2006); *Surfvivor Media, Inc. v. Survivor Productions*, 406 F.3d 625 (9th Cir. 2005). *But see M2 Software, Inc. v. Madacy Entm't*, 421 F.3d 1073 (9th Cir. 2005) (conducting a standard mark strength analysis in a case involving claims of both forward and reverse confusion). For additional examples from the district courts illustrating variations in the mark strength analysis, *see Playmakers, LLC v. ESPN, Inc.*, 297 F. Supp. 2d 1277 (W.D. Wash. 2003) (finding that plaintiff's mark—PLAYMAKERS for a sports agency—was suggestive, and therefore conceptually "somewhat weak," and that defendant ESPN's mark—PLAYMAKERS as the title of a sports-related television series—was commercially "exceptionally strong," and concluding that the strength factor tipped slightly in plaintiff's favor), *aff'd*, 376 F.3d 894 (2004); *Macia v. Microsoft Corp.*, 335 F. Supp. 2d 507, 511-12 (D. Vt. 2004) (observing that the commercial strength of the senior user's mark deserves little weight in a reverse confusion case, but failing to analyze the commercial strength of the junior user's mark, where Microsoft was the junior user).

5. *Reverse confusion and the actual confusion factor.* In a reverse confusion case, who precisely is the relevant consumer? The senior user's customer base? Customers of both the senior and junior users? Potential customers of both? Consider how your answers might affect the admissibility of confusion evidence. Suppose that your opponent in a trademark case conducted a survey to attempt to show reverse confusion, but the senior user's customers were not among the survey population. Would this constitute an inadmissible survey? *See Citizens Fin. Grp., Inc. v. Citizens Nat'l Bank of Evans City*, 383 F.3d 110 (3d Cir. 2004). According to the *A & H* court, a showing of actual confusion in a reverse confusion case may rest in part on evidence of *forward* actual confusion. The *A & H* court declines to create a "strict bar" to the use of evidence of forward actual confusion in a reverse confusion case, instead predicting that cases may well involve evidence of both forward and reverse actual confusion. Do you agree?

6. *Combining forward and reverse confusion theories.* Given that the *A & H* court counsels against creating any "rigid division" between forward and reverse confusion *evidence*, should courts also be advised against creating any such division overall, between forward and reverse confusion *theories*? In *Freedom Card, Inc. v. JPMorgan Chase & Co.*, 432 F.3d 463 (3d Cir. 2005), JPMorgan sought a declaration that its use of CHASE FREEDOM CARD for credit cards did not infringe a senior user's rights in FREEDOM CARD for credit cards. After using the mark for a short time, the senior user (Urban Television Network) stopped promoting its cards in December 2001. JPMorgan began promoting the mark CHASE FREEDOM CARD in January 2003. The senior user claimed that it had planned to partner with other firms to expand efforts to market its cards, but that potential partners lost interest once JPMorgan entered the market. If you were representing the senior user, would you frame an infringement counterclaim as a claim of forward confusion? Reverse confusion? Both? In the actual case, the district court granted summary judgment of no likelihood of confusion, applying the standard multi-factor test for forward confusion, and not mentioning reverse confusion. Has the district court committed error by failing to invoke reverse confusion and failing to apply the altered multi-factor test for reverse confusion?

7. *Is reverse confusion a "likelihood of" theory?* The *A & H* court, quoting a prior decision, describes reverse confusion as a phenomenon occurring when the junior user "saturates the market with a similar trademark and overwhelms the senior user." *A & H Sportswear*, 237 F.3d at 228. Does this imply that reverse confusion is not really a "likelihood of" theory, but rather a theory calling for evidence of consummated confusion? If not, then perhaps the description should be refined: Reverse confusion occurs when the evidence shows that the junior user is likely to saturate the market with a similar trademark and is likely to overwhelm the senior user. Are you satisfied with this refinement? Is it problematic for courts to speculate about the likelihood of saturation? Or is this no more speculative than forward confusion? For a practical take on this debate, *see M2 Software, Inc. v. Madacy Entm't*, 421 F.3d 1073 (9th Cir. 2005) (analyzing whether a jury instruction on reverse confusion using the "saturate the market" language erroneously suggests that reverse confusion requires a showing of existing market saturation). If a mark owner is unable to make a plausible allegation of actual reverse confusion, should a court dismiss on the pleadings under Rule 12(b)(6)? *See Fortres Grand Corp. v. Warner Bros. Entm't Inc.*, 763 F.3d 696 (7th Cir. 2014) (upholding a motion to dismiss a reverse confusion allegation based on the lack of a plausible actual confusion allegation and an analysis of other confusion factors).

8. *Reverse confusion in the Section 2(d) context.* The Federal Circuit and TTAB have employed reverse confusion theories to sustain oppositions under Section 2(d) and to uphold the denial of registrations under Section 2(d). *See, e.g., Hilson Research Inc. v. Soc'y for Human Res. Mgmt.*, 27 U.S.P.Q.2d (BNA) 1423 (TTAB 1993) (sustaining opposition on the ground of reverse confusion); *In re Shell Oil Co.*, 992 F.2d 1204 (Fed. Cir. 1993) (affirming denial of registration on ground of reverse confusion).

   9.   *Reverse confusion: examples.* For cases finding reverse confusion, *see, e.g., Big O Tire Dealers, Inc. v. Goodyear Tire & Rubber Co.*, 561 F.2d 1365 (10th Cir. 1977) (Goodyear's use of the mark BIGFOOT is likely to cause reverse confusion with the products from the plaintiff dealer); *Sands, Taylor & Wood Co. v. Quaker Oats Co.*, 978 F.2d 947 (7th Cir. 1992) (defendant Quaker Oats' use of the mark GATORADE IS THIRST AID is likely to cause confusion with senior user's registered mark, THIRST-AID); *Banff, Ltd. v. Federated Dep't Stores, Inc.*, 841 F.2d 486 (2d Cir. 1988) (Bloomingdale's "B Wear" women's clothing line likely to cause reverse confusion with Banff's women's apparel line called "Bee Wear"). *See also Commerce Nat'l Ins. Servs., Inc. v. Commerce Ins. Agency, Inc.*, 214 F.3d 432 (3d Cir. 2000) (use of COMMERCE by bank's insurance services division is likely to cause reverse confusion with the COMMERCE mark owned by Commerce Insurance Agency); *Dreamwerks Prod. Grp., Inc. v. SKG Studio*, 142 F.3d 1127 (9th Cir. 1998) (summary judgment for defendant is reversed and remanded because defendant studio's mark "DreamWorks" could constitute reverse confusion with plaintiff's mark "Dreamwerks" used for science fiction conventions).

   For cases recognizing the reverse confusion theory but finding no reverse confusion on the facts presented, *see, e.g., Cohn v. Petsmart, Inc.*, 281 F.3d 837 (9th Cir. 2002) (pet supply store's use of the mark WHERE PETS ARE FAMILY is not likely to cause reverse confusion with a veterinarian's use of the same phrase); *MicroStrategy Inc. v. Motorola, Inc.*, 245 F.3d 335 (4th Cir. 2001) (defendant Motorola's use of mark INTELLIGENCE EVERYWHERE not likely to cause reverse confusion with software company's use of the same phrase); *Walter v. Mattel, Inc.*, 210 F.3d 1108 (9th Cir. 2000) ("Pearl Beach Barbie" is not likely to cause reverse confusion with plaintiff's mark "Pearl Beach" used in commercial illustrations for advertisements, brochures, and product packaging); *W.W.W. Pharm. Co. v. Gillette Co.*, 984 F.2d 567 (2d Cir. 1993) (plaintiff's use of SPORTSTICK for lip balm not likely to cause reverse confusion with junior user's mark RIGHT GUARD SPORT STICK); *Chattanoga Mfg, Inc. v. Nike, Inc.*, 140 F. Supp. 2d 917 (N.D. Ill. 2001) (defendant Nike's use of JORDAN for apparel line named after Michael Jordan not likely to cause reverse confusion with plaintiff's use of JORDAN for women's clothing line), *aff'd as modified*, 301 F.3d 789 (2002).

F.   INDIRECT AND VICARIOUS THEORIES OF INFRINGEMENT LIABILITY

INWOOD LABORATORIES, INC. v. IVES LABORATORIES, INC.

456 U.S. 844 (1982)

Justice O'CONNOR delivered the opinion of the Court:

   This action requires us to consider the circumstances under which a manufacturer of a generic drug, designed to duplicate the appearance of a similar drug marketed by a competitor under a registered trademark, can be held vicariously liable for infringement of that trademark by pharmacists who dispense the generic drug.

I

In 1955, respondent Ives Laboratories, Inc. (Ives), received a patent on the drug cyclandelate, a vasodilator used in long-term therapy for peripheral and cerebral vascular diseases. Until its patent expired in 1972, Ives retained the exclusive right to make and sell the drug, which it did under the registered trademark CYCLOSPASMOL. Ives marketed the drug, a white powder, to wholesalers, retail pharmacists, and hospitals in colored gelatin capsules. Ives arbitrarily selected a blue capsule, imprinted with "Ives 4124," for its 200 mg dosage and a combination blue-red capsule, imprinted with "Ives 4148," for its 400 mg dosage.

After Ives' patent expired, several generic drug manufacturers, including petitioners Premo Pharmaceutical Laboratories, Inc., Inwood Laboratories, Inc., and MD Pharmaceutical Co., Inc. (collectively the generic manufacturers), began marketing cyclandelate. They intentionally copied the appearance of the CYCLOSPASMOL capsules, selling cyclandelate in 200 mg and 400 mg capsules in colors identical to those selected by Ives.

The marketing methods used by Ives reflect normal industry practice. Because cyclandelate can be obtained only by prescription, Ives does not direct its advertising to the ultimate consumer. Instead, Ives' representatives pay personal visits to physicians, to whom they distribute product literature and "starter samples." Ives initially directed these efforts toward convincing physicians that CYCLOSPASMOL is superior to other vasodilators. Now that its patent has expired and generic manufacturers have entered the market, Ives concentrates on convincing physicians to indicate on prescriptions that a generic drug cannot be substituted for CYCLOSPASMOL.

The generic manufacturers also follow a normal industry practice by promoting their products primarily by distribution of catalogs to wholesalers, hospitals, and retail pharmacies, rather than by contacting physicians directly. The catalogs truthfully describe generic cyclandelate as "equivalent" or "comparable" to CYCLOSPASMOL. In addition, some of the catalogs include price comparisons of the generic drug and CYCLOSPASMOL and some refer to the color of the generic capsules. The generic products reach wholesalers, hospitals, and pharmacists in bulk containers which correctly indicate the manufacturer of the product contained therein.

A pharmacist, regardless of whether he is dispensing CYCLOSPASMOL or a generic drug, removes the capsules from the container in which he receives them and dispenses them to the consumer in the pharmacist's own bottle with his own label attached. Hence, the final consumer sees no identifying marks other than those on the capsules themselves.

II

A

Ives instituted this action in the United States District Court for the Eastern District of New York under §§32 and 43(a) of the Trademark Act of 1946 (Lanham Act), and under New York's unfair competition law, N.Y. Gen. Bus. Law §368-d (McKinney 1968).

Ives' claim under §32, derived from its allegation that some pharmacists had dispensed generic drugs mislabeled as CYCLOSPASMOL. Ives contended that the generic manufacturers' use of look-alike capsules and of catalog entries comparing prices and revealing the colors of the generic capsules induced pharmacists illegally to substitute a generic drug for CYCLOSPASMOL and to mislabel the substitute drug CYCLOSPASMOL. Although Ives did not allege that the petitioners themselves applied the Ives trademark to the drug products they produced and distributed, it did allege that the petitioners contributed to the infringing activities of pharmacists who mislabeled generic cyclandelate.

Ives' claim under §43(a), alleged that the petitioners falsely designated the origin of their products by copying the capsule colors used by Ives and by promoting the generic products as equivalent to CYCLOSPASMOL. In support of its claim, Ives argued that the colors of its capsules were not functional and that they had developed a secondary meaning for the consumers.

Contending that pharmacists would continue to mislabel generic drugs as CYCLOSPASMOL so long as imitative products were available, Ives asked that the court enjoin the petitioners from marketing cyclandelate capsules in the same colors and form as Ives uses for CYCLOSPASMOL. In addition, Ives sought damages pursuant to §35 of the Lanham Act.

B

The District Court denied Ives' request for an order preliminarily enjoining the petitioners from selling generic drugs identical in appearance to those produced by Ives. [cit.] Referring to the claim based upon §32, the District Court stated that, while the "knowing and deliberate instigation" by the petitioners of mislabeling by pharmacists would justify holding the petitioners as well as the pharmacists liable for trademark infringement, Ives had made no showing sufficient to justify preliminary relief. [cit.] Ives had not established that the petitioners conspired with the pharmacists or suggested that they disregard physicians' prescriptions.

The Court of Appeals for the Second Circuit affirmed. [cit.] To assist the District Court in the upcoming trial on the merits, the appellate court defined the elements of a claim based upon §32 in some detail. Relying primarily upon *Coca-Cola Co. v. Snow Crest Beverages, Inc.*, 64 F. Supp. 980 (Mass. 1946), *aff'd*, 162 F.2d 280 [(1st Cir.)], *cert. denied*, 332 U.S. 809 (1947), the court stated that the petitioners would be liable under §32 either if they suggested, even by implication, that retailers fill bottles with generic cyclandelate and label the bottle with Ives' trademark or if the petitioners continued to sell cyclandelate to retailers whom they knew or had reason to know were engaging in infringing practices.

C

After a bench trial on remand, the District Court entered judgment for the petitioners. 488 F. Supp. 394 (1980). Applying the test approved by the Court of Appeals to the claim based upon §32, the District Court found that the petitioners had not suggested, even by implication, that pharmacists should dispense generic drugs incorrectly identified as CYCLOSPASMOL.[12]

In reaching that conclusion, the court first looked for direct evidence that the petitioners intentionally induced trademark infringement. Since the petitioners' representatives do not make personal visits to physicians and pharmacists, the petitioners were not in a position directly to suggest improper drug substitutions. *Cf. William R. Warner & Co. v. Eli Lilly & Co.*, 265 U.S. 526, 530-531 (1924); *Smith, Kline & French Laboratories v. Clark & Clark*, 157 F.2d 725, 731 (CA3), *cert. denied*, 329 U.S. 796 (1946). Therefore, the court

---

12. The District Court also found that the petitioners did not continue to provide drugs to retailers whom they knew or should have known were engaging in trademark infringement. The Court of Appeals did not discuss that finding, and we do not address it.

concluded, improper suggestions, if any, must have come from catalogs and promotional materials. The court determined, however, that those materials could not "fairly be read" to suggest trademark infringement. [cit.]

The trial court next considered evidence of actual instances of mislabeling by pharmacists, since frequent improper substitutions of a generic drug for CYCLOSPASMOL could provide circumstantial evidence that the petitioners, merely by making available imitative drugs in conjunction with comparative price advertising, implicitly had suggested that pharmacists substitute improperly. After reviewing the evidence of incidents of mislabeling, the District Court concluded that such incidents occurred too infrequently to justify the inference that the petitioners' catalogs and use of imitative colors had "impliedly invited" druggists to mislabel. Moreover, to the extent mislabeling had occurred, the court found it resulted from pharmacists' misunderstanding of the requirements of the New York Drug Substitution Law, rather than from deliberate attempts to pass off generic cyclandelate as CYCLOSPASMOL. *Ibid.*

. . .

Without expressly stating that the District Court's findings were clearly erroneous, and for reasons which we discuss below, the Court of Appeals concluded that the petitioners violated §32. The Court of Appeals did not reach Ives' other claims. We granted certiorari [cit.], and now reverse the judgment of the Court of Appeals.

III

A

As the lower courts correctly discerned, liability for trademark infringement can extend beyond those who actually mislabel goods with the mark of another. Even if a manufacturer does not directly control others in the chain of distribution, it can be held responsible for their infringing activities under certain circumstances. Thus, if a manufacturer or distributor intentionally induces another to infringe a trademark, or if it continues to supply its product to one whom it knows or has reason to know is engaging in trademark infringement, the manufacturer or distributor is contributorily responsible for any harm done as a result of the deceit.[13] *See William R. Warner & Co. v. Eli Lilly & Co., supra; Coca-Cola Co. v. Snow Crest Beverages, Inc., supra.*

It is undisputed that those pharmacists who mislabeled generic drugs with Ives' registered trademark violated §32. However, whether these petitioners were liable for the pharmacists' infringing acts depended upon whether, in fact, the petitioners intentionally induced the pharmacists to mislabel generic drugs or, in fact, continued to supply cyclandelate to pharmacists whom the petitioners knew were mislabeling generic drugs. The District Court concluded that Ives made neither of those factual showings.

. . .

---

13. Justice WHITE, in his opinion concurring in the result, voices his concern that we may have "silently acquiesce[d] in a significant change in the test for contributory infringement." *Post*, at 2192. His concern derives from his perception that the Court of Appeals abandoned the standard enunciated by Judge Friendly in its first opinion, a standard which both we and Justice WHITE approve, *post*, at 2191. The Court of Appeals, however, expressly premised its second opinion on "the governing legal principles . . . set forth in Judge Friendly's opinion upon the earlier appeal, 601 F.2d 631 (2d Cir. 1979)," and explicitly claimed to have rendered its second decision by "[a]pplying those principles. . . ." 638 F.2d 538, 542 (1981). Justice WHITE's concern is based on a comment by the Court of Appeals that the generic manufacturers "could reasonably anticipate" illegal substitution of their drugs. *Id.*, at 543. If the Court of Appeals had relied upon that statement to define the controlling legal standard, the court indeed would have applied a "watered down" and incorrect standard. As we read the Court of Appeals' opinion, however, that statement was intended merely to buttress the court's conclusion that the legal test for contributory infringement, as earlier defined, had been met. [cit.]

IV

In reversing the District Court's judgment, the Court of Appeals initially held that the trial court failed to give sufficient weight to the evidence Ives offered to show a "pattern of illegal substitution and mislabeling in New York. . . ." 638 F.2d, at 543. By rejecting the District Court's findings simply because it would have given more weight to evidence of mislabeling than did the trial court, the Court of Appeals clearly erred. Determining the weight and credibility of the evidence is the special province of the trier of fact. Because the trial court's findings concerning the significance of the instances of mislabeling were not clearly erroneous, they should not have been disturbed.

Next, after completing its own review of the evidence, the Court of Appeals concluded that the evidence was "clearly sufficient to establish a §32 violation." *Ibid*. In reaching its conclusion, the Court of Appeals was influenced by several factors. First, it thought the petitioners reasonably could have anticipated misconduct by a substantial number of the pharmacists who were provided imitative, lower priced products which, if substituted for the higher priced brand name without passing on savings to consumers, could provide an economic advantage to the pharmacists. *Ibid*. Second, it disagreed with the trial court's finding that the mislabeling which did occur reflected confusion about state law requirements. *Id.*, at 544. Third, it concluded that illegal substitution and mislabeling in New York are neither *de minimis* nor inadvertent. *Ibid*. Finally, the Court of Appeals indicated it was further influenced by the fact that the petitioners did not offer "any persuasive evidence of a legitimate reason unrelated to CYCLOSPASMOL" for producing an imitative product. *Ibid*.

Each of those conclusions is contrary to the findings of the District Court. An appellate court cannot substitute its interpretation of the evidence for that of the trial court simply because the reviewing court "might give the facts another construction, resolve the ambiguities differently, and find a more sinister cast to actions which the District Court apparently deemed innocent." *United States v. Real Estate Boards*, 339 U.S. 485 (1950).

. . .

Reversed and remanded.

Justice WHITE, with whom Justice MARSHALL joins, concurring in the result:

I . . . concur in reversal because I believe that the Court of Appeals has watered down to an impermissible extent the standard for finding a violation of §32 of the Lanham Act, 15 U.S.C. §1114.

In its first opinion in this litigation, the Court of Appeals indicated that a "manufacturer or wholesaler would be liable under §32 if he suggested, even if only by implication, that a retailer fill a bottle with the generic capsules and apply Ives' mark to the label, or continued to sell capsules containing the generic drug which facilitated this to a druggist whom he knew or had reason to know was engaging in the practices just described." 601 F.2d 631, 636 (1979) (*Ives II*). The District Court applied this test but concluded that no violation of §32 had been shown. On appeal after trial, a majority of the Second Circuit found defendants liable for contributory infringement by revising and expanding the doctrine of contributory trademark infringement. 638 F.2d 538 (1981) (*Ives IV*):

> By using capsules of identical color, size, and shape, together with a catalog describing their appearance and listing comparable prices of CYCLOSPASMOL and generic cyclandelate, appellees *could reasonably anticipate* that their generic drug product would by a substantial number of druggists be substituted illegally. . . . This amounted to a suggestion, at least by implication, that the druggists take advantage of the opportunity to engage in such misconduct. *Id.*, [sic] at 543 (emphasis added).

Ives II required a showing that petitioners intended illegal substitution or knowingly continued to supply pharmacists palming off generic cyclandelate as CYCLOSPASMOL; *Ives IV* was satisfied merely by the failure to "reasonably anticipate" that illegal substitution by some pharmacists was likely. In my view, this is an erroneous construction of the statutory law governing trademark protection.

The mere fact that a generic drug company can anticipate that some illegal substitution will occur to some unspecified extent, and by some unknown pharmacists, should not by itself be a predicate for contributory liability. I thus am inclined to believe that the Court silently acquiesces in a significant change in the test for contributory infringement.

Diluting the requirement for establishing a prima facie case of contributory trademark infringement is particularly unjustified in the generic drugs field. Preventing the use of generic drugs of the same color to which customers had become accustomed in their prior use of the brand name product interferes with the important state policy, expressed in New York and 47 other States, of promoting the substitution of generic formulations. *See* Warner, *Consumer Protection and Prescription Drugs: The Generic Drug Substitution Laws,* 61 Ky. L.J. 384 (1978-1979).

TIFFANY (NJ) INC. v. eBAY INC.

600 F.3d 93 (2d Cir. 2010), cert. denied, 131 S. Ct. 647 (2010)

SACK, Circuit Judge:

BACKGROUND

[eBay operates an Internet-based auction site where sellers can list goods for sale. More than 6 million new listings are posted on eBay's site daily, and the site contains some 100 million listings at any given time. eBay charges sellers an initial fee for listed items (based on a percentage of the starting price), another fee for completed sales (based on a percentage of the final sale price), and a fee for each transaction that it processes through its PayPal system (again based on a percentage of the transaction amount).

Tiffany sells branded jewelry exclusively through its own outlets. Sometime before 2004, Tiffany became aware that counterfeit Tiffany merchandise was being sold on eBay's site. Tiffany attempted to assess the extent of the problem by instituting two "Buying Programs" in which Tiffany bought purported Tiffany goods on eBay and inspected them. According to Tiffany, about 75 percent of the purchased items were counterfeits.

eBay never inspected the merchandise sold via its site (and might not have been able to detect counterfeits if it had), but eBay did engage in various methods to address counterfeiting problems on its site. eBay claimed to have spent as much as $20 million per year on "tools to promote trust and safety on its website." It established a "Trust and Safety" department staffed with some 4,000 employees, 200 of whom focused exclusively on infringement issues. It created a "fraud engine" that conducted automatic searches for counterfeiting activity, including searches specifically targeting Tiffany counterfeits. It set up a notice-and-takedown system (the "Verified Rights Owner," or VeRO, program) where IP rights owners could notify eBay of potentially infringing listings by filing a "Notice of Claimed Infringement" (NOCI) form, and eBay would respond by removing the notified listing within twelve to twenty-four hours. eBay also invited rights owners to create "About Me" warning pages (Tiffany stated that most of the purported Tiffany jewelry sold on eBay was counterfeit). eBay suspended sellers who were suspected of offering infringing goods, often employing a "three-strikes" rule, and delayed the listing of certain brand-name articles for a few hours (including Tiffany products) to give the mark owner more time to review the listing. Finally, eBay instituted certain Tiffany-specific measures, such as displaying automated warning messages to sellers who listed purported Tiffany items.

On the other hand, eBay also advertised to potential buyers that Tiffany merchandise was available on the eBay site, and urged potential sellers to "take advantage of the demand for Tiffany merchandise" on eBay.

Tiffany sued eBay on numerous Lanham Act claims. The District Court decided in favor of eBay on all issues.]

DISCUSSION

I.   DIRECT TRADEMARK INFRINGEMENT

[The Court of Appeals agreed with the District Court that eBay had not engaged in direct infringement when it used the TIFFANY mark to refer to Tiffany on the eBay website. The use of another's mark is permissible where the mark is necessary to identify the other's products and the use does not imply endorsement or affiliation. Some courts identify this principle as "nominative fair use," which we discuss in Chapter 9. The Second Circuit endorsed the principle, concluding therefore that eBay had not engaged in direct infringement. The Second Circuit avoided ruling on the appropriateness of the label "nominative fair use."]

II.   CONTRIBUTORY TRADEMARK INFRINGEMENT

The more difficult issue, and the one that the parties have properly focused our attention on, is whether eBay is liable for contributory trademark infringement—i.e., for culpably facilitating the infringing conduct of the counterfeiting vendors. Acknowledging the paucity of case law to guide us, we conclude that the district court correctly granted judgment on this issue in favor of eBay.

A.   Principles

. . .

Inwood's test for contributory trademark infringement applies on its face to manufacturers and distributors of goods. Courts have, however, extended the test to providers of services.

. . .

[T]he Ninth Circuit concluded that *Inwood*'s test for contributory trademark infringement applies to a service provider if he or she exercises sufficient control over the infringing conduct. *Lockheed Martin Corp. v. Network Solutions, Inc.*, 194 F.3d 980, 984 (9th Cir. 1999); *see also id.* ("Direct control and monitoring of the instrumentality used by a third party to infringe the plaintiff's mark permits the expansion of *Inwood Lab.*'s 'supplies a product' requirement for contributory infringement.").

B.   Discussion

1.   Does *Inwood* Apply?

In the district court, the parties disputed whether eBay was subject to the *Inwood* test. [cit.] eBay argued that it was not because it supplies a service while *Inwood* governs only manufacturers and distributors of products. [cit.] The district court rejected that distinction. It adopted instead the reasoning of the Ninth Circuit in *Lockheed* to conclude that *Inwood* applies to a service provider who exercises sufficient control over the means of the infringing conduct. [cit.] Looking "to the extent of the control exercised by eBay over its sellers' means of infringement," the district court concluded that *Inwood* applied in light of the "significant control" eBay retained over the transactions and listings facilitated by and conducted through its website. [cit.]

On appeal, eBay no longer maintains that it is not subject to *Inwood*.[10] We therefore assume without deciding that *Inwood*'s test for contributory trademark infringement governs.

2.   Is eBay Liable Under *Inwood*?

The question that remains, then, is whether eBay is liable under the *Inwood* test on the basis of the services it provided to those who used its website to sell counterfeit Tiffany products. As noted, when applying *Inwood* to service providers, there are two ways in which a defendant may become contributorily liable for the infringing conduct of another: first, if the service provider "intentionally induces another to infringe a trademark," and second, if the service provider "continues to supply its [service] to one whom it knows or has reason to know is engaging in trademark infringement." *Inwood*, 456 U.S. at 854. Tiffany does not argue that eBay induced the sale of counterfeit Tiffany goods on its website — the circumstances addressed by the first part of the *Inwood* test. It argues instead, under the second part of the *Inwood* test, that eBay continued to supply its services to the sellers of counterfeit Tiffany goods while knowing or having reason to know that such sellers were infringing Tiffany's mark.

The district court rejected this argument. First, it concluded that to the extent the NOCIs that Tiffany submitted gave eBay reason to know that particular listings were for counterfeit goods, eBay did not continue to carry those listings once it learned that they were specious. The court found that eBay's practice was promptly to remove the challenged listing from its website, warn sellers and buyers, cancel fees it earned from that listing, and direct buyers not to consummate the sale of the disputed item. The court therefore declined to hold eBay contributorily liable for the infringing conduct of those sellers. On appeal, Tiffany does not appear to challenge this conclusion. In any event, we agree with the district court that no liability arises with respect to those terminated listings.

Tiffany disagrees vigorously, however, with the district court's further determination that eBay lacked sufficient knowledge of trademark infringement by sellers behind other, non-terminated listings to provide a basis for *Inwood* liability. Tiffany argued in the district court that eBay knew, or at least had reason to know, that counterfeit Tiffany goods were being sold ubiquitously on its website. As evidence, it pointed to, *inter alia*, the demand letters it sent to eBay in 2003 and 2004, the results of its Buying Programs that it shared with eBay, the thousands of NOCIs it filed with eBay alleging its good faith belief that certain listings were counterfeit, and the various complaints eBay received from buyers claiming that they had purchased one or more counterfeit Tiffany items through eBay's website. Tiffany argued that taken together, this evidence established eBay's knowledge of the widespread sale of counterfeit Tiffany products on its website. Tiffany urged that eBay be held contributorily liable on the basis that despite that knowledge, it continued to make its services available to infringing sellers.

The district court rejected this argument. It acknowledged that "[t]he evidence produced at trial demonstrated that eBay had *generalized* notice that some portion of the Tiffany

---

10. Amici do so claim. *See Electronic Frontier Foundation et al.* Amici Br. 6 (arguing that *Inwood* should "not govern where, as here, the alleged contributory infringer has no direct means to establish whether there is any act of direct infringement in the first place"). We decline to consider this argument. . . .

goods sold on its website might be counterfeit" (emphasis in original). The court characterized the issue before it as "whether eBay's *generalized* knowledge of trademark infringement on its website was sufficient to meet the 'knowledge or reason to know' prong of the *Inwood* test" (emphasis in original). eBay had argued that "such generalized knowledge is insufficient, and that the law demands more specific knowledge of individual instances of infringement and infringing sellers before imposing a burden upon eBay to remedy the problem."

The district court concluded that "while eBay clearly possessed general knowledge as to counterfeiting on its website, such generalized knowledge is insufficient under the *Inwood* test to impose upon eBay an affirmative duty to remedy the problem." The court reasoned that *Inwood*'s language explicitly imposes contributory liability on a defendant who "continues to supply its product[— in eBay's case, its service —]to *one* whom it knows or has reason to know is engaging in trademark infringement" (emphasis in original). The court also noted that plaintiffs "bear a high burden in establishing 'knowledge' of contributory infringement," and that courts have

> been reluctant to extend contributory trademark liability to defendants where there is some uncertainty as to the extent or the nature of the infringement. In *Inwood*, Justice White emphasized in his concurring opinion that a defendant is not "require[d] . . . to refuse to sell to dealers who merely *might* pass off its goods."

(quoting *Inwood*, 456 U.S. at 861 (White, J., concurring) (emphasis and alteration in original)).

Accordingly, the district court concluded that for Tiffany to establish eBay's contributory liability, Tiffany would have to show that eBay "knew or had reason to know of specific instances of actual infringement" beyond those that it addressed upon learning of them. Tiffany failed to make such a showing.

On appeal, Tiffany argues that the distinction drawn by the district court between eBay's general knowledge of the sale of counterfeit Tiffany goods through its website, and its specific knowledge as to which particular sellers were making such sales, is a "false" one not required by the law. Tiffany posits that the only relevant question is "whether all of the knowledge, when taken together, puts [eBay] on notice that there is a substantial problem of trademark infringement. If so and if it fails to act, [eBay] is liable for contributory trademark infringement."

We agree with the district court. For contributory trademark infringement liability to lie, a service provider must have more than a general knowledge or reason to know that its service is being used to sell counterfeit goods. Some contemporary knowledge of which particular listings are infringing or will infringe in the future is necessary.

We are not persuaded by Tiffany's proposed interpretation of *Inwood*. Tiffany understands the "lesson of *Inwood*" to be that an action for contributory trademark infringement lies where "the evidence [of infringing activity] — direct or circumstantial, taken as a whole — . . . provide[s] a basis for finding that the defendant knew or should have known that its product or service was being used to further illegal counterfeiting activity." We think that Tiffany reads *Inwood* too broadly. Although the *Inwood* Court articulated a "knows or has reason to know" prong in setting out its contributory liability test, the Court explicitly declined to apply that prong to the facts then before it. *See Inwood*, 456 U.S. at 852 n.12 ("The District Court also found that the petitioners did not continue to provide drugs to retailers whom they knew or should have known were engaging in trademark infringement. The Court of Appeals did not discuss that finding, and we do not address it.") (internal citation omitted). The Court applied only the inducement prong of the test. *See id.* at 852-59.

We therefore do not think that *Inwood* establishes the contours of the "knows or has reason to know" prong. Insofar as it speaks to the issue, though, the particular phrasing that the Court used — that a defendant will be liable if it "continues to supply its product to *one* whom it knows or has reason to know is engaging in trademark infringement," [cit.] (emphasis added)—supports the district court's interpretation of *Inwood*, not Tiffany's.

We find helpful the Supreme Court's discussion of *Inwood* in a subsequent *copyright* case, *Sony Corp. of America v. Universal City Studios, Inc.*, 464 U.S. 417 (1984). There, defendant Sony manufactured and sold home video tape recorders. [cit.] Plaintiffs Universal Studios and Walt Disney Productions held copyrights on various television programs that individual tele-vision-viewers had taped using the defendant's recorders. [cit.] The plaintiffs contended that this use of the recorders constituted copyright infringement for which the defendants should be held contributorily liable. *Id.* at 419-20. In ruling for the defendants, the Court discussed *Inwood* and the differences between contributory liability in trademark versus copyright law.

> If *Inwood*'s *narrow standard* for contributory trademark infringement governed here, [the plaintiffs'] claim of contributory infringement would merit little discussion. Sony certainly does not "intentionally induce[]" its customers to make infringing uses of [the plaintiffs'] copy-rights, nor does it supply its products to *identified individuals known by it* to be engaging in continuing infringement of [the plaintiffs'] copyrights.

Id. at 439 n.19 (quoting *Inwood*, 456 U.S. at 855; emphases added).

Thus, the Court suggested, had the *Inwood* standard applied in *Sony*, the fact that Sony might have known that some portion of the purchasers of its product used it to violate the copyrights of others would not have provided a sufficient basis for contributory liability. *Inwood*'s "narrow standard" would have required knowledge by Sony of "identified indi-viduals" engaging in infringing conduct. Tiffany's reading of *Inwood* is therefore contrary to the interpretation of that case set forth in *Sony*.

Although the Supreme Court's observations in *Sony*, a copyright case, about the "knows or has reason to know" prong of the contributory trademark infringement test set forth in *Inwood* were dicta, they constitute the only discussion of that prong by the Supreme Court of which we are aware. We think them to be persuasive authority here.[12]

Applying *Sony*'s interpretation of *Inwood*, we agree with the district court that "Tiffany's general allegations of counterfeiting failed to provide eBay with the knowledge required under *Inwood*." Tiffany's demand letters and Buying Programs did not identify particular sellers who Tiffany thought were then offering or would offer counterfeit goods. [cit.] And although the NOCIs and buyer complaints gave eBay reason to know that cer-tain sellers had been selling counterfeits, those sellers' listings were removed and repeat offenders were suspended from the eBay site. Thus Tiffany failed to demonstrate that eBay was supplying its service to individuals who it knew or had reason to know were selling counterfeit Tiffany goods.

Accordingly, we affirm the judgment of the district court insofar as it holds that eBay is not contributorily liable for trademark infringement.

3. Willful Blindness

Tiffany and its amici express their concern that if eBay is not held liable except when specific counterfeit listings are brought to its attention, eBay will have no incentive to root out such listings from its website. They argue that this will effectively require Tiffany and similarly situated retailers to police eBay's website—and many others like it—"24 hours a

---

12. In discussing *Inwood*'s "knows or has reason to know" prong of the contributory infringe-ment test, *Sony* refers to a defendant's knowledge, but not to its constructive knowledge, of a third party's infringing conduct. *Sony*, 464 U.S. at 439 n. 19. We do not take the omission as altering the test *Inwood* articulates.

day, and 365 days a year." *Council of Fashion Designers of America, Inc.* Amicus Br. 5. They urge that this is a burden that most mark holders cannot afford to bear.

First, and most obviously, we are interpreting the law and applying it to the facts of this case. We could not, even if we thought it wise, revise the existing law in order to better serve one party's interests at the expense of the other's.

But we are also disposed to think, and the record suggests, that private market forces give eBay and those operating similar businesses a strong incentive to minimize the counterfeit goods sold on their websites. eBay received many complaints from users claiming to have been duped into buying counterfeit Tiffany products sold on eBay. [cit.] The risk of alienating these users gives eBay a reason to identify and remove counterfeit listings.[14] Indeed, it has spent millions of dollars in that effort.

Moreover, we agree with the district court that if eBay had reason to suspect that counterfeit Tiffany goods were being sold through its website, and intentionally shielded itself from discovering the offending listings or the identity of the sellers behind them, eBay might very well have been charged with knowledge of those sales sufficient to satisfy *Inwood*'s "knows or has reason to know" prong. [cit.] A service provider is not, we think, permitted willful blindness. When it has reason to suspect that users of its service are infringing a protected mark, it may not shield itself from learning of the particular infringing transactions by looking the other way. *See, e.g., Hard Rock Café Licensing Corp. v. Concession Servs., Inc.*, 955 F.2d 1143, 1149 (7th Cir. 1992) ("To be willfully blind, a person must suspect wrongdoing and deliberately fail to investigate."); *Fonovisa, Inc. v. Cherry Auction*, 76 F.3d 259, 265 (9th Cir. 1996) (applying *Hard Rock Café*'s reasoning to conclude that "a swap meet can not disregard its vendors' blatant trademark infringements with impunity").[15] In the words of the Seventh Circuit, "willful blindness is equivalent to actual knowledge for purposes of the Lanham Act." *Hard Rock Café*, 955 F.2d at 1149.

eBay appears to concede that it knew as a general matter that counterfeit Tiffany products were listed and sold through its website. [cit.] Without more, however, this knowledge is insufficient to trigger liability under *Inwood*. The district court found, after careful consideration, that eBay was not willfully blind to the counterfeit sales. [cit.] That finding is not clearly erroneous.[17] eBay did not ignore the information it was given about counterfeit sales on its website.

[*Affirmed* as to trademark infringement.]

---

14. At the same time, we appreciate the argument that insofar as eBay receives revenue from undetected counterfeit listings and sales through the fees it charges, it has an incentive to permit such listings and sales to continue.

15. To be clear, a service provider is not contributorily liable under *Inwood* merely for failing to anticipate that others would use its service to infringe a protected mark. *Inwood*, 456 U.S. at 854 n. 13 (stating that for contributory liability to lie, a defendant must do more than "reasonably anticipate" a third party's infringing conduct (internal quotation marks omitted)). But contributory liability may arise where a defendant is (as was eBay here) made aware that there was infringement on its site but (unlike eBay here) ignored that fact.

17. Tiffany's reliance on the "flea market" cases, *Hard Rock Café* and *Fonovisa*, is unavailing. eBay's efforts to combat counterfeiting far exceeded the efforts made by the defendants in those cases. *See Hard Rock Café*, 955 F.2d at 1146 (defendant did not investigate any of the seizures of counterfeit products at its swap meet, even though it knew they had occurred); *Fonovisa*, 76 F.3d at 265 (concluding that plaintiff stated a claim for contributory trademark infringement based on allegation that swap meet "disregard[ed] its vendors' blatant trademark infringements with impunity"). Moreover, neither case concluded that the defendant was willfully blind. The court in *Hard Rock Café* remanded so that the district court could apply the correct definition of "willful blindness," 955 F.2d at 1149, and the court in *Fonovisa* merely sustained the plaintiff's complaint against a motion to dismiss, 76 F.3d at 260-61, 265.

NOTES AND QUESTIONS

1.   *Indirect infringement and the patent statute.* Contributory trademark infringement is a species of "indirect" infringement. Indirect infringement claims appear in many settings in intellectual property. In U.S. patent law, indirect infringement standards are better developed than in U.S. trademark law. For example, patent law has relatively detailed indirect infringement statutory provisions:

35 U.S.C. §271 INFRINGEMENT OF PATENT

. . .

(b) Whoever actively induces infringement of a patent shall be liable as an infringer.

(c) Whoever offers to sell or sells within the United States or imports into the United States a component of a patented machine, manufacture, combination or composition, or a material or apparatus for use in practicing a patented process, constituting a material part of the invention, knowing the same to be especially made or especially adapted for use in an infringement of such patent, and not a staple article or commodity of commerce suitable for substantial noninfringing use, shall be liable as a contributory infringer.

How does the patent law standard differ from the trademark standard articulated in *Inwood*? The Lanham Act includes no statutory provision for indirect infringement; standards are entirely the product of case law development. Should Congress develop a contributory infringement provision for the Lanham Act? Should the provision simply codify the common law standard articulated in *Inwood*? Should such a provision track the patent statute?

2.   *Indirect infringement and copyright law.* Claims of indirect copyright infringement are adjudicated under common law indirect infringement standards. *See, e.g., Sony Corp. of Am. v. Universal City Studios, Inc.*, 464 U.S. 417 (1984) (borrowing standards from the patent statute for contributory infringement liability); *Fonovisa, Inc. v. Cherry Auction, Inc.*, 76 F.3d 259 (9th Cir. 1996) (analyzing contributory and vicarious liability); *A&M Records, Inc. v. Napster, Inc.*, 239 F.3d 1004 (9th Cir. 2001) (same). In *Metro-Goldwyn-Mayer Studios Inc. v. Grokster*, 545 U.S. 913 (2005), the Supreme Court invoked an inducement theory to impose liability on distributors of peer-to-peer file sharing software that was being used to share copyrighted works. In a unanimous opinion, the Court announced that "one who distributes a device with the object of promoting its use to infringe copyright, as shown by clear expression or other affirmative steps taken to foster infringement, is liable for the resulting acts of infringement by third parties." *Id.* at 919. Grokster had communicated a clear "inducing message" to its customers, and additional circumstances suggested inducement. In particular, Grokster was responding to a known source of demand for infringing materials; Grokster had failed to develop filtering software to minimize infringing activity; and Grokster's very business model (ad revenue linked to the extent of the software's use) appeared to be built around widespread infringement. Does the *Grokster* approach—in particular, the set of considerations listed above—also reflect (or illuminate) the *Inwood* standard for secondary liability in trademark law? If competitors purchase rivals' trademarks using Google's Adwords program, and Google's liability for trademark infringement is treated as inducement of the primary infringement of the competitors, would *Grokster* affect whether Google should be held secondarily liable?

There is some residual controversy in the cases about whether copyright and trademark indirect infringement standards stand on common ground. In *Sony*, the Supreme Court had distinguished between the copyright and trademark standards, refusing to apply *Inwood. Sony Corp. of Am.*, 464 U.S. at 439 n.19. Would the Court draw such a distinction today? In answering the question, consider how the Second Circuit in *Tiffany v. eBay* made use of the *Sony* discussion.

3. *Evolution of the contributory infringement standard in trademark law.* The contributory infringement standard enunciated in *Inwood* had been articulated many years earlier. In *Coca-Cola Co. v. Snow Crest Beverages, Inc.*, 64 F. Supp. 980, 989 (D. Mass. 1946), cited in *Inwood*, the court explained the standard for contributory trademark infringement as follows:

> It is, of course, defendant's duty to avoid intentionally inducing bars to market defendant's products as products of plaintiff. [cit.] It is also defendant's duty to avoid knowingly aiding bars which purchase defendant's products from marketing those products in such a manner as to infringe plaintiff's trade-mark. [cit.]

The court proceeded to explain how the standard would apply:

> Under the principles just stated, it would have been a breach of duty if defendant's salesmen had induced bars to buy defendant's product for the stated or implied purpose of serving it when Coca-Cola was called for. It would also have been a breach of duty for defendant to have continued sales to bars without taking some precautionary measures it if [sic.] had known or a normal bottler would have known that most bar customers specifically ordered Coca-Cola and that consequently a normal bottler would infer from defendant's large volume of sales that many bars which bought defendant's product were using defendant's product as a substitute in the case of specific orders of Coca-Cola and were not merely using it as an ordinary cola when a customer placed a general order for a "Cuba Libre" or a "rum (or whiskey) and cola." Likewise, it would have been a breach of duty if defendant had known that many bar customers specifically ordered Coca-Cola and had also known that some particular bars were in fact using defendant's product as a substitute in the case of specific orders for Coca-Cola.

Id. The court emphasized, however, that the law of contributory infringement did not go so far as to make the defendant "his brother's or his customer's keeper." *Id.* Instead,

> [b]efore he can himself be held as a wrongdoer or contributory infringer one who supplies another with the instruments by which that other commits a tort, must be shown to have knowledge that the other will or can reasonably be expected to commit a tort with the supplied instrument.

Id.

The Restatement (Third) of Unfair Competition adopts a similar indirect infringement standard:

> One who markets goods or services to a third person who further markets the goods or services in a manner that subjects the third person to liability to another for infringement under the rule stated in §20 is subject to liability to that other for contributory infringement if:
> (a) the actor intentionally induces the third person to engage in the infringing conduct; or
> (b) the actor fails to take reasonable precautions against the occurrence of the third person's infringing conduct in circumstances in which the infringing conduct can be reasonably anticipated.

Restatement (Third) of Unfair Competition §27 (1995). Does the Restatement standard restate *Inwood*? Or does it resurrect the "watered down" standard that the *Inwood* majority dismisses in its opinion, n.13?

4. *The COCO-QUININE case.* The Court in *Inwood* cited *William R. Warner & Co. v. Eli Lilly & Co.*, 265 U.S. 526 (1924). In that case, Lilly manufactured "a liquid preparation of quinine, in combination with other substances, including yerbasanta and chocolate," under the mark COCO-QUININE, and sold it to druggists. Subsequently, Warner began manufacturing a substantially similar product under the mark QUIN-COCO, which it also sold to druggists, albeit at a lower price. According to the Court, the evidence showed that Warner's sales personnel induced druggists to substitute QUIN-COCO for COCO-QUININE, and did so "either in direct terms or by suggestion or insinuation." *Id.* at 530. Specifically, the evidence showed that some of Warner's sales personnel

> suggested that, without danger of detection, prescriptions and orders for Coco-Quinine could be filled by substituting Quin-Coco. More often, however, the feasibility of such a course was brought to the mind of the druggist by pointing out the identity of the two preparations and the enhanced profit to be made by selling Quin-Coco because of its lower price.

Id. The Court noted that whereas the retail druggists "knew exactly what they were getting," Warner had still engaged in wrongful conduct by "designedly enabling" the druggists to palm off the Warner product as being the Lilly product. *Id.* Is *Inwood* distinguishable on its facts from *Lilly*? If not, why did the Court in *Inwood* reverse?

    5. *Applying the* Inwood *standard (first prong): intentional inducement.* What types of evidence of intent might a trademark owner muster to satisfy *Inwood*'s first prong? If intent may be inferred from circumstantial evidence, what evidence? For examples in which the alleged contributory infringer was found to lack the requisite intent for purposes of the *Inwood* standard, *see, e.g., Rolex Watch USA, Inc. v. Michel Co.*, 179 F.3d 704 (9th Cir. 1999); *Rolex Watch USA, Inc. v. Meece*, 158 F.3d 816 (5th Cir. 1998). *Cf. Rescuecom Corp. v. Google Inc.*, 562 F.3d 123 (2d Cir. 2009) (noting relevance of Google's Keyword Suggestion Tool to the question whether it had engaged in actionable use).

    6. *Applying the* Inwood *standard (second prong): continued supply with knowledge or reason to know.* The second prong of the *Inwood* standard requires that the plaintiff show that the defendant (indirect infringer) continued to supply the direct infringer, knowing or having reason to know of the direct infringer's infringement. Certainly, these requirements are satisfied where the indirect infringer "foresaw and intended" that a particular direct infringer would infringe. *See Sealy, Inc. v. Easy Living, Inc.*, 743 F.2d 1378, 1382 (9th Cir. 1984) (manufacturer was contributory infringer under second prong of *Inwood* test where manufacturer "foresaw and intended" that distributor would pass off manufacturer's goods as originating from trademark owner). By contrast, according to the *Tiffany v. eBay* decision, a defendant's "generalized" knowledge of direct infringements in the aggregate does not suffice. Do you agree with the *Tiffany v. eBay* court's approach of distinguishing between generalized and particularized knowledge? Some subsequent cases have appeared to accept the distinction, but have distinguished *Tiffany v. eBay. See, e.g., Rosetta Stone Ltd. v. Google, Inc.*, 676 F.3d 144, 163-65 (4th Cir. 2012) (sufficient evidence of specialized knowledge where Rosetta Stone allegedly had notified Google of approximately 200 instances in which a website associated with a keyword-triggered "sponsored link" was advertising counterfeit Rosetta Stone products, and Google had allowed the same advertisers to continue to use Rosetta Stone's marks for sponsored links connected with those advertisers' other websites); *Coach, Inc. v. Goodfellow*, 717 F.3d 498 (6th Cir. 2013) (flea market operator had "actual knowledge that the infringing activity was occurring at his flea market over a lengthy period of time and even knew that particular vendors were selling counterfeit Coach products" but "failed to deny access to offending vendors or take other reasonable measures to prevent use of flea market resources for unlawful purposes, and failed even to undertake a reasonable investigation," instead merely distributing pamphlets and holding a voluntary meeting with some vendors). Notwithstanding the ruling in *Tiffany v. eBay*, are there some scenarios in which contributory infringement should be found under the second prong of the *Inwood* test even if a service provider only has generalized knowledge that its customers are engaged in infringing activities? For example, suppose the evidence shows that if the service provider had sent an email blast to all of its customers advising them to stop using a particular mark, the customers would have complied, at least to a large degree.

If the service provider did not take that step, and continued to supply services to its customers, is such a situation distinguishable from that in *Tiffany v. eBay*? *See 1-800 Contacts, Inc. v. Lens.com, Inc.*, 722 F.3d 1229 (10th Cir. 2013).

Do you agree with the *Tiffany v. eBay* court's separate point that a defendant should be deemed to have sufficient knowledge if the evidence shows that the defendant was willfully blind to the infringement? In *Global-Tech Appliances, Inc. v. SEB, S.A.*, 563 U.S. 754 (2011), a case involving allegations of induced patent infringement under 35 U.S.C. §271(b), the Supreme Court held that evidence of willful blindness as to the existence of patent rights sufficed to show that the alleged inducer knew of those rights. How important, if at all, should that ruling be for application of the *Inwood* standard in trademark law?

7. *Applying the* Inwood *standard (second prong) to service providers.* The second prong of the *Inwood* standard refers to continued supply of a *product*, but, as *Tiffany v. eBay* illustrates, questions about secondary liability for trademark infringement may also arise where the supply of *services* allegedly facilitates others' infringement. The *Tiffany v. eBay* court cited the Ninth Circuit's *Lockheed* decision for the proposition that the *Inwood* standard applies to the provision of services—after modifying *Inwood*'s second prong to require an additional showing that the service provider exercised "direct control and monitoring of the instrumentality used by a third party to infringe. . . ." *Tiffany (NJ) Inc.*, 600 F.3d at 105. *See also Perfect 10, Inc. v. Visa Int'l Serv. Ass'n*, 494 F.3d 788 (9th Cir. 2007) (citing and endorsing *Lockheed*). Do you agree with this adaptation of *Inwood* from a policy perspective? Is it akin to a judicially-created analog to the statutory notice-and-takedown regime that exists in the U.S. Copyright Act? For a case exploring the direct control and monitoring issue, *see Louis Vuitton Malletier, S.A. v. Akanoc Solutions, Inc.*, 658 F.3d 936 (9th Cir. 2011). The defendants ran a web-hosting business in which they operated servers and provided server space and IP addresses to their customers, some of whom operated websites where allegedly counterfeit Louis Vuitton merchandise was offered for sale. What do you think of the argument that on these facts, the defendant might be exercising "control," but is not "monitoring"?

8. *Applying the* Inwood *standard in other factual contexts.* Should *Inwood* apply when a franchisor induces a franchisee to infringe? Should it apply when a landlord provides space that a tenant uses for carrying out an infringement? *See Habeeba's Dance of the Arts Ltd. v. Knoblauch*, 430 F. Supp. 2d 709 (S.D. Ohio 2006) (fact issue as to YWCA's contributory infringement liability where YWCA permitted Knoblauch to use YWCA premises to hold dance symposium using allegedly infringing mark). Should it apply when a corporate officer or director induces his company to infringe? Does liability in the latter situation depend upon an analysis of "piercing the corporate veil"? What if a *retailer* persuades a *manufacturer* to infringe? If a court declines to apply *Inwood* in these situations, should there be other avenues for finding secondary liability? We continue this discussion below in the note on other vicarious liability theories.

9. *The relevance of contract restrictions under the* Inwood *standard.* Should a supplier be able to protect itself contractually from charges that it knew or had reason to know of its customers' infringement or intentionally induced infringement? In *Medic Alert Foundation United States, Inc. v. Corel Corp.*, 43 F. Supp. 2d 933 (N.D. Ill. 1999), Corel's "CorelDRAW 4" software included a library of "clip art" images, one of which resembled the "Medic Alert" logo, a registered trademark owned by the Medic Alert Foundation for use in connection with nonprofit services relating to the emergency identification of medical conditions. At least one purchaser of the software used the clip art image in connection with promotion of a vitamin product. Medic Alert sued Corel, alleging that Corel contributorily infringed by continuing to sell its inventory of software containing the disputed image, rather than immediately pulling the software from distribution.

In assessing whether Corel continued to supply the software when it knew or should have known of customer infringement, the court looked to the language of Corel's end user agreement accompanying Corel's software, which stated that users could not use images in such a way as to suggest "their association with or endorsement of any product or service." *Id.* at 935. In light of this agreement, Corel could not be charged with having the requisite mental state for contributory infringement until it had received actual information that its end users were acting in contravention with the end user agreement. *Id.*

Did the court draw a fair inference from the existence of the end user agreement? Or does the existence of the provision in that agreement indicate that Corel indeed did have reason to know of probable infringements by its customers?

10.   *Exception for "innocent" printers/broadcasters.* Should printers and publishers who reproduce a mark on labels, advertising, or goods on behalf of another be liable for infringement? Suppose, for example, that a real estate broker who was at one time licensed to use the CENTURY 21 mark continues to use the mark in phone book advertisements even after the expiration of the license agreement. Should the phone book publisher be liable for trademark infringement? If so, under what circumstances? *See* Lanham Act §32(2)(A) (as amended 1989); *Century 21 Real Estate Corp. v. R.M. Post, Inc.*, 8 U.S.P.Q.2d (BNA) 1614 (N.D. Ill. 1988).

11.   *Immunity for domain name registrars.* Under what circumstances should a domain name registrar be contributorily liable for registering or maintaining a domain name for another? The Lanham Act supplies an answer in Section 32(2)(D)(iii) (no liability for damages absent a showing of bad faith intent to profit from such registration or maintenance), an element of the Anticybersquatting Consumer Protection Act, enacted in 1999. *See Baidu, Inc. v. Register.com*, 760 F. Supp. 2d 312 (S.D.N.Y. 2010) (discussing this provision). We discuss the ACPA in more detail in Chapter 8.

12.   *Other vicarious liability theories.* We have noted that contributory infringement is simply one species of indirect infringement. Indirect infringement, in turn, is simply one species of the broad concept of joint liability for torts. In view of this hierarchy of theories, a trademark plaintiff who fails on a contributory infringement theory might not have exhausted all possibilities for showing indirect liability. Might the plaintiff assert alternative theories that also draw from general principles of vicarious liability for torts? *See Hard Rock Cafe Licensing Corp. v. Concession Servs., Inc.*, 955 F.2d 1143 (7th Cir. 1992) (flea market operator could be vicariously liable for vendors' infringing activities, but only where "the defendant and the infringer have an apparent or actual partnership, have authority to bind one another in transactions with third parties or exercise joint ownership or control over the infringing product"). *See also American Tel. & Tel. Co. v. Winback & Conserve Program, Inc.*, 42 F.3d 1421 (3d Cir. 1994) (potential vicarious liability for Winback for the foreseeable acts of Winback's sales representatives, under an agency theory); *1-800 Contacts, Inc. v. Lens.com, Inc.*, 722 F.3d 1229 (10th Cir. 2013) (asserting that vicarious liability under trademark law on the part of a principal requires a showing that the agent is acting within the scope of the principal's authority, which in turn requires a showing that the agent subjectively believed that the principal's grant of authority encompassed the agent's conduct, and that this belief was reasonable). What are the limits of vicarious liability theories? Would a credit card company be vicariously liable for online infringements if the evidence shows that the websites cannot practically operate without the cooperation of credit card companies to process customers' payments, and the credit card companies profit by their arrangement with the websites on a transaction-by-transaction basis? *See Perfect 10, Inc. v. Visa Int'l Serv. Ass'n*, 494 F.3d 788 (9th Cir. 2007) (discussing the issue).

13.   *Other causes of action against eBay?* Is there a viable dilution cause of action against the sellers in *eBay*—and if so, is there a viable contributory dilution cause of action against eBay? *See* Chapter 8 for a discussion of the dilution cause of action. As a matter of law, should courts recognize a contributory dilution cause of action? Alternatively, was eBay engaged in false advertising in violation of Lanham Act §43(a)(1)(B)? We discuss the relevant analysis in Chapter 10.

14. *A comparative reference.* Controversies over whether to impose secondary liability for online trademark infringement have also flared up overseas in recent years. eBay has itself been the target of much of this litigation. Within Europe, different national courts reached different results, leading to a reference from the UK courts to the European Court of Justice. In *L'Oreal SA v. eBay International AG* (C-324/09), [2011] E.T.M.R. 52, the Court of Justice held that potential secondary liability was a matter for national laws and was not addressed by the EU Trademark Directive. However, the EU E-Commerce Directive may offer Internet service providers with EU-wide immunity against liability under such national law in a range of circumstances that correspond roughly to those conferred in the United States by the Digital Millennium Copyright Act (now Section 512 of the U.S. Copyright Act). Unlike the U.S. statute, immunity under the EU Directive is not confined to copyright, and thus applies to potential claims of indirect trademark liability. Would you support extension of the DMCA to trademark law? The *L'Oreal* Court also offered an interpretation of the EU Enforcement Directive, Article 11 of which requires that "rightholders are in a position to apply for an injunction against intermediaries whose services are used by a third party to infringe an intellectual property right." Thus, even when the E-Commerce Directive immunizes Internet intermediaries from liability, they may be subject to court orders designed to assist in the prevention of infringement. Although it remains for the national court to devise the precise relief, the Court of Justice suggested that intermediaries may be ordered to "suspend the perpetrator of the infringement of intellectual property rights in order to prevent further infringements of that kind by the same seller in respect of the same trademarks" or may be ordered to take measures to make it easier to identify its customer-sellers. Would you support the adoption of a similar provision to Article 11 in U.S. law?

15. *The five-or-more rule.* In the *eBay* litigation, the district court had dismissed Tiffany's efforts to establish a "five-or-more" rule—a presumption that a seller who lists five or more Tiffany items is dealing in counterfeit goods. Is the five-or-more rule, or a similar bright-line rule, a wise approach for resolving disputes over secondary liability in trademark law? Would you favor legislation establishing such a rule? Of course, as the *eBay* case shows, some intermediaries have developed their own policies to deal with claims of alleged infringement. As we saw in the context of the sale of keywords by search engines, these policies play a substantial part in determining the uses of trademarks online. What are the advantages of allowing such disputes to be resolved in the first instance by application of intermediary-developed policies? Do you favor greater private ordering in this area?

16. *Legislative fixes?* The district court in *eBay* commented that

> [t]he result of the application of this legal standard is that Tiffany must ultimately bear the burden of protecting its trademark. Policymakers may yet decide that the law as it stands is inadequate to protect rights owners in light of the increasing scope of Internet commerce and the concomitant rise in potential trademark infringement. Nevertheless, under the law as it currently stands, it does not matter whether eBay or Tiffany could more efficiently bear the burden of policing the eBay website for Tiffany counterfeits—an open question left unresolved by this trial. Instead, the issue is whether eBay continued to provide its website to sellers when eBay knew or had reason to know that those sellers were using the website to traffic in counterfeit Tiffany jewelry.

Tiffany (NJ) Inc. v. eBay, Inc., 576 F. Supp. 2d 463, 470 (S.D.N.Y. 2008). Should the law be changed to reflect some overt consideration of "whether eBay or Tiffany could more efficiently bear the burden of policing the eBay website for Tiffany counterfeits"?

PROBLEM 7-10:   BROTHER BILLY AND THE BAPTISTS' BATHROOMS

Suppose that the Northwest Kentucky Paper Co. ("P") manufactures disposable paper towels (e.g., for use in public restrooms), and also manufactures dispensers that hold and dispense the towels. The dispensers bear P's "Kentuckian" logo, the exact appearance of which doesn't matter for purposes of this Problem and is best left to your imagination anyway. The towels aren't marked with the logo, but they come in a bulk package that is marked with P's logo. Suppose that P sells a dispenser and a bulk package of towels to the Tick Ridge Separate Baptist Church of Tick Ridge, Kentucky. Brother Billy, as chair of the church's Board of Trustees, is in charge of ensuring that the dispenser is full of towels, which he does by tearing open the bulk package wrapper and discarding it, stuffing the dispenser full of towels, and leaving the extras in a stack near the dispenser. A lot of towels get used. Soon, the supply dwindles. Brother Billy (acting on behalf of the church) decides to buy a new supply of towels from Cousin Clem's Cut-Rate Janitorial Emporium. Cousin Clem's towels don't bear any trademark, and they come packaged in a plain brown wrapper. The towels are of generally lousy quality, although the people at church tend not to complain. Suppose that P finds out about Brother Billy's purchases and threatens action for trademark infringement. What's the possibility that Cousin Clem's Cut-Rate Janitorial Emporium is liable? What about the Tick Ridge Separate Baptist Church? Does it matter to your analysis whether the Baptists who attend regularly and use the towels are likely to be confused? (For that matter, what about those who don't attend religiously but sometimes use the towels?) *See Georgia-Pacific Consumer Prods., LP v. Von Drehle Corp.*, 618 F.3d 441, 452 (4th Cir. 2010) and *Georgia-Pacific Consumer Prods., LP v. Myers Supply, Inc.*, 621 F.3d 771 (8th Cir. 2010).

PROBLEM 7-11:   TRADEMARK "DISPARAGEMENT"?

The Freecycle Network (TFN) operates a website aimed at encouraging the reuse and recycling of goods by allowing individuals to advertise and exchange unwanted goods. A member of the group, Oey, encouraged TFN to secure trademark rights in the mark FREECYCLE for a recycling network, but subsequently decided that the term should remain in the public domain. Eventually Oey began posting messages on the Internet encouraging others to use the term "freecycle" in a generic sense and to initiate opposition proceedings against TFN at the USPTO.

TFN eventually sued Oey, alleging contributory infringement, and in the alternative, "trademark disparagement" under Section 43(a), meaning (according to TFN) that Oey had made false statements, with malice, about TFN's operations and the validity of the FREECYCLE mark.

(1) Analyze TFN's contributory infringement claim. Does TFN have a viable claim?

(2) As a policy matter, should courts recognize a non-confusion-based claim of "trademark disparagement"? You may wish to revisit this question after you have studied the materials in Chapter 8. *See Freecycle Network, Inc. v. Oey*, 505 F.3d 898 (9th Cir. 2007).

8

Non–Confusion-Based Trademark Liability Theories

In this chapter we discuss trademark enforcement theories that do not rely on confusion. We consider dilution protection under Lanham Act §43(c) (section A of this chapter) and anticybersquatting protection under §43(d) (section B of this chapter). As you study the materials in this chapter, consider the assumptions about the nature of trademark rights that are reflected in confusion theory and whether departing from confusion theory means dispensing with those assumptions.

A. Dilution Protection

1. The Concept of Dilution

Suppose you are shopping for a musical instrument—say a viola. You go to your local high-quality musical instrument store, where they sell a variety of violas, ranging in quality from very good to professional, and in price from several hundred dollars to several thousand. One viola in particular catches your eye. It is in the "very good" quality range, selling for $900. A large logo is engraved in the viola body:

Even though you may not be particularly hip, you are well aware that the logo is identical to the famous "swoosh" logo of the Nike Corporation, used on shoes, apparel, and sports equipment.

To the shopkeeper, you say, "I assume that this viola is not made by the Nike Corporation, because it would be ridiculous to think that Nike has expanded into fine musical instruments. But I am surprised to see the 'swoosh' logo on a product that is totally unrelated to Nike."

The shopkeeper says, "Yes, everyone says that. Of course, it's getting less and less surprising. There's a company in Alabama that makes solid rocket boosters that have the 'swoosh' logo. There's another company in North Dakota that makes printer toner cartridges that also have the 'swoosh' logo. There's another company in Hills, Iowa, that produces soybean seed and uses the logo on the seed bags. . . ."

Is Nike harmed in this scenario? If so, how—immediately by the use of the logo on violas, or eventually, when the logo becomes prevalent on many unrelated products produced by many unrelated firms? Are consumers harmed? If so, how, considering that there is no evidence of confusion?

Suppose, alternatively, that you are shopping for a nice bottle of wine for an intimate dinner with your significant other. Being generally a cheapskate, you go to your local grocery store (this could be your first mistake, but read on). In the "Cheapskate" section, you discover a wine labeled "WINE—CHEAP" packaged in recycled plastic milk jugs for $1 a gallon. The labels also feature a "swoosh" logo that is crudely printed but identical to the famous Nike logo. You assume that Nike doesn't make the wine.

Is Nike harmed by the use of the logo on the cheap wine? How? If the use isn't confusing, and doesn't even create the false impression that Nike endorses or is otherwise affiliated with the product or its producer, should Nike nonetheless have a cause of action under the Lanham Act? If we do give Nike a cause of action, are we giving Nike absolute anti-copying protection—or, put another way, property rights in gross in the "swoosh" logo, unattached to any particular goods or services?

In the 1920s, Frank Schechter grappled with these questions. In articles and a book, he articulated various formulations of a different type of harm. Thus, he wrote that the "real injury" in cases like the NIKE hypotheticals we posed above was not consumer confusion, but "the gradual whittling away or dispersion of the identity and hold upon the public mind of the mark or name by its use upon non-competing goods." Frank I. Schechter, *The Rational Basis of Trademark Protection*, 40 HARV. L. REV. 813, 825 (1927). And he alternatively defined this harm as occurring when a mark's "uniqueness or singularity is vitiated or impaired by its use upon either related or non-related goods." *Id*. at 831-32. As the phrase "uniqueness" might suggest, Schechter appeared to want to protect "coined, arbitrary or fanciful words or phrases that have . . . from the very beginning, been associated in the public mind with a particular product." *Id*. at 829. But the examples that he used to illustrate the problem were not fully confined to such marks; for example, he used the example of the DUPONT mark for plastics, which was a name mark and not inherently distinctive. Loss of uniqueness would occur through "*any* junior use of the unique mark, on the rationale that any such use would necessarily have the whittling-away effect. *Id*. at 825. Preserving the uniqueness of the mark from this effect was "the only rational basis" for trademark protection, Schechter asserted. *Id*. at 831. In later work, he called this harm "dilution," a term purportedly borrowed from the German *Odol* case. He also further elaborated on the function of the mark he was seeking to protect, describing it as the "selling power" of the mark (another phrase drawn from the German *Odol* case).

While Schechter's proposal was never adopted in the form set out in *Rational Basis*, starting in the mid-twentieth century a number of states enacted anti-dilution protections that were doubtlessly inspired by his article. These provisions received a mixed response in the courts. *See Ringling Bros.-Barnum & Bailey Combined Shows, Inc. v. Utah Div. of Travel Dev.*, 170 F.3d 449 (4th Cir. 1999) (summarizing state legislation and jurisprudence); Restatement (Third) of Unfair Competition §25, cmt. b (1995) (same). Congress considered anti-dilution protection in the debates that culminated in the 1988 Trademark Law Revision Act, but it was only in 1995 that federal anti-dilution protection was enacted. The dilution provisions were codified primarily in new Section 43(c) of the Lanham Act. The 1995 legislation (H.R. 1295) passed the House with little debate, was introduced in the Senate on December 29, 1995 (as S. 1513), and passed the Senate the same day on a voice vote, and shortly thereafter was signed into law, as the Federal Trademark Dilution Act (FTDA).

Like its state law predecessors, the FTDA garnered a skeptical reception in the courts. *See generally* Clarissa Long, *Dilution*, 106 COLUM. L. REV. 1029 (2006) (offering empirical support for this proposition). In 2006, Congress revised the dilution provisions significantly in the Trademark Dilution Revision Act (TRDA). The federal provisions form the basis for our study of dilution in this chapter.

NOTES AND QUESTIONS

1. *Dilution and consumers' interests.* Is the dilution action solely about protection of trademark owners' interests? Can you fashion any argument that the dilution action has an additional, consumer protection role? *See* Shahar J. Dilbary, *Famous Trademarks and the Rational Basis for Protecting "Irrational Beliefs,"* 14 Geo. Mason L. Rev. 605 (2007) (offering a consumer protection argument).

2. *Dilution and the traditional model of trademarks as limited property rights.* Schechter's proposed dilution remedy unabashedly challenged a core assumption of traditional trademark law—that the trademark right is not an in-gross right, but rather is limited in the sense that the trademark right inheres in the use of the mark in connection with particular goods and services. Judges applying state anti-dilution provisions may have been reluctant to part with that assumption, which may explain why courts approached those provisions with some skepticism. As you study the modern dilution provisions, consider whether they likewise require courts to recognize something akin to in-gross property rights in trademarks, and whether this continues to affect how courts apply the provisions.

3. *Relationship between dilution and confusion causes of action.* If adopted in the form Schechter proposed, would anti-dilution protection have become the principal theory of trademark enforcement, displacing likelihood of confusion? Must any dilution provision be carefully limited lest it become the trademark owner's remedy of choice in every routine case? Alternatively, should dilution instead be viewed as an expression of frustration over the apparent failings of confusion law, rather than an independently formed concept? *See* Gerard N. Magliocca, *One and Inseparable: Dilution and Infringement in Trademark Law,* 85 Minn. L. Rev. 949 (2001) (exploring the proposition). If so, is dilution very different from variant approaches to confusion, such as initial interest confusion and post-sale confusion? (You might note how often opinions in the last chapter resisting the expansion of the confusion action complained that such expansions sought to provide relief for dilution).

4. *Dilution's uncertain pedigree.* As noted, Schechter looked to German law in fashioning his dilution proposal. In the *Odol* case, a German firm owned the mark ODOL for mouthwash and sought to enforce it against another firm that used ODOL for various steel products. As Schechter described it, the German court opined that

> the use of the mark, "Odol" even on non-competing goods was *"gegen die guten Sitten,"* pointing out that, when the public hears or reads the word "Odol," it thinks of the complainant's mouth wash, and that an article designated with the name "Odol" leads the public to assume that it is of good quality. Consequently, concludes the court, complainant has "the utmost interest in seeing that its mark is not diluted [*verwassert*]: it would lose in selling power if everyone used it as the designation of his goods."

Frank I. Schechter, *The Rational Basis of Trademark Protection,* 40 Harv. L. Rev. 813, 831-32 (1927). What do you think Schechter (or the German court) meant by the "selling power" of a mark that was not protected by conventional forms of protection?

Barton Beebe has pointed out that Schechter's account of the *Odol* case omits a critical passage in which the German court justifies its holding by saying that it is "opposed to good morals to appropriate thus the fruits of another's labors. . . ." Barton Beebe, *The Suppressed Misappropriation Origins of Trademark Antidilution Law: The Landgericht Elberfeld's* Odol *Decision and Frank Schechter's* The Rational Basis of Trademark Protection, *in* Intellectual Property at the Edge: The Contested Contours of IP (Dreyfuss & Ginsburg eds., Cambridge Univ. Press 2014). This is the language of misappropriation, perhaps even misappropriation in the style of the *INS* case (excerpted in Chapter 1). Beebe speculates that Schechter may have been trying to distance his *Rational Basis* argument from *INS*, which had been decided only a few years earlier but was already attracting criticism. To Beebe, the indeterminacy surrounding dilution is a consequence of these efforts. *See also* Graeme B. Dinwoodie, *Dilution as Unfair Competition: European Echoes, in* INTELLECTUAL PROPERTY AT THE EDGE: THE CONTESTED CONTOURS OF IP (Dreyfuss & Ginsburg eds., Cambridge Univ. Press 2014) (assessing Beebe's analysis in terms of European developments). For an earlier analysis situating Schechter's work in the context of the legal realist movement, *see* Robert Bone, *Schechter's Ideas in Historical Context and Dilution's Rocky Road*, 24 SANTA CLARA COMPUTER & HIGH TECH. L.J. 469 (2008).

   5. *Resources on dilution.* For a comprehensive treatment of the history and evolution of the dilution cause of action, *see* David S. Welkowitz, TRADEMARK DILUTION: FEDERAL, STATE, AND INTERNATIONAL LAW (2002 and supplement). For comparative references, *see* INTERNATIONAL TRADEMARK DILUTION (Daniel R. Bereskin ed., 2013); *International and Comparative Aspects of Dilution Symposium*, 17 TRANSNAT'L L. & CONTEMP. PROBS. 603 (2008).

2.   Anatomy of the Federal Trademark Dilution Provisions

LANHAM ACT
Section 43(c) [15 U.S.C. §1125(c)] (2006) (as amended 2012)

   (c) Dilution by Blurring; Dilution by Tarnishment—
   (1) INJUNCTIVE RELIEF—Subject to the principles of equity, the owner of a famous mark that is distinctive, inherently or through acquired distinctiveness, shall be entitled to an injunction against another person who, at any time after the owner's mark has become famous, commences use of a mark or trade name in commerce that is likely to cause dilution by blurring or dilution by tarnishment of the famous mark, regardless of the presence or absence of actual or likely confusion, of competition, or of actual economic injury.
   (2) DEFINITIONS—
      (A) For purposes of paragraph (1), a mark is famous if it is widely recognized by the general consuming public of the United States as a designation of source of the goods or services of the mark's owner. In determining whether a mark possesses the requisite degree of recognition, the court may consider all relevant factors, including the following:
         (i) The duration, extent, and geographic reach of advertising and publicity of the mark, whether advertised or publicized by the owner or third parties.
         (ii) The amount, volume, and geographic extent of sales of goods or services offered under the mark.
         (iii) The extent of actual recognition of the mark.
         (iv) Whether the mark was registered under the Act of March 3, 1881, or the Act of February 20, 1905, or on the principal register.
      (B) For purposes of paragraph (1), dilution by blurring is association arising from the similarity between a mark or trade name and a famous mark that impairs the distinctiveness of the famous mark. In determining whether a mark or trade name is likely to cause dilution by blurring, the court may consider all relevant factors, including the following:
         (i) The degree of similarity between the mark or trade name and the famous mark.

(ii) The degree of inherent or acquired distinctiveness of the famous mark.

(iii) The extent to which the owner of the famous mark is engaging in substantially exclusive use of the mark.

(iv) The degree of recognition of the famous mark.

(v) Whether the user of the mark or trade name intended to create an association with the famous mark.

(vi) Any actual association between the mark or trade name and the famous mark.

(C) For purposes of paragraph (1), dilution by tarnishment is association arising from the similarity between a mark or trade name and a famous mark that harms the reputation of the famous mark.

(3) EXCLUSIONS—The following shall not be actionable as dilution by blurring or dilution by tarnishment under this subsection:

(A) Any fair use, including a nominative or descriptive fair use, or facilitation of such fair use, of a famous mark by another person other than as a designation of source for the person's own goods or services, including use in connection with—

(i) advertising or promotion that permits consumers to compare goods or services; or

(ii) identifying and parodying, criticizing, or commenting upon the famous mark owner or the goods or services of the famous mark owner.

(B) All forms of news reporting and news commentary.

(C) Any noncommercial use of a mark.

(4) BURDEN OF PROOF—In a civil action for trade dress dilution under this Act for trade dress not registered on the principal register, the person who asserts trade dress protection has the burden of proving that—

(A) the claimed trade dress, taken as a whole, is not functional and is famous; and

(B) if the claimed trade dress includes any mark or marks registered on the principal register, the unregistered matter, taken as a whole, is famous separate and apart from any fame of such registered marks.

(5) ADDITIONAL REMEDIES—In an action brought under this subsection, the owner of the famous mark shall be entitled to injunctive relief as set forth in section 34. The owner of the famous mark shall also be entitled to the remedies set forth in sections 35(a) and 36, subject to the discretion of the court and the principles of equity if—

(A) the mark or trade name that is likely to cause dilution by blurring or dilution by tarnishment was first used in commerce by the person against whom the injunction is sought after the date of enactment of the Trademark Dilution Revision Act of 2006; and

(B) in a claim arising under this subsection—

(i) by reason of dilution by blurring, the person against whom the injunction is sought willfully intended to trade on the recognition of the famous mark; or

(ii) by reason of dilution by tarnishment, the person against whom the injunction is sought willfully intended to harm the reputation of the famous mark.

(6) OWNERSHIP OF VALID REGISTRATION A COMPLETE BAR TO ACTION—The ownership by a person of a valid registration under the Act of March 3, 1881, or the Act of February 20, 1905, or on the principal register under this chapter shall be a complete bar to an action against that person, with respect to that mark, that—

(A) is brought by another person under the common law or a statute of a State; and

(B)(i) seeks to prevent dilution by blurring or dilution by tarnishment; or

(ii) asserts any claim of actual or likely damage or harm to the distinctiveness or reputation of a mark, label, or form of advertisement.

(7) SAVINGS CLAUSE—Nothing in this subsection shall be construed to impair, modify, or supersede the applicability of the patent laws of the United States.

NOTES AND QUESTIONS

1.   *Section 43(c)(1) — "likely to cause dilution."* Section 43(c)(1) calls for a showing of likely dilution, not actual dilution, a distinction that should remind you of our discussion of likely versus actual confusion in Chapter 7. Does the use of a likelihood-of-dilution standard in Section 43(c)(1) make sense given that the primary remedy for dilution is injunctive relief? Does it reflect the view that dilution is an inherently forward-looking phenomenon, designed to forestall the "gradual whittling away" of a mark's distinctiveness? (The harm has been called "death by a thousand cuts." Can you articulate a narrative involving use of a protected mark that captures that phenomenon?) The 1995 version of Section 43(c) afforded liability if the defendant's use "causes dilution" of the mark's distinctive quality. In *Moseley v. V Secret Catalogue, Inc.*, 537 U.S. 418 (2003), the Supreme Court ruled that this language called for a showing of actual dilution, alluding to the possibility of proving actual dilution by survey evidence or circumstantial evidence, but without specifying which forms of circumstantial evidence might suffice. To a great extent, the *Moseley* case supplied the impetus for legislative reform proposals that became the TDRA.

2.   *Section 43(c)(1)—entitlement to injunctive relief.* Why is injunctive relief the primary remedy afforded by Section 43(c)(1)? Note that Section 43(c)(5) specifies that additional remedies, such as damages, are available in cases of willful dilution. Does this menu of remedies reflect a continuing reluctance to embrace the concept of dilution?

3.   *Section 43(c)(1)—marks that are "distinctive, inherently or through acquired distinctiveness."* The dilution provision is not limited to inherently distinctive marks. Is this departure from Schechter's proposal good trademark policy? This language also abrogates some 1995 Act decisions, notably *TCPIP Holding Co. v. Haar Comms. Inc.*, 244 F.3d 88 (2d Cir. 2001), ruling that only inherently distinctive marks could qualify for protection against dilution under the 1995 version of Section 43(c). The language also opens up the possibility of asserting a dilution claim for product design trade dress, which would have been unavailable had the dilution provision been restricted only to inherently distinctive marks. *See* Section 43(c)(4) (specifying the burden of proof for "trade dress dilution"). Does the application of Section 43(c) to trade dress comport with the "limited times" proviso of Article I, Section 8, Clause 8? Note that Section 43(c)(7) provides that nothing in the dilution subsection "shall be construed to impair, modify, or supersede the applicability of the patent laws of the United States." Does this language suggest that a product configuration trade dress claim should be precluded as a matter of federal/federal preemption? If a mark owner sought to avoid this outcome by asserting dilution under state law, would federal/state preemption preclude the state law claim? *See Adidas America, Inc. v. Payless Shoesource, Inc.*, 546 F. Supp. 2d 1029 (D. Or. 2008) (concluding that it would). For discussions of the constitutionality issue under the 1995 Act, *see, e.g., I.P. Lund Trading ApS v. Kohler Co.*, 163 F.3d 27 (1st Cir. 1998) (discussing but not resolving the issue in a 1995

Act case); *see also* Katherine J. Strandburg, *Rounding the Corner on Trade Dress*, 29 YALE J. REG. 387 (2012) (analyzing Judge Cudahy's important dissent in the *Kohler* case).

4.   *Section 43(c)(1)—actionable use.* Section 43(c) requires that the alleged diluter make "use of a mark or trade name in commerce." It dispenses with the 1995 Act language that had required the alleged diluter to make a "commercial use in commerce" of the mark. Does the current language require the mark owner to show that the alleged diluter is using the mark as a brand for its own product/services? *See Nat'l Bus. Forms & Printing, Inc. v. Ford Motor Co.*, 671 F.3d 526 (5th Cir. 2012) (adopting such a requirement). *But cf. Rosetta Stone Ltd. v. Google, Inc.*, 676 F.3d 144, 168-69 (4th Cir. 2012) (rejecting such a requirement). An early draft of the 2006 legislation would have included additional language in Section 43(c)(1) requiring the trademark owner to show that the alleged diluter's use of the famous mark in commerce was "as a designation of source of [the alleged diluter's] goods or services." Does this legislative history change your interpretation of the current statute? For a debate over the meaning of the relevant language, and opposing views on the legislative history, *see* Stacey L. Dogan & Mark A. Lemley, *The Trademark Use Requirement in Dilution Cases*, 24 SANTA CLARA COMPUTER & HIGH TECH. L.J. 541 (2008); William G. Barber, *Dumping the "Designation of Source" Requirement from the TDRA: A Response to the Alleged "Trademark Use Requirement in Dilution Cases,"* 24 SANTA CLARA COMPUTER & HIGH TECH. L.J. 559 (2008). In arriving at your interpretation, what weight would you give to Section 43(c)(3), which excludes from dilution liability "[a]ny fair use, including a nominative or descriptive fair use, or facilitation of such fair use, of a famous mark by another person *other than as a designation of source for the person's own goods or services*" (emphasis supplied). We will study Section 43(c)(3) alongside other fair use doctrines in Chapter 9.

5.   *Sections 43(c)(1) and 43(c)(2)(A)—the fame requirement.* Section 43(c)(1) specifies that only owners of "famous" marks can obtain a remedy against dilution—specifically, marks that have become famous before the alleged dilutive use commenced. *See Rosetta Stone Ltd. v. Google, Inc.*, 676 F.3d 144, 171-73 (4th Cir. 2012) (ruling that mark fame for purposes of Section 43(c) must be measured as of the time when the defendant's alleged diluting use began). Section 43(c)(2)(A) defines fame, calling for the dilution plaintiff's mark to be "widely recognized" by the general consuming public of the United States and providing factors to assist in the determination of whether the mark possesses the requisite "degree of recognition." Is the fame requirement wrongheaded? Are the owners of famous marks most in need of a dilution cause of action because they have the most to lose in terms of diminished unique association and in money invested in goodwill? Or least in need, because famous marks—by virtue of their very fame—are more likely to be resistant to dilution than less famous marks? For a variation on this theme, *see* Sara Stadler Nelson, *The Wages of Ubiquity in Trademark Law*, 88 IOWA L. REV. 731 (2003) (arguing that when mark owners market so vigorously that their marks become ubiquitous in the marketplace, those mark owners be *denied* recourse to the dilution remedy).

Does Section 43(c)(2)(A)'s preamble language and factor test ensure that the dilution remedy extends only to marks that are "household names"? *See Coach Servs., Inc. v. Triumph Learning LLC*, 668 F.3d 1356, 1373 (Fed. Cir. 2012) (yes). Does this indicate that the dilution remedy is unlikely to replace trademark infringement as the predominant vehicle for trademark enforcement? In cases decided under the 1995 Act, it was not clear that the fame requirement supplied this threshold filtering function. While some cases seemed to construe fame as limited to a select group of elite brands, others appeared to set the threshold much lower. *See, e.g., Nailtiques Cosmetic Corp. v. Salon Scis., Corp.*, 41 U.S.P.Q.2d (BNA) 1995 (S.D. Fla. 1997) (extending the dilution remedy to NAILTIQUES, DOUBLE N DESIGN, and FORMULA 2 PLUS for fingernail care products).

The current version of Section 43(c)(2)(A) is understood as addressing two additional important requirements as to the scope of fame:

- *Regional versus national fame*: By requiring recognition among the general consuming public "of the United States," the statute is generally understood to require national fame. Some cases under the 1995 Act had appeared to accept proof of regional fame, and the 1995 Act multi-factor definition of fame had included "the geographical extent of the trading area in which the mark is used" as one applicable factor. That factor is omitted from current Section 43(c)(2)(A).
- *Niche market versus general market fame*: The requirement for recognition among the "general" consuming public appears to reject the proposition that fame in a niche market could suffice for Section 43(c) purposes. Cases under the 1995 Act had hinted that niche market fame might be satisfactory. *Syndicate Sales, Inc. v. Hampshire Paper Corp.*, 192 F.3d 633 (7th Cir. 1999) (discussing the issue). To understand the concept of "niche fame," consider how well known the mark LEXIS for electronic legal retrieval services would be to attorneys and, alternatively, to the "general consuming public."

6. *Section 43(c)(6)—effect of a federal registration on state law dilution claims.* Section 43(c)(6), as revised in 2012, provides that ownership of a federal registration shields the owner from dilution claims brought under state law. The revision was necessary to correct a drafting error that could have been construed to make ownership of a federal registration a defense to even a *federal* dilution action.

7. *Sections 43(c)(2)(B) and (C)—dilution by blurring and dilution by tarnishment.* Section 43(c)(2) defines two forms of dilution: dilution by blurring and dilution by tarnishment. These labels designating forms of dilution were recognized before the 1995 Act came into being. The 1995 Act defined dilution as "the lessening of the capacity of a famous mark to identify and distinguish goods or services, regardless of the presence or absence of (1) competition between the owner of the famous mark and other parties, or (2) likelihood of confusion, mistake, or deception." *See* 15 U.S.C. §1127 (1995). The definition did not confine the concept of dilution to blurring and tarnishment, and evidence from the legislative history suggested that the definition was deliberately left open-ended. H.R. Rep. No. 104-374 (1995) (stating that the Section 45 definition of dilution "was designed to encompass all forms of dilution recognized by the courts, including dilution by blurring, by tarnishment and disparagement, and by diminishment"). Courts were thus left free to recognize new forms of dilution on a case-by-case basis—as the Ninth Circuit did in a case excerpted later in this chapter, *Panavision Int'l v. Toeppen*, 141 F.3d 1316 (9th Cir. 1998) (dilution by cybersquatting). *But see Ty Inc. v. Perryman*, 306 F.3d 509 (7th Cir. 2002) (discussing, then dismissing, a theory of dilution by genericide under the 1995 Act, where the mark owner had sought to "forbid commercial uses that accelerate the transition" toward genericness, even in the absence of any tarnishment or blurring). The current dilution provision appears to leave no room for judicial freelancing of this sort. Is this an improvement or an unwise limitation on judicial discretion? The case law on the meaning of "tarnishment" and "blurring" warrants closer scrutiny. We now turn to that.

3.   The Forms of Dilution: Dilution by Tarnishment and Dilution by Blurring

The Nike viola hypothetical presented at the outset of this chapter is a canonical example of dilution by blurring, while the Nike wine hypothetical offers an example of dilution by "tarnishment." We encountered similar assertions of harm in the *Ferrari* case in Chapter 7 (in the context of post-sale confusion). To the extent that Ferrari was arguing that the sheer proliferation of vehicles shaped like a Testarossa diminished the luxury image of its brand, it was arguing a harm akin to that caused in cases of dilution by blurring. To the extent that Ferrari was arguing that the kit car was of dubious quality, it was arguing something like dilution by tarnishment.

Judge Posner elaborated on these concepts in a case decided under the 1995 Act:

> [The] concern [motivating one form of dilution is] that consumer search costs will rise if a trademark becomes associated with a variety of unrelated products. Suppose an upscale restaurant calls itself "Tiffany." There is little danger that the consuming public will think it's dealing with a branch of the Tiffany jewelry store if it patronizes this restaurant. But when consumers next see the name "Tiffany" they may think about both the restaurant and the jewelry store, and if so the efficacy of the name as an identifier of the store will be diminished. Consumers will have to think harder—incur as it were a higher imagination cost—to recognize the name as the name of the store. [cit.] So "blurring" is one form of dilution.
>
> Now suppose that the "restaurant" that adopts the name "Tiffany" is actually a striptease joint. Again, and indeed even more certainly than in the previous case, consumers will not think the striptease joint under common ownership with the jewelry store. But because of the inveterate tendency of the human mind to proceed by association, every time they think of the word "Tiffany" their image of the fancy jewelry store will be tarnished by the association of the word with the strip joint. [cit.] So "tarnishment" is a second form of dilution. Analytically it is a subset of blurring, since it reduces the distinctness of the trademark as a signifier of the trademarked product or service.

Ty Inc. v. Perryman, 306 F.3d 509 (7th Cir. 2002).

As you study the materials in this section about the two statutory forms of dilution, keep these examples in mind, and consider both the threshold notion of "association" and the additional harm beyond association that must be proved before courts are willing to find actionable tarnishment or blurring.

a.   *Tarnishment*

The following two cases, both involving the TOYS "R" US mark for retail toy stores, arose under the 1995 Act. To what extent is the standard of dilution by tarnishment expressed in these cases still good law under the 2006 Act?

TOYS "R" US, INC. v. AKKAOUI

40 U.S.P.Q.2d (BNA) 1836 (N.D. Cal. 1996)

WILKEN, District Judge:

Plaintiffs [Toys "R" Us] seek a preliminary injunction against [Defendant Adults "R" Us] for trademark dilution and infringement. Plaintiffs hold an array of trademarks ending with the phrase "R Us." [Defendant was operating an Internet site featuring a variety of sexual devices and clothing under the name "adultsrus." Toys "R" Us sued to shut down the site, asserting a variety of Lanham Act theories, including dilution.]

. . .

B.   PROBABILITY OF SUCCESS ON THE MERITS

1.   *Dilution*

[The court found that the Toys "R" Us family of marks was famous, and had become famous before Adults "R" Us set up its website, citing extensive Toys "R" Us advertising, registrations of multiple "R" Us marks, and evidence of litigation to enforce rights in the marks.]

. . . In authorizing courts to enjoin dilution, Congress intended "to protect famous marks from subsequent uses that blur the distinctiveness of the mark or tarnish or disparage it." H.R. Rep. No. 374, 104th Cong., 1st Sess. 3 (1995). . . . "Adults R Us" tarnishes the "R Us" family of marks by associating them with a line of sexual products that are inconsistent with the image Toys "R" Us has striven to maintain for itself. [cit.]

Plaintiffs have therefore established a strong likelihood that they will prevail on the merits of their trademark dilution cause of action.

[The court granted the motion for preliminary injunction.]

TOYS "R" US, INC. v. FEINBERG

26 F. Supp. 2d 639 (S.D.N.Y. 1998), vacated, 1999 WL 1069999 (2d Cir. 1999) (unpub.) *

SCHWARTZ, District Judge:

BACKGROUND

[The court found that the TOYS "R" US mark was "one of the most famous and widely known marks in the world."]Toys "R" Us has also worked diligently to maintain its reputation as a family oriented store with a wholesome image. Toys "R" Us has sought to project the image of a store where children are the first concern, and was one of the first stores to refuse to carry or sell toy guns—a fact widely publicized.

[The court found that the plaintiff had registered many "R" US marks in addition to TOYS "R" US—for example: Babies "R" Us, Bikes "R" Us, Books "R" Us, Computers "R" Us, Dolls "R" Us, Games "R" Us, Mathematics "R" Us, Movies "R" Us, Parties "R" Us, Portraits "R" Us, Shoes "R" Us, and Sports "R" Us. The plaintiff also asserted common law rights in various other "R" US marks, such as Treats "R" Us, Gifts "R" Us, and 1-800-Toys-R-Us. In addition, the plaintiff owned various Internet domain names including tru.com, toysrus.com, kidsrus.com, boysrus.com, dollsrus.com, galsrus.com, girlsrus.com, babiesrus.com, computersrus.com, guysrus.com, mathematicsrus.com, moviesrus.com, opportunitiesrus.com, partiesrus.com, poolsrus.com, portraitsrus.com, racersrus.com, supervaluesrus.com, treatsrus.com, tykesrus.com, sportsrus.com, giftsrus.com, and toysrusregistry.com. Toys "R" Us also operated a website located at www.toysrus.com.]

Defendant Richard Feinberg is the sole proprietor of codefendant We Are Guns, a firearms store. . . . Feinberg runs his business predominantly in Massachusetts, but also sells products on the internet and has, "on occasion, shipped products to New York firearms dealers." Feinberg's business had been previously known as "Guns Are Us." The business's name was changed to "Guns Are We" and then to "We Are Guns" in response to objections by plaintiffs. Feinberg maintains a website located at www.gunsareus.com and has registered the domain name "gunsareus.com". . . .

---

* *Ed. Note:* The Second Circuit vacated this decision, in an unpublished disposition available at 1999 WL 1069999 (2d Cir. 1999), on procedural grounds: The lower court had (1) granted summary judgment sua sponte without proper notice to the plaintiff; and (2) failed to draw factual inferences against the defendant as regards intent, consumer sophistication, and the defendant's continued use of the plaintiff's marks, all of which were pertinent to the plaintiff's infringement claim.

Plaintiffs brought this suit seeking damages and an injunction prohibiting defendants from operating the website at gunsareus.com and from reverting back to either of the trade names "Guns Are Us" or "Guns Are We."

DISCUSSION

[The court granted summary judgment in favor of defendants on likelihood of confusion, then analyzed dilution, applying the 1995 version of Section 43(c).]

B.   PLAINTIFF'S DILUTION CLAIMS (COUNTS IV AND V)

. . .

[T]he Court . . . finds an absence of a triable issue of fact as to whether defendants have diluted plaintiffs' mark by tarnishment. Dilution by tarnishment occurs when "a famous mark is improperly associated with an inferior or offensive product or service." [cit.] Courts have found such negative connotations in situations where a mark was used in the context of drugs, nudity, and sex. *See e.g., Dallas Cowboys Cheerleaders, Inc. v. Pussycat Cinema, Ltd.*, 467 F. Supp. 366 (S.D.N.Y. 1979) (pornography); *Coca-Cola Co. v. Gemini Rising, Inc.*, 346 F. Supp. 1183 (E.D.N.Y. 1972) (cocaine); *Eastman Kodak Co. v. Rakow*, 739 F. Supp. 116, 118 (W.D.N.Y. 1989) (crude comedy routine).

The Court, however, finds it unlikely that defendants' website will be associated with plaintiffs' stores and products at all . . . the differing product areas, absence of the single letter "R" in the name, and peculiarities of an internet domain name make any association with plaintiffs' products extremely unlikely. In addition, defendant does not sell to the general public outside of Massachusetts. Its internet site is used almost exclusively to sell to firearms dealers.

[Summary judgment granted in favor of defendants.]

Many of the definitional problems with tarnishment presented in the *Toys "R" Us* cases—cases decided under the 1995 Act—continue under the 2006 Act, as the following decision illustrates.

V SECRET CATALOGUE, INC. v. MOSELEY

605 F.3d 382 (6th Cir. 2010)

MERRITT, Circuit Judge:

In this trademark "dilution by tarnishment" case, brought under the Trademark Dilution Revision Act of 2006, the question is whether the plaintiff, an international lingerie company that uses the trade name designation "Victoria's Secret," has a valid suit for injunctive relief against the use of the name "Victor's Little Secret" or "Victor's Secret" by the defendants, a small retail store in a mall in Elizabethtown, Kentucky, that sells assorted merchandise, including "sex toys" and other sexually oriented products. The District Court issued the injunction. Since then the shop has been operating under the name of "Cathy's Little Secret." The District Court concluded that even though the two parties do not compete in the same market, the "Victor's Little Secret" mark—because it is sex related—disparages and tends to reduce the positive associations and the "selling power" of the "Victoria's Secret" mark. The question is whether the plaintiff's case meets the definitions and standards for "dilution by tarnishment" set out in the new Act. . . .

The new Act was expressly intended to overrule the Supreme Court interpretation of the old Act in this very same case. [cit.] The Supreme Court reversed a panel of this Court that had affirmed an injunction against "Victor's Little Secret." [On remand, the District Court again issued the injunction, this time under the 2006 Act.] We conclude that the new Act creates a kind of rebuttable presumption, or at least a very strong inference, that a new mark used to sell sex related products is likely to tarnish a famous mark if there is a clear semantic association between the two. That presumption has not been rebutted in this case.

I.   THE SUPREME COURT OPINION AND THE NEW ACT

The Supreme Court explained that this case started when an Army Colonel at Fort Knox saw an ad for "Victor's Secret" in a weekly publication. It advertised that the small store in Elizabethtown sold adult videos and novelties and lingerie.[3] There was no likelihood of confusion between the two businesses or the two marks, but the Army Colonel was offended because the sexually-oriented business was semantically associating itself with "Victoria's Secret." The Court explained that the concepts of "dilution by blurring" and "dilution by tarnishment" originated with an article in the Harvard Law Review, Frank Schechter, "Rational Basis of Trademark Protection," 40 HARV. L. REV. 813 (1927), and that the history and meaning of the concepts were further well explained in Restatement (Third) of Unfair Competition, Section 25 (1995). The Restatement section referred to by the Supreme Court explains this new intellectual property tort and contains in §25 a comprehensive statement of "Liability Without Proof of Confusion: Dilution and Tarnishment." "Tarnishment," as distinguished from "dilution by blurring," was the only claim before the Supreme Court and is the only claim before us in this new appeal. We quote at length the relevant Restatement explanation of "tarnishment" in the footnote below.[4]

[The court recited the Supreme Court's holding that a showing of likelihood of dilution was insufficient to establish liability under the 1995 Act. Then the court turned to the 2006 legislation.] In the new law Congress rejected the Court's view that a simple "likelihood" of an association in the consumer's mind of the Victoria's Secret mark with the sexually-oriented videos and toys of "Victor's Secret" is insufficient for liability.

---

3. The Supreme Court explained:

> In the February 12, 1998, edition of a weekly publication distributed to residents of the military installation at Fort Knox, Kentucky, petitioners advertised the "GRAND OPENING just in time for Valentine's Day!" of their store "VICTOR'S SECRET" in nearby Elizabethtown. The ad featured "Intimate Lingerie *for every woman*," "Romantic Lighting"; "Lycra Dresses"; "Pagers"; and "Adult Novelties/Gifts." An army colonel, who saw the ad and was offended by what he perceived to be an attempt to use a reputable company's trademark to promote the sale of "unwholesome, tawdry merchandise," sent a copy to respondents. Their counsel then wrote to petitioners stating that their choice of the name "Victor's Secret" for a store selling lingerie was likely to cause confusion with the well-known VICTORIA'S SECRET mark and, in addition, was likely to "dilute the distinctiveness" of the mark. They requested the immediate discontinuance of the use of the name "and any variations thereof." In response, petitioners changed the name of their store to "Victor's Little Secret." Because that change did not satisfy respondents, they promptly filed this action in Federal District Court. [cit.] (internal citations omitted).

4. [The relevant section asserts that "[t]he selling power of a trademark also can be undermined by a use of the mark with goods or services such as illicit drugs or pornography that 'tarnish' the mark's image through inherently negative or unsavory associations. . . ." Comment (g) includes the following illustration: "3. *A*, a bank, uses the designation "Cookie Jar" to identify its automatic teller machine. *B* opens a topless bar across the street from *A* under the trade name "Cookie Jar." Although prospective customers of *A* are unlikely to believe that *A* operates or sponsors the bar, *B* is subject to liability to *A* for tarnishment under an applicable antidilution statute if the customers are likely to associate *A's* mark or *A's* business with the images evoked by *B's* use."]

The House Judiciary Committee Report states the purpose of the new 2006 legislation as follows:

> The *Moseley* standard *creates an undue burden* for trademark holders who contest diluting uses and should be revised.
>
> . . .
>
>   The new language in the legislation [provides] . . . specifically that the standard for proving a dilution claim is "likelihood of dilution" and that both dilution by blurring and dilution by tarnishment are actionable.

(emphasis added). [cit.] . . . The drafters of the Committee Report also called special attention to the "burden" of proof or persuasion placed on "trademark holders" by the Supreme Court's opinion in *Moseley*, suggesting a possible modification in the burden of proof. The question for us then is whether "Victor's Little Secret" with its association with lewd sexual toys creates a "likelihood of dilution by tarnishment" of Victoria's Secret mark.

II.   APPLICATION OF STATUTORY STANDARD

The specific question in this case is whether, without consumer surveys or polls or other evidence, a semantic "association" is equivalent to a liability-creating mental "association" of a junior mark like "Victor's Little Secret" with a famous mark like "Victoria's Secret" that constitutes dilution by tarnishment when the junior mark is used to sell sexual toys, videos and similar soft-core pornographic products. There appears to be a clearly emerging consensus in the case law, aided by the language of §25 of the Restatement of Trademarks 3d, quoted in footnote 4, *supra*, that the creation of an "association" between a famous mark and lewd or bawdy sexual activity disparages and defiles the famous mark and reduces the commercial value of its selling power. This consensus stems from an economic prediction about consumer taste and how the predicted reaction of conventional consumers in our culture will affect the economic value of the famous mark.

There have been at least eight federal cases in six jurisdictions that conclude that a famous mark is tarnished when its mark is semantically associated with a new mark that is used to sell sex-related products. We find no exceptions in the case law that allow such a new mark associated with sex to stand. [cit.]

The phrase "likely to cause dilution" used in the new statute significantly changes the meaning of the law from "causes actual harm" under the preexisting law. The word "likely" or "likelihood" means "probably," WEBSTER'S THIRD NEW INTERNATIONAL DICTIONARY 1310 (1963); BLACK'S LAW DICTIONARY 1076 (1968). It is important to note also that the Committee Report quoted above seeks to reduce the "burden" of evidentiary production on the trademark holder. The burden-of-proof problem, the developing case law, and the Restatement (Third) of Trademarks in §25 (particularly subsection g) should now be interpreted, we think, to create a kind of rebuttable presumption, or at least a very strong inference, that a new mark used to sell sex-related products is likely to tarnish a famous mark if there is a clear semantic association between the two. This *res ipsa loquitur*-like effect is not conclusive but places on the owner of the new mark the burden of coming forward with evidence that there is no likelihood or probability of tarnishment. The evidence could be in the form of expert testimony or surveys or polls or customer testimony.

In the present case, the Moseleys have had two opportunities in the District Court to offer evidence that there is no real probability of tarnishment and have not done so. They did not offer at oral argument any suggestion that they could make such a showing or wanted the case remanded for that purpose. The fact that Congress was dissatisfied with the *Moseley* result and the *Moseley* standard of liability, as well as apparently the *Moseley* burden of proof, supports the view of Victoria's Secret that the present record—in the eyes of the legislative branch—shows a likelihood of tarnishment. Without evidence to the contrary or a persuasive defensive theory that rebuts the presumption, the defendants have given us no basis to reverse the judgment of the District Court. We do not find sufficient the defendants' arguments that they should have the right to use Victor Moseley's first name and that the effect of the association is *de minimis*. The Moseleys do not have a right to use the word "secret" in their mark. They use it only to make the association with the Victoria's Secret mark. We agree that the tarnishing effect of the Moseley's mark on the senior mark is somewhat speculative, but we have no evidence to overcome the strong inference created by the case law, the Restatement, and Congressional dissatisfaction with the burden of proof used in this case in the Supreme Court. The new law seems designed to protect trademarks from any unfavorable sexual associations. Thus, any new mark with a lewd or offensive-to-some sexual association raises a strong inference of tarnishment. The inference must be overcome by evidence that rebuts the probability that some consumers will find the new mark both offensive and harmful to the reputation and the favorable symbolism of the famous mark.

Our dissenting colleague, in relying on the Supreme Court treatment of the proof in this case—for example, the long quotation from the Supreme Court concerning the legal effect of the evidence—fails to concede what seems obvious: Congress overruled the Supreme Court's view of the burden of proof. As quoted above, it said, "the Moseley standard creates an undue burden for trademark holders who contest diluting uses." It seems clear that the new Act demonstrates that Congress intended that a court should reach a different result in this case if the facts remain the same. We do not necessarily disagree with our dissenting colleague that the policy followed by the Supreme Court in such cases may be better. We simply believe that the will of Congress is to the contrary with regard to the proof in this case and with regard to the method of allocating the burden of proof.

[*Affirmed*.]

JULIA SMITH GIBBONS, Circuit Judge, concurring:

I fully concur in the majority opinion with the exception of one small quibble. I would not use the term "rebuttable presumption" to describe the inference that a new mark used to sell sex-related products is likely to tarnish a famous mark if there is a clear semantic association between the two. Practically speaking, what the inference is called makes little difference. I agree with the majority opinion that the inference is a strong one and that, to counter it, some evidence that there is no likelihood or probability of tarnishment is required. But because we are endeavoring to interpret a new law and because the legislative history is not explicit on the point of modification of the burden of proof, I think it best to end our analysis by characterizing the inference as an inference.

KAREN NELSON MOORE, Circuit Judge, dissenting:

Because I believe that Victoria's Secret has failed to produce sufficient evidence to show that the Moseleys' use of the name "Victor's Little Secret" is likely to tarnish the VICTORIA'S SECRET mark, I would reverse the judgment of the district court and must respectfully dissent.

Under the Trademark Dilution Revision Act of 2006 ("TDRA"), Victoria's Secret is entitled to injunctive relief if the Moseleys' use of "Victor's Little Secret" as the name of their adult-oriented novelty store[1] "is likely to cause dilution . . . by tarnishment of

---

1. Victor's Little Secret "sell[s]" a wide variety of items, including adult videos, adult novelties, and lingerie." [cit.] "Victor Moseley stated in an affidavit that women's lingerie represented only about five percent of their sales." [cit.]

the" VICTORIA'S SECRET mark. 15 U.S.C. §1125(c)(1). "[D]ilution by tarnishment" is defined as an "association arising from the similarity between a mark or trade name and a famous mark that harms the reputation of the famous mark." *Id*. §1125(c)(2)(C). Thus, under the terms of the statute, to determine whether the VICTORIA'S SECRET mark is likely to be tarnished by the Moseleys' use, this court must inquire as to both the "association" between the two marks and the "harm" that the association causes to the senior mark.

Because I agree that there is a clear association between the two marks, the determinative inquiry in this dilution-by-tarnishment case is whether that association is likely to harm Victoria's Secret's reputation. *See id*. §1125(c)(2)(C) ("that harms the reputation of the famous mark"). Contrary to the majority's conclusion, however, given the record before the panel, I would hold that Victoria's Secret has failed to meet its burden to show that the Moseleys' use of "Victor's Little Secret" is likely to dilute Victoria's Secret's mark.[2]

Victoria's Secret's evidence of tarnishment includes nothing more than the following: (1) an affidavit from Army Colonel John E. Baker stating that he "was . . . offended by [the] defendants' use of [Victoria's Secret's] trademark to promote . . . unwholesome, tawdry merchandise," such as "'adult' novelties and gifts," and that since his "wife . . . and . . . daughter . . . shop at Victoria's Secret, [he] was further dismayed by [the] defendants' effort to associate itself with, trade off on the image of, and in fact denigrate a store frequented by members of [his] family"; and (2) a statement from one of Victoria's Secret's corporate officers that Victoria's Secret strives to "maintain[] an image that is sexy and playful" and one that "avoid[s] sexually explicit or graphic imagery."

Reviewing Baker's affidavit, I believe that it is plain that Baker made a "mental association" between "Victor's Little Secret" and "Victoria's Secret." It is also clear that Baker held a negative impression of "Victor's Little Secret." But despite the clear negative association of this *one* individual when confronted with "Victor's Little Secret," Victoria's Secret has presented *no* evidence that Baker's, or anyone else's, distaste or dislike of "Victor's Little Secret" is likely to taint their positive opinion or perception of Victoria's Secret. Yet evidence that the junior mark is likely to undermine or alter the positive associations of the senior mark—i.e., evidence that the junior mark is likely to harm the reputation of the senior mark—is precisely the showing required under the plain language of 15 U.S.C. §1125(c)(2)(C) to prove dilution by tarnishment. As the Second Circuit recently noted in *Starbucks Corp. v. Wolfe's Borough Coffee, Inc.*, 588 F.3d 97 (2d Cir. 2009):

> That a consumer may associate a negative-sounding junior mark with a famous mark says little of whether the consumer views the junior mark as harming the reputation of the famous mark. The more relevant question, for purposes of tarnishment, would have been how a hypothetical coffee [with a negative-sounding name] would affect the positive impressions about the coffee sold by Starbucks.

Starbucks Corp., 588 F.3d at 110; *see also* J. Thomas McCarthy, 4 McCarthy on Trademarks and Unfair Competition §24:89 (4th ed.) [hereinafter McCarthy on Trademarks]

---

2. I respectfully disagree with the majority's conclusion that in dilution-by-tarnishment cases involving new marks "with lewd or offensive-to-some sexual association[s]" the TDRA establishes a presumption or inference of tarnishment that the Moseleys must rebut. To be sure, the House Judiciary Committee Report highlights Congress's concern with the pre-TDRA actual-dilution standard, but I do not read its concern that the previous standard created "an undue burden" to mean that Congress envisioned a modification of the party that bears the burden of proof as opposed to simply a lightening of the evidentiary showing. *See* H.R. Rep. No. 109-23, at 5 (2005) ("Witnesses at the [] [legislative] hearings focused on the standard of harm threshold articulated in *Mosely* [sic]. . . . The *Mosely* [sic] standard creates an undue burden for trademark holders who contest diluting uses and should be revised."). The burden to show tarnishment remains with Victoria's Secret.

(discussing tarnishment claims as being premised on the notion that "positive associations" of the senior mark will be displaced or degraded by the negative associations of the junior mark); Restatement (Third) of Unfair Competition §25 cmt. g (1995) ("To prove a case of tarnishment, the prior user must demonstrate that the subsequent use is likely to . . . undermine or damage the positive associations evoked by the mark."). In fact, when reviewing the exact same evidentiary record, the Supreme Court explicitly noted that Victoria's Secret's offer of proof included no evidence that "Victor's Little Secret" affected Baker's positive impressions of Victoria's Secret:

> The record in this case establishes that an army officer . . . did make the mental association with "Victoria's Secret," but it also shows that *he did not therefore form any different impression of the store that his wife and daughter had patronized*. There is a complete absence of evidence of any lessening of the capacity of the VICTORIA'S SECRET mark to identify and distinguish goods or services sold in Victoria's Secret stores or advertised in its catalogs. The officer was offended by the ad, *but it did not change his conception of Victoria's Secret*. His offense was directed entirely at [the Moseleys], not at [Victoria's Secret]. Moreover, the expert retained by respondents had nothing to say about the impact of [the Moseleys'] name on the strength of [Victoria's Secret's] mark.

[cit.] (emphases added).[3]

---

3. The majority mischaracterizes my citation to the Supreme Court's decision as evidencing a refusal to follow the "will of Congress" and a desire to follow the pre-TDRA "policy [of the] . . . Supreme Court." Maj. Op. at 389. My citation to the Supreme Court's decision, however, does no such thing. First, as stated previously, I believe that the majority's conclusion that Congress intended to change which party has the burden of proof—i.e., the framework governing which party must put forth evidence in support of its position—as opposed to the standard of harm—i.e., actual harm versus a likelihood of harm—is not supported by the statute or the legislative history. In fact, the only evidence that the majority cites in support of its belief that Congress intended to place the burden of proof on the defendant is the House Committee Report, but even that Report undercuts the majority's argument. The full paragraph from which the majority draws its quotation states:

> Witnesses at the [ ] [legislative] hearings focused on the *standard of harm threshold* articulated in *Mosely* [sic]. For example, a representative of the International Trademark Association observed that "[b]y the time measurable, provable damage to the mark has occurred much time has passed, the damage has been done, and the remedy, which is injunctive relief, is far less effective." The Committee endorses this position. The *Mosely* [sic] standard creates an undue burden for trademark holders who contest diluting uses and should be revised.

H.R. Rep. No. 109-23, at 5 (internal footnote omitted and emphasis added). It was the "standard of harm threshold," i.e., the showing of actual harm that the Supreme Court employed, that was Congress's concern, not the party bearing the burden of proof. This conclusion is supported by the hearings to which the Committee Report refers. During those hearings, the focus of both the House of Representatives and the witnesses was whether Congress should "maintain an actual dilution standard, as the Supreme Court held in the Victoria's Secret case," or adopt a "likelihood of dilution standard." [cit.]

I certainly recognize that Congress changed the law concerning dilution in response to the Supreme Court's decision in *Moseley*, but the Supreme Court in *Moseley* said nothing about changing the party bearing the burden of proof and neither does the amended statute. Instead, the statute explicitly states that "dilution by tarnishment" is an "association arising from the similarity between a mark or trade name and a famous mark *that harms the reputation of the famous mark*." 15 U.S.C. §1125(c)(2)(C) (emphasis added). In concluding that Victoria's Secret has failed to prove a likelihood of tarnishment because it has failed to present evidence that Victor's Little Secret is likely to harm the reputation of its mark, I am doing nothing more than applying the plain language of the statute that Congress enacted after the Supreme Court's decision. This approach certainly reflects the "will of Congress."

In short, Victoria's Secret has presented *no* probative evidence that anyone is likely to think less of Victoria's Secret as a result of "Victor's Little Secret" and cannot therefore prevail on its claim of dilution by tarnishment. [cit.] Instead of developing a record on remand that contains at least some evidence that Victoria's Secret's reputation is likely to suffer because of the negative response that "Victor's Little Secret" engendered, the record before the panel indicates only that a single individual thinks poorly of "Victor's Little Secret." On this record, it is simply no more probable that Victoria's Secret will suffer reputational harm as a result of the Moseleys' use of "Victor's Little Secret" than it is probable that those who are offended by "Victor's Little Secret" will limit their negative impressions to the Moseleys and refrain from projecting those negative associations upon Victoria's Secret. Baker's affidavit does nothing to contradict this conclusion, and given the absence of any indication that his or his family's opinion of Victoria's Secret changed following the Moseleys' use of "Victor's Little Secret," his affidavit may, in fact, provide evidence that individuals are likely to confine their distaste to the Moseleys. *See id.* ("The officer was offended by the ad, but it did not change his conception of Victoria's Secret. His offense was directed entirely at [the Moseleys], not at [Victoria's Secret].").

Certainly, it is *possible* that the Moseleys' use of "Victor's Little Secret" to sell adult-oriented material and other novelties could reflect poorly on the VICTORIA'S SECRET mark and could cause Victoria's Secret to suffer damage to its "sexy and playful" reputation, but the evidentiary standard set forth in the statute is one of likelihood, *not* mere possibility. Likelihood is based on probable consequence and amounts to more than simple speculation as to what might possibly happen. [cit.] Yet, as the majority notes, on the instant record, the "tarnishing effect of the Moseley's mark on the senior mark" is nothing more than "speculative."

Despite the absence of evidence, the majority is willing to assume that Victoria's Secret has met its burden to prove the essential element of "harm to reputation" based on the fact that numerous cases from other jurisdictions conclude, without much inquiry, "that a famous mark is tarnished when its mark is semantically associated with a new mark that is used to sell sex-related products." *Id.* at 388. I do not agree. Although it is true that courts have concluded that a finding of tarnishment is likely when a mark's "likeness is placed in the context of sexual activity, obscenity, or illegal activity," [cit.], a court cannot ignore the showing of reputational harm that the statute requires.[4]

Even assuming that "Victor's Little Secret" is plainly unwholesome when compared to Victoria's Secret and that this case is completely analogous to those cases on which the majority relies, I still maintain that it is improper simply to assume likelihood of harm to the reputation of a senior mark when dealing with a junior mark of sexual character. As recounted above, there is *no* evidence connecting Victor's Little Secret's "unwholesome"

---

4. Nor can the court ignore the character of the senior mark when applying the majority's "rule." Victoria's Secret sells women's lingerie, and, as Victoria's Secret readily admits, its own mark is already associated with sex, albeit not with sex novelties. *See* ROA at 90 (Kriss Aff.) (noting that Victoria's Secret attempts to maintain a "sexy and playful" image); *see also, e.g., id.* at 156-57 (depicting Victoria's Secret advertisements for "sexy little things" lingerie, which urge customers to "[b]e bad for goodness sake[] [i]n peek-a-boo's, bras and sexy Santa accessories"; to "[g]ive flirty panties" as gifts, and participate in the store's "panty fantasy," which it describes as "Very racy. Very lacy"); *id.* at 209 (reproducing an article in Redbook magazine entitled "46 Things to Do to a Naked Man," which highlights Victoria's Secret's role in the sexual activities of one of the contributors).

In essence, the VICTORIA'S SECRET mark is not entirely separate from the sexual context within which the junior mark, "Victor's Little Secret," operates. This fact makes the instant case unlike many of the cases that the majority cites. [The dissenting judge cited *Toys "R" Us Inc. v. Akkaoui*, 40 U.S.P.Q.2d (BNA) 1836, 1838 (N.D. Cal. 1996), among others.]

or "tawdry" sexual character to the senior mark's reputation, and there is nothing in the language of the TDRA that would allow the court to forgive a party's obligation present proof as to an element of the tarnishment cause of action—i.e., the likelihood of harm to reputation.[5] *See* McCarthy on Trademarks §24:115 ("Even after the 2006 revision when only a likelihood of dilution is required, . . . judges should demand persuasive evidence that dilution is likely to occur. Even the probability of dilution should be proven by evidence, not just by theoretical assumptions about what possibly could occur or might happen.").

With its conclusion that there is sufficient evidence of harm to the reputation of the VICTORIA'S SECRET mark based solely on the sexual nature of the junior mark, the majority sanctions an almost non-existent evidentiary standard and, in the process, essentially eliminates the requirement that a plaintiff provide some semblance of proof of likelihood of reputational harm in order to prevail on a tarnishment claim, despite the plain language of 15 U.S.C. §1125(c)(2). Because I believe that Victoria's Secret has not met its burden to show that "Victor's Little Secret" is likely to dilute the famous mark by way of tarnishment, I respectfully dissent.

NOTES AND QUESTIONS

1. *Contradictory or predictable?* Are the two *Toys "R" Us* decisions in tension? Or can they readily be harmonized? Do they apply the same legal standard for tarnishment? Suppose that the cases had arisen after the passage of the 2006 legislation. Would the outcomes have been the same under the 2006 standard for dilution by tarnishment? In *Louis Vuitton Malletier S.A. v. Haute Diggity Dog, LLC*, 507 F.3d 252 (4th Cir. 2007) (excerpted *infra* in Chapter 9), the court discussed dilution by tarnishment under the 2006 provisions. Louis Vuitton, the manufacturer of high-end handbags, alleged that the defendant's sale of dog chew toys that imitated (and allegedly parodied) Louis Vuitton's mark and handbag design amounted to tarnishment. In support of that assertion, Louis Vuitton sought to rely on what the court called a "logical concession that a $10 dog toy made in China was of 'inferior quality' to the $1190 LOUIS VUITTON handbag." Is this sufficient harm to support a tarnishment claim under the 2006 statutory standard? If not, would evidence that a dog could choke on the defendant's toys cause actionable "harm to reputation"? Or is tarnishment under the 2006 standard limited to uses that evoke "drugs, sex, or nudity" as in the *Adults "R" Us* and *V Secret* cases?

2. *The* V Secret *presumption.* Is the *V Secret* presumption (or, as the court puts it, "a kind of rebuttable presumption, or at least a very strong inference") reasonably grounded in the statute? Are you persuaded by the *V Secret* court's use of legislative history? If you were an appellate judge in a different jurisdiction, would you adopt the *V Secret* presumption?

3. *Is dilution by tarnishment unconstitutional?* Is tarnishment a potentially potent mechanism through which a trademark owner (acting through the courts) might restrain "undesirable" speech about the trademark owner's product, the trademark owner's

---

5. The potential problem with simply assuming tarnishment when the junior mark places the senior mark in a sexual context becomes apparent if one considers a different case. What if the holder of a sex-related senior mark levied a claim of dilution by tarnishment against the holder of a junior mark that was similarly associated with sex? Would the court be willing to assume without further proof that despite their similar sexual origins the junior mark necessarily tarnishes the senior mark? Under the majority's reasoning, such an assumption would be appropriate. This cannot be the law.

corporate practices, or the trademark owner itself? If so, can dilution by tarnishment survive First Amendment scrutiny after *Tam*? For purposes of the First Amendment categories canvassed in *Tam*, how would you classify a rule that use on "sex-related" products was presumptively tarnishment? How would that affect your assessment of whether the majority or dissent had the better of the argument in *V Secret*? We consider First Amendment limitations on the scope of trademark protection further in Chapter 9.

In *S.F. Arts & Athletics, Inc. v. U.S. Olympic Comm.*, 483 U.S. 522 (1987), the U.S. Supreme Court held that the U.S. Olympic Committee, as owners of the mark OLYMPICS under the Amateur Sports Act, had the right to restrain use of the term GAY OLYMPICS notwithstanding the lack of consumer confusion. The Court rejected (by 6-3) the defendant's First Amendment challenge to the enforcement of the U.S.O.C.'s statutory rights, which approximate dilution protection under the Lanham Act.

PROBLEM 8-1:   DILUTION BY BURNISHING?

Suppose that Professor Janis' cousin, Clem, opened a nationwide chain of PINK DIVAS gentlemen's clubs, featuring nude dancing, pornographic videos, and the like. When Cousin Clem was heard to boast that "the PINK DIVAS trademark alone is worth millions," a women's rights group, Women Revolting Against Pornography, devised a protest measure: They immediately adopted PINK DIVAS as the name of their local chapter and assiduously promoted the PINK DIVAS name in connection with rape counseling services, the local girls' club, and other charitable fundraising activities focusing on women's issues. Does Clem have a viable cause of action for dilution by tarnishment because of the unwelcome burnishing of the PINK DIVAS mark? If not, are there some marks (i.e., those already associated with drugs, nudity, and sex) for which tarnishment is impossible?

b. Blurring

In decisions preceding the 1995 Act, courts in some states recognized a concept of dilution by blurring, but struggled to lay out a test for it. In *Mead Data Cent. v. Toyota Motor Sales U.S.A., Inc.*, 875 F.2d 1026, 1035 (2d Cir. 1989), decided under New York law, Judge Sweet, concurring, suggested that blurring be analyzed in view of: (1) similarity of the marks; (2) similarity of the products covered by the marks; (3) sophistication of consumers; (4) predatory intent; (5) renown of the senior mark; and (6) renown of the junior mark. These became known as the "Sweet" factors.

After the passage of Section 43(c), litigants frequently invoked the Sweet factors as a basis for analyzing dilution by blurring. Courts gave the factors a mixed reception, pointing out various flaws, including that unlike the federal law, New York law did not impose a fame requirement, perhaps explaining why Judge Sweet included "renown of the senior mark" as a blurring factor. In *Nabisco, Inc. v. PF Brands, Inc.*, 191 F.3d 208 (2d Cir. 1999), the court went even further, resisting the adoption of any multi-factor test—at least at that time—and instead arguing that "courts would do better to feel their way from case to case, setting forth in each those factors that seem to bear on the resolution of that case, and, only eventually to arrive at a consensus of relevant factors on the basis of this accumulated experience."

Courts were still feeling their way along as of 2006. No definitive test for dilution by blurring had emerged when Congress passed the TDRA, which defined dilution by blurring by reference to an open-ended multi-factor test that appears to have been inspired by the Sweet factors. The courts then took up the difficult task of applying the statutory factors, as the following cases and materials illustrate.

STARBUCKS CORP. v. WOLFE'S BOROUGH COFFEE, INC.
736 F.3d 198 (2d Cir. 2013)

LOHIER, Circuit Judge:

. . .

BACKGROUND

We assume familiarity with the underlying facts and long procedural history of the case, which are set forth in our previous opinions, *Starbucks Corp. v. Wolfe's Borough Coffee, Inc.*, 477 F.3d 765 (2d Cir. 2007) ("*Starbucks II*"), and *Starbucks Corp. v. Wolfe's Borough Coffee, Inc.*, 588 F.3d 97 (2d Cir. 2009) ("*Starbucks IV*"). We recount them here only as necessary to explain our disposition of this appeal.

As of 2005, when the bench trial occurred, Starbucks had grown from a single coffee shop in Seattle in 1971 to a singularly prominent global purveyor of specialty coffee and coffee products, with 8,700 retail locations worldwide and revenues of $5.3 billion for fiscal year 2004. Starbucks U.S. Brands is the owner, and Starbucks Corporation a licensee, of at least 56 valid United States trademark registrations that include the Starbucks Marks. The Starbucks Marks are displayed on signs and at multiple locations in each Starbucks store, as well as on the Starbucks website.

Starbucks has devoted substantial time, effort, and money to advertising and promoting the Starbucks Marks. From fiscal year 2000 to 2003, Starbucks spent over $136 million on advertising, promotion, and related marketing activities, essentially all of which featured the Starbucks Marks. Starbucks actively polices the Starbucks Marks, demanding that infringing uses be terminated and, where necessary, commencing litigation. Well before Black Bear used the term "Charbucks" as part of any product name, the Starbucks Marks were "famous" within the meaning of the FTDA.

Black Bear manufactures and sells roasted coffee beans and related goods via mail and internet order, at a limited number of New England supermarkets, and at a single New Hampshire retail outlet. In 1997 Black Bear developed a coffee blend named "Charbucks Blend"; it now sells a dark-roast coffee called "Mister Charbucks" or "Mr. Charbucks." When Black Bear began manufacturing coffee using the Charbucks Marks, it was aware of the Starbucks Marks. One of the reasons Black Bear used the term "Charbucks" was the public perception that Starbucks roasted its beans unusually darkly. Soon after Black Bear began to sell Charbucks Blend, Starbucks demanded that it cease using the Charbucks Marks. Black Bear nevertheless continued to sell coffee under the Charbucks Marks, and in 2001 Starbucks started this action claiming, among other things, trademark dilution in violation of 15 U.S.C. §§1125(c), 1127.[3]

The District Court held a two-day bench trial in March 2005. At trial, two matters of significance to this appeal occurred. First, Black Bear's founder, James O. Clark III, testified that the name "Charbucks" had previously been used during "the coffee wars in Boston between Starbucks and the Coffee Connection," a Boston-based company.[4]

---

3. Starbucks also asserted claims of [trademark infringement and unfair competition under the Lanham Act and related state law causes of action, all of which were dismissed during the course of the suit.]

Second, Starbucks introduced the testimony of Warren J. Mitofsky, a scientist in the field of consumer research and polling. Mitofsky explained the results of a telephone survey he had conducted of six hundred participants, designed to be representative of the United States population. The survey found that when asked, "What is the first thing that comes to your mind when you hear the name 'Charbucks,' spelled C-H-A-R-B-U-C-K-S?," 30.5 percent of participants answered "Starbucks," while 9 percent answered "coffee."[5] When the participants were asked, "Can you name any company or store that you think might offer a product called 'Charbucks'?," 3.1 percent responded "Starbucks," and another 1.3 percent responded "coffee house."[6] Mitofsky concluded that "[t]he number one association of the name 'Charbucks' in the minds of consumers is with the brand 'Starbucks.'" Commenting on the scope of his survey, Mitofsky also stated: "[I]f you want to know the reaction to the name Charbucks, then the telephone is perfectly adequate. If you want to measure the reaction or the familiarity with other visual cues, then it's not the right method."

In December 2005 the District Court ruled in favor of Black Bear and dismissed Starbucks' complaint. *See Starbucks Corp. v. Wolfe's Borough Coffee, Inc.*, No. 01 Civ. 5981, 2005 WL 3527126 (S.D.N.Y. Dec. 23, 2005) ("*Starbucks I*"). . . .

Starbucks appealed. While the appeal was pending, Congress passed the Trademark Dilution Revision Act of 2006 ("TDRA"). . . . In light of this change in the governing law, we vacated the judgment of the District Court and remanded for further proceedings. *Starbucks II*, 477 F.3d at 766.

On remand, after further briefing, the District Court again ruled in Black Bear's favor for substantially the same reasons set forth in its earlier opinion, but it also analyzed the federal dilution claim in light of the TDRA. *See Starbucks Corp. v. Wolfe's Borough Coffee, Inc.*, 559 F. Supp. 2d 472, 475-79 (S.D.N.Y. 2008) ("*Starbucks III*"). In particular, the District Court considered the six non-exclusive factors listed in the statute and made the following findings: (1) the marks were minimally similar, which the court deemed alone sufficient to defeat Starbucks' claim; (2) (a) the distinctiveness of the Starbucks Marks, (b) the exclusivity of their use by Starbucks, and (c) their high degree of recognition, all weighed in favor of Starbucks; (3) the intent factor weighed in Black Bear's favor because Black Bear's intent to create an association with the Starbucks Marks did not constitute bad faith; and (4) evidence from Mitofsky's survey was "insufficient to make the actual confusion factor weigh in [Starbucks'] favor to any significant degree." Balancing all six factors, the District Court held that the record was "insufficient to demonstrate the requisite likelihood that the association arising from the similarity of the core terms is likely to impair the distinctiveness of Starbucks' mark, and Plaintiff is not entitled to injunctive relief under that statute."

Starbucks appealed again, arguing that the District Court erred in finding that the Charbucks Marks are not likely to dilute the Starbucks Marks. In *Starbucks IV*, we examined the District Court's findings as to the first, fifth, and sixth factors, as well as its balancing of the statutory factors that bear on the likelihood of dilution by blurring. We held that "the District Court did not clearly err in finding that the Charbucks Marks were minimally similar to the Starbucks Marks," because the context of the Charbucks Marks (on Black Bear's packaging, on its website, and in the phrases "Charbucks Blend" and "Mister Charbucks") differentiated them from the famous marks. We concluded, however, that "the District Court erred to the extent it required 'substantial' similarity between the marks," and we suggested that the District Court had overemphasized the similarity factor. In particular,

---

4. The Coffee Connection apparently no longer exists as an independent company. *See Starbucks Plans to Acquire Coffee Connection*, New York Times (March 16, 1994), *available at http://www. nytimes.com/1994/03/16/business/company-news-starbucks-plans-to-acquire-coffee-connection.html.*

we stated that the inclusion of "the degree of similarity" as only one of six factors in the revised statute indicates that even a low degree of similarity would not categorically bar a dilution-by-blurring claim.

Turning to the fifth and sixth factors—intent to associate and actual association—we held that the District Court had erred by requiring "bad faith" to find that the intent to associate factor favored Starbucks. Noting the survey results, which demonstrated some degree of association between "Charbucks" and "Starbucks," we also held that the District Court erred by relying on evidence supporting the absence of "actual *confusion*" to conclude that the actual *association* factor did not weigh in Starbucks' favor "to any significant degree." The absence of actual or likely confusion, we reasoned, does not bear directly on whether dilution is likely.

Emphasizing that the analysis of a dilution by blurring claim must ultimately focus on "whether an *association*, arising from the similarity between the subject marks, 'impairs the distinctiveness of the famous mark,'" we vacated the judgment of the District Court and remanded for reconsideration of the claim in light of our discussions of the first, fifth, and sixth statutory factors.

In its opinion and order following that remand, ("*Starbucks V*"), the District Court recognized that the second through fifth statutory factors favored Starbucks. But the court again found that the first factor (the similarity of the marks) favored Black Bear because the marks were only minimally similar when presented in commerce—that is, when the Charbucks Marks are viewed on the packaging, which includes the phrases "Charbucks Blend" or "Mister Charbucks."

As for the sixth factor (actual association), the District Court acknowledged that the results of the Mitofsky survey "constitute evidence of actual association," but it then significantly discounted those results on the ground that the survey inquired into associations only with the isolated word "Charbucks" and failed to present the Charbucks Marks in full context. The court also compared the survey results in this case with those in other cases. Here, it noted, only 30.5 percent of respondents associated "Charbucks" with "Starbucks," while in other trade dilution cases 70 percent to 90 percent of survey respondents associated the relevant marks. The District Court also compared the 3.1 percent of respondents who thought a product called "Charbucks" would be made by Starbucks to the 28 percent of respondents who made a similar origin association in a Ninth Circuit trademark dilution case (citing *Jada Toys, Inc. v. Mattel, Inc.*, 518 F.3d 628, 636 (9th Cir. 2008)). With the benefit of these comparisons, the District Court found that the actual association factor weighs "no more than minimally" in Starbucks' favor.

In evaluating the likelihood of dilution, the District Court emphasized the "association" and "similarity" factors. Citing the TDRA's definition of dilution by blurring as "*association arising from the similarity* between a mark or trade name and a famous mark that impairs the distinctiveness of the famous mark," the District Court explained that "[t]he statutory language leaves no doubt" that these two factors are "obviously important." After balancing all six factors, the District Court held that Starbucks had failed to meet its burden of showing that it was entitled to injunctive relief:

> [T]he Charbucks marks are only weakly associated with the minimally similar Starbucks marks and, thus, are not likely to impair the distinctiveness of the famous Starbucks marks. In other words, [Starbucks] has failed to carry its burden of proving that [Black Bear's] use of its marks, as evidenced on the record before the Court, is likely to cause dilution by blurring.

[cit.]

On appeal, Starbucks challenges both the factual findings of minimal similarity and weak association and the conclusion that it failed to demonstrate a likelihood of dilution.

DISCUSSION

. . .

B.   Standard of Review

After a bench trial on a claim for trademark dilution by blurring, where the district court evaluates and balances the factors listed in the TDRA, we review the court's determinations as to each factor for clear error and its balancing of those factors *de novo*. *See [Tiffany (NJ) Inc. v. eBay Inc.*, 600 F.3d 93,101 (2d Cir. 2010)]; *Starbucks IV*, 588 F.3d at 105.[10] Accordingly, the District Court's factual findings regarding each factor bearing on the likelihood of trademark dilution by blurring will not be disturbed unless "on the entire evidence [we are] left with the definite and firm conviction that a mistake has been committed," [cit.] while the balancing of those factors to determine the likelihood of dilution is a legal exercise subject to de novo review. To determine how to conduct the balancing, we look first to the language of the statute. [cit.]

We previously have declined to treat the factors pertinent to a trademark dilution analysis as an inflexible, mechanical test, suggesting instead that the importance of each factor will vary with the facts. *Nabisco, Inc. v. PF Brands, Inc.*, 191 F.3d 208, 227-28 (2d Cir. 1999), *abrogated on other grounds by Moseley*, 537 U.S. at 433. Accordingly, we need not consider all six statutory factors listed in 15 U.S.C. §1125(c)(2)(B)(i)-(vi) if some are irrelevant to the ultimate question; nor are we limited to those six factors. *See Louis Vuitton Malletier S.A. v. Haute Diggity Dog, LLC*, 507 F.3d 252, 266 (4th Cir. 2007) ("Not every factor will be relevant in every case, and not every blurring claim will require extensive discussion of the factors."). Instead, we employ a "cautious and gradual approach," which favors the development of a nonexclusive list of trademark dilution factors over time. *Nabisco*, 191 F.3d at 217.

C.   Factual Findings: The Statutory Factors

On appeal, Starbucks challenges two of the District Court's findings: (1) that there is only a minimal degree of similarity between the Starbucks Marks and the Charbucks Marks; and (2) that Starbucks demonstrated only a weak association between the marks. The District Court did not clearly err with regard to either finding.

1.   Degree of Similarity

In *Starbucks IV* we held that "[w]ith respect to the first factor—the degree of similarity between the marks—the District Court did not clearly err in finding that the Charbucks Marks were minimally similar to the Starbucks Marks." We highlighted the difference between the Starbucks Marks and Charbucks Marks when the latter are placed in the context of Black Bear's packaging and the word "Charbucks" is incorporated into the phrases "Charbucks Blend" and "Mister Charbucks." "The law of the case ordinarily forecloses relitigation of issues expressly or impliedly decided by the appellate court." [cit.] Although not binding, the doctrine "counsels a court against revisiting its prior rulings in subsequent stages of the same case absent 'cogent' and 'compelling' reasons such as 'an intervening

---

10. We employ the same standard here that we use in the context of trademark infringement. . . . The statutory factors enumerated in §1125(c)(2)(B) are similar in kind to the [likelihood of confusion] factors. For example, both lists include the "similarity between" the two marks; "strength" of the mark in [the likelihood of confusion factors test] is akin to "distinctiveness" in §1125; and "actual confusion" in [the likelihood of confusion factors test] mirrors "actual association" in §1125.

change of controlling law, the availability of new evidence, or the need to correct a clear error or prevent manifest injustice.'" [cit.] Starbucks advances no compelling reason for us to revisit our ruling on the issue of similarity. It urges that the holding in *Starbucks IV* applied only to our "likelihood of confusion" analysis, and that the District Court erred by considering the contexts in which consumers encounter the Charbucks Marks. We reject such a crabbed view of the holding and adhere to our prior ruling that the District Court did not clearly err in finding minimal similarity.

2.   *Actual Association*

Starbucks next contends that the District Court's finding that actual association "weighs no more than minimally" in Starbucks' favor, was error for two reasons. First, Starbucks argues, Black Bear's admitted intent to create an association—the fifth statutory factor—raises a "presumption of association," or at least is strong evidence of actual association—the sixth statutory factor. Second, it argues that the District Court improperly discounted the Mitofsky survey evidence, which, in Starbucks' view, proves a high degree of actual association. We reject both arguments.

a.   Intent to Create an Association

As an initial matter, an intent to create an association is a separate factor under the TDRA and does not constitute per se evidence that the actual association factor weighs in favor of the owner of the famous mark. In support of its argument to the contrary, Starbucks quotes McCarthy's treatise, which states, "If the junior [user] intended to create an association, the law may assume that it succeeded." McCarthy §24:119. Starbucks similarly relies on *Federal Express Corp. v. Federal Espresso, Inc.*, 201 F.3d 168 (2d Cir. 2000), a dilution case in which we stated that the trier of fact "may well find that the marks are of sufficient similarity so that, in the mind of the consumer, the junior mark will conjure an association with the senior, especially in light of the testimony of [Federal Espresso's founder] that she chose the name Federal Espresso, in part, precisely because it would call to mind Federal Express." *Id.* at 177 (quotation marks omitted).

Both *Federal Espresso* and McCarthy's treatise acknowledge the importance of the intent factor in determining likelihood of dilution. This makes sense, as district courts must evaluate whether a junior mark is "likely to cause" "association arising from the similarity" between the marks "that impairs the distinctiveness of the famous mark," 15 U.S.C. §§1125(c)(1), (c)(2)(B), and the intent to associate may bear directly on the likelihood that the junior mark will cause such an association.

That said, "we interpret statutes to give effect, if possible, to every clause and word and to avoid statutory interpretations that render provisions superfluous." [cit.] Adopting Starbucks' presumption argument would effectively merge the intent to associate and the actual association factors, by making the former determinative of the latter, rather than treating them as distinct but related considerations. We therefore conclude that the District Court did not clearly err in finding that Clark's testimony concerning the origin of the Charbucks Marks was not an "admission" of actual association and that his intentions were not definitive proof of an actual association between the marks.

b.   Mitofsky Survey

Nor did the District Court err when it discounted the Mitofsky survey evidence because the survey measured only how respondents reacted to the isolated word "Charbucks," rather than to the Charbucks Marks in context, and because the share of respondents who indicated an association between the marks was "relatively small." We arrive at this conclusion for two reasons.

First, it coheres with our decision in *Starbucks IV*, in which we discerned no clear error in the District Court's consideration of context—including the addition of "Mister" or "Blend" to "Charbucks" and Black Bear's packaging—in assessing the marks' similarity, as consumers are likely to experience the product only in the context of those full phrases and Black Bear's packaging or website. *Starbucks IV*, 588 F.3d at 106. In our analysis of Starbucks' infringement claim, we similarly determined that the District Court did not clearly err when it found (1) that the survey failed to demonstrate significant actual confusion, "[p]articularly in light of the fact that the survey was administered by telephone and did not present the term 'Charbucks' in the context in which Black Bear used it," and (2) that the survey should have examined the effects of "a hypothetical coffee named either 'Mister Charbucks' or 'Charbucks Blend'" on the respondents' impressions of Starbucks coffee as a measure of dilution by tarnishment.

Second, our conclusion also comports with our prior precedents and other cases unrelated to Starbucks. In *Playtex Products, Inc. v. Georgia-Pacific Corp.*, 390 F.3d 158 (2d Cir. 2004), a case interpreting the pre-revision FTDA, we held that the results of a consumer survey showing an association between the marks "Moist-Ones" and "Wet Ones" were inadmissible as evidence of actual dilution because the defendant's product was "presented and packaged" as "*Quilted Northern* Moist-Ones." *Id*. at 168 (emphasis added). District courts within our Circuit have applied the same reasoning in evaluating surveys in the infringement context. [cit.] In the dilution context, the language of the FTDA, which requires a plaintiff to show the defendant's "*use of a mark . . . in commerce* that is likely to cause dilution by blurring . . . ," 15 U.S.C. §1125(c)(1) (emphasis added), clarifies that the way the defendant's mark is used in commerce is central to the dilution inquiry. As in *Playtex*, the District Court was within its rights to conclude that the Mitofsky survey had limited probative value because the defendant's marks were not presented to survey respondents as they are actually "presented and packaged" in commerce.

Citing our decision in *Nabisco*, Starbucks nevertheless argues that consumers are likely to hear and view the term "Charbucks" outside the context of Black Bear's packaging and without the full phrases "Mister Charbucks" and "Charbucks Blend." *Nabisco*, 191 F.3d at 218 (rejecting an argument under the pre-revision FTDA that packaging made two marks dissimilar, because many consumers would see the marks outside of the packaging). But Starbucks presented no record evidence that "Charbucks" is ever read or heard in isolation,[13] and in the absence of such evidence, we are not persuaded by the argument. To the contrary, as we noted in *Starbucks IV*, "it is unlikely that 'Charbucks' will appear to consumers outside the context of its normal use," and "it was not clearly erroneous for the District Court to find that the 'Mister' prefix or 'Blend' suffix lessened the similarity between the [marks]."

Starbucks also challenges the District Court's finding that the association between "Charbucks" and Starbucks was "relatively small." It contends that the Mitofsky survey in fact provided evidence of substantial actual association. We disagree.

It is true that in response to Mitofsky's question most probative of actual association— "What is the FIRST THING that comes to your mind when you hear the name 'Charbucks,'

---

13. Although the name "Mr. Charbucks" is presented in plain text on at least one page of Black Bear's website, all other record uses of the Charbucks Marks situate them in Black Bear's distinct color scheme, font, and layout.

spelled C-H-A-R-B-U-C-K-S?"—30.5 percent of respondents said "Starbucks," and 9 percent said "coffee." Both of these responses suggest an association between "Charbucks" and the Starbucks Marks. In *Jada Toys*, 518 F.3d at 636, for example, the Ninth Circuit held that a survey demonstrated actual association because it showed that 28 percent of respondents thought Jada's product was made by Mattel when asked who they thought produced the item. Here, however, the equivalent question in Mitofsky's survey was: "Can you name any company or store that you think might offer a product called 'Charbucks'?"[14] In response to that question concerning source on the Mitofsky survey, however, only 3.1 percent of respondents answered "Starbucks" and 1.3 percent answered "coffee house." These percentages are far below that for the equivalent question in *Jada Toys* and fail to demonstrate anything more than minimal actual association.[15]

Ultimately, on this factor, we consider only whether the District Court clearly erred when it found that the Mitofsky survey tilts the "actual association" factor "no more than minimally in [Starbucks'] favor." Had the Mitofsky survey presented the Charbucks Marks as they appear in commerce, we might well conclude that the District Court erred. But the word "Charbucks" was presented outside of its marketplace context, and Starbucks, which bears the burden of proof, *see Jada Toys*, 518 F.3d at 634, failed to show that this flaw did not materially impact the survey results. We therefore conclude that the record supports the District Court's decision to discount the survey and consider the actual association factor as weighing only minimally in Starbucks' favor.

D.   BALANCING

We next balance the factors enumerated in §1125(c)(2)(B), along with any other factors that bear on a likelihood of dilution, *de novo*. In balancing these factors, we are again mindful that the test is not an inflexible one, and that the ultimate question is whether the Charbucks Marks are likely to cause an association arising from their similarity to the Starbucks Marks, which impairs the Starbucks Marks' tendency to identify the source of Starbucks products in a unique way.

We have already affirmed the District Court's finding of minimal similarity between the Charbucks Marks and the Starbucks Marks. That finding weighs heavily in Black Bear's favor. Certainly, a plaintiff may show a likelihood of dilution notwithstanding only minimal similarity. But here, minimal similarity strongly suggests a relatively low likelihood of an association diluting the senior mark. The statute itself emphasizes the similarity of marks. *See* §1125(c)(2)(B) (defining "dilution by blurring" as "association arising from the similarity between a mark or a trade name and a famous mark that impairs the distinctiveness of the famous mark" (emphasis added)). Indeed, in *Starbucks IV*, we stated that "'similarity' is an integral element in the definition of 'blurring'" under the TDRA and suggested that, without *any* similarity, there could be no dilution by blurring.[17]

---

14. Both that question and the question discussed in *Jada Toys* test not merely *association* but also source *confusion*. Source confusion may be probative of association, because to confuse Charbucks with Starbucks, the word "Charbucks" must call "Starbucks" to mind. *See Nabisco*, 191 F.3d at 221 ("Confusion lessens distinction.").

15. Although some other respondents gave answers consistent with an association with Starbucks—18.3 percent answered "grocery store," 16.9 percent answered "discount store," 7 percent answered "restaurant," and 4.8 percent answered "department store"—these responses are also consistent with other views of what "Charbucks" could be, including meat or a charcoal grilling product, as 38.5 percent of respondents suggested.

17. Of course, in *Starbucks IV*, we rejected a *per se* or threshold requirement of "substantial similarity" between the marks at issue in federal dilution actions. In doing so, however, we did not suggest that a finding of *minimal* similarity could not be highly probative of the likelihood of dilution.

The next three factors—the degrees of distinctiveness, exclusive use, and recognition—are features of the senior mark itself that do not depend on the use of the junior mark. "[T]he *degree* of distinctiveness of the senior mark has a considerable bearing on the question whether a junior use will have a diluting effect. . . . [T]he more distinctiveness the mark possesses, the greater the interest to be protected." *Nabisco*, 191 F.3d at 217. There is no question that "Starbucks"—an arbitrary mark as applied to coffee—is highly distinctive. *See id.* at 216. Moreover, because, as the District Court found, the Starbucks Marks are in substantially exclusive use "the mark's distinctiveness is more likely to be impaired by the junior use," 2005 Hearing, at 14 (statement of Anne Gundelfinger). Lastly, as 79 percent of Mitofsky survey respondents were familiar with Starbucks, it is undisputed that Starbucks constitutes a widely recognized mark, and that this factor favors Starbucks.

Although the three factors of distinctiveness, recognition, and exclusivity favor Starbucks and bear to some degree on our assessment of the likelihood of dilution by blurring, the more important factors in the context of this case are the similarity of the marks and actual association. We agree with the District Court that the distinctiveness, recognition, and exclusive use of the Starbucks Marks do not overcome the weak evidence of actual association between the Charbucks and Starbucks marks. To the contrary, viewed in light of Starbucks' fame, both globally and among the Mitofsky survey participants more particularly, the fact that more survey participants did not think of "Starbucks" upon hearing "Charbucks" reinforces the District Court's finding that the marks are only minimally similar, and therefore unlikely to prompt an association that impairs the Starbucks Marks. Likewise, although the distinctiveness and exclusive use of the Starbucks Marks help Starbucks prove *susceptibility* to dilution by association arising from similarity between the Charbucks and Starbucks marks, they do not demonstrate that such an association is likely to arise, as Starbucks needed to show to obtain an injunction. Accordingly, these factors weigh only weakly in Starbucks' favor.

In this case, we attribute a moderate amount of significance to the fifth factor, intent to create an association. Clark's testimony indicated that Black Bear was capitalizing on an historic connection between the word "Charbucks" and "Starbucks," which arose out of the so-called "coffee-wars" in Boston, Massachusetts, *see Starbucks IV*, 588 F.3d at 111, and that he "meant to evoke an image of dark-roasted coffee of the type offered by Starbucks[.]" "[W]here, as here, the allegedly diluting mark was created with an intent to associate with the famous mark," *Starbucks IV*, 588 F.3d at 109, we agree with the District Court that this factor favors a finding of a likelihood of dilution.

The final, disputed factor, actual association, is highly relevant to likelihood of association. In the analogous context of determining the "likelihood of confusion" for trademark infringement claims, we have noted that "[t]here can be no more positive or substantial proof of the likelihood of confusion than proof of actual confusion," even though a showing of actual confusion is not necessary to prevail on such a claim. [cit.] The same principle obtains with respect to proof of actual association in dilution claims. And as noted, the Mitofsky survey demonstrated weak actual association, at best.

Weighing the factors above *de novo*, we agree with the District Court that Starbucks did not demonstrate a likelihood of dilution by blurring. Ultimately what tips the balance in this case is that Starbucks bore the burden of showing that it was entitled to injunctive relief on this record. Because Starbucks' principal evidence of association, the Mitofsky survey, was fundamentally flawed, and because there was minimal similarity between the marks at issue, we agree with the District Court that Starbucks failed to show that Black Bear's use of its Charbucks Marks in commerce is likely to dilute the Starbucks Marks.

[*Affirmed.*]

VISA INT'L SERVICE ASSOC. v. JSL CORP.

610 F.3d 1088 (9th Cir. 2010)

Kozinski, Chief Judge:

She sells sea shells by the sea shore. That's swell, but how about Shell espresso, Tide motor oil, Apple bicycles and Playboy computers? We consider the application of anti-dilution law to trademarks that are also common English words.

FACTS

Joseph Orr runs eVisa, a "multilingual education and information business that exists and operates exclusively on the Internet," at *www.evisa.com*. At least he did, until the district court enjoined him. Orr traces the name eVisa back to an English language tutoring service called "Eikaiwa Visa" that he ran while living in Japan. "Eikaiwa" is Japanese for English conversation, and the "e" in eVisa is short for Eikaiwa. The use of the word "visa" in both eVisa and Eikaiwa Visa is meant to suggest "the ability to travel, both linguistically and physically, through the English-speaking world." Orr founded eVisa shortly before his return to America, where he started running it out of his apartment in Brooklyn, New York.

Visa International Service Association sued JSL Corporation, through which Orr operates eVisa, claiming that eVisa is likely to dilute the Visa trademark. The district court granted summary judgment for Visa, and JSL appeals.

ANALYSIS

A plaintiff seeking relief under federal anti-dilution law must show that its mark is famous and distinctive, that defendant began using its mark in commerce after plaintiff's mark became famous and distinctive, and that defendant's mark is likely to dilute plaintiff's mark. *See Jada Toys, Inc. v. Mattel, Inc.*, 518 F.3d 628, 634 (9th Cir. 2008). JSL does not dispute that the Visa mark is famous and distinctive or that JSL began using the eVisa mark in commerce after Visa achieved its renown. JSL claims only that the district court erred when it found as a matter of law that eVisa was likely to dilute the Visa trademark.

There are two types of dilution, but here we are concerned only with dilution by blurring, which occurs when a mark previously associated with one product also becomes associated with a second. [cit.] This weakens the mark's ability to evoke the first product in the minds of consumers. "For example, Tylenol snowboards, Netscape sex shops and Harry Potter dry cleaners would all weaken the 'commercial magnetism' of these marks and diminish their ability to evoke their original associations." *Mattel*, 296 F.3d at 903. Dilution isn't confusion; quite the contrary. Dilution occurs when consumers form new and different associations with the plaintiff's mark. "Even if no one suspects that the maker of analgesics has entered into the snowboard business, the Tylenol mark will now bring to mind two products, not one." *Id.*

Whether a defendant's mark creates a likelihood of dilution is a factual question generally not appropriate for decision on summary judgment. *See Jada Toys, Inc.*, 518 F.3d at 632. Nevertheless, summary judgment may be granted in a dilution case, as in any other, if no reasonable fact-finder could fail to find a likelihood of dilution. Congress has enumerated factors courts may use to analyze the likelihood of dilution, including the similarity between the two marks and the distinctiveness and recognition of the plaintiff's mark. 15 U.S.C. §1125(c)(2)(B)(i), (ii), (iv); [cit.]. And, in an appropriate case, the district court may conclusively determine one or more of these factors before trial.

The marks here are effectively identical; the only difference is the prefix "e," which is commonly used to refer to the electronic or online version of a brand. That prefix does no more to distinguish the two marks than would the words "Corp." or "Inc." tacked onto the end. *See Horphag Research Ltd. v. Garcia*, 475 F.3d 1029, 1036 (9th Cir. 2007) (use of identical mark provides "circumstantial evidence" of dilution).

And Visa is a strong trademark. "In general, the more unique or arbitrary a mark, the more protection a court will afford it." *Nutri/System, Inc. v. Con-Stan Indus., Inc.*, 809 F.2d 601, 605 (9th Cir. 1987). The Visa mark draws on positive mental associations with travel visas, which make potentially difficult transactions relatively simple and facilitate new opportunities and experiences. Those are good attributes for a credit card. But those associations are sufficiently remote that the word visa wouldn't make people think of credit cards if it weren't for the Visa brand. "This suggests that any association is the result of goodwill and deserves broad protection from potential infringers." *Dreamwerks Prod. Grp., Inc. v. SKG Studio*, 142 F.3d 1127, 1130 n.7 (9th Cir. 1998). Visa also introduced uncontroverted evidence that Visa is the world's top brand in financial services and is used for online purchases almost as often as all other credit cards combined. This was enough to support the district court's summary judgment.

JSL vigorously contests the validity of market surveys and expert testimony introduced by Visa to show that eVisa dilutes the Visa mark, and it claims that evidence should have been excluded under *Daubert v. Merrell Dow Pharm., Inc.*, 509 U.S. 579 (1993). But a plaintiff seeking to establish a likelihood of dilution is not required to go to the expense of producing expert testimony or market surveys; it may rely entirely on the characteristics of the marks at issue. *See* 15 U.S.C. §1125(c)(2)(B) (listing relevant factors). Expert testimony and survey evidence may be necessary in marginal cases, or where a defendant introduces significant evidence to show that dilution is unlikely. But JSL presented nothing, other than Orr's statement that he did not intend to dilute the Visa mark, to rebut the inference of likely dilution created by the strength and similarity of the marks. Good intentions alone do not negate a showing of a likelihood of dilution. We therefore need not reach the admissibility of Visa's expert testimony and market survey evidence.

JSL claims the eVisa mark cannot cause dilution because, in addition to being an electronic payment network that's everywhere you want to be, a visa is a travel document authorizing the bearer to enter a country's territory. When a trademark is also a word with a dictionary definition, it may be difficult to show that the trademark holder's use of the word is sufficiently distinctive to deserve anti-dilution protection because such a word is likely to be descriptive or suggestive of an essential attribute of the trademarked good. Moreover, such a word may already be in use as a mark by third parties. For example, we rejected a dilution claim by Trek Bicycle Corporation for its "Trek" mark in part because it played heavily off the dictionary meaning of "trek," suggesting that the bicycles were designed for long or arduous journeys. *Thane Int'l, Inc. v. Trek Bicycle Corp.*, 305 F.3d 894, 912 n.14 (9th Cir. 2002). Additionally, the creators of the Star Trek series had already "incorporated this common English language word into their trademark," and the "glow of this celebrity ma[de] it difficult for Trek to obtain fame using the same word." *Id.* In our case, Visa's use of the word visa is sufficiently distinctive because it plays only weakly off the dictionary meaning of the term and JSL presented no evidence that a third party has used the word as a mark.

It's true that the word visa is used countless times every day for its common English definition, but the prevalence of such non-trademark use does not undermine the uniqueness of Visa as a trademark. *See* 2 McCarthy on Trademarks and Unfair Competition §11:87 (4th ed. 2010). "The significant factor is not whether the word itself is common, but whether the way the word is used in a particular context is unique enough to warrant trademark protection." *Wynn Oil Co. v. Thomas*, 839 F.2d 1183, 1190 n.4 (6th Cir. 1988). In the context of anti-dilution law, the "particular context" that matters is use of the word in commerce to identify a good or service. There are, for instance, many camels, but just one

Camel; many tides, but just one Tide. Camel cupcakes and Tide calculators would dilute the value of those marks. Likewise, despite widespread use of the word visa for its common English meaning, the introduction of the eVisa mark to the marketplace means that there are now two products, and not just one, competing for association with that word. This is the quintessential harm addressed by anti-dilution law.

JSL is not using the word visa for its literal dictionary definition, and this would be a different case if it were. Visa does not claim that it could enforce its Visa trademark to prevent JSL from opening "Orr's Visa Services," any more than Apple could shut down Orr's Apple Orchard or Camel could fold up Orr's Camel Breeders. Visa doesn't own the word "visa" and may not "deplete the stock of useful words" by asserting otherwise. *New Kids on the Block v. News America Publ'g, Inc.*, 971 F.2d 302, 306 (9th Cir. 1992); *cf. Kellogg Co. v. Nat'l Biscuit Co.*, 305 U.S. 111, 116-17 (1938). Conferring anti-dilution rights to common English words would otherwise be untenable, as whole swaths of the dictionary could be taken out of circulation. Nor would a suit against Orr's Visa Services advance the purpose of anti-dilution law. Such use of the word would not create a new association for the word with a product; it would merely evoke the word's existing dictionary meaning, as to which no one may claim exclusivity.

JSL argues that its use of the word "visa" is akin to Orr's Visa Services because the eVisa mark is meant to "connote the ability to travel, both linguistically and physically, through the English-speaking world" and therefore employs the word's common English meaning. JSL's site depicted the eVisa mark next to a booklet that looks like a passport, and it divided the services offered into the categories "Travel Passport," "Language Passport" and "Technology Passport." But these allusions to the dictionary definition of the word visa do not change the fact that JSL has created a novel meaning for the word: to identify a "multilingual education and information business." This multiplication of meanings is the essence of dilution by blurring. Use of the word "visa" to refer to travel visas is permissible because it doesn't have this effect; the word elicits only the standard dictionary definition. Use of the word visa in a trademark to refer to a good or service other than a travel visa, as in this case, undoubtedly does have this effect; the word becomes associated with two products, rather than one. This is true even when use of the word also gestures at the word's dictionary definition.

JSL's allusions to international travel are more obvious and heavy-handed than Visa's, and JSL claims that its use of the word is therefore "different" from Visa's. That's true; Visa plays only weakly off the word's association with international travel, whereas JSL embraced the metaphor with gusto. But dilution always involves use of a mark by a defendant that is "different" from the plaintiff's use; the injury addressed by anti-dilution law in fact occurs when marks are placed in new and different contexts, thereby weakening the mark's ability to bring to mind the plaintiff's goods or services. See *Mattel*, 296 F.3d at 903. The only context that matters is that the marks are both used in commerce as trademarks to identify a good or service, as they undoubtedly are in this case.

The district court was quite right in granting summary judgment to Visa and enjoining JSL's use of the mark.

Affirmed.

NOTES AND QUESTIONS

1. *The "quintessential harm" of blurring.* Exactly how will Starbucks be harmed by the defendant's use of CHARBUCKS for its product? What of Visa? According to the *Visa* opinion, the case exemplifies the "quintessential harm addressed by anti-dilution law" because "the introduction of the eVisa mark to the marketplace means that there are now two products, and not just one, competing for association with that word." Do you agree that this is the quintessential harm that Section 43(c) addresses? Elsewhere, the opinion refers to the "multiplication of meanings" as constituting "the essence of dilution by blurring." This might suggest that the risk of blurring is higher when the defendant's goods or services are more remote from the plaintiff's. Does this help explain the outcomes in *Starbucks* and *Visa*? Contrast this reasoning to Judge Posner's in *Hugunin v. Land O' Lakes, Inc.*, 815 F.3d 1064 (7th Cir. 2016), upholding the dismissal of a dilution claim brought by the owner of the mark LAND O LAKES for dairy products against a seller of fishing tackle (Hugunin) who was using LAND O LAKES for his products. Judge Posner was "puzzled that the dairy company should have been worried by Hugunin's use of the same trademark," because the dairy company did not sell fishing tackle, and "[i]t would be strange indeed for a dairy company to manufacture a product so remote from milk, butter, and cream." *Id.* at 1066. Judge Posner elaborated that:

> Many consumers would recognize the name "LAND O LAKES" as referring to the dairy company, but we can't see how the company could be hurt by the use of the same name by a seller just of fishing tackle. The products of the two companies are too different, and the sale of fishing tackle is not so humble a business [that it might give rise to harm in the form of tarnishment]. And so it is beyond unlikely that someone dissatisfied with LAND O LAKES fishing tackle would take revenge on the dairy company by not buying any of its products. . . .

Id. at 1067. Should Judge Posner instead have concluded that the unauthorized use of one's mark on "remote" products is the very epitome of dilution by blurring?

According to one prominent commentator, the harm of dilution by blurring may be described as the reduction in a mark's capacity to cut through the informational "clutter" of the marketplace. Jerre B. Swann, *The Evolution of Dilution in the United States from 1927 to 2013*, 103 TRADEMARK REP. 721, 761 (2013). Would the blurring analyses in *Starbucks*, *Visa*, and *Hugunin* have benefited from incorporating the idea of blurring as "clutter"?

2. *Blurring factors versus confusion factors.* Are the statutory blurring factors so similar to the confusion factors as to give the unwelcome impression that a blurring claim is little more than a second shot at establishing confusion? *See* Graeme B. Dinwoodie & Mark D. Janis, *Dilution's (Still) Uncertain Future*, 105 MICH. L. REV. FIRST IMPRESSIONS 98 (2006) (predicting that courts may view the statutory blurring test as little more than "confusion analysis with a different paint job"). Consider the *Visa* case. Does *Visa* seem to be an "easy" case of likely confusion? Does it follow that it is an easy case likely dilution by blurring? Do you think that the blurring determination in *Starbucks* reflects the court's perception that confusion is unlikely? If so, how does this square with Section 43(c)(1), which offers a dilution remedy "regardless of the presence or absence of actual or likely confusion, of competition, or of actual economic injury."

3. *Shortcutting the blurring factors?* In *Starbucks*, the court (eventually, after many efforts) focused primarily on a subset of the blurring factors: similarity of the marks; intent to create association; and actual association. While the court alluded to the remaining statutory factors ((ii) through (iv)—distinctiveness, recognition, and exclusivity), it found them to be less important than the other factors in the context of the case. Is this because the court had already determined that the STARBUCKS mark was famous, a determination that surely overlaps with factors (ii)-(iv)? If so, should we expect blurring analyses regularly to turn on the remaining factors—similarity, intent, and actual association? In all instances of alleged dilution by blurring? Consider *Louis Vuitton Malletier S.A. v. Haute Diggity Dog, LLC*, 507 F.3d 252 (4th Cir. 2007), excerpted in Chapter 9, suggesting that factors (ii)-(iv) might cut *against* dilution by blurring in a parody case. If the blurring analysis turns on similarity, intent, and association, what do the factors add to the definition of "blurring"?

4. *Adding to the blurring factors?* The list of statutory blurring factors is open-ended. Which additional factors (if any) beyond those expressly listed should be considered in a blurring analysis? Do you expect that courts routinely will take advantage of the statute's invitation to consider "all relevant factors" in analyzing blurring?

5. *Factor tests overseas.* The European Trademark Directive includes a form of dilution protection. Under the Directive, a party may be liable for using a mark in a way that takes "unfair advantage of, or is detrimental to, the distinctive character or repute of an earlier mark." In Case C-252/07, *Intel Corporation Inc. v. CPM United Kingdom Limited*, 2009 E.T.M.R. 13, the Court of Justice of the European Union set forth the factors relevant in assessing whether a link between the two marks had been established, which is a precondition to a dilution claim. (The concept of a "link" approximates "association" in the U.S. statute.) The factors to be considered include:

- the degree of similarity between the conflicting marks;
- the nature of the goods or services for which the conflicting marks were registered, including the degree of closeness or dissimilarity between those goods or services, and the relevant section of the public;
- the strength of the reputation of the earlier mark;
- the degree of the distinctive character of the earlier mark (whether inherent or acquired through use); and
- the existence of the likelihood of confusion on the part of the public.

As to the last factor, the CJEU noted that a showing of likely confusion was not a requirement, but only a factor. How do these factors compare to analysis under U.S. law?

6. *The similarity factor: degree of similarity or near identity?* Did the court in *Starbucks* impose a requirement for substantial similarity or near identity between the plaintiff's and defendant's marks, instead of assessing the degree of similarity in accordance with statutory factor (i)? In *Visa*, Judge Kozinski mentions that the plaintiff's and defendant's marks are "effectively identical." Is this a prerequisite, or merely an observation that the degree of similarity is high?

Under the pre-2006 Section 43(c), the Ninth Circuit had developed a line of cases that arguably did impose a threshold requirement of identity. Applying those cases post-2006, a trial judge found that the plaintiff's mark (Levi's "arcuate" design, above left) was not identical to, and could not be diluted by, the defendant's mark (Abercrombie & Fitch's "Ruehl" design, above right). Suppose that Levi's appeals, contesting whether, as a matter of law, the modern version of Section 43(c) requires identity. How would you decide the question? *See Levi Strauss & Co. v. Abercrombie & Fitch Trading Co.*, 633 F.3d 1158 (9th Cir. 2011); *see also Rolex Watch U.S.A., Inc. v. AFP Imaging Corp.*, 101 U.S.P.Q.2d (BNA) 1188, 1194 (TTAB 2011) (rejecting an identity of marks requirement in the Section 2(f) context).

7. *Mark alteration as blurring?* Suppose that the alleged diluter has appropriated the mark owner's mark and altered it, and then argues that by virtue of the alterations, the marks are not similar. Should lack of similarity necessarily cut against blurring? For a sample fact pattern from a case decided under New York state dilution law, *see Deere & Co. v. MTD Prods., Inc.*, 41 F.3d 39 (2d Cir. 1994) (MTD aired a commercial in featuring a John Deere "Deer" logo that had been altered in appearance and shown as an animated, cartoonish figure jumping and running in apparent fear as if pursued by MTD's yard tractor). How would you decide a dilution by blurring claim brought by Deere under Section 43(c)?

8. *The intent-to-associate factor.* The court in *Starbucks* rejects the proposition that evidence of intent to associate triggers a presumption of actual association. Do you agree? How does intent to associate as a factor in dilution by blurring differ (if at all) from intent to trade off goodwill as a factor in likelihood of confusion?

9. *The actual association factor: the importance of survey evidence.* If you were a judge deciding a blurring claim, would you place great weight on the presence (or absence) of survey evidence in assessing the actual association factor? Consider *Starbucks.* Do you agree with the court's analysis of the Mitofsky telephone survey? Was the court correct to criticize the survey for failing to place the marks within their marketplace context (which here seems to mean failing to display the marks visually)? Should the court have placed more weight on the fact that 30.5 percent of survey respondents said that hearing the name "Charbucks" called to mind Starbucks?

For an example of a successful effort to establish actual association (and, ultimately, a success in showing likelihood of dilution by blurring), *see Louis Vuitton Malletier, S.A. v. Hyundai Motor America*, No. 10 Civ. 1611 (PKC), 2012 WL 1022247 (S.D.N.Y. 2012). Hyundai had aired an advertisement called "Luxury" that depicted "policemen eating caviar in a patrol car; large yachts parked beside modest homes; blue-collar workers eating lobster during their lunch break; a four-second scene of an inner-city basketball game played on a lavish marble court with a gold hoop; and a ten-second scene of the Sonata driving down a street lined with chandeliers and red-carpet crosswalks." (quoting Hyundai's brief). The idea, according to Hyundai, was to "pok[e] fun at the silliness of luxury-as-exclusivity by juxtaposing symbols of luxury with everyday life," *id.*, communicating that the modestly-priced Hyundai Sonata automobile offered "luxury for all." The advertisement aired during the post-game show of the 2010 Super Bowl. (Professor Janis was too busy mourning the Indianapolis Colts' loss to notice it, and he wouldn't have gotten Hyundai's message anyway.) The advertisement's basketball scene included a one-second shot of a basketball bearing "a distinctive pattern resembling the famous trademarks" of Louis Vuitton. So, Louis Vuitton sued, claiming dilution. Study the district court's discussion of the dilution evidence, particularly the actual association evidence. Would you have found a likelihood of dilution by blurring? Are you satisfied that you have a clearer understanding of what dilution by blurring is, and how it differs from confusion, after studying the evidence in this case? Or not?

10. *Standard of review of blurring determinations; summary disposition.* In *Starbucks*, the court rules that the lower court's determinations on the individual blurring factors will be treated as factual and reviewed for clear error, while the balancing of the factors will be treated as legal and reviewed de novo. Does it explain the outcome of the case? In *Visa*, the court labels dilution a factual question and remarks that, as such, dilution is often not amenable to summary judgment (though the court ultimately affirms the grant of summary judgment). Are the *Visa* and *Starbucks* courts applying different standards of review? If so, which is preferable as a matter of trademark policy?

4.   Dilution Under Lanham Act §2(f)

In the Trademark Amendments Act of 1999, Pub. L. No. 106-43, 113 Stat. 218, Congress amended Lanham Act §2(f) to provide that dilution is a ground for opposition or cancellation proceedings before the Board. *See* Chapter 5 for a discussion of the procedural aspects of oppositions under Section 13 and cancellations under Section 14. By providing that dilution could be a basis for refusing registration only in proceedings brought under Section 13, or in Section 14 cancellation proceedings, Congress ensured that trademark examiners could not use dilution as a basis for rejecting an application in ex parte examination proceedings. Why might Congress have adopted this approach?

When Congress amended Section 43(c) in 2006, it made conforming amendments to Sections 2(f), 13, and 14. The dilution language in Section 2(f) now provides that:

> [a] mark which would be likely to cause dilution by blurring or dilution by tarnishment under section 43(c), may be refused registration only pursuant to a proceeding brought under section 13. A registration for a mark which would be likely to cause dilution by blurring or dilution by tarnishment under section 43(c), may be canceled pursuant to a proceeding brought under either section 14 or section 24.

Likewise, the amendments to Sections 13 and 14 expressly incorporate the likelihood-of-dilution standard.

As the statutory language indicates, the law developed under Section 43(c) in litigation matters as the point of reference for Section 2(f) determinations. Nonetheless, Section 2(f) dilution determinations sometimes involve issues peculiar to the opposition/cancellation context. For example:

- The filing of an ITU application satisfies the actionable use requirement for dilution, such that an opposition or cancellation proceeding can be brought against such an application. *New York Yankees Partnership v. IET Prods. & Services, Inc.*, 114 U.S.P.Q.2d (BNA) 1497 (TTAB 2015); *Toro Co. v. ToroHead Inc.*, 61 U.S.P.Q.2d (BNA) 1164 (TTAB 2001) (same, decided under the FTDA).
- In petitioning to oppose or cancel ITU-based applications or registrations, the petitioner must show that its mark became famous before the applicant's (or registrant's) effective filing date (i.e., the constructive use date). *Inter IKEA Sys. B.V. v. Akea, LLC*, 110 U.S.P.Q.2d (BNA) 1734 (TTAB 2014).
- For challenges to use-based registrations, the petitioner must show that its mark became famous before the applicant's (or registrant's) first use of the mark, *Citigroup Inc. v. Capital City Bank Group, Inc.*, 94 U.S.P.Q.2d (BNA) 1645 (TTAB 2010), *aff'd*, 637 F.3d 1344 (Fed. Cir. 2011), meaning the first use on any goods or services (or as a trade name), not just use on the goods or services specified in the application, *Omega Sa v. Alpha Phi Omega*, 118 U.S.P.Q.2d (BNA) 1289 (TTAB 2016), and meaning *any* first use, even if that use is confined to a limited

geographic area. *Enterprise Rent-A-Car Co. v. Advantage Rent-A-Car, Inc.*, 330 F.3d 1333 (Fed. Cir. 2003) (further ruling that the statute does not authorize the PTO to issue concurrent registrations in such scenarios).

B. Protection Against Cybersquatting

Throughout the book, we have at different stages noted the important differences between trademark rights and domain names. In particular, we have discussed the different ways in which rights in trademarks and domain names are acquired and maintained. But, as you will have seen from several cases, trademark owners value highly the control of domain names that are identical or similar to their trademarks. Branding strategy now often suggests owning and investing not only in a trademark but also in the domain name that corresponds to that trademark. Because trademark owners are, in the most popular generic top-level domains, accorded no preference in the acquisition of the domain name registration that corresponds to their trademark, there exists the possibility that the corresponding domain name could be registered by a third party. Some enterprising individuals did just that and then sought to exploit the value that trademark owners attach to those domain name registrations by demanding large sums of money for the transfer of the domain name registration to the trademark owner. This activity came to be known as cybersquatting. Eventually, it was proscribed through a number of different laws, which we consider below. As you read the materials that follow, consider (1) the range of activity by domain name registrants that should fall within the proscription, (2) whether existing trademark law provided adequate solutions to remedy the problem, (3) whether the enactment of cybersquatting-specific laws is an appropriate response, and (4) what policy objectives are being furthered by the proscription in question. Finally, does the pervasiveness of cybersquatting suggest any changes that we should make to the means by which trademark rights or domain name registrations are acquired?

1. Protection Under the Dilution Statute

When the practice of cybersquatting first occurred, the most effective weapon for trademark owners was the dilution cause of action, which was introduced into the Lanham Act in 1995. The following case was one of the leading early appellate endorsements of the use of Section 43(c) to combat cybersquatting. The court is discussing the language in the 1995 version of Section 43(c), some of which was revised by the 2006 TDRA reforms.

PANAVISION INTERNATIONAL v. TOEPPEN
141 F.3d 1316 (9th Cir. 1998)

David R. Thompson, Circuit Judge:

[Panavision owned the registered trademarks "Panavision" and "Panaflex" in connection with motion picture camera equipment. Panavision was unable to register the domain name Panavision.com because Toeppen had already established a website using Panavision's trademark as his domain name. Toeppen's web page for this site displayed photographs of the City of Pana, Illinois. After Panavision sent Toeppen a letter telling him to stop using their trademark and the domain name Panavision.com, Toeppen responded in a letter stating he had the right to use the name Panavision.com as his domain name. Toeppen offered to "settle the matter" if Panavision would pay him $13,000 in exchange for the domain name. Additionally, Toeppen stated that if Panavision agreed to his offer, he would not "acquire any other Internet addresses which are alleged by Panavision Corporation to be its property." After Panavision refused Toeppen's demand, he registered the domain name Panaflex.com (reflecting Panavision's other trademark) with NSI. Toeppen's web page for Panaflex.com simply displayed the word "Hello." Toeppen has registered domain names for various other companies, including Delta Airlines, Neiman Marcus, Eddie Bauer, Lufthansa, and over 100 other marks. Toeppen has attempted to "sell" domain names for other trademarks such as intermatic.com to Intermatic, Inc. for $10,000 and americanstandard.com to American Standard, Inc. for $15,000. Panavision sued, alleging, inter alia, dilution under the pre-TDRA version of Section 43(c) of the Lanham Act. The case also arose before the enactment of the ACPA, now codified at Section 43(d) of the Lanham Act. The district court granted summary judgment in Panavision's favor, and Toeppen appealed.]

B.   Trademark Dilution Claims

. . .

Toeppen does not challenge the district court's determination that Panavision's trademark is famous, that his alleged use began after the mark became famous, or that the use was in commerce. Toeppen challenges the district court's determination that he made "commercial use" of the mark and that this use caused "dilution" in the quality of the mark.

1.   Commercial Use

Toeppen argues that his use of Panavision's trademarks simply as his domain names cannot constitute a commercial use under the Act. Case law supports this argument. *See Panavision International, L.P. v. Toeppen*, 945 F. Supp. 1296, 1303 (C.D. Cal. 1996) ("Registration of a trade[mark] as a domain name, without more, is not a commercial use of the trademark and therefore is not within the prohibitions of the Act."); [cit.].

Developing this argument, Toeppen contends that a domain name is simply an address used to locate a web page. He asserts that entering a domain name on a computer allows a user to access a web page, but a domain name is not associated with information on a web page. If a user were to type Panavision.com as a domain name, the computer screen would display Toeppen's web page with aerial views of Pana, Illinois. The screen would not provide any information about "Panavision," other than a "location window" which displays the domain name. Toeppen argues that a user who types in Panavision.com, but who sees no reference to the plaintiff Panavision on Toeppen's web page, is not likely to conclude the web page is related in any way to the plaintiff, Panavision.

Toeppen's argument misstates his use of the Panavision mark. His use is not as benign as he suggests. Toeppen's "business" is to register trademarks as domain names and then sell them to the rightful trademark owners. He "act[s] as a 'spoiler,' preventing Panavision and others from doing business on the Internet under their trademarked names unless they pay his fee." *Panavision*, 938 F. Supp. at 621. This is a commercial use. *See Intermatic Inc. v. Toeppen*, 947 F. Supp. 1227, 1230 (N.D. Ill. 1996) (stating that "[o]ne of Toeppen's business objectives is to profit by the resale or licensing of these domain names, presumably to the entities who conduct business under these names").

As the district court found, Toeppen traded on the value of Panavision's marks. So long as he held the Internet registrations, he curtailed Panavision's exploitation of the value of its trademarks on the Internet, a value which Toeppen then used when he attempted to sell the Panavision.com domain name to Panavision.

[The court favorably recognized a decision of a federal district court in Illinois which upheld a dilution claim against Toeppen for his registration of the domain name intermatic. com for the purpose of selling that name to the owner of the INTERMATIC trademark. The court there found that Toeppen's intention to arbitrage the domain name constituted a commercial use of the mark.]

Toeppen's reliance on *Holiday Inns, Inc. v. 800 Reservation, Inc.*, 86 F.3d 619 (6th Cir. 1996), *cert. denied*, 519 U.S. 1093 (1997), is misplaced. In *Holiday Inns*, the Sixth Circuit held that a company's use of the most commonly misdialed number for Holiday Inns' 1-800 reservation number was not trademark infringement.

Holiday Inns is distinguishable. There, the defendant did not use Holiday Inns' trademark. Rather, the defendant selected the most commonly misdialed telephone number for Holiday Inns and attempted to capitalize on consumer confusion.

A telephone number, moreover, is distinguishable from a domain name because a domain name is associated with a word or phrase. A domain name is similar to a "vanity number" that identifies its source. Using Holiday Inns as an example, when a customer dials the vanity number "1-800-Holiday" she expects to contact Holiday Inns because the number is associated with that company's trademark. A user would have the same expectation typing the domain name HolidayInns.com. The user would expect to retrieve Holiday Inns' web page.

Toeppen made a commercial use of Panavision's trademarks. It does not matter that he did not attach the marks to a product. Toeppen's commercial use was his attempt to sell the trademarks themselves.[5] Under the Federal Trademark Dilution Act . . . , this was sufficient commercial use.

2. Dilution

"Dilution" is defined as "the lessening of the capacity of a famous mark to identify and distinguish goods or services, regardless of the presence or absence of (1) competition between the owner of the famous mark and other parties, or (2) likelihood of confusion, mistake or deception." 15 U.S.C. §1127.

Trademark dilution on the Internet was a matter of Congressional concern. Senator Patrick Leahy (D-Vt.) stated:

> [I]t is my hope that this anti-dilution statute can help stem the use of deceptive Internet addresses taken by those who are choosing marks that are associated with the products and reputations of others.

141 Cong. Rec. §19312-01 (daily ed. Dec. 29, 1995) (statement of Sen. Leahy); [cit.].

To find dilution, a court need not rely on the traditional definitions such as "blurring" and "tarnishment." Indeed, in concluding that Toeppen's use of Panavision's trademarks diluted the marks, the district court noted that Toeppen's conduct varied from the two standard dilution theories of blurring and tarnishment. The court found that Toeppen's conduct diminished "the capacity of the Panavision marks to identify and distinguish Panavision's goods and services on the Internet." [cit.]

[The court noted that this view was also supported by *Teletech Customer Care Mgmt., Inc. v. Tele-Tech Co.*, 911 F. Supp. 1407 (C.D. Cal. 1997), where, in a case involving similar facts, the district court found that the plaintiff had demonstrated a likelihood of success on the merits on its dilution claim. That court "found that [the owner of the mark

---

5. *See Boston Pro. Hockey Assoc., Inc. v. Dallas Cap & Emblem* (1975). . . .

TELETECH] had invested great resources in promoting its servicemark and Teletech's registration of the domain name teletech.com on the Internet would most likely dilute [the TELETECH] mark."]

Toeppen argues he is not diluting the capacity of the Panavision marks to identify goods or services. He contends that even though Panavision cannot use Panavision.com and Panaflex.com as its domain name addresses, it can still promote its goods and services on the Internet simply by using some other "address" and then creating its own web page using its trademarks.

We reject Toeppen's premise that a domain name is nothing more than an address. A significant purpose of a domain name is to identify the entity that owns the web site. "A customer who is unsure about a company's domain name will often guess that the domain name is also the company's name." *Cardservice Int'l v. McGee*, 950 F. Supp. 737, 741 (E.D. Va. 1997). "[A] domain name mirroring a corporate name may be a valuable corporate asset, as it facilitates communication with a customer base." *MTV Networks, Inc. v. Curry*, 867 F. Supp. 202, 203-04 n.2 (S.D.N.Y. 1994).

Using a company's name or trademark as a domain name is also the easiest way to locate that company's web site. Use of a "search engine" can turn up hundreds of web sites, and there is nothing equivalent to a phone book or directory assistance for the Internet. *See Cardservice*, 950 F. Supp. at 741.

Moreover, potential customers of Panavision will be discouraged if they cannot find its web page by typing in "Panavision.com," but instead are forced to wade through hundreds of web sites. This dilutes the value of Panavision's trademark. We echo the words of Judge Lechner, quoting Judge Wood: "Prospective users of plaintiff's services who mistakenly access defendant's web site may fail to continue to search for plaintiff's own home page, due to anger, frustration or the belief that plaintiff's home page does not exist." *Jews for Jesus v. Brodsky*, 993 F. Supp. 282, 306-07 (D.N.J. 1998) (Lechner, J., quoting Wood, J., *in Planned Parenthood v. Bucci*, 1997 WL 133313 at *4); *see also Teletech*, 977 F. Supp. at 1410 (finding that use of a search engine can generate as many as 800 to 1000 matches and it is "likely to deter web browsers from searching for Plaintiff's particular web site").

Toeppen's use of Panavision.com also puts Panavision's name and reputation at his mercy. *See Intermatic*, 947 F. Supp. at 1240 ("If Toeppen were allowed to use 'intermatic. com,' Intermatic's name and reputation would be at Toeppen's mercy and could be associated with an unimaginable amount of messages on Toeppen's web page.").

We conclude that Toeppen's registration of Panavision's trademarks as his domain names on the Internet diluted those marks within the meaning of the Federal Trademark Dilution Act, 15 U.S.C. §1125(c), and the California Anti-dilution statute, Cal. Bus. & Prof. Code §14330.

[Affirmed.]

NOTES AND QUESTIONS

1. *Dilution by cybersquatting? Toeppen* is a canonical case of cybersquatting. Are you persuaded that the court's effort to combat cybersquatting with a dilution theory was a proper construction of the pre-TDRA Section 43(c)? From the perspective of a trademark owner, what problems do you foresee in relying on a dilution theory to proceed against cybersquatters? Could a claim be pursued against a cybersquatter under the current version of Section 43(c)? In what ways, if any, do the 2006 revisions make it easier to assert a dilution claim against Mr. Toeppen? Harder?

2.   *Inadequacy of traditional trademark remedies?* What additional problems do you foresee in litigating against cybersquatters under traditional trademark infringement theories? *Compare People for the Ethical Treatment of Animals v. Doughney*, 263 F.3d 359 (4th Cir. 2001) ("To use [plaintiff's] mark 'in connection with' goods or services, [defendant] need not have actually sold or advertised goods or services on [his allegedly infringing] website. Rather, [he] need only have prevented users from obtaining or using [plaintiff's] goods or services, or need only have connected the website to other's goods or services.") *with Taubman Co. v. Webfeats*, 319 F.3d 770 (6th Cir. 2003) (defendant who established a website using a domain name that incorporated the plaintiff's mark along with the epithet "sucks" and contained links only to noncommercial sites not using in connection with the advertising of goods or services). Procedural problems? Remedial problems? Consider these questions as you study the materials in the following section.

3.   *Harms of cybersquatting.* What harm does protection against cybersquatting prevent? That is, who or against what does this form of protection protect? Does the rationalization of harm by the *Panavision* court fit with the rationales for either classical trademark protection or dilution protection that we have considered in earlier cases? Do you detect any other motivations for ensuring that a remedy is available to the trademark owner?

2.   Anticybersquatting Consumer Protection Act: Section 43(d) of the Lanham Act

In late 1999, Congress enacted additional legislation aimed at the problem of cybersquatting. Section 3002(a) of the Anticybersquatting Consumer Protection Act (ACPA), Pub. L. No. 106-113, tit. III, now codified at Section 43(d) of the Lanham Act, created two related causes of action: Subsection (1) of Section 43(d) provides an action *in personam* against the cybersquatter, grounded in bad faith registration or use of the domain name; and subsection (2) creates an action *in rem* against the domain name itself in circumstances where in personam jurisdiction is lacking.

SPORTY'S FARM L.L.C. v. SPORTSMAN's MARKET, INC.

202 F.3d 489 (2d Cir.), cert. denied, 530 U.S. 1262 (2000)

CALABRESI, Circuit Judge:

BACKGROUND

. . .

I

. . .

For consumers to buy things or gather information on the Internet, they need an easy way to find particular companies or brand names. The most common method of locating an unknown domain name is simply to type in the company name or logo with the suffix. com. If this proves unsuccessful, then Internet users turn to a device called a search engine. A search engine will find all web pages on the Internet with a particular word or phrase. Given the current state of search engine technology, that search will often produce a list of hundreds of web sites through which the user must sort in order to find what he or she is looking for. As a result, companies strongly prefer that their domain name be comprised of the company or brand trademark and the suffix.com [cit.]. . . .

Until recently, domain names with the .com top level domain could only be obtained from Network Solutions, Inc. ("NSI"). Now other registrars may also assign them. But all these registrars grant such names primarily on a first-come, first-served basis upon payment of a small registration fee. They do not generally inquire into whether a given domain name request matches a trademark held by someone other than the person requesting the name [cit.]. . . .

Due to the lack of any regulatory control over domain name registration, an Internet phenomenon known as "cybersquatting" has become increasingly common in recent years. *See, e.g., Panavision Int'l, L.P. v. Toeppen*, 141 F.3d 1316 (9th Cir. 1998). . . .

II

Sportsman's is a mail order catalog company that is quite well-known among pilots and aviation enthusiasts for selling products tailored to their needs. In recent years, Sportsman's has expanded its catalog business well beyond the aviation market into that for tools and home accessories. The company annually distributes approximately 18 million catalogs nationwide, and has yearly revenues of about $50 million. Aviation sales account for about 60% of Sportsman's revenue, while non-aviation sales comprise the remaining 40%.

In the 1960s, Sportsman's began using the logo "sporty" to identify its catalogs and products. In 1985, Sportsman's registered the trademark SPORTY's with the United States Patent and Trademark Office. Since then, Sportsman's has complied with all statutory requirements to preserve its interest in the SPORTY's mark. Sporty's appears on the cover of all Sportsman's catalogs; Sportsman's international toll free number is 1-800-4sportys; and one of Sportsman's domestic toll free phone numbers is 1-800-Sportys. Sportsman's spends about $10 million per year advertising its sporty's logo.

Omega is a mail order catalog company that sells mainly scientific process measurement and control instruments. In late 1994 or early 1995, the owners of Omega, Arthur and Betty Hollander, decided to enter the aviation catalog business and, for that purpose, formed a wholly-owned subsidiary called Pilot's Depot, IXC ("Pilot's Depot"). Shortly thereafter, Omega registered the domain name sportys.com with NSI. Arthur Hollander was a pilot who received Sportsman's catalogs and thus was aware of the sporty's trademark.

In January 1996, nine months after registering sportys.com, Omega formed another wholly-owned subsidiary called Sporty's Farm and sold it the rights to sportys.com for $16,200. Sporty's Farm grows and sells Christmas trees, and soon began advertising its Christmas trees on a sportys.com web page. When asked how the name Sporty's Farm was selected for Omega's Christmas tree subsidiary, Ralph S. Michael, the CEO of Omega and manager of Sporty's Farm, explained, as summarized by the district court, that

> in his own mind and among his family, he always thought of and referred to the Pennsylvania land where Sporty's Farm now operates as *Spotty's farm*. The origin of the name . . . derived from a childhood memory he had of his uncle's farm in upstate New York. As a youngster, Michael owned a dog named Spotty. Because the dog strayed, his uncle took him to his upstate farm. Michael thereafter referred to the farm as Spotty's farm. The name Sporty's Farm was . . . a subsequent derivation.

Joint Appendix ("JA") at 277 (emphasis added). There is, however, no evidence in the record that Hollander was considering starting a Christmas tree business when he registered sportys.com or that Hollander was ever acquainted with Michael's dog Spotty.

In March 1996, Sportsman's discovered that Omega had registered sportys.com as a domain name. Thereafter, and before Sportsman's could take any action, Sporty's Farm brought this declaratory action seeking the right to continue its use of sportys.com. Sportsman's counterclaimed and also sued Omega as a third-party defendant for, inter alia, (1) trademark infringement, (2) trademark dilution pursuant to the [1995 version of Section 43(c), which the court refers to as the "FTDA"], and (3) unfair competition under state law. Both sides sought injunctive relief to force the other to relinquish its claims to sportys.com. While this litigation was ongoing, Sportsman's used "sportys-catalogs.com" as its primary domain name.

After a bench trial, the court rejected Sportsman's trademark infringement claim and all related claims that are based on a "likelihood of [consumer] confusion" since "the parties operate wholly unrelated businesses [and t]herefore, confusion in the marketplace is not likely to develop." *Id.* at 282-83. But on Sportsman's trademark dilution action, where a likelihood of confusion was not necessary, the district court found for Sportsman's. The court concluded (1) that sporty's was a famous mark entitled to protection under the FTDA since "the 'Sporty's' mark enjoys general name recognition in the consuming public," *id.* at 288, and (2) that Sporty's Farm and Omega had diluted sporty's because "registration of the 'sportys.com' domain name effectively compromises Sportsman's Market's ability to identify and distinguish its goods on the Internet . . . [by] preclud[ing] Sportsman's Market from using its 'unique identifier,'" *id.* at 289. The court also held, however, that Sportsman's could only get injunctive relief and was not entitled to "punitive damages . . . profits, and attorney's fees and costs" pursuant to the FTDA since Sporty Farm and Omega's conduct did not constitute willful dilution under the FTDA. *Id.* at 292-93.

        . . .

III

[W]hile this appeal was pending, Congress passed the ACPA. That law was passed "to protect consumers and American businesses, to promote the growth of online commerce, and to provide clarity in the law for trademark owners by prohibiting the bad-faith and abusive registration of distinctive marks as Internet domain names with the intent to profit from the goodwill associated with such marks—a practice commonly referred to as 'cybersquatting.'" S. Rep. No. 106-140, at 4. In particular, Congress viewed the legal remedies available for victims of cybersquatting before the passage of the ACPA as "expensive and uncertain." H.R. Rep. No. 106-412, at 6. The Senate made clear its view on this point:

> While the [FTDA] has been useful in pursuing cybersquatters, cybersquatters have become increasingly sophisticated as the case law has developed and now take the necessary precautions to insulate themselves from liability. For example, many cybersquatters are now careful to no longer offer the domain name for sale in any manner that could implicate liability under existing trademark dilution case law. And, in cases of warehousing and trafficking in domain names, courts have sometimes declined to provide assistance to trademark holders, leaving them without adequate and effective judicial remedies. This uncertainty as to the trademark law's application to the Internet has produced inconsistent judicial decisions and created extensive monitoring obligations, unnecessary legal costs, and uncertainty for consumers and trademark owners alike.

S. Rep. No. 106-140, at 7. In short, the ACPA was passed to remedy the perceived shortcomings of applying the FTDA in cybersquatting cases such as this one.

The new act accordingly amends the Trademark Act of 1946, creating a specific federal remedy for cybersquatting. New 15 U.S.C. §1125(d)(1)(A) reads:

> A person shall be liable in a civil action by the owner of a mark, including a personal name which is protected as a mark under this section, if, without regard to the goods or services of the parties, that person—
>   (i) has a bad faith intent to profit from that mark, including a personal name which is protected as a mark under this section; and
>   (ii) registers, traffics in, or uses a domain name that—

(I) in the case of a mark that is distinctive at the time of registration of the domain name, is identical or confusingly similar to that mark;

(II) in the case of a famous mark that is famous at the time of registration of the domain name, is identical or confusingly similar to or dilutive of that mark; . . . .

The Act further provides that "a court may order the forfeiture or cancellation of the domain name or the transfer of the domain name to the owner of the mark," 15 U.S.C. §1125(d)(1)(C), if the domain name was "registered before, on, or after the date of the enactment of this Act," Pub. L. No. 106-113, §3010. It also provides that damages can be awarded for violations of the Act, but that they are not "available with respect to the registration, trafficking, or use of a domain name that occurs before the date of the enactment of this Act." *Id.*

DISCUSSION

[The court concluded that the ACPA was applicable to this case even though the district court had made its holding based on the federal dilution statute. The court noted that the ACPA "was adopted specifically to provide courts with a preferable alternative to stretching federal dilution law when dealing with cybersquatting cases." Moreover, the court concluded that because the record enabled the court to apply the new law to the case without difficulty, it would do so rather than remand to the district court to decide the case under the new law.]

B.   "Distinctive" or "Famous"

Under the new Act, we must first determine whether sporty's is a distinctive or famous mark and thus entitled to the ACPA's protection. *See* 15 U.S.C. §1125(d)(1)(A)(ii) (I), (II). The district court concluded that sporty's is both distinctive and famous. We agree that sporty's is a "distinctive" mark [for the purposes of §1125(d)(1)(A)(ii)(I)]. As a result, and without casting any doubt on the district court's holding in this respect, we need not, and hence do not, decide whether sporty's is also a "famous" mark.

. . .

C.   "Identical and Confusingly Similar"

The next question is whether domain name sportys.com is "identical or confusingly similar to" the sporty's mark.[11] [cit.] [A]postrophes cannot be used in domain names. [cit.] As a result, the secondary domain name in this case (sportys) is indistinguishable from the Sportsman's trademark (sporty's). *Cf. Brookfield Communications, Inc. v. West Coast Entertainment Corp.*, 174 F.3d 1036, 1055 (9th Cir. 1999) (observing that the differences between the mark "MovieBuff" and the domain name "moviebuff.com" are "inconsequential in light of the fact that Web addresses are not caps-sensitive and that the '.com' top-level domain signifies the site's commercial nature"). We therefore conclude that, although the domain name sportys.com is not precisely identical to the sporty's mark, it is certainly "confusingly similar" to the protected mark under §1125(d)(1)(A)(ii)(I). [cit.].

D.   "Bad Faith Intent to Profit"

We next turn to the issue of whether Sporty's Farm acted with a "bad faith intent to profit" from the mark sporty's when it registered the domain name sportys.com. 15 U.S.C.

---

11. We note that "confusingly similar" is a different standard from the "likelihood of confusion" standard for trademark infringement adopted by this court in *Polaroid Corp. v. Polarad Electronics Corp.*, 287 F.2d 492 (2d Cir. 1961). [cit.] . . .

§1125(d)(1)(A)(i). The statute lists nine factors to assist courts in determining when a defendant has acted with a bad faith intent to profit from the use of a mark. But we are not limited to considering just the listed factors when making our determination of whether the statutory criterion has been met. The factors are, instead, expressly described as indicia that "may" be considered along with other facts. *Id.* §1125(d)(1)(B)(i).

We hold that there is more than enough evidence in the record below of "bad faith intent to profit" on the part of Sporty's Farm (as that term is defined in the statute), so that "no reasonable factfinder could return a verdict against" Sportsman's. [cit.] First, it is clear that neither Sporty's Farm nor Omega had any intellectual property rights in sportys.com at the time Omega registered the domain name. *See id.* §1125(d)(1)(B)(i)(I). Sporty's Farm was not formed until nine months after the domain name was registered, and it did not begin operations or obtain the domain name from Omega until after this lawsuit was filed. Second, the domain name does not consist of the legal name of the party that registered it, Omega. *See id.* §1125(d)(1)(B)(i)(II). Moreover, although the domain name does include part of the name of Sporty's Farm, that entity did not exist at the time the domain name was registered.

The third factor, the prior use of the domain name in connection with the bona fide offering of any goods or services, also cuts against Sporty's Farm since it did not use the site until after this litigation began, undermining its claim that the offering of Christmas trees on the site was in good faith. *See id.* §1125(d)(1)(B)(i)(III). Further weighing in favor of a conclusion that Sporty's Farm had the requisite statutory bad faith intent, as a matter of law, are the following: (1) Sporty's Farm does not claim that its use of the domain name was "noncommercial" or a "fair use of the mark," *see id.* §1125(d)(1)(B)(i)(IV), (2) Omega sold the mark to Sporty's Farm under suspicious circumstances, *see Sporty's Farm v. Sportsman's Market*, No. 96CV0756 (D. Conn. Mar. 13, 1998), *reprinted in* Joint Appendix at A277 (describing the circumstances of the transfer of sportys.com); 15 U.S.C. §1125(d)(1) (B)(i)(VI), and, (3) as we discussed above, the sporty's mark is undoubtedly distinctive, *see id.* §1125(d)(1)(B)(i)(IX).

The most important grounds for our holding that Sporty's Farm acted with a bad faith intent, however, are the unique circumstances of this case, which do not fit neatly into the specific factors enumerated by Congress but may nevertheless be considered under the statute. We know from the record and from the district court's findings that Omega planned to enter into direct competition with Sportsman's in the pilot and aviation consumer market. As recipients of Sportsman's catalogs, Omega's owners, the Hollanders, were fully aware that sporty's was a very strong mark for consumers of those products. It cannot be doubted, as the court found below, that Omega registered sportys.com for the primary purpose of keeping Sportsman's from using that domain name. Several months later, and after this lawsuit was filed, Omega created another company in an unrelated business that received the name Sporty's Farm so that it could (1) use the sportys.com domain name in some commercial fashion, (2) keep the name away from Sportsman's, and (3) protect itself in the event that Sportsman's brought an infringement claim alleging that a "likelihood of confusion" had been created by Omega's version of cybersquatting. Finally, the explanation given for Sporty's Farm's desire to use the domain name, based on the existence of the dog Spotty, is more amusing than credible. Given these facts and the district court's grant of an equitable injunction under the FTDA, there is ample and overwhelming evidence that, as a matter of law, Sporty's Farm acted with a "bad faith intent to profit" from the domain name sportys.com as those terms are used in the ACPA. [cit.]

E.   REMEDY

Based on the foregoing, we hold that under §1125(d)(1)(A), Sporty's Farm violated Sportsman's statutory rights by its use of the sportys.com domain name. The question that remains is what remedy is Sportsman's entitled to. The Act permits a court to "order the forfeiture or cancellation of the domain name or the transfer of the domain name to the owner of the mark," §1125(d)(1)(C) for any "domain name [] registered before, on, or after the date of the enactment of [the] Act," Pub. L. No. 106-113, §3010. That is precisely what the district court did here, albeit under the pre-existing law, when it directed a) Omega and Sporty's Farm to release their interest in sportys.com and to transfer the name to Sportsman's, and b) permanently enjoined those entities from taking any action to prevent and/or hinder Sportsman's from obtaining the domain name. That relief remains appropriate under the ACPA. We therefore affirm the district court's grant of injunctive relief.

We must also determine, however, if Sportsman's is entitled to damages either under the ACPA or pre-existing law. Under the ACPA, damages are unavailable to Sportsman's since sportys.com was registered and used by Sporty's Farm prior to the passage of the new law. *See id.* (stating that damages can be awarded for violations of the Act but that they are not "available with respect to the registration, trafficking, or use of a domain name that occurs before the date of the enactment of this Act.").

But Sportsman's might, nonetheless, be eligible for damages under the FTDA since there is nothing in the ACPA that precludes, in cybersquatting cases, the award of damages under any pre-existing law. *See* 15 U.S.C. §1125(d)(3) (providing that any remedies created by the new act are "in addition to any other civil action or remedy otherwise applicable"). [The court concluded, however, that damages were not available to Sportsman's under the FTDA because the defendant's conduct did not meet the then-prevailing standard for dilution damages.]

[Affirmed.]

DSPT INT'l, INC. v. NAHUM

624 F.3d 1213 (9th Cir. 2010)

KLEINFELD, Circuit Judge:

We address the scope of the Anticybersquatting Consumer Protection Act.

I.   FACTS

. . .

DSPT, founded and owned by Paolo Dorigo, designs, manufactures, and imports men's clothing. The company sells clothes to between 500 and 700 retailers. It sells mostly shirts, but also some knitwear, trousers, and t-shirts. Its brand name since 1988 had been Equilibrio. To serve a younger market with somewhat "trendier, tighter fitting fashion," the company created the EQ brand name in 1999.

At about that time, Dorigo brought his friend Lucky Nahum into the business. Dorigo lived in Los Angeles, Nahum in Rochester, New York. They decided to set up a site on what was then the fledgling internet, and Nahum's brother, a hairdresser, was doing part-time website design, so DSPT had Nahum arrange to have his brother prepare the site. The website, "www.eq-Italy.com" (eq for the brand, Italy for Dorigo's and the style's origin), was created solely for DSPT for the purpose of showing DSPT clothes. Nahum's brother designed the website in consultation with Dorigo, though Nahum registered the site to himself. This seemed trivial at the time, since Nahum was working exclusively for DSPT and registration cost only $25. Dorigo, who was not knowledgeable or interested in computer matters, was unaware that the registration was in Nahum's name.

The importance of the website grew with the importance of the internet. By 2005, the website served as DSPT's catalog. Customers accessed it 24 hours a day, chose designs from it, and sent in orders through it. DSPT e-mailed them about new items on the site. Salesmen sold DSPT clothes to retailers by referring them to pictures on the website and soliciting their orders based on the pictures.

Unfortunately, during the same period, the friendship between Dorigo and Nahum soured. Nahum's DSPT contract was up for renewal August 31, 2005, so Dorigo sent him a proposal in mid-August. At the same time, DSPT paid Nahum's airfare, hotel, and meals for a trip to Las Vegas for the West Coast Exclusive Wear show, an offshoot of the largest menswear show in the world (MAGIC, Men's Apparel Guild in California) which was taking place in Las Vegas. But while there, Nahum spent time in a competitor's booth, and arranged employment with that DSPT competitor. Though Dorigo was also at the show and asked Nahum whether he would be renewing his contract, Nahum only informed Dorigo by e-mail after the show that he was not renewing his contract.

At the beginning of October, DSPT's website mysteriously disappeared. If a customer typed "eq-Italy.com" into his web browser, instead of seeing DSPT's clothing line, all he saw was a screen saying "All fashion related questions to be referred to Lucky Nahum at: lnahum@yahoo.com." Nahum had no use for the website, but he told his new boss at DSPT's competitor that "he had inserted that sentence in order to get Equilibrio [DSPT's older brand] to pay him funds that were due to him." DSPT repeatedly but unsuccessfully asked Nahum to give back the website.

This created a crisis for DSPT. Retailers do around three fourths of their business during the last quarter of the year, so wholesalers and manufacturers, like DSPT, do a large percentage of their business supplying retailers during October, November, and the first part of December. DSPT's website in the fall also generated the orders for the upcoming spring. Without its website, DSPT could not sell anything in a manner approaching its previous efficiency. It was forced to go back to the old way of sending out samples, but retailers did not want to deal with DSPT using the old method. Sales plummeted and inventory was left over in the spring from the very bad fall. 2004 had been good, and the first quarter of 2005 was the best ever, but the last quarter of 2005, and all of 2006, were disastrous. A lot of inventory had to be sold below cost. DSPT spent $31,572.72, plus a great deal of time, writing to customers to explain the situation and replacing its website and the stationery that referred customers to "eq-Italy.com."

DSPT sued Nahum [*inter alia*] for "cybersquatting" . . . in violation of the Lanham Act. . . .

The case was tried to a jury. The jury returned a special verdict, finding, among other things, that "EQ" and "Equilibrio" were valid trademarks owned by DSPT; that "Lucky Nahum registered, trafficked in, or used the www.eq-Italy.com domain name"; that the name was identical or confusingly similar to DSPT's distinctive trademark; and that "Lucky Nahum commit[ed] the acts with a bad faith intent to profit from DSPT's mark." The jury found that DSPT's damages were $152,000. . . . [Nahum appealed.]

II. ANALYSIS

. . .

The Anti-Cybersquatting Consumer Protection Act establishes civil liability for "cyberpiracy" where a plaintiff proves that (1) the defendant registered, trafficked in, or used a domain name; (2) the domain name is identical or confusingly similar to a protected mark owned by the plaintiff; and (3) the defendant acted "with bad faith intent to profit from that mark."

Nahum first argues that as a matter of law, this statute does not apply to what he did. He argues that the statute applies only to one who registers a well-known trademark as a domain name, and then attempts to profit in bad faith by either (1) selling the domain name back to the trademark holder, or (2) using the domain name to divert business from the trademark holder. He argues that he cannot owe damages under the statute because the evidence shows only that he used DSPT's mark to gain leverage over DSPT in bargaining for money he claimed he was owed, not to sell under DSPT's mark or sell the mark to DSPT. He argues that even if in some sense he had a bad-faith intent to profit, any "intent to profit" under the act must be an intent to profit from the goodwill associated with the mark rather than to gain some other benefit. The core of his argument is that he did not register the domain name in bad faith, and used it only to get what he was entitled to.

His arguments are not implausible, but we conclude that they are mistaken. True, the statute was intended to prevent cybersquatters from registering well-known brand names as internet domain names in order to make the trademark owners buy the ability to do business under their own names. Nahum cites a remark in a Senate Committee report mentioning the intent to profit from the goodwill associated with someone else's trademark. And the Sixth Circuit noted that "[t]he paradigmatic harm that the [Anticybersquatting Consumer Protection Act] was enacted to eradicate [was] the practice of cybersquatters registering several hundred domain names in an effort to sell them to the legitimate owners of the mark."

But the statute, like so many, is written more broadly than what may have been the political catalyst that got it passed. As in *Bosley Medical Institute v. Kremer*, we conclude that the words of the statute are broader than this political stimulus that led to its enactment. Though there was no evidence of anything wrong with Nahum's registration of the domain name to himself, the evidence supported a verdict that Nahum subsequently, years later, used the domain name to get leverage for his claim for commissions. The statute says "registers, traffics in, or uses," with "or" between the terms, so use alone is enough to support a verdict, even in the absence of violative registration or trafficking.

As for whether use to get leverage in a business dispute can establish a violation, the statutory factors for "bad faith intent" establish that it can. "Evidence of bad faith may arise well after registration of the domain name."[16] The statute contains a safe harbor provision, excluding a finding of "bad faith intent" for persons who reasonably believed that use of the domain name was fair use or otherwise lawful,[17] but that safe harbor has no application here. Nahum could not have reasonably believed that he could lawfully use "eq-Italy" when he no longer worked for DSPT. The safe harbor protects uses such as parody and comment,[18] and use by persons ignorant of another's superior right to the mark.[19]

The statute provides that a court "may consider factors such as, but not limited to" the . . . enumerated list of nine. Nahum does not challenge the jury instruction, which listed all of the factors, even though some have no bearing on this case, and some do not offer either side much support. One of the factors, number VI in the statute, strongly supports DSPT's claim. That factor notes that it is "indicative" of a "bad faith intent to profit" from the mark if the person offering to transfer the domain name to the owner of the mark has never actually used or intended to use the domain name for bona fide sales of goods.

---

16. *Lahoti v. VeriCheck, Inc.*, 586 F.3d 1190, 1202 (9th Cir. 2009) (citation omitted).

17. 15 U.S.C. §1125(d)(1)(B)(ii).

18. *See, e.g., Mattel, Inc. v. MCA Records, Inc.*, 296 F.3d 894, 906-07 (9th Cir. 2002).

19. *See, e.g.*, 15 U.S.C. §1114 (innocent infringement by publishers); 15 U.S.C. §1115 (innocent infringement as a defense to right to use a mark).

Factor VI may fairly be read to mean that it is bad faith to hold a domain name for ransom,[22] where the holder uses it to get money from the owner of the trademark rather than to sell goods. The jury had evidence that Nahum was using the "eq-Italy.com" domain name as leverage to get DSPT to pay him the disputed commissions, not for the bona fide sale of clothes. Though there was no direct evidence of an explicit offer to sell the domain to DSPT for a specified amount, the jury could infer the intent to give back the site to DSPT only if DSPT paid Nahum the disputed commissions.

The "intent to profit," as factor VI shows, means simply the intent to get money or other valuable consideration. "Profit" does not require that Nahum receive more than he is owed on his disputed claim. Rather, "[p]rofit includes an attempt to procure an advantageous gain or return." Thus, it does not matter that, as the jury concluded, Nahum's claim for unpaid commissions was meritless, because he could not hold the domain name for ransom even if he had been owed commissions.

In this case, shortly after DSPT's content disappeared from eq-Italy.com, Nahum e-mailed Dorigo stating that the eq-Italy.com website would be back up under a new format. Nahum testified that he would transfer the domain to DSPT after Nahum and DSPT were able to resolve the "monetary issues regarding [Nahum's] commissions." Nahum's subsequent employer testified that Nahum told him that DSPT wanted the website returned to them, but Nahum was keeping it to use it as leverage in order to get the money he said DSPT owed him. This is evidence of an "intent to profit" under the Act.

C.   Distinctive and Confusingly Similar

Nahum's second argument is that there was no evidence from which a jury could conclude that "www. eq-Italy. com" was a distinctive mark, or that it was confusingly similar to DSPT's "EQ" mark. The latter point is meritless, since the evidence showed that only DSPT used the mark "EQ" for a men's shirts line, and used the Italian fashion connection as a selling point. Even though DSPT had not registered the "EQ" mark, ownership of common law trademark "is obtained by actual use of a symbol to identify the goods or services of one seller and distinguish them from those offered by others." The evidence shows that DSPT used the mark in commerce in fall 1999, when it exhibited EQ at the New York fashion shows[25] and thereafter used the "EQ" symbol. Although Nahum showed that others used an "EQ" mark in subsequent years for other sorts of goods, such as online publications, engine cylinder heads, and bicycles, no one would likely confuse these goods with DSPT's. The only other use that was even arguably confusingly similar was EQ equestrian clothing, but the jury could conclude that retailers shopping for men's shirts are unlikely to be confused by a mark also used for equestrian clothing, and that the style in which the marks were displayed was too different to foster confusion. The shirts were marked by the letters EQ, whereas the equestrian apparel was marked by a rectangle inside another rectangle.

---

22. *See Bosley Med. Inst., Inc. v. Kremer,* 403 F.3d 672, 680 (9th Cir. 2005) (stating that cybersquatting "occurs when a person other than the trademark holder registers the domain name of a well known trademark and then attempts to profit from this by either *ransoming the domain name back* to the trademark holder or by using the domain name to divert business from the trademark holder to the domain name holder." (emphasis added) (quoting *DaimlerChrysler v. The Net Inc.,* 388 F.3d 201, 204 (6th Cir. 2004))).

25. *See Chance [v. Pac-Tel Teletrac Inc.,* 242 F.3d 1151, 1156-59 (9th Cir. 2001)] (applying totality of the circumstances test and determining that pre-sales activity could qualify mark for trademark protection); *New West Corp. v. NYM Co. of Cal., Inc.,* 595 F.2d 1194, 1199 (9th Cir. 1979) (holding "that appellee established a prior use of the mark without an actual sale").

As for whether "eq-Italy.com" is "confusingly similar" to EQ, a jury could reasonably conclude that in the context of men's shirts, it was. The jury could have concluded that, at the time Nahum used it, the mark was distinctive and his use of the site after leaving DSPT would confuse retailers trying to shop DSPT's catalog at the website where they had done so before.[28] In fact, as Dorigo testified, several customers were actually confused by the alteration of the website. "Now, people would still call and say, what happened? Where is it? You know, they wanted to know what's this screen?" By 2005, eq-Italy.com was identified with EQ and Equilibrio. The similarity of "EQ" and "eq-Italy" is considerably greater than "perfumebay.com" and "ebay.com," which we held were similar, and thus the jury's finding should be upheld.

. . .

III.   CONCLUSION

Even if a domain name was put up innocently and used properly for years, a person is liable under 15 U.S.C. §1125(d) if he subsequently uses the domain name with a bad faith intent to profit from the protected mark by holding the domain name for ransom. The evidence sufficiently supported the jury's verdict that Nahum did so, causing $152,000 in damages to DSPT.

Affirmed.

NEWPORT NEWS HOLDINGS CORP. v. VIRTUAL CITY VISION, INC.

650 F.3d 423 (4th Cir. 2011)

DUNCAN, Circuit Judge:

This appeal raises numerous issues arising out of the grant of summary judgment to Newport News Holdings Corporation ("NNHC") on its claims against Virtual City Vision and its owner Van James Bond Tran (collectively, "VCV") under the Anticybersquatting Consumer Protection Act ("ACPA"). . . .

I.

A.

. . .

NNHC is a women's clothing and accessories company that has been in existence for over twenty years. It owns five federally registered trademarks for the mark "Newport News." These trademarks cover the sale of women's clothing and accessories and the offering of these items for sale through catalogs and the Internet. The trademarks also cover the domain name newport-news.com, which NNHC purchased in November 1997. NNHC attempted to acquire the domain name newportnews.com as well, but VCV had already purchased that domain name in October 1997. NNHC began offering its goods for sale over the Internet in 1999 using the newport-news.com domain name.

---

28. The usual eight factors from *AMF Inc. v. Sleekcraft Boats* for determining whether passing off one's goods as another is "confusingly similar" are a poor fit in this context, because they are designed to address a different social harm than the cybersquatting statute. 599 F.2d 341, 348-49 (9th Cir. 1979).

VCV, an Alabama corporation, owns at least thirty-one domain names that incorporate the names of geographic locations. Newportnews.com, which initially focused on Newport News, Virginia, is one such example. VCV's "original intent . . . was to create websites . . . where residents of, and visitors to, these cities could find information and advertising related to th[e] cities." [cit.]

VCV's organization is skeletal. Tran is its president, sole employee, and the only participating member of its board of directors. He operates the business from his home.

NNHC and VCV first clashed in a private dispute resolution forum. In 2000, NNHC brought a complaint against VCV under the Uniform Domain Name Dispute Resolution Policy of the Internet Corporation for Assigned Names and Numbers ("ICANN"). NNHC alleged that VCV's newportnews.com website was "confusingly similar to [NNHC's] family of registered trademarks for the mark 'Newport News'"; that "any rights [VCV] has in the domain name in contention are illegitimate"; and that VCV "registered this domain name in bad faith." [cit.]

The ICANN panel rejected NNHC's arguments and dismissed its complaint. In doing so, it found that, although the mark and the domain name are identical, "visitors to [NNHC's] branded web site, who seek out the latest women's clothing and home fashions would clearly not be confused when seeing a home page of another web site, bearing an identical mark, that explicitly provides city information . . . with no connection whatsoever to women's and home fashions." [cit.] The panel further held that VCV's website provided "bona fide service offerings," which included "disseminat[ing] city information in an effort to increase tourism and other visitor traffic to the city." [cit.] Significantly, with respect to NNHC's claim of bad faith, the panel noted that "given the total absence of competition between the businesses of [NNHC and VCV] . . . [VCV] did not register the contested domain name in an effort to cause any likelihood of confusion." [cit.]

Between 2000 and 2004, newportnews.com remained relatively unchanged. It continued to provide information about the city of Newport News and link visitors to local businesses, such as hotels, movie theaters, real estate companies, and entertainment venues. In 2004, the website began running occasional advertisements for women's clothing.

In the summer of 2007, NNHC made an offer to purchase the newportnews.com domain name, which VCV rejected. VCV responded that it would sell the domain name for a "seven-figure" amount, or, in the alternative, sell NNHC goods on its website for a commission. [cit.]

A substantive evolution in the VCV website began in the fall of 2007. The site shifted from a city focus, similar to that of VCV's other locality sites, to one emphasizing women's fashions. By February of 2008, the homepage was dominated by advertisements for women's apparel.

At about the same time, the management of the site changed as well. Tran began managing the newportnews.com website personally, taking control away from Local Matters, the company that ran VCV's locality sites. The changes to the website were lucrative. Tran would later testify that most of VCV's revenue during that time came from the newportnews.com website instead of the locality sites, either individually or in total.

II

[VCV challenged the district court's grant of summary judgment in favor of NNHC on its claim under the ACPA.]

1.

[The court first considered the issue of bad faith under the ACPA.] VCV challenges the district court's finding of bad faith in several respects. It attacks the court's determination that VCV did not provide legitimate services that would constitute a fair use of the domain name. VCV also asserts that the evidence does not support a finding that it intended to create a likelihood of confusion. Finally, it challenges the court's reliance on the ICANN ruling as evidence that VCV knew it was acting unlawfully when it changed its website.

a.

VCV claims that, contrary to the district court's conclusion, its website offered a legitimate service by providing information about the city of Newport News.

The ACPA permits a registered trademark to be used by someone other than the mark owner if it is a "use, otherwise than as a mark, . . . of a term or device which is descriptive of and used fairly and in good faith only to describe the goods or services of such party, or their geographic origin." 15 U.S.C. §1115(b)(4). The district court found that this provision did not apply here because "[o]n VCV's website, Newport News is no longer used to describe VCV's goods or services, or their geographic origin, because the site is dedicated primarily to women's fashion." [cit.] VCV disputes this characterization, contending to the contrary that its website offered the legitimate service of providing information about the city of Newport News. We disagree.

The record conclusively shows that in making changes to its website in 2007, VCV shifted its focus away from the legitimate service of providing information related to the city of Newport News and became instead a website devoted primarily to women's fashion. Most of the items on its homepage, as well as those most prominently placed, related to women's attire. Not only was the site dominated by advertisements for apparel, it also contained dozens of links to shopping websites. The website's references to the city of Newport News became minor in comparison to the fashion-related content. VCV cannot escape the consequences of its deliberate metamorphosis. VCV would apparently have us hold that as long as it provided any information about the city of Newport News, it continued to provide a "bona fide" service. Such a formalistic approach would allow a cybersquatter seeking to profit from another company's trademark to avoid liability by ensuring that it provides some minimal amount of information about a legitimate subject. It would also undermine the purpose of the ACPA, which seeks to prevent "the bad-faith and abusive registration of distinctive marks as Internet domain names with the intent to profit from the goodwill associated with such marks." *Barcelona.com, Inc. v. Excelentisimo Ayuntamiento de Barcelona*, 330 F.3d 617, 624 (4th Cir. 2003) (quoting S. Rep. No. 106-140, at 4 (1999)).

As we have noted, in analyzing bad faith, we "view the totality of the circumstances." [*Virtual Works, Inc. v. Volkswagen of Am., Inc.*, 238 F.3d 264, 270 (4th Cir. 2001).] Here, even drawing all reasonable inferences in favor of VCV, the record is clear that after November 2007, VCV was no longer in the business of providing information about the city of Newport News. The contrast between the newportnews.com website and VCV's other locality websites, which were dominated by links and advertisements for businesses and activities in those cities, is stark. Unlike those websites, newportnews.com went from being a website about a city that happened to have some apparel advertisements to a website about women's apparel that happened to include minimal references to the city of Newport News. The district court correctly held that, once VCV largely abandoned its city information service, it ceased to have a right to use the name of Newport News to describe such service.

b.

VCV argues that the district court failed to properly analyze whether there was a likelihood of confusion between NNHC's website and VCV's website. Its argument, however, mischaracterizes the nature of an ACPA claim. The standard under the ACPA is not whether there is a likelihood of confusion between the two websites but rather whether the allegedly offending website "creat[es] a likelihood of confusion as to the source, sponsorship, affiliation, or endorsement of the site." 15 U.S.C. §1125(d)(1)(B)(v). The ACPA provides for liability "without regard to the goods or services of the parties." *Id*. §1125(d)(1)(A).

VCV argues that, under our precedent in *Lamparello v. Falwell*, 420 F.3d 309 (4th Cir. 2005), we must "determine whether a likelihood of confusion exists by 'examin[ing] the allegedly infringing use in the context in which it is seen by the ordinary consumer.'" *Id*. at 316 (alteration in original). However, the court in Lamparello made that statement in the context of trademark infringement, not the ACPA. *See id*. As the Eighth Circuit court has noted, "[t]he inquiry under the ACPA is . . . narrower than the traditional multifactor likelihood of confusion test for trademark infringement." *Coca-Cola Co. v. Purdy*, 382 F.3d 774, 783 (8th Cir. 2004); *see also N. Light Tech., Inc. v. N. Lights Club*, 236 F.3d 57, 66 n.14 (1st Cir. 2001) ("[T]he likelihood of confusion test of trademark infringement is more comprehensive than the identical or confusingly similar requirement of ACPA, as it requires considering factors beyond the facial similarity of the two marks." (internal quotations omitted)). "The question under the ACPA is . . . whether the domain names which [the defendant] registered . . . are identical or confusingly similar to a plaintiff's mark." *Coca-Cola Co.*, 382 F.3d at 783. Here VCV's domain name was identical to NNHC's mark.

VCV further alleges that its disclaimer, "We are Newport News, Virginia," which appeared near the top of the new version of the website, eliminated any likelihood of confusion. Again, VCV misinterprets the applicable law. For ACPA purposes, "[t]he fact that confusion about a website's source or sponsorship could be resolved by visiting the website is not relevant to whether the domain name itself is identical or confusingly similar to a plaintiff's mark." *Id*.; *see also Virtual Works*, 238 F.3d at 271 (finding that the domain name vw.net was confusingly similar to the Volkswagen "VW" mark for purposes of the ACPA, even though the domain name was being used as an internet service provider's website); [cit.]. Given that VCV's domain name was identical to NNHC's mark, we find that the district court correctly held that VCV created a likelihood of confusion as to the source of the site.

c.

VCV argues that the district court erred in finding that the ICANN decision was further proof of VCV's bad faith in making the November 2008 changes to its website. It asserts that, because the ICANN decision did not prohibit any of the changes made by VCV, VCV's awareness of the decision does not support a finding that it made the changes in bad faith.

VCV's argument misses the mark here as well. What the court deemed most significant was that the ICANN decision found VCV's use proper precisely because its business of providing city information was unrelated to NNHC's clothing business. The ICANN decision found that VCV was not in competition with NNHC precisely because of their disparate business models. Indeed, in holding that there was no evidence of bad faith on the part of VCV, the ICANN relied on "*the total absence of competition between the businesses of [NNHC and VCV].*" [cit.] (emphasis added). The fact that, in the face of this cautionary language, VCV later purposefully transformed its website into one that competed with NNHC by advertising women's apparel is a legitimate factor within the totality of the circumstances supporting the district court's finding of bad faith.[9]

[*Affirmed.*]

LAMPARELLO v. FALWELL

420 F.3d 309 (4th Cir. 2005), cert. denied, 547 U.S. 1069 (2006)

Diana Gribbon Motz, Circuit Judge:

. . .

Reverend Falwell is "a nationally known minister who has been active as a commentator on politics and public affairs." [cit.] He holds the common law trademarks "Jerry Falwell" and "Falwell," and the registered trademark "Listen America with Jerry Falwell." Jerry Falwell Ministries can be found online at "www.falwell.com," a website which receives 9,000 hits (or visits) per day.

Lamparello registered the domain name "www.fallwell.com" on February 11, 1999, after hearing Reverend Falwell give an interview "in which he expressed opinions about gay people and homosexuality that [Lamparello] considered . . . offensive." Lamparello created a website at that domain name to respond to what he believed were "untruths about gay people." Lamparello's website included headlines such as "Bible verses that Dr. Falwell chooses to ignore" and "Jerry Falwell has been bearing false witness (Exodus 20:16) against his gay and lesbian neighbors for a long time." The site also contained in-depth criticism of Reverend Falwell's views. . . .

Although the interior pages of Lamparello's website did not contain a disclaimer, the homepage prominently stated, "This website is NOT affiliated with Jerry Falwell or his ministry"; advised, "If you would like to visit Rev. Falwell's website, you may click here"; and provided a hyperlink to Reverend Falwell's website.

At one point, Lamparello's website included a link to the Amazon.com webpage for a book that offered interpretations of the Bible that Lamparello favored, but the parties agree that Lamparello has never sold goods or services on his website. The parties also agree that "Lamparello's domain name and web site at www.fallwell.com," which received only 200 hits per day, "had no measurable impact on the quantity of visits to [Reverend Falwell's] web site at www.falwell.com."

Nonetheless, Reverend Falwell sent Lamparello letters in October 2001 and June 2003 demanding that he cease and desist from using www.fallwell.com or any variation of Reverend Falwell's name as a domain name. Ultimately, Lamparello filed this action against Reverend Falwell and his ministries (collectively referred to hereinafter as "Reverend Falwell"), seeking a declaratory judgment of noninfringement. Reverend Falwell counterclaimed, [alleging various Lanham Act violations. Lamparello lost at the district court and

---

9. VCV's argument that the district court failed to consider the safe-harbor fair use defense fails as well. Under the ACPA's safe-harbor provision, "[b]ad faith intent . . . shall not be found in any case in which the court determines that the person believed and had reasonable grounds to believe that the use of the domain name was a fair use or otherwise lawful." 15 U.S.C. §1125(d)(1)(B)(ii). The district court's specific finding that "VCV knew or should have known" that the November 2007 changes to its website "would give rise to some type of liability," [cit.], defeats any contention that VCV "believed and had reasonable grounds to believe" that its use of the domain name was lawful.

appealed. In addition to a claim under Section 43(a), Falwell alleged that Lamparello had engaged in cybersquatting under Section 43(d). The court evaluated Falwell's cybersquatting claim separately because the elements of a cybersquatting violation differ from those of traditional Lanham Act violations. The court stressed that "'[t]he paradigmatic harm that the ACPA was enacted to eradicate' is 'the practice of cybersquatters registering several hundred domain names in an effort to sell them to the legitimate owners of the mark.' *Lucas Nursery & Landscaping, Inc. v. Grosse*, 359 F.3d 806, 810 (6th Cir. 2004)."]

To distinguish abusive domain name registrations from legitimate ones, the ACPA directs courts to consider nine nonexhaustive factors. . . . These factors attempt "to balance the property interests of trademark owners with the legitimate interests of Internet users and others who seek to make lawful uses of others' marks, including for purposes such as comparative advertising, *comment, criticism*, parody, news reporting, fair use, etc." H.R. Rep. No. 106-412, 1999 WL 970519, at *10 (emphasis added). . . .

After close examination of the undisputed facts involved in this case, we can only conclude that Reverend Falwell cannot demonstrate that Lamparello "had a bad faith intent to profit from using the [www.fallwell.com] domain name." [*People for the Ethical Treatment of Animals v. Doughney*, 263 F.3d 359, 367 (4th Cir. 2001) (*PETA*).] Lamparello clearly employed www.fallwell.com simply to criticize Reverend Falwell's views. Factor IV of the ACPA, 15 U.S.C. §1125(d)(1)(B)(i)(IV), counsels against finding a bad faith intent to profit in such circumstances because "use of a domain name for purposes of . . . comment, [and] criticism," H.R. Rep. No. 106-412, 1999 WL 970519, at *11, constitutes a "bona fide noncommercial or fair use" under the statute, 15 U.S.C. §1125(d)(1)(B)(i)(IV).[7] That Lamparello provided a link to an Amazon.com webpage selling a book he favored does not diminish the communicative function of his website. The use of a domain name to engage in criticism or commentary "even where done for profit" does not alone evidence a bad faith intent to profit, H.R. Rep. No. 106-412, 1999 WL 970519, at *11, and Lamparello did not even stand to gain financially from sales of the book at Amazon.com. Thus factor IV weighs heavily in favor of finding Lamparello lacked a bad faith intent to profit from the use of the domain name.

Equally important, Lamparello has not engaged in the type of conduct described in the statutory factors as typifying the bad faith intent to profit essential to a successful cybersquatting claim. First, we have already held, [cit.], that Lamparello's domain name does not create a likelihood of confusion as to source or affiliation. Accordingly, Lamparello has not engaged in the type of conduct—"creating a likelihood of confusion as to the source, sponsorship, affiliation, or endorsement of the site," 15 U.S.C. §1125(d)(1)(B)(i)(V)—described as an indicator of a bad faith intent to profit in factor V of the statute.

Factors VI and VIII also counsel against finding a bad faith intent to profit here. Lamparello has made no attempt—or even indicated a willingness—"to transfer, sell, or otherwise assign the domain name to [Reverend Falwell] or any third party for financial gain." 15 U.S.C. §1125(d)(1)(B)(i)(VI). Similarly, Lamparello has not registered "multiple

---

7. We note that factor IV does not protect a faux noncommercial site, that is, a noncommercial site created by the registrant for the sole purpose of avoiding liability under the FTDA, which exempts noncommercial uses of marks, *see* 15 U.S.C. §1125(c)(4)(B), or under the ACPA. As explained by the Senate Report discussing the ACPA, an individual cannot avoid liability for registering and attempting to sell a hundred domain names incorporating famous marks by posting noncommercial content at those domain names. *See* S. Rep. No. 106-140, 1999 WL 594571, at *14 (citing *Panavision Int'l v. Toeppen*, 141 F.3d 1316 (9th Cir. 1998)). But Lamparello's sole purpose for registering www.fallwell.com was to criticize Reverend Falwell, and this noncommercial use was not a ruse to avoid liability. Therefore, factor IV indicates that Lamparello did not have a bad faith intent to profit.

domain names," 15 U.S.C. §1125(d)(1)(B)(i)(VIII); rather, the record indicates he has registered only one. Thus, Lamparello's conduct is not of the suspect variety described in factors VI and VIII of the Act.

Notably, the case at hand differs markedly from those in which the courts have found a bad faith intent to profit from domain names used for websites engaged in political commentary or parody. For example, in *PETA* we found the registrant of www.peta.org engaged in cybersquatting because www.peta.org was one of *fifty* to *sixty* domain names Doughney had registered, *PETA*, 263 F.3d at 362, and because Doughney had evidenced a clear intent to sell www.peta.org to PETA, stating that PETA should try to "'settle' with him and 'make him an offer.'" *Id*. at 368. *See also Virtual Works*, 238 F.3d at 269-70. Similarly, in *Coca-Cola Co. v. Purdy*, 382 F.3d 774 (8th Cir. 2004), the Eighth Circuit found an anti-abortion activist who had registered domain names incorporating famous marks such as "Washington Post" liable for cybersquatting because he had registered almost *seventy* domain names, had offered to stop using the Washington Post mark if the newspaper published an opinion piece by him on its editorial page, and posted content that created a likelihood of confusion as to whether the famous markholders sponsored the anti-abortion sites and "ha[d] taken positions on hotly contested issues." *Id*. at 786. In contrast, Lamparello did not register multiple domain names, he did not offer to transfer them for valuable consideration, and he did not create a likelihood of confusion.

Instead, Lamparello, like the plaintiffs in two cases recently decided by the Fifth and Sixth Circuits, created a gripe site. Both courts expressly refused to find that gripe sites located at domain names nearly identical to the marks at issue violated the ACPA. In *TMI, Inc. v. Maxwell*, 368 F.3d 433, 434-35 (5th Cir. 2004), Joseph Maxwell, a customer of homebuilder TMI, registered the domain name "www.trendmakerhome.com," which differed by only one letter from TMI's mark, TrendMaker Homes, and its domain name, "www.trendmakerhomes.com." Maxwell used the site to complain about his experience with TMI and to list the name of a contractor whose work pleased him. After his registration expired, Maxwell registered "www.trendmakerhome.info." TMI then sued, alleging cybersquatting. The Fifth Circuit reversed the district court's finding that Maxwell violated the ACPA, reasoning that his site was noncommercial and designed only "to inform potential customers about a negative experience with the company." *Id*. at 438-39.

Similarly, in *Lucas Nursery & Landscaping*, a customer of Lucas Nursery registered the domain name "www.lucasnursery.com" and posted her dissatisfaction with the company's landscaping services. Because the registrant, Grosse, like Lamparello, registered a single domain name, the Sixth Circuit concluded that her conduct did not constitute that which Congress intended to proscribe—i.e., the registration of multiple domain names. *Lucas Nursery & Landscaping*, 359 F.3d at 810. Noting that Grosse's gripe site did not create any confusion as to sponsorship and that she had never attempted to sell the domain name to the markholder, the court found that Grosse's conduct was not actionable under the ACPA. The court explained: "One of the ACPA's main objectives is the protection of consumers from slick internet peddlers who trade on the names and reputations of established brands. The practice of informing fellow consumers of one's experience with a particular service provider is surely not inconsistent with this ideal." *Id*. at 811.

Like Maxwell and Grosse before him, Lamparello has not evidenced a bad faith intent to profit under the ACPA. To the contrary, he has used www.fallwell.com to engage in the type of "comment[] [and] criticism" that Congress specifically stated militates against a finding of bad faith intent to profit. *See* S. Rep. No. 106-140, 1999 WL 594571, at *14. And he has neither registered multiple domain names nor attempted to transfer www.fallwell.com for valuable consideration. We agree with the Fifth and Sixth Circuits that, given these circumstances, the use of a mark in a domain name for a gripe site criticizing the markholder does not constitute cybersquatting.

IV.

For the foregoing reasons, Lamparello, rather than Reverend Falwell, is entitled to summary judgment on all counts. Accordingly, the judgment of the district court is reversed and the case is remanded for entry of judgment for Lamparello.

Reversed and remanded.

NOTES AND QUESTIONS

1. *A range of options for the trademark holder.* Causes of action under the ACPA are in addition to any other civil action or remedy otherwise applicable. Indeed, the statute does not preempt state law, and thus state causes of action are also available. Should the ACPA be the exclusive cause of action under the Lanham Act for an alleged act of cybersquatting? What advantages does the ACPA provide trademark owners over other possible causes of action? When might other causes of action usefully supplement the ACPA cause of action? When might they provide relief that the ACPA does not?

2. *The premises underlying each cause of action.* What assumptions regarding consumer behavior are made by the courts in *Panavision* and *Sporty's Farm*? Do you agree with those assumptions? To what extent are the legal conclusions in those cases dependent on assumptions about consumer behavior?

3. *Confusing similarity.* The *Sporty's Farm* court noted that "confusingly similar" is a different standard from the "likelihood of confusion" standard for trademark infringement. As we saw in Chapter 7, courts have spent a substantial amount of time developing the test of "likelihood of confusion." Which considerations should guide courts in determining whether a domain name registration is "confusingly similar" to a trademark such that element of an action under the ACPA is satisfied? Why did the question present little difficulty for the *Sporty's Farm* court? What should courts do in closer cases? To what extent did you think that trademark owners will bring such cases? *See also Coca-Cola Co. v. Purdy,* 382 F.3d 774, 783 (8th Cir. 2004) (noting that "the question under the ACPA is not whether the domain names [that were registered] are likely to be confused with a plaintiff's *domain name,* but whether they are identical or confusingly similar to a plaintiff's *mark* "). Is mycoke.com confusingly similar to COKE? Drinkcoke.org? *See id.* (also noting that the fact that "confusion about a website's source or sponsorship could be resolved by visiting the website is not relevant to whether the domain name itself is identical or confusingly similar to a plaintiff's mark"). *Contra Smith v. Wal-Mart Stores, Inc.,* 537 F. Supp. 2d 1302, 1315-16 (N.D. Ga. 2008) (quoting statutory language but applying same "likelihood of confusion" test to infringement and ACPA claim).

4. *Bad faith.* In determining the bad faith of the registrant, the statute instructs courts to consider whether the defendant owns any trademark or other intellectual property rights in the domain name. Assume that the domain name registrant owns no U.S. intellectual property rights in the domain name but has a trademark corresponding to the domain name in Argentina. Should this count against a finding of bad faith? *See Harrods Ltd. v. Sixty Internet Domain Names,* 302 F.3d 214, 234 (4th Cir. 2002). Should legitimate ownership of one domain name registration (e.g., gopet.com) count in favor of a finding of good faith when the registrant registers additional related domain names (e.g., gopet. org) in order to increase the selling price of the legitimate domain name registration? *See GoPets Ltd. v. Hise,* 657 F.3d 1024, 1032-33 (9th Cir. 2011). Is it bad faith if a domain name registrant registered the domain name hoping (or believing) that the ACPA would be declared unconstitutional? *See E. & J. Gallo Winery v. Spider Webs Ltd.*, 286 F.3d 270 (5th Cir. 2002). Review the "bad faith" factors. Should it favor the defendant that the site using the domain name in question did not generate profit for the defendant but instead linked to sites at which political causes (e.g., the anti-abortion movement) solicited funds? What about an offer to stop using the domain name of a newspaper that was at issue in return for space on the editorial page of the newspaper? *See Coca-Cola Co. v. Purdy*, 382 F.3d 774, 786 (8th Cir. 2004). How do First Amendment values affect your analysis of these questions? What if the defendant converts content to a commentary on plaintiffs after a dispute arises? *See Audi AG v. D'Amato*, 469 F.3d 534 (6th Cir. 2006). In *Flat Rate Movers, Ltd. v. FlatRate Moving & Storage, Inc.*, 104 F. Supp. 3d 371 (S.D.N.Y. 2015), the court held that the bad faith required under the ACPA was a bad faith intent to profit from its cybersquatting activity. Does this reading comport with the purpose or text of the legislation?

   5. *ACPA remedies.* The ACPA provides that damages and injunctive relief will be available under the statute, as will statutory damages under Section 35(d) of the Lanham Act, which provides that "in a case involving a violation of section 43(d)(1), the plaintiff may elect, at any time before final judgment is rendered by the trial court, to recover, instead of actual damages and profits, an award of statutory damages in the amount of not less than $1,000 and not more than $100,000 per domain name, as the court considers just." *See* 15 U.S.C. §1117(d). In December 2008, Verizon was awarded $33.15 million in damages against a cybersquatter by a federal court in California, which is thought to be the largest-ever damages award for cybersquatting. *See* Michelle Meyers, *Verizon Awarded "Largest-Ever" Cybersquatting Judgment*, CNet News, Dec. 24, 2008.

   6. *Damages under the ACPA for domain names registered pre-ACPA.* Damages can be awarded for violations of the ACPA but they are not "available with respect to the registration, trafficking, or use of a domain name that occurs before the date of the enactment of [the] Act." Should damages be available where a domain name was first registered in 1998, but re-registered (or registration renewed) after the effective date of the ACPA? *Cf. Schmidheiny v. Weber*, 319 F.3d 581 (3d Cir. 2003) (discussing scope of 15 U.S.C. §1129 and finding it applicable to re-registrations because "to conclude otherwise would permit the domain names of living persons to be sold and purchased without the living person's consent, ad infinitum, so long as the name was first registered before the effective date of the Act"); *Jysk Bed'N Linen v. Dutta-Roy*, 117 U.S.P.Q.2d (BNA) 1200 (11th Cir. 2015) (same). *See contra GoPets Ltd. v. Hise*, 657 F.3d 1024 (9th Cir. 2011) (registration does not include re-registration). To what extent should the answer to the re-registration question depend on whether initial registrations that predate the ACPA are covered by the Act? *See id.* at 1031-32.

   7. *Protection of personal names.* The ACPA also created a cause of action intended to offer additional protections for individuals. *See* 15 U.S.C. §1129. This provides that "any person who registers a domain name [on or after December 2, 1999] that consists of the name of another living person, or a name substantially and confusingly similar thereto, without that person's consent, with the specific intent to profit from such name by selling the domain name for financial gain to that person or any third party, shall be liable in a civil action by such person." *See* 15 U.S.C. §1129. Examine that provision: what must a registrant do to fall within its scope? *See Schmidheiny v. Weber*, 319 F.3d 581, 582 (3d Cir. 2003) ("the provision does not define what a person who registers must do to fall within the scope of the statute, and the legislative history does not provide an explanation"); *see also Philbrick v. eNom, Inc.*, 593 F. Supp. 2d 352 (D.N.H. 2009) (differing basis for rejection of claim based on registration of domain name which was similar to mark, on the one hand, and registration of domain name which was similar to personal name, on the other); 15 U.S.C. §1129(1)(A). If a plaintiff is successful under Section 47, a court may award injunctive relief, including the forfeiture or cancellation of the domain name or the transfer of the domain name to the plaintiff (or, in its discretion, award costs and attorney's fees to the prevailing party). What is the purpose of this cause of action? What objectives does it further?

No cause of action will exist under this separate provision if registration of such a name is made in good faith and is used in, affiliated with, or related to a protected work of authorship, and the person registering the domain name is the copyright owner or licensee of the work, the person intends to sell the domain name in conjunction with the lawful exploitation of the work, and such registration is not prohibited by a contract between the registrant and the named person. (This exception applies only to causes of action under Section 47 and does not limit other, more traditional trademark or other causes of action.) What is the purpose of this exception?

8. *"Commercial use" and the ACPA.* In *Bosley Medical Inst., Inc. v. Kremer*, 403 F.3d 672 (9th Cir. 2005), the Ninth Circuit noted that "to the extent the [Fourth Circuit in *PETA v. Doughney*] held that the Lanham Act's commercial use requirement is satisfied because the defendant's use of the plaintiff's mark as the domain name may deter customers from reaching the plaintiff's site itself, we respectfully disagree with that rationale." *Bosley Med. Inst. v. Kremer*, 403 F.3d 672, 679 (9th Cir. 2005); *see also Lucas Nursery & Landscaping, Inc. v. Grosse*, 359 F.3d 806 (6th Cir. 2004) (distinguishing *PETA*). Regardless of which approach to the question of commercial use is more persuasive, note that the *Bosley* court disagreed with the *PETA* court's commercial use analysis in the context of dismissing infringement and dilution claims (where the *Bosley* court held that a "commercial use" was required). The plaintiff in *Bosley* fared better in its ACPA claim:

> The district court dismissed Bosley's ACPA claim for the same reasons that it dismissed the infringement and dilution claims—namely, because Kremer did not make commercial use of Bosley's mark. However, the ACPA does not contain a commercial use requirement, and we therefore reverse.
>
> Kremer argues that the "noncommercial use" proviso that appears in the dilution portion of §1125 applies to cybersquatting claims with equal force. Admittedly, the language in §1125 is confusing. 15 U.S.C. §1125(c)(4) reads: "The following shall not be actionable under this section: . . . (B) Noncommercial use of a mark." 15 U.S.C. §1125(c)(4)(B). Kremer asserts that by using the word "section," rather than the more precise term "subsection," Congress meant for the proviso to apply to all of §1125, as opposed to subsection (c).
>
> This argument fails for two reasons. The noncommercial use exception, which appears in a different part of the Lanham Act, is in direct conflict with the language of the ACPA. The ACPA makes it clear that "use" is only one possible way to violate the Act ("registers, traffics in, *or* uses"). Allowing a cybersquatter to register the domain name with a bad faith intent to profit but get around the law by making noncommercial use of the mark would run counter to the purpose of the Act. "[T]he use of a domain name in connection with a site that makes a noncommercial or fair use of the mark does not necessarily mean that the domain name registrant lacked bad faith." *Coca-Cola Co. v. Purdy*, 382 F.3d 774, 778 (8th Cir. 2004) (internal quotation marks and citation omitted); *see also* H.R. Rep. No. 106-412 at 11 (1999) ("This factor is not intended to create a loophole that otherwise might swallow the bill, however, by allowing a domain name registrant to evade application of the Act by merely putting up a non-infringing site under an infringing domain name."). "It is a well-established canon of statutory construction that a court should go beyond the literal language of a statute if reliance on that language would defeat the plain purpose of the statute." [cit.]
>
> Additionally, one of the nine factors listed in the statute that courts must consider is the registrant's "bona fide noncommercial or fair use of the mark in a site accessible under the domain name." 15 U.S.C. §1125(d)(1)(B)(i)(IV). This factor would be meaningless if the statute exempted all noncommercial uses of a trademark within a domain name. We try to avoid,

where possible, an interpretation of a statute "that renders any part of it superfluous and does not give effect to all of the words used by Congress." [cit.]

Finally, other courts that have construed the ACPA have not required commercial use. In *DaimlerChrysler*, the Sixth Circuit held that a

> trademark owner asserting a claim under the ACPA must establish the following: (1) it has a valid trademark entitled to protection; (2) its mark is distinctive or famous; (3) the defendant's domain name is identical or confusingly similar to, or in the case of famous marks, dilutive of, the owner's mark; and (4) the defendant used, registered, or trafficked in the domain name (5) with a bad faith intent to profit.

388 F.3d at 204; [cit.].

The district court erred in applying the commercial use requirement to Bosley's ACPA claim. Rather, the court should confine its inquiry to the elements of the ACPA claim listed in the statute, particularly to whether Kremer had a bad faith intent to profit from his use of Bosley's mark in his site's domain name. Bosley has met the first prong of the ACPA (that the domain name is identical to the mark) because Kremer used an unmodified version of Bosley's mark as his domain name.

Concluding that all of Bosley's claims, including the ACPA claim, were subject to a commercial use requirement, the district judge granted summary judgment in Kremer's favor. . . . It remains to be seen whether Bosley can establish that Kremer registered the domain name in bad faith or can authenticate other letters that Bosley alleges were written and sent by Kremer.

9. *Extensions of the cybersquatting cause of action?* Would you support the extension of prohibitions against cybersquatting to unauthorized use of usernames consisting of trademarks on social networking sites such as Facebook and Twitter? (At present, most of these sites do have policies relating to the use of trademarks.) If you had to modify the ACPA rule, what modifications might you make?

10. *Contributory cybersquatting.* Trademark owners have filed many individual complaints against cybersquatters. To make enforcement efficient, should courts consider a cause of action for contributory cybersquatting? *Compare Transamerica Corp. v. Moniker Online Servs.*, 672 F. Supp. 2d 1353 (S.D. Fla. 2009) *with Petroliam Nasional Berhad v. GoDaddy.com, Inc.*, 737 F.3d 546 (9th Cir. 2013) (denying the possibility of a claim for contributory cybersquatting). Against whom would such a cause of action be brought? What would be the standard, and what conduct would meet that standard?

The *in rem* cause of action created by Section 43(d)(2) has proved to be an invaluable instrument by which the owners of U.S. trademarks can secure the return of domain names from cybersquatters (and, arguably, from other domain name registrants that have registered the domain name without authority of the trademark owner). The scope of the provision, both in terms of its geographic reach and in terms of the types of conduct over which it establishes jurisdiction, has, however, been the subject of substantial litigation. Indeed, its very constitutionality has been questioned. The following case touches on all these issues, and also allows us to consider further the element of bad faith central to liability under Section 43(d)(1).

HARRODS LTD. v. SIXTY INTERNET DOMAIN NAMES
302 F.3d 214 (4th Cir. 2002)

MICHAEL, Circuit Judge:

This case involves a dispute over Internet domain names between two companies named "Harrods," both with legitimate rights to the "Harrods" name in different parts of the world. The plaintiff, Harrods Limited ("Harrods UK"), is the owner of the well-known Harrods of London department store. The defendants are 60 Internet domain names ("Domain Names" or "Names") registered in Herndon, Virginia, by Harrods (Buenos Aires) Limited ("Harrods BA"). Harrods BA, once affiliated with Harrods UK, is now a completely separate corporate entity that until recently operated a "Harrods" department store in Buenos Aires, Argentina. Harrods UK sued the 60 Domain Names under 15 U.S.C. §1125(d)(2). . . . Harrods UK alleged that the Domain Names infringed and diluted its American "Harrods" trademark and that Harrods BA registered the Names in bad faith as prohibited by 15 U.S.C. §1125(d)(1). The district court dismissed the infringement and dilution claims, holding that in rem actions could only be maintained for bad faith registration claims under §1125(d)(1). As discovery was just beginning, the district court granted summary judgment to six of the Domain Names on Harrods UK's bad faith registration claim. After full discovery and a bench trial, the court awarded judgment to Harrods UK against the remaining 54 Domain Names and ordered those names to be transferred to Harrods UK. Both sides now appeal. For the reasons that follow, we affirm the judgment as to the 54 Domain Names, reverse the dismissal of Harrods UK's infringement and dilution claims, reverse the grant of summary judgment to the six Domain Names, and remand for further proceedings.

I

Harrods UK and its predecessors have operated a department store named "Harrods" in the Knightsbridge section of London, England, since 1849. In 1912 Harrods UK created a wholly owned subsidiary Harrods South America Limited, to carry on business in South America. Harrods South America Limited created Harrods BA as an independent company, and in 1914 Harrods BA opened a department store under the name "Harrods" in a new building in downtown Buenos Aires designed to look like Harrods UK's historic London building. Over the following decades Harrods BA registered "Harrods" as a trademark in Argentina, Brazil, Paraguay, Venezuela, and a number of other South American countries. Harrods UK and Harrods BA quickly drifted apart: by the 1920s Harrods BA was operating largely independently of Harrods UK, and the last remaining legal ties between the two companies were severed in 1963.

In the early 1990s Harrods UK and Harrods BA entered into negotiations for Harrods UK to buy Harrods BA's South American trademark rights in the name "Harrods." At one point Harrods UK offered $10 million for the rights, but the parties never reached agreement. . . . It appears . . . that Harrods BA has the right to use the name "Harrods" in Argentina and much of South America, and for the limited purposes of this litigation Harrods UK does not attempt to prove otherwise.

Harrods UK, for its part, has exclusive trademark rights in the name "Harrods" in much of the rest of the world, including the United States, where retail catalog and Internet sales generate millions of dollars in revenue each year. Harrods UK's retail business has thrived in recent years, but Harrods BA's business has been in decline since the early 1960s. . . . Harrods BA's only current revenue is about $300,000 annually from the continued operation of [its] building's parking garage.

In February of 1999 Harrods UK launched a website at the domain name harrods. com, and the website became a functioning online retail store in November of 1999. Harrods BA executives testified that sometime in 1999 they also began planning to launch a Harrods store on the Internet. Toward that end, Harrods BA hired a consultant, a Mr. Capuro, to prepare a proposal for an online business. In the fall of 1999, around the same time that Harrods UK was launching its Internet business (and announcing this in the press), Harrods BA began registering the first of what eventually became around 300

Harrods-related domain names. The 60 Domain Names that are defendants in this case were registered with Network Solutions, Inc. (NSI), a domain name registry located in Herndon, Virginia. At that time NSI served as the exclusive worldwide registry for domain names using .com, .net, and .org. [Harrods BA registered 20 distinct second-level domain names (e.g., harrodsbrasil, harrodsfinancial), each registered under the three top-level domains .com, .net, and .org, for a total of 60 defendant Domain Names.]

. . .

On February 16, 2000, Harrods UK sued 60 of the Harrods-related domain names in the United States District Court for the Eastern District of Virginia. Harrods UK sued under 15 U.S.C. §1125(d)(2), which permits the owner of a protected mark to bring an in rem action against domain names that violate "any right of the owner of a mark," subject to certain limitations. For example, the in rem action is available only when the plaintiff cannot find or cannot obtain personal jurisdiction over the domain name registrant. Harrods UK claimed that the Domain Names violated 15 U.S.C. §1125(d)(1), which prohibits bad faith registration of domain names with intent to profit, and 15 U.S.C. §§1114, 1125(a) & (c), which together prohibit trademark infringement and dilution. Harrods BA was easily identified as the registrant of the defendant Domain Names, but the mere act of registering the Domain Names in Virginia was deemed insufficient to provide personal jurisdiction over Harrods BA. [cit.] Because Harrods UK could not obtain personal jurisdiction over Harrods BA, the suit was filed in rem against the 60 Domain Names themselves.

. . .

II

[Before addressing the question of bad faith, the court considered several preliminary issues raised by the parties.]

A

On appeal the Domain Names claim that the district court's exercise of in rem jurisdiction over them violates the Due Process Clause because they lack sufficient minimum contacts with the forum. The Due Process clause of the Fifth Amendment permits a federal court to exercise personal jurisdiction over a defendant only if that defendant has "certain minimum contacts with [the forum] such that the maintenance of the suit does not offend 'traditional notions of fair play and substantial justice.'" *Int'l Shoe Co. v. Washington*, 326 U.S. 310, 316 (1945). . . . "[T]he minimum contacts rule of *International Shoe* . . . applie[s] to actions *in rem* and *quasi in rem*, as well as to actions *in personam*." *Pittsburgh Terminal Corp. v. Mid Allegheny Corp.*, 831 F.2d 522, 526 (4th Cir. 1987) (construing *Shaffer v. Heitner*, 433 U.S. 186 (1977)). Accordingly, we apply the minimum contacts test to the district court's exercise of in rem jurisdiction over the Domain Names. Under this test we ask whether there has been "some act by which the defendant purposefully avail[ed] itself of the privilege of conducting activities within the forum State, thus invoking the benefits and protections of its laws." *Hanson v. Denckla*, 357 U.S. 235, 253 (1958). . . .

In the case of disputes involving property, the presence of the property in the jurisdiction does not *always* justify the exercise of in rem jurisdiction, but "when claims to the property itself are the source of the underlying controversy between the plaintiff and the defendant, it would be unusual for the State where the property is located not to have jurisdiction." *Shaffer*, 433 U.S. at 207 (internal footnote omitted). *See also* 4A Charles A. Wright & Arthur R. Miller, *Federal Practice & Procedure* §1072 (3d ed. 2002). Specifically, the Supreme Court said in *Shaffer* that in rem jurisdiction is appropriate in "suits for injury suffered on the land of an absentee owner, where the defendant's ownership of the property is conceded but the cause of action is otherwise related to rights and duties growing out of that ownership." *Shaffer*, 433 U.S. at 208. The dispute in this case is roughly analogous to such a suit. Harrods UK has allegedly suffered injury by way of property, the Domain Names, owned by Harrods BA, an absentee owner. Harrods BA's initial ownership of the Names is conceded, but the cause of action is related to Harrods BA's rights and duties arising out of that ownership.

Likewise, Virginia's "interests in assuring the marketability of property within its borders and in providing a procedure for peaceful resolution of disputes about the possession of that property" also support the exercise of in rem jurisdiction in this case. *Id.* (internal footnote omitted). Moreover, Virginia's interest in not permitting foreign companies to use rights emanating from, and facilities located in, its territory to infringe U.S. trademarks also supports the exercise of in rem jurisdiction. By registering these Domain Names in Virginia, Harrods BA exposed those Names to the jurisdiction of the courts in Virginia (state or federal) at least for the limited purpose of determining who properly owns the Domain Names themselves. This is not a case where "the only role played by the property is to provide the basis for bringing the defendant into court." *Id.* at 209. Rather, because "claims to the property itself are the source of the underlying controversy," *id.* at 207, and because Virginia has important interests in exercising jurisdiction over that property (the Names), we conclude that courts in Virginia, the state where the Domain Names are registered, may constitutionally exercise in rem jurisdiction over them. Thus, the district court's exercise of in rem jurisdiction over the Domain Names was constitutional.

. . .

C

The final issue we must consider before reaching the question of bad faith is the scope of the in rem provision of the ACPA, 15 U.S.C. §1125(d)(2). Harrods UK argues that §1125(d)(2) provides for in rem jurisdiction against domain names for traditional infringement and dilution claims under §§1114, 1125(a) & (c) as well as for claims of bad faith registration with the intent to profit under §1125(d)(1). The Domain Names argue that the district court correctly limited the scope of the in rem provision to claims under §1125(d)(1) for bad faith registration of a domain name with the intent to profit. This argument has not yet been settled by any federal circuit court. . . . While we consider this to be a close question of statutory interpretation, we ultimately conclude that §1125(d)(2) is not limited to violations of §1125(d)(1); it also authorizes in rem actions for certain federal infringement and dilution claims.

We begin our analysis with the text of the statute. Section 1125(d)(2)(A) provides that the "owner of a mark" may file an in rem action against a domain name if:

> (i) the domain name violates any right of the owner of a mark registered in the Patent and Trademark Office, or protected under subsection (a) [infringement] or (c) [dilution]; and
>> (ii) . . . the owner—
>>> (I) is not able to obtain in personam jurisdiction over a person who would have been a defendant in a civil action under paragraph (1) [§1125(d)(1)]; or
>>> (II) through due diligence was not able to find a person who would have been a defendant in a civil action under paragraph (1). . . .

15 U.S.C. §1125(d)(2)(A). We start with the first clause, subsection (d)(2)(A)(i), which provides that an in rem action is available if "(i) the domain name violates *any right* of the owner of a mark registered in the Patent and Trademark Office, or protected under subsection (a) or (c)." 15 U.S.C. §1125(d)(2)(A)(i) (emphasis added). The broad language "any right of the owner of a mark" does not look like it is limited to the rights guaranteed by subsection (d)(1), but appears to include any right a trademark owner has with respect to

the mark. This language, by itself, would include rights under §1125(d)(1), and it would also include, for example, rights under §1125(a) against trademark infringement and rights under §1125(c) against trademark dilution. If Congress had intended for subsection (d)(2) to provide in rem jurisdiction only for subsection (d)(1) claims, it could easily have said so directly. For example, Congress could have said that an in rem action is available if "the domain name violates subsection (d)(1)." . . .

According to the Domain Names, the problem with interpreting subsection (d)(2) as covering more than just bad faith claims under subsection (d)(1) is that subsection (d)(2)(A)(ii) conditions the availability of in rem jurisdiction on proof that the plaintiff is unable to find or obtain personal jurisdiction over the "person who would have been a defendant in a civil action [for bad faith registration] under paragraph (1)," that is, §1125(d)(1). As the district court explained, "because Congress chose to include in the *in rem* action the definition of potential defendants used in paragraph (1), we must therefore conclude that Congress intended for the 'bad faith intent to profit' element to be part of any *in rem* action." [cit.] We realize that it is possible to get the impression from reading subsection (d)(2)(A)(ii) that the in rem action is available only for subsection (d)(1) violations. But it is important to distinguish between the language discussing the subject matter covered by the in rem provision and the language discussing the proper defendant in a cybersquatting case. Subsection (d)(2)(A)(i) deals with the former, and subsection (d)(2)(A)(ii) deals with the latter. Subsection (d)(2)(A)(i) identifies the substantive rights actionable under the in rem provision, stating in broad terms that the in rem provision protects "any right of the owner of a mark" that is registered in the PTO or "protected under subsection (a) or (c)." Subsection (d)(2)(A)(ii) deals with the proper defendant to a cybersquatting claim, stating that in rem jurisdiction is available only when personal jurisdiction over the registrant is lacking. It would be odd for Congress to have placed a significant limitation on the scope of the substantive rights identified in subsection (d)(2)(A)(i), which deals with the subject matter of in rem actions, by indirectly tacking something on to subsection (d)(2)(A)(ii), which deals with the proper defendant in cybersquatting actions.

If the only way to understand the phrase "a person who would have been a defendant in a civil action under paragraph (1)" was as a reference to subsection (d)(1)'s bad faith requirement, we would be forced to confront the tension between this language and subsection (d)(2)(A)(i)'s broad language of "any right of the owner of a mark." However, the phrase "a person who would have been a defendant in a civil action under paragraph (1)" can fairly be understood as a shorthand reference to the current registrant of the domain name. [cit.] This reading avoids tension with subsection (d)(2)(A)(i)'s reference to "any right of the owner of a mark," which does not appear to be limited to rights protected by subsection (d)(1).

[Because of the ambiguity in the statutory language, the court looked to the legislative history for further guidance. The court read the legislative history as confirming that the phrase "a person who would have been a defendant in a civil action under paragraph (1)" should be read as a shorthand reference to the domain name registrant.]

The Domain Names do not give up easily. They point to other legislative history that describes the general purpose of the ACPA in terms of outlawing "cybersquatting," which is always discussed as bad faith registration with intent to profit. . . . [T]his might suggest that the entire bill, including both subsection (d)(1) and subsection (d)(2), is aimed solely at bad faith registration with the intent to profit. [cit.] . . .

This reading of the language describing the general purpose of the ACPA is trumped, however, by the language Congress used when it discussed the purpose of subsection (d)

(2) specifically. . . . Thus, when the legislative history addresses subsection (d)(2) specifically, it speaks in terms of violations of trademark law generally and of subsections (a) and (c); it does not repeat the references to bad faith registration that appear elsewhere. Just like the text of subsection (d)(2)(A)(i), this language in the legislative history suggests that the in rem action is available to enforce several of the substantive provisions of Federal trademark law.

On balance, we . . . conclude that the best interpretation of §1125(d)(2) is that the in rem provision not only covers bad faith claims under §1125(d)(1), but also covers infringement claims under §1114 and §1125(a) and dilution claims under §1125(c).

In light of this conclusion, we reverse the district court's dismissal of Harrods UK's claims for infringement and dilution and remand for further proceedings on those claims. However, the district court need not consider Harrods UK's infringement and dilution claims as against the 54 Domain Names because we affirm the court's order requiring the transfer of the 54 Names to Harrods UK. Transfer or cancellation of the defendant domain names is the only remedy available under §1125(d)(2)'s in rem provision, so Harrods UK could gain no additional relief if the court considered and ruled on its infringement and dilution claims against the 54 Names. Thus, on remand the district court need only consider Harrods UK's infringement and dilution claims against the six Argentina Names.

III

With the preliminary issues out of the way, we turn at last to Harrods UK's claim alleging bad faith on the part [of] Harrods BA in registering the 60 defendant Domain Names. . . . We first consider the district court's finding of bad faith with respect to the 54 Names, and after that we consider the court's award of summary judgment to the six Argentina Names.

A

. . .

Before we look at the nine bad faith factors, we stop for a moment to note that this case presents the unusual situation of two companies named "Harrods," both with legitimate rights to use the "Harrods" name in different geographical regions. The use of an identical mark by two different companies is sometimes allowed in trademark law under the concept of "concurrent use.". . . As we explain below, a concurrent user of a mark that registers a domain name incorporating that mark will always trigger a number of the nine bad faith factors listed in the ACPA. However, the legislative history of the ACPA demonstrates that Congress recognized the legitimacy of concurrent use when it enacted the ACPA and did not intend to disrupt the rights of legitimate concurrent users of a mark. *See, e.g.*, 145 Cong. Rec. S14,713 (daily ed. Nov. 17, 1999) ("[T]here may be concurring uses of the same name that are noninfringing, such as the use of the 'Delta' mark for both air travel and sink faucets. Similarly, the registration of the domain name 'delta-force.com' by a movie studio would not tend to indicate a bad faith intent on the part of the registrant to trade on Delta Airlines' or Delta Faucets' trademarks."); [cit.]. Accordingly, we should apply the bad faith factors in a manner that will not lead to a finding of bad faith registration every time a concurrent user registers a mark. Of course, even recognizing the rights of concurrent users of a mark, a legitimate concurrent user still violates the other user's trademark rights if it uses the shared mark in a manner that would cause consumer confusion, such as by using the mark in the other's geographic area. [cit.] Thus, if a concurrent user registers a domain name with the intent of expanding its use of the shared mark beyond its geographically restricted area, then the domain name is registered in bad faith as outlined in the ACPA.[9] With these points noted, we are finally ready to review the district court's evaluation of the 54 Domain Names in light of the nine bad faith factors listed in §1125(d)(1)(B)(i). . . .

Factor (I): "the trademark or other intellectual property rights of [the defendant], if any, in the domain name." 15 U.S.C. §1125(d)(1)(B)(i)(I). The district court found that this factor favored the Domain Names because while Harrods BA does not own any United States trademarks, it does own trademarks for the name "Harrods" (and various permutations thereof, such as "Harrods Magazine") throughout South America. We agree. The language of Factor (I) does not speak in terms of United States trademark rights, but refers generally to "intellectual property rights." This encompasses intellectual property rights irrespective of their territorial origin.[10] Thus, Factor (I) favors the Domain Names.

[The Court found that the second factor also favored the Domain Names because Harrods BA is commonly known throughout Argentina and South America as "Harrods."].

Factor (III): "the person's prior use, if any, of the domain name in connection with the bona fide offering of any goods or services." 15 U.S.C. §1125(d)(1)(B)(i)(III). [The court agreed that Factor (III), by its terms, favors Harrods UK because Harrods BA has never offered goods or services online through these domain names.] However, in this case Factor (III) does not sufficiently take into account the legitimacy of Harrods BA's use of Harrods-related names. As noted above, the nine factors from subsection (d)(1)(B)(i) are not exclusive, so we may consider other factors that are relevant given the particular facts of this case. [cit.]

In this case, Harrods BA has a long history of providing goods and services under the "Harrods" mark, so it is not surprising that it would want to register Harrods-related domain names to provide such goods and services online. Whenever a decades-old company seeks to launch an online retail store, there will likely be a startup period after domain name registration during which the company does not use the domain name to offer goods and services online. During this time, the company will not be able to show any "prior use . . . of the domain name in connection with the bona fide offering of any goods or services," and thus it will not get the benefit of Factor (III). Here, for example, Harrods UK registered "harrods.com" in early 1999, but by October of that year it still had not offered goods or services through that domain name. In the circumstance where a domain name registrant has a longstanding history of using a trademark to provide goods and services (as Harrods BA has here), legitimate plans to offer such goods and services online in the future should be considered as a factor that mitigates against a finding of bad faith. . . . Thus, Factor (III) does not reliably indicate bad faith on the part of Harrods BA. Instead, Harrods BA's long

---

9. A more difficult problem, one not presented in this case, is created when a concurrent mark user registers a domain name incorporating the shared mark with the intent only to use the domain name within its limited geographic area, but the registrant's site is nonetheless accessed by users outside the permissible geographic area. If the registrant in this situation is deemed to violate the other user's trademark, then it is unclear how (territorial) concurrent users of a mark can maintain an Internet presence using their mark. This is one of the difficulties that courts and legislatures will eventually have to face as they work to harmonize the geographically limited nature of trademark law with the global nature of the Internet as a medium. *See generally* Graeme B. Dinwoodie, *(National) Trademark Laws and the (Non-National) Domain Name System,* 21 U. Pa. J. Int'l Econ. L. 495 (2000).

10. Harrods UK raises the specter of cybersquatters registering trademarks identical to American marks in obscure locales—registering the name Nike in Burma, for example—and then using those foreign trademark rights as a shield against legal action by the American trademark holder. This case, however, does not involve a newly minted foreign trademark registered solely with the aim to defend against cybersquatting claims. That is a problem for another day.

history of using the "Harrods" name to offer goods and services is a factor that favors the Domain Names.

[*Factors (IV) and (V):* The court concluded that the fourth factor was not relevant because Harrods BA registered the Domain Names for a commercial purpose. It also agreed with the district court that the fifth factor weighed very heavily in favor of Harrods UK because Harrods BA's online business plan was to use these Domain Names to profit by deliberately confusing and diverting non–South American customers seeking to shop at Harrods UK. Three items of evidence supported this conclusion. Harrods BA had registered almost 300 Harrods-related domain names covering a wide variety of good and services offered by Harrods UK but not by Harrods BA (such as harrodsinsurance).]

[Moreover], the district court found it "highly suspect" that Harrods BA's domain name registrations almost always used English words rather than Spanish words, noting that Harrods BA was not authorized to conduct business outside of South America. However, the use of English language terms in domain names by non–English speakers, standing alone, does not constitute much evidence of an intent to market to American or British consumers. English is by far the most common language of the Internet. *See* Sharon K. Horn & Eric K. Yamamoto, *Collective Memory, History, and Social Justice*, 47 U.C.L.A. L. Rev. 1747, 1750 (2000) (noting that "[a]lthough only 10 percent of people worldwide speak English, 80 percent of internet websites appear in English"). And of course Spanish is not the national language in every South American country. Nonetheless, in this case Harrods BA registered domain names containing large numbers of English words but *not* their Spanish counterparts, and those English words describe many of the goods and services offered by Harrods UK but not by Harrods BA. These facts, taken together, do offer support for the district court's finding that Harrods BA was intending to target non–South American consumers.

[The court also agreed with the district court's reliance, in its analysis of the fifth factor, on the "incriminating business proposal" prepared for Harrods BA by Capuro, which contained an illustration of a proposed transaction over the Harrods BA website involving a "UK citizen" purchasing a Burberry sweater with funds from Barclays Bank. Harrods BA had no right to do business in Great Britain and had never done business there. Harrods BA's intent was to use at least some of the domain names to sell to non–South American consumers who were seeking Harrods UK's website and who would think they were buying from Harrods UK.]

Factor (VI): [The district court found that this factor favored Harrods UK because] while there was no evidence that Harrods BA offered to sell or transfer the domain names to Harrods UK, "[t]he history of [Harrods BA's] efforts to sell its business supports plaintiff's argument that [Harrods BA's] registration of the Domain Names was intended to 'drive up the price [Harrods BA] can command from [Harrods UK] for the sale of [the "Harrods"] name.'" However, while Harrods BA clearly had some interest in selling out its South American trademarks and store to Harrods UK, this is neither inappropriate nor all that incriminating. Harrods BA has a legitimate right to use the Harrods name, albeit in a limited geographic area. The Congressional Record's section-by-section analysis of the ACPA states that Factor (VI) "does not suggest that a court should consider the mere offer to sell a domain name to a mark owner . . . as sufficient to indicate bad faith. . . . [S]omeone who has a legitimate registration of a domain name that mirrors someone else's domain name, such as a trademark owner that is a lawful concurrent user of that name with another trademark owner, may, in fact, wish to sell that name to the other trademark owner." 145 Cong. Rec. S14,714 (daily ed. Nov. 17, 1999).

To the extent that Harrods BA had planned to use these Domain Names in a legitimate attempt to offer goods and services in South America (an assumption undermined by the evidence recounted in our discussion of Factor (V)), Harrods BA's registration of these names would be no more indicative of bad faith than its registration of a number of Harrods-related trademarks throughout South America, such as "Harrods Magazine," "Harrods Department Store," and "Harrodscard." There is nothing wrong with acquiring property, such as legitimate domain names or additional trademarks, for the express purpose of increasing the value (and therefore the potential sales price) of a business. Cybersquatting is considered wrong because a person can reap windfall profits by laying claim to a domain name that he has no legitimate interest in or relationship to. [cit.] It is not wrong, however, for a business to seek to profit from the sale of its legitimate assets.

Still, to the extent that Harrods BA intended to improperly divert non–South American Harrods UK customers, *see* Factor (V), and to the extent that the sale of the Domain Names would be based on the value to Harrods UK of preventing this practice, then Factor (VI) does demonstrate bad faith intent to profit and weighs in favor of Harrods UK. Because ample evidence supports the district court's determination under Factor (V) that Harrods BA intended to use the "Harrods" name to divert Harrods UK's customers, the evidence also supports the court's conclusion that Harrods BA intended to use these Domain Names to improperly leverage a higher price from Harrods UK. Factor (VI) therefore weighs in favor of Harrods UK. . . .

[*Factor (VII):* The district court properly found this factor favored the Domain Names because Harrods BA never provided false or misleading contact information.]

Factor (VIII): . . . This factor was intended by Congress to target the "practice known as 'warehousing,' in which a cyberpirate registers multiple domain names—sometimes hundreds, even thousands—that mirror the trademarks of others." H.R. Rep. No. 106-412, at 13. *See also* Sen. Rep. No. 106-140, at 16. While the registration of multiple domain names is a factor that a court may consider in determining bad faith, Congress warned that the ACPA "does not suggest that the mere registration of multiple domain names is an indication of bad faith." H.R. Rep. No. 106-412, at 13. *See also* Sen. Rep. No. 106-140, at 16. This is presumably because many companies legitimately register many, even hundreds, of domain names consisting of various permutations of their own trademarks in combination with other words. "Just as they can have several telephone numbers, companies can register multiple domain names in order to maximize the chances that customers will find their web site." [cit.]

Factor (VIII) nominally favors Harrods UK because Harrods BA did register multiple domain names that it knew were identical or confusingly similar to the mark of another, Harrods UK. We say "nominally favors" because Factor (VIII) will be triggered whenever there are concurrent users of a trademark. For example, Delta Airline's registration of delta.com constitutes the registration of a mark that it knows is identical to the mark of another, namely, Delta Faucets. But the legislative history of the ACPA show's that Congress recognized the legitimacy of concurrent uses of trademarks. [cit.] In the case of legitimate concurrent users, Factor (VIII) does not reliably indicate anything about the bad faith (or lack thereof) of the domain name registrant. Thus, standing alone, the fact that a company named Harrods of Buenos Aires with trademark rights in the name "Harrods" registers hundreds of Harrods-related domain names does not indicate bad faith.[13]

---

13. As the district court noted, Harrods BA is not generally in the business of cybersquatting, that is, it has not registered hundreds of non–Harrods-related domain names, such as names incorporating marks like "Bloomingdale's" or "Saks Fifth Avenue." The domain names it has registered only incorporate its own name.

Nonetheless, the district court found that this factor "heavily favored" Harrods UK. The court reasoned that because Harrods BA intended to use the names outside of South America and because it "[had] trademark rights only in South America, [Harrods BA's] registrations of these Domain Names in the United States amount to registrations of 'others' marks.'" We disagree with the suggestion that either the registrant's planned future use of a domain name or the physical location of the domain name registry influences whether that name incorporates "marks of others." Factor (VIII) simply asks a court to compare the domain name in question with the marks of the ACPA plaintiff.[14]

In sum, because Harrods BA is a concurrent user of the mark "Harrods," its registration of Harrods-related domain names nominally satisfies Factor (VIII) because Harrods BA registered multiple names identical or confusingly similar to the marks of others. This is true, however, for all concurrent users of marks who register domain names incorporating their marks. Factor (VIII) therefore cannot be weighed against the Domain Names in the bad faith calculus.

[*Factor (IX):* The court noted that, like Factor (VIII), this factor is triggered in many instances involving concurrent users of a mark, and because Harrods BA also has trademark rights in "Harrods," this factor cannot be given much weight.]

As noted at the outset, this case presents us with the unusual situation of two companies named "Harrods," both with legitimate rights to use the "Harrods" name in different geographic regions. It is not surprising that concurrent users of a shared mark would resort to litigation under the recently enacted ACPA in an attempt to gain through the courts what they failed to obtain by speedy registration. In situations like these, many of the bad faith factors under the ACPA will have been triggered; for example, the first registrant may have offered to sell the disputed names to its competitor (Factor (VI)), and one or both of the companies may have registered many, perhaps even hundreds, of domain names incorporating the shared mark of the competitor (Factors (VIII) and (IX)). For two concurrent users of a mark, however, this sort of behavior is not cybersquatting; it is simply part of legitimate competition. The ACPA was not designed to provide a battlefield for legitimate concurrent trademark users. *See* 145 Cong. Rec. S14,713 ("[T]here may be concurring uses of the same name that are non-infringing . . . [and that] would not tend to indicate a bad faith intent on the part of the registrant."). Nonetheless, while trademark law permits concurrent use of the same mark under certain conditions, a concurrent user of a mark may still violate the other user's trademark rights in certain cases. For example, if Delta Airlines wished to expand its business into the kitchen faucet market, it would have to do so under a name other than "Delta."

[The court held that the evidence supported the district court's conclusion that Harrods BA registered these names with the intent to divert and confuse non–South American customers seeking to do business with Harrods UK, and that Harrods BA sought to extract a higher price for the sale of the Domain Names from Harrods UK as a result.

---

14. Harrods UK places great weight on the fact that Harrods BA registered these domain names in the United States. This demonstrates, it argues, that Harrods BA intended to use the names to market to American consumers. We seriously doubt that the registration of a domain name in a registry located in the United States says *anything* about the intended audience for the registrant's website. In 1999, when these names were registered, NSI in Herndon, Virginia, was the exclusive worldwide registry for .com, .net, and .org domain names. Thus, Harrods UK would have us believe that anyone, anywhere in the world, who registers a .com, .net, or .org domain name is presumptively trying to reach an American market. The evidence presented at trial does not come close to establishing this proposition, and a presumption to that effect is not supported by either the text or legislative history of the ACPA.

Harrods BA had crossed the line from a permissible intent to use Harrods BA's own South American "Harrods" trademark on the Internet to an impermissible intent to profit online from the protected mark of Harrods UK.] Accordingly, we affirm the judgment of the district court as to the 54 Domain Names.[15]

B

[The court reversed the district court's grant of summary judgment to the six Argentina Names and remanded for further proceedings. On the basis of the evidence presented to the district court, the Fourth Circuit agreed that no reasonable factfinder could have found bad faith intent on the part of Harrods BA: Harrods BA's use of a United States–based domain name registry was not, standing alone, indicative of an intent on the part of Harrods BA to market to U.S. consumers, and the registration of multiple Harrods-related domain names by a company long known by the name Harrods (Buenos Aires) Limited was not indicative of bad faith. Harrods UK also relied heavily on a news article, in which a Harrods BA manager states that Harrods BA had registered more than 100 Harrods-related domain names "which the British Harrods will now be unable to use." Harrods UK claimed that this statement indicates that Harrods BA's purpose in registering these domain names was to prevent Harrods UK from registering them. According to Harrods UK, this purpose indicates bad faith, citing *Sporty's Farm L.L.C. v. Sportsman's Market, Inc.*, 202 F.3d 489, 499 (2d Cir. 2000). But, unlike the facts in that case, both Harrods BA and Harrods UK had used the "Harrods" mark for decades. The fact that the two would race to register Harrods-related domain names was not surprising, nor did it indicate bad faith to the court. Although the court agreed that the evidence presented by Harrods UK failed to create a genuine issue of material fact on the question of bad faith intent sufficient to withstand summary judgment for the six Argentina Names, it concluded that the district court granted summary judgment to the Argentina Names prematurely, before Harrods UK had an adequate opportunity through discovery to find evidence in the sole possession of Harrods BA that might indicate bad faith.]

NOTES AND QUESTIONS

1.   *The substantive scope of* in rem *jurisdiction.* What are the elements of an action brought *in rem*? From where are these elements imported? Early courts interpreting the statute concluded that the language of the provision appears to suggest that the elements of the cause of action are the same as where jurisdiction is *in personam* under Section 43(d)(1). If this is correct, when the defendant is a domain name rather than a legal person, should "bad faith" be an element of the cause of action? Can it be? *See BroadBridge Media, L.L.C. v. Hypercd.com*, 106 F. Supp. 2d 505, 511 (S.D.N.Y. 2000). The *Harrods* court held that Section 43(d)(2) authorizes an *in rem* action for the violation of Sections 43(a) and 43(c), as well as Section 43(d)(1). Does this answer (or render moot) the questions posed

---

15. The Domain Names seek refuge in the safe harbor provision of the ACPA, which provides that "[b]ad faith intent . . . shall not be found in any case in which . . . the person believed and had reasonable grounds to believe that the use of the domain name was a fair use or otherwise lawful." 15 U.S.C. §1125(d)(1)(B)(ii). This provision might be significant in some cases, such as when the site of a registrant with pure intent is accessed by a user beyond the registrant's geographically permissible area. See *supra*, footnote 9. But when the evidence demonstrates an express intent to use a shared mark in another's territory, as here, the registrant cannot claim a reasonable ground to believe that the intended use of the domain name was lawful.

above and addressed in *BroadBridge*? Is the analysis of the *Harrods* court on the scope of *in rem* jurisdiction persuasive as a matter of statutory interpretation? As a matter of congressional intent?

2. *Courts with jurisdiction in* in rem *causes of action (I)*. Section 43(d)(2)(A) of the Lanham Act authorizes an *in rem* action in the judicial district in which the "registrar, registry, or other domain-name authority that registered or assigned the disputed domain name is located." Early commentary on the *in rem* provision arguably did not recognize the scope of the provision, and focused primarily on the likelihood that suit would be brought in the district in which the *registrar* was located. The registrar is the entity licensed by ICANN to grant domain name registrations to applicants. Although at one point the exclusive registrar of .com domains was NSI, ICANN introduced a competitive registration system, and domain names in the .com domain are now available from a number of registrars in different states (and in different countries around the world). This suggested that fears of the Eastern District of Virginia (where NSI was based) becoming the "global cybersquatting court" would dissipate over time. But when *in rem* jurisdiction may be asserted in the jurisdiction of the *registry*, the scope of the *in rem* provision appears far broader. *See Cable News Network L.P. v. CNNnews.com*, 177 F. Supp. 2d 506 (E.D. Va. 2002), *aff'd*, 66 U.S.P.Q.2d (BNA) 1057 (4th Cir. 2003). The registry is the single official entity that maintains a list of all top-level domain names in a particular domain and maintains all official records regarding the registration of such domains. The registry for all .com domain names (Verisign) is based in Virginia, as is the registry for the .org domain.

3. *Courts with jurisdiction in* in rem *causes of action (II)*. Section 43(d)(2)(C) provides that "[i]n an in rem action under this paragraph, a domain name shall be deemed to have its situs in the judicial district in which (i) the domain name registrar, registry, or other domain name authority that registered or assigned the domain name is located, or (ii) documents sufficient to establish control and authority regarding the disposition of the registration and use of the domain name are deposited with the court." Does Section 43(d)(2)(C) enable a court other than a court in the judicial district where the domain name registrar, registry, or other domain name authority that registered or assigned the domain name is located to exercise *in rem* jurisdiction? That is, does it expand the jurisdictional grant of Section 43(d)(2)(A)? *See Mattel, Inc. v. Barbie-Club.com*, 310 F.3d 293 (2d Cir. 2002). If not, what is the purpose of Section 43(d)(2)(C)? Should it matter whether the cybersquatter is a U.S. resident? *See* 145 Cong. Rec. H10,823, H10,826 (Oct. 26, 1999) (*in rem* action jurisdiction provided in part to address the situation where "a non–U.S. resident cybersquats on a domain name that infringes on a U.S. trademark").

4. *Constitutional analysis.* Should the holding of the *Harrods* court on the scope of the *in rem* action affect the court's constitutional analysis? That is, even if *in rem* jurisdiction is constitutional where an action is predicated on Section 43(d)(1), would the exercise of *in rem* jurisdiction be constitutional when the plaintiff alleged a violation of the dilution provision in Section 43(c) or the unfair competition provision of Section 43(a)? Should the effective geographic reach of the statute affect whether the *in rem* provision is a constitutional violation of due process?

5. *Domain names as property.* The Domain Names in *Harrods* had also argued that domain names do not constitute a form of property over which *in rem* jurisdiction can be exercised, but the Fourth Circuit held that the Domain Names had waived this objection by failing to raise it before the district court. The Fourth Circuit dismissed a challenge to the constitutionality of the *in rem* action on similar grounds in *Porsche Cars N. Am., Inc. v. Porsche.net*, 302 F.3d 248 (4th Cir. 2002).

6. *At what time must there be a lack of* in personam *jurisdiction?* A court's jurisdiction *in rem* is intended to be used as a backup, triggered only when the court is not seized of personal jurisdiction. In *Porsche Cars N. Am., Inc. v. Porsche.net*, 302 F.3d 248 (4th Cir. 2002), three days before the trial of an action *in rem* against the domain names was scheduled to commence in the District Court for the Eastern District of Virginia, the court was notified that the alleged cybersquatter had submitted to personal jurisdiction in California. Should the court asserting jurisdiction *in rem* dismiss the action before it? *Cf. Lucent Technologies, Inc. v. Lucentsucks.com*, 95 F. Supp. 2d 528, 531-34 (E.D. Va. 2000) (dismissing an *in rem* ACPA case after the plaintiff located the U.S.-based registrant five days after suing).

7. *Where must there be a lack of* in personam *jurisdiction?* Does a plaintiff seeking to assert *in rem* jurisdiction have to show that no *in personam* jurisdiction exists anywhere in the United States, or merely in the district in which it asserts jurisdiction *in rem*? *See Alitalia-Linee Aaree Italiane S.p.A. v. casinoalitalia.com*, 61 U.S.P.Q.2d (BNA) 1490, 1495 n.14 (E.D. Va. 2001).

8. *Alternative bases for transfer of domain names.* In *Porsche, supra*, the plaintiff trademark owner argued that a district court would independently of the ACPA have jurisdiction under 28 U.S.C.A. §1655 (taken together with the dilution provision in Section 43(c)) to order transfer of the domain name registration at issue. Section 1655 authorizes *in rem* jurisdiction "to enforce any lien upon, or claim to" property, or to remove an "incumbrance or lien" on property. 28 U.S.C.A. §1655. The Fourth Circuit rejected this argument, finding that a dilution claim under §1125(c) does not give Porsche a "lien upon, or claim to" the offending property; it entitles the plaintiff only to certain (other) specified forms of relief. The court commented:

> Nor will we stretch the trademark-dilution statute to afford Porsche the remedy it seeks. Because of the importance of domain names and the possibility of using them to do substantial damage to valuable trademarks, it might have been tempting, before the enactment of the ACPA, to try to provide such a remedy to holders of marks in cases involving domain names held by foreign registrants. *Cf. Washington Speakers Bureau, Inc. v. Leading Authorities, Inc.*, 33 F. Supp. 2d 488, 504-05 (E.D. Va. 1999) (ordering a trademark infringer to "relinquish all rights" to infringing domain names), *aff'd*, Nos. 99-1440 & 99-1442, 2000 WL 825881 (4th Cir. June 27, 2000).
>
> To ensure a remedy in anticybersquatting cases, however, Congress chose not to amend §1655, but to create a separate statutory provision, §1125(d). . . . We may and do conclude that the enactment of the ACPA eliminated any need to force trademark-dilution law beyond its traditional bounds in order to fill a past hole, now otherwise plugged, in protection of trademark rights.

9. *Deferring to foreign institutions?* In *Heathmount A.E. Corp. v. Technodome.com*, 60 U.S.P.Q.2d (BNA) 2018 (E.D. Va. 2000), a Canadian corporation brought an *in rem* action under the ACPA against domain names that had been registered with NSI in Virginia by a Canadian citizen. The defendant sought to dismiss the action on *forum non conveniens* grounds. Should the court dismiss the action?

10. *Using technological control.* To what extent does the ability of U.S. courts to enforce U.S. norms through the assertion of *in rem* jurisdiction depend upon the de facto control that the United States has over the domain name system? In *Globalsantafe Corp. v. Globalsantafe.com*, 250 F. Supp. 2d 610 (E.D. Va. 2003), the plaintiff trademark owner obtained an order from the Eastern District of Virginia exercising *in rem* jurisdiction directing a Korean registrar to transfer a confusingly similar domain name in the .com domain (for which the registry was based in Virginia) to the trademark owner. The Korean domain name registrant responded by obtaining an order from the Korean courts directing the Korean registrar not to comply with the order of the U.S. court (on the ground that Korean

choice-of-law rules identified the law of the server as the applicable law and thus U.S. courts should not have applied U.S. law to the case). When the Korean registrar chose to comply with the Korean court order rather than the U.S. court order, the plaintiff then sought an order against Verisign (the registry for the .com domain) compelling it to disable the domain name registration in question. The court granted the relief sought by plaintiff. If you were hearing this case on appeal, what considerations would you take into account in determining whether to affirm the court's order? *See also Am. Online, Inc. v. AOL.org*, 259 F. Supp. 2d 449 (E.D. Va. 2003) (in circumstances similar to *Globalsantafe*, but without a competing court order, holding that the court had power to order the registry to transfer the infringing domain name registration even if that conduct might be in violation of the agreements between the registrar that had refused to comply with the U.S. court decision and the registry). Should such an order be analyzed under the *Steele v. Bulova Watch* test, *supra* Chapter 6? *See id.* at 456-57. The *AOL.org* court explained as follows:

> [T]he foreign registrants in this case, like all registrants, had a choice of top-level domains in which to register a domain name. By choosing to register a domain name in the popular ".org" top-level domain, these foreign registrants deliberately chose to use a top-level domain controlled by a United States registry. They chose in effect to play Internet ball in American cyberspace. Had they wished to avoid an American ACPA suit and transfer order and American jurisdiction altogether, they might have chosen to register the infringing domain name in top-level domains with solely foreign registries and registrars, such as ".kr".

Is this reasoning persuasive? Is this a fair assessment of the choices facing foreign registrants?

    11. *ACPA safe harbor.* In footnote 15, the *Harrods* court references the safe harbor in Section 43(d)(1)(B)(ii). However, the courts have stressed that this should be used "very sparingly and only in the most unusual cases." *See GoPets Ltd. v. Hise*, 657 F.3d 1024 (9th Cir. 2011); *Lahoti v. VeriCheck, Inc.*, 586 F.3d 1190, 1123 (9th Cir. 2009).

3.   ICANN Uniform Domain Name Dispute Resolution Policy (UDRP)

FINAL REPORT OF THE WIPO INTERNET DOMAIN NAME PROCESS (EXECUTIVE SUMMARY, APRIL 30, 1999)

http://www.wipo.int/amc/en/processes/process1/report/finalreport.html

BACKGROUND

. . .

On the proposal of the Government of the United States of America, and with the approval of its Member States, WIPO has since July 1998 undertaken an extensive international process of consultations ("the WIPO Process"). The purpose of the WIPO Process was to make recommendations to the corporation established to manage the domain name system, the Internet Corporation for Assigned Names and Numbers (ICANN), on certain questions arising out of the interface between domain names and intellectual property rights. . . .

[T]he present document [the Final Report] is being submitted to ICANN and to the Member States of WIPO. The main recommendations in the Final Report are summarized below.

. . .

Administrative Procedure Concerning Abusive Domain Name Registrations

(v) ICANN should adopt a dispute-resolution policy under which a uniform administrative dispute-resolution procedure is made available for domain name disputes in all generic top level domains (gTLDs). In the Interim Report, it was recommended that domain name applicants should be required to submit to the procedure in respect of any intellectual property dispute arising out of a domain name registration. The Final Report recommends that the scope of the administrative procedure be limited to cases of bad faith, abusive registration of domain names that violate trademark rights ("cybersquatting," in popular terminology). Domain name holders would thus be required to submit to the administrative procedure only in respect of allegations that they are involved in cybersquatting, which was universally condemned throughout the WIPO Process as an indefensible activity that should be suppressed.

(vi) The administrative procedure would be quick, efficient, cost-effective and conducted to a large extent on-line. Determinations under it would be limited to orders for the cancellation or transfer of domain name registrations. . . . Determinations would be enforced by registration authorities under the dispute-resolution policy.

. . .

New gTLDs

(x) The evidence shows that the experience of the last five years in gTLDs has led to numerous instances of abusive domain name registrations and, consequently, to consumer confusion and an undermining of public trust in the Internet. It has also led to the necessity for intellectual property owners to invest substantial human and financial resources in defending their interests. This arguably wasteful diversion of economic resources can be averted by the adoption of the improved registration practices, administrative dispute-resolution procedure and exclusion mechanism recommended in the Final Report of the WIPO Process.

(xi) In view of past experience, intellectual property owners are very apprehensive about the introduction of new gTLDs and the possible repetition in the new gTLDs of that experience.

(xii) Many issues other than intellectual property protection are involved in the formulation of a policy on the introduction of new gTLDs. Insofar as intellectual property is concerned, it is believed that the introduction of new gTLDs may be envisaged on the condition that the recommendations of the WIPO Final Report with respect to improved registration practices, dispute resolution and an exclusion mechanism for famous and well-known marks are adopted, and on the further condition that any new gTLDs are introduced in a slow and controlled manner that allows for experience with the new gTLDs to be monitored and evaluated.

First Steps and Outstanding Issues

The recommendations of the Final Report of the WIPO Process have been directed at the most egregious problems between intellectual property and domain names and at obtaining effective solutions to those problems. Other issues remain outstanding and require further reflection and consultation. . . .

UNIFORM DOMAIN NAME DISPUTE RESOLUTION POLICY (AS APPROVED BY ICANN ON OCTOBER 24, 1999)

. . .

4.   MANDATORY ADMINISTRATIVE PROCEEDING

This Paragraph sets forth the type of disputes for which you are required to submit to a mandatory administrative proceeding. These proceedings will be conducted before one of the administrative-dispute-resolution service providers listed at www.icann.org/udrp/approved-providers.htm (each, a "Provider").

a. Applicable Disputes. You are required to submit to a mandatory administrative proceeding in the event that a third party (a "complainant") asserts to the applicable Provider, in compliance with the Rules of Procedure, that

(i) your domain name is identical or confusingly similar to a trademark or service mark in which the complainant has rights; and

(ii) you have no rights or legitimate interests in respect of the domain name; and

(iii) your domain name has been registered and is being used in bad faith.

In the administrative proceeding, the complainant must prove that each of these three elements [is] present.

b. Evidence of Registration and Use in Bad Faith. For the purposes of Paragraph 4(a)(iii), the following circumstances, in particular but without limitation, if found by the Panel to be present, shall be evidence of the registration and use of a domain name in bad faith:

(i) circumstances indicating that you have registered or you have acquired the domain name primarily for the purpose of selling, renting, or otherwise transferring the domain name registration to the complainant who is the owner of the trademark or service mark or to a competitor of that complainant, for valuable consideration in excess of your documented out-of-pocket costs directly related to the domain name; or

(ii) you have registered the domain name in order to prevent the owner of the trademark or service mark from reflecting the mark in a corresponding domain name, provided that you have engaged in a pattern of such conduct; or

(iii) you have registered the domain name primarily for the purpose of disrupting the business of a competitor; or

(iv) by using the domain name, you have intentionally attempted to attract, for commercial gain, Internet users to your web site or other on-line location, by creating a likelihood of confusion with the complainant's mark as to the source, sponsorship, affiliation, or endorsement of your web site or location or of a product or service on your web site or location.

c. How to Demonstrate Your Rights to and Legitimate Interests in the Domain Name in Responding to a Complaint. When you receive a complaint, you should refer to Paragraph 5 of the Rules of Procedure in determining how your response should be prepared. Any of the following circumstances, in particular but without limitation, if found by the Panel to be proved based on its evaluation of all evidence presented, shall demonstrate your rights or legitimate interests to the domain name for purposes of Paragraph 4(a)(ii):

(i) before any notice to you of the dispute, your use of, or demonstrable preparations to use, the domain name or a name corresponding to the domain name in connection with a bona fide offering of goods or services; or

(ii) you (as an individual, business, or other organization) have been commonly known by the domain name, even if you have acquired no trademark or service mark rights; or

(iii) you are making a legitimate noncommercial or fair use of the domain name, without intent for commercial gain to misleadingly divert consumers or to tarnish the trademark or service mark at issue.

d. Selection of Provider. The complainant shall select the Provider from among those approved by ICANN by submitting the complaint to that Provider. The selected Provider will administer the proceeding, except in cases of consolidation as described in Paragraph 4(f).

e. Initiation of Proceeding and Process and Appointment of Administrative Panel. The Rules of Procedure state the process for initiating and conducting a proceeding and for appointing the panel that will decide the dispute (the "Administrative Panel").

. . .

g. Fees. All fees charged by a Provider in connection with any dispute before an Administrative Panel pursuant to this Policy shall be paid by the complainant, except in cases where you elect to expand the Administrative Panel from one to three panelists as provided in Paragraph 5(b)(iv) of the Rules of Procedure, in which case all fees will be split evenly by you and the complainant.

. . .

i. Remedies. The remedies available to a complainant pursuant to any proceeding before an Administrative Panel shall be limited to requiring the cancellation of your domain name or the transfer of your domain name registration to the complainant.

. . .

k. Availability of Court Proceedings. The mandatory administrative proceeding requirements set forth in Paragraph 4 shall not prevent either you or the complainant from submitting the dispute to a court of competent jurisdiction for independent resolution before such mandatory administrative proceeding is commenced or after such proceeding is concluded. If an Administrative Panel decides that your domain name registration should be canceled or transferred, we will wait ten (10) business days (as observed in the location of our principal office) after we are informed by the applicable Provider of the Administrative Panel's decision before implementing that decision. We will then implement the decision unless we have received from you during that ten (10) business day period official documentation (such as a copy of a complaint, file-stamped by the clerk of the court) that you have commenced a lawsuit against the complainant in a jurisdiction to which the complainant has submitted under Paragraph 3(b)(xiii) of the Rules of Procedure. (In general, that jurisdiction is either the location of our principal office or of your address as shown in our Whois database. See Paragraphs 1 and 3(b)(xiii) of the Rules of Procedure for details.) If we receive such documentation within the ten (10) business day period, we will not implement the Administrative Panel's decision, and we will take no further action, until we receive (i) evidence satisfactory to us of a resolution between the parties; (ii) evidence satisfactory to us that your lawsuit has been dismissed or withdrawn; or (iii) a copy of an order from such court dismissing your lawsuit or ordering that you do not have the right to continue to use your domain name.

. . .

WORLD WRESTLING FEDERATION ENTERTAINMENT, INC. v. BOSMAN

Case No. D-99-0001 (WIPO Arb. and Mediation Center, 2000)

M. Scott Donahey, Panelist:

1.   THE PARTIES

The complainant is World Wrestling Federation Entertainment, Inc., f/k/a Titan Sports, Inc., a corporation organized under the laws of the State of Delaware, United

States of America, having its principal place of business at Stamford, Connecticut, United States of America. The respondent is Michael Bosman, an individual resident in Redlands, California, United States of America.

2.   THE DOMAIN NAME(S) AND REGISTRAR(S)

The domain name at issue is worldwrestlingfederation.com, which domain name is registered with MelbourneIT, based in Australia.

3.   PROCEDURAL HISTORY

. . .

The policy in effect at the time of the original registration of the domain name at issue provided that "Registrant agrees to be bound by the terms and conditions of this Registration Agreement"[which] provides in pertinent part:

> Registrant agrees, as a condition to submitting this Registration Agreement, and if the Registration Agreement is accepted by MelbourneIT, that the Registrant is bound by MelbourneIT's current Dispute Policy ("Dispute Policy"). Registrant agrees that MelbourneIT, in its sole discretion, may change or modify the Dispute Policy, incorporated by reference herein, at any time. Registrant agrees that Registrant's maintaining the registration of a domain name after changes or modifications to the Dispute Policy become effective constitutes Registrant's continued acceptance of these changes or modifications. Registrant agrees that if Registrant considers any such changes or modifications to be unacceptable, Registrant may request that the domain name be deleted from the domain name database. Registrant agrees that any dispute relating to the registration or use of its domain name will be subject to the provisions specified in the Dispute Policy.

Effective December 1, 1999, MelbourneIT adopted the [UDRP]. There is no evidence that respondent ever requested that the domain name at issue be deleted from the domain name database. Accordingly, respondent is bound by the provisions of the Policy.

. . .

The Administrative Panel shall issue its Decision based on the Complaint, the e-mails exchanged, the Policy, the Uniform Rules, the WIPO Supplemental Rules, and without the benefit of any Response from respondent.

4.   FACTUAL BACKGROUND

The complainant has provided evidence of the registration of the following marks:

1. Service Mark: WORLD WRESTLING FEDERATION, registered for a term of 20 years from January 29, 1985, with the United States Patent and Trademark Office;
2. Trademark: WORLD WRESTLING FEDERATION, registered for a term of 20 years from November 7, 1989, with the United States Patent and Trademark Office.

The respondent registered the domain name worldwrestlingfederation.com for a term of two years from October 7, 1999. [cit.] The respondent is not a licensee of complainant, nor is he otherwise authorized to use complainant's marks. [cit.]

. . .

On October 10, 1999, three days after registering the domain name at issue, respondent contacted complainant by e-mail and notified complainant of the registration and stated that his primary purpose in registering the domain name was to sell, rent or otherwise transfer it to complainant for a valuable consideration in excess of respondent's out-of-pocket expenses. . . .

Respondent has not developed a Web site using the domain name at issue or made any other good faith use of the domain name. [cit.] The domain name at issue is not, nor could it be contended to be, a nickname of respondent or other member of his family, the name of a household pet, or in any other way identified with or related to a legitimate interest of respondent. [The Respondent did not contest the allegations of the Complaint.]

6.   DISCUSSION AND FINDINGS

Paragraph 15(a) of the Rules instructs the Panel as to the principles the Panel is to use in determining the dispute: "A Panel shall decide a complaint on the basis of the statements and documents submitted in accordance with the Policy, these Rules and any rules and principles of law that it deems applicable." Since both the complainant and respondent are domiciled in the United States, and since United States' courts have recent experience with similar disputes, to the extent that it would assist the Panel in determining whether the complainant has met its burden as established by Paragraph 4(a) of the Policy, the Panel shall look to rules and principles of law set out in decisions of the courts of the United States.

Paragraph 4(a) of the Policy directs that the complainant must prove *each* of the following:

> 1) that the domain name registered by the respondent is identical or confusingly similar to a trademark or service mark in which the complainant has rights; *and,*
> 2) that the respondent has no legitimate interests in respect of the domain name; *and,*
> 3) the domain name has been registered and used in bad faith.

It is clear beyond cavil that the domain name <worldwrestlingfederation.com> is identical or confusingly similar to the trademark and service mark registered and used by complainant, WORLD WRESTLING FEDERATION. It is also apparent that the respondent has no rights or legitimate interests in respect of the domain name. Since the domain name was registered on October 7, 1999, and since respondent offered to sell it to complainant three days later, the Panel believes that the name was registered in bad faith.

However, the name must not only be registered in bad faith, but it must also be *used* in bad faith. The issue to be determined is whether the respondent used the domain name in bad faith. It is not disputed that the respondent did not establish a Web site corresponding to the registered domain name. Accordingly, can it be said that the respondent "used" the domain name?

It is clear from the legislative history that ICANN intended that the complainant must establish not only bad faith registration, but also bad faith use.

> These comments point out that cybersquatters often register names in bulk, but do not use them, yet without use the streamlined dispute-resolution procedure is not available. While that argument appears to have merit on initial impression, it would involve a change in the policy adopted by the Board. The WIPO report, the DNSO recommendation, and the registrars-group recommendation all required both registration *and* use in bad faith before the streamlined procedure would be invoked. Staff recommends that this requirement not be changed without study and recommendation by the DNSO.

Second Staff Report on Implementation Documents for the Uniform Dispute Resolution Policy, submitted for Board meeting of October 24, 1999, para. 4.5,a.

Paragraph 4,b,i of the Policy, provides that:

> the following circumstances . . . shall be evidence of the registration and *use* of a domain name in bad faith:

. . . circumstances indicating that you have registered or you have acquired the domain name primarily for the purpose of selling, renting or otherwise transferring the domain name registration to the complainant who is the owner of the trademark or service mark . . . for valuable consideration in excess of the documented out-of-pocket costs directly related to the domain name. (Emphasis added.)

Because respondent offered to sell the domain name to complainant "for valuable consideration in excess of" any out-of-pocket costs directly related to the domain name, respondent has "used" the domain name in bad faith as defined in the Policy.

Although it is therefore unnecessary to consult decisions of United States' courts, the panel notes that decisions of those courts in cases which determine what constitutes "use" where the right to a domain name is contested by a mark owner support the panel's conclusion. For example, in the case of *Panavision International, L.P. v. Dennis Toeppen*, 141 F.3d 1316 (9th Cir. 1998), the Court of Appeals held that the defendant's intention to sell the domain name to the plaintiff constituted "use" of the plaintiff's mark.

. . .

7.   DECISION

For all of the foregoing reasons, the Panel decides that the domain name registered by respondent is identical or confusingly similar to the trademark and service mark in which the complainant has rights, and that the respondent has no rights or legitimate interests in respect of the domain name, and that the respondent's domain name has been registered and is being used in bad faith. Accordingly, pursuant to Paragraph 4,i of the Policy, the Panel requires that the registration of the domain name <worldwrestlingfederation.com> be transferred to the complainant.

TELSTRA CORP. LTD. v. NUCLEAR MARSHMALLOWS

Case No. D2000-0003 (WIPO Arb. and Mediation Center, 2000)

ANDREW F. CHRISTIE, Panelist:

The Complainant is Telstra Corporation Limited, a company incorporated in Australia, with its registered office in Melbourne, Australia. The Respondent is Nuclear Marshmallows. Nuclear Marshmallows is an unregistered business name of an unidentifiable business entity. The address of the Respondent as contained in the domain name registration is a post office box in Gosford, NSW, Australia. . . .

[The Complainant is the largest company on the Australian Stock Exchange, is the proprietor of more than 50 registrations in Australia of trademarks consisting of or containing the word TELSTRA, and is the registrant of the following domain names containing the word TELSTRA: telstra.com, telstra.net, telstra.com.au, telstra-inc.com, and telstrainc.com. The Respondent is the registrant of the domain name <telstra.org>, the Registrar of which is Network Solutions, Inc. of Herndon, Virginia, USA.]

Paragraph 4(b) of the Uniform Policy identifies, in particular but without limitation, four circumstances which, if found by the Administrative Panel to be present, shall be evidence of the registration and use of a domain name in bad faith. [The panelist quoted paragraph 4(b).]

It is worthy of note that *each* of the four circumstances in paragraph 4(b), if found, is an instance of "registration and use of a domain name in bad faith," notwithstanding the fact that circumstances (i), (ii), and (iii) are concerned with the primary intention or purpose of the registration of the domain name, whilst circumstance (iv) is concerned with an act of use of the domain name. The significance of this point is discussed . . . below.

. . .

[Although the first two elements of Paragraph 4(a) are clearly made out,] [i]t is less clear-cut whether the Complainant has proved the third element in paragraph 4(a) of the Uniform Policy, namely that the domain name "has been registered and is being used in bad faith" by Respondent. . . .

The significance of the use of the conjunction "and" is that paragraph 4(a)(iii) requires the Complainant to prove use in bad faith as well as registration in bad faith. That is to say, bad faith registration alone is an insufficient ground for obtaining a remedy under the Uniform Policy. This point is acknowledged in [*World Wrestling Federation v. Bosman*], the first case decided under the Uniform Policy. [The panelist, Prof. Christie, noted with approval that the *Bosman* panelist referred to the legislative history of the UDRP.]

. . .

This interpretation is confirmed, and clarified, by the use of both the past and present tenses in paragraph 4(a)(iii) of the Uniform Policy. The use of both tenses draws attention to the fact that, in determining whether there is bad faith on the part of the Respondent, consideration must be given to the circumstances applying both at the time of registration and thereafter. So understood, it can be seen that the requirement in paragraph 4(a)(iii) that the domain name "has been registered and is being used in bad faith" will be satisfied only if the Complainant proves that the registration was undertaken in bad faith *and* that the circumstances of the case are such that Respondent is continuing to act in bad faith.

Has the Complainant proved that the domain name "has been registered in bad faith" by the Respondent? [T]he Administrative Panel finds that the Respondent does not conduct any legitimate commercial or noncommercial business activity in Australia. [T]he Administrative Panel further finds that the Respondent has taken deliberate steps to ensure that its true identity cannot be determined and communication with it cannot be made. Given the Complainant's numerous trademark registrations for, and its wide reputation in, the word TELSTRA, . . . it is not possible to conceive of a plausible circumstance in which the Respondent could legitimately use the domain name telstra.org. It is also not possible to conceive of a plausible situation in which the Respondent would have been unaware of this fact at the time of registration. These findings, together with the finding . . . that the Respondent has no rights or interests in the domain name, lead the Administrative Panel to conclude that the domain name <telstra.org> has been registered by the Respondent in bad faith.

Has the Complainant proved the additional requirement that the domain name "is being used in bad faith" by the Respondent? The domain name <telstra.org> does not resolve to a web site or other on-line presence. There is no evidence that a web site or other on-line presence is in the process of being established which will use the domain name. There is no evidence of advertising, promotion or display to the public of the domain name. Finally, there is no evidence that the Respondent has offered to sell, rent or otherwise transfer the domain name to the Complainant, a competitor of the Complainant, or any other person. In short, there is no positive action being undertaken by the Respondent in relation to the domain name.

This fact does not, however, resolve the question. [T]he relevant issue is not whether the Respondent is undertaking a positive action in bad faith in relation to the domain name, but instead whether, in all the circumstances of the case, it can be said that the Respondent is acting in bad faith. The distinction between undertaking a positive action in bad faith and acting in bad faith may seem a rather fine distinction, but it is an important one. The significance of the distinction is that the concept of a domain name "being used in bad faith" is not limited to positive action; inaction is within the concept. That is to say, it is possible, in certain circumstances, for inactivity by the Respondent to amount to the domain name being used in bad faith.

This understanding of paragraph 4(a)(iii) is supported by the actual provisions of the Uniform Policy. Paragraph 4(b) of the Uniform Policy identifies, without limitation, circumstances that "shall be evidence of the registration and use of a domain name in bad faith," for the purposes of paragraph 4(a)(iii). Only one of these circumstances (paragraph 4(b)(iv)), by necessity, involves a positive action post-registration undertaken in relation to the domain name (using the name to attract custom to a web site or other on-line location). The other three circumstances contemplate either a positive action or inaction in relation to the domain name. That is to say, the circumstances identified in paragraphs 4(b)(i), (ii) and (iii) can be found in a situation involving a passive holding of the domain name registration. Of course, these three paragraphs require additional facts (an intention to sell, rent or transfer the registration, for paragraph 4(b)(i); a pattern of conduct preventing a trade mark owner's use of the registration, for paragraph 4(b)(ii); the primary purpose of disrupting the business of a competitor, for paragraph 4(b)(iii)). Nevertheless, the point is that paragraph 4(b) recognises that inaction (eg. passive holding) in relation to a domain name registration can, in certain circumstances, constitute a domain name being used in bad faith. Furthermore, it must be recalled that the circumstances identified in paragraph 4(b) are "without limitation" — that is, paragraph 4(b) expressly recognises that *other* circumstances can be evidence that a domain name was registered and is being used in bad faith.

The question that then arises is what circumstances of inaction (passive holding) other than those identified in paragraphs 4(b)(i), (ii) and (iii) can constitute a domain name being used in bad faith? This question cannot be answered in the abstract; the question can only be answered in respect of the particular facts of a specific case. That is to say, in considering whether the passive holding of a domain name, following a bad faith registration of it, satisfies the requirements of paragraph 4(a)(iii), the Administrative Panel must give close attention to all the circumstances of the Respondent's behavior. A remedy can be obtained under the Uniform Policy only if those circumstances show that the Respondent's passive holding amounts to acting in bad faith.

The Administrative Panel has considered whether, in the circumstances of this particular Complaint, the passive holding of the domain name by the Respondent amounts to the Respondent acting in bad faith. It concludes that it does. The particular circumstances of this case which lead to this conclusion are:

i. the Complainant's trademark has a strong reputation and is widely known, as evidenced by its substantial use in Australia and in other countries,
ii. the Respondent has provided no evidence whatsoever of any actual or contemplated good faith use by it of the domain name,
iii. the Respondent has taken active steps to conceal its true identity, by operating under a name that is not a registered business name,
iv. the Respondent has actively provided, and failed to correct, false contact details, in breach of its registration agreement, and
v. taking into account all of the above, it is not possible to conceive of any plausible actual or contemplated active use of the domain name by the Respondent that would not be illegitimate, such as by being a passing off, an infringement of consumer protection legislation, or an infringement of the Complainant's rights under trademark law.

In light of these particular circumstances, the Administrative Panel concludes that the Respondent's passive holding of the domain name in this particular case satisfies the requirement of paragraph 4(a)(iii) that the domain name "is being used in bad faith" by Respondent.

The Administrative Panel decides that the Complainant has proven each of the three elements in paragraph 4(a) of the Uniform Policy. Accordingly, the Administrative Panel requires that the domain name <telstra.org> be transferred to the Complainant.

NOTES AND QUESTIONS

1. *The UDRP and the ACPA.* In what ways does the cause of action established by the UDRP differ from that under the ACPA? Does the *Telstra* opinion respect that difference? For what reasons might a trademark owner pursue an action under the ACPA, and when might an action under the UDRP seem more attractive? *See* Barbara A. Solomon, *Two New Tools to Combat Cyberpiracy—A Comparison*, 90 TRADEMARK REP. 679 (2000).

2. *The elements of a UDRP cause of action.* Rule 4 of the UDRP sets out three elements of a cause of action under the Policy. The first requirement is that the complainant possess trademark rights. Must these rights be registered? Does it matter in which country these rights exist? Similarly, the respondent may defend its registration on the basis that it has legitimate interests in the domain name. Under which law must those interests exist? *See* Graeme B. Dinwoodie, *Private International Aspects of the Protection of Trademarks*, WIPO Doc. No. WIPO/PIL/01/4 (2001). Is the "confusing similarity" required by the UDRP the same as that required by the ACPA?

3. *The UDRP in new gtlds.* To what extent, in light of the expansion in the number and nature of generic top-level domains in recent years, is it appropriate to take into account the top-level suffix of a domain name in determining any elements of a UDRP claim? *See Canyon Bicycles GmbH v. Domains By Proxy, LLC*, Case No. D2014-0206 (Mar. 14, 2014) (action by owner of mark CANYON for bicycles against registrant of canyon.bike).

4. *"Private" lawmaking.* The transfer of domain name registrations by registrars pursuant to decisions of panelists convened under the UDRP by ICANN-authorized dispute settlement providers occurs without the intervention of any national or conventional international institution. It is heavily dependent on the web of contracts involved (between the registrant and registrar, between ICANN and dispute settlement providers, and between ICANN and the registrar and registries) and the technological power that ICANN possesses by virtue of its control of the root server that is essential for mapping domain names to corresponding Internet protocol addresses. Does this lack of national political involvement concern you?

5. *Personal names.* Should the UDRP protect against domain name registrants who register domain names identical to the names of celebrities? What rights might this implicate? Does the UDRP offer protection in such circumstances? What additional facts might you need to answer that question?

6. *"Dot sucks" cases.* Would the registration of the domain name *fordsucks.com* by a disgruntled Ford automobile owner violate the trademark rights of the Ford Motor Co. in the mark FORD for cars? What additional facts, if any, would you want to know before answering that question?

7. *Generic terms.* How would you approach the registration of a term that has trademark significance in one context but is a generic term in another context? For example, J. Crew, Inc. owns the registration J. CREW for clothing, but the term CREW is generic in describing, for example, a form of varsity rowing. Can a per se rule be adopted? Or will your decision depend on other factors? If so, which factors?

8.   *The extent of use of the UDRP.* In the fourteen years since its inception, the UDRP has become the international standard for resolving cybersquatting disputes, whether the dispute involves international actors or purely U.S. parties. Trademark owners have been successful in a large majority of cases that have been filed. What might explain this success rate?

9.   *Critiques of the UDRP.* Despite (or perhaps because of) its success in quickly resolving numerous disputes, the UDRP has attracted substantial scholarly and critical attention. In addition to criticism of particular decisions (a phenomenon not unique to the UDRP, of course), critics have focused on procedural details that arguably affect the impartiality (or, at least, the appearance of impartiality) that the UDRP and ICANN aim to foster. For example, the selection of the dispute settlement provider (from among the few authorized by ICANN) is always made by the complainant, and it has been demonstrated that the success rate of complaints varies among providers. Moreover, use of a dispersed dispute settlement system (not only among providers, but also among an increasing roster of panelists) inevitably gives rise to inconsistent decisions. (But is this a feature of any dispute settlement system?) Some of the criticisms of the UDRP also no doubt reflect a broader dissatisfaction with the role of ICANN in regulation of the domain name system. *See generally* Laurence R. Helfer & Graeme B. Dinwoodie, *Designing Non-National Systems: The Case of the Uniform Domain Name Dispute Resolution Policy*, 43 WM. & MARY L. REV. 141 (2001).

10.   *Country code domains and new generic top-level domains.* The UDRP applies in all disputes regarding registrations in the most commercially lucrative generic top-level domains (.com, .net, and .org). Modified versions of the UDRP were also used for some of the new generic top-level domains later introduced (e.g., .biz). Although some country code domains (such as .uk or .ca) have created their own dispute settlement systems, which differ in some respects from the UDRP, many others have been attracted by the turnkey nature of the UDRP model and have made disputes in their domains subject to resolution under the UDRP. For the .us policy, *see www.us/policies/docs/usdrp.pdf.*

11.   *Uniform Rapid Suspension.* The Uniform Rapid Suspension ("URS") procedure complements the UDRP by offering a lower-cost, faster path to relief for rights holders in the most clear-cut cases of infringement. The current version of the URS was effective March 2013. For full details, *see http://newgtlds.icann.org/en/applicants/urs.* How often, and in what circumstances, would you expect the URS to be used? How would you improve the procedure?

12.   *Additional rights protection mechanisms (RPMs) for new generic top-level domains.* As ICANN creates new generic top-level domains, it has offered the same dispute resolution options (i.e., UDRP) as were established in 1999. But it was felt necessary to augment the possibility of post-registration proceedings with some form of preventive mechanism that allows trademark owners to forestall bad faith registration. Thus, ICANN created a pre-delegation procedure for so-called legal rights objections, (LROs) available with respect to new generic top-level domains. *See* New gTLD Applicant Guidebook, Version 4 (June 4, 2012), *at http://newgtlds.icann.org/en/applicants/agb.* Such objections had to be filed by March 2013, and in that month WIPO released a number of decisions (so-called expert determinations) relating to LROs. The next case is a prominent example of one such decision.

COACH, INC. v. KOKO ISLAND

LLC Case No. LRO2013-0002 (WIPO 2013)

1. THE PARTIES

The Objector/Complainant ("Objector") is Coach, Inc. of New York, New York, United States of America, represented internally.

The Applicant/Respondent ("Respondent") is Koko Island, LLC, of Bellevue, Washington, United States, represented by the IP & Technology Legal Group, United States.

2. THE APPLIED-FOR GTLD STRING

The applied-for gTLD string is <.coach>.

. . .

4. FACTUAL BACKGROUND

Founded in 1941, the Objector is a well-known United States company that manufactures and retails handbags, other leather goods and complementary accessories on a worldwide basis. The Objector has registered its COACH trademark with many national authorities, including the United States Patent and Trademark Office. . . .

The Respondent has applied to register the opposed string <.coach> in compliance with the Internet Corporation for Assigned Names and Numbers ("ICANN") guidelines. . . .

6. DISCUSSION AND FINDINGS

To have standing to file the Legal Rights Objection, the Objector must submit documentation of its existing legal rights, which may include registered trademarks. The Objector has duly submitted copies of some of its trademark registrations, and the Respondent has not disputed the Objector's standing, so the Panel finds that the Objector has standing to bring this Objection.

Pursuant to the Applicant Guidebook, Section 3.5.2, in deciding whether the Objector will prevail in its objection to the Respondent's application for the opposed string <.coach>, the Panel will determine whether the potential use of the applied-for gTLD:

(i)   takes unfair advantage of the distinctive character or the reputation of the objector's registered or unregistered trademark or service mark ("mark"); or

(ii) unjustifiably impairs the distinctive character or the reputation of the objector's mark; or

(iii) otherwise creates an impermissible likelihood of confusion between the applied-for gTLD and the objector's mark.

. . .

For an objector to prevail, "there must be something more than mere advantage gained, or mere impairment, or mere likelihood of confusion." See *Right at Home v. Johnson Shareholdings, Inc.*, WIPO Case No. LRO2013-0030. Although the terms "unfair, "unjustifiably," and "impermissible" are not uniformly defined or understood in the trademark context, their use here suggests that, in order to sustain the Objection, the Panel must find something untoward about the Respondent's behavior or something intolerable about the Respondent being permitted to keep the string in dispute, even if the Respondent's conduct or motives do not rise to the level of bad faith.

The Procedure sets forth eight non-exclusive factors to aid the Panel in its analysis. In rendering its Determination, the Panel shall, among other things, consider:

i. Whether the applied-for gTLD is identical or similar, including in appearance, phonetic sound, or meaning, to the objector's existing mark.

ii. Whether the objector's acquisition and use of rights in the mark has been bona fide.

iii. Whether and to what extent there is recognition in the relevant sector of the public of the sign corresponding to the gTLD, as the mark of the objector, of the applicant or of a third party.

iv. Applicant's intent in applying for the gTLD, including whether the applicant, at the time of application for the gTLD, had knowledge of the objector's mark, or could not have reasonably been unaware of that mark, and including whether the applicant has engaged in a pattern of conduct whereby it applied for or operates TLDs or registrations in TLDs which are identical or confusingly similar to the marks of others.

v. Whether and to what extent the applicant has used, or has made demonstrable preparations to use, the sign corresponding to the gTLD in connection with a bona fide offering of goods or services or a bona fide provision of information in a way that does not interfere with the legitimate exercise by the objector of its mark rights.

vi. Whether the applicant has marks or other intellectual property rights in the sign corresponding to the gTLD, and, if so, whether any acquisition of such a right in the sign, and use of the sign, has been bona fide, and whether the purported or likely use of the opposed string by the respondent is consistent with such acquisition or use.

vii. Whether and to what extent the applicant has been commonly known by the sign corresponding to the gTLD, and if so, whether any purported or likely use of the gTLD by the applicant is consistent therewith and bona fide.

viii. Whether the applicant's intended use of the gTLD would create a likelihood of confusion with the objector's mark as to the source, sponsorship, affiliation, or endorsement of the gTLD.

These factors are not exclusive, nor are they meant to function as a scorecard, to see which party has more factors in its favor. Rather, the Panel is to consider these factors, along with any others that the Panel deems relevant, in considering the ultimate issues, as highlighted above, that is, whether the proposed string takes unfair advantage or unjustifiably impairs the distinctive character or the reputation of the Objector's mark; and/or whether it otherwise creates an impermissible likelihood of confusion.

A. The Eight Factors

i. Identical or Similar

The Panel believes that the Objector has established its ownership of trademark rights in the mark COACH by submitting to the Panel appropriate evidence of its valid USPTO registrations for said mark. . . . The Panel finds that the opposed string, <.coach>, is identical in appearance and sound to the Objector's COACH trademark. The string and the mark contain exactly the same word, pronounced the same way, and the initial dot (or period) in the string is inconsequential in this determination because it is a requirement of all such top level domain strings.

The string does not, however, necessarily have the same meaning as Objector's trademark. Objector's mark is not descriptive of its goods or services; rather, it is at least a suggestive if not an arbitrary mark. The meaning of the trademark COACH is thus as a brand name signifying the source of Objector's goods. The string might be understood to have the same meaning by some Internet viewers, but others may ascribe to it one of its several dictionary meanings. . . .

Accordingly, the Panel finds that the first factor weighs in the Objector's favor as to appearance and sound, and is neutral as to meaning.

ii.   Acquisition and Use of Rights

The Respondent concedes the validity of the Objector's assertions that it has legitimately acquired its COACH trademark and uses it for the bona fide purpose of commerce. . . . Accordingly, the Panel finds that the second factor weighs in the Objector's favor.

iii.   Public Recognition of the String as a Mark

The third factor in the Legal Rights Analysis asks the Panel to consider the extent of recognition of the mark "in the relevant sector of the public." It is not clear to the Panel what "sector" is relevant, but that may not matter since the Objector does not purport to limit the sector that is relevant. Instead, the Objector argues that its mark is famous even outside its traditional market segment (presumably leather goods, handbags and accessories), and that its mark is "known across many jurisdictions, many market segments and many diverse trademark classes."

The evidence of record supports the Objector's argument that its mark has achieved public recognition in at least some relevant sectors of the public. But that mark has achieved such recognition when it is used in connection with certain goods. The Objector has not submitted evidence that persuasively establishes that the letter string <.coach>, when used as a gTLD, will necessarily be seen as a reference to the Objector's mark as contrasted with a reference to the word "coach" for its dictionary meaning.

The evidence also supports the Respondent's argument that the dictionary word "coach" would be recognized for its dictionary meaning across a wide variety of sectors. "Coach" is not an obscure dictionary word rarely used for its dictionary meaning and mostly used solely for its trademark meaning; rather, "coach" is a common word which the general public may well associate with transportation, sport team leaders, academic tutors, artistic trainers, or goods or services other than those provided by the Objector under its mark. Other members of the public may associate the string "coach" with the television series named "Coach" that ran from 1989-1997 (according to the IMDb database), which series was listed on the first page of the search results when the Panel searched for the word "coach" on the Yahoo! and Google search engines.

Accordingly, the Panel finds that the third factor is neutral and favors neither party.

iv.   Intent, Awareness and Pattern of Conduct

The Respondent does not dispute that it was aware of the Objector's trademark prior to applying for the opposed string. The Respondent does dispute that it in any way intends to infringe on the COACH trademark. The Respondent claims that it will use the opposed string in a manner that conforms to the common dictionary meaning of the English language word "coach." Moreover, the Respondent represents that it will put in place measures designed to prevent those applying for domain names attached to that string from infringing the Objector's COACH trademark. The Objector counters that the Respondent's proposed measures, and the funding available to the Respondent to implement them, will be insufficient to protect the Objector's rights from likely scammers and cybersquatters. As both of these lines of contention depend upon subjective projections into the future, the Panel is disinclined to favor either position over the other. The Panel does note that the threat of cybersquatting behavior with respect to the creation of new TLDs probably is as likely as in connection with the older gTLDs, which have been subject to thousands of Uniform Domain Name Dispute Resolution Policy ("UDRP") dispute resolution proceedings. The Panel further notes that, if the Respondent allows a new registry operated at the gTLD <.coach> to be used for cybersquatting, the Respondent itself may be challenged under the Trademark Post-Delegation Dispute Resolution Procedure.

As to the Respondent's pattern of conduct, the Objector contends, and the Respondent admits, that the Respondent has applied for some 307 new TLD strings. This appears to be more than any other applicant. However, that fact alone does not mean necessarily that the Respondent intends to engage in illegitimate use of trademark rights. Furthermore, the Panel notes that a number of the strings for which the Respondent has applied appear to consist of common dictionary words or abbreviations thereof (although the Panel notes that it has not reviewed evidence relating to other strings and could only make a finding as to a specific string after reviewing the relevant evidence). On the other hand, as the Objector claims, the opportunity for illegitimate use does exist when a string corresponds both to a dictionary word and a trademark. Indeed, as the Objector notes, among the strings the Respondent has applied for are <.express>, <.limited> and <.direct>, all of which are also identical to third party trademarks. However, panels have already rejected Legal Rights Objections filed against the first two of those strings, which shows that other panels also have recognized that the Respondent's business model does not automatically translate into a finding of bad intent. . . . Indeed, as the Panel found in the *Express, LLC* case, this risk is an inherent function of the Objector's decision to use a dictionary word as its brand name.

In sum, the Panel recognizes that the opposed string <.coach> consists of a common word that can readily be put to use to describe goods and services and activities other than those related to the Objector's mark. On this record, the Panel cannot conclude that the Respondent has engaged in a pattern of abusive TLD string applications.

Accordingly, the Panel finds that the fourth factor favors the Respondent.

v.   Use of or Preparations to Use

The Respondent has submitted no evidence to the Panel that it has used a sign or name that corresponds to the opposed string <.coach> in a bona fide offering of goods or services. Also, other than stating its plans, the Respondent has not presented any other evidence that it is preparing to use such a sign for those purposes. Moreover, the Respondent does not claim to represent or belong to any group or community to which such a sign might apply.

However, the Respondent has averred its intent and plans to use the opposed string with respect to third party registration of domain names that correspond to one or more of the dictionary meanings of the word "coach." The Respondent asserts that such registration will increase international commerce and otherwise conform to the ICANN goals of expanding the number of TLDs available for public use. Moreover, the Respondent has, in its application for the opposed string, put forth several procedures that it intends to employ to curb potential abusive domain name registration and potential harm to the Objector's trademark rights. These procedures include eight specific mechanisms and resources to be adopted by the Respondent. These are in addition to the 14 protective measures developed by ICANN, to which the Respondent is also prepared to adhere. The Respondent contends, without counter from the Objector except a contention the amount is inadequate, that it has raised in excess of USD 100 Million to acquire and administer the TLDs for which it has applied, including the opposed string. That investment, the Respondent contends, will enable it to carry out its planned programs of TLD string usage and abuse protection.

[T]he Objector contends that such anti-abuse measures will be insufficient—in large part because the funding to which the Respondent refers will not be enough to administer adequately the volume of TLDs for which the Respondent has applied. However, the Panel feels constrained to view the Objector's contentions in this regard as conjecture. While the Panel believes that there is always the possibility for abusive domain name registrations, the Panel is not in a position to conclude that the Respondent has failed to put forth reasonable plans to mitigate those possibilities, or that such plans could not be modified in the future—possibly in conjunction with the Objector—to achieve that goal.

As a result, the Panel believes that, although the Respondent has not shown demonstrable preparations for a direct bona fide offering of goods, services or information by use of a sign corresponding to the opposed string, the Respondent does have preparations in place for offerings on an indirect basis through third-party domain name registrations in connection with the opposed string. Furthermore, the Panel finds that the Respondent is preparing to do so in a way so as not to interfere with the Objector's legitimate exercise of its mark rights.

Accordingly, the Panel finds that the fifth factor favors the Respondent.

vi.   Marks or Intellectual Property Rights

The Respondent claims that it "has rights in the <.coach> gTLD by virtue of its Application." That, however, is not the test under the sixth element. Rather, the Applicant Guidebook directs the Panel to consider "whether the applicant has marks or other intellectual property rights in the sign corresponding to the gTLD."

The Respondent has not presented any evidence to the Panel that the Respondent owns valid rights in any marks or any intellectual property rights that might pertain to a sign that corresponds to the opposed string. The Respondent contends that, as a member of the public, it is entitled to claim equal rights in the use of the common, descriptive, dictionary word "coach," which corresponds to the opposed string. However, that does not give the Respondent any intellectual property rights in the opposed string <.coach>. On the other hand, there was no obligation on applicants for new gTLDs to show that they have intellectual property rights in strings for which they applied.

Accordingly, although the Panel finds that the sixth element favors the Objector, to the extent that the Respondent has not shown that it has marks or intellectually property in the sign, the Panel does not believe that this militates against the Respondent's overall position in this proceeding.

vii.   Commonly Known By

The seventh factor asks whether "the applicant has been commonly known by the sign corresponding to the gTLD." The Respondent claims this factor favors it because its "proposed bona fide use of a <.coach> gTLD is consistent with the rights it has acquired by its Application." The Panel rejects that argument; otherwise, every application would automatically be proof that the applicant was commonly known by the applied-for string. Rather, the question is whether, outside of the application, the Respondent has been commonly known by the name "Coach." The Respondent has presented no evidence that it has ever been commonly known as a sign that would correspond to the opposed string. The Panel thus concludes that the Respondent has not been so commonly known.

Accordingly, the Panel finds that the seventh factor favors the Objector.

viii.   Likelihood of Confusion

The Objector contends that the Respondent's purported use of the opposed string would cause a likelihood of confusion with the Objector's trademark as to source, sponsorship, affiliation or endorsement of that string. The Objector argues that the general public will believe that the second-level domain names that the Respondent allows to be registered in the registry corresponding to the string will necessarily be associated with the Objector's business because the Objector's mark is identical to the string. The Objector points out that this likelihood of confusion will be heightened because other holders of famous trademarks and/or service marks are also seeking to obtain gTLD strings that correspond to their marks, setting a pattern to which consumers will expect the Objector to conform and causing them to see the <.coach> gTLD as a branded gTLD registry as well.

In response, the Respondent argues that, because the common word "coach" has meanings diverse from the Objector's main area of commerce, the relevant public will not likely believe that the opposed string is sourced from, sponsored by, affiliated with or endorsed by the Objector. To support its argument, the Respondent has submitted evidence, in the form of a survey that found that only a small percentage of those surveyed identified the word "coach" primarily with the Objector. [T]he Objector has disputed the methodological validity of the survey. Rather than permit further briefing on this point, thus delaying a resolution, the Panel has elected to disregard the survey since it need not rely on the survey results to rule on the Legal Rights Objection.

The Panel agrees with the Respondent that there are several definitions of the word "coach," and that many Internet users may equate that word with goods, services or activities other than those related to the Objector or its trademark. The Panel does not need survey evidence to know that "coach" is a common dictionary word, and is used frequently in reference to the various definitions listed above. As also noted above, this does not preclude the Panel from ascertaining that the Objector's trademark is also well- established within the relevant public. The Panel is thus of the belief that some Internet users may assume that a domain name found at <.coach> will relate directly to merchandise offered under the COACH trademark by the Objector, whereas others may associate the string with one of the various dictionary meanings of "coach."

On balance, the Panel cannot conclude that, given the many definitions of "coach," an appreciable number of Internet users will confuse the proposed string with the Objector's mark. Had the survey measured consumers' perceptions of a <.coach> gTLD, that might have provided more relevant evidence, but neither party submitted such evidence. Considering the available evidence, however, the Panel finds that it is unclear whether the intended use of the opposed string would create a likelihood of confusion with the Objector's mark as to the source, sponsorship, affiliation, or endorsement of that string.

Accordingly, the Panel finds that the eighth factor is neutral.

B.   Conclusion

Taking into consideration all of the eight factors mandated by Section 3.5.2 of the Applicant Guidebook, the Panel now turns to the ultimate question of whether the Objector has sustained its burden of proving the grounds for the Objection as listed in Section 3.5.2. Those grounds are referred to in Section 3.5.2 as Standards and Principles and it is clear from that terminology that those who drafted the Guidebook intended them to be regarded as pivotal in this proceeding. In any event, Section 3.5 goes on to make this determination mandatory by providing that the Panel "will determine" the three grounds, to which the Panel will now turn.

(I)   Takes Unfair Advantage of the Objector's Mark

The first circumstance the Panel must address is whether the potential use of the opposed string takes unfair advantage of the distinctive character or the reputation of the Objector's trademark. As reasoned in element iii above, the Panel recognizes that the Objector's COACH mark is relatively well-known throughout the world. Moreover, the distinctive character and reputation of the Objector's mark are of a high order, as the Objector's products appear to be considered by the relevant public to be of excellent quality. As a result, the Panel believes that there is the distinct potential that the Respondent will gain some advantage in using the opposed string <.coach> due to the distinction and reputation of that mark if the gTLD registry is operated to permit registration of domain names related to leather goods, handbags, accessories, and the other products sold by the Objector, or if the websites to which domain names registered in this registry discuss, advertise, promote, sell or otherwise address such products.

However, the Panel also believes that, if the Respondent sets rules that prohibit such confusing uses and instead promotes use of the gTLD for information, goods and services related to the dictionary meanings attached to the common word "coach," confusion with the Objector's trademark would be no more likely than any confusion caused when consumers use the word "coach" for its dictionary meaning in other real-world contexts. As noted above, this is a risk that the Objector assumed when it adopted as its trademark a common dictionary word.

The opposed string can—and, according to the Respondent, will—be used for domain names that reflect those alternative meanings. For example, the opposed string can be applied in the realms of team coaching, travel, mentoring, etc. Those areas of commerce are far afield from the sector for which the Objector mark is best known: leather goods, handbags, and other accessories. Although there may be some overlap in areas of offerings in which the Objector engages, but for which it is not so well known, the Panel is persuaded that this will constitute a relatively minor advantage to the Respondent in the potential use of the opposed string, and to the extent it does give rise to confusion, the Objector will be able to rely on any rights granted by the UDRP and the Trademark Post-Delegation Dispute Resolution Procedure ("TMPDDRP"). What is crucial, in the Panel's opinion, is that there is no reason to believe that the potential use of the opposed string takes unfair advantage of the Objector's mark.

In short, the Panel finds that the Objector has failed to provide sufficient evidence to conclude that the Respondent will gain an advantage that is unfair—in using the opposed string to register domain names—due solely and directly to the connection between the fame of the Objector's COACH trademark and the unrelated goods and services likely available under those names.

Accordingly, the Panel finds that the Objector has failed to satisfy this circumstance that would require a denial of the Respondent's application for the opposed string.

(II)   Unjustifiably Impairs Objector's Mark

Next, the Panel must determine whether the potential use of the opposed string <.coach> unjustifiably impairs the distinctive character or the reputation of the Objector's mark. Again, the Panel agrees with the Objector's contentions with respect to the considerable consumer regard held for the character and reputation of the goods sold under the Objector's mark. Consequently, there is little doubt, in the Panel's view, that there exists a possibility that the potential use to which the opposed string may be put—the registration of domain names under which goods and/or services may be marketed—may impair or tarnish that character or reputation. Simply put, those third party goods and/or services may be considered by the relevant public to be of lesser quality than the products offered under the Objector's trademark.

However, once again, the Panel is mindful that any such impairment must be considered unjustifiable for the Objector to prevail on this issue. The Panel believes that the intent of ICANN in soliciting applications for new TLDs was to stimulate expansion and competition in connection with the provision of goods, services and information through the Internet. As a result, some impairment of established trademark and service mark rights is to be expected as the field of marks becomes more crowded. But, in this case, the mark in question, COACH, is also a common dictionary word and there is the potential for many uses on the Internet that would relate to the dictionary meaning of the word rather than the source-identifying meaning of the mark. Thus, the Panel is unconvinced that any resulting impairment to the COACH mark on account of the mere registration of the <.coach> gTLD by the Respondent is likely to be so great as to be classified as "unjustifiable" (bearing in mind, once again, the Objector's rights under the TMPDDRP should the Respondent fail to manage the registry in a way that avoids undue impairment of the Objector's trademark rights).

Accordingly, the Panel finds that the Objector has failed to satisfy this circumstance that would require a denial of the Respondent's application for the opposed string.

(III) Creates an Impermissible Likelihood of Confusion

Finally, the Panel must decide whether the potential use of the opposed string <.coach> otherwise creates an impermissible likelihood of confusion between the opposed string and the Objector's mark. In factor i above, the Panel found that the opposed string, <.coach>, is identical to the COACH trademark. Thus, there is a possibility of some confusion between the opposed string and the Objector's mark.

What is not clear is whether confusion will be likely, let alone whether any such likelihood of confusion would be impermissible, given the goals and intents of ICANN in promulgating the process for creating new gTLDs. In setting forth significant protections against abusive registrations that might result from use of the new strings, ICANN seems, in the Panel's view, to have anticipated the risk of confusion between the use of those strings and existing trademark and service mark rights. In this case, as noted in the analysis of factor v above, the Respondent has even added eight more protective measures to ICANN's protective scheme. Moreover, as reasoned in factor viii above, the Panel is uncertain as to the likelihood of confusion in the minds of the relevant Internet user group between the opposed string and the Objector's mark, because the various definitions of the descriptive word "coach" would probably lead to uses of that string that do not coincide at all with the principal goods sold under that mark. Thus, while some confusion is possible, the Objector has not sustained its burden of proving that the potential use of the gTLD will create an impermissible likelihood of confusion. Further, to the extent that some low-level confusion may be created, the Panel believes that that degree of confusion is permissible within the structure that ICANN contemplates and can be resolved on a case-by-case basis as genuine complaints or concerns arise.

Accordingly, the Panel finds that the Objector has failed to satisfy this circumstance that would require a denial of the Respondent's application for the opposed string.

7. DECISION

For the foregoing reasons, the Objection is denied.

4. The Relationship Between the UDRP and the ACPA

The ACPA also amended Section 32 of the Lanham Act, introducing a provision permitting a domain name registrant whose domain name has been canceled or transferred pursuant to the UDRP (or any similar policy) to file a civil action in U.S. federal court against the prevailing party to establish that the registration and use of the domain name was lawful (under the Lanham Act). The case law under this provision (15 U.S.C. §1114(2) (D)(v)) remains surprisingly sparse.

BARCELONA.COM, INC. v. EXCELENTISIMO AYUNTAMIENTO DE BARCELONA

330 F.3d 617 (4th Cir. 2003)

NIEMEYER, Circuit Judge:

Barcelona.com, Inc. ("Bcom, Inc."), a Delaware corporation, commenced this action under the Anticybersquatting Consumer Protection Act against Excelentisimo Ayuntamiento de Barcelona (the City Council of Barcelona, Spain) for a declaratory judgment that Bcom, Inc.'s registration and use of the domain name <barcelona.com> is not unlawful under the Lanham Act. The district court concluded that Bcom, Inc.'s use of <barcelona.com> was confusingly similar to Spanish trademarks owned by the City Council that include the word "Barcelona." Also finding bad faith on the basis that Bcom, Inc. had attempted to sell the <barcelona.com> domain name to the City Council for a profit, the court ordered the transfer of the domain name to the City Council.

Because the district court applied Spanish law rather than United States law . . . we reverse the judgment of the district court denying Bcom, Inc. relief under the Anticybersquatting Consumer Protection Act, vacate its memorandum opinion and its order to transfer the domain name <barcelona.com> to the City Council, and remand for further proceedings consistent with this opinion.

I

In 1996, Mr. Joan Nogueras Cobo ("Nogueras"), a Spanish citizen, registered the domain name <barcelona.com> in the name of his wife, also a Spanish citizen, with the domain registrar, Network Solutions, Inc., in Herndon, Virginia. In the application for registration of the domain name, Nogueras listed himself as the administrative contact. When Nogueras met Mr. Shahab Hanif, a British citizen, in June 1999, they developed a business plan to turn <barcelona.com> into a tourist portal for the Barcelona, Spain, region. A few months later they formed Bcom, Inc. under Delaware law to own <barcelona.com> and to run the website, and Nogueras, his wife, and Hanif became Bcom, Inc.'s officers. Bcom, Inc. was formed as an American company in part because Nogueras believed that doing so would facilitate obtaining financing for the development of the website. Although Bcom, Inc. maintains a New York mailing address, it has no employees in the United States, does not own or lease office space in the United States, and does not have a telephone listing in the United States. Its computer server is in Spain.

[Although Nogueras placed some Barcelona-related information on the site, lack of financing prevented much development. Nogueras e-mailed the Mayor of Barcelona to negotiate the acquisition of the domain name by the City Council; the City demanded transfer of the domain name.]

. . . The City Council owned about 150 trademarks issued in Spain, the majority of which included the word Barcelona, such as "Teatre Barcelona," "Barcelona Informacio I Grafic," and "Barcelona Informacio 010 El Tlefon Que Ho Contesta Tot." Its earlier effort in 1995 to register the domain name <barcelona.es>, however, was unsuccessful. The City Council's representative explained, "It was denied to Barcelona and to all place names in Spain." . . . The City Council now took the position with Bcom, Inc. that its domain name

<barcelona.com> was confusingly similar to numerous trademarks that the City Council owned.

A couple of days after the City Council sent its letter, Nogueras had the domain name <barcelona.com> transferred from his wife's name to Bcom, Inc., which he had neglected to do in 1999 when Bcom, Inc. was formed.

Upon Bcom, Inc.'s refusal to transfer <barcelona.com> to the City Council, the City Council invoked the Uniform Domain Name Dispute Resolution Policy ("UDRP") promulgated by the Internet Corporation for Assigned Names and Numbers ("ICANN") to resolve the dispute. . . . The complaint sought transfer of the domain name <barcelona.com> to the City Council and relied on Spanish law in asserting that Bcom, Inc. had no rights to the domain name while the City Council had numerous Spanish trademarks that contained the word "Barcelona." As part of its complaint, the City Council agreed "to be subject to the jurisdiction of the registrant[']s residence, the Courts of Virginia (United States), only with respect to any challenge that may be made by the Respondent to a decision by the Administrative Panel to transfer or cancel the domain names that are [the] subject of this complaint."

The administrative complaint was resolved by a single WIPO panelist who issued a ruling in favor of the City Council on August 4, 2000, . . . [and] ordered that Bcom, Inc. transfer the domain name <barcelona.com> to the City Council.

In accordance with the UDRP's provision that required a party aggrieved by the dispute resolution process to file any court challenge within ten business days, Bcom, Inc. commenced this action on August 18, 2000, under the provision of the Anticybersquatting Consumer Protection Act (the "ACPA") that authorizes a domain name owner to seek recovery or restoration of its domain name when a trademark owner has overstepped its authority in causing the domain name to be suspended, disabled, or transferred. *See* 15 U.S.C. §1114(2)(D)(v). Bcom, Inc.'s complaint sought a declaratory judgment that its use of the name <barcelona.com> "does not infringe upon any trademark of defendant or cause confusion as to the origin, sponsorship, or approval of the website <barcelona.com>; . . . [and] that [the City Council] is barred from instituting any action against [Bcom, Inc.] for trademark infringement." . . .

Following a bench trial, the district court entered a memorandum opinion and an order dated February 22, 2002, denying Bcom, Inc.'s request for declaratory judgment and directing Bcom, Inc. to "transfer the domain name barcelona.com to the [City Council] forthwith." 189 F. Supp. 2d 367, 377 (E.D. Va. 2002). Although the district court concluded that the WIPO panel ruling "should be given no weight and this case must be decided based on the evidence presented before the Court," the court proceeded in essence to apply the WIPO panelist opinion as well as Spanish law. *Id.* at 371. The court explained that even though the City Council did not own a trademark in the name "Barcelona" alone, it owned numerous Spanish trademarks that included the word Barcelona, which could, under Spanish law as understood by the district court, be enforced against an infringing use such as <barcelona.com>. *Id.* Adopting the WIPO panelist's decision, the court stated that "the WIPO decision was correct in its determination that [Bcom, Inc.] took 'advantage of the normal confusion' of an Internet user by using the 'Barcelona route' because an Internet user would 'normally expect to reach some official body . . . for . . . the information.'" *Id.* at 372. [The court also found a bad faith intent on the part of the Plaintiff.] At bottom, the court concluded that Bcom, Inc. failed to demonstrate, as required by 15 U.S.C. §1114(2)(D)(v), that its use of <barcelona.com> was "not unlawful." *Id.* at 373.

. . .

From the district court's order of February 22, 2002, Bcom, Inc. filed this appeal.

II

Bcom, Inc. contends that when it "sought a declaration under 15 U.S.C. §1114(2) (D)(v), it was entitled to have its conduct judged by U.S. trademark law, not Spanish trademark law." It argues that even if Spanish law applies, however, a party cannot, under Spanish law, "get a registration for a term that is only geographically descriptive, such as the word 'Barcelona.'" Finally, it maintains that its use of the domain name was not unlawful under United States trademark law because it could not be found to have acted in bad faith under §1125, as the district court concluded.

The City Council contends that the WIPO panelist's decision, including its reference to Spanish law, must be considered to decide this case. It argues:

> [T]rial courts may consider rights in foreign trademarks which were asserted in the transfer decision under review. The [WIPO] administrative transfer proceeding itself gives the district court both subject matter and personal jurisdiction; jurisdiction is not dependent upon allegations of U.S. trademark rights. Therefore, failure to consider the basis for the administrative decision would remove the basis for jurisdiction, and require dismissal of the case. The statute language does not limit the marks considered to U.S. marks. . . .
>
> To hold otherwise would be to strip a trademark owner of its foreign rights whenever it is haled into court by a U.S. domain name owner who has lost a UDRP administrative proceeding. Without the ability to assert their rights, foreign trademark owners would automatically lose such proceedings, creating an unintended and unjust result.

The City Council also maintains that the district court's conclusions of confusing similarity and bad faith were factually supported and justified.

. . .

The district court had subject matter jurisdiction based on the fact that this case was brought under the Lanham Act, as amended by the ACPA, and that §§1331 and 1338 of Title 28 confer jurisdiction over such claims.

Apparently, the City Council does not dispute these jurisdictional observations as far as they go. It contends, however, that jurisdiction to hear a claim under §1114(2)(D) (v) rests on a recognition of the WIPO proceeding and the law that the WIPO panelist applied. Although we agree with the City Council that the WIPO proceeding is relevant to a claim under §1114(2)(D)(v), it is not jurisdictional; indeed, the WIPO panelist's decision is not even entitled to deference on the merits. A brief review of the scheme established by ICANN in adopting the UDRP and by Congress in enacting the ACPA informs our resolution of this issue.

. . .

. . . The UDRP is intended to provide a quick process for resolving domain name disputes by submitting them to authorized panels or panel members operating under rules of procedure established by ICANN and under "any rules and principles of law that [the panel] deems applicable." ICANN, Rules for Uniform Domain Name Dispute Resolution Policy, 115(a), *at* http://www.icann.org/dndr/udrp/uniform-rules.htm (Oct. 24, 1999).

Because the administrative process prescribed by the UDRP is "adjudication lite" as a result of its streamlined nature and its loose rules regarding applicable law, the UDRP itself contemplates judicial intervention, which can occur before, during, or after the UDRP's dispute-resolution process is invoked. *See* ICANN, UDRP ¶3(b), at http://www.icann. org/dndr/udrp/policy.htm (Oct. 24, 1999) (stating that the registrar will cancel or transfer the domain name upon the registrar's "receipt of an order from a court or arbitral tribunal, in each case of competent jurisdiction, requiring such action"); *id.* at ¶4(k) ("The mandatory administrative proceeding requirements set forth in Paragraph 4 shall not prevent either you or the complainant from submitting the dispute to a court of competent jurisdiction for independent resolution before such mandatory administrative proceeding is commenced or after such proceeding is concluded."); *id.* (providing that the registrar will stay implementation of the administrative panel's decision if the registrant commences "a lawsuit against the complainant in a jurisdiction to which the complainant has submitted" under the applicable UDRP rule of procedure). As ICANN recognized in designing the UDRP, allowing recourse to full-blown adjudication under a particular nation's law is necessary to prevent abuse of the UDRP process. *See id.* at ¶1 (defining "reverse domain name hijacking" as use of the UDRP "in bad faith to attempt to deprive a registered domain-name holder of a domain name"). Thus, when a person obtains a domain name, the person agrees, in the registration contract with the registrar, to follow the UDRP as established by ICANN.

In 1999, Congress amended the Trademark Act of 1946 (the Lanham Act) with the Anticybersquatting Consumer Protection Act (ACPA). . . . Although the ACPA was enacted primarily to redress cyberpiracy or "cybersquatting," . . . to balance the rights given to trademark owners against cybersquatters, the ACPA also provides some protection to domain name registrants against "overreaching trademark owners." S. Rep. No. 106-140, at 11; *see also* 15 U.S.C. §1114(2)(D)(iv)-(v). Thus, §1114(2)(D)(v) authorizes a domain name registrant to sue trademark owners for "reverse domain name hijacking."[1] Under that reverse domain name hijacking provision, a domain name registrant who is aggrieved by an overreaching trademark owner may commence an action to declare that the domain name registration or use by the registrant is not unlawful under the Lanham Act. This section provides that the court may "grant injunctive relief to the domain name registrant, including the reactivation of the domain name or transfer of the domain name to the domain name registrant." 15 U.S.C. §1114(2)(D)(v).

In sum, domain names are issued pursuant to contractual arrangements under which the registrant agrees to a dispute resolution process, the UDRP, which is designed to resolve a large number of disputes involving domain names, but this process is not intended to interfere with or modify any "independent resolution" by a court of competent jurisdiction. Moreover, the UDRP makes no effort at unifying the law of trademarks among the nations served by the Internet. Rather, it forms part of a contractual policy developed by ICANN for use by registrars in administering the issuance and transfer of domain names. Indeed, it explicitly anticipates that judicial proceedings will continue under various nations' laws applicable to the parties.

The ACPA recognizes the UDRP only insofar as it constitutes a part of a policy followed by registrars in administering domain names, and the UDRP is relevant to actions brought under the ACPA in two contexts. First, the ACPA limits the liability of a registrar in respect to registering, transferring, disabling, or cancelling a domain name if it is done in the "implementation of *a reasonable policy*" (including the UDRP) that prohibits registration of a domain name "identical to, confusingly similar to, or dilutive of another's mark." 15 U.S.C. §1114(2)(D)(ii)(II) (emphasis added). Second, the ACPA authorizes a suit by a domain name registrant whose domain name has been suspended, disabled, or transferred *under that reasonable policy* (including the UDRP) to seek a declaration that the registrant's

---

1. If a domain-name registrant cybersquats in violation of the ACPA, he "hijacks" the domain name from a trademark owner who ordinarily would be expected to have the right to use the domain name involving his trademark. But when a trademark owner overreaches in exercising rights under the ACPA, he "reverse hijacks" the domain name from the domain-name registrant. Thus, §1114(2)(D)(v), enacted to protect domain-name registrants against overreaching trademark owners, may be referred to as the "reverse domain name hijacking" provision.

registration and use of the domain name involves no violation of the Lanham Act as well as an injunction returning the domain name.

Thus, while a decision by an ICANN-recognized panel might be a condition of, indeed the reason for, bringing an action under 15 U.S.C. §1114(2)(D)(v), its recognition *vel non* is not jurisdictional. Jurisdiction to hear trademark matters is conferred on federal courts by 28 U.S.C. §§1331 and 1338, and a claim brought under the ACPA, which amended the Lanham Act, is a trademark matter over which federal courts have subject matter jurisdiction.

Moreover, any decision made by a panel under the UDRP is no more than an agreed-upon administration that is *not* given any deference under the ACPA. To the contrary, because a UDRP decision is susceptible of being grounded on principles foreign or hostile to American law, the ACPA authorizes reversing a panel decision if such a result is called for by application of the Lanham Act.

In sum, we conclude that we have jurisdiction over this dispute brought under the ACPA and the Lanham Act. Moreover, we give the decision of the WIPO panelist no deference in deciding this action under §1114(2)(D)(v). [cit.] Thus, for our purposes, the WIPO panelist's decision is relevant only to serve as the reason for Bcom, Inc.'s bringing an action under §1114(2)(D)(v) to reverse the WIPO panelist's decision.

III

Now we turn to the principal issue raised in this appeal. Bcom, Inc. contends that in deciding its claim under §1114(2)(D)(v), the district court erred in applying the law of Spain rather than the law of the United States. Because the ACPA explicitly requires application of the Lanham Act, not foreign law, we agree.

Section 1114(2)(D)(v), the reverse domain name hijacking provision, states:

> A domain name registrant whose domain name has been suspended, disabled, or transferred under a policy described under clause (ii)(II) may, upon notice to the mark owner, file a civil action to establish that the registration or use of the domain name by such registrant is not unlawful under this chapter. The court may grant injunctive relief to the domain name registrant, including the reactivation of the domain name or transfer of the domain name to the domain name registrant.

15 U.S.C. §1114(2)(D)(v). Thus, to establish a right to relief against an "overreaching trademark owner" under this reverse hijacking provision, a plaintiff must establish (1) that it is a domain name registrant; (2) that its domain name was suspended, disabled, or transferred under a policy implemented by a registrar as described in 15 U.S.C. §1114(2)(D) (ii)(II); (3) that the owner of the mark that prompted the domain name to be suspended, disabled, or transferred has notice of the action by service or otherwise; and (4) that the plaintiff's registration or use of the domain name is not unlawful under the Lanham Act, as amended.

The parties do not dispute that the first two elements are satisfied. . . . Although the domain name had not actually been transferred from Bcom, Inc. as of the time that Bcom, Inc. commenced this action, the WIPO panelist had already ordered the transfer, and as a result of this order the transfer was certain to occur absent the filing of this action to stop it. By filing this suit, Bcom, Inc. obtained an automatic stay of the transfer order by virtue of paragraph 4(k) of the UDRP, which provides that the registrar will stay implementation of the administrative panel's decision if the registrant commences "a lawsuit against the complainant in a jurisdiction to which the complainant has submitted" under the applicable UDRP rule of procedure. *See* ICANN, UDRP ¶4(k). Moreover, this suit for declaratory judgment and injunctive relief under §1114(2)(D)(v) appears to be precisely the mechanism designed by Congress to empower a party whose domain name is subject to a transfer order like the one in the present case to prevent the order from being implemented. [cit.]

There also can be no dispute that Bcom, Inc. provided notice of this §1114(2)(D)(v) action to the City Council.

It is the last element that raises the principal issue on appeal. Bcom, Inc. argues that the district court erred in deciding whether Bcom, Inc. satisfied this element by applying Spanish law and then by concluding that Bcom, Inc.'s use of the domain name violated Spanish law.

It appears from the district court's memorandum opinion that it indeed did resolve the last element by applying Spanish law. Although the district court recognized that the City Council did not have a registered trademark in the name "Barcelona" alone, either in Spain or in the United States, it observed that "[u]nder Spanish law, when trademarks consisting of two or more words contain one word that stands out in a predominant manner, that dominant word must be given decisive relevance." *Barcelona.com, Inc.*, 189 F. Supp. 2d at 371-72. The court noted that "the term 'Barcelona' has been included in many trademarks consisting of two or more words owned by the City Council of Barcelona. In most of these marks, the word 'Barcelona' is clearly the dominant word which characterizes the mark." *Id.* at 372. These observations regarding the substance and effect of Spanish law led the court to conclude that the City Council of Barcelona "owns a legally valid Spanish trademark for the dominant word 'Barcelona.'" *Id.* The district court then proceeded to determine whether Bcom's "use of the Barcelona trademark is 'not unlawful.'" *Id.* In this portion of its analysis, the district court determined that there was a "confusing similarity between the barcelona.com domain name and the marks held by the Council," *id.*, and that "the circumstances surrounding the incorporation of [Bcom, Inc.] and the actions taken by Nogueras in attempting to sell the domain name evidence[d] a bad faith intent to profit from the registration of a domain name containing the Council's mark," *id.* Applying Spanish trademark law in this manner, the court resolved that Bcom, Inc.'s registration and use of <barcelona.com> were unlawful.

It requires little discussion to demonstrate that this use of Spanish law by the district court was erroneous under the plain terms of the statute. The text of the ACPA explicitly requires application of the Lanham Act, not foreign law, to resolve an action brought under 15 U.S.C. §1114(2)(D)(v). Specifically, it authorizes an aggrieved domain name registrant to "file a civil action to establish that the registration or use of the domain name by such registrant is *not unlawful under this chapter.*" 15 U.S.C. §1114(2)(D)(v) (emphasis added).[2] It is thus readily apparent that the cause of action created by Congress in this portion of the ACPA requires the court adjudicating such an action to determine whether the registration or use of the domain name violates the Lanham Act. Because the statutory language has a plain and unambiguous meaning that is consistent with the statutory context and application of this language in accordance with its plain meaning provides a component of a coherent statutory scheme, our statutory analysis need proceed no further. [cit.]

By requiring application of United States trademark law to this action brought in a United States court by a United States corporation involving a domain name administered by a United States registrar, 15 U.S.C. §1114(2)(D)(v) is consistent with the fundamental doctrine of territoriality upon which our trademark law is presently based. Both the United

---

2. The ACPA actually provides that the registrant may sue to declare that the domain name's use by such registrant is "not unlawful under this Act." 113 Stat. 1501A-550, §3004. "Act" is defined to refer to the Trademark Act of 1946 (the Lanham Act). *Id.* Upon codification, the term "this Act" became "this chapter," Chapter 22 of Title 15, which contains the Lanham Act.

States and Spain have long adhered to the Paris Convention for the Protection of Industrial Property. [cit.] . . . The relevant substantive provision in this case is Article 6(3) of the Paris Convention, which implements the doctrine of territoriality by providing that "[a] mark duly registered in a country of the [Paris] Union shall be regarded as independent of marks registered in the other countries of the Union, including the country of origin." Paris Convention, *supra*, art. 6(3). . . .

It follows from incorporation of the doctrine of territoriality into United States law . . . that United States courts do not entertain actions seeking to enforce trademark rights that exist only under foreign law. *See Person's Co., Ltd. v. Christman*, 900 F.2d 1565, 1568-69 (Fed. Cir. 1990) ("The concept of territoriality is basic to trademark law; trademark rights exist in each country solely according to that country's statutory scheme."). Yet the district court's application of foreign law in this declaratory judgment action did precisely this and thereby neglected to apply United States law as required by the statute.

When we apply the Lanham Act, not Spanish law, in determining whether Bcom, Inc.'s registration and use of <barcelona.com> is unlawful, the ineluctable conclusion follows that Bcom, Inc.'s registration and use of the name "Barcelona" is not unlawful. Under the Lanham Act, and apparently even under Spanish law, the City Council could not obtain a trademark interest in a purely descriptive geographical designation that refers only to the City of Barcelona. *See* 15 U.S.C. §1052(e)(2); *see also* Spanish Trademark Law of 1988, Art. 11(1)(c) (forbidding registration of marks consisting exclusively of "geographical origin"). Under United States trademark law, a geographic designation can obtain trademark protection if that designation acquires secondary meaning. *See, e.g., Resorts of Pinehurst, Inc. v. Pinehurst Nat'l Corp.*, 148 F.3d 417, 421 (4th Cir. 1998). On the record in this case, however, there was no evidence that the public—in the United States or elsewhere—associates "Barcelona" with anything other than the City itself. Indeed, the Chief Director of the City Council submitted an affidavit stating that "[t]he City does not own and is not using any trademarks in the United States, to identify any goods or services." Therefore, under United States trademark law, "Barcelona" should have been treated as a purely descriptive geographical term entitled to no trademark protection. *See* 15 U.S.C. §1052(e)(2). It follows then that there was nothing unlawful about Nogueras' registration of <barcelona. com>, nor is there anything unlawful under United States trademark law about Bcom, Inc.'s continued use of that domain name.

For these reasons, we conclude that Bcom, Inc. established entitlement to relief under 15 U.S.C. §1114(2)(D)(v) with respect to the domain name <barcelona.com>, and accordingly we reverse the district court's ruling in this regard.

. . .

Reversed, Vacated, and Remanded.

NOTES AND QUESTIONS

1.   *Use of national appeals.* Thus far, only the United States has enacted a specific provision expressly designed to facilitate so-called national appeals from decisions of UDRP panelists. But, as the Fourth Circuit notes in *Barcelona.com*, several provisions of the UDRP clearly contemplate the use of national courts where domain name registrants (or trademark owners) are dissatisfied with the outcome before UDRP panelists. Despite this, very few losing parties under the UDRP have had recourse to national courts. Although precise numbers are hard to determine, it is estimated that less than 1 percent of decisions are "appealed." What might explain this small number?

2.   *Treatment of UDRP decisions in national court proceedings.* As the *Barcelona.com* court notes, U.S. courts have given no deference (and indeed have declined to give any weight) to UDRP decisions in actions between the same parties under the Lanham Act. *See, e.g., Dluhos v. Strasberg*, 321 F.3d 365, 371-74 (3d Cir. 2003) (UDRP proceedings should not be treated as arbitral decisions under the Federal Arbitration Act and should thus be reviewed de novo under the ACPA). To what extent should courts afford deference to decisions of the UDRP panels? To what extent should courts hearing an action under Section 32(2)(D)(v) have regard to actions in foreign courts regarding the same domain name dispute? *Cf. Hawes v. Network Solutions, Inc.*, 337 F.3d 377 (4th Cir. 2003) (declining to give weight to proceedings in French court); *Globalsantafe Corp. v. Globalsantafe.com*, 250 F. Supp. 2d 610, 624-27 (E.D. Va. 2003) (discussing comity concerns in context of action under Section 43(d)(2), but deciding not to defer to competing Korean decision). To what extent, if any, should a court give weight to the factual findings of the UDRP panelist? *See Victoria's Secret Stores v. Artco Equip. Co.*, 194 F. Supp. 2d 704 (S.D. Ohio 2002).

3.   *The protection of foreign marks: congressional intent and practical policymaking.* What geographic scope did Congress intend to give the ACPA? The district court in *Barcelona.com* reasoned:

> In the text of the statute Congress makes no distinction between United States or foreign marks, even though trademark law has historically been governed and regulated on a national level. However, this law was framed to govern the registration of domain names on the Internet, and the framers were perfectly aware of the international nature of the Internet when enacting the law. . . . It is untenable to suppose that Congress, aware of the fact that the Internet is so international in nature, only intended for U.S. trademarks to be protected under the Anticybersquatting statute. . . . For these reasons, this Court is of the opinion that the Spanish trademark "Barcelona" is valid for purposes of the ACPA.

The Fourth Circuit disagreed. Is the district court's reasoning persuasive? If the district court is correct, what problems would such an approach create? What problems might it solve?

4.   *Foreign marks: procedural requirements.* In *Sallen v. Corinthians Licenciamentos LTDA*, 273 F.3d 14 (1st Cir. 2001), the First Circuit confronted a dispute not unlike that addressed by the Fourth Circuit in *Barcelona.com*. There, a Brazilian trademark owner, who held a trademark registration for CORINTHIANS for soccer entertainment in Brazil but had not used or registered the CORINTHIANS mark in the United States, prevailed in a UDRP proceeding against a U.S.-based cybersquatter. The cybersquatter brought an action against the Brazilian trademark owner under Section 32(2)(D)(v). The Brazilian company challenged the court's subject matter jurisdiction, arguing that the plaintiff's action did not arise under Section 32(2)(D)(v) because the plaintiff had not provided notice to a "mark owner" as required by that provision. The First Circuit rejected this argument, noting that the term "'mark owner' must be understood against the backdrop of U.S. trademark law, which provides some protections to unregistered marks." The court continued:

> In addition, interpreting "mark owner" to apply only to registered U.S. marks would create a perverse result at odds with our view of the ACPA as granting relief to registrants who have wrongly lost domain names in UDRP proceedings. It would be very odd if Congress, which was well aware of the international nature of trademark disputes, protected Americans against reverse domain name hijacking only when a registered American mark owner was doing the hijacking. Such a policy would permit American citizens, whose domain names are subject to WIPO transfer orders, to get relief against abusive mark owners that have registered in the U.S., but not against abusive mark owners that have not registered (including both foreign mark owners and domestic mark owners that have not registered). It would leave registrants unprotected against reverse domain name hijackers so long as the hijackers are not registered with the PTO.

Are you persuaded by the reasoning of the First Circuit? *Cf.* H.R. Rep. No. 106-412, at 15 (discussing the meaning of "reasonable policy" as that term is used in Section 32(2)(D)(ii)(II), and noting that "the act anticipates a reasonable policy against cyberpiracy will apply only to marks registered on the Principal Register of the Patent and Trademark Office"). Is it consistent with the philosophy underlying *Barcelona.com*? In other contexts, the U.S. courts have read this part of the ACPA to refer only to American institutions. *See, e.g., Hawes v. Network Solutions, Inc.*, 337 F.3d 377 (4th Cir. 2003) (interpreting reference, in provision setting out an exception to a registrar's general exemption from liability for transferring a domain name, to the transfer of a domain name "during the pendency of an action" to mean an action in U.S. courts). Might there be reasons for the U.S. courts to read these provisions in ways that restrict U.S. jurisdiction? In the cases you have read thus far, what are those limits?

5.   *Scope of the Section 32(2)(D)(v) action.* Even if the Fourth Circuit is correct about the nonprotection of foreign marks under the Lanham Act, are there any facts in *Barcelona.com* suggesting that the ACPA should not have been applied? If the defendant in *Barcelona.com* had sought to dismiss the action on grounds of *forum non conveniens*, should that motion have been granted?

6.   *The "trumping" of the UDRP.* The First Circuit in *Sallen* found support for its conclusion that "a declaration of compliance with the ACPA trumps the panel's finding of noncompliance with the UDRP" in the overlap between the two provisions, in the extent to which a panel's application of the UDRP requires it to resolve issues of U.S. law, and in the fact that the UDRP "does not create new law—it applies existing law." In fact, the application of the "lowest common denominator of internationally agreed and accepted principles concerning the abuse of trademarks," rather than the creation of new law, is part of the UDRP's fundamental structure. Which of these reasons are most persuasive in support of supplanting the UDRP decision by a decision under the ACPA?

7.   *The possibility of tit-for-tat legislation.* Consider again the facts in *Sallen, supra* note 4. What would happen if the Brazilian legislature enacted the same type of provision as Section 32(2)(D)(v)? Or, what if the Brazilian trademark owner brought an action under Brazilian trademark law seeking a declaration that Mr. Sallen's use violates its rights under Brazilian law? Does your answer to that question affect whether you think the *Sallen* court is correct in its interpretation of the ACPA?

8.   *Attempted reverse domain name hijacking?* If a trademark owner institutes an allegedly ungrounded UDRP proceeding, and the domain name owner responds with an action under Section 32(2)(D)(v) of the Lanham Act, what should happen next? Assuming that the UDRP dispute resolution provider dismisses the UDRP claim without prejudice upon receiving notice of the U.S. lawsuit, does the domain name owner have a cause of action under the Lanham Act for attempted reverse domain name hijacking (assuming that the UDRP claim was indeed meritless)? *See Frayne v. Chicago 2016*, 90 U.S.P.Q.2d (BNA) 1055 (N.D. Ill. 2009).

9

Permissible Uses of Another's Trademarks

In order to establish liability for trademark infringement, a mark owner must prove that the alleged infringer's unauthorized activities amount to the type of use actionable under the Lanham Act. *See* Chapter 7 (section B). Unauthorized use is also an element of dilution and cybersquatting, though the nature of the use required may vary depending upon the cause of action. *See* Chapter 8.

In this chapter, we focus on another issue concerning the concept of use: whether some unauthorized uses of another's mark should be deemed permissible as a matter of law. That is, consider a case in which the defendant's activities do constitute actionable "use," and arguably cause a likelihood of confusion or of dilution. Should liability automatically follow, or might there be some cases in which considerations of the *nature* of the use should compel a finding that the defendant's use be immunized from liability, despite the confusion or dilution? If there are such cases, which uses should be deemed permissible? And which party should have the burden of invoking a permissible-use doctrine — the defendant, invoking the doctrine as an affirmative defense, or the mark owner, establishing as part of the infringement or dilution case that the defendant's use should *not* be deemed permissible? More broadly, should a doctrine of permissible use be seen as another limitation on the scope of trademark rights, to be added to geographic limitations (Chapter 6) and goods/services limitations (Chapter 7)? Consider each of these questions as you study the materials in this chapter.

We first take up the doctrine of "fair" use (section A). We then turn to a doctrine most commonly called the "first sale" doctrine, in which the purchaser of genuine trademarked goods seeks to continue using the trademark in connection with resale of the purchased goods, sometimes after having altered the goods or their packaging (section B). Finally, we take up cases in which the unauthorized user of a trademark claims that its use is expressive — i.e., for parody, criticism, or other purposes in which speech interests may require trademark interests to give way (section C).

A. Fair Use of Another's Trademark

In this section, we consider trademark fair use. The trademark fair use doctrine reflects the limited nature of trademark rights, ensuring that trademark rights do not become in-gross property rights that result in the removal of words from the language. Fair use originated at common law. It is among the defenses that may be asserted against both unregistered or registered marks. *See* Lanham Act §33(a). Indeed, fair use, in the form articulated in Lanham Act §33(b)(4), can be asserted even as a defense against Lanham Act claims that are based on incontestable registrations. Fair use can also be asserted against dilution claims under the terms specified in Lanham Act §43(c)(3)(A).

We first consider a threshold question about how trademark fair use relates to likelihood of confusion. Then, following the lead of some courts, we discuss two strands of fair use law: one covering "descriptive" or "classic" fair use, and a second covering "nominative" fair use. We urge you to consider the possibility that the distinction between these two categories of case law is not as clear as some courts suggest, and that unintended consequences may flow from insisting on such a distinction.

1.   Relationship Between Fair Use and Confusion

If a use is likely to cause confusion, can the use nonetheless be a fair use? That is, if a trademark owner can prove that an alleged infringer's use was likely to confuse, should the alleged infringer be precluded from invoking the protections of the fair use doctrine? Courts had split on the question before the Supreme Court took it up in the next case.

KP PERMANENT MAKE-UP, INC. v. LASTING IMPRESSION I, INC.

543 U.S. 111 (2004)

Justice SOUTER delivered the opinion of the Court:

The question here is whether a party raising the statutory affirmative defense of fair use to a claim of trademark infringement, 15 U.S.C. §1115(b)(4), has a burden to negate any likelihood that the practice complained of will confuse consumers about the origin of the goods or services affected. We hold it does not.

I

Each party to this case sells permanent makeup, a mixture of pigment and liquid for injection under the skin to camouflage injuries and modify nature's dispensations, and each has used some version of the term "micro color" (as one word or two, singular or plural) in marketing and selling its product. Petitioner KP Permanent Make-Up, Inc., claims to have used the single-word version since 1990 or 1991 on advertising flyers and since 1991 on pigment bottles. [In 1992, Respondent Lasting applied to register "Micro Colors" in white letters separated by a green bar within a black square. The PTO registered the mark in 1993, and the registration became incontestable in 1999.]

It was also in 1999 that KP produced a 10-page advertising brochure using "microcolor" in a large, stylized typeface, provoking Lasting to demand that KP stop using the term. Instead, KP sued Lasting in the Central District of California, seeking, on more than one ground, a declaratory judgment that its language infringed no such exclusive right as Lasting claimed.[3] Lasting counterclaimed, alleging, among other things, that KP had infringed Lasting's "Micro Colors" trademark.

---

3. We summarize the proceedings in this litigation only as they are relevant to the question before us. The District Court's findings as to the generic or descriptive nature of the term "micro color" and any secondary meaning that term has acquired by any of the parties are not before us. Nor are the Court of Appeals's holdings on these issues. See 328 F.3d 1061, 1068-1071 (C.A.9 2003). Nor do we address the Court of Appeals's discussion of "nominative fair use." *Id.*, at 1071-1072.

KP sought summary judgment on the infringement counterclaim, based on the statutory affirmative defense of fair use, 15 U.S.C. §1115(b)(4). After finding that Lasting had conceded that KP used the term only to describe its goods and not as a mark, the District Court held that KP was acting fairly and in good faith because undisputed facts showed that KP had employed the term "microcolor" continuously from a time before Lasting adopted the two-word, plural variant as a mark. Without inquiring whether the practice was likely to cause confusion, the court concluded that KP had made out its affirmative defense under §1115(b)(4) and entered summary judgment for KP on Lasting's infringement claim.

On appeal, the Court of Appeals for the Ninth Circuit thought it was error for the District Court to have addressed the fair use defense without delving into the matter of possible confusion on the part of consumers about the origin of KP's goods. The reviewing court took the view that no use could be recognized as fair where any consumer confusion was probable, and although the court did not pointedly address the burden of proof, it appears to have placed it on KP to show absence of consumer confusion. *Id.*, at 1072 ("Therefore, KP can only benefit from the fair use defense if there is no likelihood of confusion between KP's use of the term 'micro color' and Lasting's mark"). Since it found there were disputed material facts relevant under the Circuit's eight-factor test for assessing the likelihood of confusion, it reversed the summary judgment and remanded the case.

We granted KP's petition for certiorari to address a disagreement among the Courts of Appeals on the significance of likely confusion for a fair use defense to a trademark infringement claim, and the obligation of a party defending on that ground to show that its use is unlikely to cause consumer confusion. [cit.] We now vacate the judgment of the Court of Appeals.

II

A

The Trademark Act of 1946 . . . provides the user of a trade or service mark with the opportunity to register it with the PTO, §§1051, 1053. If the registrant then satisfies further conditions including continuous use for five consecutive years, "the right . . . to use such registered mark in commerce" to designate the origin of the goods specified in the registration "shall be incontestable" outside certain listed exceptions. §1065.

The holder of a registered mark (incontestable or not) has a civil action against anyone employing an imitation of it in commerce when "such use is likely to cause confusion, or to cause mistake, or to deceive." §1114(1)(a). Although an incontestable registration is "conclusive evidence . . . of the registrant's exclusive right to use the . . . mark in commerce," §1115(b), the plaintiff's success is still subject to "proof of infringement as defined in section 1114," *ibid.* And that, as just noted, requires a showing that the defendant's actual practice is likely to produce confusion in the minds of consumers about the origin of the goods or services in question. *See Two Pesos, Inc. v. Taco Cabana, Inc.*, 505 U.S. 763, 780 (1992) (STEVENS, J., concurring); *Lone Star Steakhouse & Saloon, Inc. v. Alpha of Virginia, Inc.*, 43 F.3d 922, 935 (C.A.4 1995); Restatement (Third) of Unfair Competition §21, Comment *a* (1995) (hereinafter Restatement). This plaintiff's burden has to be kept in mind when reading the relevant portion of the further provision for an affirmative defense of fair use, available to a party whose

> "use of the name, term, or device charged to be an infringement is a use, otherwise than as a mark, . . . of a term or device which is descriptive of and used fairly and in good faith only to describe the goods or services of such party, or their geographic origin. . . ." §1115(b)(4).

Two points are evident. Section 1115(b) places a burden of proving likelihood of confusion (that is, infringement) on the party charging infringement even when relying on an incontestable registration. And Congress said nothing about likelihood of confusion in setting out the elements of the fair use defense in §1115(b)(4).

Starting from these textual fixed points, it takes a long stretch to claim that a defense of fair use entails any burden to negate confusion. It is just not plausible that Congress would have used the descriptive phrase "likely to cause confusion, or to cause mistake, or to deceive" in §1114 to describe the requirement that a markholder show likelihood of consumer confusion, but would have relied on the phrase "used fairly" in §1115(b)(4) in a fit of terse drafting meant to place a defendant under a burden to negate confusion. "'[W]here Congress includes particular language in one section of a statute but omits it in another section of the same Act, it is generally presumed that Congress acts intentionally and purposely in the disparate inclusion or exclusion.'" [cit.][4]

Nor do we find much force in Lasting's suggestion that "used fairly" in §1115(b)(4) is an oblique incorporation of a likelihood-of-confusion test developed in the common law of unfair competition. Lasting is certainly correct that some unfair competition cases would stress that use of a term by another in conducting its trade went too far in sowing confusion, and would either enjoin the use or order the defendant to include a disclaimer. *See, e.g., Baglin v. Cusenier Co.*, 221 U.S. 580, 602 (1911) ("[W]e are unable to escape the conclusion that such use, in the manner shown, was to serve the purpose of simulation . . ."); *Herring-Hall-Marvin Safe Co. v. Hall's Safe Co.*, 208 U.S. 554, 559 (1908) ("[T]he rights of the two parties have been reconciled by allowing the use, provided that an explanation is attached."). But the common law of unfair competition also tolerated some degree of confusion from a descriptive use of words contained in another person's trademark. *See, e.g., William R. Warner & Co. v. Eli Lilly & Co.*, 265 U.S. 526, 528 (1924) (as to plaintiff's trademark claim, "[t]he use of a similar name by another to truthfully describe his own product does not constitute a legal or moral wrong, even if its effect be to cause the public to mistake the origin or ownership of the product"); *Canal Co. v. Clark*, 13 Wall. 311, 327, 20 L. Ed. 581 (1872) ("Purchasers may be mistaken, but they are not deceived by false representations, and equity will not enjoin against telling the truth"); [cit.]. While these cases are consistent with taking account of the likelihood of consumer confusion as one consideration in deciding whether a use is fair, see Part II-B, *infra*, they do not stand for the proposition that an assessment of confusion alone may be dispositive. Certainly one cannot get out of them any defense burden to negate it entirely.

Finally, a look at the typical course of litigation in an infringement action points up the incoherence of placing a burden to show nonconfusion on a defendant. If a plaintiff succeeds in making out a prima facie case of trademark infringement, including the element of likelihood of consumer confusion, the defendant may offer rebutting evidence to undercut the force of the plaintiff's evidence on this (or any) element, or raise an affirmative defense to bar relief even if the prima facie case is sound, or do both. But it would make no sense to give the defendant a defense of showing affirmatively that the plaintiff cannot succeed in proving some element (like confusion); all the defendant needs to do is to leave the factfinder unpersuaded that the plaintiff has carried its own burden on that point. A defendant has no need of a court's true belief when agnosticism will do. Put another way, it

---

4. Not only that, but the failure to say anything about a defendant's burden on this point was almost certainly not an oversight, not after the House Subcommittee on Trademarks declined to forward a proposal to provide expressly as an element of the defense that a descriptive use be "'[un]likely to deceive the public.'" Hearings on H.R. 102 et al. before the Subcommittee on Trade-Marks of the House Committee on Patents, 77th Cong., 1st Sess., 167-168 (1941) (hereinafter Hearings) (testimony of Prof. Milton Handler).

is only when a plaintiff has shown likely confusion by a preponderance of the evidence that a defendant could have any need of an affirmative defense, but under Lasting's theory the defense would be foreclosed in such a case. "[I]t defies logic to argue that a defense may not be asserted in the only situation where it even becomes relevant." *Shakespeare Co. v. Silstar Corp.*, 110 F.3d, at 243. Nor would it make sense to provide an affirmative defense of no confusion plus good faith, when merely rebutting the plaintiff's case on confusion would entitle the defendant to judgment, good faith or not.

Lasting tries to extenuate the anomaly of this conception of the affirmative defense by arguing that the oddity reflects the "vestigial" character of the fair use defense as a historical matter. [cit.] Lasting argues that, because it was only in 1988 that Congress added the express provision that an incontestable markholder's right to exclude is "subject to proof of infringement," Trademark Law Revision Act of 1988, §128(b)(1), 102 Stat. 3944, there was no requirement prior to 1988 that a markholder prove likelihood of confusion. Before 1988, the argument goes, it was sensible to get at the issue of likely confusion by requiring a defendant to prove its absence when defending on the ground of fair use. When the 1988 Act saddled the markholder with the obligation to prove confusion likely, §1115(b), the revision simply failed to relieve the fair use defendant of the suddenly strange burden to prove absence of the very confusion that a plaintiff had a new burden to show in the first place.

But the explanation does not work. It is not merely that it would be highly suspect in leaving the claimed element of §1115(b)(4) redundant and pointless. *Hibbs v. Winn*, 542 U.S. 88, 101 (2004) (noting "rule against superfluities" in statutory construction). The main problem of the argument is its false premise: Lasting's assumption that holders of incontestable marks had no need to prove likelihood of confusion prior to 1988 is wrong. *See, e.g., Beer Nuts, Inc. v. Clover Club Foods Co.*, 805 F.2d 920, 924-925 (C.A.10 1986) (requiring proof of likelihood of confusion in action by holder of incontestable mark); *United States Jaycees v. Philadelphia Jaycees*, 639 F.2d 134, 137, n.3 (C.A.3 1981) ("[I]ncontestability [does not] mak[e] unnecessary a showing of likelihood of confusion . . ."); 5 J. McCarthy, Trademarks and Unfair Competition §32:154, p. 32-247 (4th ed. 2004) ("Before the 1988 Trademark Law Revision Act, the majority of courts held that while incontestability grants a conclusive presumption of the 'exclusive right to use' the registered mark, this did not relieve the registrant of proving likelihood of confusion").

B

Since the burden of proving likelihood of confusion rests with the plaintiff, and the fair use defendant has no free-standing need to show confusion unlikely, it follows (contrary to the Court of Appeals's view) that some possibility of consumer confusion must be compatible with fair use, and so it is. The common law's tolerance of a certain degree of confusion on the part of consumers followed from the very fact that in cases like this one an originally descriptive term was selected to be used as a mark, not to mention the undesirability of allowing anyone to obtain a complete monopoly on use of a descriptive term simply by grabbing it first. *Canal Co. v. Clark*, 13 Wall., at 323-324, 327. The Lanham Act adopts a similar leniency, there being no indication that the statute was meant to deprive commercial speakers of the ordinary utility of descriptive words. "If any confusion results, that is a risk the plaintiff accepted when it decided to identify its product with a mark that uses a well known descriptive phrase." *Cosmetically Sealed Industries, Inc. v. Chesebrough-Pond's USA Co.*, 125 F.3d, at 30. See also *Park 'N Fly, Inc. v. Dollar Park and Fly, Inc.*, 469 U.S. 189, 201 (1985) (noting safeguards in Lanham Act to prevent commercial monopolization of language); *Car-Freshner Corp. v. S.C. Johnson & Son, Inc.*, 70 F.3d 267, 269 (C.A.2 1995) (noting importance of "protect[ing] the right of society at large to use words or images in their primary descriptive sense").[5] This right to describe is the reason that descriptive terms qualify for registration as trademarks only after taking on secondary meaning as "distinctive of the applicant's goods," 15 U.S.C. §1052(f), with the registrant getting an exclusive right not in the original, descriptive sense, but only in the secondary one associated with the markholder's goods, 2 McCarthy, *supra*, §11:45, p. 11-90 ("The only aspect of the mark which is given legal protection is that penumbra or fringe of secondary meaning which surrounds the old descriptive word").

While we thus recognize that mere risk of confusion will not rule out fair use, we think it would be improvident to go further in this case, for deciding anything more would take us beyond the Ninth Circuit's consideration of the subject. It suffices to realize that our holding that fair use can occur along with some degree of confusion does not foreclose the relevance of the extent of any likely consumer confusion in assessing whether a defendant's use is objectively fair. Two Courts of Appeals have found it relevant to consider such scope, and commentators and *amici* here have urged us to say that the degree of likely consumer confusion bears not only on the fairness of using a term, but even on the further question whether an originally descriptive term has become so identified as a mark that a defendant's use of it cannot realistically be called descriptive. See *Shakespeare Co. v. Silstar Corp.*, 110 F.3d, at 243 ("[T]o the degree that confusion is likely, a use is less likely to be found fair . . ." (emphasis deleted)); *Sunmark, Inc. v. Ocean Spray Cranberries, Inc.*, 64 F.3d, at 1059; Restatement §28; [cit.].

Since we do not rule out the pertinence of the degree of consumer confusion under the fair use defense, we likewise do not pass upon the position of the United States, as *amicus*, that the "used fairly" requirement in §1115(b)(4) demands only that the descriptive term describe the goods accurately. [cit.] Accuracy of course has to be a consideration in assessing fair use, but the proceedings in this case so far raise no occasion to evaluate some other concerns that courts might pick as relevant, quite apart from attention to confusion. The Restatement raises possibilities like commercial justification and the strength of the plaintiff's mark. Restatement §28. As to them, it is enough to say here that the door is not closed.

III

In sum, a plaintiff claiming infringement of an incontestable mark must show likelihood of consumer confusion as part of the prima facie case, 15 U.S.C. §1115(b), while the defendant has no independent burden to negate the likelihood of any confusion in raising the affirmative defense that a term is used descriptively, not as a mark, fairly, and in good faith, §1115(b)(4).

Because we read the Court of Appeals as requiring KP to shoulder a burden on the issue of confusion, we vacate the judgment and remand the case for further proceedings consistent with this opinion.[6]

It is so ordered.

---

5. See also Hearings 72 (testimony of Wallace Martin, Chairman, American Bar Association Committee on Trade-Mark Legislation) ("Everybody has got a right to the use of the English language and has got a right to assume that nobody is going to take that English language away from him").

6. The record indicates that on remand the courts should direct their attention in particular to certain factual issues bearing on the fair use defense, properly applied. The District Court said that Lasting's motion for summary adjudication conceded that KP used "microcolor" descriptively and not as a mark. [cit.] We think it is arguable that Lasting made those concessions only as to KP's use of "microcolor" on bottles and flyers in the early 1990's, not as to the stylized version of "microcolor" that appeared in KP's 1999 brochure. [cit.] We also note that the fair use analysis of KP's employment of the stylized version of "microcolor" on its brochure may differ from that of its use of the term on the bottles and flyers.

NOTES AND QUESTIONS

1. *Did* KP Permanent *leave a lasting impression?* Predictably, opinions varied widely on the likely long-term significance of *KP Permanent*:

(a) *KP Permanent* was a disappointing non-event. The Court chose a timid and ambiguous middle ground—rejecting the requirement that a fair use proponent prove the absence of likelihood of confusion, but also rejecting the proposition that the presence of likelihood of confusion is irrelevant to the fair use defense.

(b) *KP Permanent* was a crucial antidote to *Park 'N Fly*. Whereas *Park 'N Fly* upheld the incontestability provisions, even as to arguably descriptive marks (*see* Chapter 5), *KP Permanent* effectively limited the enforceable scope of incontestable registrations by making the fair use defense easier to sustain. As a result, *KP Permanent* lessened "the potential damaging impact that a clearly descriptive incontestable trademark granted through error will have on commercial speech." Michael Machat, *The Practical Significance of the Supreme Court Decision in* KP Permanent Make-Up, Inc. v. Lasting Impression I, Inc., 95 TRADEMARK REP. 825, 826 (2005).

(c) *KP Permanent* left many issues unresolved, yet might still serve "as a bridge of sorts" between inquiries currently treated as distinct, such as inquiries into nominative fair use, parodic fair use, fair use applied to inherently distinctive marks, and so on. Jonathan Moskin, *Frankenlaw: The Supreme Court's Fair and Balanced Look at Fair Use*, 95 TRADEMARK REP. 848, 851 (2005). Moskin argues that such a harmonization is needed because "trademark fair use 'doctrine' is not a coherent doctrine at all but a body loosely stitched together from many different sources: a 'Frankenlaw,'" *id.* at 872, and that harmonization might be effectuated by reading *KP Permanent* as establishing a presumption that truthful speech falls outside the scope of Lanham Act liability. *Id.* at 851.

What is your view?

2. *Roles of the courts and Congress.* Should Congress or the courts take the lead in articulating permissible use doctrines in trademark law? Consider this question at the outset of your study of permissible use doctrines, and then again after you have read the materials in this chapter. For some pertinent scholarship, *see* Graeme B. Dinwoodie, *Lewis & Clark Law School Ninth Distinguished IP Lecture: Developing Defenses in Trademark Law*, 13 LEWIS & CLARK L. REV. 99 (2009) (asserting that *KP Permanent* and other cases covered in this chapter may be seen as part of a larger judicial project to refine and develop defenses to liability in trademark law); *see also* William McGeveran, *The Trademark Fair Use Reform Act*, 90 B.U. L. REV. 2267 (2010) (proposing legislation).

2. Descriptive Fair Use

Descriptive fair use claims arise when a defendant has used a term to describe its own goods or services, and the plaintiff has used the same term as a source-identifier for its goods and services. For example, a candy manufacturer would presumably be free to use the term "sweet" to describe its own candy products despite the fact that a car manufacturer owned rights in the mark SWEET for cars. *See Car-Freshner Corp. v. S.C. Johnson & Son, Inc.*, 70 F.3d 267, 270 (2d Cir. 1995) (offering this example). We have already seen issues of descriptive fair use in cases from earlier chapters—for example, whether the defendant's use of "fish fry" on its product packaging was a descriptive fair use in *Zatarain's* (Chapter 2). The following cases and materials articulate and apply the elements of the fair use analysis.

FORTUNE DYNAMIC, INC. v. VICTORIA'S SECRET STORES BRAND MANAGEMENT, INC.

618 F.3d 1025 (9th Cir. 2010)

Bybee, Circuit Judge:

. . .

I

Since 1987 Fortune has been in the business of designing and selling footwear for women, young women, and children. In 1997, Fortune began using DELICIOUS as a trademark on its footwear for young women. Two years later, in 1999, Fortune registered the DELICIOUS trademark for footwear on the principal register of the U.S. Patent and Trademark Office. For most of the time relevant to this appeal, Fortune depicted DELICIOUS in standard block lettering with a capital "D."[1]

Fortune spends approximately $350,000 a year advertising its footwear. In the three-year period from 2005 to 2007, Fortune sold more than 12 million pairs of DELICIOUS shoes. DELICIOUS shoes are featured on Fortune's website and in its catalogs, and have appeared in fashion magazines directed specifically to young women, including *Cosmo girl, Elle girl, Teen People, Twist, In Touch, Seventeen, Latina, ym, Shop, CB, marie claire,* and *Life & Style.* DELICIOUS footwear is available in authorized retail outlets throughout the United States.

Victoria's Secret is a well-known company specializing in intimate apparel. It sells a wide variety of lingerie, beauty products, and personal care products in its 900 retail stores. In February 2007, Victoria's Secret launched a line of personal care products under the trademark BEAUTY RUSH. At the same time, it started a promotion that included giving away a gift package of BEAUTY RUSH lip gloss and—most importantly for our case—a pink tank top to anyone who purchased $35 of beauty product.[3] The tank top was folded inside a clear plastic pouch with the lip gloss and a coupon for a future BEAUTY RUSH purchase. Across the chest of the tank top was written, in silver typescript, the word "Delicious" with a capital "D." On the back, in much smaller lettering, there appeared the word "yum," and the phrase "beauty rush" was written in the back collar. Victoria's Secret models were featured wearing the tank top, as were mannequins on in-store display tables. Victoria's Secret distributed 602,723 "Delicious" tank tops in connection with its BEAUTY RUSH promotion, which lasted until March 2007. Those tank tops not sold or given away during the promotion were sold at Victoria's Secret's semi-annual sale a few months later.

Victoria's Secret executives offered two explanations for using the word "Delicious" on the tank top. First, they suggested that it accurately described the taste of the BEAUTY RUSH lip glosses and the smell of the BEAUTY RUSH body care. Second, they thought that the word served as a "playful self-descriptor," as if the woman wearing the top is saying, "I'm delicious." No one at Victoria's Secret conducted a search to determine whether DELICIOUS was a registered trademark, but Victoria's Secret had run a very similar promotion several months earlier, this one in conjunction with the launch of its VERY SEXY makeup. That promotion also included a tank top, but that tank top was "black ribbed"

---

1. In June 2007 (after this lawsuit was filed), Fortune applied to register DELICIOUS in a stylized font for use on clothing.

3. Forty-four Victoria's Secret stores sold the tank top for $10 with any purchase of beauty product.

with "Very Sexy" written in hot pink crystals across the chest. VERY SEXY is a Victoria's Secret trademark.

[Fortune sued, and the district court granted summary judgment in favor of Victoria's Secret on fair use. Fortune appealed.]

. . .

III

[The court analyzed confusion under the *Sleekcraft* factors, finding multiple fact issues that should have precluded the grant of summary judgment.]

B

We next turn to Victoria's Secret's argument that its use of the word "Delicious" was protected by the Lanham Act's fair use defense. 15 U.S.C. §1115(b)(4). Long before the Lanham Act was enacted, the Supreme Court explained that "[t]he use of a similar name by another to truthfully describe his own product does not constitute a legal or moral wrong, even if its effect be to cause the public to mistake the origin . . . of the product." *William R. Warner & Co. v. Eli Lilly & Co.*, 265 U.S. 526, 529 (1924). Congress codified this common law principle in the Lanham Act's fair use defense, which allows a party to use a descriptive word "otherwise than as a mark . . . [and] fairly and in good faith only to describe the goods or services of such party, or their geographic origin." 15 U.S.C. §1115(b)(4). In establishing that its use was fair, the defendant is not required to "negate confusion." *KP Permanent I*, 543 U.S. at 118. This is because, although the Lanham Act is less than clear on the subject, the Supreme Court recently clarified that, consistent with *Eli Lilly*, "some possibility of consumer confusion must be compatible with fair use." *Id.* at 121. Finally, Victoria's Secret's subjective good faith is relevant to the inquiry, but the overall analysis focuses on whether Victoria's Secret's use of "Delicious" was "objectively fair." *Id.* at 123.

The fair use defense stems from the "undesirability of allowing anyone to obtain a complete monopoly on use of a descriptive term simply by grabbing it first." *Id.* at 122; [cit.]. To avoid monopolization, a company such as Victoria's Secret may invoke a trademark term in its descriptive sense "regardless of [the mark's] classification as descriptive, suggestive, arbitrary, or fanciful." *Brother Records, Inc. v. Jardine*, 318 F.3d 900, 907 (9th Cir. 2003). In other words, how Fortune's DELICIOUS mark is categorized as a matter of conceptual strength has no bearing on whether Victoria's Secret is entitled to the fair use defense.

According to Victoria's Secret, it should prevail on the fair use defense because, as the Lanham Act provides, it used the term "Delicious" "otherwise than as a mark," "only to describe [its] goods or services," and "in good faith." 15 U.S.C. §1115(b)(4). We think there is some merit to Victoria's Secret's argument, but ultimately conclude that the question of "fair use," like the question of likelihood of confusion, should be resolved by a jury. We consider each of the "fair use" factors in turn.

1

We first consider whether the district court correctly ruled, as a matter of law, that Victoria's Secret used "Delicious" "otherwise than as a mark." 15 U.S.C. §1115(b)(4). The Lanham Act defines a trademark as something used "to identify and distinguish . . . goods . . . and to indicate the source of the goods." *Id.* §1127. To determine whether a term is being used as a mark, we look for indications that the term is being used to "associate it with a manufacturer." *Sierra On-Line, Inc. v. Phoenix Software, Inc.*, 739 F.2d 1415, 1423 (9th Cir. 1984). Indications of trademark use include whether the term is used as a "symbol to attract public attention," *JA Apparel Corp. v. Abboud*, 568 F.3d 390, 400 (2d Cir. 2009), which can be demonstrated by "the lettering, type style, size and visual placement and prominence of the challenged words," [MCCARTHY ON TRADEMARKS AND UNFAIR COMPETITION] §11:46. Another indication of trademark use is whether the allegedly infringing user undertook "precautionary measures such as labeling or other devices designed to minimize the risk that the term will be understood in its trademark sense." RESTATEMENT (THIRD) OF UNFAIR COMPETITION §28 cmt. c (1995) ("RESTATEMENT"); [cit.].

Here, there is evidence from which a reasonable jury could conclude that Victoria's Secret was using "Delicious" as a trademark. "Delicious" was written in large letters, with a capital "D," and in silver typescript across the chest, suggesting that Victoria's Secret used the word to attract public attention. Further, there is little evidence that Victoria's Secret employed "precautionary measures" to avoid confusion with Fortune's mark. It is true that the word "yum" appeared on the back of the tank top and "beauty rush" appeared in its back collar. But a jury could reasonably conclude that those hard-to-find words did not detract from the overall message broadcast loudly on the front of the shirt, "Delicious." Perhaps most important, Victoria's Secret's used "Delicious" in a remarkably similar way to how it uses two of its own trademarks—PINK and VERY SEXY. PINK is written in bold capital letters on different items of Victoria's Secret clothing, while VERY SEXY was written, in hot pink crystals, across the chest of a similar black-ribbed tank top during a very similar promotion. The fact that Victoria's Secret used "Delicious" in the same way that it uses other Victoria's Secret trademarks could be persuasive evidence to a jury that Victoria's Secret used, or at least intended to establish, "Delicious" as a trademark.

In support of its argument that Victoria's Secret used "Delicious" as a trademark, Fortune attempted to introduce the testimony of expert Dean K. Fueroghne, a forty-year advertising and marketing professional, who would have testified that Victoria's Secret used "Delicious" as a trademark. We think the district court acted within its discretion to exclude this portion of Fueroghne's testimony. The basis of his knowledge regarding trademark use is not entirely clear. More important, Fueroghne's opinion does not "assist" the jury because the jury is well equipped "'to determine intelligently and to the best possible degree'" the issue of trademark usage "'without enlightenment from those having a specialized understanding of the subject involved in the dispute.'" FED. R. EVID. 702 advisory committee's note (quoting Mason Ladd, *Expert Testimony*, 5 VAND. L. REV. 414, 418 (1952)). Even though we agree that this portion of Fueroghne's proffered testimony was properly excluded, we believe that there still remains a genuine issue of material fact as to whether Victoria's Secret used "Delicious" as a trademark.

2

A genuine issue of material fact also remains with respect to whether Victoria's Secret used the word "Delicious" "only to describe [its] goods or services." 15 U.S.C. §1115(b) (4). To prevail on this factor, we have held, a defendant must establish that it used the word "in [its] primary, descriptive sense" or "primary descriptive meaning." *Brother Records*, 318 F.3d at 906. As a practical matter, "it is sometimes difficult to tell what factors must be considered to determine whether a use . . . is descriptive." *EMI Catalogue P'ship v. Hill, Holliday, Connors, Cosmopulos Inc.*, 228 F.3d 56, 64 (2d Cir. 2000). We agree with the Restatement, however, that the scope of the fair use defense varies with what we will call the descriptive purity of the defendant's use and whether there are other words available to do the describing. *See* RESTATEMENT §28, cmt. c.

Victoria's Secret makes two points—one factual and one legal—in support of its argument that it used "Delicious" descriptively. As to facts, Victoria's Secret says that it used "Delicious" merely to "describe the flavorful attributes of Victoria's Secret's BEAUTY RUSH lip gloss and other products that feature the same popular fruit flavors." A jury, however, could reasonably conclude otherwise. For one thing, in its advertisements, Victoria's Secret described its BEAUTY RUSH lip gloss as "deliciously sexy," not delicious. For another, Victoria's Secret's executives testified that they wanted "Delicious" to serve as a "playful self-descriptor," as if the wearer of the pink tank top is saying, "I'm delicious." These examples suggest that a jury could reasonably decide that Victoria's Secret did not use "Delicious" "only to describe its goods." *See* RESTATEMENT §28, cmt. c. ("If the original meaning of the term is not in fact descriptive of the attributes of the user's goods, services, or business, the [fair use] defense is not applicable.").

As to law, Victoria's Secret argues that it used "Delicious" in a permissible "descriptive sense," even if its use of the word was not technically descriptive. Victoria's Secret points to the Second Circuit's decision in *Cosmetically Sealed Industries, Inc. v. Chesebrough-Pond's USA Co.*, 125 F.3d 28 (2d Cir. 1997), in which the court noted that the statutory requirement that a defendant use the term "only to describe [its] goods or services" "has not been narrowly confined to words that describe a characteristic of the goods, such as size or quality." *Id.* at 30. Instead, that court observed, "the phrase permits use of words or images that are used . . . in their 'descriptive sense.'" *Id.* Under that standard, the court held that although the defendants' use of the phrase "Seal it With a Kiss" "d[id] not describe a characteristic of the defendants' product," it was used in its "'descriptive sense'—to describe an action that the sellers hope consumers will take, using their product." *Id.* Other Second Circuit cases have followed the same general approach. *See Car-Freshner Corp. v. S.C. Johnson & Son, Inc.*, 70 F.3d 267, 270 (2d Cir. 1995) (concluding that the defendant had established fair use because its "pinetree shape" air freshener "describes . . . the pine scent" and "refers to the Christmas season, during which Johnson sells th[e] item"); *B & L Sales Assocs. v. H. Daroff & Sons, Inc.*, 421 F.2d 352, 353 (2d Cir. 1970) (upholding the defendant's use of the phrase "Come on Strong" because it "describe[d] the manner in which [the] clothing would assist the purchaser in projecting a commanding, confident, 'strong' image to his friends and admirers"). *But see EMI*, 228 F.3d at 65 (holding that, although the word "Swing" "undoubtedly describes both the action of using a golf club and the style of music on the soundtrack," "Swing, Swing, Swing [wa]s not necessarily [descriptive]").

We have no quarrel with the general proposition that the fair use defense may include use of a term or phrase in its "descriptive sense," which in some instances will describe more than just "a characteristic of the [defendant's] goods." MCCARTHY §11:49; *see Brother Records*, 318 F.3d at 907. We also agree that a capacious view of what counts as descriptive supports Victoria's Secret's argument that its use of "Delicious" qualifies as fair use. Even under this view of whether a use counts as descriptive, however, we think that a jury could reasonably conclude that Victoria's Secret's use was not fair under this factor, for three reasons.

First, although we accept some flexibility in what counts as descriptive, we reiterate that the scope of the fair use defense varies with the level of descriptive purity. Thus, as a defendant's use of a term becomes less and less purely descriptive, its chances of prevailing on the fair use defense become less and less likely. *See* RESTATEMENT §28, cmt. c. And here, a jury could reasonably conclude, for the same reasons it might conclude that DELICIOUS as applied to footwear is not descriptive, *see supra* Part III.A.2, that Victoria's Secret's use of "Delicious" on a pink tank top did not qualify as sufficiently descriptive for Victoria's Secret to prevail on the fair use defense.

Second, even if a jury thought that there was some evidence of descriptive use, it could still reasonably conclude that the lack of "precautionary measures" on Victoria's

Secret's pink tank top outweighs that evidence. Indeed, the same Second Circuit decisions upon which Victoria's Secret relies support this view. In *Cosmetically Sealed*, for example, "[t]he product name 'Color Splash'"—the defendant's trademark—"appeared in the center of the display in red block letters, at least twice the size of the lettering for 'Seal it with a Kiss.'" 125 F.3d at 29-30. And "the brand name 'CUTEX'[appeared] in block letters three times the size of the 'Seal it' instruction." *Id.* at 30. *B & L Sales* describes a similar layout: "Directly below this phrase ['Come on Strong'], in somewhat smaller, yet readily visible, block-type print appears the phrase 'With Botany 500.' Thus the copy reads 'COME ON STRONG with Botany 500.'" 421 F.2d at 353. Here, by contrast, the word "Delicious" appeared all by itself on the front of a tank top. Even though other words, such as "beauty rush" and "yum yum," appeared elsewhere on the top, a jury could reasonably conclude that in order to prevail on the fair use defense, Victoria's Secret should have been more careful about "indicating [Victoria's Secret] as the source." *Packman*, 267 F.3d at 639.

Finally, there is little doubt that Victoria's Secret had at its disposal a number of alternative words that could adequately capture its goal of providing a "playful self-descriptor" on the front of its tank top. An abundance of alternative words is important because it suggests that Victoria's Secret's use was more suggestive than descriptive. *See* McCarthy §11:45 ("[T]o be eligible for . . . fair use, [a] defendant must be using the challenged designation in a descriptive, not merely suggestive, sense."). If so, restricting Victoria's Secret's use of "Delicious" does not implicate the same concerns regarding the monopolization of the lexicon that lie at the heart of the fair use defense. [cit.] Overall, we think a genuine issue of material fact remains as to whether Victoria's Secret used "Delicious" only to describe its goods or services.

3

The last factor of the fair use defense asks whether the defendant has exercised "good faith." We have not given this factor of the fair use defense much attention, but we agree with the Second Circuit that it involves the same issue as the intent factor in the likelihood of confusion analysis: "whether defendant in adopting its mark intended to capitalize on plaintiff's good will." *EMI*, 228 F.3d at 66. Fortune argues that a jury could construe Victoria's Secret's failure to investigate the possibility that DELICIOUS was being used as a mark as evidence of bad faith. For support, Fortune offers the other portion of Fueroghne's expert testimony, in which Fueroghne opines that "[i]t is standard practice in the advertising and marketing industry . . . to perform at least a cursory search on the Internet and with the United State[s] Trademark Office to see what else is out in the market . . . to avoid possible conflicts or confusion." The district court excluded this evidence for the same reasons it excluded Fueroghne's other testimony, because Fueroghne "is not an expert in any field relevant to this case."

With respect to this portion of Fueroghne's testimony, the district court is plainly wrong. Fueroghne has forty years of experience in the marketing and advertising industry, strongly suggesting that he is familiar with what companies within the industry do when placing words on a product. . . . More important, Fueroghne's testimony "will assist the trier of fact . . . to determine a fact in issue," Fed. R. Evid. 702, as it supports an inference that Victoria's Secret acted in bad faith. Therefore, we conclude that the district court abused its discretion in excluding this portion of Fueroghne's testimony.

On the whole, we think that the evidence of malicious intent on the part of Victoria's Secret, even with Fueroghne's expert testimony, is thin at best. But Victoria's Secret's failure to investigate whether someone held a DELICIOUS trademark, combined with the other evidence discussed above, provides support for a jury's potential finding that

Victoria's Secret's carelessness in its use of the word "Delicious" rendered its use of that word "objectively [un]fair." *KP Permanent I*, 543 U.S. at 123.

. . .

Reversed and remanded.

KELLY-BROWN v. WINFREY

717 F.3d 295 (2d Cir. 2013)

STRAUB, Circuit Judge:

BACKGROUND

Kelly-Brown owns a motivational services business organized around the concept "Own Your Power." Kelly-Brown hosts a radio show, holds conferences and retreats, and writes a blog promoting the concept of "owning" one's power. She also has a federally registered service mark in the phrase "Own Your Power."

The service mark registered with the United States Patent and Trademark Office is displayed in a distinctive font that Kelly-Brown uses on her website and other materials, as follows:

own your power

The service mark states, "THE COLOR(S) LIGHT BLUE IS/ARE CLAIMED AS A FEATURE OF THE MARK. THE MARK CONSISTS OF LIGHT BLUE SCRIPTED LETTERS WHICH CREATE THE WORDS OWN YOUR 'POWER.'" Kelly-Brown's service mark was registered May 27, 2008.

Defendant Oprah almost needs no introduction, but warrants one in this context. She runs a vast media empire, which consists of, *inter alia*, a magazine, and a website, which is run by Harpo, and (until recently) a television program. Oprah's name and images figure prominently in the branding of these enterprises.

At roughly the same time that Kelly-Brown was seeking to register her service mark in "Own Your Power," the defendants also sought to register a trademark in a new Oprah venture, the Oprah Winfrey Network, to be known as "OWN." During the creation of OWN, Harpo arranged for the transfer of a trademark in "OWN ONYX WOMAN NETWORK" from its original owner to Harpo to avoid an infringement action from that mark's original owner. Defendants would likely have been aware of Kelly-Brown's pending registration for the service mark in "Own Your Power," since the same search defendants would have run to locate and negotiate the transfer of the trademark in "OWN ONYX WOMAN NETWORK" would have also revealed Kelly-Brown's mark.

Kelly-Brown alleges that the defendants infringed upon her service mark by producing a bevy of publications, events, and online content all using the phrase, "Own Your Power." For example, the October 2010 issue of O, the Oprah Magazine (the "Magazine"), which was distributed on or about September 13, 2010, prominently featured the words "Own Your Power" on its front cover. Beneath these words were the sub-headings "How to Tap Into Your Strength"; "Focus Your Energy"; and "Let Your Best Self Shine." It also contained the following headline set off to the right side: "THE 2010 O POWER LIST! 20 Women Who Are Rocking the World."

The Power List therein consisted of a list of people who were influential in various fields, with each serving as an example of a particular "kind" of power. For example, one page contained a photograph of the actress Julia Roberts and a paragraph describing her. Set off from the text is a red circle containing the phrase "THE POWER OF . . . living large."

On September 16, 2010, the Magazine, in connection with various other businesses, including defendants Wells Fargo, Clinique, and Chico's, held an "Own Your Power" event (the "Event"). At the Event, various celebrities posed for promotional photographs in front of an "Own Your Power" backdrop that also contained trademarks for Chico's, Wells Fargo, Clinique, and the Magazine. The Event involved a seminar and workshop offering motivational advice regarding self-awareness, self-realization, and entrepreneurship, under the aegis of the theme "Own Your Power." The Event was subsequently described in the December 2010 issue of the Magazine as the "FIRST-EVER OWN YOUR POWER EVENT."

Following the Event, the Harpo website (the "Website") contained video clips from the Event and placed "Own Your Power" banners and content on at least 75 different individual webpages. Each page containing the "Own Your Power" banner displayed the same header image, with font and graphics that resembled the layout of the October issue of the Magazine. In the center of the banner were the words "Own Your Power!" in a large italicized font. On either side of these words were truncated, colored circles, each containing text. The text inside the leftmost circle contained the words, "The Power of . . ." To the right were arrayed other circles containing ellipses followed by the words, ". . . heart," ". . . vision," ". . . one voice," and ". . . seizing the moment."

The October issue contained pages with a similar format, with the phrase "the power of . . ." surrounded by various concepts written in colored circles, each beginning with an ellipsis. The "Own Your Power" bannered pages of the website included articles such as, "How to Tap Into Your True Power," "Motivation: One Entrepreneur's Fabulous Story," and "The Secrets of Success." Each page is accompanied by banner advertisements.

Approximately two weeks after the Event occurred, the Magazine's Facebook page displayed photographs taken that evening. On September 27, 2010, Oprah appeared on her television show and displayed the cover of the October 2010 issue of the Magazine. In addition, the December 2010 issue of the Magazine, circulated around November 13, 2010, contained information encouraging readers to view the videos from the Event online at the Website.

Following the Magazine's Own Your Power cover, Kelly-Brown and Own Your Power Communications, Inc. received numerous inquiries from people who appear to have confused Kelly-Brown's services with Oprah's Event, Website, and Magazine. Competition from Oprah has been detrimental to Kelly-Brown's brand.

[Kelly-Brown sued, alleging Lanham Act violations and other causes of action. Kelly-Brown argued reverse confusion. As to the Lanham Act claims, the District Court held in favor of defendants. *Inter alia*, the District Court concluded that defendants' use of the phrase "Own Your Power" was a fair use.]

DISCUSSION

. . .

II.   FAIR USE

In order to assert a successful fair use defense to a trademark infringement claim, the defendant must prove three elements: that the use was made (1) other than as a mark, (2) in a descriptive sense, and (3) in good faith. *See* 15 U.S.C. §1115(b)(4); *EMI Catalogue P'ship*, 228 F.3d at 64. Because fair use is an affirmative defense, it often requires consideration of facts outside of the complaint and thus is inappropriate to resolve on a motion to dismiss. Affirmative defenses may be adjudicated at this stage in the litigation, however, where the facts necessary to establish the defense are evident on the face of the complaint. [cit.] Plaintiffs, in rebutting defendants' arguments, are held only to the usual burden of a motion to dismiss, *id.*, which is to say they must plead sufficient facts to plausibly suggest that they are entitled to relief, *Iqbal*, 556 U.S. at 678.

Defendants here note that the mere fact that someone owns a mark that contains a particular word or phrase does not grant the holder the exclusive right to use that word or phrase commercially. *See Sands, Taylor & Wood Co. v. Quaker Oats Co.*, 978 F.2d 947, 951 (7th Cir. 1992) ("The fair use doctrine is based on the principle that no one should be able to appropriate descriptive language through trademark registration."). "[T]he owner's rights in a mark extend only to its significance as an identifying source, not to the original descriptive meanings of a mark," *EMI Catalogue P'ship*, 228 F.3d at 64, and so where another person uses the words constituting that mark in a purely descriptive sense, this use may qualify as permissible fair use.

We now consider whether the defendants have satisfied each element of a fair use defense in turn.

A.   *Trademark Use*

. . . In determining whether the defendants were using the words "Own Your Power" as a mark, we ask whether they were using the term "as a symbol to attract public attention." [cit.] Kelly-Brown alleges that the defendants used the phrase "Own Your Power" in several unique instances and that these collectively constitute use as a mark. She provides allegations regarding several such uses, including: (1) the October Issue of the Magazine, featuring the phrase in the center of the Issue's cover; (2) the Own Your Power Event, billed as the "first ever," that featured motivational content; (3) promotion of the Event through social media; and (4) the online video from the Event and other motivational articles provided on an "Own Your Power" section of Oprah's website. Kelly-Brown argues that, taken together, these uses suggest that the defendants were attempting to build an association with consumers between the phrase "Own Your Power" and Oprah.

At this stage in the litigation, this array of uses is sufficient for us to infer a pattern of use. We thus conclude that Kelly-Brown has plausibly alleged that Oprah was attempting to build a new segment of her media empire around the theme or catchphrase "Own Your Power," beginning with the October Issue and expanding outward from there. We have recognized that established companies are allowed to seek trademarks in sub-brands. *See Abercrombie & Fitch Co. v. Hunting World, Inc.*, 537 F.2d 4, 14 (2d Cir. 1976). Kelly-Brown's complaint implies that Oprah is a brand and is therefore the ultimate source of all things related to that brand, but that defendants sought to use the phrase "Own Your Power" to denote a particular line of services and content within the larger Oprah brand.

Defendants counter that this case is on all fours with *Packman v. Chicago Tribune Co.*, 267 F.3d 628, 633 (7th Cir. 2001). There, the Chicago Tribune published a newspaper with the headline "The Joy of Six" after the Chicago Bulls won their sixth basketball championship. *Id.* at 634. Plaintiff claimed she had a trademark in the phrase. *Id.* The Tribune later reproduced this front page on various promotional items. *Id.* The Seventh Circuit concluded that this use was merely a headline, rather than a use as a mark, because the Tribune's masthead clearly identified the source of the newspaper, and because the sports memorabilia at issue in the case was more readily identifiable with the Tribune brand name than with the phrase "Joy of Six." *Id.* at 639-40. Defendants rely on *Packman* to argue that their use of the phrase "Own Your Power" was similarly only a headline and that the subsequent use in connection with the Event and on the Website were derivative of this use.

Defendants' use of the phrase "Own Your Power" was much different than the Chicago Tribune's use of the phrase "The Joy of Six." Defendants' use was far more wide-ranging and varied. At least with respect to the Website, the content was not merely derivative of the October Issue in the sense that the promotional items in *Packman* were derivative of the original headline. In *Packman*, the promotional hats and T-shirts plaintiff alleged infringed her trademark merely reproduced the front page of a particular issue of the Chicago Tribune. By contrast, the articles on the Website here contained unique content that was not previously published in the October Issue of the Magazine. The webpages attached to the complaint do not even directly reference the October Issue, its cover page, or its content. A viewer of these pages could easily read their copy without realizing that an issue of the Magazine had ever so much as used the phrase "Own Your Power."

The Complaint provides few allegations regarding what happened at the Event. It was, however, referred to as the "first-ever" of its kind, suggesting that it was not directly tied to a particular issue of the Magazine, but instead was to be a recurring enterprise within the Oprah media empire.

Courts are more likely to treat recurring themes or devices as entitled to protection as a mark, even where a single iteration might not enjoy such protection. The titles of literary series enjoy more protection as marks than single works of artistic expression. *Compare EMI Catalogue P'ship*, 228 F.3d at 63 (holding that a single work of artistic expression is entitled to protection if the title has acquired secondary meaning) *with* 2 J. THOMAS MCCARTHY, MCCARTHY ON TRADEMARKS AND UNFAIR COMPETITION §10:7 (4th ed. 2012) ("[S]econdary meaning need not be proven for an inherently distinctive title of a literary series, newspaper, periodical, television series or the like."). Similarly, courts have protected advertising slogans under the theory that companies have devoted a great deal of time and expense into creating an association in the minds of consumers between a slogan and a particular product. [cit.]

Repetition is important because it forges an association in the minds of consumers between a marketing device and a product. When consumers hear a successful slogan, for example, they immediately think of a particular product without even being prompted by the product's actual name. When they encounter the title of a popular literary series, they will recognize, just based on the name, that the work is one of that series and is therefore the work of a particular author. The slogan or title becomes a symbolic identifier of a product or product line through repetition.

It is adequately alleged in the complaint that the defendants were trying to create, through repetition across various forms of media, a similar association between Oprah and the phrase "Own Your Power." The defendants began to create the association between that phrase and Oprah with the cover of the October Issue of the Magazine, and continued to encourage it through both the Event and the Website. Each of these employed usages of the phrase "Own Your Power" involved separate content and context, and thus it is plausible that the defendants were attempting to build up a line of wide-ranging content all denoted by the phrase "Own Your Power." "Own Your Power," through these interrelated uses, would thus become symbolic shorthand for the products and message as a whole, meant to remind consumers of a particular kind of Oprah-related content. Thus, plaintiffs have alleged that this repeated and wide-ranging usage of the phrase "Own Your Power" functioned as a mark. Of course, further information may emerge during discovery that undermines Kelly-Brown's theory that Oprah's use was an attempt to create a sub-brand, but her allegations are sufficient at this stage.

The fact that Oprah's (household) name was also attached to the Magazine, the Website, and the Event does not suffice to demonstrate that "Own Your Power" was not also employed as a mark in each of its uses by defendants. It is well established law that both a slogan and a single brand name can serve as co-existent marks. *See Grotrian, Helfferich, Schulz, Th. Steinweg Nachf. v. Steinway & Sons,* 523 F.2d 1331, 1338-39 (2d Cir. 1975) (holding that "Steinway The Instrument of Immortals" was a properly "registered slogan" notwithstanding the fact that Steinway itself was also a protected mark); *see also Sands, Taylor & Wood Co. v. Quaker Oats Co.,* 978 F.2d 947, 954 (7th Cir. 1992) ("Nor is a defendant's use of a term in conjunction with its own trademark *per se* a use other than as a trademark." (internal quotation marks omitted)); 1 McCarthy on Trademarks §7.21 ("The fact that a slogan is used in conjunction with a previously existing trademark does not mean that the slogan does not also function as a mark, for a product can bear more than one trademark.").

To be sure, we have previously noted that "the prominent display of the defendants' own trademarks" can contribute to a finding that the defendants were not using a different distinct phrase as a mark. *See Cosmetically Sealed Indus., Inc. v. Chesebrough-Pond's USA Co.,* 125 F.3d 28, 30-31 (2d Cir. 1997). In *Cosmetically Sealed,* a lipstick manufacturer had a display of trial-sized lipsticks as well as complimentary postcards that customers were encouraged to use to test the lipsticks. *Id.* at 29. The display featured the words, "Seal it with a Kiss!!" which another lipstick manufacturer, the plaintiff, used as a slogan, and in which the plaintiff held a valid trademark. *Id.* We there held that such use was not done "as a mark." But *Cosmetically Sealed* did not announce a rule that all use was other than "as a mark" if the defendant also displayed a different mark, such as Oprah's name in this case, in close proximity. Rather, this fact was one of several considerations in a fact-intensive analysis. Also crucial to our finding there was the fact that "[t]he challenged phrase [did] not appear on the lipstick itself, on its packaging, or in any other advertising or promotional materials related to [the defendant's] product." *Id.* at 31. The words "Seal it with a Kiss!!" thus did not help to identify the product in any context but a single advertising campaign. The defendants' use of the phrase "Own Your Power" here was not similarly tangential.

Kelly-Brown therefore has plausibly alleged that the defendants intended to create a new line of products and services offered by Oprah under the mark "Own Your Power." Defendants thus have not met their burden at this stage in the litigation in demonstrating that their use of the phrase "Own Your Power" in its various iterations was use other than as a mark.

B.   Descriptive Sense

The next element of a fair use defense is that the disputed use was in a descriptive sense. Defendants argue that the use of the phrase "Own Your Power" was descriptive of the publications to which that phrase was attached. They argue that the use of the phrase on the Magazine's cover describes its contents and also "served as an exhortation for readers to take action to own their power and described a desired benefit of reading the Magazine Issue." They further assert that subsequent uses of the phrase in connection with the Event, on the Website, etc., were merely referring back to this original, approved use.

At the outset, it should be noted that the phrase "Own Your Power" differs from the sort of phrase which courts usually find to be used descriptively. Courts more readily find a phrase descriptive when it is in common usage. For example, we have found the instruction "Seal it with a Kiss!!" to be descriptive where lipstick testers were to kiss a postcard wearing the lipstick and then send it to a loved one. *Cosmetically Sealed Indus.,* 125 F.3d at 30. In so holding, we noted, "The phrase 'sealed with a kiss' is a fixture of the language, used by generations of school girls, who have given it such currency that it is readily recognized when communicated only as an acronym — SWAK." *Id*. Similarly, the Seventh Circuit held that the phrase "The Joy of Six" was descriptive after noting that the phrase "is a play on the 1970s book series *The Joy of Sex*" and "has been used to describe positive feelings associated with six of anything." *Packman*, 267 F.3d at 641. By contrast, we have held that the slogan "Swing Swing Swing" for golf clubs, playing on the title of the Benny Goodman song "Sing Sing Sing," was not descriptive because golfers "swing" their clubs, not "swing swing swing" them. *EMI Catalogue P'ship*, 228 F.3d at 65.

Defendants have not argued that the phrase "Own Your Power" was in popular usage. Nor indeed could they in a motion to dismiss. Doing so would surely require defendants to reference material beyond the four corners of the complaint. Of course, discovery may reveal that the phrase has some wider currency than is immediately apparent.

To be sure, there is no requirement that a usage be immediately recognizable as a popular phrase for it to be descriptive. *See Sands, Taylor & Wood Co.*, 978 F.2d at 952-53. In *Sands*, the court held that a material issue of fact existed regarding whether the tagline "Gatorade is Thirst Aid" was descriptive notwithstanding the fact that it was not a "common phrase." *Id*. at 953. It so held because "the average consumer [could] perceive[] 'Thirst Aid' as describing a characteristic of Gatorade — its ability to quench thirst." *Id*.

But here the phrase "Own Your Power" does not describe the contents of the Magazine. The words are prominently displayed in the center of the Magazine with the subtitles "How to Tap Into Your Strength"; "Focus Your Energy"; and "Let Your Best Self Shine" in smaller type below. Along the edges of the magazine are specific headlines for articles, including "THE 2010 O POWER LIST! 20 Women Who Are Rocking the World." Although both the center phrase and the article headline make use of the word "power," it does not appear that the phrase "Own Your Power" is meant to describe the contents of a particular item in the Magazine. For example, the "Power List" inside the Magazine contains a list of admirable people, accompanied by biographical information about each. But the list does not provide specific advice regarding how a reader can follow in the footsteps of any of these individuals, nor does it provide advice regarding how a reader can become more powerful in general.

The Table of Contents of the Magazine further underscores the fact that the phrase is not used as a headline for a particular article or content. The bottom left corner of the page contains a smaller picture of the cover and a list describing where the articles referenced on the cover can be found. It does not list any article corresponding to the phrase "Own Your Power."

It is the defendants' burden here to show that their use of the phrase "Own Your Power" was descriptive. At this stage in the litigation, defendants have not made that showing.

C.   Good Faith

The final element of a fair use defense is a showing that the use was made in good faith. We "equate a lack of good faith with the subsequent user's intent to trade on the good will of the trademark holder by creating confusion as to source or sponsorship." *EMI Catalogue P'ship*, 228 F.3d at 66. Even where there is no direct evidence of intent, "if there is additional evidence that supports the inference that the defendant sought to confuse consumers as to the source of the product, . . . the inference of bad faith may fairly be drawn." *Id*. (internal quotation marks omitted).

Defendants, who bear the burden in establishing a fair use defense, assert that their good faith is evident from the face of the complaint. They argue, in essence, that it is implausible that someone as well-known as Oprah would attempt to trade on the goodwill of someone relatively obscure like Kelly-Brown. *See Star Indus.*, 412 F.3d at 389 (finding good faith based in part on "the implausibility of the notion that a premier international rum manufacturer would seek to conflate its products with those of a regional discount vodka manufacturer"). The defendants further observe that the phrase "Own Your Power" was comingled with other Oprah-related marks, suggesting both that no consumer would be confused as to the origin of their "Own Your Power" publications and that they were not trading on Kelly-Brown's good will.

The defendants are correct that we have found good faith where a defendant prominently displayed its own marks in a way that overshadows the plaintiff's mark, reasoning that the prominent placement demonstrates that the defendant had no intent to trade on the plaintiff's good will. *Cosmetically Sealed Indus.*, 125 F.3d at 30-31. But a plaintiff may also show absence of good faith where a junior user had knowledge or constructive knowledge of the senior user's mark and chose to adopt a similar mark. *Star Indus.*, 412 F.3d at 389.

Kelly-Brown argues that she has pleaded facts sufficient to plausibly suggest that the defendants had knowledge of her mark and chose to go forward with the "Own Your Power" campaign anyway. Indeed, she alleges that prior to the rollout of Oprah's new Oprah Winfrey Network, to be known as "OWN," the defendants bought the rights to use the acronym "OWN" from a woman who had previously registered it as an acronym for the "Onyx Woman Network." Kelly-Brown argues that this transaction plausibly suggests that the defendants conducted a trademark registration search for the word "Own," and that such a search would have turned up her then-pending service mark in the phrase "Own Your Power." We agree that these allegations do plausibly suggest that the defendants had knowledge of Kelly-Brown's mark, liked it, and decided to use it as their own. In other words, defendants' allegations that they did not intend to trade on Kelly-Brown's good will, even if true, do not preclude a finding of bad faith. *See Cadbury Beverages, Inc. v. Cott Corp.*, 73 F.3d 474, 483 (2d Cir. 1996) (declining to decide good faith as a matter of law where defendant used a mark, which happened to be the name of defendant's parent company, knowing it was identical to plaintiff's registered mark); *see also Kiki Undies Corp. v. Promenade Hosiery Mills, Inc.*, 411 F.2d 1097, 1101 (2d Cir. 1969) (explaining that defendant has the burden of persuasion in such circumstances).

At bottom, the defendants ask us to weigh their averments that they did not use the phrase "Own Your Power" in order to trade on Kelly-Brown's good will against Kelly-Brown's allegations that they were aware of her registered mark before launching the "Own Your Power" campaign. Our role in considering a motion to dismiss is not to resolve these sorts of factual disputes. Accordingly, the District Court erred in holding that the defendants have conclusively demonstrated good faith in their use of the phrase "Own Your Power."

[The court's discussion affirming the dismissal of the vicarious infringement and counterfeiting claims is omitted.]

[*Vacated and remanded.*]

MARKETQUEST GROUP, INC. v. BIC CORP.

862 F.3d 927 (9th Cir. 2017)

M. SMITH, Circuit Judge:

FACTS AND PRIOR PROCEEDINGS

Marketquest produces and sells promotional products, and has used its United States Patent and Trademark Office registered trademarks "All-in-One" and "The Write Choice" since 1999 and 2000, respectively. In 2009, BIC Corp. and BIC USA, Inc. (collectively,

BIC) acquired Norwood, a promotional products company, and in 2010 Norwood published a promotional products catalogue for 2011 that featured the phrase "All-in-One" on the cover of and in the catalogue. The 2011 catalogue consolidated all of Norwood's eight "hard goods" catalogues "in one" catalogue, whereas they were previously published in separate catalogues. In 2010, BIC also used the phrase "The WRITE Pen Choice for 30 Years" in advertising and packaging for its pens, in connection with its thirtieth anniversary promotion.

[Marketquest sued and sought a preliminary injunction, which the district court denied, concluding that the defendants were likely to prevail on fair use. Subsequently, the parties filed cross-motions for summary judgment.] The district court granted summary judgment for Defendants, holding that there was "some likelihood of confusion and therefore the potential for trademark infringement liability," but that further analysis of likelihood of confusion was unnecessary because fair use provided Defendants a complete defense to allegations of infringement of both the "All-in-One" and "The Write Choice" trademarks. Marketquest timely appealed.

ANALYSIS. . .

III. THE DISTRICT COURT ERRED BY GRANTING SUMMARY JUDGMENT IN FAVOR OF DEFENDANTS BASED UPON ON THE FAIR USE DEFENSE REGARDING THEIR USE OF "ALL-IN-ONE"

Applying the "classic fair use" defense, "[a] junior user is always entitled to use a descriptive term in good faith in its primary, descriptive sense other than as a trademark." *Cairns v. Franklin Mint Co.*, 292 F.3d 1139, 1150 (9th Cir. 2002). A defendant must show that its use is (1) other than as a trademark, (2) descriptive of the defendant's goods, and (3) in good faith. 15 U.S.C. §1115(b)(4). Additionally, "the degree of customer confusion [is] a factor in evaluating fair use." *KP Permanent II*, 408 F.3d at 609.

The district court considered the elements of the fair use defense, and concluded that Defendants' use of "All-in-One" in connection with the 2011 catalogue was completely protected by the fair use defense. As discussed below, genuine issues of material fact exist regarding the elements of fair use in this case, thereby precluding summary judgment. While summary judgment on the fair use defense in a trademark case is *possible*, we reiterate that "summary judgment is generally disfavored" in trademark cases, due to "the intensely factual nature of trademark disputes." *Fortune Dynamic*, 618 F.3d at 1031.

A.   Non-Catalogue Uses of All-in-One

Marketquest first argues that the district court erred by not specifically analyzing all of the uses of "All-in-One" employed by Defendants, since the fair use analysis often varies when a defendant uses the same mark in different ways. The "other uses" of "All-in-One" included (1) promotional materials that featured an image of the 2011 catalogue; (2) promotional materials that directed customers to look for products or information in "the 2011 Norwood All in ONE catalogue"; and (3) an online advertisement that said "Put Your Drinkware Needs . . . in a Norwood ALL in ONE Basket," which included a photo of a basket containing several different types of drinkware. Defendants respond that there was no need to conduct a design-by-design review because all of these uses connected to the 2011 catalogue, and there is no basis for the claim that the district court did not consider all the evidence, even if other uses were not specifically referenced by the district court.

It appears from its summary judgment order that the district court focused on Defendants' use of "All-in-One" on the 2011 catalogue, and perhaps did not consider other uses. While a design-by-design review of promotional materials that merely included a picture of the 2011 catalogue was not required, references to "the 2011 Norwood All in ONE catalogue" and "a Norwood ALL in ONE Basket" are sufficiently distinct to require analysis for fair use. These uses are considered below, along with the 2011 catalogue use.

B.   Use Other Than as a Trademark

A fair use must be a use other than as a trademark. 15 U.S.C. §1115(b)(4). A trademark is used "to identify and distinguish . . . goods . . . from those manufactured or sold by others and to indicate the source of the goods." *Id.* §1127. "To determine whether a term is being used as a mark, we look for indications that the term is being used to associate it with a manufacturer," and "whether the term is used as a symbol to attract public attention." *Fortune Dynamic*, 618 F.3d at 1040 (internal quotation marks omitted). We also consider "whether the allegedly infringing user undertook precautionary measures . . . to minimize the risk that the term will be understood in its trademark sense." *Id.* (internal quotation marks omitted).

A genuine issue of fact exists regarding whether Defendants used "All-in-One" as a trademark. Defendants did take "precautionary measures" when featuring "All-in-One" on the 2011 catalogue: Norwood was printed at the top in large, bold, capital letters with a trademark symbol, while "All-in-One" was located further down on the page, in smaller letters, without a trademark symbol, and positioned as a heading over a list of all the products consolidated "in one" catalogue. This suggests that Norwood was used to indicate the source of the goods, rather than "All-in-One" (although it is possible for more than one trademark to appear on a catalogue cover). However, when considering all of Defendants' uses of "All-in-One," a jury could potentially find trademark use. The "precautionary measures" listed above were *not* present when Defendants referred to "the 2011 Norwood All in ONE catalogue" and "a Norwood ALL in ONE Basket." In these uses, there is no obvious distinction between Norwood and "All-in-One," and both could reasonably be understood to indicate source.

C.   Descriptive Use

To prevail on fair use, a defendant must show that it used the mark "in its primary, descriptive sense." *Fortune Dynamic*, 618 F.3d at 1041 (quoting *Brother Records, Inc. v. Jardine*, 318 F.3d 900, 906 (9th Cir. 2003) (alteration omitted)); *see* 15 U.S.C. §1115(b)(4). While "we accept some flexibility in what counts as descriptive," *Fortune Dynamic*, 618 F.3d at 1042, "the scope of the fair use defense varies with . . . the descriptive purity of the defendant's use and whether there are other words available to do the describing." *Id.* at 1041. Even when "there [is] some evidence of descriptive use, [a jury] could still reasonably conclude that [a defendant's] lack of 'precautionary measures' " outweighs such evidence. *Id.* at 1042.

There is a strong argument that Defendants' use of "All-in-One" on the 2011 catalogue was descriptive, because it was used as a heading for a list of the products consolidated "all in one" catalogue. Moreover, as discussed above, Defendants took "precautionary measures" on their catalogue cover by using a design that indicated descriptive use. However, Defendants' other uses of "All-in-One" were arguably not descriptive, and "precautionary measures" were not taken with these uses. While Defendants' use of "All-in-One" as a heading on the 2011 catalogue strongly indicates descriptive use, such use is not apparent in decontextualized references to "the 2011 Norwood All in ONE catalogue." Additionally, "Put Your Drinkware Needs . . . in a Norwood ALL in ONE Basket" does not fall under the descriptive use explanation that Defendants advance because it does not refer to a consolidated catalogue. It may descriptively refer to consolidating drinkware in a basket, but the "descriptive purity" of such use is questionable because it is unclear if the basket is literal or suggestive. *See id.* at 1041. Uses of "All-in-One" in ways that stripped it of its possible descriptive meaning undermine Defendants' descriptive use argument, such that a finder of fact could determine that the use was not descriptive. Moreover, a finder of fact could determine that Defendants "had at [their] disposal a number of alternative words [or phrases] that could adequately capture [their] goal," limiting the scope of the fair use defense in this case. *Id.* at 1042.

D.   In Good Faith

A defendant asserting fair use must also show that it used the mark in good faith. 15 U.S.C. §1115(b)(4). When considering forward confusion, this element "involves the same issue as the intent factor in the likelihood of confusion analysis"; that is, "whether defendant in adopting its mark intended to capitalize on plaintiff's good will." *Fortune Dynamic*, 618 F.3d at 1043. The shift in focus discussed in Part II above for assessing intent when considering likelihood of confusion under a reverse confusion theory generally applies when considering good faith as part of the fair use defense in a case that presents reverse confusion. However, the good faith inquiry differs somewhat from the *Sleekcraft* intent factor, regardless of the underlying theory of confusion. In fair use, good faith is an element of the defense, not merely a factor to consider when it is relevant in a given case.

As with intent in *Sleekcraft*, there is no bright-line rule or required piece of evidence to establish good or bad faith. While the focus may differ when considering forward or reverse confusion, generally the same types of evidence will be relevant to this inquiry. This includes evidence such as whether the defendant intended to create confusion, whether forward or reverse; intended to push the plaintiff out of the market; remained ignorant of the plaintiff's mark when it reasonably should have known of the mark; knew of the mark and showed bad faith in its disregard of the plaintiff's rights; or any other evidence relevant to whether the defendant's claimed "objectively fair" use of the mark was done in good faith. *See KP Permanent I*, 543 U.S. at 123, 125 S. Ct. 542; *see also, e.g., Fortune Dynamic*, 618 F.3d at 1043 (holding that a material question of fact existed regarding defendant's good faith when the plaintiff introduced evidence that the defendant carelessly failed to investigate the trademark at issue, along with expert testimony that a trademark search would have been standard practice in the relevant industry).

Marketquest argues that because this case presents reverse confusion, mere knowledge of Marketquest's ownership and use of the "All-in-One" mark establishes bad faith on the part of Defendants, and fair use is thus unavailable as a matter of law. That is incorrect. An inference of bad faith does not arise from mere knowledge of a mark when the use is otherwise objectively fair, even in a case presenting reverse confusion. Marketquest also argues that Defendants' use of two of its marks in the same year supports an inference of bad faith. This fact by itself, coupled with Marketquest's knowledge of the marks, is thin evidence of bad faith. However, we cannot say on summary judgment that no reasonable finder of fact could infer bad faith from these facts.

E.   Degree of Consumer Confusion

"The fair use defense only comes into play once the party alleging infringement has shown by a preponderance of the evidence that confusion is likely." *KP Permanent II*, 408 F.3d at 608-09. This is because if there is no likelihood of consumer confusion, then there is no trademark infringement, making an affirmative defense to trademark infringement irrelevant. *KP Permanent I*, 543 U.S. at 120, 125 S. Ct. 542. After the plaintiff meets the threshold showing, in the fair use analysis "the degree of customer confusion [is] a factor" to consider. *KP Permanent II*, 408 F.3d at 609. However, a defendant raising the defense does not have the burden to negate any likelihood of consumer confusion. *KP Permanent*

I, 543 U.S. at 114, 125 S. Ct. 542. Some consumer confusion is compatible with fair use, and when a plaintiff chooses "to identify its product with a mark that uses a well known descriptive phrase" it assumes the risk of some confusion. *Id*. at 121-22, 125 S. Ct. 542.

The district court held that Marketquest met the threshold requirement for fair use by showing that there is some likelihood of confusion, relying upon its previous *Sleekcraft* analysis in the order denying Marketquest's motion for a preliminary injunction. However, the district court held that any further *Sleekcraft* analysis was "unnecessary" because fair use provided Defendants a complete defense.

Marketquest argues that the district court's holding was incomplete because it did not conduct a full *Sleekcraft* analysis, nor did it consider the additional factors that we stated in *KP Permanent II* would be relevant to the jury's consideration of fair use in that case. Defendants counter that a court may grant summary judgment on the fair use defense without deciding the likelihood of confusion because confusion is not the focus of fair use; the focus is objective fairness, and some confusion is accepted.

We emphasize that the degree of consumer confusion is a *factor* in the fair use analysis, not an *element* of fair use. *See KP Permanent I*, 543 U.S. at 118, 125 S. Ct. 542 ("Congress said nothing about likelihood of confusion in setting out the elements of the fair use defense."). This factor is useful in considering whether, overall, the use was objectively fair. A use that is likely to confuse consumers, or that has caused actual confusion, is less likely to be objectively fair (although some confusion is permissible). *Accord Shakespeare Co. v. Silstar Corp. of Am.*, 110 F.3d 234, 243 (4th Cir. 1997) ("While it is true that *to the degree* that confusion is likely, a use is less likely to be found fair, it does not follow that a determination of likely confusion precludes considering the fairness of use."). The *Sleekcraft* factors and additional factors that we identified as relevant in *KP Permanent II* may also be relevant in a given case where fair use is at issue. A court is not required in every case to recite and analyze all the factors identified in *Sleekcraft* and *KP Permanent II* one-by-one for a fair use analysis to be complete. A court *may* do so, but these are merely factors to facilitate a court's analysis, to the degree they are relevant in a given case.

In this case, the district court referenced its previous *Sleekcraft* analysis at the preliminary injunction phase. The district court was not required to conduct this analysis again and determine all potential issues of fact as a matter of law before considering summary judgment on fair use. However, because we reverse summary judgment on fair use for the reasons indicated above, we leave it to the district court to determine on remand the relevance of the degree of consumer confusion in this case.

. . .

[*Reversed and remanded.*]

NOTES AND QUESTIONS

1.   *A three-element test for descriptive fair use.* The cases above read Section 33(b)(4) as establishing a three-element test for descriptive fair use. Do you agree with this construction? Is there a meaningful difference between use "otherwise as a mark" (element 1) and use "only to describe [one's] goods or services" (element 2)? How does descriptive fair use under this three-element test differ from the test for copyright fair use? *See* 17 U.S.C. §107 (providing a four-factor test for copyright fair use).

2.   *Role of confusion in the three-part descriptive fair use analysis?* In cases involving the fair use defense, could a court assume likely confusion *arguendo* and then analyze fair use, potentially avoiding the need to engage in a full multi-factor likelihood-of-confusion analysis? Or, since *KP Permanent* declined to "rule out the pertinence of the degree of

consumer confusion under the fair use defense," must a court always analyze confusion first, and fair use afterward? Under this second approach, might courts find it harder to dispose of trademark cases on summary judgment? This might be problematic if the cost of trial itself imposes a chilling effect on activities that might ultimately be deemed fair. For an analysis and proposals for a solution, *see* William McGeveran, *Rethinking Trademark Fair Use*, 94 IOWA L. REV. 49 (2008).

On remand in *KP Permanent*, the Ninth Circuit confirmed that "the degree of customer confusion remains a factor in evaluating fair use," and listed "the relevant factors for consideration by the jury" in determining descriptive fair use:

> the degree of likely confusion, the strength of the trademark, the descriptive nature of the term for the product or service being offered by KP and the availability of alternate descriptive terms, the extent of the use of the term prior to the registration of the trademark, and any differences among the times and contexts in which KP has used the term.

KP Permanent Make-Up, Inc. v. Lasting Impression I, Inc., 408 F.3d 596, 609 (9th Cir. 2005). Are the *KP Permanent* factors very much different from the multi-factor likelihood-of-confusion test itself? *Marketquest* explicitly incorporates the degree of confusion into its fair use analysis (as a factor, and not an element, the court emphasizes), while *Fortune Dynamic* and *Kelly-Brown* do not—at least not explicitly.

3.   *Element (1)—"use otherwise than as a mark."* According to the *Fortune Dynamic* court, a defendant may be using a term as a mark if the defendant is using the term as a "symbol to attract public attention," or if the defendant has failed to take "precautionary measures" (such as including labels that minimize the risk that the term will be perceived as a source indicator, or juxtaposing the term with the defendant's house mark). It is apparent from the cases that this inquiry is highly contextual. Should it be? What are the drawbacks of such an approach? Should expert testimony be permitted, or do you agree with the *Fortune Dynamic* opinion that the fact finder is well equipped to make this determination without hearing from experts? Does *Marketquest* help you understand what might be required for acceptable precautionary measures?

4.   *Element (1)—"use otherwise than as a mark" versus actionable trademark use.* How does the element (1) inquiry differ from the actionable trademark use requirement discussed in Chapter 7? *See generally* Margreth Barrett, *Reconciling Fair Use and Trademark Use*, 28 CARDOZO ARTS & ENT. L.J. 1 (2010) (exploring the issue).

5.   *Element (2)—use in a descriptive sense, applied in* Fortune Dynamic. The court in *Fortune Dynamic* explained that use in a "descriptive sense" is not narrowly confined to terms that describe the physical attributes of the goods. Elsewhere, the court suggested that the analysis be framed as a matter of "descriptive purity," where uses that are less purely descriptive are less likely to be adjudged fair uses. The court also considered whether terms other than the trademark at issue could have been used. Does any of this clarify what "use in a descriptive sense" means? In view of this apparent flexibility, are you surprised that the court treated the argument that DELICIOUS was descriptive because it was a playful reference to the qualities of the wearer of the tank top? Does the reasoning or language of *KP Permanent* contemplate the application of the fair use concept to uses of inherently distinctive marks?

6.   *Element (2)—use in a descriptive sense, applied in* Kelly-Brown. Was the court in *Kelly-Brown* applying the notion of descriptive purity? Was it considering available alternatives? If not, what *was* it considering? And was it undertaking these inquiries with respect to each individual use by defendants, or with respect to the collective whole? Suppose that you analyzed the use of OWN YOUR POWER on the O magazine cover individually? How

would your analysis for use in a descriptive sense come out, and would it be different from your analysis of the website use? In general, should courts analyze the defendant's uses individually or as a whole?

7. *Element (2) — use in a descriptive sense, applied in* Marketquest. The court in *Marketquest* distinguishes between the defendant's use of the "All-in-One" heading on the catalogue and other uses, such as the use of the phrase "Put Your Drinkware Needs . . . in a Norwood ALL in ONE Basket." Should descriptive fair use be quite so fact-sensitive? If so, what are the lessons for the development of the defense?

8. *Element (2) — use in a descriptive sense, applied to non-verbal marks.* Suppose that the mark at issue is a non-verbal mark, such as a pine-scented, pine tree–shaped cardboard air freshener for automobiles. Defendant makes a pine-scented, pine tree–shaped room air freshener designed to be plugged into electrical outlets and sold at Christmas time. Is the defendant's use a use in a descriptive sense? Can it be, as a matter of law? *See Car-Freshener Corp. v. S.C. Johnson & Son, Inc.,* 70 F.3d 267, 269 (2d Cir. 1995). Does the fair use defense as articulated in Lanham Act §33(b)(4) apply only to cases involving word marks?

9. *Element (3) — good faith.* In both *Fortune Dynamic* and *Kelly-Brown*, the courts equate the good faith inquiry in fair use to the intent factor in the likelihood-of-confusion test. *See also International Stamp Art, Inc. v. United States Postal Service,* 456 F.3d 1270 (11th Cir. 2006) (same; suggesting that the inquiry is whether the alleged infringer intended to trade on the mark owner's goodwill). Is this sensible, even if it has the effect of further entangling fair use with confusion? In *Fortune Dynamic*, the appellate court concluded that the trial judge should have admitted Fortune's expert testimony on lack of good faith — in particular, testimony that Victoria's Secret's had failed "to investigate whether someone held a DELICIOUS trademark," contrary to standard industry practice. Is this circumstantial evidence of intent, or mere negligence? Should courts develop a rule that effectively imposes an affirmative duty to investigate? Should businesses be required to obtain a formal clearance opinion from trademark counsel in order to satisfy the element of good faith?

10. *Summary resolution of descriptive fair use?* In the above cases, the courts declined to resolve the descriptive fair use issue summarily. Does this underscore a problem with the structure of the fair use doctrine? On the other hand, grants of summary judgment sustaining a fair use defense are not entirely unknown. *See, e.g., Sorensen v. WD-40 Co.,* 792 F.3d 712 (7th Cir. 2015) (upholding a determination on summary judgment that defendant's use of the term "inhibitor" was a descriptive fair use). Should courts be reluctant to grant summary judgment in fair use cases?

PROBLEM 9-1: FAIR USE OF NAMES

Cases presenting fair use claims for name marks arise frequently. For one thing, many people share surnames. In addition, family members operating a business under the family name may decide to split up and compete. The Lanham Act specifically recognizes the fair use of one's name as a species of the fair use defense. Lanham Act §33(b)(4) preserves as a defense to incontestable registrations the "use, otherwise than as a mark, of the party's individual name in his own business, or of the individual name of anyone in privity with such party. . . ."

In *L.E. Waterman Co. v. Modern Pen Co.,* 235 U.S. 88 (1914), Modern Pen sought to use the name "A.A. Waterman" on its fountain pens, claiming that an individual named Arthur A. Waterman had been affiliated with its business. L.E. Waterman, owner of the mark WATERMAN for pens, sued for an injunction, which the Supreme Court upheld, dispensing with the argument that Arthur A. Waterman should have an absolute right to use his own name in business. Whether Modern Pen could use the Waterman name depended on whether its use created a likelihood of confusion.

While the Court did not frame its decision in terms of "fair use," the *Waterman* case is nonetheless instructive on the scope of fair use of one's own name. The lower court's injunction did not forbid Modern Pen from any use of the term "Waterman" whatsoever; rather, it ordered that Modern Pen use "Arthur A. Waterman & Co." (instead of A.A. Waterman & Co.), and that Modern Pen include an express statement disclaiming any affiliation with the L.E. Waterman Company.

This approach of providing carefully limited injunctive relief, which treats name marks like any other trademarks, but recognizes the policy interest in permitting some breathing space for "fair" uses of one's own name, is now the dominant approach in the courts. For example, one court enjoined Paolo Gucci (grandson of the famous designer) from using his grandfather's famous GUCCI mark on various leather goods because the use created a likelihood of confusion, but allowed him to include text such as "Designed by Paolo Gucci" on the labels. *Gucci v. Gucci Shops, Inc.*, 688 F. Supp. 916 (S.D.N.Y. 1988).

The extent of allowable breathing space—if any—is informed by a range of equitable considerations. For example, in *Levitt Corp. v. Levitt*, 593 F.2d 463 (2d Cir. 1979), William J. Levitt, who founded the Levitt Corporation and its "Levittown" real estate developments, left the company after signing an agreement in which the company retained rights to the use of the Levitt name. Subsequently, William J. Levitt started a real estate development in Florida under the "Levittown" name. The company sued and procured a wide-ranging injunction banning William J. Levitt from using the "Levittown" name in connection with the new development, forbidding any advertisements or other publicity that connected William J. Levitt with the new development, and prohibiting William J. Levitt from publicizing his prior connection to the famous company.

Of course, in some cases, the court will not even reach a fair use analysis because of the absence of any evidence of confusion. *See, e.g.*, *Brennan's, Inc. v. Brennan's Restaurant, L.L.C.*, 360 F.3d 125 (2d Cir. 2004) (denying relief to owner of trademark BRENNAN'S in connection with a New Orleans restaurant, who sought preliminary injunction against use of TERRANCE BRENNAN'S SEAFOOD AND CHOP HOUSE in connection with New York restaurant).

(1) Suppose that Professors Dinwoodie and Janis decide to open a chain of fast-food hamburger restaurants. We want to call our restaurants McDONALD'S. Clearly, we can't: Even though "McDonald" might indicate a common surname, it also clearly has trademark significance and is registrable for fast-food restaurants under the rules that we discussed for obtaining trademark rights in names in Chapter 5. Suppose, however, that Professor Dinwoodie (who is, after all, Scottish) can prove that his legal surname is actually McDonald; he only adopted "Dinwoodie" as a nom de plume. Is Dinwoodie a.k.a. McDonald likely to succeed in claiming that his use of McDONALD'S in connection with his restaurant is a "fair use" of his own name in connection with his business? *McDonald's Takes Issue with Rugby's McBrat Pack*, ABC NEWS (Mar. 11, 2005), *http://www.abc.net.au/news/2005-03-11/mcdonalds-takes-issue-with-rugbys-mcbrat-pack/2592756* (reporting on a similar dispute from Australia).

(2) Consider the advertisement on the following page. The advertiser, Ramada, operates the Renaissance Hotels. Ramada's competitor, the Marriott Corporation, owns the mark MARRIOTT for hotels. The ad text in the left-hand column of the page purports to quote "Frank and Cindy Marriott from Florida" while the two are supposedly "staying at the Los Angeles Renaissance Hotel." At the foot of the page, beneath the phone number, is the line "Frank and Cindy Marriott are not related to the Marriott Hotels and the advertisement does not constitute an endorsement of the Renaissance Hotels by Marriott

Hotels." Suppose that Marriott sues Ramada under the Lanham Act. Are the references to "Marriott" in the advertisement fair uses? *See Marriott Corp. v. Ramada Inc.*, 826 F. Supp. 726 (S.D.N.Y. 1993).

(3) Given the long tradition of lawyers using their last names in connection with law firm partnerships, should the trademark law recognize an absolute right to use one's name in connection with a law firm? The issue arises when the name partner of a firm breaks off to start a competing firm and wants to use his or her name in connection with the competing firm. *See Suisman, Shapiro, Wool, Brennan, Gray & Greenberg PC v. Suisman*, 80 U.S.P.Q.2d (BNA) 1072 (D. Conn. 2006); *see also Jones Day v. Blockshopper LLC*, 89 U.S.P.Q.2d (BNA) 1623 (N.D. Ill. 2008) (alleged Lanham Act violations where defendant's website made references to Jones Day real estate lawyers and links to Jones Day's website).

(4) One day, Dinwoodie and Janis decided to start their own law school. Having no prior experience in such things as constructing law school facilities, we opted for an online law school. Initially, we called it the Dinwoodie & Janis Electronic School of Law. This proved to be a marketing failure. So we picked a name with more cachet: the Sonia Sotomayor Electronic School of Law. Under Lanham Act principles, do we need the Justice's permission?

PROBLEM 9-2:   FAIR USE OF GEOGRAPHIC INDICATORS

Lanham Act §33(b)(4) mentions fair use of geographic terms as a species of fair use. This should not surprise you. Even where a geographic term takes on trademark significance for particular goods and services—*see* Chapter 5—others may routinely need access to the geographic term to describe truthfully the geographic origin of their own products or services. For example, suppose that Joe, the Beer Guy, acquires trademark rights in LONE TREE for beer brewed in Lone Tree, Iowa, and Joe's competitor, Jill, brews PRAIRIE beer, also in Lone Tree, Iowa. If Jill wants to include text on her bottle labels stating that PRAIRIE beer "is brewed proudly in Lone Tree, Iowa," is Joe likely to prevail in a suit for injunctive relief? *See Schafer Co. v. Innco Mgmt. Corp.*, 797 F. Supp. 477 (E.D.N.C. 1992), *aff'd*, 995 F.2d 1064 (4th Cir. 1993); *see also Leelanau Wine Cellars, Ltd. v. Black & Red, Inc.*, 502 F.3d 504 (6th Cir. 2007) (likelihood of confusion claim by owner of LEELANAU CELLARS for wine against owner of CHATEAU DE LEELANAU for wine, where both wines were produced in Michigan's Leelanau Peninsula).

3.   Nominative Fair Use

The *Chanel* case, which follows, lays out the standard policy arguments for recognizing a nominative fair use doctrine, albeit without invoking that doctrine explicitly.

R. G. SMITH v. CHANEL, INC.
402 F.2d 562 (9th Cir. 1968)

BROWNING, Circuit Judge:

Appellant R. G. Smith, doing business as Ta'Ron, Inc., advertised a fragrance called "Second Chance" as a duplicate of appellees' "Chanel No. 5," at a fraction of the latter's price. Appellees were granted a preliminary injunction prohibiting any reference to Chanel No. 5 in the promotion or sale of appellants' product. This appeal followed.

The action rests upon a single advertisement published in "Specialty Salesmen," a trade journal directed to wholesale purchasers. The advertisement offered "The Ta'Ron Line of Perfumes" for sale. It gave the seller's address as "Ta'Ron Inc., 26 Harbor Cove, Mill Valley, Calif." It stated that the Ta'Ron perfumes "duplicate 100% perfect the exact scent of the world's finest and most expensive perfumes and colognes at prices that will zoom sales to volumes you have never before experienced!" It repeated the claim of exact duplication in a variety of forms.

The advertisement suggested that a "Blindfold Test" be used "on skeptical prospects," challenging them to detect any difference between a well known fragrance and the Ta'Ron "duplicate." One suggested challenge was, "We dare you to try to detect any difference between Chanel #5 (25.00) and Ta'Ron's 2nd Chance. $7.00."

In an order blank printed as part of the advertisement each Ta'Ron fragrance was listed with the name of the well known fragrance which it purportedly duplicated immediately beneath. Below "Second Chance" appeared "*(Chanel #5)." The asterisk referred to a statement at the bottom of the form reading "Registered Trade Name of Original Fragrance House."

Appellees conceded below and concede here that appellants "have the right to copy, if they can, the unpatented formula of appellees' products." Moreover, for the purposes of these proceedings, appellees assume that "the products manufactured and advertised by [appellants] are *in fact* equivalents of those products manufactured by appellees."

(Emphasis in original.) Finally, appellees disclaim any contention that the packaging or labeling of appellants' "Second Chance" is misleading or confusing.

I

The principal question presented on this record is whether one who has copied an unpatented product sold under a trademark may use the trademark in his advertising to identify the product he has copied. We hold that he may, and that such advertising may not be enjoined under either the Lanham Act, 15 U.S.C. §1125(a) (1964), or the common law of unfair competition, so long as it does not contain misrepresentations or create a reasonable likelihood that purchasers will be confused as to the source, identity, or sponsorship of the advertiser's product.

This conclusion is supported by direct holdings in *Saxlehner v. Wagner*, 216 U.S. 375 (1910); [cit.], and *Societe Comptoir de L'Industrie Cotonniere Etablissements Boussac v. Alexander's Dept. Stores, Inc.*, 299 F.2d 33 (2d Cir. 1962).

In *Saxlehner* the copied product was a "bitter water" drawn from certain privately owned natural springs. The plaintiff sold the natural water under the name "Hunyadi Janos," a valid trademark. The defendant was enjoined from using plaintiff's trademark to designate defendant's "artificial" water, but was permitted to use it to identify plaintiff's natural water as the product which defendant was copying.

Justice Holmes wrote:

> We see no reason for disturbing the finding of the courts below that there was no unfair competition and no fraud. The real intent of the plaintiff's bill, it seems to us, is to extend the monopoly of such trademark or tradename as she may have to a monopoly of her type of bitter water, by preventing manufacturers from telling the public in a way that will be understood, what they are copying and trying to sell. But the plaintiff has no patent for the water, and the defendants have a right to reproduce it as nearly as they can. They have a right to tell the public what they are doing, and to get whatever share they can in the popularity of the water by advertising that they are trying to make the same article, and think that they succeed. . . .

216 U.S. at 380-381.

. . .

In *Societe Comptoir de L'Industrie Cotonniere Etablissements Boussac v. Alexander's Dept. Stores, Inc.*, the defendant used plaintiff's registered trademarks "Dior" and "Christian Dior" in defendant's advertising in identifying plaintiff's dresses as the original creations from which defendant's dresses were copied. The district court refused to grant a preliminary injunction.

. . .

The [*Alexander's Dept. Store*] court weighed the underlying interests in this language:
> Involved in the instant case is a conflict of values which necessarily arises in an economy characterized by competition and private property. The courts have come to recognize the true nature of the considerations often involved in efforts to extend protection of common law trade names so as to create a shield against competition. . . . The interest of the consumer here in competitive prices of garments using Dior designs without deception as to origin, is at least as great as the interest of plaintiff's in monopolizing the same.

299 F.2d at 37.

We have found no holdings by federal or California appellate courts contrary to the rule of these . . . cases. Moreover, the principle for which they stand—that use of another's trademark to identify the trademark owner's product in comparative advertising is not prohibited by either statutory or common law, absent misrepresentation regarding the products or confusion as to their source or sponsorship—is also generally approved by secondary authorities.

The rule rests upon the traditionally accepted premise that the only legally relevant function of a trademark is to impart information as to the source or sponsorship of the product. Appellees argue that protection should also be extended to the trademark's commercially more important function of embodying consumer good will created through extensive, skillful, and costly advertising. The courts, however, have generally confined legal protection to the trademark's source identification function for reasons grounded in the public policy favoring a free, competitive economy.

Preservation of the trademark as a means of identifying the trademark owner's products, implemented both by the Lanham Act and the common law, serves an important public purpose.[13] It makes effective competition possible in a complex, impersonal marketplace by providing a means through which the consumer can identify products which please him and reward the producer with continued patronage. Without some such method of product identification, informed consumer choice, and hence meaningful competition in quality, could not exist.

On the other hand, it has been suggested that protection of trademark values other than source identification would create serious anti-competitive consequences with little compensating public benefit. This is said to be true for the following reasons.

The object of much modern advertising is "to impregnate the atmosphere of the market with the drawing power of a congenial symbol," *Mishawaka Rubber & Woolen Mfg. Co. v. S. S. Kresge Co.*, 316 U.S. 203, 205 (1942), rather than to communicate information as to quality or price. The primary value of the modern trademark lies in the "conditioned reflex developed in the buyer by imaginative or often purely monotonous selling of the mark itself." Derring, Trademarks on Noncompetitive Products, 36 Or. L. Rev. 1, 2 (1956). To the extent that advertising of this type succeeds, it is suggested, the trademark is endowed with sales appeal independent of the quality or price of the product to which it is attached; economically irrational elements are introduced into consumer choices; and the trademark owner is insulated from the normal pressures of price and quality competition. In consequence the competitive system fails to perform its function of allocating available resources efficiently.

Moreover, the economically irrelevant appeal of highly publicized trademarks is thought to constitute a barrier to the entry of new competition into the market. "[T]he presence of irrational consumer allegiances may constitute an effective barrier to entry. Consumer allegiances built over the years with intensive advertising, trademarks, trade names, copyrights and so forth extend substantial protection to firms already in the market. In some markets this barrier to entry may be insuperable." Papandreou, The Economic Effects of Trademarks, 44 Cal. L. Rev. 503, 508-09 (1956). High barriers to entry tend, in turn, to produce "high excess profits and monopolistic output restriction" and "probably . . . high and possibly excessive costs of sales promotion." J. Bain, Barriers to New Competition 203 (1955).

A related consideration is also pertinent to the present case. Since appellees' perfume was unpatented, appellants had a right to copy it, as appellees concede. There was a strong public interest in their doing so, "[f]or imitation is the life blood of competition. It is the unimpeded availability of substantially equivalent units that permits the normal operation of supply and demand to yield the fair price society must pay for a given commodity." *American Safety Table Co. v. Schreiber*, 269 F.2d 255, 272 (2d Cir. 1959). But this public benefit might be lost if appellants could not tell potential purchasers that appellants'

---

13. It also serves two substantial private interests of the owner: It protects him from diversion of sales through a competitor's use of his trademark or one confusingly similar to it; and it protects his reputation from the injury that could occur if the competitor's goods were inferior.

product was the equivalent of appellees' product. "A competitor's chief weapon is his ability to represent his product as being equivalent and cheaper. . . ." Alexander, Honesty and Competition, 39 So. Cal. L. Rev. 1, 4 (1966). The most effective way (and, where complex chemical compositions sold under trade names are involved, often the only practical way) in which this can be done is to identify the copied article by its trademark or trade name. To prohibit use of a competitor's trademark for the sole purpose of identifying the competitor's product would bar effective communication of claims of equivalence. Assuming the equivalence of "Second Chance" and "Chanel No. 5," the public interest would not be served by a rule of law which would preclude sellers of "Second Chance" from advising consumers of the equivalence and thus effectively deprive consumers of knowledge that an identical product was being offered at one third the price.

As Justice Holmes wrote in *Saxlehner v. Wagner*, the practical effect of such a rule would be to extend the monopoly of the trademark to a monopoly of the product. The monopoly conferred by judicial protection of complete trademark exclusivity would not be preceded by examination and approval by a governmental body, as is the case with most other government-granted monopolies. Moreover, it would not be limited in time, but would be perpetual.

Against these considerations, two principal arguments are made for protection of trademark values other than source identification.

The first of these, as stated in the findings of the district court, is that the creation of the other values inherent in the trademark require "the expenditure of great effort, skill and ability" and that the competitor should not be permitted "to take a free ride" on the trademark owner's "widespread goodwill and reputation."

A large expenditure of money does not in itself create legally protectable rights. Appellees are not entitled to monopolize the public's desire for the unpatented product, even though they themselves created that desire at great effort and expense. As we have noted, the most effective way (and in some cases the only practical way) in which others may compete in satisfying the demand for the product is to produce it and tell the public they have done so, and if they could be barred from this effort appellees would have found a way to acquire a practical monopoly in the unpatented product to which they are not legally entitled.

Disapproval of the copyist's opportunism may be an understandable first reaction, "[b]ut this initial response to the problem has been curbed in deference to the greater public good." *American Safety Table Co. v. Schreiber*, 269 F.2d at 272. By taking his "free ride," the copyist, albeit unintentionally, serves an important public interest by offering comparable goods at lower prices. On the other hand, the trademark owner, perhaps equally without design, sacrifices public to personal interests by seeking immunity from the rigors of competition.

Moreover, appellees' reputation is not directly at stake. Appellants' advertisement makes it clear that the product they offer is their own. If it proves to be inferior, they, not appellees, will bear the burden of consumer disapproval. *Cf. Prestonettes, Inc. v. Coty*, 264 U.S. 359, 369 (1924).

The second major argument for extended trademark protection is that even in the absence of confusion as to source, use of the trademark of another "creates a serious threat to the uniqueness and distinctiveness" of the trademark, and "if continued would create a risk of making a generic or descriptive term of the words" of which the trademark is composed.

The contention has little weight in the context of this case. Appellants do not use appellees' trademark as a generic term. They employ it only to describe appellees' product, not to identify their own. They do not label their product "Ta'Ron's Chanel No. 5," as they might if appellees' trademark had come to be the common name for the product to which it is applied. Appellants' use does not challenge the distinctiveness of appellees' trademark, or appellees' exclusive right to employ that trademark to indicate source or sponsorship. For reasons already discussed, we think appellees are entitled to no more. The slight tendency to carry the mark into the common language which even this use may have is outweighed by the substantial value of such use in the maintenance of effective competition.

We are satisfied, therefore, that both authority and reason require a holding that in the absence of misrepresentation or confusion as to source or sponsorship a seller in promoting his own goods may use the trademark of another to identify the latter's goods. The district court's contrary conclusion cannot support the injunction.

. . .

[*Reversed and remanded.*]

NOTES AND QUESTIONS

1. Chanel *and the doctrine of "nominative" fair use.* The *Chanel* case is often cited for the proposition that truthful "comparative" advertising is permissible. However, in retrospect, the case might also be understood as an illustration of the defense of "nominative" fair use later articulated in numerous cases, including the cases excerpted below.

2. Chanel *and false advertising.* The *Chanel* case may also be understood as an application of false advertising principles. The Lanham Act does contain a false advertising cause of action, now articulated as Section 43(a)(1)(B). We discuss that cause of action *infra* in Chapter 10.

In *New Kids on the Block v. News Am. Publ'g Inc.*, 971 F.2d 302, 308 (9th Cir. 1992), the court adopted a three-part test for nominative fair use that has proven influential, as the cases below illustrate. In *New Kids*, the defendant newspaper had referred to the plaintiff band "New Kids on the Block" in the course of conducting a telephone poll about the most popular member of the band. Descriptive fair use was not necessarily a good fit because the defendant was using the plaintiff's mark to refer to the *plaintiff's* product. Accordingly, the Ninth Circuit adopted a three-part test for nominative fair use, under which a defendant could establish fair use by proving (1) that the product or service in question was one not readily identifiable without use of the trademark; (2) that only so much of the mark or marks was used as was reasonably necessary to identify the product or service; and (3) that the user did nothing that would suggest sponsorship or endorsement by the trademark holder. In *Cairns v. Franklin Mint Co.*, 292 F.3d 1139, 1151 (9th Cir. 2002), the Ninth Circuit explained the distinction between "nominative" fair use and "classic" (descriptive) fair use:

> The nominative fair use analysis is appropriate where a defendant has used the plaintiff's mark to describe the plaintiff's product, *even if the defendant's ultimate goal is to describe his own product.* Conversely, the classic fair use analysis is appropriate where a defendant has used the plaintiff's mark *only* to describe his own product, *and not at all to describe the plaintiff's product.*

The Ninth Circuit also seemed to suggest that in a nominative fair use case, the *New Kids* test should replace the likelihood-of-confusion factors analysis.

The following cases take up the tasks of clarifying the test for nominative fair use and explaining how it relates to confusion. On the latter point, recall that the Court in

KP Permanent addressed the relationship between descriptive fair use and confusion, but declared (in footnote 3) that it was not addressing "the [Ninth Circuit's] discussion of 'nominative fair use.'" As the cases below illustrate, no uniform approach to nominative fair use has yet emerged.

CENTURY 21 REAL ESTATE CORP. v. LENDINGTREE, INC.

425 F.3d 211 (3d Cir. 2005)

RENDELL, Circuit Judge:

. . .

Appellees, Century 21, Coldwell Banker and ERA ("CCE") complain that Appellant LendingTree ("LT"), in the process of marketing its mortgage services, improperly referenced CCE's trademarked services. LT contends that its use was nominative and fair, and permitted as a matter of law.

. . .

Traditionally, we have looked to whether a trademark is likely to cause confusion in order to determine whether a violation of the Lanham Act has occurred and, thus, whether the use should be enjoined and prohibited. However, it is unclear what role "likelihood of confusion" plays in the analysis when "fair use" is asserted as a defense. Recently, the United States Supreme Court provided guidance to the courts regarding the test for classic fair use in *KP Permanent Make-Up, Inc. v. Lasting Impression I, Inc.*, 543 U.S. 111 (2004). The issue before us is the extent to which its reasoning applies to the nominative fair use analysis as well.

I.   FACTUAL AND PROCEDURAL BACKGROUND

[CCE are real estate companies that operate extensive franchise systems. Franchisees (real estate brokers) are licensed to use the CCE companies' various marks, albeit only in conjunction with the franchisee's brokerage name.

LT runs a web-based real estate referral service. LT's website invites customers to input a desired location and various other real estate criteria. The website responds with a list of brokers, and also includes various references to the CCE firms. For example, the website states that LT gives consumers access to "a national network of brokers" representing companies like "Coldwell Banker, ERA and Century 21." The website also states that LT is "[r]epresented by large independent real estate companies" and lists the companies by name. Marketing material for LT's website claims that LT is "affiliated with" real estate brokers, again listing the CCE firms by name.

CCE sued LT for trademark infringement. The District Court granted CCE's motion for preliminary injunction, rejecting LT's nominative use argument. LT appealed.]

. . .

IV.   FAIR USE

[The court discussed Ninth Circuit nominative fair use doctrine and recited the holding of *KP Permanent*, and noted that the issue of nominative fair use was one of first impression in the Third Circuit.]

While we agree with the Ninth Circuit Court of Appeals that a distinct analysis is needed for nominative fair use cases, we do not accept the legal basis or advisability of supplanting the likelihood of confusion test entirely. First, we do not see nominative fair use as so different from classic fair use as to warrant such different treatment. The Ninth Circuit Court of Appeals believed that the two types of fair use could be distinguished on the basis that nominative fair use makes it clear to consumers that the plaintiff, not the defendant, is the source of the trademarked product or service, while classic fair use does not. Thus, the Ninth Circuit Court of Appeals believed that a different analysis was appropriate for nominative fair use and that it could abandon the need for proof of confusion in these circumstances. *New Kids on the Block*, 971 F.2d at 307-08.[1] Yet, it is clear to us that even a defendant's nominative use has the potential of confusing consumers with respect to its products or services. Since the defendant ultimately uses the plaintiff's mark in a nominative case in order to describe its own product or services, *Cairns*, 292 F.3d at 1151 & n.8, even an accurate nominative use could potentially confuse consumers about the plaintiff's endorsement or sponsorship of the defendant's products or services. Thus, we disagree with the fundamental distinction the Ninth Circuit Court of Appeals drew between classic and nominative fair use.

In addition, the approach of the Court of Appeals for the Ninth Circuit would relieve the plaintiff of the burden of proving the key element of a trademark infringement case—likelihood of confusion—as a precondition to a defendant's even having to assert and demonstrate its entitlement to a nominative fair use defense. The Supreme Court in *KP Permanent Make-Up* clearly established that it was plaintiff's burden in a classic fair use case to prove likelihood of confusion. There, the Court noted the difference between fair use and other trademark infringement claims, opining, as we stated above, that likelihood of confusion and fair use can coexist. This does not mean that we should remove the need for finding confusion in the first instance. Instead, once the plaintiff proves likelihood of confusion, defendant only had to show that defendant's use, even if confusing, was "fair."

This view finds support not only in the Supreme Court's recent opinion, but also in the relevant statutory framework. The very language of the Lanham Act leads us to conclude that likelihood of confusion is an essential indicator of whether or not trademark infringement has occurred. Both §§32 and 43(a) of the Lanham Act, allegedly violated in this case, forbid use of words or marks in a way which is likely to cause confusion as to the origin, sponsorship, or approval of goods or services. Surely the plaintiff's success in its claim must rely on a finding in this regard. Given this, we decline to read this requirement out of a case alleging trademark infringement.

We are thus left with the firm conviction that the burden of proving likelihood of confusion should remain with the plaintiff in a trademark infringement case—including one where the defendant claims nominative fair use. As detailed below, we will devise a modified likelihood of confusion test to be employed in nominative fair use cases that takes into account the concerns expressed by the Court of Appeals for the Ninth Circuit. Then, we will determine the extent to which we would adopt the test for nominative fair use that the Ninth Circuit Court of Appeals established in light of our disagreement with that court's view that nominative fair use is fundamentally different from classic fair use.

---

1. Interestingly, the thinking of the Ninth Circuit Court of Appeals appears to have evolved in this regard. The court reasoned in *New Kids on the Block* that nominative use does not risk consumer confusion and is "outside the strictures of trademark law." 971 F.2d at 308. Ten years later, however, it justified replacing the likelihood of confusion test by arguing that the test would be inaccurate in the nominative use context. *Playboy Enters.*, 279 F.3d at 801. As explained below, we believe that neither rationale requires us to abandon the likelihood of confusion test in the nominative use context, and particularly not since the Supreme Court's decision in *KP Permanent Make-Up*.

V.   THE PROPER ANALYTICAL APPROACH FOR NOMINATIVE FAIR USE CASES

A.   Overview

Today we adopt a two-step approach in nominative fair use cases. The plaintiff must first prove that confusion is likely due to the defendant's use of plaintiff's mark. As we discuss more fully below, because our traditional likelihood of confusion test does not apply neatly to nominative fair use cases, we suggest eliminating those factors used to establish confusion in other trademark infringement cases that do not "fit" in the nominative use context. Once plaintiff has met its burden of proving that confusion is likely, the burden then shifts to defendant to show that its nominative use of plaintiff's mark is nonetheless fair. To demonstrate fairness, the defendant must satisfy a three-pronged nominative fair use test, derived to a great extent from the one articulated by the Court of Appeals for the Ninth Circuit. Under our fairness test, a defendant must show: (1) that the use of plaintiff's mark is necessary to describe both the plaintiff's product or service and the defendant's product or service; (2) that the defendant uses only so much of the plaintiff's mark as is necessary to describe plaintiff's product; and (3) that the defendant's conduct or language reflect the true and accurate relationship between plaintiff and defendant's products or services.

. . .

B.   The Proper Test for Likelihood of Confusion

As we have noted, and as the Ninth Circuit in *New Kids on the Block* also stated, the "likelihood of confusion" test does not lend itself nicely to a nominative fair use fact pattern. The traditional likelihood of confusion test has been set forth [in the factors recited in the Third Circuit's *Lapp* decision].

. . . In the context of a nominative use of a mark, such as the one we are presented with here, certain *Lapp* factors are either unworkable or not suited or helpful as indicators of confusion in this context. That is because, by definition, nominative use involves the use of *another's* trademark in order to describe the trademark owner's *own* product. Further, certain of the *Lapp* factors applied mechanically would inevitably point towards likelihood of confusion where no likelihood of confusion may actually exist. Thus, we must tailor the test and measure only those factors that are meaningful and probative in the context of nominative fair use.

Specifically, the first two *Lapp* factors [mark similarity and mark strength] would indicate a likelihood of confusion in a case such as this one simply *because* the mark is being employed in a nominative manner. By way of example, looking at the similarity of the mark would automatically lead to the conclusion that the use is likely to confuse simply because the mark is not merely similar, it is identical. The first *Lapp* factor does not leave any room for the consideration of the context of the use—i.e., that the mark is being used to describe the plaintiff's own product. Therefore, it is not appropriate for analysis in a nominative use case.

Looking at the strength of CCE's marks in this case, and in most nominative use cases, would also weigh in favor of a finding that the use is likely to confuse. However, defendants in nominative use cases, like LT in this case, feel they need to use the actual mark to describe the plaintiff's product *because* of its very strength and what it has come to represent. In reality, in many such cases, the use of the name may be the only way for defendant to easily and precisely refer to plaintiff's product in a way that will be understood by consumers. Accordingly, the marks' strength is not really probative of confusion here, whereas it would be if defendant were passing off its goods under a similar mark.

We find that all of the other *Lapp* factors, while perhaps not appropriate for analysis in this particular case, could be analyzed in future nominative use cases, depending on the factual situation. For example, in this case, looking at whether the goods are marketed through the same channels or advertised in the same media would be a misleading indicator in determining the true likelihood of confusion. It would be of little relevance in this case whether LT marketed its services through the same channels as CCE because LT is not attempting to use CCE's marks to refer to LT's own services, but rather is using the marks to refer to CCE's services. Therefore, it would almost be expected that LT and most other defendants in a nominative use case would market themselves through a media in which the marks to which they are referring would be easily recognized and have meaning or relevance, namely channels similar to those used by plaintiff. However, there may be certain situations, such as that encountered in *New Kids* (where newspapers used the New Kids' mark to inquire of readers, for a price, their feelings about the group), where the channels of marketing are so dissimilar that evidence as to this factor could mitigate against a finding of likelihood of confusion. Similarly, in looking at whether the targets of the parties' marketing efforts are the same, one could expect a fair use defendant to be reaching out to a group of consumers who are likely to recognize the mark. The fact that LT markets its services to real estate consumers makes sense. These are the very people who are likely to recognize and appreciate CCE's marks and be able to evaluate the benefit that CCE's purported association with LT could bring to them in the search for a home. This is not likely to confuse in the same way as would be the case if the defendant is passing off plaintiff's goods as its own or using a similar mark to that of the plaintiff, but this factor should not be completely eliminated from a district court's arsenal in evaluating likelihood of confusion in a nominative use case.

In the context of the facts of the case before us, we will turn our focus to those *Lapp* factors that appear most relevant in assessing likely confusion. These include:

(1) the price of the goods and other factors indicative of the care and attention expected of consumers when making a purchase;
(2) the length of time the defendant has used the mark without evidence of actual confusion;
(3) the intent of the defendant in adopting the mark; and
(4) the evidence of actual confusion.

In focusing on these factors, the court will be better able to assess whether consumers are likely to be confused by the use *not* because of its nominative nature, but rather because of the manner in which the mark is being nominatively employed. Of course the determination of which factors are relevant and probative in a given factual setting should be made in the first instance by the District Court, but here we provide our view on this issue as guidance. . . .

Viewed in the context of the present case, it is apparent why these factors are appropriate: they analyze the likelihood that a consumer will be confused as to the relationship or affiliation between LT and CCE, the heart of the nominative fair use situation. Focusing on the care and attention expected of consumers when making a purchase or using a service allows the court to understand the true risk that consumers may be confused merely because of their own inattention. Moreover, focusing on evidence of actual confusion (factors 2 and 4) will allow the District Court to truly understand whether this is merely a theoretical or hypothetical fear of the plaintiff or whether there is real danger that consumers are likely to be confused.

Lastly, analyzing the intent of the defendant in using the mark will allow the court to understand the defendant's reason for utilizing the mark in the manner that it did. That is, if the court finds that the defendant made use of the plaintiff's mark with the very purpose of causing consumers to think the plaintiff endorses or sponsors plaintiff's good or service, then the likelihood that consumers will be confused as to endorsement/affiliation is greater. Whereas the traditional "intent" prong looks at intent to adopt a similar mark, here the key inquiry is whether the mark is being used so as to convey a connection between the parties that may not exist.

We hold today that the burden of proving likelihood of confusion, even in a nominative use case, should remain with the plaintiff and that these four factors are the essence of the inquiry, although others may prove useful in certain contexts. [While the District Court had likewise placed the burden on CCE, the Third Circuit nonetheless remanded, instructing the District Court to reconsider its confusion analysis. The District Court had analyzed *all* of the confusion factors, not just the four factors deemed to be the essence of the inquiry, and, moreover, the District Court's analysis of those four factors was "somewhat imprecise," thus necessitating a remand.]

C.   THE AFFIRMATIVE DEFENSE OF NOMINATIVE FAIR USE

Under the nominative fair use test adopted by the Court of Appeals for the Ninth Circuit, a defendant must prove: (1) that the product or service in question is one not readily identifiable without use of the trademark; (2) that only so much of the mark or marks is used as is reasonably necessary to identify the product or service; and (3) that the user did nothing that would, in conjunction with the mark, suggest sponsorship or endorsement by the trademark holder. *New Kids on the Block*, 971 F.2d at 308. In the Ninth Circuit, if these elements are proven, the use is "fair" and defendant will prevail. Further, this nominative fair use test, as discussed above, replaces the likelihood of confusion test in the Court of Appeals for the Ninth Circuit. We must decide the extent to which we should adopt this test as our own, mindful that we will employ it as an affirmative defense to be proven by defendant after likelihood of confusion has been demonstrated by the plaintiff.

. . .

[W]e conclude that the [Ninth Circuit's] test as written suffers from a lack of clarity. . . . We will adjust the test to include a slightly different set of considerations:

1. Is the use of plaintiff's mark necessary to describe (1) plaintiff's product or service and (2) defendant's product or service?
2. Is only so much of the plaintiff's mark used as is necessary to describe plaintiff's products or services?
3. Does the defendant's conduct or language reflect the true and accurate relationship between plaintiff and defendant's products or services?

The following discussion explains how these factors should be applied.

1.   First Prong

The first element of the Ninth Circuit Court of Appeals' test involved an inquiry *only* into the necessity of using plaintiff's trademark to describe plaintiff's product. Here, the District Court instead—probably mistakenly—examined the necessity of the use of plaintiff's trademark in order to describe defendant's product. [cit.] The first prong of *New Kids on the Block* is at best confusing and at worst incomplete. While it should be asked whether plaintiff's product needs to be described by reference to its mark, should it not also be examined whether defendant's use of it, at all, is necessary to accurately describe what defendant does or sells, or whether its reference to plaintiff's mark is actually gratuitous? The District Court's inquiry into the latter aspect was not called for under the *New Kids on the Block* test, but it actually seems entirely appropriate.

The focus on the necessity of the mark in order for defendant to describe plaintiff's product makes sense in the context of nominative fair use, where the plaintiff's mark is being used because it identifies the plaintiff's product. We further note that the court need not find that the use of the mark is indispensable in order to find this factor fulfilled. For, as we have stated before, "[t]he Lanham Act does not compel a competitor to resort to second-best communication." . . . Therefore, the court need only be satisfied that the identification by the defendant of plaintiff's product or service would be rendered significantly more difficult without use of the mark.

Additionally, we believe that it is important for a court to understand how necessary the use of the mark is to the identification of defendant's product. That is, the more dependent the ready identification of defendant's product is on the description of plaintiff's product through the employment of plaintiff's mark, the more likely it is that the use is a fair one.

In this case, the District Court looked at this test only in regard to *defendant's* product. On remand the Court should additionally focus on whether requiring LT to describe plaintiff CCE's services without using its mark is a forced reversion to second-best communications. Considerations such as the simplicity of description and the likelihood that consumers will understand a given reference to plaintiff's services without use of the mark are appropriate to this analysis. [cit.]

2.   Second Prong

Here again, the *New Kids on the Block* test focuses on the "amount" of plaintiff's mark that is used, asking whether only so much is used as is necessary to describe plaintiff's product. That focus on limiting the quantum use of the attributes of plaintiff's marks is appropriate, for it is the use of plaintiff's marks that concerns us. Yet, the case law of the Ninth Circuit Court of Appeals has expanded on this prong to inquire, at this stage, about the defendant's need to use . . . the mark, stating:

> [W]hat is "reasonably necessary to identify the plaintiff's product["] differs from case to case. . . . Where, as in the present case, the description of the defendant's product depends on the description of the plaintiff's product, more use of the plaintiff's trademark is "reasonably necessary to identify the plaintiff's product" than in cases where the description of the defendant's product does *not* depend on the description of the plaintiff's product.

Cairns, 292 F.3d at 1154. Since we have positioned the assessment of the defendant's need to use plaintiff's mark as part of the first inquiry, we eliminate the confusion inherent in inquiring into "need" at the second step. Thus, under our approach, the second prong tests only whether the *quantum* of the plaintiff's mark used by the defendant was appropriate.

In analyzing this factor, the District Court essentially predetermined the outcome of the second prong by its finding as to the first prong. The District Court found that because the use of CCE's marks was not necessary to identify LT's services as a whole under the first prong, the use could not possibly be only so much as was necessary. But the proper focus under this prong is on whether *only so much* of plaintiff's *mark* as is reasonably necessary to identify plaintiff's product or service has been used by defendant. Consideration should be given at this stage to the manner in which the mark is portrayed. For example, did the defendant use plaintiff's distinctive lettering when using the plaintiff's mark or did the defendant, as in this case, simply use block letters to spell out plaintiffs' names?

. . .

3.   Third Prong

The *New Kids* test at this stage asks whether the user did anything that would, in conjunction with the mark, suggest sponsorship or endorsement by the trademark holder. However, we believe the appropriate question should be a bit broader: does the defendant's conduct or language reflect the true and accurate relationship between plaintiff and defendant's products or services? We believe that the Ninth Circuit Court of Appeals' focus on whether the user's conduct implies endorsement may not truly reflect whether the use is fair because sometimes the plaintiff's relationship with defendant may be one of endorsement, but the nature of the endorsement as reflected by defendant's employment of plaintiff's marks may not be accurate. A defendant's purposeful portrayal of plaintiff's endorsement of its product through defendant's conduct or language does not necessarily render the use unfair, as long as the depiction of the endorsement is accurate. In addition, our version suggests that we can consider the defendant's failure to state or explain some aspect of the relationship, whereas the *New Kids* version focuses on affirmative acts, i.e., what the defendant *did* to suggest sponsorship.

In this case, the District Court concluded that an ordinary consumer would look at LT's website and conclude that there was some affiliation between LT and the enumerated companies. Further, the Court inferred from the mere presence of the marks an intent on the part of LT to convey endorsement or affiliation. On remand, the District Court should specifically determine in analyzing this prong whether the portrayal of the relationship was accurate, and what more the defendant could have done to prevent an improper inference regarding the relationship. The mere presence or use of the mark does not suggest unfairness under this prong. Here, LT added a disclaimer, the significance of which the District Court downplayed, stating that "LendingTree is not sponsored by or affiliated with the parent franchisor companies of any of the participating members of its network." Far from unimportant, such a disclaimer must be considered in determining whether the alleged infringer accurately portrayed the relationship that existed between plaintiff and defendant. [cit.] Therefore, the District Court on remand should look at the precise way in which what the defendant said, or did not say, other than the mere presence of the mark on the website, may have inaccurately implied endorsement or sponsorship by CCE. The District Court should consider whether the disclaimer was an affirmative action by LT that effectively negated an inaccurate implication of sponsorship or endorsement by CCE.

The Ninth Circuit's test for nominative fair use does not explicitly include accuracy within the analysis, but the Supreme Court has recognized that "[a]ccuracy of course has to be a consideration in assessing fair use." *KP Permanent Make-Up, Inc.*, 125 S. Ct. at 551. In examining the conduct of the defendant to determine whether the defendant has done anything to affirmatively cause consumer confusion, it is only reasonable to consider the precision with which the defendant has described its relationship with plaintiff. In this case, the evaluation of accuracy would necessarily include consideration of LT's characterization of the nature and extent of its relationship with CCE and its agents. This would include the District Court's consideration of LT's reference to its affiliation with CCE brokers in general, rather than referencing each more accurately by their "d/b/a/" title and whether this rendered the use inaccurate or was somehow misleading as to any endorsement or relationship.

V.   CONCLUSION*

In sum, we hold today that the *Lapp* test for likelihood of confusion still has an important place in a trademark infringement case in which the defendant asserts the nominative

---

* *Ed. Note:* The conclusion is designated "V" in the original, but it probably should be "VI."

fair use defense. In this case, the test should focus on the four relevant factors: (1) the price of the goods and other factors indicative of the care and attention expected of consumers when making a purchase; (2) the length of time the defendant has used the mark without evidence of actual confusion; (3) the intent of the defendant in adopting the mark; and (4) the evidence of actual confusion.

Once plaintiff has met its burden of proving that confusion is likely, the burden then shifts to defendant to show that its nominative use of plaintiff's marks is nonetheless fair. In this Circuit, we have today adopted a test for nominative fair use in which a court will pose three questions: (1) Is the use of the plaintiff's mark necessary to describe both plaintiff's product or service and defendant's product or service? (2) Is only so much of the plaintiff's mark used as is necessary to describe plaintiff's products or services? (3) Does the defendant's conduct or language reflect the true and accurate relationship between plaintiff and defendant's products or services? If each of these questions can be answered in the affirmative, the use will be considered a fair one, regardless of whether likelihood of confusion exists.

We adopt a bifurcated approach that tests for confusion and fairness in separate inquiries in order to distribute the burden of proof appropriately between the parties at each stage of the analysis. The defendant has no burden to show fairness until the plaintiff first shows confusion. Furthermore, by properly treating nominative fair use as an affirmative defense, our approach allows for the possibility that a district court could find a certain level of confusion, but still ultimately determine the use to be fair. By contrast, a unified likelihood of confusion test would require a defendant to negate likelihood of confusion by undercutting the *Lapp* factors. Because the Supreme Court explicitly rejected such a proposition in *KP Permanent Make-Up*, we decline to adopt it.

[*Reversed and remanded.*]

[Judge Fisher's opinion, concurring in part and dissenting in part, is omitted.]

TOYOTA MOTOR SALES, U.S.A., INC. v. TABARI
610 F.3d 1171 (9th Cir. 2010)

KOZINSKI, Chief Judge:

In this trademark infringement case, we consider the application of the nominative fair use doctrine to internet domain names.

FACTS

Farzad and Lisa Tabari are auto brokers—the personal shoppers of the automotive world. They contact authorized dealers, solicit bids and arrange for customers to buy from the dealer offering the best combination of location, availability and price. Consumers like this service, as it increases competition among dealers, resulting in greater selection at lower prices. For many of the same reasons, auto manufacturers and dealers aren't so keen on it, as it undermines dealers' territorial exclusivity and lowers profit margins. Until recently, the Tabaris offered this service at buy-a-lexus.com and buyorleaselexus.com.

Toyota Motor Sales U.S.A. ("Toyota") is the exclusive distributor of Lexus vehicles in the United States, and jealous guardian of the Lexus mark. A Toyota marketing executive testified at trial that Toyota spends over $250 million every year promoting the Lexus brand. In the executive's estimation, "Lexus is a very prestigious luxury brand and it is an indication of an exclusive luxury experience." No doubt true.

Toyota objected to the Tabaris' use on their website of copyrighted photography of Lexus vehicles and the circular "L Symbol Design mark." Toyota also took umbrage at the

Tabaris' use of the string "lexus" in their domain names, which it believed was "likely to cause confusion as to the source of [the Tabaris'] web site." The Tabaris removed Toyota's photography and logo from their site and added a disclaimer in large font at the top. But they refused to give up their domain names. Toyota sued, and the district court found infringement after a bench trial. It ordered the Tabaris to cease using their domain names and enjoined them from using the Lexus mark in any other domain name. Pro se as they were at trial, the Tabaris appeal.

NOMINATIVE FAIR USE

When customers purchase a Lexus through the Tabaris, they receive a genuine Lexus car sold by an authorized Lexus dealer, and a portion of the proceeds ends up in Toyota's bank account. Toyota doesn't claim the business of brokering Lexus cars is illegal or that it has contracted with its dealers to prohibit selling through a broker. Instead, Toyota is using this trademark lawsuit to make it more difficult for consumers to use the Tabaris to buy a Lexus.

The district court applied the eight-factor test for likelihood of confusion articulated in [*Sleekcraft*], and found that the Tabaris' domain names—buy-a-lexus.com and buyor-leaselexus.com—infringed the Lexus trademark. But we've held that the *Sleekcraft* analysis doesn't apply where a defendant uses the mark to refer to the trademarked good itself. *See Playboy Enters., Inc. v. Welles*, 279 F.3d 796, 801 (9th Cir. 2002); *New Kids on the Block v. News Am. Publ'g, Inc.*, 971 F.2d 302, 308 (9th Cir. 1992).[1] The Tabaris are using the term Lexus to describe their business of brokering Lexus automobiles; when they say Lexus, they mean Lexus. We've long held that such use of the trademark is a fair use, namely nominative fair use. And fair use is, by definition, not infringement. The Tabaris did in fact present a nominative fair use defense to the district court.

In cases where a nominative fair use defense is raised, we ask whether (1) the product was "readily identifiable" without use of the mark; (2) defendant used more of the mark than necessary; or (3) defendant falsely suggested he was sponsored or endorsed by the trademark holder. *Welles*, 279 F.3d at 801 (*quoting New Kids*, 971 F.2d at 308-09). This test "evaluates the likelihood of confusion in nominative use cases." *Id*. It's designed to address the risk that nominative use of the mark will inspire a mistaken belief on the part of consumers that the speaker is sponsored or endorsed by the trademark holder. The third factor speaks directly to the risk of such confusion, and the others do so indirectly: Consumers may reasonably infer sponsorship or endorsement if a company uses an unnecessary trademark or "more" of a mark than necessary. But if the nominative use satisfies the three-factor *New Kids* test, it doesn't infringe. If the nominative use does not satisfy all the *New Kids* factors, the district court may order defendants to modify their use of the mark so that all three factors are satisfied; it may not enjoin nominative use of the mark altogether.

A.   The district court enjoined the Tabaris from using "any . . . domain name, service mark, trademark, trade name, meta tag or other commercial indication of origin that includes the mark LEXUS." A trademark injunction, particularly one involving nominative fair use, can raise serious First Amendment concerns because it can interfere with truthful communication between buyers and sellers in the marketplace. *See Va. State Bd. of Pharmacy v. Va. Citizens Consumer Council, Inc.*, 425 U.S. 748, 763-64 (1976). Accordingly, "we must [e]nsure that [the injunction] is tailored to eliminate only the specific harm alleged." *E. & J. Gallo Winery v. Gallo Cattle Co.*, 967 F.2d 1280, 1297 (9th Cir. 1992). To uphold

---

1. This is no less true where, as here, "the defendant's ultimate goal is to describe his own product." *Cairns v. Franklin Mint Co.*, 292 F.3d 1139, 1151 (9th Cir. 2002) (emphasis omitted). . . .

the broad injunction entered in this case, we would have to be convinced that consumers are likely to believe a site is sponsored or endorsed by a trademark holder whenever the domain name contains the string of letters that make up the trademark.

In performing this analysis, our focus must be on the "'reasonably prudent consumer' in the marketplace." *Cf. Dreamwerks Prod. Grp., Inc. v. SKG Studio*, 142 F.3d 1127, 1129 (9th Cir. 1998) (describing the test for likelihood of confusion in analogous *Sleekcraft* context). The relevant marketplace is the online marketplace, and the relevant consumer is a reasonably prudent consumer accustomed to shopping online; the kind of consumer who is likely to visit the Tabaris' website when shopping for an expensive product like a luxury car. *See, e.g., Interstellar Starship Servs., Ltd. v. Epix, Inc.*, 304 F.3d 936, 946 (9th Cir. 2002). Unreasonable, imprudent and inexperienced web-shoppers are not relevant.

The injunction here is plainly overbroad—as even Toyota's counsel grudgingly conceded at oral argument—because it prohibits domain names that on their face dispel any confusion as to sponsorship or endorsement. The Tabaris are prohibited from doing business at sites like independent-lexus-broker.com and we-are-definitely-not-lexus.com, although a reasonable consumer wouldn't believe Toyota sponsors the websites using those domains. Prohibition of such truthful and non-misleading speech does not advance the Lanham Act's purpose of protecting consumers and preventing unfair competition; in fact, it undermines that rationale by frustrating honest communication between the Tabaris and their customers.

Even if we were to modify the injunction to exclude domain names that expressly disclaim sponsorship or endorsement (like the examples above), the injunction would still be too broad. The Tabaris may not do business at lexusbroker.com, even though that's the most straightforward, obvious and truthful way to describe their business. The nominative fair use doctrine allows such truthful use of a mark, even if the speaker fails to expressly disavow association with the trademark holder, so long as it's unlikely to cause confusion as to sponsorship or endorsement. *See Welles*, 279 F.3d at 803 n.26. In *New Kids*, for instance, we found that use of the "New Kids on the Block" mark in a newspaper survey did not infringe, even absent a disclaimer, because the survey said "nothing that expressly or by fair implication connotes endorsement or joint sponsorship." 971 F.2d at 309. Speakers are under no obligation to provide a disclaimer as a condition for engaging in truthful, non-misleading speech.

Although our opinion in *Volkswagenwerk Aktiengesellschaft v. Church* remarked on that defendant's "prominent use of the word 'Independent' whenever the terms 'Volkswagen' or 'VW' appeared in his advertising," 411 F.2d 350, 352 (9th Cir. 1969), it isn't to the contrary. The inclusion of such words will usually negate any hint of sponsorship or endorsement, which is why we mentioned them in concluding that there was no infringement in *Volkswagenwerk*. *Id.* But that doesn't mean such words are required, and *Volkswagenwerk* doesn't say they are. Our subsequent cases make clear they're not. *See Welles*, 279 F.3d at 803 n.26; *New Kids*, 971 F.2d at 309.

The district court reasoned that the fact that an internet domain contains a trademark will "generally" suggest sponsorship or endorsement by the trademark holder. When a domain name consists only of the trademark followed by .com, or some other suffix like .org or .net, it will typically suggest sponsorship or endorsement by the trademark holder. *Cf. Panavision Int'l, L.P. v. Toeppen*, 141 F.3d 1316, 1327 (9th Cir. 1998).[4] This

---

4. Of course, not every trademark.com domain name is likely to cause consumer confusion. *See Interstellar Starship*, 304 F.3d at 944-46. For instance, we observed in *Interstellar Starship* that an apple orchard could operate at the website apple.com without risking confusion with Apple Computers, in light of the vast difference between their products. *Id.* at 944. "If, however, the apple

is because "[a] customer who is unsure about a company's domain name will often guess that the domain name is also the company's name." *Id.* [cit.]; *see also Brookfield Commc'ns, Inc. v. W. Coast Entm't Corp.*, 174 F.3d 1036, 1045 (9th Cir. 1999). If customers type in trademark.com and find the site occupied by someone other than the trademark holder, they may well believe it *is* the trademark holder, despite contrary evidence on the website itself. Alternatively, they may become discouraged and give up looking for the trademark holder's official site, believing perhaps that such a website doesn't exist. *Panavision*, 141 F.3d at 1327.

But the case where the URL consists of nothing but a trademark followed by a suffix like .com or .org is a special one indeed. *See Brookfield*, 174 F.3d at 1057. The importance ascribed to trademark.com in fact suggests that far less confusion will result when a domain making nominative use of a trademark includes characters in addition to those making up the mark. *Cf. Entrepreneur Media, Inc. v. Smith*, 279 F.3d 1135, 1146-47 (9th Cir. 2002). Because the official Lexus site is almost certain to be found at lexus.com (as, in fact, it is), it's far less likely to be found at other sites containing the word Lexus. On the other hand, a number of sites make nominative use of trademarks in their domains but are not sponsored or endorsed by the trademark holder: You can preen about your Mercedes at mercedes forum.com and mercedestalk.net, read the latest about your double-skim-no-whip latte at starbucksgossip.com and find out what goodies the world's greatest electronics store has on sale this week at fryselectronics-ads.com. Consumers who use the internet for shopping are generally quite sophisticated about such matters and won't be fooled into thinking that the prestigious German car manufacturer sells boots at mercedesboots.com, or homes at mercedeshomes.com, or that comcastsucks.org is sponsored or endorsed by the TV cable company just because the string of letters making up its trademark appears in the domain.

When people go shopping online, they don't start out by typing random URLs containing trademarked words hoping to get a lucky hit. They may start out by typing trademark.com, but then they'll rely on a search engine or word of mouth. If word of mouth, confusion is unlikely because the consumer will usually be aware of who runs the site before typing in the URL. And, if the site is located through a search engine, the consumer will click on the link for a likely-relevant site without paying much attention to the URL. Use of a trademark in the site's domain name isn't materially different from use in its text or metatags in this context; a search engine can find a trademark in a site regardless of where exactly it appears. In *Welles*, we upheld a claim that use of a mark in a site's metatags constituted nominative fair use; we reasoned that "[s]earchers would have a much more difficult time locating relevant websites" if the law outlawed such truthful, non-misleading use of a mark. 279 F.3d at 804. The same logic applies to nominative use of a mark in a domain name.

Of course a domain name containing a mark cannot be nominative fair use if it suggests sponsorship or endorsement by the trademark holder. We've already explained why

---

grower . . . competed directly with Apple Computer by selling computers, initial interest confusion probably would result," as the apple grower would be using the apple.com domain to appropriate the goodwill Apple Computer had developed in its trademark. *Id.*

When a website deals in goods or services related to a trademarked brand, as in this case, it is much closer to the second example, where apple.com competes with Apple Computers. If a company that repaired iPods, iPads and iPhones were to set up at apple.com, for instance, consumers would naturally assume that the company was sponsored or endorsed by Apple (or, more likely, that it *was* Apple). Where a site is used to sell goods or services related to the trademarked brand, a trademark. com domain will therefore suggest sponsorship or endorsement and will not generally be nominative fair use.

trademark.com domains have that effect. Sites like trademark-USA.com, trademark-of-glendale.com or e-trademark.com will also generally suggest sponsorship or endorsement by the trademark holder; the addition of "e" merely indicates the electronic version of a brand, and a location modifier following a trademark indicates that consumers can expect to find the brand's local subsidiary, franchise or affiliate. *See Visa Int'l Serv. Ass'n v. JSL Corp.*, [610 F.3d 1088 (9th Cir. 2010)]. For even more obvious reasons, domains like official-trademark-site.com or we-are-trademark.com affirmatively suggest sponsorship or endorsement by the trademark holder and are not nominative fair use. But the district court's injunction is not limited to this narrow class of cases and, indeed, the Tabaris' domain names do not fall within it.

When a domain name making nominative use of a mark does not actively suggest sponsorship or endorsement, the worst that can happen is that some consumers may arrive at the site uncertain as to what they will find. But in the age of FIOS, cable modems, DSL and T1 lines, reasonable, prudent and experienced internet consumers are accustomed to such exploration by trial and error. *Cf. Interstellar Starship*, 304 F.3d at 946. They skip from site to site, ready to hit the back button whenever they're not satisfied with a site's contents. They fully expect to find some sites that aren't what they imagine based on a glance at the domain name or search engine summary. Outside the special case of trademark.com, or domains that actively claim affiliation with the trademark holder, consumers don't form any firm expectations about the sponsorship of a website until they've seen the landing page—if then. This is sensible agnosticism, not consumer confusion. *See* Jennifer E. Rothman, *Initial Interest Confusion: Standing at the Crossroads of Trademark Law*, 27 Cardozo L. Rev. 105, 122-24, 140, 158 (2005). So long as the site as a whole does not suggest sponsorship or endorsement by the trademark holder, such momentary uncertainty does not preclude a finding of nominative fair use.

Toyota argues it is entitled to exclusive use of the string "lexus" in domain names because it spends hundreds of millions of dollars every year making sure everyone recognizes and understands the word "Lexus." But "[a] large expenditure of money does not in itself create legally protectable rights." *Smith v. Chanel, Inc.*, 402 F.2d 562, 568 (9th Cir. 1968); [cit.]. Indeed, it is precisely because of Toyota's investment in the Lexus mark that "[m]uch useful social and commercial discourse would be all but impossible if speakers were under threat of an infringement lawsuit every time they made reference to [Lexus] by using its trademark." *New Kids*, 971 F.2d at 307.

It is the wholesale prohibition of nominative use in domain names that would be unfair. It would be unfair to merchants seeking to communicate the nature of the service or product offered at their sites. And it would be unfair to consumers, who would be deprived of an increasingly important means of receiving such information. As noted, this would have serious First Amendment implications. The only winners would be companies like Toyota, which would acquire greater control over the markets for goods and services related to their trademarked brands, to the detriment of competition and consumers. The nominative fair use doctrine is designed to prevent this type of abuse of the rights granted by the Lanham Act.

B.   Toyota asserts that, even if the district court's injunction is overbroad, it can be upheld if limited to the Tabaris' actual domain names: buyorleaselexus.com and buy-a-lexus.com. We therefore apply the three-part *New Kids* test to the domain names, and we start by asking whether the Tabaris' use of the mark was "necessary" to describe their business. Toyota claims it was not, because the Tabaris could have used a domain name that did not contain the Lexus mark. It's true they could have used some other domain name like autobroker.com or fastimports.com, or have used the text of their website to explain their business. But it's enough to satisfy our test for necessity that the Tabaris needed to communicate that they specialize in Lexus vehicles, and using the Lexus mark in their domain names accomplished this goal. While using Lexus in their domain names wasn't the only way to communicate the nature of their business, the same could be said of virtually any choice the Tabaris made about how to convey their message: Rather than using the internet, they could publish advertisements in print; or, instead of taking out print ads, they could rely on word of mouth. We've never adopted such a draconian definition of necessity, and we decline to do so here. In *Volkswagenwerk*, for instance, we affirmed the right of a mechanic to put up a sign advertising that he specialized in repairing Volkswagen cars, although he could have used a sandwich board, distributed leaflets or shouted through a megaphone. 411 F.2d at 352. One way or the other, the Tabaris need to let consumers know that they are brokers of Lexus cars, and that's nearly impossible to do without mentioning Lexus, [cit.], be it via domain name, metatag, radio jingle, telephone solicitation or blimp.

The fact that the Tabaris also broker other types of cars does not render their use of the Lexus mark unnecessary. Lisa Tabari testified: "I in my conviction and great respect for the company always try to convince the consumer to first purchase a Lexus or Toyota product." If customers decide to buy some other type of car, the Tabaris may help with that, but their specialty is Lexus. The Tabaris are entitled to decide what automotive brands to emphasize in their business, and the district court found that the Tabaris do in fact specialize in Lexus vehicles. Potential customers would naturally be interested in that fact, and it was entirely appropriate for the Tabaris to use the Lexus mark to let them know it.

Nor are we convinced by Toyota's argument that the Tabaris unnecessarily used domain names containing the Lexus trademark as their trade name. [cit.] The Tabaris' business name is not buyorleaselexus.com or buy-a-lexus.com; it's Fast Imports. Toyota points out that the Tabaris' domain names featured prominently in their advertising, but that by no means proves the domain names were synonymous with the Tabaris' business. The Tabaris may have featured their domain names in their advertisements in order to tell consumers where to find their website, as well as to communicate the fact that they can help buy or lease a Lexus. Toyota would have to show significantly more than "prominent" advertisement to establish the contrary. We therefore conclude that the Tabaris easily satisfy the first *New Kids* factor.

As for the second and third steps of our nominative fair use analysis, Toyota suggests that use of the stylized Lexus mark and "Lexus L" logo was more use of the mark than necessary and suggested sponsorship or endorsement by Toyota. This is true: The Tabaris could adequately communicate their message without using the visual trappings of the Lexus brand. *New Kids*, 971 F.2d at 308 n.7. Moreover, those visual cues might lead some consumers to believe they were dealing with an authorized Toyota affiliate. Imagery, logos and other visual markers may be particularly significant in cyberspace, where anyone can convincingly recreate the look and feel of a luxury brand at minimal expense. It's hard to duplicate a Lexus showroom, but it's easy enough to ape the Lexus site.

But the Tabaris submitted images of an entirely changed site at the time of trial: The stylized mark and "L" logo were gone, and a disclaimer appeared in their place. The disclaimer stated, prominently and in large font, "We are not an authorized Lexus dealer or affiliated in any way with Lexus. We are an Independent Auto Broker." While not required, such a disclaimer is relevant to the nominative fair use analysis. *See Welles*, 279 F.3d at 803. Toyota claims the Tabaris' disclaimer came too late to protect against confusion caused by their domain names, as such confusion would occur before consumers saw the site or the disclaimer. *See Brookfield*, 174 F.3d at 1057. But nothing about the Tabaris' domains would give rise to such confusion; the Tabaris did not run their business at lexus.com, and their domain names did not contain words like "authorized" or "official." Reasonable consumers would arrive at the Tabaris' site agnostic as to what they would find. Once there, they would immediately see the disclaimer and would promptly be disabused of any notion that the Tabaris' website is sponsored by Toyota. Because there was no risk of confusion as to sponsorship or endorsement, the Tabaris' use of the Lexus mark was fair.

This makeover of the Tabaris' site is relevant because Toyota seeks only forward-looking relief. In *Volkswagenwerk*, we declined to order an injunction where the defendant had likewise stopped all infringing activities by the time of trial, [cit.], although we've said that an injunction may be proper if there's a risk that infringing conduct will recur, [cit.]. Even assuming some form of an injunction is required to prevent relapse in this case, the proper remedy for infringing use of a mark on a site generally falls short of entirely prohibiting use of the site's domain name, as the district court did here. *See Interstellar Starship*, 304 F.3d at 948. "[O]nly upon proving the rigorous elements of cyber-squatting . . . have plaintiffs successfully forced the transfer of an infringing domain name." *Id*. Forced relinquishment of a domain is no less extraordinary.

The district court is in a better position to assess in the first instance the timing and extent of any infringing conduct, as well as the scope of the remedy, if any remedy should prove to be required. We therefore vacate the injunction and remand for reconsideration. The important principle to bear in mind on remand is that a trademark injunction should be tailored to prevent ongoing violations, not punish past conduct. Speakers do not lose the right to engage in permissible speech simply because they may have infringed a trademark in the past.

C.   When considering the scope and timing of any infringement on remand, the district court must eschew application of *Sleekcraft* and analyze the case solely under the rubric of nominative fair use. *Cairns*, 292 F.3d at 1151. The district court treated nominative fair use as an affirmative defense to be established by the Tabaris only after Toyota showed a likelihood of confusion under *Sleekcraft*. This was error; nominative fair use "replaces" *Sleekcraft* as the proper test for likely consumer confusion whenever defendant asserts to have referred to the trademarked good itself. *Id*. (emphasis omitted); *see also Welles*, 279 F.3d at 801.

On remand, Toyota must bear the burden of establishing that the Tabaris' use of the Lexus mark was *not* nominative fair use. A finding of nominative fair use is a finding that the plaintiff has failed to show a likelihood of confusion as to sponsorship or endorsement. *See Welles*, 279 F.3d at 801; *New Kids*, 971 F.2d at 308 ("Because [nominative fair use] does not implicate the source-identification function that is the purpose of trademark, it does not constitute unfair competition.").[11] And, as the Supreme Court has unambiguously instructed, the Lanham Act always places the "burden of proving likelihood of confusion . . . on the party charging infringement." *KP Permanent Make-Up, Inc. v. Lasting Impression I, Inc.*, 543 U.S. 111, 118 (2004); *see also id*. at 120-21. In this case, that party is Toyota. "[A]ll the [Tabaris] need[ ] to do is to leave the factfinder unpersuaded." *Id*. at 120.

We have previously said the opposite: "[T]he nominative fair use defense shifts to the defendant the burden of proving no likelihood of confusion." [*Brother Records, Inc. v. Jardine*, 318 F.3d 900, 909 n.5 (9th Cir. 2003).] But that rule is plainly inconsistent with *Lasting Impression* and has been "effectively overruled." [cit.]; *see also* 4 McCarthy on

---

11. This is necessarily so because, unlike classic fair use, nominative fair use is not specifically provided for by statute. A court may find classic fair use despite "proof of infringement" because the Lanham Act authorizes that result. *See* 15 U.S.C. §1115(b)(4). Nominative fair use, on the other hand, represents a finding of no liability under that statute's basic prohibition of infringing use. *See id*. §1114.

Trademarks and Unfair Competition §23:11 at 82 n.5 (4th ed. 2010). A defendant seeking to assert nominative fair use as a defense need only show that it used the mark to refer to the trademarked good, as the Tabaris undoubtedly have here. The burden then reverts to the plaintiff to show a likelihood of confusion.

. . .

We vacate and remand for proceedings consistent with this opinion. At the very least, the injunction must be modified to allow some use of the Lexus mark in domain names by the Tabaris. Trademarks are part of our common language, and we all have some right to use them to communicate in truthful, non-misleading ways.

Many of the district court's errors seem to be the result of unevenly-matched lawyering, as Toyota appears to have taken advantage of the fact that the Tabaris appeared pro se. [cit.] To avoid similar problems on remand, the district court might consider contacting members of the bar to determine if any would be willing to represent the Tabaris at a reduced rate or on a volunteer basis.

Vacated and remanded.

FERNANDEZ, Circuit Judge, concurring:

I concur in the majority's conclusion that the district court erred in its handling of the nominative fair use defense. I write separately, however, because I cannot concur in all that is said by the majority.

First, and principally, I feel compelled to disassociate myself from statements by the majority which are not supported by the evidence or by the district court's findings. I simply cannot concur in essentially factual statements whose provenance is our musings rather than the record and determinations by trier of fact. For example, on this record I do not see the basis for the majority's assertion that the "relevant consumer is . . . accustomed to shopping online"; or that "[c]onsumers who use the internet for shopping are generally quite sophisticated" so that they are not likely to be misled; or that "the worst that can happen is that some consumers may arrive at [a] site uncertain as to what they will find"; or that, in fact, consumers are agnostic and, again, not likely to be misled; or that "[r]easonable consumers would arrive at the Tabaris' site agnostic as to what they would find."

Second, I am unable to join the gratuitous slap at counsel for Toyota in the majority opinion, which I see as entirely unnecessary to our decision or even to the upholding of the marmoreal* surface of the law.

Finally, I do not join the final textual paragraph, which nudges the district court to find pro bono counsel for the Tabaris, who have neither chosen to retain their own counsel nor demonstrated that they cannot do so. To the extent that the majority sees their activities as especially socially worthy and above reproach, I do not agree.

Thus, I respectfully concur in the result.

INT'L INFO. SYS. SECURITY CERT. CONSORTIUM, INC. v. SECURITY UNIV., LLC

823 F.3d 153 (2d Cir. 2016)

POOLER, Circuit Judge:

Plaintiff-appellant International Information Systems Security Certification Consortium, Inc. ["ISC"] filed suit against defendants-appellees Security University ("SU")

---

* *Ed. Note:* "Marmoreal" means "suggestive of marble." (We didn't know that, either.)

[alleging, *inter alia*, various Lanham Act violations. The district court granted a motion for summary judgment in favor of SU, and ISC appealed.]

BACKGROUND

I. THE CISSP® MARK

A. ISC's Mark

ISC is a non-profit organization that was formed in 1989 to develop standards for the information security industry. In March 1990, ISC developed a certification program and began using the certification mark "CISSP®" to denote a "Certified Information Systems Security Professional" who has met certain requirements and standards of competency in the information security field, including passing the CISSP® certification examination that ISC administers.

On March 18, 1997, the United States Patent and Trademark Office registered ISC's CISSP® certification mark. The registration stated: "The [CISSP®] certification mark is used by persons authorized by the certifier [ISC] to certify completion of appropriate work experience and/or successfully passing examinations as established by the certifier in the field of security of information systems."

B. SU's Alleged Infringement

SU is a for-profit company that was formed in 1999 by defendant-appellee Sondra Schneider, a CISSP®-certified individual, to provide information security training. SU offers various classes, including a class to prepare individuals for ISC's CISSP® certification examination. SU has used the CISSP® mark in connection with certification-specific training courses since 2001. It is undisputed that SU is allowed to use the CISSP® certification mark to indicate that its services are directed at preparing students for the CISSP® certification examination. Furthermore, given the nature of ISC's certification mark, SU instructors may accurately identify themselves as being CISSP®-certified, so long as they follow ISC's regulations governing the use of the mark.[1]

However, ISC objects to some of SU's advertisements, run between 2010 and 2012, which, ISC argues, misleadingly suggested that SU's instructor, Clement Dupuis, had attained some higher level of certification as a "Master CISSP" or "CISSP Master." These advertisements include the following statements:

- "MASTER THE 10 CISSP DOMAINS with the Master CISSP® Clement Dupuis."
- "REGISTER NOW to Master the CISSP® Certification with Master CISSP® Instructor Clement Dupuis of www.ccure.org!"
- "Register for CISSP® Prep class with Master CISSP Clement Dupuis today!"
- "You are taught by CISSP Master Clement Dupuis, the father of www.ccure.org website."

---

1. Upon meeting ISC's certification standards, ISC licenses an individual to use the CISSP® mark in accordance with the "(ISC) ® Regulations Governing Use of Certification/Collective Marks." The Regulations provide that, in using the mark, certified individuals "*may not combine the Logo with any other object,* including, but not limited to, other logos, icons, words, graphics, photos, [or] slogans . . . (i.e., Mixing another Logo with the CISSP[®] Logo to create a variation.)" *Int'l Info. Sys. Sec. Certification Consortium, Inc. v. Sec. Univ., LLC,* No. 3:10-CV-01238 (MPS), 2014 WL 3891287, at *2 (D. Conn. Aug. 7, 2014) (alterations in original) (emphasis added). Another rule provides that "[t]he Logo may not be used in any manner that expresses or might imply (ISC) 2's affiliation, sponsorship, endorsement, certification, or approval, other than as set forth by the (ISC) 2 Application Agreement." *Id.* (alteration in original).

- "Security University's CISSP® Prep Class[.] Register for CISSP® Prep class with Master CISSP Clement Dupuis today!"
- "Attend the BEST CISSP® Prep Class in Europe[.] Master CISSP June 27-30 AMERSTERDAM with MASTER CISSP® Instructor Clement Dupuis[.]"

SU began using the term "Master" in May 2010. On June 9, 2010, ISC's counsel wrote to Schneider asking that she cease using the phrase "Master CISSP" in SU's advertisements. On June 13, 2010, Schneider emailed Marc Thompson, an employee of a third party entity that oversees seminars on ISC's behalf, stating that "SU will continue to use the word Master. Master Clement Dupuis is a Male Teacher [and] thus he is a Master according to the dictionary." . . . On July 15, 2010, ISC's counsel "again wrote to Ms. Schneider requesting that she and SU cease and desist their improper advertising." *Id*. Although ISC's exhibits reveal that SU continued using this terminology at least through February of 2012, SU submitted declarations in support of its motion for summary judgment stating that it no longer uses these terms in its advertising materials.

[ISC asserted claims under Lanham Act §§32, 43(a), and 43(c), along with state law claims. The district court granted summary judgment to SU on the ground that its uses were shielded under the doctrine of nominative fair use.]

DISCUSSION

[The court noted that because certification marks are generally not used to designate source, it should be expected that confusion (if any) would involve confusion over sponsorship or affiliation in a certification mark case.]

C.   *Likelihood of Confusion in Nominative Use Cases*

. . .

To this point, this Court has not adopted either the Ninth Circuit or the Third Circuit's rule on nominative fair use. [cit.] Nonetheless, district courts within our Circuit frequently use the Ninth Circuit's formulation. [cit.] Further, as discussed below we have endorsed the principles underlying the nominative fair use doctrine. *See Tiffany (NJ) Inc.*, 600 F.3d at 102-03; *Dow Jones & Co. v. Int'l Sec. Exch., Inc.*, 451 F.3d 295, 308 (2d Cir. 2006).

Having considered the case law, as well as the positions of the United States Patent and Trademark Office,[5] we reject the Third Circuit's treatment of nominative fair use as an affirmative defense. The Lanham Act sets forth numerous affirmative defenses to infringement claims that can be asserted even if the plaintiff has established likelihood of confusion. *See* 15 U.S.C. §1115(b). The Third Circuit's basis for treating nominative fair use as an affirmative defense is that the Supreme Court has treated classic, or descriptive, fair use as an affirmative defense. *See Century 21 Real Estate Corp.*, 425 F.3d at 222 (citing *KP Permanent Make-Up, Inc. v. Lasting Impression I, Inc.*, 543 U.S. 111, 118-20, 125 S. Ct. 542, 160 L. Ed. 2d 440 (2004)). But in treating descriptive fair use as an affirmative defense, the Supreme Court was interpreting [Section 33(b)(4)] [cit.]. That is, under the Supreme Court's interpretation, the Lanham Act explicitly provides that descriptive fair use is an affirmative defense. And nominative fair use cannot fall within §1115(b)(4)'s language, as nominative fair use is not the use of a name, term, or device otherwise than as a

---

5. We invited the United States Patent and Trademark Office to submit a letter brief regarding several issues to be decided in this appeal. It did so on August 14, 2015 and August 31, 2015, through submissions signed by the United States Patent and Trademark Office and the Department of Justice. "We consider the views expressed therein for persuasive value." [cit.]

mark which is descriptive of and used merely to describe the goods or services of the alleged infringer. *See Cosmetically Sealed Indus., Inc. v. Chesebrough-Pond's USA Co.*, 125 F.3d 28, 30 (2d Cir. 1997) (finding descriptive fair use when the alleged infringer engaged in a "non-trademark use of words in their descriptive sense"). Nominative use involves using the mark at issue *as a mark* to specifically invoke the mark-holder's mark, rather than its use, other than as a mark, to describe the alleged infringer's goods or services. If Congress had wanted nominative fair use to constitute an additional affirmative defense, it would have provided as such. We therefore hold that nominative fair use is not an affirmative defense to an infringement claim.

We turn next to the question of whether we should adopt a nominative fair use test, either to supplant or to replace the *Polaroid* test. Although we see no reason to replace the *Polaroid* test in this context, we also recognize that many of the *Polaroid* factors are a bad fit here and that we have repeatedly emphasized that the *Polaroid* factors are non-exclusive. And although we have not expressly rejected or accepted other circuits' nominative fair use tests, we "have recognized that a defendant may lawfully use a plaintiff's trademark where doing so is necessary to describe the plaintiff's product and does not imply a false affiliation or endorsement by the plaintiff of the defendant." *Tiffany (NJ) Inc.*, 600 F.3d at 102-03. *See also Dow Jones & Co.*, 451 F.3d at 308 ("While a trademark conveys an exclusive right to the use of a mark in commerce in the area reserved, that right generally does not prevent one who trades a branded product from accurately describing it by its brand name, so long as the trader does not create confusion by implying an affiliation with the owner of the product.").

Because we believe that the nominative fair use factors will be helpful to a district court's analysis, we hold that, in nominative use cases, district courts are to consider the Ninth Circuit and Third Circuit's nominative fair use factors, in addition to the *Polaroid* factors.[6] When considering a likelihood of confusion in nominative fair use cases, *in addition to* discussing each of the *Polaroid* factors, courts are to consider: (1) whether the use of the plaintiff's mark is necessary to describe both the plaintiff's product or service and the defendant's product or service, that is, whether the product or service is not readily identifiable without use of the mark; (2) whether the defendant uses only so much of the plaintiff's mark as is necessary to identify the product or service; and (3) whether the defendant did anything that would, in conjunction with the mark, suggest sponsorship or endorsement by the plaintiff holder, that is, whether the defendant's conduct or language reflects the true or accurate relationship between plaintiff's and defendant's products or services.

When assessing the second nominative fair use factor, courts are to consider whether the alleged infringer "step[ped] over the line into a likelihood of confusion by using the senior user's mark too prominently or too often, in terms of size, emphasis, or repetition." McCarthy §23:11; [cit.]. Additionally, when considering the third nominative fair use factor, courts must not, as the district court did here, consider only source confusion, but rather must consider confusion regarding affiliation, sponsorship, or endorsement by the mark holder. *See Courtenay Commc'ns Corp. v. Hall*, 334 F.3d 210, 213 n. 1 (2d Cir. 2003) (vacating dismissal of Lanham Act claims and holding nominative fair use did not supply alternative grounds for dismissal because defendant's "hyperlink connection to a page of endorsements suggests affiliation, sponsorship, or endorsement by" the plaintiff (internal quotation marks omitted)).

---

6. As we have emphasized with reference to the *Polaroid* factors, this combination of factors is not exclusive, and other factors may be considered where relevant.

We therefore remand for reconsideration of the *Polaroid* factors in addition to the nominative fair use factors, keeping in mind the numerous types of confusion that are relevant to an infringement analysis other than mere source confusion and the numerous ways in which a certification mark may be infringed.

[*Vacated and remanded.*]

NOTES AND QUESTIONS

1. *Nominative fair use and the statute.* The court in *Century 21* did not see nominative fair use "as so different from classic fair use as to warrant such different treatment . . . [s]ince the defendant ultimately uses the plaintiff's mark in a nominative case in order to describe its own product or services. . . ." Thus, the nominative fair use defense could conceivably rest on Section 33(b)(4) as its foundation. The court in *ISC* disagreed, holding that nominative fair use "is not an affirmative defense to an infringement claim." Which court has the better of the argument? How does the Ninth Circuit's approach to nominative fair use deal with this problem? Does this statutory interpretation question matter, given that the Second Circuit in *ISC* still recognizes a nominative fair use doctrine anyway (even though the court is not willing to call it an affirmative defense)?

2. *Relationship between nominative fair use and confusion analysis.* As *Tabari* indicates, in the Ninth Circuit, nominative fair use operates as a replacement for the likelihood-of-confusion factors test, and the three-part *New Kids* test governs the nominative fair use inquiry. By contrast, the Sixth Circuit rejected the Ninth Circuit's nominative fair use test and asserted that the standard multi-factor test for confusion should govern nominative fair use claims. *See Paccar Inc. v. Telescan Techs., L.L.C.*, 319 F.3d 243, 256 (6th Cir. 2003). In *Century 21*, the Third Circuit offered yet a different approach, first applying an (abbreviated) likelihood-of-confusion test and then separately considering whether the defendant's use should be permitted under the nominative fair use "defense." In *ISC*, the Second Circuit avoids adopting any particular approach to nominative fair use, joining the First and (arguably) Fourth Circuits. *Swarovski Aktiengesellschaft v. Building #19, Inc.*, 704 F.3d 44, 53 (1st Cir. 2013); *Rosetta Stone Ltd. v. Google, Inc.*, 676 F.3d 144, 153-55 (4th Cir. 2012). Which of these approaches aligns best with the statute (or, put more pointedly, which approach best circumnavigates the statute given that there is no explicit nominative fair use doctrine in Section 33(b)(4))? Which approach aligns best with fair use precedent, particularly *KP Permanent*? Which party bears the burden of proof under the respective tests? (Note particularly *Tabari* in this regard, and pay close attention to the court's restatement of the *New Kids* test in *Tabari*, presumably to account for the use of that test as part of the plaintiff's case-in-chief rather than as an affirmative defense.) Which approach best strikes a balance between private and public interests? For relevant commentary, *see* Peter M. Brody & Alexandra J. Roberts, *What's in a Domain Name? Nominative Fair Use Online After* Toyota v. Tabari, 100 TRADEMARK REP. 1290 (2010).

3. *Deciding nominative use as a threshold matter.* Under both the Third Circuit and Ninth Circuit approaches to nominative fair use, a court must decide as a threshold matter that it is dealing with a nominative use case. At that point, the Third Circuit would apply an abbreviated likelihood-of-confusion test followed by its nominative fair use test, whereas the Ninth Circuit would proceed directly to its nominative fair use test. How easy do you expect it will be for courts to decide at the outset that the case is a nominative use case? How different are the nominative fair use inquiries from the threshold determination of nominative use?

4. *Evaluating the* Century 21 *abbreviated likelihood-of-confusion analysis.* The *Century 21* court rules that the mark similarity and mark strength factors of the

likelihood-of-confusion analysis are not appropriate for nominative fair use cases because they would invariably point in favor of likely confusion if a defendant is undertaking a nominative use. Does this justification make sense? What of the argument that a party who chooses to use another's similar and strong mark *should* be at greater risk of a finding of likely confusion (even if the party's use ultimately is deemed permissible as a fair use)? The *Century 21* court's solution is to drop those factors from the likelihood-of-confusion analysis for nominative fair use cases. In general, what is the effect of dropping factors from the likelihood-of-confusion analysis?

5.   *The role of intent in the nominative fair use analysis.* How should evidence of the defendant's intent factor into nominative fair use cases? Does the *Century 21* majority's approach give intent too prominent a role? In general, should trademark law invite more emphasis on intent-based standards, or should trademark law resist those standards, giving greater prominence to other objective criteria?

6.   *Fair use under and the dilution cause of action.* The 1995 version of the dilution legislation contained fair use protections. The statute imposed liability for a person's "commercial use in commerce" of a famous mark, but also provided that the following "shall not be actionable":

> (A) Fair use of a famous mark by another person in comparative commercial advertising or promotion to identify the competing goods or services of the owner of the famous mark.
> (B) Noncommercial use of a mark.
> (C) All forms of news reporting and news commentary.

Lanham Act §43(c)(4) (1995). As we have seen, Congress amended the dilution provision in 2006, imposing liability for a person's "use of a mark . . . in commerce," but excluding

> (A) Any fair use, including a nominative or descriptive fair use, or facilitation of such fair use, of a famous mark by another person other than as a designation of source for the person's own goods or services, including use in connection with—
> (i) advertising or promotion that permits consumers to compare goods or services; or
> (ii) identifying and parodying, criticizing, or commenting upon the famous mark owner or the goods or services of the famous mark owner.
> (B) All forms of news reporting and news commentary.
> (C) Any noncommercial use of a mark.

Lanham Act §43(c)(3) (2006). What is the significance of the new language regarding the "facilitation of such fair use"? What is the significance of the language "other than as a designation of source for the person's own goods"? Do the principles of *KP Permanent* apply to fair use under the dilution provision? For example, is the degree of dilution (if there is such a thing) a factor in deciding whether a use is fair under Section 43(c)(3)(A)? Does this dilution provision tell us anything about how to understand the scope of Section 33(b)(4) (and particularly the status of the nominative fair use defense)?

PROBLEM 9-3:   APPLYING NOMINATIVE FAIR USE TESTS

How would you analyze the following scenarios under the *Century 21* approach to nominative fair use? Under the Ninth Circuit's approach as exemplified by *Tabari*? Under the Second Circuit's approach articulated in *ISC*? Under the Sixth Circuit's approach from *Paccar* (which calls for applying the standard likelihood-of-confusion analysis)?

(1) Franklin Mint produced collectibles (jewelry, plates, dolls) bearing the name and likeness of Princess Diana, without authority from Diana's successors (her estate and a fund established to manage charitable activities relating to Diana after her death and to manage

uses of Diana's name and likeness). Treat Princess Diana as the fund's "product" and her name and likeness as the "marks" at issue. Franklin Mint's advertisements referred extensively to Princess Diana. Nominative fair use? The facts are from *Cairns v. Franklin Mint Co.*, 292 F.3d 1139 (9th Cir. 2002).

(2) Scott Fetzer Co. owns the mark KIRBY for vacuum cleaners. House of Vacuums is a retailer selling many brands of new and used vacuum cleaners. Although House of Vacuums is not an authorized KIRBY retailer, House of Vacuums does sell reconditioned KIRBY vacuum cleaners, along with some new vacuum cleaners received in trades from dealers. House of Vacuums' print advertisement includes the banner "New—Used—Rebuilt" and lists thirteen brands of vacuum cleaners, one of which is Kirby. Is House of Vacuums' use a nominative fair use? The facts are drawn from *Scott Fetzer Co. v. House of Vacuums Inc.*, 381 F.3d 477 (5th Cir. 2004).

(3) Suppose a car manufacturer (Opel) owned trademark rights in a logo mark that it used, inter alia, on its ASTRA car. A toy company manufactured and sold remote-controlled scale models of the ASTRA car bearing the Opel logo (as well as the defendant's mark). Is the defendant's use a nominative use? *See Adam Opel AG v. Autec AG*, [2007] E.T.M.R. 33 (ECJ 2007); *see also LG Nürnberg-Fürth*, May 11, 2007, NJOZ 2007, 4377 (on remand to the German courts).

(4) Suppose that an enterprising (but possibly misguided) Indiana University student sells crimson-colored T-shirts bearing the phrase BANNER UP in cream-colored lettering. Indiana University's school colors are cream and crimson, and "Banner Up" is understood among basketball cognoscenti (that is, among everyone in Indiana) as a reference to hoisting championship banners celebrating the school's basketball national championships—and also as a not particularly subtle dig at in-state rival Purdue University, where the catchphrase "Boiler Up" is used. If Indiana University sues the student, asserting rights in the combination of the colors and the phrase, could the student successfully claim nominative fair use? *See Bd. of Supervisors for Louisiana State Univ. v. Smack Apparel Co.*, 550 F.3d 465 (5th Cir. 2008) (noted in Chapter 2). What result if Purdue sues the Indiana student? (We mean what result in court, not what result in the unfiltered blogosphere.)

(5) Keurig makes KEURIG single-serve coffee machines, which use Keurig's K-CUP coffee cartridges. (Coffee sophisticates such as Professor Dinwoodie know what these are. For the benefit of coffee novices—e.g., Professor Janis—a coffee cartridge consists of a sealed container containing a filter and ground coffee. The cartridge fits on a coffee machine, and pins from the machine pierce the cartridge so that water can be admitted in order to brew the coffee.) Suppose that another firm, Strum, makes coffee cartridges that fit on KEURIG coffee machines. Appearing on the bottom left-hand corner of Strum's cartridge is the text: "For use by owners of Keurig® coffee makers." On the bottom of the package, next to the product directions, the following text appears: "Strum has no affiliation with Keurig." Analyze nominative fair use. *See Keurig, Inc. v. Strum Foods, Inc.*, 769 F. Supp. 2d 699 (D. Del. 2011). Should there be a special rule of nominative fair use for cases involving complementary products? If so, should the rule make it easier to show nominative fair use or harder?

PROBLEM 9-4:   NOMINATIVE FAIR USE IN MOVIES AND TV

(1) Once upon a time . . .

. . . at a gathering of many thousands in New York's Times Square for the "World Unity Festival," the crowd was murderously attacked by the jet-powered Green Goblin, who was, however, eventually put to flight by the timely arrival of Spider-Man. This event was memorialized on film, which swept the almost totally advertising-encrusted buildings surrounding Times Square. . . .

Sherwood 48 Assocs. v. Sony Corp. of Am., 213 F. Supp. 2d 376 (S.D.N.Y. 2002), *aff'd in part, vacated in part, and remanded,* 76 Fed. Appx. 389 (2d Cir. 2003).

The owners of some of the Times Square buildings apparently were not amused by the depiction of their buildings in the movie *Spiderman.* To make the movie, Sony took digital pictures of Times Square, then made certain digital modifications, including digitally removing some of the existing advertisements on the Times Square buildings and replacing them with other advertisements. The building owners claimed Lanham Act violations. Identify the issues. How would you rule?

(2) And also in Times Square . . . The Naked Cowboy is a street performer who generally appears in New York City's Times Square wearing underwear, cowboy boots, and a cowboy hat, and playing a guitar. The words "Naked Cowboy" appear on his underwear. CBS broadcasts a daytime television series called "The Bold and the Beautiful." In one episode, a character appeared for a few seconds clad in underwear, a cowboy hat, and cowboy boots, and played a guitar. The words "Naked Cowboy" did not appear on the underwear and were not used in the script. CBS later posted a clip of the episode on its YouTube channel, labeling the clip "The Bold and the Beautiful—Naked Cowboy." CBS also purchased the phrase "naked cowboy" as a keyword term from YouTube. Is CBS's use a fair use under any of the cases discussed in this chapter? Is it an actionable use under the principles of the *Rescuecom* case discussed in Chapter 7? *See Naked Cowboy v. CBS,* 844 F. Supp. 2d 510 (S.D.N.Y. 2012).

B.   USE OF ANOTHER'S TRADEMARK ON GENUINE GOODS: "FIRST SALE" DOCTRINE

The doctrine known variously as the "first sale" doctrine or the "exhaustion of rights" doctrine addresses a common conundrum in intellectual property law. The conundrum arises when an intellectual property rights holder sells products or services embodying intellectual property to a purchaser without including an express license of the intellectual property rights as part of the sales transaction. This characterizes the vast majority of consumer transactions where intellectual property rights are involved—e.g., the purchase of an authentic copyrighted music CD, the purchase of a genuine patented device, or the purchase of an item legitimately bearing a genuine trademark. In the absence of an express intellectual property license, the scope of the purchaser's permission to exploit the purchased item may be unclear. For example, we assume that the purchaser of a patented golf club would be authorized to use the club to play a round of golf, but what is the basis for that assumption, given the fact that patents confer exclusive rights to block others' use of the patented invention?

One way to address the problem is to employ the rubric of implied license: i.e., to declare that an intellectual property license in favor of the purchaser should be implied from the sales transaction. Subsequent litigation between the rights holder and the purchaser is likely to focus on divining the terms of this implied license. Another way to address the problem is to hold that upon the first authorized sale of the physical item, some or all of the intellectual property owner's exclusionary rights vanish (are "exhausted") as applied to that physical item. *See, e.g., Denbicare U.S.A. Inc. v. Toys "R" Us, Inc.,* 84 F.3d 1143, 1151 (9th Cir. 1996) (employing the "first sale" rubric); *Osawa & Co. v. B&H Photo,* 589 F. Supp. 1163, 1173 (S.D.N.Y. 1984) ("After the first sale, the brandholder's control is deemed exhausted."). Here, the litigation ordinarily focuses on which events constitute an exhaustion-triggering "sale" and which rights precisely are "exhausted" upon sale. *See generally* Mark D. Janis, *A Tale of the Apocryphal Axe: Repair, Reconstruction, and the Implied*

License in Intellectual Property Law, 58 MD. L. REV. 423 (1999) (discussing the implied license and exhaustion rubrics).

In trademark law, the exclusionary rights are less absolute than in patents or copyrights, and, correspondingly, the need for a "first sale" or exhaustion doctrine may be less keen. Thus, unlike copyright law, where the "first sale" doctrine is a matter of statute, 17 U.S.C. §109, the Lanham Act includes no explicit "first sale" defense.

The need to consider a "first sale" concept in trademark law commonly arises in cases where one party purchases genuine trademarked goods—genuine in the sense that the mark was applied to the goods, and the goods put on the market, by or under authority of the mark owner—and the purchaser wishes to resell the original goods or altered goods, under the trademark. In a leading case, *Prestonettes, Inc. v. Coty*, 264 U.S. 359 (1924), Prestonettes purchased Coty's powders and perfumes from authorized sources. As to the perfumes, Prestonettes rebottled and resold them, indicating on the label that Prestonettes was not connected with Coty, that Prestonettes had independently rebottled the product in New York, and that the contents of the bottle were specified Coty products. All of these assertions were true. As to the powders, Prestonettes added binder and subjected the powders to pressure, then sold the resulting product in a metal compact, again indicating on the label that Prestonettes was not affiliated with Coty and that Prestonettes had independently compounded the product from the original Coty product. The label also specified the constituents of the new product and their relative proportions.

Justice Holmes reversed a lower court decision of trademark infringement. His argument started from the proposition that Prestonettes had certain rights by virtue of its ownership of the physical chattels:

> The defendant of course by virtue of its ownership had a right to compound or change what it bought, to divide either the original or the modified product, and to sell it so divided. The plaintiff could not prevent or complain of its stating the nature of the component parts and the source from which they were derived if it did *not* use the trade-mark in doing so.

Id. at 368 (emphasis supplied). Having established that Prestonettes would have been free to make truthful representations about the product so long as Prestonettes did not refer to Coty's trademark, Justice Holmes proceeded to ask what new prohibition was triggered when Prestonettes went one step further, actually naming Coty as the original source. None, according to Justice Holmes, as long as the reference was truthful:

> When the mark is used in a way that does not deceive the public we see no such sanctity in the word as to prevent its being used to tell the truth. It is not taboo.

Id. (internal citation omitted). That is, a seller should be entitled to refer "collaterally" to another's trademark in a label that did not attempt to deceive consumers by emphasizing the other's trademark, but instead merely indicated "that the trade-marked product is a constituent in the article now offered as new and changed." *Id.* at 369.

What general principle was Justice Holmes applying? Is it simply an application of the notion of nominative fair use—i.e., a reseller using another's trademark to refer truthfully to the mark owner's product? Or was Justice Holmes crafting a separate doctrine—i.e., a "first sale" doctrine, insulating resellers and repackagers from liability for the use of the original trademark on genuine goods, with a possible exception where the reseller or repackager uses the original trademark in a manner that *does* deceive the public? The *Coty* opinion does not provide clear answers. Justice Holmes merely said that he arrived at his conclusion from "the general ground that we have stated"—whatever that might mean—and *not* "because of a license implied from the special facts." *Id.*

In the remaining materials in this section, we consider the ways in which courts have applied the first sale doctrine in three main classes of cases: those (like *Coty*) involving the use of another's trademark on genuine goods that are repackaged for resale; those involving the use of another's trademark on genuine goods that have been refurbished for resale; and those involving parallel imports of goods put on foreign markets by or under the authority of the mark owner (i.e., gray goods). Of course, the first sale doctrine operates without controversy in many other common situations—for example, when a golf club retailer purchases genuine trademarked golf clubs and resells them to customers without any alteration of the packaging or products.

NOTES AND QUESTIONS

1.   *"Quality control" exception to "first sale" doctrine.* The *Coty* case might be characterized as creating an exception to the protections ordinarily accorded by the "first sale" doctrine. That is, the defendant in *Coty* succeeded in invoking the protections of first sale, but only because the defendant clearly placed consumers on notice of the fact of the repackaging. Perhaps, then, the *Coty* court was articulating not only a "first sale" doctrine, but also a "repackaging" exception to that doctrine. A defendant who fails to give adequate notice about repackaging loses the benefits of the "first sale" doctrine. There is also a "quality control" exception to the "first sale" doctrine. In *Enesco Corp. v. Price/Costco Inc.*, 146 F.3d 1083 (9th Cir. 1998), the court conceptualized the "exception" as, in fact, a limitation on the definition of "genuine" goods:

> Under the quality control theory, largely developed by the Second Circuit, "[d]istribution of a product that does not meet the trademark holder's quality control standards may result in the devaluation of the mark by tarnishing its image." *Warner-Lambert Co. v. Northside Dev. Corp.*, 86 F.3d 3, 6 (2d Cir. 1996); *see also El Greco Leather Prods. Co., Inc. v. Shoe World, Inc.*, 806 F.2d 392, 395 (2d Cir. 1986) ("One of the most valuable and important protections afforded by the Lanham Act is the right to control the quality of the goods manufactured and sold under the holder's trademark."). If this occurs, "the non-conforming product is deemed for Lanham Act purposes not to be the genuine product of the holder, and its distribution constitutes trademark infringement." *Warner-Lambert*, 86 F.3d at 6 (citations omitted).
>
>   Courts have recognized the quality control argument in cases where there is "some defect (or potential defect) in *the product itself* that the customer would not be readily able to detect." *Matrix Essentials, Inc. v. Emporium Drug Mart, Inc.*, 988 F.2d 587, 591 (5th Cir. 1993) (emphasis in original); *see, e.g., Shell Oil Co. v. Commercial Petroleum, Inc.*, 928 F.2d 104 (4th Cir. 1991) (defendant prohibited from selling oil under Shell trademarks because Shell's stringent tank and pump cleaning requirements not observed); *El Greco*, 806 F.2d 392 (infringement found where shoes sold by defendant did not go through plaintiff's quality inspection); *Adolph Coors*, 486 F. Supp. 131 (beer not genuine Coors product where unauthorized distributor did not maintain required refrigeration).

Id. at 1087. In *Enesco*, defendants (Price/Costco) had repackaged PRECIOUS MOMENTS porcelain figurines for resale in clear, blister-pack packaging rather than resell them in plaintiff's packaging. Plaintiff Enesco, the trademark owner, claimed that the new packaging did not adequately protect the figurines from breakage or chipping. According to Enesco, even if Price/Costco had provided an appropriate *Coty*-type notice on the new packaging, consumers might still mistakenly attribute the breakage to Enesco. The Ninth Circuit would not accept this argument for invoking the "quality control" exception to the "first sale" doctrine:

> [Enesco's] contention seeks to push the quality control exception beyond its reasonable limit. The critical issue is whether the public is likely to be confused as a result of the lack of quality

control. As noted above, the "quality control" cases where trademark infringement has been found all involved some defect (or potential defect) in the product itself that the customer would not be readily able to detect.

> The oil, shoes, and beer from *Shell*, *El Greco*, and *Coors* all contained or could potentially contain a latent product defect due to the unauthorized distributor's failure to observe the manufacturer and mark owner's rigorous quality control standards. Most importantly, a consumer would not necessarily be aware of the defective condition of the product and would thereby be confused or deceived.

Matrix, 988 F.2d at 591.

If the public were adequately informed that Price/Costco repackaged the figurines and the figurines were subsequently chipped, the public would not likely be confused as to the cause of the chipping. *See Coty*, 264 U.S. at 369 ("If the defendant's rebottling the plaintiff's perfume deteriorates it and the public is adequately informed who does the rebottling, the public, with or without plaintiff's assistance, is likely to find it out."). In light of the unlikelihood of consumer confusion, the quality control exception to the "first sale" doctrine does not apply to this case.

Id. at 1087.

2. *Repackaging and mark owner private quality control procedures.* In *Zino Davidoff SA v. CVS Corp.*, 571 F.3d 238 (2d Cir. 2009), the defendant, a retail drugstore chain, purchased plaintiff's trademarked COOL WATER fragrances, removed the plaintiff's so-called unique production codes ("UPCs") from the packages and labels affixed to the fragrance bottles, and then resold the fragrances in its stores. The fragrance was sold in its original packaging with the plaintiff's marks clearly visible and unaltered. The plaintiff argued that the UPCs acted as a quality control mechanism which enables it to protect the reputation of its marks (which it used on high-end products, sold only through luxury retailers) by identifying counterfeits and by protecting against defects (for example, the UPC helps the plaintiff to recall already distributed products that may share any discovered defect and to prevent further recurrence of the defect). The defendant argued that it was selling genuine goods sold by the mark owner through authorized channels in other countries and subsequently imported by others into the United States. The Second Circuit accepted that:

> [A]s a general rule, the Lanham Act does not impose liability for the sale of genuine goods bearing a true mark even though the sale is not authorized by the mark owner because such a sale does not inherently cause confusion or dilution. However, . . . goods are not genuine if they do not conform to the trademark holder's quality control standards, or if they differ materially from the product authorized by the trademark holder for sale.
>
> Where the alleged infringer has interfered with the trademark holder's ability to control quality, the trademark holder's claim is not defeated because of failure to show that the goods sold were defective. That is because the interference with the trademark holder's legitimate steps to control quality unreasonably subjects the trademark holder to the risk of injury to the reputation of its mark.

Id. at 243 (citations omitted). Invoking *Warner-Lambert Co. v. Northside Dev. Corp.*, 86 F.3d 3 (2d Cir. 1996), the court held that the plaintiff was entitled to an injunction because (i) the asserted quality control procedures were established, legitimate, substantial, and nonpretextual, (ii) the plaintiff abided by these procedures, and (iii) sales of products that failed to conform to these procedures will diminish the value of the mark. Does this standard, or the court's application of it, undermine the policy objectives of the first sale rule? Should it matter whether the retailer offered to assist the mark owner in detecting counterfeits through procedures other than reliance on UPCs? Should it matter that legislation expressly creating liability for tampering with product identification codes has been introduced, but not passed, by Congress? *See* Proposed Antitampering Act of 1999, H.R. 2100,

106th Cong. (1st Sess. 1999) (proposing civil and criminal remedies for unauthorized changes to product identification codes).

3.   *Repackaging notice and post-sale confusion.* Suppose that a reseller of genuine trademarked goods includes a notice as to the fact of repackaging, as contemplated by *Prestonettes.* Even if the notice effectively dispels confusion among the reseller's customers at the point of sale, would the notice dispel post-sale confusion? If not, should the protections of the "first sale" doctrine disappear, as a matter of law, where the confusion at issue is post-sale confusion among the public? *See Au-Tomotive Gold Inc. v. Volkswagen of Am., Inc.*, 603 F.3d 1133 (9th Cir. 2010) (addressing the question in a case in which the defendant purchased genuine "VW" badges from Volkswagen, adapted and mounted them on "marquee" license plates, and sold the plates).

4.   *Discount resales.* Suppose that a reseller sells genuine goods, but at a steep discount—say, 50 percent off. Does the first sale doctrine shield the reseller under these circumstances? Does your answer depend upon the nature of the goods? For example, would it matter if the goods at issue are dietary nutritional supplements? *See Brain Pharma, LLC v. Scalini*, 858 F. Supp. 2d 1349 (S.D. Fla. 2012).

5.   *Deconstructing first sale.* Is the proliferation of doctrine laid out in the preceding notes helpful? Or would courts and commentators be better off discarding the rhetoric of a first sale "defense" and "exceptions" to that defense, and analyzing these cases as simply another set of factual variations affecting likelihood of confusion? Is the "first sale" doctrine a defense in any event? Do you agree with the view expressed in *Taylor Made Golf Co. v. MJT Consulting Group, LLC*, 265 F. Supp. 2d 732, 739 (N.D. Tex. 2003), that the "first sale" rule is "not an affirmative defense" but instead "defines an area of commerce beyond the reach of trademark law"?

6.   *Repackaging as dilution by tarnishment?* *Coty* and its progeny allow a purchaser to repackage and resell trademarked goods under conditions that minimize the risk of consumer confusion. Broadly speaking, the case allows a purchaser to change the context in which the trademark is presented to consumers, as long as no confusion is likely to ensue as a result. What if a purchaser repackages and resells trademarked goods in such a way as to cause dilution, even in the absence of likelihood of confusion? What result? What if the purchaser makes no alteration whatsoever, but merely presents the genuine trademark or good in an unsavory context? *See Parfum Christian Dior v. Evora BV*, 1998 R.P.C. 166 (ECJ 1997) (sale of select perfume in discount drug stores along with mass market products).

Professor Landes offers the following hypothetical involving Ty, the owner of the mark BEANIE BABIES for pellet-filled plush toys, and Perryman, a would-be reseller of the toys:

> Suppose a fire or flood has severely damaged a large number of Beanies in Perryman's inventory. The damage includes tattered costumes, faces that are no longer recognizable and even limbs that have been torn from their bodies and destroyed. Assume further that the Beanies are sufficiently rare and valuable to make restoration worthwhile. In some cases, [Perryman works with the original materials, while in others, Perryman] essentially starts from scratch but closely follows the original design. The end result is a restored Beanie that an expert cannot distinguish from a brand new one. Perryman promotes her goods as "restored and repaired authentic Beanies" in "like-new" condition, and offers them at prices comparable to second-hand Beanies that have never been repaired. Perryman calls her business "Bargain Beanies" but disclaims any connection to Ty and provides on request a detailed description of her restoration work. In these circumstances, does Perryman risk infringing or diluting the Beanies' mark by naming her firm "Bargain Beanies" and designating her goods as "authentic" and "restored Beanies"? Stated differently, can the extent of repair be so great that Perryman is no longer selling an authentic Beanie but a lower quality and possibly different product altogether?

William M. Landes, *Posner on Beanie Babies*, 74 U. Chi. L. Rev. 1761, 1773-74 (2007). For Landes' analysis of a dilution claim arising from the hypothetical, *see id.* at 1777-78. The hypothetical is a modification of *Ty Inc. v. Perryman*, 306 F.3d 509 (7th Cir. 2002).

   7.   *Copyright "first sale" versus trademark "first sale."* Copyright law confers on the copyright owner exclusive rights including, but not limited to, the exclusive rights

   (1)   to reproduce the copyrighted work in copies or phonorecords;
   (2)   to prepare derivative works based upon the copyrighted work;
   (3)   to distribute copies or phonorecords of the copyrighted work to the public by sale or other transfer of ownership. . . .

17 U.S.C. §106(1)-(3). In 17 U.S.C. §109, the copyright law imposes a "first sale" limitation on the copyright owner's exclusive rights:

   Notwithstanding the provisions of section 106(3), the owner of a particular copy or phonorecord lawfully made under this title, or any person authorized by such owner, is entitled, without the authority of the copyright owner, to sell or otherwise dispose of the possession of that copy or phonorecord. . . .

17 U.S.C. §109(a); *see generally Kirtsaeng v. John Wiley & Sons, Inc.*, 568 U.S. 519 (2013). The "first sale" limitation in copyright applies only to the distribution right of 17 U.S.C. §106(3), and Section 109 also contains a number of refinements to, and limitations on, the copyright "first sale" doctrine. However, the contours of the first sale doctrine are clearer in copyright than in trademark. Where a good is protected by copyright and trademark, should the exhaustion of rights under copyright law be coextensive with that which occurs under trademark law? *See, e.g., Denbicare U.S.A. Inc. v. Toys "R" Us, Inc.*, 84 F.3d 1143 (9th Cir. 1996) (involving assertions of copyright in the package labeling of diaper packages and trademark in the name used in connection with the diapers); *see also Evora, supra.*

   8.   *"First sale" and express contract restrictions on distribution.* Can a trademark owner—or any IP owner—contract around the "first sale" doctrine? Suppose, for example, that *Y*, a manufacturer of trademarked hair care products, sells the products to *Z*, a distributor, under an express contract that provides that *Z* may resell the products only to salons for professional use, and not to consumers for home use. If *Z* resells the trademarked goods to consumers, what result if *Y* sues *Z* for trademark infringement? Specifically, could *Z* successfully deflect trademark infringement liability by asserting a "first sale" defense? In answering this question, does it matter how seriously we take Justice Holmes' comment that the doctrine does not sound in "implied license"?

   Presumably, *Y* could sue on the contract as an alternative to the trademark infringement suit. Might a court deny trademark infringement relief, on "first sale" grounds, in the knowledge that the mark owner would have a contract remedy anyway? Are the trademark and contract remedies interchangeable?

   Suppose that a manufacturer of paper towel dispensers (and paper towels) sells the dispensers to customers under a contract that provides that customers may only use the manufacturer's towels in the dispenser. When customers refill the dispensers with towels that are not made by the manufacturer, thus violating the lease restriction, can the customers nonetheless invoke the first sale doctrine? *See Georgia-Pacific Consumer Prods., LP v. Von Drehle Corp.*, 618 F.3d 441, 452 (4th Cir. 2010); *see also Georgia-Pacific Consumer Prods., LP v. Myers Supply, Inc.*, 621 F.3d 771 (8th Cir. 2010).

   9.   *State law prohibitions on resale of altered trademarked goods.* Some state statutes purport to limit the rule in the *Coty* case by placing severe restrictions (or even prohibitions) on the resale of repackaged trademarked goods. *See, e.g.*, N.Y. Arts & Cult. Aff. Law §33.09(6) (McKinney 2006):

A person who . . .
> 6. Knowingly sells, offers or exposes for sale, any goods which are represented in any manner, by word or deed, to be the manufacture, packing, bottling, boxing or product of any person, firm or corporation, other than himself, unless such goods are contained in the original package, box or bottle and under the labels, marks or names placed thereon by the manufacturer who is entitled to use such marks, names, brands or trade-marks . . .

is guilty of a misdemeanor.

10. *First sale and the goods/services distinction.* Plaintiff retrofits school buses with gymnastics equipment and uses the buses to provide gymnastics instructional services, using the mark TUMBLEBUS in connection with both the buses and the services. Plaintiff sells a retrofitted bus that eventually ends up in the possession of defendant competitor. Defendant uses the bus to provide identical services, using the TUMBLEBUS mark, and plaintiff sues. Does the "first sale" doctrine insulate defendant? Should courts observe a distinction between products and services here? That is, should a court say that the sale of the bus exhausted plaintiff's trademark rights in the sold bus (such that defendant could resell it using the name TUMBLEBUS without plaintiff's authorization), but that the sale of the bus did not exhaust plaintiff's rights in the accompanying services? Or should a court say that when plaintiff sold the bus, the implicit understanding of the plaintiff and the buyer was that the buyer would use the bus to provide gymnastics instruction, such that the sale of the bus did exhaust plaintiff's rights in both the sold bus and services provided with the use of the bus? In general, should we approach "first sale" questions by imposing clear default rules, or should we apply a less predictable (but potentially more equitable) case-by-case determination of the parties' probable understanding?

CHAMPION SPARK PLUG CO. v. SANDERS
331 U.S. 125 (1947)

Mr. Justice DOUGLAS delivered the opinion of the Court:

Petitioner is a manufacturer of spark plugs which it sells under the trade mark "Champion." Respondents collect the used plugs, repair and recondition them, and resell them. Respondents retain the word "Champion" on the repaired or reconditioned plugs. The outside box or carton in which the plugs are packed has stamped on it the word "Champion," together with the letter and figure denoting the particular style or type. They also have printed on them "Perfect Process Spark Plugs Guaranteed Dependable" and "Perfect Process Renewed Spark Plugs." Each carton contains smaller boxes in which the plugs are individually packed. These inside boxes also carry legends indicating that the plug has been renewed. But respondent company's business name or address is not printed on the cartons. It supplies customers with petitioner's charts containing recommendations for the use of Champion plugs. On each individual plug is stamped in small letters, blue on black, the word "Renewed," which at time[s] is almost illegible.

Petitioner brought this suit in the District Court, charging infringement of its trade mark and unfair competition. [cit.] The District Court found that respondents had infringed the trade mark. It enjoined them from offering or selling any of petitioner's plugs which had been repaired or reconditioned unless (a) the trade mark and type and style marks were removed, (b) the plugs were repainted with a durable grey, brown, orange, or green paint, (c) the word "Repaired" was stamped into the plug in letters of such size and depth as to retain enough white paint to display distinctly each letter of the word, (d) the cartons in which the plugs were packed carried a legend indicating that they contained used spark plugs originally made by petitioner and repaired and made fit for use up to 10,000 miles by respondent company.[2] The District Court denied an accounting. [cit.]

The Circuit Court of Appeals held that respondents not only had infringed petitioner's trade mark but also were guilty of unfair competition. It likewise denied an accounting but modified the decree in the following respects: (a) it eliminated the provision requiring the trade mark and type and style marks to be removed from the repaired or reconditioned plugs; (b) it substituted for the requirement that the word "Repaired" be stamped into the plug, etc., a provision that the word "Repaired" or "Used" be stamped and baked on the plug by an electrical hot press in a contrasting color so as to be clearly and distinctly visible, the plug having been completely covered by permanent aluminum paint or other paint or lacquer; and (c) it eliminated the provision specifying the precise legend to be printed on the cartons and substituted therefor a more general one.[3] The case is here on a petition for certiorari which we granted because of the apparent conflict between the decision below and *Champion Spark Plug Co. v. Reich*, 121 F.2d 769, decided by the Circuit Court of Appeals for the Eighth Circuit.

There is no challenge here to the findings as to the misleading character of the merchandising methods employed by respondents, nor to the conclusion that they have not only infringed petitioner's trade mark but have also engaged in unfair competition. The controversy here relates to the adequacy of the relief granted, particularly the refusal of the Circuit Court of Appeals to require respondents to remove the word "Champion" from the repaired or reconditioned plugs which they resell.

We put to one side the case of a manufacturer or distributor who markets new or used spark plugs of one make under the trade mark of another. . . .

We are dealing here with second-hand goods. The spark plugs, though used, are nevertheless Champion plugs and not those of another make. There is evidence to support what one would suspect, that a used spark plug which has been repaired or reconditioned does not measure up to the specifications of a new one. But the same would be true of a second-hand Ford or Chevrolet car. And we would not suppose that one could be enjoined from selling a car whose valves had been reground and whose piston rings had been replaced unless he removed the name Ford or Chevrolet. [The Court quoted from *Prestonettes, Inc. v. Coty.*]

Cases may be imagined where the reconditioning or repair would be so extensive or so basic that it would be a misnomer to call the article by its original name, even though the words "used" or "repaired" were added. *Cf. Ingersoll v. Doyle*, D.C., 247 F. 620. But no such practice is involved here. The repair or reconditioning of the plugs does not give them a new design. It is no more than a restoration, so far as possible, of their original condition. The type marks attached by the manufacturer are determined by the use to which the plug is to be put. But the thread size and size of the cylinder hole into which the plug is fitted

---

2. The prescribed legend read:

"Used spark plug(s) originally made by Champion Spark Plug Company repaired and made fit for use up to 10,000 miles by Perfect Recondition Spark Plug Co., 1133 Bedford Avenue, Brooklyn, N.Y."

The decree also provided: "the name and address of the defendants to be larger and more prominent than the legend itself, and the name of plaintiff may be in slightly larger type than the rest of the body of the legend."

3. "The decree shall permit the defendants to state on cartons and containers, selling and advertising material, business records, correspondence and other papers, when published, the original make and type numbers provided it is made clear that any plug referred to therein is used and reconditioned by the defendants, and that such material contains the name and address of defendants."

are not affected by the reconditioning. The heat range also has relevance to the type marks. And there is evidence that the reconditioned plugs are inferior so far as heat range and other qualities are concerned. But inferiority is expected in most second-hand articles. Indeed, they generally cost the customer less. That is the case here. Inferiority is immaterial so long as the article is clearly and distinctively sold as repaired or reconditioned rather than as new. The result is, of course, that the second-hand dealer gets some advantage from the trade mark. But under the rule of *Prestonettes, Inc. v. Coty, supra,* that is wholly permissible so long as the manufacturer is not identified with the inferior qualities of the product resulting from wear and tear or the reconditioning by the dealer. Full disclosure gives the manufacturer all the protection to which he is entitled.

The decree as shaped by the Circuit Court of Appeals is fashioned to serve the requirements of full disclosure. . . . We cannot say that the conduct of respondents in this case, or the nature of the article involved and the characteristics of the merchandising methods used to sell it, called for more stringent controls than the Circuit Court of Appeals provided.

. . .

Affirmed.

NOTES AND QUESTIONS

1. *Established markets for rebuilt goods.* Suppose that a distributor deals in heavily rebuilt goods that bear another's trademark. How should the rule from *Champion* be applied if the market for those rebuilt goods is a well-developed, long-standing market, populated by highly knowledgeable buyers who are fully aware that the goods are, in fact, extensively rebuilt, with parts that might not originate from the trademark owner? *See, e.g., Brandtjen & Kluge, Inc. v. Prudhomme,* 765 F. Supp. 1551 (N.D. Tex. 1991) (concerning trademarks on commercial printing presses).

2. *Case-by-case determination?* Lanham Act liability in cases involving resale of refurbished goods is highly contextual. Should courts nonetheless strive to set forth bright-line rules—e.g., a rule that would impose liability whenever the extent of replacement activity exceeded some predetermined level? Consider a case involving a trademarked watch, in which defendants substitute replacement watch movements or watch cases, or add diamonds to lower-level models, while leaving the trademark indicia (on the watch face) intact. Should a court find liability here, notwithstanding the protections afforded by *Champion?* Should a court find liability based on the extent of the replacement activity? *See, e.g., Bulova Watch Co. v. Allerton Co.,* 328 F.2d 20 (7th Cir. 1964); *Rolex Watch USA, Inc. v. Meece,* 158 F.3d 816 (5th Cir. 1998) (applying *Bulova); see also Cartier, A Div. of Richemont N. Am., Inc. v. Aaron Faber Inc.,* 396 F. Supp. 2d 356 (S.D.N.Y. 2005) (distinguishing *Prestonettes* and *Champion* in a case involving the addition of diamonds to stainless steel Cartier watches so that they would resemble the more expensive, white-gold models).

3. *Advertising one's repair services.* Cases such as *Champion* deal with a repair service provider's freedom to resell refurbished goods that still bear the original trademark. To what extent can a repair services provider truthfully *advertise* that he or she provides such services, using the mark in the advertising? The answer would seem to depend only indirectly, if at all, on the "first sale" doctrine; the issue could be resolved by resort to general principles of confusion, dilution, or, potentially, false advertising. In general, courts tend to scrutinize such advertisements carefully to ensure that the repair service provider is not giving a misleading or confusing impression that the provider is a manufacturer's authorized service provider. *See, e.g., Porsche Cars N. Am., Inc. v. Manny's Porshop, Inc.,* 972 F. Supp.

1128 (N.D. Ill. 1997) (enjoining repair shop from using PORSHOP for repair services for Porsche automobiles). Otherwise a strict approach restricting advertising would threaten to eviscerate the freedoms provided by the "first sale" doctrine. If so, how might judges best balance the parties' interests?

The Fifth Circuit has warned trademark owners sternly about dilution claims asserted against aftermarket service providers who use brand names in their advertisements:

> Trademark law does not entitle markholders to control the aftermarket in marked products. *Ty, Inc. v. Perryman*, 306 F.3d 509, 513 (7th Cir. 2002). Granted, consumers will naturally associate a used, repaired, or rebuilt product with the mark it bears. As a quick glance at any classifieds section shows, reference to a used or repaired item's trademark will often be the only feasible way to announce the item's availability for sale. *See id.* at 512. Moreover, consumers will often base their opinion of a product on the product's performance after months or years of use and periodic repairs. These phenomena are necessary and unremarkable offshoots of a robust aftermarket in trademarked products, not evidence of dilution.

Scott Fetzer Co. v. House of Vacuums Inc., 381 F.3d 477, 489-90 (5th Cir. 2004).

4. *Replacement parts and compatibility.* Suppose that a manufacturer makes automobile grilles that are designed to serve as replacement parts for certain Chevrolet vehicles. The grilles have indentations in the shape of the Chevrolet "bow-tie" logo. The manufacturer purchases plastic bow-tie emblems, places them in the indentations, and sells the grilles as replacement parts to collision repair shops. Suppose that General Motors, owner of the Chevrolet trademarks, sues for trademark infringement. Should the reasoning of *Champion* be extended to this case—i.e., should the replacement part manufacturer be entitled to use the original equipment manufacturer's mark to show that the replacement part is indeed a replacement part, as long as the packaging indicates that the replacement part was not manufactured by the original equipment manufacturer? *See Gen. Motors Corp. v. Keystone Auto. Indus., Inc.*, 453 F.3d 351 (6th Cir. 2006). Should it matter whether the grille manufacturer in this case purchased the bow-tie emblem from Chevrolet, or from an unauthorized source?

Suppose that Cousin Clem manufactures COUSIN CLEM paper towel dispensers, sized such that the dispensers will only accept non-standard towels, which Cousin Clem also makes. A third party (Brother Billy) who wants to sell towels that fit into the COUSIN CLEM dispensers advertises the towels as being "compatible with COUSIN CLEM dispensers." If Brother Billy sells towels to the Cheap Sleep Motel, where a legitimate COUSIN CLEM dispenser has been installed in the restrooms, is there a risk of trademark infringement liability on the part of Cheap Sleep? Would your answer change if Cheap Sleep has leased (rather than purchased) the dispenser from Cousin Clem, assuming no other pertinent lease restrictions?

5. *"Material differences."* Some courts have adopted the "material differences" standard in determining whether the "first sale" doctrine shields the resale of altered or modified new goods. *See Brilliance Audio, Inc. v. Haights Cross Commc'ns, Inc.*, 474 F.3d 365, 369-70 (6th Cir. 2007) (identifying two situations in which the "first sale" doctrine does not shield resellers: (1) "when the notice that the item has been repackaged is inadequate," citing *Coty* and *Enesco*; and (2) when the resold goods are materially different from those sold by the trademark owner, citing *Davidoff*). Suppose that a firm resells genuine goods without their original serial numbers. Is this alteration a "material difference"? If so, why? *See Beltronics USA, Inc. v. Midwest Inventory Distribution, LLC*, 562 F.3d 1067 (10th Cir. 2009); *see also Zino Davidoff SA v. CVS Corp.*, 571 F.3d 238 (2d Cir. 2009) (removal of unique production code ("UPC") from cologne product). The "material differences" standard is often at issue in cases involving gray goods, the topic of the next set of materials.

The "first sale" analysis becomes somewhat more complicated when the first sale of the product bearing the trademark (and with respect to which a defendant claims trademark rights are exhausted) occurred outside the United States. (For a debate in copyright involving construction of several relevant provisions of the Copyright Act, *see Kirtsaeng v. John Wiley & Sons, Inc.*, 568 U.S. 519 (2013) (sale of a lawfully made copy outside the United States triggers the first sale doctrine).) Should a purchaser of that product be able to resell the product in the United States without infringing the U.S. trademark rights? Because of the principle of territoriality of trademark rights, enshrined in the Paris Convention and TRIPS, one might expect that the sale would have to occur in the United States because there is no guarantee that the trademark owner in the United States is the same as or related to the trademark owner in the foreign country. *See A. Bourjois & Co. v. Katzel*, 260 U.S. 689 (1923). But what if the goods *are* placed on the market abroad by the U.S. rights owner, or by a company in an economic relationship with the rights owner? What legitimate interests of the trademark owner are being protected if we allow the trademark owner to stop the sale of goods that were put on the market abroad by itself or with its authorization? Do consumers benefit from such imports? In all circumstances? If not, what considerations should determine whether such imports should be permitted? What changes in global marketing, whether those now occurring or those that may soon occur, might alter the importance of the markets for these imports? How does this affect your analysis of the appropriate approach to such importing? For a useful discussion of these points, *see American Circuit Breaker Corp. v. Oregon Breakers Inc.*, 406 F.3d 577, 581-85 (9th Cir. 2005).

The territorial nature of intellectual property rights clashes with an absolutist vision of free international trade in goods. The exhaustion doctrine mediates to some extent that clash, by determining whether and to what extent a rights holder in country *A* can assert its rights and thus prevent the entry into country *A* of genuine goods put on the market in country *B* by the mark owner. (These goods imported from country *B* are called "parallel imports" or "gray goods.") In this area, however, international law imposes no rule. Article 6 of TRIPS expressly permits WTO member states to adopt a rule of national exhaustion (i.e., the sale must occur in the member state) or international exhaustion (i.e., an authorized sale anywhere exhausts rights).

In the United States, issues concerning gray goods arise not only in the infringement context, but also in the context of Customs enforcement. Litigation over the question of when Customs is obliged to stop the importation of gray goods has arisen both under the Tariff Act, *see K Mart Corp. v. Cartier, Inc.*, 486 U.S. 281 (1988) (and *Gamut*, excerpted *infra*), and under Section 42 of the Lanham Act. Section 42 provides that:

> no article of imported merchandise which shall copy or simulate the name of any domestic manufacture, or manufacturer, or trader, . . . or which shall copy or simulate a trademark registered in accordance with the provisions of this chapter or shall bear a name or mark calculated to induce the public to believe that the article is manufactured in the United States, or that it is manufactured in any foreign country or locality other than the country or locality in which it is in fact manufactured, shall be admitted to entry at any customhouse of the United States. . . .

However, the Customs Service took the view, as embodied in its so-called affiliate exception, that goods are genuine—and thus neither "copy nor simulate" a domestic trademarked good—when they bear trademarks valid in their country of origin and the foreign manufacturer is affiliated with the domestic trademark holder. In *Lever Brothers Co. v. United States*, 877 F.2d 101 (D.C. Cir. 1989), a U.S. trademark owner challenged the application of this exception. The Court of Appeals for the District of Columbia struck down the affiliate exception, holding that Section 42 "bars foreign goods bearing a trademark identical to a valid US trademark but physically different, regardless of the trademarks' genuine character abroad or affiliation between the producing firms." *Id.* at 111. The court reasoned that:

> On its face the section appears to aim at deceit and consumer confusion; when identical trade-marks have acquired different meanings in different countries, one who imports the foreign version to sell it under that trademark will (in the absence of some specially differentiating feature) cause the confusion Congress sought to avoid. The fact of affiliation between the producers in no way reduces the probability of that confusion; it is certainly not a constructive consent to the importation.

Id.; *see also later proceeding*, 981 F.2d 1330 (D.C. Cir. 1993).

GAMUT TRADING CO. v. U.S.I.T.C.

200 F.3d 775 (Fed. Cir. 1999)

NEWMAN, Circuit Judge:

    . . .

BACKGROUND

Kubota-Japan manufactures in Japan a large number of models of agricultural trac-tors, for use in Japan and other countries. Various tractor models are custom-designed for a particular use in a particular country. For example, tractor models that are designed for rice paddy farming are constructed for traction and maneuverability under wet, muddy condi-tions; these tractors have smaller tire separation in order to make tight turns in rice paddies, and are designed to function with rice paddy tillers, which contain narrow, light-weight blades. No corresponding model is designed for export to the United States.

In contrast, some tractor models that are intended to be used in the United States are specially constructed for lifting and transporting earth and rocks, and to function with rear cutters that contain heavy blades capable of cutting rough undergrowth; these models do not have a direct Japanese counterpart. The tractor models intended for sale and use in the United States bear English-language controls and warnings, and have English-language dealers and users manuals. They are imported by Kubota-US and sold through a nation-wide dealership network which provides full maintenance and repair service and maintains an inventory of parts for these specific tractor models. Kubota-US conducts training classes for its dealership employees, instructing them on service and maintenance procedures.

Gamut purchases used Kubota tractors in Japan and imports them into the United States. The majority of the imported tractors are described as between 13 and 25 years old. All bear the mark "Kubota." The Kubota companies state that the importation and its extent came to their attention when United States purchasers sought service and repair or maintenance from Kubota-US dealerships.

[Kubota initiated a so-called Section 337 action against Gamut—that is, an action before the U.S. International Trade Commission seeking an order excluding importation of the allegedly infringing goods, under authority of 19 U.S.C. §1337, the Tariff Act. That section provides, in relevant part, that

> [t]he importation into the United States, the sale for importation, or the sale within the United States after importation by the owner, importer, or consignee, of articles that infringe a valid and enforceable United States trademark registered under the Trademark Act of 1946.

19 U.S.C. §1337(a)(1)(C). The I.T.C. granted the exclusion order, and Gamut appealed to the Federal Circuit.]

The Gray Market

The term "gray market goods" refers to genuine goods that in this case are of foreign manufacture, bearing a legally affixed foreign trademark that is the same mark as is registered in the United States; gray goods are legally acquired abroad and then imported without the consent of the United States trademark holder. *See K Mart Corp. v. Cartier, Inc.*, 486 U.S. 281, 286-87 (1987) (discussing various gray-market conditions); 4 *McCarthy on Trademark and Unfair Competition* §29.46 (4th ed. 1997). The conditions under which gray-market goods have been excluded implement the territorial nature of trademark registration, and reflect a legal recognition of the role of domestic business in establishing and maintaining the reputation and goodwill of a domestic trademark.

Until the Supreme Court's decision in *A. Bourjois & Co. v. Katzel*, 260 U.S. 689 (1923), the prevailing rule in the United States was that the authorized sale of a validly trademarked product, anywhere in the world, exhausted the trademark's exclusionary right; thus the holder of the corresponding registered United States trademark was believed to have no right to bar the importation and sale of authentically marked foreign goods. However, in the *Bourjois* case the Court recognized the territorial boundaries of trademarks, stressing that the reputation and goodwill of the holder of the corresponding United States mark warrants protection against unauthorized importation of goods bearing the same mark, although the mark was validly affixed in the foreign country. In *Bourjois* the foreign-origin goods were produced by an unrelated commercial entity and imported by a third person, although the goods themselves were related in that the United States trademark owner bought its materials from the foreign producer. *See id.* at 692.

Since the *Bourjois* decision, the regional circuits and the Federal Circuit have drawn a variety of distinctions in applying gray market jurisprudence, primarily in consideration of whether the foreign source of the trademarked goods and the United States trademark holder are related commercial entities and whether the imported goods bearing the foreign mark are the same as (or not materially different from) the goods that are sold under the United States trademark, applying a standard of materiality suitable to considerations of consumer protection and support for the integrity of the trademarks of domestic purveyors, all with due consideration to the territorial nature of registered trademarks in the context of international trade.

Gamut directs our attention to cases in which the courts have refused to exclude gray market goods. For example, in *NEC Electronics v. CAL Circuit Abco*, 810 F.2d 1506 (9th Cir. 1987), the court held that the importation of genuine NEC computer chips by the defendant, an entity unrelated to any NEC company, did not constitute infringement of the United States "NEC" trademark when there was no material difference between the NEC product imported by the defendant and the NEC product imported by the NEC United States subsidiary; the court distinguished *Bourjois* on the ground that in *Bourjois* the United States trademark owner could not control the quality of the unaffiliated foreign producer's goods, whereas when the companies are commonly controlled there is a reasonable assurance of similar quality. *Id.* at 1510.

A similar refusal to exclude was reached in *Weil Ceramics & Glass, Inc. v. Dash*, 878 F.2d 659 (3d Cir. 1989), wherein the court held that the United States trademark "Lladro" was not infringed by importation and sale of authentic "Lladro" figurines by one other than the trademark holder. The court reasoned that there is no need to protect the consumer against confusion when the goods imported by the defendant are identical to the goods imported by the United States trademark holder. *Id.* at 672, 878 F.2d 659. The court also reasoned that when the foreign manufacturer and the United States trademark holder are related companies, there is no need to protect the domestic company's investment in goodwill based on the quality of the trademarked goods, for the foreign manufacturer has control over their quality and the goods (porcelain figurines) are unchanged from their original quality.

However, when there are material differences between the domestic product and the foreign product bearing the same mark, most of the courts that have considered the issue have excluded the gray goods, even when the holders of the domestic and foreign trademarks are related companies, on grounds of both safeguarding the goodwill of the domestic enterprise, and protecting consumers from confusion or deception as to the quality and nature of the product bearing the mark. Thus in *Societe Des Produits Nestle v. Casa Helvetia, Inc.*, 982 F.2d 633 (1st Cir. 1992) the court held that the foreign owner of the United States trademark "Perugina" and its Puerto Rican subsidiary that imported Italian-made "Perugina" chocolate could prevent the importation of "Perugina" chocolate made under license in Venezuela, because the product is materially different in taste; the court referred to the likelihood of consumer confusion and loss of goodwill and integrity of the mark.

Similarly in *Original Appalachian Artworks v. Granada Electronics*, 816 F.2d 68, 73 (2d Cir. 1987) the court held that the United States owner of the "Cabbage Patch" mark can prevent importation of "Cabbage Patch" dolls that were made and sold abroad under license from the United States owner, on the ground that the foreign dolls were materially different from the dolls authorized for sale in the United States because their instructions and adoption papers were in the Spanish language. *See also Martin's Herend Imports, Inc. v. Diamond & Gem Trading USA, Co.*, 112 F.3d 1296 (5th Cir. 1997) (foreign owner of United States trademark and domestic distributor can prevent the importation of authentic "Herend" porcelain that is materially different in color, pattern, or shape from the "Herend" porcelain made for sale in the United States); *Lever Brothers Co. v. United States*, 981 F.2d 1330 (D.C. Cir. 1993) (in action against Customs Service, "Sunlight" brand dishwashing liquid sold in Great Britain by Lever-UK was required to be excluded because materially different from the "Sunlight" dishwashing liquid sold in the United States by Lever-US; third party importation was an act of trademark infringement).

These decisions implement the reasoning that the consuming public, associating a trademark with goods having certain characteristics, would be likely to be confused or deceived by goods bearing the same mark but having materially different characteristics; this confusion or deception would also erode the goodwill achieved by the United States trademark holder's business. Thus the basic question in gray market cases concerning goods of foreign origin is not whether the mark was validly affixed, but whether there are differences between the foreign and domestic product and if so whether the differences are material.

The courts have applied a low threshold of materiality, requiring no more than showing that consumers would be likely to consider the differences between the foreign and domestic products to be significant when purchasing the product, for such differences would suffice to erode the goodwill of the domestic source. As explained in *Nestle*, "[a]ny higher threshold would endanger a manufacturer's investment in product goodwill and unduly subject consumers to potential confusion by severing the tie between a manufacturer's protected mark and its associated bundle of traits." 982 F.2d at 641. This criterion readily reconciles cases that have permitted parallel importation of identical goods, such as the Lladro figurines in *Weil Ceramics* (consumers not deceived, and no erosion of goodwill) and those that have barred importation based on material differences, such as the "Perugina" chocolate in *Nestle*. This criterion was applied by the Commission in reviewing the used "Kubota" tractor importations.

The "Kubota" Importations

The ALJ [Administrative Law Judge] found that twenty-four models of the "Kubota" Japanese tractors imported by Gamut were materially different from any corresponding tractor imported by Kubota-US, and that one model was substantially the same. The ALJ found that the twenty-four tractor models differed in at least one of the following characteristics: structural strength, maximum speed, power take-off speed, wheel-base and tread-width dimensions, existence of a power take-off shield, and existence of a hydraulic block outlet. The ALJ found that certain parts for these models were not available in the United States, that the service necessary for these tractors differed from the service available for the United States models, that the used Japanese tractors lacked English warning labels and instructions, and that the Kubota-US dealers did not have English-language operator or service manuals for the Japanese models. Finding these differences to be material, the ALJ found that these used tractors bearing the trademark "Kubota" infringed the United States "Kubota" trademark.

The ALJ found that one used tractor model, the Kubota L200, was not materially different from a corresponding model imported and sold by Kubota-US, and that although the labels and instructions on the tractor were in Japanese, the English -language instruction and service manuals, warning labels, and parts available for the corresponding United States model were applicable to the Japanese Kubota L200. The ALJ concluded that the imported used Kubota L200 tractor did not infringe the "Kubota" United States trademark.

The Commission adopted the ALJ's Initial Decision as to the twenty-four models found to be infringing, and reversed the determination of no infringement by the Kubota L200. The Commission also found infringement by twenty additional tractor models not reviewed by the ALJ. For the Kubota L200 and the twenty additional models, the Commission found that the absence of English-language warning and instructional labels constituted a material difference from the "Kubota" brand tractors sold in the United States by Kubota-US, giving rise to trademark infringement by these unauthorized imports and violation of Section 337.

The Question of Material Differences

Gamut argues that the ITC erred in finding that there are material differences between their imported tractors and those imported by Kubota-US. Gamut points out that materiality of product differences is determined by the likelihood of confusion of those whose purchasing choice would be affected by knowledge of the differences, *see Nestle*, 982 F.2d at 643, and that its purchasers know that they are purchasing a used Japanese tractor. Gamut states that a purchaser of a used tractor bearing Japanese labels would not be deceived into thinking that he/she is buying a new tractor designed for the United States market. Gamut states that any differences between the imported models and the United States models are readily apparent, and thus cannot be . . . material difference[s].

The ITC rejected this argument, finding that it is not reasonable to expect that purchasers of used Kubota tractors will be aware of structural differences from the United States models and of the consequences of these differences for purposes of maintenance, service, and parts. This finding was supported by substantial evidence. Indeed, the marking of these tractors with the "Kubota" mark weighs against an inference that purchasers would be expected to be aware of or expect structural differences.

As precedent illustrates, differences that may be readily apparent to consumers may nevertheless be material. In *Nestle* the court found differences in quality, composition, and packaging to be material. In *Martin's Herend* the court found differences in the color, pattern, or shape of porcelain figures to be material, although they would be apparent to an observer of the products side-by-side. Differences in labeling and other written materials have been deemed material, on the criteria of likelihood of consumer confusion and concerns for the effect of failed consumer expectations on the trademark holder's reputation and goodwill. [cit.]

The Commission found that the imported used "Kubota" tractors lacked English instructional and warning labels, operator manuals, and service manuals. Labels are attached at various places on the tractor to instruct the user on the proper operation of the tractor and to warn of potential hazards, and include instructions on the direction of the engine speed hand throttle, the function of the transmission, the four-wheel drive, the power take-off speed, hydraulic power lift, and other controls on the tractor. The Commission found that such labels are necessary to safe and effective operation. The authorized "Kubota" tractors bear these labels in English; the permanent labels on the used imported tractors are in Japanese.

While it would be obvious to the purchaser that the warning and instructional labels are in Japanese, there was evidence before the ITC of consumer belief that the used tractors were sponsored by or otherwise associated with the Kubota-US distributorship/service system. The ALJ heard evidence that a purchaser of such a used tractor knew the tractor bore Japanese labels, but did not realize that he was not buying an authorized tractor or that service and parts were not available from the Kubota-US dealerships. Gamut contends that Kubota-Japan and Kubota-US form a single enterprise and thus that Kubota-US can and should provide any parts, service, maintenance, and repairs required by these used tractors. The ALJ found that in order to service the Gamut-imported tractors in the same manner as Kubota-US provides for its authorized tractors, the dealerships and service agencies would require an additional inventory of parts for the various Japan-only models, English-language operator manuals and service manuals that do not now exist, and additional service training as to the different models. There was testimony from a Kubota-US dealer that he had tried to service several of the imported used tractors in order to preserve the reputation and goodwill of the mark, but that he was unable to do so satisfactorily since he had neither technical information nor replacement parts. He testified to customer dissatisfaction and anger with his dealership. The ALJ heard testimony that it would cost millions of dollars to provide equivalent support in the United States for the tractors that are made for use only in Japan. Gamut disputes these assertions and argues that most of the used tractors could be readily serviced without extraordinary effort. However, the record contains substantial evidence in support of the ALJ's findings. Further, materiality does not turn on whether extraordinary effort would be required for Kubota to service the Gamut-imported tractors; the threshold is not so high or the burden of establishing materiality so heavy.

The Kubota companies are not required to arrange to provide service to Gamut's imports in order to ratify these importations by mitigating their injury to the goodwill associated with the "Kubota" trademark. Whether or not the Kubota companies could arrange to service these tractors does not convert an otherwise infringing activity into an authorized importation. *See Osawa*, 589 F. Supp. at 1167-68 (trademark holder incurred damage from the unauthorized importation of gray market cameras because it voluntarily bore the warranty expenses for servicing them).

In addition to the differences in labeling, service, and parts, the ALJ found that many of the tractors designed by Kubota for use in the United States are stronger structurally than the corresponding tractors made for use in Japan. For example, the ALJ found that some of the intended United States tractors were made with stronger front and rear axles, front axle brackets, chassis, power trail, and parts contained in the transmission, such as gears. The ALJ found that the stronger gears increase load-bearing capacity and bending strength, thereby reducing wear and tear. The ALJ found that some of the tractor models designed for the United States market have a stronger power take-off shaft, installed to accommodate the heavy load placed on the shaft by implements often used in the United States such as a rear cutter. The ALJ heard evidence that these structural differences significantly increase the likelihood of breakdowns of the less strong Japanese models. Although Gamut points to the absence of evidence of actual breakdown, the conceded or established differences in structural strength are relevant to the finding of material differences, and were properly considered by the Commission, along with the evidence concerning labelling [sic], warnings, service, and parts.

Gamut raises the additional argument that in all events the Commission erred in law by applying the material differences test with the low threshold of precedent, because the imported tractors are not new but used. Gamut states that the Commission should have applied a more stringent test, namely, that differences which are easily ascertained by the consumer can not be material. Gamut also argues that the Commission erred in ruling that differences that are easily apparent to the consumer, such as differences in structural strength and availability of parts and service, are material. We conclude that the Commission applied the correct standard, for this standard implements the two fundamental policies of trademark law: to protect the consumer and to safeguard the goodwill of the producer. The Commission did not err in finding no factual basis for assuming, as Gamut proposes, that the purchaser of a used tractor should be charged with the knowledge or awareness that replacement parts may not be available.

Substantial evidence supports the Commission's finding that consumers would consider the differences between the used imported tractors and the authorized Kubota-US tractors to be important to their purchasing decision, and thus material.

EFFECT OF THE FACT THAT THE GOODS ARE USED

Gamut argues that this is not a "gray market" case because the imported tractors are simply durable used goods, rendering it irrelevant whether the trademark owner authorized their sale in the United States. Gamut also argues that imported goods must be sold in competition with the goods of the owner of the United States trademark in order for authentic foreign-marked goods to infringe any trademark rights, citing *K Mart v. Cartier*, 486 U.S. at 286. Gamut asserts that because Kubota-US sells new tractors in the United States and the respondents sell only used tractors, the goods are not in direct competition and the imported used tractors can not be held to be infringing gray market goods.

Direct competition between substantially identical goods is a factor to be considered, but it is not a prerequisite to trademark infringement. In *Safety-Kleen Corp. v. Dresser Indus.*, 518 F.2d 1399, 1404 (CCPA 1975) the court explained that "[w]hile the similarity or dissimilarity of the goods or service should, in appropriate cases, be considered in determining likelihood of confusion . . . the law has long protected the legitimate interests of trademark owners from confusion among noncompetitive, but related, products bearing confusingly similar marks." Similar reasoning applies to products of the gray market.

As we have discussed, trademark law as applied to gray market goods embodies a composite of likelihood of consumer confusion as to the source of the goods, likelihood of consumer confusion arising from differences between the foreign and the domestic goods, impositions on the goodwill and burdens on the integrity of the United States trademark owner due to consumer response to any differences, and recognition of the territorial scope of national trademarks. Various of these factors acquire more or less weight depending on the particular situation. Although it is relevant to consider whether the imported product is new or used, other factors that may affect the reputation and the goodwill enuring to the holder of a trademark are not overridden by the fact that the product is known to be second-hand.

Courts that have considered the question and concluded that used goods can be gray market goods include *Red Baron-Franklin Park, Inc. v. Taito Corp.*, 883 F.2d 275, 11 USPQ2d 1548 (4th Cir. 1989) (used circuit boards purchased abroad and imported into the United States without the copyright holder's consent were gray market goods); [cit.].

The ALJ found that Kubota-US has established a reputation for safety, reliability, and service that consumers associate with the "Kubota" mark, and that the used tractors bearing the "Kubota" mark undermine the investment that Kubota-US made in consumer goodwill for "Kubota" products. These findings are supported by substantial evidence. The fact that the imported tractors are used does not prevent a finding of infringement of the United States "Kubota" trademark.

[*Affirmed.*]

NOTES AND QUESTIONS

1.   *More on the meaning of "gray goods."* What if a firm manufactures a product in the United States (and applies its trademark to the product) and ships the product abroad for sale, only to find that third parties are re-importing the product into the United States, outside the authorized distribution channels? Is such a product a gray good, or do gray good rules apply only where the product was manufactured outside the United States with the trademark owner's authorization, and then imported into the United States without the trademark owner's authorization? In *K Mart*, in which customs regulations were at issue, the Supreme Court noted that a gray market good is "a foreign-manufactured good, bearing a valid United States trademark, that is imported without the consent of the United States trademark holder." *K Mart Corp. v. Cartier, Inc.*, 486 U.S. 281, 285 (1988). The Court identified three cases in which a product might be deemed a gray market good:

> The prototypical gray-market victim (case 1) is a domestic firm that purchases from an independent foreign firm the rights to register and use the latter's trademark as a United States trademark and to sell its foreign-manufactured products here. . . . The second context (case 2) is a situation in which a domestic firm registers the United States trademark for goods that are manufactured abroad by an affiliated manufacturer . . . [and i]n the third context (case 3), the domestic holder of a United States trademark *authorizes* an independent foreign manufacturer to use it. Usually the holder sells to the foreign manufacturer an exclusive right to use the trademark in a particular foreign location, but conditions the right on the foreign manufacturer's promise not to import its trademarked goods into the United States.

Id. at 286-87.

2.   *Are "material differences" limited to physical differences?* Suppose that the imported tractors in *Gamut* had been physically identical to the tractors sold in the United States, but the warranty conditions for the imported tractors were less generous. Or, what if Kubota forbids its authorized dealers from providing post-sale repair and maintenance service for imported Kubota tractors? Are these cognizable "material differences"? *See SKF USA Inc. v. I.T.C.*, 423 F.3d 1307 (Fed. Cir. 2005), *cert. denied*, 548 U.S. 904 (2006). Should the analysis for material differences depend on where the goods at issue are being sold? In particular, where the goods at issue are sold on eBay, should courts presume that eBay consumers are bargain hunters who expect that the goods that they are purchasing differ materially from the genuine goods? *See Bose Corp. v. Ejaz*, 732 F.3d 17 (1st Cir. 2013). Should differences in production potentially be material? *See Hokto Kinoko Co. v. Concord Farms, Inc.*, 738 F.3d 1085 (9th Cir. 2013) (involving trademarks on mushrooms; the genuine mushrooms were produced under certified organic standards but the imported mushrooms were not).

3. *Mark owner's authorized domestic sales.* The gray market theory posits that domestic consumers will be confused when confronted with both a mark owner's authorized trademarked goods and imported goods that bear the mark owner's trademark but are materially different from the domestic goods. But the theory seems to assume that the mark owner observes a strict division between goods intended for its U.S. market and goods intended for its overseas market; that is, it authorizes only the sale of the U.S. goods in the U.S. market. What if the division is not quite so strict? For example, what if the mark owner authorizes its U.S. dealers to sell, in the United States, some goods that were manufactured for the overseas market? Is the mark owner itself contributing to consumer confusion? Should third parties be free to place gray goods into the stream of U.S. commerce if the mark owner is allowing some of it to occur through its own distribution channels? *See SKF USA Inc.*, 423 F.3d at 1315; *Bourdeau Bros., Inc. v. I.T.C.*, 444 F.3d 1317 (Fed. Cir. 2006); *Deere & Co. v. I.T.C.*, 605 F.3d 1350 (Fed. Cir. 2010). If the mark owner authorizes the sale of even a single import, should that be dispositive against the mark owner, or should the court take into account the number of sales and factor it into the ultimate determination of Section 337 compliance?

C.   EXPRESSIVE USE OF ANOTHER'S TRADEMARK

ANHEUSER-BUSCH, INC. v. BALDUCCI PUBLICATIONS
28 F.3d 769 (8th Cir. 1994), cert. denied, 513 U.S. 1112 (1995)

JOHN R. GIBSON, Senior Circuit Judge:

. . .

Anheuser-Busch operates a brewery in St. Louis. Its products include the Michelob family of beers: Michelob, Michelob Dry, Michelob Light and Michelob Classic Dark. For use in its marketing of these products, Anheuser-Busch owns several federally-registered trademarks: (1) Michelob; (2) Michelob Dry; (3) A & Eagle Design; (4) Bottle and Label Configuration; (5) Bottle Configuration; (6) Vertical Stripe Design; (7) the phrase "ONE TASTE AND YOU'LL DRINK IT DRY"; and (8) Vertical Stripe and A & Eagle Design. Of these, (1) and (3) are also registered Missouri trademarks.

Balducci Publications is a publishing business owned by Richard and Kathleen Balducci, also defendants in this case. Balducci Publications has published *Snicker*, a humor magazine, since April 1987. The back cover of issue 5 ½, published in April 1989, contains a mock advertisement for the fictitious product "Michelob Oily." [Images reproduced at end of case.] The advertisement states in bold type, "ONE TASTE AND YOU'LL DRINK IT OILY" immediately above "MICHELOB OILY®." The accompanying graphics include a partially-obscured can of Michelob Dry pouring oil onto a fish, an oil-soaked rendition of the A & Eagle design (with the eagle exclaiming "Yuck!") below a Shell Oil symbol, and various "Michelob Oily" products bearing a striking resemblance to appellants' Michelob family. This resemblance was quite intentional, as evidenced by the admitted use of actual Anheuser-Busch "clip-art" in replicating several of the protected trademarks. In smaller text the ad opines, "At the rate it's being dumped into our oceans, lakes and rivers, you'll drink it oily sooner or later, anyway." Finally, the following disclaimer is found in extremely small text running vertically along the right side of the page: "Snicker Magazine Editorial by Rich Balducci. Art by Eugene Ruble. Thank goodness someone still cares about quality (of life)." [See appendixes at the end of the case for reproductions of the allegedly infringing advertisements.]

Balducci continues to sell back issues of *Snicker*—including Issue 5 ½. Advertising for back issues of the magazine has included the words "Michelob Oily" and a blue ribbon design associated with Anheuser-Busch.

Mr. Balducci stated at trial that he used the parody to comment on: (1) the effects of environmental pollution, including a specific reference to the then-recent Shell oil spill in the Gasconade River—a source of Anheuser-Busch's water supply; (2) Anheuser-Busch's subsequent decision to temporarily close its St. Louis brewery; and (3) the proliferation of Anheuser-Busch beer brands and advertisements. The defendants concede they possessed no knowledge that any Anheuser-Busch product actually contained oil.

Anheuser-Busch, displeased with Balducci's extensive use of its trademarks and the possible implication that its products were tainted with oil, brought this suit in May 1989. It asserted five causes of action: (1) infringement of federally-registered trademarks, 15 U.S.C. §1114(1); (2) federal unfair competition, 15 U.S.C. §1125(a); (3) state trademark infringement, Mo. Rev. Stat. §417.056; (4) common law unfair competition; and (5) state law trademark dilution, Mo. Rev. Stat. §417.061. It sought one dollar in nominal damages and injunctive relief.

Other than the Balducci ad itself, the primary evidence offered by Anheuser-Busch was a study designed by Jacob Jacoby, Ph.D., and conducted under the supervision of Leon B. Kaplan, Ph.D. This survey, conducted in St. Louis shopping malls, involved 301 beer drinkers or purchasers who claimed to periodically review magazines or newspapers. The surveyors showed the Balducci ad to 200 participants and a Michelob Dry ad to the remaining 101. Of those viewing the Balducci ad, many expressed an impression of Anheuser-Busch's role in its creation. For example, fifty-eight percent felt the creators "did have to get permission to use the Michelob name." Fifty-six percent believed permission would be required for the various symbols and logos. Six percent of the classified responses construed the Balducci ad to be an actual Anheuser-Busch advertisement. Almost half (45%) found nothing about the parody which suggested it was an editorial, and seventy-five percent did not perceive it as satirical. Virtually none (3.5%) noticed the tiny disclaimer on the side of the ad. Fifty-five percent construed the parody as suggesting that Michelob beer is or was in some way contaminated with oil. As a result, twenty-two percent stated they were less likely to buy Michelob beer in the future.

After a bench trial, the district court ruled in favor of Balducci on each of the five theories. Although the court found that "Defendants clearly used Plaintiff's marks in their ad parody, they used some of those marks without alteration, and they did so without Plaintiff's permission," it dismissed the trademark claims because "Defendants' use of [the] marks did not create a likelihood of confusion in the marketplace." *Anheuser-Busch, Inc. v. Balducci Publications*, 814 F. Supp. 791, 793. In reaching this decision, the court expressed the need to give "special sensitivity" to the First Amendment aspects of the case. *Id*. at 796. Accordingly, the court concluded that although "Plaintiff's statistical evidence [might] well be persuasive in the context of a classic trademark infringement case, . . . where the allegedly infringing use occurs in an editorial context," more persuasive evidence of confusion is required. *Id*. at 797. The court similarly dismissed the state law dilution claim, stating that "because Defendant's use of Plaintiff's marks occurred in an editorial context, there is no threat of tarnishment through association with shoddy or disharmonious products." *Id*. at 799. Finally, the court rejected the unfair competition claims because the "parody was not in any way connected with the sale of a product and because Plaintiff has failed to establish a likelihood of confusion in the marketplace." *Id*. at 798.

On appeal, Anheuser-Busch contends the district court gave inordinate weight to Balducci's First Amendment claims and erred in finding no likelihood of confusion. Balducci contends the court correctly found no likelihood of confusion and, furthermore, argues the ad parody is absolutely protected by the First Amendment.

I

This case involves the tension between the protection afforded by the Lanham Act to trademark owners and the competing First Amendment rights of the parodist. Our analysis of the district court's decision encompasses two related, but distinct steps. We begin by considering whether the district court erred in finding no likelihood of confusion. Since a trademark infringement action requires a likelihood of confusion, this finding, if upheld, decides this case. If we conclude the court erred in finding no likelihood of confusion, we must consider Balducci's additional argument that the First Amendment protects it from liability.

. . . Rather than first considering whether Balducci's ad parody was likely to confuse the public and then considering the scope of First Amendment protection, the district court conflated the two. The court essentially skewed its likelihood of confusion analysis in an attempt to give "special sensitivity" to the First Amendment, holding Anheuser-Busch to a higher standard than required in a "classic trademark infringement case." *Balducci*, 814 F. Supp. at 796-97. Since we cannot separate the court's factual finding of confusion from its legal conclusions, we conduct a de novo review of the well-developed record before us. *Calvin Klein*, 815 F.2d at 504.

Many courts have applied, we believe correctly, an expansive interpretation of likelihood of confusion, extending "protection against use of [plaintiff's] mark on any product or service which would reasonably be thought by the buying public to come from the same source, or thought to be affiliated with, connected with, or sponsored by, the trademark owner." McCarthy, *Trademarks and Unfair Competition* §24.03, at 24-13 (3d ed. 1992); [cit.]. This approach seems consistent with congressional intent, as evidenced by the express inclusion during the 1989 revision of the Lanham Act of protection against confusion as to "origin, sponsorship, or approval." 15 U.S.C. §1125(a). This court enumerated several factors pertinent to the finding of likelihood of confusion in *SquirtCo*. . . .

Anheuser-Busch possessed several very strong trademarks that Balducci displayed virtually unaltered in the ad parody. Thus, the first two *SquirtCo* factors [strength and similarity] weigh heavily in favor of Anheuser-Busch. The third factor, competitive proximity, is less one-sided. Balducci does not directly compete with Anheuser-Busch. Confusion, however, may exist in the absence of direct competition. *SquirtCo*, 628 F.2d at 1091. Moreover, Balducci published the parody on the back cover of a magazine — a location frequently devoted to real ads, even in *Snicker*. This location threatens to confuse consumers accustomed to seeing advertisements on the back cover of magazines.

Our analysis of Balducci's intent relies, of necessity, on circumstantial evidence. According to Richard Balducci, he sought to comment on certain social conditions through parody. "An intent to parody is not an intent to confuse." *Jordache Enters., Inc. v. Hogg Wyld, Ltd.*, 828 F.2d 1482, 1486 (10th Cir. 1987). Other factors, however, suggest Balducci had, if not an intent to confuse, at least an indifference to the possibility that some consumers might be misled by the parody. For example, no significant steps were taken to remind readers that they were viewing a parody and not an advertisement sponsored or approved by Anheuser-Busch. Balducci carefully designed the fictitious ad to appear as authentic as possible. Several of Anheuser-Busch's marks were used with little or no alteration. The disclaimer is virtually undetectable. Balducci even included a ® symbol after the words Michelob Oily. These facts suggest that Balducci sought to do far more than just "conjure up" an image of Anheuser-Busch in the minds of its readers. *Cf. Walt Disney Productions v. Air Pirates*, 581 F.2d 751, 758 (9th Cir. 1978), *cert. denied*, 439 U.S. 1132 (1979) (in copyright context, "fair use" doctrine does not entitle parodist to copy everything needed to create the "best parody"; rather, the parodist may copy only that portion of the protected work necessary to "conjure up the original"). These factors limit the degree to which Balducci's intent to parody weighs in favor of a finding of no likelihood of confusion.

Balducci's desired message, or humor, presumably hinged on consumers' ultimate realization that although this "advertisement" was based on the painstaking duplication of Anheuser-Busch's marks, it was in fact a parody or editorial parody. We have significant doubt as to whether many consumers would develop this understanding of Balducci's true purpose. There is a distinct possibility, accepted by the district court, "that a superficial observer might believe that the ad parody was approved by Anheuser-Busch." *Balducci*, 814 F. Supp. at 797. The back cover of magazines is frequently used for advertisements and cannot be expected to command the thoughtful deliberation of all or even most of the viewing public. The district court downplayed this fact, observing that "[o]nce again . . . the First Amendment concerns at issue in this litigation require a closer examination of Plaintiff's claims." *Id*. When objectively viewed, the fourth and sixth *SquirtCo* factors (i.e., intent and degree of care) may not fully support Anheuser-Busch, but they are consistent with a finding that the parody presented a significant likelihood of confusing consumers.

The survey evidence, whether considered as direct or indirect evidence of actual confusion, tilts the analysis in favor of Anheuser-Busch. Over half of those surveyed thought Balducci needed Anheuser-Busch's approval to publish the ad. Many of these presumably felt that such approval had in fact been obtained. Six percent thought that the parody was an actual Anheuser-Busch advertisement. Other courts have accepted similar survey findings. *See Novak*, 836 F.2d at 400; *Nat'l Football League Props., Inc. v. New Jersey Giants, Inc.*, 637 F. Supp. 507, 517 (D.N.J. 1986) (citing decisions relying on surveys showing 8.5% to 15% confusion); *Schieffelin & Co. v. Jack Company of Boca*, 850 F. Supp. 232, 247-48 (S.D.N.Y. 1994). In *Novak*, for example, "approximately ten percent of all the persons surveyed thought that Mutual 'goes along' with Novak's product." 836 F.2d at 400. The court found this persuasive despite the existence of "some ambiguity" in the survey question. *Id*. Thus, we are left with evidence, obtained by means of a valid consumer survey, that strongly indicates actual consumer confusion.

Our review of the record before the district court, including the Balducci ad and the survey evidence, convinces us that the court erred in finding no likelihood of confusion. The court reached its finding only after it mistakenly weighted its analysis in favor of Balducci in an effort to satisfy the limits set by the First Amendment. We believe the better course would have been to analyze the likelihood of confusion first and then proceed to an analysis of the First Amendment issues.

Having determined that a likelihood of confusion exists, we must next consider Balducci's argument that the First Amendment protects it from liability for its ad parody. Parody does implicate the First Amendment's protection of artistic expression. *Cliffs Notes, Inc. v. Bantam Doubleday Dell Pub. Group*, 886 F.2d 490, 493 (2d Cir. 1989). Based on this, Balducci argues it has an absolute First Amendment right to use plaintiff's trademarks in its parody. No such absolute right exists. *See id*. at 493-94 ("Trademark protection is not lost simply because the allegedly infringing use is in connection with a work of artistic expression.") (quoting *Silverman v. CBS Inc.*, 870 F.2d 40, 49 (2d Cir.), *cert. denied*, 492 U.S. 907 (1989)); *Nike*, 6 F.3d at 1228; *Dallas Cowboys Cheerleaders*, 604 F.2d at 206 (defendant liable for using cheerleader uniform in X-rated film); *Pillsbury Co. v. Milky Way Productions, Inc.*, 215 U.S.P.Q. 124, 135 (N.D. Ga. 1981) (defendant liable for dilution for publishing cartoon of "Poppin' Fresh" and "Poppie Fresh" doughpersons engaging in sexual intercourse and fellatio); *Edgar Rice Burroughs, Inc. v. Manns Theaters*, 195 U.S.P.Q. 159, 162 (C.D. Cal. 1976) (defendant liable for using TARZAN mark in X-rated film).

In arguing against the reasoning of these many cases, Balducci relies on this court's opinion in *Mutual of Omaha Ins. Co. v. Novak*, 836 F.2d 397 (8th Cir. 1987), *cert. denied*,

488 U.S. 933 (1988). In *Novak*, a panel of this court upheld an injunction against Novak's continued sale of anti-war T-shirts, coffee mugs and other products containing words such as "Mutants of Omaha" and bearing symbols with a likeness to plaintiff's Indian head logo. *Id.* at 398. In dicta, the court stated that the injunction "in no way infringes upon the constitutional protection the First Amendment would provide were Novak to present an editorial parody in a book, magazine, or film." *Id.* at 402. This language does not support absolute protection for editorial parody, but merely reflects the fact that a parody contained in an obvious editorial context is less likely to confuse, and thus more deserving of protection than those displayed on a product. *See Nike*, 6 F.3d at 1228; *Jordache Enters., Inc. v. Hogg Wyld, Ltd.*, 625 F. Supp. 48, 55 (D.N.M. 1985), aff'd, 828 F.2d 1482 (10th Cir. 1987); 3 J.T. McCarthy §31:38 at 31-213. A parody creating a likelihood of confusion may be subject to a trademark infringement action. *Cliffs Notes*, 886 F.2d at 494 (confusing parodies are "vulnerable under trademark law"); *L.L. Bean, Inc. v. Drake Publishers, Inc.*, 811 F.2d 26, 32 n.3 (1st Cir.) (confusing parodies "implicate[] the legitimate commercial and consumer protection objectives of trademark law"), *cert. denied and appeal dismissed*, 483 U.S. 1013 (1987).

There is no simple, mechanical rule by which courts can determine when a potentially confusing parody falls within the First Amendment's protective reach. Thus, "in deciding the reach of the Lanham Act in any case where an expressive work is alleged to infringe a trademark, it is appropriate to weigh the public interest in free expression against the public interest in avoiding consumer confusion." *Cliffs Notes*, 886 F.2d at 494. "This approach takes into account the ultimate test in trademark law, namely, the likelihood of confusion as to the source of the goods in question." *Id.* at 495 (internal quotations omitted).

In applying this balancing test, we begin with the recognition that parody serves as a "humorous form of social commentary and literary criticism that dates back as far as Greek antiquity." *Bean*, 811 F.2d at 28. Balducci purports to comment on several matters, including environmental pollution and Anheuser-Busch's brand proliferation. The First Amendment's protection of social commentary generally, and parody in particular, is certainly implicated in this case. "The fact that parody can claim legitimacy for some appropriation does not, of course, tell either parodist or judge much about where to draw the line." *Campbell v. Acuff-Rose Music, Inc.*, 114 S. Ct. 1164, 1172 (1994). "The benefit to the one making the parody . . . arises from the humorous association, not from public confusion as to the source of the marks." *Jordache Enters.*, 828 F.2d at 1486. Thus, we must weigh the public interest in protecting Balducci's expression against the public interest in avoiding consumer confusion.

Applying this standard, we are convinced that the First Amendment places no bar to the application of the Lanham Act in this case. As we have discussed, Balducci's ad parody was likely to confuse consumers as to its origin, sponsorship or approval. This confusion might have to be tolerated if even plausibly necessary to achieve the desired commentary—a question we need not decide. In this case, the confusion is wholly unnecessary to Balducci's stated purpose. By using an obvious disclaimer, positioning the parody in a less-confusing location, altering the protected marks in a meaningful way, or doing some collection of the above, Balducci could have conveyed its message with substantially less risk of consumer confusion. Other courts have upheld the use of obvious variations of protected marks. *See, e.g., Cliffs Notes*, 886 F.2d at 496 ("Spy Notes" held not to infringe "Cliffs Notes" mark); *Jordache Enters.*, 828 F.2d at 1485-88 (comparing "Jordache" and "Lardashe" jeans). The First Amendment does not excuse Balducci's failure to do so. As the Second Circuit observed:

> A parody must convey two simultaneous—and contradictory—messages: that it is the original, but also that it is *not* the original and is instead a parody. To the extent that it does only the

former but not the latter, it is not only a poor parody but also vulnerable under trademark law, since the customer will be confused.

Cliffs Notes, 886 F.2d at 494; *see Nike*, 6 F.3d at 1228. Balducci's ad, developed through the nearly unaltered appropriation of Anheuser-Busch's marks, conveys that it is the original, but the ad founders on its failure to convey that it is not the original. Thus, it is vulnerable under trademark law since the customer is likely to be confused, as the record before the district court demonstrated.

We believe it is important to acknowledge the limits of our holding today. We do not hold that Balducci's extensive borrowing of Anheuser-Busch's trademarks amounts to a per se trademark violation. Unlike copyright and patent owners, trademark owners have no right in gross. *See McCarthy* §24.03[4][d]; *Jordache*, 625 F. Supp. at 56 (trademark owner "does not own in gross the penumbral customer awareness of its name, nor the fallout from its advertising"). By taking steps to insure that viewers adequately understood this was an unauthorized editorial, Balducci might have avoided or at least sharply limited any confusion, and thereby escaped from liability. Absent such measures, Balducci's ad parody was likely to confuse consumers and fall subject to federal trademark law.

[*Reversed.*] . . .

APPENDIX A

LOUIS VUITTON MALLETIER S.A. v. HAUTE DIGGITY DOG, LLC

507 F.3d 252 (4th Cir. 2007)

NIEMEYER, Circuit Judge:

Louis Vuitton Malletier S.A., a French corporation located in Paris, that manufactures luxury luggage, handbags, and accessories, commenced this action against Haute Diggity Dog, LLC, a Nevada corporation that manufactures and sells pet products nationally, alleging trademark infringement under 15 U.S.C. §1114(1)(a), trademark dilution under 15 U.S.C. §1125(c), copyright infringement under 17 U.S.C. §501, and related statutory and common law violations. Haute Diggity Dog manufactures, among other things, plush toys on which dogs can chew, which, it claims, parody famous trademarks on luxury products, including those of Louis Vuitton Malletier. The particular Haute Diggity Dog chew toys in question here are small imitations of handbags that are labeled "Chewy Vuiton" and that mimic Louis Vuitton Malletier's LOUIS VUITTON handbags.

On cross-motions for summary judgment, the district court concluded that Haute Diggity Dog's "Chewy Vuiton" dog toys were successful parodies of Louis Vuitton Malletier's trademarks, designs, and products, and on that basis, entered judgment in favor of Haute Diggity Dog on all of Louis Vuitton Malletier's claims.

On appeal, we agree with the district court that Haute Diggity Dog's products are not likely to cause confusion with those of Louis Vuitton Malletier and that Louis Vuitton Malletier's copyright was not infringed. On the trademark dilution claim, however, we reject the district court's reasoning but reach the same conclusion through a different analysis. Accordingly, we affirm.

I

Louis Vuitton Malletier S.A. ("LVM") is a well known manufacturer of luxury luggage, leather goods, handbags, and accessories, which it markets and sells worldwide. In connection with the sale of its products, LVM has adopted trademarks and trade dress that are well recognized and have become famous and distinct. Indeed, in 2006, *BusinessWeek* ranked LOUIS VUITTON as the 17th "best brand" of all corporations in the world and the first "best brand" for any fashion business.

LVM has registered trademarks for "LOUIS VUITTON," in connection with luggage and ladies' handbags (the "LOUIS VUITTON mark"); for a stylized monogram of "LV," in connection with traveling bags and other goods (the "LV mark"); and for a monogram canvas design consisting of a canvas with repetitions of the LV mark along with four-pointed stars, four-pointed stars inset in curved diamonds, and four-pointed flowers inset in circles, in connection with traveling bags and other products (the "Monogram Canvas mark"). In 2002, LVM adopted a brightly-colored version of the Monogram Canvas mark in which the LV mark and the designs were of various colors and the background was white (the "Multicolor design"), created in collaboration with Japanese artist Takashi Murakami. For the Multicolor design, LVM obtained a copyright in 2004. In 2005, LVM adopted another design consisting of a canvas with repetitions of the LV mark and smiling cherries on a brown background (the "Cherry design").

As LVM points out, the Multicolor design and the Cherry design attracted immediate and extraordinary media attention and publicity in magazines such as *Vogue, W, Elle, Harper's Bazaar, Us Weekly, Life and Style, Travel & Leisure, People, In Style,* and *Jane.* The press published photographs showing celebrities carrying these handbags, including Jennifer Lopez, Madonna, Eve, Elizabeth Hurley, Carmen Electra, and Anna Kournikova, among others. When the Multicolor design first appeared in 2003, the magazines typically reported, "The Murakami designs for Louis Vuitton, which were the hit of the summer, came with hefty price tags and a long waiting list." *People Magazine* said, "the wait list is in the thousands." The handbags retailed in the range of $995 for a medium handbag to $4500 for a large travel bag. The medium size handbag that appears to be the model for the "Chewy Vuiton" dog toy retailed for $1190. The Cherry design appeared in 2005, and the handbags including that design were priced similarly—in the range of $995 to $2740. LVM does not currently market products using the Cherry design.

The original LOUIS VUITTON, LV, and Monogram Canvas marks, however, have been used as identifiers of LVM products continuously since 1896.

During the period 2003-2005, LVM spent more than $48 million advertising products using its marks and designs, including more than $4 million for the Multicolor design.

It sells its products exclusively in LVM stores and in its own in-store boutiques that are contained within department stores such as Saks Fifth Avenue, Bloomingdale's, Neiman Marcus, and Macy's. LVM also advertises its products on the Internet through the specific websites www.louisvuitton.com and www.eluxury.com.

Although better known for its handbags and luggage, LVM also markets a limited selection of luxury pet accessories—collars, leashes, and dog carriers—which bear the Monogram Canvas mark and the Multicolor design. These items range in price from approximately $200 to $1600. LVM does not make dog toys.

Haute Diggity Dog, LLC, which is a relatively small and relatively new business located in Nevada, manufactures and sells nationally—primarily through pet stores—a line of pet chew toys and beds whose names parody elegant high-end brands of products such as perfume, cars, shoes, sparkling wine, and handbags. These include—in addition to Chewy Vuiton (LOUIS VUITTON)—Chewnel No. 5 (Chanel No. 5), Furcedes (Mercedes), Jimmy Chew (Jimmy Choo), Dog Perignonn (Dom Perignon), Sniffany & Co. (Tiffany & Co.), and Dogior (Dior). The chew toys and pet beds are plush, made of polyester, and have a shape and design that loosely imitate the signature product of the targeted brand. They are mostly distributed and sold through pet stores, although one or two Macy's stores carries Haute Diggity Dog's products. The dog toys are generally sold for less than $20, although larger versions of some of Haute Diggity Dog's plush dog beds sell for more than $100.

Haute Diggity Dog's "Chewy Vuiton" dog toys, in particular, loosely resemble miniature handbags and undisputedly evoke LVM handbags of similar shape, design, and color. In lieu of the LOUIS VUITTON mark, the dog toy uses "Chewy Vuiton"; in lieu of the LV mark, it uses "CV"; and the other symbols and colors employed are imitations, but not exact ones, of those used in the LVM Multicolor and Cherry designs.

. . . On cross-motions for summary judgment, the district court granted Haute Diggity Dog's motion and denied LVM's motion, entering judgment in favor of Haute Diggity Dog on all of the claims. It rested its analysis on each count principally on the conclusion that Haute Diggity Dog's products amounted to a successful parody of LVM's marks, trade dress, and copyright. [cit.]

LVM appealed and now challenges, as a matter of law, virtually every ruling made by the district court.

II

LVM contends first that Haute Diggity Dog's marketing and sale of its "Chewy Vuiton" dog toys infringe its trademarks because the advertising and sale of the "Chewy Vuiton" dog toys is likely to cause confusion. *See* 15 U.S.C. §1114(1)(a). LVM argues:

> The defendants in this case are using almost an exact imitation of the house mark VUITTON (merely omitting a second "T"), and they painstakingly copied Vuitton's Monogram design mark, right down to the exact arrangement and sequence of geometric symbols. They also used the same design marks, trade dress, and color combinations embodied in Vuitton's Monogram Multicolor and Monogram Cerises [Cherry] handbag collections. Moreover, HDD did not add any language to distinguish its products from Vuitton's, and its products are not "widely recognized."

Haute Diggity Dog contends that there is no evidence of confusion, nor could a reasonable factfinder conclude that there is a likelihood of confusion, because it successfully markets its products as parodies of famous marks such as those of LVM. It asserts that "precisely because of the [famous] mark's fame and popularity . . . confusion is avoided, and it is this lack of confusion that a parodist depends upon to achieve the parody." Thus, responding to LVM's claims of trademark infringement, Haute Diggity Dog argues:

The marks are undeniably similar in certain respects. There are visual and phonetic similarities. [Haute Diggity Dog] admits that the product name and design mimics LVM's and is based on the LVM marks. It is necessary for the pet products to conjure up the original designer mark for there to be a parody at all. However, a parody also relies on "equally obvious dissimilarit[ies] between the marks" to produce its desired effect.

Concluding that Haute Diggity Dog did not create any likelihood of confusion as a matter of law, the district court granted summary judgment to Haute Diggity Dog. [cit.] We review its order *de novo*. [cit.]

[The court noted that to determine whether the "Chewy Vuiton" product line creates a likelihood of confusion it would look to the Fourth Circuit's *Pizzeria Uno* factors.] These *Pizzeria Uno* factors are not always weighted equally, and not all factors are relevant in every case. [cit.]

Because Haute Diggity Dog's arguments with respect to the *Pizzeria Uno* factors depend to a great extent on whether its products and marks are successful parodies, we consider first whether Haute Diggity Dog's products, marks, and trade dress are indeed successful parodies of LVM's marks and trade dress.

For trademark purposes, "[a] 'parody' is defined as a simple form of entertainment conveyed by juxtaposing the irreverent representation of the trademark with the idealized image created by the mark's owner." *People for the Ethical Treatment of Animals v. Doughney* ("*PETA*"), 263 F.3d 359, 366 (4th Cir. 2001) (internal quotation marks omitted). "A parody must convey two simultaneous—and contradictory—messages: that it is the original, but also that it is *not* the original and is instead a parody." *Id.* (internal quotation marks and citations omitted). This second message must not only differentiate the alleged parody from the original but must also communicate some articulable element of satire, ridicule, joking, or amusement. Thus, "[a] parody relies upon a difference from the original mark, presumably a humorous difference, in order to produce its desired effect." *Jordache Enterprises, Inc. v. Hogg Wyld, Ltd.*, 828 F.2d 1482, 1486 (10th Cir. 1987) (finding the use of "Lardashe" jeans for larger women to be a successful and permissible parody of "Jordache" jeans).

When applying the *PETA* criteria to the facts of this case, we agree with the district court that the "Chewy Vuiton" dog toys are successful parodies of LVM handbags and the LVM marks and trade dress used in connection with the marketing and sale of those handbags. First, the pet chew toy is obviously an irreverent, and indeed intentional, representation of an LVM handbag, albeit much smaller and coarser. The dog toy is shaped roughly like a handbag; its name "Chewy Vuiton" sounds like and rhymes with LOUIS VUITTON; its monogram CV mimics LVM's LV mark; the repetitious design clearly imitates the design on the LVM handbag; and the coloring is similar. In short, the dog toy is a small, plush imitation of an LVM handbag carried by women, which invokes the marks and design of the handbag, albeit irreverently and incompletely. No one can doubt that LVM handbags are the target of the imitation by Haute Diggity Dog's "Chewy Vuiton" dog toys.

At the same time, no one can doubt also that the "Chewy Vuiton" dog toy is not the "idealized image" of the mark created by LVM. The differences are immediate, beginning with the fact that the "Chewy Vuiton" product is a dog toy, not an expensive, luxury LOUIS VUITTON handbag. The toy is smaller, it is plush, and virtually all of its designs differ. Thus, "Chewy Vuiton" is not LOUIS VUITTON ("Chewy" is not "LOUIS" and "Vuiton" is not "VUITTON," with its two Ts); CV is not LV; the designs on the dog toy are simplified and crude, not detailed and distinguished. The toys are inexpensive; the handbags are expensive and marketed to be expensive. And, of course, as a dog toy, one must buy it with pet supplies and cannot buy it at an exclusive LVM store or boutique within a department store. In short, the Haute Diggity Dog "Chewy Vuiton" dog toy undoubtedly and deliberately conjures up the famous LVM marks and trade dress, but at the same time, it communicates that it is not the LVM product.

Finally, the juxtaposition of the similar and dissimilar—the irreverent representation and the idealized image of an LVM handbag—immediately conveys a joking and amusing parody. The furry little "Chewy Vuiton" imitation, as something to be *chewed by a dog*, pokes fun at the elegance and expensiveness of a LOUIS VUITTON handbag, which must *not* be chewed by a dog. The LVM handbag is provided for the most elegant and well-to-do celebrity, to proudly display to the public and the press, whereas the imitation "Chewy Vuiton" "handbag" is designed to mock the celebrity and be used by a dog. The dog toy irreverently presents haute couture as an object for casual canine destruction. The satire is unmistakable. The dog toy is a comment on the rich and famous, on the LOUIS VUITTON name and related marks, and on conspicuous consumption in general. This parody is enhanced by the fact that "Chewy Vuiton" dog toys are sold with similar parodies of other famous and expensive brands—"Chewnel No. 5" targeting "Chanel No. 5"; "Dog Perignonn" targeting "Dom Perignon"; and "Sniffany & Co." targeting "Tiffany & Co."

We conclude that the *PETA* criteria are amply satisfied in this case and that the "Chewy Vuiton" dog toys convey "just enough of the original design to allow the consumer to appreciate the point of parody," but stop well short of appropriating the entire marks that LVM claims. *PETA*, 263 F.3d at 366 (quoting *Jordache*, 828 F.2d at 1486).

Finding that Haute Diggity Dog's parody is successful, however, does not end the inquiry into whether Haute Diggity Dog's "Chewy Vuiton" products create a likelihood of confusion. *See* 6 J. Thomas McCarthy, *Trademarks and Unfair Competition* §31:153, at 262 (4th ed. 2007) ("There are confusing parodies and non-confusing parodies. All they have in common is an attempt at humor through the use of someone else's trademark."). The finding of a successful parody only influences the way in which the *Pizzeria Uno* factors are applied. *See, e.g., Anheuser-Busch, Inc. v. L & L Wings, Inc.*, 962 F.2d 316, 321 (4th Cir. 1992) (observing that parody alters the likelihood-of-confusion analysis). Indeed, it becomes apparent that an effective parody will actually diminish the likelihood of confusion, while an ineffective parody does not. We now turn to the *Pizzeria Uno* factors.

A

As to the first *Pizzeria Uno* factor, the parties agree that LVM's marks are strong and widely recognized. They do not agree, however, as to the consequences of this fact. LVM maintains that a strong, famous mark is entitled, as a matter of law, to broad protection. While it is true that finding a mark to be strong and famous usually favors the plaintiff in a trademark infringement case, the opposite may be true when a legitimate claim of parody is involved. As the district court observed, "In cases of parody, a strong mark's fame and popularity is precisely the mechanism by which likelihood of confusion is avoided." [cit.] "An intent to parody is not an intent to confuse the public." *Jordache*, 828 F.2d at 1486.

We agree with the district court. It is a matter of common sense that the strength of a famous mark allows consumers immediately to perceive the target of the parody, while simultaneously allowing them to recognize the changes to the mark that make the parody funny or biting. *See Tommy Hilfiger Licensing, Inc. v. Nature Labs, LLC*, 221 F. Supp. 2d 410, 416 (S.D.N.Y. 2002) (noting that the strength of the "TOMMY HILFIGER" fashion mark did not favor the mark's owner in an infringement case against "TIMMY HOLEDIGGER" novelty pet perfume). In this case, precisely because LOUIS VUITTON is so strong a mark and so well recognized as a luxury handbag brand from LVM, consumers readily recognize that when they see a "Chewy Vuiton" pet toy, they see a parody. Thus, the strength of LVM's marks in this case does not help LVM establish a likelihood of confusion.

B

With respect to the second *Pizzeria Uno* factor, the similarities between the marks, the usage by Haute Diggity Dog again converts what might be a problem for Haute Diggity Dog into a disfavored conclusion for LVM.

Haute Diggity Dog concedes that its marks are and were designed to be somewhat similar to LVM's marks. But that is the essence of a parody—the invocation of a famous mark in the consumer's mind, so long as the distinction between the marks is also readily recognized. While a trademark parody necessarily copies enough of the original design to bring it to mind as a target, a successful parody also distinguishes itself and, because of the implicit message communicated by the parody, allows the consumer to appreciate it. *See PETA*, 263 F.3d at 366 (citing *Jordache*, 828 F.2d at 1486); *Anheuser-Busch*, 962 F.2d at 321.

In concluding that Haute Diggity Dog has a successful parody, we have impliedly concluded that Haute Diggity Dog appropriately mimicked a part of the LVM marks, but at the same time sufficiently distinguished its own product to communicate the satire. The differences are sufficiently obvious and the parody sufficiently blatant that a consumer encountering a "Chewy Vuiton" dog toy would not mistake its source or sponsorship on the basis of mark similarity.

This conclusion is reinforced when we consider how the parties actually use their marks in the marketplace. [cit.] The record amply supports Haute Diggity Dog's contention that its "Chewy Vuiton" toys for dogs are generally sold alongside other pet products, as well as toys that parody other luxury brands, whereas LVM markets its handbags as a top-end luxury item to be purchased only in its own stores or in its own boutiques within department stores. These marketing channels further emphasize that "Chewy Vuiton" dog toys are not, in fact, LOUIS VUITTON products.

C

Nor does LVM find support from the third *Pizzeria Uno* factor, the similarity of the products themselves. It is obvious that a "Chewy Vuiton" plush imitation handbag, which does not open and is manufactured as a dog toy, is not a LOUIS VUITTON handbag sold by LVM. Even LVM's most proximate products—dog collars, leashes, and pet carriers—are fashion accessories, not dog toys. As Haute Diggity Dog points out, LVM does not make pet chew toys and likely does not intend to do so in the future. Even if LVM were to make dog toys in the future, the fact remains that the products at issue are not similar in any relevant respect, and this factor does not favor LVM.

D

[With respect to the fourth and fifth *Pizzeria Uno* factors, the court noted that, although both LVM handbags and "Chewy Vuiton" dog toys are sold at a Macy's department store in New York, as a general matter, there is little overlap in the individual retail stores selling the brands.]

Likewise with respect to advertising, there is little or no overlap. LVM markets LOUIS VUITTON handbags through high-end fashion magazines, while "Chewy Vuiton" products are advertised primarily through pet-supply channels.

The overlap in facilities and advertising demonstrated by the record is so minimal as to be practically nonexistent. "Chewy Vuiton" toys and LOUIS VUITTON products are neither sold nor advertised in the same way, and the *de minimis* overlap lends insignificant support to LVM on this factor.

E

The sixth factor, relating to Haute Diggity Dog's intent, again is neutralized by the fact that Haute Diggity Dog markets a parody of LVM products. As other courts have recognized, "An intent to parody is not an intent to confuse the public." *Jordache*, 828 F.2d at 1486. Despite Haute Diggity Dog's obvious intent to profit from its use of parodies, this action does not amount to a bad faith intent to create consumer confusion. To the contrary, the intent is to do just the opposite—to evoke a humorous, satirical association that *distinguishes* the products. This factor does not favor LVM.

F

[The court found no actual confusion, dismissing incidents where retailers misspelled "Chewy Vuiton" on invoices or order forms, using two Ts instead of one, as "confusion over how to spell the product name [rather] than any confusion over the source or sponsorship of the 'Chewy Vuiton' dog toys."]

In sum, the likelihood-of-confusion factors substantially favor Haute Diggity Dog. But consideration of these factors is only a proxy for the ultimate statutory test of whether Haute Diggity Dog's marketing, sale, and distribution of "Chewy Vuiton" dog toys is likely to cause confusion. Recognizing that "Chewy Vuiton" is an obvious parody and applying the *Pizzeria Uno* factors, we conclude that LVM has failed to demonstrate any likelihood of confusion. Accordingly, we affirm the district court's grant of summary judgment in favor of Haute Diggity Dog on the issue of trademark infringement.

III

LVM also contends that Haute Diggity Dog's advertising, sale, and distribution of the "Chewy Vuiton" dog toys dilutes its LOUIS VUITTON, LV, and Monogram Canvas marks, which are famous and distinctive, in violation of the Trademark Dilution Revision Act of 2006 ("TDRA"), 15 U.S.C.A. §1125(c) (West Supp. 2007). . . . [T]he TDRA defines "dilution by blurring" as the "association arising from the similarity between a mark or trade name and a famous mark that impairs the distinctiveness of the famous mark." *Id.* §1125(c)(2)(B). . . .

. . .

A

We address first LVM's claim for dilution by blurring.

The first three elements of a trademark dilution claim are not at issue in this case. LVM owns famous marks that are distinctive; Haute Diggity Dog has commenced using "Chewy Vuiton," "CV," and designs and colors that are allegedly diluting LVM's marks; and the similarity between Haute Diggity Dog's marks and LVM's marks gives rise to an association between the marks, albeit a parody. The issue for resolution is whether the association between Haute Diggity Dog's marks and LVM's marks is likely to impair the distinctiveness of LVM's famous marks.

In deciding this issue, the district court correctly outlined the six factors to be considered in determining whether dilution by blurring has been shown. *See* 15 U.S.C.A. §1125(c)(2)(B). But in evaluating the facts of the case, the court did not directly apply those factors it enumerated. It held simply:

[The famous mark's] strength is not likely to be blurred by a parody dog toy product. Instead of blurring Plaintiff's mark, the success of the parodic use depends upon the continued association with LOUIS VUITTON.

[cit.] The amicus supporting LVM's position in this case contends that the district court, by not applying the statutory factors, misapplied the TDRA to conclude that simply because Haute Diggity Dog's product was a parody meant that "there can be no *association* with the famous mark as a matter of law." Moreover, the amicus points out correctly that to rule in favor of Haute Diggity Dog, the district court was required to find that the "association" did not impair the distinctiveness of LVM's famous mark.

. . .

To determine whether a junior mark is likely to dilute a famous mark through blurring, the TDRA directs the court to consider all factors relevant to the issue, including six factors that are enumerated in the statute:

   (i)   The degree of similarity between the mark or trade name and the famous mark.
   (ii)   The degree of inherent or acquired distinctiveness of the famous mark.
   (iii) The extent to which the owner of the famous mark is engaging in substantially exclusive use of the mark.
   (iv)   The degree of recognition of the famous mark.
   (v)   Whether the user of the mark or trade name intended to create an association with the famous mark.
   (vi)   Any actual association between the mark or trade name and the famous mark.

15 U.S.C.A. §1125(c)(2)(B). Not every factor will be relevant in every case, and not every blurring claim will require extensive discussion of the factors. But a trial court must offer a sufficient indication of which factors it has found persuasive and explain why they are persuasive so that the court's decision can be reviewed. The district court did not do this adequately in this case. Nonetheless, after we apply the factors as a matter of law, we reach the same conclusion reached by the district court.

We begin by noting that parody is not automatically a complete *defense* to a claim of dilution by blurring where the defendant uses the parody as its own designation of source, i.e., *as a trademark*. Although the TDRA does provide that fair use is a complete defense and allows that a parody can be considered fair use, it does not extend the fair use defense to parodies used as a trademark. As the statute provides:

> The following shall not be actionable as dilution by blurring or dilution by tarnishment under this subsection:
>   (A) Any fair use . . . *other than as a designation of source for the person's own goods or services*, including use in connection with . . . parodying. . . .

15 U.S.C.A. §1125(c)(3)(A)(ii) (emphasis added). Under the statute's plain language, parodying a famous mark is protected by the fair use defense only if the parody is *not* "a designation of source for the person's own goods or services."

The TDRA, however, does not require a court to ignore the existence of a parody that is used as a trademark, and it does not preclude a court from considering parody as part of the circumstances to be considered for determining whether the plaintiff has made out a claim for dilution by blurring. Indeed, the statute permits a court to consider "all relevant factors," including the six factors supplied in §1125(c)(2)(B).

Thus, it would appear that a defendant's use of a mark as a parody is relevant to the overall question of whether the defendant's use is likely to impair the famous mark's distinctiveness. Moreover, the fact that the defendant uses its marks as a parody is specifically relevant to several of the listed factors. For example, factor (v) (whether the defendant intended to create an association with the famous mark) and factor (vi) (whether there exists an actual association between the defendant's mark and the famous mark) directly invite inquiries into the defendant's intent in using the parody, the defendant's actual use of the parody, and the effect that its use has on the famous mark. While a parody intentionally creates an association with the famous mark in order to be a parody, it also intentionally communicates, if it is successful, that it is *not* the famous mark, but rather a satire of the famous mark. *See PETA*, 263 F.3d at 366. That the defendant is using its mark as a parody is therefore relevant in the consideration of these statutory factors.

Similarly, factors (i), (ii), and (iv)—the degree of similarity between the two marks, the degree of distinctiveness of the famous mark, and its recognizability—are directly implicated by consideration of the fact that the defendant's mark is a successful parody. Indeed, by making the famous mark an object of the parody, a successful parody might actually enhance the famous mark's distinctiveness by making it an icon. The brunt of the joke becomes yet more famous. *See Hormel Foods*, 73 F.3d at 506 (observing that a successful parody "tends to increase public identification" of the famous mark with its source); *see also Yankee Publ'g Inc. v. News Am. Publ'g Inc.*, 809 F. Supp. 267, 272-82 (S.D.N.Y. 1992) (suggesting that a sufficiently obvious parody is unlikely to blur the targeted famous mark).

In sum, while a defendant's use of a parody as a mark does not support a "fair use" defense, it may be considered in determining whether the plaintiff-owner of a famous mark has proved its claim that the defendant's use of a parody mark is likely to impair the distinctiveness of the famous mark.

In the case before us, when considering factors (ii), (iii), and (iv), it is readily apparent, indeed conceded by Haute Diggity Dog, that LVM's marks are distinctive, famous, and strong. The LOUIS VUITTON mark is well known and is commonly identified as a brand of the great Parisian fashion house, Louis Vuitton Malletier. So too are its other marks and designs, which are invariably used with the LOUIS VUITTON mark. It may not be too strong to refer to these famous marks as icons of high fashion.

While the establishment of these facts satisfies essential elements of LVM's dilution claim, *see* 15 U.S.C.A. §1125(c)(1), the facts impose on LVM an increased burden to demonstrate that the distinctiveness of its famous marks is likely to be impaired by a successful parody. Even as Haute Diggity Dog's parody mimics the famous mark, it communicates simultaneously that it is not the famous mark, but is only satirizing it. [cit.] And because the famous mark is particularly strong and distinctive, it becomes more likely that a parody will not impair the distinctiveness of the mark. In short, as Haute Diggity Dog's "Chewy Vuiton" marks are a successful parody, we conclude that they will not blur the distinctiveness of the famous mark as a unique identifier of its source.

It is important to note, however, that this might not be true if the parody is so similar to the famous mark that it likely could be construed as actual use of the famous mark itself. Factor (i) directs an inquiry into the "degree of similarity between the junior mark and the famous mark." If Haute Diggity Dog used the actual marks of LVM (as a parody or otherwise), it could dilute LVM's marks by blurring, regardless of whether Haute Diggity Dog's use was confusingly similar, whether it was in competition with LVM, or whether LVM sustained actual injury. *See* 15 U.S.C.A. §1125(c)(1). Thus, "the use of DUPONT shoes, BUICK aspirin, and KODAK pianos would be actionable" under the TDRA because the unauthorized use of the famous marks *themselves* on unrelated goods might diminish the capacity of these trademarks to distinctively identify a single source. [*Moseley v. V Secret Catalogue, Inc.*, 537 U.S. 418, 431 (2003)] (quoting H.R. Rep. No. 104-374, at 3 (1995)). This is true even though a consumer would be unlikely to confuse the manufacturer of KODAK film with the hypothetical producer of KODAK pianos.

But in this case, Haute Diggity Dog mimicked the famous marks; it did not come so close to them as to destroy the success of its parody and, more importantly, to diminish the LVM marks' capacity to identify a single source. Haute Diggity Dog designed a pet chew toy to imitate and suggest, but not *use*, the marks of a high-fashion LOUIS VUITTON handbag. It used "Chewy Vuiton" to mimic "LOUIS VUITTON"; it used "CV" to mimic "LV"; and it adopted *imperfectly* the items of LVM's designs. We conclude that these uses by Haute Diggity Dog were not so similar as to be likely to impair the distinctiveness of LVM's famous marks.

In a similar vein, when considering factors (v) and (vi), it becomes apparent that Haute Diggity Dog intentionally associated its marks, but only partially and certainly imperfectly, so as to convey the simultaneous message that it was not in fact a source of LVM products. Rather, as a parody, it separated itself from the LVM marks in order to make fun of them.

In sum, when considering the relevant factors to determine whether blurring is likely to occur in this case, we readily come to the conclusion, as did the district court, that LVM has failed to make out a case of trademark dilution by blurring by failing to establish that the distinctiveness of its marks was likely to be impaired by Haute Diggity Dog's marketing and sale of its "Chewy Vuiton" products.

. . .

The judgment of the district court is *Affirmed*.

MATTEL, INC. v. MCA RECORDS, INC.

296 F.3d 894 (9th Cir. 2002), cert. denied, 537 U.S. 1171 (2003)

KOZINSKI, Circuit Judge:

If this were a sci-fi melodrama, it might be called Speech-Zilla meets Trademark Kong.

I

Barbie was born in Germany in the 1950s as an adult collector's item. Over the years, Mattel transformed her from a doll that resembled a "German street walker," as she originally appeared, into a glamorous, long-legged blonde. Barbie has been labeled both the ideal American woman and a bimbo. She has survived attacks both psychic (from feminists critical of her fictitious figure) and physical (more than 500 professional makeovers). She remains a symbol of American girlhood, a public figure who graces the aisles of toy stores throughout the country and beyond. With Barbie, Mattel created not just a toy but a cultural icon.

With fame often comes unwanted attention. Aqua is a Danish band that has, as yet, only dreamed of attaining Barbie-like status. In 1997, Aqua produced the song Barbie Girl on the album *Aquarium*. In the song, one bandmember impersonates Barbie, singing in a high-pitched, doll-like voice; another bandmember, calling himself Ken, entices Barbie to "go party." (The lyrics are in the Appendix.) Barbie Girl singles sold well and, to Mattel's dismay, the song made it onto Top 40 music charts.

Mattel brought this lawsuit against the music companies who produced, marketed and sold Barbie Girl: MCA Records, Inc. . . . [asserting trademark infringement and trademark dilution].

[The District Court granted summary judgment for Aqua on the trademark-related counts. Mattel appealed.]

III

A

A trademark is a word, phrase or symbol that is used to identify a manufacturer or sponsor of a good or the provider of a service. *See New Kids on the Block v. News Am. Publ'g, Inc.*, 971 F.2d 302, 305 (9th Cir. 1992). It's the owner's way of preventing others from duping consumers into buying a product they mistakenly believe is sponsored by the trademark owner. A trademark "inform[s] people that trademarked products come from the same source." *Id.* at 305 n.2. Limited to this core purpose—avoiding confusion in the marketplace—a trademark owner's property rights play well with the First Amendment. "Whatever first amendment rights you may have in calling the brew you make in your bathtub 'Pepsi' are easily outweighed by the buyer's interest in not being fooled into buying it." *Trademarks Unplugged*, 68 N.Y.U. L. Rev. 960, 973 (1993).

The problem arises when trademarks transcend their identifying purpose. Some trademarks enter our public discourse and become an integral part of our vocabulary. How else do you say that something's "the Rolls Royce of its class"? What else is a quick fix, but a Band-Aid? Does the average consumer know to ask for aspirin as "acetyl salicylic acid"? *See Bayer Co. v. United Drug Co.*, 272 F. 505, 510 (S.D.N.Y. 1921). Trademarks often fill in gaps in our vocabulary and add a contemporary flavor to our expressions. Once imbued with such expressive value, the trademark becomes a word in our language and assumes a role outside the bounds of trademark law.

Our likelihood-of-confusion test, *see AMF Inc. v. Sleekcraft Boats*, 599 F.2d 341, 348-49 (9th Cir. 1979), generally strikes a comfortable balance between the trademark owner's property rights and the public's expressive interests. But when a trademark owner asserts a right to control how we express ourselves—when we'd find it difficult to describe the product any other way (as in the case of aspirin), or when the mark (like Rolls Royce) has taken on an expressive meaning apart from its source-identifying function—applying the traditional test fails to account for the full weight of the public's interest in free expression.

The First Amendment may offer little protection for a competitor who labels its commercial good with a confusingly similar mark, but "[t]rademark rights do not entitle the owner to quash an unauthorized use of the mark by another who is communicating ideas or expressing points of view." *L.L. Bean, Inc. v. Drake Publishers, Inc.*, 811 F.2d 26, 29 (1st Cir. 1987). Were we to ignore the expressive value that some marks assume, trademark rights would grow to encroach upon the zone protected by the First Amendment. *See Yankee Publ'g, Inc. v. News Am. Publ'g, Inc.*, 809 F. Supp. 267, 276 (S.D.N.Y. 1992) ("[W]hen unauthorized use of another's mark is part of a communicative message and not a source identifier, the First Amendment is implicated in opposition to the trademark right."). Simply put, the trademark owner does not have the right to control public discourse whenever the public imbues his mark with a meaning beyond its source-identifying function. *See Anti-Monopoly, Inc. v. Gen. Mills Fun Group*, 611 F.2d 296, 301 (9th Cir. 1979) ("It is the source-denoting function which trademark laws protect, and nothing more.").

B

There is no doubt that MCA uses Mattel's mark: Barbie is one half of Barbie Girl. But Barbie Girl is the title of a song about Barbie and Ken, a reference that—at least today—can only be to Mattel's famous couple. We expect a title to describe the underlying work, not to identify the producer, and Barbie Girl does just that.

The Barbie Girl title presages a song about Barbie, or at least a girl like Barbie. The title conveys a message to consumers about what they can expect to discover in the song itself; it's a quick glimpse of Aqua's take on their own song. The lyrics confirm this: The female singer, who calls herself Barbie, is "a Barbie girl, in [her] Barbie world." She tells her male counterpart (named Ken), "Life in plastic, it's fantastic. You can brush my hair, undress me everywhere/Imagination, life is your creation." And off they go to "party." The song pokes fun at Barbie and the values that Aqua contends she represents. *See Cliffs Notes, Inc. v. Bantam Doubleday Dell Publ'g Group*, 886 F.2d 490, 495-96 (2d Cir. 1989). The female singer explains, "I'm a blond bimbo girl, in a fantasy world/Dress me up, make it tight, I'm your dolly."

The song does not rely on the Barbie mark to poke fun at another subject but targets Barbie herself. *See Campbell v. Acuff-Rose Music, Inc.*, 510 U.S. 569, 580 (1994); *see also Dr. Seuss Ents., L.P. v. Penguin Books USA, Inc.*, 109 F.3d 1394, 1400 (9th Cir. 1997). This case is therefore distinguishable from *Dr. Seuss*, where we held that the book *The Cat NOT in the Hat!* borrowed Dr. Seuss's trademarks and lyrics to get attention rather than to mock *The Cat in the Hat!* The defendant's use of the Dr. Seuss trademarks and copyrighted works had "no critical bearing on the substance or style of" *The Cat in the Hat!*, and therefore could not claim First Amendment protection. *Id.* at 1401. *Dr. Seuss* recognized that, where an artistic work targets the original and does not merely borrow another's property to get attention, First Amendment interests weigh more heavily in the balance. *See id.* at 1400-02; *see also Harley-Davidson, Inc. v. Grottanelli*, 164 F.3d 806, 812-13 (2d Cir. 1999) (a parodist whose expressive work aims its parodic commentary at a trademark is given considerable leeway, but a claimed parodic use that makes no comment on the mark is not a permitted trademark parody use).

The Second Circuit has held that "in general the [Lanham] Act should be construed to apply to artistic works only where the public interest in avoiding consumer confusion outweighs the public interest in free expression." *Rogers v. Grimaldi*, 875 F.2d 994, 999 (2d Cir. 1989); *see also Cliffs Notes*, 886 F.2d at 494 (quoting *Rogers*, 875 F.2d at 999). *Rogers* considered a challenge by the actress Ginger Rogers to the film *Ginger and Fred*. The movie told the story of two Italian cabaret performers who made a living by imitating Ginger Rogers and Fred Astaire. Rogers argued that the film's title created the false impression that she was associated with it.

At first glance, Rogers certainly had a point. Ginger was her name, and Fred was her dancing partner. If a pair of dancing shoes had been labeled Ginger and Fred, a dancer might have suspected that Rogers was associated with the shoes (or at least one of them), just as Michael Jordan has endorsed Nike sneakers that claim to make you fly through the air. But *Ginger and Fred* was not a brand of shoe; it was the title of a movie and, for the reasons explained by the Second Circuit, deserved to be treated differently.

A title is designed to catch the eye and to promote the value of the underlying work. Consumers expect a title to communicate a message about the book or movie, but they do not expect it to identify the publisher or producer. *See Application of Cooper*, 45 C.C.P.A. 923, 254 F.2d 611, 615-16 (C.C.P.A. 1958) (A "title . . . identifies a specific literary work, . . . and is not associated in the public mind with the . . . manufacturer." (internal quotation marks omitted)). If we see a painting titled "Campbell's Chicken Noodle Soup," we're unlikely to believe that Campbell's has branched into the art business. Nor, upon hearing Janis Joplin croon "Oh Lord, won't you buy me a Mercedes-Benz?," would we suspect that she and the carmaker had entered into a joint venture. A title tells us something about the underlying work but seldom speaks to its origin:

> Though consumers frequently look to the title of a work to determine what it is about, they do not regard titles of artistic works in the same way as the names of ordinary commercial products. Since consumers expect an ordinary product to be what the name says it is, we apply the Lanham Act with some rigor to prohibit names that misdescribe such goods. But most consumers are well aware that they cannot judge a book solely by its title any more than by its cover.

Rogers, 875 F.2d at 1000 (citations omitted).

Rogers concluded that literary titles do not violate the Lanham Act "unless the title has no artistic relevance to the underlying work whatsoever, or, if it has some artistic relevance, unless the title explicitly misleads as to the source or the content of the work." *Id.* at 999 (footnote omitted). We agree with the Second Circuit's analysis and adopt the *Rogers* standard as our own.

Applying *Rogers* to our case, we conclude that MCA's use of Barbie is not an infringement of Mattel's trademark. Under the first prong of *Rogers*, the use of Barbie in the song title clearly is relevant to the underlying work, namely, the song itself. As noted, the song is about Barbie and the values Aqua claims she represents. The song title does not explicitly mislead as to the source of the work; it does not, explicitly or otherwise, suggest that it was produced by Mattel. The *only* indication that Mattel might be associated with the song is the use of Barbie in the title; if this were enough to satisfy this prong of the *Rogers* test, it would render *Rogers* a nullity. We therefore agree with the district court that MCA was entitled to summary judgment on this ground. We need not consider whether the district court was correct in holding that MCA was also entitled to summary judgment because its use of Barbie was a nominative fair use.

IV

[Mattel also alleged dilution by blurring and tarnishment, invoking the 1995 dilution legislation, which governed at the time. The 1995 legislation carved out an exemption from liability for "noncommercial" uses. 15 U.S.C. §1125(c)(4)(B) (1995). The court agreed that there was dilution by blurring, but then turned to the noncommercial use exemption. Here the court considered the First Amendment underpinnings of the exemption. Parts of the discussion, reproduced below, remain relevant today, because the TDRA likewise exempts noncommercial uses. 15 U.S.C. §1125(c)(3)(C) (2006).]

We consider next the applicability of the FTDA's three statutory exemptions. These are uses that, though potentially dilutive, are nevertheless permitted: comparative advertising; news reporting and commentary; and noncommercial use. 15 U.S.C. §1125(c)(4)(B). The first two exemptions clearly do not apply; only the exemption for noncommercial use need detain us.

[The court pointed out that the 1995 legislation limited dilution to acts of "commercial" use in commerce, but then exempted "noncommercial" uses from liability. That statutory structure seemed to leave no role for the exemption, because a mark owner who failed to prove that the defendant's uses were commercial would fail to establish prima facie dilution.]

[However, reading the noncommercial use exemption out of the statute] would be a serious problem because the primary (usually exclusive) remedy for dilution is an injunction. As noted above, tension with the First Amendment also exists in the trademark context, especially where the mark has assumed an expressive function beyond mere identification of a product or service. *See . . .* [*New Kids on the Block v. News Am. Publ'g, Inc.*, 971 F.2d 302, 306-08 (9th Cir. 1992)]. These concerns apply with greater force in the dilution context because dilution lacks two very significant limitations that reduce the tension between trademark law and the First Amendment.

First, depending on the strength and distinctiveness of the mark, trademark law grants relief only against uses that are likely to confuse. *See* 5 *McCarthy* §30:3 at 30-8 to 30-11; *Restatement* §35 cmt. c at 370. A trademark injunction is usually limited to uses within one industry or several related industries. Dilution law is the antithesis of trademark law in this respect, because it seeks to protect the mark from association in the public's mind with wholly unrelated goods and services. The more remote the good or service associated with the junior use, the more likely it is to cause dilution rather than trademark infringement. A dilution injunction, by contrast to a trademark injunction, will generally sweep across broad vistas of the economy.

Second, a trademark injunction, even a very broad one, is premised on the need to prevent consumer confusion. This consumer protection rationale—averting what is essentially a fraud on the consuming public—is wholly consistent with the theory of the First Amendment, which does not protect commercial fraud. *Cent. Hudson Gas & Elec. v. Pub. Serv. Comm'n*, 447 U.S. 557, 566 (1980); *see Thompson v. W. States Med. Ctr.*, 535 U.S. 357 (2002) (applying *Central Hudson*). Moreover, avoiding harm to consumers is an important interest that is independent of the senior user's interest in protecting its business.

Dilution, by contrast, does not require a showing of consumer confusion, 15 U.S.C. §1127, and dilution injunctions therefore lack the built-in First Amendment compass of trademark injunctions. In addition, dilution law protects only the distinctiveness of the mark, which is inherently less weighty than the dual interest of protecting trademark owners and avoiding harm to consumers that is at the heart of every trademark claim.

[Reviewing the legislative history of the 1995 legislation, the court concluded that noncommercial use "refers to a use that consists entirely of noncommercial, or fully constitutionally protected, speech." The court then considered whether the defendant's song title should be exempted.]

To determine whether Barbie Girl falls within this exemption, we look to our definition of commercial speech under our First Amendment caselaw. *See* H.R. Rep. No. 104-374, at 8, *reprinted in* 1995 U.S.C.C.A.N. 1029, 1035 (the exemption "expressly incorporates the concept of 'commercial' speech from the 'commercial speech' doctrine"); 141 Cong. Rec. S19306-10, S19311 (daily ed. Dec. 29, 1995) (the exemption "is consistent with existing [First Amendment] case law"). "Although the boundary between commercial and noncommercial speech has yet to be clearly delineated, the 'core notion of commercial speech' is that it 'does no more than propose a commercial transaction.'" *Hoffman v. Capital Cities/ABC, Inc.*, 255 F.3d 1180, 1184 (9th Cir. 2001) (quoting *Bolger v. Youngs Drug Prods. Corp.*, 463 U.S. 60, 66 (1983)). If speech is not "purely commercial"—that is, if it does more than propose a commercial transaction—then it is entitled to full First Amendment protection. *Id.* at 1185-86 (internal quotation marks omitted).

In *Hoffman*, a magazine published an article featuring digitally altered images from famous films. Computer artists modified shots of Dustin Hoffman, Cary Grant, Marilyn Monroe and others to put the actors in famous designers' spring fashions; a still of Hoffman from the movie "Tootsie" was altered so that he appeared to be wearing a Richard Tyler evening gown and Ralph Lauren heels. Hoffman, who had not given permission, sued under the Lanham Act and for violation of his right to publicity. *Id.* at 1183.

The article featuring the altered image clearly served a commercial purpose: "to draw attention to the for-profit magazine in which it appear[ed]" and to sell more copies. *Id.* at 1186. Nevertheless, we held that the article was fully protected under the First Amendment because it included protected expression: "humor" and "visual and verbal editorial comment on classic films and famous actors." *Id.* at 1185 (internal quotation marks omitted). Because its commercial purpose was "inextricably entwined with [these] expressive elements," the article and accompanying photographs enjoyed full First Amendment protection. *Id.*

Hoffman controls: Barbie Girl is not purely commercial speech, and is therefore fully protected. To be sure, MCA used Barbie's name to sell copies of the song. However, as we've already observed, [cit.], the song also lampoons the Barbie image and comments humorously on the cultural values Aqua claims she represents. Use of the Barbie mark in the song Barbie Girl therefore falls within the noncommercial use exemption to the FTDA. For precisely the same reasons, use of the mark in the song's title is also exempted.

. . .

VI

After Mattel filed suit, Mattel and MCA employees traded barbs in the press. When an MCA spokeswoman noted that each album included a disclaimer saying that Barbie Girl was a "social commentary [that was] not created or approved by the makers of the doll," a Mattel representative responded by saying, "That's unacceptable. . . . It's akin to a bank robber handing a note of apology to a teller during a heist. [It n]either diminishes the severity of the crime, nor does it make it legal." He later characterized the song as a "theft" of "another company's property."

MCA filed a counterclaim for defamation based on the Mattel representative's use of the words "bank robber," "heist," "crime" and "theft." But all of these are variants of the invective most often hurled at accused infringers, namely "piracy." No one hearing this accusation understands intellectual property owners to be saying that infringers are nautical cutthroats with eyepatches and peg legs who board galleons to plunder cargo. In context, all these terms are nonactionable "rhetorical hyperbole". . . . The parties are advised to chill.

Affirmed.

APPENDIX

"Barbie Girl" by Aqua
-Hiya Barbie!
-Hi Ken!
-You wanna go for a ride?
-Sure, Ken!
-Jump in!
-Ha ha ha ha!
(CHORUS:)
I'm a Barbie girl, in my Barbie world
Life in plastic, it's fantastic
You can brush my hair, undress me everywhere
Imagination, life is your creation
Come on Barbie, let's go party!
(CHORUS)
I'm a blonde bimbo girl, in a fantasy world
Dress me up, make it tight, I'm your dolly
You're my doll, rock and roll, feel the glamour in pink
Kiss me here, touch me there, hanky-panky
You can touch, you can play
If you say "I'm always yours," ooh ooh
(CHORUS)
(BRIDGE:)
Come on, Barbie, let's go party, ah ah ah yeah
Come on, Barbie, let's go party, ooh ooh, ooh ooh
Come on, Barbie, let's go party, ah ah ah yeah
Come on, Barbie, let's go party, ooh ooh, ooh ooh
Make me walk, make me talk, do whatever you please
I can act like a star, I can beg on my knees
Come jump in, be my friend, let us do it again

Hit the town, fool around, let's go party
You can touch, you can play
You can say "I'm always yours"
You can touch, you can play
You can say "I'm always yours"
(BRIDGE)
(CHORUS x2)
(BRIDGE)
-Oh, I'm having so much fun!
-Well, Barbie, we're just getting started!
-Oh, I love you Ken!

NOTES AND QUESTIONS

1.   *What is expressive use?* *Balducci*, *Louis Vuitton*, and *Mattel* all involve claims of parodic use. In the lexicon of this casebook—not necessarily mirrored in the courts—parody is one type of "expressive use." Artistic uses and political uses are other common types of expressive uses, as the next set of main cases will illustrate. We have chosen the umbrella term "expressive use" to denote all varieties of uses that may implicate First Amendment speech values. The label is imperfect, given that virtually any use of a trademark might be characterized as expressing some message. But the label does reflect the wide diversity of uses that might warrant special attention as bearing on protected speech. For a further example illustrating the breadth of the notion of expressive use.

2.   *Relationship between expressive use and confusion.* Just as the jurisprudence of nominative fair use is divided about whether nominative fair use is an affirmative defense to likelihood of confusion or a replacement for the confusion factors test, the expressive use case law is split on the role of confusion. Considering the three parody cases excerpted above. Which approach best balances trademark policy interests and speech interests—considering whether to immunize parody as a constitutionally-grounded defense that might outweigh a determination of infringement (*Balducci*), using the parodic nature of a work to inform many of the confusion factors (*Louis Vuitton*), or deciding that the parodic nature of the use rendered it artistic, thus triggering a test (discussed more fully below) that replaces the confusion test in determining infringement? Recall that this issue also arose in *Elvis Presley Enterprises* (*see* Chapter 1).

3.   *Tests for parody.* To what extent does the ultimate conclusion (or the test applied) in each of these cases turn on the characterization of the defendant's use as parody? How does the *Louis Vuitton* court define "parody" for purposes of its analysis? Do you agree that Haute Diggity's use is a "successful parody" under the definition? Would the defendant's use in *Balducci* fall within the definition? Aqua's use of "Barbie" in the Barbie Girl song in *Mattel*? In a leading copyright case, the Court distinguished between parody (as an art form that borrows from the original for purposes of targeting the original for critique or ridicule) and satire (as an art form that may use others' work as a vehicle to make a general social commentary or critique, but borrows from others' work to draw attention, not to target the work). *Campbell v. Acuff-Rose Music, Inc.*, 510 U.S. 569 (1994). Would the parody/satire distinction enhance the analysis in *Balducci*, *Louis Vuitton*, or *Mattel*? Or would it put judges in the unenviable position of making complex, subjective aesthetic judgments

about the "message" embedded in an alleged infringer's work? *See, e.g.*, *Dallas Cowboys Cheerleaders, Inc. v. Pussycat Cinema, Ltd.*, 604 F.2d 200 (2d Cir. 1979) (in which the court evaluates whether an adult film was conveying a message about the Dallas Cowboys football franchise—or any message at all, for that matter). Would the parody/satire approach also force courts into making artistic determinations about whether the accused infringer borrowed more than was necessary to carry off the alleged parody? Does the *Louis Vuitton* test also require such determinations? This may also call to mind the "necessity" criterion found in descriptive and nominative fair use tests.

    4. *The* Rogers *test applied to parody.* The *Mattel* court relies on a test from *Rogers v. Grimaldi* to address Aqua's claim of parody. Is *Rogers* suitable for this purpose? Note that the *Rogers* case itself was not a parody case, but, like *Mattel*, it did involve the title of an artistic work. *Rogers* has become the leading test for a variety of expressive uses beyond parody, as we will see in the next set of main cases.

    5. *Framing the likelihood-of-confusion analysis in parody cases.* In *Balducci*, the court asserts that it is error to "skew" the likelihood-of-confusion analysis in cases where parody or other speech interests are arguably implicated. In *Louis Vuitton*, the very purpose of the threshold analysis of parody is to inform the standard confusion analysis (and presumably affect the outcome). How does the determination in *Louis Vuitton* that the defendant's use is parodic affect the court's factors analysis? Once a court has decided that a defendant's use is a parody under the *Louis Vuitton* approach, is the case decided for all practical purposes? That is, does the adapted factors analysis become an elaborate exercise in vindicating *ex post* the threshold parody determination?

    6. *Trade dress parody?* Suppose that Mattel claims trade dress protection for the overall appearance of the Barbie doll. Would the analysis of parody as a defense to trade dress infringement follow the same rules as the analysis of parody as a defense to trademark infringement? For the Ninth Circuit's answer, in a case involving a photographer who sold photographs of Barbie dolls in "various absurd and often sexualized positions," *see Mattel Inc. v. Walking Mountain Productions*, 353 F.3d 792 (9th Cir. 2003).

    7. *The relationship between dilution and parody: "other than as a designation of source for the person's own goods or services." Louis Vuitton* is the leading case on the application of the parody defense to dilution under the modern dilution provision, Section 43(c)(3)(A). That provision shields a defendant's fair uses, but only where the defendant is using the mark "other than as a designation of source" for the defendant's own goods or services. The *Louis Vuitton* court concludes that Haute Diggity's use of the logo and trade dress fails to satisfy this limitation, because Haute Diggity is using the marks at issue as brands for its own goods. Do you agree with the court's construction of the statute? Compare the language of current Section 43(c)(3)(A) to the language in the 1995 version of the provision (Section 43(c)(4)(A) (1995)), which made non-actionable the "fair use of a famous mark by another person in comparative commercial advertising or promotion to identify the competing goods or services of the owner of the famous mark." Does it make sense that Congress would have narrowed the fair use defense to dilution by adding the "designation of source" language? If Congress was not trying to narrow the defense, what was it doing when it added the language?

    Suppose that your client makes the following bag, which includes the legend "My Other Bag" on one side and a copy of the Louis Vuitton "toile" monogram on the other:

Is your client using the Louis Vuitton monogram as a designation of source for its own products, such that the fair use protection of Section 43(c)(3)(A) does not apply? *See Louis Vuitton Malletier, S.A. v. My Other Bag, Inc.*, 156 F. Supp. 3d 425 (S.D.N.Y. 2016), *aff'd*, 674 Fed. Appx. 16 (Dec. 22, 2016).

8. *The relationship between dilution and parody: parody as a threshold consideration in the dilution by blurring analysis.* Given that Haute Diggity's activity failed to fall within the protections of the Section 43(c)(3)(A) parody defense, should the *Louis Vuitton* court have concluded that the parodic nature of Haute Diggity's use could not be relevant in the dilution by blurring analysis? The court, of course, did just the opposite. Is the court's conclusion as to blurring a *fait accompli* once it has determined that the defendant's use is a successful parody? If not, what is the independent significance of analyses for blurring factors such as intent (factor (v)) and actual association (factor (vi)) once the court has concluded that defendant is engaging in a successful parody? Do you agree that the existence of a successful parody should subject the mark owner to "an increased burden to demonstrate that the distinctiveness of its famous marks is likely to be impaired"? Did parody differently affect the *Louis Vuitton* court's analysis of confusion and dilution claims?

9. *Commercial versus noncommercial.* In *Mattel*, the court relies on the distinction between commercial and noncommercial uses in analyzing the dilution claim. Under the dilution provision in force at the time (the provision from the 1995 Act), "noncommercial use of a mark" was not actionable as dilution, and the legislative history suggested that the commercial/noncommercial distinction was a crude proxy for First Amendment considerations, particularly considerations of First Amendment commercial speech doctrine. Does the modern dilution provision embody the same principle? How so? Should courts interpret Sections 32 and 43(a) to incorporate the commercial/noncommercial distinction? Via what language? We will return to this point in the next set of main cases. For the moment, you may wish to consider the difficulty of drawing the line between commercial and noncommercial activity using the subject matter of the *Balducci* and *Mattel* cases. Is the defendant's use of MICHELOB trademarks in *Balducci* commercial or noncommercial? What of *Barbie Girl*—does the court's conclusion that the use is not "purely" commercial apply to defendant's use of BARBIE in the song lyrics? Song title? Title of the music CD? Other uses of Barbie imagery in the music video?

10. *Parody and Section 2(d) confusion or 2(f) dilution analysis.* Suppose that the applicant in an opposition (or a registrant in a cancellation proceeding) claims to be making parodic use of its mark? Is the applicant's claim sufficient to defeat an opposition (or cancellation) based on Section 2(f) dilution? *See New York Yankees Partnership v. IET Prods. & Services, Inc.*, 114 U.S.P.Q.2d (BNA) 1497 (TTAB 2015) (no; Section 43(c)(3)(A) shields parodies only when they are not being used as a designation of source, but an applicant's or registrant's claim to be entitled to registration requires a showing that the mark *is* being used as a designation of source). Could the TTAB rely on applicant's claim of parodic use for any other purpose in adjudicating a Section 2(f) dilution question?

PROBLEM 9-5: WALOCAUST

How would you apply the *Louis Vuitton* parody analysis to a case in which Wal-Mart asserts that its registered mark (WAL-MART for discount stores) is infringed and diluted by the following, found on the websites www.walocaust.com and www.walqaeda.com and available for reproduction on T-shirts, bumper stickers, and the like:

See Smith v. Wal-Mart Stores, Inc., 537 F. Supp. 2d 1302 (N.D. Ga. 2008).

UNIVERSITY OF ALABAMA BOARD OF TRUSTEES v. NEW LIFE ART, INC.

683 F.3d 1266 (11th Cir. 2012)

ANDERSON, Circuit Judge:

. . .

I. FACTS

From 1979 to 1990, Moore painted historical Alabama football scenes without any kind of formal or informal relationship with the University. From 1991 to 1999, Moore signed a dozen licensing agreements with the University to produce and market specific items, which would often include additional Alabama trademarks on the border or packaging, or would come with a certificate or stamp saying they were officially licensed products.

From 1991 to 2002, Moore produced other Alabama-related paintings and prints that were not the subject of any licensing agreements. He also continued to sell paintings and prints of images that had originally been issued before 1991. He did not pay royalties for any of these items, nor did the University request that he do so. Moore said that he would enter into a licensing agreement if he felt that it would help increase the sales of that particular product, or if he wanted the University—his alma mater—to benefit from royalties.

During this time, the University issued Moore press credentials so he could obtain material for his work. The University also asked Moore to produce an unlicensed painting on live television during a football game.

However, in January 2002, the University told Moore that he would need to license all of his Alabama-related products because they featured the University's trademarks. In particular, the University asserted that Moore needed permission to portray the University's uniforms, including the jersey and helmet designs and the crimson and white colors.

Moore contended that he did not need permission to paint historical events and that there was no trademark violation so long as he did not use any of the University's trademarks outside of the "image area" of the painting (i.e., outside the original painting). Despite this disagreement, the University still sold Moore's unlicensed calendars in its campus stores for several years. It also displayed unlicensed paintings at its Bryant Museum and athletic department office.

[The University sued under Lanham Act §43(a) on the basis of its unregistered trade dress, and both parties moved for summary judgment.]

The only issues on appeal in this case are those decided by Judge Propst, who concluded in November 2009 that (1) the prior licensing agreements did not require that Moore receive permission to portray the University's uniforms because the uniforms were not included in the agreements' definition of "licensed indicia"; (2) the University's colors had some secondary meaning but were not especially strong marks on the trademark spectrum; (3) Moore's depiction of the uniforms in paintings and prints was protected by the First Amendment and also was a fair use; and (4) Moore's depiction of the uniforms on mugs, calendars, and other "mundane products" was not protected by the First Amendment, was not a fair use, and would likely result in consumer confusion.

In accordance with these findings, the district court granted summary judgment to Moore on the paintings and prints, and to the University on the calendars, mugs, and other "mundane products." Both parties appealed the conclusions of the district court, which certified under Rule 54(b). . . .

. . .

We believe that the simplest way to address all of the arguments in this appeal is to divide the opinion based on the two categories of objects produced by Moore. With respect to both categories, we address only objects which were never the subject of a specific, written licensing agreement. First we address the arguments of the respective parties with respect to a category of objects composed of paintings, prints, and calendars. Then we address the arguments of the parties with respect to a second category of objects composed of mugs and other "mundane products."

II.   PAINTINGS, PRINTS, AND CALENDARS

In accordance with the district court's rulings, the University is appellant with respect to paintings and prints that "are of the same or larger sizes and of the same or better quality of such paintings and prints previously created, produced, manufactured and distributed by [Moore]." Moore is appellant for calendars. We address these items together.

The University first argues that it is unnecessary to reach the trademark issues in this appeal because the language of Moore's prior licensing agreements prohibits his unlicensed portrayal of the University's uniforms. We disagree.

[The court's discussion of the licensing agreements is omitted.]

B.   Trademark Claims

Because we find that the licensing agreements were not intended to prohibit Moore's depiction of the University's uniforms in unlicensed paintings, prints, or calendars, we proceed to address the University's trademark claims with respect to these items. The University's claim is that Moore's unlicensed paintings, prints, and calendars infringe on the University's trademarks because the inclusion in these products of the University's football uniforms (showing the University's crimson and white colors) creates a likelihood of confusion on the part of buyers that the University sponsored or endorsed the product.

The University argues that its uniforms are "strong" trademarks and that its survey provides strong evidence of confusion sufficient to establish a likelihood of confusion to sustain a Lanham Act violation by Moore. [cit.] Contrary to the University's argument, the district court concluded there was a "weak mark and [merely] some likelihood of confusion." And contrary to the University's argument that its trademarks triggered the sales of Moore's products, the district court concluded with respect to the paintings and prints that "the plays and Moore's reputation established during a period when his art was agreeably not licensed are what predominantly trigger the sales." Similarly, with respect to the University's survey upon which the University relies to support likelihood of confusion, the district court concluded "that the survey lacks strength because of its manner of taking, the form of the questions, the nature of the surveyed customers, and the number of responders. It involved only one print. The questions are loaded with suggestions that there is a 'sponsor' other than the artist." We note that Moore's signature was prominent on the paintings, prints, and calendars, clearly telegraphing that he was the artist who created the work of art. We also note that the one print used in the survey was in fact specifically licensed, and thus had an actual, historical sponsorship association with the University. Although we are in basic agreement with the district court's evaluation of the mark and the degree of confusion as to the source and sponsorship of the paintings, prints, and calendars, we need not in this case settle upon a precise evaluation of the strength of the mark or the degree of likelihood of confusion. As our discussion below indicates, we conclude that the First Amendment interests in artistic expression so clearly outweigh whatever consumer confusion that might exist on these facts that we must necessarily conclude that there has been no violation of the Lanham Act with respect to the paintings, prints, and calendars.

The First Amendment's protections extend beyond written and spoken words. "[P]ictures, films, paintings, drawings, and engravings . . . have First Amendment protection[.]" [cit.]

The University argues that Moore's paintings, prints, and calendars "are more commercial than expressive speech and, therefore, entitled to a lower degree" of First Amendment protection. *See Cent. Hudson Gas & Elec. Corp. v. Pub. Serv. Comm'n of N.Y.*, 447 U.S. 557, 562-63 (1980) ("The Constitution . . . accords a lesser protection to commercial speech than to other constitutionally guaranteed expression."). However, these items certainly do more than "propos[e] a commercial transaction." *Id.* at 562. Naturally, Moore sells these items for money, but it "is of course no matter that the dissemination [of speech] takes place under commercial auspices." *Smith v. California*, 361 U.S. 147, 150 (1959). Like other expressive speech, Moore's paintings, prints, and calendars are entitled to full protection under the First Amendment. *Accord ETW Corp. v. Jireh Pub., Inc.*, 332 F.3d 915, 925 (6th Cir. 2003).

Thus, we must decide whether Moore's First Amendment rights will give way to the University's trademark rights. We are not the first circuit to confront this issue. In 1989, the Second Circuit decided *Rogers v. Grimaldi*, 875 F.2d 994 (2d Cir. 1989), which is the landmark case for balancing trademark and First Amendment rights. [According to Judge Anderson, the court in *Rogers* "concluded that the Lanham Act should be read narrowly to avoid impinging on speech protected by the First Amendment." Judge Anderson then invoked the *Rogers* balancing test.]

Circuit courts have also applied *Rogers* in cases where trademark law is being used to attack the content—as opposed to the title—of works protected by the First Amendment. In *Cliffs Notes, Inc. v. Bantam Doubleday Dell Publishing Group*, 886 F.2d 490 (2d Cir. 1989), the defendant published humorous versions of "Cliffs Notes" study books and had imitated the plaintiff's trademarked black and yellow covers. *Id.* at 492. The court held that the *Rogers* test was "generally applicable to Lanham Act claims against works of artistic expression" and found that the parody books were protected by the First Amendment because the defendant had not explicitly misled consumers as to the source or content of the books. *Id.* at 495-96.

In *ESS Entertainment 2000, Inc. v. Rock Star Videos, Inc.*, 547 F.3d 1095 (9th Cir. 2008), a scene in the defendant's video game featured the trademark of the plaintiff's entertainment club located in Los Angeles. *Id.* at 1096-98. The Ninth Circuit held that there "is no principled reason why [*Rogers*] ought not also apply to the use of a trademark in the body of the work." *Id.* at 1099. The court found that the defendant's use of the trademark did not explicitly mislead as to the source or content of the video game, and thus the First Amendment protected the defendant's use of the plaintiff's trademark. *Id.* at 1099-1101.

In the case perhaps most similar to the one *sub judice*, the Sixth Circuit addressed a claim of false endorsement under the Lanham Act where an artist had painted a collage of Tiger Woods images. *ETW Corp. v. Jireh Publ'g, Inc.*, 332 F.3d 915, 918-19 (6th Cir. 2003). Woods's publicity company sued the artist, and the court applied the *Rogers* balancing test and found that Woods's image on the painting had artistic relevance to the underlying work and did not explicitly mislead as to the source of the work. *Id.* at 936-37. As a result, the painting was protected by the First Amendment against a claim of false endorsement. *Id.* at 937.

The University contends that none of those cases are analogous to our current set of facts. It argues that *Cliffs Notes* and *ESS Entertainment* are not applicable because those cases involved parody, whereas Moore's paintings do not. However, neither *Rogers* nor *ETW* dealt with parody, yet the courts in those cases still read the Lanham Act narrowly to avoid First Amendment concerns. *See Rogers*, 875 F.2d at 999-1000; *ETW*,

332 F.3d at 937. Additionally, courts adopting *Rogers* have noted that it is "generally applicable to works of artistic expression," not just parodies. *Cliffs Notes*, 886 F.2d at 495; *see also ESS Entm't*, 547 F.3d at 1099 ("artistic works"); *ETW*, 332 F.3d at 937 ("artistic works").

The University responds by saying that we should not consider *Rogers* or *ETW* because those cases dealt with rights of publicity, which the University contends are much weaker than trademark rights. However, *Rogers* and *ETW* both dealt also with Lanham Act false endorsement claims, and we have never treated false endorsement and trademark infringement claims as distinct under the Lanham Act. *See Tana v. Dantanna's*, 611 F.3d 767, 777 n.9 (11th Cir. 2010) ("[W]e have . . . never recognized a separate claim of false endorsement, distinct from trademark infringement under §43(a). . . ."); *see also Landham v. Lewis Galoob Toys, Inc.*, 227 F.3d 619, 626 (6th Cir. 2000) ("A false designation of origin claim . . . under §43(a) of the Lanham Act . . . is equivalent to a false association or endorsement claim. . . .").

Therefore, we have no hesitation in joining our sister circuits by holding that we should construe the Lanham Act narrowly when deciding whether an artistically expressive work infringes a trademark. This requires that we carefully "weigh the public interest in free expression against the public interest in avoiding consumer confusion." *Cliffs Notes*, 886 F.2d at 494. An artistically expressive use of a trademark will not violate the Lanham Act "unless the use of the mark has no artistic relevance to the underlying work whatsoever, or, if it has some artistic relevance, unless it explicitly misleads as to the source or the content of the work." *ESS Entm't*, 547 F.3d at 1099 (quotations and alterations omitted); *see also Rogers*, 875 F.2d at 999.

In this case, we readily conclude that Moore's paintings, prints, and calendars are protected under the *Rogers* test. The depiction of the University's uniforms in the content of these items is artistically relevant to the expressive underlying works because the uniforms' colors and designs are needed for a realistic portrayal of famous scenes from Alabama football history. Also there is no evidence that Moore ever marketed an unlicensed item as "endorsed" or "sponsored" by the University, or otherwise explicitly stated that such items were affiliated with the University. Moore's paintings, prints, and calendars very clearly are embodiments of artistic expression, and are entitled to full First Amendment protection. The extent of his use of the University's trademarks is their mere inclusion (their necessary inclusion) in the body of the image which Moore creates to memorialize and enhance a particular play or event in the University's football history. Even if "some members of the public would draw the incorrect inference that [the University] had some involvement with [Moore's paintings, prints, and calendars,] . . . that risk of misunderstanding, not engendered by any overt [or in this case even implicit] claim . . . is so outweighed by the interest in artistic expression as to preclude" any violation of the Lanham Act. *Rogers*, 875 F.2d at 1001.

Because Moore's depiction of the University's uniforms in the content of his paintings, prints, and calendars results in no violation of the Lanham Act, we affirm the district court with respect to paintings and prints, and reverse with respect to calendars.

III.   MUGS AND OTHER "MUNDANE PRODUCTS"

We now proceed to the issues related to Moore's depiction of the University's uniforms on "mini-prints, mugs, cups, . . . flags, towels, t-shirts, or any other mundane products." Moore is appellant for these items, which we will refer to as "mugs and other 'mundane products.'"

[The court's discussion of the trademark licensing agreements is omitted.]

B.   MOORE'S COPYRIGHT ARGUMENT

Moore argues that because his original paintings do not infringe the University's trademarks, he has an unfettered right to produce derivative works featuring those paintings. We disagree with this broad contention. "[T]he defendant's ownership of or license to use a copyrighted image is no defense to a charge of trademark infringement. It should be remembered that a copyright is not a 'right' to use: it is a right to exclude *others* from using the copyrighted work." 1 J. Thomas McCarthy, *McCarthy on Trademarks and Unfair Competition* §6:14 (4th ed. 2011) (emphasis added); [cit.].

If it were otherwise, a person could easily circumvent trademark law by drawing another's trademark and then placing that drawing on various products with impunity. Selling the copyrighted drawing itself may not amount to a trademark infringement, but its placement on certain products very well might. *See, e.g., Nova Wines, Inc. v. Adler Fels Winery LLC*, 467 F. Supp. 2d 965, 983 (N.D. Cal. 2006) (holding that the copyright holder of a Marilyn Monroe photograph could not use the photo on wine bottles because it would infringe the trademark rights of another winery that sold wine in bottles that prominently featured images of Monroe); McCarthy, *supra*, §6:14. Thus, we reject Moore's argument that his copyright in the paintings gives him an automatic defense to any trademark claims made by the University.

C.   TRADEMARK CLAIMS

Because the district court ruled against Moore with respect to the mugs and other "mundane products," Moore is appellant for these items. However, he has waived any challenge to the district court's conclusions that his use of the uniforms on these products was not a fair use and was not protected by the First Amendment. . . .

Acquiescence is the only remaining trademark argument that Moore has preserved on appeal for these items. Acquiescence is a statutory defense under 15 U.S.C. §1115(b)(9). "The defense of acquiescence requires proof of three elements: (1) the plaintiff actively represented it would not assert a right or claim; (2) the delay between the active representation and assertion of the right or claim was not excusable; and (3) the delay caused the defendant undue prejudice." *Angel Flight of Ga., Inc. v. Angel Flight Am., Inc.*, 522 F.3d 1200, 1207 (11th Cir. 2008) (citation and quotation omitted). "The difference between acquiescence and laches is that laches denotes passive consent and acquiescence denotes active consent." *Id*. Thus, the relevant evidence for acquiescence would be active behavior by the University during the time that Moore has been portraying the University's uniforms (i.e., since 1979).

"Active consent" does not necessarily mean an explicit promise not to sue. It only requires "conduct on the plaintiff's part that amounted to an assurance to the defendant, express or implied, that plaintiff would not assert his trademark rights against the defendant." *Creative Gifts, Inc. v. UFO*, 235 F.3d 540, 547-48 (10th Cir. 2000); [cit.].

Here, a finding of acquiescence on the mugs or other "mundane products" would estop the University from prosecuting its action against Moore with respect to those items, [cit.], unless the University can show that "'inevitable confusion' arises from the continued dual use of the marks." *SunAmerica Corp. v. Sun Life Assurance Co. of Can.*, 77 F.3d 1325, 1334 (11th Cir. 1996). As we noted in our discussion *supra* at Part III.A, the record is not clear with respect to the parties' course of conduct towards Moore's sale of mugs and other "mundane products." The record relevant to acquiescence on these items is similarly undeveloped. Accordingly, we remand this acquiescence issue for the district court to conduct further proceedings, if necessary.

IV.   CONCLUSION

As evidenced by the parties' course of conduct, Moore's depiction of the University's uniforms in his unlicensed paintings, prints, and calendars is not prohibited by the prior licensing agreements. Additionally, the paintings, prints, and calendars do not violate the Lanham Act because these artistically expressive objects are protected by the First Amendment, by virtue of our application of the *Rogers* balancing test. The uniforms in these works of art are artistically relevant to the underlying works, Moore never explicitly misled consumers as to the source of the items, and the interests in artistic expression outweigh the risk of confusion as to endorsement. Accordingly, we affirm the judgment of the district court with respect to the paintings and prints, and reverse with respect to the prints as replicated on calendars.[42]

With respect to the licensing agreements' coverage of the mugs and other "mundane products," we reverse the district court because disputed issues of fact remain. [cit.] Moore has not argued on appeal that his actions with respect to these items constituted fair use or were protected by the First Amendment, and therefore any such protection has been waived, and we need not address those issues with respect to the mugs and other "mundane products." We remand this case to the district court for further proceedings, consistent with this opinion.

Affirmed in part, reversed in part, and remanded.

TWENTIETH CENTURY FOX TELEVISION v. EMPIRE DIST., INC.

875 F.3d 1192 (9th Cir. 2017)

M. Smith, Circuit Judge:

FACTUAL AND PROCEDURAL BACKGROUND

Empire Distribution, founded in 2010, is a well-known and respected record label that records and releases albums in the urban music genre, which includes hip hop, rap, and R&B. Empire Distribution has released many albums by established and lesser-known artists as well as music compilations with titles such as *EMPIRE Presents: Ratchet Music*, *EMPIRE Presents: Yike 4 Life*, and *EMPIRE Presents: Triple X-Mas*.

In 2015, Fox premiered a television show titled *Empire*, which portrays a fictional hip hop music label named "Empire Enterprises" that is based in New York. The show features songs in every episode, including some original music. Under an agreement with Fox, Columbia Records releases music from the show after each episode airs, as well as soundtrack albums at the end of each season. Fox has also promoted the *Empire* show and its associated music through live musical performances, radio play, and consumer goods such as shirts and champagne glasses bearing the show's "Empire" brand.

In response to a claim letter from Empire Distribution, Fox filed suit on March 23, 2015, seeking a declaratory judgment that the *Empire* show and its associated music releases do not violate Empire Distribution's trademark rights under either the

---

42. We disagree with the district court with respect to such calendars for several reasons. First, the First Amendment interests in expressive art apply with equal (or near equal) force to prints used in Moore's calendars. Second, prints replicated on calendars would be of a size more comparable to other prints, and would be more analogous to those than to the smaller replications on mugs or post-card-sized mini-prints, where the artistic work is much less likely to have been considered significant by the purchaser. Finally, as noted above, the course of conduct of the parties with respect to the calendars establishes acquiescence.

Lanham Act or California law. Empire Distribution counterclaimed for trademark infringement, trademark dilution, unfair competition, and false advertising under the Lanham Act and California law, and sought both injunctive and monetary relief. Fox moved for summary judgment, and Empire Distribution's opposition to Fox's motion included a request for a continuance under Federal Rule of Civil Procedure 56(d) in order to complete discovery. On February 1, 2016, the district court denied Empire Distribution's request, and granted summary judgment to Fox on all claims and counterclaims. Empire Distribution moved for reconsideration, which was denied. Empire Distribution timely appealed.

. . .

ANALYSIS

In general, claims of trademark infringement under the Lanham Act are governed by a likelihood-of-confusion test. *See Mattel, Inc. v. MCA Records, Inc.*, 296 F.3d 894, 900 (9th Cir. 2002). When the allegedly infringing use is in the title of an expressive work, however, we instead apply a test developed by the Second Circuit in *Rogers v. Grimaldi*, 875 F.2d 994 (2d Cir. 1989), to determine whether the Lanham Act applies. *Mattel*, 296 F.3d at 902. Like the Second Circuit, we have identified two rationales for treating expressive works differently from other covered works: because (1) they implicate the First Amendment right of free speech, which must be balanced against the public interest in avoiding consumer confusion; and (2) consumers are less likely to mistake the use of someone else's mark in an expressive work for a sign of association, authorship, or endorsement. *See Rogers*, 875 F.2d at 997-1000; *Mattel*, 296 F.3d at 900, 902.

Under the *Rogers* test, the title of an expressive work does not violate the Lanham Act "unless the title has no artistic relevance to the underlying work whatsoever, or, if it has some artistic relevance, unless the title explicitly misleads as to the source or the content of the work." *Mattel*, 296 F.3d at 902 (internal quotation marks omitted) (quoting *Rogers*, 875 F.2d at 999). We have extended this test from titles to allegedly infringing uses within the body of an expressive work. *See E.S.S. Entm't 2000, Inc. v. Rock Star Videos, Inc.*, 547 F.3d 1095, 1099 (9th Cir. 2008).

DOES THE ROGERS TEST APPLY TO FOX'S USE OF THE MARK "EMPIRE"?

We must first determine whether the *Rogers* test applies to Fox's use of the mark "Empire." We decide this legal question de novo. *See Brown v. Elec. Arts, Inc.*, 724 F.3d 1235, 1240-41 (9th Cir. 2013).

Empire Distribution argues that at least some of Fox's uses of the mark "Empire" fall outside the title or body of an expressive work, and therefore outside the scope of the *Rogers* test. The *Empire* television show itself is clearly an expressive work, *see Charles v. City of Los Angeles*, 697 F.3d 1146, 1151-52 (9th Cir. 2012), as are the associated songs and albums, *see Mattel*, 296 F.3d at 902, but Empire Distribution asserts that Fox's use of the mark "Empire" extends well beyond the titles and bodies of these expressive works. Specifically, Empire Distribution points to Fox's use of the "Empire" mark "as an umbrella brand to promote and sell music and other commercial products." These promotional activities under the "Empire" brand include appearances by cast members in other media, radio play, online advertising, live events, and the sale or licensing of consumer goods.

Although it is true that these promotional efforts technically fall outside the title or body of an expressive work, it requires only a minor logical extension of the reasoning of *Rogers* to hold that works protected under its test may be advertised and marketed by name, and we so hold. Indeed, the *Rogers* case itself concerned both a movie with an allegedly infringing title and its advertising and promotion, although the majority opinion did not deal separately with the latter aspect. *See Rogers*, 875 F.2d at 1005 (Griesa, J., concurring in the judgment). The balance of First Amendment interests struck in *Rogers* and *Mattel* could be destabilized if the titles of expressive works were protected but could not be used to promote those works. In response, Empire Distribution raises the specter of a pretextual expressive work meant only to disguise a business profiting from another's trademark, but the record in this case makes clear that the *Empire* show is no such thing. Fox's promotional activities, including those that generate revenue, are auxiliary to the television show and music releases, which lie at the heart of its "Empire" brand.

Empire Distribution also claims that Fox's uses of the "Empire" mark fall within the Lanham Act due to a footnote in *Rogers*, which stated that *Rogers*' "limiting construction would not apply to misleading titles that are confusingly similar to other titles [because the] public interest in sparing consumers this type of confusion outweighs the slight public interest in permitting authors to use such titles." 875 F.2d at 999 n.5. This footnote has been cited only once by an appellate court since *Rogers*, in a case in which the Second Circuit itself rejected its applicability and applied the *Rogers* test. *See Cliffs Notes, Inc. v. Bantam Doubleday Dell Publ'g Grp., Inc.*, 886 F.2d 490, 494-95 (2d Cir. 1989). The exception the footnote suggests may be ill-advised or unnecessary: identifying "misleading titles that are confusingly similar to other titles" has the potential to duplicate either the likelihood-of-confusion test or the second prong of *Rogers*, which asks whether a title "explicitly misleads as to the source or the content of the work." *Mattel*, 296 F.3d at 902 (quoting *Rogers*, 875 F.2d at 999). More importantly, it conflicts with our precedents, which "dictate that we apply the *Rogers* test in [Lanham Act] §43(a) cases involving expressive works." *Brown*, 724 F.3d at 1241-42. We therefore examine Fox's use of the "Empire" mark under that test.

APPLYING THE ROGERS TEST

I

Under the two prongs of the *Rogers* test, "the Lanham Act should not be applied to expressive works 'unless the [use of the trademark or other identifying material] has no artistic relevance to the underlying work whatsoever, or, if it has some artistic relevance, unless the [trademark or other identifying material] explicitly misleads as to the source or the content of the work.'" *Brown*, 724 F.3d at 1242 (alterations in original) (quoting *Rogers*, 875 F.2d at 999). In addition to these two prongs, Empire Distribution argues that the *Rogers* test incudes a threshold requirement that a mark have attained a meaning beyond its source-identifying function.

What Empire Distribution identifies as a threshold requirement is merely a consideration under the first prong of the *Rogers* test. Trademark suits often arise when a brand name enters common parlance and comes to signify something more than the brand itself, but we apply the *Rogers* test in other cases as well. In *Mattel*, we noted that some trademarks, such as Rolls-Royce or Band-Aid, "enter our public discourse and become an integral part of our vocabulary." 296 F.3d at 900. The ordinary likelihood-of-confusion test provides insufficient protection against a trademark owner's ability to control public discourse in these cases — but not *only* in these cases. *Mattel* focused on these examples, in which "the mark (like Rolls Royce) has taken on an expressive meaning apart from its source-identifying function," as part of a larger class of cases in which "a trademark owner asserts a right to control how we express ourselves." *Id.* In other words, the only threshold requirement for the *Rogers* test is an attempt to apply the Lanham Act to First Amendment expression.

Of course, the cultural significance of a mark may often be relevant to the first prong of the *Rogers* test. Trademarks that "transcend their identifying purpose," *id.*, are more likely to be used in artistically relevant ways. For example, at issue in *Mattel* was a song titled "Barbie Girl," which poked fun at the shallow materialism identified with Mattel's trademarked Barbie brand of dolls. Barbie's status as a "cultural icon" helped explain the artistic relevance of Mattel's doll to the song. A mark that has no meaning beyond its source-identifying function is more likely to be used in a way that has "no artistic relevance to the underlying work whatsoever," *id.* at 902 (quoting *Rogers*, 875 F.2d at 999), because the work may be "merely borrow[ing] another's property to get attention," *id.* at 901. *See, e.g.*, *Dr. Seuss Ents., L.P. v. Penguin Books USA, Inc.*, 109 F.3d 1394, 1401 (9th Cir. 1997) (holding that an account of the O.J. Simpson murder trial titled *The Cat NOT in the Hat!* borrowed Dr. Seuss's trademark and poetic style only "'to get attention' or maybe even 'to avoid the drudgery in working up something fresh.'" (citation omitted)).

In this case, Fox used the common English word "Empire" for artistically relevant reasons: the show's setting is New York, the Empire State, and its subject matter is a music and entertainment conglomerate, "Empire Enterprises," which is itself a figurative empire. Because we cannot say that Fox's use of the "Empire" mark "has no artistic relevance to the underlying work whatsoever," the first prong of the *Rogers* test is satisfied.

Empire Distribution does not dispute that the title "Empire" is relevant to Fox's work in this sense, but it argues that the first prong of the *Rogers* test includes a requirement that the junior work refer to the senior work. In this case, Empire Distribution argues that the *Empire* show fails the test because its use of the word "Empire" does not refer to Empire Distribution. This referential requirement does not appear in the text of the *Rogers* test, and such a requirement would be inconsistent with the purpose of the first prong of *Rogers*.

The first prong of *Rogers* distinguishes cases in which the use of the mark has some artistic relation to the work from cases in which the use of the mark is arbitrary. In these latter cases, the First Amendment interest is diminished. The bar is set low: "the level of relevance merely must be above zero." *E.S.S. Entm't*, 547 F.3d at 1100. Empire Distribution argues that cases like *Parks v. LaFace Records*, 329 F.3d 437 (6th Cir. 2003), show that this prong contains a referential requirement. In *Parks*, the Sixth Circuit held that a district court erred in concluding as a matter of law that the title of the song "Rosa Parks" by the hip hop duo OutKast was artistically relevant to the work. *Id.* at 452-59. Despite the song's use of the civil rights figure's name, "[t]he composers did *not* intend it to be about Rosa Parks, and the lyrics are *not* about Rosa Parks." *Id.* at 452. There was no question, however, that the title *did* refer to Parks; no one contended the name was a coincidence. The Sixth Circuit suggested that OutKast had chosen an irrelevant title that "unquestionably enhanced the song's potential sale to the consuming public." *Id.* at 453. A reasonable person could find that the song "Rosa Parks" failed the *Rogers* test not because of a lack of relationship between the title "Rosa Parks" and the person Rosa Parks, but because of the "highly questionable" artistic relevance of the title "Rosa Parks" to the song itself—the underlying work. *Id.* at 459.

This is how a work fails the first prong of the *Rogers* test: by bearing a title which has no artistic relevance to the work. A title may have artistic relevance by linking the work to another mark, as with "Barbie Girl," or it may have artistic relevance by supporting the themes and geographic setting of the work, as with *Empire*. Reference to another work may be a component of artistic relevance, but it is not a prerequisite. Accordingly, the relevance of the word "empire" to Fox's expressive work is sufficient to satisfy the first prong of the *Rogers* test.

II

If the use of a mark is artistically relevant to the underlying work, the Lanham Act does not apply "unless the title explicitly misleads as to the source or the content of the work." *Mattel*, 296 F.3d at 902 (quoting *Rogers*, 875 F.2d at 999) (internal quotation mark omitted). Empire Distribution argues that the "relevant inquiry . . . is whether the defendant's use of the mark would confuse consumers as to the source, sponsorship or content of the work." But this test conflates the second prong of the *Rogers* test with the general *Sleekcraft* likelihood-of-confusion test, which applies outside the *Rogers* context of expressive works. *See Mattel*, 296 F.3d at 900 (citing *AMF, Inc. v. Sleekcraft Boats*, 599 F.2d 341, 348-49 (9th Cir. 1979)).

To fail the second prong of the *Rogers* test, "[i]t is key . . . that the creator must *explicitly* mislead consumers." *Brown*, 724 F.3d at 1245. We must ask not only about the likelihood of consumer confusion but also "whether there was an 'explicit indication,' 'overt claim,' or 'explicit misstatement' that caused such consumer confusion." *Id.* (quoting *Rogers*, 875 F.2d at 1001). As "the use of a mark alone is not enough to satisfy this prong of the *Rogers* test," *id.*, Fox's *Empire* show, which contains no overt claims or explicit references to Empire Distribution, is not explicitly misleading, and it satisfies the second *Rogers* prong.

[*Affirmed.*]

NOTES AND QUESTIONS

1. Rogers *extended to the content of expressive uses?* The *Rogers* test was formulated to assess whether a defendant's use of a mark in a title of an artistic work should be deemed permissible. In *Alabama* and *Empire* (and other cases cited in those opinions), the court extends the *Rogers* test to uses of marks within the body of artistic works. Is this a sensible extension? Or do cases such as *Alabama* and *Empire* extend the *Rogers* test too far beyond its original domain?

2. *Does* Rogers *extend to "mundane" products?* Should the "mundane" products mentioned in the *Alabama* case—products such as mugs depicting Alabama football scenes—be considered expressive works that benefit from the protection of the *Rogers* test? Should Moore's use of the Alabama trade dress on those products have been deemed permissible under the *Rogers* test, had the court reached the question? Does *Empire* answer the question by extending the *Rogers* test to the defendant's references to "Empire" in its promotional materials? Or is *Empire* distinguishable from *Alabama* in this respect?

3. Rogers *part 1—artistic relevance merely above zero.* An expressive use can fail the *Rogers* test if it has "no artistic relevance" to the work. By concluding that expressive uses pass this part of the *Rogers* test by any showing of artistic relevance "above zero," have courts successfully taken themselves out of the business of making difficult judgments about art? Or have they rendered the "artistic relevance" aspect of the *Rogers* test a virtual nullity? For a rare example of an expressive use that might fail the artistic relevance prong of the *Rogers* test even under the current "merely above zero" approach, consider the use by the rap group OutKast of "Rosa Parks" as a song title. Rosa Parks, of course, is famed for her role in the civil rights movement as a result of refusing to vacate her seat in the "Whites Only" section of a bus. The OutKast song lyrics briefly mention a bus ("Ah ha, hush that fuss/Everybody move to the back of the bus") but do not mention Rosa Parks, the bus incident for which she is known, or the civil rights movement in general. *See Parks v. LaFace Records,* 329 F.3d 437 (6th Cir. 2003) (concluding that it was at a minimum "open to debate" whether the use of the name "Rosa Parks" in the title was artistically relevant to the work).

4. Rogers *part 2 — "explicitly misleading."* An expressive use that is artistically relevant to the work (and thus passes *Rogers* part 1) might still fail the *Rogers* test if it "explicitly misleads as to the source or content of the work." By emphasizing that the misleading must be explicit, do cases such as *Empire* all but guarantee that expressive uses will pass this part of the *Rogers* test? Put another way, what would it take to explicitly mislead? Is OutKast's use of "Rosa Parks" discussed in the preceding note explicitly misleading? Suppose that in the Alabama case, the university had survey evidence that over 60 percent of respondents who were shown the Moore paintings thought that the university had an affiliation with the painting or had authorized or sponsored it. Explicit misleading? Or just, at best, a lot of implicit misleading? *See ETW Corp. v. Jireh Publ'g, Inc.*, 332 F.3d 915 (6th Cir. 2003) (involving similar survey evidence regarding paintings that depicted golfer Tiger Woods); *see also Brown v. Electronic Arts, Inc.*, 724 F.3d 1325 (9th Cir. 2013) (discussing *ETW* in a case that likewise involved consumer survey evidence; concluding that the survey evidence did not even raise a triable issue of fact as to explicit misleading). Suppose that the "explicitly" modifier were eliminated. If the *Rogers* test largely boils down to the part 2 inquiry into whether the use is misleading, would the *Rogers* test do any more than restate the likelihood of confusion inquiry that it supposedly replaces?

5. *Should all "noncommercial uses" be shielded from Lanham Act liability?* How useful (if at all) would be the distinction between commercial and noncommercial uses in cases involving artistic uses? To what extent was that distinction given weight in *Alabama* and *Empire*? What of cases involving expressive uses that are overtly political in nature? Should commerciality be relevant? Consider *Radiance Foundation, Inc. v. Nat'l Ass'n for the Advancement of Colored People*, 786 F.3d 316 (4th Cir. 2015), involving the Radiance Foundation's use of the acronym NAACP juxtaposed with "National Association for the Abortion of Colored People," in the headline of an article asserting that the NAACP supports abortion. The court reasoned that the language in Section 32 specifying that the alleged infringer's use be "in connection with the sale, offering for sale, distribution, or advertising of any goods or services" required "sufficient nexus between the unauthorized use of the protected mark and clear transactional activity." The court observed that First Amendment commercial speech doctrine (which defines commercial speech as an activity that does no more than propose a commercial transaction) could be used to guide the "in connection with" inquiry. Applying its approach, the court held that the fact that Radiance accepted donations for its advocacy via the website was insufficient to connect the activity to the provision of goods and services. The "in connection with" element was not met, the court concluded, which presumably was enough by itself to dispose of the NAACP's Lanham Act claim. However, the court proceeded to undertake an apparently separate inquiry that mixed elements of confusion analysis with reliance on *Mattel* and *Rogers*. Do you expect that the "in connection with" language, and the commercial/noncommercial distinction generally, will prove useful as an alternative path for balancing trademark policy interests and speech interests, especially in cases involving political expression?

6. *Effect of* Tam? Recall from Chapter 5 the Court's decision in *Tam*, concluding that the Section 2(a) disparagement bar violated the First Amendment. Does the Court's reasoning in *Tam* affect any of the analyses of expressive use that we have seen in this chapter?

7. *Comparative notions of free speech.* The Constitutional Court of the Republic of South Africa overturned a lower court's finding of trademark infringement and held that the protection afforded by the Trademarks Act had to be balanced with freedom of expression guaranteed by the Bill of Rights in South Africa's constitution. In the case, the defendant had produced T-shirts that bore decoration resembling the trademarks of a brewer. The T-shirts mimicked the logo for CARLING BLACK LABEL beer but replaced the words "America's Lusty, Lively Beer, CARLING BLACK LABEL BEER, enjoyed by men around the world" with "Black Labour, White Guilt, Africa's Lusty, Lively Exploitation Since 1652, no regard given worldwide." *Laugh It Off Promotions CC v. S. Afr. Breweries Int'l (Finance) B.V.* 2006 (1) SA 144 (CC) (S. Afr.).

You may find the following problems to be useful for reviewing the analysis for assessing speech-related defenses to confusion and dilution claims. Some involve speech that is explicitly political, while others involve speech that has a stronger commercial nexus.

PROBLEM 9-6:   TRADEMARKS AND VIRTUAL WORLDS

Although it's hard to imagine that Dinwoodie and Janis could be any more awesome than we already are (just ask us), let's just hypothesize that in a virtual world, we *could* be even more awesome—and, on top of that, we could walk around wearing outlandish body armor and carrying magical swords and stuff and possibly fly. This brings us to the virtual world known as "Second Life." Second Life is a 3D online digital world "where everyone you see is a real person and every place you visit is built by people just like you." *See http://secondlife.com.* Second Life claims to have several million registered users, and, honestly, we find it pretty unsettling that there are that many people "just like us," but, whatever. These users create "avatars" (their personae in the digital world) and (with a premium membership) can purchase land, open businesses, and make digital money, which can be exchanged in the digital economy.

Suppose that one day, while we (actually, our avatars) were virtually walking around in Second Life, Professor Dinwoodie's avatar needed to get a coffee, thereby demonstrating that Professor Dinwoodie's avatar truly is a virtual embodiment of his persona. Professor Janis's avatar suggested stopping at a Starbucks, but one didn't exist. So we quickly bought land and opened a virtual Starbucks, complete with authentic reproductions of the marks and logos of the real-world Starbucks.

(1) Is our use a cognizable use in commerce or use in connection with goods or services under either Section 32 or Section 43? *See* Chapter 7.

(2) Even if our use is a cognizable use causing a likelihood of confusion, is it nonetheless a permissible use? Under what theory? To the extent that speech interests are relevant, would you apply the *Rogers* test to assess those interests?

(3) Suppose that the real-world Starbucks decides to enter Second Life to get a piece of the action. Could we succeed in a claim that we have priority of use over the real-world Starbucks in the mark STARBUCKS for retail (virtual) coffee sales? As you consider this question, consider the Second Life "Terms of Service" agreement, *http://lindenlab.com/tos.*

(4) Suppose that business at our Starbucks was booming, especially after we hit upon a very effective promotion. We designed five glowing purple orbs and hid them in our virtual Starbucks store. Orb finders were entitled to various wonderful and valuable prizes—such as free virtual Starbucks coffee for a year. A few weeks after the contest ended, we were startled to discover that one of the orbs was being auctioned on eBay (the real-world one) for several hundred (real-world) dollars, identified as "Second Life Starbucks Orbs." Analyze the trademark issues.

PROBLEM 9-7: TRADEMARKS AND POLITICAL SPEECH

(1) A political action committee calling itself Americans for Jeb Bush organized during Jeb Bush's 2002 reelection campaign for governor of Florida. Americans for Jeb Bush established a website (formerly located at *www.americansforjebbush.com*) that advocated Jeb Bush's candidacy, solicited financial contributions for the committee, and allegedly included various attacks against Bush's likely rival, former U.S. Attorney General Janet Reno. Mailings sent out by Americans for Jeb Bush also allegedly included similar attacks. The website included a disclaimer stating that Americans for Jeb Bush was "independent of any other committee, not approved by any candidate."

Jeb Bush publicly disavowed any affiliation with Americans for Jeb Bush and stated that the committee was a "scam" that misrepresented his views. Eventually, Bush sued to enjoin the committee from using his name and likeness. *See Bush v. Ams. for Jeb Bush Political Comm.*, No. 02-22275, 2002 WL 32672121 (S.D. Fla. July 30, 2002) (complaint).

    a.   Evaluate Bush's likelihood of success on the merits of this claim.

    b.   Suppose that Bush has procured federal trademark registrations for JEB BUSH FOR GOVERNOR and JEB! used in connection with his political campaign. Does this affect your analysis? In general, would it be advisable for political candidates to obtain similar trademark protection as a matter of course?

    c.   In press reports, the organizer of Americans for Jeb Bush stated that he originally intended to call the organization the Committee to Stop Janet Reno. Suppose that he had done so. Would Janet Reno have a trademark-related cause of action? Would Jeb Bush?

(2) Suppose the Bi-Partisan T-Shirt Company offers T-shirts bearing the following graphic:

Assume that the GOP has authorized neither of these uses of its "elephant" logo. Assess the likelihood that Bi-Partisan's uses are permissible. Is it more likely to be at risk of liability for one use than for the other? If so, why?

(3) Barack Obama's 2008 presidential campaign featured the slogan "Yes We Can!" Suppose that a group supporting the legalization of marijuana begins to use the slogan YES

WE CANNABIS! for T-shirts and other promotional items connected with the movement to legalize marijuana. Lanham Act liability? Suppose that a group protesting surreptitious government monitoring activities creates and distributes promotional materials as shown below:

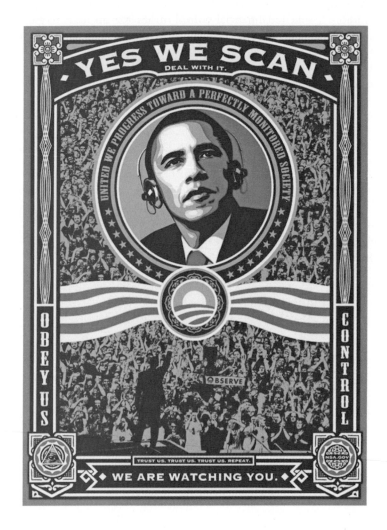

Lanham Act liability? Is there even a plausible risk of such liability?

PROBLEM 9-8: "DUMB" STARBUCKS

In February 2014, at 1802 Hillhurst Avenue in Los Angeles, a coffee shop opened. The shop used signs and logos that were pretty much identical to those used by Starbucks, with the addition of the word "dumb" before "Starbucks." The store mimicked the Starbucks menu, store layout, and associated merchandise, right down to the "Dumb

Nora Jones Duets" CDs. A letter answering "Frequently Asked Questions" about DUMB STARBUCKS indicated that "[b]y adding the word 'dumb,' we are technically 'making fun' of Starbucks, which allows us to use their trademarks under a law known as 'fair use.'" The letter proceeded to refer to *copyright* fair use, which may itself be dumb, but we get the point.

A Twitter frenzy followed. People waited in line for an hour to buy coffee at the DUMB STARBUCKS. A commenter advised his Twitter followers to "go buy some @ dumbstarbucks before dumb lawyers get to it," which strikes us as sage advice. In time, the DUMB STARBUCKS shop was revealed to be the work of a Comedy Central comedian, who eventually claimed that the shop would be featured in an upcoming episode of his television show. For a promotional video also making the claim of parody (but at the same time claiming that the shop is a real business, not a comedy skit, which strikes us as possibly a dumb move), *see https://www.youtube.com/watch?v=Bo_deCOd1HU.*

In the meantime, the Los Angeles Health Department had shut the shop down for health code violations.

(1) Is the DUMB STARBUCKS shop a "successful parody" under the *Louis Vuitton* analysis?

(2) Suppose that Dinwoodie and Janis—always looking to make a quick buck (or, euphemistically, always "entrepreneurial")—make and sell DUMB STARBUCKS merchandise on eBay. We don't get permission from Starbucks, or from the Comedy Central comedian. What's our risk of liability to the comedian? (For that matter, what if Starbucks starts selling DUMB STARBUCKS merchandise?)

10

FALSE ADVERTISING

A. INTRODUCTION: THE EVOLUTION OF SECTION 43(A) FALSE ADVERTISING CLAIMS

Before the 1988 amendments, Lanham Act §43(a) did not single out false advertising as a form of unfair competition. Instead, it contained general language proscribing false descriptions and representations:

> Any person who shall affix, apply, or annex, or use in connection with any goods or services, or any container or containers for goods, a false designation of origin, or any false description or representation, including words or other symbols tending falsely to describe or represent the same, and shall cause such goods or services to enter into commerce, and any person who shall with knowledge of the falsity of such designation of origin or description or representation cause or procure the same to be transported or used in commerce or deliver the same to any carrier to be transported or used, shall be liable to a civil action by any person doing business in the locality falsely indicated as that of origin or in the region in which said locality is situated, or by any person who believes that he is or is likely to be damaged by the use of any such false description or representation.

15 U.S.C. §1125 (1987). Courts construed this language to provide the basis for a false designation of origin cause of action based on a likelihood-of-confusion test, as discussed in Chapter 7. Courts also construed this language to provide the basis for a narrow false advertising cause of action—specifically, false advertising about one's own goods or services. *See, e.g., Coca-Cola Co. v. Procter & Gamble Co.*, 822 F.2d 28, 31 (6th Cir. 1987) ("Protecting consumers from false or misleading advertising, moreover, is an important goal of the statute and a laudable public policy to be served. . . . Public policy . . . is indeed well served by permitting misrepresentation of quality claims to be actionable under section 43(a)."); *U-Haul Int'l, Inc. v. Jartran, Inc.*, 681 F.2d 1159, 1161 (9th Cir. 1982) ("False statements of fact in a defendant's advertising concerning his product fit comfortably within the language of section 43(a)."). Courts generally incorporated false advertising concepts that had been developed under the common law tort of false advertising, except that a majority of courts dispensed with the common law requirement that the false advertising plaintiff prove direct injury through actual lost sales. *See, e.g.,* J. Thomas McCarthy, *Lanham Act §43(a): The Sleeping Giant Is Now Wide Awake*, 59 LAW & CONTEMP. PROBS. 45, 54-57 (1996). One district court set out the dominant standard for adjudicating false advertising claims under the pre-1988 Section 43(a):

(1) In its comparison advertisements, defendant made false statements of fact about its own product;

(2) Those advertisements actually deceived or have the tendency to deceive a substantial segment of their audience;

(3) Such deception is material, in that it is likely to influence the purchasing decision;

(4) Defendant caused its falsely advertised goods to enter interstate commerce; and

(5) Plaintiff has been or is likely to be injured as the result of the foregoing either by a direct diversion of sales from itself to defendant, or by lessening of the goodwill which its products enjoy with the buying public.

Skil Corp. v. Rockwell Int'l Corp., 375 F. Supp. 777, 783 (N.D. Ill. 1974).

Notably, the pre-1988 Section 43(a) false advertising action as articulated in the *Skil* test above is limited to an advertiser's false statements about *its own* goods or services. Before 1988, courts declined to extend the Section 43(a) false advertising action to an advertiser's false statements about *others'* goods or services. *See, e.g., Bernard Food Indus., Inc. v. Dietene Co.*, 415 F.2d 1279 (7th Cir. 1969), *cert. denied*, 397 U.S. 912 (1970) ("False advertising or representations made by a defendant about a plaintiff's product are not covered by section 43(a)."); *L'Aiglon Apparel, Inc. v. Lana Lobell, Inc.*, 214 F.2d 649 (3d Cir. 1954). This refusal was not altogether surprising. The common law had already developed the tort variously labeled "trade libel," "injurious falsehood," "product disparagement," or the like, to deal with deceptive misrepresentations about another's goods or services. For example, according to the Restatement (Second) of Torts, one who publishes a false statement of fact about the product or service of another is liable for "injurious falsehood" if:

> (a) he intends for publication of the statement to result in harm to the interests of the other having a pecuniary value, or either recognizes or should recognize that it is likely to do so, and
>
> (b) he knows that the statement is false or acts in reckless disregard of its truth or falsity.

Restatement (Second) of Torts §632A. In addition, decisions required a showing of specific, customer-by-customer damages directly caused by the false statement, typically from evidence that particular purchasers declined to purchase from the injured party due to the false statement. *See Porous Media Corp. v. Pall Corp.*, 110 F.3d 1329, 1337-41 (8th Cir. 1997) (noting requirement for proof of special damages for product disparagement tort under Minnesota law, but concluding that evidence of particular lost sales and "lost growth opportunities" sufficed to support verdict for plaintiff on disparagement claim). These high-level scienter and special damages requirements obviously differ quite substantially from the pre-1988 standards for Lanham Act false advertising.

As described in previous chapters, Congress made numerous changes to the Lanham Act in the 1988 Trademark Law Revision Act. Among these were revisions to Section 43(a): Congress divided Section 43(a) into two subsections, (1)(A) and (1)(B), placing the language pertinent to false advertising claims into (1)(B) and leaving the "false designation of origin" language in Section 43(a)(1)(A). Under the post-1988 version of Section 43(a):

> (1) Any person who, on or in connection with any goods or services, or any container for goods, uses in commerce any word, term, name, symbol, or device, or any combination thereof, or any false designation of origin, false or misleading description of fact, or false or misleading representation of fact, which— . . .
>
> (B) in commercial advertising or promotion, misrepresents the nature, characteristics, qualities, or geographic origin of his or her or another person's goods, services, or commercial activities, shall be liable in a civil action by any person who believes that he or she is or is likely to be damaged by such act.

Although the legislative history explains the changes as an effort "to codify the interpretation that [Section 43(a)] has been given by the courts," S. Rep. No. 100-515 at 40

(1988), this claim must be evaluated critically. First, the post-1988 language clearly covers an advertiser's misrepresentations about *others'* products and services, previously the realm of the product disparagement tort. The legislative history notes simply that "the public policy of deterring acts of unfair competition will be served if Section 43(a) is amended to make clear that misrepresentations about another's products are as actionable as misrepresentations about one's own." *Id.; see also U.S. Healthcare, Inc. v. Blue Cross of Greater Philadelphia*, 898 F.2d 914, 921 (3d Cir. 1990) (noting the statutory revision).

Second, as is often the case, Congress' language left many unresolved questions about exactly which judicial interpretations were being codified. *See generally* Jean Wegman Burns, *Confused Jurisprudence: False Advertising Under the Lanham Act*, 79 B.U. L. REV. 807 (1999) (identifying many such questions). Most fundamentally, Congress did not take the opportunity to expressly codify the multifactor *Skil* test, leaving courts to fashion a test for post-1988 false advertising. The cases in this chapter reflect the courts' efforts to fashion and refine the test.

In this chapter, we will analyze judicial decisions that interpret the language of the Section 43(a)(1)(B) false advertising provision, first examining selected threshold issues, then turning to the judicially crafted elements of the Section 43(a)(1)(B) false advertising claim.

NOTES AND QUESTIONS

1. *Splitting Section 43(a) false advertising from Section 43(a) false designation of origin*. When it broke out false advertising separately as Section 43(a)(1)(B), was Congress simply trying to make the point that Section 43(a) embraced false advertising claims, as courts had already decided under the pre-1988 statute? Or was Congress trying to create significant conceptual space between the false designation of origin claim and the false advertising claim? *See Dastar, supra* Chapter 2. Recall that courts had construed the false designation of origin claim, which Congress shifted to Section 43(a)(1)(A) in revising the provision, as requiring evidence of likelihood of confusion (even though likelihood of confusion was not explicit in the pre-1988 text). Did the 1988 revision signal that false advertising claims did not require evidence of likelihood of confusion, since Congress did not include that language in Section 43(a)(1)(B)?

2. *False advertising versus product disparagement*. As explained above, at common law, misrepresentations about one's own product fell into the realm of the false advertising tort, while misrepresentations about another's product fell into the realm of the product disparagement tort. The modern false advertising provision, Section 43(a)(1)(B), clearly encompasses both. But should courts construe Section 43(a)(1)(B) as applying the same standard to both? Does the "plain" language of Section 43(a)(1)(B) draw any distinction between traditional false advertising and traditional product disparagement? If not, should courts recognize a distinction nonetheless? *See, e.g., Procter & Gamble Co. v. Amway Corp.*, 242 F.3d 539, 558 (5th Cir. 2001) (refusing to adopt a standard that "would result in differing amounts of protection for false commercial speech depending on whether the speaker discusses his own goods or those of another").

Consider two grounds for recognizing distinct standards for "false advertising" and "product disparagement." First, when Congress expanded Lanham Act false advertising to embrace acts formerly in the realm of the "product disparagement" tort, perhaps it intended to incorporate the common law elements that had been developed for analyzing that tort, at least when Section 43(a)(1)(B) was invoked in a case involving misrepresentations about another's products. Second, perhaps the common law limitations on the product disparagement tort derived from constitutional concerns. *See, e.g.*, 5 J. Thomas McCarthy, McCarthy on Trademarks and Unfair Competition §27:104 (4th ed. 2013) (observing that the scienter limitations on product disparagement claims were held to "coincide" with the *New York Times* "actual malice" limitation on libel actions). *But cf. U.S. Healthcare, Inc. v. Blue Cross of Greater Philadelphia*, 898 F.2d 914, 939 (3d Cir. 1990) (refusing to require proof of actual malice in a Section 43(a)(1)(B) claim concerning misrepresentations about another's product). Are you persuaded that courts must incorporate common law limitations to keep Section 43(a)(1)(B) within First Amendment bounds? Or did Congress take care of such concerns by adding the word "commercial" before "advertising or promotion" and requiring that the "misrepresentations" be misrepresentations of "fact"? Recall from Chapter 9 that Congress has frequently resorted to the relatively clumsy commercial/noncommercial distinction in an effort to minimize conflicts between Lanham Act causes of action and First Amendment values.

3. *"Commercial activities."* The post-1988 language reaches misrepresentations about "goods" and "services," and about "commercial activities." Conceptually, this change takes the false advertising provision further afield from the traditional confusion-based trademark model. Do you think that the change is significant as a practical matter?

4. *FTC and state law remedies for false advertising.* Although our focus in this chapter is solely on Lanham Act remedies for false advertising, other remedies do exist. The Federal Trade Commission has the authority to act against "unfair or deceptive acts or practices," including false or misleading statements in advertising, where those statements harm consumers. The law in some states provides for similar remedies, frequently under the state's version of the Uniform Deceptive Trade Practices Act.

5. *Alternative dispute resolution.* Where rivals in a given market can predict that they will routinely take exception to one another's advertisements, might a low-cost, rapid alternative dispute resolution mechanism seem attractive? The National Advertising Division of the Council of Better Business Bureaus offers a voluntary dispute resolution mechanism that is described as "the industry's main self-regulatory program for national ads." *See* Stephanie Clifford, *Best Soup Ever? Suits over Ads Demand Proof*, N.Y. Times, Nov. 21, 2009, at A1.

B.   Threshold Issues

We turn first to a pair of threshold questions, which we explore through the problems that follow. First, who has standing to pursue Section 43(a)(1)(B) false advertising claims? Second, when do a party's statements constitute "advertising" for purposes of a Section 43(a)(1)(B) claim?

PROBLEM 10-1: STANDING

Suppose that firm *A*, a brewer, makes allegedly false statements in advertising about firm *B*, a competing brewer. Brewer *A* is likely to have standing to pursue a Section 43(a)(1)(B) false advertising claim against brewer *B*—but why? Is it because of *B*'s status as a competitor of *A*? But what about firms that are not direct competitors? What about consumers, or organizations purporting to act on behalf of consumers?

In *Lexmark Int'l, Inc. v. Static Control Components, Inc.*, 134 S. Ct. 1377 (2014), the Supreme Court resolved a three-way circuit split on the test for standing under Section 43(a)(1)(B). Writing for a unanimous Court, Justice Scalia first distinguished Article III standing from statutory standing. Article III standing requires a showing that the plaintiff has suffered, or is imminently threatened with, "a concrete and particularized 'injury in fact' that is fairly traceable to the challenged action of the defendant and likely to be redressed by a favorable judicial decision." *Id*. at 1386 (citing *Lujan v. Defenders of Wildlife*, 504 U.S. 555, 560 (1992)). An allegation of lost sales and damage to business reputation will generally suffice to show Article III standing.

By contrast, statutory standing requires an additional showing: that the plaintiff falls "within the class of plaintiffs whom Congress has authorized to sue" under the relevant statutory provision. *Lexmark*, 134 S. Ct. at 1387. Lanham Act §43(a)(1) authorizes suit by "any person who believes that he or she is likely to be damaged" by a defendant's acts. According to the Court, this language, albeit expansive, did not merely confer standing on any plaintiff who could make the Article III showing. *Id*. at 1388. Rather, the language was limited by two "background principles": the zone of interests and proximate causality.

To fall within the zone of interests in a false advertising suit under Section 43(a)(1)(B), a plaintiff must allege "an injury to a commercial interest in reputation or sales," the Court held. *Id*. at 1390. Accordingly, a consumer who relied on an allegedly false advertisement in purchasing a product would not fall within the relevant zone of interests, nor would "a business misled by a supplier into purchasing an inferior product," even though both might have suffered injuries-in-fact that would be cognizable under Article III. *Id*.

To satisfy the proximate cause inquiry, a false advertising plaintiff "ordinarily must show economic or reputational injury flowing directly from the deception wrought by the defendant's advertising; and that that occurs when deception of consumers causes them to withhold trade from the plaintiff. That showing is generally not made when the deception produces injuries to a fellow commercial actor that in turn affect the plaintiff." *Id*. at 1391. A firm forced out of business by its competitor's false advertising ordinarily would satisfy the inquiry, while the firm's utility company, for example, ordinarily would not. *Id*.

In adopting the zone of interest and proximate cause inquiries, the Court rejected all three of the tests that had developed in the circuits. In particular, the Court rejected

(1) the "direct competitor" test, because it was "a mistake to infer that because the Lanham Act treats false advertising as a form of unfair competition, it can protect *only* the false-advertiser's direct competitors." *Id*. at 1392 (emphasis in original);

(2) the "reasonable interest" test, because, *inter alia*, it addressed the wrong question—the reasonableness of the plaintiff's interest and basis for believing that the interest was likely to be damaged—rather than asking what the statute provided; and

(3) the multi-factor balancing test from *Conte Bros. Automotive, Inc. v. Quaker State-Slick 50, Inc.*, 165 F.3d 221, 225 (3d Cir. 1998), because, *inter alia*, it was unpredictable in application, it treated the zone of interest and proximate cause as mere factors to be weighed rather than requirements in every case, and it permitted courts to deny standing based on the difficulty of quantifying damages, even though the plaintiff might conceivably be entitled to various forms of equitable relief.

Consider whether the *Lexmark* standing inquiry is satisfied in the following scenarios:

(1) Brewer *B* buys barley from supplier *S*. Suppose that competing brewer *A* advertises falsely that S's barley contains a constituent that may be toxic to humans when the barley is subjected to the brewing process. Under the *Lexmark* test, does *B* have standing to bring a Section 43(a)(1)(B) action against *A*? Does *S* have standing to bring a Section 43(a)(1)(B) action against *A*? Compare the facts of this hypothetical to those of *Lexmark*. Lexmark sold laser printers containing toner cartridges. To encourage consumers to return empty cartridges to Lexmark (and to purchase new, full ones from Lexmark), Lexmark placed a microchip in each cartridge that disabled the cartridge when empty, and included a shrinkwrap license on the cartridge packaging. Under the license terms, purchasers agreed

to return the empty cartridge to Lexmark and received a 20 percent discount on the purchase of a new cartridge. Static Control developed a chip that mimicked the functions of Lexmark's chip and sold the chips to refurbishers who refurbished and resold Lexmark cartridges. Customers could thereby avoid the need to purchase a new cartridge from Lexmark. Lexmark then allegedly sent letters to customers asserting that the use of refurbished cartridges (and particularly the use of Static Control's chip) was illegal. These statements were the basis for Static Control's claim of false advertising. Lexmark and Static Control are not direct competitors in the laser printer market. Under the *Lexmark* test, does Static Control have standing? (Yes, the Court concluded in *Lexmark*. 132 S. Ct. at 1395.) For another example, *see Syngenta Seeds, Inc. v. Bunge North America, Inc.*, 762 F.3d 795 (8th Cir. 2014) (remanding to allow district court to apply *Lexmark* rule to false advertising claim).

(2) Anna Kournikova was a famous professional tennis player. Penthouse is an adult magazine. In the June 2002 issue (we're told), Penthouse published a series of photographs of a topless woman sunbathing. Captions accompanying the photos indicated that the woman was Kournikova, which, in fact, was false. A headline on the cover of the June issue proclaimed, "EXCLUSIVE ANNA KOURNIKOVA CAUGHT UP CLOSE ON NUDE BEACH." Kournikova sued for false advertising under Section 43(a)(1)(B). Penthouse argued that Kournikova lacked standing. How would the issue be decided under the *Lexmark* test? What alternative theories, if any, might Kournikova pursue if she is held to lack standing to bring a Section 43(a)(1)(B) action?

(3) During the late 1990s, McDonald's offered (and heavily promoted) various promotional games in which customers at its fast-food restaurants could win a variety of cash awards or other prizes. McDonald's advertisements represented that customers had a fair and equal opportunity to win prizes, and published the odds of winning specific prizes. As it turned out, at least according to the FBI, a few individuals (employed by the marketing firm that McDonald's had hired) had illegally diverted winning game pieces to "winners" who then claimed the prizes. Subsequently, Phoenix, a Burger King franchisee, filed an action on behalf of itself and a proposed class of 1,100 other Burger King franchisees alleging Lanham Act false advertising. Phoenix alleged that McDonald's falsely advertised that each player in its promotional games had a fair and equal chance of winning prizes, and falsely advertised the specific odds of winning particular prizes. Phoenix also alleged that "during the run of the games, McDonald's experienced an 'unnatural spike' in its sales while Burger King experienced a decrease in its sales; and [that] Burger King franchisees incurred counter-promotion costs in an effort to 'lure back customers who frequented McDonald's while the fraudulent games were running.'" *See Phoenix of Broward, Inc. v. McDonald's Corp.*, 489 F.3d 1156, 1168 (11th Cir. 2007). Does Phoenix have standing to assert the false advertising claim? *See also Natural Answers, Inc. v. SmithKline Beecham Corp.*, 529 F.3d 1325 (11th Cir. 2008) (applying *Phoenix* test to deny standing to a plaintiff that had ceased producing the goods that were allegedly impacted by the defendant's supposedly false statements).

(4) All of the above scenarios involve allegations of false advertising under Section 43(a)(1)(B). Should the *Lexmark* test for standing be applied to all Section 43(a) actions—including, for example, Section 43(a)(1)(A) false designation of origin claims? *See Bayer v. Belmora*, discussed in Chapter 6.

PROBLEM 10-2:   COMMERCIAL "ADVERTISING OR PROMOTION"

Section 43(a)(1)(B) prohibits specified misrepresentations "in commercial advertising or promotion." Whether any given communication should be deemed to be "advertising or promotion" is not always obvious. Seventh Circuit cases require that the communication appear in "promotional material disseminated to anonymous recipients." *First Health Grp. Corp. v. BCE Emergis Corp.*, 269 F.3d 800, 804 (7th Cir. 2001); *see also Sanderson v. Culligan Int'l Co.*, 415 F.3d 620, 623 (7th Cir. 2005). In *Gordon & Breach Science Publishers, S.A. v. American Institute of Physics*, 859 F. Supp. 1521 (S.D.N.Y. 1994), the court proposed a four-part test, holding that communications constitute commercial advertising or promotion under Section 43(a)(1)(B) if they are:

(1) commercial speech;

(2) by a defendant who is in commercial competition with plaintiff;

(3) for the purpose of influencing consumers to buy defendant's goods or services; and

(4) disseminated sufficiently to the relevant purchasing public to constitute advertising or promotion within that industry.

See, e.g., Suntree Techs., Inc. v. Ecosense Int'l, Inc., 693 F.3d 1338, 1348-49 (11th Cir. 2012) (applying the *Gordon & Breach* test). *See also Tobinick v. Novella*, 848 F.3d 935 (11th Cir. 2017) (concluding that a doctor's blog posts did not constitute commercial advertising or promotion).

Consider whether either of the following scenarios presents instances of commercial speech (prong 1) that constitutes "advertising or promotion" (prong 4) under the *Gordon & Breach* test. Is the *Gordon & Breach* test effective? Is it in conformity with the statute? If you were a judge deciding the issue as a matter of first impression, would you favor adopting the *Gordon & Breach* test? If not, consider what alternative test you would propose.

(1) For several years, Bill's Racing Supplies of Speedway, Indiana, was the exclusive Indianapolis-area dealer of JOE SLICK racing tires. Recently, a competitor, Ann's Fabulous World of Speed, acquired a distributorship and also began selling JOE SLICK tires. Ann instructed her sales personnel ("Speed Consultants") to "bad-mouth" Bill's to racing clientele and other customers who came into Ann's shop. For example, Ann told the Speed Consultants to say that Bill's sold "bogus" JOE SLICK tires that were "inferior" for professional racing and should be used only "by teenagers racing on dirt tracks in Terre Haute." All of these claims were demonstrably false.

Ann's Speed Consultants made the statements to at least two dozen customers during the month of May. Bill's Racing Supplies promptly sued for false advertising under Section 43(a)(1)(B). Do the statements constitute commercial "advertising or promotion"?

(2) Same as above, except that the Speed Consultants convey the false information in the form of product reviews on Amazon.com and the like.

C. ELEMENTS OF THE SECTION 43(A)(1)(B) FALSE ADVERTISING CLAIM

UNITED INDUSTRIES CORP. v. CLOROX CO.

140 F.3d 1175 (8th Cir. 1998)

WOLLMAN, Circuit Judge:

. . .

I

Clorox and United Industries are competing producers of roach bait insecticide products. Clorox manufactures and sells Combat, the top-selling brand of roach bait, while United Industries manufactures and sells the Maxattrax brand of roach bait, a small and relatively new participant in this market. . . .

[United Industries sought a declaratory judgment that certain of its advertisements did not violate Section 43(a); Clorox counterclaimed, asserting that a specific United Industries television commercial did constitute Section 43(a) false advertising.]

The commercial at issue, entitled "Side by Side" by the advertising firm that produced it, depicts a split-screen view of two roach bait products on two kitchen countertops. The lighting is dark. On the left, one sees the Maxattrax box; on the right, a generic "Roach Bait" box that is vaguely similar to the packaging of the Combat brand sold by Clorox. An announcer asks the question: "Can you guess which bait kills roaches in 24 hours?" The lights then come up as the camera pans beyond the boxes to reveal a clean, calm, pristine kitchen, uninhabited by roaches, on the Maxattrax side. On the other side, the kitchen is in a chaotic state: cupboards and drawers are opening, items on the counter are turning over, paper towels are spinning off the dispenser, a spice rack is convulsing and losing its spices, all the apparent result of a major roach infestation. At the same time, the message "Based on lab tests" appears in small print at the bottom of the screen. The two roach bait boxes then reappear on the split-screen, and several computer-animated roaches on the "Roach Bait" side appear to kick over the generic box and dance gleefully upon it. The final visual is of the Maxattrax box only, over which the announcer concludes, "To kill roaches in 24 hours, it's hot-shot Maxattrax. Maxattrax, it's the no-wait roach bait." The final phrase is also displayed in print on the screen. The entire commercial runs fifteen seconds.

Clorox filed a motion for a preliminary injunction against this commercial. After expedited discovery and a two-day hearing, the district court denied the motion.

II

. . .

SECTION 43(A) OF THE LANHAM ACT

. . .

To establish a claim under the false or deceptive advertising prong of the Lanham Act, a plaintiff must prove: (1) a false statement of fact by the defendant in a commercial advertisement about its own or another's product; (2) the statement actually deceived or has the tendency to deceive a substantial segment of its audience; (3) the deception is material, in that it is likely to influence the purchasing decision; (4) the defendant caused its false statement to enter interstate commerce; and (5) the plaintiff has been or is likely to be injured as a result of the false statement, either by direct diversion of sales from itself to defendant or by a loss of goodwill associated with its products. *See Southland Sod Farms v. Stover Seed Co.*, 108 F.3d 1134, 1139 (9th Cir. 1997); *Johnson & Johnson-Merck Consumer Pharm. Co. v. Rhone-Poulenc Rorer Pharm., Inc.*, 19 F.3d 125, 129 (3d Cir. 1994). In addition, to recover money damages under the Act, a "[p]laintiff must prove both actual damages and a causal link between defendant's violation and those damages." *Rhone-Poulenc*, 93 F.3d at 515.

The false statement necessary to establish a Lanham Act violation generally falls into one of two categories: (1) commercial claims that are literally false as a factual matter; and (2) claims that may be literally true or ambiguous but which implicitly convey a false impression, are misleading in context, or likely to deceive consumers. *See Southland*, 108 F.3d at 1139; *National Basketball Ass'n v. Motorola, Inc.*, 105 F.3d 841, 855 (2d Cir. 1997); *Abbott Lab. v. Mead Johnson & Co.*, 971 F.2d 6, 13 (7th Cir. 1992). . . .

1.   Literally False Claims

If a plaintiff proves that a challenged claim is literally false, a court may grant relief without considering whether the buying public was actually misled; actual consumer confusion need not be proved. *See Rhone-Poulenc*, 93 F.3d at 516; *Johnson & Johnson-Merck*, 19 F.3d at 129; *McNeil-P.C.C., Inc. v. Bristol-Myers Squibb Co.*, 938 F.2d 1544, 1549 (2d Cir. 1991) (where advertisement is shown to be literally false, court may enjoin it without reference to its impact on consumers). In assessing whether an advertisement is literally false, a court must analyze the message conveyed within its full context. *See Rhone-Poulenc*, 93 F.3d at 516; *Southland*, 108 F.3d at 1139. In some circumstances, even a visual image, or a visual image combined with an audio component, may be literally false:

> We find, therefore, that the squeezing-pouring sequence in the Jenner commercial is false on its face. The visual component of the ad makes an explicit representation that Premium Pack is produced by squeezing oranges and pouring the freshly squeezed juice directly into the carton. This is not a true representation of how the product is prepared. Premium Pack juice is heated and sometimes frozen prior to packaging.

Coca-Cola Co. v. Tropicana Products, Inc., 690 F.2d 312, 318 (2d Cir. 1982); *see also Rhone-Poulenc*, 93 F.3d at 516 (drug manufacturer's advertisements featuring images such as two similar gasoline pumps or airline tickets with dramatically different prices, accompanied by slogan, "Which one would you choose?" was literally false message that competing drugs could be indiscriminately substituted). The greater the degree to which a message relies upon the viewer or consumer to integrate its components and draw the apparent conclusion, however, the less likely it is that a finding of literal falsity will be supported. Commercial claims that are implicit, attenuated, or merely suggestive usually cannot fairly be characterized as literally false.

The district court determined that the Maxattrax commercial conveyed an explicit message that the product killed roaches in 24 hours and found that this message was literally true. The court concluded that scientific testing performed both by United Industries and Clorox sufficiently demonstrated that Maxattrax, which contains the fast-acting nerve toxin known as chlorpyrifos or Dursban, will actually kill a roach within 24 hours of its coming into contact with the product. In response, Clorox argues that the district court erroneously "ignored the explicit visual statements in United's advertising that, as a matter of law, combine with its express audio statements to determine its literal meaning." Clorox contends that the Maxattrax commercial conveyed three additional explicit messages that are literally false: (1) that Maxattrax controls roach infestations in consumers' homes within 24 hours; (2) that Combat and other roach baits are entirely ineffective in consumers' homes within 24 hours; and (3) that Maxattrax provides superior performance in consumers' homes in comparison to Combat and other roach baits.

Our review of the record satisfies us that the district court's determination that the commercial was literally true is not clearly erroneous. The court was clearly correct in its assessment that the audio and print components of the advertisement are literally true. The scientific evidence and expert testimony contained in the record satisfactorily established that Maxattrax roach bait "kills roaches in 24 hours." Clorox protests that this statement is literally true only in circumstances where a particular roach actually comes into the contact with the product. This complaint rings hollow. The requirement that roaches must come into contact with the poison for it to be effective is the central premise of the roach bait line of products. We will not presume the average consumer to be incapable of comprehending the essential nature of a roach trap.

Similarly, we conclude that the district court did not err in determining that the Maxattrax commercial did not convey explicit visual messages that were literally false. The depiction of a Maxattrax box in a pristine, roach-free kitchen, coupled with the depiction of a kitchen in disarray in which animated roaches happily dance about on a generic roach trap, is not sufficient, in our view, to constitute literal falsity in the manner in which it was presented. When the context is considered as a whole, moreover, the audio component of the advertisement, emphasizing only the 24-hour time frame and quick roach kill with no mention of complete infestation control, fosters ambiguity regarding the intended message and renders the commercial much more susceptible to differing, plausible interpretations. Thus, in our view, the district court's finding that the commercial did not explicitly convey a literally false message that Maxattrax will completely control a home roach infestation within 24 hours is not clearly erroneous.

Clorox also contends that the commercial conveys an explicit message of comparative superiority that is literally false. We have recently distinguished between two types of comparative advertising claims brought under the Lanham Act: (1) "my product is better than yours" and (2) "*tests prove* that my product is better than yours." *Rhone-Poulenc*, 93 F.3d at 514 (emphasis in original). When challenging a claim of superiority that does not make express reference to testing, a plaintiff must prove that the defendant's claim of superiority is actually false, not simply unproven or unsubstantiated. *See id.* Under a "tests prove" claim, in which a defendant has buttressed a claim of superiority by attributing it to the results of scientific testing, a plaintiff must prove only "that the tests [relied upon] were not sufficiently reliable to permit one to conclude with reasonable certainty that they established the proposition for which they were cited." *Id.* at 514-15 (quoting *Castrol, Inc. v. Quaker State Corp.*, 977 F.2d 57, 62-63 (2d Cir. 1992)). However, "[t]o ensure vigorous competition and to protect legitimate commercial speech, courts applying this standard should give advertisers a fair amount of leeway, at least in the absence of a clear intent to deceive or substantial consumer confusion." *Rhone-Poulenc*, 93 F.3d at 515.

The Maxattrax commercial indicates in small print at the bottom of the screen that its implied answer to the posed question, "Can you guess which bait kills roaches in 24 hours?" is, "Based on lab tests." In order for this claim to be considered literally false, then, Clorox must establish that the tests to which the commercial referred were not sufficiently reliable to support its claims with reasonable certainty. *See id.* at 514-15. The district court determined that the scientific research provided by United Industries was reliable and supported the commercial's claims. We agree with this conclusion. Laboratory testing indicates that the toxin contained in Maxattrax kills within 24 hours those roaches that come into contact with it. Some other roach bait products will not kill a roach within that interval and, in fact, are not even intended to do so.

Any additional messages in the Maxattrax commercial perceived by Clorox, visual or otherwise, are not sufficiently explicit or unambiguous so as to constitute specific false claims of a literal nature. Thus, we cannot say that the court committed clear error in its determinations regarding the scope of the commercial's explicit claims of superiority (that it kills roaches within 24 of [sic.] hours and that a generic competitor does not), or in finding that claim to be literally true. *See L & F Products, a Div. of Sterling Winthrop, Inc. v. Procter & Gamble Co.*, 45 F.3d 709, 712 (2d Cir. 1995) (district court's determination with respect to facial falsity was not clearly erroneous).[6]

2.   *Implicitly False or Misleading Claims*

Statements that are literally true or ambiguous but which nevertheless have a tendency to mislead or deceive the consumer are actionable under the Lanham Act. *See Southland,*

---

6. Clorox places reliance on *S.C. Johnson*, 930 F. Supp. at 753, in which a district court issued a preliminary injunction against a Clorox commercial that claimed "testing proves" that its product killed 98 percent of roaches, while its competitors' products killed only 60 percent. In that case, however, the court found that these numeric, measurable claims, expressly attributed to scientific testing, were unsubstantiated and therefore literally false. *See id.* at 782-83.

108 F.3d at 1140. [cit.] Where a commercial claim is not literally false but is misleading in context, proof that the advertising actually conveyed the implied message and thereby deceived a significant portion of the recipients becomes critical. [cit.]

> If a plaintiff does not prove the claim to be literally false, he must prove that it is deceptive or misleading, which depends on the message that is conveyed to consumers. Public reaction is the measure of a commercial's impact. As the district court noted, the success of the claim usually turns on the persuasiveness of a consumer survey.

Johnson & Johnson-Merck, 19 F.3d at 129-30 (internal citations omitted).

In affirming a jury verdict awarding damages under a Lanham Act claim, we recently held that a manufacturer was not required to provide consumer surveys or reaction tests in order to prove entitlement to damages in a false comparative advertising action against its competitor where the jury found that the competitor had violated the Lanham Act willfully and in bad faith. *See Porous Media Corp. v. Pall Corp.*, 110 F.3d 1329, 1337 (8th Cir. 1997). Where, as here, there has been no finding of a willful violation or an intent to deceive, evidence of consumer impact is essential. *See William H. Morris*, 66 F.3d at 258-59; [cit.]. Therefore, unless a commercial claim is literally false, or a trier of fact has determined that a competitor acted willfully with intent to deceive or in bad faith, a party seeking relief under this section of the Lanham Act bears the ultimate burden of proving actual deception by using reliable consumer or market research. *See Smithkline Beecham*, 960 F.2d at 297 ("It is not for the judge to determine, based solely upon his or her intuitive reaction, whether the advertisement is deceptive."); [*American Tel. & Tel. Co. v. Winback & Conserve Program, Inc.*, 42 F.3d 1421 (3d Cir. 1994),] at 1443 (quoting *Sandoz*, 902 F.2d at 228-29) ("[I]t cannot obtain relief by arguing how consumers *could* react; it must show how consumers *actually* do react.").

At the preliminary injunction stage, however, full-blown consumer surveys or market research are not an absolute prerequisite, and expert testimony or other evidence may at times be sufficient to obtain preliminary injunctive relief in cases involving implicitly false or misleading claims. *See Abbott*, 971 F.2d at 15; 3 McCarthy §27:55 at 27-81 ("However, on a motion for a preliminary injunction, a survey is not always necessary and it is sufficient if plaintiff introduces expert testimony or any other evidence showing that a significant number of consumers received the claimed message from the advertisement.").

Clorox contends that when one assesses the comparative visuals and implicit messages in the commercial, a consumer might be misled to construe them as a claim that Maxattrax will completely control an infestation by killing all of the roaches in one's home within 24 hours, while its competitors will fail to do the same. In fact, Maxattrax will kill only those roaches which come into contact with the product; actual control of a roach problem may take several weeks. Whether one accepts the district court's more literal interpretation of the commercial's message or Clorox's proposed construction, however, is highly dependent upon context and inference, and Clorox's view is unsupported at this point by expert testimony, surveys, or consumer reaction evidence of any kind. It is, in other words, a classic question of fact, the resolution of which we will not disturb absent a showing of clear error by the district court. Clorox has not made such a showing.

In sum, then, the district court did not err in concluding that Clorox had not shown a likelihood of success on the merits of the claim.

. . .

[Denial of preliminary injunction motion affirmed.]

NOTES AND QUESTIONS

1. *Expressly literally false statements versus ambiguous but misleading statements.* In *Castrol Inc. v. Pennzoil Co.*, 987 F.2d 939 (3d Cir. 1993), the Third Circuit enunciated the fundamental distinction between advertisements that are "literally false" (and hence trigger liability whether or not they actually deceived or had a tendency to deceive consumers) and those that are literally true but arguably misleading (and hence trigger liability only upon a showing that they actually deceived or had a tendency to deceive consumers). How might an advocate prove—and a court analyze—literal falsity?

Judge Posner has observed that "what is 'literally' false is often a semantic question," and that it might be more effective simply to ask whether a representation is obviously, blatantly misleading. *See Schering-Plough Healthcare Prods., Inc. v. Schwarz Pharma, Inc.*, 586 F.3d 500, 512 (7th Cir. 2009). According to Judge Posner,

> [w]hat the cases mean when they say that proof of literal falsity allows the plaintiff to dispense with evidence that anyone was misled or likely to be misled is that the seller who places an indisputably false statement in his advertising or labeling probably did so for a malign purpose, namely to sell his product by lies, and if the statement is false probably at least some people were misled, and since it was a lie why waste time on costly consumer surveys? [cit.] When this is stated as the doctrine of "literal falsity," "literal" must be understood in the common colloquial sense in which Americans . . . say things like "I am literally out of my mind." A "literal" falsehood is bald-faced, egregious, undeniable, over the top.
>
> We *know* this is what the cases are driving at because they add to "literal falsity" such qualifiers as that the meaning of the alleged literal falsehood must be considered in context and with reference to the audience to which the statement is addressed. . . .
>
> The proper domain of "literal falsity" as a doctrine that dispenses with proof that anyone was misled or likely to be misled is the patently false statement that means what it says to any linguistically competent person. . . .

Id. at 512-13. Do you agree with Judge Posner's attempt to illuminate the meaning of literal falsity in this context? Is it easier to resolve cases under Judge Posner's approach?

2. *The role of survey evidence in proving (or disproving) literal falsity.* Instead of treating the question of literal falsity as a pure semantic question, should courts conduct the analysis in context, with some evidence as to how consumers would perceive the advertisement? Notice that as courts turn to contextual evidence to resolve the question of literal falsity, the distinction between literally false advertisements and literally true but misleading advertisements may become more theoretical than real. The dissenting judge in *Castrol*, questioning the wisdom of creating a separate category of literally false advertisements, argued that "consumer survey evidence is particularly relevant to the threshold determination of what message an advertisement conveys to consumers." Do you agree? If you do, can you distinguish meaningfully between literal and nonliteral falsity?

3. *Liability without confusion.* Should the Lanham Act ever impose liability in the absence of a showing of likely consumer confusion? We have seen instances in which it does—Section 43(c) dilution and Section 43(d) cybersquatting, for example. We can now add to the list Section 43(a)(1)(B) false advertising liability for literally false advertisements. Does Section 43(a)(1)(B) liability present the same concerns about awarding property rights in gross that we encountered in connection with Section 43(c)? Or is Section 43(a)(1)(B) liability inherently different?

4. *Express literal falsity: examples.* In *S.C. Johnson & Son, Inc. v. Clorox Co.*, 241 F.3d 232 (2d Cir. 2001), the court considered whether Clorox's "Goldfish I and II" television commercials and print advertisements were literally false. As the court described them:

In August 1999, Clorox introduced a 15-second and a 30-second television commercial ("Goldfish I"), each depicting an S.C. Johnson Ziploc Slide-Loc resealable storage bag side-by-side with a Clorox Glad-Lock bag. The bags are identified in the commercials by brand name. Both commercials show an animated, talking goldfish in water inside each of the bags. In the commercials, the bags are turned upside-down, and the Slide-Loc bag leaks rapidly while the Glad-Lock bag does not leak at all. In both the 15- and 30-second Goldfish I commercials, the Slide-Loc goldfish says, in clear distress, "My Ziploc slider is dripping. Wait a minute!," while the Slide Loc bag is shown leaking at a rate of approximately one drop per one to two seconds. In the 30-second Goldfish I commercial only, the Slide-Loc bag is shown leaking while the Slide-Loc goldfish says, "Excuse me, a little help here," and then, "Oh, dripping, dripping." At the end of both commercials, the Slide-Loc goldfish exclaims, "Can I borrow a cup of water!!!"

. . .

In February 2000, Clorox released a modified version of the Goldfish I television commercials as well as a related print advertisement ("Goldfish II"). In the 15-second Goldfish II television commercial, a Ziploc Slide-Loc bag and Glad-Lock bag are again shown side-by-side, filled with water and containing an animated, talking goldfish. The bags are then rotated, and a drop is shown forming and dropping in about a second from the Slide-Loc bag. During the approximately additional two seconds that it is shown, the Slide-Loc goldfish says, "My Ziploc slider is dripping. Wait a minute." The two bags are then off-screen for approximately eight seconds before the Slide-Loc bag is again shown, with a drop forming and falling in approximately one second. During this latter depiction of the Slide-Loc bag, the Slide-Loc goldfish says, "Hey, I'm gonna need a little help here." Both bags are identified by brand name, and the Glad-Lock bag does not leak at all. The second-to-last frame shows three puddles on an orange background that includes the phrase "Don't Get Mad."

In the print advertisement, a large drop is shown forming and about to fall from an upside-down Slide-Loc bag in which a goldfish is partially out of the water. Bubbles are shown rising from the point of the leak in the Slide-Loc bag. Next to the Slide-Loc bag is a Glad-Lock bag that is not leaking and contains a goldfish that is completely submerged. Under the Slide-Loc bag appears: "Yikes! My Ziploc© Slide-Loc™ is dripping!" Under the Glad-Lock bag is printed: "My Glad is tight, tight, tight." On a third panel, three puddles and the words "Don't Get Mad" are depicted on a red background. In a fourth panel, the advertisement recites: "Only Glad has the Double-Lock™ green seal. That's why you'll be glad you got Glad. Especially if you're a goldfish."

Id. at 234-36. S.C. Johnson's expert testified that he tested the Slide-Loc bags by filling them with water, rotating them for ten seconds, and holding them upside down for twenty seconds; the tests showed that 37 percent of the tested bags did not leak at all, and of the remainder, most leaked "at a rate between two and twenty times slower than that depicted in the Goldfish I commercials." Only a "small percentage" of the tested bags leaked at a rate that compared with depictions in the Goldfish I commercials. On the basis of this evidence, should a court find literal falsity? *Cf. Innovation Ventures, LLC v. N.V.E., Inc.*, 694 F.3d 723, 735-37 (6th Cir. 2012) (presenting a "close question" as to literal falsity).

5. *Literal falsity by necessary implication: standard.* In determining what constitutes a "literally false" statement, should courts include only *expressly* literally false statements, or should they also include statements that are literally false by necessary implication? *See Novartis Consumer Health, Inc. v. Johnson & Johnson-Merck Consumer Pharm. Co.*, 290 F.3d 578, 586-87 (3d Cir. 2002) ("A 'literally false' message may be either explicit or 'conveyed by necessary implication when, considering the advertisement in its entirety, the audience would recognize the claim as readily as if it had been explicitly stated.'") (citing *Clorox Co. v. Procter & Gamble Commercial Co.*, 228 F.3d 24, 35 (1st Cir. 2000)).

In *Time Warner Cable, Inc. v. DirecTV, Inc.*, 497 F.3d 144 (2d Cir. 2007), a Second Circuit panel approved of the doctrine of literal falsity by necessary implication. As the Second Circuit saw it, the doctrine required that courts analyze the alleged literal falsity of the advertisement by considering "the message conveyed in full context" (quoting *Castrol Inc. v. Pennzoil Co.*, 987 F.2d 939, 946 (3d Cir. 1993)) and by avoiding any "disputatious dissection" (quoting *Avis Rent A Car Sys., Inc. v. Hertz Corp.*, 782 F.2d 381, 385 (2d Cir. 1986)). The Second Circuit also warned that only "unambiguous" advertisements could be deemed literally false, so that "if the language or graphic is susceptible to more than one reasonable interpretation, the advertisement cannot be literally false," and the court must look to consumer data. *Time Warner Cable*, 497 F.3d at 158.

By recognizing a doctrine of literal falsity by necessary implication, do courts threaten the integrity of the dichotomy between literally false statements and ambiguous but misleading statements? In particular, in attempting to apply this doctrine, will courts be able to distinguish satisfactorily between statements that are literally false by necessary implication and statements that are ambiguous but misleading?

What evidence would you find helpful in determining whether a statement in an advertisement is literally false by necessary implication? Evidence of consumers' actual or likely reaction to the statements? Isn't this the very evidence—evidence of deception—that is presumed to exist once we conclude that a statement is literally false? *See Hickson Corp. v. N. Crossarm Co.*, 357 F.3d 1256, 1261 (11th Cir. 2004) (requiring "evidence of deception" in the form of "consumer surveys, market research, expert testimony, or other evidence"). A Second Circuit case indicates that in cases of implied falsity where there is also evidence of the advertiser's intent to deceive, the court may presume consumer deception and shift to the advertiser the burden of overcoming this presumption with evidence showing the absence of deception. *Merck Eprova AG v. Gnosis S.p.A.*, 760 F.3d 247 (2d Cir. 2014).

6. *Literal falsity by necessary implication: examples.* The court in *Novartis Consumer Health, Inc. v. Johnson & Johnson-Merck Consumer Pharm. Co.*, 290 F.3d 578, 587-88 (3d Cir. 2002), discussed a number of examples in which courts concluded that an advertiser's statements were literally false by necessary implication:

> [I]n *Breathasure* [*Warner-Lambert Co. v. Breathasure, Inc.*, 204 F.3d 87 (3d Cir. 2000)], the defendant claimed that its capsules would freshen breath when swallowed, and that they were more effective at freshening breath than other products like gum, mints, and mouthwash because the capsule would "[f]ight the problem at its source." *Breathasure*, 204 F.3d at 89. During the course of litigation it became clear that the capsules had no effect on bad breath because in fact bad breath originates in the mouth, not in the stomach. *See id.* at 90. The District Court found that the BreathAsure product claim was therefore misleading because it "implie[d] assurance where there [was] no basis for it," and we concurred. *Id.* at 96. In addition, because "[t]he name [BreathAsure] falsely tells the consumer that he or she has assurance of fresher breath . . . ," *id.* at 97, we enjoined use of that name.
>
> In *Castrol* [*Castrol Inc. v. Pennzoil Co.*, 987 F.2d 939 (3d Cir. 1993)], the defendant's advertisements claimed that motor oil viscosity breakdown leads to engine failure. The advertising also claimed that the defendant's brand of motor oil outperformed any leading motor oil against viscosity breakdown. We affirmed the District Court's conclusion that these two claims taken together necessarily implied that "Pennzoil outperforms the other leading brands with respect to protecting against engine failure, because it outperforms them in protecting against viscosity breakdown, the cause of engine failure." *Castrol*, 987 F.2d at 947. Because this implied message of superior protection against engine failure was false, the defendant, Pennzoil, was permanently enjoined from using these challenged advertisements. *See id.* at 948.
>
> In *Cuisinarts* [*Cuisinarts, Inc. v. Robot-Coupe Int'l Corp.*, 1982 WL 121559 (S.D.N.Y. June 9, 1982)], the defendant's advertisement stated: "Robot-Coupe: 21, Cuisinart: 0. WHEN ALL 21 OF THE THREE-STAR RESTAURANTS IN FRANCE'S MICHELIN GUIDE CHOOSE THE SAME PROFESSIONAL MODEL FOOD PROCESSOR, SOMEBODY KNOWS THE SCORE—SHOULDN'T YOU?" *Cuisinarts*, 1982 WL 121559, at *2. The District Court for the Southern District of New York found that the advertisement necessarily implied a message that both Robot-Coupe and Cuisinart built professional model food processors and that restaurateurs presented with two existing alternatives had chosen the Robot-Coupe model. This implied message was false because Cuisinart did not in fact make a professional model food processor. The Court therefore issued a preliminary injunction prohibiting the use of this advertisement. *See id.* at *2-3.

Do these examples illuminate what courts mean by literal falsity by necessary implication? Or do they demonstrate that the concept resists easy definition?

7. *Literally true, but ambiguous and misleading: proof by survey evidence.* On the question of whether consumer survey evidence is important to the threshold determination of what message an advertisement conveys (especially when the allegation is that the statement is literally true but misleading), *see Pernod Ricard USA, LLC v. Bacardi U.S.A., Inc.*, 653 F.3d 241 (3d Cir. 2011). The case involved Bacardi's HAVANA CLUB rum. The bottle's label says "Puerto Rican Rum" on the front, and elsewhere says that the rum is "distilled and crafted in Puerto Rico," which, we understand, is a literally true statement. Pernod sued for false advertising, claiming that the label misleadingly implied that the rum was made in Havana (when, in fact, the rum was made in Puerto Rico, albeit from a recipe that originated in Havana). Pernod submitted a consumer survey that allegedly supported its view. The district court determined that it need not consider the survey, and the Third Circuit agreed. According to the Third Circuit, when the words "Havana Club" were read in the context of the entire label, including the references to Puerto Rico, no reasonable consumer could be misled into thinking that the rum was manufactured in Havana. Under such circumstances, "a district court can properly disregard survey evidence as immaterial, because, by definition, §43(a)(1) does not forbid language that reasonable people would have to acknowledge is not false or misleading. . . . A contrary holding would not only be out of keeping with the language of §43(a)(1), it would undermine the purpose of subsection (a)(1)(B) by subjecting advertisers to a level of risk at odds with consumer protection." *Id.* at 253-54. Do you agree with the court's approach? The court acknowledged that its rule might appear to give "license to lightly disregard survey evidence about consumer reactions to challenged advertisements." *Id.* at 254. The court cautioned that:

> [b]efore a defendant or a district judge decides that an advertisement could not mislead a reasonable person, serious care must be exercised to avoid the temptation of thinking, "my way of seeing this is naturally the only reasonable way." Thoughtful reflection on potential ambiguities in an advertisement, which can be revealed by surveys and will certainly be pointed out by plaintiffs, will regularly make it the wisest course to consider survey evidence.

Id. at 254-55. Does this allay any concerns you might have about the court's rule—or does it magnify them?

8. *Falsity versus lack of substantiation.* In deciding the falsity element of a false advertising claim, should a court presume that consumers always expect that advertisers have some substantiation for the claims in their advertisements? Consider the implications of such a presumption. Suppose that firm *A*, a soft-drink producer, alleges that statements in firm *B*'s advertisements are false under Section 43(a)(1)(B). Firm *B* presents no evidence of any substantiation for the statements. Should a court hold that firm *A* has met its burden of proving falsity under the first prong of the false advertising test, on the ground that consumers expect that substantiation exists, so that a completely unsubstantiated statement is per se misleading to consumers? In *Novartis Consumer Health, Inc. v. Johnson & Johnson-Merck Consumer Pharm. Co.*, 290 F.3d 578, 590 (3d Cir. 2002), the court held that "although the plaintiff normally has the burden to demonstrate that the defendant's advertising claim is false, a court may find that a completely unsubstantiated advertising claim by the defendant is *per se* false without additional evidence from the plaintiff to that effect." Should the *Novartis* exception be read narrowly to apply only when the defendant declines to submit any evidence in support of the allegedly false advertisement, to guard against the exception swallowing the rule? Or could it apply in a case where the defendant does submit some evidence, but the evidence is not persuasive? *See Groupe SEB USA, Inc. v. Euro-Pro Operating LLC*, 744 F.3d 192 (3d Cir. 2014) (adopting the latter approach).

9. *Truth and falsity of comparative statements.* Comparative statements are so ubiquitous in advertising that some courts have developed tests for analyzing the truth or falsity of specific types of comparisons. In the *Clorox* case, the court distinguished between "better than" comparisons and "tests prove" comparisons, and indicated that "tests prove" comparisons will be viewed with greater suspicion—meaning that the plaintiff's burden of showing falsity is more easily met in those cases. *See also C.B. Fleet Co. v. SmithKline Beecham Consumer Healthcare, L.P.*, 131 F.3d 430, 435-36 (4th Cir. 1997) (designating the distinction between "better than" and "tests prove" claims a question of fact, and concluding that in the absence of an express assertion of test validation in the advertisement, the claim should be treated as a "better than" claim). Do you agree with this approach? Are there other categories of comparative statements that courts should recognize?

The impulse to scrutinize comparative statements closely must be counterbalanced against free speech values. As we saw in the *Chanel* case in Chapter 9, courts have recognized that *true* comparative statements in advertisements receive broad protection from Lanham Act liability, either as "fair uses" or sometimes under the specific label of a fair "comparative advertising" defense.

PROBLEM 10-3:   THIS CASEBOOK ROCKS

Aspen Publishers, the publisher of this casebook, routinely sends out tasteful and professionally prepared flyers to law professors to advertise the arrival of new casebooks. Professors Dinwoodie and Janis proposed the following ad text for the flyer advertising this casebook:

> "Two thumbs up . . . way up!! Bring on the sequel!" — *Good Morning America*
> "The blockbuster hit of the year! A sure-fire winner." — *Wall Street Journal*
> "Gutsy—compelling—intense—a white-knuckle roller coaster ride!" — *Rolling Stone*
> "Quite possibly Dinwoodie and Janis' best performance! Stunning!" — *Entertainment Tonight*
> "Dinwoodie and Janis have put the 'fun' back in 'functionality'!" — *People*

When Aspen's crack production team raised its collective eyebrows, Dinwoodie and Janis admitted that the testimonials were "patently false." Asked for their legal opinion as to the likelihood that Aspen would be sued by competing publishers under Section 43(a) for false advertising, Dinwoodie and Janis said, "Nah." (Actually, only Janis, a Hoosier, said, "Nah." Dinwoodie, who is Scottish, said, "Nae.") Read the next case, and then decide whether Aspen (or Dinwoodie and Janis) should be concerned.

PIZZA HUT, INC. v. PAPA JOHN'S INTERNATIONAL, INC.

227 F.3d 489 (5th Cir. 2000), cert. denied, 532 U.S. 920 (2001)

JOLLY, Circuit Judge:

. . .

I

A

Pizza Hut is a wholly owned subsidiary of Tricon Global Restaurants. With over 7000 restaurants (both company and franchisee-owned), Pizza Hut is the largest pizza chain in the United States. In 1984, John Schnatter founded Papa John's Pizza in the back of his father's tavern. Papa John's has grown to over 2050 locations, making it the third largest pizza chain in the United States.

In May 1995, Papa John's adopted a new slogan: "Better Ingredients. Better Pizza." In 1996, Papa John's filed for a federal trademark registration for this slogan with the United States Patent & Trademark Office ("PTO"). Its application for registration was ultimately granted by the PTO. Since 1995, Papa John's has invested over $300 million building customer goodwill in its trademark "Better Ingredients. Better Pizza." The slogan has appeared on millions of signs, shirts, menus, pizza boxes, napkins and other items, and has regularly appeared as the "tag line" at the end of Papa John's radio and television ads, or with the company logo in printed advertising.

On May 1, 1997, Pizza Hut launched its "Totally New Pizza" campaign. This campaign was the culmination of "Operation Lightning Bolt," a nine-month, $50 million project in which Pizza Hut declared "war" on poor quality pizza. From the deck of a World War II aircraft carrier, Pizza Hut's president, David Novak, declared "war" on "skimpy, low quality pizza." National ads aired during this campaign touted the "better taste" of Pizza Hut's pizza, and "dared" anyone to find a "better pizza."

In early May 1997, Papa John's launched its first national ad campaign. The campaign was directed towards Pizza Hut, and its "Totally New Pizza" campaign. In a pair of TV ads featuring Pizza Hut's co-founder Frank Carney, Carney touted the superiority of Papa John's pizza over Pizza Hut's pizza. Although Carney had left the pizza business in the 1980's, he returned as a franchisee of Papa John's because he liked the taste of Papa John's pizza better than any other pizza on the market. The ad campaign was remarkably successful. During May 1997, Papa John's sales increased 11.7 percent over May 1996 sales, while Pizza Hut's sales were down 8 percent.

. . .

Papa John's [also] ran a series of ads comparing specific ingredients used in its pizzas with those used by its "competitors." During the course of these ads, Papa John's touted the superiority of its sauce and its dough. During the sauce campaign, Papa John's asserted that its sauce was made from "fresh, vine-ripened tomatoes," which were canned through a process called "fresh pack," while its competitors—including Pizza Hut—make their sauce from remanufactured tomato paste. During the dough campaign, Papa John's stated that it used "clear filtered water" to make its pizza dough, while the "biggest chain" uses "whatever comes out of the tap." Additionally, Papa John's asserted that it gives its yeast "several days to work its magic," while "some folks" use "frozen dough or dough made the same day." At or near the close of each of these ads, Papa John's punctuated its ingredient comparisons with the slogan "Better Ingredients. Better Pizza."

Pizza Hut does not appear to contest the truthfulness of the underlying factual assertions made by Papa John's in the course of these ads. Pizza Hut argues, however, that its own independent taste tests and other "scientific evidence" establishes that filtered water makes no difference in pizza dough, that there is no "taste" difference between Papa John's "fresh-pack" sauce and Pizza Hut's "remanufactured" sauce, and that fresh dough is not superior to frozen dough. In response to Pizza Hut's "scientific evidence," Papa John's asserts that "each of these 'claims' involves a matter of common sense choice (fresh versus frozen, canned vegetables and fruit versus remanufactured paste, and filtered versus unfiltered water) about which individual consumers can and do form preferences every day without 'scientific' or 'expert' assistance."

In November 1997, Pizza Hut filed a complaint regarding Papa John's "Better Ingredients. Better Pizza." advertising campaign with the National Advertising Division of the Better Business Bureau, an industry self-regulatory body. This complaint, however, did not produce satisfactory results for Pizza Hut.

B

On August 12, 1998, Pizza Hut filed a civil action in the United States District Court for the Northern District of Texas charging Papa John's with false advertising in violation of Section 43(a)(1)(B) of the Lanham Act. The suit sought relief based on the above described TV ad campaigns, as well as on some 249 print ads. . . .

. . .

[The district court submitted the liability issue to the jury through several special interrogatories, including one inquiring whether the slogan "Better Ingredients. Better Pizza." gave rise to liability. The jury found that it did. Reviewing the verdict, the district court determined that the slogan alone constituted non-actionable "puffery," but nevertheless found for Pizza Hut on other grounds. Papa John's appealed.]

III

. . .

B

(1)

(a)

Essential to any claim under Section 43(a) of the Lanham Act is a determination of whether the challenged statement is one of fact—actionable under Section 43(a)—or one of general opinion—not actionable under Section 43(a). Bald assertions of superiority or general statements of opinion cannot form the basis of Lanham Act liability. *See Presidio Enters., Inc. v. Warner Bros. Distrib. Corp.*, 784 F.2d 674, 685 (5th Cir. 1986); *Groden v. Random House, Inc.*, 61 F.3d 1045, 1051 (2d Cir. 1995) (citing Restatement (Third) of Unfair Competition §3 (1993)). Rather the statements at issue must be a "specific and measurable claim, capable of being proved false or of being reasonably interpreted as a statement of objective fact." *Coastal Abstract Serv., Inc. v. First Am. Title Ins. Co.*, 173 F.3d 725, 731 (9th Cir. 1999); *see also American Council*, 185 F.3d at 614 (stating that "a Lanham Act claim must be based upon a statement of fact, not of opinion"). As noted by our court in *Presidio*: "[A] statement of fact is one that (1) admits of being adjudged true or false in a way that (2) admits of empirical verification." *Presidio*, 784 F.2d at 679; *see also Southland Sod Farms v. Stover Seed Co.*, 108 F.3d 1134, 1145 (9th Cir. 1997) (stating that in order to constitute a statement of fact, a statement must make "a specific and measurable advertisement claim of product superiority").

(b)

One form of non-actionable statements of general opinion under section 43(a) of the Lanham Act has been referred to as "puffery." Puffery has been discussed at some length by other circuits. The Third Circuit has described "puffing" as "advertising that is not deceptive for no one would rely on its exaggerated claims." *U.S. Healthcare, Inc. v. Blue Cross of Greater Philadelphia*, 898 F.2d 914 (3d Cir. 1990). Similarly, the Ninth Circuit has defined "puffing" as "exaggerated advertising, blustering and boasting upon which no reasonable buyer would rely and is not actionable under 43(a)." *Southland Sod Farms v. Stover Seed Co.*, 108 F.3d 1134, 1145 (9th Cir. 1997) (quoting 3 J. Thomas McCarthy, McCarthy on Trademarks and Unfair Competition §27.04[4][d] (3d ed. 1994)); *see also Cook*, 911 F.2d at 246 (stating that "[p]uffing has been described by most courts as involving outrageous generalized statements, not making specific claims, that are so exaggerated as to preclude reliance by consumers").[6]

These definitions of puffery are consistent with the definitions provided by the leading commentaries in trademark law. A leading authority on unfair competition has defined "puffery" as an "exaggerated advertising, blustering, and boasting upon which no reasonable buyer would rely," or "a general claim of superiority over a comparative product that is so vague, it would be understood as a mere expression of opinion." 4 J. Thomas McCarthy, McCarthy on Trademarks and Unfair Competition §27.38 (4th ed. 1996).[7] Similarly, Prosser and Keeton on Torts defines "puffing" as "a seller's privilege to lie his head off, so long as he says nothing specific, on the theory that no reasonable man would believe him, or that no reasonable man would be influenced by such talk." W. Page Keeton, et al., Prosser and Keeton on the Law of Torts §109, at 757 (5th ed. 1984).

Drawing guidance from the writings of our sister circuits and the leading commentators, we think that non-actionable "puffery" comes in at least two possible forms: (1) an exaggerated, blustering, and boasting statement upon which no reasonable buyer would be justified in relying; or (2) a general claim of superiority over comparable products that is so vague that it can be understood as nothing more than a mere expression of opinion.

. . .

IV

We turn now to consider the case before us. Reduced to its essence, the question is whether the evidence, viewed in the most favorable light to Pizza Hut, established that Papa John's slogan "Better Ingredients. Better Pizza." is misleading and violative of section 43(a) of the Lanham Act. In making this determination, we will first consider the slogan "Better Ingredients. Better Pizza." standing alone to determine if it is a statement of fact capable of deceiving a substantial segment of the consuming public to which it was directed. . . .

A

The jury concluded that the slogan itself was a "false or misleading" statement of fact, and the district court enjoined its further use. Papa John's argues, however, that this statement "quite simply is not a statement of fact, [but] rather, a statement of belief or opinion, and an argumentative one at that." Papa John's asserts that because "a statement of fact is either true or false, it is susceptible to being proved or disproved. A statement of opinion or belief, on the other hand, conveys the speaker's state of mind, and even though it may be used to attempt to persuade the listener, it is a subjective communication that may be accepted or rejected, but not proven true or false." Papa John's contends that its slogan "Better Ingredients. Better Pizza." falls into the latter category, and because the phrases

---

6. In the same vein, the Second Circuit has observed that "statements of opinion are generally not the basis for Lanham Act liability." *Groden v. Random House*, 61 F.3d 1045, 1051 (2d Cir. 1995). When a statement is "obviously a statement of opinion," it cannot "reasonably be seen as stating or implying provable facts." *Id.* "The Lanham Act does not prohibit false statements generally. It prohibits only false or misleading description or false or misleading representations of fact made about one's own or another's goods or services." *Id.* at 1052.

7. McCarthy on Trademarks goes on to state: "[V]ague advertising claims that one's product is 'better' than that of competitors' can be dismissed as mere puffing that is not actionable as false advertising." 4 J. Thomas McCarthy, McCarthy on Trademarks and Unfair Competition §27:38 (4th ed. 1997).

"better ingredients" and "better pizza" are not subject to quantifiable measures, the slogan is non-actionable puffery.

We will therefore consider whether the slogan standing alone constitutes a statement of fact under the Lanham Act. Bisecting the slogan "Better Ingredients. Better Pizza.," it is clear that the assertion by Papa John's that it makes a "Better Pizza." is a general statement of opinion regarding the superiority of its product over all others. This simple statement, "Better Pizza.," epitomizes the exaggerated advertising, blustering, and boasting by a manufacturer upon which no consumer would reasonably rely. *See, e.g., In re Boston Beer Co.*, 198 F.3d 1370, 1372 (Fed. Cir. 1999) (stating that the phrase "The Best Beer in America" was "trade puffery" and that such a general claim of superiority "should be freely available to all competitors in any given field to refer to their products or services"); *Atari Corp. v. 3DO Co.*, 1994 WL 723601, *2 (N.D. Cal. 1994) (stating that a manufacturer's slogan that its product was "the most advanced home gaming system in the universe" was non-actionable puffery); *Nikkal Indus., Ltd. v. Salton, Inc.*, 735 F. Supp. 1227, 1234 n.3 (S.D.N.Y. 1990) (stating that a manufacturer's claim that its ice cream maker was "better" than competition ice cream makers is non-actionable puffery). Consequently, it appears indisputable that Papa John's assertion "Better Pizza." is non-actionable puffery.[8]

Moving next to consider separately the phrase "Better Ingredients.," the same conclusion holds true. Like "Better Pizza.," it is typical puffery. The word "better," when used in this context, is unquantifiable. What makes one food ingredient "better" than another comparable ingredient, without further description, is wholly a matter of individual taste or preference not subject to scientific quantification. Indeed, it is difficult to think of any product, or any component of any product, to which the term "better," without more, is quantifiable. As our court stated in *Presidio*:

> The law recognizes that a vendor is allowed some latitude in claiming merits of his wares by way of an opinion rather than an absolute guarantee, so long as he hews to the line of rectitude in matters of fact. Opinions are not only the lifestyle of democracy, they are the brag in advertising that has made for the wide dissemination of products that otherwise would never have reached the households of our citizens. If we were to accept the thesis set forth by the appellees, [that all statements by advertisers were statements of fact actionable under the Lanham Act,] the advertising industry would have to be liquidated in short order.

Presidio, 784 F.2d at 685. Thus, it is equally clear that Papa John's assertion that it uses "Better Ingredients." is one of opinion not actionable under the Lanham Act.

Finally, turning to the combination of the two non-actionable phrases as the slogan "Better Ingredients. Better Pizza.," we fail to see how the mere joining of these two statements of opinion could create an actionable statement of fact. Each half of the slogan amounts to little more than an exaggerated opinion of superiority that no consumer would be justified in relying upon. It has not been explained convincingly to us how the combination of the two phrases, without more, changes the essential nature of each phrase so as to make it actionable. We assume that "Better Ingredients." modifies "Better Pizza." and consequently gives some expanded meaning to the phrase "Better Pizza," i.e., our pizza is better because our ingredients are better. Nevertheless, the phrase fails to give "Better Pizza." any more quantifiable meaning. Stated differently, the adjective that continues to

---

8. It should be noted that Pizza Hut uses the slogan "The Best Pizza Under One Roof." Similarly, other nationwide pizza chains employ slogans touting their pizza as the "best": (1) Domino's Pizza uses the slogan "Nobody Delivers Better."; (2) Danato's uses the slogan "Best Pizza on the Block."; (3) Mr. Gatti's uses the slogan "Best Pizza in Town: Honest!"; and (4) Pizza Inn uses the slogans "Best Pizza Ever." and "The Best Tasting Pizza."

describe "pizza" is "better," a term that remains unquantifiable, especially when applied to the sense of taste. Consequently, the slogan as a whole is a statement of non-actionable opinion. Thus, there is no legally sufficient basis to support the jury's finding that the slogan standing alone is a "false or misleading" statement of fact.

. . .

Reversed, vacated, and remanded for entry of judgment for Papa John's.

NOTES AND QUESTIONS

1. *Whose burden?* Does the defendant advertiser bear the burden of proving facts to establish that statements in the advertisement constitute non-actionable puffery? Or does the false advertising plaintiff bear the burden of showing that the challenged statements are *not* puffery, as part of the requirement to show that the challenged statements are statements "of fact"?

2. *Proving puffery.* In *Pizza Hut*, the court did not point to specific items of evidence in its review of the jury's determination as to puffery. Indeed, the appellate court seemed to have performed its own linguistic analysis. If you were representing a party in a false advertising case where puffery was at issue, what evidence would you offer? Consumer perception surveys? Dictionary definitions of the phrases at issue? Both?

Suppose that survey evidence on puffery points against finding puffery, and dictionary evidence points in the other direction. As a policy matter, should a court favor one type of evidence over the other? Or should both types of evidence be considered probative, and the issue resolved by weighing the evidence? As you analyze this matter, consider the following argument against the use of survey evidence to establish puffery:

> To allow a consumer survey to determine a claim's benchmark would subject any advertisement or promotional statement to numerous variables, often unpredictable, and would introduce even more uncertainty into the market place. A manufacturer or advertiser who expended significant resources to substantiate a statement or forge a puffing statement could be blindsided by a consumer survey that defines the advertising statement differently, subjecting the advertiser or manufacturer to unintended liability for a wholly unanticipated claim the advertisement's plain language would not support. The resulting unpredictability could chill commercial speech, eliminating useful claims from packaging and advertisements. As the Seventh Circuit noted, the Lanham Act protects against misleading and false statements of fact, not misunderstood statements. [*Mead Johnson & Co. v. Abbott Laboratories*, 201 F.3d 883, 886 (7th Cir.), *amended*, 209 F.3d 1032 (7th Cir. 2000).]

Am. Italian Pasta Co. v. New World Pasta Co., 371 F.3d 387, 393-94 (8th Cir. 2004).

Do you agree with the argument? Do you agree with the court's general pronouncement in the last quoted sentence? For relevant commentary, *see* Richard J. Leighton, *Making Puffery Determinations in Lanham Act False Advertising Cases: Surveys, Dictionaries, Judicial Edicts, and Materiality Tests*, 95 TRADEMARK REP. 615 (2005); Richard J. Leighton, *Materiality and Puffing in Lanham Act False Advertising Cases: The Proofs, Presumptions, and Pretexts*, 94 TRADEMARK REP. 585, 616-33 (2004).

3. *Taint?* Can a statement that is insulated from liability as "puffery" in one context be tainted—and lose its insulation from liability—if placed alongside other, admittedly false statements? Suppose that the slogan "Better Ingredients. Better Pizza." appears in numerous Papa John's advertisements. In many of the print advertisements the slogan simply appears alongside menu and location information. However, suppose that the slogan also appears as a tagline in a few of Papa John's television commercials, and that these commercials contain statements that have been determined to be "false" in the sense of Section

43(a)(1)(B) (i.e., they are either literally false, or literally true but misleading). What is the effect, if any, on your analysis of Papa John's "puffery" defense? Should the false statements be considered to "taint" the slogan? If there is a "taint," does it justify an injunction (or damages award) directed at all uses of the slogan, or just those uses in connection with the false television ads?

4. *Being careful what you ask for. . .* From a litigation perspective, puffery may appear to be an attractive defense against false advertising claims. But from a business perspective, how attractive is it for Papa John's to establish in court that its claim of "Better Ingredients. Better Pizza." is mere exaggerated bluster? In a television commercial that aired in early 2010, Papa John's competitor Domino's mocked Papa John's for admitting that the "Better Ingredients. Better Pizza." slogan was puffery. The spot featured shots of the courthouse where the Fifth Circuit sits, depicted a "lawyer" reading a definition of puffery, and claimed that Domino's descriptions of its own pizza certainly were *not* puffery. Ouch.

5. *Puffery: examples.* For additional examples of litigation over the "puffery" issue, *see, e.g., Verisign, Inc. v. XYZ.Com LLC*, 848 F.3d 292 (4th Cir. 2017) (statements by XYZ. Com that "all of the good [.com] real estate is taken," and similar statements, constituted puffery); *Hall v. Bed Bath & Beyond, Inc.*, 705 F.3d 1357, 1368 (Fed. Cir. 2013) (advertising that a towel had "performance that lasts the useful lifetime of the towel"); *id.* at 1374 (Lourie, J., dissenting); *Newcal Indus., Inc. v. Ikon Office Solution*, 513 F.3d 1038 (9th Cir. 2008) (advertising that Ikon could deliver "flexibility" in its customer contracts and lower photocopying costs for customers); *Southland Sod Farms v. Stover Seed Co.*, 108 F.3d 1134 (9th Cir. 1997) (advertising grass seed as "Less is More," and advertising that grass required "50% less mowing"); *Syncsort Inc. v. Sequential Software, Inc.*, 50 F. Supp. 2d 318 (D.N.J. 1999) (advertising software as "the fastest commercial sort product in the world"). You have undoubtedly encountered countless other examples. For example, what of the once-famous beer slogan TASTES GREAT; LESS FILLING?

CASHMERE & CAMEL HAIR MFRS. INST. v. SAKS FIFTH AVENUE

284 F.3d 302 (1st Cir. 2002)

TORRUELLA, Circuit Judge:

. . .

BACKGROUND

The Institute is a trade association of cashmere manufacturers dedicated to preserving the name and reputation of cashmere as a speciality fiber. [Co-plaintiff] Packard is a member of the Institute and a manufacturer of cashmere and cashmere-blend fabric.

In 1993, defendant-appellee Harve Benard, Ltd. ("Harve Benard") began manufacturing a line of women's blazers that were labeled as containing 70 percent wool, 20 percent nylon, and 10 percent cashmere. Its labels also portrayed the blazers as "A Luxurious Blend of Cashmere and Wool," "Cashmere and Wool," or "Wool and Cashmere." Harve Benard sold large quantities of these cashmere-blend garments to retail customers, including defendants Saks Fifth Avenue ("Saks") and Filene's Basement.

In 1995, plaintiffs began purchasing random samples of the Harve Benard garments and giving them to Professor Kenneth Langley and Dr. Franz-Josef Wortmann, experts in the field of cashmere identification and textile analysis. After conducting separate tests on the samples, the experts independently concluded that, despite Harve Benard's labels to the contrary, the garments contained no cashmere. In addition, Dr. Wortmann found that approximately 10 to 20% of the fibers in the Harve Benard garments were recycled—that is, reconstituted from the deconstructed and chemically-stripped remnants of previously used or woven garments.

Relying on their experts' findings, plaintiffs filed this suit in district court claiming that defendants falsely advertised their garments in violation of §43(a) of the Lanham Act, 15 U.S.C. §1125(a), the Massachusetts Unfair and Deceptive Trade Practices Act, Mass. Gen. Laws ch. 93A, and the common law of unfair competition. More specifically, plaintiffs claim that the garments were mislabeled in two material respects: (1) the Harve Benard blazers contained significantly less than the 10% cashmere they were represented as having ("cashmere content claim"); and (2) any cashmere that the blazers did contain was not virgin, as the unqualified word "cashmere" on the label suggests, but recycled ("recycled cashmere claim"). . . .

[The Institute sought an injunction against future mislabeling; Packard sought damages for alleged lost sales caused by the mislabeling. The district court granted summary judgment in favor of defendants, and plaintiff appealed. For purposes of appeal, defendants conceded that there were genuine issues of material fact concerning prong (1) of the analysis, whether the advertising statements were false statements of fact, and prong (4), whether the statements had been placed into interstate commerce. However, as to the remaining elements of the false advertising claim, defendants argued that plaintiffs had not raised a genuine issue of material fact. The court analyzed those remaining elements of the claim in its discussion below.]

DISCUSSION

II

. . .

B. *Materiality*

The materiality component of a false advertising claim requires a plaintiff to prove that the defendant's deception is "likely to influence the purchasing decision." *Clorox*, 228 F.3d at 33 n.6. One method of establishing materiality involves showing that the false or misleading statement relates to an "inherent quality or characteristic" of the product. *Nat'l Basketball Ass'n v. Motorola, Inc.*, 105 F.3d 841, 855 (2d Cir. 1997).[10]

On their first claim, plaintiffs argue that overstating the cashmere content of cashmere-blend blazers is material because the misrepresentation relates to an inherent characteristic of the product sold. Indeed, it seems obvious that cashmere is a basic ingredient of a cashmere-blend garment; without it, the product could not be deemed a cashmere-blend garment or compete in the cashmere-blend market. Thus, it seems reasonable to conclude that defendants' misrepresentation of the blazers' cashmere content is material because it relates to a characteristic that defines the product at issue, as well as the market in which it is sold.

Moreover, defendants prominently labeled their garments as "Cashmere and Wool," "A Luxurious Blend of Cashmere and Wool," "Cashmere Blend," or "Wool and Cashmere,"

---

10. Whether a misrepresentation is material has nothing to do with the nature of the relief sought or the defendant's intent. Rather, materiality focuses on whether the false or misleading statement is likely to make a difference to purchasers. *See* 4 J. Thomas McCarthy, McCarthy on Trademarks and Unfair Competition §27:35 (4th ed. 2001). Thus, even when a statement is literally false or has been made with the intent to deceive, materiality must be demonstrated in order to show that the misrepresentation had some influence on consumers.

and their garments were conspicuously advertised in stores and catalogues as "Cashmere Blazers." It seems reasonable to infer from defendants' aggressive marketing strategy highlighting the "cashmere" nature of the blazers that defendants themselves believed cashmere to be an inherent and important characteristic of the blazers.

With respect to their second claim, plaintiffs argue that defendants' misrepresentation of the recycled nature of their cashmere also relates to an inherent characteristic of the garments. To substantiate this point, plaintiffs offer the affidavit of Karl Spilhaus, the Institute's president, in which he explains:

> The process of recycling . . . involves the use of machinery to tear apart existing garments, during or after which they are subjected to a wet processing with the resulting wool fibers dried out, frequently carbonized (subjected to heat and sulphuric acid), and then re-used in the manufacture of other fabric.
>
> In the process of tearing apart existing garments, considerable damage is inevitably done to the fibers in those garments, and additional damage is also done by the acid or other chemical treatments applied to them during the recycling process. The result is that recycled fibers frequently have substantial surface damage to their scale structure which effects [sic] their ability to felt, or bind together, thereby effecting [sic] the ability of a recycled fiber fabric to hold together as well or as long as fibers which are being used in the fabric for the first time. Such fabric will be rougher to the touch and lack "handle," plushness or softness normally associated with quality woolen or cashmere products.

Given the degree to which recycled fibers affect the quality and characteristics of a garment, a rational factfinder could conclude that consumers, especially experienced ones like retail stores, would likely be influenced in their purchasing decisions by labeling that gave the false impression that the garments contained virgin cashmere.[11]

In fact, plaintiffs offer anecdotal evidence as corroboration for this very assertion. In January 1996, Saks, one of Harve Benard's largest customers, learned that the cashmere blazers it had purchased from Harve Benard might contain recycled cashmere. Shortly thereafter, Lynne Ronon, the merchandise manager at Saks, met with representatives of Harve Benard to inform them that Saks did not wish to sell garments containing recycled cashmere. After the meeting, Carole Sadler, the associate counsel for Saks, sent Harve Benard a letter restating Saks' position as set forth by Ronon: "Saks does not wish to sell jackets containing recycled cashmere."

Rather than viewing this anecdote as evidence of how an actual consumer's purchasing decision was influenced by the misrepresentation, defendants draw the opposite conclusion by focusing on Saks' ultimate purchasing decision. Notwithstanding its earlier position, Saks eventually decided to sell Harve Benard garments containing recycled cashmere. Moreover, Sadler testified that Saks' initial refusal to sell recycled cashmere garments was merely a strategic move on an issue "that could ripen into a negotiation or a renegotiation" between the parties.

The problem with defendants' rebuttal argument, however, is that it ignores what a rational juror could find after drawing all reasonable inferences in plaintiffs' favor. Saks' initial refusal to sell the recycled cashmere garments; Saks' belief that the matter could lead

---

11. The relevant "consumers" are those groups of people to whom the advertisement was addressed. *See Johnson & Johnson-Merck Consumer Pharm. Co. v. Smithkline Beecham Corp.*, 960 F.2d 294, 297 (2d Cir. 1992) (noting that "[t]he question in such cases is—what does the person to whom the advertisement is addressed find to be the message?") (internal quotations and citations omitted). In this case, the relevant consumers include, but are not limited to, the retail stores that purchased Harve Benard garments instead of buying from Packard's garment manufacturer customers and individual purchasers.

to a negotiation; and the actual negotiations that took place before Saks agreed to continue selling the garments are competent evidence from which a reasonable juror could conclude that the issue related to an inherent quality or characteristic of the garment. Indeed, it makes little sense that Saks and Harve Benard would spend so much time and effort resolving a matter they deemed immaterial.

Furthermore, it is important to reiterate, as the caselaw explicitly states, that plaintiffs are not required to present evidence that defendants' misrepresentation actually influenced consumers' purchasing decisions, but that it was *likely* to influence them. *See Clorox*, 228 F.3d at 33 n.6. Given the significant degree to which using recycled fibers adversely impacts the quality, texture, and characteristics of cashmere, and considering Saks' erratic behavior upon learning of the mislabeling, we find that plaintiffs have presented sufficient evidence to demonstrate that defendants' recycled cashmere misrepresentation was material.

C.   *Consumer Deception*

The next element of a false advertising claim under the Lanham Act requires plaintiffs to demonstrate that the alleged misrepresentation deceived a substantial portion of the consuming public. *See Clorox*, 228 F.3d at 33 n.6.[12] Usually consumer deception is demonstrated through surveys, which establish that consumers were misled by the alleged misrepresentations. *See Johnson & Johnson-Merck*, 960 F.2d at 298. Plaintiff-appellant Packard argues, however, that it does not have to shoulder the burden of presenting this evidence because existing caselaw allows plaintiffs like it who allege claims that are literally false to avail themselves of a presumption of consumer deception. [cit.]

In response, defendants recognize that a presumption of consumer deception is available to plaintiffs seeking injunctive relief for literal falsity claims; however, they argue that the presumption does not apply, without more, to plaintiffs seeking money damages for literal falsity claims.

Though there was once support for the assertion that consumer deception cannot be presumed simply because a plaintiff alleges a literal falsity claim for money damages, *see PPX*, 818 F.2d at 272 (noting that as of 1987 the presumption had only been applied to literal falsity claims for injunctive relief), it has become the practice of most circuits to apply the presumption to all literal falsity claims. *See Pizza Hut, Inc. v. Papa John's Int'l, Inc.*, 227 F.3d 489, 497 (5th Cir. 2000) (holding, on a claim for damages and injunctive relief, that "when the statements of fact at issue are shown to be literally false, the plaintiff need not introduce evidence on the issue of the impact the statements had on consumers. . . . [However,] [p]laintiffs looking to recover monetary damages for false or misleading advertising that is not literally false must prove actual deception"); [cit.].

In fact, defendants' argument contradicts this Court's explicit pronouncements on the issue. In assessing whether a Lanham Act claim for injunctive relief and money damages had been properly dismissed, we stated, "If the advertisement is literally false, the court may grant relief without considering evidence of consumer reaction. In the absence of such literal falsity, an additional burden is placed upon plaintiff to show that the advertisement . . . conveys a misleading message to the viewing public." *Clorox*, 228 F.3d at 33 (internal citations omitted).

Moreover, applying a presumption of consumer deception to all literal falsity claims, irrespective of the type of relief sought, makes sense. When a plaintiff demonstrates that a

---

12. Since Packard is seeking monetary damages, it must demonstrate that consumers were actually deceived by the misrepresentations. Only plaintiffs seeking injunctive relief face the lesser burden of demonstrating a tendency to deceive.

defendant has made a material misrepresentation that is literally false, there is no need to burden the plaintiff with the onerous task of demonstrating how consumers perceive the advertising. *See Balance Dynamics*, 204 F.3d at 693 (noting that "[b]ecause proof of 'actual confusion' may be difficult to obtain, most of the circuits have ruled that when a statement is literally false, a plaintiff need not demonstrate actual customer deception in order to obtain relief under the Lanham Act"). Common sense and practical experience tell us that we can presume, without reservation, that consumers have been deceived when a defendant has explicitly misrepresented a fact that relates to an inherent quality or characteristic of the article sold. To presume as much requires neither a leap of faith nor the creation of any new legal principle.[13]

Because defendants do not dispute that overstating cashmere content is a literal falsity claim, we apply a presumption of consumer deception in plaintiffs' favor on this claim. Based on this presumption, and defendants' failure to present evidence to rebut it, Packard has satisfied its burden of demonstrating consumer deception on its cashmere content claim. . . .

[The court discussed whether the "recycled cashmere" claim involved literal falsity, concluding that it did. Then the court proceeded with the alternative analysis below.]

Even if plaintiffs' recycled cashmere claim did not involve literal falsity, plaintiffs would still be able to avail themselves of a presumption of consumer deception on alternative grounds. It is well established that if there is proof that a defendant intentionally set out to deceive or mislead consumers, a presumption arises that customers in fact have been deceived. *See Porous Media Corp. v. Pall Corp.*, 110 F.3d 1329, 1333 (8th Cir. 1997) (approving of a presumption of consumer deception upon a finding that defendant acted deliberately to deceive); *see also U-Haul Int'l, Inc. v. Jartran, Inc.*, 793 F.2d 1034, 1041 (9th Cir. 1986) (same).

As evidence of defendants' intentional mislabeling of the blazers' recycled cashmere, plaintiffs introduced a letter dated January 13, 1995, addressed to Harve Benard's president, Bernard Holtzman, from one of Harve Benard's testing laboratories. On the top of the letter, there is a handwritten note from "L. Pedell," an agent for Harve Benard, which states, "Also see note from mill below. This is an on-going saga." The note that Pedell is referring to reads, in pertinent part, "FOR YOUR INFO PLS NOTE MILL IS USING RECICLED CHASMERE [sic]." Despite receiving notice that its blazers were being made from recycled cashmere, Harve Benard continued to market its garments without any "recycled" designation, as required by law, until months after the commencement of this lawsuit in 1996. Thus, Harve Benard's unwillingness to comply with the law, despite being on notice of its violation, can be seen as an attempt deliberately to deceive the consuming public.

In response, defendants offer several factual and legal arguments, none of which we find persuasive. First, defendants argue that a presumption of consumer deception cannot be triggered on an implied falsity claim, even if there is evidence of an intent to deceive.

---

13. Defendants also argue that before the presumption of consumer deception can apply to a literal falsity claim for damages, the plaintiff must demonstrate that the defendant intentionally deceived the consuming public. None of the . . . circuit cases cited *supra*, however, speaks of the intent to deceive as a prerequisite to applying a presumption of consumer deception on a literal falsity claim. As discussed in more detail below, the intent to deceive is an independent basis for triggering a presumption of consumer deception. *See William H. Morris Co. v. Group W, Inc.*, 66 F.3d 255, 258 (9th Cir. 1995) (ruling, on an implied falsity claim, that "[i]f [defendant] intentionally misled consumers, we would presume consumers were in fact deceived and [defendant] would have the burden of demonstrating otherwise").

Defendants' claim, however, is undermined by several circuit cases that have explicitly held otherwise. [cit.] The justification for applying the presumption whenever there is evidence of intentional deception is perspicuous: "The expenditure by a competitor of substantial funds in an effort to deceive customers and influence their purchasing decisions justifies the existence of a presumption that consumers are, in fact, being deceived." *U-Haul*, 793 F.2d at 1041. This reasoning holds true regardless of whether the claim that plaintiffs allege involves an implied or literal falsity.

Second, defendants argue that the fact that an Italian mill stated that it was using recycled cashmere has little bearing on whether the mill was using cashmere that would be considered recycled under the definitions of the Wool Products Labeling Act. Defendants seem to misunderstand or underestimate the import of the letter. One of Harve Benard's mills informed the president of the company that its cashmere-blend garments contained recycled fabric. Rather than investigating the matter to determine whether Harve Benard was violating the law by not properly labeling its cashmere as "recycled," Harve Benard did nothing. It did not finally change the garments' labels until more than one year later when plaintiffs sought a temporary restraining order on the issue. One reasonable explanation, which a juror may choose to credit, for Harve Benard's refusal to investigate or act on the letter is that Harve Benard intended to deceive the consuming public about the recycled nature of its cashmere. [cit.]

Lastly, defendants argue that Harve Benard's failure to act on the letter for one year does not meet the intent requirement set forth in applicable precedent. Defendants read *Resource Developers*, 926 F.2d at 140, as standing for the proposition that a defendant's failure to dispel confusion caused by its advertising circular for four months is insufficient evidence of intent. Since Harve Benard's failure to act is comparable to the defendant's in *Resource Developers*, defendants conclude that there is insufficient evidence to support a finding of intent.

Even if we were to adopt defendants' reading of *Resource Developers*, we remain unpersuaded by their argument because the circumstances of this case are far more compelling. First, the fact that defendants waited for more than a year before changing the blazers' mislabeling is far more probative of intentional deceit than waiting for four months. Second, when referring to the Italian mill's use of recycled cashmere, Pedell noted on the top of the letter, "This is an on-going saga." Drawing all reasonable inferences in plaintiffs' favor, a rational juror could conclude from this sentence that the recycled cashmere issue had been encountered before and—as the word "saga" suggests—on a continuing basis. Because this "saga" probably began or could have begun a considerable amount of time before January 1995, we decline defendants' invitation to place a time constraint on plaintiffs' evidence of intent.

With respect to the Institute's recycled cashmere claim for injunctive relief, the district court dismissed the claim because the Institute failed to demonstrate evidence of consumer deception. Because the foregoing analysis applies with equal force to the Institute's recycled cashmere claim, we rule that the Institute can avail itself of a presumption of consumer deception. Thus, the district court erred in granting defendants' motion for summary judgment on the Institute's recycled cashmere claim.

Nothing in this opinion, however, is meant to preclude defendants from rebutting the presumption of consumer deception at trial by showing that the labeling did not actually deceive consumers.

D.   Causation and Damages

. . .

In order to prove causation under §1125(a) of the Lanham Act, the aggrieved party must demonstrate that the false advertisement actually harmed its business. "A precise showing is not required, and a diversion of sales, for example, would suffice." *Quabaug*, 567 F.2d at 161 (internal citations omitted).

To satisfy this requirement, plaintiffs present two pieces of interrelated evidence. First, plaintiffs point to Harve Benard's purchase orders which demonstrate that Harve Benard was paying $5 per yard less for the fabric it was using to make its garments than Packard's customers, who were paying for legitimate 10% cashmere fabric. Next, plaintiffs offer uncontradicted evidence that Packard's customers actually reduced their purchases of Packard's cashmere-blend fabric because they could not compete with Harve Benard's lower-priced garments. Specifically, Peter Warshaw, a sales agent for Packard, testified that three of Packard's customers—Gilmore, RCM, and Perfect Petite—notified him that they could no longer purchase Packard's cashmere-blend fabric because Harve Benard's lower-priced garments were driving them out of the market. This evidence supports the plaintiffs' claim that Harve Benard's low prices caused Packard lost sales.

The critical question, then, is what enabled Harve Benard to lower its prices to the point that prospective competitors refused to purchase Packard fabric. Based on the evidence presented, a rational factfinder could reasonably infer that the substantial cost savings Harve Benard enjoyed from using non-cashmere or recycled cashmere fabric allowed Harve Benard to lower the price of its blazers, thereby preventing Packard's customers from competing in the market. Indeed, using inexpensive materials that are represented as something more valuable would generally create a substantial competitive advantage by undercutting competitors who correctly represent their products. *See Camel Hair*, 799 F.2d at 13 (approving the district court's commonsense "inference that the sale of cashmere-blend coats which overstated their cashmere content could cause a loss of sales of cashmere-blend coats which correctly stated their cashmere content"). This reasonable inference, to which plaintiffs are entitled at summary judgment, enables plaintiffs to demonstrate the causal link between the harm they suffered and defendants' misrepresentations.

In response, defendants argue that it is unreasonable to infer that Harve Benard's lower fabric costs translated into lower garment prices given that evidence in the record suggests otherwise. In his affidavit, Harve Benard's vice-president Harvey Schutzbank stated that Harve Benard's garment prices would have remained the same even if it had used the more expensive Packard fabric to manufacture its garments. Based on this evidence, Harve Benard claims it would still have enjoyed the same price advantage that prevented Packard's customers from competing in the market even if the garments had been properly labeled and manufactured with legitimate 10% cashmere fabric. In short, defendants cite Schutzbank's affidavit as proof that it was Harve Benard's low prices—not its mislabeling—that caused Packard's lost sales.

We agree with defendants that if they were to present undisputed evidence establishing that their garment prices would have remained the same even if they had used Packard fabric, it would be unreasonable to infer that Harve Benard's lower fabric costs translated into lower garment prices. However, plaintiffs present competent evidence which casts serious doubt on Schutzbank's testimony. Packard's president John Glidden testified to the relationship between fabric cost and garment price:

> Because Harve Benard was not putting the cashmere in the fabric, they had a tremendously reduced cost. . . . [T]he added expense of putting cashmere in a garment or in a fabric increases the garment's cost; and when [Packard] legitimately labeled [its] fabrics, [the fabrics] were too expensive for the marketplace which Harve Benard was selling to.

Moreover, Warshaw, who has years of experience working with garment manufacturers, testified that "Harve Benard had an unfair competitive advantage in fabric that is the major component of a garment. . . . *[B]y far and away the largest component of the total costs of a garment is the fabric*" (emphasis added). He also testified to Harve Benard's comparative advantage:

> [T]he garment manufacturers that are available to compete with Harve Benard are savvy, smart, sharp manufacturers who have at their disposal cheap labor, cheap trim, cheap transportation. They have available to them the same range of possibilities for plugging in to a garment, except that if those sharp competitors use a Packard product that's $11.25, they're going to get blown out of the water by Harve Benard['s use of] inexpensive [] fabric.

After weighing all of this evidence, a rational jury could choose to discredit Schutzbank's affidavit, especially considering (1) the commonsense inference that a lower fabric cost translates into a price advantage; (2) the fact that Schutzbank does not provide any quantitative analysis to substantiate his bald assertion that the garments' prices would have remained the same even if Harve Benard were to have used the more expensive Packard fabric; (3) several "savvy, smart, sharp" garment manufacturers could not do what Harve Benard claims it can—that is, use Packard fabric and still keep its low prices; and (4) two of plaintiffs' witnesses assert that fabric cost has a substantial impact on garment price.

In the end, the parties present witnesses who hold inconsistent positions on a crucial issue of fact. Rather than weighing in on the matter, we conclude that this dispute is one which a jury is best suited to resolve.

. . .

Reversed and remanded.

NOTES AND QUESTIONS

1. *Deception prong: actual consumer deception versus tendency to deceive.* In cases where evidence of consumer deception is relevant (i.e., cases in which the advertisement in question is ambiguous, but arguably misleading), some courts take the position that evidence of actual consumer deception is required if the plaintiff seeks damages, while evidence of a tendency to deceive consumers suffices if the plaintiff seeks only injunctive relief. *See Pizza Hut, Inc. v. Papa John's Int'l, Inc.*, 227 F.3d 489, 497-98 (5th Cir. 2000). Recall that in the law of trademark infringement, many courts hold that a plaintiff who seeks damages must show actual confusion, while a plaintiff who merely seeks an injunction need only show likelihood of confusion. *See* Chapter 7.

2. *Deception prong: proving deception.* Ordinarily, a false advertising plaintiff who cannot prove literal falsity, and hence does not enjoy the presumption of deception, uses consumer survey evidence to establish deception. *See Clorox Co. Puerto Rico v. Procter & Gamble Comm. Co.*, 228 F.3d 24 (1st Cir. 2000). In *Novartis Consumer Health, Inc. v. Johnson & Johnson-Merck Consumer Pharm. Co.*, 290 F.3d 578 (3d Cir. 2002), the Third Circuit reviewed the plaintiff's survey evidence in some detail, concluding that the district court had properly accepted the plaintiff's survey evidence as demonstrating likely deception, where the survey showed that 25 percent of consumer respondents were likely deceived by the advertising. In evaluating the survey evidence, the Third Circuit drew freely from survey evaluations in other Lanham Act contexts, notably surveys establishing confusion. Is "deception" for Section 43(a)(1)(B) purposes equivalent to actual confusion? If not, what are the differences?

3. *Materiality prong: rationale.* The false advertising standard as articulated by most courts includes a materiality prong. That requirement does not appear on the face of Section 43(a)(1)(B), but nonetheless is firmly fixed in the law of false advertising. Why should courts require materiality? Why not impose liability for all statements of fact in

advertisements that are false, whether literally false or ambiguous but misleading? If you think that this rule sweeps too broadly, what of an alternative rule that presumes materiality for literally false statements? (Under this approach, a plaintiff who proves literal falsity would earn not only a presumption of consumer deception under the third prong, but also a presumption of materiality under the second prong.) Note that we have seen other instances in which judges have imposed a materiality requirement as a gloss on Lanham Act requirements—in connection with marks excluded from registration under Section 2's deceptiveness prong, discussed in Chapter 5 *supra*. For an argument that materiality should play a prominent role in the confusion analysis, *see* Mark A. Lemley & Mark McKenna, *Irrelevant Confusion*, 62 STAN. L. REV. 413 (2010).

4. *Materiality prong: puffery and the materiality requirement.* Suppose that a court analyzes the puffery question in connection with the "statement of fact" prong of the false advertising test. In general, puffery might fall outside the realm of "fact" because of its content (e.g., it might be "opinion," not "fact") or its presentation (e.g., it might be so vague as to be unverifiable). In either event, the statement is one on which a reasonable consumer would not rely.

Does this inquiry overlap substantially with the materiality inquiry? If a statement is one on which no reasonable consumer would rely, isn't the statement immaterial (i.e., not one that would influence the purchasing decision)? What is the purpose of having separate inquiries for "puffery" and immateriality?

5. *Materiality prong: proof.* In the *Pizza Hut* case, the plaintiff Pizza Hut's survey evidence was deemed inadequate to demonstrate materiality, so Pizza Hut turned to other avenues of proof, including evidence that Papa John's executives allegedly had the subjective intent to deliver a message of ingredient superiority through its advertisements. Should evidence of defendant's subjective intent be admissible on the issue of materiality? If not, why not?

In *Skydive Arizona, Inc. v. Quattrocchi*, 673 F.3d 1105 (9th Cir. 2012), plaintiff did not submit survey evidence as proof of materiality. Instead, plaintiff relied on a declaration from a disgruntled consumer. Apparently, the declaration stated that the declarant "had personally bought [defendant's] SKYRIDE certificates based on the [defendant's] online representations and advertisements that he could redeem the certificates at Skydive Arizona [the plaintiff's business]." Should this alone suffice to establish materiality? The Ninth Circuit also looked to evidence concerning "numerous consumers who had telephoned or came to Skydive Arizona's facility after having been deceived into believing there was an affiliation between Skydive Arizona and [defendant]." Is this evidence probative as to materiality? Or as to deception? Or both? How likely is it that materiality will serve a significant role in filtering out unwarranted claims of false advertising?

The court in *Cashmere* notes that one method of establishing materiality is to show that the false or misleading statement relates to an inherent quality of the product at issue. Should courts accept this approach? *See Church & Dwight Co., Inc. v. SPD Swiss Precision Diagnostics, GMBH*, 843 F.3d 48 (2d Cir. 2016) (expressing confusion about whether proof that the advertisement misrepresents an "inherent characteristic" is a requirement for materiality or simply one cognizable method for showing it).

6. *Injury and causation.* In *Cashmere*, the court states that in order to show causation, the plaintiff must show that the allegedly false advertising caused the plaintiff actual harm. In *Hall v. Bed Bath & Beyond, Inc.*, 705 F.3d 1357, 1367-68 (Fed. Cir. 2013), the court ruled that a false advertising claim need not include a pleading of actual harm; Section 43(a) only calls for a likelihood of damage. *Id.* at 1367. Where plaintiff's and defendant's products were competitive and plaintiff alleged that one of his customers believed that defendant was selling plaintiff's product for nearly half the price, this was sufficient to avoid dismissal on the pleadings. *Id*. at 1367-68 (advocating a "flexible approach" to injury and causation). As a policy matter, what are the best arguments against a "flexible approach"?

7.   *Damages—actual loss of sales.* When a plaintiff establishes a claim of Section 43(a)(1)(A) false advertising, what is the appropriate remedy? As is true for other Lanham Act causes of action, the plaintiff is entitled to a range of remedies, including both injunctive relief and damages.

How should a court measure money damages for false advertising? One option, discussed in *Cashmere* case, is for the plaintiff to show that the false advertising caused actual losses of sales, often by diversion of those sales to the false advertiser. Where the plaintiff can show that the false advertiser made certain sales that the plaintiff would have made but for the false advertising, the plaintiff may be entitled to claim the false advertiser's profits on the diverted sales. *See, e.g., BASF Corp. v. Old World Trading Co.*, 41 F.3d 1081, 1092 (7th Cir. 1994) (awarding $2.5 million in profits on lost sales). *See also Retractable Techs., Inc. v. Becton Dickinson & Co.*, 842 F.3d 883 (5th Cir. 2016) (discussing the disgorgement of profits remedy). Showing that the false advertising caused the damage is likely to be difficult, although in some circuits, plaintiffs who show intentionally deceptive advertising obtain the benefit of a presumption of causation. *See Porous Media Corp. v. Pall Corp.*, 110 F.3d 1329 (8th Cir. 1997) (recognizing presumption of causation in false comparative advertising case). In a comparative advertising case, it may be reasonable to presume that any sales that defendant makes have come at the plaintiff's expense. Is this true of other types of false advertising cases?

8.   *Damages—reputational loss; cost of corrective advertising.* A plaintiff in a false advertising case may also attempt to show monetary damages attributable to the cost of corrective advertising or the cost of lost reputational value. In *Skydive Arizona, Inc. v. Quattrocchi*, 673 F.3d 1105 (9th Cir. 2012), a divided panel of the Ninth Circuit upheld an award of $1 million in actual damages for false advertising. The damages evidence (which was offered to support damages claims for both trademark infringement and false advertising) consisted of exhibits showing "the hundreds of thousands of dollars Skydive Arizona spent in developing and advertising its business," and "multiple declarations and witness testimony proving that customers were very angry with, and blamed Skydive Arizona for, problems caused by [defendant]," along with an argument that corrective advertising was needed. The panel majority found this showing sufficient; plaintiff did not need to provide a "specific mathematical formula" for the jury to use in calculating actual damage to the plaintiff's goodwill. Judge Noonan, dissenting as to the damages judgment, called for a more rigorous quantitative approach to measuring goodwill, and asserted that Skydive Arizona's expenditures might be relevant to computing the value of its goodwill, but did not provide a measure of the damage to that goodwill that defendant's activities had caused. *Id*. at 1116-17 (Noonan, J., dissenting in part).

In *Callaway Golf Co. v. Dunlop Slazenger*, 384 F. Supp. 2d 735 (D. Del. 2005), Dunlop had advertised that its A10 golf ball was "the Longest Ball on Tour." A jury determined that the claim was literally false and awarded Callaway $1.1 million for corrective advertising. On post-trial review, the trial court vacated the award. Damages for corrective advertising might be appropriate where a party incurred advertising costs before trial in attempting to combat a competitor's falsehoods. Damages might also be appropriate for advertising costs anticipated to be incurred after trial—i.e., prospective corrective advertising. Here, Callaway had not provided sufficient evidence of pre-trial costs to justify the award, and because both parties had ceased selling the golf balls at issue, an award based on prospective corrective advertising appeared to be a windfall. *Id*. at 1718-19 (also noting that the jury had awarded Callaway an additional $1.1 million for unjust enrichment, even though Callaway had presented the corrective advertising and unjust enrichment theories as alternative theories of relief).

9. *Contributory false advertising?* Should courts recognize a cause of action for contributory false advertising? If so, should the *Inwood* test for contributory trademark infringement (discussed in Chapter 7) be extended to govern contributory false advertising claims? In *Duty Free Americas, Inc. v. Estee Lauder Cos., Inc.*, 797 F.3d 1248, 1278-79 (11th Cir. 2015), the court considered such a claim. DFA and its rivals were participating in competitive bidding processes to open duty-free stores at airports. During the bidding, DFA's rivals questioned whether DFA had permission to sell Estee Lauder products at its proposed stores. After losing the bids, DFA alleged that the statements from the rivals constituted false advertising and that Estee Lauder had facilitated those false statements. DFA sued Estee Lauder, alleging contributory false advertising. Assuming that such a cause of action is recognized, what facts should DFA be required to allege in order state a claim? Can DFA simply allege that its rivals who won the bids sold Estee Lauder products from their stores, and that Estee Lauder continued to supply product to the rivals?

TRAFFICSCHOOL.COM, INC. v. EDRIVER, INC.

653 F.3d 820 (9th Cir. 2011)

KOZINSKI, Chief Judge:

Defendants own and manage DMV.org, a for-profit website with a mission to save you "time, money and even a trip to the DMV!" DMV.org, Home Page, http://www.dmv.org (last visited Feb. 28, 2011). Consumers visit DMV.org for help renewing driver's licenses, buying car insurance, viewing driving records, beating traffic tickets, registering vehicles, even finding DUI/DWI attorneys. The more eyeballs DMV.org attracts, the more money defendants earn from selling sponsored links and collecting fees for referring site visitors to vendors of traffic school courses, driver's ed lessons and other driver-related services. This seems like a legitimate and useful business, except that some visitors mistakenly believe the site is run by their state's department of motor vehicles (DMV).

Plaintiffs TrafficSchool.com, Inc. and Drivers Ed Direct, LLC market and sell traffic school and driver's ed courses directly to consumers. They also compete with DMV.org for referral revenue. Plaintiffs claim that defendants violated federal and state unfair competition and false advertising laws by actively fostering the belief that DMV.org is an official state DMV website, or is affiliated or endorsed by a state DMV.

[Plaintiff won at trial on the Lanham Act false advertising claim, and the court issued an injunction ordering DMV.org to present every site visitor with a splash screen bearing a disclaimer. Defendant appealed. Judge Kozinski's analysis of the scope of the injunction follows.]

B. By way of a remedy, the district court ordered DMV.org to present every site visitor with a splash screen stating, "YOU ARE ABOUT TO ENTER A *PRIVATELY OWNED* WEBSITE THAT IS *NOT* OWNED OR OPERATED BY ANY STATE GOVERNMENT AGENCY." Visitors can't access DMV.org's content without clicking a "CONTINUE" button on the splash screen. Defendants argue that the district court abused its discretion by fashioning a "blanket injunction" that's overbroad—i.e., restrains conduct not at issue in plaintiffs' complaint—and violates the First Amendment.

Overbreadth. The district court reasoned that the splash screen was necessary to: (1) "remedy any confusion that consumers have already developed before visiting DMV.ORG for the first time," (2) "remedy the public interest concerns associated with [confused visitors'] transfer of sensitive information to Defendants," and (3) "prevent confusion among DMV.ORG's consumers." Defendants argue that the splash screen doesn't effectuate these stated goals. But their only evidence is a declaration from DMV.org's CEO stating that defendants tested several alternative disclaimers and found them to be more effective than the splash screen in preventing consumers from emailing DMV.org with sensitive personal information. To the extent we credit a self-serving declaration, [cit.], defendants' evidence doesn't prove that the splash screen is ineffective in this respect, and says nothing about whether the alternative disclaimers serve the other two interests identified by the district court. Defendants haven't carried their "heavy burden" of showing that their alternative disclaimers reduce DMV.org's likelihood of confusing consumers. [cit.] The scope of an injunction is within the broad discretion of the district court, [cit.], and the district court here didn't abuse that discretion when it concluded that the splash screen was the optimal means of correcting defendants' false advertising.

First Amendment. Courts routinely grant permanent injunctions prohibiting deceptive advertising. *See* 1 Charles E. McKenney & George F. Long III, Federal Unfair Competition: Lanham Act §43(a) §10:5 (17th ed. 2010). Because false or misleading commercial statements aren't constitutionally protected, *see Cent. Hudson Gas & Elec. Corp. v. Pub. Serv. Comm'n of N.Y.*, 447 U.S. 557, 563 (1980); [cit.], such injunctions rarely raise First Amendment concerns.

The permanent injunction here does raise such concerns because it erects a barrier to *all* content on the DMV.org website, not merely that which is deceptive. Some of the website's content is informational and thus fully protected, such as guides to applying for a driver's license, buying insurance and beating traffic tickets. *See Mattel, Inc. v. MCA Records, Inc.*, 296 F.3d 894, 906 (9th Cir. 2002). The informational content is commingled with truthful commercial speech, which is entitled to significant First Amendment protection. *See Cent. Hudson*, 447 U.S. at 564. The district court was required to tailor the injunction so as to burden no more protected speech than necessary. [cit.]

The district court does not appear to have considered that its injunction would permanently and unnecessarily burden access to DMV.org's First Amendment-protected content. The splash screen forces potential visitors to take an additional navigational step, deterring some consumers from entering the website altogether.[5] It also precludes defendants from tailoring DMV.org's landing page to make it welcoming to visitors, and interferes with the operation of search engines, making it more difficult for consumers to find the website and its protected content.[6] All of these burdens on protected speech are, under the current injunction, permanent.

The district court premised its injunction on its findings that defendants' "search engine marketing" and "non-sponsored natural listings, including the DMV.ORG domain name," caused consumers to be confused even before they viewed DMV.org's content. The court also identified specific misleading statements on the website. The splash screen is justified to remedy the harm caused by such practices so long as they continue. But website content and advertising practices can and do change over time. Indeed, the court found that defendants had already "made some changes to DMV.ORG and how they marketed it."

---

5. Defendants' website usability expert submitted a declaration stating that splash screens typically drive away up to a quarter of potential site visitors. Plaintiffs cite nothing to rebut this evidence.

6. Defendants introduced unrebutted evidence that splash screens commonly interfere with the automated "spiders" that search engines deploy to "crawl" the Internet and compile the indexes of web pages they use to determine every page's search ranking. And splash screens themselves don't have high search rankings: Search engines commonly base these rankings on the web page's content and the number of other pages linking to it, and splash screens lack both content and links.

The splash screen is also justified so long as it helps to remedy lingering confusion caused by defendants' past deception. But the splash screen will continue to burden DMV. org's protected content, even if all remaining harm has dissipated. At that point, the injunction will burden protected speech without justification, thus burdening more speech than necessary. [cit.]; *see also E. & J. Gallo Winery v. Gallo Cattle Co.*, 967 F.2d 1280, 1298 (9th Cir. 1992) (permanent injunction can't burden future non-misleading business practices); *U-Haul Int'l, Inc. v. Jartran, Inc.*, 793 F.2d 1034, 1042-43 (9th Cir. 1986) ("U-Haul II") (permanent injunction can't burden future truthful advertising).

On remand, the district court shall reconsider the duration of the splash screen in light of any intervening changes in the website's content and marketing practices, as well as the dissipation of the deception resulting from past practices. If the district court continues to require the splash screen, it shall explain the continuing justification for burdening the website's protected content and what conditions defendants must satisfy in order to remove the splash screen in the future. In the alternative, or in addition, the court may permanently enjoin defendants from engaging in deceptive marketing or placing misleading statements on DMV.org. *See U-Haul II*, 793 F.2d at 1043 (modifying injunction to prohibit only false or misleading advertising).

[*Affirmed in part, reversed in part, and remanded.*]

NOTES AND QUESTIONS

1. *The* eBay *factors for injunctive relief; irreparable harm.* Regarding the grant of injunctive relief for false advertising, should courts apply the factor test from the Supreme Court's patent decision, *eBay Inc. v. MercExchange, L.L.C.*, 547 U.S. 388, 391 (2006)? Why or why not? *See PBM Prods., LLC v. Mead Johnson & Co.*, 639 F.3d 111 (4th Cir. 2011). Should courts presume irreparable harm upon a showing of false advertising (or, in the context of preliminary injunctive relief, upon a showing of likelihood of success on the merits)? In *Groupe SEB USA, Inc. v. Euro-Pro Operating LLC*, 774 F.3d 192 (3d Cir. 2014), the court declined to apply a presumption but observed that the reasons offered for the presumption under pre-*eBay* law might still inform the court's exercise of equitable discretion. *Id.* at 205 n.8 (false statement in advertising necessarily diminishes product value, and corresponding harm to reputation and goodwill may be difficult to quantify). We return to the issue of injunctive relief, and remedies more generally, in Chapter 12.

2. *Injunctive relief and the requirement to use a "splash screen."* The court in *Trafficschool.com* remands so that the trial court can determine how long the defendant should be required to use the splash screen. But if it's the dmv.org domain name that lies at the root of the defendant's deception of consumers, then it would seem that the splash screen would always be needed, unless the defendant stops using the domain name. Thus, it may be a little odd to suggest that the splash screen only need be in place for as long as the deception continues. Professor Rebecca Tushnet has pointed this out. *See* Rebecca Tushnet & Eric Goldman, *Joint post: Kozinski on DMV.org*, Rebecca Tushnet's 43(B)log (Aug. 2, 2011), *http://tushnet.blogspot.com/2011/08/joint-post-kozinski-on-dmvorg.html.* Suppose that defendant's dmv.org website includes no splash screen, but does include a banner stating in capital letters that "DMV.ORG IS A **PRIVATELY OWNED** WEBSITE THAT IS **NOT** OWNED OR OPERATED BY ANY STATE GOVERNMENT AGENCY." Is this adequate to dispel consumer deception?

3. *First Amendment implications of injunctive relief.* Does anything in the *Tam* decision affect the First Amendment analysis in *Trafficschool.com*?

PROBLEM 10-4: "AMBUSH" ADVERTISING

Suppose that Coca-Cola produces a drink for athletes called QUENCH. Coca-Cola has entered into a multimillion-dollar contract with the National Basketball Association (NBA) naming Coca-Cola the "official sponsor" and QUENCH the "official drink" of the NBA.

Suppose that Coca-Cola's main rival, Pepsi, produces POWER JUICE, a competing drink for athletes. Alarmed by Coca-Cola's arrangement with the NBA, Pepsi produces a major advertising campaign for POWER JUICE, timed to air during the NBA playoffs. Pepsi's POWER JUICE campaign features numerous former NBA greats, college basketball coaches, and sportscasters professing their love of POWER JUICE and making references to "the drink of real pros" while film clips of basketball games run in the background. Pepsi has made no arrangements with the NBA in connection with its advertisements.

What are the prospects that Coca-Cola would prevail against Pepsi in a suit for false advertising? Should courts recognize a special subcategory of false advertising claims in situations of "ambush" advertising?

For more on the practice of ambush advertising, *see* Brian Steinberg, *Ambush Ads Hitch a Ride on Super Bowl*, WALL ST. J., Jan. 15, 2004, at B1; *see also* 112 Sports Illustrated (No. 27) at 18 (June 28, 2010) (reporting ejection from ground of fans dressed in colors of rival of exclusive World Cup advertiser). For commentary in favor of regulations directed specifically against ambush marketing, *see* Carolina Pina & Ana Gil-Roble, *Sponsorship of Sports Events and Ambush Marketing*, 27 EUR. INTELL. PROP. REV. 93 (2005). The authors describe Greek Law No. 3254 on the Regulation of the 2004 [Athens] Olympic and Paralympic Games and other provisions, 137/22.7.04, which reportedly

> barred the dissemination of all types of advertising in the city and the Olympic stadium, as well as other venues used for the sports events and public and private buildings within a 200-metre radius of those areas. It also barred advertising on buses, trains, subways and cars visible from the Olympic Games' vicinity and the airspace of the stadium unless consent was obtained from the organisers of the event. Advertising through promotional goods (free gifts, leaflets, etc.) was subject to prior authorisation by the organiser. Advertising in ports and airports was also reserved for official sponsors.

Id. at 96. Would a similar regulation pass constitutional muster in the United States?

PROBLEM 10-5: LANHAM ACT FALSE ADVERTISING VERSUS OTHER FEDERAL LABELING REGULATIONS

The U.S. Food and Drug Administration (FDA) regulates the labels that may appear on many food and beverage products under the Food, Drug, and Cosmetic Act (FDCA), 21 U.S.C. §§301 *et seq*. For example, food and beverage labels that are "false or misleading in any particular" violate 21 U.S.C. §343(a)(1), and may trigger action by the FDA or Department of Justice. The FDA has promulgated regulations that address in detail the content of labels for many products. *See, e.g.*, 21 C.F.R. 102.33(c), (d) (labels for juice beverages).

Suppose that Coca-Cola distributes a juice product that is labeled, as shown below, as "Pomegranate Blueberry Flavored Blend of 5 Juices." The product actually contains 99.4 percent apple and grape juices, 0.3 percent pomegranate juice, 0.2 percent blueberry juice, and 0.1 percent raspberry juice. Assume that the content and size of the text on the labels comply with the applicable FDA regulations for juice labels (which do specify how juice blends may be labeled, among other things). Should a competitor of Coca-Cola still be able to assert a Lanham Act false advertising cause of action based on the labeling? If a court permits the Lanham Act allegation to go forward, does this undermine the FDA's regulatory authority? If a wide array of products are subject to various federal labeling regulations, should a Lanham Act false advertising cause of action be barred in all of these circumstances? *See Pom Wonderful LLC v. Coca-Cola Co.*, 134 S. Ct. 2228 (2014). Would it matter to your analysis that the FDCA and its regulations rely almost exclusively on federal government enforcement actions, while the Lanham Act relies predominantly on civil suits brought by private parties? Would it matter which aspects of the label are at issue in the Lanham Act action? In particular, should the courts distinguish between the name of the product (which the FDCA and its regulations specifically reach) and other aspects of the label (which the FDCA and its regulations don't explicitly reach)?

11

TRADE IDENTITY RIGHTS IN ONE'S PERSONA: ENDORSEMENT, ATTRIBUTION, AND PUBLICITY

We sometimes think of the power of celebrity—and of celebrity endorsements—as strictly a late–twentieth-century phenomenon. Certainly, the term "right of publicity" traces back only to the 1950s. *See* Melville Nimmer, *The Right of Publicity*, 19 LAW & CONTEMP. PROBS. 203 (1954); *Haelan Labs, Inc. v. Topps Chewing Gum, Inc.*, 202 F.2d 866 (2d Cir.), *cert. denied*, 346 U.S. 816 (1953). However, the phenomenon of celebrity endorsement, and the unauthorized exploitation of that endorsement in the U.S. marketplace, has deeper historical roots. Consider, for example, the plight of aviator Charles Lindbergh in 1927, upon returning from his historic solo flight across the Atlantic in the *Spirit of St. Louis:*

> Then came the wave of requests for his endorsement of products—not just from cigarette and cereal companies but from: Thomas D. Murphy Company of Red Oak, Iowa, which manufactured calendars . . . ; the German firm selling Lindbergh Razor Blades in Turkey; the New York outfit producing bronze *Spirit of St. Louis* letter openers; the Hookless Fastener Company of Meadville, Pennsylvania, which wanted to boast that Lindbergh's new flying suits would use their zippers.
>
> Countless manufacturers did not wait for his approval. Clothiers could outfit men and women from head to toe in Lindbergh fashions: The Bruck-Weiss Company, for example, manufactured the "Lucky Lindy Lid"—a lady's hat of gray felt trimmed with black felt, with flaps on the side simulating plane wings and a propeller appliqued in the front; a company in Haverhill produced the "Lucky Lindbergh" shoe for women, which featured the design of the Spirit of St. Louis sewn in patent leather with a propeller on the toe and a photograph of Lindbergh inserted in a leather horseshoe on the side. One of the salesmen of the Thompson Manufacturing Company in Belfast, Maine, realized they could move their boys' breeches faster if they started calling it the "Lindy" pant. A baker in Elkhart, Indiana, renamed his product "Lucky Lindy Bread." Toys and games, watches and clocks, pencils and rulers, and almost any paper product could be adapted to include a Lindbergh theme; anything packaged—from cigars to canned fruit—became fair game for a logo of a single-engined monoplane. . . .

A. SCOTT BERG, LINDBERGH 161-62 (1998).

How should the law respond to such unbridled adulation . . . or exploitation, as the case may be? Should the law respond at all? If it should, does trademark and unfair competition law provide the model? Or should the unauthorized exploitation of personal identity be deemed purely a matter of privacy? Or should the law create a separate mechanism designed specifically to deal with the commercial exploitation of personal identity?

In this chapter, we take up these questions in two parts. First, we consider attempts to use Lanham Act §43(a) to protect against the unauthorized exploitation of personal identity (section A). Second, we consider the right of publicity (section B). It is common for plaintiffs to plead both theories in a personal identity case brought in federal court.

A.   Section 43(a) and the Protection of Personal Identity

§1125.   (§43) FALSE DESIGNATIONS OF ORIGIN AND FALSE DESCRIPTIONS . . .

(a) Civil action

(1) Any person who, on or in connection with any goods or services, or any container for goods, uses in commerce any word, term, name, symbol, or device, or any combination thereof, or any false designation of origin, false or misleading description of fact, or false or misleading representation of fact, which—

(A) is likely to cause confusion, or to cause mistake, or to deceive as to the affiliation, connection, or association of such person with another person, or as to the origin, sponsorship, or approval of his or her goods, services, or commercial activities by another person, or

(B) in commercial advertising or promotion, misrepresents the nature, characteristics, qualities, or geographic origin of his or her or another person's goods, services, or commercial activities,

shall be liable in a civil action by any person who believes that he or she is or is likely to be damaged by such act.

We have studied the language of Section 43(a) in previous chapters. In Chapter 7, we noted that trademark owners frequently invoke Section 43(a)(1)(A) as a companion cause of action to Section 32 trademark infringement claims. In Chapter 10, we noted that firms may invoke Section 43(A)(1)(B) to combat false advertising by competitors. In this section of the casebook, we consider whether Section 43(a) is a suitable vehicle for adjudicating claims involving the unauthorized commercial exploitation of an individual's personal identity. This is an important question in its own right, but it is also important as an illustration of a broader conceptual issue: whether Section 43(a) is (or should be) limited strictly to its traditional roles of protecting against confusion and false advertising, or whether it is (or should be) a general unfair competition provision.

The cases employing Section 43(a) to protect personal identity may be divided into two loose groups. The first group includes cases of unwanted attribution (or "over-attribution"), in which a person's identity is used without permission in connection with another's product or service. Two Section 43(a) theories might be asserted against unwanted attribution: (1) a Section 43(a)(1)(A) claim for confusion or passing off, frequently labeled "false endorsement" or "false association"; and (2) a Section 43(a)(1)(B) claim for false advertising.

The second group of cases includes cases involving misleading omissions of attribution ("under-attribution"). Here, two Section 43(a) theories have traditionally been asserted: (1) a Section 43(a)(1)(A) claim for reverse passing off and (2) a Section 43(a)(1)(B) claim for false advertising. We discuss each of these theories in the following pages.

1.   False Over-Attribution

Waits v. Frito-Lay, Inc., 978 F.2d 1093 (9th Cir. 1992), *cert. denied*, 506 U.S. 1080 (1993), presents one example of a claim of over-attribution in violation of Section 43(a). Tom Waits, a professional singer, songwriter, and actor, asserted claims against Frito-Lay under Section 43(a) and various other theories for the use of a sound-alike in Frito-Lay's advertisements. Waits has a raspy voice, described in the case as "how you'd sound if you drank a quart of bourbon, smoked a pack of cigarettes and swallowed a pack of razor blades. . . . Late at night. After not sleeping for three days." *Id.* at 1097 (quoting an unnamed Waits fan). Waits is a "prestige artist" who maintains a consistent policy against adopting any endorsement deals.

Frito-Lay's advertising agency produced commercials for Frito-Lay "SalsaRio Doritos" corn chips in which a professional musician named Stephen Carter (not Stephen Carter the law professor—to our knowledge, anyway) performed an imitation of Waits. There was evidence that the defendants knew of Waits' policy against doing commercials but proceeded anyway on the premise that Waits' musical "style" could not be protected.

The court characterized Waits' Section 43(a) theory as one of "false endorsement" and observed that "courts have recognized false endorsement claims brought by plaintiffs, including celebrities, for the unauthorized imitation of their distinctive attributes, where those attributes amount to an unregistered commercial 'trademark.'" *Id.* at 1106. According to the court, the trial court had been correct in instructing the jury to consider the likelihood-of-confusion factors in assessing the false endorsement claim, and the evidence was sufficient to support the jury's determination that consumers were likely to be confused. That evidence included a comparison of recordings of Tom Waits' voice and a recording of the Frito-Lay's commercial, along with actual confusion evidence (witnesses who testified that they believed that Tom Waits was singing the endorsement).

Similarly, in *Abdul-Jabbar v. General Motors Corp.*, 75 F.3d 1391, 1393-94 (9th Cir. 1996), *amended on denial of rehearing*, 85 F.3d 407 (9th Cir. 1996), the Ninth Circuit assessed a false endorsement claim under Section 43(a) by applying the multi-factor likelihood-of-confusion test. General Motors ran a television advertisement that aired during the 1993 telecasts of the NCAA men's basketball tournament. In the advertisement a voice asked, "Who holds the record for being voted the most outstanding player of this tournament?" A response appeared on the screen: "Lew Alcindor, UCLA, '67, '68, '69." The voice proceeded to ask, "Has any car made the 'Consumer Digest's Best Buy' list more than once?" The response indicated that "[t]he Oldsmobile Eighty-Eight has" and, while a film clip of the car was shown, noted, "In fact, it's made that list three years in a row. And now you can get this Eighty-Eight special edition for just $18,995." General Motors did not obtain Lew Alcindor's consent to use his name in the advertisement. According to the court, there was at least a fact question for trial on the confusion issue.

In other cases as well, courts have employed the confusion factors to adjudicate claims of over-attribution. *See, e.g., Tin Pan Apple, Inc. v. Miller Brewing Co., Inc.*, 737 F. Supp. 826 (S.D.N.Y. 1990) (rap group known as the "Fat Boys" stated a false endorsement claim arising from defendant's beer advertisement featuring look-alikes); *King v. Ames*, 179 F.3d 370 (5th Cir. 1999) (no showing of confusion where packaging of recording falsely credited a party as "producer").

By contrast, in *King v. Innovation Books*, 976 F.2d 824 (2d Cir. 1992), the court addressed a claim of over-attribution using an analysis that borrowed from tests for false advertising. Defendants had produced a movie that they advertised as "Stephen King's *The Lawnmower Man*" and as "based upon" the short story of the same title by Stephen King. Defendants had licensed the movie rights to King's story, but King had not been involved in writing the screenplay or producing the movie. The movie also differed from the short story in certain particulars. King objected to both the "possessory" and "based upon" credits, and sought a preliminary injunction that the crediting violated Section 43(a).

The Second Circuit found that King was likely to succeed on the merits of the possessory credit claim given his lack of involvement in the screenplay and movie production. Although there was a question over whether King had introduced any evidence of confusion, the court found that no evidence of confusion was required "where, as is the case with the possessory credit, the attribution is false on its face"—a false advertising analysis. *Id.* at 829. Indeed, the court cited a false advertising case involving an attribution claim, *PPX Enters., Inc. v. Audiofidelity Enters., Inc.*, 818 F.2d 266 (2d Cir. 1987) (false advertising claim arising from packaging of defendant's recordings, which exaggerated contribution of

Jimi Hendrix to the recordings). However, the court proceeded to recite a confusion standard in its analysis of the "based upon" credit and rejected King's claim that this credit was false. Thus, *King* is a useful—albeit ambivalent—illustration of the possibility of asserting a false advertising theory against over-attribution.

NOTES AND QUESTIONS

1.   *Name and likeness as "mark."* What is the mark at issue in cases like *Waits* and *Abdul-Jabbar*? For that matter, what are the mark owner's "goods"? In *Amazon Inc. v. Cannondale Inc.*, 56 U.S.P.Q.2d (BNA) 1568 (D. Colo. 2000), Amazon, owner of the publicity rights of professional mountain bike racer Melissa Giove, asserted that Cannondale's depictions of Giove in the Cannondale cycling catalog gave rise to a Section 43(a) false endorsement claim. The court treated Giove's name and likeness as the mark at issue, and her skill and fame as a mountain bike racer as the "goods." Is this a sensible approach? Does it call into question the treatment of over-attribution claims as analogous to trademark infringement claims? Would you suggest that courts turn more frequently to a false advertising theory? Or would you recommend that the confusion test be retained, but with adaptations to make it more amenable to personal identity cases? *See Downing v. Abercrombie & Fitch*, 265 F.3d 994 (9th Cir. 2001) (suggesting adaptations to the confusion test).

The court in *Amazon* found that the mark at issue was distinctive because Giove was a celebrity among mountain bike enthusiasts and that the mark owner's "goods" were closely similar to Cannondale's goods (mountain bike products). However, there was little evidence of actual confusion, and Cannondale had used Giove's name and image on only four of ninety-six catalog pages. On balance, the court found, Cannondale was entitled to summary judgment of no false endorsement violation.

Contrast the *Amazon* case with the Sixth Circuit's approach to personal identity as a trademark in *ETW Corp. v. Jireh Publ'g, Inc.*, 332 F.3d 915 (6th Cir. 2003). The court rejected professional golfer Tiger Woods' claim to trademark rights in his likeness:

> ETW claims protection under the Lanham Act for any and all images of Tiger Woods. This is an untenable claim. ETW asks us, in effect, to constitute Woods himself as a walking, talking trademark. Images and likenesses of Woods are not protectable as a trademark because they do not perform the trademark function of designation. They do not distinguish and identify the source of goods. They cannot function as a trademark because there are undoubtedly thousands of images and likenesses of Woods taken by countless photographers, and drawn, sketched, or painted by numerous artists, which have been published in many forms of media, and sold and distributed throughout the world. No reasonable person could believe that merely because these photographs or paintings contain Woods's likeness or image, they all originated with Woods.
>
>   We hold that, as a general rule, a person's image or likeness cannot function as a trademark.

Id. at 922 (footnote omitted). Do you agree with the court's general rule? Do you agree with the court's reasoning? In another part of the opinion, the court addressed Woods' claim of registered trademark rights in the name "Tiger Woods" without raising any question of trademark validity. Why should Tiger Woods be entitled to claim trademark protection in his name but not in his likeness? *Cf. Nova Wines, Inc. v. Adler Fels Winery LLC*, 467 F. Supp. 2d 965, 977 (N.D. Cal. 2006) (distinguishing *ETW* in a case involving the use of images of Marilyn Monroe on bottles of MARILYN MERLOT wine and other "Marilyn" wines).

We will discuss the right of publicity and First Amendment aspects of the case in more detail in section B.

2.   *Section 43(a) as a vehicle for protecting moral rights.* Are cases such as *Waits* and *King* best explained as cases about protecting artists' moral rights? *Gilliam v. Am. Broad. Cos., Inc.*, 538 F.2d 14 (2d Cir. 1976), is widely viewed as such a case. There, the court upheld a Lanham Act claim on the part of British comedy group Monty Python against ABC when ABC aired a truncated and "mutilated" version of a Monty Python program.

Tom Waits has reportedly invoked moral rights (and copyright claims) in litigation against sound-alikes in Spain (against the auto manufacturer Audi, for using a sound-alike in a commercial), and has initiated litigation in Germany as well (against the auto manufacturer Opel, for using a sound-alike in a commercial). *See* Ben Sisario, *Still Fighting for the Right to His Voice*, N.Y. TIMES, Jan. 20, 2006, at B3 (quoting Waits, who says that an artist's voice is "kind of like your face, your identity" and that he regrets that he has "these unscrupulous dopplegangers out there — my evil twin who is undermining every move I make"). The suit in Spain was apparently grounded in claims of copyright infringement and the violation of moral rights.

Is the following over-attribution allegation a disguised claim of "moral rights" to preserve a work in its original state? Choe, a law student at Fordham, wrote a comment. The *Fordham International Law Journal* published Choe's comment, although the final version appeared in print some time after Choe had graduated from law school. Upon reviewing the published comment, Choe professed horror at alleged substantive and typographical errors that, he said, so mangled the comment that attaching his name to it constituted a false affiliation in violation of Lanham Act §43(a). *See Choe v. Fordham Univ. School of Law*, 920 F. Supp. 44 (S.D.N.Y. 1995), *aff'd*, 81 F.3d 319 (2d Cir. 1996).

3.   *False over-attribution by coincidence.* Suppose that your given name is T.J. Hooker. You discover that a television show producer has created a show using a character named T.J. Hooker. Assume that you are not a celebrity, or even particularly notorious; the producer's selection of your name appears to be pure coincidence. Do you nevertheless have a Section 43(a) cause of action for either false endorsement or false over-attribution? Actually, no. *See Hooker v. Columbia Pictures Indus., Inc.*, 551 F. Supp. 1060 (N.D. Ill. 1982) (no Section 43(a) violation from use of name "T.J. Hooker" as character in TV series, despite fact that plaintiff's name was T.J. Hooker); *Newton v. Thomason*, 22 F.3d 1455 (9th Cir. 1994) (same). Do you agree with these outcomes? *Cf. Albert v. Apex Fitness Inc.*, 44 U.S.P.Q.2d (BNA) 1855 (S.D.N.Y. 1997) (no implied false endorsement where defendant used picture of relatively unknown model in advertisement).

4.   *Adapting the confusion factors for false over-attribution cases.* In *Century 21 v. LendingTree*, discussed in Chapter 9, the court tailored the multi-factor confusion test in order to apply it in a case involving nominative fair use. Should courts tailor the test in order to apply it in a false over-attribution case? In *Facenda v. N.F.L. Films, Inc.*, 542 F.3d 1007 (3d Cir. 2008), the same court agreed to the following adaptations to its multi-factor test (the "*Lapp*" factors, reproduced in Chapter 7, Figure 7-1):

1. the level of recognition that the plaintiff has among the segment of the society for whom the defendant's product is intended;
2. the relatedness of the fame or success of the plaintiff to the defendant's product;
3. the similarity of the likeness used by the defendant to the actual plaintiff;
4. evidence of actual confusion;
5. marketing channels used;
6. likely degree of purchaser care;
7. defendant's intent [in] selecting the plaintiff; and
8. likelihood of expansion of the product lines.

Id. at 1019 (citing *Downing v. Abercrombie & Fitch*, 265 F.3d 994 (9th Cir. 2001)). Do you agree with this approach? If not, what adaptations would you suggest? Do you agree with the general concept of tailoring the likelihood-of-confusion factors to fit particular classes of cases? From your reading of cases in Chapter 7, do you think that courts already do that? *See also Fifty-Six Hope Road Music, Ltd. v. A.V.E.L.A., Inc.*, 778 F.3d 1059 (9th Cir. 2015) (applying the tailored likelihood-of-confusion factors and upholding the determination that the defendant's unauthorized use of a Bob Marley image on T-shirts and other merchandise constituted a false endorsement in violation of Section 43(a)).

2.   False Under-Attribution

One important theory that has surfaced repeatedly in cases involving authors' and performers' attribution in artistic works is the theory of "reverse passing off." *See generally* John T. Cross, *Giving Credit Where Credit Is Due: Revisiting the Doctrine of Reverse Passing Off in Trademark Law*, 72 WASH. L. REV. 709 (1997). "Passing off" or "palming off" refers to acts that we have been studying throughout much of this book, in which a party seeks to represent that its own products actually originate with another by appropriating the other's mark.

The Ninth Circuit distinguished passing off and reverse passing off, and further explained that either variety of passing off could occur through express or implied representations:

> [We define] "passing off" as the practice of selling one person's product or service under the name or mark of another. Passing off may be either "express" or "implied." Express passing off occurs when a business labels its goods or services with a mark identical to that of another enterprise, or otherwise expressly misrepresents the origin of the goods or services. Implied passing off involves the use of a competitor's advertising material, or a sample or photograph of the competitor's product, to impliedly represent that the product being sold is made by the competitor. . . . Express reverse passing off is "accomplished . . . when the wrongdoer removes the name or trademark on another party's product and sells that product under a name chosen by the wrongdoer." Implied reverse passing off is accomplished simply by removing or obliterating the name of the source and then selling the product in an unbranded state.

Lamothe v. Atlantic Recording Corp., 847 F.2d 1403, 1406 (9th Cir. 1988) (citations omitted). In *Lipton v. Nature Co.*, 71 F.3d 464, 473 (2d Cir. 1995), the Second Circuit articulated a four-part test for reverse passing off, requiring a plaintiff to show:

> (1) that the work at issue originated with the plaintiff;
> (2) that the origin of the work was falsely designated by the defendant;
> (3) that the false designation of origin was likely to cause consumer confusion; and
> (4) that the plaintiff was harmed by the defendant's false designation of origin.

Id. at 473.

Prior to the Supreme Court's 2003 *Dastar* decision, some courts found the reverse passing off theory persuasive in cases involving performer's or author's credits—particularly, cases involving a failure to give credit where credit was (allegedly) due. In an oft-cited example, an actor named Paul Smith starred in a movie called *Convoy Buddies*. *Smith v. Montero*, 648 F.2d 602, 603 (9th Cir. 1981). Before the film was released, defendant substituted the name "Bob Spencer" in the credits for Paul Smith. Smith sued under Section 43(a), and the Ninth Circuit concluded that Smith had stated a cause of action for "express reverse passing off," explaining that defendant's behavior implicated both producer interests (in this case the interests of the performer, who was deprived of whatever goodwill may have emanated from his association with *Convoy Buddies*) and consumer interests (consumers being deprived of knowing the true source of the talent that they were viewing in *Convoy Buddies*).

In a few subsequent cases in which the Ninth Circuit applied the reverse passing off theory to cases involving author and performer attribution, the potential overlap between the reverse passing off theory and copyright infringement became evident. In *Shaw v. Lindheim*, 919 F.2d 1353 (9th Cir. 1990), Lou Shaw, an experienced and successful television writer, wrote a pilot script for a television show called "The Equalizer" and submitted it to Lindheim, a television executive, in 1978. In 1982 Lindheim wrote a television series "treatment" called "The Equalizer," which was later revised and expanded into a pilot script and broadcast beginning in 1985. Shaw sued for copyright infringement and for Lanham Act violations. On the basis of a lengthy analysis, the Ninth Circuit concluded that Shaw had presented a triable fact issue on copyright infringement, and reversed the trial court's judgment. However, on the Lanham Act reverse passing off claim, the court affirmed the grant of summary judgment against Shaw. According to the court, the reverse passing off claim was limited to cases of "bodily appropriation"—i.e., cases in which the defendant removes the plaintiff's name from the plaintiff's own work and passes that identical work off as the defendant's own—and does not apply to cases where the defendant passes off a *substantially similar work* as originating with the defendant. *Id.* at 1364. The court took the view that

> Shaw's claim is not consistent with the Lanham Act's purpose of preventing individuals from misleading the public by placing their competitors' work forward as their own. In spite of the similarities between Shaw's script and defendants' pilot, the likelihood that the two works will be confused is minimal. We decline to expand the scope of the Lanham Act to cover cases in which the Federal Copyright Act provides an adequate remedy.

Id. at 1364-65.

Similarly, in *Cleary v. News Corp.*, 30 F.3d 1255 (9th Cir. 1994), plaintiff James Cleary had substantially contributed revisions to *Robert's Rules of Order*, and defendant publisher had credited Cleary on the title page of the 1970 and 1980 editions but had omitted his name from the 1990 edition. In reviewing Cleary's Section 43(a) claim, using reverse passing off rhetoric, the court noted that it had adopted a "bodily appropriation" test without offering a definition of the concept. The court borrowed from copyright law, finding that "bodily appropriation" in copyright law signified copying of "substantially the entire item," and concluding that this definition would be "useful" in Lanham Act cases because "it recognizes that slight modifications of a product might cause customer confusion, while products which are merely generally similar will not." *Id.* at 1261. Applying the test, the court once again found no "bodily appropriation" despite "many" similarities.

This line of cases eventually produced the Ninth Circuit's opinion (and subsequently the Supreme Court's opinion) in *Dastar*, which we examined in Chapter 2. Recall that the dispute that gave rise to the *Dastar* case originated when defendant Dastar distributed a videotape set—"World War II Campaigns in Europe"—that Dastar had created by copying and editing tapes of a television series, "Crusade in Europe." Dastar's packaging for its video set made no reference to the television series, nor was any mention of the series given in the screen credits.

Plaintiff Fox, who was distributing its own set of videotapes based on the television series, sued under both copyright and Lanham Act theories. As for the copyright theory, Fox had owned the copyright in the television series but had failed to renew it, and the copyright had expired, so the copyright claim was based on the copyright in the underlying book from which the television series was made. The Lanham Act theory was a reverse passing off theory: Defendant's packaging falsely omitted crediting the original television series, thus creating the false impression that Dastar was the origin of the content of the videotapes.

The Ninth Circuit rendered its decision in rather summary fashion, in an unpublished opinion, *Twentieth Century Fox Film Corp. v. Entm't Distrib.*, 34 Fed. Appx. 312 (9th Cir. 2002). In contrast to its usual pattern in reverse passing off cases, the Ninth Circuit concluded that the plaintiff had satisfied the "bodily appropriation" test. That is, instead of using the "bodily appropriation" test as an obstacle to keep the Lanham Act out of the purported domain of copyright, the Ninth Circuit declared that the test relieved the plaintiff from proving confusion because the test "subsumes the less demanding 'consumer confusion' standard." *Id.* at 314 (quoting *Cleary*).

The Supreme Court granted *certiorari* and reversed, as we noted in Chapter 2. *Dastar Corp. v. Twentieth Century Fox Film Corp.*, 539 U.S. 23 (2003). The Court's *Dastar* opinion does not fit easily within the existing jurisprudence of Section 43(a) false endorsement and false attribution. The Court acknowledged the existence of the reverse passing off theory and the bodily appropriation test, but did not frame its opinion in terms of either the theory or the test, leaving the question of the role of reverse passing off and bodily appropriation for cases post-*Dastar*. Instead, the Court veered off unexpectedly into a disquisition on the proper interpretation of "origin" in Section 43(a). As we have previously discussed (*see* Chapter 2), the Court concluded that "origin" as used in Section 43(a) "refers to the producer of the tangible goods that are offered for sale, and not to the author of any idea, concept, or communication embodied in those goods." *Id.* at 37.

The Court also cited practical and theoretical problems with applying a Section 43(a) reverse passing off theory beyond the confines of the Court's narrow conception of the meaning of "origin." Many of these problems deal with the trademark-copyright interface, and we have explored those elsewhere (again, Chapter 2). However, the Court also cited a supposed doctrinal dilemma within the Lanham Act: On the one hand, manufacturers like

Dastar "would face Lanham Act liability for *failing* to credit the creator of a work on which their lawful copies are based; and on the other hand they could face Lanham Act liability for *crediting* the creator if that should be regarded as implying the creator's 'sponsorship or approval' of the copy." *Id.* at 36 (*citing* Section 43(a)(1)(A)). Is this a dilemma at all? If Dastar's packaging had indicated that the videotape series was "prepared from the original television series 'Crusade in Europe'" and noted that "Dastar is not affiliated with the producers of the original television series," what is the likelihood that Dastar would have been found liable for false over-attribution under Section 43(a)? Is the Court's "dilemma" a straw man?

Unfortunately, the opinion contained very few hints about how false attribution cases were to be decided. The Court opined that Fox's claim "undoubtedly" would have been sustained had Dastar simply bought some of the Fox videotapes "and merely repackaged them as its own." Dastar's behavior, said the Court, was "vastly different." Dastar "took a creative work in the public domain—the Crusade television series—copied it, made modifications (arguably minor), and produced its very own series of videotapes." *Id.* at 31. What is it precisely that makes the two acts "vastly different"? When "copying" is grouped together with "producing one's very own" work, don't these concepts begin to lose meaning? What one person characterizes as "mere repackaging" another might just as plausibly characterize as copying and producing as one's very own (with minor modifications). So is it the fact that the "Crusade" television series was no longer under copyright that creates space between prohibited repackaging and allowable repackaging? If so, does this mean that *Dastar* applies only when a defendant appropriates an uncopyrighted work? But doesn't the *Dastar* interpretation of "origin" in Section 43(a) apply to all Section 43(a) actions, not just actions involving alleged false attribution in uncopyrighted communicative works?

NOTES AND QUESTIONS

1.   *The scope of* Dastar. Courts have applied *Dastar* broadly in a variety of under-attribution cases involving reverse passing off claims. For example, in *Zyla v. Wadsworth*, 360 F.3d 243 (1st Cir. 2004), Zyla and Struble co-authored a textbook. After a dispute involving preparation of the fourth edition of the text, Zyla withdrew from the project and insisted that any work she had done for the fourth edition not be included in the final product. The publisher used her work anyway, and Zyla sued under various theories, including a Section 43(a) reverse passing off theory based on the fact that the book credits for the fourth edition omitted mention of Zyla's contributions. In perfunctory fashion, the court concluded that Zyla's claim was of the same type as the claim in *Dastar*—"false authorship," according to the court's characterization—and therefore was barred just as Fox's claim in *Dastar* had been barred. *See also Bretford Mfg., Inc. v. Smith Sys. Mfg. Corp.*, 419 F.3d 576 (7th Cir. 2005); *Monsanto Co. v. Syngenta Seeds, Inc.*, 443 F. Supp. 2d 648 (D. Del. 2006). In the latter case, Syngenta's inbred corn contained the valuable "GA21" trait (imparting herbicide tolerance); Monsanto had crossed its own inbred corn line with Syngenta's inbred and had sold the resulting hybrid (which contained the GA21 trait) as its own. This was not reverse passing off, because Monsanto was correctly representing that it was the physical origin of the hybrid, even though it was not the originator of the GA21 trait contained in the hybrid.

Should *Dastar* also preclude claims of false over-attribution (passing off claims), or should it be limited to false under-attribution (reverse passing off claims)? Consider, for example, the *Waits* case. Is the false statement there—the implication that Tom Waits endorses Frito-Lay's products—a representation about the physical origin of the goods?

If it isn't, is it outside the scope of Section 43(a) and therefore shielded from liability after *Dastar*? *But cf. Facenda v. N.F.L. Films, Inc.*, 542 F.3d 1007 (3d Cir. 2008) (addressing a false over-attribution claim after *Dastar*). What about the false possessory credit in the *Stephen King* case? For example, after *Dastar*, would we (or our casebook publisher) be subject to liability under Section 43(a) if we called this casebook "Stephen King's *Trademark and Unfair Competition Law*"? (Before you respond that we would escape liability under Section 43(a)(1)(A) but be subject to false advertising liability under Section 43(a)(1)(B), take a look at Problem 11-1 below.) For an unusual view on post-*Dastar* false over-attribution cases, *see Schlotzsky's, Ltd. v. Sterling Purchasing and Nat'l Dist. Co., Inc.*, 520 F.3d 393 (5th Cir. 2008) (citing *Dastar* for the proposition that Section 43(a)(1)(A) applies broadly, even to some cases in which no trademark is involved). In the case, Schlotzsky's, a restaurant franchisor, had approved defendant Sterling as a temporary nonexclusive purchasing agent to interface with Schlotzsky's franchisees, but even after Schlotzsky's had terminated the relationship, Sterling allegedly held itself out to various manufacturers and distributors as the exclusive purchasing agent for the Schlotzsky's franchise system.

　　2. Dastar *and the language of Section 43(a).* In answering questions in the preceding note about the scope of *Dastar*, perhaps a return to the statutory language is in order. The *Dastar* Court focuses on the term "origin," but Section 43(a) imposes liability for a false representation that is likely to cause confusion "as to the affiliation, connection, or association" of one person with another, "*or* as to the origin, sponsorship, or approval" of one person's commercial activities as those of another (emphasis supplied). Statements of false over-attribution surely may be said to cause confusion as to affiliation, connection, or association, even if they may not be considered statements about "origin" after *Dastar*. Indeed, statements of false over-attribution may be considered statements about "sponsorship or approval," even if they cannot be considered statements about "origin."

　　Nonetheless, some courts seem to be unwilling to recognize such distinctions. For example, in *Antidote Int'l Films v. Bloomsbury Publ'g, PLC*, 467 F. Supp. 2d 394 (S.D.N.Y. 2006), an author wrote a novel under the name "J.T. Leroy" and, with the assistance of others, including her publisher (Bloomsbury), created an elaborate fictional persona for Leroy suggesting that the novel was based on events in Leroy's life. Apparently taken in by these representations, a film producer (Antidote) purchased an option to create a film based on the book. When the press eventually revealed "Leroy" as a hoax, Antidote sued under various theories, including a Lanham Act §43(a) claim.

　　Without considering whether the claim was for reverse passing off (is it?), the court concluded that *Dastar* precluded liability, because any false representation was about authorship, not about "origin." Although the plaintiff had asserted only the "origin" language in Section 43(a), the court indicated that it would have ruled the same way even if Antidote had alleged a violation of the "association, affiliation, or connection." According to the court, this would have been a mere restatement of the cause of action precluded by *Dastar*. How would you rule on these points if they came before you on appeal?

　　3. Dastar *and trademark theories of attribution.* In the section on false over-attribution, we noted that courts (before *Dastar*) routinely analogized to trademark infringement in assessing over-attribution claims, relying expressly on the likelihood-of-confusion factors and treating personal names and likenesses as the relevant marks. Does *Dastar* effectively reject this analogy? Suppose you go into a bookstore and pick up a book by wildly successful author Danielle Steel. The author's name appears in large print in a distinctive font on the cover and the book spine; the title appears in much smaller print. Is the author's name functioning as a trademark? Are you surprised, or do you find it rather obvious that an author's name might function as a trademark? Now, review the *Dastar* opinion. Does *Dastar* cast into doubt the proposition that an author's name could be recognized as serving a trademark function? If so, does *Dastar* have it wrong? For interesting scholarly explications of this and related points, *see, e.g.*, Laura A. Heymann, *The Birth of the Authornym: Authorship, Pseudonymity, and Trademark Law*, 80 Notre Dame L. Rev. 1377 (2005); F. Gregory Lastowka, *The Trademark Function of Authorship*, 85 B.U. L. Rev. 1171 (2005); Jane C. Ginsburg, *The Author's Name as a Trademark: A Perverse Perspective on the Moral Right of "Paternity"?*, 23 Cardozo Arts & Ent. L.J. 379 (2005). For other relevant commentary, *see, e.g.*, Jane C. Ginsburg, *The Right to Claim Authorship in U.S. Copyright and Trademark Law*, 41 Hous. L. Rev. 263 (2004); Roberta Rosenthal Kwall, *The Attribution Right in the United States: Caught in the Crossfire Between Copyright and Section 43(a)*, 77 Wash. L. Rev. 985 (2002).

4. *Dastar and moral rights.* Whose interests are at stake in the debate over whether to craft intellectual property law protection against false under-attribution? Primarily the unattributed author? If so, is the debate best framed as one involving author's moral rights, finding roots in both copyright and (perhaps) unfair competition law? Primarily the author's publisher? If so, is the debate then best framed in terms of trademark law's incentive effects, on the ground that publishers will have greater incentives to invest in authors' works, and in maintaining consistent quality in those works, if the law ensures that the works carry the authors' names? What of consumers? If consumer interests in minimizing search costs are implicated, should the debate be framed in trademark terms? For one view, *see* Justin Hughes, *American Moral Rights and Fixing the* Dastar *"Gap,"* 2007 Utah L. Rev. 659.

5. *Norms against plagiarism.* We have shown how courts have viewed under-attribution through the lens of trademark and unfair competition law, using theories such as reverse passing off. But more commonly, when someone fails to give attribution to another's work, we view the matter through the lens of commonly held norms of behavior, and call the under-attribution plagiarism. What relevance, if any, should the norms of plagiarism have in shaping the Lanham Act law of false attribution? Consider whether you agree with the following:

> Attribution norms vary widely from one field to another, and even within the same field, depending on the content's audience. This wide variance suggests that plagiarism is better left to the community or professional associations, which are capable of considering the nuances of context, than the far more rigid legal system. And when plagiarism rises beyond *de minimis* copying, copyright law may be invoked, where appropriate. The *Dastar* Court, therefore, reached the proper policy outcome; it did not impose costly attribution requirements on authors in situations where attribution does not benefit the market.

Jonathan Band & Matt Schruers, Dastar, *Attribution, and Plagiarism*, 33 AIPLA Q.J. 1, 22-23 (2005).

While you ponder this, recall the *Dastar* opinion. Remember the pungent phrase "mutant copyright law"? We thought you would. And how about the passage comparing rigorous attribution to a search for the "source of the Nile"? The Court apparently lifted these colorful passages from the briefs—without attribution. But who cares? (And lest there be any question, we got this information from Band & Schruers, 33 AIPLA Q.J. at 15-16, who say that they got it from David Nimmer, *The Moral Imperative Against Academic Plagiarism (Without a Moral Right Against Reverse Passing Off)*, 54 DePaul L. Rev. 1 (2004), who wrote the brief in question.)

6. *Dastar and state law unfair competition claims.* Does *Dastar*'s restrictive ruling apply to reverse passing off claims grounded in state unfair competition law? On remand in *Dastar*, the trial court held that California state unfair competition law was substantially congruent with Lanham Act §43(a), because both depended on a showing of likelihood of confusion. *See Twentieth Century Fox Film Corp. v. Dastar Corp.*, 68 U.S.P.Q.2d (BNA) 1536 (C.D. Cal. 2003) (dismissing the state law claim).

7.   *Proving harm from reverse passing off: materiality?* Courts are sometimes skeptical about reverse passing off claims even when those claims are premised on misrepresentations about the physical origin of the goods. In *Syngenta Seeds, Inc. v. Delta Cotton Co-operative, Inc.*, 457 F.3d 1269 (Fed. Cir. 2006), defendant Delta, operator of a grain elevator, purchased large quantities of wheat from various local farmers and stored the wheat in a common storage bin. Periodically, Delta withdrew wheat from storage and resold it as "feed wheat" (which means, for those of you not from Iowa, that it was sold for use as feed for animals, not as seed to propagate crops). Delta sold its feed wheat in bags marked DELTA COTTON CO-OPERATIVE and FEED WHEAT. Some of the feed wheat bags contained plaintiff Syngenta's COKER wheat seed, presumably because farmers who had sold wheat to the elevator had grown COKER seed.

These facts surely fit the typical pattern for express reverse passing off cases: Delta was applying its own mark to products that had not originated with it. The jury found Delta liable under that theory, but the Federal Circuit overturned the verdict. The Federal Circuit was willing to acknowledge the existence of the reverse passing off cause of action, but found no sufficient evidence of reputational injury to Syngenta. According to the court,

> A person who purchased Coker 9663 that was marked as "Delta Co-Op Feed" could never know that it had purchased the trademarked product, and could thus have drawn no conclusions about the merits or quality of that product. The parties have not directed this court to any record evidence of lost advertising value, the value of lost goodwill, or any similar injury. Given that these were the only kinds of harm on which the jury received instructions, we cannot conclude that the jury's verdict was supported by sufficient evidence.

Id. at 1278. In *Dastar*, if Dastar had merely repackaged Fox tapes with Dastar packaging, would a consumer have known that it was purchasing Fox's product? If not, doesn't the Federal Circuit's reasoning effectively gut any claim of reverse passing off? Perhaps, instead, the court is instinctively attempting to add a materiality requirement to the reverse passing off analysis. Should reverse passing off claims be subject to such a requirement? Recall that materiality is typically recited as an element of a Section 43(a)(1)(B) false advertising claim.

PROBLEM 11-1:   *DASTAR* AND FALSE ADVERTISING THEORIES IN UNDER-ATTRIBUTION CASES . . . FEATURING PARIS HILTON

At the end of the *Dastar* opinion, the Court remarked that even though Fox's reverse passing off claim failed under Section 43(a)(1)(A), Fox might have a false advertising claim under Section 43(a)(1)(B). The following exercises explore how such a claim might (or might not) work.

(1) Few people know this, but this casebook was actually written by hotel heiress Paris Hilton. Just before publication, the publisher deleted Paris Hilton's name from the credits and substituted Dinwoodie and Janis, citing "market factors." Paris Hilton sued under Section 43(a)(1)(A) for reverse passing off. We cited *Dastar*. Paris amended her complaint, transforming her reverse passing off allegation into a Section 43(a)(1)(B) false advertising allegation. Is Paris likely to survive a motion to dismiss on the newly minted false advertising allegation? Will most plaintiffs facing *Dastar*-inspired dismissal of false attribution claims reformulate them successfully as false advertising claims, as the *Dastar* opinion invites? What about the problem of standing (discussed above, in the notes following the cases on over-attribution)? Does Paris have standing to assert a false advertising

claim against us? For a relevant discussion, *see, e.g., Radolf v. Univ. of Connecticut*, 364 F. Supp. 2d 204, 221-22 (D. Conn. 2005). (Paris, if you're reading this, we're just kidding.)

(2) To supplement our incomes, we (Dinwoodie and Janis) market a line of high-fashion athletic shoes using "dual-cushion technology." We describe the technology in our advertisements, and claim that the shoes are "innovative." In fact, Paris Hilton developed the dual-cushion technology. We ripped it off, and nowhere credit Paris Hilton for it. Suppose that Ms. Hilton sues under Section 43(a)(1)(B). Even if Ms. Hilton has standing, does her false advertising claim survive *Dastar*? A key question may be whether the claim that the shoes are innovative is essentially a claim of false authorship. Is it? Should that matter? *See, e.g., Baden Sports, Inc. v. Molten USA, Inc.*, 556 F.3d 1300 (Fed. Cir. 2009) (applying Ninth Circuit law); *Sybersound Records, Inc. v. UAV Corp.*, 517 F.3d 1137, 1144 (9th Cir. 2008); *Antidote Int'l Films v. Bloomsbury Publ'g, PLC*, 467 F. Supp. 2d 394 (S.D.N.Y. 2006). If you're weary of Paris Hilton and would prefer other fact settings, try *Wilchcombe v. Teevee Toons, Inc.*, 515 F. Supp. 2d 1297 (N.D. Ga. 2007) (CD insert and other materials allegedly failed to credit plaintiff and instead credited recording artist Lil Jon for track "Tha Weedman" on CD *Kings of Crunk*), *aff'd*, 555 F.3d 949 (2009); *Monsanto Co. v. Syngenta Seeds, Inc.*, 443 F. Supp. 2d 648 (D. Del. 2006) (advertising concerning genetically modified seed).

B. RIGHT OF PUBLICITY

We now leave the Lanham Act behind and turn to state law, currently the only source of rights of publicity. Most states have recognized either statutory or common law rights of publicity. In the remaining jurisdictions, right-of-publicity claims have not been asserted in recent reported decisions; i.e., there are no recent cases in which courts have refused to recognize the right of publicity. For an analysis of the current state of the right of publicity, see JENNIFER E. ROTHMAN, THE RIGHT OF PUBLICITY: PRIVACY REIMAGINED FOR A PUBLIC WORLD (Harvard Univ. Press 2018).

The first subsection (B.1) introduces both statutory and common law right-of-publicity regimes, and sketches out some of the issues that commonly arise under those regimes. The next subsection (B.2) explores the key issue of defining the scope of the right of publicity, an exercise that entails determining which aspects of a rights holder's persona lie within the ambit of the right of publicity as defined either by local statute or common law. The final subsection (B.3) considers limitations on the right of publicity.

1. Overview of Statutory and Common Law Regimes

In this section we first present an overview of statutory rights of publicity, using the Indiana statute as an example. We chose the Indiana statute because it is comprehensive and serves as a good introduction to many of the issues that arise in right of publicity litigation. The notes following the statute examine some of those issues and draw comparisons between the Indiana statute and statutes in more active right-of-publicity jurisdictions, such as California.

Consider the following fact pattern as you read the Indiana statute. Larry Bird, a basketball star who played for Indiana State University and the Boston Celtics, and coached the Indiana Pacers, is from French Lick, Indiana. Suppose that Larry Bird returns to French Lick to coach basketball at his high school alma mater, Springs Valley High. Immediately, a few interesting things happen:

(1) The French Lick City Fathers immediately erect a new, ten-foot-tall bronze statue of Larry Bird in front of the entrance to the high school gymnasium. The plaque on the statue reads, "Larry Bird: The Greatest of All Time."

(2) In the nearby town of Paoli, a local bar owner constructs a giant billboard featuring a photograph of Larry Bird, a testimonial ("After the ball game, meet me at Joe's Sports Bar, the best sports bar in Paoli"), and some other references implying that people who spend their time in French Lick are boring losers.

(3) The local newspapers run a ten-part series on Larry Bird, commencing with a front-page photo of Larry Bird under the headline "The Second Coming."

(4) The local newspaper laminates copies of the front page and gives them away at Springs Valley High basketball games. Later, the newspaper begins selling the laminated copies at a gift shop at the Paoli International Airport for $5 apiece.

(5) Using a sophisticated color printing process, the local newspaper prints a color reproduction of the front page on a towel set. The "Larry Bird—The Second Coming" souvenir towel set retails for $55, although people in places like Terre Haute and Martinsville will pay upwards of $125.

(6) In a comedy segment using local newspaper headlines during *The Tonight Show*, comedian Jimmy Fallon displays a copy of the front page of the *French Lick Times*. The page includes a large photo of Larry Bird.

(7) A French Lick resident converts his garage into "The Larry Bird Museum." The museum features many photographs of Larry Bird, a towel once used by Larry Bird in a high school game, a jar containing toenail clippings from Larry Bird, and oil drained from a truck that Larry Bird drove during college.

Assume that Larry Bird has not consented to any of these uses, at least not in writing. Read the Indiana right-of-publicity statute and determine whether any of the uses raise right-of-publicity problems.

INDIANA CODE TITLE 32 (PROPERTY)—ART. 36 (PUBLICITY), CHAP. 1 (RIGHTS OF PUBLICITY)

[SELECTED EXCERPTS]

32-36-1-1 APPLICATION OF CHAPTER

Sec. 1. (a) This chapter applies to an act or event that occurs within Indiana, regardless of a personality's domicile, residence, or citizenship.

(b) This chapter does not affect rights and privileges recognized under any other law that apply to a news reporting or an entertainment medium.

(c) This chapter does not apply to the following:

(1) The use of a personality's name, voice, signature, photograph, image, likeness, distinctive appearance, gestures, or mannerisms in any of the following:

(A) Literary works, theatrical works, musical compositions, film, radio, or television programs.

(B) Material that has political or newsworthy value.

(C) Original works of fine art.

(D) Promotional material or an advertisement for a news reporting or an entertainment medium that:

(i) uses all or part of a past edition of the medium's own broadcast or publication; and

(ii) does not convey or reasonably suggest that a personality endorses the news reporting or entertainment medium.

(E) An advertisement or commercial announcement for a use described under this subdivision.

(2) The use of a personality's name to truthfully identify the personality as:

    (A) the author of a written work; or

    (B) a performer of a recorded performance;

under circumstances in which the written work or recorded performance is otherwise rightfully reproduced, exhibited, or broadcast.

(3) The use of a personality's:

    (A) name;

    (B) voice;

    (C) signature;

    (D) photograph;

    (E) image;

    (F) likeness;

    (G) distinctive appearance;

    (H) gestures; or

    (I) mannerisms;

in connection with the broadcast or reporting of an event or a topic of general or public interest.

32-36-1-2 "Commercial Purpose" Defined

Sec. 2. As used in this chapter, "commercial purpose" means the use of an aspect of a personality's right of publicity as follows:

(1) On or in connection with a product, merchandise, goods, services, or commercial activities.

(2) For advertising or soliciting purchases of products, merchandise, goods, services, or for promoting commercial activities.

(3) For the purpose of fundraising.

32-36-1-3 "Name" Defined

Sec. 3. As used in this chapter, "name" means the actual or assumed name of a living or deceased natural person that is intended to identify the person.

   . . .

32-36-1-5 "Person" Defined

Sec. 5. As used in this chapter, "person" means a natural person, a partnership, a firm, a corporation, or an unincorporated association.

32-36-1-6 "Personality" Defined

Sec. 6. As used in this chapter, "personality" means a living or deceased natural person whose:

    (1) name;

    (2) voice;

    (3) signature;

    (4) photograph;

    (5) image;

    (6) likeness;

    (7) distinctive appearance;

    (8) gesture; or

    (9) mannerism;

has commercial value, whether or not the person uses or authorizes the use of the person's rights of publicity for a commercial purpose during the person's lifetime.

32-36-1-7 "Right of Publicity" Defined

Sec. 7. As used in this chapter, "right of publicity" means a personality's property interest in the personality's:

(1) name;

(2) voice;

(3) signature;

(4) photograph;

(5) image;

(6) likeness;

(7) distinctive appearance;

(8) gestures; or

(9) mannerisms.

32-36-1-8 Use of Personality's Right of Publicity

Sec. 8. (a) A person may not use an aspect of a personality's right of publicity for a commercial purpose during the personality's lifetime or for one hundred (100) years after the date of the personality's death without having obtained previous written consent from a person specified in section 17 of this chapter. . . .

32-36-1-9 Submission to Court Jurisdiction

Sec. 9. A person who:

(1) engages in conduct within Indiana that is prohibited under section 8 of this chapter;

(2) creates or causes to be created within Indiana goods, merchandise, or other materials prohibited under section 8 of this chapter;

(3) transports or causes to be transported into Indiana goods, merchandise, or other materials created or used in violation of section 8 of this chapter; or

(4) knowingly causes advertising or promotional material created or used in violation of section 8 of this chapter to be published, distributed, exhibited, or disseminated within Indiana;

submits to the jurisdiction of Indiana courts.

32-36-1-10 Damages

Sec. 10. A person who violates section 8 of this chapter may be liable for any of the following:

(1) Damages in the amount of:

(A) one thousand dollars ($1,000); or

(B) actual damages, including profits derived from the unauthorized use; whichever is greater.

(2) Treble or punitive damages, as the injured party may elect, if the violation under section 8 of this chapter is knowing, willful, or intentional.

. . .

32-36-1-12 Attorney's Fees; Injunctions

Sec. 12. In addition to any damages awarded under section 10 of this chapter, the court:

(1) shall award to the prevailing party reasonable attorney's fees, costs, and expenses relating to an action under this chapter; and

(2) may order temporary or permanent injunctive relief, except as provided by section 13 of this chapter.

32-36-1-13 UNENFORCEABLE INJUNCTIONS

Sec. 13. Injunctive relief is not enforceable against a news reporting or an entertainment medium that has:

(1) contracted with a person for the publication or broadcast of an advertisement; and

(2) incorporated the advertisement in tangible form into material that has been prepared for broadcast or publication.

32-36-1-14 ORDER FOR IMPOUNDMENT

Sec. 14. (a) This section does not apply to a news reporting or an entertainment medium.

(b) During any period that an action under this chapter is pending, a court may order the impoundment of:

(1) goods, merchandise, or other materials claimed to have been made or used in violation of section 8 of this chapter; and

(2) plates, molds, matrices, masters, tapes, negatives, or other items from which goods, merchandise, or other materials described in subdivision (1) may be manufactured or reproduced.

(c) The court may order impoundment under subsection (b) upon terms that the court considers reasonable.

32-36-1-15 ORDER FOR DESTRUCTION

Sec. 15. (a) This section does not apply to a news reporting or an entertainment medium.

(b) As part of a final judgment or decree, a court may order the destruction or other reasonable disposition of items described in section 14(b) of this chapter.

32-36-1-16 PROPERTY RIGHTS

Sec. 16. The rights recognized under this chapter are property rights, freely transferable and descendible, in whole or in part, by the following:

(1) Contract.

(2) License.

(3) Gift.

(4) Trust.

(5) Testamentary document.

(6) Operation of the laws of intestate succession applicable to the state administering the estate and property of an intestate deceased personality, regardless of whether the state recognizes the property rights set forth under this chapter.

32-36-1-17 WRITTEN CONSENT

Sec. 17. (a) The written consent required by section 8 of this chapter and the rights and remedies set forth in this chapter may be exercised and enforced by:

(1) a personality; or

(2) a person to whom the recognized rights of a personality have been transferred under section 16 of this chapter.

(b) If a transfer of a personality's recognized rights has not occurred under section 16 of this chapter, a person to whom the personality's recognized rights are transferred under section 18 of this chapter may exercise and enforce the rights under this chapter and seek the remedies provided in this chapter.

32-36-1-18 Exercise of Rights and Remedies Post-Mortem

Sec. 18. (a) Subject to sections 16 and 17 of this chapter, after the death of an intestate personality, the rights and remedies of this chapter may be exercised and enforced by a person who possesses a total of not less than one-half (1/2) interest of the personality's recognized rights.

(b) A person described in subsection (a) shall account to any other person in whom the personality's recognized rights have vested to the extent that the other person's interest may appear.

32-36-1-19 Termination of Deceased Person's Rights

Sec. 19. If:

(1) a deceased personality's recognized rights under this chapter were not transferred by:

(A) contract;
(B) license;
(C) gift;
(D) trust; or
(E) testamentary document; and

(2) there are no surviving persons as described in section 17 of this chapter to whom the deceased personality's recognized rights pass by intestate succession;

the deceased personality's rights set forth in this chapter terminate.

. . .

NOTES AND QUESTIONS

1.   *Lanham Act right of publicity?* Although a Lanham Act §43(a) violation is sometimes alleged in cases of unauthorized exploitation of identity (*see supra* section A), the Lanham Act contains no right-of-publicity provision. The right of publicity is strictly a creature of state law. Should Congress adopt a federal right of publicity? For proposals, *see* Symposium, *Rights of Publicity: An In-Depth Analysis of the New Legislative Proposal to Congress*, 16 Cardozo Arts & Ent. L.J. 209 (1998); Barbara A. Solomon, *Can the Lanham Act Protect Tiger Woods? An Analysis of Whether the Lanham Act Is a Proper Substitute for a Federal Right of Publicity*, 94 Trademark Rep. 1202 (2004) (concluding that existing Lanham Act remedies are inadequate and discussing a 2001-02 ABA IP section proposal for a federal right of publicity); *cf.* Usha Rodrigues, *Race to the Stars: A Federalism Argument for Leaving the Right of Publicity in the Hands of the States*, 87 Va. L. Rev. 1201 (2001).

2.   *Property rights in gross?* In connection with our discussions of trademark rights, we routinely confronted questions about the nature of the trademark as property, characterizing the trademark right as a limited property right and questioning whether the presence of a Section 43(c) dilution cause of action extended trademark rights to something approaching property rights in gross. The right of publicity is an in-gross property right as normally conceptualized. Is this true of the Indiana right of publicity? To which provisions would you look in answering this question?

Another way to approach the question is to ask whether liability for violation of a right of publicity is based on a confusion-oriented theory. For example, in reference to the scenario at the beginning of this section, if Larry Bird sued the sports bar under Indiana right-of-publicity law over the billboard, would Bird have to show that consumers were likely confused about Bird's possible endorsement of or affiliation with the sports bar? To which Indiana statutory provisions would you look in answering this question? If right-of-publicity rules do not currently incorporate limiting concepts such as confusion or dilution, should they be limited to conform to those trademark concepts? *See* Stacey L. Dogan & Mark A. Lemley, *What the Right of Publicity Can Learn from Trademark Law*, 58 Stan. L. Rev. 1161 (2006).

If the right of publicity is a true property right in gross, we would expect to see rules on alienability. Does the Indiana statute contain such rules? What are they? If the right of publicity is a freely alienable property right, is it subject to *involuntary* transfer—for example, seizure by creditors, or in the course of a bankruptcy proceeding? *See* Melissa B. Jacoby & Diane Leenheer Zimmerman, *Foreclosing on Fame: Exploring the Uncharted Boundaries of the Right of Publicity*, 77 N.Y.U. L. Rev. 1322 (2002) (arguing that the right of publicity should be subject to certain types of involuntary transfers). *Should* the right of publicity be freely alienable? Under which circumstances might free alienability run counter to the interests of the personality who initially holds the rights? *See* Jennifer E. Rothman, *The Inalienable Right of Publicity*, 101 Geo. L.J. 185 (2012).

3.   *What is the* res? It is typical to characterize property as a set of rights attaching to some *res.* Consider the Larry Bird example. What is the *res* for purposes of Larry Bird's right of publicity as defined in the Indiana statute? It may be helpful generally to consider the *res* to constitute the rights holder's "persona," and then to define the components of that persona in order to delineate the precise scope of the right of publicity in any case. Many of the right-of-publicity cases can be understood as engaging in this exercise, even if the courts do not always define the exercise specifically in these terms. We explore such cases in subsection B.2 *infra.*

4.   *Obtaining rights: is use required?* In most intellectual property systems, a body of rules (both substantive and procedural) governs the creation of rights, and another body of rules governs the enforcement of rights. Consider whether the Indiana statute on the right of publicity reflects that typical division. Look first for rules governing the creation of rights, and consider the following issue. Under U.S. trademark law, rights are acquired through use. Should persons have a right of publicity only if they can show that they have exploited it? Or are the rights inchoate? The issue is certainly important as a theoretical matter. As a practical matter, the issue might arise, e.g., if a person's estate asserts a postmortem right of publicity, and the person had never exploited his or her publicity rights during his or her lifetime.

5.   *Obtaining rights: who may be a "personality"?* Does the Indiana right of publicity extend only to human persons—or might it extend further? Would Lassie, the celebrity dog, have a right of publicity under the Indiana statute? If not, should the statute be amended to provide for such a right? What of Garfield the cat, a famous cartoon character drawn by Jim Davis (of Indiana)?

Should the right of publicity extend beyond natural persons, to nonhuman entities? For example, the University of Notre Dame is located in South Bend, Indiana. Does Notre Dame have a right of publicity under the Indiana statute as currently formulated? Should it? What about the Indianapolis Motor Speedway, operated by a privately owned business organization and located in Speedway, Indiana?

Should the right of publicity extend to communities? For example, could members of the Miami Indian Native American community in Indiana assert a collective right of publicity against, say, a basket weaver who advertises baskets that are allegedly "inspired by styles first noted among the Miami tribes" and who uses numerous Miami Indian references and imagery in promoting the baskets? *See* Antony Taubman, *Is There a Right of Collective Personality?*, 28 Eur. Intell. Prop. Rev. 485 (2006).

6.   *Term.* What is the term of a right of publicity in Indiana? What should the term of a right of publicity be—an arbitrary term of years? A term coextensive with the subject's life, such that the right of publicity would not extend postmortem? For a view from a common law jurisdiction, *see, e.g., McFarland v. Miller*, 14 F.3d 912 (3d Cir. 1994) (noting that under New Jersey state law, civil actions for trespass survive the property owner's death, and analogizing the right of publicity to trespass actions). If courts recognize a post-mortem right of publicity in a common law jurisdiction, should they require evidence that the personality exploited the right during the personality's lifetime? *See Hebrew Univ. of Jerusalem v. General Motors L.L.C.*, 878 F. Supp. 2d 1021 (C.D. Cal. 2012) (involving use of Albert Einstein image in an automobile advertisement) (applying New Jersey law). Moreover, if courts recognize post-mortem rights of publicity, how long should those rights last? Should courts look to statutes from other states? (Statutes that recognize post-mortem rights specify durations as low as twenty years after death to an indefinite duration.) Should courts analogize to copyright duration (life of the author plus seventy years, where the author is a natural person)? *See Hebrew Univ. of Jerusalem v. General Motors L.L.C.*, 903 F. Supp. 2d 932, 942 (C.D. Cal. 2012) (ruling that a duration of fifty years after death "appropriately reflects the balance between meaningful enforcement of the right of publicity after a famous individual's death and the public's interest in free expression") (applying New Jersey law). *See generally* John W. Branch, David H. Green & Karl A. Hefter, *No Respect for the Dead: Protecting Deceased Celebrity Personality Rights in the United States*, 22 WORLD INTELL. PROP. REP. (No. 10) (Oct. 2008).

7.   *Limitations and defenses.* Does the right of publicity raise First Amendment concerns? If so, how are those concerns addressed in the Indiana statute, if at all? What statutory defenses or limitations does the Indiana statute provide?

8.   *Commercial purpose.* Internet booksellers, such as Amazon.com, typically display cover images of the books that they offer for sale. One day, while shopping for books online, we (Dinwoodie and Janis) came across a murder mystery, *The Case of the Larcenous Law Professors*. The book cover contained an unauthorized photograph of the two of us looking, well, furtive. Assuming that jurisdictional requirements are satisfied, do we have a case under the Indiana right-of-publicity statute against the book publisher? Do we have a right-of-publicity claim against the online bookseller for displaying an image of the book cover? *See Almeida v. Amazon.com, Inc.*, 456 F.3d 1316 (11th Cir. 2006) (applying Florida right-of-publicity law).

9.   *Remedies.* If the right of publicity is a true property right in gross, we would expect that to be reflected in the available remedies for right-of-publicity violations. What are the available remedies under the Indiana statute? Do they reinforce or undermine the proposition that the Indiana right of publicity is a property right in gross?

In a dispute between former Harlem Globetrotters players and firms that were licensing the players' names, likenesses, and jersey numbers, the parties litigated the question of the measure of damages for a right-of-publicity violation. The plaintiffs sought disgorgement of the defendants' profits, but defendants contended that damages in right-of-publicity cases were measured by determining the fair market value of the right to use the plaintiff's identity. According to the court:

> Fair market value of the unauthorized use is simply one measure of damages available in right of publicity cases. *See* Restatement (Third) of Unfair Competition ("Restatement") §49 cmt. d (stating that "courts *sometimes* apply a measure of damages based on the fair market value of the unauthorized use") (emphasis added). The Restatement makes clear that "the plaintiff may recover the proportion of the defendant's net profits that is attributable to the unauthorized use." *Id.* Once the plaintiff establishes the defendant's sales, "the defendant has the burden of establishing any portion of the sales that is attributable to factors other than the appropriation of the plaintiff's identity and any expenses properly deducted in determining net profits." *Id.* Because this law clearly makes disgorgement of profits available as a remedy in this case, the Court will deny Defendants' request for summary judgment on this issue.

Lemon v. Harlem Globetrotters Int'l, Inc., 437 F. Supp. 2d 1089, 1103 (D. Ariz. 2006).

Suppose that a publicity rights owner prevailed in an action under the Indiana statute and sought injunctive relief. Should the court limit the injunction to Indiana? Can you fashion an argument on behalf of the rights owner that the court should order a nationwide injunction? *See John W. Carson v. Here's Johnny Portable Toilets, Inc.*, 810 F.2d 104 (6th Cir. 1987) (addressing the remedy issue). The court's prior decision on the merits is excerpted *infra* in this subsection of the casebook.

10.   *Jurisdiction.* Study the jurisdictional provision in the Indiana statute, §32-36-1-9. Suppose that we (Dinwoodie and Janis) create a website promoting this casebook. The website features photographs of singer Britney Spears and quotations indicating that the casebook is "the best one she's ever read." It turns out that we used the photographs without Britney's consent, and we made up the quotations. Could Britney Spears establish jurisdiction under the Indiana statute for a right-of-publicity violation?

11.   *Choice of law.* Even if it is proper for a court in a particular state to exercise jurisdiction in a right-of-publicity case, the court must engage in a separate analysis to determine which state's law should apply—or which country's law, for that matter. For a case analyzing a conflict between California and English law, *see Love v. Associated Newspapers, Ltd.*, 611 F.3d 601 (9th Cir. 2010).

Choice of law, and the existence of a post-mortem right of publicity in California, New York, and Indiana, were major issues in litigation involving actress Marilyn Monroe's estate. Marilyn Monroe died in 1962, and whether she was domiciled in New York or California at the time was a matter of dispute, of importance in determining whether the will should be construed under New York or California law. Monroe's will did not expressly purport to dispose of her rights of publicity, but her beneficiaries claimed that those rights passed implicitly through a residuary clause. However, in *Shaw Family Archives Ltd. v. CMG Worldwide, Inc.*, 486 F. Supp. 2d 309 (S.D.N.Y. 2007) and in *Milton H. Greene Archives, Inc. v. CMG Worldwide, Inc.*, 568 F. Supp. 2d 1152 (C.D. Cal. 2008), courts held that neither California nor New York publicity rights laws recognized a descendible, post-mortem right of publicity as of 1962, so Monroe would have had no rights to pass in her will. In response, both the New York and California legislatures introduced legislation to amend their respective publicity rights provisions. The California legislation, S.B. 711, became law in October 2007, and amended California Civil Code Section 3344.1 to provide that publicity rights will be deemed to have existed at the time of death of anyone who died prior to 1985. Monroe's beneficiaries then took the position that Monroe was a domiciliary of California when she died, such that the amended Section 3344.1 applied. The court concluded that the beneficiaries had previously argued that Monroe had been domiciled in New York when she died, so the beneficiaries were now judicially estopped from making the California domicile claim. *See Milton H. Greene Archives, Inc. v. Marilyn Monroe LLC*, 692 F.3d 983 (9th Cir. 2012). As for the involvement of Indiana law (in case you're wondering), CMG Worldwide, licensee of Monroe's beneficiaries (and headquartered in Indiana), argued that Monroe's right of publicity posthumously vested in the beneficiaries under Indiana's right-of-publicity statute. However, the court ruled that under Indiana choice-of-law rules, the law of Monroe's domicile must apply, and the beneficiaries were estopped from claiming that California was the domicile. *Id.* at 993 n.12.

12.   *New York versus California right-of-publicity regimes.* Figure 11-1 compares the Indiana statute to the right-of-publicity regimes in New York and California. Look for variations in (1) the protectable aspects of "persona," including the issue of whether the rights extend to look-alikes and sound-alikes as well as actual photographs, voice recordings, and the like; (2) any scienter requirements for liability; (3) the term of protection and whether rights are available postmortem; and (4) restrictions on alienability.

13.   *Right of publicity and "first sale" defense.* Should the "first sale" defense apply to the right of publicity? *See Allison v. Vintage Sports Plaques*, 136 F.3d 1443 (11th Cir. 1998) (yes).

14.   *Names as domain names.* For a discussion of the use of celebrity (and other) names in domain names, *see supra* Chapter 8 (discussing rights under the ACPA).

FIGURE 11-1

	NY Civ. Rts §50	NY Civ. Rts §51	CA Civil §3344	CA Civil §3344.1	IN §§32-36-1-1 to -20
Knowingly use			X		
Use of:					
name	X	X	X	X	X
portrait	X	X			
picture	X	X			
voice		X	X	X	X
signature			X	X	X
photograph			X	X	X
image					X
likeness			X	X	X
distinctive appearance					X
gestures					X
mannerisms					X
On or in:					
products			X	X	
merchandise			X	X	
goods			X	X	
Purposes:					
advertising	X	X	X	X	
trade			X	X	
selling			X	X	
soliciting			X	X	
commercial purpose					X
Consent:					
consent			X	X	
written	X	X			
Protected:					
living	X	X	X		X
deceased				X	X
Remedies:					
equity		X			X (may)
damages		X	X	X	X
atty fees/costs			X (shall)	X (shall)	X (shall)
exemplary		X (with knowledge)	X (may)	X (may)	X (knowing, willful, intentional)
Transfer of right				X	X
Term				70 y after death	life + 100y

PROBLEM 11-2: COPYRIGHT PREEMPTION OF THE RIGHT OF PUBLICITY

Brother Billy is renowned in the greater French Lick, Indiana, metropolitan area for his bass fishing exploits. He is known locally as the "Bassin' Man," especially after he stenciled the phrase in large white block letters on the back window of his pickup.

Cousin Clem, a local entrepreneur and collector of discarded automobile parts, negotiated to have Brother Billy appear in a series of fishing videos, to be distributed throughout the southwestern Indiana area and other areas where fine fishing equipment is sold. Cousin Clem shot some initial photographs of Brother Billy for use in advertising the video series. However, shortly thereafter, negotiations broke down when Cousin Clem asked Brother Billy to engage in obscene behavior in the videos (such as appearing with live Democrats, driving a Ford pickup, and other behavior too horrible to print here). Brother Billy never actually appeared in any of the videos.

Nevertheless, Cousin Clem used photographs of Brother Billy on the advertisements for the videos and on the video boxes. Brother Billy sued for a right-of-publicity violation in Indiana state court, under the Indiana statute.

Cousin Clem argued that the Indiana statute is preempted by U.S. copyright law under 17 U.S.C. §301, the preemption provision in the 1976 Copyright Act. Identify the principal steps in the preemption analysis under 17 U.S.C. §301 (reproduced below), and consider the policy issues that Cousin Clem's preemption argument raises. If you are familiar with copyright law, you may wish to proceed further to formulate an answer to the ultimate question of preemption.

17 U.S.C. §301. PREEMPTION WITH RESPECT TO OTHER LAWS

(a) On and after January 1, 1978, all legal or equitable rights that are equivalent to any of the exclusive rights within the general scope of copyright as specified by section 106 in works of authorship that are fixed in a tangible medium of expression and come within the subject matter of copyright as specified by sections 102 and 103, whether created before or after that date and whether published or unpublished, are governed exclusively by this title. Thereafter, no person is entitled to any such right or equivalent right in any such work under the common law or statutes of any State.

(b) Nothing in this title annuls or limits any rights or remedies under the common law or statutes of any State with respect to—

(1) subject matter that does not come within the subject matter of copyright as specified by sections 102 and 103, including works of authorship not fixed in any tangible medium of expression; or

(2) any cause of action arising from undertakings commenced before January 1, 1978;

(3) activities violating legal or equitable rights that are not equivalent to any of the exclusive rights within the general scope of copyright as specified by section 106; or

(4) State and local landmarks, historic preservation, zoning, or building codes, relating to architectural works protected under section 102(a)(8). . . .

(d) Nothing in this title annuls or limits any rights or remedies under any other Federal statute.

(e) The scope of Federal preemption under this section is not affected by the adherence of the United States to the Berne Convention or the satisfaction of obligations of the United States thereunder. . . .

Note that the Section 301 inquiry essentially has two major prongs: (1) whether the subject matter that is allegedly preempted is fixed in tangible form and comes within the subject matter of copyright as specified in Sections 102 and 103 of the Copyright Act; and (2) whether the rights asserted in the subject matter are equivalent to at least one of the rights specified in Section 106 of the Copyright Act. *See, e.g., Baltimore Orioles, Inc. v. Major League*

Baseball Players Ass'n, 805 F.2d 663, 674 (7th Cir. 1986), *cert. denied*, 480 U.S. 941 (1987). This analysis is not a simple one. Both prongs draw on central concepts of copyright law, including fixation, copyrightability, and the scope of exclusive rights. In addition, the issue of "equivalency" under prong (2) has been the subject of some dispute. For a helpful primer on copyright preemption, *see* MARSHALL LEAFFER, UNDERSTANDING COPYRIGHT LAW ch. 11 (6th ed. 2014). *See also Maloney v. T3 Media, Inc.*, 853 F.3d 1004 (9th Cir. 2017) (upholding a determination that copyright preempted former collegiate athletes' right-of-publicity claims); *Dryer v. National Football League*, 814 F.3d 938 (8th Cir. 2016) (upholding a determination that copyright preempted retired NFL football player's right-of-publicity claim).

For two views of the copyright/right-of-publicity preemption issue, *see Laws v. Sony Music Entm't, Inc.*, 448 F.3d 1134 (9th Cir. 2006) (copyright law preempts California right-of-publicity claim); *Toney v. L'Oreal USA, Inc.*, 406 F.3d 905 (7th Cir. 2005) (copyright law does not preempt Illinois right-of-publicity claim).

The following case illustrates the common law right of publicity and its relationship with the right of privacy. Consider how, or if, the common law right of publicity under Kentucky law differs from the statutory rights of publicity discussed *supra*.

CHEATHAM v. PAISANO PUBLICATIONS, INC.

891 F. Supp. 381 (W.D. Ky. 1995)

HEYBURN, District Judge:

I

Plaintiff creates "unique" clothing designs and displays these designs at bikers' events. At a Chillicothe, Ohio, bikers' festival, Plaintiff wore one of her distinctive creations, which displayed her bottom through fishnet fabric that replaced cut out portions of her blue jeans. In May of 1993, Paisano Publications' ("Paisano's") *In the Wind* magazine published a picture of Plaintiff's backside as part of a photo essay of the Chillicothe festival. The picture does not identify Plaintiff. A year and a half later, in December of 1994, Paisano's *Easyriders* magazine published T-Shurte's advertisement for a T-shirt with a similarly-clad backside, which Plaintiff claims portrayed her likeness. T-Shurte's may have sold several hundred or more of the shirts.

Plaintiff alleges that Paisano's provided the *In the Wind* photo to T-Shurte's to display her likeness on T-shirts and that Paisano's received part of the income from the sale of each T-shirt. Plaintiff asserts five causes of action arising out of this appropriation: (1) invasion of privacy; (2) commercial exploitation of a likeness; (3) negligent licensing of an image without the owner's consent; (4) misappropriation of an image for commercial gain; and (5) unjust enrichment. Plaintiff also seeks leave to file a Second Amended Complaint adding claims for interference with prospective business relations and for intentional infliction of emotional distress.

II

When considering a motion for dismissal, the Court must determine if a reasonable jury could find for Plaintiff under any set of facts. The Court also must accept the allegations of the complaint as true and should dismiss a claim only if it appears that the record as a whole could not lead a rational trier of fact to give Plaintiff the relief requested. *Street v. J.C. Bradford & Co.*, 886 F.2d 1472, 1479-80 (6th Cir. 1989).

Plaintiff asserts that her designs are unique and that, because of their uniqueness, her friends and customers recognize them. When evaluating Defendants' Motions to Dismiss, the Court must examine Plaintiff's claim, therefore, in light of the assumption that her designs are unique and that she sells these designs to customers who recognize them as hers.

All of Plaintiff's claims center around her allegation that Defendants appropriated her image. Kentucky has long recognized the invasion of privacy as an actionable tort. *Foster-Milburn Co. v. Chinn*, 134 Ky. 424, 120 S.W. 364 (1909). Over the years since *Foster-Milburn*, this theory of law has evolved, and in 1981, the Kentucky Supreme Court formally adopted the definition from the Restatement (Second) of Torts (1976). *McCall v. Courier-Journal & Louisville Times*, 623 S.W.2d 882, 887 (Ky. 1981). Under the Restatement definition, four distinct causes of action exist, each of which is classified loosely as invasion of privacy:

> (2) The right of privacy is invaded by
> (a) unreasonable intrusion upon the seclusion of another . . . ; or
> (b) appropriation of the other's name or likeness . . . ; or
> (c) unreasonable publicity given to the other's private life; or
> (d) publicity that unreasonably places the other in a false light before the public. . . .

Restatement (Second) of Torts (1976). In determining if Plaintiff states a meritorious claim for invasion of privacy, this Court must examine each of the four possible causes of action for invasion of privacy.

A

First, the Court must consider whether Defendants unreasonably intruded upon Plaintiff's seclusion. This is not a case where Plaintiff sought to keep her designs secret and wore them only to very private functions.[3] Instead, Plaintiff wore her unusual clothing at large public events, namely bikers' conventions, and in front of large crowds of people. If Plaintiff believed these designs were truly unique, she certainly might have expected that someone might photograph her in this clothing. Consequently, no reasonable jury could possibly conclude that Paisano's taking of these photos was an unreasonable intrusion upon her seclusion.

Second, the Court must consider whether Defendants gave unreasonable publicity to Plaintiff's private life. Plaintiff has stated that her friends and *customers* recognize her designs. If Plaintiff wears the clothing designs to attract attention to herself as well as the designs, then she has voluntarily taken them out of her private life and injected them into public view. Given the facts of this case, no reasonable jury could construe any attention given to Plaintiff's wearing of these designs as unreasonable publicity of Plaintiff's private life.

Third, the Court must consider whether the publicity placed Plaintiff in a false light. The two basic requirements to sustain this action are: (1) the false light in which the other was placed would be highly offensive to a reasonable person; and (2) the publisher has knowledge or acted in reckless disregard of the falsity of the publicized matter. *McCall v. Courier-Journal & Louisville Times*, 623 S.W.2d at 888. It is sufficient that the publicity attributes to the plaintiff characteristics, conduct or beliefs that are false. *Id.* Plaintiff voluntarily wore this clothing to public events. Defendant photographed her exactly as she appeared at the bikers' event. Paisano's made no assertions about her character; in fact, they did not identify her. Plaintiff's own conduct and Defendant's unoffensive characterization

---

3. Indeed, in his affidavit, Plaintiff's husband noted that Plaintiff never wore her designs in their home.

leads [sic] to the certain conclusion that there was no false light invasion of privacy in this matter.

B

In her motion for summary judgment, Plaintiff concentrates on the fourth possible cause of action for invasion of privacy—Defendants' unauthorized appropriation of her likeness. Restatement (Second) of Torts, §652A(2)(b). Among Plaintiff's claims are those for commercial exploitation of her likeness, negligent licensing of her image without her consent, and misappropriation of her image for commercial gain. These claims merely recast the claim for damages based on the improper appropriation of another's name or likeness.

Not all jurisdictions recognize the tort of unauthorized appropriation of likeness. But the Kentucky Supreme Court has suggested that it is available by adopting the Restatement view of invasion of privacy. Kentucky courts have not specifically addressed the elements of proof required to support this cause of action, however. Other courts have referred to the unauthorized use of another's likeness as the "appropriation of the right of publicity." *Waits v. Frito-Lay, Inc.*, 978 F.2d 1093, 1098 (9th Cir. 1992) (appropriation of a voice is "a species of violation of the 'right of publicity,' the right of a person whose identity has commercial value—most often a celebrity—to control the use of that identity"); *Lerman v. Flynt Distributing Co., Inc.*, 745 F.2d 123, 133 (2d Cir. 1984) ("[T]he right to publicity is essentially identical to the right to be free from commercial appropriation"); *see also* Restatement (Third) of Unfair Competition §46, comment a ("The interest protected by these rules is often described as the 'right of publicity.'"). . . .

[Plaintiff] alleges that Defendants have deprived her of the commercial benefit of her "image" by appropriating the image for their own commercial gain. The Second Circuit has defined this issue as one in which the "plaintiff is not so concerned that the use occurs; [s]he simply wants to be the one to decide when and where, and to be paid for it." *Lerman v. Flynt Distributing Co., Inc.*, 745 F.2d at 134. This statement perfectly articulates Plaintiff's position in this case. She merely wants to be compensated for the use of her likeness by Defendants for their own commercial gain.

Two distinct uses of Plaintiff's likeness could be the source of a claim under a right of publicity: (1) Paisano's printed her photograph in their photo essay of the bikers' event; and (2) T-Shurte's used a similar likeness on their T-shirts. The Court need only concern itself with the second use.[5] As to that issue, Defendants argue that such claims belong only to persons of celebrity status and that "plaintiff is no Elvis Presley, Muhammad Ali or Bruce Springsteen."

Having reviewed §652A(2)(b) of the Restatement (Second) of Torts and the cases that discuss a right of publicity claim, the Court concludes the following principles should govern Plaintiff's claim for appropriation of likeness. Plaintiff must prove that she has developed a property interest in her likeness or her designs by proving that her image has commercial value and that she intended to profit from that value. Without such proof, Plaintiff cannot show that Defendants exploited the fame or fortune that Plaintiff has developed. *Id.* To be sure, such proof is normally found in cases involving celebrities. But celebrity

---

5. The law protects the first use under an exception for newsworthy items, *Zacchini v. Scripps-Howard Broadcasting Co.*, 433 U.S. 562, 574 (1977). Paisano's merely took photos at the event and published them as part of their photo essay of the event. In doing so, Paisano's invaded no rights of Plaintiff's. This Court finds that publishing Plaintiff's photo as part of the photo essay is a newsworthy item and is entitled to First Amendment protection.

status should not be an absolute prerequisite.[6] This Court concludes the best rule is that the remedy available in right of publicity claims belongs to those whose identity has commercial value. Commercial value may be established by proof of (1) the distinctiveness of the identity and by (2) the degree of recognition of the person among those receiving the publicity. *Waits v. Frito-Lay, Inc.*, 978 F.2d at 1098, 1101-02. In order to succeed in her claim, Plaintiff must have a notoriety which is strong enough to have commercial value within an identifiable group.

The Court has grave doubts that Plaintiff can establish the proof necessary to show a sufficiently wide notoriety for this case to go forward. The photographic replica does not display Plaintiff's face; because the photo was taken from behind and includes only her backside from her waist to her thighs. Plaintiff's cause of action under a right of publicity claim may arise only if her image is distinctive enough that her friends and customers recognized the replica drawing on the T-shirt and identified this drawing as her "image."

Plaintiff's assertions that friends and customers recognize her designs and that these unique designs have commercial value overcomes Defendants' motions to dismiss at this early stage. If the recognition of Plaintiff's image is sufficiently clear and sufficiently broad-based, it may be an unlawful appropriation for which Plaintiff could receive damages. For these reasons, Defendants' Motions to Dismiss the claim for appropriation of image are denied at this time.[7]

NOTES AND QUESTIONS

1. *Relationship with right of privacy. Cheatham* provides us with a first glance at the right of publicity in a common law jurisdiction. As is typical, the court in *Cheatham* looks to rights of privacy as defined by the Restatement of Torts to find authority for a common law right of publicity. Section 2(c) of the Restatement definition supports recognition of a right of publicity, even though it is not separately labeled as such. Clearly, the common law right of publicity springs from right-of-privacy notions.

But how closely related is the right of publicity to right-of-privacy concerns? Is the right of publicity as understood at common law a personal right? Is the damage from invasion of the right of publicity psychic damage to the invaded individual, as it surely is when rights of privacy are invaded? For example, in the Larry Bird scenario is the damage from the billboard merely psychic — e.g., damage to Bird's psyche from seeing his identity connected to negative statements about French Lick and its populace? Are your answers to these questions, given in the context of a common law right of publicity, consistent with

---

6. In *Waits v. Frito Lay*, the Ninth Circuit rejected a requirement for superstar status, instead defining the standard as "known to a *large number* of people throughout a *relatively large* geographical area." *Waits v. Frito-Lay*, 978 F.2d at 1102. In reaching its decision, the court opined that the amount of damages awarded would reflect the extent of celebrity. *Id.* (citing *Motschenbacher v. R.J. Reynolds Tobacco Co.*, 498 F.2d 821, 824-25 (9th Cir. 1974) ("Generally the greater the fame or notoriety of the identity appropriated, the greater will be the extent of the economic injury suffered.")); *see also* Restatement (Third) of Unfair Competition §46 comment d ("Private persons may also recover damages measured by the value of the use by establishing the market price that the defendant would have been required to pay to secure similar services from other private persons or from professional models.").

7. Plaintiff also has asserted a claim for unjust enrichment. However, unjust enrichment in this circumstance merely forms a measure of damages in a right of publicity claim. It is not a separate cause of action. . . .

your answers to similar questions given in the context of the statutory right of publicity? For additional discussion of these issues, *see, e.g., Rose v. Triple Crown Nutrition, Inc.*, 82 U.S.P.Q.2d (BNA) 1222 (M.D. Pa. 2007).

2. *Obtaining common law rights: should celebrity status be a prerequisite?* Under Kentucky common law, celebrity status is "not an absolute prerequisite" for receiving rights of publicity, according to the *Cheatham* court. Should it be? *See Bullard v. MRA Holding, L.L.C.*, 740 S.E.2d 622, 628 (Ga. 2013) (asserting that plaintiff "need not show that her likeness had inherent commercial value before [defendant] used it in order for her to collect damages," and that "the fact that [defendant] chose to use [plaintiff's] specific image would suggest that it believed that the image held some value with respect to advancing the company's goal of selling more *College Girls Gone Wild* videos"). If celebrity status isn't required, does everyone potentially have a right of publicity? Should celebrity status merely be an indicator of how large a damage award a rights holder might collect for a right-of-publicity violation, rather than a prerequisite for obtaining the right of publicity? Should celebrities and noncelebrities alike have the power of injunctive relief under the right of publicity? For example, suppose that the billboard in the Larry Bird example also features pictures of Professors Dinwoodie and Janis, and the top line says, "After the ball game, Dinwoodie and Janis always meet me at Joe's Sports Bar, the best sports bar in Paoli." Assuming that we gave no consent, should we have a right-of-publicity cause of action?

3. *Statutory versus common law.* Are there major differences between the statutory right-of-publicity regime set forth in the Indiana statute and the common law right-of-publicity regime outlined in the *Cheatham* case? What are they?

4. *Restatement approach.* The Restatement of Unfair Competition also sets forth its own version of a common law right of publicity. *See* Restatement (Third) of Unfair Competition §§46-49 (1996).

2.   Protectable Aspects of Persona

We have noted that the exclusive rights that constitute the right of publicity attach to a person's "persona." To determine the scope of the right of publicity in any given case, we must define precisely the contours of protectable "persona." Recall that the Indiana statute attempts to do so by means of a laundry list of personal qualities and the like. IND. CODE §32-36-1-7. The following cases all present issues about the aspects of persona that may be protected against unauthorized appropriation under the right of publicity as implemented in various states' statutes and common law.

JOHN W. CARSON v. HERE'S JOHNNY PORTABLE TOILETS, INC.

698 F.2d 831 (6th Cir. 1983)

BAILEY BROWN, Senior Circuit Judge:

Appellant, John W. Carson (Carson), is the host and star of "The Tonight Show," a well-known television program broadcast five nights a week by the National Broadcasting Company. Carson also appears as an entertainer in night clubs and theaters around the country. From the time he began hosting "The Tonight Show" in 1962, he has been introduced on the show each night with the phrase "Here's Johnny." This method of introduction was first used for Carson in 1957 when he hosted a daily television program for the American Broadcasting Company. The phrase "Here's Johnny" is generally associated with Carson by a substantial segment of the television viewing public. In 1967, Carson first authorized use of this phrase by an outside business venture, permitting it to be used by a chain of restaurants called "Here's Johnny Restaurants."

Appellant Johnny Carson Apparel, Inc. (Apparel), formed in 1970, manufactures and markets men's clothing to retail stores. Carson, the president of Apparel and owner of 20% of its stock, has licensed Apparel to use his name and picture, which appear on virtually all of Apparel's products and promotional material. Apparel has also used, with Carson's consent, the phrase "Here's Johnny" on labels for clothing and in advertising campaigns. In 1977, Apparel granted a license to Marcy Laboratories to use "Here's Johnny" as the name of a line of men's toiletries. The phrase "Here's Johnny" has never been registered by appellants as a trademark or service mark.

Appellee, Here's Johnny Portable Toilets, Inc., is a Michigan corporation engaged in the business of renting and selling "Here's Johnny" portable toilets. Appellee's founder was aware at the time he formed the corporation that "Here's Johnny" was the introductory slogan for Carson on "The Tonight Show." He indicated that he coupled the phrase with a second one, "The World's Foremost Commodian," to make "a good play on a phrase."

[Carson sued on both Lanham Act and right-of-publicity theories, among others. The trial court held for defendants, and Carson appealed.]

I

[On the Lanham Act theory, the court affirmed the trial court's finding on likelihood of confusion. The mark "Here's Johnny" was "not such a strong mark that its use for other goods should be entirely foreclosed"; defendant had not intended to deceive the public, even if defendant did intend to capitalize on the phrase that Carson had popularized; and there was "little evidence" of actual confusion.]

Appellants' first claim alleges unfair competition from appellee's business activities in violation of §43(a) of the Lanham Act, 15 U.S.C. §1125(a) (1976). . . .

II

[The court next turned to the right of publicity theory.]

. . .

The district court dismissed appellants' claim based on the right of publicity because appellee does not use Carson's name or likeness. 498 F. Supp. at 77. It held that it "would not be prudent to allow recovery for a right of publicity claim which does not more specifically identify Johnny Carson." 498 F. Supp. at 78. We believe that, on the contrary, the district court's conception of the right of publicity is too narrow. The right of publicity, as we have stated, is that a celebrity has a protected pecuniary interest in the commercial exploitation of his identity. If the celebrity's identity is commercially exploited, there has been an invasion of his right whether or not his "name or likeness" is used. Carson's identity may be exploited even if his name, John W Carson, or his picture is not used.

In *Motschenbacher v. R.J. Reynolds Tobacco Co.*, 498 F.2d 821 (9th Cir. 1974), the court held that the unauthorized use of a picture of a distinctive race car of a well known professional race car driver, whose name or likeness were not used, violated his right of publicity. In this connection, the court said:

> We turn now to the question of "identifiability." Clearly, if the district court correctly determined as a matter of law that plaintiff is not identifiable in the commercial, then in no sense has plaintiff's identity been misappropriated nor his interest violated.
>
> Having viewed a film of the commercial, we agree with the district court that the "likeness" of plaintiff is itself unrecognizable; however, the court's further conclusion of law to the effect that the driver is not identifiable as plaintiff is erroneous in that it wholly fails to attribute proper significance to the distinctive decorations appearing on the car. As pointed out earlier,

these markings were not only peculiar to the plaintiff's cars but they caused some persons to think the car in question was plaintiff's and to infer that the person driving the car was the plaintiff.

Id. at 826-827 (footnote omitted).

In *Ali v. Playgirl, Inc.*, 447 F. Supp. 723 (S.D.N.Y. 1978), Muhammad Ali, former heavyweight champion, sued Playgirl magazine under the New York "right of privacy" statute and also alleged a violation of his common law right of publicity. The magazine published a drawing of a nude, black male sitting on a stool in a corner of a boxing ring with hands taped and arms outstretched on the ropes. The district court concluded that Ali's right of publicity was invaded because the drawing sufficiently identified him in spite of the fact that the drawing was captioned "Mystery Man." The district court found that the identification of Ali was made certain because of an accompanying verse that identified the figure as "The Greatest." The district court took judicial notice of the fact that "Ali has regularly claimed that appellation for himself." *Id.* at 727.

In *Hirsch v. S.C. Johnson & Son, Inc.*, 280 N.W.2d 129 (1979), the court held that use by defendant of the name "Crazylegs" on a shaving gel for women violated plaintiff's right of publicity. Plaintiff, Elroy Hirsch, a famous football player, had been known by this nickname. . . .

In this case, Earl Braxton, president and owner of Here's Johnny Portable Toilets, Inc., admitted that he knew that the phrase "Here's Johnny" had been used for years to introduce Carson. Moreover, in the opening statement in the district court, appellee's counsel stated:

> Now, we've stipulated in this case that the public tends to associate the words "Johnny Carson," the words "Here's Johnny" with plaintiff, John Carson and, Mr. Braxton, in his deposition, admitted that he knew that and probably absent that identification, he would not have chosen it.

App. 68. That the "Here's Johnny" name was selected by Braxton because of its identification with Carson was the clear inference from Braxton's testimony irrespective of such admission in the opening statement.

We therefore conclude that, applying the correct legal standards, appellants are entitled to judgment. The proof showed without question that appellee had appropriated Carson's identity in connection with its corporate name and its product. . . .

[Vacated and remanded.]

VANNA WHITE v. SAMSUNG ELECTRONICS AMERICA, INC.

971 F.2d 1395 (9th Cir. 1992), cert. denied, 508 U.S. 951 (1993)

Goodwin, Senior Circuit Judge:

This case involves a promotional "fame and fortune" dispute. In running a particular advertisement without Vanna White's permission, defendants Samsung Electronics America, Inc. (Samsung) and David Deutsch Associates, Inc. (Deutsch) attempted to capitalize on White's fame to enhance their fortune. White sued, alleging infringement of various intellectual property rights, but the district court granted summary judgment in favor of the defendants. We affirm in part, reverse in part, and remand.

Plaintiff Vanna White is the hostess of "Wheel of Fortune," one of the most popular game shows in television history. An estimated forty million people watch the program daily. Capitalizing on the fame which her participation in the show has bestowed on her, White markets her identity to various advertisers.

The dispute in this case arose out of a series of advertisements prepared for Samsung by Deutsch. The series ran in at least half a dozen publications with widespread, and in some cases national, circulation. Each of the advertisements in the series followed the same theme. Each depicted a current item from popular culture and a Samsung electronic product. Each was set in the twenty-first century and conveyed the message that the Samsung product would still be in use by that time. By hypothesizing outrageous future outcomes for the cultural items, the ads created humorous effects. For example, one lampooned current popular notions of an unhealthy diet by depicting a raw steak with the caption: "Revealed to be health food. 2010 A.D." Another depicted irreverent "news"-show host Morton Downey Jr. in front of an American flag with the caption: "Presidential candidate. 2008 A.D."

The advertisement which prompted the current dispute was for Samsung video-cassette recorders (VCRs). The ad depicted a robot, dressed in a wig, gown, and jewelry which Deutsch consciously selected to resemble White's hair and dress. The robot was posed next to a game board which is instantly recognizable as the Wheel of Fortune game show set, in a stance for which White is famous. The caption of the ad read: "Longest-running game show. 2012 A.D." Defendants referred to the ad as the "Vanna White" ad. Unlike the other celebrities used in the campaign, White neither consented to the ads nor was she paid.

Following the circulation of the robot ad, White sued Samsung and Deutsch in federal district court under: (1) California Civil Code §3344; (2) the California common law right of publicity; and (3) §43(a) of the Lanham Act, 15 U.S.C. §1125(a). The district court granted summary judgment against White on each of her claims. White now appeals.

I.   SECTION 3344

White first argues that the district court erred in rejecting her claim under section 3344. Section 3344(a) provides, in pertinent part, that "[a]ny person who knowingly uses another's name, voice, signature, photograph, or likeness, in any manner, . . . for purposes of advertising or selling, . . . without such person's prior consent . . . shall be liable for any damages sustained by the person or persons injured as a result thereof."

White argues that the Samsung advertisement used her "likeness" in contravention of section 3344. In *Midler v. Ford Motor Co.*, 849 F.2d 460 (9th Cir. 1988), this court rejected Bette Midler's section 3344 claim concerning a Ford television commercial in which a Midler "sound-alike" sang a song which Midler had made famous. In rejecting Midler's claim, this court noted that "[t]he defendants did not use Midler's name or anything else whose use is prohibited by the statute. The voice they used was [another person's], not hers. The term 'likeness' refers to a visual image not a vocal imitation." *Id*. at 463.

In this case, Samsung and Deutsch used a robot with mechanical features, and not, for example, a manikin molded to White's precise features. Without deciding for all purposes when a caricature or impressionistic resemblance might become a "likeness," we agree with the district court that the robot at issue here was not White's "likeness" within the meaning of section 3344. Accordingly, we affirm the court's dismissal of White's section 3344 claim.

II.   RIGHT OF PUBLICITY

White next argues that the district court erred in granting summary judgment to defendants on White's common law right of publicity claim. In *Eastwood v. Superior Court*, 149 Cal. App. 3d 409 (1983), the California court of appeal stated that the common law right of publicity cause of action "may be pleaded by alleging (1) the defendant's use of the plaintiff's identity; (2) the appropriation of plaintiff's name or likeness to defendant's advantage, commercially or otherwise; (3) lack of consent; and (4) resulting injury." *Id*. at 417, 198 Cal. Rptr. 342 (citing Prosser, Law of Torts (4th ed. 1971) §117, pp. 804-807). The district court dismissed White's claim for failure to satisfy *Eastwood*'s second prong, reasoning that defendants had not appropriated White's "name or likeness" with their robot ad. We agree that the robot ad did not make use of White's name or likeness. However, the common law right of publicity is not so confined.

The *Eastwood* court did not hold that the right of publicity cause of action could be pleaded only by alleging an appropriation of name or likeness. *Eastwood* involved an unauthorized use of photographs of Clint Eastwood and of his name. Accordingly, the *Eastwood* court had no occasion to consider the extent beyond the use of name or likeness to which the right of publicity reaches. That court held only that the right of publicity cause of action "may be" pleaded by alleging, *inter alia*, appropriation of name or likeness, not that the action may be pleaded *only* in those terms.

The "name or likeness" formulation referred to in *Eastwood* originated not as an element of the right of publicity cause of action, but as a description of the types of cases in which the cause of action had been recognized. The source of this formulation is Prosser, *Privacy*, 48 Cal. L. Rev. 383, 401-07 (1960), one of the earliest and most enduring articulations of the common law right of publicity cause of action. In looking at the case law to that point, Prosser recognized that right of publicity cases involved one of two basic factual scenarios: name appropriation, and picture or other likeness appropriation. *Id*. at 401-02, nn.156-57.

Even though Prosser focused on appropriations of name or likeness in discussing the right of publicity, he noted that "[i]t is not impossible that there might be appropriation of the plaintiff's identity, as by impersonation, without the use of either his name or his likeness, and that this would be an invasion of his right of privacy." *Id*. at 401, n.155. At the time Prosser wrote, he noted however, that "[n]o such case appears to have arisen." *Id*.

. . .

In *Midler*, this court held that, even though the defendants had not used Midler's name or likeness, Midler had stated a claim for violation of her California common law right of publicity because "the defendants . . . for their own profit in selling their product did appropriate part of her identity" by using a Midler sound-alike. *Id*. at 465-64.

[The court also cited *Carson* and *Motschenbacher*, the race car case discussed in *Carson*.]

These cases teach not only that the common law right of publicity reaches means of appropriation other than name or likeness, but that the specific means of appropriation are relevant only for determining whether the defendant has in fact appropriated the plaintiff's identity. The right of publicity does not require that appropriations of identity be accomplished through particular means to be actionable. It is noteworthy that the *Midler* and *Carson* defendants not only avoided using the plaintiff's name or likeness, but they also avoided appropriating the celebrity's voice, signature, and photograph. The photograph in *Motschenbacher* did include the plaintiff, but because the plaintiff was not visible the driver could have been an actor or dummy and the analysis in the case would have been the same.

Although the defendants in these cases avoided the most obvious means of appropriating the plaintiffs' identities, each of their actions directly implicated the commercial interests which the right of publicity is designed to protect. . . .

It is not important *how* the defendant has appropriated the plaintiff's identity, but *whether* the defendant has done so. *Motschenbacher*, *Midler*, and *Carson* teach the impossibility of treating the right of publicity as guarding only against a laundry list of specific means of appropriating identity. A rule which says that the right of publicity can be infringed only through the use of nine different methods of appropriating identity merely challenges the clever advertising strategist to come up with the tenth.

Indeed, if we treated the means of appropriation as dispositive in our analysis of the right of publicity, we would not only weaken the right but effectively eviscerate it. The right would fail to protect those plaintiffs most in need of its protection. Advertisers use celebrities to promote their products. The more popular the celebrity, the greater the number of people who recognize her, and the greater the visibility for the product. The identities of the most popular celebrities are not only the most attractive for advertisers, but also the easiest to evoke without resorting to obvious means such as name, likeness, or voice.

Consider a hypothetical advertisement which depicts a mechanical robot with male features, an African-American complexion, and a bald head. The robot is wearing black hightop Air Jordan basketball sneakers, and a red basketball uniform with black trim, baggy shorts, and the number 23 (though not revealing "Bulls" or "Jordan" lettering). The ad depicts the robot dunking a basketball one-handed, stiff-armed, legs extended like open scissors, and tongue hanging out. Now envision that this ad is run on television during professional basketball games. Considered individually, the robot's physical attributes, its dress, and its stance tell us little. Taken together, they lead to the only conclusion that any sports viewer who has registered a discernible pulse in the past five years would reach: the ad is about Michael Jordan.

Viewed separately, the individual aspects of the advertisement in the present case say little. Viewed together, they leave little doubt about the celebrity the ad is meant to depict. The female-shaped robot is wearing a long gown, blond wig, and large jewelry. Vanna White dresses exactly like this at times, but so do many other women. The robot is in the process of turning a block letter on a game-board. Vanna White dresses like this while turning letters on a game-board but perhaps similarly attired Scrabble-playing women do this as well. The robot is standing on what looks to be the Wheel of Fortune game show set. Vanna White dresses like this, turns letters, and does this on the Wheel of Fortune game show. She is the only one. Indeed, defendants themselves referred to their ad as the "Vanna White" ad. We are not surprised.

Television and other media create marketable celebrity identity value. Considerable energy and ingenuity are expended by those who have achieved celebrity value to exploit it for profit. The law protects the celebrity's sole right to exploit this value whether the celebrity has achieved her fame out of rare ability, dumb luck, or a combination thereof. We decline Samsung and Deutch's invitation to permit the evisceration of the common law right of publicity through means as facile as those in this case. Because White has alleged facts showing that Samsung and Deutsch had appropriated her identity, the district court erred by rejecting, on summary judgment, White's common law right of publicity claim.

III.   THE LANHAM ACT

[Regarding White's Lanham Act claim, the court treated White's persona as the "mark" and applied the likelihood-of-confusion analysis, finding that the evidence sufficed to raise a fact issue, though the court carefully pointed out that it reached its conclusion "in light of the peculiar facts of this case," including the fact that Samsung's commercial was part of a series of commercials featuring celebrities, and the other celebrities were paid for endorsements while White was not.]

IV.   THE PARODY DEFENSE

In defense, defendants cite a number of cases for the proposition that their robot ad constituted protected speech. The only cases they cite which are even remotely relevant to this case are *Hustler Magazine v. Falwell*, 485 U.S. 46 (1988) and *L.L. Bean, Inc. v. Drake Publishers, Inc.*, 811 F.2d 26 (1st Cir. 1987). Those cases involved parodies of advertisements run for the purpose of poking fun at Jerry Falwell and L.L. Bean, respectively. This case involves a true advertisement run for the purpose of selling Samsung VCRs. The ad's spoof of Vanna White and Wheel of Fortune is subservient and only tangentially related to the ad's primary message: "buy Samsung VCRs." Defendants' parody arguments are better addressed to non-commercial parodies. The difference between a "parody" and a "knock-off" is the difference between fun and profit.

V.   CONCLUSION

In remanding this case, we hold only that White has pleaded claims which can go to the jury for its decision.

Affirmed in part, reversed in part, and remanded. . . .

VANNA WHITE v. SAMSUNG ELECTRONICS AMERICA, INC.

989 F.2d 1512 (9th Cir. 1993), cert. denied, 508 U.S. 951 (1993)

The petition for rehearing is *denied* and the suggestion for rehearing en banc is *rejected*.

KOZINSKI, Circuit Judge, with whom Circuit Judges O'SCANNLAIN and KLEINFELD join, dissenting from the order rejecting the suggestion for rehearing en banc.

I

Saddam Hussein wants to keep advertisers from using his picture in unflattering contexts. Clint Eastwood doesn't want tabloids to write about him. Rudolf Valentino's heirs want to control his film biography. The Girl Scouts don't want their image soiled by association with certain activities. George Lucas wants to keep Strategic Defense Initiative fans from calling it "Star Wars." Pepsico doesn't want singers to use the word "Pepsi" in their songs. Guy Lombardo wants an exclusive property right to ads that show big bands playing on New Year's Eve. Uri Geller thinks he should be paid for ads showing psychics bending metal through telekinesis. Paul Prudhomme, that household name, thinks the same about ads featuring corpulent bearded chefs. And scads of copyright holders see purple when their creations are made fun of.

Something very dangerous is going on here. Private property, including intellectual property, is essential to our way of life. It provides an incentive for investment and innovation; it stimulates the flourishing of our culture; it protects the moral entitlements of people to the fruits of their labors. But reducing too much to private property can be bad medicine. Private land, for instance, is far more useful if separated from other private land by public streets, roads and highways. Public parks, utility rights-of-way and sewers reduce the amount of land in private hands, but vastly enhance the value of the property that remains.

So too it is with intellectual property. Overprotecting intellectual property is as harmful as underprotecting it. Creativity is impossible without a rich public domain. Nothing today, likely nothing since we tamed fire, is genuinely new: Culture, like science and technology, grows by accretion, each new creator building on the works of those who came before. Overprotection stifles the very creative forces it's supposed to nurture.

The panel's opinion is a classic case of overprotection. Concerned about what it sees as a wrong done to Vanna White, the panel majority erects a property right of remarkable and dangerous breadth: Under the majority's opinion, it's now a tort for advertisers to *remind* the public of a celebrity. Not to use a celebrity's name, voice, signature or likeness; not to imply the celebrity endorses a product; but simply to evoke the celebrity's image in the public's mind. This Orwellian notion withdraws far more from the public domain than prudence and common sense allow. It conflicts with the Copyright Act and the Copyright Clause. It raises serious First Amendment problems. It's bad law, and it deserves a long, hard second look.

II

Samsung ran an ad campaign promoting its consumer electronics. Each ad depicted a Samsung product and a humorous prediction: One showed a raw steak with the caption "Revealed to be health food. 2010 A.D." Another showed Morton Downey, Jr. in front of an

American flag with the caption "Presidential candidate. 2008 A.D."[12] The ads were meant to convey—humorously—that Samsung products would still be in use twenty years from now.

The ad that spawned this litigation starred a robot dressed in a wig, gown and jewelry reminiscent of Vanna White's hair and dress; the robot was posed next to a Wheel-of-Fortune-like game board. *See* Appendix. The caption read "Longest-running game show. 2012 A.D." The gag here, I take it, was that Samsung would still be around when White had been replaced by a robot.

Perhaps failing to see the humor, White sued, alleging Samsung infringed her right of publicity by "appropriating" her "identity." Under California law, White has the exclusive right to use her name, likeness, signature and voice for commercial purposes. Cal. Civ. Code §3344(a); *Eastwood v. Superior Court*, 149 Cal. App. 3d 409, 417 (1983). But Samsung didn't use her name, voice or signature, and it certainly didn't use her likeness. The ad just wouldn't have been funny had it depicted White or someone who resembled her—the whole joke was that the game show host(ess) was a robot, not a real person. No one seeing the ad could have thought this was supposed to be White in 2012.

The district judge quite reasonably held that, because Samsung didn't use White's name, likeness, voice or signature, it didn't violate her right of publicity. 971 F.2d at 1396-97. Not so, says the panel majority: The California right of publicity can't possibly be limited to name and likeness. If it were, the majority reasons, a "clever advertising strategist" could avoid using White's name or likeness but nevertheless remind people of her with impunity, "effectively eviscerat[ing]" her rights. To prevent this "evisceration," the panel majority holds that the right of publicity must extend beyond name and likeness, to any "appropriation" of White's "identity"—anything that "evoke[s]" her personality. *Id.* at 1398-99.

III

But what does "evisceration" mean in intellectual property law? Intellectual property rights aren't like some constitutional rights, absolute guarantees protected against all kinds of interference, subtle as well as blatant. They cast no penumbras, emit no emanations: The very point of intellectual property laws is that they protect only against certain specific kinds of appropriation. I can't publish unauthorized copies of, say, *Presumed Innocent*; I can't make a movie out of it. But I'm perfectly free to write a book about an idealistic young prosecutor on trial for a crime he didn't commit. So what if I got the idea from *Presumed Innocent*? So what if it reminds readers of the original? Have I "eviscerated" Scott Turow's intellectual property rights? Certainly not. All creators draw in part on the work of those who came before, referring to it, building on it, poking fun at it; we call this creativity, not piracy.[15]

The majority isn't, in fact, preventing the "evisceration" of Vanna White's existing rights; it's creating a new and much broader property right, a right unknown in California law. It's replacing the existing balance between the interests of the celebrity and those of the public by a different balance, one substantially more favorable to the celebrity. Instead of having an exclusive right in her name, likeness, signature or voice, every famous person now has an exclusive right to *anything that reminds the viewer of her*. After all, that's all Samsung did: It used an inanimate object to remind people of White, to "evoke [her identity]." 971 F.2d at 1399.

. . .

---

12. I had never heard of Morton Downey, Jr., but I'm told he's sort of like Rush Limbaugh, but not as shy.

15. In the words of Sir Isaac Newton, "[i]f I have seen further it is by standing on [the shoulders] of Giants." Letter to Robert Hooke, Feb. 5, 1675/1676.

Newton himself may have borrowed this phrase from Bernard of Chartres, who said something similar in the early twelfth century. Bernard in turn may have snatched it from Priscian, a sixth century grammarian. [cit.]

This is entirely the wrong place to strike the balance. Intellectual property rights aren't free: They're imposed at the expense of future creators and of the public at large. Where would we be if Charles Lindbergh had an exclusive right in the concept of a heroic solo aviator? If Arthur Conan Doyle had gotten a copyright in the idea of the detective story, or Albert Einstein had patented the theory of relativity? If every author and celebrity had been given the right to keep people from mocking them or their work? Surely this would have made the world poorer, not richer, culturally as well as economically.

This is why intellectual property law is full of careful balances between what's set aside for the owner and what's left in the public domain for the rest of us: [t]he relatively short life of patents; the longer, but finite, life of copyrights; copyright's idea-expression dichotomy; the fair use doctrine; the prohibition on copyrighting facts; the compulsory license of television broadcasts and musical compositions; federal preemption of overbroad state intellectual property laws; the nominative use doctrine in trademark law; the right to make soundalike recordings. All of these diminish an intellectual property owner's rights. All let the public use something created by someone else. But all are necessary to maintain a free environment in which creative genius can flourish.[18]

The intellectual property right created by the panel here has none of these essential limitations: [n]o fair use exception; no right to parody; no idea-expression dichotomy. It impoverishes the public domain, to the detriment of future creators and the public at large. Instead of well-defined, limited characteristics such as name, likeness or voice, advertisers will now have to cope with vague claims of "appropriation of identity," claims often made by people with a wholly exaggerated sense of their own fame and significance. Future Vanna Whites might not get the chance to create their personae, because their employers may fear some celebrity will claim the persona is too similar to her own.[21] The public will be robbed of parodies of celebrities, and our culture will be deprived of the valuable safety valve that parody and mockery create.

Moreover, consider the moral dimension, about which the panel majority seems to have gotten so exercised. Saying Samsung "appropriated" something of White's begs the question: *Should* White have the exclusive right to something as broad and amorphous as her "identity"? Samsung's ad didn't simply copy White's schtick—like all parody, it created something new. True, Samsung did it to make money, but White does whatever she does to

---

18. Once the right of publicity is extended beyond specific physical characteristics, this will become a recurring problem: Outside name, likeness and voice, the things that most reliably remind the public of celebrities are the actions or roles they're famous for. A commercial with an astronaut setting foot on the moon would evoke the image of Neil Armstrong. Any masked man on horseback would remind people (over a certain age) of Clayton Moore. And any number of songs—"My Way," "Yellow Submarine," "Like a Virgin," "Beat It," "Michael, Row the Boat Ashore," to name only a few—instantly evoke an image of the person or group who made them famous, regardless of who is singing.

See also Carlos V. Lozano, *West Loses Lawsuit over Batman TV Commercial*, L.A. Times, Jan. 18, 1990, at B3 (Adam West sues over Batman-like character in commercial); *Nurmi v. Peterson*, 10 U.S.P.Q.2d 1775, 1989 WL 407484 (C.D. Cal. 1989) (1950s TV movie hostess "Vampira" sues 1980s TV hostess "Elvira"); . . . (lawsuits brought by Guy Lombardo, claiming big bands playing at New Year's Eve parties remind people of him, and by Uri Geller, claiming psychics who can bend metal remind people of him.). . . *Cf. Motschenbacher*, where the claim was that viewers would think plaintiff was actually in the commercial, and not merely that the commercial reminded people of him.

21. If Christian Slater, star of "Heathers," "Pump up the Volume," "Kuffs," and "Untamed Heart"—and alleged Jack Nicholson clone—appears in a commercial, can Nicholson sue? Of 54 stories on LEXIS that talk about Christian Slater, 26 talk about Slater's alleged similarities to Nicholson. Apparently it's his nasal wisecracks and killer smiles, St. Petersburg Times, Jan. 10, 1992, at 13, his eyebrows, Ottawa Citizen, Jan. 10, 1992, at E2, his sneers, Boston Globe, July 26, 1991, at 37, his menacing presence, USA Today, June 26, 1991, at 1D, and his sing-song voice, Gannett News Service, Aug. 27, 1990 (or, some say, his insinuating drawl, L.A. Times, Aug. 22, 1990, at F5). That's a whole lot more than White and the robot had in common.

make money, too; the majority talks of "the difference between fun and profit," 971 F.2d at 1401, but in the entertainment industry fun *is* profit. Why is Vanna White's right to exclusive for-profit use of her persona—a persona that might not even be her own creation, but that of a writer, director or producer—superior to Samsung's right to profit by creating its own inventions? Why should she have such absolute rights to control the conduct of others, unlimited by the idea-expression dichotomy or by the fair use doctrine?

To paraphrase only slightly *Feist Publications, Inc. v. Rural Telephone Service Co.*, 499 U.S. 340 (1991), it may seem unfair that much of the fruit of a creator's labor may be used by others without compensation. But this is not some unforeseen byproduct of our intellectual property system; it is the system's very essence. Intellectual property law assures authors the right to their original expression, but encourages others to build freely on the ideas that underlie it. This result is neither unfair nor unfortunate: It is the means by which intellectual property law advances the progress of science and art. We give authors certain exclusive rights, but in exchange we get a richer public domain. The majority ignores this wise teaching, and all of us are the poorer for it.

APPENDIX

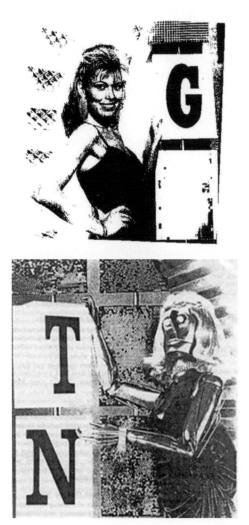

VANNA WHITE

NOTES AND QUESTIONS

1. *Intent, identifiability, and the right of publicity.* In the *Vanna White* case, suppose that Samsung had depicted a blonde-wigged robot without the letters in the background and without the "longest-running game show" tagline. Suppose that there was no evidence that Samsung intended to invoke Vanna White, but survey evidence showed that a significant number of respondents identified the robot with Vanna anyway. Right of publicity violation?

Compare *Vanna White* to *Burck v. Mars, Inc.*, 571 F. Supp. 2d 446 (S.D.N.Y. 2008). Burck performed in Times Square in New York City as the "Naked Cowboy." *See http://www.nakedcowboy.com.* Mars ran video advertisements in Times Square showing M&M candy characters substituted for various New York City icons. One such ad showed an M&M character dressed (or not dressed) in a manner reminiscent of the "Naked Cowboy." How would you analyze identifiability? The *Burck* case arose under the New York statute, which prohibits unauthorized uses of a person's "name, portrait, picture or voice." Is the New York statute less generous than California law? Is *Burck* distinguishable from *Vanna White* on this basis? *See also Lohan v. Take-Two Interactive Software, Inc.*, 30 N.Y.3d 1055 (2018) (computer-generated avatar in a video game constituted a "portrait" for purposes of the New York statute, but the avatar was not identifiable as plaintiff actress Lindsay Lohan).

2. *Proving identifiability.* Should we require right-of-publicity plaintiffs to present survey evidence indicating that some threshold number of respondents could identify the plaintiff from the allegedly infringing use? Suppose that in the survey, respondents are shown only the allegedly infringing picture and asked the identification question. Alternatively, suppose that respondents are shown a picture of plaintiff, and then shown the allegedly infringing picture and asked the identification question. Which method is more likely to achieve a correct outcome? *See also Estate of Mercer K. Ellington v. Gibson Piano Ventures Inc.*, 75 U.S.P.Q.2d (BNA) 1724 (S.D. Ind. 2005) (discussing the use of surveys to assess whether consumers confronted with the name ELLINGTON on defendant's pianos would identify the persona of Duke Ellington); *Pesina v. Midway Mfg. Co.*, 948 F. Supp. 40 (N.D. Ill. 1996) (identifiability issue where martial artist was used as model for video game MORTAL KOMBAT).

3. *Parody defense?* Did the *Vanna White* court give short shrift to the parody defense? Recall the materials in Chapter 9, dealing with the parody defense as it arises in trademark infringement and trademark dilution cases. Does the parody claim in *Vanna White* fit well with successful parody claims in trademark infringement/dilution cases? Should the same analysis apply to parody claims in the right-of-publicity context? Why or why not?

4. *Rejoinder to Kozinski.* Does Judge Kozinski have it right? Consider Professor McCarthy's rejoinder:

> Kozinski asks why Vanna White's right to profit from her professional identity should be superior to "Samsung's right to profit by creating its own inventions." The problem with this view is that the Vanna-robot ad was almost wholly derivative and non-inventive. The only appeal of the Samsung ad lies in the viewer's immediate recognition that this is not just any game show robot, this is a *Vanna White* robot. Without the ability to derive recognition and gain from Vanna White, this advertisement would be worthless. The Ninth Circuit's opinion will not, as Kozinski argues, chill an ad agency's inventiveness. Rather, it will chill the temptation to be wholly derivative of a prominent personality without pay and will stimulate ad agency creative juices to produce something truly original. Both Vanna White and the consumer will benefit from that result.

J. Thomas McCarthy, The Rights of Publicity and Privacy App. A (2000).

PROBLEM 11-3: THE RIGHT OF PUBLICITY AND PORTRAYALS OF FICTIONAL CHARACTERS

Problem Statement

In a long-running television situation comedy called *Cheers*, George Wendt portrayed the character "Norm" and John Ratzenberger portrayed "Cliff."

Host International, which runs bars in airports, decided to decorate various bars with a *Cheers* theme, and secured certain copyright and trademark permissions from the producers of the show, but not from Ratzenberger or Wendt. Host also decided to create animatronic robots of the Norm and Cliff characters and seat them at the bars, where they could greet customers and the like. The robots were not named Norm and Cliff.

Wendt and Ratzenberger sued for a violation of their rights of publicity. Evaluate the likelihood of success, applying general principles of the common law right of publicity. The following case excerpts may be helpful in your analysis.

Background Readings

McFarland v. Miller, 14 F.3d 912, 920-21 (3d Cir. 1994):

> Where an actor plays a well-defined part which has not become inextricably identified with his own person, it has been suggested the actor receives no right of exploitation in his portrayal of the character. *See Lugosi v. Universal Pictures*, 603 P.2d 425, 432 (Cal. 1979) (Mosk, J., concurring) ("Merely playing a role [such as Bela Lugosi as Dracula] . . . creates no inheritable property right in an actor, absent a contract so providing."). *But see Id.* at 344, 603 P.2d at 444 (Bird, C.J., dissenting) ("Substantial publicity value exists in the likeness of [famous actors] in their character roles. The professional and economic interests in controlling the commercial exploitation of their likenesses while portraying these characters are identical to their interest in controlling the use of their own 'natural' likeness.").
>
> In his concurrence in *Lugosi*, Justice Mosk recognized another distinct situation where the actor could obtain proprietary interests in a screen persona: "An original creation of a fictional figure played exclusively by its creator may well be protectible." *Id.* at 330, 603 P.2d at 432 (Mosk, J., concurring).[14] We are inclined to agree, but we think the difference between the two situations Justice Mosk contrasts is not wholly dependent on originality as his concurrence suggests. While originality plays a role, a court should also consider the association with the real life actor. Where an actor's screen persona becomes so associated with him that it becomes inseparable from the actor's own public image, the actor obtains an interest in the image which gives him standing to prevent mere interlopers from using it without authority.[15] This principle may be seen in a number of other cases. *See, e.g., Allen v. Men's World Outlet, Inc.*, 679 F. Supp. 360, 362, 371 (S.D.N.Y. 1988) (enjoining

---

14. Justice Mosk contrasted that case with Gregory Peck's role as General MacArthur, George C. Scott's role as General Patton, James Whitmore playing Will Rogers and Charlton Heston playing Moses, as well as Bela Lugosi as Dracula. Justice Mosk believed these actors had no proprietary interest in their roles.

15. We think the case in which an actor becomes known for a single role such as Batman is different. *See Carlos V. Lozano, West Loses Lawsuit Over Batman TV Commercial*, L.A. Times, Jan. 18, 1990, at B3 (Actor Adam West failing in bid to stop retail chain from using a Batman in a commercial that West argued invoked his portrayal). West's association with the role of Batman or Johnny Weismuller's with the role of Tarzan is different than McFarland's identification with Spanky. West's identity did not merge into Batman and Weismuller did not become indistinguishable from Tarzan. McFarland, like Groucho Marx, may have become indistinguishable in the public's eye from his stage persona of Spanky.

look-alike's misappropriation of "schlemiel" persona of Woody Allen cultivated in the film *Annie Hall*); *Groucho Marx Prod. Inc. v. Day & Night Co.*, 523 F. Supp. 485, 491 (S.D.N.Y. 1981) (Marx Brothers had protected right in on-screen images and actions), *rev'd on other grounds*, 689 F.2d 317 (2d Cir. 1982); *Price v. Hal Roach Studios, Inc.*, 400 F. Supp. 836, 843-44 (S.D.N.Y. 1975) (comic duo Stan Laurel and Oliver Hardy had common law right of publicity in on-screen images). Much as the court observed in *Price*, "we deal here with actors portraying themselves and developing their own characters. . . ." *Price*, 400 F. Supp. at 845. A misappropriation took place in *Allen* and *Price* because the performers were identified with the image developed on-screen. Thus, the actor who developed the image had the right to exploit it as superior to third parties which had nothing to do with the actor or the character identified with the actor.

Landham v. Lewis Galoob Toys, Inc., 227 F.3d 619 (6th Cir. 2000):

Landham is a fringe actor who has played supporting roles in several motion pictures, including *48 Hours, Action Jackson*, and *Maximum Force*, as well as several unrated, pornographic films. This suit concerns the role of "Billy, the Native American Tracker" that Landham portrayed in Fox's 1987 action film *Predator*. Landham's employment was initially memorialized in a March 3, 1986, "Standard Cast Deal Memo" ("Memo"), which detailed only the salary, starting date, and an agreement that Landham would pay for a bodyguard for himself. Fox later delivered a "Deal Player Employment Agreement" ("Agreement") which, among other things, assigned all merchandising rights for the Billy character to Fox. The Agreement was never signed, however, and there is a dispute between the parties as to how long after Landham left for filming in Mexico the Agreement was received by his agent in the United States. Landham testified that the only contractual understanding he had with Fox was that he would act in the movie for a specified amount of money and that he would be required to pay for the bodyguard. In 1995, Fox licensed to Galoob the rights to produce and market a line of its "Micro Machines" toys based on *Predator*. One of these three sets of toys contained a "Billy" action figure. Because the toy is only 1.5 inches tall and has no eyes or mouth, it bears no personal resemblance to Landham. Moreover, Eric Shank, the Galoob employee who designed the toy, purposefully avoided any such resemblance. Nonetheless, Landham argues that the toy violates his right of publicity under Kentucky law and amounts to a false endorsement under the Lanham Act. The district court disagreed, finding insufficient evidence to suggest that consumers would associate the toy with Landham. . . .

We decline Landham's invitation to extend *White* to this case. First, the holding is factually distinguishable, as White used her own name in her television role, and also produced evidence that her identity was invoked and had commercial value. More importantly, we share, as we think the Kentucky courts would, Judge Kozinski's unwillingness to give every individual who appears before a television or movie camera, by occupation or happenstance, the right as a matter of law to compensation for every subtle nuance that may be taken by someone as invoking his identity without first being required to prove significant commercial value and identifiability. Such a holding would upset the careful balance that courts have gradually constructed between the right of publicity and the First Amendment and federal intellectual property laws, undermining the right's viability. We therefore decline to give Landham "an exclusive right not in what [he] looks like or who [he] is, but in what [he] does for a living." *White*, 989 F.2d at 1515. To the extent that *White* may be read to require a contrary result, we reject its reasoning.

Stanford v. Caesar's Entertainment, Inc., 430 F. Supp. 2d 749 (W.D. Tenn. 2006):

[Plaintiff Stanford had agreed to play the character "Loose Slot Louie" in television, radio, and print commercials advertising defendant's casinos. Stanford had signed a release granting defendant certain rights in the use of Stanford's image, likeness, and voice in the commercials. When a dispute arose over Stanford's compensation, Stanford sued, claiming that some of his portrayals of "Loose Slot Louie" fell outside the scope of the release and hence constituted right-of-publicity violations.

The court accepted defendant's argument that Stanford's right-of-publicity claim was preempted by copyright law. The court distinguished *Landham* and a handful of other right-of-publicity cases involving portrayals of fictional characters, finding that the subject matter of the right of publicity claim fell within the subject matter of copyright.]

In this case . . . Plaintiff's claims do not involve the exploitation or misappropriation of "the very identity or persona of [Plaintiff] as a human being." Despite Plaintiff's attempt to characterize his claims as such, it is clear that the claims actually involve Plaintiff's dramatic portrayal of a fictional character named "Loose Slot Louie"—a character featured in Defendants' advertisements. The advertisement campaign features "Loose Slot Louie," not Crisper Stanford. The fact that Plaintiff is disputing Defendants' use of his image, not as Crisper Stanford, but as Crisper Stanford playing "Loose Slot Louie," makes his case unlike those in which courts have found that federal copyright law does not preempt a state-law right of publicity.

. . .

[B]ecause Plaintiff appeared in Defendants' advertisements not as himself, but as a fictional character, the facts of this case are distinguishable. . . .

[O]nce Plaintiff willingly dressed up in the "Loose Slot Louie" costume and knowingly appeared as this character in Defendants' advertisements, his performance became a "dramatic work" that was "fixed in a tangible medium of expression" and "perceived, reproduced, or otherwise communicated" through the various media outlets in which Defendants' advertisement campaign was run. . . .

[In addition, the court found that the exclusive rights conferred under the right-of-publicity claim at issue were equivalent to those conferred under copyright. Accordingly, the two elements for copyright preemption were satisfied, and copyright law preempted the state right-of-publicity claim. (See Problem 11-2 for more on the preemption analysis.)]

3. Limitations on the Right of Publicity

As we have seen, right-of-publicity claims frequently arise in cases where a party appropriates another's identity for use on products or services, or for use in advertising those products or services. How should the right of publicity operate outside this paradigmatic setting? For example, suppose that a novelist (say, Professor Janis) writes a book that invokes a famous personality (say, a book called "MJ and MJ," which details the mysterious connection between Professor Janis and Michael Jordan, purportedly attributable to the fact that they share the same initials). Does Michael Jordan have a right-of-publicity claim? For that matter, does Michael Jordan have a right-of-publicity claim based on the use of his name in this paragraph of this book?

We have encountered similar issues in our study of trademark rights. In Chapter 9, we found that the First Amendment's Speech Clause, and other concepts closely intertwined with speech interests (such as parody), marked out a zone in which anyone was free to use another's trademarks without permission. In this section we consider how those concepts limit the right of publicity. Before you arrive too quickly at the conclusion that the limiting concepts developed in trademark jurisprudence do (or should) carry over to right-of-publicity law, consider two points. First, the doctrine in trademark law is thin; courts have shown solicitude for speech interests but have not developed robust general tests for mediating the clash between trademark rights and speech interests. Second, rights of publicity differ from trademark rights in that rights of publicity are in gross property rights. When evaluating a trademark claim that implicates speech issues, a court may take advantage of the fluidity of the confusion or dilution doctrines to absolve a defendant of liability—avoiding the need to speak directly to the parameters of speech-related defenses. By contrast, when adjudicating a right-of-publicity claim in which speech interests are at stake, a court's options for balancing interests are different, and arguably more constrained: the court might craft limitations on protectable aspects of identity; it might distinguish between commercial and non-commercial uses; or the court might speak directly to the speech limitations on the right of publicity.

The main cases in this section attempt to formulate a general approach for balancing speech interests against the right of publicity. The accompanying materials explore how those approaches, and others, may be applied.

HART v. ELECTRONIC ARTS, INC.

717 F.3d 141 (3d Cir. 2013)

GREENAWAY, JR., Circuit Judge:

I.   FACTS

Hart was a quarterback, player number 13, with the Rutgers University NCAA Men's Division I Football team for the 2002 through 2005 seasons. As a condition of participating in college-level sports, Hart was required to adhere to the National Collegiate Athletic Association's ("NCAA") amateurism rules as set out in Article 12 of the NCAA bylaws. *See, e.g.,* NCAA, *2011-12 NCAA Division I Manual* §12.01.1 (2011) ("Only an amateur student-athlete is eligible for inter-collegiate athletics participation in a particular sport."). In relevant part, these rules state that a collegiate athlete loses his or her "amateur" status if (1) the athlete "[u]ses his or her athletics skill (directly or indirectly) for pay in any form in that sport," *id.* §12.1.2, or (2) the athlete "[a]ccepts any remuneration or permits the use of his or her name or picture to advertise, recommend or promote directly the sale or use of a commercial product or service of any kind," *id.* §12.5.2.1.[2] In comporting with these bylaws, Hart purportedly refrained from seizing on various commercial opportunities. On the field, Hart excelled. At 6'2", weighing 197 pounds, and typically wearing a visor and armband on his left wrist, Hart amassed an impressive list of achievements as the Scarlet Knights' starting quarterback. As of this writing, Hart still holds the Scarlet Knights' records for career attempts, completions, and interceptions. Hart's skill brought success to the team and during his senior year the Knights were invited to the Insight Bowl, their first Bowl game since 1978.

Hart's participation in college football also ensured his inclusion in EA's successful *NCAA Football* videogame franchise. . . . New editions in the series are released annually, and "allow[] users to experience the excitement and challenge of college football" by interacting with "over 100 virtual teams and thousands of virtual players."

A typical play session allows users the choice of two teams. "Once a user chooses two college teams to compete against each other, the video game assigns a stadium for the match-up and populates it with players, coaches, referees, mascots, cheerleaders and fans."[5] In addition to this "basic single-game format," EA has introduced a number of additional game modes that allow for "multi-game" play. . . .

In no small part, the *NCAA Football* franchise's success owes to its focus on realism and detail—from realistic sounds, to game mechanics, to team mascots. This focus on realism also ensures that the "over 100 virtual teams" in the game are populated by digital avatars that resemble their real-life counterparts and share their vital and biographical information. Thus, for example, in *NCAA Football 2006*, Rutgers' quarterback, player number 13, is 6'2" tall, weighs 197 pounds and resembles Hart. Moreover, while users can change

---

2. The NCAA Manual also states that where a collegiate athlete's

> name or picture appears on commercial items . . . or is used to promote a commercial product sold by an individual or agency without the student-athlete's knowledge or permission, the student athlete (or the institution acting on behalf of the student-athlete) is required to take steps to stop such an activity in order to retain his or her eligibility for intercollegiate athletics.

NCAA, *2011-12 NCAA Division I Manual* §12.5.2.2 (2011).

5. Appellee licenses, from the Collegiate Licensing Company (the NCAA's licensing agent), "the right to use member school names, team names, uniforms, logos, stadium fight songs, and other game elements." Unlike certain of its other videogame franchises, EA does not license the likeness and identity rights for intercollegiate players.

the digital avatar's appearance and most of the vital statistics (height, weight, throwing distance, etc.), certain details remain immutable: the player's home state, home town, team, and class year.

[Appellee Hart sued, alleging that appellant EA had violated his right of publicity.] Specifically, Appellant alleges that (1) Appellee replicated his likeness in *NCAA Football 2004, 2005*, and *2006* (complete with biographical and career statistics)[8] and that (2) Appellee used Appellant's image "in the promotion for [*NCAA Football*] wherein [Appellant] was throwing a pass with actual footage from Rutgers University's Bowl Game against Arizona State University."

[The District Court granted summary judgment in favor of EA Sports on the ground that the First Amendment shielded EA Sports from the right of publicity claim. Hart appealed.]

. . .

III. DISCUSSION

[The court noted that it was "self-evident" that video games are protected as expressive speech under the First Amendment, citing *Brown v. Entm't Merch. Ass'n*, 131 S. Ct. 2729 (2011).] To resolve the tension between the First Amendment and the right of publicity, we must balance the interests underlying the right to free expression against the interests in protecting the right of publicity. *See Zacchini v. Scripps–Howard Broad. Co.*, 433 U.S. 562, 574-75 (1977).[11]

Courts have taken varying approaches in attempting to strike a balance between the competing interests in right of publicity cases, some more appealing than others. In our discussion below, we first consider the nature of the interests we must balance and then analyze the different approaches courts have taken to resolving the tension between the First Amendment and the right of publicity.

[The court discussed the fundamentals of the First Amendment and right-of-publicity interests. Then it turned to New Jersey right-of-publicity law. Noting that New Jersey courts had not set out any definitive methodology for balancing First Amendment interests against the right of publicity, the court stated that it would evaluate authority from other jurisdictions.]

B. How Courts Balance the Interests

We begin our inquiry by looking at [*Zacchini*], the only Supreme Court case addressing the First Amendment in a right of publicity context. In this case, the Court called for a balancing test to weigh the interest underlying the First Amendment against those underpinning the right of publicity. [cit.] This decision sets the stage for our analysis of three systematized analytical frameworks that have emerged as courts struggle with finding a standardized way for performing this balancing inquiry.

1. *Zacchini and the Need for Balance*

In *Zacchini*, an Ohio television news program recorded and subsequently broadcast Mr. Hugo Zacchini's entire "human cannonball" act from a local fair. The daredevil

---

8. Appellant alleges that the physical attributes exhibited by the virtual avatar in *NCAA Football* are his own (i.e., he attended high school in Florida, measures 6'2" tall, weighs 197 pounds, wears number 13, and has the same left wrist band and helmet visor) and that the avatar's speed, agility, and passer rating reflected actual footage of Appellant during his tenure at Rutgers.

11. While it is true that the right of publicity is a creature of state law and precedent, its intersection with the First Amendment presents a federal issue, and, thus, permits us to engage in the sort of balancing inquiry at issue here. *See, e.g., Zacchini*, 433 U.S. at 566-68.

brought suit alleging a violation of his right of publicity as recognized by Ohio law. *Id.* at 563-66. The Ohio courts held that Zacchini's claim was barred on First Amendment grounds, and the case then came before the Supreme Court.

In setting out the interests at issue in the case, the Supreme Court noted . . . that "the State's interest in permitting a 'right of publicity' is in protecting the proprietary interest of the individual in his act in part to encourage such entertainment." *Id.* at 573. This aspect of the right, the Court noted, was "analogous to the goals of patent and copyright law," given that they too serve to protect the individual's ability to "reap the reward of his endeavors." *Id.* In *Zacchini*, the performance was the "product of [Zacchini's] own talents and energy, the end result of much time, effort and expense." *Id.* at 575. Thus much of its economic value lay "in the right of exclusive control over the publicity given to his performance." *Id.* Indeed, while the Court noted that "[a]n entertainer such as petitioner usually has no objection to the widespread publication of his act as long as [he] gets the commercial benefit of such publication," *id.* at 573, the claim at issue in the *Zacchini* concerned "the strongest case for a 'right of publicity,'" because it did not involve the "appropriation of an entertainer's reputation to enhance the attractiveness of a commercial product," but instead involved "the appropriation of the very activity by which the entertainer acquired his reputation in the first place," *id.* at 576.

Ultimately, the Court ruled in favor of the human cannonball, and held that

> [w]herever the line in particular situations is to be drawn between media reports that are protected and those that are not, we are quite sure that the First and Fourteenth Amendments do not immunize the media when they broadcast a performer's entire act without his consent. The Constitution no more prevents a State from requiring respondent to compensate petitioner for broadcasting his act on television than it would privilege respondent to film and broadcast a copyrighted dramatic work without liability to the copyright owner.

Id. at 574-75. Thus, while the Court did not itself engage in an explicit balancing inquiry, it did suggest that the respective interests in a case should be balanced against each other.

In the wake of *Zacchini*, courts began applying a balancing inquiry to resolve cases where a right of publicity claim collided with First Amendment protections. While early cases approached the analysis from an ad hoc perspective, [cit.], courts eventually began developing standardized balancing frameworks. Consequently, we now turn our attention to more standardized balancing tests to see whether any of them offer a particularly compelling methodology for resolving the case at hand and similar disputes.[14]

---

14. We reject as inapplicable in this case the suggestion that those who play organized sports are not significantly damaged by appropriation of their likeness because "players are rewarded, and handsomely, too, for their participation in games and can earn additional large sums from endorsement and sponsorship arrangements." *C.B.C. Distrib. & Mktg., Inc. v. Major League Baseball Advanced Media, L.P.*, 505 F.3d 818, 824 (8th Cir. 2007) (discussing Major League Baseball players); *see also, e.g., Cardtoons, L.C. v. Major League Baseball Players Ass'n*, 95 F.3d 959, 974 (10th Cir. 1996) ("[T]he additional inducement for achievement produced by publicity rights are often inconsequential because most celebrities with valuable commercial identities are already handsomely compensated."). If anything, the policy considerations in this case weigh in *favor* of Appellant. As we have already noted, intercollegiate athletes are forbidden from capitalizing on their fame while in school. Moreover, the NCAA most recently estimated that "[l]ess than one in 100, or 1.6 percent, of NCAA senior football players will get drafted by a National Football League (NFL) team." NCAA, Estimated Probability of Competing in Athletics Beyond the High School Interscholastic Level, available at *http://www.ncaa. org/wps/wcm/connect/public/ncaa/pdfs/2012/estimated+probability+of+competing+in+athletics+beyon d+the+high+school+interscholastic+level*. Despite all of his achievements, it should be noted that Ryan Hart was among the roughly ninety-nine percent who were not drafted after graduation.

2.   *The Modern Balancing Tests*

. . . [T]hree [balancing] tests are of particular note: the commercial-interest-based Predominant Use Test, the trademark-based *Rogers* Test, and the copyright-based Transformative Use Test. . . .

a.   Predominant Use Test

Appellant urges us to adopt the Predominant Use Test, which first appeared in *Doe v. TCI Cablevision*, 110 S.W.3d 363 (Mo. 2003) (en banc), a case that considered a hockey player's right of publicity claim against a comic book publishing company. In *TCI*, Anthony "Tony" Twist, a hockey player, brought suit against a number of individuals and entities involved in producing and publishing the *Spawn* comic book series after the introduction of a villainous character named Anthony "Tony Twist" Twistelli.

In balancing Twist's property interests in his own name and identity against the First Amendment interests of the comic book creators, the *TCI* court rejected both the Transformative Use and *Rogers* tests, noting that they gave "too little consideration to the fact that many uses of a person's name and identity have both expressive and commercial components." [cit.] The Supreme Court of Missouri considered both tests to be too rigid, noting that they operated "to preclude a cause of action whenever the use of the name and identity is in any way expressive, regardless of its commercial exploitation." *Id.* The court instead applied what it called a "sort of predominant use test":

> If a product is being sold that predominantly exploits the commercial value of an individual's identity, that product should be held to violate the right of publicity and not be protected by the First Amendment, even if there is some "expressive" content in it that might qualify as "speech" in other circumstances. If, on the other hand, the predominant purpose of the product is to make an expressive comment on or about a celebrity, the expressive values could be given greater weight.

Id. (quoting Mark S. Lee, *Agents of Chaos: Judicial Confusion in Defining the Right of Publicity–Free Speech Interface*, 23 Loy. L.A. Ent. L. Rev. V. 471, 500 (2003)). The *TCI* court considered this to be a "more balanced balancing test [particularly for] cases where speech is both expressive and commercial." *Id.* After applying the test, the court ruled for Twist, holding that "the metaphorical reference to Twist, though a literary device, has very little literary value compared to its commercial value." *Id.*

We decline Appellant's invitation to adopt this test. By our reading, the Predominant Use Test is subjective at best, arbitrary at worst, and in either case calls upon judges to act as both impartial jurists and discerning art critics. These two roles cannot co-exist. Indeed, Appellant suggests that pursuant to this test we must evaluate "what value [Appellee is] adding to the First Amendment expressiveness [of *NCAA Football*] by appropriating the commercially valuable likeness?" Since "[t]he game would have the exact same level of First Amendment expressiveness if [Appellee] didn't appropriate Mr. Hart's likeness," Appellant urges us to find that *NCAA Football* fails the Predominant Use Test and therefore is not shielded by the First Amendment. Such reasoning, however, leads down a dangerous and rightly-shunned road: adopting Appellant's suggested analysis would be tantamount to admitting that it is proper for courts to analyze select elements of a work to determine how much they contribute to the entire work's expressiveness. Moreover, as a necessary (and insidious) consequence, the Appellant's approach would suppose that there exists a broad range of seemingly expressive speech that has no First Amendment value.

Appellee rightly argues that the Predominant Use Test is antithetical to our First Amendment precedent, and we likewise reject the Test. We instead turn our attention to the *Rogers* Test, which was proposed by Appellee and which draws its inspiration from trademark law.

b.   The *Rogers* Test

The *Rogers* Test looks to the relationship between the celebrity image and the work as a whole. As the following discussion demonstrates, however, adopting this test would potentially immunize a broad swath of tortious activity. We therefore reject the *Rogers* Test as inapposite in the instant case.

I.   Origins and Scope of the Rogers Test

[The court discussed the test from *Rogers v. Grimaldi*, 875 F.2d 994 (2d Cir. 1989). Recall from the discussion in Chapter 9 that under the *Rogers* test, the use of a celebrity's name in a movie title was deemed to be permissible unless the title had no artistic relevance to the underlying work or if the title was explicitly misleading as to the source or content of the work. EA argued that the test should be applied to the use of a celebrity's name or likeness in any part of a work, not just in the title. The court noted that the Sixth Circuit had applied the *Rogers* test to the content of the work in *Parks v. LaFace Records*, but that it had subsequently applied a different test (the transformative use test, discussed below) in *ETW Corp. v. Jireh Publishing, Inc.* The court also observed that one of its own prior cases expressed hesitation about extending the *Rogers* test beyond titles. *Facenda v. N.F.L. Films, Inc.*, 542 F.3d 1007, 1018 (3d Cir. 2008).]

II.   Analysis of the *Rogers* Test

Ultimately, we find that the *Rogers* Test does not present the proper analytical approach for cases such as the one at bar. While the Test may have a use in trademark-like right of publicity cases, it is inapposite here. We are concerned that this test is a blunt instrument, unfit for widespread application in cases that require a carefully calibrated balancing of two fundamental protections: the right of free expression and the right to control, manage, and profit from one's own identity.

[The court expressed dissatisfaction with the "no artistic relevance" prong as applied here. According to the court, EA's use of Hart's likeness would be shielded under the *Rogers* test if Hart's likeness was relevant to the content of the video game   which it presumably was. (Note that the court's analysis here seems to assume away the second prong of the *Rogers* test.) Such a result would tip the balance too far in favor of free expression, according to the court. Indeed, the court stated, it would "turn the right of publicity on its head" to say that Hart's very stature as a recognizable college football player ensured that his likeness was artistically relevant to the content of the game.]

On the other hand, we do agree with the *Rogers* court in so far as it noted that the right of publicity does not implicate the potential for consumer confusion and is therefore potentially broader than the protections offered by the Lanham Act. [cit.] Indeed, therein lies the weakness of comparing the right of publicity to trademark protections: the right of publicity is broader and, by extension, protects a greater swath of property interests. Thus, it would be unwise for us to adopt a test that hews so closely to traditional trademark principles. Instead, we need a broader, more nuanced test, which helps balance the interests at issue in cases such as the one at bar. The final test—the Transformative Use Test—provides just such an approach.

c.   The Transformative Use Test

Looking to intellectual property law for guidance on how to balance property interests against the First Amendment has merit. We need only shift our gaze away from trademark, to the broader vista of copyright law. Thus, we come to the case of *Comedy III Prods., Inc. v. Gary Saderup, Inc.*, which imported the concept of "transformative" use from copyright law into the right of publicity context. 21 P.3d 797, 804-08 (Cal. 2001). This concept lies at the core of a test that both Appellant and Appellee agree is applicable to this case: the Transformative Use Test.

I.   GENESIS OF THE TRANSFORMATIVE USE TEST

The Transformative Use Test was first articulated by the Supreme Court of California in *Comedy III*. That case concerned an artist's production and sale of t-shirts and prints bearing a charcoal drawing of the Three Stooges. The California court determined that while "[t]he right of publicity is often invoked in the context of commercial speech," it could also apply in instances where the speech is merely expressive. *Id.* at 802-803. The court also noted, however, that when addressing expressive speech, "the very importance of celebrities in society means that the right of publicity has the potential of censoring significant expression by suppressing alternative versions of celebrity images that are iconoclastic, irreverent or otherwise attempt to redefine the celebrity's meaning." *Id.* at 803. Thus, while the "the right of publicity cannot, consistent with the First Amendment, be a right to control the celebrity's image by censoring disagreeable portrayals," *id.* at 807, the right, like copyright, nonetheless offers protection to a form of intellectual property that society deems to have social utility, *id.* at 804.

After briefly considering whether to import the "fair use" analysis from copyright, the *Comedy III* court decided that only the first fair use factor, "the purpose and character of the use," was appropriate. *Id.* at 808. Specifically, the *Comedy III* court found persuasive the Supreme Court's holding in *Campbell v. Acuff-Rose Music, Inc.* that

> the central purpose of the inquiry into this fair use factor 'is to see . . . whether the new work merely "supercede[s] the objects" of the original creation, or instead adds something new, with a further purpose or different character, altering the first with new expression, meaning, or message; it asks, in other words, whether and to what extent the new work is "*transformative*."'

Id. (emphasis added) (citing *Campbell v. Acuff-Rose Music, Inc.*, 510 U.S. 569, 579 (1994)).

Going further, the court explained that works containing "significant transformative elements" are less likely to interfere with the economic interests implicated by the right of publicity. For example, "works of parody or other distortions of the celebrity figure are not, from the celebrity fan's viewpoint, good substitutes for conventional depictions of the celebrity and therefore do not generally threaten markets for celebrity memorabilia that the right of publicity is designed to protect." *Id.* The court was also careful to emphasize that "the transformative elements or creative contributions" in a work may include—under the right circumstances—factual reporting, fictionalized portrayal, heavy-handed lampooning, and subtle social criticism. *Id.* at 809 ("The inquiry is in a sense more quantitative than qualitative, asking whether the literal and imitative or the creative elements predominate in the work.").[24]

---

24. The court in *Comedy III* also added an ancillary question to its inquiry: "does the marketability and economic value of the challenged work derive primarily from the fame of the celebrity depicted?" *Comedy III*, 21 P.3d at 810. If not, then "there would generally be no actionable right of publicity." *Id.* However, the inverse is not necessarily true: even if the work does derive its value principally from the celebrity's depiction, "it may still be a transformative work." *Id.*

Restating its newly-articulated test, the Supreme Court of California held that the balance between the right of publicity and First Amendment interests turns on

> [w]hether the celebrity likeness is one of the "raw materials" from which an original work is synthesized, or whether the depiction or imitation of the celebrity is the very sum and substance of the work in question. We ask, in other words, *whether the product containing a celebrity's likeness is so transformed that it has become primarily the defendant's own expression rather than the celebrity's likeness.* And when we use the word "expression," we mean expression of something other than the likeness of the celebrity.

Id. (emphasis added).

Applying this test, the court concluded that charcoal portraits of the Three Stooges did violate the Stooges' rights of publicity, holding that the court could "discern no significant transformative or creative contribution" and that "the marketability and economic value of [the work] derives primarily from the fame of the celebrities depicted." *Id.* at 811.

II.   APPLICATION OF THE TRANSFORMATIVE USE TEST

Given its relative recency, few courts have applied the Transformative Use Test, and consequently there is not a significant body of case law related to its application. Nonetheless, a handful of cases bear mention as they help frame our inquiry.

In 2003, the Supreme Court of California revisited the Transformative Use Test when two musicians, Johnny and Edgar Winter, who both possessed long white hair and albino features, brought suit against a comic book company over images of two villainous half-man, half-worm creatures, both with long white hair and albino features, named Johnny and Edgar Autumn. *Winter v. DC Comics*, 69 P.3d 473, 476 (Cal. 2003). As the brothers' right of publicity claims necessarily implicated DC Comics' First Amendment rights, the *Winter* court looked to the Transformative Use Test. In summarizing the test, the court explained that "[a]n artist depicting a celebrity must contribute something more than a 'merely trivial' variation, [but must create] something recognizably 'his own,' in order to qualify for legal protection." *Id.* at 478 (alteration in original) (quoting *Comedy III*). Thus, in applying the test, the *Winter* court held that

> [a]lthough the fictional characters Johnny and Edgar Autumn are less-than-subtle evocations of Johnny and Edgar Winter, the books do not depict plaintiffs literally. Instead, plaintiffs are merely part of the raw materials from which the comic books were synthesized. To the extent the drawings of the Autumn brothers resemble plaintiffs at all, they are distorted for purposes of lampoon, parody, or caricature. And the Autumn brothers are but cartoon characters—half-human and half-worm—in a larger story, which is itself quite expressive.

Id. at 479. The court therefore found that "fans who want to purchase pictures of [the Winter brothers] would find the drawing of the Autumn brothers unsatisfactory as a substitute for conventional depictions." *Id.*[25] Consequently, the court rejected the brothers' claims for a right of publicity violation.

Also in 2003, the Sixth Circuit decided *ETW*, a case focusing on a photograph of Tiger Woods set among a collage of other, golf-related photographs. As we previously noted, while *ETW* mentioned both the *Rogers* case and the Restatement (Third) of Unfair

---

25. The *Winter* court also found unpersuasive arguments that the comic books were marketed by "trading on [the brothers'] likenesses and reputations to generate interest in the comic book series." *Winter v. DC Comics*, 69 P.3d 473, 479 (Cal. 2003). The court held that considerations of marketing strategy were "irrelevant" because the "question is whether the work is transformative, not how it is marketed." *Id.*

Competition, the test it ultimately applied was a combination of an ad-hoc approach and the Transformative Use Test. [cit.] In holding that the collage "contain[ed] significant transformative elements," *id.* at 938, the court compared it to the Three Stooges portraits from *Comedy III*, and noted that the collage "does not capitalize solely on a literal depiction of Woods." *Id.* Instead, the "work consists of a collage of images in addition to Woods's image which are combined to describe, in artistic form, a historic event in sports history and to convey a message about the significance of Woods's achievement in that event." [cit.]

ETW presents an archetypical example of a case falling somewhere in the middle of Transformative Use Test jurisprudence, given that it focuses on the use of photographs (literal depictions of celebrities), but adds a transformative aspect to the work, thereby altering the meaning behind the use of the celebrity's likeness. Arguably, the *Comedy III* and *Winter* decisions bookend the spectrum of cases applying the Transformative Use Test. Where *Comedy III* presents a clear example of a non-transformative use (i.e., mere literal depictions of celebrities recreated in a different medium), *Winter* offers a use that is highly transformative (i.e., fanciful characters, placed amidst a fanciful setting, that draw inspiration from celebrities). As with *ETW*, however, most of the cases discussed below (along with the instant case), fall somewhere between these two decisions. This same analytical approach—focusing on whether and how the celebrity's likeness is transformed—appears in decisions by courts applying the Transformative Use Test to video games, an area of law which we consider next.

III.   THE TRANSFORMATIVE USE TEST AND VIDEO GAMES

In mid-2006, the California Court of Appeal decided *Kirby v. Sega of America, Inc.*, 50 Cal. Rptr. 3d 607 (Cal. Ct. App. 2006), which addressed a musician's right of publicity claim against a video game company. Specifically, the musician (Kierin Kirby) had claimed that Sega misappropriated her likeness and signature phrases for purposes of creating the character of Ulala, a reporter in the far flung future. In applying the Transformative Use Test, the court noted that not only did Kirby's signature phrases included "ooh la la" but that both she and the videogame character would often use phrases like "groove," "meow," "dee-lish," and "I won't give up." *Id.* at 613. The court also found similarities in appearance between Kirby and Ulala, based on hair style and clothing choice. *Id.* At the same time, the court held that differences between the two did exist—both in appearance and movement—and that Ulala was not a mere digital recreation of Kirby. *Id.* Thus, the court concluded that Ulala passed the Transformative Use Test, rejecting Kirby's argument that the differences between her and the character added no additional meaning or message to the work. *Id.* at 616-17 ("A work is transformative if it adds 'new expression.' That expression alone is sufficient; it need not convey any 'meaning or message.'"); *see also id.* at 617 ("[A]ny imitation of Kirby's likeness or identity in Ulala is not the sum and substance of that character.").

Several years later, in early 2011, the California courts again confronted the right of publicity as it related to video games in *No Doubt v. Activision Publishing, Inc.*, 122 Cal. Rptr. 3d 397 (Cal. Ct. App. 2011). The case centered on *Band Hero*, a game that allows player to "simulate performing in a rock band in time with popular songs" by selecting digital avatars to represent them in an in-game band. *Id.* at 401. Some of the avatars were digital recreations of real-life musicians, including members of the band No Doubt. After a contract dispute broke off relations between the band and the company, No Doubt sued, claiming a violation of their rights of publicity. The California Court of Appeal applied the Transformative Use Test.

The *No Doubt* court began by noting that "in stark contrast to the 'fanciful creative characters' in *Winter* and *Kirby*," the No Doubt avatars could not be altered by players and thus remained "at all times immutable images of the real celebrity musicians." *Id*. at 410. But this fact, by itself, did not end the court's inquiry since "even literal reproductions of celebrities can be 'transformed' into expressive works based on the context into which the celebrity image is placed." *Id*. [cit.] Looking to the context of the *Band Hero* game, the court found that "no matter what else occurs in the game *during the depiction of the No Doubt avatars*, the avatars perform rock songs, the same activity by which the band achieved and maintains its fame." *Id*. at 410-11 (emphasis added). The court explained:

> [T]he avatars perform [rock] songs as literal recreations of the band members. That the avatars can be manipulated to perform at fanciful venues including outer space or to sing songs the real band would object to singing, or that the avatars appear in the context of a videogame *that contains many other creative elements*, does not transform the avatars into anything other than the exact depictions of No Doubt's members doing exactly what they do as celebrities.

Id. at 411 (emphasis added).[27] As a final step in its analysis, the court noted that Activision's use of highly realistic digital depictions of No Doubt was motivated by a desire to capitalize on the band's fan-base, "because it encourages [fans] to purchase the game so as *to perform as, or alongside, the members of No Doubt*." *Id*. (emphasis added). Given all this, the court concluded that Activision's use of No Doubt's likenesses did infringe on the band's rights of publicity. *Id*. at 411-12.

IV.   ANALYSIS OF THE TRANSFORMATIVE USE TEST

Like the Predominant Use and *Rogers* tests, the Transformative Use Test aims to balance the interest protected by the right of publicity against those interests preserved by the First Amendment. In our view, the Transformative Use Test appears to strike the best balance because it provides courts with a flexible—yet uniformly applicable—analytical framework. Specifically, the Transformative Use Test seems to excel precisely where the other two tests falter. Unlike the *Rogers* Test, the Transformative Use Test maintains a singular focus on whether the work sufficiently transforms the celebrity's identity or likeness, thereby allowing courts to account for the fact that misappropriation can occur in any market segment, including those related to the celebrity.

On the other hand, unlike the Predominant Use Test, applying the Transformative Use Test requires a more circumscribed inquiry, focusing on the specific aspects of a work that speak to whether it was merely created to exploit a celebrity's likeness. This test therefore recognizes that if First Amendment protections are to mean anything in right of publicity claims, courts must *begin* by considering the extent to which a work is the creator's own expression.[29]

---

27. For support, the *No Doubt* court relied on the Ninth Circuit's decision in *Hilton v. Hallmark Cards*, where our sister court held that a greeting card depicting Paris Hilton's head on a cartoon waitress accompanied by the line "that's hot" was not transformative and thus infringed on Hilton's right of publicity. 599 F.3d 894, 911 (9th Cir. 2010) ("While a work need not be phantasmagoric as in *Winter* or fanciful as in *Kirby* in order to be transformative, there is enough doubt as to whether Hallmark's card is transformative under our case law that we cannot say Hallmark is entitled to the defense. . . .").

29. While we acknowledge that the test in *Comedy III* included a question as to whether the "marketability and economic value of [the work] derive primarily from the fame of the celebrities depicted," *Comedy III*, 21 P.3d at 810, we note that this is a secondary question. The court in *Comedy III* rightly recognized that the balancing inquiry suggested by the Supreme Court in *Zacchini* cannot start and stop with commercial purpose or value.

Additionally, the Transformative Use Test best comports with the cautionary language present in various right of publicity cases. Specifically, we believe that an initial focus on the creative aspects of a work helps address our own concern from *Facenda*, where we noted that "courts must circumscribe the right of publicity." *Facenda*, 542 F.3d at 1032. As our discussion below demonstrates, the Transformative Use Test effectively restricts right of publicity claims to a very narrow universe of expressive works. Moreover, we believe that the Transformative Use Test best exemplifies the methodology suggested by Justice Powell's dissent in *Zacchini*:

> Rather than begin with a quantitative analysis of the performer's behavior—is this or is this not his entire act?—we should direct initial attention to the actions of the news media: what use did the station make of the film footage? When a film is used, as here, for a routine portion of a regular news program, I would hold that the First Amendment protects the station from a "right of publicity" or "appropriation" suit, absent a strong showing by the plaintiff that the news broadcast was a subterfuge or cover for private or commercial exploitation.

Zacchini, 433 U.S. at 581 (Powell, J., dissenting). Consistent with Justice Powell's argument, the Transformative Use Test begins by asking "what use did the [defendant] make of the [celebrity identity]?" *Id.*

Finally, we find that of the three tests, the Transformative Use Test is the most consistent with other courts' ad hoc approaches to right of publicity cases. [cit.]

It is little wonder, then, that the *Comedy III* decision looked to all three of these cases for guidance in defining the Transformative Use Test. *See Comedy III*, 21 P.3d at 806-09. The fact that such prior holdings can be reconciled with the Test not only bolsters our views as to its propriety, but also ensures that adopting the Transformative Use Test does not result in the sort of backward-looking jurisprudential revision that might disturb prior protections for expressive speech. Quite to the contrary, adopting the Test ensures that already-existing First Amendment protections in right of publicity cases apply to video games with the same force as to "biographies, documentaries, docudramas, and other expressive works depicting real-life figures." (Dissent Op. at 6.)

In light of the above discussion, we find that the Transformative Use Test is the proper analytical framework to apply to cases such as the one at bar. Consequently, we now apply the test to the facts of the instance case.

C. APPLICATION

In applying the Transformative Use Test to the instant case, we must determine whether Appellant's identity is sufficiently transformed in *NCAA Football*. As we mentioned earlier, we use the term "identity" to encompass not only Appellant's likeness, but also his biographical information. It is the combination of these two parts—which, when combined, identify the digital avatar as an in-game recreation of Appellant—that must be sufficiently transformed.[37]

---

37. This joint focus on both likeness and identifying information avoids a conflict with *C.B.C. Distribution & Mktg., Inc. v. Major League Baseball Advanced Media, L.P.*, 505 F.3d 818 (8th Cir. 2007), which held that use of major league baseball players' records in a fantasy baseball game was protected by the First Amendment even against right of publicity claims because such information was publicly available. *Id.* at 823-24. The presence of a digital avatar that recreates Appellant in a digital medium differentiates this matter from *C.B.C.*

Having thus cabined our inquiry to the appropriate form of Appellant's identity, we note that—based on the combination of both the digital avatar's appearance and the biographical and identifying information—the digital avatar does closely resemble the genuine article. Not only does the digital avatar match Appellant in terms of hair color, hair style and skin tone, but the avatar's accessories mimic those worn by Appellant during his time as a Rutgers player. The information, as has already been noted, also accurately tracks Appellant's vital and biographical details. And while the inexorable march of technological progress may make some of the graphics in earlier editions of *NCAA Football* look dated or overly-computerized, we do not believe that video game graphics must reach (let alone cross) the uncanny valley to support a right of publicity claim. If we are to find some transformative element, we must look somewhere other than just the in-game digital recreation of Appellant. Cases such as *ETW* and *No Doubt*, both of which address realistic digital depictions of celebrities, point to the next step in our analysis: context.

Considering the context within which the digital avatar exists—effectively, looking at how Appellant's identity is "incorporated into and transformed by" NCAA Football, (Dissent Op. at 6)—provides little support for Appellee's arguments. The digital Ryan Hart does what the actual Ryan Hart did while at Rutgers: he plays college football, in digital recreations of college football stadiums, filled with all the trappings of a college football game. This is not transformative; the various digitized sights and sounds in the video game do not alter or transform the Appellant's identity in a significant way. *See No Doubt*, 122 Cal. Rptr. 3d at 410-11 ("[N]o matter what else occurs in the game during the depiction of the No Doubt avatars, the avatars perform rock songs, the same activity by which the band achieved and maintains its fame."). Indeed, the lack of transformative context is even more pronounced here than in *No Doubt*, where members of the band could perform and sing in outer space.

Even here, however, our inquiry is not at an end. For as much as the digital representation and context evince no meaningful transformative element in *NCAA Football*, a third avatar-specific element is also present: the users' ability to alter the avatar's appearance. This distinguishing factor ensures that we cannot dispose of this case as simply as the court in *No Doubt*. [cit.] Indeed, the ability for users to change the avatar accounted, in large part, for the District Court's deciding that *NCAA Football* satisfied the Transformative Use Test.[40] We must therefore consider to what extent the ability to alter a digital avatar represents a transformative use of Appellant's identity.

At the outset, we note that the mere presence of this feature, without more, cannot satisfy the Transformative Use Test. True, interactivity is the basis upon which First Amendment protection is granted to video games in the first instance. [cit.] However, the balancing test in right of publicity cases does not look to whether a particular work *loses* First Amendment protection. Rather, the balancing inquiry looks to see whether the

---

40. To be clear, the District Court focused specifically on the *ability* to alter the digital avatars, not on the alterations themselves:

> [I]t is not the user's alteration of Hart's image that is critical. What matters for my analysis of EA's First Amendment right is that EA created the mechanism by which the virtual player may be altered, as well as the multiple permutations available for each virtual player image.

Hart, 808 F. Supp. 2d at 785. That is, the court below did not look to the users' creations as proxies for Appellee's expression. While we disagree with its final decision, we agree with the District Court's careful navigation of this point.

interests protected by the right of publicity are sufficient to *surmount* the already-existing First Amendment protections. [cit.] As *Zacchini* demonstrated, the right of publicity can triumph even when an essential element for First Amendment protection is present. In that case, the human cannonball act was broadcast *as part of the newscast. See Zacchini*, 433 U.S. at 563. To hold, therefore, that a video game should satisfy the Transformative Use Test simply because it includes a particular interactive feature would lead to improper results. Interactivity cannot be an end onto itself.

Moreover, we are wary of converting the ability to alter a digital avatar from mere feature to talisman, thereby opening the door to cynical abuse. If the mere presence of the feature were enough, video game companies could commit the most blatant acts of misappropriation only to absolve themselves by including a feature that allows users to modify the digital likenesses. We cannot accept that such an outcome would adequately balance the interests in right of publicity cases. As one amicus brief noted:

> [U]nder [Appellee's] application of the transformative test [sic], presumably no infringement would be found if individuals such as the Dalai Lama and the Pope were placed within a violent "shoot-em-up" game, so long as the game include[d] a "mechanism" by which the user could manipulate their characteristics.

(Screen Actors Guild, Inc. et al., Amicus Br. at 21.) With this concern in mind, therefore, we consider whether the type and extent of interactivity permitted is sufficient to transform the Appellant's likeness into the Appellee's own expression. We hold that it does not.

In *NCAA Football*, Appellee seeks to create a realistic depiction of college football for the users. Part of this realism involves generating realistic representations of the various college teams—which includes the realistic representations of the players. Like Activision in *No Doubt*, therefore, Appellee seeks to capitalize on the respective fan bases for the various teams and players. Indeed, as the District Court recognized, "it seems ludicrous to question whether video game consumers enjoy and, as a result, purchase more EA-produced video games as a result of the heightened realism associated with actual players." *Hart*, 808 F. Supp. 2d at 783 (quoting James J.S. Holmes & Kanika D. Corley, *Defining Liability for Likeness of Athlete Avatars in Video Games, L.A. Law.*, May 2011, at 17, 20). Moreover, the realism of the games—including the depictions and recreations of the players—appeals not just to home-team fans, but to bitter rivals as well. Games such as *NCAA Football* permit users to recreate the setting of a bitter defeat and, in effect, achieve some cathartic readjustment of history; realistic depictions of the players are a necessary element to this. That Appellant's likeness is the *default* position only serves to support our conclusion that realistic depictions of the players are the "sum and substance" of these digital facsimiles. [cit.] Given that Appellant's unaltered likeness is central to the core of the game experience, we are disinclined to credit users' ability to alter the digital avatars in our application of the Transformative Use Test to this case.

We are likewise unconvinced that *NCAA Football* satisfies the Transformative Use Test because Appellee created various in-game assets to support the altered avatars (*e.g.*, additional hair styles, faces, accessories, et al.). In the first instance, the relationship between these assets and the digital avatar is predicated on the users' desire to alter the avatar's appearance, which, as we have already noted, is insufficient to satisfy the Test. The ability to make minor alterations—which substantially maintain the avatar's resemblance to Appellant (e.g., modifying only the basic biographical information, playing statistics, or uniform accessories)—is likewise insufficient, for "[a]n artist depicting a celebrity must contribute something more than a 'merely trivial' variation." *Winter*, 69 P.3d at 478-79. Indeed, the ability to modify the avatar counts for little where the appeal of the game lies in users' ability to play "as, or alongside" their preferred players or team. *See No Doubt*, 122 Cal. Rptr. 3d at 411. Thus, even avatars with superficial modifications to their appearance can count as a suitable proxy or market "substitute" for the original. *See Comedy III*, 21 P.3d at 808; *Winter*, 69 P.3d at 479; *Cardtoons*, 95 F.3d at 974. For larger potential changes, such as a different body type, skin tone, or face, Appellant's likeness is not transformed; it simply ceases to be. Therefore, once a user has made major changes to the avatar, it no longer represents Appellant, and thus it no longer qualifies as a "use" of the Appellant's identity for purposes of our inquiry. Such possibilities therefore fall beyond our inquiry into how *Appellant's likeness* is used in *NCAA Football*. That the game may lend itself to uses wholly divorced from the appropriation of Appellant's identity is insufficient to satisfy the Transformative Use Test. *See No Doubt*, 122 Cal. Rptr. 3d 397 (focusing on the use of the No Doubt avatars, not alternative avatars or custom-made characters).

In an attempt to salvage its argument, Appellee suggests that *other* creative elements of *NCAA Football*, which do not affect Appellant's digital avatar, are so numerous that the videogames should be considered transformative. We believe this to be an improper inquiry. Decisions applying the Transformative Use Test invariably look to how the *celebrity's identity* is used in or is altered by other aspects of a work. Wholly unrelated elements do not bear on this inquiry. Even *Comedy III*, in listing potentially "transformative or creative contributions" focused on elements or techniques that affect the celebrity identity. *See Comedy III*, 21 P.3d at 809 (discussing factual reporting, fictionalized portrayal, heavy-handed lampooning, and subtle social criticism); *see also Winter*, 69 P.3d at 478-79 (noting that "[a]n artist depicting a celebrity must contribute something more than a 'merely trivial' variation" before proceeding to discuss how the Winter brothers' likenesses were altered directly and through context); *Kirby*, 50 Cal. Rptr. 3d at 616-18. To the extent that any of these cases considered the broader context of the work (e.g., whether events took place in a "fanciful setting"), this inquiry was aimed at determining whether this context acted upon the celebrity identity in a way that transformed it or imbued it with some added creativity beyond providing a "merely trivial variation." Thus, while we recognize the creative energies necessary for crafting the various elements of *NCAA Football* that are not tied directly to reality, we hold that they have no legal significance in our instant decision.

To hold otherwise could have deleterious consequences for the state of the law. Acts of blatant misappropriation would count for nothing so long as the larger work, on balance, contained highly creative elements in great abundance. This concern is particularly acute in the case of media that lend themselves to easy partition such as video games. It cannot be that content creators escape liability for a work that uses a celebrity's unaltered identity in one section but that contains a wholly fanciful creation in the other, larger section.

For these reasons, we hold that the broad application of the Transformative Use Test represents an inappropriate application of the standard. Consequently, we shall not credit elements of *NCAA Football* that do not, in some way, affect the use or meaning of Appellant's identity.

As a final point, we note that the photograph of Appellant that appears in NCAA Football 2009 does not bear on our analysis above. On that subject, we agree with the District Court that the photograph is "but a fleeting component part of the montage" and therefore does not render the entire work nontransformative. *Hart*, 808 F. Supp. 2d at 786. The reasoning from *ETW* is sufficiently applicable: the context of Appellant's photograph—the montage—imbues the image with additional meaning beyond simply being a representation of the player. *See ETW*, 332 F.3d at 938 (holding that the photographs in a collage were "combined to describe, in artistic form, a historic event in sports history and to convey a message about the significance of [Tiger] Woods's achievement in that event"). Consequently, this particular use of Appellant's likeness *is* shielded by the First Amendment and therefore can contribute nothing to Appellant's claim for violation of his right of publicity.

[*Reversed and remanded.*]

[Judge Ambro's dissenting opinion is omitted.]

NOTES AND QUESTIONS

1. *Which test?* The majority opinion in *Hart* adopts the transformative use test for determining whether First Amendment interests limit the right of publicity, rejecting the predominant use test and the *Rogers v. Grimaldi* test. Do you agree with the court's choice? The transformative use test borrows from copyright law; the *Rogers v. Grimaldi* test arguably has its roots in trademark law. Should that matter? Is the right of publicity more akin to one than the other? *See In re NCAA Student-Athlete Name & Likeness Licensing Litigation*, 724 F.3d 1268, 1281 (9th Cir. 2013) (relying on the transformative use test; rejecting the use of the *Rogers* test in the right of publicity context, and commenting that "[t]he right of publicity protects the *celebrity*, not the *consumer*"). In similar litigation brought on behalf of former NFL players against EA Sports involving video games depicting historic NFL teams and avatars resembling the former players, the Ninth Circuit likewise applied the transformative use defense, and found liability. *Davis v. Electronic Arts Inc.*, 775 F.3d 1172 (9th Cir. 2015) (NFL fans of a certain age might recognize some of the named plaintiffs: Vince Ferragamo and Billy Joe Dupree, among others).

2. *Which test (again) one for merchandise, and another for expressive works?* The transformative use test derives from the California Supreme Court's decision in *Comedy III*, which involved the depiction of the Three Stooges on a T-shirt. Should the transformative use test be limited to the merchandising context? Is it unsuited for the context of expressive works, like the video games at issue in *Hart*? In *C.B.C. Distribution & Mktg., Inc. v. Major League Baseball Advanced Media, L.P.*, 505 F.3d 818 (8th Cir. 2007), the court considered a right-of-publicity claim based on CBC's use of biographical data of major league baseball players in its fantasy baseball game products. In upholding CBC's argument that the First Amendment trumped the right-of-publicity claim, the court balanced the economic interests underlying the right of publicity against the First Amendment speech interests without adopting any overarching test. Should the court in *Hart* have adopted the *CBC* ad hoc balancing approach? The fantasy game products at issue in *CBC* were expressive works, but they did not involve digital portrayals of players. The *Hart* court distinguished *CBC* on this basis. Would you have ruled similarly?

3. *Applying the transformative use test defendant's work as a whole, or celebrity's likeness alone?* Judge Ambro, dissenting in *Hart*, argued that the majority's application of the transformative use test was flawed because the majority restricted its inquiry to Hart's avatar alone, rather than taking into account other aspects of the video game. To Judge Ambro, the majority's approach to transformative use is insufficiently protective of speech interests. How so? Consider the movie *Argo* (2012), billed as a historical drama about U.S. Central Intelligence Agency operative Tony Mendez's mission to rescue six U.S. diplomats from Tehran, Iran, in 1979, during the Iran hostage crisis. Ben Affleck played the role of Tony Mendez. Suppose that in the movie, Affleck actually did look and act very much like the real Tony Mendez, which, we tend to think, is kind of the point. Would a court applying the transformative use test based strictly on the celebrity's

likeness (and not on the work as a whole) be compelled to conclude that Affleck's portrayal was non-transformative and thus potentially violated Tony Mendez's right of publicity? Does the *Hart* majority's version of the transformative use test essentially thwart anyone from creating historical dramas? Would it block any producer of a documentary that depicted a realistic reenactment of actual events? *See In re NCAA Student-Athlete Name & Likeness Licensing Litigation*, 724 F.3d 1268, 1278-79 (9th Cir. 2013) (adopting the *Hart* majority's approach). *See also Sarver v. Chartier*, 813 F.3d 891 (9th Cir. 2016) (First Amendment would have precluded a right-of-publicity claim against producers of the movie *The Hurt Locker* brought by an individual who contended that the main character in the movie was based on him).

4. *Applying the transformative use test to the work as a whole quantitatively?* If the challenged work as a whole contains at least something beyond a literal depiction of the celebrity's identity, should this be enough to justify calling the challenged work "transformative" and thus outside the reach of the right of publicity? If virtually all expressive works qualify as transformative under this application of the test, would you conclude that this application of the test tips the balance too far against the interests of the holder of the right of publicity?

5. *The transformative use test in view of prior cases.* The *Hart* majority claims obedience to prior cases in which the transformative use test was applied. Consider one such case that the court cites. In *ETW Corp. v. Jireh Publishing, Inc.*, 332 F.3d 915 (6th Cir. 2003), ETW, owners of the intellectual property rights of professional golfer Tiger Woods, sued over the marketing of "sports artist" Rick Rush's painting called "The Masters of Augusta." In the painting, Tiger Woods is featured in the foreground, with several other images of legendary golfers in the background. ETW sued on a Lanham Act false endorsement theory (as we noted in section A) and on an Ohio right-of-publicity theory. The trial court granted summary judgment to Jireh, and the Sixth Circuit affirmed in a split decision. The Sixth Circuit majority relied on the *Comedy III* test (and on other cases), but concluded that Rush's work contained "significant transformative elements. . . ." According to the court:

> Unlike the unadorned, nearly photographic reproduction of the faces of The Three Stooges in *Comedy III*, Rush's work does not capitalize solely on a literal depiction of Woods. Rather, Rush's work consists of a collage of images in addition to Woods's image which are combined to describe, in artistic form, a historic event in sports history and to convey a message about the significance of Woods's achievement in that event. Because Rush's work has substantial transformative elements, it is entitled to the full protection of the First Amendment.

Id. at 938. Was the *Hart* majority correct to say that its application of the transformative use test to the digital avatar of Hart is consistent with that in *ETW*? The majority in *Hart* also invokes *ETW* to support its conclusion that EA's use of an actual photograph of Hart as part of a photo montage in one of its games "does not render the entire work nontransformative." Are the *Hart* court's rulings contradictory?

Before we leave the topic of Tiger Woods, suppose that an artist known for sculpting cows from butter at the Iowa State Fair (yes, we're serious) sculpts a life-size and highly realistic butter rendering of Tiger Woods. Reportedly, Tiger is depicted "sitting with a golf club leaning against him" and "scratching the head" of a life-size tiger, which also will be part of the sculpture. As the artist quite reasonably points out, playing golf while petting a tiger is something that "nobody ever does," especially in Iowa. Would the artist need Tiger Woods' permission to create the sculpture if Iowa courts followed the transformative use test? Would it matter whether fair attendees had to pay admission to see Tiger Woods rendered in butter? *See Butter Cow Lady Waits for Tiger's OK*, IOWA CITY

PRESS-CITIZEN, June 29, 2005, at 1A—which shows that we're not always just making this stuff up.

Also consider a case involving the actor Dustin Hoffman, *Hoffman v. Capital Cities/ ABC, Inc.*, 255 F.3d 1180, 1182-83 (9th Cir. 2001):

> In 1982, actor Dustin Hoffman starred in the movie "Tootsie," playing a male actor who dresses as a woman to get a part on a television soap opera. One memorable still photograph from the movie showed Hoffman in character in a red long-sleeved sequined evening dress and high heels, posing in front of an American flag. [See the accompanying reproduction of the movie poster.] The still carried the text "What do you get when you cross a hopelessly straight, starving actor with a dynamite red sequined dress? You get America's hottest new actress."

In March 1997, *Los Angeles Magazine* (LAM) published the "Fabulous Hollywood Issue." An article from this issue titled "Grand Illusions" used computer technology to alter famous film stills to make it appear that the actors were wearing Spring 1997 fashions. The sixteen familiar scenes included movies and actors such as *North by Northwest* (Cary Grant), *Saturday Night Fever* (John Travolta), *Rear Window* (Grace Kelly and Jimmy Stewart), *Gone with the Wind* (Vivian Leigh and Hattie McDaniel), *Jailhouse Rock* (Elvis Presley), *The Seven Year Itch* (Marilyn Monroe), *Thelma and Louise* (Susan Sarandon and Geena Davis), and even *The Creature from the Black Lagoon* (with the Creature in Nike shoes). The final shot was the *Tootsie* still. The American flag and Hoffman's head remained as they appeared in the original, but Hoffman's body and his long-sleeved red sequined dress were replaced by the body of a male model in the same pose, wearing a spaghetti-strapped, cream-colored, silk evening dress and high-heeled sandals. [The photograph is reproduced below.] LAM omitted the original caption. The text on the page identified the still as being from the movie *Tootsie* and read, "Dustin Hoffman isn't a drag in a butter-colored silk gown by Richard Tyler and Ralph Lauren heels."

Hoffman in *Los Angeles*

Hoffman had not consented to the use of his photograph, and he sued for a right-of-publicity violation. LAM claimed a First Amendment defense. How would you evaluate the defense? Is the use "transformative"?

6. *Statutory exemptions.* The Indiana right-of-publicity statute (introduced earlier in this chapter) includes a series of statutory exemptions to liability under the right of publicity. IND. CODE §32-36-1-1 (exempting, *inter alia*, the use of protectable aspects of personality in material that has political or newsworthy value, in literary works, or in reporting on an event of public interest). The court applied the exemptions in *Daniels v. FanDuel, Inc.*, 124 U.S.P.Q.2d (BNA) 1392 (S.D. Ind. 2017) (use of aspects of former collegiate athletes' personalities in fantasy sports game is exempt from Indiana right-of-publicity liability under the statutory exemptions).

MICHAEL JORDAN v. JEWEL FOOD STORES, INC.

743 F.3d 509 (7th Cir. 2014)

SYKES, Circuit Judge:

This trademark and right-of-publicity dispute pits basketball legend Michael Jordan against Jewel Food Stores, Inc., the operator of 175 Jewel-Osco supermarkets in and around Chicago. On the occasion of Jordan['s] induction into the Naismith Memorial Basketball Hall of Fame in September 2009, Time, Inc., the publisher of *Sports Illustrated*, produced a special commemorative issue of *Sports Illustrated Presents* devoted exclusively to Jordan's remarkable career. Jewel was offered free advertising space in the issue in exchange for agreeing to stock the magazine in its stores. Jewel accepted the offer and submitted a full-page ad congratulating Jordan on his induction into the Hall of Fame. The ad ran on the inside back cover of the commemorative issue, which was available on newsstands for a three-month period following the induction ceremony.

To Jordan the ad was not a welcome celebratory gesture but a misappropriation of his identity for the supermarket chain's commercial benefit. He responded with this $5 million lawsuit alleging violations of the federal Lanham Act, the Illinois Right of Publicity Act, the Illinois deceptive-practices statute, and the common law of unfair competition. Jewel denied liability under these laws and also claimed a blanket immunity from suit under the First Amendment. The district court sided with Jewel on the constitutional defense, prompting this appeal.

Jewel maintains that its ad is "noncommercial" speech and thus has full First Amendment protection. Jordan insists that the ad is garden-variety commercial speech, which gets reduced constitutional protection and may give rise to liability for the private wrongs he alleges in this case. As the case comes to us, the commercial/noncommercial distinction is potentially dispositive. If the ad is properly classified as commercial speech, then it may be regulated, normal liability rules apply (statutory and common law), and the battle moves to the merits of Jordan's claims. If, on the other hand, the ad is fully protected expression, then Jordan agrees with Jewel that the First Amendment provides a complete defense and his claims cannot proceed. The district court held that the ad was fully protected noncommercial speech and entered judgment for Jewel.

We reverse. Jewel's ad, reproduced below, prominently features the "Jewel-Osco" logo and marketing slogan, which are creatively and conspicuously linked to Jordan in the text of the ad's congratulatory message. Based on its content and context, the ad is properly classified as a form of image advertising aimed at promoting the Jewel-Osco brand. The ad is commercial speech and thus is subject to the laws Jordan invokes here. The substance of

Jordan case remains untested, however; the district court's First Amendment ruling halted further consideration of the merits. We remand for further proceedings.

I.   BACKGROUND

On September 11, 2009, Jordan was inducted into the Basketball Hall of Fame.[1] In light of the occasion, Time, Inc., the publisher of *Sports Illustrated*, produced a special edition of *Sports Illustrated Presents* to celebrate Jordan's noteworthy career. The commemorative issue was not distributed to regular *Sports Illustrated* subscribers, but rather was sold separately in stores. The issue was titled "Jordan: Celebrating a Hall of Fame Career" and was slated to be offered for sale from late October 2009 until late January 2010.

About a month prior to publication, a Time sales representative contacted Jewel to offer free advertising space in the commemorative issue in return for a promise to stock and sell the magazines in its stores. Jewel agreed to the deal and had its marketing department design a full-page color ad. The ad combines textual, photographic, and graphic elements, and prominently includes the Jewel-Osco logo and the supermarket chain's marketing slogan, "Good things are just around the corner." The logo and slogan—both registered trademarks—are positioned in the middle of the page, above a photo of a pair of basketball shoes, each bearing Jordan's number "23." The text of the ad reads as follows:

> A Shoe In!
> After six NBA championships, scores of rewritten record books and numerous buzzer beaters, Michael Jordan's elevation in the Basketball Hall of Fame was never in doubt! Jewel-Osco salutes # 23 on his many accomplishments as we honor a fellow Chicagoan who was "just around the corner" for so many years.

Time accepted Jewel's ad and placed it on the inside back cover of the commemorative issue, which featured *Sports Illustrated* editorial content and photographs from the magazine's prior coverage of Jordan's career. Among other advertisements, the commemorative issue also contained a full-page congratulatory ad by a rival Chicago-area grocery chain. We include a copy of Jewel's ad at the end of this opinion.

Soon after the commemorative issue hit the newsstands, Jordan filed this lawsuit against Jewel in Illinois state court alleging violations of the Illinois Right of Publicity Act, [state unfair competition law, and the Lanham Act.] He sought $5 million in damages, plus punitive damages on the state-law claims and treble damages on the Lanham Act claim. Jewel removed the case to federal court.

Following discovery, Jewel moved for summary judgment raising the First Amendment as a defense and arguing that its ad qualified as "noncommercial" speech and was entitled

---

1. Jordan, of course, is the superstar former Chicago Bulls basketball player. During his fabled career, Jordan led the Bulls to six National Basketball Association championships, winning myriad awards and countless accolades as the best player in the game. *See Legends profile: Michael Jordan*, NBA HISTORY, *http://www.nba.com/history/legends/michael-jordan* (Mar. 4, 2013, 4:14 PM) (last visited Feb. 10, 2014). Although the district court did not make a factual finding on the matter, according to the NBA's website, Jordan is "[b]y acclamation . . . the greatest basketball player of all time." *Id.* For another view, see *NBA's best all-time? You be the judge*, CHI. TRIB. (Mar. 23, 2012), *http:// articles.chicagotribune.com/2012–03–23/sports/ct–spt–0324– mitchell–20120324_1_the-nba-kareem-abdul-jabbar-lebron-james* (last visited Feb. 10, 2014), suggesting that the "best ever" title should go to Kareem Abdul-Jabbar based on lifetime statistics. The Milwaukee judges on this panel would not dissent from that. [*Ed. Note*: Judge Sykes, of course, was writing in the era B.C. — "Before Curry."]

to full constitutional protection. Jordan filed a cross-motion for partial summary judgment on the issue of whether Jewel's ad was a commercial use of his identity. In a thoughtful opinion, the district court agreed with Jewel that the ad was noncommercial speech and sought further briefing on the implications of that classification. Jewel maintained that the commercial-speech ruling conclusively defeated all of Jordan's claims. Jordan agreed, accepting Jewel's position that the First Amendment provided a complete defense. The court accordingly entered final judgment in favor of Jewel, and Jordan appealed.

II.   DISCUSSION

A.   SOME CONTEXT FOR THE COMMERCIAL-SPEECH CLASSIFICATION

Jordan's appeal requires us to decide whether Jewel's ad is properly classified as commercial speech or noncommercial speech under the Supreme Court's First Amendment jurisprudence. Before addressing the substance of that question, we take a moment to place it in the context of the claims raised in this litigation, which arise from different sources of law but all center on Jordan's allegation that Jewel misappropriated his identity for its commercial benefit.

Jordan is a sports icon whose name and image are deeply embedded in the popular culture and easily recognized around the globe. His singular achievements on the basketball court have made him highly sought after as a celebrity endorser; as a retired player who continues to reap the economic value of his reputation in the history of the game, he understandably guards the use of his identity very closely. The Lanham Act and the other laws he invokes here enable him to do that.

Jewel argues that Jordan's claims can't succeed because its ad is fully protected noncommercial speech under the First Amendment. We understand this to be an argument that the First Amendment prevents the court from applying these laws to any speech that is considered "noncommercial" in the constitutional sense, thus providing a complete constitutional defense to all claims. Jordan accepts this legal premise, so we take the point as conceded. But the law in this area is considerably more complex than the parties' agreement implies.[4]

The Supreme Court has generally worked out its commercial-speech doctrine in public-law cases. *See generally City of Cincinnati v. Discovery Network, Inc.*, 507 U.S. 410 (1993) (challenging a municipal ban on distribution of commercial publications on newsstands on public property); *Bd. of Trs. of State Univ. of N.Y. v. Fox*, 492 U.S. 469 (1989) (challenging a public university's ban on "Tupperware"-style housewares parties in dormitories); *Riley v. Nat'l Fed. of the Blind of N.C.*, 487 U.S. 781 (1988) (challenging a state statute regulating fees charged by professional charitable fundraisers); *Bolger v. Youngs Drug*

---

4. The analytical ground shifted a bit during oral argument. Jewel's counsel argued that the federal and state laws at issue here, by their own terms, apply only to commercial speech as defined by First Amendment jurisprudence. So Jewel's free-speech defense might be understood as using the First Amendment commercial-speech inquiry as a proxy for determining whether the speech potentially falls within the scope of these laws. It is true that each of the statutory and common-law claims alleged here has a "commercial" element in one form or another, but it's not clear that the Supreme Court's commercial-speech doctrine should be used to define this term in each cause of action. As to the Lanham Act claim in particular, we have cautioned against interpreting the scope of the statute in this way. *See First Health Grp. Corp. v. BCE Emergis Corp.*, 269 F.3d 800, 803 (7th Cir. 2001). We don't need to address this matter further because the parties haven't briefed the extent to which the scope of the Lanham Act (or the state laws) is coextensive with the Supreme Court's constitutional commercial-speech doctrine.

Prods. Corp., 463 U.S. 60 (1983) (challenging a federal statute prohibiting the mailing of unsolicited contraceptive advertisements); *Cent. Hudson Gas & Elec. Corp. v. Pub. Serv. Comm'n of N.Y.*, 447 U.S. 557 (1980) (challenging a state regulation banning promotional advertising by utilities); *Va. State Bd. of Pharmacy v. Va. Citizens Consumer Council, Inc.*, 425 U.S. 748 (1976) (challenging a state statute prohibiting pharmacists from advertising the prices of prescription drugs). In the public-law context, the commercial/noncommercial classification determines the proper standard of scrutiny to apply to the law or regulation under review in the case.

This is not a public-law case; it's a clash of private rights. Even if Jewel's ad qualifies as noncommercial speech, it's far from clear that Jordan's trademark and right-of-publicity claims fail without further ado. According to a leading treatise on trademark and unfair-competition law, there is no judicial consensus on how to resolve conflicts between intellectual-property rights and free-speech rights; instead, the courts have offered "a buffet of various legal approaches to [choose] from." 6 J. THOMAS MCCARTHY, MCCARTHY ON TRADEMARKS AND UNFAIR COMPETITION §31.139 (4th ed. 2013). The Supreme Court has not addressed the question, and decisions from the lower courts are a conflicting mix of balancing tests and frameworks borrowed from other areas of free-speech doctrine.[5]

Jordan's litigating position allows us to sidestep this complexity. The parties have agreed that if Jewel's ad is "noncommercial speech" in the constitutional sense, then the First Amendment provides a complete defense to all claims in this suit. We're not sure that's right, but for now we simply note the issue and leave it for another day. With that large unsettled question reserved, we move to the task of classifying Jewel's ad as commercial or noncommercial speech for constitutional purposes. This is a legal question, so our review is de novo. [cit.]

B. COMMERCIAL OR NONCOMMERCIAL SPEECH?

1. *The Commercial-Speech Doctrine*

The First Amendment prohibits the government from "abridging the freedom of speech." U.S. CONST. amend. I. Because "'not all speech is of equal First Amendment importance,'" *Snyder v. Phelps*, 131 S. Ct. 1207, 1215 (2011) (quoting *Hustler Magazine, Inc. v. Falwell*, 485 U.S. 46, 56 (1988)), certain categories of speech receive a lesser degree of constitutional protection. Commercial speech was initially viewed as being outside the ambit of the First Amendment altogether. *See Valentine v. Chrestensen*, 316 U.S. 52, 54 (1942). That understanding has long since been displaced. Current doctrine holds that commercial speech is constitutionally protected but governmental burdens on this category of speech are scrutinized more leniently than burdens on fully protected noncommercial speech. [cit.]

---

5. *See, e.g., Facenda v. NFL Films, Inc.*, 542 F.3d 1007, 1015-18 (3d Cir. 2008) (canvassing the caselaw but ultimately avoiding the issue after finding that the film in question was commercial speech); *Downing v. Abercrombie & Fitch*, 265 F.3d 994, 1001-03 (9th Cir. 2001) (rejecting a First Amendment defense to right-of-publicity claim under California law); *Hoffman v. Capital Cities/ABC Inc.*, 255 F.3d 1180, 1184-86 (9th Cir. 2001) (resolving a First Amendment defense in a case raising Lanham Act and state-law right-of-publicity claims by using the "actual malice" standard applicable in defamation cases); *Cardtoons, L.C. v. Major League Baseball Players Ass'n*, 95 F.3d 959, 968-76 (10th Cir. 1996) (resolving a First Amendment defense in a state-law right-of-publicity case by balancing the free-speech interests against the intellectual-property interests).

The Court's rationale for treating commercial speech differently rests on the idea that commercial speech is "more easily verifiable by its disseminator" and "more durable"—that is, less likely to be chilled by regulations—than fully protected noncommercial speech. *Va. Pharmacy Bd.*, 425 U.S. at 771 n. 24. Other cases explain that the more deferential degree of judicial scrutiny is justified because commercial speech "'occurs in an area traditionally subject to government regulation.'" *Lorillard Tobacco Co. v. Reilly*, 533 U.S. 525, 554 (2001) (quoting *Cent. Hudson*, 447 U.S. at 562). Whatever the justification, the Court has not strayed from its commercial-speech jurisprudence despite calls for it to do so. [cit.]

To determine whether speech falls on the commercial or noncommercial side of the constitutional line, the Court has provided this basic definition: Commercial speech is "speech that proposes a commercial transaction."[6] *Fox*, 492 U.S. at 482 (emphasis deleted). . . . It's important to recognize, however, that this definition is just a starting point. Speech that does *no more than* propose a commercial transaction "fall[s] within the core notion of commercial speech," *Bolger*, 463 U.S. at 66, but other communications also may "'constitute commercial speech notwithstanding the fact that they contain discussions of important public issues,'" *Fox*, 492 U.S. at 475 (quoting *Bolger*, 463 U.S. at 67-68). [cit.]

Indeed, the Supreme Court has "'made clear that advertising which links a product to a current public debate is not thereby entitled to the constitutional protection afforded noncommercial speech.'" *Zauderer*, 471 U.S. at 637 n. 7 (quoting *Bolger*, 463 U.S. at 68) (internal quotation marks omitted). Although commercial-speech cases generally rely on the distinction between speech that proposes a commercial transaction and other varieties of speech, *id.* at 637, it's a mistake to assume that the boundaries of the commercial-speech category are marked exclusively by this "core" definition. [cit.] To the contrary, there is a "common-sense distinction" between commercial speech and other varieties of speech, and we are to give effect to that distinction. [cit.]

The Supreme Court's decision in *Bolger* is instructive on this point. *Bolger* dealt with the question of how to classify speech with both noncommercial and commercial elements. There, a prophylactics manufacturer published informational pamphlets providing general factual information about prophylactics but also containing information about the manufacturer's products in particular. *Bolger*, 463 U.S. at 62. The manufacturer brought a pre-enforcement challenge to a federal statute that prohibited the unsolicited mailing of advertisements about contraceptives. The Supreme Court held that although the pamphlets did not expressly propose a commercial transaction, they were nonetheless properly classified as commercial speech based on the following attributes: the pamphlets were a form of advertising, they referred to specific commercial products, and they were distributed by the manufacturer for economic purposes. *Id.* at 66-67.

We have read *Bolger* as suggesting certain guideposts for classifying speech that contains both commercial and noncommercial elements; relevant considerations include "whether: (1) the speech is an advertisement; (2) the speech refers to a specific product; and (3) the speaker has an economic motivation for the speech." [cit.] This is just a general framework, however; no one factor is sufficient, and *Bolger* strongly implied that all are not necessary. *See*

---

6. The Court has also defined commercial speech as "expression related solely to the economic interests of the speaker and its audience." *Cent. Hudson Gas & Elec. Corp. v. Pub. Serv. Comm'n of N.Y.*, 447 U.S. 557 (1980). This formulation has largely fallen into disuse, though it has never been expressly disavowed. *See City of Cincinnati v. Discovery Network, Inc.*, 507 U.S. 410, 422-23 (1993) (discussing the two standards).

Bolger, 463 U.S. at 67 n. 14 ("Nor do we mean to suggest that each of the characteristics present in this case must necessarily be present in order for speech to be commercial.").

2.   *Applying the Doctrine*

Jewel argues that its ad doesn't propose a commercial transaction and therefore flunks the leading test for commercial speech. As we have explained, the commercial-speech category is not limited to speech that directly or indirectly proposes a commercial transaction. Jewel nonetheless places substantial weight on this test, and the district judge did as well. Although neither relies exclusively on it, the district court's opinion and Jewel's defense of it on appeal both press heavily on the argument that the ad doesn't propose a commercial transaction, so we will start there.

It's clear that the textual focus of Jewel's ad is a congratulatory salute to Jordan on his induction into the Hall of Fame. If the literal import of the words were all that mattered, this celebratory tribute would be noncommercial. But evaluating the text requires consideration of its context, and this truism has special force when applying the commercial-speech doctrine. Modern commercial advertising is enormously varied in form and style.

We know from common experience that commercial advertising occupies diverse media, draws on a limitless array of imaginative techniques, and is often supported by sophisticated marketing research. It is highly creative, sometimes abstract, and frequently relies on subtle cues. The notion that an advertisement counts as "commercial" only if it makes an appeal to purchase a particular product makes no sense today, and we doubt that it ever did. An advertisement is no less "commercial" because it promotes brand awareness or loyalty rather than explicitly proposing a transaction in a specific product or service. Applying the "core" definition of commercial speech too rigidly ignores this reality. Very often the commercial message is general and implicit rather than specific and explicit.

Jewel's ad served two functions: congratulating Jordan on his induction into the Hall of Fame and promoting Jewel's supermarkets. The first is explicit and readily apparent. The ad contains a congratulatory message remarking on Jordan's record-breaking career and celebrating his rightful place in the Basketball Hall of Fame. Jewel points to its longstanding corporate practice of commending local community groups on notable achievements, giving as examples two public-service ads celebrating the work of Chicago's Hispanocare and South Side Community Services. The suggestion seems to be that the Jordan ad belongs in this "civic booster" category: A praise-worthy "fellow Chicagoan" was receiving an important honor, and Jewel took the opportunity to join in the applause.

But considered in context, and without the rose-colored glasses, Jewel's ad has an unmistakable commercial function: enhancing the Jewel-Osco brand in the minds of consumers. This commercial message is implicit but easily inferred, and is the dominant one.

We begin by making a point that should be obvious but seems lost on Jewel: There is a world of difference between an ad congratulating a local community group and an ad congratulating a famous athlete. Both ads will generate goodwill for the advertiser. But an ad congratulating a famous athlete can only be understood as a promotional device for the advertiser. Unlike a community group, the athlete needs no gratuitous promotion and his identity has commercial value. Jewel's ad cannot be construed as a benevolent act of good corporate citizenship.

As for the other elements of the ad, Jewel-Osco's graphic logo and slogan appear just below the textual salute to Jordan. The bold red logo is prominently featured in the center of the ad and in a font size larger than any other on the page. Both the logo and the slogan are styled in their trademarked ways. Their style, size, and color set them off from the congratulatory text, drawing attention to Jewel-Osco's sponsorship of the tribute. Apart from the basketball shoes, the Jewel-Osco brand name is the center of visual attention on the page. And the congratulatory message specifically incorporates Jewel's slogan: "as we honor a fellow Chicagoan who was 'just around the corner' for so many years." The ad is plainly aimed at fostering goodwill for the Jewel brand among the targeted consumer group — "fellow Chicagoans" and fans of Michael Jordan — for the purpose of increasing patronage at Jewel-Osco stores.

The district judge nonetheless concluded that the ad was not commercial speech based in part on his view that "readers would be at a loss to explain what they have been invited to buy," a reference to the fact that the ad features only the tribute to Jordan, the Jewel-Osco logo and slogan, and a pair of basketball shoes. Granted, Jewel does not sell basketball shoes; it's a chain of grocery stores, and this ad contains not a single word about the specific products that Jewel-Osco sells, nor any product-specific art or photography. The Supreme Court has said that the failure to reference a specific product is a relevant consideration in the commercial-speech determination. *See Bolger*, 463 U.S. at 66-67. But it is far from dispositive, especially where "image" or brand advertising rather than product advertising is concerned.

Image advertising is ubiquitous in all media. Jewel's ad is an example of a neighborly form of general brand promotion by a large urban supermarket chain. What does it invite readers to buy? Whatever they need from a grocery store — a loaf of bread, a gallon of milk, perhaps the next edition of *Sports Illustrated* — from *Jewel-Osco*, where "good things are just around the corner." The ad implicitly encourages readers to patronize their local Jewel-Osco store. That it doesn't mention a specific product means only that this is a different genre of advertising. It promotes brand loyalty rather than a specific product, but that doesn't mean it's "noncommercial."

The district judge was not inclined to put much stock in the ad's use of Jewel-Osco's slogan and graphic logo. Specifically, he considered the logo as little more than a convenient method of identifying the speaker and characterized the slogan as simply a means of ensuring "that the congratulatory message *sounded* like it was coming from Jewel." Dismissing the logo and slogan as mere nametags overlooks their value as advertising tools. The slogan is attached to the Jewel-Osco graphic logo and is repeated in the congratulatory message itself, which describes Jordan as "a fellow Chicagoan who was 'just around the corner' for so many years." This linkage only makes sense if the aim is to promote shopping at Jewel-Osco stores. Indeed, Jewel's copywriter viewed the repetition of the slogan the same way we do; she thought it was "too selly" and "hitting too over the head."

In short, the ad's commercial nature is readily apparent. It may be generic and implicit, but it is nonetheless clear. The ad is a form of image advertising aimed at promoting goodwill for the Jewel-Osco brand by exploiting public affection for Jordan at an auspicious moment in his career.

Our conclusion is confirmed by application of the *Bolger* framework, which applies to speech that contains both commercial and noncommercial elements. Again, the *Bolger* inquiry asks whether the speech in question is in the form of an advertisement, refers to a specific product, and has an economic motive. [cit.]

Jewel's ad certainly qualifies as an advertisement in form. Although the text is congratulatory, the page nonetheless promotes something to potential buyers: Jewel-Osco supermarkets. Jewel's ad is easily distinguishable from the magazine's editorial content. Although the district court properly characterized it as "embrac[ing] the issue's theme," the ad obviously isn't part of the editorial coverage of Jordan's career. It isn't an article, a column, or a news photograph or illustration. It looks like, and is, an advertisement.

We can make quick work of the second and third *Bolger* factors. As we have explained, although no *specific* product or service is offered, the ad promotes patronage at Jewel-Osco stores more generally. And there is no question that the ad serves an economic purpose: to burnish the Jewel-Osco brand name and enhance consumer goodwill. The record reflects that Jewel received Time's offer of free advertising space enthusiastically; its marketing representatives said it was a "great offer" and it "would be good for us to have our logo in *Sports Illustrated*" because "having your logo in any location where people see it is going to help your company." Indeed, Jewel gave Time valuable consideration—floor space in Jewel-Osco grocery stores—in exchange for the full-page ad in the magazine, suggesting that it expected valuable brand-enhancement benefit from it. We don't doubt that Jewel's tribute was in a certain sense public-spirited. We only recognize the obvious: that Jewel had something to gain by conspicuously joining the chorus of congratulations on the much-anticipated occasion of Jordan's induction into the Basketball Hall of Fame. Jewel's ad is commercial speech.

A contrary holding would have sweeping and troublesome implications for athletes, actors, celebrities, and other trademark holders seeking to protect the use of their identities or marks. Image advertising (also known as "institutional advertising") is commonplace in our society. Rather than expressly peddling particular products, this form of advertising features appealing images and subtle messages alongside the advertiser's brand name or logo with the aim of linking the advertiser to a particular person, value, or idea in order to build goodwill for the brand. [cit.]

To pick a current example for illustrative purposes, think of the television spots by the corporate sponsors of the Olympics. Many of these ads consist entirely of images of the American athletes coupled with the advertiser's logo or brand name and an expression of support for the U.S. Olympic team; nothing is explicitly offered for sale. Jewel's ad in the commemorative issue belongs in this genre. It portrays Jewel-Osco in a positive light without mentioning a specific product or service—in this case, by invoking a superstar athlete and a celebratory message with particular salience to Jewel's customer base. To say that the ad is noncommercial because it lacks an outright sales pitch is to artificially distinguish between product advertising and image advertising. Classifying this kind of advertising as constitutionally immune noncommercial speech would permit advertisers to misappropriate the identity of athletes and other celebrities with impunity.

Nothing we say here is meant to suggest that a company cannot use its graphic logo or slogan in an otherwise noncommercial way without thereby transforming the communication into commercial speech. Our holding is tied to the particular content and context of Jewel's ad as it appeared in the commemorative issue of *Sports Illustrated Presents*.

Before closing, we take this opportunity to clarify the proper use of the "inextricably intertwined" doctrine, which the district court relied on to support its decision. That doctrine holds that when commercial speech and noncommercial speech are inextricably intertwined, the speech is classified by reference to the whole; a higher degree of scrutiny may be applied if the relevant speech "'taken as a whole'" is properly deemed noncommercial. [cit.] The central inquiry is not whether the speech in question combines commercial and noncommercial elements, but whether it was legally or practically impossible for the speaker to separate them.

To see how this principle works in application, consider the facts at issue in the Supreme Court's decision in *Fox*. That case involved a First Amendment challenge to a public university's ban on commercial solicitations on campus. Several students and a housewares manufacturer asserted a free-speech right to hold "Tupperware parties" in the dormitories. *See id*. at 472. These gatherings consisted of demonstrations and a sales pitch for the manufacturer's products, but they also touched on other, noncommercial subjects, such as "how to be financially responsible and how to run an efficient home." *Id*. at 473-74. The plaintiffs maintained that the commercial and noncommercial elements of the speech were inextricably intertwined and the whole should be treated as noncommercial speech. *Id*. at 474.

The Supreme Court rejected this argument and analyzed the case under the standard applicable to commercial speech. In so doing, the Court clarified the limited applicability of the inextricably intertwined doctrine:

> [T]here is nothing whatever "inextricable" about the noncommercial aspects of these [Tupperware party] presentations. No law of man or of nature makes it impossible to sell housewares without teaching home economics, or to teach home economics without selling housewares. Nothing in the [university rule] prevents the speaker from conveying, or the audience from hearing, these noncommercial messages, and nothing in the nature of things requires them to be combined with commercial messages.

Id.

Properly understood, then, the inextricably intertwined doctrine applies only when it is legally or practically impossible for the speaker to separate out the commercial and noncommercial elements of his speech. In that situation the package as a whole gets the benefit of the higher standard of scrutiny applicable to noncommercial speech. But simply combining commercial and noncommercial elements in a single presentation does not transform the whole into noncommercial speech.

The district court relied on the Ninth Circuit's decision in *Hoffman v. Capital Cities/ABC, Inc.*, 255 F.3d 1180 (9th Cir. 2001), but there the court misapplied the inextricably intertwined doctrine. *Hoffman* involved a fashion article featuring popular movie stills that had been altered to make it appear as though the actors were modeling clothing from famous designers. *Id*. at 1183. One of the photoshopped images was of Dustin Hoffman in his role in the film "Tootsie." Hoffman sued the magazine publisher for misappropriating his identity. The Ninth Circuit held that the article was fully protected noncommercial speech: "[T]he article as a whole is a combination of fashion photography, humor, and visual and verbal editorial comment on classic films and famous actors. Any commercial aspects are 'inextricably entwined' with expressive elements, and so they cannot be separated out 'from the fully protected whole.'" *Id*. at 1185.

This use of the inextricably intertwined doctrine was mistaken; no law of man or nature prevented the magazine from publishing a fashion article without superimposing the latest fashion designs onto film stills of famous actors. The district court's application of *Hoffman* here made the same mistake. The commercial and noncommercial elements of Jewel's ad were not inextricably intertwined in the relevant sense. No law of man or nature compelled Jewel to combine commercial and noncommercial messages as it did here.

To wrap up, we hold that Jewel's ad in the commemorative issue qualifies as commercial speech. This defeats Jewel's constitutional defense, permitting Jordan's case to go forward. We note that the lone federal claim in the suit—a false-endorsement claim under §43(a) of the Lanham Act—requires proof that Jewel's congratulatory ad caused a likelihood of confusion that Jordan was a Jewel-Osco sponsor or endorsed its products and services. *See, e.g., Facenda v. NFL Films, Inc.*, 542 F.3d 1007, 1014-15 (3d Cir. 2008). Because the merits have not been briefed, we express no opinion on the substance of Jordan's claims under the Lanham Act or any of the state-law theories. We remand to permit the parties to address whether the Lanham Act claim warrants a trial, and if not, whether the district court should retain or relinquish supplemental jurisdiction over the state-law claims. [cit.]

[*Reversed and remanded.*]

PROBLEM 11-4: THE SCOTTISH ELVIS

Few people know this, but Professor Dinwoodie is an Elvis impersonator. He got his start playing birthday parties, retirement dinners, and wedding receptions (as well as wedding ceremonies, where he would administer the vows and then sing "Love Me Tender"). Initially, he billed himself as "The Scottish Elvis." In time, however, he sought to become a more credible Elvis, so he consulted Professor Janis, who sounds exactly like Elvis when singing in the shower. Together, they hit upon the idea of producing a stage show, THE FABULOUS EL SHOW: A TRIBUTE TO ELVIS, in which Professor Dinwoodie would perform on stage wearing the same style of clothing, jewelry, and hair as Elvis did, would imitate Elvis poses and gyrations, and would lip-sync Elvis music (Professor Janis, backstage, did the actual singing). During summer vacation, the duo toured extensively, playing Branson, Missouri; Las Vegas; and numerous NASCAR venues. Sold at the shows were T-shirts, CDs, and white scarves reminiscent of those that Elvis used to toss out to his admirers.

Is the Scottish Elvis transformative (we mean, in the sense of the transformative use test)? And, by the way, if not, what is likely to be the scope of injunctive relief? For example, would the injunctive relief extend to the stage performances? The sales of the collateral merchandise?

———————

Aside from cases involving artistic expression, clashes between First Amendment interests and the right of publicity may arise in connection with newsworthy events, and (especially) in connection with political speech. Regarding news stories, the Indiana right-of-publicity statute, for example, explicitly excludes "material that has political or newsworthy value" from the ambit of right-of-publicity protection. How far can this exclusion be pushed? *Montana v. San Jose Mercury News, Inc.*, 40 Cal. Rptr. 2d 639 (Cal. App. 1995), involved the sale of posters by a newspaper that were exact reproductions of the newspaper's various front-page stories about the San Francisco 49ers' Super Bowl championship. The posters featured photographs and sketches of Joe Montana, 49ers quarterback. Montana sued, invoking the right of publicity. The court found that the First Amendment protected the newspaper's sale of the posters because the posters depicted a newsworthy event—though the court did admit that it had been unable to find any cases "directly on point." Did the court reach the correct result? Would it depend on the venue in which the newspaper sold the posters, and the price that it asked—e.g., on a newsstand for $1, as opposed to a sporting goods store's memorabilia section for $25? Suppose the newspaper had the front pages reproduced on T-shirts. Does this raise a different First Amendment question? Does the transformative use test provide a viable approach for evaluating First Amendment claims here? *See also Toffoloni v. LFP Publ. Group, L.L.C.*, 572 F.3d 1201 (11th Cir. 2009) (publication in adult magazine of erotic photographs of ex-wife of professional wrestler and accompanying story about her murder). Should courts hesitate to grant preliminary injunctive relief in right-of-publicity cases that arguably implicate First Amendment issues, on the ground that preliminary relief would constitute a prior restraint on speech? Catherine Bosley, a news anchor from Youngstown, Ohio, went to Florida and took part in a "wet T-shirt" contest at a nightclub, apparently sans the T-shirt. Bosley's performance was immortalized in film, allegedly without her consent. Videos and photo montages featuring the "naked anchorwoman" soon appeared on the defendant's website, *WildWetT.com*. According to the trial court, "[f]or a period of time, website searches related to Catherine Bosley outnumbered those relating to Paris Hilton as the most popular search on the World Wide Web," which shows you how Americans value their television network news. Bosley asserted procured a preliminary injunction from the trial court prohibiting the defendant from using images of the plaintiff on websites, videos, DVDs, and other media. *Bosley v. WildWetT.com*, 70 U.S.P.Q.2d (BNA) 1520 (N.D. Ohio 2004). If the video likely contains First Amendment protected speech, should the court of appeals reverse on the ground that the preliminary injunction is a prior restraint? *Bosley v. WildWetT.com*, 2004 WL 1093037 (6th Cir. 2004).

The problems below explore intersections between the right of publicity and the political arena.

PROBLEM 11-5: SHERIFF ANDY GRIFFITH

As everybody knows, the actor Andy Griffith starred in the popular television series "The Andy Griffith Show," in which he played Andy Taylor, the sheriff of small town Mayberry, North Carolina. Sheriff Andy Taylor was wise, humble, fair, and generally the embodiment of all-American virtue.

Professor Janis' Cousin Clem, who is definitely *not* the embodiment of all-American virtue, decided to run for sheriff of Tick Ridge County. Hoping to enhance his appeal among qualified voters, Cousin Clem legally changed his name to Andy Griffith and then used the name (of course) on various campaign posters, stickers, and the like.

Suppose the actor Andy Griffith sues the former Cousin Clem before the election, claiming a right-of-publicity violation. Assume that the actor owns the relevant rights of publicity and that the jurisdiction recognizes a common law right of publicity. Should the First Amendment or other limitations shield Cousin Clem from liability? Alternatively, suppose that Andy Griffith waits until after the election, and then sues. Assume that Cousin Clem has lost the election but wants to keep the name. Does the timing of the lawsuit affect the analysis? *See Griffith v. Fenrick*, 486 F. Supp. 2d 848 (W.D. Wis. 2007).

PROBLEM 11-6: G.I. GEORGE

In May 2003, a Navy S-3B Viking fighter jet touched down on the flight deck of the aircraft carrier USS *Abraham Lincoln* in the Pacific Ocean. President George W. Bush, attired in a flight suit, emerged from the cockpit of the S-3B and pronounced major combat operations in the 2003 war against Iraq at an end. Aides assured the press that the president hadn't actually been flying the plane.

BBI, a toy manufacturer, markets a variety of military action figure dolls as part of its Elite Force series. BBI marketed a George W. Bush "naval aviator" action figure doll. According to the advertisement,

> [t]his fully poseable figure features a realistic head sculpt, fully detailed cloth flight suit, helmet with oxygen mask, survival vest, g-pants, parachute harness and much more. The realism and exacting attention to detail demanded by today's 12-inch action figure enthusiast are met and exceeded with this action figure.

(We're guessing that "12-inch action figure enthusiast" might really mean "enthusiast of 12-inch action figures," but that doesn't matter right now.) The toy and its packaging are depicted below:

As shown, the packaging includes a color sketch of George W. Bush and the words "George W. Bush" and below them "President and Naval Aviator." We think that the doll's "realistic head sculpt" really does look pretty much like George W. Bush, at least on a good day. Assume that BBI did not acquire George W. Bush's permission to produce the doll. Should a court find a right-of-publicity violation under a typical state law regime? Would depictions and other representations of the president ordinarily qualify as constitutionally protected speech? Is the doll "political speech" protected by the First Amendment? Is the *Montana* case (discussed in the notes above) on point?

While we're on the matter of figurines, consider the matter of the Obama daughters. Ty makes BEANIE BABIES plush toys. In early 2009, Ty introduced two "TY GIRLZ" dolls named "Marvelous Malia" and "Sweet Sasha." Sasha and Malia Obama are the daughters of Barack Obama, who was starting his first term as President in early 2009. Some would say that there is some physical resemblance between the dolls and the president's daughters. Right-of-publicity violation? Same case as the G.I. George case?

PROBLEM 11-7:   THE SOLDIER'S RIGHT OF PUBLICITY

A few states have passed statutes concerning rights of publicity for members of the U.S. armed forces. In Arizona, for example, Ariz. Rev. Stat. §12-761 provided a "soldier's right of publicity" encompassing "the right to control and to choose whether and how to use a soldier's name, portrait or picture for commercial purposes. . . ." Liability for violating a soldier's right of publicity occurred upon unconsented use of the soldier's "name, portrait or picture" for any of a series of enumerated purposes, including, among others:

1. Advertising for the sale of any goods, wares or merchandise.
2. Soliciting patronage for any business.
3. Receiving consideration for the sale of any goods, wares or merchandise.

ARIZ. REV. STAT. §12-761(B). The statute also provided that the soldier's right of publicity did not apply to activities including, among others,

1. The use of a soldier's name, portrait or picture in an attempt to portray, describe or impersonate that soldier in a live performance, a single and original work of fine art, a play, book, article, musical work or film or on radio, television or other audio or audio-visual work if the performance, musical work, play, book, article or film does not itself constitute a commercial advertisement for any goods, wares or merchandise.
2. The use of a soldier's name, portrait or picture for noncommercial purposes, including any news, public affairs or sports broadcast or account.

ARIZ. REV. STAT. §12-761(H). The statute further provided that the rights extended beyond a soldier's death, and that violations could be remedied by injunction or a claim for damages. The Arizona statute also provided for criminal penalties.

Suppose that an individual (Dan) sells T-shirts that say "Bush Lied—They Died" on the front (in reference to President George W. Bush and the Iraq War), and lists hundreds of names of deceased soldiers on the back. Suppose that Dan's sale of the T-shirts is enjoined under the Arizona statute. Does the injunction violate the First Amendment? *See Frazier v. Boomsma*, 84 U.S.P.Q.2d (BNA) 1779 (D. Ariz. 2007).

The following problem may be useful for reviewing many of the concepts introduced in this chapter.

PROBLEM 11-8:   GUITAR HERO

In the video game Guitar Hero, players use a plastic replica guitar and attempt to mimic the notes and rhythms of various songs. One version of the Guitar Hero game featured songs that were popular in the 1980s, including "What I Like about You," recorded by the Romantics. Activision, the producer of the Guitar Hero game, licensed the copyright in the musical composition and created a recording under the license for use in the Guitar Hero game. (Activision did not use the actual Romantics sound recording.) The Guitar Hero game makes some references to the Romantics—for example, identifying "What I Like About You" as "the song made famous by the Romantics."

The Romantics asserted right-of-publicity and Lanham Act violations. Analyze the following issues:

(1)   Whether copyright law should preempt the right-of-publicity claim.

(2)   Whether Activision has appropriated any protectable aspects of the Romantics' identities. Apply the Indiana statute for purposes of your analysis.

(3)   Whether the First Amendment would limit the assertion of a right-of-publicity claim.

(4)   Whether the Romantics have a viable false endorsement claim under Lanham Act §43(a).

See Romantics v. Activision Pub. Inc., 88 U.S.P.Q.2d (BNA) 1243 (E.D. Mich. 2008).

12

REMEDIES

In this chapter, we consider the range of remedies that are available in cases of trademark infringement, unfair competition, false advertising, and violation of publicity rights. In most intellectual property litigation, the principal battle is resolved by the grant or denial of injunctive relief (and often *preliminary* injunctive relief is sufficient). This is especially so in trademark and unfair competition litigation. Historically, trademark disputes have not given rise to the amount or frequency of monetary relief that is found even in copyright or patent cases. Thus, in this chapter, we first address the availability of injunctive relief and then turn to the range of monetary remedies that are available.

A. INJUNCTIVE RELIEF

Traditionally, injunctive relief was generously available in trademark actions. The first case in this section of the Chapter illustrates that traditional approach. Recent cases have focused on the effect of the U.S. Supreme Court patent decision in *eBay Inc. v. MercExchange, L.L.C.*, 547 U.S. 388 (2006) on trademark law. In that case, the Supreme Court rejected the "categorical" approach of the Court of Appeals for the Federal Circuit that as a "general rule courts will issue permanent injunctions against patent infringement absent exceptional circumstances" and instead stressed that the Patent Act indicates "that injunctive relief 'may' issue only 'in accordance with the principles of equity.'" Under *eBay*, to secure a permanent injunction, a plaintiff must demonstrate: (1) that it has suffered an irreparable injury; (2) that remedies at law, such as monetary damages, are inadequate to compensate; (3) that, considering the balance of hardships between the plaintiff and defendant, a remedy in equity is warranted; and (4) that the public interest would not be disserved by a permanent injunction. The later cases in this section address the effect of *eBay* in trademark law.

GOTO.COM, INC. v. WALT DISNEY CO.
202 F.3d 1199 (9th Cir. 2000)

O'SCANNLAIN, Circuit Judge:

[GoTo sued Disney alleging a violation of Section 43(a)(1)(A) of the Lanham Act, and sought a preliminary injunction. The district court granted GoTo's motion for a preliminary injunction. After Disney appealed, and moved the district court to modify and to stay the preliminary injunction, the district court amended its preliminary injunction order by adding language proposed by GoTo that allowed Disney to phase out its use of the infringing logo in many of its incarnations. Disney again appealed, and the Court of Appeals granted Disney's motion to stay the preliminary injunction pending an expedited appeal.]

II

We review the district court's grant of a preliminary injunction for an abuse of discretion. *See Brookfield Communications, Inc. v. West Coast Entertainment Corp.*, 174 F.3d 1036, 1045 (9th Cir. 1999). The grant of a preliminary injunction will be reversed only when the district court has based its decision on an erroneous legal standard or on clearly erroneous findings of fact. [cit.] The legal issues underlying the injunction are reviewed de novo because a "district court would necessarily abuse its discretion if it based its ruling on an erroneous view of law." *Brookfield*, 174 F.3d at 1046. As to findings of fact, we may affirm the district court "as long as 'the findings are sufficiently comprehensive and pertinent to the issues to provide a basis for the decision, or if there can be no genuine dispute about the omitted findings.'" *Ocean Garden, Inc. v. Marktrade Co.*, 953 F.2d 500, 509 (9th Cir. 1991) (quoting *Vance v. American Hawaii Cruises, Inc.*, 789 F.2d 790, 792 (9th Cir. 1986)). We review a legal and factual determination of likelihood of confusion under the trademark laws for clear error. *See Brookfield*, 174 F.3d at 1061.

A plaintiff is entitled to a preliminary injunction in a trademark[3] case when it demonstrates either (1) a combination of "probable success on the merits" and "the possibility of irreparable injury"[4] or (2) the existence of "serious questions going to the merits" and that "the balance of hardships tips sharply in his favor." *Sardi's Restaurant Corp. v. Sardie*, 755 F.2d 719, 723 (9th Cir. 1985). To prevail on a claim under the Lanham Act, GoTo must establish that Disney is using a mark confusingly similar [to] its own, which it began using a year earlier. *See AMF Inc. v. Sleekcraft Boats*, 599 F.2d 341, 348 (9th Cir. 1979). Or, as the court in *Brookfield* clarified: "[m]ore precisely, because we are at the preliminary injunction stage, [GoTo] must establish that it is likely to be able to show . . . a likelihood of confusion." 174 F.3d at 1052 n.15 (citing *Sardi's Restaurant*, 755 F.2d at 723).

The likelihood of confusion is the central element of trademark infringement, and the issue can be recast as the determination of whether "the similarity of the marks is likely to confuse customers about the source of the products."[5] . . .

. . .

III

From our analysis of the *Sleekcraft* factors, we conclude that GoTo has demonstrated a likelihood of success on its claim that Disney's use of its logo violates the Lanham Act. From this showing of likelihood of success on the merits in this trademark infringement claim, we may presume irreparable injury. *See Brookfield*, 174 F.3d at 1066; [cit.]. GoTo has therefore demonstrated the combination of success on the merits and the possibility of irreparable injury necessary to entitle it to a preliminary injunction in a trademark case. Because GoTo has prevailed under this avenue for obtaining injunctive relief, we need not decide whether there exist serious questions on the merits or whether the balance of hardships tips sharply in favor of GoTo.

---

3. Although there is some dispute among the parties concerning whether either of the marks is officially registered, "the same standard" applies to both registered and unregistered trademarks. . . .

4. The articulation of this prong as a bifurcated one is somewhat misleading. In a trademark infringement claim, "irreparable injury may be presumed from a showing of likelihood of success on the merits." *See Brookfield*, 174 F.3d at 1066 (citing *Metro Pub., Ltd. v. San Jose Mercury News*, 987 F.2d 637, 640 (9th Cir. 1993)). This presumption effectively conflates the dual inquiries of this prong into the single question of whether the plaintiff has shown a likelihood of success on the merits.

5. Because of the aforementioned conflation of the factors in this area of the law, a plaintiff is therefore entitled to a preliminary injunction in a trademark case simply when it shows a likelihood of confusion.

IV

Disney raises two equitable defenses in its attempt to stymie GoTo's preliminary injunction: laches and unclean hands. As to the first, we have certainly allowed laches to bar trademark infringement cases in the past, but "we have done so only where the trademark holder knowingly allowed the infringing mark to be used without objection for a lengthy period of time." *Brookfield*, 174 F.3d at 1061 (citing time periods of eight years and two years). Here, GoTo objected to Disney's use of its logo within a fortnight of Disney's beta launch. Although several months did pass between GoTo's filing suit in February 1999 and moving for a preliminary injunction in July 1999, the parties had entered into a tolling agreement under which Disney agreed not to raise this issue. Even without this tolling agreement, however, this delay of only a few months would not be sufficient to bar GoTo's recovery.

As to the question of unclean hands, again we disagree with Disney. We conclude that the record supports the district court's ruling, sub silentio, in favor of GoTo. . . . While the record does not necessarily demonstrate that GoTo's hands were clean as snow, it does provide evidence to support the district court's decision to ignore Disney's allegations. First, evidence exists to support GoTo's assertion that it did not alter its logo to resemble Disney's; from March 1998 until December 1998, there were approximately 240 million impressions of the GoTo logo with yellow boxes. In fact, the version of the GoTo logo that most resembles the Disney logo was published in *Time* magazine well before Disney's beta launch. As for the contention that GoTo manipulated Disney's logo shown in a press release, we recognize that the version of the Disney logo in the press release does, indeed, appear different from the usual image proffered by Disney. Nevertheless, GoTo correctly points to many available variations of the Disney logo that look less like the prototypical Disney lamp than the image used in the press release. Finally, as to GoTo's order to its public relations firm to destroy old drafts of the press release, evidence suggests that this was simply an attempt to avoid a leak of the press release to the media or to Disney. Although the district court did not catalog its findings on this issue, it did not abuse its discretion by failing to do so, because evidence in the record supports the denial of Disney's unclean hands defense.

V

Furthermore, we disregard the contention that this preliminary injunction alters the status quo ante litem. Disney's arguments to the contrary reveal its confusion as to this term of law. The status quo ante litem refers not simply to any situation before the filing of a lawsuit, but instead to "the last uncontested status which preceded the pending controversy," *Tanner Motor Livery, Ltd. v. Avis, Inc.*, 316 F.2d 804, 809 (9th Cir. 1963) (quoting *Westinghouse Elec. Corp. v. Free Sewing Mach. Co.*, 256 F.2d 806, 808 (7th Cir. 1958)). In this case, the status quo ante litem existed before Disney began using its allegedly infringing logo. The interpretation of this concept that Disney advocates would lead to absurd situations, in which plaintiffs could never bring suit once infringing conduct had begun. Disney severely mischaracterizes this concept, and we conclude that its argument is without merit.

. . .

VII

Disney contends that the district court abused its discretion by crafting the preliminary injunction too vaguely and broadly. We do not agree. *See SEC v. Interlink Data Network*, 77 F.3d 1201, 1204 (9th Cir. 1996) (holding that the scope of injunctive relief is reviewed for an abuse of discretion or application of erroneous legal principles). Although the preliminary injunction certainly does not catalog the entire universe of possible uses of Disney's logo, it is nevertheless sufficiently clear to protect GoTo's interests and to provide Disney with adequate notice. *See* Fed. R. Civ. P. 65(d); *Granny Goose Foods, Inc. v. Brotherhood of Teamsters & Auto Truck Drivers*, 415 U.S. 423, 444 (1974) (stating that the party enjoined should "receive fair and precisely drawn notice of what the injunction actually prohibits").

When the infringing use is for a similar service, a broad injunction is "especially appropriate." *Century 21 Real Estate Corp. v. Sandlin*, 846 F.2d 1175, 1181 (9th Cir. 1988). Here, we have concluded that the services are practically identical. Furthermore, we reiterate the rule in this circuit that the plaintiff should not be held to answer the infringer's subjective assertion that it cannot understand how best to comply with an injunction. *See Triad Sys. Corp. v. Southeastern Express Co.*, 64 F.3d 1330, 1337 (9th Cir. 1995) (holding that placing the burden of determining how to comply with an injunction on the defendant was "appropriate" because it was the defendant who "is the infringer").

In addition, we take comfort in the knowledge that Disney has already demonstrated that it is capable of obeying this injunction, as it did when the clock struck midnight and the preliminary injunction was first entered on November 12, 1999.

VIII

Finally, as to whether the bond [which plaintiff must post to cover any costs or damages that a defendant might incur if it is later found that the injunction was wrongfully issued] was adequate, we conclude that the district court did not abuse its discretion in requiring a bond of only $25,000. *See Walczak v. EPL Prolong, Inc.*, 198 F.3d 725 (9th Cir. Dec. 3, 1999). Disney would have us increase that bond 800 times to at least $20,000,000. We decline to do so, and look to Rule 65(c), which places within the discretion of the district court the amount of the bond. Fed. R. Civ. P. 65(c). We have rejected similar requests to raise the bond dramatically. *See, e.g., Brookfield*, 174 F.3d at 1043-44 (rejecting the defendant's request to increase the bond from $25,000 to $400,000). Were we to grant Disney's request, we would risk denying GoTo access to judicial review since the preliminary injunction would not take effect until GoTo posted the bond. We decline to do so.

IX

We conclude that the district court correctly found that two remarkably similar marks displayed commercially on the Web were likely to cause consumer confusion. We therefore confirm our order of January 27, 2000, vacating our stay of November 18, 1999, and reinstating the preliminary injunction as it was modified on November 16, 1999, by Judge Hatter.

Affirmed; Preliminary Injunction Reinstated.

NORTH AMERICAN MEDICAL CORP. v. AXIOM WORLDWIDE, INC.

522 F.3d 1211 (11th Cir. 2008)

ANDERSON, Circuit Judge:

[NAM (North American Medical Corporation) designs and manufacturers physiotherapeutic spinal devices, which are used, for example, to treat lower back pain. Adagen is an authorized distributor of NAM's devices. NAM and Adagen alleged that a competitor (Axiom) engaged in unfair competition by infringing NAM's trademarks and by issuing false advertising. The trademark infringement claims stem from Axiom's use of two of NAM's registered trademarks: the terms "Accu-Spina" and "IDD Therapy." Axiom included these terms on its website within metatags. Evidence indicated that, before Axiom removed these metatags from its website, if a computer user entered the trademarked terms into Google's Internet search engine, Google listed Axiom's website as the second most relevant search result. The district court issued a preliminary injunction in favor of NAM and Adagen, prohibiting Axiom from using NAM's trademarks within metatags and prohibiting Axiom from making the challenged statements about the DRX 9000. The Eleventh Circuit affirmed the conclusion of the District Court that the plaintiff had shown a likelihood of success on the merits both with respect to its trademark infringement and false advertising claim. However, the defendant also argued on appeal that the district court erred by categorically presuming that any plaintiff with a viable unfair competition claim will always suffer irreparable harm in the absence of a preliminary injunction.]

C.   PRESUMPTIONS OF IRREPARABLE HARM

Even though we hold that NAM and Adagen [the plaintiffs] have established a substantial likelihood of success on the merits of their trademark infringement and false advertising claims, we must still evaluate whether NAM and Adagen have demonstrated, with respect to each claim, that they will suffer irreparable harm in the absence of an injunction. In reaching its conclusion that NAM and Adagen satisfied this element of the preliminary injunction test, the district court relied on two presumptions, one regarding the infringement claims and one regarding the false advertising claims. For the reasons that follow, we vacate the preliminary injunction with respect to both the trademark claims and the false advertising claims.

1.   IRREPARABLE HARM IN FALSE ADVERTISING CASES

The district court erred when it presumed that NAM and Adagen would suffer irreparable harm in the absence of a preliminary injunction merely because Axiom's advertisements are literally false. The district court cited a case out of the Northern District of Georgia, *Energy Four, Inc. v. Dornier Medical Systems, Inc.*, 765 F. Supp. 724, 734 (N.D. Ga. 1991), for the following proposition: "In false advertising cases, '[p]roof of falsity is sufficient to sustain a finding of irreparable injury for purposes of a preliminary injunction.'" This quote, however, is an incomplete statement of the law. Proof of falsity is generally only sufficient to sustain a finding of irreparable injury when the false statement is made in the context of comparative advertising between the plaintiff's and defendant's products. *See* [J. THOMAS MCCARTHY, MCCARTHY ON TRADEMARKS AND UNFAIR COMPETITION §27:37] ("Where the challenged advertising makes a misleading comparison to a competitor's product, irreparable harm is presumed. But if the false advertising is non-comparative and makes no direct reference to a competitor's product, irreparable harm is not presumed." (internal footnotes omitted)). Although some cases, such as the one cited by the district court, employ language that may suggest a more expansive presumption, such quotes take the original principle out of context without explanation.

Once this presumption is properly stated, it becomes evident that NAM and Adagen are not entitled to the presumption's benefits because Axiom's statements, although false, do not mention NAM's products by name or in any way compare Axiom's products with NAM's products. This is not to say that NAM and Adagen could not demonstrate, absent the presumption, that they will suffer irreparable harm from Axiom's false advertising, but the district court abused its discretion by relying solely on the presumption to find irreparable harm. Accordingly, we vacate the preliminary injunction to the extent it proscribes

Axiom's false advertising, and we remand to the district court to determine whether NAM and Adagen will suffer irreparable harm in the absence of a preliminary injunction.

2.   IRREPARABLE HARM IN TRADEMARK INFRINGEMENT CASES

Regardless of whether NAM deserves a presumption of irreparable harm on its false advertising claims, our prior cases do extend a presumption of irreparable harm once a plaintiff establishes a likelihood of success on the merits of a trademark infringement claim. Our circuit has acknowledged as much on several occasions. [cit.]

Nonetheless, although established law entitles NAM and Adagen to this presumption in the trademark infringement context, a recent U.S. Supreme Court case calls into question whether courts may presume irreparable harm merely because a plaintiff in an intellectual property case has demonstrated a likelihood of success on the merits. *See generally eBay Inc. v. MercExchange, L.L.C.*, 547 U.S. 388 (2006). In *eBay*, after a jury had found patent infringement by the defendant, the district court denied the plaintiff's motion for permanent injunctive relief. [cit.] In so doing, the district court "appeared to adopt certain expansive principles suggesting that injunctive relief could not issue in a broad swath of cases." [cit.] On appeal, the Federal Circuit reversed the denial of injunctive relief, articulating a categorical rule that permanent injunctions shall issue once infringement is established. [cit.] The Supreme Court reversed the Federal Circuit and admonished both the district and appellate courts for applying categorical rules to the grant or denial of injunctive relief. [cit.] The Court stressed that the Patent Act indicates "that injunctive relief 'may' issue only 'in accordance with the principles of equity.'" [cit.] Because the Court concluded "that neither court below correctly applied the traditional four-factor framework that governs the award of injunctive relief, [it] vacated the judgment of the Court of Appeals, so that the District Court may apply that framework in the first instance." [cit.] The Supreme Court held that while "the decision whether to grant or deny injunctive relief rests within the equitable discretion of the district courts, . . . such discretion must be exercised consistent with traditional principles of equity, in patent disputes no less than in other cases governed by such standards." [cit.]

Although *eBay* dealt with the Patent Act and with permanent injunctive relief, a strong case can be made that *eBay*'s holding necessarily extends to the grant of preliminary injunctions under the Lanham Act. Similar to the Patent Act, the Lanham Act grants federal courts the "power to grant injunctions, according to the principles of equity and upon such terms as the court may deem reasonable." 15 U.S.C. §1116(a) (2006). Furthermore, no obvious distinction exists between permanent and preliminary injunctive relief to suggest that *eBay* should not apply to the latter. Because the language of the Lanham Act—granting federal courts the power to grant injunctions "according to the principles of equity and upon such terms as the court may deem reasonable"—is so similar to the language of the Patent Act, we conclude that the Supreme Court's *eBay* case is applicable to the instant case.

However, we decline to express any further opinion with respect to the effect of *eBay* on this case. For example, we decline to decide whether the district court was correct in its holding that the nature of the trademark infringement gives rise to a presumption of irreparable injury. In other words, we decline to address whether such a presumption is the equivalent of the categorical rules rejected by the Court in *eBay*. We decline to address such issues for several reasons. First, the briefing on appeal has been entirely inadequate in this regard. Second, the district court has not addressed the effect of *eBay*. Finally, the district court may well conclude on remand that it can readily reach an appropriate decision by fully applying *eBay* without the benefit of a presumption of irreparable injury, or it may well decide that the particular circumstances of the instant case bear substantial parallels to previous cases such that a presumption of irreparable injury is an appropriate exercise of its discretion in light of the historical traditions. *See eBay*, 547 U.S. at 394-97 (concurring opinions of Chief Justice Roberts and Justice Kennedy, representing the views of seven Justices). Accordingly, we also vacate the preliminary injunction as it applies to the trademark infringement claim, and remand to the district court for further proceedings not inconsistent with this opinion, and with *eBay*.

ADIDAS AMERICA, INC. v. SKECHERS USA, INC.

890 F.3d 747 (9th Cir. 2018)

Nguyen, Circuit Judge:

Skechers USA, Inc. appeals the district court's issuance of a preliminary injunction prohibiting it from selling shoes that allegedly infringe and dilute adidas America, Inc.'s Stan Smith trade dress and Three–Stripe trademark. We hold that the district court did not abuse its discretion in issuing the preliminary injunction as to adidas's claim that Skechers's Onix shoe infringes on adidas's unregistered trade dress of its Stan Smith shoe. We conclude, however, that the district court erred in issuing a preliminary injunction as to adidas's claim that Skechers's Cross Court shoe infringes and dilutes its Three–Stripe mark. Accordingly, we affirm in part and reverse in part.

I. Factual Background

adidas is a leading manufacturer of athletic apparel and footwear. Skechers is a footwear company that competes with adidas in the active footwear and apparel market. Skechers has grown to become the second largest footwear company in the United States, ahead of adidas and behind only Nike.

[The Stan Smith has become one of adidas's most successful shoes in terms of sales and influence since its release in the 1970s. adidas is also known for its Three–Stripe mark, which has been featured on its products for many years as part of its branding strategy and for which it owns federal trademark registrations.]

adidas filed the present lawsuit against Skechers on September 14, 2015, alleging, among other things, that Skechers's Onix shoe infringes on and dilutes the unregistered trade dress of adidas's Stan Smith shoe (both pictured below).

adidas further alleges that Skechers's Relaxed Fit Cross Court TR (pictured below) infringes and dilutes adidas's Three–Stripe trademark . . .

adidas filed a motion for preliminary injunction to prohibit Skechers from manufacturing, distributing, advertising, selling, or offering for sale the Onix and Cross Court. The district court granted adidas's motion and issued the preliminary injunction . . .

Skechers timely appealed. . . .

III.

ANALYSIS

A. Skechers' Onix and adidas's Stan Smith

[The Ninth Circuit concluded that, given the evidence, the district court did not clearly err in concluding that adidas was likely to succeed on its claim that Skechers's Onix shoe infringes on adidas's Stan Smith trade dress.]

Skechers also argues that the district court's finding of a likelihood of irreparable harm to the Stan Smith was erroneous.

In *Herb Reed Enterprises, LLC v. Florida Entertainment Management, Inc.*, we reaffirmed that "[e]vidence of loss of control over business reputation and damage to goodwill [can] constitute irreparable harm," so long as there is concrete evidence in the record of those things. 736 F.3d 1239, 1250 (9th Cir. 2013). Consistent with *Herb Reed*, the district court here based its finding of irreparable harm from the Onix shoe on evidence that adidas was likely to suffer irreparable harm to its brand reputation and goodwill if the preliminary injunction did not issue. adidas's Director of Sport Style Brand Marketing testified to the significant efforts his team invested in promoting the Stan Smith through specific and controlled avenues such as social media campaigns and product placement, and he stated that the Stan Smith earned significant media from various sources that was not initiated or solicited by adidas. adidas also presented evidence regarding its efforts to carefully control the supply of Stan Smith shoes and its concerns about damage to the Stan Smith's reputation if the marketplace were flooded with similar shoes. Finally, adidas produced customer surveys showing that approximately twenty percent of surveyed consumers believed Skechers's Onix was made by, approved by, or affiliated with adidas.

The extensive and targeted advertising and unsolicited media, along with tight control of the supply of Stan Smiths, demonstrate that adidas has built a specific reputation around the Stan Smith with "intangible benefits." And, the customer surveys demonstrate that those intangible benefits will be harmed if the Onix stays on the market because consumers will be confused about the source of the shoes. We find that the district court's finding of irreparable harm is not clearly erroneous. *See Herb Reed*, 736 F.3d at 1250; *Rent–A–Ctr., Inc. v. Canyon Television & Appliance Rental, Inc.*, 944 F.2d 597, 603 (9th Cir. 1991) (noting that harm to advertising efforts and goodwill constitute "intangible injuries" that warrant injunctive protection).

B. Skecher's Cross Court and adidas' Three-Stripe Mark

[The Ninth Circuit concluded that the district court did not err in finding adidas showed a likelihood of success on its trademark infringement claim or its adidas's trademark dilution claim.]

Skechers next argues that the district court abused its discretion in issuing the preliminary injunction because under [Winter v. Nat. Res. Def. Council, Inc., 555 U.S. 7, 20 (2008)] adidas has not shown that it will be irreparably harmed from sale of the Cross Court. We agree.

Both below and on appeal, adidas advanced only a narrow argument of irreparable harm as to the Cross Court: that Skechers harmed adidas's ability to control its brand image because consumers who see others wearing Cross Court shoes associate the allegedly lesser-quality Cross Courts with adidas and its Three–Stripe mark. Yet we find no evidence in the record that could support a finding of irreparable harm based on this loss of control theory.

First, adidas's theory of harm relies on the notion that adidas is viewed by consumers as a premium brand while Skechers is viewed as a lower-quality, discount brand. But even if adidas presented evidence sufficient to show its efforts to cultivate a supposedly premium brand image for itself, adidas did not set forth evidence probative of Skechers's allegedly less favorable reputation. The only evidence in the record regarding Skechers's reputation was testimony from adidas employees. First, adidas claimed that "Skechers generally sells its footwear at prices lower than adidas's"—how much lower, and for what of any number of possible reasons other than the quality of its products, we do not know. This generalized statement regarding Skechers's price point does not indicate that consumers view Skechers as a value brand. Second, one adidas employee noted that within adidas, Skechers is viewed as inferior to adidas. Again, Skechers's reputation among the ranks of adidas employees does not indicate how the general consumer views it. Thus, the district court's finding that Skechers is viewed as a "value brand" is an "unsupported and conclusory statement[ ]" that is not "grounded in any evidence or showing offered by [adidas]." *See Herb Reed*, 736 F.3d at 1250 (internal quotation marks omitted).[8]

Second, adidas's theory of harm is in tension with the theory of customer confusion that adidas has advanced to establish a likelihood of success on the merits. adidas did not argue in the district court, and has not argued on appeal, that a Cross Court purchaser would mistakenly believe he had bought adidas shoes at the time of sale. Indeed, this argument would be implausible because the Cross Court contains numerous Skechers logos and identifying features. Instead, adidas argues only that *after* the sale, *someone else* looking at a Cross Court shoe from afar or in passing might not notice the Skechers logos and thus might mistake it for an adidas.

The tension between adidas's consumer confusion and irreparable harm theories, then, boils down to this: How would consumers who confused Cross Courts for adidas shoes be able to surmise, from afar, that those shoes were low quality? If the "misled" consumers could not assess the quality of the shoe from afar, why would they think any differently about adidas's products? How could adidas's "premium" brand possibly be hurt by any confusion?

Indeed, such a claim is counterintuitive. If a consumer viewed a shoe from such a distance that she could not notice its Skechers logos, it is unlikely she would be able to reasonably assess the quality of the shoes. And the consumer could not conflate adidas's brand with Skechers's supposedly "discount" reputation if she did not know the price of the shoe and was too far away to tell whether the shoe might be a Skechers to begin with. In short, even if Skechers does make inferior products (or even if consumers tend to think so), there is no evidence that adidas's theory of post-sale confusion would cause consumers to associate such lesser-quality products with adidas. And, even if we agree with the district court that some consumers are likely to be confused as to the maker of the Cross Court shoe, we

---

8. The dissent criticizes our reliance on Herb Reed. True, there are more facts in the record here that adidas claims support a finding of likelihood of irreparable harm than there were in Herb Reed. *See* 736 F.3d at 1250 (noting there was only one email in the record that might support an inference of irreparable harm). The problem is that none of those facts actually support such a finding. Herb Reed makes clear that it is the plaintiff's burden to put forth specific evidence from which the court can infer irreparable harm. See id. ("The district court's analysis of irreparable harm is cursory and conclusory, rather than being grounded in any evidence or showing offered by [the plaintiff]."). Regardless of our deferential review, there must actually be such evidence in the record before we can uphold the district court's factual findings. Id. (overturning the district court where its "pronouncements [were] grounded in platitudes rather than evidence"). We simply disagree with the dissent that there is any such evidence supporting adidas's theory of irreparable harm on this record.

cannot simply assume that such confusion will cause adidas irreparable harm where, as here, adidas has failed to provide concrete evidence that it will.

As discussed above, adidas presented specific evidence that its reputation and goodwill were likely to be irreparably harmed by Skechers's Onix shoe based on adidas's extensive marketing efforts for the Stan Smith and its careful control of the supply of Stan Smiths available for purchase. Thus, even post-sale confusion of consumers from afar threatens to harm the value adidas derives from the scarcity and exclusivity of the Stan Smith brand. But there was no comparable argument or evidence for the Cross Court.

Because adidas failed to produce evidence that it will suffer irreparable harm due to the Cross Court, we conclude that the district court abused its discretion by issuing a preliminary injunction for the Cross Court.

Affirmed in Part, Reversed in Part.

CLIFTON, Circuit Judge, concurring in part and dissenting in part:

The preliminary injunction entered by the district court should be affirmed in full. I join with my colleagues in affirming the preliminary injunction regarding Skechers's Onix shoe based on its infringement on the trade dress of adidas's Stan Smith shoe and concur in that part of the majority opinion.

Where I part ways with the majority concerns the infringement by Skechers with its Cross Court shoe of the Three–Stripe mark owned by adidas. . . .

I. *Herb Reed*

The precedent relied upon by the part of the majority decision in question comes down essentially to a single case, *Herb Reed Enterprises, LLC v. Florida Entertainment Management, Inc.*, 736 F.3d 1239 (9th Cir. 2013). . . .

Our decision noted that the legal rule previously was that "irreparable injury may be *presumed* from a showing of likelihood of success on the merits of a trademark infringement claim." . . . Subsequent Supreme Court decisions undermined that presumption, however, and in *Herb Reed* we held that a plaintiff could not simply rely on that presumption but must establish irreparable harm in order to obtain an injunction. We went on to reverse the preliminary injunction that had been entered by the district court, noting that the finding of irreparable harm was not "grounded in *any* evidence or showing offered by" the plaintiff. *Id.* at 1250 (emphasis added). We emphasized that "missing from this record is *any* such evidence." *Id.* (emphasis added).

. . .

Our decision in *Herb Reed* did not disclaim the logic that led to the creation of the now-discarded legal presumption, however. It is not hard to understand how the presumption arose. If a plaintiff can demonstrate a likelihood that it will succeed on the merits of its trademark claim—as adidas succeeded in establishing that Skechers's Cross Court shoe infringed and diluted adidas's famous Three–Stripe mark, a conclusion we affirm—it is not a big leap to conclude that adidas would be injured by that action. The inference might not always follow, as the facts in *Herb Reed* illustrate. That one Platters tribute band might be mistaken for another did not necessarily establish that the band that had a legal right to the name suffered an injury to its reputation. But in other circumstances, including those here, the inference of injury is logical. As the Third Circuit observed in affirming a similar preliminary injunction: "Although we no longer apply a presumption, the logic underlying the presumption can, and does, inform how we exercise our equitable discretion in this particular case." *Groupe SEB USA, Inc. v. Euro–Pro Operating LLC*, 774 F.3d 192, 205 n.8 (3d Cir. 2014). Our decision in *Herb Reed* did not change that.

II. Irreparable Injury

The district court found that adidas likely suffered harm as the result of post-sale confusion. The theory of post-sale confusion in the trademark context provides that "consumers could acquire the prestige value of the senior user's product by buying the copier's cheap imitation," and that, "[e]ven though the knowledgeable buyer knew that it was getting an imitation, viewers would be confused." "Thus, the senior user suffers a loss of sales diverted to the junior user, the same as if the actual buyer were confused." In other words, sale of the Cross Court, which infringed and diluted adidas's Three–Stripe trademark, would result in post-sale confusion and harm adidas, the trademark holder, by threatening to divert potential customers who can obtain the prestige of its goods without paying its normal prices.[2]

Post-sale confusion accounts for consumers who buy imitations of a prestigious senior holder's brand at lower prices in the very hope that others will confuse their products as being manufactured by the senior holder. About thirty years ago, when I was in private practice, my law firm was retained by Louis Vuitton to combat the sale of cheaper imitations. Some were counterfeits, reproducing the distinctive "LV" mark and pattern on bags similar to those actually sold by Louis Vuitton. Others were knock-offs, such as bags with a similar looking "LW" mark or products that Louis Vuitton probably wouldn't dream of making, such as baseball caps covered with dozens of "LV" marks. Many of the items were sold at locations, like swap meets and flea markets, where few would expect to find real Louis Vuitton products. Prices were often a tiny fraction of what the real thing cost, and it was unlikely that the purchasers thought that they were walking away with genuine Louis Vuitton merchandise. Leaving the legal arguments aside, it wasn't a surprise to me (and still isn't) that Louis Vuitton was concerned and was willing to expend considerable effort to protect its trademark. As Professor McCarthy described, if the prestige of carrying a bag with the Louis Vuitton trademark could be obtained at a fraction of the price, and if viewers could not tell the difference, the value of the trademark would be in jeopardy. And, if someone did confuse the cheap imitation for the real thing, the lesser quality of the imitator could further imperil the perceived value of the Louis Vuitton products and trademark.

The Three–Stripe mark owned by adidas is one of the most famous marks in the world. There is evidence in the record that it has been heavily advertised and promoted by adidas for many years, at the cost of millions of dollars each year. adidas sells several hundred million dollars worth of products bearing the Three–Stripe mark each year in the United States and billions of dollars globally. The Three–Stripe mark is the subject of multiple trademark registrations, in this country and others. adidas has worked to protect its mark, including through litigation against Skechers, and Skechers has acknowledged, as the majority opinion notes, that adidas is the exclusive owner of the Three–Stripe mark and agreed not to use it or any confusingly similar mark.

That adidas is concerned about the impact of trademark infringement and dilution on the Three–Stripe mark, like Louis Vuitton was, is obvious. The reasons seem pretty obvious to me as well. If a shoe bearing a mark that looks like the Three Stripes cannot reliably be identified as being an adidas shoe, available at adidas prices, and made to satisfy the quality standards of adidas, then that Three–Stripe mark will lose some of its value and adidas will be harmed.

The majority opinion describes this as "counterintuitive." It seems logical to me, and it is well established in the law as a basis for a claim of dilution.

---

2. Diversion of customers is a form of irreparable harm. See McCarthy, supra, § 30:47 ("confusion may cause purchasers to refrain from buying either product and to turn to those of other competitors. Yet to prove the loss of sales due to infringement is also notoriously difficult"). . . .

The majority opinion attempts to justify its constrained consideration of the post-sale confusion harm suffered by adidas on the premise that adidas "advanced only a narrow argument of irreparable harm" as to the Skechers shoe that infringed on the Three–Stripe mark, the Cross Court shoe. The majority describes the argument as follows: "that Skechers harmed adidas's ability to control its brand image because consumers who see others wearing Cross Court shoes associate the allegedly lesser-quality Cross Courts with adidas and its Three–Stripe mark."

That argument is actually not so narrow. It is remarkably similar to the explanation provided by Professor McCarthy, as quoted above, that the majority opinion claims that adidas did not make: that "consumers could acquire the prestige value of the senior user's product by buying the copier's cheap imitation," and that, "[e]ven though the knowledge-able buyer knew that it was getting an imitation, viewers would be confused." McCarthy, *supra*, § 23:7. It is also consistent with the definition of "dilution" applied by the district court in its preliminary injunction order: "'the lessening of the capacity of a famous mark to identify and distinguish goods or services' of the owner of the famous mark such that the strong identification value of the owner's trademark whittles away or is gradually attenuated as a result of its use by another." (Quoting *adidas-Am., Inc. v. Payless Shoesource, Inc.*, 546 F.Supp.2d 1029, 1060 (D. Or. 2008) (quoting *Horphag Research Ltd. v. Garcia*, 475 F.3d 1029, 1035 (9th Cir. 2007) (quoting 15 U.S.C. § 1127)).)

The district court went on to observe that "[t]here are two types of dilution: by blurring and by tarnishment." Tarnishment appears to be the only argument the majority considers. The district court described that form of dilution: "a famous mark is considered diluted by tarnishment when the reputation of the famous mark is harmed by the association resulting from the use of the similar mark." But the district court's order described the blurring form of dilution as well, recognizing it as part of adidas's claim, and defining it as "association arising from the similarity between a mark or trade name and a famous mark that impairs the distinctiveness of the famous mark." The district court found that adidas has offered sufficient proof to support a blurring claim. It specifically found that "Skechers' infringement undermines adidas's substantial investment in building its brand and the reputation of its trademarks and trade dress" and that "Skechers' attempts to 'piggy back' off of adidas's efforts by copying or closely imitating adidas's marks means adidas loses control over its trademarks, reputation, and goodwill." There was nothing counterintuitive or narrow about the dilution claim presented by adidas and found persuasive by the district court.

. . .

IV. Evidence

Herb Reed faulted the plaintiff in that case for not producing "any" evidence in support of its claim of irreparable injury. The majority apparently concludes the same to be true here. . .

adidas, in contrast to the appellee in *Herb Reed*, provided ample evidence of this harm. The record includes the sworn declarations and live testimony by several adidas employees, including marketing executives. These employees testified that adidas has, over decades, established a reputation for itself as a premium sports brand, whereas Skechers's brand perception is as a "value brand" or "lower-end brand." They also testified to the particular steps regarding investments in advertising, promotion, and quality control that adidas has taken to achieve and maintain this positive reputation. These steps include taking special care to ensure that the Three–Stripe mark is always prevalent, whether on a shoe or in a retail location. In addition, adidas spends millions each year on promotions and brand advertising on television, in print publications, and via digital media; sponsorships of sporting events such as the FIFA World Cup and Boston Marathon; college sports programs like those at Arizona State, Miami, Nebraska, and Texas A&M; teams such as the Manchester United Football Club and the French national basketball team; professional sports leagues such as Major League Soccer; and individual professional athletes like NBA player James Harden and MLB player Kris Bryant. adidas also uses "influencer marketing," and works with celebrities like Kanye West and Pharrell Williams to ensure that they promote the adidas brand to their fans and followers.

Skechers did not rebut adidas's evidence of the brands' respective reputations, failing to cross-examine the adidas employees on these issues or to provide any counter evidence of its own. Nor did it submit any evidence denying the efforts of adidas to promote and protect the Three–Stripe mark or the sales of adidas products bearing the Three–Stripe mark. The majority opinion does not explain why the evidence of the substantial efforts of adidas to promote its brand and its Three–Stripe mark was insufficient. Nor does it explain why those efforts do not distinguish this case from the factual setting of *Herb Reed*, where the plaintiff failed to produce "any" evidence.

. . .

The record also includes evidence that adidas products were generally priced above comparable Skechers products. There was testimony by an adidas employee that "Skechers generally sells its footwear at prices lower than adidas's." It would be expected that a company would be aware of relative pricing by competitors. Skechers never disputed the competence of that testimony or provided evidence to the contrary. Beyond that, the record also contains evidence that specific adidas products sold at higher prices than their alleged Skechers's counterparts. For example, the record contains proof that the standard version of the adidas Stan Smith retailed between $85 to $75, whereas the Skechers Onix was priced at $65. The adidas Supernova was priced between $130 to $95, whereas the Skechers Supernova was $70. There is no reason why this evidence of the prices of other shoes could not be relied upon by the district court to corroborate the statement by adidas's employee that Skechers generally sold its shoes at a lower price. Again, Skechers did not contest the relative prices of the brands' shoes, leaving the evidence of its lower pricing unrebutted.

In sum, based on the record before it, the district court was well within its discretion to infer that confusion between Skechers's "lower-end" footwear and adidas's footwear was likely to harm adidas's reputation and goodwill as a premium shoe brand. This is precisely the type of harm that is "irreparable" insofar as it cannot be adequately compensated for by money damages. It was simply not the case, as the majority opinion asserts, that "the testimony did not demonstrate that Skechers is a lower-value brand." The findings by the district court were not clearly erroneous.

Finally, the district court's determination did not even depend on adidas's testimony regarding Skechers's reputation as a lower quality brand. The premise of the majority opinion that adidas had to establish that difference in reputation, stated multiple times, is wrong. Instead, the loss by adidas of control over its mark was by itself irreparably harmful. "A trademark carries with it a message that the trademark owner is controlling the nature and quality of the goods or services sold under the mark. Without quality control, this message is false because without control of quality, the goods or services are not truly 'genuine.'". 1 *McCarthy on Trademarks and Unfair Competition* § 3:11 (5th ed. 2018). "One of the most valuable and important protections afforded by the Lanham Act is the right to control the quality of the goods manufactured and sold under the holder's trademark. . . . For this purpose the actual quality of the goods is irrelevant: it is the control of quality that a trademark holder is entitled to maintain." *Id.* (quoting *El Greco Leather Prods. Co. v. Shoe World, Inc.*, 806 F.2d 392, 395 (2d Cir. 1986)). Accordingly, irreparable harm exists in a trademark case when the party seeking the injunction shows that it will lose control over the reputation of its trademark. *See, e.g.*, *La Quinta Corp. v. Heartland Props. LLC*, 603

F.3d 327, 343 (6th Cir. 2010) (explaining that a plaintiff who loses "the ability to control its brand image and reputation" loses an "intangible, but valuable . . . asset[ ].". There was substantial evidence in the record regarding the value of adidas's mark and its management of the mark through investment and quality control over its products. Though the majority ignores that evidence, it was there and could properly be relied upon by the district court to support its finding of irreparable harm. . . .

NOTES AND QUESTIONS

1. *Injunctions under the Lanham Act.* Section 34 of the Lanham Act provides that in an action for infringement of a registered mark, the courts "shall have power to grant injunctions, according to the principles of equity and upon such terms as the court may deem reasonable." The same is true in actions for infringement of unregistered marks. Although injunctive relief is indeed an equitable remedy and thus subject to judicial discretion, until recently a prevailing plaintiff in a trademark infringement, unfair competition, or false advertising case was almost automatically granted injunctive relief. *See* Restatement (Third) of Unfair Competition §35, cmts. b, h (1995). Damages were normally regarded as inadequate relief in such cases, thus triggering the need for an injunction. Why was an injunction an almost automatic remedy in the case of trademark infringement? Why might damages be inadequate? Whose interests are served by the entry of an injunction?

2. *The effect of* eBay. The effect of the Supreme Court's patent decision in *eBay* toward the award of permanent injunctions in trademark cases remains uncertain. A number of courts have now extended *eBay* to the trademark context. As indicated in *Adidas*, the Ninth Circuit has adopted the most far-reaching approach, requiring that the same factors outlined in *eBay* be considered in trademark cases. *See, e.g., Herb Reed Enterprises, LLC v. Florida Entertainment Mgmt., Inc.*, 736 F.3d 1239 (9th Cir. 2013); *see also Ferring Pharmaceuticals v. Watson Pharmaceuticals*, 765 F.3d 205, 217 (3d Cir. 2014) ("A presumption of irreparable harm that functions as an automatic or general grant of an injunction is inconsistent with these principles of equity"). In *Herb Reed Enterprises*, the Ninth Circuit recognized that "evidence of loss of control over business reputation and damage to goodwill could constitute irreparable harm." But it imposed a strict standard. In particular, it held that in the case before it "the court's pronouncements are grounded in platitudes rather than evidence, and relate neither to whether 'irreparable injury is likely in the absence of an injunction.'" Most problematically for trademark plaintiffs, the *Herb Reed* court held that proof of likely confusion was not sufficient proof of irreparable harm. Why might you support that rule? To what extent do you think the approach in *Herb Reed* might create problems? *See* Mark Lemley, *Did* eBay *Irreparably Injure Trademark Law?*, 92 NOTRE DAME L. REV. 1795 (2017) ("Trademark, however, is different. The purposes of trademark law—and who it benefits—should lead us to treat trademark injunctions differently than patent and copyright injunctions. Further, trademark courts have misinterpreted *eBay*, treating each of the four factors as a requirement rather than a consideration. That is a particular problem in trademark law, where proof of future injury can be elusive. And perhaps most remarkably, courts have expanded *eBay* in trademark cases at the same time they have denied damages relief, with the result that trademark owners can and do win their case only to receive no remedy at all. The result is a very real risk that courts will hurt rather than help consumers by allowing confusion to continue."). Despite the *Herb Reed* decision, many other courts are still feeling their way. In addition to those cases excerpted above, *see Audi AG v. D'Amato*, 469 F.3d 534 (6th Cir. 2006); *Reno Air Racing Ass'n v. McCord*, 452 F.3d 1126 (9th Cir. 2006); *Voice of the Arab World, Inc. v. Medical News Now, LLC,*

645 F.3d 26 (1st Cir. 2011). And some courts appear to adhere to the presumption despite *eBay*. *See, e.g., Abraham v. Alpha Chi Omega*, 708 F.3d 614, 627 (5th Cir. 2013). In *eBay*, Justice Kennedy partially justified the approach of the Court by noting the problem of non-practicing entities or "trolls." To what extent does trademark law already contain doctrinal devices to preclude trademark "troll" behavior?

3. *Standards for the grant of preliminary injunctions.* Although the considerations that inform analysis of whether to grant a preliminary injunction are similar throughout the country, the different federal circuits each have their own particular formulation. The Ninth Circuit standard recited in *GoTo* is not atypical. As the court notes in footnote 4, the central question in trademark cases is likelihood of success on the merits, which often determines the question of irreparable injury. *But see Winter v. Nat'l Resources Defense Council, Inc.*, 555 U.S. 7 (2008) (suggesting that in other contexts a standard of "possible" irreparable harm was too lenient to support preliminary injunctive relief). The first prong of the test for preliminary injunctions may be less certain after *eBay*. The second prong of the test is less frequently the basis on which courts rest the award of relief (at least pre-*eBay*). But the balance of hardships is clearly a factor that plaintiffs will advance forcefully where the likely success is less clear. What kind of "hardships" might be relevant? In what circumstances might the hardship to the defendant undercut the plaintiff's request? Some courts also explicitly consider "the effect on the public interest." *See, e.g., American Greetings Corp. v. Dan-Dee Imports., Inc.*, 807 F.2d 1136 (3d Cir. 1986). How might this factor inform courts' analysis? What different public interests are at stake? *See also Berkley Networks Corp. v. InMarket Media, LLC*, 114 U.S.P.Q.2d (BNA) 1169 (S.D.N.Y. 2014) (denying preliminary injunction despite plaintiff showing likelihood of success on the merits because plaintiff waited eleven months after release of allegedly infringing products to bring lawsuit undermining the claim of irreparable harm); *Wreal, LLC v. Amazon.com, Inc.*, 840 F.3d 1244 (11th Cir. 2016) (holding that unexplained five-month delay in seeking a preliminary injunction, by itself, fatally undermined any showing of irreparable injury).

4. *Preserving the status quo.* A preliminary injunction is not a final adjudication on the merits of a case (indeed, a court is not bound by its findings at the preliminary stage of the litigation). It is an equitable remedy, upon which the trial court has substantial discretion, and which is intended to preserve the status quo. Preservation of the status quo is thus often cited by courts as a factor to consider in deciding motions for a preliminary injunction. Is the supposedly exceptional nature of preliminary injunctive relief evident from the Ninth Circuit's discussion in *GoTo*? If not, why not? Why is preliminary injunctive relief arguably granted more routinely in trademark cases than in commercial disputes generally?

5. *Mandatory injunctions.* The Second Circuit has suggested that if the injunction alters the status quo, it will be treated as a "mandatory injunction," rather than a "prohibitory injunction," and granted only if the plaintiff makes a higher showing, namely either (1) a clear or substantial showing of entitlement to the relief requested, or (2) a showing that extreme or very serious damage will result from the denial of preliminary relief. *See Tom Doherty Assocs., Inc. v. Saban Entm't, Inc.*, 60 F.3d 27 (2d Cir. 1995).

> A preliminary injunction is usually prohibitory and seeks generally only to maintain the status quo pending a trial on the merits. [cit.] A prohibitory injunction is one that "forbids or restrains an act." *Black's Law Dictionary* 788 (7th ed. 1999). For example, in the typical trademark case a prohibitory injunction seeks to stop alleged infringement. A mandatory injunction, in contrast, "orders an affirmative act or mandates a specified course of conduct," [cit.], such as requiring a defendant to turn over phone numbers featuring a tradename or to assign a trademark," [cit.].

Louis Vuitton Malletier v. Dooney & Bourke, Inc., 454 F.3d 108, 114 (2d Cir. 2006). How would you classify an injunction ordering the defendant to take affirmative steps (such as labeling or adding disclaimers) that the court believes will dispel confusion? *See, e.g., Pebble Beach Co. v. Tour 18 I Ltd.*, 155 F.3d 526 (5th Cir. 1998) (ordering that defendant remove lighthouse from golf course, where its presence infringed the trade dress of plaintiff's golf course design). Corrective advertising is a remedial option often used in false advertising claims. To what extent, and in what circumstances, should a court impose such obligations? When is such an approach likely to be most effective? Most important? *See Rhone-Poulenc Rorer Pharm., Inc. v. Marion Merrell Dow, Inc.*, 93 F.3d 511 (8th Cir. 1996).

6. *Balancing equities.* If the defendant has a large inventory of goods bearing the infringing trademark, should the court allow the defendant to sell off that inventory before adopting a different trademark for its goods? What considerations might be relevant to such a condition? *See Attrezzi, LLC v. Maytag Corp.*, 436 F.3d 32 (1st Cir. 2006) (giving the defendant twelve months to sell off existing stock); *George Basch Co. v. Blue Coral, Inc.*, 968 F.2d 1532 (2d Cir. 1992) (permitting sell-off). Alternatively, some courts have ordered defendants to recall goods bearing infringing marks. *See Nikon Inc. v. Ikon Corp.*, 987 F.2d 91 (2d Cir. 1993).

7. *Injunctions without actual damage.* Injunctive relief may be granted based on a *likelihood* of confusion. It is not necessary for the plaintiff to show actual confusion, or actual damage. A plaintiff has a right to forestall damage, rather than wait for it to occur. However, how early in the defendant's manufacturing, marketing, and distribution process can a plaintiff obtain relief? What if the defendant has printed labels bearing the infringing mark but has not delivered the products bearing any such labels to its distributors? What if the defendant has not engaged in any marketing using the allegedly infringing mark? Are there any elements in the infringement cause of action that might determine the point at which an injunction is appropriate? *See Bertolli USA, Inc. v. Filippo Bertolli Fine Foods, Ltd.*, 662 F. Supp. 203 (S.D.N.Y. 1987) (allegedly infringing merchandise does not have to be available to the public); *Cognitest Corp. v. Riverside Publ'g Co.*, 36 U.S.P.Q.2d (BNA) 1363 (N.D. Ill. 1995).

8. *Scope of injunctions.* Injunctive relief allows a court equitably to fashion relief that accommodates the interests of both parties to the litigation. Thus, on occasion, a court may decline to issue an injunction absolutely prohibiting the defendant from using the trademark in dispute, but rather grant an order conditioning or limiting the type of use that the defendant can make of the mark. This occurs in particular where the defendant has a limited right to use the mark (for example, because the mark consists of the defendant's personal name, or because the defendant has rights within a remote geographical area) or where likely confusion can be dispelled by narrower remedial measures (such as the addition or display of a disclaimer). *See, e.g., E. & J. Gallo Winery v. Gallo Cattle Co.*, 12 U.S.P.Q.2d (BNA) 1657 (E.D. Cal. 1989), *aff'd*, 967 F.2d 1280 (9th Cir. 1992). In what additional circumstances might such a balancing of interests warrant the crafting of a limited injunction? *See King-Seeley Thermos Co. v. Aladdin Indus., Inc.*, 321 F.2d 577 (2d Cir. 1963), *later proceeding*, 418 F.2d 31 (2d Cir. 1969); *Forschner Grp., Inc. v. Arrow Trading Co.*, 124 F.3d 402 (2d Cir. 1997); *Abraham v. Alpha Chi Omega*, 708 F.3d 614 (5th Cir. 2013) (discussing products subject to injunction). Are there any sets of circumstances where you would expect a fully prohibitory injunction to issue without much thought being given to this more limited approach? In what circumstances might it be appropriate for a court, after a period of time, to consider modifying the terms of an injunction? *See King-Seeley Thermos Co. v. Aladdin Indus., Inc.*, 418 F.2d 31 (2d Cir. 1969), *later proceeding*, 320 F. Supp. 1156 (D. Conn. 1970) (modifying injunction). Should it matter whether the party seeking modification is requesting a reduction or expansion of the scope of the injunction?

9. *Effect of disclaimers.* In general, should courts conclude that disclaimers dispel any likelihood of confusion? Courts have often expressed skepticism, but have found disclaimers effective in some recent cases. *See, e.g., Ptak Bros. Jewelry Inc. v. Ptak*, 83 U.S.P.Q.2d (BNA) 1519, 1525 (S.D.N.Y. 2007) (defendants could use family surname along with disclaimer indicating that defendant was not affiliated with plaintiff). *Cf. Paul Frank Indus., Inc. v. Sunich*, 502 F. Supp. 2d 1094 (C.D. Cal. 2007) (defendant's proposed disclaimers to be included on clothing labels rejected as impractical and unlikely to be effective given the striking similarity between defendant's and plaintiff's marks).

10. *Geographic scope of injunctions.* A court with personal jurisdiction over a defendant can prohibit the defendant from conduct outside the territorial jurisdiction of the court. Thus, a court has the power to issue a nationwide injunction against infringing conduct. Are there circumstances where a court should decline to exercise that power fully in cases of trademark infringement, and instead enjoin activities in a more narrowly confined area? *See supra* Chapter 6. Are there circumstances where a court should consider an injunction that affects activity outside the United States? *See id.* If the defendant has infringed plaintiff's mark by using it as part of a website, but that website is hosted on a computer based in Italy (where the plaintiff has no trademark rights), what injunctive relief would be appropriate? *See Playboy Enters., Inc. v. Chuckleberry Publ'g, Inc.*, 939 F. Supp. 1032 (S.D.N.Y. 1996); *see also* World Intellectual Property Organization (WIPO) Joint Recommendation Concerning Provisions on the Protection of Marks, and Other Industrial Property Rights in Signs, on the Internet §15 (adopted September-October 2001) (discouraging "global injunctions" and suggesting that courts explore other remedies in trademark cases involving multinational Internet use); *Visible Sys. Corp. v. Unisys Corp.*, 551 F.3d 65 (1st Cir. 2008) (affirming district court's decision not to bar the defendant's use of the infringing mark on its country-specific websites based outside of the United States despite negligible overseas sales based simply on the possibility that a U.S. customer might access those sites from the United States because such an injunction would not have been "workable in the real world"). What should be the scope of an injunction where different regional circuits reach differing results on questions of liability? *Compare Georgia-Pacific Consumer Prods., LP v. Von Drehle Corp.*, 618 F.3d 441 (4th Cir. 2010) (vacating a grant of summary judgment to defendant competitor of paper towel manufacturer on trademark claims arising from supply of paper towels compatible with plaintiff's dispenser), *with Georgia-Pacific Consumer Prods., LP v. Myers Supply, Inc.*, 621 F.3d 771 (8th Cir. 2010) (affirming judgment for defendant in case brought by same plaintiff against towel distributor, as opposed to manufacturer). How should the principle of non-mutual offensive collateral estoppel work to resolve such questions?

Prior to the enactment of federal dilution legislation in 1995, dilution protection was available in most, but far from all, states. And, as we noted in Chapter 8, the federal dilution legislation leaves in place state statutes, some of which arguably are more generous to plaintiffs than the federal statute. Should this affect the geographic scope of injunctions where the plaintiff has prevailed on a dilution theory alone?

11. *The "safe distance" rule.* An injunction may prohibit the defendant from a range of uses, some of which might in themselves have been non-infringing. This creates a buffer between the defendant's use and the plaintiff's mark. What purposes does this buffer serve? *See Scandia Down Corp. v. Euroquilt, Inc.*, 772 F.2d 1423 (7th Cir. 1985). The Sixth Circuit has commented that "a competitive business, once convicted of unfair competition in a given particular, should thereafter be required to keep a safe distance away from the margin line — even if that requirement involves a handicap as compared with those who have not disqualified themselves." *Taubman Co. v. Webfeats*, 319 F.3d 770, 779 (6th Cir. 2003) (quoting *Broderick & Bascom Rope Co. v. Manoff*, 41 F.2d 353, 354 (6th Cir. 1930)).

Is this fair? The safe distance rule is frequently cited where the plaintiff files a motion for contempt for failure of the defendant to comply with the terms of the injunction. Why is such a rule particularly useful in the contempt context? *See Wolfard Glassblowing Co. v. Vanbragt*, 118 F.3d 1320 (9th Cir. 1997).

Should the safe distance rule affect the test for *liability* in a new infringement suit brought by a trademark owner alleging infringement by a defendant previously held to have infringed the plaintiff's mark? *See PRL USA Holdings, Inc. v. United States Polo Ass'n*, 520 F.3d 109, 118-19 (2d Cir. 2008); *cf. John Allan Co. v. Craig Allen Co.*, 540 F.3d 1133, 1142 (10th Cir. 2008) (stressing that the "safe distance rule" does not mandate that the court issue an injunction that eliminates "all possibilities of confusion" even though it permits a court in its discretion to grant such relief).

12. *Specificity of injunctions.* The *GoTo* court upheld the district court's injunction, although it did "not catalog the entire universe of possible uses of Disney's logo." What considerations should inform the level of detail with which a court must frame the terms of an injunction? *See* Fed. R. Civ. P. 65(d) (requiring specificity in injunctions). What are the dangers of a court simply enjoining a defendant from using a mark that is confusingly similar to plaintiff's? Conversely, what dangers flow from requiring a court specifically to list the acts from which the defendant is enjoined? *See Calvin Klein Cosmetics Corp. v. Parfums de Coeur, Ltd.*, 824 F.2d 665 (8th Cir. 1987) (requiring more specificity); *cf. Wynn Oil Co. v. Am. Way Serv. Corp.*, 943 F.2d 595 (6th Cir. 1991) (upholding generally worded injunction).

13. *Injunction requiring negative keyword activation.* In *Orion Bancorp, Inc. v. Orion Residential Finance, LLC*, No. 8:07-cv-1753-T-26, 2008 WL 816794 (M.D. Fla. Mar. 25, 2008), the plaintiff operated a banking service under the mark ORION BANCORP. It also owned the mark ORION BANK. The defendant used the term ORION in different ways as part of its real estate and financial services business. When defendant defaulted on the plaintiff's trademark infringement claim, the court entered injunctive relief largely in conventional terms, such as prohibiting the use of the plaintiff's marks or any confusingly similar term in advertising or promotional material. However, the court also instructed the plaintiff "when purchasing internet advertising using keywords, adwords or the like, [to] require the activation of the term 'Orion' as negative keywords or negative adwords in any internet advertising purchased or used." *Id.* at *3. If an advertiser purchases a "negative" adword, this ensures that its advertisement will *not* appear if the term assigned a negative status appears as part of the user's search. Thus, for example, in *Orion*, if the defendant purchased the keyword "Bank" as part of its Internet advertising strategy, the injunction requires it also to purchase "Orion" as a negative keyword, ensuring that its advertisements will not appear in response to a user search on "Orion Bank." Does the appropriateness of this sort of relief depend on whether the purchase of a keyword is a trademark use? If not, under what traditional remedial rule might this approach be justified?

14. *Laches.* The equitable defense of laches is available in Lanham Act claims. The test for laches is twofold: First, was the plaintiff's delay in bringing suit unreasonable? *See, e.g., Au-Tomotive Gold Inc. v. Volkswagen of Am., Inc.*, 603 F.3d 1133 (9th Cir. 2010) (three years' delay triggers presumption of laches, the three-year period being determined by borrowing from an analogous statute of limitations rule in the relevant state); *see also Abraham v. Alpha Chi Omega*, 708 F.3d 614, 622 (5th Cir. 2013) (phrasing in terms of "lack of excuse" and prejudice). Second, was the defendant prejudiced by the delay? In *Internet Specialties West, Inc. v. Milon-Digiorgio Enterprises, Inc.*, 559 F.3d 985 (9th Cir. 2009), the court held that the plaintiff had indeed delayed unreasonably in bringing suit, largely by virtue of the presumption of having done so that arose because the lawsuit was filed outside the California trademark statute of limitations. However, the majority also held that the defendant failed to show prejudice within the meaning of the second leg of the test. The defendant argued that it was prejudiced because it had built a valuable business around its trademark during the time that the plaintiff delayed in the exercise of its legal rights. The majority distinguished between a claim of prejudice based on "mere . . . expenditures in promoting the infringed name," and one based on an investment in its mark as the identity of the business in the minds of the public. Only the latter satisfies the prejudice test, and the majority found it was not present in the case before it.

> [The defendant in this case] did not spend the time in the interim developing brand recognition of its mark. [The vast majority of its] advertising took the form of "pay-per-click" advertisements, through which potential customers are funneled to [the defendant's] website based on their interest in a particular type of service (i.e., internet services in Southern California). Such advertising creates little to no brand awareness. Furthermore, [the defendant] typically did not even include the [mark at issue] in the pay-per-click advertisements. It is a simple premise that [the defendant] cannot create "public association" between [the mark] and the company if it does not even use the [mark] in its most prevalent form of advertising.

Id. at 992. Does the majority approach adopt too narrow a view of prejudice?

A laches defense may also be defeated by an assertion of "progressive encroachment." *See Oriental Fin. Grp., Inc. v. Cooperativa de Ahorro y Crédito Oriental*, 698 F.3d 9, 21 (1st Cir. 2012). What would be the consequence of not recognizing such a counter-argument?

15. *Declaratory judgment jurisdiction.* Suppose that parties *A* and *B* both claim that they are the first to use the mark SUREFOOT for various shoe and boot products. How might such disputes be resolved efficiently? One way involves administrative procedures, applicable if at least one of the parties has registered rights. For example, if *A* has a registration, *B* might petition to cancel the registration in an administrative proceeding at the Patent and Trademark Office. Another way involves litigation. *B* could, of course, wait to be sued for infringement and raise priority of use as a defense. But what if *A* sends a letter to *B*, making various veiled threats—arguably threats to sue *B* for trademark infringement? In order to clear the air, *B* files a lawsuit, asking for a declaratory judgment of no infringement. Suppose that a court concludes that the letter would not have put *B* in reasonable apprehension of an imminent suit for trademark infringement.

In some circuits, courts have in the past declined to exercise declaratory judgment under such circumstances. *See, e.g., Cardtoons, L.C. v. Major League Baseball Players Ass'n*, 95 F.3d 959 (10th Cir. 1996). What considerations might favor a more generous approach to the existence of jurisdiction? Are those considerations unique to trademark law? In a patent case, the Supreme Court rejected the Federal Circuit's rule that a showing of a reasonable apprehension of suit was a prerequisite for the exercise of declaratory judgment jurisdiction in a patent case. *See MedImmune, Inc. v. Genentech, Inc.*, 549 U.S. 118 (2007). In *Surefoot LC v. Sure Foot Corp.*, 531 F.3d 1236 (10th Cir. 2008), a Tenth Circuit panel applied *MedImmune* in a trademark case. In general, should courts presume that procedural rules developed in one area of intellectual property law should apply to other areas of intellectual property law? *See N. Am. Med. Corp. v. Axiom Worldwide, Inc.*, 522 F.3d 1211 (11th Cir. 2008), excerpted *supra; see also Green Edge Enters., LLC v. Rubber Mulch Etc., LLC*, 620 F.3d 1287 (Fed. Cir. 2010) (applying *MedImmune* to trademark counterclaims seeking declarations of non-infringement and invalidity).

Nike sued Already (doing business as "Yums") over trademarks relating to Nike's AIR FORCE 1 shoe. Yums filed counterclaims seeking a declaratory judgment that Nike's marks were invalid and one of its registrations should be cancelled. (Lanham Act §37 gives courts the power to order cancellation of a registration "[i]n any action involving a registered mark.") Subsequently, Nike covenanted not to sue Yums "based on the appearance of any of [Yums]'s current and/or previous footwear product designs, and any colorable imitations thereof, regardless of whether that footwear is produced, distributed, offered for sale, advertised, sold, or otherwise used in commerce before or after the Effective Date of this Covenant." Nike then voluntarily dismissed its claims and sought to have Yums' counterclaims dismissed on the ground that the court had been divested of jurisdiction. The district court dismissed the claims, invoking *MedImmune*. The Second Circuit affirmed, relying on *MedImmune* and also holding that Lanham Act §37 did not provide an independent basis for jurisdiction. *Nike, Inc. v. Already, LLC*, 663 F.3d 89 (2d Cir. 2011). How should the U.S. Supreme Court rule? *See* 133 S. Ct. 721 (2013).

16.   *Destruction of goods.* Courts may order the destruction of goods that bear infringing marks. This remedy is most often used with respect to counterfeit goods. *See Fendi S.A.S. Di Paola Fendi E Sorelle v. Cosmetic World, Ltd.*, 642 F. Supp. 1143 (S.D.N.Y. 1986). Lanham Act §45, in turn, defines a "counterfeit" as "a spurious mark which is identical with, or substantially indistinguishable from, a registered mark." It is thus a subset of trademark infringement. *See, e.g., Colgate-Palmolive Co. v. J.M.D. All-Star Import & Export Inc.*, 486 F. Supp. 2d 286 (S.D.N.Y. 2007) (COLDDATE for toothpaste not "substantially indistinguishable" from COLGATE for toothpaste, and hence not a counterfeit).

17.   *Ex parte seizures of counterfeit goods.* The Lanham Act specifically provides for courts to issue ex parte temporary restraining orders permitting seizure of counterfeit goods ("Anton Piller orders," as they are known internationally) because the nature of the alleged offenders is such that the normal civil remedies have tended to be ineffectual. *See* 15 U.S.C. §1116(d). In what ways might such orders be reconciled with the purpose of preliminary injunctive relief? It is possible, but rare, for such orders to be issued in cases of regular infringement. *See Pepe (U.K.) Ltd. v. Ocean View Factory Outlet Corp.*, 770 F. Supp. 754 (D.P.R. 1991).

18.   *Bonds.* Although the *GoTo* court declined to increase the bond that the plaintiff was obliged to deposit, substantial bonds are sometimes required. *See, e.g., Philip Morris Inc. v. Star Tobacco Corp.*, 879 F. Supp. 379 (S.D.N.Y. 1995) (bond of $5 million).

B.   Monetary Relief

As Professor McCarthy notes, "[t]here is a great deal of semantic confusion in the opinions dealing with the award of monetary recovery for trademark infringement and unfair competition." 5 J. THOMAS MCCARTHY, MCCARTHY ON TRADEMARKS AND UNFAIR COMPETITION §30:57 at 30-109 (4th ed. 2013). This confusion stems in part from different views among the judiciary regarding the underlying purpose of monetary relief in trademark cases. And it is not eased by the language of the Lanham Act addressing monetary recovery. That language often provides little guidance, and in some respects is simply hard to fathom.

LINDY PEN CO. v. BIC PEN CORP.

982 F.2d 1400 (9th Cir. 1993)

ROLL, District Judge [sitting by designation]:

This trademark infringement case brought by Lindy Pen Company, Inc. against Bic Pen Corporation returns to this court for the third time seeking review of the district court's damages order upon remand. For the reasons set forth below, we affirm the decision of the district court and deny Bic's cross-appeal.

INTRODUCTION

The origins of this case go back to the mid-1960s when Appellant Lindy Pen Company (Lindy) and Appellee Bic Pen Corporation (Bic) were competitors in the production and manufacture of ball point pens. Each marketed a fine-point tip for use by accountants and auditors. In 1965, before Lindy's trademark . . . registration issued, Bic used the mark "Auditor's" on its pen barrels. Lindy contacted Bic, making a claim to the mark, and Bic voluntarily agreed to stop using it. On September 20, 1966, United States Trademark Registration No. 815,488 was issued to Lindy for the word "Auditor's." . . .

Fourteen years later, Bic adopted the legend "Auditor's Fine Point" to describe a certain pen model. Prior to this use, Bic researched the term "Auditor's" and found that at least three other manufacturers employed a variation of the word "Auditor's" in their marketing materials. This investigation revealed that Lindy also used the term, but that Lindy exerted no proprietary interest over it in its advertising.

Lindy learned of Bic's renewed use of the mark and filed suit in 1980 alleging trademark infringement, unfair competition, breach of contract, and trademark dilution. The district court entered judgment in favor of Bic on all claims. The circuit court upheld the district court's ruling that Bic did not infringe in the major retail markets, but remanded the case to determine whether there was a likelihood of confusion in telephone order sales. *Lindy Pen Co., Inc. v. Bic Pen Corp.*, 725 F.2d 1240 (9th Cir. 1984), *cert. denied*, 469 U.S. 1188 (1985) (*Lindy I*). The court specifically found that "there is no evidence of actual confusion [and] that Bic adopted the designation 'Auditor's fine point' without intent to capitalize on Lindy's goodwill. . . ." *Id.* at 1246.

[In *Lindy II*, after remand to the district court, the circuit court] found that Lindy had established a likelihood of confusion in the telephone order market. . . . *Lindy Pen Co., Inc. v. Bic Pen Corp.*, 796 F.2d 254 (9th Cir. 1986) (*Lindy II*). In words which now comprise the nub of the current appeal, this court ordered that the case be remanded to district court "with instructions to enter an order enjoining Bic from using the word 'Auditor's' on or in connection with its pens. We additionally instruct the district court to order an accounting and to award damages and other relief as appropriate." *Id.*

The district court thereafter issued an injunction and permitted the parties to conduct discovery regarding damages and profits. The court ordered the parties to submit briefs addressing four specific points directed at the damages claim. After reviewing the parties' briefs and exhibits, the court held that an accounting of profits was inappropriate because Bic's infringement was innocent and accomplished without intent to capitalize on Lindy's trade name. The court also found that an award of damages was inappropriate because Lindy had failed to establish the amount of damages. The court granted Lindy the opportunity to resubmit written argument on damages, but found that Lindy once again failed to sustain its burden of proof.

The parties now argue, on appeal and cross-appeal, that the remand determination regarding damages is in error. A determination of damages is left to the sound discretion of the trial court. In the instant case, there has been no abuse of discretion; therefore, the judgment is affirmed.

INTERPRETATION OF LINDY II

The threshold question of this appeal is whether the language of *Lindy II* entitled Lindy to an accounting and monetary damages upon remand. Lindy maintains that the district court had no choice but to order an accounting pursuant to this court's mandate. . . .

We find that the district court established Lindy's damages upon remand in accordance with the mandate of *Lindy II*. We base this decision upon a thorough reading of the decision as a whole which quite clearly remanded the action for a "determination of damages." *Lindy II*, 796 F.2d at 255. We also draw support for this interpretation from case law that holds that a determination of damages in a trademark infringement action, including an accounting, is to be pursued in light of equitable considerations. *Maier Brewing Co. v. Fleischmann Distilling Corp.*, 390 F.2d 117, 120 (9th Cir.), *cert. denied*, 391 U.S. 966 (1968). "The equitable limitation upon the granting of monetary awards . . . would seem to make it clear that such a remedy should not be granted as a matter of right." *Id. See also Burger King Corp. v. Mason*, 855 F.2d 779, 780 (11th Cir. 1988). When fashioning a remedy in a given case, the court must rely "not merely on the legal conclusion of liability, but [must] also . . . consider the nature of the infringing actions, including the intent with which they were motivated and the actuality, if any, of their adverse effects upon the aggrieved party." *Bandag, Inc. v. Al Bolser's Tire Stores*, 750 F.2d 903, 918 (Fed. Cir. 1984) (applying Ninth Circuit law). *See also Highway Cruisers of California, Inc. v. Security Industries, Inc.*, 374 F.2d 875, 876 (9th Cir. 1967) ("One may get just enough relief to stop the evil. . . .").

The district court adhered to the spirit of *Lindy II* and the dictates of controlling precedent by proceeding with additional discovery and argument prior to ordering an accounting of Bic's profits. The district court ultimately determined that an accounting was not appropriate under the circumstances of this case and its decision will therefore be reviewed for an abuse of discretion. "There is an abuse of discretion when a judge's decision is based on an erroneous conclusion of law or when the record contains no evidence on which [s]he rationally could have based that decision." *Petition of Hill*, 775 F.2d 1037, 1040 (9th Cir. 1985).

ACCOUNTING OF PROFITS

Following the damages proceeding, the district court held that an accounting of profits was inappropriate because Bic's infringement was innocent and accomplished without intent to capitalize on Lindy's trade name. Section 35 of the Lanham Act, 15 U.S.C. §1117(a), governs the award of monetary remedies in trademark infringement cases and provides for an award of defendant's profits, any damages sustained by the plaintiff, and the costs of the action.

The Supreme Court has indicated that an accounting of profits follows as a matter of course after infringement is found by a competitor. *Hamilton-Brown Shoe Co. v. Wolf Bros. & Co.*, 240 U.S. 251, 259 (1916). Nonetheless, an accounting of profits is not automatic and must be granted in light of equitable considerations. *Champion Spark Plug Co. v. Sanders*, 331 U.S. 125, 131 (1947). Where trademark infringement is deliberate and willful, this court has found that a remedy no greater than an injunction "slights" the public. *Playboy Enterprises, Inc. v. Baccarat Clothing Co., Inc.*, 692 F.2d 1272, 1274 (9th Cir. 1982). This standard applies, however, only in those cases where the infringement is "willfully calculated to exploit the advantage of an established mark." *Id.* The intent of the infringer is relevant evidence on the issue of awarding profits and damages and the amount. *Maier Brewing Co.*, 390 F.2d at 123. When awarding profits, the court is cautioned that the "Plaintiff is not . . . entitled to a windfall." *Bandag, Inc.*, 750 F.2d at 918.

Lindy posits that Bic's actions require an accounting as a remedy for willful infringement.[3] The parties agree that as early as 1965, Bic had knowledge of Lindy's claim to trademark rights in the term "Auditor's" when Bic published a catalog advertising pens with

---

3. Intentional infringement is not at issue as the district court's initial conclusion that Bic's infringement was not intentional is law of the case and cannot be disturbed.

the mark stamped on their barrels. Bic voluntarily suspended use of the mark after Lindy informed Bic of its claim to the term. Fourteen years after this exchange, Bic began using the legend "Auditor's Fine Point" on its extra-fine point pens, the subject of the current litigation.

Willful infringement carries a connotation of deliberate intent to deceive. Courts generally apply forceful labels such as "deliberate," "false," "misleading," or "fraudulent" to conduct that meets this standard. [cit.] Cases outside this jurisdiction offer additional guidance. For instance, the Circuit for the District of Columbia equates willful infringement with bad faith. *Reader's Digest Association, Inc. v. Conservative Digest, Inc.*, 821 F.2d 800, 807 (D.C. Cir. 1987). Willfulness and bad faith "require a connection between a defendant's awareness of its competitors and its actions at those competitors' expense." *ALPO Petfoods, Inc. v. Ralston Purina Co.*, 913 F.2d 958, 966 (D.C. Cir. 1990) (court reversed trial court's finding that false advertising violation of Lanham Act was willful or in bad faith). The Sixth Circuit has stated that a knowing use in the belief that there is no confusion is not bad faith. *Nalpac, Ltd. v. Corning Glass Works*, 784 F.2d 752, 755 (6th Cir. 1986) (accounting of profits properly denied where there was no deliberate intent to cause confusion). *See also W.E. Bassett Co. v. Revlon, Inc.*, 435 F.2d 656, 662 (2d Cir. 1970) (affirming finding of willfulness based on evidence that defendant tried to buy out trademark holder prior to infringement). Indeed, this court has cautioned that an accounting is proper only where the defendant is "attempting to gain the value of an established name of another." *Maier Brewing Co.*, 390 F.2d at 123.

The present case simply does not involve willful infringement. Evidence taken at the damages proceeding shows that Lindy in general, and its Auditor's line in particular, was experiencing an overall business decline. The trial court also found that any knowledge that Bic may have had of Lindy's mark stemming from the 1965 interchange was conducted by outside counsel, thereby implying that Bic's knowledge of Lindy's interest was attenuated at best. *Lindy Pen*, 550 F. Supp. at 1059. The district court also determined that Lindy's mark was weak and that there was no evidence of actual confusion. *Id.* at 1058-60. Based on these facts, it was reasonable for the district court to conclude that Bic's actions were not "willfully calculated to exploit the advantage of an established mark," *Bandag, Inc.*, 750 F.2d at 921, and that Bic's conduct did not rise to the level of willfulness which would have mandated an award.[4]

This circuit has announced a deterrence policy in response to trademark infringement and will grant an accounting of profits in those cases where infringement yields financial rewards. *Playboy Enterprises, Inc. v. Baccarat Clothing Co., Inc.*, 692 F.2d 1272, 1274 (9th Cir. 1982) (plaintiff damaged through defendant's intentional use of counterfeit product labels). However, the policy considerations which clearly justified an award in *Playboy Enterprises* are not present in this case. Unlike the *Playboy Enterprises* plaintiff, Lindy's trademark was weak and Bic's infringement was unintentional. Moreover, Bic's major position in the pen industry makes it clear that it was not trading on Lindy's relatively obscure name. Accordingly, the policy considerations announced by *Playboy Enterprises* would be trivialized by insisting on an accounting in this case. *See ALPO Petfoods Inc.*, 913 F.2d at 969 ("deterrence is too weak and too easily invoked a justification for the severe and often cumbersome remedy of a profits award. . . ."). To award profits in this situation would

---

4. Even assuming that Bic could be termed a willful infringer, "[w]illful infringement may support an award of profits to the plaintiff, but does not require one." *Faberge, Inc. v. Saxony Products, Inc.*, 605 F.2d 426, 429 (9th Cir. 1979) (citing *Maier Brewing Co.*, 390 F.2d at 121).

amount to a punishment in violation of the Lanham Act, which clearly stipulates that a remedy "shall constitute compensation not a penalty." 15 U.S.C. §1117(a).

AWARD OF DAMAGES

15 U.S.C. §1117(a) further provides for an award, subject to equitable principles, of "any damages sustained by the plaintiff. . . ." A plaintiff must prove both the fact and the amount of damage. 2 J. Thomas McCarthy, Trademarks and Unfair Competition §30:27, at 511 (2d ed. 1984). Damages are typically measured by any direct injury which a plaintiff can prove, as well as any lost profits which the plaintiff would have earned but for the infringement. *Id.* at 509. Because proof of actual damage is often difficult, a court may award damages based on defendant's profits on the theory of unjust enrichment. *Id.* at 511. *See also Bandag, Inc.*, 750 F.2d at 918.

The district court gave Lindy the opportunity to prove its damages under both methods: actual damages in the form of its lost profits, or if that proved too difficult, through proof of Bic's unjust enrichment in the form of Bic's profits. The damages proceeding was conducted through written pleadings.[5] Based on the initial submissions, the judge held that although Lindy had established the fact of damage, it had not proven the amount of damage. However, the court directed further briefing subject to detailed instructions.[6]

After final briefing, the court concluded that Lindy had failed to show any actual damage because it did not put forth sufficient proof of its lost profits. To establish damages under the lost profits method, a plaintiff must make a "prima facie showing of reasonably forecast profits." 2 J.T. McCarthy, Trademarks and Unfair Competition §30:27, at 511 (2d ed. 1984). The court found Lindy's calculations to be irreparably flawed because Lindy did not isolate its own telephone order sales from total pen sales. Consequently, Lindy's calculations contained items in which no likelihood of confusion existed and therefore were inappropriately included. The district court reasoned that it had no rational basis upon which to estimate an award as to the infringing items and accordingly denied Lindy's request.

Trademark remedies are guided by tort law principles. *Id.* at 509 ("Plaintiff's damages should be measured by the tort standard under which the infringer-tortfeasor is liable for all injuries caused to plaintiff by the wrongful act. . . ."). As a general rule, damages which result from a tort must be established with reasonable certainty. Dan B. Dobbs, Remedies §3.3, at 151 (1973). The Supreme Court has held that "[d]amages are not rendered uncertain because they cannot be calculated with absolute exactness," yet a reasonable basis for computation must exist. *Eastman Kodak Co. v. Southern Photo Materials Co.*, 273 U.S. 359, 379 (1927). Many courts have denied a monetary award in infringement cases when damages are remote and speculative. *See generally Foxtrap, Inc. v. Foxtrap, Inc.*, 671 F.2d 636, 642 (D.C. Cir. 1982) ("any award based on plaintiff's damages requires some showing of

---

5. The court ordered the parties to file written position statements on the following issues: (1) The amount of telephone order sales of Bic pens. The parties should address the propriety and feasibility of a breakdown of sales based on orders requesting pens by manufacturer's name, model number and "AUDITOR'S." (2) Lindy's sales of its "AUDITOR'S" line before and during the period at issue. (3) Lindy's total attorneys' fees incurred in prosecuting this action and those attributable to the theory on which it has prevailed. The statement of attorneys' fees should include a brief description of the services rendered, the attorney who performed them, that attorney's applicable billing rate, the date rendered, and the time billed to the tenth of an hour. (4) Any equitable factors for the Court to consider under §1117(a).

6. The court found Lindy's initial submission to be defective because Lindy did not attempt to isolate the telephone order submarket of pens, its proposed pre-infringement period inappropriately excluded a period of loss and contained an explicable gap in the period, and because Lindy used different infringement periods depending on whether it was calculating lost sales or lost profits.

actual loss"); *Burndy Corp. v. Teledyne Industries, Inc.*, 584 F. Supp. 656, 664 (D.C. Conn.) ("no assessment of damages is authorized if it is not based on actually proven damages"), *aff'd*, 748 F.2d 767 (2d Cir. 1984); *Invicta Plastics (USA) Ltd. v. Mego Corp.*, 523 F. Supp. 619, 624 (S.D.N.Y. 1981) ("damages will not be awarded in the absence of credible evidence demonstrating injury to the plaintiff from defendant's sales"); *Vuitton et Fits, S.A. v. Crown Handbags*, 492 F. Supp. 1071, 1077 (S.D.N.Y. 1979) ("The discretionary award of either damages or profits assumes an evidentiary basis on which to rest such an award. Without such a basis there can be no recovery."), *aff'd mem.*, 622 F.2d 577 (2d Cir. 1980).

Lindy produced evidence of its total pen sales, as available,[7] for the designated time period. Although it divided its sales into total sales and specific sales of Auditor's, it failed to further subdivide its data into the category of telephone order sales. Lindy was in the best position to identify its own sales, but declined to provide the court with any evidence of its loss caused by Bic's wrong doing. Although Lindy offers excuses for this deficiency, its explanations do not negate the fact that Lindy never furnished the court any reasonable estimate of its own sales. It would have been error for the district court to select an arbitrary percentage of total sales to represent the more narrow submarket of telephone sales. The court was correct, therefore, in finding that Lindy failed to sustain its burden of proving reasonably forecast profits.

Lindy also sought an accounting of Bic's profits based on a theory of unjust enrichment. Lindy assesses as error the district court's requirement that Lindy separate Bic's telephone order sales from total sales of goods. Lindy maintains that this requirement had the effect of shifting the burden of proving infringing sales from the infringer to the trademark holder. However, an accounting is intended to award profits only on sales that are attributable to the infringing conduct. The plaintiff has only the burden of establishing the defendant's gross profits from the infringing activity with reasonable certainty. Once the plaintiff demonstrates gross profits, they are presumed to be the result of the infringing activity. *Mishawaka Rubber & Woolen Mfg. Co. v. S.S. Kresge Co.*, 316 U.S. 203, 206-07 (1942). The defendant thereafter bears the burden of showing which, if any, of its total sales are not attributable to the infringing activity, and, additionally, any permissible deductions for overhead. 15 U.S.C. 1117(a).

Lindy failed to come forward with any evidence of sales of the Bic "Auditor's Fine Point" in the infringing market. Lindy instead brought forth proof of Bic's total sales. Lindy averred to the court that a division of Bic's sales into the telephone submarket "is impossible from Bic's records since Bic never separated its pens according to telephone sales. . . ." To the contrary, Lindy had access through discovery to Bic's records from which a reasonable estimate could have been accomplished.[9]

We find that Lindy's appeal on the question of actual damages fails due to a lack of proof at the damages proceeding. The district court followed the directive of this court when it offered Lindy the opportunity to establish damages. Lindy was unable or unwilling to present competent evidence of its lost profits or Bic's unjust enrichment arising from the infringement. We affirm the trial court on this point.

---

7. Lindy admitted that it did not have records or complete records from which to calculate the lost sales for the entire period.

9. Bic offers in the alternative that its cost and deduction evidence shows that Bic made no profits on its "Auditor's Fine Point" pens. Because we find that Lindy failed to make a prima facie showing of Bic's unjust enrichment, we need not reach this argument.

AWARD OF TREBLE DAMAGES AND ATTORNEYS' FEES

In addition to challenging the district court's decision under 15 U.S.C. §§1117(a), Lindy attacks the court's refusal to award damages pursuant to the provisions of 15 U.S.C. §§1117(b).[10] Section 1117(b) mandates an award of treble damages and attorneys' fees in the case of an intentional infringement "unless the court finds extenuating circumstances." 15 U.S.C. §§1117(b). The district court specifically found and concluded that "[t]he record taken as a whole does not support a finding that the defendant's conduct or mark falls within the scope" of the subsection. The court ordered that the damages phase of the trial be conducted solely under the provisions of §§1117(a) which require a showing of exceptional circumstances as a precondition to an award of attorneys' fees.

Lindy doggedly maintains that the prerequisites of §§1117(b) are met and the court's contrary determination is clear error. Notwithstanding Lindy's protestations, the elements required to support an award are not present here. The Ninth Circuit expressly determined in both prior appeals that Bic's infringement was not intentional. [cit.] Bic's admission that it had knowledge of Lindy's claim to trademark rights in the term "Auditor's" in 1965 does not now refute the settled law of the case that Bic did not intentionally infringe upon Lindy's trademark. *See generally Chanel, Inc. v. Italian Activewear of Florida, Inc.*, 931 F.2d 1472 (11th Cir. 1991) (a plaintiff must prove an intent to infringe beyond that required to establish a violation of federal law or to obtain federal statutory remedies).

Even assuming this court were somehow to find that Bic demonstrated the requisite intent, an award under §§1117(b) is never automatic and may be limited by equitable considerations. The statute specifically states that the district court may refrain from imposing the mandatory sanctions of §§1117(b) upon a finding of extenuating circumstances. Although the district court did not make a finding on this point other than to note that the record as a whole did not justify an award under §§1117(b), extenuating circumstances may be inferred. Some of the factors the court found persuasive were that Bic was "unaware of Lindy's registered trademark" and that "[a]ll references to the earlier correspondence between Bic and Lindy were held by outside counsel and were unknown to in-house counsel." 550 F. Supp. at 1059. . . .

BIC PEN'S CROSS-APPEAL

Bic contends by way of cross-appeal that the district court's finding that Lindy had established the fact of damages was in error. . . . Bic does not challenge the court's finding of likelihood of confusion, but maintains that evidence of actual confusion is necessary in order for Lindy to recover damages. The district court found, and this court affirmed, that there has been no showing of actual confusion between the competing products.

Other jurisdictions have made a distinction between the elements necessary to establish a legal basis for liability from those required for proof of damages. *See Brunswick Corp. v. Spinit Reel Co.*, 832 F.2d 513, 525 (10th Cir. 1987). Although we recognize this distinction, "[n]evertheless, an inability to show actual damages does not alone preclude a recovery under section 1117." *Bandag, Inc.*, 750 F.2d at 919. In so holding, we express a distinct preference for those opinions permitting relief based on the totality of the circumstances. *See Burger King Corp.*, 855 F.2d at 781 (plaintiff need not demonstrate actual damage to obtain an award reflecting an infringer's profits); *PPX Enterprises, Inc. v. Audiofidelity Enterprises, Inc.*, 818 F.2d 266 (2d Cir. 1987) (consumer deception, as opposed to consumer confusion, is sufficient to state a claim for damages); *American Home Products Corp. v. Johnson & Johnson*, 577 F.2d 160, 165 (2d Cir. 1978) ("Deceptive advertising or merchandising statements may be judged in various ways. If a statement is actually false, relief can be granted on the court's own findings without reference to the reaction of the buyer or consumer of the product."). Here, Lindy's evidence that at least one wholesale distributor engaged in switching its product is credible proof of the fact of damage.

As its second point of appeal, Bic seeks a ruling specifying that injunctive relief is the sole appropriate remedy in this case. Although the use of an injunction as a sole remedy would not be an abuse of the district court's discretion, and indeed reflects the actual result in this case, it is not mandated as a matter of law. The district court is granted broad discretion within which to fashion a remedy for a violation of federal trademark law. *Maier Brewing Co.*, 390 F.2d at 121. An injunction alone may fully satisfy the equities of a case, particularly in the absence of a showing of wrongful intent. *Id.* at 124. Bic cites the court to numerous cases where an injunction alone has been held to be sufficient relief; however, none of these cases advance a rule requiring injunctive relief as a sole and exclusive remedy. We will refrain from formulating such a rule here.

CONCLUSION

The district court's order complies with the Ninth Circuit's previous mandate. We find that the district court did not abuse its discretion in denying Lindy an accounting of profits and award of damages. We also hold that the elements necessary for a grant of treble damages and attorneys' fees are not present in this case. . . . Bic's cross-appeal is denied in its entirety.

Accordingly, the decision of the district court is *affirmed* and Bic's cross-appeal is *denied*.

GEORGE BASCH CO. v. BLUE CORAL, INC.

968 F.2d 1532 (2d Cir. 1992)

WALKER, Circuit Judge:

Along with several issues regarding the particulars of injunctive relief, this case presents the general question of whether, in an action for trade dress infringement, a plaintiff may recover a defendant's profits without establishing that the defendant engaged in deliberately deceptive conduct. The district court concluded that bad faith was not a necessary predicate for an accounting. We disagree. Accordingly, we hold that in order to justify an award of profits, a plaintiff must establish that the defendant engaged in willful deception.

BACKGROUND

[The George Basch Co. ("Basch") sued Blue Coral, Inc., *inter alia*, under Section 43(a) of the Lanham Act for selling automotive products in packaging that was confusingly similar to the trade dress of its automotive products. A jury found for the plaintiff on its trade dress claim. The district court entered its judgment, which included $200,000 awarded by the jury as damages. The judgment also contained an injunction allowing Blue Coral to sell off its remaining inventory of infringing cans, but prohibiting any future use of the existing trade dress in the United States market. The district court also denied Basch's application for attorneys' fees. This appeal followed.]

DISCUSSION

I. BLUE CORAL'S APPEAL

[The court affirmed the district court's judgment that Basch sufficiently established the necessary elements to support the jury's finding of liability.]

B.   Grounds for Awarding Profits

We turn now to the issue of whether the district court correctly authorized an award of Blue Coral's profits. Section 35(a) of the Lanham Act generally provides that a successful plaintiff under the act shall be entitled, "subject to the principles of equity, to recover (1) defendant's profits, (2) any damages sustained by the plaintiff, and (3) costs of the action." 15 U.S.C. §1117(a). Clearly, the statute's invocation of equitable principles as guideposts in the assessment of monetary relief vests the district court with some degree of discretion in shaping that relief. *See id.*, (both damage and profit awards may be assessed "according to the circumstances of the case"). Nevertheless, that discretion must operate within legally defined parameters.

For example, it is well settled that in order for a Lanham Act plaintiff to receive an award of *damages* the plaintiff must prove either "'actual consumer confusion or deception resulting from the violation,'" *Getty Petroleum Corp. v. Island Transportation Corp.*, 878 F.2d 650, 655 (2d Cir. 1989) (quoting *PPX Enterprises, Inc. v. Audiofidelity Enterprises, Inc.*, 818 F.2d 266, 271 (2d Cir. 1987)), or that the defendant's actions were intentionally deceptive thus giving rise to a rebuttable presumption of consumer confusion. [cit.] Here, Basch failed to present any evidence regarding consumer confusion or intentional deception. Accordingly, prior to the jury's deliberation, the district court correctly decided that damages were not an available form of relief. Basch does not appeal from this ruling.

However, with respect to authorizing an award of Blue Coral's profits, the district judge concluded that §35(a) affords a wider degree of equitable latitude. In denying its j.n.o.v. motion, the district court rejected Blue Coral's position that, absent a finding of defendant's willfully deceptive conduct, a court may not award profits. . . . To the extent that the cases are ambiguous as to whether deceptive conduct is a necessary basis for an accounting, we take this opportunity to clarify the law.

The rule in this circuit has been that an accounting for profits is normally available "only if the 'defendant is unjustly enriched, if the plaintiff sustained damages from the infringement, or if the accounting is necessary to deter a willful infringer from doing so again.'" *Burndy Corp. v. Teledyne Industries, Inc.*, 748 F.2d 767, 772 (2d Cir. 1984) (quoting *W.E. Bassett Co. v. Revlon, Inc.*, 435 F.2d 656, 664 (2d Cir. 1970)). Courts have interpreted the rule to describe three categorically distinct rationales. *See e.g.*, *Cuisinarts, Inc. v. Robot-Coupe Intern. Corp.*, 580 F. Supp. 634, 637 (S.D.N.Y. 1984) ("These justifications are stated in the disjunctive. Any one will do.").

Thus, the fact that willfulness expressly defines the third rationale (deterrence) may suggest that the element of intentional misconduct is unnecessary in order to require an accounting based upon a theory of unjust enrichment or damages. However, the broad language contained in *Burndy Corp.* and *W.E. Bassett Co.* is in no way dispositive on this point. Indeed, a closer investigation into the law's historical development strongly supports our present conclusion that, under any theory, a finding of defendant's willful deceptiveness is a prerequisite for awarding profits.

Unjust Enrichment: The fact that an accounting may proceed on a theory of unjust enrichment is largely a result of legal institutional evolution. Prior to the fusion of law and equity under the Federal Rules of Civil Procedure, *see* Fed. R. Civ. P. 2, courts of law were the sole dispensary of damages, while the chancellor issued specific relief. However, in order to avoid piecemeal litigation, once a court of equity took jurisdiction over a case it would do complete justice—even if that entailed granting a monetary award. This resulted in the development of parallel remedial schemes.

Long ago, the Supreme Court explained the origin of profit awards in trademark infringement suits:

The infringer is required in equity to account for and yield up his gains to the true owner [of the mark], upon a principle analogous to that which charges a trustee with the profits acquired by the wrongful use of the property of the *cestui que trust*. Not that equity assumes jurisdiction upon the ground that a trust exists. . . . [T]he jurisdiction must be rested upon some other equitable ground—in ordinary cases, as in the present, the right to an injunction—but the court of equity, having acquired jurisdiction upon such a ground, retains it for the purpose of administering complete relief, rather than send the injured party to a court of law for his damages. And profits are then allowed as an equitable measure of compensation, on the theory of a trust *ex maleficio*.

Hamilton-Brown Shoe Co. v. Wolf Brothers & Co., 240 U.S. 251, 259 (1916).

Thus, a defendant who is liable in a trademark or trade dress infringement action may be deemed to hold its profits in constructive trust for the injured plaintiff. However, this results only "when the defendant's sales 'were attributable to its infringing use' of the plaintiff's" mark, *Burndy Corp.*, 748 F.2d at 772 (quoting *W.E. Bassett Co.*, 435 F.2d at 664), and when the infringing use was at the plaintiff's expense. *Id.* at 773. In other words, a defendant becomes accountable for its profits when the plaintiff can show that, were it not for defendant's infringement, the defendant's sales would otherwise have gone to the plaintiff. *Id.* at 772.

At bottom, this is simply another way of formulating the element of consumer confusion required to justify a damage award under the Lanham Act. As such, it follows that a profits award, premised upon a theory of unjust enrichment, requires a showing of actual consumer confusion—or at least proof of deceptive intent so as to raise the rebuttable presumption of consumer confusion. *See* [cit.]; *PPX Enterprises*, 818 F.2d at 273.

Moreover, the doctrine of constructive trust has traditionally been invoked to defeat those gains accrued by wrongdoers as a result of fraud. [cit.]

The rationale underlying the Supreme Court's holding in *Hamilton-Brown Shoe Co.* reflects this purpose. There, the Court upheld a profits award for trademark infringement where the "imitation of complainant's mark was fraudulent, [and] the profits included in the decree [were] confined to such as accrued to the defendant through its persistence in the unlawful simulation. . . ." 240 U.S. at 261. Thus, it would seem that for the defendant's enrichment to be "unjust" in terms of warranting an accounting, it must be the fruit of willful deception. [cit.]

Where Plaintiff Sustains Damages: Historically, an award of defendant's profits has also served as a rough proxy measure of plaintiff's damages. *Champion Plug Co. v. Sanders*, 331 U.S. 125, 131 (1947); *Mishawaka Mfg. Co. v. S.S. Kresge Co.*, 316 U.S. 203, 206 (1942); *Hamilton-Brown Shoe Co.*, 240 U.S. at 261-62; *see also, Restatement (Third) of Unfair Competition* §37 cmt. b (Tent. Draft No. 3, 1991) ("*Restatement*"). Due to the inherent difficulty in isolating the causation behind diverted sales and injured reputation, damages from trademark or trade dress infringement are often hard to establish. Recognizing this, the Supreme Court has stated that, "[i]nfringement and damage having been found, the Act requires the trademark owner to prove only the sales of articles bearing the infringing mark." *Mishawaka Mfg. Co.*, 316 U.S. at 206.

Under this rule, profits from defendant's proven sales are awarded to the plaintiff unless the defendant can show "that the infringement had no relationship" to those earnings. *Id.* This shifts the burden of proving economic injury off the innocent party, and places the hardship of disproving economic gain onto the infringer. Of course, this "does not stand for the proposition that an accounting will be ordered merely because there has been an infringement." *Champion Plug Co.*, 331 U.S. at 131. Rather, in order to award profits there must first be "a basis for finding damage." *Id.*; *Mishawaka Mfg. Co.*, 316 U.S. at 206. While a plaintiff who seeks the defendant's profits may be relieved of certain evidentiary requirements otherwise carried by those trying to prove damages, a plaintiff must nevertheless establish its general right to damages before defendant's profits are recoverable.

Thus, under the "damage" theory of profits, a plaintiff typically has been required to show consumer confusion resulting from the infringement. [cit.] Whether a plaintiff also had to show willfully deceptive conduct on the part of the defendant is not so clear. While some courts "rejected good faith as a defense to an accounting for profits," *Burger King Corp. v. Mason*, 855 F.2d 779, 781 (11th Cir. 1988) (citing *Wolfe v. National Lead Co.*, 272 F.2d 867, 871 (9th Cir. 1959), *cert. denied*, 362 U.S. 950 (1960)), others have concluded that a defendant's bad faith is the touchstone of accounting liability. *Cf. Champion Plug Co.*, 331 U.S. at 131 (accounting was unavailable where "there ha[d] been no showing of fraud or palming off"); *Carl Zeiss Stiftung v. Veb Carl Zeiss Jena*, 433 F.2d 686, 706-08 (2d Cir. 1970) (discussing monetary awards which are inclusive of both damages and profits).

Deterrence: Finally, we have held that a court may award a defendant's profits solely upon a finding that the defendant fraudulently used the plaintiff's mark. *See Monsanto Chemical Co. v. Perfect Fit Mfg. Co.*, 349 F.2d 389, 396 (2d Cir. 1965), *cert. denied*, 383 U.S. 942 (1966). The rationale underlying this holding is not compensatory in nature, but rather seeks to protect the public at large. By awarding the profits of a bad faith infringer to the rightful owner of a mark, we promote the secondary effect of deterring public fraud regarding the source and quality of consumer goods and services. *Id.*; *W.E. Bassett Co.*, 435 F.2d at 664.

. . .

Although these three theories address slightly different concerns, they do share common ground. In varying degrees, a finding of defendant's intentional deceptiveness has always been an important consideration in determining whether an accounting was an appropriate remedy. In view of this, the American Law Institute has recently concluded that a finding of willful infringement is the necessary catalyst for the disgorgement of ill-gotten profits. *See Restatement*, §37(1)(a) ("One . . . is liable for the net profits earned on profitable transactions resulting from [the infringement], if, but only if, the actor engaged in conduct with the intention of causing confusion or deception . . .").

We agree with the position set forth in §37 of the *Restatement* and therefore hold that, under §35(a) of the Lanham Act, a plaintiff must prove that an infringer acted with willful deception before the infringer's profits are recoverable by way of an accounting. Along with the *Restatement*'s drafters, we believe that this requirement is necessary to avoid the conceivably draconian impact that a profits remedy might have in some cases. While damages directly measure the plaintiff's loss, *defendant's* profits measure the defendant's gain. Thus, an accounting may overcompensate for a plaintiff's actual injury and create a windfall judgment at the defendant's expense. *See Restatement*, §37 at cmt. e. Of course, this is not to be confused with *plaintiff's* lost profits, which have been traditionally compensable as an element of plaintiff's damages.

So as to limit what may be an undue windfall to the plaintiff, and prevent the potentially inequitable treatment of an "innocent" or "good faith" infringer, most courts require proof of intentional misconduct before allowing a plaintiff to recover the defendant's profits. *Id.*; [cit.]. We underscore that in the absence of such a showing, a plaintiff is not foreclosed from receiving monetary relief. Upon proof of actual consumer confusion, a plaintiff may still obtain damages—which, in turn, may be inclusive of plaintiff's own lost profits. *See Getty Petroleum Corp.*, 878 F.2d at 655.

Neither *Burndy Corp.* [n]or *W.E. Bassett Co.* rejects the notion that willful deceptiveness is a necessary predicate for an award of defendant's profits. *See El Greco Leather Products Co.*, 726 F. Supp. at 29. To the contrary, both cases reflect the centrality of this factor. For example, defendant's profits were denied in *Burndy Corp.* because the plaintiff failed to establish that its own sales were diverted as a result of the infringement and that the defendant acted willfully. This finding precluded *both* unjust enrichment and deterrence as available grounds for relief. *See* 748 F.2d at 773. On the other hand, an accounting was ordered in *W.E. Bassett Co.* solely because the defendant had "deliberately and fraudulently infringed Bassett's mark." 435 F.2d at 664. Finally, to the extent that these cases suggest that a defendant's profits are recoverable whenever a plaintiff may obtain damages, we conclude that the language of *Burndy Corp.* and *W.E. Bassett Co.* was simply imprecise on this point, and we reject such a reading. *Cf. Carl Zeiss Stiftung*, 433 F.2d at 706-08.

Having stated that a finding of willful deceptiveness is necessary in order to warrant an accounting for profits, we note that it may not be sufficient. *See Springs Mills, Inc. v. Ultracashmere House, Ltd.*, 724 F.2d 352, 356 (2d Cir. 1983) ("an accounting may be appropriate whenever an infringer's conduct is willful"). While under certain circumstances, the egregiousness of the fraud may, of its own, justify an accounting, *see W.E. Bassett Co.*, 435 F.2d at 664, generally, there are other factors to be considered. Among these are such familiar concerns as: (1) the degree of certainty that the defendant benefited from the unlawful conduct; (2) availability and adequacy of other remedies; (3) the role of a particular defendant in effectuating the infringement; (4) plaintiff's laches; and (5) plaintiff's unclean hands. *See generally Restatement*, §37(2) at cmt. f & cases cited in the reporter's notes. The district court's discretion lies in assessing the relative importance of these factors and determining whether, on the whole, the equities weigh in favor of an accounting. As the Lanham Act dictates, every award is "subject to equitable principles" and should be determined "according to the circumstances of the case." 15 U.S.C. §1117.

In light of the foregoing legal analysis, the district court's error becomes apparent. To begin with, the district judge concluded that an accounting was warranted in order to prevent Blue Coral's unjust enrichment. However, as stated earlier, Basch produced no evidence to suggest that the infringement caused any sales diversion. As a result, there is nothing to suggest that Blue Coral's EVER BRITE sales were at Basch's expense. It follows that "an accounting based on unjust enrichment is precluded." *Burndy Corp.*, 748 F.2d at 773.

Secondly, even if Basch had shown loss of sales, it still would not have been entitled to an accounting for profits under a theory of unjust enrichment—or any other theory. The jury made no finding to the effect that Blue Coral was a bad faith infringer. Indeed, one reason why the judge refused to let the jury assess damages was the fact that Basch failed to present any evidence regarding bad faith infringement. Nevertheless, Basch argues that the court's jury instruction on liability—which suggested that the jury consider whether Blue Coral intended "to benefit" from Basch's NEVR-DULL trade dress—taken in conjunction with the special verdict finding that Blue Coral "intended to imitate Basch's NEVR-DULL trade dress," results in a constructive finding that Blue Coral engaged in intentionally deceptive conduct. We disagree.

There is an "essential distinction . . . between a deliberate attempt to deceive and a deliberate attempt to compete. Absent confusion, imitation of certain successful features in another's product is not unlawful and to that extent a 'free ride' is permitted." *Norwich Pharmacal Co. v. Sterling Drug, Inc.*, 271 F.2d 569, 572 (2d Cir. 1959) (citation omitted). Of course, even when a likelihood of confusion does arise, that does not inexorably lead to the conclusion that the defendant acted with deliberate deceit. Depending upon the circumstances, consumer confusion might as easily result from an innocent competitor who inadvertently crosses the line between a "free ride" and liability, as it could from a defendant's intentionally fraudulent conduct.

In this regard, we note that the jury specifically found that "the acts of [Blue Coral] in violation of Basch's rights [were not] done wantonly and maliciously and in reckless disregard of Basch's rights." This conclusion is buttressed by the fact this is not a case of a counterfeit trade dress from which a jury might infer that Blue Coral "intended to deceive the public concerning the origin of the goods." *WSM, Inc. v. Tennessee Sales Co.*, 709 F.2d

1084, 1087 (6th Cir. 1983). Thus, we find no merit in Basch's contention that the jury effectively concluded that Blue Coral acted with wrongful intent.

Accordingly, we reverse the district court's denial of Blue Coral's j.n.o.v. motion, insofar as it related to the availability of an accounting in this case, and we vacate the jury's profits award. . . .

. . .

CONCLUSION

Having reviewed the development of the relevant case law under §§43(a) and 35(a) of the Lanham Act, and having considered the underlying policies that the law seeks to implement, we conclude that before a defendant may be held to account for profits received in conjunction with a trade dress infringement, a plaintiff must first prove that the defendant acted with willful intent to deceive the public. Since the plaintiff in this case failed to establish this vital element, we partially reverse the district court's denial of Blue Coral's motion for judgment n.o.v., and vacate the jury award. We affirm the district court's grant of injunctive relief and denial of attorney fees.

Affirmed in part; reversed in part; and jury award vacated.

KEARSE, Circuit Judge, dissenting in part:

[Judge Kearse dissented from the reversal of the monetary award to Basch. In her view, jury findings of Blue Coral's intentional copying of a distinctive trade dress that had acquired secondary meaning, thereby creating a likelihood of consumer confusion, in order to benefit from the breach of Basch's rights, and culminating in the unfair receipt by Blue Coral of $200,000 in profits due to the infringement, sufficed to support the conclusion that Blue Coral was unjustly enriched. She would thus affirm the district court's judgment that an award of profits was justified.]

SYNERGISTIC INT'L, LLC v. KORMAN

470 F.3d 162 (4th Cir. 2006)

KING, Circuit Judge:

Defendant Jody Fine Korman appeals from the district court's award of summary judgment and damages to plaintiff Synergistic International, LLC, in this trademark dispute. [cit.] Korman makes two contentions of error: first, that the court erred in ruling that Korman's trademark, "THE WINDSHIELD DOCTOR," infringed Synergistic's trademark, "GLASS DOCTOR®"; and second, that the court erred in awarding more than $142,000 in damages to Synergistic. As explained below, we affirm on the liability ruling, but vacate the court's award of damages and remand.

. . .

B.

Korman . . . maintains that, even if she is liable under the Lanham Act, the district court erred in its award of damages to Synergistic under the Act. In this regard, she maintains that the court, in contravention of applicable law, failed to apply the appropriate equitable principles in making the damages award. Section 1117(a) of Title 15 provides, as to Lanham Act claims, that a successful plaintiff is entitled, "subject to the principles of equity, to recover (1) defendant's profits, (2) any damages sustained by the plaintiff, and (3) the costs of the action." Importantly, it also provides that such damages "shall constitute compensation and not a penalty." 15 U.S.C. §1117(a). In general, however, the Lanham

Act gives little guidance on the equitable principles to be applied by a court in making an award of damages.

[T]he district court awarded damages of more than $142,000 to Synergistic, but did not specify the equitable factors it had utilized in making such an award. The court summarily stated, however, that the equities had been balanced. [cit.] In making a damages award under the Lanham Act, the Third and the Fifth Circuits have identified six factors to guide the process. *See Banjo Buddies, Inc. v. Renosky*, 399 F.3d 168, 175 (3d Cir. 2005); *Quick Techs., Inc. v. Sage Group PLC*, 313 F.3d 338, 349 (5th Cir. 2002). As those courts have spelled out, these factors include:

> (1) whether the defendant had the intent to confuse or deceive, (2) whether sales have been diverted, (3) the adequacy of other remedies, (4) any unreasonable delay by the plaintiff in asserting his rights, (5) the public interest in making the misconduct unprofitable, and (6) whether it is a case of palming off.

Quick Techs., 313 F.3d at 349 (internal quotation marks omitted); *see also Banjo Buddies*, 399 F.3d at 175.

We agree with Korman that the district court abused its discretion in making the damages award, and that the foregoing factors are appropriate for consideration in connection with damages issues in Lanham Act litigation. And we will briefly discuss each of these factors. The first—whether the defendant had an intent to confuse or deceive—addresses whether there has been a willful infringement on the trademark rights of the plaintiff, or whether the defendant has acted in bad faith. [cit.] In her appeal, Korman contends that a willful infringement is an essential predicate for any damages award, and that, in its absence here, the court abused its discretion in making such an award. As Korman emphasizes, the court specifically found that she neither acted in "bad faith" nor was the use of her "THE WINDSHIELD DOCTOR" mark "malicious, fraudulent, willful or deceitful." [cit.] We agree, however, with the Third and Fifth Circuits that although willfulness is a proper and important factor in an assessment of whether to make a damages award, it is not an essential predicate thereto. [cit.] In other words, a lack of willfulness or bad faith should weigh against an award of damages being made, but does not necessarily preclude such an award.

The second factor identified above—whether sales have been diverted—involves the issue of whether the plaintiff lost sales as a result of the defendant's trademark infringement activities, and the extent to which the plaintiff had entered the market area where the infringement occurred. Korman contends that, in this dispute, the district court was not entitled to award damages because Synergistic had not conducted any business in the [defendant's] area [of business] during the period of infringement. *See Dawn Donut Co. v. Hart's Food Stores, Inc.*, 267 F.2d 358, 365 (2d Cir. 1959) (observing that court should not assess damages for trademark infringement if plaintiff has not entered defendant's market area). We are satisfied that, in this situation, Synergistic's non-entry into the Virginia Beach marketplace is an important factor with respect to the assessment of any damages. The fact that a plaintiff had not entered the relevant marketplace when the infringement was ongoing, in combination with the fact that no sales were diverted, should weigh against an award being made.

The third of the six factors—the adequacy of other remedies—addresses whether another remedy, such as an injunction, might more appropriately correct any injury the plaintiff suffered from the defendant's infringement activities. If an injunction is an adequate remedy, this factor should weigh against a damages award. [cit.] Here, the court granted injunctive relief against Korman, prohibiting her from using "THE WINDSHIELD DOCTOR" mark and the name "GLASS DOCTOR" with her windshield repair business. [cit.]

The fourth factor—unreasonable delay by the plaintiff in asserting its rights—addresses the temporal issue of whether the plaintiff waited too long, after the infringement activities began, before seeking court relief. A substantial delay between the commencement of infringement activities and the plaintiff seeking judicial relief should weigh against an award of damages. The fifth factor—the public interest in making the infringing misconduct unprofitable—addresses the balance that a court should strike between a plaintiff's right to be compensated for the defendant's trademark infringement activities, and the statutory right of the defendant to not be assessed a penalty.

The sixth and final factor—whether the situation involved a case of "palming off"—involves the issue of whether the defendant used its infringement of the plaintiff's mark to sell its products, misrepresenting to the public that the defendant's products were really those of the plaintiff. *See Tex. Pig Stands, Inc. v. Hard Rock Café Int'l, Inc.*, 951 F.2d 684, 695 (5th Cir. 1992) (concluding that "palming off" did not occur when there was no basis for inferring that profits received by defendant were attributable to infringement). We agree that, if "palming off" is shown, such activity should weigh in favor of a damages award.

In conclusion, a trial court, in assessing the issue of damages under [15] U.S.C. §1117(a), should weigh the equities of the dispute and exercise its discretion on whether an award is appropriate and, if so, the amount thereof. In each instance, of course, the court should explain its reasoning and the impact of the relevant factors. And, although each trademark dispute is fact specific, the foregoing factors, as well as others that may be relevant in the circumstances, should guide a court's consideration of the damages issue.

Having provided this guidance to the district court, we vacate its Opinion as to the Lanham Act damages award and remand for further proceedings. . . .

NOTES AND QUESTIONS

1. *The purpose of monetary awards.* In *Lindy Pen* and *George Basch*, the Ninth and Second Circuits identify several purposes underlying the different types of monetary recovery that the respective plaintiffs sought. What are those different purposes? To what extent do the purposes underlying the different types of award determine the conditions upon which those awards will be granted?

2. *Elements of claim for monetary relief.* According to the *Lindy Pen* court, under what conditions will the Ninth Circuit award (a) an accounting of defendant's profits, (b) an amount equal to damages sustained by plaintiff, and (c) treble damages and attorneys' fees? To what extent do the different types of award overlap? (If there is an overlap, the court must ensure that there is no double recovery. *See* Restatement (Third) of Unfair Competition §36, cmt. c (1995). How do these differ from the conditions imposed by the Second Circuit? To what extent are the conditions authoritatively established by the Lanham Act? To what extent are the limits on a plaintiff's ability to recover money substantive and to what extent are they procedural (relating to proof)?

3. *An actual damages prerequisite.* Although Lanham Act liability may be premised on proof of likelihood of confusion, some (but by no means all) courts have suggested that actual confusion is required for a party to obtain damages or an accounting of profits. Why might this be so? To what extent does the Ninth Circuit in *Lindy Pen* adhere to such a rule? *Cf. Gracie v. Gracie*, 217 F.3d 1060 (9th Cir. 2000) (a showing of actual confusion is not necessary for recovery of profits). This requirement is more frequently insisted upon in proving damages (rather than profits). What doctrinal devices might lessen the weight of this requirement? *See Boosey & Hawkes Music Publishers, Ltd. v. Walt Disney Co.*, 145 F.3d 481 (2d Cir. 1998); *cf. Conopco, Inc. v. May Dep't Stores Co.*, 46 F.3d 1556 (Fed. Cir. 1994).

4. *Notice prerequisite.* Section 29 limits monetary relief in actions for infringement of registered marks by providing that, unless the plaintiff attached the statutory notice of registration as required by the Lanham Act, no damages will be available for any period prior to the infringer's receiving actual notice of the registration. However, because similar requirements did not exist at common law, a successful plaintiff might (at least since a 1989 amendment of Section 35) be able to recover pre-notice damages by advancing a claim based on common law rights under Section 43(a). Notice requirements are also less strictly enforced in cases of counterfeiting.

5. *Measuring damages.* The Ninth Circuit in *Lindy Pen* notes that:

> Damages are typically measured by any direct injury which a plaintiff can prove, as well as any lost profits which the plaintiff would have earned but for the infringement. [cit.] Because proof of actual damage is often difficult, a court may award damages based on defendant's profits on the theory of unjust enrichment. [cit.]

What direct injury might a plaintiff prove in a trademark infringement case? Should the cost of corrective advertising be considered ahead of damage? *Cf. Big O Tire Dealers, Inc. v. Goodyear Tire & Rubber Co.*, 408 F. Supp. 1219 (D. Colo. 1976) (basing damages on the amount plaintiff would need in order to conduct corrective advertising); *Balance Dynamics Corp. v. Schmitt Indus., Inc.*, 204 F.3d 683 (6th Cir. 2000) (listing what plaintiff would need to show to obtain an award of damages based on "damage control" expenses, such as corrective advertising). *See generally* Paul J. Heald, *Money Damages and Corrective Advertising: An Economic Analysis*, 55 U. Chi. L. Rev. 629 (1988). Why might proof of damages sustained by a plaintiff be difficult? (Note that damages may not be speculative.) Might your answer to either of these questions depend on whether the plaintiff and defendant are competitors? *See Polo Fashions, Inc. v. Craftex, Inc.*, 816 F.2d 145 (4th Cir. 1987) (suggesting that where parties are competitors, the defendant's profits are a rough and best measure of plaintiff's damages); *see also* Restatement (Third) of Unfair Competition §37, cmt. b (1995); *Maier Brewing Co. v. Fleischmann Distilling Corp.*, 390 F.2d 117 (9th Cir. 1968) (explaining reasons to award profits even where the parties are not competitors). To what extent might it depend on the size of the plaintiff's business? To what extent (and in what circumstances) should the measure of damages reflect a (hypothetical) reasonable royalty? *See Sands, Taylor & Wood Co. v. Quaker Oats Co.*, 978 F.2d 947 (7th Cir. 1992). Does this measure of damages suffer from any deficiencies? *See Playboy Enters., Inc. v. Baccarat Clothing Co.*, 692 F.2d 1272 (9th Cir. 1982).

6. *Questions of proof.* In articulating what the plaintiff is required to prove to make a profits award possible, courts take into account the extent to which the item of information is available to the plaintiff and defendant. What other considerations should inform a court's allocation of the burden of proof on such matters? *See Wynn Oil Co. v. Am. Way Serv. Corp.*, 943 F.2d 595 (6th Cir. 1991); *see also* Lanham Act §35; Restatement (Third) of Unfair Competition §37, cmt. g (1995). A defendant is entitled to deduct from gross profits the costs it incurred in producing and distributing the infringing goods, but it must allocate costs that contributed to the production of both infringing and non-infringing goods.

7. *Calculating profits.* A prevailing plaintiff is not required to distinguish a defendant's infringing profits from those earned in non-infringing activities. *See WMS Gaming Inc. v. WPC Prods. Ltd.*, 542 F.3d 601 (7th Cir. 2008) (placing the burden of showing portions of income that are attributable to non-infringing activities on the defendant). Is the approach of the *Lindy Pen* court consistent with this rule?

8. *Rationales for the award of profits.* The award of the infringer's profits is not (in all courts) dependent on the ability to prove actual damages, as the Ninth Circuit notes. What rationales other than the existence of clear damages might support an award of profits? *See* Restatement (Third) of Unfair Competition §37, cmt. b (1995) (noting range of rationales). Why does the Ninth Circuit not find those rationales satisfied in *Lindy Pen*? To what extent does each of the rationales adopted for the award of profits overlap with the rationale for other monetary awards? Some courts, contrary to the view of the Ninth Circuit, adhere to the traditional view that profits should be awarded only where the parties are competitors (in terms of both geography and product similarity). *See, e.g., Aktiebolaget Electrolux v. Armatron Int'l, Inc.,* 999 F.2d 1 (1st Cir. 1993). Why might a court adopt such a view?

9. *State of mind: willfulness.* Trademark infringement, in modern times, is essentially a strict liability action. But the defendant's state of mind occasionally intrudes upon analysis of liability. When? It is raised even more frequently in the context of claims for monetary relief. But the different circuits take quite different approaches. In what circumstances does the *Lindy Pen* court reference state of mind? The Ninth Circuit has subsequently held that, while a willful intent is necessary to justify an award of profits under the unjust enrichment theory, such intent is not necessary where the claim for profits is based on the existence of actual damages. *See Adray v. Adry-Mart, Inc.,* 76 F.3d 984 (9th Cir. 1995).

The Second Circuit, in contrast, makes "willful, deceptive conduct" a prerequisite to any claim for profits. *See Banff, Ltd. v. Colberts, Inc.,* 996 F.2d 33 (2d Cir. 1993); *see also Romag Fasteners v. Fossil, Inc.,* 817 F.3d 782 (Fed. Cir. 2016) (requiring willful infringement for recovery of profits). Might this explain the Second Circuit's decision in *International Star Class Yacht Racing Ass'n v. Tommy Hilfiger, U.S.A., Inc.,* 80 F.3d 749 (2d Cir. 1996), in which the court found bad faith based on the performance of only a limited trademark search, the failure to follow legal advice to conduct broader search, and the failure to stop operations after being informed of plaintiff's mark? (Note that the Second Circuit has since held that failure to perform a search does not of itself prove bad faith, *see Streetwise Maps, Inc. v. Vandam Inc.,* 159 F.3d 739 (2d Cir. 1998), and in the *Hilfiger* case itself on remand, the district court found the evidence insufficient to support a claim of bad faith.) The D.C. Circuit, like the Second Circuit, requires proof of willfulness as a condition to the recovery of profits.

In the Third, Fourth, Fifth, Seventh, and Eleventh (and perhaps the First and Sixth) Circuits, willfulness is a factor but not a requirement. Despite the split, the Supreme Court has declined to consider whether willfulness is a prerequisite for an award of profits for violations of Section 43(a) of the Lanham Act. *See Contessa Premium Foods, Inc. v. Berdex Seafood, Inc.,* 123 Fed. Appx. 747 (9th Cir.), *cert. denied,* 546 U.S. 957 (2005). As a result, the debate continues at the circuit level, and the result hardly has been greater clarity. For example, in *Western Diversified Services, Inc. v. Hyundai Motor America, Inc.,* 427 F.3d 1269 (10th Cir. 2005), the Tenth Circuit held that an award of profits involves a two-step process: (1) a finding of willfulness or bad faith, and (2) a weighing of the equities. The Tenth Circuit also considered the existence of actual damages, which it stressed is not a prerequisite to an award of profits, as an "important factor in determining whether an award of profits is appropriate." That is, actual damages are part of the equitable analysis that the statute instructs courts to perform.

In determining whether willfulness should be a prerequisite to an award of profits in an action under Section 43(a), what weight should be given to the fact that a 1999 amendment to Section 35 of the Lanham Act makes damages available for a "willful violation under [S]ection 43(c)" of the Lanham Act, such that Section 35 now reads:

> When a violation of any right of the registrant of a mark registered in the Patent and Trademark Office, a violation under section 43(a) or (d) . . . , or a willful violation under section 43(c) . . . , shall have been established in any civil action arising under this Act, the plaintiff shall be entitled, subject to the provisions of sections 29 and 32 . . . , and subject to the principles of equity, to recover (1) defendant's profits, (2) any damages sustained by the plaintiff, and (3) the costs of the action.

See *Banjo Buddies, Inc. v. Renosky*, 399 F.3d 168, 174 (3d Cir. 2005); *Korman*, 470 F.3d at 175 n.13 (noting that the argument for a willfulness *requirement* was more persuasive prior to the amendment); *see also Nike, Inc. v. Top Brand Co.*, No.-00-Civ.-8179, 2005 WL 1654859 (S.D.N.Y. July 13, 2005) (suggesting that the 1999 amendment revised the Second Circuit rule); *Mastercard Int'l Inc. v. Nader 2000 Primary Comm., Inc.*, No. 00 Civ. 6068, 2004 WL 434404 (S.D.N.Y. Mar. 8, 2004) (adhering to pre-1999 Second Circuit requirement of willfulness). Since a reverse confusion case does not depend on an intent to trade on plaintiff's reputation, to what extent should this element be relevant in reverse confusion cases? *See Sands, Taylor & Wood Co. v. Quaker Oats Co.*, 978 F.2d 947 (7th Cir. 1992), *modified*, 44 F.3d 579 (7th Cir. 1995) (basing damages on reasonable royalty).

   10. *The standard for willfulness.* The *standard* for willfulness also remains somewhat unclear. In *Western Diversified Services, Inc.*, *supra*, the Tenth Circuit addressed the question for the first time. The court held that the willfulness necessary to support an award of profits "typically requires an intent to appropriate the goodwill of another's mark," which is the same standard that the court adopted for the willfulness component of an award of attorneys' fees (on which, see *infra*). The court formally adopted a higher standard for willfulness compared with other circuits, *see, e.g.*, *W.E. Bassett Co. v. Revlon, Inc.*, 435 F.2d 656, 662 (2d Cir. 1970) (describing willfulness as "an aura of indifference to [the] plaintiff's rights"); *ALPO Petfoods, Inc. v. Ralston Purina Co.*, 913 F.2d 958, 966 (D.C. Cir. 1990) (noting that willfulness and bad faith "require a connection between a defendant's awareness of its competitors and its actions at those competitors' expense"), because of the exceptional nature of the remedy. The Tenth Circuit explained that "we decline to adopt these standards as the general rule because 'intent' . . . requires something more than 'indifference' or a mere 'connection.' It is a conscious desire." However, the *Western Diversified* court stressed the equitable nature of the relief rather than offering a bright-line standard:

> Because an award of profits under the Lanham Act is grounded in equity, there may be other situations that constitute willful infringement even though the defendant does not intend to derive any benefit from the plaintiff's goodwill or reputation. For example, if the defendant deceives the plaintiff into thinking he has ceased infringing the trademark when in fact the illegal action continues, a finding of willfulness might be appropriate. Similarly, misrepresentation to the courts might constitute willful infringement.

   Moreover, the court was willing to extend the benefit of its presumption (developed in the context of liability determinations) that "the deliberate adoption of a similar mark may lead to an inference of an intent to pass off goods as those of another" to the remedial context. As a result, the clarity of the court's statement that a strict intent to appropriate the goodwill of another's mark is necessary to support an award of profits was obscured by the flexibilities that the court later introduced into its analysis.

   11. *Good faith infringement.* Somewhat corollary to the case law regarding *bad* faith, good faith is often said to defeat any claim for monetary relief. *Cf.* Restatement (Third) of Unfair Competition §36, cmt. j (1995) (noting that good faith is not an absolute defense to a claim for damages). But what is good faith? Is it simply the absence of bad faith? The absence of intent to trade on the goodwill of the plaintiff? To what extent should acting on the advice of counsel immunize the defendant from any or all monetary awards? *See Sands, Taylor & Wood Co. v. Quaker Oats Co.*, 978 F.2d 947 (7th Cir. 1992).

12.   *Judicial practice with respect to monetary claims.* In practice, monetary awards are far from automatic in trademark cases. This does not mean that monetary awards are never made. *See, e.g., Big O Tire Dealers, Inc. v. Goodyear Tire & Rubber Co.*, 408 F. Supp. 1219 (D. Colo. 1976), *modified*, 561 F.2d 1365 (10th Cir. 1977) (reducing jury award of $19.6 million to $4.7 million). To what extent does this reflect (or balance) the liberal attitude toward the grant of injunctive relief? What must a plaintiff demonstrate to obtain monetary relief that is not necessary for injunctive relief?

13.   *Treble damages.* The language of Section 35 regarding treble damages and upward adjustment of defendant's profits ("shall constitute compensation and not a penalty") is ambiguous. What might it mean? If no damages are proven, can this language of Section 35 be used to adjust damages upward? *See Caesars World, Inc. v. Venus Lounge, Inc.*, 520 F.2d 269 (3d Cir. 1975). In what circumstances might an adjustment of damages serve merely to compensate? (Consider to what extent monetary relief absent adjustment capacity *fails* to compensate.) Courts have largely based upward adjustments on the *mala fides* of the defendant, as the Ninth Circuit suggests in *Lindy Pen*. Does this comport with the statutory language? *Cf.* Senate-House Joint Explanatory Statement on Trademark Counterfeiting Legislation, 130 Cong. Rec. H12076, at 12083 (Oct. 10, 1984) (noting inapplicability of this language in counterfeiting cases). *See also La Quinta Corp. v. Heartland Props. LLC*, 603 F.3d 327 (6th Cir. 2010) (affirming award of treble damages).

NIGHTINGALE HOME HEALTHCARE, INC. v. ANODYNE THERAPY, LLC

626 F.3d 958 (7th Cir. 2010)

POSNER, Circuit Judge:

After Anodyne successfully defended against Nightingale's suit, [cit.], the district judge granted the defendant's request for an award of attorneys' fees in the amount of $72,747. The award was based on 15 U.S.C. §1117(a), which allows attorneys' fees to be awarded to prevailing parties in Lanham Act suits—but only in "exceptional cases," a term we shall try to clarify in this opinion because of the surprising lack of agreement among the federal courts of appeals concerning its meaning in the Act. [cit.] The judge had granted summary judgment in favor of Anodyne on Nightingale's Lanham Act claim early in the litigation. Nightingale, which had not appealed that ruling, contends that no award of attorneys' fees is justified, because the case is not "exceptional."

The Fourth, Sixth, Tenth, and D.C. Circuits apply different tests of exceptionality depending on whether it was the plaintiff or the defendant who prevailed. In the Fourth and D.C. Circuits a prevailing plaintiff is entitled to an award of attorneys' fees if the defendant's infringement (most cases under the Lanham Act charge trademark infringement) was willful or in bad faith (these terms being regarded as synonyms), while a prevailing defendant "can qualify for an award of attorney fees upon a showing of 'something less than bad faith' by the plaintiff," such as "economic coercion, groundless arguments, and failure to cite controlling law." *Retail Services Inc. v. Freebies Publishing*, 364 F.3d 535, 550 (4th Cir. 2004); *Reader's Digest Ass'n, Inc. v. Conservative Digest, Inc.*, 821 F.2d 800, 808-09 (D.C. Cir. 1987).

In the Tenth Circuit the prevailing plaintiff has to prove that the defendant acted in bad faith, while the prevailing defendant need only show "(1) . . . lack of any foundation [of the lawsuit], (2) the plaintiff's bad faith in bringing the suit, (3) the unusually vexatious and oppressive manner in which it is prosecuted, or (4) perhaps for other reasons as well." *National Ass'n of Professional Baseball Leagues, Inc. v. Very Minor Leagues, Inc.*, 223 F.3d 1143, 1147 (10th Cir. 2000). Given the fourth item in this list, the Tenth Circuit can hardly be said to have a test.

The Sixth Circuit asks in the case of a prevailing plaintiff whether the defendant's infringement of the plaintiff's trademark was "malicious, fraudulent, willful, or deliberate," and in the case of a prevailing defendant whether the plaintiff's suit was "oppressive." *Eagles, Ltd. v. American Eagle Foundation*, 356 F.3d 724, 728 (6th Cir. 2004). As factors indicating oppressiveness, *Eagles* quotes the Tenth Circuit's list but states in the alternative, quoting (see *id.* at 729) our opinion in *S Industries, Inc. v. Centra 2000, Inc.*, 249 F.3d 625, 627 (7th Cir. 2001), that "a suit is oppressive if it lacked merit, had elements of an abuse of process claim, and plaintiff's conduct unreasonably increased the cost of defending against the suit."

The Second, Fifth, and Eleventh Circuits require prevailing defendants, as well as prevailing plaintiffs, to prove that their opponent litigated in bad faith, or (when the defendant is the prevailing party) that the suit was a fraud. *Patsy's Brand, Inc. v. I.O.B. Realty, Inc.*, 317 F.3d 209, 221-22 (2d Cir. 2003); *Procter & Gamble Co. v. Amway Corp.*, 280 F.3d 519, 527-28 (5th Cir. 2002); *Lipscher v. LRP Publications, Inc.*, 266 F.3d 1305, 1320 (11th Cir. 2001); *Tire Kingdom, Inc. v. Morgan Tire & Auto, Inc.*, 253 F.3d 1332, 1335-36 (11th Cir. 2001) (per curiam). The Fifth Circuit adds that a court considering a prevailing defendant's application for an award of attorneys' fees should "consider the merits and substance of the civil action when examining the plaintiffs' good or bad faith." *Procter & Gamble Co. v. Amway Corp., supra*, 280 F.3d at 528.

The First, Third, Eighth, and Ninth Circuits, like the Second and the Eleventh, do not distinguish between prevailing plaintiffs and prevailing defendants; neither do they require a showing of bad faith. *Tamko Roofing Products, Inc. v. Ideal Roofing Co.*, 282 F.3d 23, 32 (1st Cir. 2002) ("willfulness short of bad faith or fraud will suffice when equitable considerations justify an award and the district court supportably finds the case exceptional"); *Securacomm Consulting, Inc. v. Securacom Inc.*, 224 F.3d 273, 280 (3d Cir. 2000) ("culpable conduct on the part of the losing party" is required but "comes in a variety of forms and may vary depending on the circumstances of a particular case"); *Stephen W. Boney, Inc. v. Boney Services, Inc.*, 127 F.3d 821, 827 (9th Cir. 1997) ("a finding that the losing party has acted in bad faith may provide evidence that the case is exceptional" but "other exceptional circumstances may [also] warrant a fee award"); *Hartman v. Hallmark Cards, Inc.*, 833 F.2d 117, 123 (8th Cir. 1987) ("bad faith is not a prerequisite" to an award). Yet a later Ninth Circuit decision interprets "exceptional" to mean "the defendant acted maliciously, fraudulently, deliberately, or willfully" (note the echo of the Sixth Circuit's *Eagles* decision) or the plaintiff's case was "groundless, unreasonable, vexatious, or pursued in bad faith." *Love v. Associated Newspapers, Ltd.*, 611 F.3d 601, 615 (9th Cir. 2010).

And where are we, the Seventh Circuit, in this jumble? In *Door Systems, Inc. v. Pro-Line Door Systems, Inc.*, 126 F.3d 1028, 1031 (7th Cir. 1997), we said that the test was whether the conduct of the party from which the payment of attorneys' fees was sought had been "oppressive," and that "whether the plaintiff's suit was oppressive" turned on whether the suit "was something that might be described not just as a losing suit but as a suit that had elements of an abuse of process, whether or not it had all the elements of the tort." But that, we said, "would not be the right question if the plaintiff had prevailed and was seeking the award of attorneys' fees. In such a case the focus would be on whether the defendant had lacked a solid justification for the defense or had put the plaintiff to an unreasonable expense in suing." *Id.* The quoted passage was actually discussing the award of attorneys' fees under the Illinois Consumer Fraud and Deceptive Business Practices Act.

But fees were also sought under the Lanham Act, and the opinion—seeking to make sense of one of the definitions of "exceptional" (namely, "malicious, fraudulent, deliberate, or willful") that is found, as we noted earlier, in the cases—suggests that the test is the same under both statutes: "oppressive," in the sense expounded in *Door Systems. Id.* at 1031-32.

In later cases we said that oppressive conduct by a plaintiff that might justify an award of reasonable attorneys' fees to the defendant would be conduct that "lacked merit, had elements of an abuse of process claim, and plaintiff's conduct in the litigation unreasonably increased the cost of defending against the suit," *S Industries, Inc. v. Centra 2000, Inc., supra,* 249 F.3d at 627; *see also Central Mfg., Inc. v. Brett,* 492 F.3d 876, 883-84 (7th Cir. 2007); that oppressive conduct by defendants included not only willful infringement of the plaintiff's trademark but also "vexatious litigation conduct," *TE-TA-MA Truth Foundation-Family of URI, Inc. v. World Church of the Creator,* 392 F.3d 248, 261-63 (7th Cir. 2004); and that a finding that a suit was oppressive could be "based solely on the weakness" of the plaintiff's claims, *S Industries, Inc. v. Centra 2000, Inc., supra,* 249 F.3d at 627, or the plaintiff's "vexatious litigation conduct." *TE-TA-MA Truth Foundation-Family of URI, Inc. v. World Church of the Creator, supra,* 392 F.3d at 263. So "vexatious litigation conduct" by the losing party can justify the award of attorneys' fees to the winner, regardless of which side engages in such conduct, as long as it's the losing side.

It is surprising to find *so* many different standards for awarding attorneys' fees in Lanham Act cases. The failure to converge may be an illustration of "circuit drift": the heavy caseloads and large accumulations of precedent in each circuit induce courts of appeals to rely on their own "circuit law," as if each circuit were a separate jurisdiction rather than all being part of a single national judiciary enforcing a uniform body of federal law. But whether the difference in standards generates actual differences in result is unclear because the opinions avoid commitment by using vague words and explicit escape clauses, with the Tenth Circuit's catchall ("perhaps for other reasons as well") taking the prize. To decide whether the standards differ more than semantically would require a close study of the facts of each case.

It may be helpful in the interest of clarity, simplicity, and uniformity to start with first principles, by asking why the Lanham Act makes an exception, albeit a narrow one (if "exceptional" is to be given proper force), to the "American" rule that forbids shifting the litigation expenses of the prevailing party to the loser.

The reason has been said to be that "the public interest in the integrity of marks as a measure of quality of products" is so great that it would be "unconscionable not to provide a complete remedy including attorney fees for acts which courts have characterized as malicious, fraudulent, deliberate, and willful," and the award of fees "would make a trademark owner's remedy complete in enforcing his mark against willful infringers, and would give defendants a remedy against unfounded suits." S. Rep. No. 1400, 93d Cong., 2d Sess. 5-6 (1974). In addition, the patent and copyright statutes authorize the award of attorneys' fees, *id.* at 5, and trademark law protects an analogous form of intellectual property.

A more practical concern is the potential for businesses to use Lanham Act litigation for strategic purposes—not to obtain a judgment or defeat a claim but to obtain a competitive advantage independent of the outcome of the case by piling litigation costs on a competitor. Almost all cases under the Act (this one, as we'll see, is a rare exception), whether they are suits for trademark infringement or for false advertising, 15 U.S.C. §§1114, 1125(a), are between competitors. The owner of a trademark might bring a Lanham Act suit against a new entrant into his market, alleging trademark infringement but really just hoping to drive out the entrant by imposing heavy litigation costs on him. *See, e.g., Peaceable Planet, Inc. v. Ty, Inc.,* 362 F.3d 986, 987 (7th Cir. 2004). "Trademark suits, like much other commercial litigation, often are characterized by firms' desire to heap costs on their rivals, imposing marketplace losses out of proportion to the legal merits." *Mead Johnson & Co. v. Abbott Laboratories*, 201 F.3d 883, 888 (7th Cir. 2000). "The increased ease of bringing suit in federal court and the greater availability of remedies may extend the competitive battlefield beyond the 'shelves of the supermarket' and into the halls of the courthouse. Commentators have already suggested that the availability of large damage awards will motivate firms to litigate false advertising suits aggressively in the hope of winning large damage awards and impairing the competitiveness of a business rival, particularly a new entrant." James B. Kobak Jr. & Mary K. Fleck, "Commercial Defamation Claim Added to Revised Lanham Act," *Nat'l L.J.*, Oct. 30, 1989, p. 33. Similarly, a large firm sued for trademark infringement by a small one might mount a scorched-earth defense to a meritorious claim in the hope of imposing prohibitive litigation costs on the plaintiff.

These, then, are the types of suit rightly adjudged "exceptional"; for in a battle of equals each contestant can bear his own litigation costs without impairing competition.

When the plaintiff is the oppressor, the concept of abuse of process provides a helpful characterization of his conduct. Unlike malicious prosecution, which involves filing a baseless suit to harass or intimidate an antagonist, abuse of process is the use of the litigation process for an improper purpose, whether or not the claim is colorable. "The gist of the abuse of process tort is said to be misuse of legal process primarily to accomplish a purpose for which it was not designed, usually to compel the victim to yield on some matter not involved in the suit. . . . If the plaintiff can show instigation of a suit for an improper purpose without probable cause and with a termination favorable to the now plaintiff, she has a malicious prosecution or a wrongful litigation claim, not a claim for abuse of process. . . . [T]he abuse of process claim permits the plaintiff to recover without showing the traditional want of probable cause for the original suit and without showing termination of that suit." 2 Dan B. Dobbs, *The Law of Torts* §438 (2001). Abuse of process is a prime example of litigating in bad faith.

The term "abuse of process" is not used to describe behavior by defendants. *Id*. It has been said that "while it is obvious that the torts of abuse of process and malicious prosecution are prevalent and damaging to both innocent defendants as well as the judicial process, it is not so obvious where the line is that separates an attorney's zealous advocacy from his tortious interference with the litigation processes." Leah J. Pollema, "Beyond the Bounds of Zealous Advocacy: The Prevalence of Abusive Litigation in Family Law and the Need for Tort Remedies," 75 *U. Mo.-Kan. City L. Rev.* 1107, 1117 (2007). But the need to draw that line is the same whether the plaintiff is attacking or the defendant is defending. If a defendant's trademark infringement or false advertising is blatant, his insistence on mounting a costly defense is the same misconduct as a plaintiff's bringing a case (frivolous or not) not in order to obtain a favorable judgment but instead to burden the defendant with costs likely to drive it out of the market. Predatory initiation of suit is mirrored in predatory resistance to valid claims.

We conclude that a case under the Lanham Act is "exceptional," in the sense of warranting an award of reasonable attorneys' fees to the winning party, if the losing party was the plaintiff and was guilty of abuse of process in suing, or if the losing party was the defendant and had no defense yet persisted in the trademark infringement or false advertising for which he was being sued, in order to impose costs on his opponent.

This approach captures the concerns that underlie the various tests and offers a pathway through the semantic jungle. It can account for most of the case outcomes in the various circuits with the exception of those that make it easier for prevailing defendants to obtain attorneys' fees than prevailing plaintiffs. The usual rule, notably in civil rights cases, is the reverse: a prevailing plaintiff is presumptively entitled to an award of attorneys' fees, while a prevailing defendant is entitled to such an award only if the plaintiff's suit was frivolous. [cit.] But those are cases in which the plaintiff is an individual and the defendant a corporation or other institution, implying an asymmetry of resources for litigation. Plaintiffs and defendants in Lanham Act cases usually are symmetrically situated: they are businesses. Of course they may be very different in size, but this is not a reason for a general rule favoring prevailing plaintiffs or prevailing defendants, for there is no correlation between the size of a party and which side of the litigation he's on. Big businesses sue big and small businesses for trademark infringement and false advertising, and small businesses sue big and small businesses for the same torts. Disparity in size will often be relevant in evaluating the legitimacy of the suit or defense, but it is as likely to favor the defendant as the plaintiff.

But there's a puzzle: cases such as *Chambers v. NASCO, Inc.*, 501 U.S. 32, 45-46 (1991), state that one of the inherent powers of a federal court is to "assess attorney's fees when a party has acted in bad faith, vexatiously, wantonly, or for oppressive reasons." [cit.] That sounds a lot like the abuse of process test that we think best describes the exceptional case that merits an award of attorneys' fees under the Lanham Act. But if we are right about our interpretation of "exceptional case," the question arises why Congress bothered to include a fee-shifting provision in the Act; for didn't the courts already have inherent power to award fees for abuse of process in Lanham Act cases?

Although the fee provision of the Lanham Act dates only from 1975, already by then the courts' inherent power to assess fees for abusive litigation was recognized. [cit.] But in *Fleischmann Distilling Corp. v. Maier Brewing Co.*, 386 U.S. 714, 719-20 (1967), decided eight years before the fee provision was added to the Lanham Act, the Supreme Court held that attorneys' fees could not be awarded in cases under the Act; it was that decision which prompted Congress to add the fee-shifting provision. *Fleischmann* rejected the proposition that courts could award fees in cases under the Act without explicit statutory authorization. "The recognized exceptions to the general rule [of no fee shifting] were not . . . developed in the context of statutory causes of action for which the legislature had prescribed intricate remedies. . . . [I]n the Lanham Act, Congress meticulously detailed the remedies available to a plaintiff who proves that his valid trademark has been infringed. It provided not only for injunctive relief, but also for compensatory recovery measured by the profits that accrued to the defendant by virtue of his infringement, the costs of the action, and damages which may be trebled in appropriate circumstances. . . . When a cause of action has been created by a statute which expressly provides the remedies for vindication of the cause, other remedies should not readily be implied." *Id.* This reasoning is consistent with interpreting the Lanham Act's "exceptional case" provision as having the same substantive content as the inherent power held inapplicable to Lanham Act cases. The puzzle is solved.

A procedural issue remains to be considered. Abuse of process is the name of a tort. A tort is proved in a tort suit. But a proceeding for an award of attorneys' fees is not a suit; it is a tail dangling from a suit. We don't want the tail to wag the dog, and this means that an elaborate inquiry into the state of mind of the party from whom reimbursement of attorneys' fees is sought should be avoided. It should be enough to justify the award if the party seeking it can show that his opponent's claim or defense was objectively unreasonable—was a claim or defense that a rational litigant would pursue only because it would impose disproportionate costs on his opponent—in other words only because it was extortionate in character if not necessarily in provable intention. That should be enough to make a case "exceptional."

In this case, however, there is more. Nightingale, a provider of home healthcare services, had bought several infrared lamps from Anodyne that were designed to relieve pain and improve circulation, paying $6,000 for each lamp. Its Lanham Act claim was that Anodyne's sales representative had falsely represented that the lamp had been approved by the Food and Drug Administration for treatment of peripheral neuropathy. The device *was* FDA-approved and *was* intended for the treatment of peripheral neuropathy, and though the FDA had not approved it *for that purpose* this did not preclude a physician or other healthcare provider, such as Nightingale, from prescribing the device to patients as a treatment for that condition. The decision to prescribe such "off-label usage," as it is called, is deemed a professional judgment for the healthcare provider to make. [cit.]

Nightingale told its patients that Anodyne's device was intended for treating peripheral neuropathy, but as far as appears did not tell them that it had been approved by the FDA for the treatment of that condition—a representation that could have gotten Nightingale into trouble with the agency. And when it replaced Anodyne's lamps with the virtually identical lamps of another company (apparently for reasons of price, unrelated to the scope of the FDA's approval), it advertised them just as it had advertised Anodyne's lamps—as devices for the treatment of peripheral neuropathy.

Not only had the Lanham Act claim no possible merit (which would not by itself demonstrate an abuse of process), but the district judge found that Nightingale had made the claim in an attempt to coerce a price reduction from Anodyne. Nightingale would have been content to continue buying Anodyne's lamps, as indicated by its purchasing lamps that were subject to the same limited FDA approval and advertising them the same way. The fact that the FDA had not approved Anodyne's lamps for treatment of peripheral neuropathy was thus of no consequence, for neither had it approved for that purpose the lamps that Nightingale bought to replace Anodyne's. To bring a frivolous claim in order to obtain an advantage unrelated to obtaining a favorable judgment is to commit an abuse of process.

Nightingale continues its frivolous litigation tactics in this court by arguing that Anodyne has "unclean hands" because it failed to turn over certain documents during discovery. It is apparent that the documents are not within the scope of Nightingale's discovery demand once omitted matter indicated by an ellipsis in Nightingale's quotation from the demand is restored.

Nightingale argues that even if Anodyne is entitled to reimbursement for *some* of the attorneys' fees that it incurred, the district court's award is excessive because it includes fees for defending against claims . . . that were based on state law rather than the Lanham Act. But Anodyne showed that the work that its lawyers had performed in defending against the Lanham Act claim could not be separated from their work in defending against the other claims, and Nightingale presented no rebuttal.

We not only affirm the judgment of the district court but also grant Anodyne's motion for fees and costs pursuant to Rule 38 of the appellate rules. . . .

NOTES AND QUESTIONS

1. *Attorneys' fees.* Since 1975, the Lanham Act has expressly permitted the award of attorneys' fees to the prevailing party in a case brought under the Act. *See* Section 35. These awards are far from automatic. Like many of the other "exceptional" remedies available under the Lanham Act, these awards are seen in cases of intentional infringement and counterfeiting; normally bad faith is present. The statute refers to "the prevailing party," but the language of the provision appears most directly to envisage an award to a plaintiff. What should be the circumstances in which a successful defendant obtains such an award? Should the same standard apply to plaintiffs and defendants? *Compare Conopco, Inc. v. Campbell Soup Co.*, 95 F.3d 187 (2d Cir. 1996) (same standard of bad faith applied to plaintiffs and

defendants), *with Scotch Whisky Ass'n v. Majestic Distilling Co.*, 958 F.2d 594 (4th Cir. 1992) (suggesting that standards should be different), *and Door Sys., Inc. v. Pro-Line Door Sys., Inc.*, 126 F.3d 1028 (7th Cir. 1997). *See also Banjo Buddies, Inc. v. Renosky*, 399 F.3d 168 (3d Cir. 2005) (holding that a finding of willful infringement is not a prerequisite to an award of attorneys' fees, which can be instead be awarded for the defendant's abusive litigation tactics).

   2.   *The effect of* Octane Fitness. In *Octane Fitness, LLC v. Icon Health & Fitness, Inc.*, 134 S. Ct. 1749 (2014), the Supreme Court ruled that under the attorneys' fees provision in the patent statute, 35 U.S.C. §285, "an 'exceptional' case is simply one that stands out from others with respect to the substantive strength of a party's litigating position (considering both the governing law and the facts of the case) or the unreasonable manner in which the case was litigated." *Id.* at 1756. This standard eliminates the need to show that a party acted in subjective bad faith in addition to bringing an objectively baseless claim. *Id.* The *Octane* Court also had noted that the Lanham Act contained an identical exceptional case provision. A number of circuits have now concluded that the *Octane* Court was sending a "clear message" that its standard for finding a patent case exceptional should also apply to trademark cases. *See Fair Wind Sailing, Inc. v. Dempster*, 764 F.3d 303 (3d Cir. 2014); *see also Baker v. DeShong*, 821 F.3d 620 (5th Cir. 2016) (incorporating lessons from *Octane*); *SunEarth, Inc. v. Sun Earth Solar Power Co., Ltd.*, 839 F.3d 1179 (9th Cir. 2016) (en banc) (district courts analyzing request for attorneys' fees should "examine 'totality of the circumstances' to determine if case was exceptional, exercising equitable discretion in light of the nonexclusive factors, and using a preponderance of the evidence standard"); *cf. Merck Eprova AG v. Gnosis S.p.A.*, 760 F.3d 247, 265-66 (2d Cir. 2014); *Burford v. Accounting Practice Sales, Inc.*, 786 F.3d 582, 588 (7th Cir. 2015). In *SunEarth, Inc*, the Ninth Circuit overruled *Lindy Pen* on the approach to attorneys' fees to the extent that it was inconsistent with *Octane*. In *Romag Fasteners, Inc. v. Fossil, Inc.*, the Federal Circuit vacated a denial of attorneys' fees and suggested that the "Second Circuit would hold that, in light of *Octane*, the Lanham Act should have the same standard for recovering attorney's fees as the Patent Act." *See Romag Fasteners, Inc. v. Fossil, Inc.*, 866 F.3d 1330 (Fed. Cir. 2017); *see id.* at 1335 ("Since *Octane* was decided, the Third, Fourth, Fifth, Sixth, and Ninth Circuits have all held that the *Octane* Court was sending a clear message that it was defining 'exceptional' not just for the fee provision in the Patent Act, but for the fee provision in the Lanham Act as well.").

   3.   *Punitive damages.* To what extent are any of the awards of damages under the Lanham Act punitive? *See* Restatement (Third) of Unfair Competition §36, cmt. n (1995) (noting that punitive damages are not available under the Lanham Act). The U.S. Supreme Court has held that the U.S. Constitution imposes Due Process limits on what can be awarded as punitive damages. These limits constrain courts awarding punitive damages under state trademark and unfair competition law. *See Cooper Indus., Inc. v. Leatherman Tool Grp., Inc.*, 532 U.S. 424 (2001) (requiring appellate court to review award de novo). Even if punitive damages under state trademark and unfair competition law do not violate the Due Process Clause, to what extent are they preempted by the Lanham Act? The Court of Appeals for the Seventh Circuit has addressed this question:

> The jury found Novelty liable for trademark infringement because Novelty used the words "Pull My Finger" to sell its farting Santa dolls, and this use infringed Novelty's mark for those words as related to plush dolls. The jury found that action to be willful, justifying the award of $50,000 in punitive damages under Illinois common law. On appeal, Novelty contends that the Lanham Act preempts the state law provision permitting punitive damages, although it admits that such a holding would be "an extension of the law."
>   In 1992, this court in *Zazú Designs v. L'Oréal, S.A.*, 979 F.2d 499 (7th Cir. 1992), expressed concern about the award of punitive damages in a trademark suit [because] "the

Lanham Act, although providing for the trebling of compensatory damages, forbids other penalties." *Id.* at 507 (internal citations omitted). In *Zelinski v. Columbia 300, Inc.*, 335 F.3d 633, 641 (7th Cir. 2003), we assumed that punitive damages were available under Illinois law but found that the defendant there had not acted willfully so as to merit them. . . .

Federal law preempts state law in three situations: (1) when the federal statute explicitly provides for preemption; (2) when Congress intended to occupy the field completely; and (3) "where state law stands as an obstacle to the accomplishment and execution of the full purposes and objectives of Congress." [cit.] [The court quoted Section 35(a) of the Lanham Act and emphasized the language to the effect that "[s]*uch sum in either of the above circumstances shall constitute compensation and not a penalty.*"] One could imagine characterizing the punitive damages permitted by state law as a means of reaching a "just sum," but we are not willing to strain the language this far. In reality punitive damages are intended to be a penalty. Thus federal law permits compensation, or a just sum, and not a penalty such as punitive damages. But it also does not expressly forbid punitive damages in a way that would preempt the state law remedy, and it is not clear from this passage that punitive damages would stand "as an obstacle to the accomplishment and execution of the full purposes and objectives of Congress." Indeed, punitive damages might be another useful tool in reaching those objectives. *Compare California v. ARC America Corp.*, 490 U.S. 93, 105 (1989) (holding that state antitrust suits on behalf of indirect purchasers are not preempted despite greatly increased exposure to damages, and commenting that "[o]rdinarily, state causes of action are not pre-empted solely because they impose liability over and above that authorized by federal law").

. . .

The First Circuit recently analyzed preemption of state law remedies by the Lanham Act in *Attrezzi, LLC v. Maytag Corp.*, 436 F.3d 32 (1st Cir. 2006). In that case, the remedies at issue were attorneys' fees and double damages. Under the Lanham Act, attorneys' fees are awarded only in "exceptional cases" and enhanced damages are awarded "subject to principles of equity." 15 U.S.C. §1117(a). In contrast, New Hampshire law awards attorneys' fees automatically and "offers enhanced damages automatically upon a showing that the violation was willful or knowing." [cit.] The First Circuit described the question as "whether New Hampshire's laxer standard for an award of attorneys' fees or its mandatory award of enhanced damages undermines the policy of the federal statute." [cit.] The court acknowledged that the state law "does create a stronger incentive for plaintiffs to bring unfair competition suits against trademark infringers," and that Congress intentionally used a "less favorable incentive structure for federal suits." [cit.] Nonetheless, the court pointed out, "Congress did not prohibit state unfair competition statutes that might have *substantive* terms somewhat more favorable to plaintiffs than the Lanham Act." [cit.] In the case before it, New Hampshire's law was substantively the same as the federal law, but the remedial structure was more generous. The court was unpersuaded that Congress meant to permit the former and forbid the latter: "to complain in this case about the modest deviation in remedial benefits favorable to plaintiffs is to swallow the camel but strain at the gnat." [cit.] Contrasting the Lanham Act, which "primarily provides a federal forum for what is in substance a traditional common-law claim," with other more complete federal regulatory regimes, it concluded that the state law remedies survive. [cit.]

Punitive damages are not the same as attorneys' fees, but we find the logic reflected in *Attrezzi* equally applicable here. Even the portion of the Lanham Act indicating that the compensation under federal law shall not constitute a "penalty" does not, either expressly or by necessary implication, mean that state laws permitting punitive damages under defined conditions are preempted. We agree with the First Circuit that, to the extent that state substantive law survives and is coterminous with federal law in this area, state law remedies should survive as well. In the area of trademark law, preemption is the exception rather than the rule. For example, when Congress amended the federal trademark laws to deal with cybersquatting, it left the state law regimes (including damages rules) in place. *See Sporty's Farm L.L.C. v. Sportsman's Market, Inc.*, 202 F.3d 489, 500-01 (2d Cir. 2000) (citing a legislative report indicating that the law was not designed to preempt state law remedies). In light of the fact that the Lanham Act has not been interpreted as a statute with broad preemptive reach, we conclude that Congress would have acted more clearly if it had intended to displace state punitive damage remedies. . . .

JCW Invs., Inc. v. Novelty, Inc., 482 F.3d 910, 917-19 (7th Cir. 2007). Are you persuaded by the court's reasoning?

4.   *Compulsory licenses under trademark law.* Copyright law contains several statutorily created compulsory licenses, and the U.S. Supreme Court has in recent years appeared to endorse judicially developed compulsory licenses as relief in cases of copyright infringement where the issue of infringement was close. Compulsory licenses are not an appropriate remedy in trademark cases; indeed, they are prohibited by Article 21 of the TRIPS Agreement. Why is the compulsory license disfavored as a remedy in trademark cases?

5.   *Statutory damages.* The ACPA, enacted in 1999, made statutory damages available in cybersquatting cases. *See supra* Chapter 8. The plaintiff may elect to pursue statutory rather than actual damages at any time before final judgment is rendered by the trial court. What is special about such claims that makes statutory damages appropriate? In *Newport News Holdings Corp. v. Virtual City Vision, Inc.*, 650 F.3d 423 (4th Cir. 2011), the Court of Appeals for the Fourth Circuit indicated that, in determining whether an award of statutory damages under the ACPA was excessive, it would be guided in part by considerations developed by courts applying similar provisions under the Copyright Act.

To what extent does the Seventh Amendment confer a right to jury trial on the question of statutory damages? *See GoPets Ltd. v. Hise*, 657 F.3d 1024, 1034 (9th Cir. 2011).

6.   *State immunity.* In *Board of Regents of the University of Wisconsin System v. Phoenix Software International, Inc.*, 565 F. Supp. 2d 1007 (W.D. Wis. 2008), the district court held that the Trademark Remedy Clarification Act, which allows states to be sued for trademark infringement, is unconstitutional. 15 U.S.C. §1122(b) provides:

> Any State, instrumentality of a State or any officer or employee of a State or instrumentality of a State acting in his or her official capacity, shall not be immune, under the eleventh amendment of the Constitution of the United States or under any other doctrine of sovereign immunity, from suit in Federal court by any person, including any governmental or nongovernmental entity for any violation under this chapter.

According to the court, Congress did not have authority to abrogate state immunity under the Eleventh Amendment. Congress can abrogate immunity if the abrogation is congruent and proportional with the injury (e.g., deprivation of trademark rights) that Congress seeks to remedy. But the court found that the legislation failed to meet that standard, in part because of a scant legislative record: There was little evidence of trademark infringement by States, and no consideration of whether other remedies were available to address that dilemma short of full liability under federal law. What other remedies might have been available to redress the problem?

C.   COUNTERFEITING

As trademark counterfeiting has become a more lucrative endeavor for various bad actors, Congress has over the past two decades introduced ever-tougher federal criminal sanctions against counterfeiters. *See* 18 U.S.C. §2320. This trend has probably also been motivated by the need to spur international and foreign action, which can sometimes be achieved most effectively via the criminal law. In addition to creating criminal liability, which can subject the offender to both fines (up to $15 million) and imprisonment (up to twenty years), newer amendments to the legislation have provided law enforcement officials substantial seizure remedies against the instruments of the criminal enterprise. The 1996 amendments also made counterfeiting a predicate act for the purposes of prosecution under the RICO statute.

Special statutory provisions also offer generous relief to successful plaintiffs in civil counterfeiting cases. *See* Lanham Act §35(b). Section 35(b) provides for mandatory treble damages and attorneys' fees "in the case of any violation of section 32(1)(a) of this Act . . . that consists of intentionally using a mark or designation, knowing such mark or designation is a counterfeit mark . . . in connection with the sale, offering for sale, or distribution of goods or services." Why? What is special about counterfeiting cases that warrants this differential treatment?

K & N ENGINEERING, INC. v. BULAT

510 F.3d 1079 (9th Cir. 2007)

IKUTA, Circuit Judge:

In this case we are asked to decide whether an award of statutory damages for trademark counterfeiting under 15 U.S.C. §1117(c) precludes an award of attorney's fees under 15 U.S.C. §1117(b).

[K & N filed a complaint in the Central District of California alleging trademark infringement under 15 U.S.C. §§1114(1) and 1125(a); trademark counterfeiting under 15 U.S.C. §1114(1)(a); trademark dilution under 15 U.S.C. §1125(c); and related state law statutory and common law causes of action. K & N also elected to seek statutory damages under 15 U.S.C. §1117(c). The district court granted K & N's summary judgment motion on all claims and entered judgment in favor of K & N. Pursuant to 15 U.S.C. §1117(c)(1) and (b) respectively, the district court awarded K & N statutory damages of $20,000 and attorney's fees of $100,000.]

III

. . .

Reading §1117 as a whole, the statute lays out an integrated scheme for plaintiffs in trademark infringement actions to recover damages and attorney's fees. Under §1117(a), a plaintiff seeking actual damages for trademark infringement is entitled to reasonable attorney's fees only in "exceptional cases." "A trademark case is exceptional where the district court finds that the defendant acted maliciously, fraudulently, deliberately, or willfully." *Watec Co. v. Liu*, 403 F.3d 645, 656 (9th Cir. 2005).

When counterfeit marks are involved, however, §1117(b) is also applicable. Under this subsection, a plaintiff seeking actual damages under §1117(a) is entitled to three times the actual damages plus reasonable attorney's fees in every case, except when there are "extenuating circumstances." §1117(b).

Finally, a plaintiff may eschew actual damages under §1117(a) and elect to seek statutory damages under §1117(c). . . . Section 1117(c) makes no provision for attorney's fees; nor does §1117(b) authorize such fees for a plaintiff seeking statutory damages under §1117(c). Section 1117(b)'s attorney's fees provision applies only in cases with actual damages under §1117(a).[5]

In this case, K & N elected to recover statutory damages under §1117(c). Because of K & N's election, the court did not assess or award K & N actual damages or profits under §1117(a). Therefore, there is no statutory basis to award K & N attorney's fees under §1117(b).

Notwithstanding the import of the statutory language, K & N argues that *Intel Corp. v. Terabyte International, Inc.*, 6 F.3d 614 (9th Cir. 1993), permits a plaintiff who

---

5. Because the fee award in this case was made pursuant to §1117(b), we do not reach the issue whether an election to receive statutory damages under §1117(c) precludes an award of attorney's fees for exceptional cases under the final sentence of §1117(a).

has elected to obtain statutory damages under §1117(c) to obtain attorney's fees under §1117(b). This argument is clearly wrong. *Intel* considered the availability of the attorney's fees allowed for "exceptional cases" under §1117(a), where the plaintiff was awarded actual damages under §1117(a). [cit.] Section 1117(c) was not enacted until 1996, three years after *Intel* was decided. *See* Anticounterfeiting Consumer Protection Act of 1996, Pub. L. No. 104-153, 110 Stat. 1386.

IV

Because an election to receive statutory damages under §1117(c) precludes an award of attorney's fees under §1117(b), we hold that the district court abused its discretion in awarding K & N $100,000 in attorney's fees. . . .

NOTES AND QUESTIONS

1. *Attorneys' fees under alternative argument.* The *Bulat* court did not address the possibility of a plaintiff electing statutory damages under Section 35(c) from securing attorneys' fees under Section 35(a). In *Louis Vuitton Malletier S.A. v. Ly USA, Inc.*, 676 F.3d 83 (2d Cir. 2012), the Second Circuit held that a trademark owner who elects statutory damages under Section 35(c) may still argue that the case is exceptional and attorneys' fees should be awarded. The court reasoned that an election under Section 35(c) in a trademark counterfeiting case should not preclude the trademark owner from invoking the same attorneys' fees remedy that other prevailing plaintiffs would have in any trademark infringement case that is deemed to be exceptional. (That remedy is provided for in Section 35(a).) Two of the three panel judges found it useful to consult the legislative history to arrive at this conclusion:

> Before 1996, trademark remedies were governed by sections 1117(a) and (b) alone. Section 1117(a) provided as remedies—then as now—profits, actual damages, and costs, plus attorney's fees in an "exceptional" case. Section 1117(b) provided—in cases of willful counterfeiting—for treble damages, a "reasonable attorney's fee," and prejudgment interest.
>
> In 1996, Congress passed the Anticounterfeiting Consumer Protection Act (the "Act"), which amended section 1117 to add subsection (c), providing for the alternative of statutory damages. Anticounterfeiting Consumer Protection Act of 1996, §7, Pub. L. No. 104-153, 110 Stat. 1386 (codified at 15 U.S.C. §1117(c)). Congress appears to have been motivated by a gap in the law: Plaintiffs who were victorious on their civil counterfeiting claims were often unable to obtain an adequate recovery in actual damages because counterfeiters often maintain sparse business records, if any at all. *See* S. Rep. 104-177, at 10 (1995).[27] In passing the Act, which

---

27. The Senate Report provides, with respect to section 7 of the Act:

> This section amends section 35 of the Lanham Act, allowing civil litigants the option of obtaining discretionary, judicially imposed damages in trademark counterfeiting cases, instead of actual damages. The committee recognizes that under current law, a civil litigant may not be able to prove actual damages if a sophisticated, large-scale counterfeiter has hidden or destroyed information about his counterfeiting.
>
> Moreover, counterfeiters' records are frequently nonexistent, inadequate or deceptively kept in order to willfully deflate the level of counterfeiting activity actually engaged in, making proving actual damages in these cases extremely difficult if not impossible. Enabling trademark owners to elect statutory damages is both necessary and appropriate in light of the deception routinely practiced by counterfeiters. The amounts are appropriate given the extent of damage done to business goodwill by infringement of trademarks.

S. Rep. 104-177, at 10.

allows trademark plaintiffs to elect to recover statutory damages in counterfeit cases in lieu of actual damages, Congress apparently sought to ensure that plaintiffs would receive more than *de minimis* compensation for the injury caused by counterfeiting as a result of the unprovability of actual damages despite the plain inference of damages to the plaintiff from the defendant's unlawful behavior. The Act was thus apparently designed to provide an alternative to the type of recovery provided in section 1117(a); not to all of the remedies provided for in that section. The Act was meant to expand the range of remedies available to a trademark plaintiff, not restrict them.

In light of that history, it seems to us unlikely that Congress intended to prevent a plaintiff who opts to recover statutory damages from also receiving attorney's fees. If Congress's purpose in enacting section 1117(c) was to address the problem facing a plaintiff unable to prove actual damages, denying an attorney's fee award to those plaintiffs making use of the new statutory-damages election would be inconsistent with that remedial purpose. The key legislative-history sources—the House and Senate Reports—do not indicate that Congress intended a tradeoff between statutory damages and both actual damages and attorney's fees. *See* H.R. Rep. 104-556 (2005); S. Rep. 104-177.

This case is illustrative. The district court concluded that the defendants were responsible for a "massive counterfeiting enterprise" based at least in part on plaintiff's allegations and the unavailability of records suggesting otherwise. As we have explained, a defendant facing a statutory damage award less than the actual amount of the damages he or she caused has the incentive to frustrate ascertainment of the actual amount of the damages. It makes little sense, we think, to further reward a defendant successful in defeating the plaintiff's and the court's attempts to fix the actual amount of damages by allowing him or her to avoid an award of attorney's fees. Such a scheme would only further incentivize the defendant to avoid making, keeping, or producing sales records.

Id. at 110-11.

2. *Statutory damages.* Legislation enacted in 1996 amended Section 35 of the Lanham Act to make statutory damages available in cases of counterfeiting. *See* 15 U.S.C. §1117(c). Section 35(c) specifies statutory damages amounts, ranging from $500 to $1,000,000 per type of good. *See Gabbanelli Accordions & Imports, LLC v. Ditta Gabbanelli Ubaldo di Elio Gabbanelli,* 575 F.3d 693 (7th Cir. 2009) (holding that it was error to assess statutory damages for each individual counterfeit good sold, as opposed to each *type* of counterfeit good sold). Should Section 35(c) be available in cases where the defendant is a contributory infringer? *See Louis Vuitton Malletier, S.A. v. Akanoc Solutions, Inc.,* 658 F.3d 936, 944-45 (9th Cir. 2011). Can you develop a statutory interpretation argument that supports this outcome?

3. *Freezing assets to ensure the availability of a counterfeiter's assets.* In order that a plaintiff will be able to seek the award of a counterfeiter's profits, as authorized by the Lanham Act, courts have frozen the assets of alleged counterfeiters, see Reebok Int'l, Ltd. v. Marnatech Enters., Inc., 970 F.2d 552 (9th Cir. 1992), or limited defendants' spending pending adjudication of the case. See Levi Strauss & Co. v. Sunrise Int'l Trading Inc., 51 F.3d 982 (11th Cir. 1995).

4. *Anti-counterfeiting legislation.* In March 2006, the Stop Counterfeiting in Manufactured Goods Act became law. The Act amended 18 U.S.C. §2320 in various ways, including by the addition of language prohibiting the sale of "labels, patches, stickers, wrappers, badges, emblems, medallions, charms, boxes, containers, cans, cases, hangtags, documentation, or packaging of any type or nature, knowing that a counterfeit mark has been applied thereto."

5. *"Substantially indistinguishable from . . .?"* Section 2320 defines "counterfeit mark" as a "spurious" mark that is either identical to, "or substantially indistinguishable from," a registered mark. Suppose that a defendant is accused of counterfeiting the Burberry "check" mark (a well-known plaid pattern, as you are probably aware). Suppose that the defendant's goods include a similar plaid pattern, with an equestrian figure

superimposed over it. Is the defendant's mark "substantially indistinguishable" from the registered Burberry check even if the registration does not include any equestrian figure? Would it matter if Burberry had separately registered an equestrian figure and sometimes sold products having both the check pattern and the equestrian figure? (Would you need to know how similar the respective equestrian figures were?) *See United States v. Chong Lam*, 677 F.3d 190 (4th Cir. 2012). Consider another variation: Suppose that a party receives genuine goods marked with a legitimate mark, then alters and resells the goods without altering the marks. Is this activity counterfeiting under Section 2320? Or can the accused counterfeiter defend on the basis that the mark is not "spurious"? *United States v. Cone*, 714 F.3d 197 (4th Cir. 2013).

6. *Is "substantially indistinguishable from" void for vagueness?* Would you uphold Section 2320 against a constitutional challenge that the definition of "counterfeit" is void for vagueness? In particular, is the phrase "substantially indistinguishable from" void for vagueness? *See United States v. Chong Lam*, 677 F.3d 190 (4th Cir. 2012). The relevant standard requires an assessment as to whether the relevant criminal offense is defined (1) with enough definiteness that ordinary people can understand what conduct is prohibited, and (2) in a manner that does not encourage arbitrary and discriminatory enforcement.

7. *Liability for possessing counterfeit goods?* Section 2320 provides a criminal penalty for anyone who "intentionally traffics" in goods or services and "knowingly uses" a counterfeit mark on or in connection with those goods or services. Suppose that a defendant, *D*, is arrested for driving a van loaded with counterfeit Louis Vuitton handbags. Has *D* satisfied the "knowingly uses" element of the offense by possessing the handbags? Or must the prosecution show that *D* has actively employed the mark by showing or displaying for sale the goods or services bearing the mark? *See United States v. Diallo*, 575 F.3d 252 (3d Cir. 2009). To what extent does the debate over actionable use in the civil context (discussed in Chapter 7) inform your assessment? To what extent is the Section 45 definition of "trademark" relevant?

8. *Criminal trademark counterfeiting at state law.* Some states have criminal statutes corresponding to 18 U.S.C. §2320. For an example of a prosecution for trademark counterfeiting under an Ohio state law (Ohio Rev. Code §2913.34), *see State v. Troisi*, 901 N.E.2d 856 (Ohio Ct. App. 2008) (appeal from conviction for trademark counterfeiting arising from defendant's hosting of a "purse party" where allegedly counterfeit items were offered for sale). The case discusses the requirements for proving whether the trademark affixed to the purported counterfeit item is "identical with or substantially indistinguishable from" the registered mark at issue, as required by both the Ohio law and 18 U.S.C. §2320. In general, should state courts look to interpretations of the federal statute when interpreting their corresponding state anti-counterfeiting statutes? Some sources suggest that as of 2008 there was a trend among state legislatures to expand civil and criminal penalties for trademark counterfeiting under state law. *See State Laws to Offer Enhanced Penalties, Protection for Federally Registered Marks*, Pat., Trademark & Copyright Daily, July 3, 2008 (reporting on Virginia legislation, ultimately codified at Va. Code Ann. §59-1.92).

9. *Liability under 18 U.S.C. §2318.* Federal law also makes it a crime to knowingly traffic in counterfeit or illicit labels affixed to, or designed to be affixed to, software. 18 U.S.C. §2318. *See, e.g., Microsoft Corp. v. Pronet Cyber Techs., Inc.*, 593 F. Supp. 2d 876 (E.D. Va. 2009) (holding that the requirement for knowledge means that the defendant must know that the labels are not genuine, not that the defendant must know that the activity is unlawful).

10. *A zoning approach to counterfeiting.* Trademark owners frequently complain that combating counterfeiting via civil or even criminal enforcement is only partially successful at best. A classic case in point is the sale of counterfeit apparel outside the venues of sporting events. Reportedly, some cities hosting major sporting events have enacted temporary local zoning ordinances forbidding the sale of any merchandise outside the venue for a limited time period. *See, e.g.*, Peter Page, *Bowl Games Trigger IP End Runs*, 31 Nat'l L.J. 15 (col. 1) (Dec. 22, 2008). What are the pros and cons of this zoning approach to regulating trademark counterfeiting?

D.   Other Remedies

As noted at several points throughout the book, Section 37 grants courts the power to cancel federal trademark registrations when those registrations are at issue in proceedings before them. Section 37 does not, however, create independent jurisdiction in the courts to hear cancellation claims. It is most commonly invoked by a counterclaim where the defendant in an infringement action defends the action by challenging the validity of the plaintiff's mark (and hence, plaintiff's trademark registration).

TABLE OF CASES

Main cases are in italics.

INDEX